A History of Scientific Psychology

A HISTORY OF
Scientific
Psychology

ITS ORIGINS AND
PHILOSOPHICAL BACKGROUNDS

D. B. Klein

BASIC BOOKS, INC., PUBLISHERS
New York / London

© 1970 by Basic Books, Inc.
Library of Congress Catalog Card Number: 72–94296
Manufactured in the United States of America

To Anne

PREFACE

THE PRESENT VOLUME is concerned with the history of psychology's efforts to achieve scientific status. It is a long history having its roots in a vast philosophic heritage. After all, those who first envisioned the prospect of a scientific psychology did not start from scratch in the sense of being uninformed about the nature of mind. The founding fathers of the "new" laboratory psychology were conversant with what their philosophical predecessors had had to say about mental life. Many of them wrote and lectured on both philosophy and psychology and thought of themselves as being philosophers as well as psychologists. Their sponsorship of psychology as science was an outgrowth of their familiarity with mental philosophy. The chief objective of the present volume is to survey, at least in broad outline, the philosophic backgrounds from which their prospects for a scientific psychology emerged. Thus, viewed in historical perspective, their advocacy of a scientific psychology was not the advocacy of an unphilosophical psychology any more than the earlier emergence of chemistry and physics had involved repudiation of their roots in natural philosophy.

In this connection it is relevant to note that the concept of experimentation was by no means alien to a philosophic orientation. For example, Newton referred to his scientific work as "experimental philosophy." In the subtitle to Hume's psychological *Treatise* of 1739, there is a reference to "the experimental method of reasoning." In 1812 Sir Humphry Davy published the results of his chemical experiments in a book entitled *Elements of Chemical Philosophy*. Furthermore, for years a leading journal for physicists was called the *Philosophical Magazine*. This title was retained until early in the present century. The phrase "experimental philosophy" that Newton had employed was also retained for a long time. It was still current in the 1880s; Cambridge University had a "professor of astronomy and experimental philosophy" on its faculty. Apparently, astronomy and other sciences had not yet cut loose from their philosophic moorings. As a result, the phrase did not sound as strange then as it does today when it might connote the paradoxical notion of an experimental metaphysics. In general, until the turn of the century, the domain of philosophy continued to overlap the territory of science.

Whether the later territorial independence of psychology meant complete severance of its former affiliation with philosophy is a moot question. Those who regard the philosophic quest as antithetic to the scientific quest would be disposed to argue in favor of complete severance. For them the introduction of philosophic considerations would be a hindrance to scientific progress—a muddying of the scientific waters. On the other hand, there are those for whom commitment to science is not incompatible with a philosophic outlook. Their devotion to science includes recognition of an indebtedness to the heritage of natural philosophy. Sir Lawrence Bragg, Cavendish Professor of Experimental Physics at Cambridge, once acknowledged such indebtedness in these words:

> Science used to be called Natural Philosophy, and it was a very good name. The fun in science lies not in discovering facts, but in discovering new ways of thinking about them. The test which we apply to these ideas is this—do they enable us to fit the facts to each other and see that more and more of them can be explained by fewer and fewer fundamental laws?

This formulation by Bragg might be paraphrased by noting that what is now called the science of psychology used to be called mental philosophy. As such it had to do with what many generations of philosophers had been thinking about the presumed facts of mental life and ways in which ideas about these facts might be fitted together in order to yield laws of mental life. This resulted in the accumulation of a mass of data—both factual and conjectural— pertaining to the realm of mind. It was this heritage of mental philosophy as it had taken shape by the 1870s and 1880s that the pioneering laboratory psychologists had at their disposal. It was a heritage replete with observations, concepts, and theories of psychological import, and the "new" scientific psychology had its roots in these observations, concepts, and theories. They may thus be viewed as the philosophic backgrounds of scientific psychology. Understanding of these backgrounds called for a review of the history of psychology from ancient times to the time of Wundt. It also called for consideration of relevant concomitants of that history as reflected in the history of science. Such extended consideration was required because mental philosophy did not flourish as an autonomous enterprise uninfluenced by the vicissitudes of science in the guise of natural philosophy.

Instead of restricting the presentation to a straightforward chronological sequence, it was deemed advisable on occasion to digress from this sequence in order to show the bearing of past events on contemporary issues. Anticipations of such issues were not at all uncommon in the writings of ancient, medieval, and postmedieval philosopher-psychologists.

To facilitate understanding of their anticipations and the general drift of their thinking, it was also deemed advisable to introduce verbatim quotations from their writings. In the case of the late nineteenth-century sponsors of psychology as science, rather lengthy quotations were sometimes interpolated. This was especially the case in considering the part played by William James in his role as one of the founding fathers of scientific psychology. An incidental reason for doing so was to arouse appreciation of James both as provocative thinker and as masterful expositor. Reading about James is not as informative and rewarding as direct acquaintance with his classic *Principles of Psychology* of 1890. More clearly than any other work of the period, it depicts the "new" psychology's scientific aspirations as projected against the background of a variegated heritage of mental philosophy.

In addition, as is brought out in Part Three of the present book, James dealt with some pivotal and persistent psychological problems. Taken collectively, these problems serve as a unifying nexus linking psychology's philosophic past to its scientific future; hence their direct relevance for the present undertaking.

It is also well to note that virtually all first and second generation American psychologists went to school with James via the *Principles*. This ceased to be as common among later generations, so that currently it is not exceptional to come across holders of advanced degrees in psychology for whom the *Principles* remains an unread work. This is akin to coming across professors of biology who have not read Darwin's *Origin of Species,* or coming across training analysts who have yet to read Freud's *Traumdeutung.* Accordingly, it is to be hoped that the amount of space devoted to the *Principles* in the present volume may help to transform this neglect into eager and active interest.

The search for pictures appearing in this book entailed the cooperation of many individuals and several galleries. For some helpful suggestions I want to thank Prof. Eric Lunzer of the University of Nottingham and Prof. J. C. Kenna, archivist of the British Psychological Association. I am especially grateful to Prof. R. W. Pickford for his time and effort in locating portraits of the members of the Scottish School. He not only enlisted the aid of his colleagues, Prof. McLaren Young and Mr. L. Cowper of the Fine Art Department of the University of Glasgow and of those in charge of the University of Glasgow Art Gallery, but also the aid of the curator of the National Galleries of Scotland in Edinburgh. I want also to thank the officials of the National Portrait Gallery in London for granting permission to reproduce their paintings of Thomas Hobbes, Charles Darwin, and John Stuart Mill. In the same spirit, thanks are due to the trustees of The Wellcome Institute of the History of Medicine in London for the picture of David Hartley, to

the University of Illinois for the picture of Franz Brentano, to Prof. W. De
Costa of the University of Gent for the picture of Albert Michotte, and to
Miss Pauline M. Harrold of the India Office Library in London for her help
in securing the picture of James Mill. Most of the other pictures were provided by Dr. Otto Bettmann of the Bettmann Archive in New York.

September 1969   D. B. KLEIN

CONTENTS

ILLUSTRATIONS

PART **I**

INTRODUCTION

1

Psychology and the History of Science

It is now just about a century since the possibility of subjecting mental life to experimental study began to be given serious consideration. There were no psychological laboratories in existence in the 1860s. Neither were there professors of psychology or departments of psychology. Psychological clinics and child-guidance centers were not to come for some decades. Not a single psychological journal was being published in English. Nobody had taken an intelligence test. Neither did anybody ever refer to an I.Q. or an inferiority complex or a superego, a learning curve, a correlation coefficient, or a Freudian slip. Terms such as these and hundreds similar to them were not yet known even to scholars. No rat had run a maze or pressed a bar in a learning experiment. Not a single person had obtained a Ph.D. in psychology and no undergraduate was majoring in the subject.

In brief, psychology as it is today was undreamed of at the time of the Civil War. It did not begin to emerge as a separate field of investigation until about the 1880s. In this sense scientific psychology is a late nineteenth-century product, with most of its organized or institutionalized support and development a product of the twentieth century. This might suggest that the history of psychology covers a span of less than one hundred years, a fragmentary interval in the time perspective of history. However, such an interpretation is not justified by the facts, for the past of psychology extends over many hundreds of years. The German psychologist Hermann Ebbinghaus (1850–1909) summed this up in his frequently quoted "Psychology has a long past but a short history."

Psychology's Remote Beginnings

The specific beginnings of psychology's long past are embedded in the obscurity of remote antiquity. There is no way of knowing with any degree of assurance whether preliterate man at the dawn of civilization gave any thought to or had any notions about aspects of experience that later came to be classified as mental phenomena. Articulate speech emerged before written language came into being. There is no way of finding out at what stage in preliterate man's speech development his vocabulary contained words to designate what we mean when we talk about memory or dreams or thought or imagination or being intelligent or being conscious or, in short, having minds. Even with knowledge about the early emergence of man's commonsense vocabulary of psychological terms, there would still be uncertainty regarding the beginnings of psychology. The mere existence of such a vocabulary would not necessarily serve to demonstrate a concomitant critical interest in the psychological events involved.

No science is likely to get under way without the impetus of a critical interest as manifested by some sort of reflective curiosity. The science of physiology did not develop just because a vocabulary having to do with physiological events was in common use. People talked about hunger, thirst, fevers, breathing, excretion, and other bodily processes without being curious about the what and how of such processes. Physiology is an outgrowth of the questioning attitude centering on bodily functions and dealing with the mechanism of respiration, the nature of digestion, and the function of the brain or the heart or the glands and their particular contributions to the maintenance of the life of an organism.

Similarly, psychology may be considered an outgrowth of the kind of question that prompts people to wonder about the nature of human nature. It is exemplified by such questions as: Why are some people color-blind? How do we acquire our likes and dislikes? Are we born with ideas of right and wrong? Why are some people morose and others cheerful? Is musical talent inherited? Do the sexes differ in mental ability? What is the most efficient method of teaching reading? Do all people have the same kinds of imagery? Can the speed of thinking be measured? Can memory be strengthened by practice just as muscles can be by exercise? Hundreds of such questions as raised by different investigators during the course of centuries gave rise to psychology as a separate field of study. Though psychology as a separate field is less than a hundred years old, it did not come into existence in virtual independence of the reflections of thoughtful men in the preceding centuries. It is this very dependence that accounts for the "long past" of psychology.

Aristotle wrote, "We shall not obtain the best insight into things until we actually see them growing from the beginning." Unfortunately, as we have noted, the earliest beginnings of psychology are difficult to establish. In terms of etymology the word "psychology" suggests a study of mind or soul so that the beginnings might be traced to the early emergence of the concepts of mind or soul. And yet, as E. G. Brett (1929, p. 706) has pointed out, "The origin of Western Psychology was in the study of the organism and not in speculations about a supernatural 'soul.' "

Moreover, the very early Greeks failed to entertain the notion of a soul in contradistinction to the body. According to Brett, this notion seems to have emerged with the Pythagoreans toward the end of the fifth century B.C. Prior to that era there seems to have been no speculative consideration of the nature of sensation or thinking viewed as distinctively *mental* functions or as activities of a soul. Just as very young children take the body and its functions for granted long before they have any occasion to wonder about events regarded as mental by adults, so the very early Greeks in the days before Socrates (469–399 B.C.) also failed to dwell upon mental events. As a consequence, Brett reminds us, "Aristotle considers the thinkers before Socrates were exclusively concerned with physical nature and for that reason unphilosophical."

For Aristotle, to be "unphilosophical" meant to be uncritical in one's thinking, to fail to make relevant distinctions, and consequently to be in error without realizing it. Because of their exclusive preoccupation with physical nature, so Aristotle held, the pre-Socratic Greek thinkers failed to come to grips with the nature of mental life as a "philosophical" problem. Meeting that challenge became one of the tasks of generations of post-Socratic philosophers. For this reason, well up until about the middle of the nineteenth century, the history of psychology involves consideration of much of the content of the history of philosophy. Since most of the broader implications of contemporary psychological issues originated in the latter history, the historian of psychology is obligated to consider the bearing of such origins on modern psychology. Furthermore, innumerable contemporary psychological issues in terms of their scientific or more sharply circumscribed implications are rooted in the history of several special sciences.

As a result, the history of psychology, within certain limits, overlaps portions of the history of such fields as medicine, physics, biology, physiology, anthropology, and even astronomy. To a large but by no means an exclusive extent, those fields came to influence psychology as it was emerging from its philosophical heritage and becoming a separate field in its own right. The resulting transition from mental philosophy to scientific psychology was the work of the nineteenth century founding fathers of the psychology of today. Man's critical and specialized study of his own nature is thus a relatively late development in the course of Western civilization.

Technological Origins of Science

This late development reflects an interesting sequence in the birth of separate fields of scientific investigation. Most scientific fields came into being in response to efforts to deal with practical problems. In this sense, technology or applied science, when considered historically, might be said to have preceded pure science. For example, the need to keep track of time and the need to direct the course of a ship on the open sea rendered knowledge of solar changes, lunar events, and stellar movements increasingly helpful. The practical demands of navigation account for the very early emergence of the kinds of observation characteristic of the work of astronomers. As a science, astronomy got under way among the Greeks around the seventh century B.C., who in turn were able to formulate theories based upon the accumulation of astronomical observations made by many generations of Babylonian observers. According to one historian of astronomy, A. M. Clarke (1929, p. 582), there are records dating back to the reign of a Babylonian king in 3800 B.C. which "imply that even then the varying aspects of the sky had long been under expert observation." However, astronomical *science* did not come into being until efforts were made to formulate theories to account for the facts observed.

Geometry is another example of an early science that grew out of the needs of everyday living. The word itself is derived from two Greek roots meaning "measurement of the earth." This derivation reflects the earth-measuring problems that gave rise to the kinds of observations systematized into a science by Euclid around 300 B.C. The problems in question originated in Egypt and were occasioned by the need to re-establish landmarks which had been washed away by periodic flooding of the Nile. Measurement of surface area in terms of land surveys became a practical problem. Boundaries had to be fixed in terms of measurement rather than by means of posts or rocks likely to vanish in the next flood. This required ways of determining the areas of tracts of varying size and shape. The tasks were very definite and the problems very practical. But the *science* of geometry did not come into being until such problems were stripped of their immediate concrete practical implications and viewed in the light of their abstract theoretical implications. As W. P. D. Wightman (1953, p. 4) has stated, "What distinguishes the Greeks of the seventh century before our era . . . is that their concern is not with triangular *fields* but with triangles. . . ."

Neither astronomy nor geometry is to be classified as an experimental science in the sense in which physics and chemistry are deemed to be experimental. To a large degree the experimental method did not begin to be employed by the founding fathers of physics and chemistry until the seventeenth century. This is the century of such giants as Galileo, Newton, Boyle, and Kepler. It was the century in which men like John Graunt in England and Jacob Bernoulli in Switzerland established the foundations of vital statistics and probability theory as adjuvants of scientific method. It was the century in which the first official societies for the discussion of scientific papers were organized. In the 1660s both Charles II in England and Louis XIV in France extended royal encouragement to such societies. The importance of controlled observation, mathematical checks, careful induction and deduction, and publication of data and conclusions became increasingly customary. In short, the methodology of science began to flourish in this century. It is worth noting that the deliberate cultivation and application of this methodology is thus not quite four hundred years old. Historically, this is but a brief span of time. In view of the vast technological changes brought about by this methodology, it is safe to say that no previous equivalent span of time modified the life of man so drastically.

In the first half of the nineteenth century, the methods and concepts of physics and chemistry began to be applied more systematically than in previous eras to understand the nature of plant and animal life. Botany and physiology emerged as independent fields of study. Darwin was brooding over the meaning of the diversity of plant and animal forms he had observed in various parts of the world. His epoch-making *On the Origin of Species* appeared in 1859 and marked a high point in the history of biology. Man's place in the evolutionary scheme of things became a subject of intense controversy. At the turn of the century and in the early years of the twentieth century, psychologists began to apply the concept of evolution to problems of human and animal mental development and to discuss the adaptive value of psychological phenomena.

Sequence of Scientific Development

The foregoing brief survey of the emergence of the several different special scientific fields can now be used to clarify what was earlier referred to as an interesting sequence in their emergence. If we think of the heavens as the outer part of a cosmic sphere and man as occupying the inner part of the sphere, one might say that scientific curiosity moved from without inwards. Astronomy and geometry are among the subjects that date back centuries before the Christian era. Neither of these subjects constitutes an experimental science. Although there were sporadic beginnings of what in retrospect might be construed as experimental ventures by some Greek investigators and some alchemists of the Middle Ages, the development of experimental methods in the modern sense was not ushered in until the late Renaissance. It was predominantly a seventeenth-century achievement concerned with studies of man's physical environment and resulting in the formulation of laws of motion, of gravitation, of the pendulum, of magnetism, and kindred topics that eventually came to be included in textbooks of physics. Why the scientific age came to appear on the world scene at this time will be considered later. In the present context it is more relevant to note its initial application to external events; to planetary orbits, to falling bodies, to magnetized particles, to gases under pressure, and similar changes in the world of inanimate nature. Even William Harvey's seventeenth-century demonstration of the circulation of the blood, an early application of scientific method to a physiological problem, was consonant with the physical concepts dominating the thinking of the pioneer experimentalists of the period. Not until the nineteenth century did the work of Harvey's eighteenth-century successors give rise to full-scale laboratories of physiology, botany, and other branches of biology. Study of the life sciences thus came in later than study of the physical sciences. And within the life sciences, scientific study of mental life was among the last on the scene.

To revert to a point already suggested: as a science, physics is at least three hundred years old, whereas psychology as a scientific specialty might claim an age of eighty years if 1879 be selected as a plausible beginning of its official concern with laboratory controls and experimental checks. This was the year when a German psychologist, Wilhelm Wundt of the University of Leipzig, initiated laboratory experience as an essential factor in the training of psychologists. At that time, this was regarded as a revolutionary innovation. Many regarded it as signifying the advent of psychology as a science as opposed to its prior status as a branch of philosophy. In fact, it was called the "new psychology" by way of differentiating it from the "old" philosophical psychology. At long last the methods that had been so successful in gaining understanding and control of the external world were to be applied to the inner world of human experience. In large measure the concepts and methods developed by physicists and physiologists were now adapted to problems as formulated by the advocates of the "new" psychology.

In terms of this perspective, as has already been suggested, the history of science is marked by the relatively late appearance of man's scientific study of himself. In part this very lateness may account for the fact that modern man possesses far more effective control of physical forces than he has of psychological and social forces. The nature of the latter forces is being investigated not only by psychologists but also by sociologists, anthropologists, economists, political scientists, and penologists. All these specialists represent fields which, like psychology, had their "scientific" beginnings in the nineteenth century and came to flourish more actively in the twentieth.

They are all concerned with studying man as a *person* rather than man as an organism. This means studying man as a product of his family tradition, his religious affiliation, his political organization, his educational influences, his business and industrial activities, and whatever else falls within the scope of the many social institutions characteristic of life in organized society today. Under the circumstances, just as the nineteenth century was marked by the influence of the biological sciences, so the twentieth century might be said to be showing the influences of the social sciences.

The trends in question are reflected in persistent controversy regarding the place of psychology in the family of sciences. Those who stress a biological approach to psychology are more likely to think of themselves as natural scientists, while those who view psychology as fundamentally concerned with a study of human personality are more likely to classify themselves as social scientists in the sense of doing their professional thinking in terms of methods and concepts germane to a social-science orientation. However, it is more relevant at this point to note that both sets of opponents in the controversy agree in their recognition of the importance of scientific method in the study of psychology. Why this recognition came so late in the history of psychology is a question that cannot be answered without considerable familiarity with that history. It constitutes an issue whose consideration therefore had better be postponed.

Science and the Renaissance

A related question that might be taken up at this point was mentioned a little earlier in connection with the rather dramatic rise of seventeenth-century science. Why, it might be asked, did not the scientific age come into being in previous centuries? Were seventeenth-century minds more curious or less gullible than those of earlier generations? This is not probable when we consider the minds of Greeks like Socrates, Plato, and Aristotle, of Romans like Seneca, Lucretius, and Cicero, or of men of the medieval period like Duns Scotus, Thomas Aquinas, or William of Occam. It would thus be highly questionable to argue that science arose because its seventeenth-century pioneers possessed keener intellects than the outstanding thinkers who were their nonscientific predecessors.

It is much more likely that the scientific quest got under way when it did because of the changes responsible for the "new learning" and the "new outlook" of the Renaissance. This period of history came into being gradually. It was not, as is sometimes implied, a sudden sharp rejection of the medieval outlook.

The shift in outlook was the result of various influences responsible for the transformation of the life of man in the closing centuries of the medieval period. Feudal institutions gave way to larger units of political organization. In part, the breakup of feudal estates was occasioned by the invention of gunpowder, which rendered feudal war machinery obsolete. By the fifteenth century, guns were being used in battles and the soldier was taking the place of the knight. Personal loyalty to the lord of the manor yielded to less rigid social ties as feudal estates merged into larger national units.

With the fall of Constantinople in 1453, scholars familiar with the Greek language appeared on the scene in Western Europe and set the stage for part of the "new learning." During this same century, with the invention of movable type by Laurens Coster in Holland and Johann Gutenberg in Germany, printed books appeared on the scene in place of bound manuscripts. This achievement obviously rendered the dissemination of knowledge much more efficient. Scholars in different parts of the world could more readily be informed of what was being taught in distant countries. The growth of knowledge is directly dependent on such interchange of ideas. Without communication there can be no scientific growth and no transmission of knowledge from generation to generation. Such communication was facilitated by the formation of learned societies and by the establishment of organized postal services during the seventeenth century. Scholars were meeting in person and keeping in touch by correspondence.

New geographic vistas had been opened up by the voyages of Columbus and succeeding navigators just as new intellectual vistas had been opened up by the humanists of the Renaissance. Moreover, the challenge to the authority of Rome initiated by the Protestant Reformation added to the intellectual ferment. This made for a greater readiness to doubt and to question and to explore. The system by which Aquinas had reconciled Church dogma with the teachings of Aristotle no longer held sway over the minds of critical thinkers as it had for some three hundred years.

By the sixteenth century the early consequences of this repudiation of blind confidence in dogmatic authority was becoming manifest. That was the century distinguished by the genius of men like da Vinci, Copernicus, and Vesalius. The energies of da Vinci were by no means restricted to painting. He was interested in applied science as well and made contributions to optics, to steam engineering, and to the very early anticipations of what was to become the field of aeronautical engineering. The astronomical observations of Copernicus paved the way for the later work of Galileo by directing attention to the heliocentric theory. Vesalius, the great anatomist, dared to challenge the Church's opposition to dissection of the human body and initiated the movement that eventually, after several centuries of continuing opposition, succeeded in making laboratory courses in anatomy an integral part of the medical curriculum.

It should thus be clear that the scientific enterprise was a gradual development through many decades and not the sudden creation of seventeenth-century scientific insight. Nor should the activities of the medieval schoolmen with their devotion to Aristotle's teachings be viewed as altogether antithetic to this development. After all, science is just as much an affair of devotion to knowledge and to the intellectual quest as it is an affair of careful observation and experimental controls. The schoolmen nurtured and kept alive this devotion. It became institutionalized as the first universities came into existence in the 1300s. The resulting intellectual tradition supplied subsequent generations of scholars with knowledge of mathematics, of early astronomical teachings, and of logic among other subjects. They became familiar with processes of ordered thinking and the nature of logical fallacies. Not everything taught by Aristotle has turned out to be contrary to fact. By keeping intellectual curiosity alive and by supplying some of the tools for gratifying this curiosity, the schoolmen enabled their remote pioneer scientific descendants to tackle the job of separating Aristotelian fact from Aristotelian error.

The Empiricist-Rationalist Controversy

Just as the appearance of experimental physics some three hundred or more years ago did not constitute a sharp break with the past, so the advent of experimental psychology some eighty or more years ago did not signify a sudden repudiation of what had been taught by preceding thinkers who belonged to psychology's philosophical past. Many of the broad problems of psychology had already been outlined by Plato and Aristotle. These will be reviewed in later chapters. For the present it is enough to note that modern psychology grew out of the earlier contributions not only of the Greeks but also of other philosopher-psychologists. Among the latter, by way of anticipation and example, mention might be made of such British philosophers as Hobbes, Locke, and Berkeley, of such French philosophers as Descartes, Condillac, and La Mettrie, or of such German philosophers as Leibnitz, Kant, and Herbart. A vast array of problems and concepts current in present-day psychology can be traced to the insights of such philosopher-psychologists. For an adequate understanding of the history of psychology, it thus becomes necessary to become familiar with many of the issues conventionally discussed in histories of philosophy.

Psychology's ancestral roots in philosophy shaped the growth of modern psychology, as is revealed in various characteristics of contemporary psychology. For example, just as there have been numerous schools or systems of philosophy, so there are numerous schools or systems of psychology. Unlike the older sciences of physics and chemistry, the science of psychology lacks unity of outlook and organization. There are no competing systems of physics and chemistry as there are diverse systems of psychology like Gestalt psychology, behaviorism, psychoanalysis, personalistic psychology, hormic psychology, and many others. At a later point an effort will be made to account for this continued existence of differing schools of psychology in contradistinction to the absence of schools among physicists, astronomers, geologists, or anatomists. There is no absence of controversy on particular issues among the latter group of scientists, but among them there is also sufficient agreement on fundamentals to ward off the kind of systematic cleavage that results in the formation of a multiplicity of diverse systems.

Another example of the influence of philosophy on the development of psychology can be noted in the kinds of topics incorporated in many of the traditional textbooks of general psychology. There are discussions of the nature of sensation and perception along with illustrations of the anatomy of the sense organs. Often there are diagrams or pictures to show the structural connections between the sense organs and the nervous system. There are chapters devoted to discussions of imagery, illusions, memory, association, attention, learning, and thinking. Sometimes there are fairly elaborate accounts of various theories of intelligence. All such topics are related to the acquisition of knowledge. They have to do with cognition.

Interest in cognition has been characteristic of the professional endeavor of many generations of philosophers from the days of the Greeks to the present. It is reflected in the existence of *epistemology* as a separate branch of philosophy. This is the branch concerned with the theory of knowledge. It raises questions about the origin of ideas and concepts, about the trustworthiness of sensory experience, and about the nature and consequences of illusion, hallucination, and delusion. The latter terms reflect recognition of the distinction between correct and erroneous perception and belief. Implicitly such recognition gives rise to the distinction between the rational and the irrational. Reason is stressed as a sovereign means of getting at the truth about the world of men and things; hence the epistemologists concerned themselves with examination of the dependability of this truth-finding function of reason. Those who exalted reason as a sovereign intellectual tool came to be called *rationalists*. They tended to regard man as inherently endowed with the capacity to make distinctions between the true and the false, to note likenesses and differences, to organize experience into appropriate categories, to evaluate, to judge, to understand, and to do whatever else one links up with the concept of man as a rational animal.

Contrasting with the rationalists were those epistemologists who deemed sensory experience of greater influence in the growth of knowledge than any other mental function. For them there could be no intellectual development without prior sensory experience. Because of this emphasis on the role of experience they came to be known as *empiricists,* a word whose root meaning suggests learning by trial or observation. This meaning is given popular expression in a phrase like "Experience is the best teacher."

Empiricists thus tended to argue that there can be no valid knowledge independent of sensory experience. Unless the shape of objects can be experienced by sight or touch, there can be no concept of geometrical form. Consequently, according to empiricists, a person born without either sight or touch can never grasp the distinction between a circle and a triangle. Nor could such a person detect the difference between a red ball and a yellow one, any more than the congenitally deaf can understand the difference between high and low notes. In brief, all that a baby comes to learn about its environment is dependent upon relevant sensory experience: its notions of hard and soft, of sweet and bitter, of painful and painless, of cold and warm, of light and dark, of colored and colorless, of straight and crooked, of near and far, and so on and so on. The data supplied by the sense organs constitute the raw material for the emergence of mind. This was a key teaching of the empiricists and undoubtedly had some bearing on the work of early experimental psychologists and their concern with sense organs, the nature of sensation and its attributes, and allied topics.

Rationalists did not disregard the part played by sensory data in the course of mental development, but they questioned whether such data suffice to account for achievements of the human intellect. The difference between a bright person and a stupid one is not ordinarily attributable to a difference in sensory equipment. Despite extreme sensory handicaps, some people like Helen Keller attain high levels of intellectual competence while others with no measurable sensory defects may be unable to master an elementary-school curriculum. Keen vision does not assure keen thinking. Brilliant reasoning is not just an elaboration of sensory experience. For the rationalist, how one reacts to sensory data was and is a more important consideration than analysis of the sensory data as such. Experience is a good teacher provided one is wise enough to learn from experience. Wisdom is an intellectual function operating on the products of sensory stimulation and not the passive outcome of such stimulation.

As Aristotle pointed out, there is a difference between having an experience and *observing* an experience. This is akin to the difference between relaxed reading of the morning paper and laborious study of a difficult text. The latter involves an active quest for meaning or a search for significant relationships among the ideas presented. Acquisition of nuances of meaning and the perception of relevant relationships call for active attention and close reasoning, involving the intellect as well as the sense organs. Such was part of the rationalist's answer to the claims of the empiricists. As formulated by Kant: "The understanding cannot see. The senses cannot think. Only by their union can knowledge be produced."

The Nature-Nurture Controversy

This empiricist-rationalist controversy came to be more than an epistemological argument. It developed into a group of psychological problems the implications of which continue to influence the thinking of contemporary psychologists. These problems all relate to questions of hereditary endowment. Empiricists had tended to play down the influence of heredity by stressing the crucial importance of experience. In metaphorical language, they compared the mind at birth to a blank tablet devoid of any inscriptions. No ideas whatsoever can appear until environmental impressions are recorded on the blank tablet. There are no innate or inborn notions or ideas. Everything is learned by experience, from learning what to eat to learning to walk and talk.

This may seem obviously true until one recalls that babies seem to "know" enough to make sucking movements when the mouth comes in contact with a nipple, that baby chicks peck at kernels of corn without prior training in pecking, or that birds build nests without special tutelage by parent birds. Adaptive reflexes and complex instincts suggest that the tablet of the empiricists is not altogether blank. It may possess "faint markings" that predispose the organism to react to environmental stimuli in predetermined ways. There may be differences in native endowment that enable some youngsters to become distinguished composers and others to be fascinated by the world of mathematics. Not all such differences are to be attributed to differences in experience. Talent is inborn and developed by training and not an exclusive product of experience.

What started as a philosophical debate among epistemologists, it should now be clear, developed into the nature-nurture controversy in modern psychology. This controversy, as has just been indicated, centered on questions of the relative influence of inborn factors as opposed to environmental ones in shaping both human and animal behavior. There were early experiments designed to investigate the beginnings of flight in fledgling birds in order to settle the question of flight as an instinctive performance or a product of learning. Results showed flight to be more related to maturation of the bird's musculature than to what had earlier appeared to be practice in flying by fledglings. In the experiments such practice had been prevented by confining the animals in enclosures that prevented such preflight exercises until a certain level of maturation had been attained. Then, upon release from the enclosure, appropriate flying maneuvers were executed. Flying seemed to be more a function of the bird's nature than its nurture.

Similarly, the question of spatial orientation came up for discussion and experimentation. This issue was concerned with the role of experience in judging distance. Is judgment of distance entirely a matter of learning or is it partly innate? Those who called themselves *empiricists* argued in favor of learning and experience, while those who called themselves *nativists* stressed the importance of unlearned reactions to height and distance. H. A. Carr (1935, p. 403) summarized this phase of the general problem of nativism versus empiricism in the following paragraph:

> The extensive character of the visual field is undoubtedly innate and given. It follows that the perceptible size and shape of objects in so far as they are dependent upon these attributes of the retinal image are also innately given. Perceptible size is dependent upon some of the distance factors, but we know little of the nature of these relations. Its relation to such factors as binocular disparity, and convergence and accommodation is probably innately conditioned in part. It is generally assumed that the dependence of perceptible size and shape upon pattern is empirical in origin. The nature of their relation to retinal position is a matter of opinion. The retinal theory implies an innate relation, while both conceptions are possible for the distance theory.

The preceding references to spatial orientation, the flight of birds, nest building, and other instinctive behavior might seem to be somewhat remote from the original epistemological argument about innate ideas. It might be maintained that for a creature equipped with wings, flight would be possible without the need to assume an inherited idea of flight, just as babies breathe and digest food despite complete ignorance of ideas of respiration and digestion. Nevertheless, there have been and continue to be specialists who have failed to give complete endorsement to the empiricist's repudiation of the doctrine of innate ideas. As is well known, the Swiss leader of the school of analytic psychology, Carl Jung (1875–1961), sponsored a belief in such ideas in his concept of *archetypes* experienced as "primordial images" inherent in the organization of brain tissue and serving to influence the symbolism of dreams and attitudes toward themes of universal import such as birth and death, motherhood, security, sunrise, climate, and whatever else may have a direct bearing on survival under primitive conditions.

The archetypes, as elaborated by Jung, seem to require the assumption of a belief in some mysterious process by which the experiences of remote ancestors modify genetic mechanisms so that the consequences of these experiences are not without influence on the inherited cerebral constitution of descendants born many, many generations later. Justification for this way of presenting Jung's teaching is embodied in the following excerpt from his works (1953, Vol. 8, p. 61):

> . . . although our inheritance consists in physiological paths, still it was mental processes in our ancestors that created the paths. If these traces come to consciousness again in the individual, they can do so only in the form of mental processes; and if these processes can become conscious only through individual experience and thus appear as individual acquisitions, they are none the less pre-existing traces, which are merely "filled out" by the individual experience. Every "impressive" experience is such an impression, in an ancient but unconscious stream bed.

Jung's reference to "mental processes in our ancestors" creating "physiological paths" in the brains of successive generations of their children's children presupposes endorsement of the now generally discredited teaching of the French biologist Lamarck (1744–1829). According to Lamarckian theory, offspring may inherit characteristics that a parent had acquired as a result of exercise or experience. Jung and some of his followers are among the very few modern biologists or psychologists who endorse this theory. Freud can also be listed among these few, for at one time he expressed his agreement with Jung when he wrote (1950, III, 577–578):

> I should myself be glad to know whether the primal scene in my present patient's case was a phantasy or a real experience; but taking other similar cases into account, I must admit that the answer to this question is not in reality a matter of very great importance. The scenes of observing parental intercourse in childhood and of being threatened with castration *are unquestionably an inherited endowment, a phylogenetic inheritance,* but they may just as easily be acquired by personal experience. . . .
>
> All that we find in the prehistory of neuroses is that a child catches hold of this phylogenetic experience where his own experience fails him. He fills in the gaps in individual truth with prehistoric truth; he replaces occurrences in his own life by occurrences in the life of his ancestors. *I fully agree with Jung in recognizing the existence of this phylogenetic inheritance;* but I regard it as a methodological error to seize upon a phylogenetic explanation before the ontogenetic possibilities have been exhausted. [Emphasis added.]

The fact that both Freud and Jung viewed innate ideas as products of phylogenetic inheritance should not be regarded as requiring, at least by implication, similar views by all who opposed the empiricist's rejection of the doctrine of innate ideas.

What Constitutes Knowledge?

Lamarckianism as such was not an issue in the empiricist-rationalist controversy. Futhermore, the rationalist position does not necessarily require

belief in innate ideas even though the empiricist position does call for repudiation of this belief. As mentioned earlier, the empiricist derives all knowledge
from sensory experience, while the rationalist questions this source. For the
rationalist, valid reasoning or thinking may result in knowledge that is not a
direct derivative of sensation. "The sum of the angles of a triangle have been
and always will be equal to 180 degrees" is accepted as a true statement. It
refers to triangles of the past and the future and those never experienced.
The truth of the statement is more a product of reason than of sensation.
This example illustrates the crux of the rationalist's argument. It is a venerable argument, as can be noted in this passage from Plato's dialogue,
Theaetetus, in which Socrates and Theaetetus are engaged in the following
interchange (Jowett [trans.], 1953, III, 287–288):

Soc. The simple sensations which reach the soul through the body are
given at birth to men and animals by nature, but the reflections on the
being and use of them are slowly and hardly gained, if they are ever
gained, by education and long experience.

Theaet. Assuredly.

Soc. And can a man attain truth who fails of attaining being?

Theaet. Impossible.

Soc. And can he who misses the truth of anything, have a knowledge of
that thing?

Theaet. He cannot.

Soc. Then knowledge does not consist in impressions of sense, but in
reasoning about them; in that only, and not in the mere impression, truth
and being can be attained?

Theaet. Clearly.

Soc. And would you call the two processes by the same name, when
there is so great a difference between them?

Theaet. That would certainly not be right.

Soc. And what name would you give to seeing, hearing, smelling, being
cold and being hot?

Theaet. I should call all of them perceiving—what other name could be
given to them?

Soc. Perception would be the collective name of them?

Theaet. Certainly.

Soc. Which, as we say, has no part in the attainment of truth any more
than of being?

Theaet. Certainly not.

Soc. And therefore not in science or knowledge?

Theaet. No.

Soc. Then perception, Theaetetus, can never be the same as knowledge or
science?

Theaet. Clearly not, Socrates; and knowledge has now been most distinctly proved to be different from perception.

Soc. But the original aim of our discussion was to find out rather what
knowledge is than what it is not; at the same time we have made some

By thus stressing intrinsic brain activity, Hebb is calling attention to a modern elaboration of what may be regarded as having been implicit in the antithetical viewpoints of the empiricists on the one hand and the rationalists on the other. Empiricism implied a nervous system that remained inactive until aroused by sensory impulses coming from without. As opposed to this view, rationalism implied the existence of intellectual or cerebral factors responsible for the selection and patterning of the stream of sensory impulses. In the following quotation, Hebb (1955, pp. 246–247) supplies both experimental and observational support for this assumption of the brain as an active rather than an inert organ:

A pedagogical experiment . . . had been very impressive in its indication that the human liking for work is not a rare phenomenon, but general. All of the 600-odd pupils in a city school, ranging from 6 to 15 years of age, were suddenly informed that they need do no work whatever unless they wanted to, that the punishment for being noisy and interrupting other's work was to be sent to the playground to play, and that the reward for being good was to be allowed to do more work. In these circumstances, *all* of the pupils discovered within a day or two that, within limits, they preferred work to no work (and incidentally learned more arithmetic and so forth than in previous years).

The phenomenon of work for its own sake is familiar enough to all of us, when the timing is controlled by the worker himself, when "work" is not defined as referring alone to activity imposed from without. Intellectual work may take the form of trying to understand what Robert Browning was trying to say (if anything), to discover what it is in Dali's paintings that can interest others, or to predict the outcome of a paperback mystery. We systematically underestimate the human need of intellectual activity, in one form or another, when we overlook the intellectual component in art and in games. Similarly with riddles, puzzles, and the puzzle-like games of strategy such as bridge, chess, and *go*; the frequency with which man has devised such problems for his own solution is a most significant fact concerning human motivation.

The preceding quotation may serve as a convenient point of departure for considering one additional aspect of modern psychology's claim to scientific status. This claim, as has been mentioned, started with the establishment of psychological laboratories and the introduction of experimental procedures. In the 1880s some viewed this daring innovation as signifying a repudiation of the earlier philosophic approach to psychological issues. By the turn of the century this approach came to be stigmatized as "armchair psychology." What Wundt's philosophical predecessors had to say about mental affairs came to be associated with this disparaging phrase. Armchair psychology, being nonexperimental, tended to connote questionable speculation and unverifiable metaphysical dogmatism.

At this juncture it is pertinent to ask whether this rather common view of

progress, for we no longer seek for knowledge in perception at all, but in that other process, however called, in which the mind is alone and engaged with being.

Theaet. You mean, Socrates, if I am not mistaken, what is called thinking or opining.

Soc. You conceive truly. And now, my friend, please to begin at this point; and having wiped out of your memory all that has preceded, see if you have arrived at any clearer view, and once more say what is knowledge.

Theaet. I cannot say, Socrates, that all opinion is knowledge, because there may be false opinion; but I will venture to assert, that knowledge is true opinion: let this then be my reply; and if this is hereafter disproved, I must try to find another.

Psychology's long past is clearly exemplified in this discussion of the difference between simple sensations and reflection or between perception and knowledge, with knowledge defined as "true opinion." Since Plato was born in 427 B.C. and died in 348 B.C., the empiricist-rationalist debate might be said to date back more than two thousand years. Is it consequently to be relegated to the limbo of dead issues having antiquarian value but devoid of importance for the psychologist of today? Can he dismiss it as outmoded epistemological speculation having possible relevance for the contemporary philosophy student, but of no direct concern to the contemporary psychology student?

As a matter of fact, these age-old epistemological problems continue to be considered by psychologists of the 1960s. For example, in a volume by B. B. Wolman (1960, pp. 499–500) dealing with contemporary psychological theories and systems there is a separate section concerned with "Psychology and the Scientific Method." In the early part of this section there is a discussion of what the author refers to as "Epistemological Problems." Among these problems he considers one already noted by Plato in the passage just quoted. This is the problem of the role of perception in the scientific enterprise or, as Wolman puts it, "how correct" is man's perception of the world and "to what extent" do "his propositions concerning the world . . . correspond to what the world is." In this connection Wolman refers to a modern epistemological distinction between "two basic types of truth: *immanent* and *transcendent* truth."

To understand the nature of this distinction, it might be helpful to note that the word "perception" is employed in two different ways in daily speech. One can talk about seeing or perceiving the point of a joke. To cite another example, one can perceive the words on this page and one can also perceive that 225 is the square of 15. The one kind of perception has to do with noting external sources of stimulation—the world of objects and animals and people—and the other kind refers to noting relations among the inner world of ideas. These two kinds of perception might thus be differentiated as *sensory* perception and *ideational* perception, respectively. Both kinds of perception might deal with "true" propositions, but the "truth" of the sensory kind refers to what actually exists in the external world while that of the ideational kind refers to the internal consistency or freedom from contradiction in what is asserted by the proposition in question.

There need be no external reality correspondning to what is ideationally perceived. In very technical language, the "truth" of what is perceived in this way becomes a matter of what *subsists* rather than what *exists* when sensory perception is involved. Animals are capable of sensory perception, but ideational perception is probably restricted almost exclusively to human beings. The concept of a syllogism will serve as a clarifying illustration. No animal can perceive the "truth" of the conclusion to be derived from these two premises: "All X is Y" and "This Z is X." The letters in question might be made to refer to mythical creatures so that the premises can be changed to read: "All hobgoblins have green eyes" and "This creature is a hobgoblin." To conclude that this creature has green eyes would be correct perception of what follows from these premises, but its correctness or "truth" would not be demonstrable by means of direct sensory observation. Such "truth" is immanent and not transcendent; it subsists while transcendent truth exists. Empiricism is rooted in the latter kind of truth, in what exists, or what is subject to verification by sensory perception. On the other hand, the rationalist tradition is more closely allied to the concept of immanent truth, to what subsists, or what is ideationally perceived. Mathematical "truths" tend to belong to this immanent category. They refer to pure abstractions like the concept of an infinite series of negative numbers or a geometric form having a definite shape but no other physical attribute.

Scientific progress sometimes depends on progress in mathematics. This is another way of saying that the scientist has to be both empiricist as well as rationalist. Another way of putting this is to say that science depends upon both facts and theories. Theories devoid of factual support are tantamount to futile speculation, while facts taken by themselves, no matter how rigorously established, are devoid of scientific significance unless their theoretic import becomes manifest. A telephone directory is replete with facts organized in terms of the system provided by the alphabet, and yet these facts are not "scientific" facts. They may be endowed with "scientific" implications, however, if utilized for testing some hypothesis or theory. For example, the names in the directory might be used to check on various aspects of the psychology of memory. A question having to do with the influence of organization on memory could be investigated by comparing the relative difficulty of memorizing one list of unfamiliar names arranged alphabetically with an equivalent list presented in random order, or comparing a list of names of Scotch extraction with an equivalent list made up of names representative of different nationalities. Should the results come out in favor of the items presented in organized fashion, then the theory that memory efficiency is

partly a function of ordered arrangement of items to be memoriz be given some confirmation. A finding of this sort would be conso what is already known about the relative ease of understanding presented in a well-organized lecture as opposed to the same mat sented in poorly organized fashion. The factor of organization ideational perception. Such perception involves noting relevant rel and logical implications. It exemplifies what the rationalist tra stressed as important in the acquisition of knowledge or mental gr

Many centuries have intervened between what a rationalist like to say about "true opinion" and what a modern laboratory psych to say about results of memory or learning experiments. Howe incidental references to the factor of organization suggest that cism of the laboratory is by no means altogether devoid of a setting. The learner is not just being acted on by the stimulus m *reacts* to this material; and that which makes such reaction possi the rationalist regards as more distinctively cognitive than the s being acted upon.

Rationalism and Sensory Deprivation

The importance of sensory data for the initiation of cogniti was, of course, always stressed by the empiricists. What they failed was the bearing of such data on the maintenance of cognitiv This phase of the traditional empiricist-rationalist controversy is recent development concerned with studies of sensory deprivatic reduction. In one of these studies (Bexton *et al.*, 1954, pp. 70- students served as subjects for an experiment in which they w a day for doing nothing under special conditions of enforced res tions were such as to reduce the amount of ordinary stimul experienced in daily life. Muscular sensations were reduced subjects stretched out in a horizontal position and also by havi long cuffs covering hands and forearms. A plastic shield was p eyes. This translucent device admitted light but rendered it perceive the contour of objects or recognize visual patterns. A lation was controlled by means of a foam rubber cushion pl ears. These restrictions were enforced throughout the day excep or when the subject went to the toilet. Although these stude money, few of them could tolerate this way of earning it for or three days. Six days proved to be the upper limit. The need react to the outside world became increasingly acute and th this "easy" way of earning money to jobs which paid less and physical and mental exertion. This need may be considered a or one which, as D. O. Hebb (1955, p. 246) stated, suggests " brain is built to be active, and that as long as it is supplied nutrition will continue to be active."

armchair psychology is justified. In the two paragraphs quoted from Hebb's article, the first introduces experimental evidence and the second deals with nonexperimental evidence. Do we find scientific evidence in the former and unscientific speculation in the latter? Is what Hebb had to say about efforts to understand poetry and about interest in mystery stories and chess to be viewed as less factual than what he had to say about the children in the "pedagogical experiment" summarized in the first paragraph? Was Hebb writing like a scientific psychologist in this paragraph and like an armchair psychologist in the second? To raise questions like these is to reveal the need for critical examination of the concept of armchair psychology.

The Concept of Armchair Psychology

As a matter of history, the term "armchair psychology" was coined by an American follower of Wundt, E. W. Scripture, in 1895 when Scripture was an instructor at Yale serving under Professor George Trumbull Ladd (1842–1921). In this connection E. G. Boring (1886–1968) wrote (1929, p. 514):

He [Scripture] was a great contrast to the theological and philosophical Ladd, coming into the laboratory with a strong conviction as to the scientific nature of psychology and its mission to work quantitatively upon the mind, ever approaching more and more nearly to the precision of measurement that obtains in physics . . . [His] books still carry the fervor of the '90's: a *new* psychology, soon to be as accurate as physics!

In the preface to his book entitled *The New Psychology,* Scripture referred to Wundt as the greatest psychologist. In the absence of such a tribute to his senior and academic superior, Ladd, one might hazard the guess that Scripture intended his disparagement of armchair psychology as a criticism of the kind of psychology sponsored by "the theological and philosophical" Ladd and certainly not at all the kind of psychology sponsored by Wundt.

Despite the championship of laboratory psychology, Wundt never repudiated his official ties with philosophy. Moreover, in his exposition of the methodology for the "new" psychology he did not rule out nonexperimental means of obtaining psychological data. In his opinion only the more elementary mental processes were amenable to experimental attack. The more complex ones, the so-called higher thought processes, were to be investigated by methods now associated with the field work of cultural anthropologists.

As an ardent Wundtian disciple, Scripture very likely endorsed such nonexperimental procedures as being scientifically respectable and not armchair psychology. In his *The New Psychology* (1898, p. 2) he actually stated that "simple observation of our minds" may supply "general outlines of facts." Evidently such "simple observation" was not to be equated with armchair psychology. He thus did not insist upon laboratory verification of all psychological observations. What Hebb had to say about work for its own sake and the invention of thought-provoking games might well have been accepted by Scripture as scientifically legitimate.

Of course, armchair psychology, in the sense of observations of everyday experience or interpretations based on common knowledge, does not always result in dependable data or valid conclusions. We must distinguish sound armchair psychology from poor armchair psychology. In comparable fashion, sound experimental work is to be distinguished from poor experimental work, for not all published experimental results turn out to be valid. The same applies to many published and unpublished armchair speculations, generalizations, and general impressions sometimes presented as "facts that everybody knows." In some regions there are people quite convinced that "experience" demonstrates the intellectual inferiority of Negroes. Similarly, there are others for whom "experience" has demonstrated the keener business acumen of American industrialists when compared with "foreign" competitors. There are still others who are altogether confident of the fickleness of blonds.

It is possible to add many more examples of the treacherous nature of the kind of thinking resulting in such erroneous conclusions. They all serve to illustrate the hazards of *uncritical* armchair psychology. Many of them could be used to illustrate the concept of a *social stereotype*. The latter concept, it may be noted, serves as a clarifying example of the issue under discussion. Social stereotypes have doubtless been operative in human thinking for many generations. However, their existence was not known to social psychologists until a few decades ago, when they were first described and given their present label. Nor was their detection and description the work of a professional psychologist. This was the work of Walter Lippmann, the well-known political analyst, in his *Public Opinion* (1922). By means of what Scripture called "simple observation," Lippmann succeeded in calling the attention of psychologists to a mental mechanism that had hitherto been overlooked. It was an armchair contribution and not the consequence of a laboratory demonstration. Psychologists came to accept it because, once having been alerted to its possible operation, they were able to confirm Lippmann's pioneer observation in their own experience.

This is not at all an exceptional instance of the way in which the professional outlook of the modern psychologist has been influenced. Many other mental mechanisms have been added to the technical vocabulary of the student of mental life because of keen armchair observations made by others. By way of illustration, it may suffice to mention terms like "intolerance of ambiguity," "rationalization," "scapegoating," "identification," "negativism," "projection," "paranoid thinking," and "autistic thinking." None of these terms, now in the psychologist's everyday professional vocabulary, refer to phenomena first brought to light by means of experimental controls. They are the results of armchair observations made by clinical observers and others.

The present discussion of armchair observations should not be misinterpreted as being an oblique disparagement of experimental observations. Nor is it to be viewed as endorsing all products of armchair observations or theorizing. As has been stated, such products require critical scrutiny before their value can be determined. They often turn out to be unwarranted generalizations or vague speculations or inaccurate descriptions. Occasionally they are prompted by wishful thinking rather than by a desire to adhere to the scientific standard of unprejudiced, realistic thinking; hence the need for careful consideration before accepting them as valid even if they are sponsored by renowned scholars. However, since many of them prove to be valid and enriching contributions to our understanding of mental life, it is unwise to reject such contributions just because of their nonexperimental origin.

As previously mentioned, many of the conceptual constructs employed by clinical psychologists are also of nonexperimental origin. For example, the allusion to wishful thinking in the preceding paragraph constitutes such a construct. The existence of this mode of thinking was not a laboratory discovery but the result of clinical observation. Once it was described and given a convenient name it was a relatively simple matter to confirm its existence both in one's own experience as well as in the experience of others, and before long the phrase "wishful thinking" became common in everyday speech. Analogously, terms like "delusions of grandeur" or "inferiority complex" found their way into the vocabulary of the daily conversation of educated people.

A chief reason for discussing the nature of armchair psychology in the opening chapter of a book concerned with the history of psychology is to guard against a possible failure to appreciate the significance of much of what will be considered in subsequent chapters. After all, since experimental psychology is a late development in the history of the subject, it might be argued that everything that preceded this development was nonexperimental. Consequently, many might feel inclined to characterize the more than two thousand years of such nonexperimental psychology as armchair psychology. As conventionally employed by some modern psychologists, the phrase "armchair psychology" connotes the unproved, and speculative, the unscientific, or sometimes even the mystically vague. Such an unfavorable connotation has sometimes been elicited by the phrase "philosophical psychology" when used to designate the psychological views of men like Plato, Aristotle, Descartes, Spinoza, Hobbes, Berkeley, and Kant. Under the circumstances, "armchair psychology" becomes a synonym for "philosophical psychology." Study of the latter kind of psychology may then appear a somewhat unprofitable venture involving the reading of a mass of material of questionable validity, much of which will have to be unlearned in the light of the later findings of "scientific" psychologists. It is likely to be regarded as more a matter of opinion than of fact or more a matter of faith than of tested knowledge. A view of this sort would seem to make study of the last hundred years of psychology a far more rewarding undertaking than that of the many preceding centuries of psychology.

By this time it ought to be clear that the negative connotation often aroused by references to armchair or philosophical psychology is not necessarily justified. The progress of psychology is by no means the result of resolute repudiation of nonexperimentally derived data and the concomitant pre-occupation with laboratory data. Actually, both types of data have shaped the present status of psychology. When experimental psychology was launched in the 1880s it was not as if the pioneer experimentalists started with no certain knowledge of mental functions or no familiarity with psychological fact. They had a vast number of armchair observations at their disposal. Many of them were active as professors of philosophy and consequently familiar with the philosophical heritage of psychology. They did not spurn all that this legacy implied as they applied themselves to the business of establishing an experimental foundation for psychology. As a result, many pre-experimental insights were woven into the developing pattern of laboratory psychology.

In this sense, experimental psychology did not involve a drastic divorce from philosophical psychology. There was continuity of development. By the time experimental psychology got under way, many of the philosopher-psychologists had already come to the conclusion that psychology was to concern itself with a study of experience as opposed to futile metaphysical arguments about the nature of the soul. The early experimentalists were familiar with these empiricist teachings of the philosophers and some of them viewed their laboratory endeavors as rooted in such teachings. For Wundt, psychology was the study of immediate experience. What he under-took in proposing to make psychology experimental might thus be regarded as in line with the empiricist tradition in philosophical psychology and not necessarily as a sharp break with his philosophical predecessors.

Study of psychology's philosophic past, it should now be evident, is not to be viewed as an unrewarding, antiquarian pursuit to be stigmatized as arm-chair study. As will be brought out in the subsequent chapters, this philo-sophic past is related to many current problems and deals with many mental phenomena now integrated into the body of accepted principles of general psychology. The perspective of history is thus likely to promote richer and more profound understanding of the present. It is an armchair perspective; but to recognize it as such, it can now be seen, is not tantamount to a dis-paraging statement. In fact, the discussion of the phrase "armchair psychol-ogy" in the present chapter involved consideration of the history of the phrase. When examined in the light of this history, the nonscientific or anti-scientific connotations sometimes aroused by the phrase were found to be unjustified. This minor excursion into history might in itself be used to illustrate what had just been stated regarding the way in which study of the history of psychology can promote more penetrating understanding of contemporary issues.

Of course armchair psychology involves theorizing about and reflection upon the facts of laboratory data as well as the facts of common experience. However, such theorizing and reflection are an important factor in scientific work. Creative scientific activity calls for hard thinking to guide the quest for significant observations as well as to interpret the soundness of conclusions based upon such observations. Thinking of this kind is not devoid of speculative features. This is especially true of *original* thinking. In the words of Charles Darwin: "Without speculation there is no good and original observation." If this be so, then even the speculative aspects of some armchair psychology may have scientific value. It all depends upon the observational consequences of the speculation; for the crux of scientific investigation is relevant and accurate observation. This applies to the observation or perception of fact as well as to relations among facts, to sensory perception as well as to ideational perception.

References

Bexton, W. H., Heron, W., and Scott, T. H. "Effects of Decreased Variation in the Sensory Environment," *Canadian Journal of Psychology*, 1954, *8*, 70–76.

Boring, E. G. *A History of Experimental Psychology*. New York: The Century Company, 1929.

Brett, G. S. "History of Psychology" in *Encyclopaedia Britannica*, Vol. 18, 14th ed., 1929.

Carr, H. A. *An Introduction to Space Perception*. New York: Longmans, Green and Company, 1935.

Clarke, A. M. "History of Astronomy," in *Encyclopaedia Britannica*, Vol. 2, 14th ed., 1929.

Freud, S. "From the History of an Infantile Neurosis," in *Collected Papers*. London: The Hogarth Press, 1950, III, 473–584.

Hebb, D. O. "Drives and the C.N.S." (Conceptual Nervous Systems), *Psychological Review*, 1955, *62*, 243–254.

Jowett, B. (trans.). *The Dialogues of Plato*, 4th ed. Vol. II, Vol. III. Oxford: Clarendon Press, 1953. Reprinted by permission of the Clarendon Press.

Jung, C. G. "On Psychical Energy," in *Collected Works*, Vol. 8. New York: Pantheon Press, 1953.

Lippmann, W. *Public Opinion*. New York: The Macmillan Company, 1922.

Scripture, E. W. *The New Psychology*. New York: Charles Scribner's Sons, 1898.

Wightman, W. P. D. *The Growth of Scientific Ideas*. New Haven: Yale University Press, 1953.

Wolman, B. B. *Contemporary Theories and Systems in Psychology*. New York: Harper and Brothers, 1960.

2

Foundations of Science
in Philosophy

As was mentioned in Chapter 1, the psychology of the present century is an outgrowth of the philosophy of many previous centuries. It might be more accurate to use a plural form by referring to the psychologies of the present and the philosophies of the past; for the existence of various schools or systems of psychology is not unrelated to psychology's philosophic heritage. Before considering the nature of this heritage, it is desirable to clear up some possible sources of confusion or misunderstanding regarding the relationship of philosophy to science in general and to psychology in particular.

At one time, problems of physics were discussed in lectures on *natural* philosophy, just as psychological problems were regarded as falling within the scope of *mental* philosophy. Thus both physics and psychology have historical roots in philosophy. Moreover, both fields eventually branched off and became more or less autonomous disciplines. In physics this took place much earlier. Psychology continued as a branch of philosophy in many universities until the late 1890s and in some institutions until the 1920s. Often the separation from philosophy was not signalized by an abrupt divorce marked by the establishment of a separate department of psychology. Instead there was a period of transition during which college catalogues, although supplying separate course descriptions for work in psychology—even laboratory work—nevertheless listed these courses as under the auspices of a bifurcated Department of Philosophy and Psychology. This nomenclature suggested a close relationship between the two fields, just as the catalogue reference to a Department of Botany and Zoology pointed to a close relationship between these branches of biology.

Going back to the turn of the century, when these independent departments of psychology first came into being, one finds most of them headed by men whose academic backgrounds included rather extensive work in philosophy.

26

Many of them were as well equipped to teach courses in the one area as in the other. In the early years of the American Psychological Association, there were two occasions when the psychologist elevated to its presidency was also a philosopher of sufficient eminence to be elected to the presidency of the equivalent national organization of philosophers. Also, most graduate students of the period had taken undergraduate work in philosophy as preparation for their study of the new science. The infant science of psychology was not quite ready to sever its dependence on its parental affiliation with mental philosophy.

Now some fifty or more years later, when the new science has achieved sufficient growth to be viewed as definitely postadolescent, it seems to have a need to carve out its own future on its own terms in what sometimes appears to be active defiance of the philosophic guidance of its infancy. In less metaphoric language, courses in philosophy are no longer regarded as essential prerequisites for graduate work in psychology. As a result the student is less prepared for study of the history of psychology than was his grandfather in the early 1900s. To understand a good portion of this history he has to familiarize himself with concepts which originated in psychology's philosophic past and which his grandfather had already considered in connection with the study of the history of philosophy. This may serve as a reminder of the extent to which the latter history and the history of psychology overlap.

Philosophical Versus Scientific Psychology

Philosophers have had and continue to have an active professional interest in mental life. The results of their analyses are sometimes designated as *philosophical* psychology in contrast to the *scientific* psychology of professional psychologists. Some people infer that such a contrast implies more speculative theorizing in the case of the former and more tested knowledge in the case of the latter. An inference of this sort is not altogether justified because, as was indicated at the close of the preceding chapter, scientists do not shun speculation. Incidentally, the psychological dictionary by English and English (1958, p. 516) explicitly states in its definition of "speculation" that "speculation has an important place in discovery and even in verification." The two kinds of psychology are thus not to be differentiated in terms of the philosophical being almost entirely speculative and the psychological rejecting speculation. Actually, the differentiation was not made until experimental procedures were introduced into psychology. Results obtained by such procedures were then referred to as *scientific* since they were the outcome of laboratory observations. It then became a matter of descriptive convenience to think of the earlier nonexperimental psychological observations as *philosophical*. Those who classified nonexperimental observations as armchair psychology came to use the term "philosophical psychology" in a derogatory sense.

To revert to what was discussed in the previous chapter, such disparagement, it will be recalled, is not always justified. Much of the armchair psychologizing of the pre-Wundtian philosophers was empirical in nature and not a matter of metaphysical dogmatism. Its empirical setting rendered confirmation by others possible. For example, Thomas Hobbes, one of the seventeenth-century philosophers, called attention to what is now described as the difference between free and controlled association. He described this as a difference between "guided fancy" and "unguided fancy," and his examples rendered it possible for others to note the difference in question by observing their own "fancies." In fact, the nature of most of the principles of association was noted and confirmed in this manner long before the rise of experimental psychology. By observing one's own experience, the validity of a given "armchair" teaching could be subjected to observational check. There was nothing obscurely metaphysical about such straightforward inspection of the flow of ideas, and indeed its solid grounding in what could be verified in experience made it an empirical rather than a metaphysical affair.

But it was not experimental, because it was not the result of a *measured* control of the conditions of observation. This innovation of control, stressed by Wundt and his followers, marks the distinction between empirical and experimental psychology. Both kinds of psychology appeal to experience and neither one is concerned with metaphysical questions about the ultimate nature of life or the soul or the body or God or gods. Such ultimate questions cannot be settled either by an appeal to direct experience or by means of laboratory experiments. In this sense a consideration of such themes lies outside of the scope of scientific investigation.

All such questions dealing with the nature of the cosmos and human existence in any final or ultimate sense belong to *metaphysics* and not to psychology or biology or physics or any other distinctive field of scientific investigation. When one comes across a statement by a psychologist to the effect that an opinion expressed by another psychologist is "just philosophical" and not "scientific," the derogatory implication is usually a reference to metaphysics and not to philosophy as a whole. In the previously mentioned dictionary by English and English, this view is clearly stated in connection with their definition of "metaphysics" as "that branch of philosophy concerned with the ultimate nature of existence." They then amplify the definition as follows (p. 320):

> In psychology, the term is nearly always one of reproach since the metaphysical has no place in the science of psychology; but there is no imputation that metaphysics as such is not perfectly legitimate and even necessary.

In some respects it is "even necessary" for psychologists to know something about metaphysics so that they will not blunder by defending a metaphysical proposition without recognizing its metaphysical status. For example, to maintain that all mental phenomena are ultimately reducible to what physicists describe as electrons and protons, as was done by the behaviorist A. P. Weiss (1929), would constitute such a blunder. Similarly, to base a system of psychology on the conviction that ultimately the entire universe is spiritual in nature would be to espouse a metaphysical as opposed to a scientific conviction.

Metaphysicians argue about questions of monism, dualism, and pluralism. Those who hold that fundamentally there is only one kind of ultimate "stuff" in the world are *monists* irrespective of the way in which they conceive of such an ultimate entity or principle. Some may conceive of it as inherently material or physical while others may advocate a monism inherently mental or spiritual. In contrast, *dualists* argue for recognition of the existence of both kinds of primordial "stuff," while the *pluralists* insist there are more than two kinds. There are no scientific criteria by means of which such metaphysical arguments can be settled. Consequently, as scientists, psychologists ought to be neutral on such metaphysical issues.

However, this counsel should not be interpreted to mean the refusal to note possible differences between events commonly classified as mental on the one hand and those classified as physical on the other. A scientist is not to be criticized as being metaphysically dualistic if he calls attention to such a distinction. For his purposes it may be legitimate to regard the task of translating a passage from Swedish to English as *mental* work and to regard the erosion of a cliff as a *physical* phenomenon. In doing so he would not be saying anything about the ultimate "stuff" which renders translation from one language to another possible and which is to be differentiated from some fundamental "stuff" responsible for soil erosion. His "dualism" might be a matter of descriptive convenience introduced to facilitate his study of a given problem. A clarifying example of this viewpoint is supplied by the following excerpt from a discussion of the "Brain and the Mind" in the volume by W. Penfield and L. Roberts dealing with *Speech and Brain-Mechanisms* (1959, pp. 10–11):

Theorists . . . may be able to give up a dualistic terminology. But biologists are not theorists. And there is no place in scientific medicine for the unprovable hypothesis. We must be content to study man and animal by the scientific method, using the language of "busy common sense." This is the language of dualism.

We have at present no basis for a scientific explanation of the *brain-mind relationship*. We can only continue to study the brain without philosophical prejudice. And if the day should ever dawn when scientific analysis of body and brain solves the "mystery," all men who have sought the truth in all sincerity will rejoice alike: the professing materialist and the dualist, the scientist and the philosopher, the agnostic and the convinced worshipper. Surely none need fear the truth.

As experimental neurophysiologists, Penfield and Roberts thus find the "language of dualism" useful in their application of "scientific method" applied to the study of brain functions. Such language does not commit them to any fixed metaphysical doctrine. It is a matter of descriptive convenience like references to the sun rising or setting without such a phrase implying ignorance or denial of heliocentric teachings. Similarly, the description of a field as flat and level is not to be construed as a disbelief in the earth as round. Such references and descriptions may serve as examples of the language of "busy common sense."

The very notion of "commonsense" is itself a good example of the way in which philosophy has influenced psychology. As will be brought out later, the idea of "a common sense" in contradistinction to a special sense like vision or smell stems from Aristotle. The special senses have definite receptor structures and known neural connections with the central nervous system; but there is no known anatomic basis for commonsense any more than there is for a sense of humor. However, this does not justify one in refusing to employ phrases like "commonsense" or "sense of humor" because they are unscientific locutions with dubious "dualistic" implications.

Just what constitutes scientific language and in what respects such language is to be distinguished from philosophic language raise somewhat troublesome issues. Another way of putting this is to ask whether scientific concepts are devoid of philosophic implications and, conversely, whether philosophic concepts are devoid of scientific implications. The popular stereotype of the scientist as the man in white in relentless pursuit of laboratory truth and the philosopher as the bewhiskered professor lost in profound contemplative abstractions in some ivory tower is both misleading and contrary to fact. It is misleading because it suggests that, unlike the scientist, the philosopher ignores the facts of daily experience and of laboratory data. It is also contrary to fact to imply that scientists rarely if ever become immersed in abstractions.

One reason for mentioning this stereotype has to do with its possible influence on the thinking of some psychologists. The word "science" has become a prestige term, whereas by some people the word "philosophy" tends to be used in a derogatory sense. Sixty and more years ago, many professors prided themselves on being known as both psychologists and philosophers, but in modern times a psychologist may not feel complimented by being called a philosopher. He prefers to be known as a scientist. It is almost as if he believes ignorance of philosophy to be a means of enhancing one's scientific virtue.

The "New" or "Scientific" Philosophy

In fairness to such psychologists it is well to note that some modern philosophers have themselves been decidedly critical of portions of traditional philosophy. In particular they repudiate professional concern with metaphysical speculations as meaningless or futile or both, preferring to devote their energies to problems capable of solution. In their rejection of the speculative and rationalistic systems of traditional philosophy they are as antiphilosophical as those psychologists who seem to view *all* philosophy as scientifically worthless or at least not likely to contribute to the clarification of the problems of science. But the philosophers in question do not go to such extremes. In fact, they see their professional role as more or less restricted to enhancing such clarification.

They may even refer to themselves as *scientific* philosophers, for they are chiefly interested in the analysis of the logical implications of scientific method as exemplified in the work of specialists in physics, astronomy, biology, and other special sciences. Just as those pioneers who first applied laboratory methods to the study of mental life talked about the "new" psychology, so those who think of themselves as scientific philosophers talk about the "new" philosophy. A glimpse of what this new orientation involves is supplied by what H. Reichenbach, one of its leading advocates, has to say about it in connection with a discussion (1951, p. 123) of its origin:

> Just as the new philosophy originated as a by-product of scientific research, the men who made it were hardly philosophers in the professional sense. They were mathematicians, physicists, biologists, or psychologists. Their philosophy resulted from the attempts to find solutions to problems encountered in scientific research, problems which defied the technical means thus far employed and called for a reexamination of the foundations and the goals of knowledge. . . .
>
> It was not until our generation that a new class of philosophers arose, who were trained in the technique of the sciences, including mathematics, and who concentrated on philosophical analysis. These men saw that a new distribution of work was indispensable, that scientific research does not leave a man time enough to do the work of logical analysis, and that conversely logical analysis demands a concentration which does not leave time for a scientific work—a concentration which because of its aiming at clarification rather than discovery may even impede scientific productivity. The professional philosopher of science is the product of this development.

Description Versus Explanation

In some ways it might be that Reichenbach's distinction between discovery and clarification is akin to the distinction between description and explanation. All four terms have something to do with the acquisition of knowledge and, of course, such acquisition is a core factor in the concept of science in the light of its derivation from the Latin "*scire*," meaning "to know." In present usage, science has come to refer to systematized knowledge and verifiable generalizations or laws reflecting the systematization.

Systematization by itself is not enough to establish a science. If it were, then dictionaries and telephone directories would be textbooks of science, for they are highly systematized presentations of factual data. For a science to come into being, there must be more than the artificial or conventional organization supplied by recourse to the alphabet. The organization or system must relate to relevant classification of the factual material being studied as exemplified by a botanist grouping plant life, a haematologist classifying blood types, a geologist noting resemblances and differences in rock strata, or a psychopathologist seeking to order or systematize the multiplicity of facts symptomatic of mental disorder.

All such classification involves observation and description of the items being classified. This constitutes the *descriptive* level of scientific endeavor. The first person to note and describe the four chambers of the human heart was thus making a contribution to the future science of anatomy. Later, when the structuralistic features of these chambers were described in terms of their functions in the regulation of circulation, the *explanatory* level of a particular scientific quest might be said to have been reached. From this viewpoint a scientific explanation is an elaborated description. Furthermore, to continue with this simple example, the person who first noted the existence of ventricles and auricles made a scientific *discovery,* and this discovery was *clarified* once the function of these cardiac structures was explained.

It might thus be said that description is to explanation as discovery is to clarification. Such a statement in itself requires clarification. It may become clearer once the meaning of the word "description" in this context is brought into focus. A given scene may be described from a variety of viewpoints. The description of a person, for example, will vary with the nature of the viewpoint adopted, which usually is determined by the objective to be reached. Mere enumeration of items noted about the person is not a description. This is what a young child may do if asked what it sees in connection with a visitor. The resulting list of random items like button, a finger, a shoe, glasses, and so on would constitute enumeration rather than description.

A description, to be meaningful, must be related to some purpose. Thus the medical description of a person will be different from the one supplied by the man's tailor, and this, in turn, will differ from descriptions supplied by his wife, his son, his golf instructor, an employee, or his banker. Each such differing description can be viewed as an answer to such varied questions as what is the man like as a patient, as a sartorial problem, as a husband, a father, a golfer, a boss, or a credit risk. Each one of these questions involves *selection* of items of appearance or behavior relevant to a given viewpoint and neglect of other items. The golf instructor may describe the man as clumsy while the wife may refer to her husband as a graceful dancer. This factor of selectivity renders description different from mere passive sensory impression of the man. It calls for discriminative judgment of a vast array of impressions and memories in order to determine which ones might serve to answer the question the resulting description is supposed to answer.

In some ways a good description may turn out to be an explanation. This happens when the items included in the description serve to justify some generalization implicit in the description, as when a son starts his description of a father by calling him an "impatient" man and then proceeds to refer to other characteristics and mannerisms. Not until he tells about the father's annoyance when dinner is five minutes late or when the telephone is not answered after the first ring is the son's reference to the father's impatience explained.

As stated earlier, the elaborated description becomes an explanation. It is also correct to say that the specific instances mentioned by the son *clarify* what he meant by describing the father as an impatient man. Moreover, his recall of these incidents might be viewed as "discoveries" if they are thought of as a consequence of a search for ways of answering a question like "What makes you call your father an impatient man?" The "discovered" incidents serve to clarify the original description of the father as impatient.

Origins of Scientific Reasoning

In some respects the "new philosophy" may be regarded as an outgrowth of portions of the "old philosophy." The new approach involves repudiation of futile metaphysical speculation along with eager endorsement and study of the methods and results of scientific work. It makes a specialty of examining the nature of the methods by which a scientific view of the world is achieved. This means examining the procedures which result in the growth and modification of scientific knowledge. In this restriction to scientific knowledge the advocate of the "new philosophy" continues to reflect the epistemological interests of some of his precursors, for they too applied themselves to the task of understanding the nature of scientific method. For them, such a task was a portion of the philosopher's job. In this connection we may note that histories of philosophy usually devote some space to discussions of scientific method when referring to the teachings of men like Roger Bacon and Francis Bacon.

Roger Bacon (c.1220–c.1292), although a monk of the Franciscan order, was among the first of medieval scholastics to question the authority of Aristotle. In fact, as a result of what the Church regarded as his heretical views, he suffered imprisonment for more than ten years. He urged the importance of squaring theological and philosophical teachings with the facts of experience. Moreover, he advocated the introduction of methods of critical scholarship with reference to such teachings by stressing the importance of studying original sources in the original instead of relying upon translations. Incidentally, some of the manuscripts of the period were translations of translations, as of a Greek work into Arabic and then into Latin. In the process, mistakes were made and remained uncorrected, with the result that what the original author had written came to be modified and sometimes distorted.

It is of much more direct relevance, however, to call attention to Bacon's recognition of the importance of checking casual experience by means of measurement and *experiment*. In fact, in the words of B. A. G. Fuller (1945, p. 428), Bacon "is the first thinker in recorded history to use the phrase 'experimental science' and may be regarded as the father of the experimental method."

The fruitfulness of the experimental method, as mentioned in the previous chapter, became evident in the work of the seventeenth-century scientists. This was the century of philosophers like Hobbes, Descartes, and Spinoza, of Shakespeare in good part, and of Queen Elizabeth's last years. In many ways it might be viewed as the century that ushered in the modern era. It was also the century of Francis Bacon (1561–1626). Like his namesake, Roger Bacon, Francis Bacon was also opposed to settling questions of fact by appeal to the authority of Aristotle. For him, knowledge, to be useful, must result in control over nature. The trite phrase "Knowledge is power" is of Baconian origin. This power, Bacon taught, should be exercised in planned investigation of the kind employed by a successful inventor. Successful invention depends upon understanding and mastery of the forces of nature.

He was especially concerned with factors that might interfere with correct understanding—factors of prejudiced thinking, distorted perception, and careless language. Such factors are like phantoms that predispose one to erroneous interpretations. In his *Novum Organum,* Bacon listed four classifications of what he called *idols:* those of the "tribe," the "cave," the "marketplace," and the "theater." Idols of the "tribe" referred to misconceptions so widely prevalent as to be viewed as characteristic of human nature. An example of this kind of idol might be the rather common tendency to regard personal disaster incident to an earthquake or a storm at sea as punishment for sin. An impersonal natural event is thus interpreted not in terms of purely physical causes but in terms of the way the outcome affects personal welfare. It is like the interpretation of a child who concludes that "it stopped raining so that we could have our picnic."

Idols of the "cave" are more regional or provincial than those of the "tribe." They have to do with the influence of unjustified prejudice in coloring our judgments of persons or things. Fixed notions about national or racial characteristics like the alleged stinginess of the Scots or the intellectual inferiority of Negroes might serve as convenient examples. One assimilates such erroneous ideas in the course of growing up in communities where ideas of this sort are current. Nor are such ideas restricted to prejudices about people. They may refer to things as well. In the latter case the prejudices may be classified as superstitions by the enlightened. That wearing a particular kind of ornament may ward off misfortune is an instance of such superstitious thinking.

Warped thinking may also be attributed to the idols of the "marketplace." By this metaphor Bacon was referring to the way in which error and misunderstanding may result from failure to employ language with careful attention to the meaning of words used. A common instance is the careless use of words like "always," "never," and "all." Its linkage with the marketplace is a reminder of the language of flamboyant advertising.

The fourth class of idols, the one referred to as those of the "theater," pertains to errors occasioned by uncritical allegiance to the teachings of authority. In Bacon's view, acceptance of something as valid merely because

ROGER BACON (1214?–1294)

FRANCIS BACON (1561–1626)

it was in line with Aristotelian tradition constituted a clear instance of this source of potential error, for Bacon was definitely anti-Aristotelian.

By way of warding off the distorting influence of his four classes of idols, Bacon introduced some positive recommendations that constitute an early formulation of the principles of scientific method. These principles, which later came to be called the *Baconian method,* stressed the importance of an empirical approach to knowledge by urging, first, an accurate description of the body of facts or items being studied. This was to be followed by their careful ordering into three groups: (a) those instances which showed the presence of the phenomenon being investigated; (b) those demonstrating the absence of the phenomenon; and (c) those revealing its presence in varying degrees. It is well to note this early recognition of the importance of the quest for negative instances as exemplified by the second of these three groups. This kind of quest in later experimental design came to be known as the *control* experiment.

The Baconian method emphasized the importance of inductive, as contrasted with deductive, procedures. Induction refers to the transition from a group of particular events to the unifying principle or generalization, whereas deduction refers to the transition from a generalization to some specific event. The quest for dependable scientific generalizations, Bacon held, was to be governed by his three ways of classifying items or data being investigated. Appropriate grouping, it was implied, would facilitate detection of an underlying principle or law.

In suggesting three modes of grouping, Bacon was guarding against some inductive errors. What is sometimes designated *induction by simple enumeration* is an especially familiar instance of such an error. It occurs, for example, when the mere recital of a series of incidents is supplied as proof in support of a given conclusion. Thus a tourist returning from a shopping expedition in Paris may report, "All French tradesmen try to take advantage of foreigners." Similarly, some housewife may enumerate three or four unpleasant experiences with Japanese gardeners or Italian cooks to demonstrate that "Japanese gardeners are impudent" and that Italian cooks are "splendid as cooks, but leave the kitchen in a mess." Such simple illustrations are readily recognized as instances of hasty generalizations. However, if twenty to thirty people in a group contribute incidents in support of the given conclusion and nobody can cite contradictory experiences, would this not suffice to establish the soundness of the generalization? In answer to this kind of question, Bertrand Russell (1945, p. 543) employed a parable to show that "we may go astray if we trust too implicitly in induction by simple enumeration."

The parable had to do with a census enumerator assigned to get a record of each inhabitant in a village in Wales. The first Welshman gave the name of William Williams. This also turned out to be the name of the second person interviewed. With monotonous regularity the third, fourth, fifth, sixth, and all the others questioned gave the same name. Relying on induction by enumeration, the census officer decided to dispense with further questioning and to devote the rest of the day to fishing, since by that time it was clear everybody in the village was named William Williams. But induction by enumeration failed even in this case, because there was one villager named John Jones.

In this parable the name of John Jones was an exception to the census taker's rule regarding William Williams as the exclusively prevalent name. This single exception *proved* the rule's weakness. It would have been a better rule had this exception not occurred. Exceptions prove rules in this sense of *testing* them and not, as is sometimes popularly believed, in the sense of confirming their validity by contradicting or being at variance with the rule.

As envisaged by Bacon, the inductive method may be construed as a reaction against scholastic dogmatism. It made observation and collection of facts the beginning of scientific endeavor. Accordingly, it might be said to have been the expression of a philosophic recognition of the seventeenth-century beginnings of modern science, in that science as dependable knowledge emerges from the bedrock of dependable observation. This holds true for the efforts of laboratory workers as well as for the observations of field naturalists and clinicians in hospitals and consulting rooms. Moreover, in the sense that experience refers to that which has been observed, Bacon's method may also be viewed as in harmony with the spirit of empiricism.

However, as Russell (1945, pp. 544–545) points out, Bacon's teaching was "faulty through insufficient emphasis on hypothesis." Without some guiding hypothesis, observation is likely to be random and fruitless. Merely watching children at play is not apt to result in a contribution to child psychology. Unless the observer is watching for the purpose of finding an answer to some definite question, he will not know what facts to observe. The function of hypotheses is to supply him with relevant questions to put to the scene being inspected. Hypotheses are tentative or preliminary guesses as to what might be significant. Such guesses pave the way for selective observation. They enable the investigator to watch for, pay attention to, and note down specific facts and to ignore others. A question like "Is cooperative play more common among kindergarten boys than kindergarten girls?" will involve a different set of facts from a question like "Do kindergarten children in the course of their play give evidence of what amounts to racial prejudice in the adult world?"

Bacon seemed to assume that a promising hypothesis would suggest itself once the observed facts were grouped according to some orderly scheme. What he failed to note was the need for theorizing before embarking on the collection of facts. Without this, as Russell puts it, "the mere multiplicity of facts is baffling." Even after the relevant facts have been collected in accordance with some provisional hypothesis, additional theorizing may often be necessary to account for the facts in question. Russell regards this as "the most difficult part of scientific work, and the part where great ability is indispensable." This is the crux of creative thinking in science. As yet there is no way of *teaching* this kind of thinking. In the words of Russell: "No method has been found which would make it possible to invent hypotheses by rule."

It is also well to recall that scientific thinking involves deduction as well as the Baconian kind of induction. This is especially the case once a working hypothesis has been formulated. A formulation of this sort constitutes a provisional generalization, and to test its soundness the investigator has to infer its probable consequences when applied to observable phenomena. This shift from the generalization to a concrete manifestation of its operation constitutes deductive thinking. In brief, from the viewpoint of logic, scientific thinking involves both inductive and deductive operations.

Logic and Science

As verified or verifiable knowledge, it should now be evident that science is not independent of logic. That branch of philosophy is concerned with the validity of reasoning or with the correctness of conclusions inferred from given facts, assumptions, or premises. It is related to science in the way that grammar is related to language. Grammar serves as a *normative* study in the sense of specifying rules governing standards of correct use of the parts of speech. Just as one can speak or write correctly without awareness of formal grammatical rules, so one can reason validly without knowledge of formal logic. Children learn to talk long before they are introduced to grammar as a special school subject. Analogously, scientific discoveries were and are made by investigators ignorant of the subject matter of textbooks of logic. Grammatical rules are implicit in the use of language just as logical rules are implicit in scientific reasoning. Nevertheless, by making such rules explicit one achieves clearer understanding and more effective control of the processes involved.

The separate branches of science like geology, chemistry, psychology, astronomy, and the rest came into being more or less independently of any deliberate consideration of the logic involved in their existence and development. Investigation of such logical considerations came much later when the logic of scientific method emerged as a separate field of philosophic study. The latter study has given rise to the relatively modern *unity of science movement*. R. Carnap, one of the leaders of this movement, refers to it as focused on a "logical analysis of science." He indicates the meaning of the latter phrase in the following passage (1955, p. 49):

> In any case, when we ask whether there is a unity in science, we mean this as a question of logic, concerning logical relationships between the terms and the laws of the various branches of science. Since it belongs to the logic of science, the question concerns scientists and logicians alike.

In terms of this viewpoint it would be difficult to justify the maintenance of a sharp cleavage between science and philosophy in general or between psychology and philosophy in particular. Leaders of science are no more desirous of training their students to be "unphilosophical" scientists than professors of philosophy strive to educate their students to become "unscientific" philosophers. For psychologists to divorce themselves from concern with philosophical issues may not, as some seem to hold, necessarily enhance the status of psychology as a science. This applies with especial force to logic as a branch of philosophy and to the whole unity of science movement within contemporary philosophy. Incidentally, the psychologist E. Brunswik (1955) has elaborated the "conceptual framework of psychology" in terms of the latter movement.

In reality, of course, modern psychology has not altogether ignored the subject of logic. It is reflected in mental tests in items calling for reasoning in dealing with problems of arithmetic or with the detection of absurdities or with the understanding of analogies. It is also reflected in the use of concepts like rationalization, autistic thinking, confabulation, delusional thinking, and kindred terms having to do with the pathology of thought.

The intimate relationship between such pathology and logic has become the subject of explicit interest in recent decades. For example, according to S. Arieti (1948), "The study of logic in mental illness may clarify several problems which have not yet been clarified by other methods of research." In this connection Arieti distinguishes between thinking governed by principles of ordinary logic and the thinking of primitive man whose logic is sometimes designated as *paleologic,* on the assumption that it harks back to older pre-Aristotelian ways of reasoning.[1] To illustrate this distinction, Arieti refers to studies of the thinking of schizophrenic patients with particular reference to studies undertaken by E. Von Domarus (1954).

The delusional thinking of the schizophrenic, as described by Von Domarus, is not altogether remote from some familiar, everyday modes of fallacious reasoning. Unchecked conclusions based upon the principle of "guilt by association" are the results of such reasoning. For example, to infer that a man has criminal inclinations solely because he was seen talking to a known criminal may be just as unwarranted as to infer that another man is a chemist because he and a prominent chemist are good friends. In both instances the association in question is made the basis for identification. Identification of this sort is unwarranted because it fails to consider the large number of circumstances that may bring people together. The isolated observation of a man in conversation with a criminal justifies no valid conclusion, for the conversation may have no bearing on events of interest to the police. In actuality, it may refer to a Red Cross contribution or to a request for directions to a certain hotel or to the need for a match. Such topics, being altogether devoid of any direct bearing on antisocial behavior, would not prove anything regarding the man's criminal intent. To identify him as a criminal because of being seen in association with a criminal would thus constitute an obvious fallacy.

---

[1] For a recent critique of Arieti's use of the paleologic concept, see M. Henle (1962, pp. 375–377).

The fallacy in question becomes even more obvious when reduced to the form of a syllogism. In the syllogism, the major premise states that Mr. X is a known criminal, while the minor premise states that Mr. Y was seen talking to Mr. X. For these two premises to result in a conclusion about Mr. Y being a criminal would constitute fallacious reasoning. It would be the kind of reasoning characteristic of paleologic or the sort of thinking Von Domarus found to be implicit in many schizophrenic delusions.

In the preceding major premise, "Mr. X" is the subject and the phrase "is a known criminal" constitute the logical predicate. Similarly, in the minor premise "Mr. Y" is the subject while the predicate is stated as "was seen talking to Mr. X." In reality the only conclusion justified by these premises is "So what?" There is no way of determining what the two subjects have in common. This is what makes it a poor syllogism. In a good syllogism the subject of the minor premise can be identified with the subject of the major premise. By way of illustration the following syllogism may serve:

Major premise: All dogs are mammals.
Minor premise.   Rover is a dog.
Conclusion: Rover is a mammal.

Here Rover, the subject of the minor premise, is included in "all dogs," the subject of a major premise. Rover is identified with dogs; and it is such identification of subjects, as contrasted with predicates, that promotes valid reasoning. In schizophrenic reasoning, on the other hand, it is identification with predicates that results in invalid conclusions. This hypothetical example will serve to show what is meant by identification of predicates:

Major premise: Kings have independent incomes.
Minor premise: Our senator has an independent income.
Conclusion: Our senator is a king.

To cite a less hypothetical example: one schizophrenic patient, upon learning that her doctor understood Hebrew, became very excited since she decided her doctor was Christ. She identified him with Christ because Christ also understood Hebrew. Both of these last two examples illustrate the basic teaching of Von Domarus. For purposes of descriptive convenience it might be called the *principle of Von Domarus*. This principle, as formulated by Arieti, reads as follows:

Whereas the normal person accepts identity only upon the basis of identical subjects, the paleologican accepts identity based upon identical predicates.

The bizarre nature of schizophrenic thinking or of the dreams of normal people is thus not, as is commonly held, exclusively a product of the disruption of logical controls by strong wishes. Irrational thinking does not necessarily indicate absence of logic. It may be the result of a logic different from ordinary logic. Paleologic is such a different logic and is reflected in the thinking of primitive man, of young children, of schizophrenic patients,[2] and often in the dreams of normal adults.

Logic, traditionally a branch of philosophy, it can now be seen, has contributed not only to scientific method in general but to current psychological research in particular. Furthermore, much that would otherwise remain inexplicable in the psychology of mental disturbance may be resolved by application of the Von Domarus principle. In terms of a broader perspective, Arieti has made the same point: ". . . the study of logic in mental illnesses may clarify several problems which have not yet been clarified by other methods of research." He does not mean this in the sense of having the investigator become a specialist in logic, but rather in the more restricted sense of having him become familiar with "a few elementary principles" of logic.

Rapprochement of Philosophy and Psychology

As a matter of fact, the antiphilosophical attitudes of many psychologists is no longer as pronounced and as prevalent as it once was.[3] This became clearly evident a few years ago when the philosopher H. Feigl was invited to address the members of the American Psychological Association at one of their annual conventions. The address dealt with what he called the "philosophical embarrassments of psychology," and some of his observations may serve as a helpful summary of what has already been mentioned in this chapter regarding the past and present status of psychology's relations with philosophy. Early in his address Feigl had this to say (1959, p. 115):

---

[2] This need not be taken to mean that schizophrenic patients will necessarily have recourse to paleologic when tested by means of syllogisms of the formal, academic sort. For details see L. Gottesman and L. J. Chapman, "Syllogistic Reasoning in Schizophrenia," *Journal of Consulting Psychology,* 1960, *24,* 250–255.

It is well to note that syllogisms as such, while enshrined in textbooks of logic, do not ordinarily characterize the deductive operations of mathematicians, scientists, or working detectives. Furthermore, modern logicians have demonstrated shortcomings and inadequacies in Aristotelian accounts of the syllogism. For details see Russell (1945, pp. 195–202).

[3] As a matter of fact, what amounts to a pro-philosophical attitude has now emerged within the structure of the American Psychological Association. The Association's structure involves more than twenty divisions reflecting the diverse interests of its membership. Division 24, called the Division of Philosophical Psychology, is one of the newest. It became a constituent division of the Association in 1962 in response to a request by a group of sponsoring psychologists who had complained: "There is presently no provision within APA for the facilitation of philosophical sophistication among its interested members, no forum in which the problems of logic and morals, religion and social theory, epistemology and metaphysics, or even philosophy of science, all becoming so visibly a part of psychology's widening horizons, can be productively discussed."

Let me say immediately that the embarrassments are mutual, they go both ways. Important philosophical issues keep bothering the psychologists; and many significant developments in psychology have baffled the philosophers. It is true that the same holds also for mathematics, physics, biology, and the social sciences; but the philosophical issues have a very special poignancy in connection with psychology.

Philosophy and psychology, only some 40 or 50 years ago, appeared so intimately related that these two fields were even administratively conjoined in one department in many colleges and universities. But with the development of the experimental techniques in psychology, there came a long series of separations and divorces. The sort of emancipations which had occurred much earlier in all the other fields of science, had finally been achieved also by psychology. But, now that the divorce is fully accepted by both parties, and remarriage is clearly out of the question, there are signs that a good friendship may be mutually profitable. This seems all the more possible and hopeful because philosophy itself has thoroughly mended its ways.

In explaining how philosophy has "mended its ways" Feigl alluded to the repudiation of futile speculation by contemporary philosophers. Unlike many of their predecessors, they no longer brood over insoluble metaphysical issues. They recognize the difference between answerable and unanswerable questions. As Feigl mentions, "There are ways of stating and handling problems that make them 100 per cent guaranteed insoluble." "Speculative thinking," he writes, "can produce completely unanswerable questions." This implies, of course, that speculative thinking may also result in completely answerable questions.

Speculation may be either fruitful or fruitless. The antiphilosophical bias of psychology, from the vantage point of history, can now be seen as disenchantment with fruitless speculation. The methodology of science as rooted in laboratory and field operations was expected to reduce or eliminate dependence on speculation. However, as already suggested, fruitful speculation is an intrinsic factor in the elaboration of scientific hypotheses. This merits special emphasis because in some quarters preoccupation with strict laboratory controls seems to be equated with rigorous exclusion of speculation. As a useful corrective it might help to reflect upon what R. S. Peters has to say about this issue. In the very last page of his long and scholarly revision of *Brett's History of Psychology* (1953, p. 725), Peters ends the survey of the subject in the following passage, in which the final paragraph is quoted from the philosopher Alfred North Whitehead's book on *The Function of Reason:*

Speculation is the life-blood of science; too much methodological purism may tend to dry it up. The day may soon dawn when psychologists will tackle the problems that interest them, whether scientific or technological or historical, in their own way, combining imagination in formulating hypotheses with ingenuity in testing them. And they may forbear to write those tedious introductory chapters, so common in textbooks of the first forty years of the twentieth century, in which they maintained that their way of doing psychology was the only scientifically respectable one. One bright idea which is testable is worth a whole book of advice on how to make psychology scientific.

"Some of the major disasters of mankind have been produced by the narrowness of men with a good methodology. . . . To set limits to speculation is treason to the future."

This recognition of the value of speculation, it may be recalled, was discussed at the end of Chapter 1 in connection with consideration of the implications of armchair psychology. Mention was made of what Charles Darwin said regarding the need for speculation if there is to be "good and original observation." Speculation or theory guides observation; in turn, observation confirms or modifies theory. It is a reciprocal relationship. How this relationship influenced the development of psychology will become increasingly evident in the light of the speculations and observations of the long line of thinkers responsible for psychology's philosophic heritage. This was the heritage bequeathed to the founding fathers of modern "scientific" psychology, and the trend of its teachings will be taken up in the next few chapters. In view of what has already been introduced in these first two chapters, it should be obvious that the "philosophic" origin of these teachings does not necessarily render them devoid of "scientific" import. Becoming familiar with them will enhance one's understanding of contemporary psychology.

References

Arieti, S. "Special Logic of Schizophrenic and Other Types of Autistic Thinking," *Psychiatry*, 1948, *11*, 325–338.

Brunswik, E. "The Conceptual Framework of Psychology," in *International Encyclopedia of Unified Science*. Chicago: The University of Chicago Press, 1955, pp. 655–750.

Carnap, R. "Logical Foundations of the Unity of Science," in *International Encyclopedia of Unified Science*. Chicago: The University of Chicago Press, 1955, pp. 42–62.

English, H. B., and English, A. C. *A Comprehensive Dictionary of Psychological and Psychoanalytical Terms*. New York: Longmans, Green and Company, 1958.

Feigl, H. "Philosophical Embarrassments of Psychology," *American Psychologist*, 1959, *14*, 115–128.

Fuller, B. A. G. *A History of Philosophy*. New York: Henry Holt and Company, 1945.

Henle, M. "The Relation between Logic and Thinking," *Psychological Review*, 1962, *69*, 366–377.

Penfield, W., and Roberts, L. *Speech and Brain-Mechanisms*. Princeton, New Jersey: Princeton University Press, 1959.

Peters, R. S. *Brett's History of Psychology*. London: George Allen and Unwin, 1953.

Reichenbach, H. *The Rise of Scientific Philosophy*. Berkeley: University of California Press, 1951.

Russell, B. *A History of Western Philosophy*. New York: Simon and Schuster, 1945.

Von Domarus, E. "The Specific Laws of Logic in Schizophrenia," in J. S. Kasanin (ed.). *Language and Thought in Schizophrenia*. Berkeley: University of California Press, 1954, pp. 104–113.

Weiss, A. P. *A Theoretical Basis of Human Behavior*. Columbus: R. G. Adams and Company, 1929.

PART  **II**

GRECIAN AND MEDIEVAL BACKGROUNDS

3

From Plato to Freud

HISTORIES OF PSYCHOLOGY customarily devote space to the contributions of Greek philosophers to this history. No one of these philosophers actually wrote a book or treatise entitled *Psychology*. In fact, as G. S. Brett (1912, p. 150) pointed out, it was not until the sixteenth century that the word appeared in the title of a book. It was written by Rudolf Goeckel, a professor in Germany, and was first published in 1590 under the title *Psychologia* along with a Latin subtitle to indicate that it had to do with the perfectibility of man.[1] Brett's concern with the volume was limited to the fact of its priority in the use of the term *"psychology,"* for, as he suggests, it was more theological than psychological in content. However, in the case of the Greeks to be considered in this chapter, there were numerous references to what would be classified as psychological topics today, even though the word "psychology" was not employed. The Greeks exhibited interest in such topics as sensation, perception, reasoning, feeling, dreaming, memory, and similar aspects of mental life. They also revealed the beginnings of what in later centuries was to become physiological psychology. Of course much that falls

---

[1] In some histories the name of Goeckel appears in its Latinized form as Goclenius. His introduction of the word *"psychologia"* may have been due to a blunder. Merz refers to one scholar who thinks that Goeckel had come across the term *psychologonia* in the writings of Proclus, a Neoplatonic philosopher of the fifth century A.D. The latter term refers to the genesis of the soul; and Goeckel, having misread the word, subsumed the question of "the generation of the soul" under what he spelled as *psychologia*. Accordingly, in the opinion of the scholar in question, if Goeckel had been influenced by Proclus in this way, then the later use of the word "psychology" as a designation for the science of mind is the result of a "sort of historical accident." Furthermore, as noted by Merz, the word "psychology" as a familiar term "did not become current in French or English literature before the nineteenth century, and seems to have been introduced into the latter through Coleridge's connection with Germany, and into the former in the school of Victor Cousin." (J. T. Merz, *A History of European Thought in the Nineteenth Century* [New York: Dover, 1965], III, 200–201.)

within the scope of modern psychology was not even touched upon. In this connection it is of interest that, as noted by Fuller (1945, p. 19), the Greek language lacked equivalents for terms like "personality," "self-conscious-ness," "ego," "conscience," and similar words dealing with the private, the unique, and distinctively personal in the life of man.

Beginnings of Typology

In general, the Greeks were more concerned with phases of psychology common to all men than with those now stressed in fields like differential psychology and the psychology of personality. This is not to be construed as total neglect of the fact of individual differences. Modern efforts to deal with such differences by classifying people into types may be viewed as outgrowths of early Greek efforts to do the same. For example, Hippocrates (460?– 357? B.C.), commonly referred to as the father of medicine, introduced a typology by calling attention to differences in physique of persons subject to apoplectic seizures as contrasted with those likely to become victims of tuber-culosis. In body build the latter were noted to be slender, frail, and under-nourished, while the former were more likely to be obese and thick-set, like Shakespeare's Falstaff. The distinction in question is thus a forerunner of Ernst Kretschmer's asthenic and pyknic body types as well as of W. H. Sheldon's ectomorphic and endomorphic body types. Present-day investiga-tions of possible relationships between habitus and personality or habitus and proneness to disease may consequently be viewed as elaborations of the typology initiated by Hippocrates.

Another kind of typology also has historical roots in the teachings of Hip-pocrates and his followers. Just as commonsense psychology has always recognized individual differences in physique, so it has recognized individual differences in temperament. People come to be classified as tall or short just as they may be classified as melancholy or irritable. Differences of the latter kind are now often related to biochemical factors, especially those belonging to the endocrine system. In fact, Robert S. Woodworth (1869–1962) once suggested the introduction of *chemique* as a correlative of *physique* as a suitable designation for the variables of temperament. The current view, in other words, renders temperament a function of endocrine secretions.

As a concept, however, this current view is of ancient origin in the sense that, long before the existence of endocrine glands was suspected, differences in temperament were attributed to differences in the juices or humors of the body. In the physiology of early medicine, fluids like blood, bile, and phlegm were referred to as *humors*. This ancient usage is still reflected in everyday speech in phrases like "being in a good humor" or "being in a bad humor." Everyday speech also reflects the influence of early humoral physiology in describing varieties of temperament by words like "sanguine," "melancholic," or "phlegmatic." These are references to blood, black bile, and viscid fluids, respectively. The relation between such fluids and temperamental differences was emphasized in the writings of another Greek physician whose teachings in the field of medicine, like Aristotle's teachings in the field of philosophy, came to be regarded as authoritative for many medical generations from the period of his life in the second century A.D. on up to the end of the medieval period. This was Galen (130?– A.D. 200?), who in histories of medicine is often mentioned as the next key figure after Hippocrates. His doctrine of the four temperaments is not unrelated to the emphasis Hippocrates placed upon the four humors of blood, black bile, yellow bile, and phlegm. In Hippocratic medicine, the maintenance of health required a correct balance among these humors.

They were regarded as important elements in the composition of the body and as derivatives of the elements supposed to account for the fundamental "stuff" of the world. They constituted one answer to the question many children have asked: "What is the world made of?" A twentieth-century chemist might answer by reference to the long list of known chemical elements. Long before the rise of chemistry, ancient thinkers also tried to answer this by reference to one or more elements. Thales, who lived some seven or eight hundred years before Galen, regarded water as the one fundamental element, while one of his successors, Heraclitus, regarded fire as the basic element. Others thought it might be air or earth. Empedocles, a contemporary of Hippocrates, relinquished the quest for a single basic substance by recognizing all four—air, fire, water, earth—as basic or, in his own words, as "the four roots of all things" (Nahm, 1947, p. 129). A distinctive quality was supposed to characterize each of these four elementary substances: water being moist and air dry with fire hot and earth cold. In the work of Hippocrates these qualities were attributed to the four humors: black bile being regarded as moist and yellow bile as dry with blood associated with warmth and phlegm with cold. Centuries later, Galen made this humoral account the basis for his typology of temperament.

In the writings of Empedocles it is of interest to mention his view of the mind-body relationship. For him, the heart was the most important organ, for, as he stated, "It lies in seas of blood which darts in opposite directions, and there most of all intelligence centers for men; for blood about the heart is intelligence in the case of men" (Nahm, p. 138). Even Aristotle continued to entertain this belief in the heart as the bodily basis for mental functions. It was by no means obvious to these pioneer "physiological psychologists" that the brain is the chief organ of intellect. Aristotle knew of the brain's existence but regarded it as a device for cooling or regulating body temperature. Plato, Aristotle's predecessor, came closer to modern teaching by regarding the head as the locus of intellectual functions, but his reason for so regarding it was more aesthetic than scientific. For him, circles and spheres were ideal forms and reason was man's noblest faculty; hence it seemed appropriate for the head as the most nearly spherical portion of the body to be the habitat of intellect.

Mythology in Plato and Freud

This poetic fancy was related to some of Plato's other less fanciful ideas regarding the nature of man. If there is a poetic quality about his writings, it may be, as H. C. Drake (1958, p. 13) suggests, that "Plato never forgot that he had been a poet" and that he was sensitive to the importance of effective use of language in the clarification of ideas and the promotion of understanding. His use of the dialogue as a means of philosophic teaching is suggestive of his concern with the pedagogic importance of literary form. Like Freud, whose expository style has also been praised for its excellence, Plato's writings are replete with metaphors and vivid imagery of a kind some might deem poetic. In fact, as will soon become evident, Plato and Freud have more in common than elegance of literary style.

Both Plato and Freud have presented some of their key concepts as myths. In Freud's writings the theory of instincts is, of course, a central feature of the psychoanalytic system. And yet Freud (1933, p. 131) wrote:

> The theory of instincts is, as it were, our mythology. The instincts are mythical beings, superb in their indefiniteness.

In commenting on this passage, Sandor Rado (1950, p. 174) credited Freud with being admirably self-critical for making it and proceeded to extend the recognition of mythological features to Freud's picture of the family drama. With specific reference to such mythological features Rado had this to say:

> The same applies to the so-called "structural theory" in which a jealous father (the superego) drives a wedge (repression) between a seductive mother (the id) and an opportunistic son (the ego) who would wish to get along with everybody: father, mother, and the rest of the world.

Whether Freud was self-critical, as Rado maintains, in acknowledging the mythological nature of the instinct theory may be open to question. Myths are not always to be equated with entertaining fiction like fairy tales for children. They may serve as expository devices to portray some insight or teaching as happens in serious drama or in the instructional use of parable and fable. This is not to deny that myths may also mislead and distort, as in the Nazi myth of Nordic superiority.

The issues involved are far too complex to lend themselves to summary presentation. In the recent *Myth and Mythmaking,* edited by H. A. Murray (1960), this complexity is well revealed in a collection of papers by some seventeen contributors. In the present context the paper by Murray is particularly relevant, for in it he takes issue with dictionary definitions of myths as "wholly fictitious" stories. Such emphasis on the fictitious, Murray points out, is not justified in terms of what myths were intended to accomplish in

PLATO (427?–347 B.C.)

SIGMUND FREUD (1856–1939)

ancient times, when they served as a means of giving expression to what was taken to be the manifestation of some "superhuman psychic determinant of a critical event." Myths, historically considered, were the sacred truths of pagans in much the same sense in which nonpagans may refer to scriptural episodes as "gospel truth." As Murray sees it, many myths of antiquity served as explanations of natural events and human events just as scientific theories do for us. Moreover, he does not regard this as justification for calling *all* myths false (1960, p. 336):

> The fact that animistic nature myths and primitive myths generally have been invalidated by science is not sufficient reason for asserting that *all* myths are false, by definition. Countless scientific theories have been similarly invalidated, but this does not lead us to assert that *all* theories are false. We say that theories are the best things science has invented, even though the latest and best of these best things are not considered to be wholly and precisely true.

In referring to scientific theories as not necessarily "wholly and precisely true," Murray touches upon a view already manifest in Plato's *Gorgias* and *Phaedrus* and cited by Irwin Edman (1928, p. XXXII) in a discussion of Plato's use of myth. In the *Gorgias,* Plato attributes these words to Socrates, who has just recounted a myth:

> Perhaps this may appear to you to be only an old wife's tale, which you will condemn. And there might be reason in contemning such tales, if by searching we could find anything better or truer.

That Plato was mindful of the distinction between the "whole truth" and and "approximation" to truth is evident in this excerpt from the *Phaedrus:*

> . . . a man of sense ought not to say, nor will I be very confident that the description which I have given of the soul and her mansions is exactly true. But I do say that, inasmuch as the soul is shown to be immortal, he may venture to think not improperly or unworthily that something of the kind is true.

A famous myth in the *Phaedrus* may serve as a convenient introduction to Plato's psychology. Before we consider this myth, we should guard against hasty rejection of its implications simply because Plato employs it to explain the "nature of the soul," where the word *soul* may strike the modern reader as "unscientific" in view of its connotation of superstitious, ghostlike apparitions. In Plato's writings, however, the word is often used to designate what the modern psychologist may call a motive or drive or impulse, or what in popular psychology is intended by the word *spirit* in phrases like "the spirit of patriotism" or "school spirit" or "team spirit." The latter phrases are recognized as ways of referring to motivating factors that enhance group morale and promote group endeavor. In such contexts there is no implication that "spirit" refers to external spiritual beings. Instead the reference is to internal stirrings, to what one feels like accomplishing or bringing to pass. Lifeless objects are devoid of such stirrings. In Plato's words: "For the body which is moved from without is soulless; but that which is moved from within has a soul, for such is the nature of the soul."

The Myth of the Charioteer

In the light of this explanation it may be easier to understand the psychological implications of Plato's myth of the charioteer as presented in the following quotation (Jowett, 1953, III, 153, 160–161):

> Of the nature of the soul, though her true form may be ever a theme of large and more than mortal discourse, let me speak briefly, and in a figure. And let the figure be composite—a pair of winged horses and a charioteer. Now the winged horses and the charioteers of the gods are all of them noble and of noble descent, but those of other races are mixed; the human charioteer drives his in a pair; and one of them is noble and of noble breed, and the other is ignoble and of ignoble breed; and the driving of them of necessity gives a great deal of trouble to him. . . .
>
> . . . As I said at the beginning of this tale, I divided each soul into three—two horses and a charioteer; and one of the horses was good and the other bad: the division may remain, but I have not yet explained in what the goodness or badness of either consists, and to that I will now proceed. The right-hand horse is upright and cleanly made; he has a lofty neck and an aquiline nose; his colour is white, and his eyes dark; he is a lover of honour and modesty and temperance, and the follower of true glory; he needs no touch of the whip, but is guided by word and admonition only. The other is a crooked lumbering animal, put together anyhow; he has a short thick neck; he is flat-faced and of dark colour, with gray and bloodshot eyes; the mate of insolence and pride, shag-eared and deaf, hardly yielding to whip and spur.

In the detailed elaboration of the myth from which the preceding excerpts were selected, it is clear that Plato, like Freud, is concerned with the conflict between reason and desire or between self-control and the imperiousness of instinctual urges. Plato actually depicts the charioteer as coping with sexual temptation. The division of the soul into three parts is not unlike Freud's tripartite scheme of ego, id, and superego. Just as id and superego refer to two antithetic sources of goads to behavior, so the dark and white horses symbolize noble and ignoble desires. In his struggle to gain control over the steeds, the charioteer plays a role akin to that of the ego in the Freudian drama. The dark or "wanton steed" is governed by the pleasure principle, while the charioteer, if successful in gaining mastery over his team, would be exemplifying what Freud called the reality principle.

Orexis, Cognition, and Integration

On an earlier page it was pointed out that traditional, academic psychology with its emphasis on sensation, perception, memory, learning, association, illusion, intelligence, and similar themes having to do with cognition might be said to have been dealing with epistemological themes. Emphasis on problems of motivation, desire, and conation was not prominent until the post-Freudian phase of academic psychology.

Freud's psychology is not much concerned with optical illusions, intelligence, theories of learning, and kindred topics of epistemological import. Instead there is emphasis on man as a creature of desire, impulse, and yearning. He is viewed as the victim of conflict in the clash between id impulses on the one hand and superego imperatives on the other. The craving for immediate gratification is balked by frustrations imposed by unaccommodating reality. Man is presented as being more of a driven, wishing creature than a contemplative, rational one.

Wishes have to do with fulfillment of desire, and objects of desire increase in value as desire increases. Value fluctuates with intensity of need. Sleep becomes precious to the exhausted soldier just as food does for one who is famished. When desires conflict, there is a conflict of values. The exhausted soldier on guard duty has to decide between the value of sleep and the value of obedience to military duty. Similarly, the famished soldier may have to struggle with his conscience when tempted to steal food. Violation of one's conscience engenders feelings of guilt. Resolution of conflict thus frequently involves ethical considerations or the maintenance of self-respect. Ethical values loom large in the clash between Freudian id impulses and superego standards. The competing wishes arouse rival inclinations to behavior and the emotional turbulence incident to wrestling with strong temptation.

In technical language, temptation of this kind is more a matter of *orexis* than of cognition. Just as cognition refers to knowledge, understanding, and whatever pertains to intellect so orexis refers to desiring, wishing, and whatever pertains to conation or purposive striving. When the striving is concerned with important goals, emotional or affective changes are experienced. In taking an important examination, the student is not just considering the meaning of the questions but is also anxious or excited as he *strives* to write down his answers in the allotted time. Considering the meaning of the questions illustrates the *cognitive* aspect of coming to terms with the examination situation, while the anxious or excited striving exemplifies the *orectic* aspect. In contrast to the cognitive or epistemological emphasis of pre-Freudian academic psychology, the psychology of Freud placed more emphasis on orectic aspects of mental life. In the language of grammar, it might be said that Freud was more optative and academic psychology more indicative.

Reverting to Plato's myth of the charioteer, it can now be seen that Plato's psychology was also stressing orectic aspects. The dark and white horses with divergent inclinations had to be brought under the driver's control. In Plato's symbolism the charioteer represented the rational soul and the horses the irrational souls. The white horse symbolized the higher irrational soul and the dark horse the lower. In terms of anatomic location the lower irrational soul was placed below the diaphragm, the higher in the heart region, and the rational soul, as already mentioned, in the head region. This, however, is of minor significance. What is more significant is the relation between Freud's concept of the unconscious and Plato's concept of the two irrational souls. Both concepts refer to noncognitive or orectic aspects of human nature. Furthermore, just as Plato attributed higher and lower impulses to the irrational side of human nature, so Freud attributed both id and superego forces to man's unconscious.[2]

What the modern psychologist describes as an integrated personality involves the reconciliation of contradictory desires. Persistent failure to effect such reconciliation may impress him and his psychiatric colleague as having neurotic or psychotic implications. Coping with conflicting desires has come to be viewed as important for understanding and evaluating such implications. And yet this modern Freudian contribution to psychopathology can be said to have been anticipated by Plato. The struggle between good and evil desires, between reason and instinct, between disciplined self-control and unbridled impulsiveness, is clearly presented in Plato's account of what happens to the charioteer when meeting with or coping with sexual conflict (Jowett, 1953, III, 163):

> When they meet, the wanton steed of the lover has a word to say to the charioteer; he would like to have a little pleasure in return for many pains, but the wanton steed of the beloved says not a word, for he is bursting with passion which he understands not,—he throws his arms round the lover and embraces him as his dearest friend; and, when they are side by side, he is not in a state in which he can refuse the lover anything, if he ask him; although his fellow-steed and the charioteer oppose him with arguments of shame and reason. After this their happiness depends upon their self-control; if the better elements of the mind which lead to order and philosophy prevail, then they pass their life here in happiness and harmony—masters of themselves and orderly—enslaving the vicious and emancipating the virtuous elements of the soul. . . .

From the foregoing it is obvious that for Plato the attainment of "happiness and harmony" demands self-control, which in turn requires subordination of the irrational soul to the sovereignty of the rational soul. Presumably without such sovereignty, the unhappiness and disharmony of irrational impulsiveness or persistent conflict would result.

As mentioned earlier, the issues involved here have to do with what the modern psychopathologist describes in terms of personality integration and disintegration. As the victim of conflicting desires, the neurotic patient is

---

[2] The use of the term "irrational" in this context might well be questioned. Students of Plato are accustomed to employ this term in referring to that which Plato opposed to the rational soul. However, a term like "nonrational" would be preferable, since wishes, desires, urges, and similar orectic factors are not necessarily at variance with the demands of logic, reason, intelligence, and whatever else is meant by *rational* behavior.

not well integrated. Part of him craves what another part of him repudiates; hence his anxiety, uncertainty, indecisiveness, and neurotic distress. He is like a house divided against itself. In the language of Freud, instinctual id forces are urging one course of action while those of the superego urge an opposite course of action. What Plato described in terms of an irrational soul Freud described in terms of the unconscious or the amoral id or the dynamism of repression.

All these Platonic and Freudian concepts suggest the nonrational and the impulsive. But the similarity and agreement goes beyond this; for just as Plato elevated the rational soul to one of controlling influence so Freud came to recognize the intellect or rationality as essential in the resolution of neurotic conflict. This was evident when he wrote (1934, p. 77): "The time has probably come to replace the consequence of repression by the results of *rational* mental effort . . ." (italics supplied). Furthermore, in arguing for what he called "the primacy of the intellect," he stated (1934, p. 93):

> We may insist as much as we like that the human intellect is weak in comparison with human instincts, and be right in doing so. But nevertheless there is something peculiar about this weakness. The voice of the intellect is a soft one, but it does not rest until it has gained a hearing. Ultimately, after endlessly repeated rebuffs, it succeeds.

Dreams, Eros, and Insight

As is well known, Freud came to regard the dream as "the royal road to the unconscious." The controls exercised by the inhibiting vigilance of the "censor" were regarded as held in abeyance during sleep; and in the absence of such controls, repressed unconscious wishes could find expression in dream imagery. Freud published the first extensive account of his dream theory at the turn of the century. Both he and many others viewed the publication as an altogether novel, pioneering approach to the psychology of dream life. And yet a few students of Plato called attention to a striking anticipation of this approach more than two thousand years before Freud. For example, Will Durant (1926, p. 33), in a work on philosophy that was a best-seller in the 1920s, referred to Plato's view of dreaming as "a remarkable anticipation" of Freud's view. This anticipation is also noted by A. L. Woods (1947, p. 179) in the following quotation from Plato's *Republic*:

> Such as are excited in sleep, when the rest of the soul—which is rational, mild, and its governing principle—is asleep, and when that part which is savage and rude, being satisfied with food and drink, frisks about, drives away sleep, and seeks to go and accomplish its practices: in such an one, you know, it dares to do everything, because it is loosed and disengaged from all modesty and prudence: for, if it pleases, it scruples not at the embraces, even of a mother, or of any-

one else, whether gods, men, or beasts; nor to commit murder, nor abstain from any sort of meat—and in one word, it is wanting neither in folly nor shamelessness. . . . in every one resides a certain species of desires that are terrible, savage, and irregular, even in some that we deem ever so moderate; and this indeed becomes manifest in sleep.

Plato's reference to desires which find expression in dreams as "terrible, savage, and irregular" is somewhat reminiscent of Freud's description of the id as "a caldron of seething excitement." Both descriptions suggest amoral impulsiveness. For Freud, such impulsiveness was identified with the pleasure-seeking lusts of the libido or what he sometimes referred to as Eros. The latter allusion to the Greek god of love is another indication of Plato's anticipation of Freudian psychology: just as Freud devoted much of his theorizing to an elaboration of the influence of libidinal or erotic forces, so Plato was much concerned with the description and analysis of different ways in which love or Eros may shape the character of men. In fact, this was the central theme of the *Symposium*, Plato's famous dialogue dealing with what he called "speeches in praise of love." Furthermore, just as Freud came to view libidinal energy as sublimated into the *creative*, socially constructive activity of poets, writers, inventors, and artists, so Plato appears to have entertained a similar view as evidenced by the following excerpt from the *Symposium* (Edman, 1928, p. 376, with italics supplied):

> Those who are pregnant in the body only, betake themselves to women and beget children—this is the character of their love. . . . But souls which are pregnant—for there certainly are men who are more *creative* in their souls than in their bodies —conceive that which is proper for the soul to conceive or contain. And what are these conceptions?—wisdom and virtue in general. And such *creators* are poets and all artists who are deserving of the name inventor.

Neither Freud nor Plato restricted the energy of libido or Eros to sex behavior as a mere biological phenomenon. For them, as just indicated, this energy may activate behavior which might be described as desexualized creative achievement. Activation of this kind involves goal-directed striving or conation. Such striving, for Plato, was the means of organizing the three parts or levels of the soul into unified efficiency. In the words of G. S. Brett (1912, p. 95), the "parts are knit together by the conative element, the Eros which is an impulse toward the attainment of a desired end."

In this connection Brett also points out that Plato's tripartite division of the soul is not to be taken to mean three separate souls. There is just one soul in the life of each individual, and Plato is primarily interested in life as conduct. Just as in the field of government one can recognize different divisions of the state even though there is but one state, so one can recognize different levels of divisions of conduct manifested by the unitary soul.

This analogy between man and the state is characteristically Platonic. It constitutes the central theme of Plato's *Republic,* which takes its point of departure from an examination of the concept of justice. In his utopian Republic justice involves cooperative endeavor on the part of the three groups constituting the body politic: the philosopher-kings, the military, and the workers. Each of these groups has its analogue in the life of man as revealed by the activity of the rational soul, the higher irrational soul, and the lower irrational soul, respectively.

Plato equates these groups and activities with reason, spirit, and desire, and both in the state as well as in the individual, a distinctive contribution to the welfare of the whole is to be made by each part. Reason is to contribute wisdom; spirit is to add courage, and desire is to donate temperance. For justice to prevail, there must be due balance and unified fusion of these virtues of wisdom, courage, and temperance. In the life of the individual, such balance and fusion is not very different from what psychologists call an integrated personality.

An integrated personality may also be described as a balanced personality. As a concept it refers to the reduction or elimination of inner conflict along with or as a result of the achievement of a balanced, harmonious organization of impulse, wish, desire, and whatever else belongs to the notion of motivation and purpose. It implies a hierarchy of values or a philosophy of life to facilitate disposition of personal conflict. This, in turn, implies knowledge of the nature and significance of one's needs and values. For Plato, such knowledge, in line with the Socratic "Know thyself," included knowledge of goals or ends to be desired. In the interests of successful living, intelligent planning has to replace blind impulsiveness. Such planning requires self-knowledge. What Freud called *insight* is another way of referring to self-knowledge.

Furthermore, both Plato and Freud recognized the hazards of excess. There can be an excess of reason, resulting in what the modern clinician describes as overintellectualization, just as there can be an excess of passion in the absence of superego controls. To guard against such excess, Plato proposed an educational program that was to provide development of all three aspects of the soul. The program called for bodily exercise as well as intellectual exercise, with appropriate balancing of the needs of mind, spirit, and body. Freud never worked out an equivalent scheme of education, but he did make clear the importance of coming to terms with the demands of id, ego, and superego.

The difference in descriptive vocabulary may obscure some of these similarities in the respective psychologies of Plato and Freud. To digress slightly, it might be well to note that popular psychology today recognizes three broad divisions of human nature to which allusion was just made in connection with the needs of mind, spirit, and body. This classification, long part of the everyday vocabulary, is also manifest in the commonsense view of man as a creature capable of thinking, feeling, and willing. This triad of terms, it can readily be seen, was foreshadowed in the myth of the charioteer as symbolic of reason or thought, with the dark horse as the embodiment of feeling or passion and the white horse as the embodiment of noble impulse or courageous devotion to duty. Put still more simply, the tripartite division going back to Plato[3] is summed up in three common phrases: I think, I want, I ought. Taken in order, these three phrases refer to functions which Freud labeled ego, id, and superego, respectively.

Did Plato Influence Freud?

The points of resemblance between Plato and Freud that have just been discussed are not to be regarded as direct ways in which Freud's thinking was influenced by study of Plato's writings. Even the emphasis on the wish-fulfilling nature of dreams in which the resemblance is especially striking may not be the result of such influence. At all events there is no reference to Plato in the first edition of *The Interpretation of Dreams*.[4] Freud does refer to Plato's *Symposium* in one of his later writings (1922, p. 47). This citation may not mean very much, for Freud once explicitly disclaimed having been influenced by the writings of other philosophers some of whose ideas have been regarded as anticipations of Freudian concepts. For example, in his history of the psychoanalytic movement Freud wrote as follows about the origin of his concept of repression (1950, p. 297):

> The doctrine of repression quite certainly came to me independently of any other source; I know of no outside impression which might have suggested it to me, and for a long time I imagined it to be entirely my own, until Otto Rank showed us the passage in Schopenhauer's *World as Will and Idea* in which the philosopher is trying to give an explanation of insanity. What he says there about the struggle against acceptance of a painful part of reality fits my conception of repression so completely that I am again indebted for having made a discovery to not being a wide reader.

The latter point is emphasized in the same article when, in discussing the origin of his dream theory, Freud stated (1950, p. 302) that he has "held fast to the habit of always studying things themselves before looking for

---

[3] This tripartite division is merely suggested by the Platonic myth. The division in question did not become explicit until the eighteenth century, as a result of a booklet on sensation written by the philosopher Moses Mendelsschn (1729–1786). As noted by Brett (1912, p. 319), "The 'three faculty' doctrine, according to which all activities of the soul come under the heads of knowing, feeling and willing, may be regarded as established by this work of Mendelssohn," published in 1755.

[4] The first edition appeared in 1900. Not until the fourth edition, which was published in 1914, was there any mention of Plato. This was limited to a single sentence from the *Republic* to the effect that "the best men are those who only *dream* what other men *do* in their waking life." In Freud's wording: *"diejenigen seien die besten, denen das, was endere tun, nur im Traume einfalle."*

information about them in books" and consequently had worked out his own views independently of similar views advanced by other writers. Even the "close connection" between psychoanalytic and ancient dream-interpretation, he wrote, "only became clear to me much later."

There is no reason to question Freud's sincerity in disclaiming "wide" reading as the source of his original ideas. As a person of exemplary integrity, he would not consciously give himself unmerited credit for ideas borrowed from others. However, it is possible that he was unconsciously influenced by such ideas. Knowing the source of our ideas involves recognition of their origin, but everybody employs concepts and uses phrases with no knowledge of how they were acquired, one recalls them without recognizing their origin. In the fields of writing and musical composition, such recall without recognition is classified as unconscious plagiarism. The author or composer makes unwitting use of what he has read or heard, believes it to be original with him, and may be chagrined when he subsequently learns of his mistake.

It is thus possible that the resemblances between some of Plato's ideas and those of Freud may be instances of recall without recognition. Freud did have some exposure to Greek philosophy during his years as a medical student when he attended the lectures of Franz Brentano (1838–1917), a philosopher-psychologist possessed of a scholarly Aristotelian background. In fact, as P. Merlan (1945 and 1949) has shown, the only nonmedical sources Freud took during his eight semesters at medical school were six taught by Brentano, between 1874 and 1876. This was some twenty-five years before the publication of Freud's volume on dream interpretation. Since details of college lectures often elude active recall within a matter of days or even of hours, it is hardly likely that Freud would have been able to recall and recognize what he had gleaned from Brentano so many years earlier. And yet, considering the number of semesters he spent with Brentano, it seems plausible to believe that the general drift of Brentano's teachings was not without some permanent effect—enough to account for its possible unrecognized reactivation in the 1890s.

In the biography of Freud by Ernest Jones (1953, Vol. I, p. 56) there is a brief reference to Brentano in connection with the translation of one of John Stuart Mill's books. It appears that Brentano had suggested Freud's name as translator of the book of essays. One of the essays that Freud translated, Jones notes, dealt with Plato. The translation was made around the year 1880. Long afterward, in 1933, Freud remarked to Jones that his knowledge of Plato's philosophy was "very fragmentary"; this little knowledge may have come from the essay by Mill. Freud admitted having been "much impressed by Plato's theory of reminiscence" and having "had at one time given it a great deal of thought."

At just which period in his life Freud gave "a great deal of thought" to Plato's theory of reminiscence is a question Jones did not raise. Seemingly he was content to dispose of the issue by reference to Freud's 1933 recollection. This, as just mentioned, induced Freud to describe his knowledge of Plato as "very fragmentary." However, more than fifty years earlier one of Freud's letters suggests that this "fragmentary" knowledge supplied him "with unexpected parallels" to his own views. This letter, dated January 1, 1899, contains this statement (Bonaparte *et al.,* p. 275): "For relaxation I am reading Burckhardt's *History of Greek Civilization,* which is providing me with unexpected parallels." In other words, at the time Freud was developing his theories of hysteria, unconscious motivation, and the dynamics of memory he was finding some support for his theorizing in this reading.

Aside from what he had to say years later about having been so "impressed by Plato's theory of reminiscence," there is no mention of the specific nature of the parallels in question. Why this particular theory should have been so impressive may not be immediately obvious. As employed today, the word "reminiscence" has several meanings. In fact, what was previously described as unconscious plagiarism may be regarded as one of these meanings. This is different from the reminiscences indulged in by the author of personal memoirs. Here there need be no distortion of memory as there is in unconscious plagiarism. It involves the recall of significant incidents in the author's life.

Nor is recall of significant incidents restricted to the writing of memoirs. It is an everyday occurrence when the examining physician requests a patient to tell about his medical past: what illnesses he and his close relatives have had, whether he has ever undergone surgery, what his present complaints are, etc. In his medical notes of the case the physician may label this account by the patient by the term "anamnesis," the word that Plato employed to designate what has been translated as "reminiscence." In fact, "anamnesis" is still used in clinical reports, along with a contrasting word "catamnesis" to refer to the history of a patient's disorder. "Anamnesis" refers to the events the patient recalls as leading up to his disorder and "catamnesis" to the subsequent events or the follow-up history.

In current experimental psychology, the term "reminiscence" is employed to describe a somewhat paradoxical phenomenon of memory in which the subject has initial difficulty in recalling memorized material but later, with no intervening presentation of the material, is successful in his efforts at recall. It is a paradoxical phenomenon because ordinarily retention suffers with the lapse of time, but in this instance delay results in improved retention. However, as should be obvious, neither Plato nor Freud was directly concerned with this restricted, technical meaning of reminiscence.

Platonic Ideas as Archetypes

Plato's theory of reminiscence involves his theory of ideas and actually is more metaphysical or quasi-mystical than factual. It may be recalled that in Chapter 1, in order to clarify the nature of the empiricist-rationalist controversy, a distinction was made between sensory perception and ideational perception. By way of showing the antiquity of the controversy, a quotation from Plato's *Theaetetus* was introduced. The quotation included a statement by Socrates to the effect that sensory impressions as such do not result in knowledge; that only "by reasoning about them" can knowledge and truth come into being.

The mere sight of a circle is not sufficient to give the observer knowledge of the computation of its area. Moreover, the particular circle as drawn or as embodied in a wheel or hoop will not be a *perfect* circle. Such perfection eludes the world of sensory experience. Similarly, there can never be an individualized manifestation of ideal health or of flawless beauty or unblemished character. At best there may be approximations to such ideal standards, but their realization in the individual is impossible. This means, Plato held, that our knowledge of such standards or ideals is not a product of direct sensory experience. Nor is it a product of abstracting elements or details common to a multiplicity of similar experiences. For Plato, such knowledge, being independent of experience, must be inherent in the soul of man. It is as if the soul had some prenatal vision or acquaintance with the universe of perfect ideas, ideals, forms, and standards. Reminiscence or revival of such vision or acquaintance facilitates understanding of particular experiences and may highlight the discrepancy between the latter and their unrealizable idealization in Plato's universe of perfect ideas.

Like valid scientific laws, such perfect ideas are universally true even though never fully demonstrable in any concrete situation. A modern Platonist might venture to defend this interpretation of Plato's distinction between universals and particulars by noting that careful measurements in the precision laboratory are usually not absolutely fixed determinations but approximations expressed in terms of averages as qualified by some index of the variations around this average. The generalization or law inferred from such "approximations" may nevertheless be regarded as universally valid and not just approximately valid. In the "ideal" scientific universe it is assumed that frictionless machines, culture-free human beings, flawless recording instruments, or a really perfect vacuum would eliminate errors of measurements; but, taken strictly, this remains assumption rather than demonstrated fact. Often the assumption is concealed by a protective phrase like "other things being equal" or "all other factors being kept constant."

In brief, in some such admittedly strained fashion might Plato's distinction between universals and particulars be given a modicum of plausibility. His rejection of sense perception as the source of knowledge is harder to justify. For him, the pursuit of knowledge is tantamount to the quest for certainty. Mathematical propositions constitute his models of genuine knowledge. The theorems of Euclid could be held up as instances of this kind of certain knowledge. Their truth could be grasped by reason alone without direct sensory observation. Such truth is *a priori*, universal, and free from the errors of the senses. The very existence of illusions and hallucinations points to the fallibility of sense perception. This kind of argument may suffice to supply an inkling of the rationalist tradition stemming from Plato.

At the beginning of this section, Plato's theory of ideas or ideals was said to be metaphysical or quasi-mystical. This, it can now be seen, is due to his doctrine of reminiscence and the somewhat related doctrine of metempsychosis. These Platonic doctrines not only endowed man with innate concepts of truth, justice, loyalty, friendship, and innumerable other abstractions but also attributed their acquisition to what occurred to the soul during some existence or existences prior to its present incarnation. The innate concepts or ideals are sometimes referred to as *essences* or *archetypes* by students of Plato.

In terms of archetypes Plato's notion of universal and innate concepts or ideas is not altogether outmoded, as has been mentioned in Chapter 1, for archetypes are key factors in Carl Jung's analytic psychology. Jung, it may be recalled, regards the archetypes as unconscious but manifesting themselves in the form of "primordial images." Interestingly, Jung borrowed the latter phrase from the writings of Jacob Burckhardt, the Swiss historian mentioned on an earlier page in connection with the "unexpected parallels" noted by Freud in the course of reading Burckhardt's account of Greek civilization. For Jung, these primordial images or archetypes have to do with such universal themes as birth, death, motherhood, the quest for food, the threat of danger, sunrise and sunset, the change of seasons, and other recurrent, awe-inspiring events in the life of man throughout the ages. Such themes have become the subject matter of myths and folklore among all people. Jung regarded them as factors in what he termed the "collective unconscious." Along with Freud, as indicated in Chapter 1, he conceived of them as phylogenetically inherited and thus part of man's innate endowment.

In other words, to account for such general ideas or thought forms, Jung and Freud, implicitly relying on the generally discredited Lamarckian genetics, traced their origin to ancestral experience. Plato, on the other hand, with explicit reliance on a mystical belief in metempsychosis, traced their origin to the soul's experiences in prior incarnations. Thus, although separated in time by more than two thousand years, all three of them derived these "universals" from experiences undergone by ancestors or souls in the remote past. The innate archetypes of Plato and Jung, in terms of this perspective, are not altogether devoid of empirical roots.

Moreover, as will be brought out later, even ardent champions of the empiricist position might be said to have entertained an incipient rationalist orientation. For example, John Locke, the seventeenth-century English empiricist, likened the mind at birth to a blank slate—a *tabula rasa*—upon which the consequences of experience were inscribed. For Locke, sensory impressions came to be linked together or associated in experience to result in ideas, concepts, and understanding. He expressly denied the existence of ideas or "knowledge" prior to such sensory impressions. However, he did endow man with capacity for "reflection." This attribute was independent of the realm of sensation and made possible the detection of resemblances, differences, and the classification of the stream of sensory impressions. By means of reflection, concepts or general ideas were brought into being. They were not, like Plato's universals, prior to experience but subsequent to the influence of reflection. Nevertheless, by endowing man with capacity for reflection, or what amounts to ability to organize or reason about experience, Locke, it would seem, was postulating an inherent readiness to group sensory impressions into ordered forms. Viewed in this light, Locke's "reflection" suggests an inborn readiness to form or welcome ideas Plato and other rationalists deemed to be innate. If this be so, then the age-old empiricist-rationalist controversy becomes less drastic and less irreconcilable.

Atomistic Analysis Versus Holism

As was just mentioned, empiricists like Locke regarded simple sensory impressions as the raw material of mind. According to them, in the course of experience these impressions or sensations come to be organized into more complex mental structures such as percepts and concepts. The concepts include abstractions like notions of negative numbers, Utopias, ideal beauty, hobgoblins, geometric points, the end of time, omniscience, and similar products of creative imagination. Analysis was presumed to reveal the sensationistic basis or origin of such products. As a consequence of this analysis, sensations were regarded as the building blocks of mind in the sense of coming first in experience and by suitable compounding eventually developing into organized patterns of ideation. This is akin to arguing that since every substance, upon chemical analysis, is found to consist of chemical elements or atoms, every substance came into existence by union of pre-existing elements or atoms. Such an argument is decidedly dubious when applied to psychological phenomena, as was long ago made clear by Brett (1912, p. 85):

> The fallacy of sensationalism lies in its persistent habit of constructing the history of mind backward; it finds in sensation the last product of analysis, and then makes it the first element of construction. The truth rather is that sensations are the occasions for our mental activities.

Broadly considered, Plato's universals or archetypes may be construed as opposed to the sensationistic reductionism of empiricists. "Atomistic analysis" is often employed as a descriptive phrase by contemporary psychologists in their critiques of reductionism. This is especially true of Gestalt psychologists, who, as is well known, stress the importance of organized forms or wholes or patterns as controlling factors in perception, learning, thinking, and motor behavior. They regard such *holistic* controlling factors as dominant over the "elements" of traditional empiricists. This means the whole is different from and not a mere sum of its constituent parts. The elements or "parts" of words like "GOD" and "DOG" are the same, but the words differ in appearance and meaning. Organization or arrangement or Gestalt is prior to the emergence of the parts in the sense that intentions and plans precede their execution. The intention or idea of writing a business letter will result in the appearance of different series of words from those produced by the intention to write a letter of condolence. In the present context there is no need to dwell upon the nature and scope of Gestalt psychology's emphasis on the priority of wholes and the concomitant attack on atomism. It is more relevant to note that, although this attack was launched around 1912, Plato's theory of ideas can be construed as an early recognition of what was to become a key Gestaltist principle. Incidentally, as we shall see in the next chapter, this recognition becomes even more explicit in the writings of Aristotle. Müller-Freienfels (1935, pp. 113–114) noted this years ago:

> The notion of *Gestalt* is by no means new to psychology. Should one attempt to write a history of *Gestalt* psychology, one could begin with Plato and Aristotle. . . .
> It is apparent that the problem of psychic *Gestalt* is ancient; and the controversy between psychologists who accept psychic *Gestalt* and those who want to construct it out of "elements" extends throughout the entire history of psychology.

Democritus and Atomism

In line with the foregoing, it might be said that if one were to venture to write a history of the "elementaristic" or atomistic approach to psychology, one might also begin with the time of Plato. Not that Plato espoused such a view, but one of his contemporaries, Democritus, did. In fact, it is customary to trace the underlying conceptual framework of some twentieth-century behaviorists back to Democritus. For example, the behavioristic theory of A. P. Weiss (1929), to which reference was made early in Chapter 2, is consonant with such a framework. Weiss, it may be recalled, defended a metaphysical thesis to the effect that "psychic" events are fundamentally reducible to the whirlings of electrons and protons. This sort of thesis is but a refinement of the atomism of Democritus, for the atoms of the ancients have become the electrons of the moderns. Democritus also conceived of "psychic" events as products of the whirlings of tiny, invisible particles or atoms. Like Weiss, he regarded all objects, animate as well as inanimate, as composed of the ultimate constituents of "material" substance. His general viewpoint is well summarized in the following pages from Aristotle quoted in Nahm (1947, p. 169):

> Democritus considers the eternal objects to be small substances infinite in number. For these he posits a place infinite in magnitude, and he calls place by such names as void, nothing, and infinite, but each of the substances he calls something, solid, and existent. He thinks the substances are so small that we cannot perceive them,

yet they have all sorts of forms and shapes, and differences in size. . . . The coherence up to a certain point of substances he explains by the gripping and intermingling of the bodies, for some of them are scalene in shape, some are barbed, some concave, some convex and others have countless other differences.

The preceding quotation explains why Democritus has been classified as a "physical philosopher." Unlike Plato, he viewed both soul and body in mechanical terms, with "soul atoms" being more mobile and finer and more spherical than the "body atoms." Differences in the qualities of sensations were attributed to variations in size and shape of the atoms. This can be illustrated by his views of gustatory sensations as described by Theophrastus, one of Aristotle's successors (Nahm, 1947, p. 189):

Democritus in assigning a shape to each quality made sweet to consist of fairly large, spherical atoms. To the quality of sour he assigned very large, rough shapes with many angles and no curves. The sharp [in taste], as its name implied, he regarded as consisting of atoms sharp in mass, angular, crooked, thin, and unrounded. The pungent needs atoms which are thin, angular, and bent, but rounded also. Salt is angular, fairly large, twisted, although symmetrical. Bitter is rounded and smooth, unsymmetrical, and small in size.

At first reading, such a passage may seem unworthy of serious attention. What Democritus has to say about the size and shape of his supposititious atoms is little more than vague guesswork devoid of any factual support. In fact, in terms of his presuppositions it was impossible to mobilize any evidential support; for by hypothesis the atoms were invisible and the manufacture of microscopes was still centuries away. Nevertheless, the passage is not altogether lacking in psychological interest, for it supplies evidence of a modicum of accurate observation in contradistinction to arbitrary guesswork. Put a little differently, what Democritus lists as important gustatory sensations is essentially correct. When laboratory investigations were launched by the nineteenth-century pioneers of experimental psychology one of the studies had to do with determining the number of elementary taste sensations. Systematic stimulation of the tongue surface revealed four qualitatively different sensations: sweet, salt, sour, and bitter. These are the four mentioned by Democritus, and they were also known to Plato. Consequently, one might be inclined to say that the experimental investigation merely confirmed what ancient philosophers had already discovered by nonexperimental means.

However, in only a very restricted sense would it be correct to say Plato and Democritus had anticipated the laboratory discovery made so many centuries later. For one thing, what Democritus had regarded as the atomic basis of each distinctive gustatory quality was not confirmed. Furthermore, the laboratory investigation enlarged the scope of the psychological issues involved far beyond the speculative horizons of the ancients. For example, the experimentalists discovered that the surface of the tongue is not uniformly sensitive to all four kinds of gustatory stimuli, some parts being responsive to sugar solutions and unresponsive to the other three modes of stimulation. It also found that to be effective the stimulating substances have to be in solution. Measurement revealed facts pertaining to sensory thresholds, and histological studies revealed the structure of the gustatory receptors. Control of concurrent olfactory stimulation demonstrated the extent to which much that commonsense attributes to taste is really a function of aroma. This was not known to Democritus, who, as the preceding quotation shows, regarded pungency as an attribute of taste. Nor did he have any inkling of the neurophysiological issues emerging from the nineteenth-century laboratory studies: Are there separate neural tracts for each gustatory sensation, or just a single one for all four? What part of the brain cortex is most directly activated by gustatory impulses? Quite obviously his early recognition of the four taste sensations cannot be interpreted as more than a fragmentary anticipation of later more systematic and controlled elaborations of the psychological implications of such recognition.

Priority Versus Achievement

Here let us consider other aspects of this question of the significance of early historical anticipation of later scientific discoveries. The matter of establishing personal credit for priority of discovery is of less importance than that of noting how and by whom the discovery became the focus of subsequent theorizing and research. For example, the concept of biological evolution was not original with Darwin. His grandfather Erasmus had entertained the idea and so had others before him. Even his contemporary, Alfred Russel Wallace, outlined the same idea in a paper at about the same time that Darwin was about ready to publish his book. Despite this, the doctrine of evolution has come to be thought of as Darwin's discovery; for he it was who devoted himself to the arduous task of marshalling a mass of evidence in support of the doctrine and in setting the stage for a new emphasis not only in biological studies, but also in the scientific work of paleontologists, psychologists, anthropologists, and others. Before his time the "discovery" was an inert item in the archives of history. After his time it became a dynamic influence in the daily work of men of science.

In analogous fashion, it should now be evident, Plato's anticipations of psychoanalytic teachings are not to be construed as disparagement of Freud's discoveries. It may even be, as was suggested on previous pages, that Freud had become familiar with some of the views of Plato and other Greek philosophers. Even though he claimed not to have been a "wide reader," his bibliographic references are so extensive as to render this a decidedly questionable self-estimate. *Traumdeutung* (1900), the original German edition of his *The Interpretation of Dreams,* ends with ten closely printed pages of references to books and articles in German, English, and French. There are references to Aristotle and Hippocrates but none to Plato. Moreover, the readiness with which Freud expressed his theories by recourse to symbols derived from the legends of Oedipus, Electra, and Narcissus indicates more than superficial familiarity with Greek mythology. In reality he seems to have been a very "wide reader." However, the extent to which the development of his own views was a product of "unconscious plagiarism" of some anticipations of these views in the writings of his predecessors is difficult to determine. The fact that the historian ferrets out such anticipations is more indicative of the possible soundness of the ideas than of proof for the direct influence of the earlier writer on the later one.

In the light of history, Plato was not the only one to have glimpsed what can now be classified as Freudian insights. The doctrine of unconscious mental influences was touched upon by Leibnitz in the time of Locke as well as by Herbart and Schopenhauer in the nineteenth century. Spinoza, some two hundred years before Freud, anticipated the theory of unconscious motivation when he wrote, "Men are generally ignorant of the causes of their desires." What is particularly striking as an anticipation of psychoanalytic teaching is an observation made by Christian Friedrich Hebbel (1813–1863), a German dramatist and poet who lived in Vienna during his later years. In 1850, six years before Freud was born, in connection with a discussion of his childhood memories, he, as quoted in an excerpt from one of Adler's articles (H. L. and R. R. Ansbacher, 1956, p. 357), had this to say about dreams and about what Freudians later called "free association" to dream material:

If a man would collect his dreams and examine them, and would add to the dreams which he is now having all the thoughts he has in association with them, all the reminiscences, all the pictures he can grasp from them, and if he would combine these with the dreams he has had in the past, he would be able to understand himself much better by this than by means of any other kind of psychology.

This passage was written fifty years before Freud's classic work on dreams was published. There is no evidence that Freud had ever come across this particular passage, even though there is evidence of his having read some of Hebbel's plays. Even if a direct connection between Hebbel's psychological views and those of Freud could be established, it would not diminish the significance of Freud's work.

Like Darwin, Freud mobilized a vast amount of data in support of his theorizing, and it was this body of data which aroused interest and attention. His predecessors from Plato to Hebbel may have anticipated some of his insights, but neither they nor their followers grasped the implications of such insights sufficiently to work them out as Freud did. Indeed, had it not been for Freud, these anticipations of his teachings might not have been "discovered" by the historians of psychology, for they too might have been blind to what they came to signify for Freud. Furthermore, in fairness to Freud, it should be noted that the broad sweep of his work included much in the way of historical precedent. This applies to such concepts as condensation and displacement in his dream theory; to projection, repression, and the whole array of defense mechanisms; to his theory of dynamic factors operative in forgetting; to his theory of infantile sexuality and the vicissitudes of the libido; and to his characterology and much else bearing on personality differences and the nature of neurotic conflict.

Significance of Historical Perspectives

In the light of what was just said about the vast difference between fragmentary anticipations of fruitful ideas and their elaboration decades or centuries later, one might well question the value of the historian's quest for such anticipations. Of what good is it to learn the views of Democritus regarding the relationship between taste sensations and the movements of atoms of varied shape? By modern standards such views are not to be classified as scientific teachings, any more than Plato's view of universal ideas as entities possessing independent, permanent existence merits scientific endorsement. And yet, in terms of the history of psychology, this is of secondary importance. What is of primary significance is the conceptual perspective involved in such teachings.

In the case of Democritus we have the beginnings of what in later centuries gave rise to so-called objective or behavioristic psychologies. Such psychologies regard man as an object to be studied in the same spirit in which botanists study plants or astronomers study the motion of planets. Man is viewed as an organism rather than as a person. It is a detached, impersonal approach to psychology comparable to an engineer's effort to understand the workings of an electronic computer. Input of stimuli as related to output of reactions is the chief focus of study. In figurative language it may be described as a slot-machine psychology. Output in the form of words or actions is viewed as a consequence of stimulus input, just as the output of chewing gum or chocolate is viewed as a consequence of differences in the input of coins. In terms of such a machinelike approach there is no need to consider such "subjective" factors as feelings, hopes, intentions, guilt, sensations, thoughts, or even consciousness.

In contrast to the kind of psychology initiated by the outlook of Democritus, the rationalism of Plato paves the way for the study of man as a creature striving for excellence in his own person by the acquisition of disciplined self-control and the organization of political institutions calculated to promote such excellence. To oversimplify somewhat, the differences between these two orientations can be summed up by saying that Democritus was concerned with *behavior* and Plato with *conduct*. Both men and monkeys exhibit varied behavior, but conduct is unique to human beings. In other words, both men and animals have impulses, but only man has ideals. To be governed by ideals means to behave in accordance with certain principles of conduct. These are principles of right and wrong, of justice and injustice, of sin and virtue, and all that falls within the purview of ethical values.

Plato's psychology was chiefly concerned with the enhancement of such values. His rationalism is not to be equated with a passionless, value-free "intellectualism." As mentioned earlier and as phrased by Brett (1912, p. 94), "For Plato life is essentially conduct." The function of the rational soul is to bring impulse into line with the attainment of ethically approved goals. What Freud called the "voice of the intellect" is reminiscent of Plato's rational soul. In his efforts to understand neurotic distress, Freud was also prompted to consider ethical issues, as is shown by his references to feelings of guilt and to conflicts between a tyrannical superego and repressed instinctual desires. In ordinary language, he was concerned with the clash between duty and desire.

Whether his psychoanalytic followers were fully cognizant of such ethical implications need not be considered at this point. It is probably correct, as O. H. Mowrer (1961) has pointed out, that both Freud and his followers made too much of the tyranny of the superego and overlooked its nontyrannical, constructive, guiding functions. It is probably also correct to say that, had it not been for Freud's introduction of problems of conscience into modern psychological discussions, Mowrer might not have been prompted to consider such problems. In reacting against what he takes to be the Freudian solution to problems of neurotic conflict, Mowrer had to work out his own ethical solution. Furthermore, in terms of others who have also reacted against some of Freud's views, one can note the introduction of ethical issues into their psychological writings. Adler was concerned with the value of community ties or social interest, Jung with the importance of religious ideals, and Erich Fromm with the development of a "humanistic conscience" and becoming an ethically responsible "productive" character. There is no need to add more names. It suffices to call attention to this twentieth-century interest in psychology as a science of conduct and not just a science of behavior.

In many ways this interest goes beyond psychology as an academic subject. It lies at the heart of what the Cornell University historian Erich Kahler has called (1943) "the basic problem of our time." For him, this takes the form of asking, "Is there a human quality common to men and distinguishing man from the animal?" Should the final answer turn out to be in the negative, then the verdict would be in support of a tradition going back to Democritus. But should the final answer turn out to be in the affirmative, then the verdict would be a vindication of the tradition we have traced back to Plato. Be this as it may, both traditions continue to be operative in the thinking of contemporary psychologists.

References

Ansbacher, H. L., and Ansbacher, R. R. *The Individual Psychology of Alfred Adler*. New York: Basic Books, 1956.

Bonaparte, M., Freud, A., and Kris, E. (eds.). *The Origins of Psycho-Analysis*. New York: Basic Books, 1954.

Brett, G. S. *A History of Psychology*, Vol. I. London: George Allen and Unwin, Ltd., 1912.

Brett, G. S. *A History of Psychology*, Vol. II. London: George Allen and Unwin, Ltd., 1912.

Drake, H. C. *The People's Plato*. New York: The Philosophical Library, 1958.

Durant, W. *The Story of Philosophy*. New York: Simon and Schuster, 1926.

Edman, I. (ed.). *The Works of Plato*. New York: The Modern Library, 1928.

Freud, S. *Beyond the Pleasure Principle*. New York: Albert and Charles Boni, 1922.

Freud, S. *The Future of an Illusion*. London: The Hogarth Press, 1934.

Freud, S. *New Introductory Lectures on Psychoanalysis*. New York: W. W. Norton and Company, 1933.

Freud, S. "On the History of the Psycho-Analytic Movement," in *Collected Papers*. Vol. I. London: The Hogarth Press, 1950.

Fuller, B. A. G. *A History of Philosophy*. New York: Henry Holt and Company, 1945.

Jones, E. *The Life and Work of Sigmund Freud*. Vol. I, 1953; Vol. II, 1955; Vol. III, 1957. New York: Basic Books.

Jowett, B. (trans.). *The Dialogues of Plato,* 4th ed. Vol. II, Vol. III. Oxford: Clarendon Press, 1953. Reprinted by permission of the Clarendon Press.

Kahler, E. *Man the Measure*. New York: Pantheon Books, 1943.

Merlan, P. "Brentano and Freud," *Journal of History of Ideas*, 1945, *VI*, 375–377; and "Brentano and Freud—A Sequel," 1949, *X*, 451.

Mowrer, O. H. *The Crisis in Psychiatry and Religion*. New York: D. Van Nostrand and Company, 1961.

Müller-Freienfels, R. *The Evolution of Modern Psychology*. New Haven: Yale University Press, 1935.

Murray, H. A. (ed.). *Myths and Mythmaking*. New York: George Braziller, 1960.

Nahm, M. C. (ed.). *Selections from Early Greek Philosophy*. New York: F. S. Crofts and Company, 1947.

Rado, S. "Emergency Behavior," in P. H. Hoch, and J. Zubin (eds.). *Anxiety*. New York: Grune and Stratton, 1950.

Weiss, A. P. *A Theoretical Basis of Human Behavior*. Columbus: R. G. Adams and Company, 1929.

Woods, A. L. (ed.). *The World of Dreams*. New York: Random House, 1947.

4

The Aristotelian Background

ARISTOTLE DIED IN 322 B.C. at the age of sixty-two. In the three or four decades of mature scholarly activity allotted to him he shaped the foundations of many subjects: logic, ethics, biology, government, education, metaphysics, and psychology. The encyclopedic range of his writings and the impact of his teachings on later generations have induced some to regard him as the possessor of the greatest intellect in the history of mankind. His erudition became legendary and was reinforced by the halo of theological endorsement surrounding his teachings during the later Middle Ages. Until the emergence of the scientific era in the seventeenth century he continued to be the revered and dominating authority. Disputes were settled by quoting Aristotle in a manner not altogether different from the way in which some ardent psychoanalysts venture to dispose of a controversial issue by quoting Freud.

Eminence Versus Evidence

Confidence in the soundness of what an authority or an expert has to say is thus not to be regarded as unique to the medieval mind. In general, such confidence may be justified in the sense that experts in a given subject are more likely to possess more dependable knowledge of that subject than dilettantes and nonexperts. The presumption is that the expert has examined the relevant evidence and bases his verdict on the evidence. If called upon, he ought to be able to justify his verdict in the light of such evidence. The soundness of the conclusion is a function of the evidence and not a consequence of the expert's eminence. When eminence is equated with evidence, intellectual progress is impeded.

The notion that scientific experts base their conclusions on an unbiassed examination of the relevant evidence was just stated to be a *presumption*. One reason for calling it a presumption is that the history of science is replete with instances of the rejection by experts of important findings for reasons unrelated to the evidence submitted. Some of these instances have been discussed by B. Barber (1961, pp. 596–602) in an article entitled "Resistance by Scientists to Scientific Discovery." By way of example, he mentions Max Planck's difficulties with distinguished physicists of his day. Men like Helmholtz and Kirchoff balked at accepting changes in the interpretation of thermodynamics proposed by Planck. In this connection Barber cites the following revealing passage from Planck's autobiography:

> This experience gave me also an opportunity to learn a new fact—a remarkable one, in my opinion: A new scientific truth does not triumph by convincing its opponents and making them see the light, but rather because its opponents eventually die, and a new generation grows up that is familiar with it.

According to Barber, when Roentgen's discovery of X rays was first reported, Lord Kelvin dismissed the report as a hoax. Barber also calls attention to Lord Kelvin's objections to James Clerk Maxwell's theory of light, and to the failure of distinguished contemporary botanists who failed to appreciate the epoch-making discoveries in plant genetics reported by Gregor Mendel; not until forty-odd years after their publication and almost twenty years after Mendel's death was their significance recognized by geneticists.

That institutionalized religion has sometimes been in active opposition to the teachings of science is common knowledge. Both Galileo and Darwin were victims of such opposition. However, it is not commonly known that sometimes the religious convictions of scientists may interfere with dispassionate evaluation of a new scientific formulation regarded as in conflict with such convictions. As reported by Barber, in the 1840s scientists as eminent as Lyell, Sedgwick, and Whewell all give expression to their opposition to a book by Robert Chambers dealing with a geological theory of the origin or development of the universe. They opposed the theory because it "was so at variance with the religious views which all scientists accepted." Moreover, the internationally famous Harvard naturalist Louis Agassiz was not only a member of this group, but also later became "the leading critic of Darwinism on religious grounds."

Sometimes authorities or experts in one field of science have spurned contributions to their field if it is proposed by a member of some other scientific group. A stock instance of this is the opposition to the germ theory of disease by the medical profession. In large measure the fact that Pasteur, the advocate of the theory, was a chemist and not a physician accounted for the resistance to his theory. A less familiar example of the same sort of intergroup resistance is also cited by Barber in connection with the reception accorded Helmholtz's theory of the conservation of energy. At the time Helmholtz was a young man whose academic training had been in medicine. Accordingly, he was not thought of as a physicist and what he had to present to specialists in physics was viewed disparagingly as the theory of an "outsider" not genuinely competent to deal with the subject.

There is no need to add more examples of these conflicts between established views and new ideas. What is important in the present context is to note that the conflict is not always due to lack of adequate supporting evidence mobilized by the advocate of the new. As the preceding examples suggest, even within science itself the "authorities" may quite unwittingly be blocking progress because their minds are not as open to impartial evaluation of new data as the ideal of scientific openmindedness might lead one to expect. Entrenched ideas are likely to be resistant to change. Even in the great "scientific" seventeenth century, leading scientists endorsed belief in witchcraft. Presumably their prestige as scientific authorities militated against due evaluation of contrary evidence. And, as stated earlier, when such prestige is equated with evidence, scientific progress is impeded. This is a chief danger of uncritical reliance on the voice of authority. To a certain extent such reliance may have accounted for the stagnation of science during the centuries when questions of fact or principle were disposed of by consulting the authority of Aristotle.

In contrast to Plato, Aristotle was an empiricist and a systematist. He was more interested in the collection and classification of facts, and in this sense exhibited more of the scientist's outlook than that of his philosophic predecessors. But it was more the outlook of the scientist as field naturalist than as experimentalist. Aristotle's scientific data were the results of ordinary observation unaided by the instrumentation of microscopes, telescopes, and other laboratory equipment. There were no laboratories, no traditions of experimental investigation, and no established canons of scientific evidence. All such developments were not to appear for some two thousand years. Under the circumstances it is not astonishing to find nonsense mingled with sense in the teachings of Aristotle. With reference to the human body, much of the nonsense was due to the fact that anatomic dissection had not yet been introduced. Mention has already been made of Aristotle's view regarding the heart as the center of mental life and the brain as a cooling mechanism. He knew nothing of the circulation of the blood and failed to note the difference between veins and arteries. Even so simple a question as the number of ribs possessed by man was answered incorrectly. Instead of twenty-four, Aristotle taught there are sixteen ribs. Such an error might be attributable to the fact that ribs are not directly visible. However, teeth can be rendered observable with little effort, and yet Aristotle was wrong in maintaining women have fewer teeth than men.

Aristotle's Genetic Viewpoint

The preceding examples of poor observation will suffice to demonstrate how wrong an "authority" can be with reference to matters of fact. It would be misleading, though, to cite these examples as representative of the general drift of Aristotle's scientific observations. In many ways he was an astute observer. In fact, one can even detect the beginnings of systematic, experimental observation in some of his writings. This applies particularly to his contributions to what the modern biologist views as the separate science of embryology. Aristotle's predecessor Hippocrates had demonstrated a method for noting embryological development by inspecting the contents of eggs that had been incubated for varying lengths of time. By employing this technique, Aristotle succeeded in noting developmental changes with keen attention to important details, as is evident in the following excerpts from Aristotle's report on his findings (W. D. Ross [ed.], 1938, pp. 149–151):

> Generation from the egg proceeds in an identical manner with all birds, but the full periods from conception to birth differ. . . . With the common hen after three days and three nights there is the first indication of the embryo; with larger birds the interval being longer, with smaller birds shorter. Meanwhile the yolk comes into being, rising towards the sharp end, where the primal element of the egg is situated, and where the egg gets hatched; and the heart appears, like a speck of blood, in the white of the egg. This point beats and moves as though endowed with life, and from it two vein-ducts with blood in them trend in a convoluted course as the egg-substance goes on growing, towards each of the two circumjacent integuments; and a membrane carrying bloody fibers now envelopes the yolk, leading off from the vein-ducts. A little afterwards the body is differentiated, at first very small and white. The head is clearly distinguished, and in it the eyes, swollen out to a great extent. This condition of the eyes lasts on for a good while, as it is only by degrees that they diminish in size and collapse. . . .
>
> When the egg is now ten days old the chick and all its parts are distinctly visible. The head is still larger than the rest of its body, and the eyes larger than the head, but still devoid of vision. . . . At this time also the larger internal organs are visible, as also the stomach and the arrangement of the viscera; and the veins that seem to proceed from the heart are now close to the navel. . . .
>
> About the twentieth day, if you open the egg and touch the chick, it moves inside and chirps; and it is already coming to be covered with down, when, after the twentieth day is past, the chick begins to break the shell.

A report like the foregoing has a modern ring. It is very different from what one would expect from an ancient philosopher in terms of the popular stereotype as a person preoccupied with vague abstractions divorced from the realities of concrete events. In fact, a modern professor of biology would be elated if one of his beginning students were to submit a report like this when given the assignment to investigate the development of the chick embryo.

In making such pioneer observations, Aristotle was not just contributing to the foundations of embryology. He was calling attention to the importance of becoming familiar with developmental changes as a means of enriched understanding. In his own words: "He who sees things grow from their beginning will have the finest view of them." The significance of this insight was lost to psychologists until the impact of Darwin's elaboration of the concept of evolution influenced the thinking of those who initiated studies of animal and child psychology in the closing decades of the nineteenth century. Their studies emphasized the importance of the *genetic method.* This method, as just indicated, had been utilized and advocated by Aristotle millennia earlier. In this sense one might say that Aristotle rather than Darwin was the first to recognize its value.

Being Contrasted with Becoming

Aristotle employed the genetic method to find out how the egg *becomes* a chick or how roe *become* fish. He was especially concerned with this phenomenon of *becoming* as contrasted with the phenomenon of *being.* The nature of being has been made the object of study in a special branch of metaphysics called *ontology.* The ontologist tries to determine the essential characteristics of existence. For example, what Plato had to say about the independent reality of ideas constituted an ontological teaching. Just as epistemology is concerned with the nature of knowledge, so ontology is concerned with the intrinsic nature of that which comes to be known.

In many respects Aristotle was more interested in the transitions from one state or level of existence to succeeding states or levels. This interest in growth or development is especially manifest in present-day psychological studies of personality development, which place more emphasis on the dynamics of personality growth than on the statics of personality as a finished product. An emphasis of this kind characterizes a central teaching of existential psychology. For example, Rollo May (1958, p. 17) has described existentialism as "an attitude which accepts man as always becoming, which means potentially in Crisis." A similar emphasis is to be found in Gordon Allport's volume entitled *Becoming.* In a section dealing with the bearing of personal values on what the individual becomes or makes of himself, Allport (1897–1967) wrote (1955, pp. 90–91):

> Philosophically speaking, values are the termini of our intentions. We never fully achieve them. Some writers make much of this fact. Jung, for example, defines personality in terms of the ideal state of integration toward which the individual is tending. Personality is not what one has, but rather the projected outcome of his growth. . . . It is the orientation that is important. From this point of view we may modify slightly our contention that complex levels of structure influence becoming. More precisely stated, it is the unfinished structure that has this dynamic power. A finished structure is static; but a growing structure, tending toward a given direction of closure, has the capacity to subsidiate and guide conduct in conformity with its movement.

Implicit in this quotation from Allport is a characteristic Aristotelian distinction; namely, the difference between the potential and the actual. To regard personality as the "projected outcome" of one's growth or development is to interpret the present status of the individual in terms of his unrealized potentialities. An interpretation of this sort may be viewed as a modern application of ontological distinctions recognized by Aristotle. By way of illustration, these sentences from Aristotle's discussion of the nature of being may prove clarifying (Ross, 1938, pp. 60–61):

> "Being" and "is" mean that a statement is true, "not being" that it is not true but false,—and this alike in affirmation and negation; e.g., "Socrates *is* musical" means that this is true, or "Socrates *is* not white" means that this is true; but "the diagonal of the square *is not* commensurate with the side" means that it is false to say it is.
>
> Again, "being" and "that which is" . . . sometimes mean being potentially, and sometimes being actually. For we say both of that which sees potentially and of that which sees actually, that it is "seeing," and both of that which can use knowledge and of that which is using it, that it knows. . . .

In less abstract terms, this last statement by Aristotle is a reference to such a commonplace observation as the fact that a chemist may be said to "know" chemistry even if he should be asleep or swimming at the time the statement is made. Not until he reaches his laboratory will his chemical knowledge be actualized. Analogously, when people are described as orators, sprinters, pitchers, or nurses there is no uncertainty about what is meant. It is understood that given the appropriate setting of lecture platform, track, diamond, or sickroom the respective skills of the individuals in question will become manifest.

The preceding examples illustrate one of the ways in which Aristotle distinguished between being and becoming, or between the potential and the actual. He employed the same terms in discussing questions of biological growth and those of artistic creativity as manifested in the work of a sculptor. As might be expected, these terms are not used in precisely the same way in such different contexts; hence the two contexts merit separate discussion.

As viewed by Aristotle, the development of complete animal forms from eggs or of complete plants from seeds was not accounted for by the mere assimilation of nutrient materials from without. Such materials are necessary to account for the increase in mass but are not sufficient to account for the emergence of unique structures or the final form upon completion of development. Factors within the egg or seedling must be assumed to govern the shape or direction of development. Such internal factors regulate the disposition of absorbed nutrient materials. Because of such factors, acorns become oak trees, the elephant ovum becomes a baby elephant, and the human embryo emerges as an infant.

In Aristotelian language the acorn is a potential tree, the ovum a potential elephant, and the embryo a potential human being. The realization of their respective potentialities constitutes their actualization. Inner forces are responsible for the transformation. This is suggested by the Greek terms used by Aristotle: "*dunamis*" for potentiality and "*energeia*" for actuality. He also employed the term "entelecheia" to designate actuality or complete development. This last word, anglicized as "entelechy," is Aristotle's expression for "inherent purpose" or, more literally, "that which has its purpose or goal within." In brief, the entelechy of the acorn is different from that of the egg; hence the inherent pattern of development for the one predestines it to become an oak and that of the other to become a chick. In each case the final actualization may be described as the entelechy of that which had been potential in the seed or egg.

Entelechy and the Concept of Cause

The word "entelechy," then, has to do with what is ordinarily regarded as the influence of purpose or planned action or predetermined ends in development and on creative endeavor. The second syllable of the word is derived from "*telos*," the Greek term for "end" or "goal." This term is also embodied in the word "teleology," the study of acts in the light of purposive striving. Aristotle's discussion of the sculptor's creation of a statue is focused on the causal influence of teleological factors. Confronted with a block of marble, the sculptor knows in general what result he intends to get when the carving is completed. In part this intention of the end sought or the final result to be attained determines which fragments of marble are to be chipped off in order to establish the contours of the finished statue.

As a determining factor, the intention or purpose serves as a cause of the carving. In Aristotle's terminology, it constitutes a *final* cause. Obviously the marble itself is necessary for bringing the statue into existence and thus can be listed as a *material* cause. But intention and a block of marble are not enough to bring the statue into being. The cutting instrument must be put into action, and this action would serve as the *efficient* cause of the final outcome. What enables the sculptor to know the latter outcome has been reached? It is reached when the form of the statue impresses him as exhibiting the *essence,* to use Aristotle's word, of what was intended or what characterizes the model. This depends on an adequate synthesis of the parts of the statue so as to endow the whole with the form required. For Aristotle this constituted a separate causal influence that he called the *formal* cause. The formal cause is not to be confused with the final cause. If the sculptor's purpose is to win a prize or to enhance his professional reputation, that purpose might be classified as a final cause, while the need to have the finished product conform to or resemble a given model would exemplify a formal cause. For a sculptor to express the "essence" of Lincoln's character would mean to be governed by what Aristotle designated as a formal cause, while the desire to pay homage to Lincoln's memory might be a final cause.

In this fourfold analysis of the concept of causation, there are issues that came to have and continue to have considerable significance for psychology. The whole question of causation as applied to human and animal behavior is bound up with the motivation of behavior. Motivation is intimately related to the question of purpose. Just how the concepts of cause, motive, and purpose are to be considered continues to be a subject of controversy among contemporary psychologists. While all of them would probably regard behavior as caused, they would not agree with respect to the operation of motives and purposes in their analyses of behavior. Aristotle's notion of final causes would be especially subject to criticism nowadays. So would his notion of entelechy as applied to growth and development. The word "entelechy" seems to be obsolescent among modern biologists and psychologists. Nevertheless, as a little reflection will show, the term has to do with current problems of maturation, of instinct, and even of learning.

In other words, present-day psychology reflects Aristotle's recognition of the complexity of causation. There are some psychologists like B. F. Skinner (1953) who rule out the relevance of motive and purpose and by implication venture to account for the instigation of behavior by what Aristotle called efficient causes. Others like E. C. Tolman (1932) place more emphasis on the importance of purposive factors. These are suggestive of the final causes in the sense of having to do with goal-directed striving. Still others like the Gestaltists can be viewed as giving due recognition to formal and material causes, for they stress the importance of organization and pattern and the visibility of significant cues in their accounts of learning and behavior.

Finally, the psychobiological issues implicit in the concept of entelechy have been elaborated in modern studies of the instinct concept by those like Knight Dunlap (1919), who question the very existence of instincts; by those like William McDougall (1923), who endow them with basic importance; by those like Abraham Maslow (1948), who recognize their value when suitably qualified; and by those like D. S. Lehrman (1953) and F. A. Beach (1955), who call attention to the need for critical examination of the whole concept of instinctive or unlearned behavior. In fact, in the article by Beach there is a statement reminiscent of the Aristotelian teaching regarding the value of seeing "things grow from their beginning." Beach has expressed the same idea in modern formulation (1955, p. 407): "No bit of behavior can be fully understood until its ontogenesis has been described."

Self-Actualization as a Mode of Becoming

Aristotle's recognition of the influence of final causes is also implicit in the thinking of those present-day personality theorists who stress the importance of self-actualization. The latter term is obviously related to what Aristotle had to say about the transition from being to becoming or the shift from the potential to the actual. Such transitions or shifts constitute the focus of the theorizing in the writings of Kurt Goldstein (1939). For Goldstein, behavior is to be understood as a continuing process of self-actualization, of realizing one's potentialities. In fact, he regards self-actualization as the fundamental source of motivation. All seemingly independent drives or motives like hunger, sex, curiosity, and others are viewed as self-actualizing trends. The person strives to become what he potentially might be in the sense that one who is endowed with mathematical aptitude will organize his life around the goal of becoming a mathematician. Similarly, one with innate musical potentialities will strive to actualize these by becoming a musician. Professional aspirations reflect aptitudes and interests. People like to do what they can do well, whether it be cooking or selling or playing golf. Whether one becomes a chef or a salesman or a professional golfer will thus be a function of the way in which aptitudes and interests as potential skills are organized in the service of self-actualizing aspirations.

Goals or aspirations have to do with what lies in the future as objectives one hopes to attain. To the extent that they influence behavior as present intentions, they can be classified as causes of behavior or, more specifically, as final causes. What Aristotle called a final cause is thus implicit in Goldstein's concept of self-actualization. Nor is Goldstein alone in emphasizing the psychological importance of this concept. Maslow (1954), for example, has equated psychological health with being a self-actualizing person. Somewhat related to this is Erich Fromm's discussion (1947) of the *productive* person as the ideal of a well-integrated personality. His account of the nature of a productive person is entirely harmonious with the concept of the self-actualizing person. Furthermore, as interpreted by the Ansbachers (1956, p. 105), Alfred Adler's recognition of the striving for superiority or mastery as a determinant of personality development is also consonant with the latter concept.

The striving for superiority, like all conative effort, is characterized by an *intention* to achieve some objective. This intention may be conscious or unconscious or subconscious. To put it in another way, a final cause may be explicit, implicit, or just dimly apprehended. In this sense, actualization of a potentiality can thus be considered as the execution of an intention or the effect of a final cause. Stated less abstractly, the sculptor can be said to intend to carve a particular figure, just as a novelist as he starts his first chapter might say, "I intend to write a short historical novel." Intentions go beyond the immediate present and point to the future or what has yet to come into being.

Intentionalism and Brentano's Act Psychology

The chief reason for introducing a discussion of the factor of intentionalism inherent in Aristotle's concept of actualization is the role this factor came to play in the psychology of Franz Brentano (1838–1917), Freud's professor of philosophy.[1] In his student days Brentano had immersed himself in the writings of Aristotle. As a result, according to E. G. Boring (1950, p. 356), Aristotle came to be "a dominating influence throughout the rest of his life." Furthermore, having been trained as a priest, Brentano was thoroughly familiar with the elaborations of Aristotelian thought introduced by medieval scholastics. According to R. Müller-Freienfels (1935, p. 82), for Brentano this scholastic tradition became the source of important ideas, for "the old Schoolmen had known something about consciousness which was later forgotten or disregarded."

What the "old Schoolmen had known" had to do with an obvious but commonly overlooked characteristic of consciousness; namely, its objective reference. To be conscious always means to be conscious *of* something. One is never just conscious in the abstract. In the act of judging there is something to be judged; in loving, something to be cherished; and in the act of thinking, something to which thought is being directed. All mental acts involve this kind of transitive relationship in the same sense in which all transitive verbs involve objective reference. Verbs like "purchase," "throw," and "find" point to objects purchased, thrown, and found. For Brentano, the transitive nature of consciousness became the hallmark of the psychical in contradistinction to the physical. He employed scholastic terminology in his definition of psychical phenomena, as is evident in the following translation of some of his key sentences (1874, pp. 115–116):

> Every psychical phenomenon is characterized by that which the scholastics of the Middle Ages called the intentional (also mental) inexistence of an object and what we, although not without altogether ambiguous expressions, would call the relationship to a content, the orientation toward an object (which is not to be understood as a reality), or immanent objectivity. Every psychical phenomenon contains something as object within itself, although not in the same way. . . . This intentional inexistence is exclusively peculiar to psychical phenomena. No physical phenomenon reveals anything like it. And so we can define psychical phenomena by saying they are such phenomena as intentionally contain an object within themselves.

The phrase "intentional inexistence" calls for clarification. It is a scholastic reference to the implicit or inherent existence of an objective in every mental act. By way of simple illustration, the act of wishing for a new coat may be

---

[1] At the time university lectures on psychology were under the aegis of the faculty of philosophy. Consequently, during his student days Freud was introduced to academic psychology as that psychology was viewed by Brentano. Moreover, as suggested by a recent publication, interest in Brentano's views has not vanished from contemporary psychology. See A. C. Rancurello, *A Study of Franz Brentano—His Psychological Standpoint and His Significance in the History of Psychology* (New York: Academic Press, 1968).

ARISTOTLE (384–322 B.C.)

FRANZ BRENTANO (1838–1917)

considered. The wish *qua* wish intends or points to an article to be found in a clothing store. It may be represented in consciousness by the visual image of a coat; but the image is not the object of the wish. The object is the coat symbolized by the image. Similarly, in reading a word like "DOG" the act of perceiving it goes beyond the bare visual sensation to the animal itself. One who has not learned to read may experience such a visual sensation but will be incapable of the perceptual act of "intending" the dog. In technical language, images and sensations are conventionally called *mental content.* However, for Brentano such content is not mental but physical; just as the image of a printed word on a photographic plate is a physical phenomenon. What converts the image or sensation into a psychical phenomenon is the reference to something beyond itself. Such transcendent reference is the crux of what Brentano called "intentional inexistence."

Intentionalism as discussed by Brentano in his publication of 1874 might be regarded as the fruit of a subjective analysis. It was an "inside" view or one that was obtained by subjecting one's own experience to analytic scrutiny. However, it may be possible to get a better understanding of what he meant by introducing an "outside" view. This can be done by subjecting the concept of a conditioned reaction to analytic scrutiny as Brentano might have done if such a concept had been prevalent in the 1870s.

Why should a conditioned reaction be regarded as a psychological phenomenon? It was not so regarded by I. P. Pavlov (1849–1936). In getting a dog to salivate at the sound of a buzzer, he believed himself to be working as a physiologist and not as a psychologist. Nevertheless, his technique commended itself to behaviorists as a means of studying the *psychology* of the dog. Brentano might have agreed with them, but for different reasons. In his view, salivation in response to the buzzer would mean that food is intentionally inexistent in the sound as the animal hears it and salivation is the outward sign of the intention to eat. In the very process of establishing the conditioned reaction, this intention has to be activated. This is done by seeing to it that the animal is hungry during the training sessions. Even after the reaction has been dependably established, it will not be elicited should the animal suffer from a digestive upset, which would militate against the arousal of the intention. In everyday speech, the dog might be said to have an aversion to food. The aversion or negative intention would, of course, be temporary; since upon recovery the customary conditioned reaction would once again be manifested. Furthermore, Brentano could readily have accounted for experimental extinction by pointing out that salivation is inhibited because the underlying intention cannot be realized in the absence of food as the intended object.

Intended objects need not be physical objects; they may be concepts, ideas, fancies, laws, or what, in brief, is to be classified as an object of thinking. In his work *The Meaning of Truth* (1909), William James clarified the meaning of intentionality by means of this simple example:

Suppose, to fix our ideas, that we take first a case of conceptual knowledge; and let it be our knowledge of the tigers in India, as we sit here. Exactly what do we *mean* by saying that we know the tigers? . . .

Most men would answer that what we mean by knowing the tigers is having them, however absent in body, become in some way present to our thought; or that our knowledge of them is known as presence of our thought to them. A great mystery is usually made of this peculiar presence in absence; and the scholastic philosophy, which is only common sense grown pedantic, would explain it as a peculiar kind of existence, called intentional inexistence, of the tigers in our mind. At the very least, people would say that what we meant by knowing the tigers is mentally *pointing* towards them as we sit here.

The previously mentioned description of intentionalism in terms of transcendent reference was an anticipation of what James had to say in terms of *pointing*. In going beyond or transcending a fragment of mental content like the letters of the word TIGER, one is pointing to what is beyond in far-off India. In this instance the intended object—the tiger—is not only present as an *idea* but may at the same time be *judged* dangerous and *hated* because of his viciousness. This somewhat forced elaboration of the tiger example is for the purpose of indicating the classes of psychical acts recognized by Brentano. It might be a more accurate statement of Brentano's teaching to describe them as aspects of any single psychical act. Such aspects are to be discussed separately only in the interests of descriptive convenience. In Brentano's terminology, these aspects of ideating, of judging, and of loving-hating have reference to the unified complexity of any mental act. In reading the preceding sentence, for example, the ideational aspect has to do with understanding its meaning, the judgmental aspect with accepting or rejecting it as a valid statement, and the loving-hating aspect with the pleasant or unpleasant concomitants of the reading.

Act Psychology Versus Associationism

The process of reading serves as a helpful means of illustrating many psychological problems as construed by advocates of differing psychological systems; since all would agree in regarding reading as being *mental* rather than purely optical or physiological in nature. In the present context this can be clarified by once again considering the tigers introduced by James.

Just what occurs in reading the word TIGERS? For Brentano, as already explained, it involves the pointing relationship or the intentionality of transcendent reference. A more familiar account would involve recourse to the psychology of the associationists. This is the psychology often designated as British associationism because a long line of scholars in Britain contributed to its development. They include Hobbes and Locke in the seventeenth century; Berkeley, Hume, and Hartley in the eighteenth; and James Mill, John Stuart Mill, and Alexander Bain in the nineteenth. Details of their specific teachings will be considered in later chapters. Here it is enough to note that they all stressed the importance of experience in establishing the connections by virtue of which ideas follow one another in sequence. The basic principle was that of *contiguity* or togetherness. Lightning touches off the thought of thunder and the pangs of hunger the idea of eating, because the events in question had so frequently been contiguous in experience in the past. As applied to reading the word TIGER, the associationists would maintain that in the course of learning the sight of the word had been linked to a picture of the animal and thus an association had been established between the word and picture. Consequently, reading might be described as a process of having relevant associated images come to mind in response to the visual presentation of verbal symbols. In the practiced reader it is an automatic, passive process.

This account of the reading process makes no mention of intentional inexistence or transcendent reference. Even in this simple example, however, an intentional factor can be shown to be operative, for the arousal of the associated image of the animal is to be attributed to a set or intention to get the meaning of the word. Had there been instructions to check the spelling or the legibility of the type or to find a rhyme for TIGER, then no visual image of the animal need have obtruded itself. The instructions in question would have aroused different intentions; hence a shift in the outcome. Reading is not an altogether passive process but rather an active quest the nature of which varies with the purpose or intention governing one's reading. Sometimes, of course, as every student knows, reading may be altogether mechanical and passive, as happens when one is thinking of a topic unrelated to the text he is supposed to be studying. Under the circumstances there is no comprehension of the material upon which his eyes have been focused. In the absence of an appropriate intention, meaning fails to be actualized.

Brentano's act psychology, it should now be clear, was different from that of the British associationists. He was familiar with their writings but evidently did not regard their associationistic accounts of mental life as adequate. His act psychology differed from the general drift of British associationism in placing more emphasis on transcendent reference as an active process as contrasted with association construed as a passive process.

Another way of indicating the difference is to say that associationism tends to stress external events as the source of our ideas, while act psychology tends to stress the selective influence of intentions in determining which external events are to be of ideational significance. In part this distinction is akin to Aristotle's distinction between having an experience and observing an experience. This is the familiar distinction between the attitude of the passive, indifferent spectator and that of the vitally interested participant observer. A foreigner viewing his first baseball game fails to have the same experience as the ardent fan viewing the same game. The latter knows what to look for, while the former, in his ignorance and bewilderment, may not; hence being at the game constitutes very different experiences for the two men.

Both British associationism and act psychology were rooted in experience, as is reflected in the facts that both tried to account for mind by means of an analysis of experience, that a synonym for "British associationism" is "British empiricism," and that the title of Brentano's first important book is *Psychology from the Empirical Standpoint*. However, as we have just seen, despite this agreement on the empirical foundations of psychology, there was disagreement with respect to the kind of psychology to be established on these foundations.

The associationistic emphasis of British empiricism, although not shared by Brentano, did find a sympathetic reception in the "new" psychology of Wilhelm Wundt. In defining psychology as the study of immediate experience he, like Brentano, was repudiating a metaphysical approach to psychology. Unlike Brentano, however, he proposed to study immediate experience under conditions of laboratory control. Just how he proposed to do this will be considered later. For the present it is enough to note that he subjected associationism to *experimental* study. This is what made Wundt's a "new" psychology. One of his early books in which he first projected his plan for an experimental psychology was published in 1874, the year of Brentano's *Psychology from the Empirical Standpoint*.

Thus the year 1874 is an important date in the history of psychology. It marks the emergence in Germany of two differing orientations toward psychology, Wundt's "new" experimental approach and Brentano's "old" revived Aristotelian approach, with both approaches focused on the concept of experience. Wundt sought laboratory support for his analyses of experience, while Brentano was content to base his conclusions on evidence derived from an appeal to analyses of everyday experiences. What has been said in the section about the psychology of reading may be regarded as an example of the kind of nonexperimental but nevertheless cogent evidence that Brentano might have endorsed. An appeal to ordinary experience suffices to demonstrate that reading a passage for meaning is different from reading it to check on the spelling. Even the most ardent experimentalist would doubtless acknowledge the existence of such a difference.

Brentano's Influence on Later Psychology

As a consequence, one ought to hesitate before stigmatizing Brentano's act psychology as nonscientific. Actually, like the tradition initiated by Wundt, it had important consequences for the subsequent development of psychology. The Austrian psychologist and philosopher Alexius Meinong (1833–1920) was greatly influenced by it. So was Edmund Husserl (1839–1938) in Germany, who developed a separate discipline called *phenomenology* to designate his way of analyzing "pure" experience. Since Husserl was more of a logician than a psychologist, his phenomenology might not be an unambiguous instance of Brentano's influence on psychology. A better instance is to be found in the contributions of Carl Stumpf (1848–1936), a distinguished German psychologist. Nor was the influence of Brentano restricted to Austria and Germany, for British psychologists such as James Ward (1843–1925), George Frederick Stout (1860–1944), and even William McDougall (1871–1938) incorporated principles of act psychology into their respective psychological systems. Through Brentano, in other words, some Aristotelian insights were woven into the pattern of twentieth-century psychology. Nor should his emphasis on the *empirical* standpoint be construed as a lack of interest in or a repudiation of the *experimental* standpoint. Actually, as E. B. Titchener (1929, p. 21) pointed out, as far back as 1874 Brentano "urged the establishment at Vienna of a psychological laboratory" and later "brought the Müller-Lyer illusion to the attention of psychologists."

In addition to his influence on segments of academic psychology, Brentano may have had some indirect influence on psychoanalytic psychology. As has been mentioned, during his student days Freud took six courses with Brentano. Accordingly, the existence of a possible relationship between act psychology and psychoanalysis merits consideration even though Freud himself makes no mention of Brentano in his semiautobiographical history of psychoanalysis (1950).

Quite obviously a good deal of psychoanalytic theory is altogether devoid of any relationship to Brentano's thinking. The libido theory, Oedipal problems, defenses against anxiety, psychosexual development, the notions of superego in conflict with the id, the concept of defense mechanisms, and other distinctively psychoanalytic concepts are not to be construed as derivatives of act psychology. But what about Brentano's understanding of the nature of a psychical act? Is there not something dynamic implicit in the intentionalism of such acts? As already explained, in pointing to something beyond mental content they involve transcendent references.

Freud's dream theory can also be said to involve transcendent reference: the symbolism of the manifest content points to the latent content. Furthermore, as envisaged by Freud, the "free" associations of his patients were not just passively aroused chance connections between contiguous ideas but intentionally directed sequences by virtue of unconscious forces. The emphasis on the unconscious was, of course, unrelated to act psychology; but the emphasis on the directional outcome of "free" associations is reminiscent of Brentano's notion of the "intentional inexistence" of psychical acts.

Whether the way in which Brentano's intentionalism may have influenced Freud's thinking, as just suggested, is in accord with fact may well be questioned. At best it is to be regarded as plausible conjecture. In the absence of supporting evidence from Freud's writings, there is no way of demonstrating it to be historically accurate. Both those who write history and those who read history ought to be mindful of the hazards incident to tracing the history of ideas. In the words of H. C. Warren (1921, p. v), "A sympathetic historian is ever in danger of reading into earlier writers the more definite results of later analysis, or of attributing to them his own ideas."

In the present instance, consequently, it is important to minimize this danger by calling attention to the conjectural nature of what Freud said about intentional factors. Although the existence of such factors can be indicated, there is no assured way of proving a direct line of influence from Brentano to Freud with respect to the factors in question. There is always the possibility that the intentionalism implicit in the Freudian wish emerged independently of what Freud had gleaned from Brentano's lectures. A similar statement can be made about a possible relationship between what Brentano had to say regarding loving and hating as psychical acts and the importance that such acts came to have in Freudian theory.

Although the bearing of Aristotelian factors in Brentano's psychology on Freud's psychology must remain conjectural, this does not hold true for a more direct relationship between Aristotle and Freud with respect to the latter's dream theories. In the very first chapter of *The Interpretation of Dreams* (1913, p. 2), Freud refers to Aristotle as the first man to subject dreaming to psychological study by divesting such study of supernatural beliefs in dreams as divine revelations. He also cites Aristotle's definition of a dream along with mention of Aristotle's knowledge of some of the characteristics of dream life. There can thus be no question of Freud's familiarity with this segment of Aristotle's teachings.

Aristotle as Phenomenologist

Aristotle's discussion of dreams is of particular psychological interest not so much because of what he said about dreams but because he includes numerous references to facts and concepts that have come to be included in the subject matter of general psychology as it is presented to the modern student. Even though the account was written more than two thousand years ago, it contains references to psychological facts of which many people are ignorant unless they chance to read a textbook of general psychology or chance to come across the relevant section in Aristotle's works. Fortunately, the latter section is readily accessible in a volume, *Readings in the History of Psychology* as edited by Wayne Dennis (1948, pp. 10–16).

Aristotle's empiricism is clearly evident in his recognition of the perseverative efforts of sensory stimulation. He refers to the persistence of brightness when "we have turned our gaze from sunlight to darkness" and also refers to the results of prolonged fixation of a color such as "white or green, that to which we next transfer our gaze appears to be of the same color." The existence of *afterimages* was thus definitely known to Aristotle. He also knew about *sensory adaptation,* as is evidenced by his reference to the impairment of the "power of smelling" as a consequence of "smelling very strong odours."

In addition he calls attention to the need for a distinction between perception and judgment and to the existence of illusions. In this connection he mentions what current textbooks often refer to as *Aristotle's illusion.* This, it may be recalled, refers to the tactual impression of duality when a single object such as a pencil is placed in the crotch formed by having the middle finger crossed over the index finger. In the words of Aristotle: "When the fingers are crossed, the one object is felt by the touch as two, but yet we deny that it is two; for sight is more authoritative than touch." Yet, if touch stood alone, we should actually have pronounced the one object to be two. An act of judgment is needed to dispose of the conflict between tactual and visual impressions; hence the distinction between perception and judgment. The distinction is also suggested by Aristotle's description of illusion as "false judgment." He cites the familiar *illusion of relative movement* as an example of such as "false judgment" by noting that "to persons sailing past, the land seems to move when it is really the eye that is being moved by something else [the moving ship]."

In some ways these descriptions of sensory events prove Aristotle to have been an early phenomenologist. In addition to the preceding phenomenological observations, he noted what in modern terminology would be called *flight of colors*: "If, after having looked at the sun or some other brilliant object, we close the eyes, then, if we watch carefully, it appears in a right line with the direction of vision, at first in its own colour; then it changes to crimson, next to purple, until it becomes black and disappears." Nor did the phenomenon of *diplopia* elude his observation: "If a finger be inserted beneath the eyeball, . . . one object will not only present two visual images, but will create an opinion of its being two objects." Furthermore, he anticipated modern teachings regarding perceptual distortions occasioned by strong emotion or the delirium of fever (Dennis [ed.], 1948, p. 13):

> . . . we are easily deceived respecting the operations of sense perception when we are excited by emotions; for example, the coward when excited by fear, the amorous person by amorous desire; to that, with but little resemblance to go upon, the former thinks he sees his foes approaching, the latter that he sees the object of his desire; and the more deeply one is under the influence of the emotion, the less similarity is required to give rise to these illusory impressions. Thus, too, both in fits of anger, and also in all states of appetite, all men become easily deceived, and more so the more their emotions are excited. This is the reason too why persons in the delirium of fever sometimes think they see animals on their chamber walls, an illusion arising from the faint resemblance to animals of the markings thereon when put together in patterns; and this sometimes corresponds with the emotional states of the sufferers, in such a way that, if the latter be not very ill, they know well enough that it is an illusion; but if the illness is more severe they actually move according to the appearances.

Motion and Process as Key Concepts

As G. S. Brett (1912, p. 122) pointed out, motion or activity supplies the key concept to Aristotle's psychology. It is a *process* psychology, just as Brentano's psychical acts were found to be processes. In fact, in translations of Aristotle one finds the word "process" employed in connection with psychological topics. For instance, in a passage concerned with the "common sense," Aristotle wrote that "the actualization of the object of sense and of the sense itself is one and the same process," even though "their essential nature" is different just as an "actual sound and actual hearing" are different (Brett, 1912, p. 63). The sound that fails to eventuate in a sensation is regarded as a stimulus, and for Aristotle, like all stimuli when objectively considered, it is to be viewed as some form of motion. In this emphasis on motion he might be said to have foreshadowed the psychology of Thomas Hobbes (1588–1679), for whom motion also became the fundamental psychological category. The following quotation from Hobbes (B. Rand [ed.], 1912, p. 152) dealing with the sound of a bell will serve as an elaboration of the preceding Aristotelian distinction between sound and hearing:

> Nothing can make any thing which is not in itself: the *clapper* hath no *sound* in it, but *motion,* and maketh motion in the internal parts of the bell; so the *bell* hath motion, and not sound, that imparteth motion to the *air*; and the *air* hath motion, but not sound; the *air* imparteth motion by the *ear* and *nerve* unto the *brain*; and the brain hath motion but not sound; from the *brain*, it reboundeth back into the *brain*, it reboundeth back into the nerves *outward,* and thence it becometh an *apparition without,* which we call *sound.*

By the time of Hobbes, it should be evident, the brain rather than the heart had come to be viewed as the "organ" of mind; but in the present context this is of minor significance. What merits special emphasis is the agreement between Aristotle and Hobbes regarding motion and process as fundamental concepts. For Aristotle, as Brett has stated (1912, p. 123), "*All* sensation implies activity on the part of the sentient organ; and perception implies activity of the percipient person." A similar statement would apply to the teachings of Hobbes. This emphasis on the concepts of motion, activity, or process is important because it marks early recognition of the transitional, as opposed to the substantive, nature of mental events. Similar recognition is embodied in the notion of streaming, as suggested by the famous phrase "*stream* of consciousness" when William James introduced it in the 1890s. Recognition of this kind serves to guard against intrusion of the fallacy of reification incident to the hazards of regarding abstract words like sensation, perception, attention, image, and other psychological terms as references to things or entities akin to objects like tables or shoes.

Anticipation of Locke: Origin of "Common Sense"

In addition to anticipating a central teaching of Hobbes, Aristotle also anticipated a central teaching of another British empiricist, John Locke (1632–1704). Locke's analysis of the origin and nature of "our simple ideas of sensation" introduced a distinction between what he termed *primary* qualities on the one hand and *secondary* ones on the other. By the former term Locke designated characteristics he deemed to be "utterly inseparable" from perceived objects, while the term "secondary qualities" was reserved for sensations produced by primary qualities but not inherent properties of the perceived objects. In Locke's own words (Rand [ed.], pp. 242–243):

> To discover the nature of our *ideas* the better, and to discourse of them intelligibly, it will be convenient to distinguish them, as they are ideas or perceptions in our minds: and as they are modifications of matter in the bodies that cause such perceptions in us; that so we may not think (as perhaps is usually done) that they are exactly the images and resemblances of something inherent in the subject; most of those of sensation being in the mind no more the likeness of something existing without us than the names that stand for them are the likeness of our ideas, which yet upon hearing they are apt to excite in us.

In Locke's view, the color, taste, odor, temperature, and sound of an object would constitute secondary characteristics. Its primary qualities, or what he also called its "original" qualities, would be its "solidity, extension, figure, motion or rest, and number." There is a striking resemblance between this list of Locke's primary qualities and a list of what Aristotle called *common sensibles*. According to Aristotle, these are (Rand, 1912, p. 61): "motion, rest, form, magnitude, number, unity."

The two lists are similar but not identical. Solidity is not mentioned by Aristotle as it is by Locke. This may seem to be a curious oversight until it is pointed out that Aristotle regarded tactual sensations as fundamental. He even recognized the complexity of cutaneous sensations by writing that "all the qualities of the tangible as such are apprehended by touch."[2] For him the "common sensibles" were functions of touch; hence solidity, it would seem, was implicit in the tactual apprehension of form, magnitude, and motion of objects.

However, such characteristics can also be apprehended visually. The sphericity of a red ball can be both felt and seen, but its redness is exclusively a function of vision. Its roundness is thus *common* to two sense modalities. As Aristotle put it, there is "a 'common sense' for the perception of common qualities." This, of course, is the origin of the familiar, everyday reference to "common sense" as the equivalent of sound, practical judgment. Aristotle, as shown in the following quotation from his discussion of the common sense, refers to the "judging subject" who notes similarities and differences (Rand, 1912, p. 65):

> Now inasmuch as we distinguish white, sweet, and every sense-quality by its relation to a particular sense, by what instrument do we perceive that these qualities

---

[2] The qualities in question included "the tangible, the hot and cold, and the fluid and the solid."

differ from one another? We must do so by means of sensation, for they are sense-qualities. Is it not plain that the flesh is not the final organ of sense? For the judging subject would then necessarily distinguish an object by contact. Neither is it possible by means of the distinct senses to judge that sweet is different from white, but it is necessary that both these qualities be cognized by some one faculty; otherwise it would be like my perceiving one thing and you another, and so proving that they are different. A single faculty must, therefore, say that they are different. For the sweet is actually different from the white. One and the same faculty, then, must affirm this. And as this faculty affirms, so do thought and perception agree.

Aristotle's notion of a "common sense" is thus a reference to judgments or thoughts aroused by sensory impressions involving sight, smell, taste, hearing, and the complexities of touch. Locke, as will be brought out in a later chapter, also recognized the need for such a notion in order to account for human understanding. In Locke's terminology, our world of ideas is a resultant of two sets of factors: sensations on the one hand and reflection on the other. What Locke called *reflection* Aristotle called *the common sense*. Both these terms serve as reminders of the fact that man is not only acted upon *by* external events but also reacts *to* them. As already mentioned, Aristotle alluded to this fact when he called attention to the differences between having and observing an experience.

Aristotle's Associationism

British empiricism was ushered in by Hobbes and Locke, and because of its stress on the doctrine of association it also came to be known as British associationism. However, Aristotle's empiricism is not unrelated to the latter doctrine. In discussing the nature of recollection he refers to association as a concept even though he fails to employ the word itself. Incidentally, as Warren (1921, p. 23) noted, Plato preceded Aristotle in suggesting "the function of *contiguity* and *similarity* in the act of recollection." What centuries later came to be called the principles of frequency, uniqueness, similarity, contrast, and contiguity were all anticipated by Aristotle. In the following excerpt from Aristotle's discussion of recollection these principles, as indicated by the italicized words, can be recognized readily, since the sequence of the latter words is the same as the preceding list of principles (Ross [ed.], pp. 216–217):

Acts of recollection, as they occur in experience, are due to the fact that one movement has by nature another that succeeds it in regular order.

If this order be necessary, whenever a subject experiences the former of two movements thus connected, it will experience the latter; if, however, the order be not necessary, but customary, only in the *majority* of cases will the subject experience the latter of the two movements. But it is a fact that there are some movements, by a single experience of which persons take the impress of custom more deeply than they do by experiencing others many times; hence upon seeing some things but *once* we remember them better than others which we may have seen frequently.

Whenever, therefore, we are recollecting, we are experiencing certain of the antecedent movements until finally we experience the one after which customarily comes that which we seek. This explains why we hunt up the series, having started in thought either from a present intuition or some other, and from something either *similar*, or *contrary*, to what we seek, or else from that which is *contiguous* with it.

It should now be evident that Aristotle's empiricism had several striking points of agreement with the empiricism of the British associationists. By way of review and summary: motion or process was stressed both by Aristotle and Hobbes; Locke's notion of primary qualities and Aristotle's common sensibles are virtually synonymous in meaning; the judgmental aspect of what Aristotle called *the common sense* has much in common with what Locke called *reflection*; and finally, association psychology's principles of contiguity, similarity, and several others were already recognized by Aristotle.

Anticipation of the Gestalt Viewpoint

Unlike Aristotle's British successors in the associationist tradition, he himself did not venture to account for the development of ideas and concepts by exclusive reliance on principles of association. As is well known, in the modern era Gestalt psychologists have been especially critical of this phase of the tradition. They have stigmatized it as an "atomistic" psychology because of its reduction of experience to sensory elements which, genetically considered, were then regarded as having preceded the emergence of their eventual organization into percepts and concepts.

The elements, like atoms, were assumed to form more or less complex ideational compounds in the course of mental development. This, so Gestaltist critics pointed out, implied that the parts or elements or "atoms" had to be fitted together in order for knowledge and understanding to emerge. According to these critics, it was as if the elements of language were to be reduced to the letters of the alphabet and then the creation of a novel were to be described as the product of one letter being added to another until the last word of the last chapter is written. From this viewpoint the whole novel would be conceived of as an arrangement of its constituent elements or parts.

In this hypothetical instance the parts would be the letters of the alphabet. The parts would then be regarded as having existed *prior* to the planning of the novel. In opposition to such a view, the Gestaltist would insist the plan or general idea of the novel must be prior to selection of the appropriate parts. Knowledge of the *whole* word must precede selection of the correct letters. In the language of Gestalt psychologists: the whole is *prior* to the parts.

The Gestaltist emphasis on the priority of wholes was introduced into psychology some fifty years ago. However, as a concept it may be said to date back to the time of Aristotle,[3] for there is a passage in Aristotle's *Politics* concerned with this phase of part-whole relationships. The passage in question deals with the origin of the state. In this connection Aristotle noted that "man is more of a political animal than bees or any other gregarious animals" and that "he alone has any sense of good and evil, of just and unjust, and the like, and the association of living beings who have this sense makes a family and a state." He continues with this paragraph (Ross, 1938, pp. 288–289):

> Further, the state is by nature clearly prior to the family and to the individual, since the whole is of necessity prior to the part; for example, if the whole body be destroyed, there will be no foot or hand, except in an equivocal sense, as we might speak of a stone hand; for when destroyed the hand will be no better than that. But things are defined by their working and power; and we ought not to say that they are the same when they no longer have their proper quality, but only that they have the same name. The proof that the state is a creation of nature and prior to the individual is that the individual, when isolated, is not self-sufficing; and therefore he is like a part in relation to the whole. But he who is unable to live in society, or who has no need because he is sufficient for himself, must be either a beast or a god: he is no part of a state. A social instinct is implanted in all men by nature, and yet he who first founded the state was the greatest of benefactors. For man, when perfected, is the best of animals, but, when separated from law and justice, he is the worst of all; since armed injustice is the more dangerous, and he is equipped at birth with arms, meant to be used by intelligence and virtue, which he may use for the worst ends. Wherefore, if he have not virtue, he is the most unholy and the most savage of animals, and the most full of lust and gluttony. But justice is the bond of men in states, for the administration of justice, which is the determination of what is just, is the principle of order in political society.

---

[3] The concept in question was not unique to Aristotle. According to the distinguished classicist Edith Hamilton (1867–1963), sensitivity to whole-part relationships was a characteristic "way of the Greeks." She demonstrates this by references to the structure of Greek drama and architecture which reveals the "necessity of the Greek mind to see everything in relation to a whole." On the first page of her chapter concerned with this issue (1930, p. 221) she indicates its importance for psychology:

> To us a man's character is that which is peculiarly his own; it distinguishes each one from the rest. To the Greeks it was a man's share in qualities all men partake of; it united each one to the rest. We are interested in people's special characteristics, the things in this or that person which are different from the general. The Greeks, on the contrary, thought what was important in a man were precisely the qualities he shared with all mankind.
> The distinction is a vital one. Our way is to consider each separate thing alone by itself; the Greeks always saw things as parts of a whole, and this habit of mind is stamped upon everything they did. It is the underlying cause of the difference between their art and ours.

Functional, Adlerian, and Social Psychology

More than an anticipation of a central teaching of Gestalt psychology is revealed by the preceding paragraph. It is also revelatory of teachings advocated by functional psychologists at the turn of the century. The functionalist viewpoint is definitely implicit in Aristotle's statement to the effect that "things are defined by their working and power." This is tantamount to saying they are to be defined by what they accomplish or what functions they subserve. In terms of Aristotle's example, a hand detached from the body ceases to be a real or full-fledged hand, since it can no longer function as a prehensile organ. To introduce a more modern example: the meaning of a term like "carburetor" is not supplied by mere observation of an isolated carburetor on the floor of a garage. Not until its function as an integral part of an automobile's fuel-feed system is explained to us do we possess adequate understanding of the term. How parts articulate with wholes is thus a basic issue both from the viewpoint of Gestalt psychology as well as from the functionalist viewpoint. In other words, both the beginnings of Gestaltism and of functionalism might be traced back to this Aristotelian source. So might a central teaching of Adlerian psychology; namely, the importance for individual development of intrafamilial and community relationships. Such a teaching is implicit in Aristotle's contention that "the individual, when isolated, is not self-sufficing; and therefore he is like a part in relation to the whole."

Moreover, the same quotation from Aristotle's *Politics* can be viewed as supplying an early glimpse of a problem which, as elaborated in the present era, has developed into the field of social psychology. McDougall, as one of the founding fathers of this field, attributed man's need for human fellowship to the driving force of a gregarious instinct. Quite manifestly a view of this kind is altogether consistent with Aristotle's reference to a "social instinct" being implanted in all men. However, Aristotle was not content to regard such an instinct as sufficient to account for man's social behavior. A careful reading of the paragraph makes clear that by stressing the priority of family and communal organization he was calling attention to the significance of man's cultural heritage, with its emphasis on "law and justice," as the means of preventing an "isolated" or feral child from becoming "the most savage of animals, and the most full of lust and gluttony." In the light of this perspective, social psychology can be said to have Aristotelian roots.

The "Golden Mean" and Personality Differences

Aristotelian roots can also be found for other sectors of modern psychology. For example, contemporary discussions of behavior often refer to people as "well adjusted" or having "balanced personalities" or being "weak characters." Such ways of describing people are little more than modifications of concepts already considered by Aristotle. In fact, his *Nicomachaean Ethics* is replete with ideas now commonly included in courses bearing titles like "Mental Hygiene," "Psychology of Adjustment," or "Psychology of Personality."

One of the key ideas frequently mentioned in such courses concerns individual differences as variables on a continuum from small through medium to large or from deficit through average to excess. It is now customary to represent such differences by means of frequency-distribution curves symbolizing the transitions from low to high scores on tests of intelligence or spelling ability or strength of grip or whatever else is deemed to be a significant and measurable trait, skill, aptitude, or achievement. The statistical procedures involved belong to the modern era, but the underlying concept dates back to Aristotle. Both the notion of a continuum and of quantitative differences can be gleaned from this Aristotelian statement (Ross, 1938, p. 232):

> In everything that is continuous and divisible it is possible to take more, less, or an equal amount, and that either in terms of the thing itself or relatively to us; and the equal is an intermediate between excess and defect.

Aristotle proceeds to clarify this statement by calling attention to the difference between absolute and relative measures of the "intermediate." The absolute refers to an impersonal and objective measure "which is one and the same for all men," as illustrated by regarding 6 as intermediate between 2 and 10. This, Aristotle states, "is intermediate according to arithmetical proportion." However, the quest for the *golden mean* in daily-life situations is not to be disposed of by such simple arithmetic. The optimal "intermediate" will be relative to the needs of the individual. Aristotle illustrates this conclusion by reference to training for athletic events by suitable control of diet. The trainer does not order six pounds of food for each of his athletes just because he regards ten pounds as too much and two pounds as too little; instead, he adjusts the estimate in accordance with the individual athlete's requirements. As a general principle, such adjustment to individual needs ought to govern all human endeavor; hence "a master of any art avoids excess and defect, but seeks the intermediate and chooses this—the intermediate not in object but" in relation to himself.

The same principle is operative in the development of what a present-day psychiatrist would call a "balanced personality" and what Aristotle designated as the pursuit of "virtue" in the interest of praiseworthy character development. He recognized two kinds of virtue: intellectual and moral. These are not to be cultivated by the same procedures, for the intellectual virtues are products of teaching and experience while the moral virtues are products of habit formation. In fact, as he points out (Ross, 1938, p. 230), the term "ethics" is derived from "ēthos," the Greek word for "habit."

Interestingly enough, in anticipation of modern educational psychology Aristotle writes that "we learn by doing" and that "we become just by doing

just acts, temperate by doing temperate acts, brave by doing brave acts."
Achievement of such individual virtues as justice, temperance, bravery, and
the rest calls for practice in selecting the mean between deficiency and excess.

Every virtue or character trait may be warped either by underdevelopment
or overdevelopment. As examples Aristotle mentions the stinginess of the
mean-spirited and the extravagance of the prodigal in their handling of
money. They both fail to approximate "the mean of liberality." Similarly, with
respect to honor or self-respect one has to guard against an excessive humility
on the one hand and overweening pride on the other. For Aristotle, in short,
becoming a well-integrated or balanced personality is the equivalent of becoming what he calls an "intermediate person" or one who avoids the extremes
of not enough and of too much (Ross, 1938, pp. 236–237) :

> . . . in all things the mean is praiseworthy, and the extremes neither praiseworthy
> nor right, but worthy of blame. . . . With regard to pleasantness in the giving of
> amusement the intermediate person is ready-witted and the disposition ready
> wit, the excess is buffoonery and the person characterized by it a buffoon, while
> the man who falls short is a sort of boor and his state is boorishness. With regard
> to the remaining kind of pleasantness, that which is exhibited in life in general, the
> man who is pleasant in the right way is friendly and the mean is friendliness,
> while the man who exceeds is an obsequious person if he has no end in view, a
> flatterer if he is aiming at his own advantage, and the man who falls short and is
> unpleasant in all circumstances is a quarrelsome and surly sort of person.

Review

What Hermann Ebbinghaus regarded as psychology's "long past" ought
now to be seen more clearly in the light of the psychological issues already
considered by Aristotle some two thousand years before the establishment of
the first laboratory of psychology. By way of summary, looking back upon
these issues as presented in the present chapter, mention might first be made
of Aristotle's recognition of the relevance of a biologically oriented empiricism for psychology, as exemplified by his interest in the facts of embryology
and his study of the sequence of changes in the developing chick embryo.
In turn it was pointed out that this interest is to be equated with modern
emphasis on the value of the genetic method. Closely related on a conceptual
level was Aristotle's introduction of a distinction between being and becoming
or between the potential and the actual. Current personality theorists who
stress self-actualization and becoming as key concepts were found to be making
use of this distinction. Among such theorists mention was made of Rollo May,
Gordon Allport, Kurt Goldstein, Abraham Maslow, Erich Fromm, and Alfred
Adler.

Actualization of potentialities was also discussed in terms of the characteristic Aristotelian concept of entelechy. This concept was considered in conjunc-

tion with Aristotle's fourfold analysis of causation and was found to be most
closely related to the notion of a final cause. The latter notion, it was pointed
out, involves teleological considerations. Such considerations have to do with
questions of intention and purpose as psychological issues, especially as they
have come to be viewed in discussions of the bearing of instinct and maturation
in human and animal development.

Aristotle's intentionalism as a distinctly psychological issue was found to
be particularly prominent in Brentano's act psychology of the 1870s. Despite
its empiricist standpoint, his psychology with intentionalism as a core concept
differed both from British empiricism as well as from the kind of psychology
sponsored by Wundt in the same decade.

In order to clarify the meaning of intentionalism as a concept it was discussed by reference to the conditioned-response paradigm. In this way the
scholastic phrase "intentional inexistence" with its implication of transcendent
reference could be explained in terms of a pointing relationship. For Pavlov's
conditioned animal, it is as if a buzzer as conditioned stimulus signalizes or
points to anticipated food and concomitantly arouses an intention to eat.

Brentano's act psychology had far-reaching consequences. With its Aristotelian heritage it came to have a bearing on later psychology through the
influence of Brentano's teachings on men like Ward and Stout in England,
Stumpf and Husserl in Germany, and possibly Freud in Austria.

Consideration of Aristotle's discussion of dreaming revealed him to be a
pioneer phenomenologist. In this connection attention was called to what he
had to say about afterimages, sensory adaptation, visual and tactual illusions,
and perceptual distortion. With its emphasis on motion and activity his
psychology was described as a *process* psychology, or one that avoids the not
uncommon tendency to reify psychological terms by thinking of vision,
memory, ideas, and motives as things or entities.

What Aristotle called *common sensibles* were noted to constitute an anticipation of Locke's distinction between primary and secondary qualities just as
his notion of a *common sense* appeared to be the equivalent of what Locke
termed *reflection*. In addition, reference to Aristotle's discussion of "acts of
recollection" served to demonstrate his anticipation of what Locke and other
associationists came to regard as laws or principles of association. In the latter
discussion Aristotle alluded to the principles of frequency, uniqueness, similarity, contrast, and contiguity.

Anticipation of still other aspects of later psychology was suggested by
passages in his *Politics* and in the *Nicomachaean Ethics*. The *Politics* revealed
a clear formulation of the Gestaltist stress on the priority of wholes and the
general significance of part-whole relationships. It also served to reveal foreshadowings of insights that millennia later came to be central in the teachings
of functional, Adlerian, and social psychologists. The passage from the
Nicomachaean Ethics dealt with Aristotle's elaboration of the concept of the
"golden mean." As thus elaborated it was found to be an early recognition of

characterological differences now the subject of study by personality theorists as well as a recognition of the contemporary mental-health ideal of a balanced personality.

In view of the range and variety of these insights, it is easy to understand why later ages came to venerate Aristotle as a profound thinker whose writings justified study by successive generations of scholars. By the late medievel period the veneration was such that questions of fact were often settled by consulting Aristotle rather than by independent investigation.[4] However, as was mentioned at the beginning of this chapter, Aristotle was by no means an invariably accurate observer; hence *uncritical* reliance on his writings retarded intellectual progress. Reliance of this kind on any authority in any age makes for such retardation. It is the consequence of confusing eminence with evidence—one of the hazards of dogmatic reliance on the voice of authority. Avoidance of such hazards is not to be obtained by repudiation of suggestions and conclusions coming from an authority but by consideration of the evidence given in their support. In terms of this perspective, what Aristotle had to say about psychological issues is not to be dismissed as idle speculation wholly unrelated to the contemporary scene.

---

[4] It would be more accurate to say that to a large extent not Aristotle but commentaries on Aristotle were consulted. As McKeon (1947, p. xxviii) has pointed out: "During the thirteenth century and increasingly during the later Middle Ages, commentaries on Aristotle became the major medium for philosophic disputation and independent investigation. . . . Disciples were won not so much to the philosophy of Aristotle as to interpretations of that philosophy."

References

Allport, G. *Becoming.* New Haven: Yale University Press, 1955.

Ansbacher, H. L., and Ansbacher, R. R. *The Individual Psychology of Alfred Adler.* New York: Basic Books, 1956.

Barber, B. "Resistance by Scientists to Scientific Discovery," *Science,* 1961, *134,* 596–602.

Beach, F. A. "The Descent of Instinct," *Psychological Review,* 1955, *62,* 401–410.

Boring, E. G. *A History of Experimental Psychology.* New York: Appleton-Century-Crofts, 1950.

Brentano, F. *Psycholgie vom Empirischen Standpunkte.* Leipzig: Duncker and Humboldt, 1874.

Brett, G. S. *A History of Psychology,* Vol. I. London: George Allen and Unwin, Ltd., 1912.

Dennis, W. (ed.). *Readings in the History of Psychology.* New York: Appleton-Century-Crofts, 1948.

Dunlap, K. "Are There Any Instincts?" *Journal of Abnormal Psychology,* 1919, *14,* 35–50.

Freud, S. *The Interpretation of Dreams.* New York: The Macmillan Company, 1913.

Freud, S. "On the History of the Psycho-Analytic Movement," in *Collected Papers,* Vol. I. London: The Hogarth Press, 1950.

Fromm, E. *Man for Himself*. New York: Rinehart, 1947.

Goldstein, K. *The Organism*. New York: American Book Company, 1939.

Hamilton, E. *The Greek Way to Western Civilization*. New York: W. W. Norton and Company, 1930.

James, W. *The Meaning of Truth*. New York: Longmans, Green and Company, 1909.

Lehrman, D. S. "Problems Raised by Instinct Theories," *Quarterly Review of Biology*, 1953, *28*, 337–365.

McDougall, W. *Outline of Psychology*. New York: Charles Scribner's Sons, 1923.

McKeon, R. *Introduction to Aristotle*. New York: The Modern Library, 1947.

Maslow, A. "The Instinctoid Nature of Basic Needs," *Journal of Personality*, 1948, *16*, 402–416.

Maslow, A. *Motivation and Personality*. New York: Harper and Brothers, 1954. Chapter 12.

May, R., Angel E., and Ellenberger, H. F. (eds.). *Existence: A New Dimension in Psychiatry and Psychology*. New York: Basic Books, 1958.

Müller-Freienfels, R. *The Evolution of Modern Psychology*. New Haven: Yale University Press, 1935.

Rand, B. (ed.). *The Classical Psychologists*. Boston: Houghton Mifflin Company, 1912.

Ross, W. D. (ed.). *Aristotle—Selections*. New York: Charles Scribner's Sons, 1938. Originally published as *The Oxford Translation of Aristotle*. Reprinted by permission of the Clarendon Press, Oxford. The translators include E. S. Forster, B. Jowett, W. D. Ross, D. W. Thompson.

Skinner, B. E. *Science and Human Behavior*. New York: The Macmillan Company, 1953.

Titchener, E. B. *Systematic Psychology: Prolegomena*. New York: The Macmillan Company, 1929.

Tolman, E. C. *Purposive Behavior in Animals and Man*. New York: D. Appleton-Century Company, 1932.

Warren, H. C. *A History of the Association Psychology*. New York: Charles Scribner's Sons, 1921.

5

Ancient Roots of Scientific
and Mental-Health Concepts

THE FOURTH CENTURY B.C., during which Plato and Aristotle conducted their schools, was the high point of Greek philosophic development. The preceding century had marked the zenith of Greek contributions to literature, while the culmination of Greek science came a century later, following the conquests of Alexander the Great. Alexander died in 323 B.C., a year before the death of Aristotle. As a result of Alexander's far-ranging military expeditions, Egyptian and Oriental teachings came to influence post-Aristotelian scholars. The city of Alexandria in Egypt emerged as a great center of intellectual activity. This marked the beginning of the Hellenistic Age and its third-century scientific achievements. However, before discussing some of these achievements it might be well to set the stage for their consideration by a review of the traditional historical epochs in terms of which historians commonly discuss the rise of Western civilization from the Hellenistic to the modern period.

Chronological Perspectives

The *Hellenistic Age,* as just mentioned, began shortly after the death of Alexander the Great and lasted until Rome conquered Macedonia with the defeat of King Perseus in 170 B.C. Actually Roman life had been exposed to Greek culture long before this, since there had been a great deal of Graeco-Roman interchange during the fourth and third centuries.

The years from about 200 B.C. to A.D. 476 cover the rise and decline of Rome. It was in the year A.D. 476 that the last of the Roman emperors, the youth Romulus Augustulus, was deposed by the barbarian Odoacer. Moreover, by the fifth century the Church had already become a regnant influence in the turbulence of the times. In some ways it was this turbulence and the concomitant decay of civilization in the succeeding centuries which gave rise to the notion of the *Dark Age* as descriptive of the period from 476 to the beginnings of the Italian Renaissance in the thirteenth century. The *medieval period* also began with the fall of the Roman Empire in 476 and lasted until about the year 1500. Feudalism and scholasticism emerged during the latter period in the ninth century and prevailed for some six hundred years.

As mentioned in Chapter I, the seventeenth century, with the establishment of scientific societies and the monumental contributions of men like Galileo, Newton, and Harvey, is often recognized as the time when the modern scientific outlook came into being. Some historians of science would prefer to date the beginnings of this outlook to about the middle of the sixteenth century; also a time of notable scientific achievements. As a forerunner of modern science, mention might be made of the Swiss physician, alchemist, and chemist Paracelsus (1493?–1541), who, despite his adherence to occult beliefs like the existence of a philosopher's stone, nevertheless was a daring innovator in medical thinking and practice. He opposed the humoral theories of disease stemming from Galen and was among the first to advocate the use of specific chemicals in the treatment of illness in place of the widespread, indiscriminate practice of purging and bleeding. His activity serves to mark the transition from the magical thinking of alchemists to the more realistic thinking of experimental chemists.

During the same period human anatomy became the subject of direct and independent study. This was not always easy because of the need to circumvent theological opposition to dissection and the consequent difficulty of securing cadavers. Furthermore, there was even opposition from some professors of medicine who regarded such study as useless or unnecessary. Nevertheless, despite such opposition, significant headway was made. For example, the existence of the spinal cord's central canal was discovered by Charles Estienne (1504–1564), the Fallopian tubes by Gabriello Fallopio (1523–1562), and the Eustachian tubes by Bartolommeo Eustachio (1528?–1574). The most influential of these pioneer anatomists was the Belgian physician, Andreas Vesalius (1514–1564), commonly regarded as the founder of modern anatomic studies. His great book with its superb illustrations, *Fabric of the Human Body,* was published in 1543. This was the same year in which the Polish astronomer, Nicolaus Copernicus (1473–1543) made his heliocentric views known by publication of his great book in which the earth is described as one of the planets moving in`its orbit about a central sun. This Copernican system became the foundation for modern astronomy. A historian of science, Charles Singer (1957, p. 131), referred to Copernicus and Vesalius as being "among the practical exponents of the new experimental method" and as two of its "brilliant practitioners." He added:

By a curious coincidence these two—both men of one book—published the great works with which their names are associated in the same year, 1543, which perhaps better than any other may be regarded as the birth-year of modern science.

Selecting specific dates for given historical epochs is a somewhat arbitrary procedure. To select the year 476, for example, as marking the end of one and the beginning of another period is more a matter of descriptive convenience than a reference to any sudden transformation in the daily routine and outlook of the people living in 476. For them, there was no awareness of a shift from Roman to medieval life. Dethronement of the emperor in 476 was not regarded by citizens of Rome as the end of the Roman Empire. In the perspective of time, historians many generations later found 476 a convenient reference point. In analogous fashion, selecting a particular date for the birth of modern science is also a somewhat arbitrary matter.[1] Shall it be dated from the sixteenth century or the seventeenth century? By noting the significance of 1543, Singer seems to prefer to date it from the former century. However, as is shown by the following passage, he has sound reasons for selecting the year 1600 as an alternative key date (1957, pp. 134–135):

> Giordano [Bruno] was burned at the stake at Rome, after seven years imprisonment, on February 17, 1600. In the same year the experimental era was ushered in with the work of William Gilbert, "On the Magnet," in which he not only demonstrates experimentally the properties of magnets but also shows that the earth itself is a magnet. In the same year Tycho Brahe handed over the torch to Johannes Kepler. Tycho was the last of the older astronomers who worked on the Aristotelian view of circular and uniform movements of heavenly bodies. Kepler was the real founder of the modern astronomical system. The period from 1600 onward lies with new men, Galileo and Kepler among astronomers and physicists, Harvey among biologists, Descartes among philosophers. The year 1600 thus represents as real a division as any that we can expect in the history of thought.

Singer's reference to the burning of Bruno serves as a reminder of the difficulties encountered by the founding fathers of modern science. Teachings that the Church might deem heretical, as Galileo and others found out, had to be advanced cautiously or surreptitiously. The heliocentric theory could not be discussed freely in terms of relevant scientific evidence, for the Church authorities examined such evidence in the light of scriptural texts. For example, the Biblical account of Joshua's command for the sun to stand still was cited as contrary evidence and as support for the geocentric

---

[1] Selecting specific dates and men for the discovery of particular scientific phenomena such as a chemical element or a planet may also involve some degree of arbitrariness on the part of the historian of science. In the words of T. S. Kuhn (1962, p. 760), "To the historian discovery is seldom a unit event attributable to some particular man, time, and place."

theory. Not until 1822 were books endorsing the Copernican theory removed from the list of the Index of forbidden works. In addition to encountering theological resistance, new theories and teachings met with opposition from scholars wedded to the dogmas of Aristotelian philosophy and Galenic medicine.

In some respects what we have been calling the modern scientific outlook might be described as a revival and elaboration of scientific thinking already manifest during the Hellenistic Age. That period was also characterized by developments in philosophy which ought to be considered in terms of their bearing on the history of psychology. The scientific developments, as contrasted with those in philosophy, have no direct bearing on the history of psychology. Nevertheless they merit some consideration because they exemplify the kind of thinking that centuries later came to be applied to psychological problems and eventually resulted in the emergence of experimental psychology. Indeed, the methodology of science adopted by the first experimental psychologists during the nineteenth century had grown out of fields of scientific endeavor having no immediate relationship to psychology. For the most part it had to do with concepts and methods belonging to such fields as physics and physiology and was largely a product of the scientific heritage stemming from the modern period. But this heritage, in turn, owed something to Greek science.

The Rise of Hellenistic Science

As has been mentioned, the foundations for the modern scientific age were laid by such men as Copernicus, Galileo, Kepler, Vesalius, Harvey, and Newton. It is well to realize, however, that their achievements were not altogether independent of scientific work done by men of earlier generations who had put mathematical procedures, conceptual models, and some dependable observational data at their disposal. Examples of such work are to be found in the history of the Hellenistic Age. The geometry of Euclid belongs to this period, for Euclid was active around 300 B.C. Progress in astronomy, physics, and engineering was obviously facilitated by Euclidian contributions. Incidentally, according to tradition, when Euclid was asked for an easy way to master geometry, he replied, "There is no royal road." Somewhat related to geometrical study is the study of conic sections, which also got under way at the instigation of Euclid and his Hellenistic successors. Terms like "ellipse," "hyperbola," and "parabola" were introduced at this time, and the curves to which they refer continue to be important in various branches of contemporary science.

An especially noteworthy scientific achievement belonging to the Hellenistic period has to do with the determination of the earth's circumference, an instructive example of creative scientific thinking as the outcome of focused curiosity, sound reasoning, and appropriate measurement. Many generations of schoolchildren have been taught that the circumference of the earth is about 25,000 miles, but it is the rare child who puzzles over the way in which this was determined or asks about when it was done or by whom. The vast majority of youngsters do not have their curiosity directed to such questions in their studies of geography. They might be fascinated by the history of this achievement as they learn of its occurrence around the year 200 B.C. Credit for the achievement goes to Eratosthenes, head of the library at Alexandria. There was a narrow well in a town some 500 miles from Alexandria and Eratosthenes learned that the entire shaft of the well was illuminated at noon of the summer solstice when the sun was directly overhead. At the same instant an obelisk in Alexandria cast a shadow whose length enabled Eratosthenes to determine the sun to be 7.5 degrees away from the zenith. Assuming the earth to be a sphere would mean a circumference of 360 degrees. Once Eratosthenes had determined that an arc of 7.5 degrees equals 500 miles, simple arithmetic enabled him to compute the circumference of the earth by dividing 360 by 7.5 and multiplying the quotient by 500, giving 24,000 miles. Actually, that figure is to be regarded as a crude approximation of what Eratosthenes concluded, since his unit of distance was not the mile but the *stadium,* which equaled about 607 feet. For present purposes this deviation from his actual results is not important. What is significant is the kind of thinking it reveals. It is a precursor of the kind of thinking that centuries later came to be recognized as belonging to the methodology of science.

During this period there was even an anticipation of the Copernican theory. Tradition credits Aristarchus, an astronomer of the third century B.C. with advancing the heliocentric theory; Copernicus mentions him as an early proponent of this view. Aristarchus also anticipated much later teachings when he accounted for the sequence of day and night by attributing rotation to the earth in place of the common belief in the actual rising and setting of the sun.

The use of the word *"eureka,"* as an interjection originated as a result of the well-known story of the discovery made by Archimedes (287–212 B.C.) as he dashed into the street from his bath crying "Eureka!" meaning "I have found it!" What he had found was a way of finding an answer to the problem assigned to him by King Hiero II of Syracuse. As many schoolboys have been told, the king had given an artisan a certain amount of gold to be made into a crown. When the crown was delivered it was found to weigh as much as the original amount of gold. However, the king suspected the artisan of having substituted some silver in place of a portion of the gold and Archimedes was asked to determine whether such deception had occurred. To determine the possible admixture of silver at a time when nothing was known of the chemistry of metals was a baffling challenge. Archimedes was preoccupied with the problem for many days. Such preoccupation is the equivalent of what was earlier called focused curiosity. Another way of putting this is to say that scientific discoveries are made by minds prepared or set to make them. In the case of Archimedes the crucial observation came as he stepped into the tub at a public bath: more water spilled over the rim as more of his body was immersed and his submerged limbs felt lighter. This observation was the instigation for what has become known as the *principle of Archimedes*. According to this principle, when a solid body is immersed in water it displaces a certain amount of water and is buoyed up by a force equal to the weight of the displaced water. In the light of this principle Archimedes found that a given weight of silver displaces more water than the same weight in gold because the volume of the latter is less than the former. When submerged, the king's crown was found to displace more water than a piece of gold of equal weight. All that remained was to substitute fragments of silver for bits of gold from the comparison weight until it displaced precisely as much water as the crown. The method demonstrated both the fact and the amount of the theft. It also provided the world of physics with the concept of specific gravity as a measurable characteristic of substances.

Histories of physics also list Archimedes as the one who first formulated the principle of the lever, and histories of mathematics mention him in connection with his demonstration of formulas for measuring the volumes of cylinders and spheres. The foundations of hydraulics, mechanics, and mathematics were thus markedly influenced by the genius of this third-century scientist.

In addition to advances made in astronomy, mathematics, and physics, Hellenistic science also made progress in such fields as botany, anatomy, physiology, and medicine. With respect to botany the work of Theophrastus, another third-century philosopher, merits attention. He was Aristotle's successor as head of the Peripatetic school and was the guardian of Aristotle's children. According to Will Durant (1939, p. 637), to a large extent "he was more scientific than his master, more careful of his facts, and more orderly in his exposition." He noted plant structure in terms of roots, stalks, branches, leaves, and so on. Our commonsense placement of plant forms into classes like trees, bushes, and herbs goes back to his work. His studies covered such varied topics as the influence of climate and geography on plant forms, their minute structural differences, and the medicinal virtues of some of them.

Theophrastus wrote on many other subjects besides botany. Of especial psychological interest is his series of character sketches, which, as Allport (1961, pp. 42–44) points out, constitutes an early form of "literary characterology" in which "Theophrastus is propounding an important theory of personality." By implication this refers to views of personality as expressive of some inherently basic or dominant trait or value forming the core of the individual's being and supplying the chief clue for understanding him as a person. Common references to people in terms of their being misers or perfectionists or Don Juans or tyrants or playboys reflect this kind of approach to personality theory. In his *History of Science*, G. Sarton (1952, pp. 548–559) discusses the part played by Theophrastus in developing this approach by writing sketches of people whose behavior can be described in the light of some key characteristic such as arrogance or stinginess or boorishness. Theophrastus dealt with thirty such characteristics, and each one had to do with

some human weakness or shortcoming. Presumably he deemed it more important or interesting to dwell on vice and weakness than on virtue and strength,
just as our newspapers devote more space to crime and scandal than to
instances of exemplary citizenship and moral excellence.

Historically considered, Theophrastus was not the originator of this style
of writing. As Sarton reminds us, he had predecessors in the work of Greeks
like Aristophanes, Herodotus, Plato, and Aristotle; but instead of contenting
himself, as they did, with an incidental sketch, he elaborated a whole series
of them. In this sense he might well be regarded as having established characterology as a distinctive literary art. By way of illustrating the nature of
this art as developed by Theophrastus, Sarton not only quotes the complete
text of the sketch concerned with *Superstitiousness* but also reminds us of
the presence of "superstitious people in Athens close to the Academy and
even to the Lyceum, even as there are superstitious people today in the shadow
of our own academies and colleges." The following excerpts from this sketch
will serve as an example of the style of literary characterology and illustrate
the universality of the themes discussed by Theophrastus in the sense that,
as in the present instance, the superstitious person in all ages is prone to
groundless fears and magical rituals:

> Superstitiousness . . . would seem to be a sort of cowardice with respect to the divine;
> and your Superstitious man such as will not sally forth for the day till he have
> washed his hands and sprinkled himself at the Nine Springs. . . . And if a cat cross
> his path he will not proceed on his way till someone else be gone by, or he have
> cast three stones across the street. . . . When he passes one of the smooth stones
> set up at crossroads he anoints it with oil from his flask, and will not go his ways
> til he have knelt down and worshipped it. . . . Should owls hoot when he is abroad, he
> is much put about, and will not on his way till he have cried "Athena forfend!"
> Set foot on a tomb he will not, nor come nigh a dead body nor a woman in child-
> bed; he must keep himself unpolluted. . . . He never has a dream but he flies to a
> diviner, or a soothsayer, or an interpreter of visions, to ask what God or Goddess
> he should appease. . . . If he catch sight of a madman or an epilept, he shudders
> and spits in his bosom.

Medical studies were also advanced during the Hellenistic period. Greek
physicians living in Alexandria were influenced by Egyptian medical tradition.
Moreover, anatomic studies were furthered by official sanction of dissection
of cadavers as well as of animals. Herophilus was probably the outstanding
anatomist of the time, and Erasistratus was the leading physiologist. In the
words of Brett (1912, p. 283): "These two doctors live in history as the
discoverers of nerves." However, recognition of the function of nerves was
delayed by the opposition of those who held to the Aristotelian teaching regarding the heart as the seat of mental life.

In the writings of Aristotle, as Brett points out (1912, pp. 117–119), there
are repeated references to the "connatural spirits" or what later came to be

implicit in the doctrine of "animal spirits." This use of the word "spirit" in connection with the air breathed is not to be confused with any notion of ghostlike apparitions. Instead, as Brett makes clear, Aristotle and other sponsors of the doctrine of the pneuma "looked upon the air as the scientist of today might look upon steam in the locomotive: its laws of expansion and contraction were the explanation of life as a mechanical system of activities." It was held that the "natural" heat of the body is maintained by the pneuma just as gusts of air seem to feed the flames of a burning building. All living things possess such vital heat as an attribute of the connatural spirit.

Among his many errors Aristotle held that sensations are transmitted to the heart via the veins containing blood and pneuma. This was an erroneous teaching which Erasistratus opposed. He not only recognized the brain as the chief center for the soul's activities, but also noted the existence of what later came to be classified as the cranial nerves. Furthermore, by regarding some nerves as sensory in function and others as motor in function he anticipated the early nineteenth-century work of Sir Charles Bell (1774–1842) and François Magendie (1783–1855).

As an anatomist, Herophilus dissected the eye and described the retina, the vitreous humor, and the ciliary body. His studies of the nervous system enabled him to note the existence of gross features of brain structure such as the cerebellum, the cerebrum, and the meninges. One feature of meningeal anatomy is still named after him. This is the convergence of blood sinuses in the dura mater of the occipital region known as the *torcular Herophili,* which means "winepress of Herophilus." Like Erasistratus, he noted the distinction between sensory and motor nerves as well as the division between cranial and spinal nerves. According to C. Singer (1957, p. 29), "He was the first to grasp the nature of nerves other than those of the special senses." In addition Singer credits him with being the first to describe lymphatic structures. The scope of his anatomic investigations is also reflected by the fact that terms like "prostate" and "duodenum" have their origin in words he introduced. This does not exhaust the list of his anatomic discoveries, but these suffice to indicate why he is sometimes called the father of anatomy.

Although universities as educational and research centers did not exist prior to the twelfth century, the Museum of Alexandria served as a forerunner of such a center, for it was more than a repository for objects of interest. As described by H. J. Muller (1958, p. 153), it not only housed a great library but also served as a center for research. There was an observatory for astronomical observations as well as a zoo and botanical collections for biological studies. Anatomy could be studied in special dissecting rooms and, in the words of Muller, the whole institution was "staffed by a hundred professors to train scholars, scientists, and technicians."

Hellenistic science, it should now be evident, involved far more than speculative elaboration of the teachings handed down by Greeks of the classical period. Much of the research was systematic, experimental, and even quantitative. The fundamentals of the methodology of science might thus be said to have come into being nineteen centuries before the time of Galileo and Newton. Moreover, the investigations had to be conducted in virtual independence of instrumental aids. Telescopes, microscopes, chemical reagents, barometers, galvanometers, thermometers, and even watches had not yet been invented. Nevertheless, as already indicated, sound observations and valid generalizations were being reported. It was as if the empirically grounded teachings of Aristotle were being extended and receiving more recognition than his speculative flights of fancy. In part this may have been due to the indirect influence of Alexander himself. Having been tutored by Aristotle in his youth, he may be presumed to have been exposed to what his tutor regarded as educationally important. At all events, men of learning were included in the military entourage on Alexander's campaigns of conquest. In this sense he gave support and encouragement to scholarly activity, just as in later centuries scientific studies were advanced when kings authorized establishment of scientific academies like the Royal Society and Napoleon brought archaeologists to Egypt. The rise of Hellenistic science was very likely also facilitated by the effect of Egyptian and Babylonian traditions on the scholars accompanying Alexander's invading armies. Exposure to "foreign" ideas or beliefs may provoke critical examination of notions at variance with such ideas or beliefs. Such examination may then result in the modification of hitherto unquestioned teachings as well as in the quest for new teachings to replace rejected ones.

The factors just mentioned are among the reasons commonly assigned for the emergence of Hellenistic science. Nevertheless, despite what in long-range retrospect can be recognized as successful scientific work, this work failed to develop into an established mode of investigation. Unlike that of seventeenth-century science, the success of Hellenistic science did not initiate an active scientific tradition in succeeding generations. With the rise of Roman power and the concomitant decline of Hellenic influence, there were no successors to men like Eratosthenes, Archimedes, Herophilus, Erasistratus, and other scientists of the period.

Decline of Hellenistic Science

Why did Hellenistic science come to an end? Why the failure to appreciate the value of controlled investigation in promoting mastery of nature and placing its forces at the disposal of man? The opposite happened when seventeenth-century science set the stage for technological developments that in the course of time made for the industrial revolution and the changes associated with the introduction of steam engines, railroads, illuminating gas, and an increasing number of labor-saving inventions.

According to one hypothesis, such technological advances failed to emerge from Hellenistic science because of slavery. With the routine chores of farming, building, sewing, transporting, and cooking all being performed by slaves, this hypothesis assumes there would be little or no motivation to seek labor-saving devices. Technology in the sense of applied science would not be encouraged. Furthermore, it may actually have been discouraged by being regarded as beneath the dignity of gentlemen or aristocrats. In fact, Muller (1958, p. 153) refers to the "mentality of the Hellenistic Greeks" as characterized by "aristocratic indifference to utility," which "might seem loftier had they not depended on slave labor, and sufficiently enjoyed material wealth and ease" to render them content with existing conditions.

As an outgrowth of Greek philosophy, Hellenistic science was more concerned with knowing than with doing, more interested in theory than in practice, and more devoted to the quest for understanding nature as contrasted with the quest for control over nature. Bertrand Russell (1951, p. 21) has pointed out that "the Greeks, with the exception of Archimedes, were only interested in science as enabling us to know things." Their scientific curiosity did not extend to fostering that function of science which "enables us to *do* things." This latter function, according to Russell, owes more to early Arabian than to Greek sources. Moreover, these sources were more superstitious and magical than scientific in the sense that they had to do with efforts to find the elixir of life or to make gold out of baser metals—efforts that continued for centuries in the activities of the alchemists.

In the course of their mystical quests the alchemists discovered many facts that subsequently came to be incorporated into chemistry. This, of course, is in line with what is now a commonplace observation; namely, that technology may influence pure science just as pure science sets the stage for technological applications. Despite this reciprocal relationship, status differences continue to be reflected in the attitudes of those who endow the physicist with a brighter halo of scientific prestige than the engineer or regard the chemist as more of a scientist than the pharmacist or those who, in general, view the technologist or practitioner as somewhat less devoted to science than the theoretician or research man. In the light of historical perspective, it might be that these status differences at least in part reflect the aristocratic Greek origin of the *knowing* function of science as contrasted with the more lowly Arabian origin of the *doing* function of science.

Another reason for the persistence of these status differences lies in the fact that, in general, for the doing function to be scientific there must be knowledge of the laws or principles being utilized. Successful doing as such is not necessarily scientific. People learned to keep warm by building fires long before there was any understanding of the chemistry of combustion. Savages were successful in shooting poisoned arrows without thereby either knowing or contributing to the sciences of ballistics or toxicology. Plumbers are not sanitary engineers nor are carpenters structural engineers. One may be altogether ignorant of the chemistry of cooking and baking and still succeed in preparing a superb meal. Unless informed and guided by the knowing function of science, the successes of the efficient workman are not to be classified as scientific successes. A laborer may wield a crowbar with great skill despite his ignorance of the law of the lever.

To revert to the question of accounting for the decline of Hellenistic science and the relative absence of applied science, it should be obvious that what was said about slave labor and status differences is hardly a complete or altogether satisfactory answer. In reviewing this matter, H. G. Wells (1921, pp. 404–410) called attention to the weakness of the administration of the great museum at Alexandria. No provision was made to enable the scholars or philosophers working there to provide for continuation of their investigations by training and selecting their successors. Professors were appointed by the reigning monarch. Under the early Ptolemies, who were of Greek origin and consequently familiar with criteria of scholarly competence, wise appointments were made and the work of the museum flourished. Their descendants, however, more influenced by the "tradition of Egyptian priestcraft" than the Greek scientific outlook, failed to staff the museum with devotees of that outlook. As a result, within about a hundred years the museum ceased to be a vital center of scientific investigation.

Alexandrian scientific influence was hampered by restrictions in addition to poor administration of the museum's affairs. One such restriction had to do with library limitations even though Ptolemy I (367?–283 B.C.), founder of the museum, had also established a famous library in Alexandria. This was some seventeen centuries before the invention of printing and long before China provided the Western world with paper. There were no books in the library. Instead there were hundreds of scrolls written on papyrus. To look up a reference it was necessary to unroll a scroll and then roll it up again once the reference had been located. This was tedious, time-consuming, and damaging to the papyrus. Dissemination of the new knowledge was thus hampered not only by such limitations but also by limitations due to the absence of learned societies, of scientific journals, of a postal service, and other means of effective communication. Moreover, ability to read the scrolls was limited to those few students who could journey to a center of learning and spend years in association with the scribes and sages. The masses were illiterate and the attainment of even a modest education involved either independent means or willingness to endure the privations and hardships of the indigent student. Under the circumstances, as Wells suggests, those who learned to use the library at Alexandria in the course of time reacted to this hard-won achievement by substituting the worship of books for the use of books. The written word tended to replace experiment, independent thought, and original observation and after some three generations of scholarly activity, "wisdom passed away from Alexandria and left pedantry behind."

War, Anxiety, and Philosophy

As mentioned earlier, not until the rediscovery of the Greek classics by the humanists of the Renaissance did the "wisdom" of Hellenism come to challenge pedantic dependence on revered texts. It might also be well to note that this "wisdom" was not the product of peaceful contemplation in a peaceful world. From the golden age of Pericles of Athens (died 429 B.C.) through the turbulence of Alexander's conquests followed by the disruption of his empire, Greek philosophy flourished and declined in a chronic setting of war and political upheaval. The war between Athens and Sparta, the Peloponnesian War, lasted for twenty-seven years, from 431 B.C. to 404 B.C. In addition to the turmoil of war, Athens suffered from the outbreak of two plagues during this period, with Pericles a victim of the first one. The war ended with the defeat of Athens and replacement of its democracy by the oligarchic authority of the thirty tyrants. Both Socrates and Plato developed their philosophic views during this period. Nor can Aristotle be said to have enjoyed the blessing of life in a country at peace with the world, for the military campaigns of Philip of Macedon and those of his son, Alexander, were being waged during the lifetime of Aristotle. Stock references to Poe's "the glory that was Greece" tend to obscure the cruelty and social chaos incident to battle and the lust for conquest. In this connection Wells (1921, pp. 352–353) cites an illuminating comment by Gilbert Murray (1866–1957), the distinguished student of Greek civilization and translator of Euripides, as reflected in the following excerpts:

As soon as you get to Alexander you get, of course, the Oriental despotic touch—fantastic vanity and cruelty; and at length the recurrence of human sacrifice.

The greatness of Greece comes out only in the art and literature and thought; not in the political and social history—except in dim flashes. By all means emphasize clearly to start with that the Greeks of, say, the ninth century, were practically savages, and those of even the sixth and in places right on to the fifth and fourth were in many things on the "Lower Cultures" level. Clothes like Polynesians; tools very poor; religion . . . fragments of the Polynesian all about, when you got outside the educated Attic world. But the *characteristic* is that, on this very low level, you have extraordinary flashes of very high inspiration, as the poetry and art and philosophy witness. Also, an actual achievement in social life —what one calls "Hellenism," *i.e.*, republicanism, simplicity of life, sobriety of thought, almost complete abolition of torture, mutilation, etc., and an amazing emancipation of the individual and of the human intellect. It is impossible to speak, really, of the "Greek view" of anything. Because all the different views are put forward and represented: polytheism, monotheism, atheism; pro-slavery, anti-slavery; duty to animals, no duty to animals; democracy, monarchy, aristocracy. The characteristic is that *human thought got free.* (Not absolutely, of course; only to an amazing extent.) This emancipation was paid for by all sorts of instability; awful political instability, because stability in such things is produced exactly by the opposite—by long firm tradition and cohesiveness.

What Murray describes as "an amazing emancipation of the individual and of the human intellect" or as the freeing of human thought might thus be viewed as a distinctive outcome of the general import of the Greek philosophic tradition. It is not unrelated to what Russell had to say regarding Greek preoccupation with the knowing as contrasted with the doing function of science. Moreover, as applied to Greek philosophy as a whole it may be misleading to suggest that Greek thinkers were exclusively preoccupied with theory and altogether unconcerned with doing or with practice. In fact, from the time of Socrates to the time of the Roman Emperor Marcus Aurelius (A.D. 121–180)—a span of some six hundred years—there was a continuing interest in using philosophic or ethical insights as a means of enhancing individual welfare. Broadly considered, the issues involved are consonant with many that fall within the scope of what contemporary psychology classifies as problems of adjustment or mental hygiene. Just as the modern mental hygienist is concerned with promoting mental health and in developing a satisfactory concept of it, so these ancient thinkers were engaged in discussions of the nature of the good life, how to cope with adversity, and what should be the goals of human endeavor.

There are some interesting parallels between these modern and ancient efforts to deal with the worries, sorrows, and fears of suffering humanity. The twentieth century has been characterized as the age of anxiety because of the devastating impact on emotional security of two global wars, one major and several minor economic upheavals, and unresolved international tensions in a setting of atomic explosiveness. In addition there is said to be widespread insecurity as a result of loss of religious faith, disruption of family life incident to domestic friction, making for an increase in divorce, and the persistent evils of poverty, unemployment, racial prejudice, and disease. The present century, unlike previous centuries, is characterized by concerted attacks by professional groups and governmental agencies on the prevention and treatment of mental disorder, of criminal behavior, of domestic discord, and other kinds of social pathology. Terms like "neurosis," "psychosis," "schizophrenia," "psychotherapy," "psychoanalysis," and "defense mechanism" have become part of the routine vocabulary of the average educated man. People whose grandparents when troubled turned to priest, minister, rector, or rabbi now when overwhelmed by emotional crises make appointments with psychiatrists, psychoanalysts, psychologists, or marriage counselors. So much for the century of anxiety.

In many ways the six hundred years from the age of Socrates to the zenith of the Roman Empire might also be designated as centuries of anxiety. These were centuries of war, from the Peloponnesian War in the days of Socrates to the domination of Greece by Roman legions around 140 B.C. One of the charges brought against Socrates was the allegation that he had corrupted the youth of Athens. In large measure this referred to an increase in religious skepticism, which his accusers attributed to his teachings. This skepticism was the beginning of a probing into the fundamentals of belief and knowledge that became deeper and broader under Platonic and Aristotelian auspices. The increase in philosophic sophistication, coupled with social and political upheaval, undermined acceptance of and trust in the traditional Greek pantheon.

This loss of faith by Greek citizens resulted in a quest for a compensatory substitute for the religion of their fathers. It was manifested by a change in the general drift of Greek philosophy in the period following Aristotle. There was less interest in epistemology, or the knowing function of philosophy, and more concern with its practical or doing function as a means of helping individuals come to terms with the hazards of life in a world of threat and disaster. Like the modern psychoanalyst, the philosopher ventured to suggest ways in which the troubled individual might learn to cope with his troubles instead of being overwhelmed by them. It was as if the philosopher was usurping a priestly role by trying to supply a substitute for religious consolation.

In general, these very early precursors of the "psychology of adjustment" embraced two initially independent but later somewhat overlapping schemes of living. One had to do with Epicureanism and the other with Stoicism. The latter was an outgrowth of the views of the Cynics as developed by Antisthenes and his followers in the days of Socrates, while the former was a derivative of the teachings of Aristippus, head of the rival school of the Cyrenaics. The rivalry in question involved opposing attitudes on this question: How can a person best promote his own welfare? To ask what should be the fundamental goal of human effort would be a variant of this question. In line with current psychoanalytic terminology, it might be said that Antisthenes answered the question by stressing superego demands while Aristippus emphasized gratification of id impulses. In the language of Freud, the Cynics urged conduct governed by the reality principle as contrasted with the Cyrenaic preference for indulgence of the pleasure principle. For the Cynics this meant the acquisition of virtue as the best protection against the vicissitudes of fate in a world of strife and uncertain fortune. On the other hand, the Cyrenaics believed the pursuit of pleasure and the concomitant avoidance of pain are a better way of coming to terms with such a world. A differentiation of this sort serves to bring out the central issue in somewhat oversimplified fashion and of course overlooks its elaboration by adherents of the rival schools. Nevertheless, it serves as sufficient background for understanding the subsequent elaboration of the issue as considered by the later rival Epicurean and Stoic movements.

As already implied, both of these movements as philosophic enterprises were more concerned with ethics than with logic or metaphysics. Concern with ethics made philosophy a practical undertaking in the sense of giving guidance with respect to everyday conduct. Both Epicureans and Stoics might thus be said to have regarded philosophy as the art of achieving happiness, but they differed from one another regarding the means to be employed.

Epicurean Teachings

Although the Epicureans equated happiness with the attainment of pleasure, they did not advocate thoughtless or impulsive self-indulgence. They were aware of the fact that today's pleasure may cause tomorrow's distress, just as today's self-denial may set the stage for tomorrow's joy. What they advocated was a regimen of life likely to result in a maximum of pleasure, not in terms of immediate gratification, but in terms of a long-range view of one's goals and aspirations. This regimen involved reflections upon the probable consequences of given courses of action and evaluation of relative degrees of pleasure as well as their duration. Epicurean insistence upon such reflection or reasoning introduced the need for self-control, as part of a philosophy that recognized the value of obedience to standards of virtue when such obedience meant enhancement of pleasure. This attitude toward virtue constituted a point of divergence from the Stoic doctrine. For the Stoics, virtuous conduct was a self-justifying end in itself; for the Epicureans it was a means to an end.

Here it might be pointed out that the English word "epicure," although derived from the philosophy under discussion, has come to denote and connote something somewhat different from the gustatory preferences of Epicurus (341–270 B.C.), one of the leaders of the school. If the word "epicure" is taken to mean one with discriminating taste for and enjoyment of fine food and drink, then Epicurus himself, a victim of digestive disturbances, was probably not an epicure. Because of his ailment, he came to view possession of a sound digestion as the acme of pleasure, exemplifying the common tendency for maximal appreciation of values when deprived of them or threatened with their loss. Freedom becomes precious to the prisoner, just as easy breathing becomes the supreme value for a man choking on a fishbone; the pleasure of easy breathing occurs when the distress of choking is removed. Similarly, Epicurus identified a sound digestion with the removal or absence of digestive distress. He was thus led to think both of the pleasures of eating as well as of pleasure in general as the absence of pain or distress. This is an essentially negative formulation. It is akin to equating mental health with freedom from worry, anxiety, confusion, delirium, or other indications of mental disorder.

In current psychiatric practice it is fairly routine to prescribe so-called tranquilizing drugs to relieve the emotional distress of patients. The technical term for such drugs is "ataraxic drugs." When effective they may be said to induce a state of *ataraxia,* a Greek word meaning serenity, tranquillity, calmness of mind, or freedom from agitation or disturbance. This is the word that Epicurus used to describe the condition of one conforming to the Epicurean philosophy. Ataraxia was not the pleasure of excited victory or thrilling sensuous experience or even sensual gratification. Instead it was the serenity of freedom from any kind of distress or discomfort. Such inner calm was to be a bulwark against fear and a help in learning to endure unavoidable troubles.

Like Freud, Epicurus was skeptical of the role of religion in promoting human welfare. For him, Greek religious beliefs were more of a hindrance than a help in attaining ataraxia. Belief in the gods as arbiters of man's fortune in this world and of his destiny in the next was viewed as a source of needless worry and panic. According to Epicurus, such worry and panic can be eliminated once one comes to realize the groundlessness of such beliefs. There is no evidence that the gods have any interest in human affairs, nor is the soul likely to survive the disintegration of a dead body; hence there is no reason to fear the gods or to appeal to them for help. Man must learn to depend upon his own resources for salvation. Attainment of philosophic calm was to serve in place of the consolation of religion.

In his views of psychology, Epicurus endorsed the atomism of Democritus. In summarizing these views, A. W. Mair (1929, Vol. 8, pp. 646–649) refers to the Epicurean notion of the soul as a material body whose minute atoms are distributed throughout the body. These soul-atoms render sensation possible. At death they leave the body not as an entity but as dissipated or scattered particles. The soulless body is no longer capable of sensation. Perception of the external world of objects is an entirely material process. Each object was supposed to have an image or replica of itself emanate from its surface. This emanation entered the body through an appropriate sense organ and gave rise to sense-perception upon reaching the soul. In line with empiricist theory, such sensory experience was regarded as the foundation for all knowledge. Error or delusion was regarded as the consequence of failure to form a correct opinion of that which is given in sensation. Mistakes or errors might also occur as a result of chance distortion of the pictures or images responsible for perception. In the final analysis, sensory experience became the criterion of truth and of good and evil, or, in the language of an Epicurean aphorism cited by Mair: "If you reject any sensation absolutely and do not distinguish opinion in regard to that which awaits confirmation from that which is already given by sensation and feelings and every imaginative apprehension of the mind, you will confound all other sensations as well and so reject every criterion."

As a separate school, Epicureanism was not limited to the Hellenic period. In an era of change and turmoil it seemed to serve as a consoling way of life for several generations of men. In Roman times, Lucretius (96?–55 B.C.) became an eminent advocate of this philosophy and its naturalistic outlook. As a school it survived until the fourth century A.D. and in terms of some of its teachings it continues to influence present-day thinking. At least the tranquilizers of today have revived the ataraxia extolled by Epicurus.

The Stoic Philosophy

By way of contrast to the ataraxia of the Epicureans, the Stoics extolled the ideal of *apatheia,* or emotional detachment in the sense of a cultivated indifference to changing events whether good or bad. It would be misleading to confuse this use of the Greek word "*apatheia*" with its English derivative "apathy," meaning "listlessness" or "ambitionless lethargy," Stoics were anything but listless or lethargic. Their chief concern was to foster an inner life of rugged personal integrity that would be immune to the lusts, hungers, and cravings associated with pleasure-seeking impulsiveness. They were apathetic with respect to the pleasures of the table, the thrills of becoming wealthy or famous, and the joys of gratified desire. But they were not apathetic about resolute devotion to the cultivation of virtue. For them, such cultivation called for suppression of desire and emotion by disciplined thinking and willing.

The Stoic way of life was obviously austere and somewhat ascetic. Some historians have attributed this ascetic factor to the suspected Semitic origin of Zeno (c. 320–c. 250 B.C.), the founder of the Stoic school. Asceticism is often held to be more characteristically Oriental than Greek. Zeno was not a native of Greece, having come to Athens from Cyprus. He lectured to his pupils under a colonnade. The Greek word for colonnade or porch is "*stoa*"; hence the adjective"Stoic" in referring to Zeno's school.

Like Epicurus and his followers, Zeno and his followers were interested in the practical, or doing, functions of philosophy. Knowledge divorced from the exigencies of daily living did not appeal to them. Instead they occupied themselves with the kind of knowledge directly related to problems of conduct, to the making of intelligent choices, and to the mastery of fear and other emotions.

Because of their negative attitude toward the place of emotion in the economy of mental life what was just referred to as the Stoics' interest in the mastery of emotions calls for some qualification. In their view, a life governed by the quest for virtue must be a life governed by reason. Since hate, terror, love, and excitement of any kind militate against efficient thinking, they regarded such emotional upheavals as threats to virtue. As forerunners of what has come to be known as the mental-hygiene viewpoint, they sought to eliminate such threats. In line with this viewpoint, the Stoic, aiming at improvement of his mental health—what he called the health of his soul—found himself at war with his emotions.

The resulting psychology of emotion was different from that of Plato and Aristotle, both of whom included desires and emotions as normal constituents of life. Plato, we recall, localized these nonrational "souls" within the trunk by placing "higher" strivings like courage above the diaphragm and "lower" ones like lust below the diaphragm. On the other hand, Aristotle subsumed desire and emotion under the general caption of the "psychic power" of *appetite.* He used the latter word as a generic designation for craving or striving, to include all special modes of conation, or as he put it "appetite is the genus of which desire, passion, and wish are the species" (R. McKeon [ed.], 1947, p. 177).

For Aristotle as well as for Plato, these conative and affective impulses were to be used constructively under the regulative control of reason. Their function as instigators of action—as motives—was recognized. However, this was not the view of the Stoics. They regarded such impulses as maladaptive hindrances to the rule of reason and its service in behalf of virtue. Like disease, emotion and feeling were to be eschewed and eliminated. Hate, love, pity, terror, sadness, elation, and all other emotions were viewed as disturbances of the mind; because they disrupted the impassive ideal state of *apatheia*.

What they advocated was not indifference to the needs of others, but clear thinking with respect to meeting such needs. A competent physician, they might have argued, does not have to feel sorry for his patient in order to prescribe appropriate treatment; pity or sorrow might actually warp his judgment. Analogously, because of love for a child, a parent's judgment might be warped, with consequent overprotection or overindulgence. Stoic austerity was thus intended to safeguard intelligent behavior in the execution of duty and the discharge of responsibility.

What the Stoic philosophy came to mean to its more ardent devotees is well exemplified by the following quotation from Seneca (4 B.C.–A.D. 65) as cited by A. K. Rogers (1915, pp. 147–148):

> I will look upon death or upon comedy with the same expression of countenance. I will submit to labors however great they may be, supporting the strength of my body by that of my mind. I will despise riches when I have them as much as when I have them not. Whether fortune comes or goes, I will take no notice of her. I will view all lands as though they belonged to all mankind. I will so live as to remember that I was born for others, and will thank nature on this account; for in what fashion could she have done better for me? She has given me alone to all, and all to me alone. Whatever I may possess, I will neither hoard it greedily, nor squander it recklessly. I will think that I have no possessions so real as those which I have given away to deserving people. I will never consider a gift to be a large one if it be bestowed upon a worthy object. I will do nothing because of public opinion, but everything because of conscience. Whenever I do anything alone by myself, I will believe that the eyes of the Roman people are upon me while I do it. In eating and drinking, my object shall be to quench the desires of nature, not to fill and empty my belly. I will be agreeable with my friends, gentle and mild to my foes. I will grant pardon before I am asked for it, and will meet the wishes of honorable men halfway. I will bear in mind that the world is my native city, that its governors are the Gods, and that they stand above and around me criticising whatever I do or say. When either nature demands my breath again, or reason bids me dismiss it, I will quit this life, calling all to witness that no one's freedom, my own least of all, has been impaired through me.

The Stoic ideal as embodied in Seneca's account can be regarded as an early formulation of what the modern personality theorists calls an *autonomous* personality. Some mental-health experts contrast such a personality with that of one in need of psychiatric help. As they see it, to be mentally healthy is not the equivalent of being free from symptoms of mental illness any more than good citizenship as an ideal is to be equated with absence of a police record. In their view, absence of mental symptoms is a negative criterion. Instead they stress the importance of positive criteria such as being problem-centered rather than self-centered, being prudent and reasonably cautious as opposed to being paralyzed by timidity, and having absorbing interests as contrasted with bored listlessness. These are but a few of the many positive criteria that have been introduced in discussions of the subject. Although an increasing number of specialists agree that the concept of mental health is to be defined in terms of such criteria, they do not agree on the criteria to be listed. The issues involved are decidedly complex. As a consequence Marie Jahoda, in her monograph dealing with *Current Concepts of Positive Mental Health* (1958, p. 76), concluded that "The relation of mental health to mental disease remains one of the most urgent areas for future research."

The Stoic as Psychotherapist

The research to which Jahoda refers has to do with problems which in some respects, when viewed in historical perspective, are related to Epicureanism and Stoicism. As mentioned earlier, both of these movements constitute proposals for what in modern terminology would be called psychologies of adjustment. They both illustrate the applied or practical aspects of philosophy, just as courses in the psychology of adjustment can be classified as applied psychology. As noted by Rogers (1915, p. 120) with the emergence of these movements "philosophy assumes an intensely practical aspect; it aims to be nothing more nor less than a complete art of living." Moreover, as we have seen, this practical philosophy emerged, at least in part, as a reaction against the turbulence of the times and the breakdown of traditional religion.

The philosophy in question served as a substitute for lost confidence in the gods, with the philosopher taking over those priestly functions having to do with bolstering self-confidence, aiding in the solution of personal problems, and assuaging guilt. In short, he served as counselor and psychotherapist. Mention has been made of the contemporary parallel to this state of affairs in the sense that many whose forebears turned to clergymen for relief from anxiety now, having despaired of benefit from religion, turn to psychoanalysts or other mental-health specialists. In the time of Roman domination of the world, the Stoic philosophy was especially influential and its "practitioners" functioned as psychotherapists. B. A. G. Fuller (1945, p. 268), for example, points out that for Epictetus, a leading Stoic during the latter part of the first century, "the philosopher was primarily the healer of souls." This role of the Stoic philosopher is clearly revealed in the following account as formulated by Rogers (1915, p. 170):

> Stoicism in particular, among the philosophical schools of the period, had attempted to act the part of a substitute for religion, and to meet the needs for satisfying which the national religion had long since lost any real capacity.

Alongside the priest, who was absorbed in the ceremonial and political duties of his office, the philosopher was generally recognized as the real spiritual guide of his time. He occupied a position similar in many respects to that of the modern clergyman. Peculiarities of dress and appearance—his cloak and long beard—marked him off from the rest of men. He was called on for advice in difficult moral problems. A philosopher was attached to many of the Roman families as a sort of family chaplain. He was called in along with the physician at a deathbed. The discourses which he was accustomed to deliver had a close analogy to the modern sermon, and, indeed, are historically related to it.

Stoicism and Epicureanism were not altogether in opposition to one another as philosophic substitutes for religion. There was agreement regarding the maintenance of inner calm as the optimal state of psychological health. Neither movement counted on the gods to help in the achievement of this condition. In fact, as already indicated, the Epicureans regarded belief in the gods as a hindrance to individual well-being. Despair or terror aroused by fear of divine disapproval was to cease to plague man once belief in the existence of divine beings was eliminated. The atomistic naturalism of Democritus was accepted as a more satisfactory means of accounting for the vicissitudes of life.

Stoic metaphysics was opposed to such an atomistic outlook. Instead there was recognition of underlying uniformities operative throughout nature and making the world an organic whole as if governed by a rational soul. For the Stoics, soul or *pneuma* was not something qualitatively different from matter being conceived to be a very rarefied or subtle form of matter. This was held to be diffused throughout nature, accounting for its lawfulness and goal-directedness. Nature so conceived was the Stoic God: the *Logos,* or principle of rationality, inherent in the cosmos and making it a cosmos rather than a chaos. God so conceived was not a transcendent being separated from the universe but an intrinsic or immanent universal process, in the sense in which so-called laws of nature like those of gravitation or thermodynamics are universal. Nature or God was not subject to caprice or chance or blind mechanism. In a world governed by the dependability of natural law, there is no place for the whim of a god or demon to interfere with such dependability. For the Stoic, God was the equivalent of impersonal intelligence or reason operative in the universe. Being impersonal, such a God exercises no influence on the destiny of individual men; hence both Epicureans and Stoics can be said to have eliminated fear of divine punishment from the systems of belief. Nor was there any support for a belief in divine favors or rewards. Whatever belief in Greek or Roman gods that survived left the gods interested in one another and utterly indifferent to the affairs of men.

Personal immortality was also a rejected belief: the injustices of the world were not to be righted by a posthumous divine court. Man was thrown upon his own resources in working out a satisfactory pattern of living and in meeting the crises of existence. This meant that man had to know himself and his needs. Of course earlier philosophers like Plato and Aristotle had also considered the importance of this kind of knowledge; but as Brett (1912, p. 162) suggested, "The creed of the Stoic or Epicurean differs from the Platonic and Aristotelian in tone and character." Brett held that it is not quite accurate to account for the difference by calling the platonic practical and the Aristotelian theoretic teachings or doctrines. After all, both Plato and Aristotle made positive recommendations to promote sound government and the good life. To this extent they were mindful of the practical implications of their theorizing. The quest for such implications was incidental to the dominant quest for enhanced understanding of the nature of man and his world. However, for Epicurus, Zeno, and their followers, the emphasis was reversed: the quest for understanding was subordinate to or a function of the quest for ways of enhancing individual human welfare. In this sense their philosophy was more practical than that of Plato and Aristotle. Their thinking was focused on human needs, and this emphasis, Brett pointed out, gave rise to "the humanism of the new era" and its recognition of the centrality of feeling and emotion and that "man's whole being is concentrated in his passions." How to deal with surging desire becomes an intensely practical issue, with the Epicureans urging a modicum of indulgence, the Stoics advocating a maximum of restraining self-denial, and both striving to free man from the tyranny of imperious craving. This, in the words of Brett, constituted "a subtle innovation by which man's thoughts were turned again from the heavens to the earth, from the gods to themselves."

Some Psychological Issues

As might be expected, in their accounts of man as a psychological being both Epicureans and Stoics were much influenced by teachings current in the time of Aristotle. Much of what they included were vague and, in the light of modern knowledge, unprofitable speculation. Mention has already been made of the Epicurean view of visual perception as due to the emanation of images of external objects entering his eye. A modification of this naïve theory is found in the Stoic account of vision as a sort of searchlight process: rays coming from the eye in the form of a cone were held to bring objects into view. Enlargement of the visual field with distance vision and its narrowing with near vision was explained by reference to the cone-shaped nature of the hypothetical rays.

As a contribution to optics, such theorizing can be dismissed without comment; but it may be regarded as possibly being a contribution to the psychology of perception by suggesting the role of an active searching process in many perceptual acts. This is clearly exemplified when we are looking *for* something or scanning the faces of approaching people when we are waiting for a friend at a busy street corner. Perception thus often involves active attention and control by present interests or a given mental set. It is not just the passive consequence of sensory stimulation as was already implicit in Aristotle's distinction between having and observing an experience. Some of the Stoics had reference to this by noting the *reactive* nature of perception: objects impress the mind and the mind reacts to the impression.

In general, the Stoics anticipated Locke's empiricism by regarding the soul at birth as akin to a blank slate—a *tabula rasa*—upon which experience has yet to write in order to produce knowledge. Furthermore, in their recognition of reason as an inherently or innate reactive propensity they might be said to have anticipated Leibnitz and Kant in regarding the intellect as independent of and different from the summation of sensory impressions in the course of mental development. In some respects this was but a dim foreshadowing of the seventeenth-century Locke-Leibnitz controversy rather than a clear-cut, explicit formulation of the central issue. As G. S. Brett (1912, p. 173) brought out in the following passage, the Stoic position on these issues was somewhat uncertain and vacillating:

> The Stoic could say (with Leibnitz) that everything comes through the senses except the intellect itself. But that is a great reservation and the Stoics were never quite clear how far knowledge was the product of experience, and how far it was the upcoming of a reason embedded in man's nature. This ambiguity shows itself even in the theory of sensation; for Stoic writings vacillate between the idea of sensation going inward to the central reason, and a central reason going out through sense-organs which it used as its channels.

In connection with the *tabula rasa* notion of the development of perceptual knowledge, an important contribution was made by Chrysippas (c. 280–206 B.C.), one of the Stoic philosophers. Initially it had been held that a sensory impression literally *impresses* the mind just as a seal impressed upon a wax surface leaves a design on the surface. This implies a copy theory of perception: sensory impressions leave pictorial copies of external objects. It is a presentational as opposed to a representational or symbolic theory. The latter constitutes the more sophisticated view held by the Stoic Chrysippas. According to this view, a sensory process does not result in a photographic copy of objects or a mental facsimile of external events. Instead it brings about changes regarded as representative of such events. To employ a simple example: when we say that the street looks wet, is wetness as a tactual event being experienced? The visual appearance of the street serves as a *sign* of what would be felt if the skin were brought into contact with the pavement.

This means that past experience governs present perceptions. We continue to see a coin as circular irrespective of the angle from which it is viewed. In other words, perception may be the same even though sensory processes are different: perceptual recognition for one who can read is the same even though a familiar phrase be written in longhand, printed in italics, set in Roman type, or sometimes even abbreviated. Sensation and perception are not fixed, static affairs. To call them *processes* is to refer to them as ongoing proceedings. They are not objects or entities. Terms like "a sensation" or "a perception" are really references to convenient abstractions. Titchener (1927, Vol. I, p. 129) put this rather strikingly:

> . . . *we never have a perception*. Consciousness is a shifting tangle of processes, themselves inconstant, and the perception is a little bit of pattern raveled out from the tangle and artificially fixed for scientific scrutiny. . . .

This statement of Titchener's may be regarded as a twentieth-century elaboration of what was implicit in the ancient Stoic repudiation of the copy theory of perception. Such repudiation does not involve rejection of the empiricist teaching regarding the intellect's dependence on sensory events as supplying the raw material for the acquisition of knowledge. The *tabula rasa* view of the empiricists is retained, with the mind at birth being compared to a blank surface upon which experience has yet to leave its mark. Moreover, what merits explicit notice is that Stoic psychology also provided for recognitition of what Leibnitz stressed so many centuries later; namely, that there are inherent modes of coming to terms with sensory experience. Instead of a theory that views the growth of knowledge as a purely passive process, this Stoic recognition makes provision for such growth to be viewed in accordance with an activity theory. According to the Stoic view, mind is not only acted upon by sensory events but also *reacts* to them. Knowledge results as an outcome of such conjoint activity.

These references to Stoic anticipations of the Locke-Leibnitz controversy should not be construed as implying a thorough grasp of the details of the controversy as they developed in the seventeenth century. The anticipations were more in the nature of unelaborated suggestions, with little interest in their bearing on abstract psychological theory. There was more interest in the practical implications of psychological theory.

In particular, the bearing of such theory on the acquisition and promotion of virtue received special treatment. From one viewpoint, virtue or right conduct may be thought of as a system of habits; and habits, in turn, may be thought of as products of mechanical repetition or drill. A trained animal can be said to exemplify such a system of habits as it responds to the trainer's signals during a circus performance. And yet trained horses, lions, or dogs would not be described as virtuous animals. Such a description would be at variance with the Stoic conception of the psychology of virtue. As envisaged by the Stoics, virtue is a product of the intellect in the sense of being the outcome of rational choice. Confronted with alternative courses of action, the man of virtue chooses that which commends itself to his reason.

Only by governing one's life by such rational insight can the inner harmony suggested by the Stoic ideal of *apatheia* be achieved. Wisdom is the hall-mark of such achievement. In the words of Seneca:

> Wisdom does not show itself so much in percept as in life—in firmness of mind and mastery of appetite. It teaches us to do as well as to talk; and to make our words and actions all of a color.

Individual well-being for the Stoic was thus contingent upon the sovereignty of reason or upon insight into the probable consequences of yielding to given impulses. Self-mastery was seen as a function of such insight. Broadly con-sidered, such a Stoic teaching is in line with some modern views regarding the promotion of individual well-being. At all events, it is not uncommon for psychotherapists to stress attainment of insight as a *sine qua non* of therapeutic progress. As used in modern psychology, the term "insight" has several meanings, but they all have to do with cognitive or intellectual functions. This is clearly exemplified in a recent dictionary definition (English and English, 1958, p. 264) of the term as meaning "reasonable understanding and evaluation of one's own mental processes, reactions, abilities; self-knowledge." In the present context it is relevant to point out that, contrary to what some have regarded as an anti-intellectualistic tendency reflected in psychoanalytic preoccupation with the unconscious, Freud himself did not repudiate the soverign role of intellect in the mastery of neurotic conflict. This has already been brought out in Chapter 3, page 55, by citing Freud's belief in what he called "the primacy of the intellect" along with his comment regarding the eventual success of the soft "voice of the intellect."

There may thus be something in common between Freud's reference to "the voice of the intellect" and the ancient Greek injunction "Know thyself" inscribed in golden letters on the Temple of Delphos. There may also be something in common between Freud's concept of repression and what the Stoic Seneca has in mind when he stated, "Other men's sins are before our eyes; our own are behind our back." In brief, modern man's quest for mental health and the good life continues to reflect insights dating back to the similar quest of Stoic and Epicurean philosophers. Seen in this light, it is an open question whether the past is illuminating the present or the present is illuminating the past. It is probably safer to conclude that the applied psychology of the ancient "healer of souls" and the applied psychology of the modern psychotherapist reflect what is common to all human beings—especially when they are troubled, anxious, confused, and possibly in search of the *apatheia* of the Stoics or the *ataraxia* of the Epicureans or the *integrated personality* of the moderns.

References

Allport, G. *Pattern and Growth in Personality*. New York: Holt, Rinehart and Winston, 1961.

Brett, G. S. *A History of Psychology,* Vol. I. London: George Allen and Unwin, Ltd., 1912.

Durant, W. *The Life of Greece.* New York: Simon and Schuster, 1939.

English, H. B., and English, A. C. *A Comprehensive Dictionary of Psychological and Psychoanalytical Terms*. New York: Longmans, Green and Company, 1958.

Fuller, B. A. G. *A History of Philosophy*. New York: Henry Holt and Company, 1945.

Jahoda, M. *Current Concepts of Positive Mental Health*. New York: Basic Books, 1958.

Kuhn, T. S. "Historical Structure of Scientific Discovery," *Science*, 1962, *136*, 760–764.

McKeon, R. (ed.). *Introduction to Aristotle*. New York: The Modern Library, 1947.

Mair, A. W. "Epicurus," in *Encyclopaedia Britannica,* Vol. 8, 14th ed., 1929.

Muller, H. J. *The Loom of History*. New York: Harper and Brothers, 1958.

Rogers, A. K. *A Student's History of Philosophy*. New York: The Macmillan Company, 1915.

Russell, B. *The Impact of Science on Society*. New York: Columbia University Press, 1951.

Sarton, G. *A History of Science—Ancient Science through the Golden Age of Greece*. Cambridge: Harvard University Press, 1952.

Singer, C. "Historical Relations of Religion and Science," in J. Needhan (ed.). *Science, Religion and Reality*. New York: George Braziller, 1955, pp. 90–152.

Singer, C. *A Short History of Anatomy and Physiology from the Greeks to Harvey*. New York: Dover Publications, 1957.

Titchener, E. B. *Experimental Psychology, Student's Manual,* Vol. I. New York: The Macmillan Company, 1927.

Wells, H. G. *The Outline of History,* Vol. I. New York: The Macmillan Company, 1921.

6

The Earlier Medieval Background

DURING THE MEDIEVAL PERIOD there was little if any consideration of psychological topics in the spirit of pure science as one thinks of pure science today. Instead such topics were enmeshed in theological and metaphysical settings. Much of the literature that has come down to us is dreary verbiage. At first arguments of the Church fathers and schoolmen about the salvation of the soul, the impact of Adam's fall, the attributes of God, and kindred theological issues might well seem devoid of interest for the student of scientific psychology. Many of these arguments may properly be stigmatized as logomachies—tediously futile disputes about words. They reflect the negative connotation often aroused by reference to a person as being "medieval-minded" and thus by inference dogmatic, narrow in outlook, and uninfluenced by postmedieval scientific developments. In terms of this connotation, the historian of psychology might feel justified in virtually ignoring the centuries from the decline of Rome to the beginnings of the Renaissance. In fact, as inspection of such scholarly works as those of Boring or J. C. Flugel or Gardner Murphy will show, it is possible to present the history of psychology without devoting space to the medieval period.

Nevertheless such a dismissal of the medieval period ought to be questioned. Can one obtain an adequate grasp of psychology's past without some acquaintance with post-Hellenic and medieval thought? Was the medieval period barren of psychological insights of historical import? Was the period stagnant with respect to general scientific developments of a kind that might be said to have paved the way for the rise of the seventeenth-century science, which in turn eventually set the stage for the emergence of laboratory psychology in the nineteenth century? If questions of this kind were to be answered in the affirmative, there would be no need for the present chapter; but such is not the case.

124

Preliminary Orientation

By way of initial orientation it is well to note that medieval psychological teachings were not just echoes of Aristotelian views as endorsed by the Church. Instead until the time of Aquinas the psychology of Plato as elaborated by St. Augustine (354–430) was more influential than that of Aristotle. At one time there was even official Church opposition to Aristotle. For example, as A. C. Crombie (1959, p. 61) reminds us, in 1210 an ecclesiastical council in Paris refused to sanction the teaching of Aristotle's ideas about natural philosophy. It also prohibited the teaching of commentaries on these ideas. Such uneasiness regarding danger to orthodoxy to be feared by exposure to Aristotle's views was not an isolated event. It was expressed both in the time of Innocent III, Pope from 1198 to 1216, and of that of Gregory IX, Pope from 1227 to 1241, during the lifetime of St. Thomas Aquinas (1225–1274). As is pointed out by Anne Fremantle (1962, Vol. 1, pp. 118–119), Gregory assigned three theologians the task of determining changes to be made in Aristotle's teachings in order to harmonize them with the doctrines of the Church.

Not until about the middle of the thirteenth century did Thomistic interpretations of Aristotle win Church approval. In the preceding eight centuries, Augustinian interpretations of Plato's philosophy were more acceptable to the ecclesiastical hierarchy. Some of these interpretations have a direct bearing on the history of psychology. With reference to this Augustinian period, Brett (1912, p. 19) wrote: "To pass over this period in silence would be to ignore the real beginning of many important inquiries, though that beginning was indeed obscure and veiled in curious terms." It may thus prove enlightening to consider some of these "inquiries" in broad perspective. Before doing so, however, it is advisable to give preliminary consideration to the work of Plotinus (205–270), whose interpretations and modification of Plato's teachings had a direct bearing on the views of Augustine.

Plotinus as Neoplatonist

The major teachings of Plotinus are to be found in a work entitled *The Enneads*. This work was edited by a Greek scholar, Porphyry, who had studied philosophy under Plotinus. Its title is derived from *ennea*, the Greek word for the number nine; the book is divided into six *enneads*, each of which is divided into nine parts. Its importance in the history of philosophy and theology may be indicated by the fact that it has been translated into Latin, Italian, French, German, and English. Probably the best English translation is that of Stephen MacKenna, who devoted more than twenty years of dedicated effort to the task.

Very little is known about the life of Plotinus. According to Porphyry

(MacKenna, p. 1), Plotinus "could never be induced to tell of his ancestry, his parentage, or his birthplace." It seems that he was born in Egypt and may have been of Roman ancestry. As a young man he joined a military expedition headed for Mesopotamia in order to learn something of Indian and Persian philosophy. Eventually he settled in Rome as the head of a school that became rather influential.

Despite the fact that his teachings eventually came to have a strong appeal for St. Augustine, Plotinus himself was opposed to Christianity. His philosophy, although largely based upon Plato, is different enough to merit separate classification. It includes Stoic and other philosophic viewpoints along with some original insights, all organized into a conceptual system requiring such classification. This differentiation is usually indicated by referring to the system as Neoplatonic, just as departures from and modifications of Freud's system of psychology are often classified as neo-Freudian. Furthermore, just as some of the neo-Freudians did not regard their systems as being in opposition to Freud's, so Plotinus does not seem to have viewed his teachings as being opposed to Plato's. As has been pointed out by A. H. Armstrong (1962, pp. 19–21), Plotinus thought of himself more the expositor of Plato's philosophy than an innovating head of a new school. However, in the words of Armstrong, Plato never had "the sort of fully worked-out system of thought which lies behind the *Enneads.*" Like William James, Plato was more the penetrating topical thinker than the systematic thinker. In the strict sense of the word "system," James never developed a system of psychology and Plato failed to develop a system of philosophy. Plotinus, in contrast, did succeed in organizing his views into a definite system. In doing so he introduced ideas that are not found in Plato and also reinterpreted some of Plato's teachings in order to fit them into his system. As a consequence his Neoplatonic system is more than a mere elaboration of Plato's philosophy.

Plotinus as Mystic

Detailed consideration of the ways in which Plotinus agreed with and differed from Plato is more germane to the history of philosophy than the history of psychology.[1] Here it suffices to note that, unlike Plato, Plotinus stressed the vital and intensely personal significance of mystical experience. He himself seems to have undergone such experiences from time to time. Like all mystics, he alludes to the ineffable nature of the core of the mystical experience. One can never know it by reading about it, for it defies verbal

---

[1] For a discussion of ways in which the philosophy of Plotinus differed from its foundations in Platonism, see E. Bréhier, *The Philosophy of Plotinus* (Chicago: University of Chicago Press, 1958). Chapter VII, entitled "The Orientalism of Plotinus," is particularly informative by calling attention to non-Hellenic influences, especially those stemming from Indian philosophy and its emphasis on asceticism and disciplined contemplation as means of promoting mystical insights.

description. It becomes a source of deep conviction for those who, like Plotinus, have come to know it by direct experience. For him, it engendered a metaphysical outlook in which mystical terminology is conspicuously present. For example, there are repeated references to The One as that which transcends Being. The One is also called The Good or The Absolute or The Infinite or even The Transcendence. Emanations from The One are held to influence a receptive soul, and the aspiring soul yearns for increasing closeness and spiritual merging with The One. As transcendent being, The One is unknowable and eludes human comprehension. Even the term "being" may be inappropriate if taken to refer to the ordinary meaning of the word as a designation for experienced existence or reality, since The One can never be experienced. It is a conceptual construct, psychologically akin to the religionist's concept of God. The very privacy of mystical experiences along with their ineffability renders it impossible to bring them within the scope of scientific verification.[2]

From one viewpoint this mystical phase of Plotinian philosophy has no direct bearing on the history of psychology. This viewpoint would apply to a history restricted to an account of psychology's eventual emergence as a laboratory science. In terms of a broader viewpoint, however, mysticism as a special topic along with religion as a special topic has aroused the interest of some professional psychologists. A classical examination of these topics was initiated by James, whose *The Varieties of Religious Experience* (1902), was the forerunner of many subsequent studies of the psychology of religion. Some years later Freud, as summarized by Ernest Jones (1957, Vol. 3, Chapter 13), concerned himself with the role of religion and mysticism in the life of man. An even more positive concern with this role is reflected in the writings of Jung (1933 and 1938). More recently, D. Bakan (1958), in a carefully documented study, traced the influence of "Jewish mystical tradition" on Freud's psychoanalytic concepts. It should thus be evident that mysticism is not altogether alien to the history of psychology.

Mysticism readily falls within the scope of psychology's interest in the vagaries of human behavior. The mystical outlook constitutes one of the ways in which man has endeavored to cope with critical life situations, especially those which arouse feelings of despairing impotence. Under such circumstances the mystic reaches out for some external source of help. In

---

[2] It is possible to argue that verification might nevertheless be attempted. Much depends on what is to be regarded as a mystical experience. The literature of Zen Buddhism supplies accounts of changes in consciousness induced by prescribed meditation exercises that seem to come close to the mystical tranquillity mentioned by Plotinus. Some contemporary psychologists have taken a great interest in this literature. (For details and relevant bibliography see E. W. Maupin, "Zen Buddhism: A Psychological Review," *Journal of Consulting Psychology,* 1962, *26,* 362–378.) Moreover, Maupin has subjected Zen meditation exercises to systematic laboratory investigation. (See E. W. Maupin, "Individual Differences in Response to a Zen Meditation Exercise," *Journal of Consulting Psychology,* 1965, *29,* 139–145.)

the case of Plotinus this great need, after intense self-examination along with devoted study of Plato and other philosophers, gave rise not only to adoration of The One but also to something of more immediate psychological significance; namely, insights into the nature of man as a self-conscious being.

Man as a Self-Conscious Being

As a religious mystic, Plotinus developed many of these insights in the course of his reflections upon such varied metaphysical issues as the relation of the soul to mind and matter, immortality of the soul and its possible reincarnation, how to reconcile the benevolence of The One with the existence of evil, and, of course, the perennial problem of sinful impulses and their control. As with Plato, his concern with such issues centered on the achievement of moral excellence. In his view, that ideal is not to be achieved by a divided soul or one disunited by antagonistic impulses. On the contrary, as he put it (MacKenna, p. 614): "Moral excellence is of a soul acting as a concordant total, brought to unity." It is tempting to regard this observation as an early glimpse of what we moderns refer to as an integrated personality. At all events, from the context in which the quotation occurs it is clear that Plotinus was mindful of the principle of unity or integration as a key factor in the nature of being. Further, the quotation is preceded by the following explicit recognition of this principle:

> It is in virtue of unity that beings are beings. This is equally true of things whose existence is primal and of all that are in any degree to be numbered among beings. What could exist at all except as one thing? Deprived of unity, a thing ceases to be what it is called: no army unless as a unity: a chorus, a flock, must be one thing. Even a house and ship demand unity, one house, one ship; unity gone, neither remains: thus even continuous magnitudes could not exist without an inherent unity; break them apart and their very being is altered in the measure of the breach of unity.
>
> Take plant and animal; the material form stands a unity; fallen from that into a litter of fragments, the things have lost their being; what was is no longer there; it is replaced by quite other things—as many others, precisely, as possesses unity.
>
> Health, similarly, is the condition of a body acting as a co-ordinate unity. Beauty appears when limbs and features are controlled by the principle, unity.

Although, as has been mentioned, both Plato and Plotinus made the achievement of moral excellence the dominating ideal of their respective philosophies, they differed in what they proposed for the realization of this ideal. Plato, who viewed man as a political animal, regarded moral excellence as a function of wise administration of governmental affairs calculated to promote sound citizenship. In contrast, Plotinus made the pursuit of moral excellence a matter of individual responsibility—a solitary quest involving concentration on or contemplation of one's inner life that will culminate in a mystical trance as the soul reached out for identification with The One. The solitariness of the venture is aptly described by Plotinus as a "flight of the alone to the Alone." However, such mystical language is not to be construed as a repudiation of the importance of reason or intellect as the sovereign regulator of the moral life. Plotinus and Plato were in agreement on recognizing this importance; they differed only in the ways in which they would have reason promote moral excellence. To oversimplify somewhat, it might be said that Platonism, in the light of its concept of the philosopher-king, provided for the sovereignty of reason in the life of community or state organization and administration, while in Neoplatonism as developed by Plotinus there was more concern with the role of reason as sovereign in the life of the individual. For Plotinus, individual salvation was to be achieved by a Stoic indifference toward cravings of the flesh along with ardent devotion to the task of so ordering one's life as to promote unity of the soul. In short, he was concerned with life as it is experienced by one in quest of intelligent or reasoned control of its vicissitudes. It is this concern rather than his metaphysical views that accounts for his place in the history of psychology, for his concern prompted him to take note of the impact of experience on man's awareness of himself. As Brett wrote (1912, p. 302): "In Plotinus, for the first time in its history, psychology becomes the science of the phenomena of consciousness, conceived as self-consciousness."

The references to consciousness and self-consciousness are scattered through *The Enneads* and not made the subject of separate treatment divorced from the metaphysics sponsored by Plotinus. This dispersion renders it difficult to summarize his views of mental life as if they constituted an independent system of psychology. It might be more accurate to regard his psychological views as potential background for a system. There are some striking observations which from the vantage point of historical perspective can be construed as foreshadowings of what centuries later came to be regarded as new teachings or novel interpretations. Let us consider a few of these observations.

The Mind-Body Problem

In connection with his reflections upon the relationship of the body to the soul or mind, Plotinus presents a view which in broad outline is substantially like a view suggested by William James in one of his Harvard lectures. Like all theories of the relationship in question, this one is also speculative. James, it should be added, developed his theory independently of any reference to the writings of Plotinus. What Plotinus proposed will be more readily understood if the theory of James is first presented.

In 1898 James delivered the "Ingersoll Lecture on the Immortality of Man" which was published under the title *Human Immortality: Two Supposed*

Objections to the Doctrine. In this lecture he raised the question of the validity of the opinion of those who reject the notion of immortality on the ground that mind is a function of the brain and consequently would have to perish with dissolution of the brain in death. According to James, the facts of physiological psychology do not necessarily restrict one to this interpretation of the mind-body relationship. The latter relationship, theoretically considered, might be either a productive or creative one or else a transmissive one, depending on what meaning is attributed to the phrase "functional dependence." In terms of one meaning, mental events can be conceived of as dependent on brain tissue in the sense of being a *product* of the brain's metabolic activity, just as shoes are a product of a shoe factory. However, functional dependence is subject to an alternative interpretation. Instead of producing or creating mental events, the brain's neurones might be serving as a *transmissive* mechanism, facilitating the flow of conscious data just as the Atlantic cable transmits messages from New York to London.

This latter interpretation involves a bold assumption that James did not hesitate to entertain; namely, that there may be a "mother-sea" of consciousness in the universe which is canalized in individual experience via brain mechanisms. As Ralph Barton Perry (1954, p. 206) pointed out in his discussion of this hypothesis, it is, of course, altogether devoid of experimental support and yet James regarded it as having "dramatic probability." What endowed it with "probability" in the opinion of James was its consonance with some reports of mystical experience. The idea of a "mother-sea of consciousness" existing as a reservoir of "cosmic consciousness" is discussed at some length in the chapter on "Mysticism" in James's *The Varieties of Religious Experience* (1902). Of particular relevance is the account James gives of the description of "cosmic consciousness" supplied by Dr. R. M. Bucke, a Canadian psychiatrist, who not only had undergone such a mystical experience but had also investigated it in others. In fact, the very phrase "cosmic consciousness" was original with Bucke as an appropriate designation for the experience in question. In its experiential immediacy this mode of consciousness, like all mystical phenomena, does not lend itself to satisfactory verbal description. Nevertheless, Bucke attempted it as indicated by the following excerpt from his writings as quoted by James (1902, p. 398):

> The prime characteristic of cosmic consciousness is a consciousness of the cosmos, that is, of the life and order of the universe. Along with the consciousness of the cosmos there occurs an intellectual enlightenment which alone would place the individual on a new plane of existence—would make him almost a member of a new species. To this is added a state of moral exaltation, an indescribable feeling of elevation, elation, and joyousness, and a quickening of the moral senses, which is fully as striking and more important than is the enhanced intellectual power. With these come what may be called a sense of immortality, a consciousness of

eternal life, not a conviction that he shall have this, but the consciousness that he has it already.

James did not dismiss descriptions such as the foregoing as mystical nonsense unworthy of serious scientific consideration. On the contrary he regarded them as important factors in the study of the psychology of religion. As he saw it, they constituted a central core of experience common to the inner life of deeply religious persons irrespective of the particular creed they chanced to espouse. He viewed this as the "common nucleus" of diverse religions. By examining accounts of mystical phenomena as reported by religious mystics through the ages, he was able to abstract such a common nucleus. It involves an initial feeling of something being amiss—a sense of uneasiness because of moral shortcomings. There is self-condemnation because of this feeling, along with recognition of a cleavage in one's being: a lower level responsible for the condemned behavior and a higher level wounded by the sense of wrongdoing. At first there is difficulty in deciding which level is characteristic of one's real self. In his final chapter James refers to this cleavage and its bearing on religious mysticism in the following passage, in which the concept of cosmic consciousness receives italicized emphasis (1902, p. 508):

> The individual, so far as he suffers from his wrongness and criticises it, is to that extent consciously beyond it, and in at least possible touch with something higher, if anything higher exist. Along with the wrong part there is thus a better part of him, even though it may be but a helpless germ. With which part he should identify his real being is by no means obvious at this stage; but when stage 2 (the stage of solution or salvation) arrives, the man identifies his real being with the germinal higher part of himself; and does so in the following way. *He becomes conscious that this higher part is conterminous and continuous with a* MORE *of the same quality, which is operative in the universe outside of him, and which he can keep in working touch with, and in a fashion get on board of and save himself when all his lower being has gone to pieces in the wreck.*

The preceding references to higher and lower parts of the self are, of course, reminiscent of Plato's levels of the soul, just as the reference to the something MORE "operative in the universe" is suggestive not only of Plato's universals but also of what Plotinus designated as The One. In this respect the phenomena of the religious consciousness as described by James at the beginning of the present century are in line with what Plotinus had already noted in the third century A.D. To use somewhat technical language, both James and Plotinus can be said to have called attention to immanent and transcendent features of mental life. What James alluded to as cosmic consciousness has to do with the transcendent implication of his notion of the brain as a transmitting organ. Such transcendence is also clearly implied in the metaphysics of Plotinus, according to which body is not only ensouled, but is also surrounded by soul. For Plotinus, this mind-body relationship is like that of light to air. What he has to say about the relationship can be more readily understood by considering these excerpts from *The Enneads* (MacKenna, pp. 277–279):

> How comes it then that everyone speaks of soul as being in body? Because the Soul is not seen and the body is: we perceive the body, and by its movement and sensation we understand that it is ensouled, and we say that it possesses a soul; to speak of residence is a natural sequence. If the soul were visible, an object of the senses, radiating throughout the entire life, if it were manifest in full force to the very outermost surface, we would no longer speak of soul as in body; we would say the minor was in the major, the contained within the container, the fleeting within the perdurable. . . .
>
> May we think that the mode of Soul's presence to body is that of the presence of light to the air?
>
> This certainly is presence with distinction: the light penetrates through and through, but nowhere coalesces; the light is the stable thing, and air flows in and out; when the air passes beyond the lit area it is dark; under the light it is lit: we have a true parallel to what we have been saying of body and soul, for the air is in the light rather than the light in the air.
>
> Plato therefore is wise when, in treating of the All he puts the body in its soul and not its soul in the body, and says that while there is a region of that soul which contains body, there is another region to which body does not enter—certain powers, that is, with which body has no concern.

Although more than a millennium and a half separates James from Plotinus, we see that their concern with the psychological import of mystical experience gave rise to substantially similar dualistic interpretations of that experience. James had to depend on other men's accounts of such experience, while for Plotinus they constituted events in his personal history. Plotinus, in other words, had knowledge of acquaintance of the "common nucleus" that James found in the widely scattered literature of mysticism. Such knowledge was not at the disposal of James; he could only know *about* the intuitively apprehended, ineffable phenomena to which mystics referred.

In some respects, knowledge of acquaintance carries more conviction than knowledge about. The congenitally deaf may learn about auditory experience, but they can never learn what listening to a symphony in its tonal richness is like. Similarly, the heart specialist who himself is free from heart disease can never have direct sensory acquaintance with the cardiac pains described by his patients. Nevertheless he knows more *about* the significance of such pains than they do. Despite their subjectivity, pains are very real phenomena and have come to have an important place in the science of medicine.

Should the subjectivity of mystical phenomena preclude their inclusion in the science of psychology? James in his day, as has been shown, did not hesitate to give them serious consideration. However, as will be shown in Chapter 9, many of his psychological successors came to question the scientific respectability of psychology's concern with subjective events. In the days of Plotinus, of course, there was no such questioning. He was content to accept subjective events as points of departure for discussions of issues which centuries later came to involve significant questions for the psychologist of the modern era. It is in this sense that, as mentioned earlier, Brett regarded Plotinus as the first one to treat psychology as "the science of the phenomena of consciousness, conceived as self-consciousness."

Plotinus as Psychologist

In addition to the mind-body question, Plotinus raised numerous others of psychological relevance. These questions are taken up in different sections of *The Enneads.* By way of showing their nature and range, a few of them will be introduced and briefly considered. For the most part it will suffice to present them as questions without introducing the answers proposed by Plotinus, since the answers are not so provocative as the questions. It is particularly provocative for the twentieth-century psychologist that some seventeen centuries ago Plotinus raised questions like the following ones: (Page citations to MacKenna.)

1. With reference to what has become an issue in the study of the psycho-physiology of emotion and the neuro-endocrine differentia of emotion, it is of interest to mention that Plotinus once asked, "Pleasure and distress, fear and courage, desire and aversion, where have these affections their seat?" (p. 21.) In this connection it should be mentioned that Plotinus recognized the brain as the chief locus for consciousness when he stated: " . . . the nerves start from the brain. The brain therefore has been considered as the centre and seat of the principle which determines feeling and impulse and the entire act of the organism as a living thing; where the instincts are found to be linked, there the operating faculty is assumed to be situated." (p. 279.)

2. Another psychophysiological issue raised by Plotinus took this form: "What of the suspension of consciousness which drugs or disease may bring about?" (p. 44.)

3. The difference between directly experienced emotional events as contrasted with their subsequent recall induced Plotinus to ask, "And what is there pleasant in the memory of pleasure? What is it to recall yesterday's excellent dinner? Still more ridiculous, one of ten years ago?" (p. 55.)

4. The psychology of love is not overlooked, for one section of the book is concerned with the question "What is Love?" In his discussion of this topic Plotinus considers both aesthetic and libidinous aspects in these words: "Now everyone recognizes that the emotional state for which we make this 'Love' responsible rises in souls aspiring to be knit in the closest union with some beautiful object,

and that this aspiration takes two forms, that of the good whose devotion is for beauty itself, and that other which seeks its consummation in some vile act." (p. 191.)

5. Man's sensitivity to beauty was another aspect of consciousness discussed by Plotinus. For example, he noted that symmetry of feature is not enough to account for one's impression of beauty when he raised this question: "Again since the one face, constant in symmetry, appears sometimes fair and sometimes not, can we doubt that beauty is something more than symmetry, that symmetry owes its beauty to a remoter principle?" (p. 57.) For Plotinus, this remoter principle involved consideration of the bearing of *nous* and *logos* on form. His discussion of these abstractions constitutes an early recognition of psychological factors included in the studies of those nineteenth-century pioneers responsible for the introduction of an experimental aesthetics as well as for present-day members of Division 10 of the American Psychological Association, the Division of Esthetics.

6. Plotinus also concerned himself with another problem that looms large in modern philosophy, namely, the meaning of the term "matter." In doing so, he was virtually asking what is involved in our consciousness of material substance, of solid bodies, of external objects. This, students of philosophy may recall, was the kind of question raised by Berkeley (1685–1753), the Irish philosopher whose subjective idealism rendered the concept of matter an affair of sensory experiences, as summed up in his famous phrase "To be is to be perceived." Our perception of what we call a material object, Berkeley argued, is thus a reference to a complex of sensations, and there is nothing aside from such a complex to be ascribed to what is commonly regarded as a *physical* substance. We never have direct experience of a substratum responsible for the complex of sensations; hence for Berkeley there is or may be no such substratum. In the light of this brief reminder of Berkeley's disposal of the concept of matter, it is of more than passing interest to note what Plotinus had to say about this concept. He seems to have anticipated Berkeley's subjective idealism when, in referring to the notion of matter, he wrote: "We must therefore refuse to it all that we find in things of sense—not merely such attributes as colour, heat or cold, but weight or weightlessness, thickness or thinness, shape and therefore magnitude. . . . " (p. 109.)

7. In addition to this anticipation of Berkeley's central teaching, Plotinus seems to have anticipated the reaction of John Stuart Mill (1806–1873) to this teaching. As Boring (1929, p. 231) has pointed out, Mill in accepting Berkeley's reduction of the concept of matter to a complex of sensory impressions was nevertheless troubled by the transitoriness of sensations as contrasted with the relative permanence of what is ordinarily called a material object. Accordingly, Mill undertook to dispose of the difficulty by means of what he called a "psychological theory of the belief in an external world." In terms of this theory, as a result of repeated experiences we learn to expect or anticipate certain organized groups of sensory impressions or perceptions when about to deal with "material" objects. In other words, such expectations serve to provide a basis for the belief or conviction for the continued existence of that which is about to be perceived.

Our belief or conviction in the existence of matter, Mill held, is a consequence of having had such expectations confirmed with dependable regularity. The concept of matter has to do with anticipations of what Mill called "Permanent Possibilities of Sensations." This view was formulated about one hundred years ago. But some sixteen hundred years earlier Plotinus seems to have arrived at a similar conclusion when he ended his discussion of the concept of matter with this statement: "If Matter is to be kept as the underlying substratum, we must keep it as Matter; that means—does it not?—that we must define it as a Potentiality and nothing more. . . . " (p. 122.)

8. Berkeley has won a place for himself in the history of psychology not so much because of his subjective idealism but more because of his theory of vision. In the latter theory he made space perception, judgments of size, and estimates of distance the results of learning, or the consequence of *experienced* associations. The theory was in line with the British empiricist tradition and was opposed to theories which, as explained in Chapter 1, accounted for space perception in line with the nativist tradition. In some respects Plotinus came close to an anticipation of this phase of Berkeley's teaching just as he came close to the doctrine of subjective idealism. At all events, he raised the question of distance vision by asking, "Why do distant objects appear small?" His answer was by no means as detailed as Berkeley's list of cues governing spatial judgments, but he did allude to a few of them clearly enough to suggest an empiricist's answer to the question. (pp. 130–131.) Incidentally, this empiricist orientation is also reflected in his discussion of the way perception is influenced by prior experience. In fact, he devotes several pages to a discussion of the relation of perception to memory. (pp. 338–341.)

There are still other topics of psychological import to be found in *The Enneads,* but there is little to be gained by enumerating them. The ones mentioned suffice to indicate the general drift of this Neoplatonic concern with phenomena of consciousness. They serve to suggest the kind of psychological issues which Plotinus bequeathed to St. Augustine, whose views, as we have noted, tended to dominate or at least to be very influential during the first eight hundred years of the medieval period. In a strict chronological sense, the views of Plotinus ought not to be made part of this chapter, since he lived some two hundred years before the onset of the medieval period. Nevertheless, by virtue of the way his views came to influence medieval thought as St. Augustine interpreted and elaborated them, one may regard them as an ideational bridge connecting some aspects of Platonic and Stoic psychology with what St. Augustine introduced into medieval psychology. The nature of this connection will be outlined in the next section.

St. Augustine: Introduction

The life of St. Augustine spanned the years from 354 to 430. These were years of strife, turmoil, and insecurity. Successive groups of barbarians attacked and pillaged cities of the Roman Empire. The Empire itself was doomed and the shadow of what historians designate as the Dark Ages was already visible. In many respects the philosophy developed by St. Augustine is to be construed as a reaction to the devastation and decadence of the Empire's decline and disintegration. He had little hope for an ordered, satisfying life in the affairs of this world. Instead he projected an ideal world for the elect in the world to come. The blessedness of life in the *City of God* was to compensate for the misery of life in the *city of the world.*

Very much more is known about the life of St. Augustine than of Plotinus. Whereas Plotinus was reticent about his early life, Augustine was relatively unreserved in his *Confessions,* a world classic of autobiography. He even refers to his infancy as the sinful beginning of his life. This, he is careful to point out, was not based upon actual recall of his own infantile behavior, but an inference derived from what he had "learnt infants to be from observing them." The autobiography is addressed to God in the form of an outpouring of his thoughts and feelings about himself as he looks back upon different periods of his life. At the time he wrote his *Confessions* he had already been ordained as a bishop and his theological views had already been crystallized.

One of these views had to do with his teaching regarding the consequences of Adam's fall. This teaching established the basis for what became the dogma of infant depravity or original sin. Its theological status is not of any direct psychological significance. What is of such significance, though, is the effect of such a teaching on what one attributes to the infant in the way of actual and potential psychological characteristics. Genetic or developmental psychology is, of course, especially concerned with this problem. Child-rearing practices, in large measure, are a function of the answers given to this problem. To regard the infant as sinful and depraved will elicit very different parental reactions from those of parents enamored of the baby's innocence.

St. Augustine on Infant and Adolescent Psychology

St. Augustine's notions of infant psychology were a product of what the modern child psychologist would stigmatize as a methodological blunder: he interpreted infant nature in the light of adult psychology. Just as reading human nature into animal nature is called an *anthropomorphic* fallacy, so St. Augustine's blunder might be called an *adultomorphic* fallacy. Both the nature of this fallacy as well as the general tone of St. Augustine's *Confessions* can be gleaned from the following quotation (Pusey translation, pp. 9–10):

Hear, O. God. Alas for man's sin! So saith man, and Thou pitiest him; for Thou madest him, but sin in him Thou madest not. Who remindeth me of the sins of my infancy? for in Thy sight none is pure from sin, not even the infant whose life is but a day upon the earth. Who remindeth me? doth not each little infant, in whom I see what of myself I remember not? When then was my sin? was it that I hung upon the breast and cried? for should I now so do for food suitable to my age, justly should I be laughed at and reproved. What I then did was worthy reproof;

ST. AUGUSTINE (354–430)

but since I could not understand reproof, custom and reason forbade me to be reproved. For those habits, when grown, we root out and cast away. Now no man, though he prunes, wittingly casts away what is good. Or was it then good, even for a while, to cry for what, if given, would hurt? bitterly to resent, that persons free, and its own elders, yea, the very authors of its birth, served it not? that many besides, wiser than it, obeyed not the nod of its good pleasure? to do its best to strike and hurt, because commands were not obeyed, which had been obeyed to its hurt? The weakness then of infant limbs, not its will, is its innocence. Myself have seen and known even a baby envious; it could not speak, yet it turned pale and looked bitterly on its foster-brother. Who knows this? Mothers and nurses tell you that they allay these things by I know not what remedies. Is that too innocence, when the fountain of milk is flowing in rich abundance, not to endure one to share it, though in extremest need, and whose very life depends thereon? We bear gently with all this, not as being no or slight evils, but because they will disappear as years increase; for, though tolerated now, the very same tempers are utterly intolerable when found in riper years.

. . . This age then, Lord, whereof I have no rememberance, which I take on others' word, and guess from other infants that I have passed, true though the guess be, I am yet loth to count in this life of mine which I live in this world. For no less than that which I spent in my mother's womb, is it hid from me in the shadows of forgetfulness. But if I was shapen in iniquity, and in sin did my mother conceive me, where, I beseech Thee, O my God, where, Lord, or when, was I Thy servant guiltless?

When St. Augustine turns to his years as a growing boy and young adolescent, when he "was no longer speechless" and could remember his past, his morbid preoccupation with his sinfulness becomes even more explicit. For example, with relentless self-condemnation and in painstaking detail he dwells upon his shame at having "joyed in the theft" of some fruit from a pear tree. This pilfering took place in his sixteenth year in the company of youthful companions. Even in retrospect he castigates himself severely and refers to the "foul soul" responsible for the "evil deed" of his youth. In commenting on this episode, Bertrand Russell (1945, p. 345) calls it a "boyish prank" to which St. Augustine had reacted with feelings of guilt of such intensity as to suggest an abnormal sense of sin. "To a modern mind," Russell points out, "this seems morbid; but in his own age it seemed right and a mark of holiness." Russell has reference to the age as one of dissension within the Church and its difficulties with heretics as well as "the stress of persecution." As already mentioned, it was an age of violence, threat, turmoil, and insecurity.

The individual growing up under such circumstances is likely to reach out for a sustaining faith to give him emotional anchorage in a world on the verge of chaos. In fact, the philosopher Charles Frankel calls attention to what he sees as a parallel between the contemporary world with its "unsettled frame of mind" in the face of threatened atomic holocaust and the world of St. Augustine. Both can be described as ages of anxiety and in both one can note a desperate search for means of coping with the anxiety. Just as St. Augustine turned to God and the hope of eternal life, many moderns are turning to faiths in the "courage to be" and to the existential philosophies calculated to foster such courage. Confidence in our ability to control events by the exercise of scientific reasoning has been shaken by the realization that recognition of the value of such reasoning is culturally limited to Western society. Frankel (1956, pp. 18–19) calls attention to this overlooked aspect of cultural relativism in these words:

> We may not have believed that we were the masters of all wisdom; but we did at least think that Western society was the school at which all men could learn rational methods of inquiry. We did not think that our fundamental intellectual methods were culturally limited in their validity. But this is precisely what we are asked to believe now. Our most fundamental conceptions of sound reasoning and sound argument are under suspicion. This turning away from traditional intellectual standards represents a loss of confidence for which it is difficult to find a parallel since the time of Saint Augustine—also a time, it will be remembered, when the long-established frontiers of the Western world were crumbling.

Growing to manhood in a crumbling world was not easy for St. Augustine. According to his *Confessions,* he was anything but saintly in his youth. He describes himself as having been obsessed with sexual desires that he failed to control. He and his wanton companions, he reports, "walked the streets of Babylon, and wallowed in the mire thereof" as one who was "easy to be seduced." To complicate matters, his parents failed to agree in their attitudes toward such profligacy. His father, a pagan, was unconcerned about unchaste conduct; but his Christian mother, Monica, warned him "not to commit fornication; but especially never to defile another man's wife." Despite this maternal admonition, his dissolute behavior continued for some years during which he acquired a mistress and fathered a son. He was on the verge of marriage in his early thirties, but was diverted from this intention by his conversion to his mother's religion. He and his son were baptized at the same time. It was then, during his thirty-second year, that at long last his mother's hopes for him were realized by his decision to devote the rest of his life to the service of God by entering the priesthood.

His Religiosity and Introspective Broodings

Some ten years after his conversion, St. Augustine became Bishop of Hippo, a town in North Africa near Carthage. As a belated celibate and as a reaction against his earlier sensuality, he extolled asceticism and denounced sinfulness. In reviewing his past life he attributed his salvation to God's grace and benevolence. For him, God was the equivalent of what Plotinus had designated as The One. However, unlike Plotinus, he had to bring his thinking into line with Catholic tradition and revelation as embodied in the

Bible. Greek rationalism as reflected in Neoplatonism thus became fused with Church doctrine and the teachings of the Gospels. In terms of such a fusion, both reason and faith were to serve as guides to the good life and individual salvation; and where they were in conflict, reason was to yield to faith. Here we have the beginnings of what centuries later became the clash between the findings of science and the dogmas of the Church.

Both Plotinus and St. Augustine with their interest in man's inner life can be thought of as early introspectionists. Their pursuit of moral excellence entailed self-examination and in the process they paved the way for the eventual emergence of the nineteenth-century interest in psychology as the science of consciousness. Recognition of consciousness as an abstract concept was a rather late development in philosophy. As Klemm (1914, pp. 166–169) points out in his review of the history of the concept: "The problem of consciousness can hardly be said to have existed for the philosophy of antiquity." Neither Plato nor Aristotle gave explicit formulation to the concept.

Although Plotinus was among the first to dwell on the topic of self-consciousness, for him the concept did not denote the current popular meaning of a distressing state of embarrassment such as stage fright. This popular usage makes self-consciousness a distinctive emotional or affective experience. As employed by Plotinus, it was more of a cognitive phenomenon having to do with his concept of the *nous,* or man's intellect. Intellectual or noetic activities involve not only sensory presentations but also the ability to reflect upon these presentations. Such reflection enables one to know that one knows, to know that one suffers, and to know one's convictions and doubts.

The very act of doubting was used by St. Augustine as proof of the existence of his own being. In doing so he was anticipating the famous seventeenth-century argument of Descartes for selfhood or psychical existence. In his quest for assured knowledge Descartes decided to divest himself of all certainty by questioning everything. The introduction of an attitude of extreme skepticism, he held, would enable him to examine the soundness of all his beliefs. Even the belief in the existence of trees, mountains, people, and animals was to be questioned. He even tried to question the reality of his own existence; but in thinking about this he realized he was thinking and the fact of this realization was too unambiguously real to be questioned; hence his famous conclusion: "I think, therefore I am."

In his anticipation of this Cartesian conclusion, St. Augustine may even have been somewhat more accurate than Descartes in his introspective description. What he noted as characteristic of the effort to be systematically skeptical was the impossibility of eliminating the attitude of doubt; hence his conclusion was the equivalent of "I doubt, therefore I am."

In thus noting the process of doubting as a self-conscious event, St. Augustine was introducing a distinction that became important in later psychology; namely, the distinction between outer and inner observation.

The traditional five senses were regarded as having to do with external or outer events, while what St. Augustine called man's internal sense (*sensus interioris hominis*) referred to inner perception or awareness of one's own mental processes.

Both Plotinus and St. Augustine, it should now be evident, were concerned with man as a reflective being—with getting to know oneself by self-observation. For them, there was no question about the possibility of such reflective knowledge, nor did the privacy of the observational act involved induce them to wonder about how to share their knowledge with others. They lived far too early to have their interest in the phenomenon of self-consciousness influenced by being self-conscious about scientific method and what it currently implies in the way of so-called operational definitions and the "public" status of scientific data. However, their failure to raise and face such issues does not necessarily render what they had to say about reflective knowledge scientifically worthless in the light of current psychology. The modernity of the issue is exemplified by the fact that as recently as 1962 it was taken up by Oliver and Landfield in an article entitled "Reflexivity: An Unfaced Issue of Psychology." In discussing the question "What is admissible evidence in psychology?" they maintain that what the psychologist "can observe as going on in himself should be regarded as data." Without overlooking the difficulties involved, they nevertheless conclude (1962, p. 122):

> The immediacies of self-consciousness constitute the very thing itself that the psychologist is investigating. That is why his hypotheses must ultimately square with them. They are data in the ultimate sense of being that which theorizing activity must start with and return to. And, what is far more troublesome, they are also what the psychologist must employ in any activity he engages in, whether of observation, calculation or theorizing.

Just how a conclusion of this sort can be squared with the need for scientific data to be "objective" or "public" and amenable to "operational" formulation will be discussed in a subsequent chapter. In the present context it is more relevant and possibly more interesting to note that what Oliver and Landfield are constrained to regard as "an unfaced issue of psychology" had already been faced by St. Augustine, as indicated in the following excerpt from his writings (Fremantle, 1962, p. 25):

> . . . For whence does a mind know another mind, if it does not know itself? For the mind does not know other's minds and not know itself, as the eye of the body sees other eyes, and does not see itself; for we see bodies through the eyes of the body, and unless we are looking into a mirror, we cannot refract and reflect the rays into themselves which shine forth through those eyes and touch whatever we discern. But whatever is the nature of the power by which we discern through the eyes, certainly, whether it be rays or anything else, we cannot discern with the eyes that power itself, but we inquire into it with the mind, and if possible,

understand even this with the mind. As the mind, then, itself gathers the knowledge of corporeal things through the senses of the body, so of incorporeal through itself. Therefore it knows itself through itself, since it is incorporeal. . . .

On the Mind-Body Problem

In referring to the mind as "knowing itself through itself" and as being "incorporeal," St. Augustine was not only alluding to the phenomenon of self-consciousness but also to the troublesome mind-body dichotomy. This was especially troublesome for him in his struggle for inner peace because of the conflict between Church doctrine and Manichaean teachings regarding this dichotomy. The latter teachings stemmed from Mani or Manes, a Persian of the third century A.D., whose religious and philosophic ideas were much influenced by Zoroastrianism and gave rise to Manichaeism as a rival to Church orthodoxy. In line with Zoroaster's fundamental belief, Manichaeism sponsored a dualistic view of the universe as the battleground of two sets of forces: those of light *versus* those of darkness. The former were regarded as good and equated with spirit while the latter were viewed as evil and equated with matter. Prior to his baptism St. Augustine had affiliated himself with the Manichaeans, but once he became a Christian he was at pains to disavow their heretical doctrine. Such disavowal was not easy for him.

In his efforts to understand "the nature of the mind" he had also to consider the nature of the body. Conceived as matter, was the body created by God as indicated by Scripture or by the forces of Darkness as taught by the Manichaeans? This was a momentous question for St. Augustine, as we see in the following passage (Pusey translation, 1949, pp. 68–69):

And I turned to the nature of the mind, but the false notion which I had of spiritual things, let me not see the truth. Yet the force of the truth did of itself flash into mine eyes, and I turned away my panting soul from incorporeal substance to lineaments, and colours, and bulky magnitudes. And not being able to see these in the mind, I thought I could not see my mind. And whereas in virtue I loved peace, and in viciousness I abhorred discord; in the first I observed a unity, but in the other, a sort of division. And in that unity I conceived the rational soul, and the nature of truth and of the chief good to consist; but in this division I miserably imagined there to be some unknown substance of irrational life, and the nature of the chief evil, which should not only be a substance, but real life also, and yet not derived from Thee, O my God, of whom are all things. And yet that first I called a Monad, as it had been a soul without sex; but the latter a Duad;—anger, in deeds of violence, and in flagitiousness, lust; not knowing whereof I spake. For I had not known or learned that neither was evil a substance, nor our soul that chief and unchangeable good.

The preceding passage with its allusion to rational and irrational features in the activity of the soul is indicative of St. Augustine's Neoplatonic heritage, and is also a reminder that his psychological observations were incidental to his longing for personal salvation or else by-products of his efforts to rid himself of morbid feelings of sinfulness. Such longing and such efforts entailed persistent self-examination of a kind that resulted in what J. W. Reeves (1958, p. 49) has called "the brilliant introspections . . . that have given him permanent status in the history of psychology."

On Volitional Control

St. Augustine's self-examination was especially concerned with his struggles to gain control over sexual impulses, or what he deplored as "carnal pleasures" to which one yields when lust is "ungoverned." Failure to gain control over lust, he pointed out, results in deeds of violence and in corruption of "the reasonable soul itself." He refers to the "errors and false opinions" stemming from such distortion of reason. This may be an early recognition of rationalization as the warped product of the conflict between desire and reason. Be this as it may, resolution of such conflict by volitional control of conduct became an important issue for St. Augustine.

He even considered the possible bearing of the stars on the determination and regulation of conduct; for astrology was taken seriously then just as it was for many succeeding centuries. He himself had consulted astrologers as a young man, and in retrospect he calls them "impostors" for misleading the sinner: they blame God, as the "Ordainer of heaven and the stars," for the sin when they say to the sinner, "The cause of thy sin is inevitably determined in heaven" (Pusey translation, p. 55). One of St. Augustine's reasons for repudiating the claims of astrologers is particularly impressive both as a demonstration of his competence as a thinker and as a cogent means of nullifying the arguments of those gullible enough to be serious about horoscopes. If one's future is determined by the position of heavenly bodies at the time of birth, then, St. Augustine noted, twins ought to have identical horoscopes; since they "for the most part come out of the womb so near one to the other, that the small interval . . . cannot be noted by human observation, or be at all expressed in those figures which the astrologer is to inspect" (Pusey translation, p. 128). By way of illustration he suggests that Esau and Jacob, although born on the same day, would have failed to confirm an astrologer's predictions.

Responsibility for sin and failure is thus not attributable to the stars but to the individual as a volitional being. This refers to man's ability to make choices and in the present context to the question of his ability to choose the good in preference to the evil when confronted with moral temptation. For St. Augustine, this question had to be considered in terms of the doctrine of original sin.

As a supporter of the doctrine, he became embroiled in the Pelagian controversy. This famous controversy was precipitated by a British monk, Pelagius, who in opposing the doctrine of original sin argued in favor of volitional freedom. Eventually the Church condemned Pelagianism as heresy.

Although the theological implications of such condemnations are not of direct psychological significance, there is some indirect significance to be noted in the fact that the Pelagian controversy involved consideration of the determinants of conduct. Pelagius seemed to argue that man possesses an independent power of will by means of which he can carve out his own moral destiny. St. Augustine, on the other hand, seems to have been more aware of the complexities of the problem. It was as if he realized that prior to his conversion he was not free to choose what he later came to regard as the path of virtue. Moreover, the act of conversion itself was not an act of will but what he attributed to "God's grace" in bringing about an inner transformation of his whole being as a necessary prelude to the shift from an evil or indifferent will to a benevolent one. The transformation in question involves a change in disposition following a profound emotional experience like falling in love. Such an emotional experience cannot be initiated by volitional fiat any more than a resolve to like cigars and to dislike ice cream can result in immediate and direct control of the affective inclinations involved.

The saintly person cannot will to become a drug addict or a vicious thug any more than the confirmed criminal can shift to the saintly role by the magic of will viewed as an independent psychic entity. To view volition as such an entity is to be guilty of the fallacy of reification. St Augustine's opposition to the free-will doctrine of Pelagius, although not based upon recognition of this fallacy, nevertheless did suggest recognition of the volitional process as being more the outcome of one's character viewed as an organized pattern of behavioral inclinations rather than an independent process governing such inclinations with autonomous sovereignty. This interpretation of the volitional process has been well expressed in this sentence by Brett (1912, p. 21): "Augustine seems to have realized that the will is really a function of the whole nature of man, and therefore dependent ultimately on that nature; the will expresses what we are, and we cannot will to be what we are not; conversion is not an act of will but a change of nature preceding any possible change of will."

In connection with his discussion of the Pelagian controversy, Brett also called attention to a "persistent fallacy" which, he maintained, continues to characterize "the average mind of the twentieth century." The fallacy results from the consequences of abstracting volitional functions from the total context of mental functions and endowing them with independent status conceived as an isolated entity or faculty of volition. Such reification of volition is analogous to the reification of intelligence. However, with respect to intelligence, from the days of antiquity it has been customary to recognize the existence of individual differences in intellectual endowment, so that there is no expectation of having all babies born equal in intellectual potential: some are "predestined" to grow up as stupid adults just as others are "predestined" to become bright adults. Strangely enough, there has not been similar recognition of individual differences in volitional endowment. This failure is reflected in the common assumption that everybody ought to have "good intentions" or a "good will" since, by implication, all men are born equal in volitional endowment. It is this notion which Brett stigmatized as a "persistent fallacy" resulting from the reification of will. In his own words (1912, p. 20): "To abstract the will from all other aspects of consciousness and assert that one can at least have good intentions, seems to be an inherent vice of human nature."

In other words, it is a fallacy to hold with the doctrine of Pelagian volitional freedom that the man of virtue is free to behave viciously and that the vicious man is free to behave virtuously, as if volitional aspects of behavior can function in complete independence of all the temperamental and experiential factors which influence character development. In terms of a non-theological interpretation of the doctrine of predestination, it might be said that the latter factors "predestine" one to volitional restrictions when confronted with moral conflicts. The man whose life history has resulted in resolute endorsement of and devotion to the principle of honest dealings finds it impossible to will to embezzle funds, to bear false witness, to cheat his customers, or, in short, to be untrue to himself.

All this can be summed up by saying that man's behavior is predestined or determined by his character. It is not will that determines character, but character that determines will. If this interpretation is sound, then a defect of will is really a character defect. This seems to be in accord with Russell's view of the meaning of St. Augustine's discussion of the will. In the words of Russell (1945, p. 359): "The vicious will has no *efficient* cause, but only a *deficient* one; it is not an e*ffect,* but a *defect.*" Of course, as a theologian, St. Augustine attributed the defect to the consequences of Adam's fall and the removal of the defect to God's grace, but this, along with his other distinctively theological views, has had little to do with his place in history as a psychologist. It is enough to be reminded of their existence by way of avoiding giving a distorted account of the extent of his psychological sophistication.

On the Nature of Memory

As just implied, St. Augustine's excursions into matters of psychological import were prompted by his preoccupation with theological affairs. A revealing example is to be found in Book X of *The Confessions* in a long discussion on the nature of memory, introduced by way of finding an answer to this question "What then do I love, when I love my God?" This discussion of memory merits special attention because it demonstrates St. Augustine's exceptional skill as an introspective observer. In fact, many centuries were to elapse before psychologists of the modern period began to note and elaborate upon some of the phenomena to which St. Augustine alluded in his fairly extensive treatment of memory (Pusey translation, pp. 203–221). His treatment, of course, lacks the technical descriptive vocabulary employed by twentieth-century students of the memory process, but it does reveal familiarity with many of the characteristics of that process as currently designated by technical terms. For example, *focalized recall* or *controlled association* is to be noted in his reference (Pusey translation, pp. 203–204) to what happens when he enters the "spacious palaces" of his memory:

> When I enter there, I require what I will to be brought forth, and something instantly comes; others must be longer sought after, which are fetched, as it were, out of some inner receptable; others rush out in troops, and while one thing is desired and required, they start forth, as who should say, "Is it perchance I?" These I drive away with the hand of my heart, from the face of my remembrance; until what I wish for be unveiled, and appear in sight, out of its secret place. Other things come up readily, in unbroken order, as they are called for; those in front making way for the following; and as they make way, they are hidden from sight, ready to come when I will. All which takes place when I repeat a thing by heart.

In several passages St. Augustine emphasizes the difference between the perception of objects and memory of such perception. He is careful to distinguish the original sensory impression from its recalled *memory image*. After enumerating the kinds of sensory impressions made on eyes, ears, nostrils, and other sensory surfaces, he comments (Pusey translation, p. 204):

> All these doth that great harbour of the memory receive . . . each entering by its own gate and there laid up. Nor yet do the things themselves enter in; only the images of the things perceived are there in readiness, for thought to recall.

His account of the relation between recall and thinking is replete with keen distinctions. In just one paragraph, it may be noted, he alludes to such distinctions as those between sensory perception and ideational perception, between perception and conception, between passive and active recall or between idle reverie and effortful thought or cogitation (Pusey translation, pp. 207–208):

> Wherefore we find, that to learn these things whereof we imbibe not the images by our senses, but perceive within by themselves, without images, as they are, is nothing else, but by conception, to receive, and by marking to take heed that those things which the memory did before contain at random and unarranged, be laid up as it were in that same memory where before the lay unknown, scattered and neglected, and so readily occur to the mind familiarised to them. And how many things of this kind does my memory bear which have been already found out, and as I said, placed as it were at hand, which we are said to have learned and come to know which were I for some short space of time to cease to call to

mind, they are again so buried, and glide back, as it were, into the deeper recesses, that they must again, as if new, be thought out thence, for other abode they have none: but they must be drawn together again, that they may be known; that is to say, they must as it were be collected together from their dispersion: whence the word "cogitation" is derived. For cogo (collect) and cogito (re-collect) have the same relation to each other as ago and agito, facio factito. But the mind hath appropriated to itself this word (cogitation), so that, not what is "collected" any how, but what is "re-collected," i.e., brought together, in the mind, is properly said to be cogitated, or thought upon.

In the course of his own "cogitations" upon what he called the "treasury of memory," St. Augustine also considered the nature of memories of emotional experiences and affective impressions. In fact, according to Klemm (1914, p. 193), "We owe the first thoroughgoing psychological description of the affective experience to Augustine." His acumen as an introspective observer is clearly manifest in the description of the difference between experienced emotion and recalled emotion (Pusey translation, p. 209): [3]

> The same memory also contains the affections of my mind, not in the same manner that my mind itself contains them, when it feels them; but far otherwise, according to a power of its own. For without rejoicing I remember myself to have joyed; and without sorrow do I recollect my past sorrow. And that I once feared, I review without fear; and without desire call to mind a past desire. Sometimes, on the contrary, with joy do I remember my fore-past sorrow, and with sorrow, joy.

Another phase of memory discussed by St. Augustine had to do with the recall of abstract knowledge originally acquired through some verbal medium such as reading or listening. In this connection he notes the importance of words as means of symbolization, as illustrated by having a word like "forgetfulness" to designate a lapse of memory which when employed in discourse does not refer to "the sound of the name, but of the thing which it signifies." Abstract knowledge, he points out, is not the direct consequence of sensory impressions; for, to cite his own formulation (Pusey translation, p. 208):

> The memory containeth also reasons and laws innumeral of numbers and dimensions, none of which hath any bodily sense impressed; seeing they have neither colour, nor sound, nor taste, nor smell, nor touch. I have heard the sound of the words whereby when discussed they are denoted: but the sounds are other than the things. For the sounds are other in Greek than in Latin; but the things are neither Greek, nor Latin, nor any other language.

---

[3] As mentioned on a previous page, this distinction had already been noted by Plotinus.

In view of the fact that these observations of the psychology of memory were made more than a millennium and half ago and centuries before mnemonic functions were subjected to laboratory control and measurement, one might be inclined to regard them as devoid of contemporary significance. At best, it might be said, along with their antiquarian interest they might serve as convenient illustrations of the nature of armchair psychology as discussed in Chapter 1. One might regard them as being good first approximations to the general phenomenology of memory. On the other hand, it would be easy from the vantage point of twentieth-century psychology to dismiss them as "unscientific." After all, much of the descriptive language is metaphoric, as exemplified by references to the "spacious palaces" and the "inner receptacle" of memory. No mention is made of curves of forgetting, of the memory span, of nonsense syllables, of memory drums, and of the pathology and physiology of memory. The whole quantitative approach to the subject of memory is conspicuous by its absence.

It is thus a far cry from what St. Augustine had to say about the phenomena of memory at the beginning of the medieval period and what constitutes the modern treatment of the subject. Nevertheless, as descriptions of such phenomena his observations in the main belong to the realm of psychological fact. They are not to be dismissed as idle philosophic speculation or as vagaries of benighted medievalism. Instead they are to be regarded as factual data to be incorporated in any adequate theory of memory.

It is also well to realize that as yet there is no altogether adequate theory to account for these data along with the many additional ones that modern psychology has gleaned from laboratory studies and clinical reports. The problem of cortical localization of memory functions, for example, continues to be refractory to clarifying theoretic formulation. Despite extensive brain damage, as the neurophysiologist R. W. Gerard (1953) has pointed out, there may be no proportionate impairment of memory. Such damage may interfere with the acquisition of new information, with reasoning and sound judgment, "but the recollection of past experience is likely to remain reasonably intact." Although Gerard believes that "memories depend on static changes left behind by the passage of nerve impulses" in the form of "memory traces" or engrams, he has difficulty in showing how such static changes can account for the dynamics of recall or, we might add, for the facts of memory as noted by St. Augustine. In his opinion, "The physiological explanation of these is certainly not yet at hand." This is not an isolated opinion, for in a still more recent article entitled "Engrams, Memory Storage, and Mnemonic Coding" the psychologist David Wechsler (1963) is constrained to introduce his discussion with this sentence: "Although the subject of memory has been investigated more than most topics in psychology, many of its basic problems remain discouragingly unsolved." Under the circumstances, the fifth-century pioneering observations of St. Augustine may now be viewed as having set the stage for the eventual emergence of twentieth-century formulation of problems being tackled by contemporary investigators interested in the psychophysiology of memory.

On the Psychology of Time

St. Augustine has also won a place in the history of psychology by another set of pioneering observations. Like his concern with the nature of memory, these observations were also prompted by a theological issue. Without going into the complexities of the issue, it will suffice to note just one question arising from its consideration. This question has to do with the meaning of a statement like "God is eternal," which suggests that God is timeless and that for Him time has neither beginning nor end. Moreover, if God be conceived as the creator of the universe, did He also create time? If He had to create time, does it make sense to say that He existed *before* this creation? Confronted with such problems of metaphysics and theology, St. Augustine found himself dealing with the consciousness of time or man's concept of duration. He was thus asking himself (Pusey translation, p. 253):

> For what is time? Who can readily and briefly explain this? But what in discourse do we mention more familiarly and knowingly, than time? And, we understand, when we speak of it; we understand also, when we hear it spoken of by another. What then is time? If no one asks me, I know: if I wish to explain it to one that asketh, I know not: yet I say boldly that I know, that if nothing passed away, time past were not; and if nothing were coming, a time to come were not; and if nothing were, time present were not. These two times then, past and to come, how are they, seeing the past now is not, and that to come is not yet?

In the course of answering the latter question, St. Augustine called attention to numerous aspects of the problem. These included the relativity of time, the transient nature of the present, and the fusion of spatial with temporal concepts as exemplified by references to time as being long or as being short. Moreover, since what we call the *present* constitutes a ceaseless flow into what we call the *past,* how does it come about, he wondered, that we talk about a "present day" or a "present month" since "present time" as experienced "passeth away in a moment?" Ideas of past and future, he noted, are nevertheless anchored in the evanescent present; for, strictly speaking, neither past nor future exists (Pusey translation, p. 258):

> What now is clear and plain is, that neither things to come nor past are. Nor is it properly said, "there be three times, past, present, and to come": yet perchance it might be properly said, "there be three times; a present of things past, a present of things present, and a present of things future." For these three do exist in some sort, in the soul, but otherwise do I not see them; present of things past, memory; present of things present, sight; present of things future, expectation.

The foregoing passage constitutes a clear formulation of what is sometimes called the subjective theory of time. By implication the passage states that consciousness of duration is restricted to creatures capable of remembering things and of expecting things. This renders time more of a psychological than a physical phenomenon, at least in the sense of making past and future dependent on man's awareness of the present. According to this subjective theory, the existence of time, like hope or perplexity or pain or any other affair of consciousness, depends on the existence of conscious beings. What time is in the abstract when divorced from such sentient beings remained a mystery for St. Augustine. In fact, toward the end of his discussion of the topic he concluded (Pusey translation, pp. 262–263):

> And I confess to Thee, O Lord, that I yet know not what time is, and again I confess to Thee, O Lord, that I know that I speak this in time, and that having long spoken of time that very "long" is not long, but by the pause of time. How then know I this, seeing I know not what time is? or is it perhaps I know not how to express what I know? Woe is me, that do not even know, what I know not.

Modern laboratory psychology has subjected many of the problems of time perception noted by St. Augustine to critical study and quantitative control. Elaboration of these problems has brought out aspects of time perception unknown to St. Augustine. Although an impressive body of relevant laboratory studies has accumulated, one might still say with St. Augustine that contemporary psychologists are not in agreement concerning the intrinsic nature of temporal experience. Some regard time as an attribute of sensation which they call *protensity*. Others emphasize the relevance of factors other than protensity in the determination of time perception. In a review of the experimental reports, H. Woodrow (1951, p. 1224) refers to "the illusive field of time perception" as well as to two of its salient trends. One of these trends has to do with lack of agreement in the findings of different investigators and the other trend has to do with "the mentalistic nature of the data." An adjective like "mentalistic" renders the findings in question consonant with St. Augustine's subjective theory of time. Moreover, despite its formulation in the early medieval period, the theory continues to elicit the respect of contemporary scholars.[4] Russell, for example, even though he rejects the theory, pays tribute to St. Augustine in these words (1945, p. 354):

> I do not agree with this theory, in so far as it makes time something mental. But it is clearly a very able theory, deserving to be seriously considered. I should go further, and say it is a great advance on anything to be found on the subject in

---

[4] For a recent account of contemporary views of subjective time see Chapter 5 of the volume by J. Cohen (1962). The chapter, entitled "Psychological Time," supplies close to forty references.

Greek philosophy. It contains a better and clearer statement than Kant's of the subjective theory of time—a theory which, since Kant, has been widely accepted among philosophers.

St. Augustine's subjectivism, Russell points out, not only gave rise to this anticipation of Kant's theory of time but also to what was previously referred to as an anticipation of a famous Cartesian argument. Like Descartes, it will be recalled, St. Augustine found it impossible to question the reality of the process of thinking or doubting in man's quest for assurance regarding his own existence as a personal being. Because of these anticipations of Kantian and Cartesian ideas, Russell concludes that "as a philosopher . . . Augustine deserves a high place." His high place as a psychologist likewise might well be conceded. A summary statement of his contributions to psychology will serve to justify such an estimate.

A Retrospective Digest

A summary review of these contributions can be listed as follows:

1. A discussion of the psychology of infancy, which, because of the adultomorphic fallacy, resulted in attributing greed and selfishness to infants. In terms of a modern outlook this constitutes a failure to note the difference between immoral and amoral behavior. Nevertheless, by calling attention to the broad question of the nature of infant behavior, the discussion might be construed as implicit recognition of what eventually emerged as a key question for genetic psychology.

2. The distinction between inner sense and outer sense foreshadowed the current distinction between introspection and inspection or between self-observation and perception of external surroundings.

3. Augustine's account of self-reflection may be viewed as a potential contribution to social psychology, for he regarded the resulting self-knowledge as the basis for one "mind to know another mind."

4. His repudiation of astrological teachings in view of the divergent life histories of twins.

5. In connection with his opposition to Pelagius it was pointed out that instead of regarding volition as an independent mental faculty he viewed it as a function of the whole nature of man. For him, it was not will that determines character but character that determines will.

6. His consideration of memory revealed definite recognition of the role of a goal idea as a selective influence in the arousal of relevant thoughts. This suggested anticipation of what is now known as focalized recall, and by implication the distinction between free and controlled association.

7. Another important contribution had to do with his observation regarding the nature of affective memories: a recalled emotional experience is different from the original experience. One can remember having been anxious about a child's illness years ago without reactivation of the anxiety.

8. Among other observations of significant import for later psychology were his allusions to the difference between sensory and ideational perception, the distinction between concepts and percepts, and the relation between language symbols and their referents.

9. A formulation of some of the basic issues to be included in a study of the psychology of time perception. Among them there is the problem of determining how we estimate the *length* of time. Here there was early anticipation of the concept of a space-time continuum. In connection with this, St. Augustine introduced a series of acute observations regarding *rhythm* as a subjective experience influencing estimates of time in music and poetry (Pusey translation, pp. 264–266).

In designating a list of observations like the foregoing as contributions to psychology, one ought to guard against a possible misinterpretation of the designation in question. At the time the observations were made, psychology as such had not come into being; hence calling them psychological contributions is a product of the historian's retrospective evaluation. It is hardly likely that St. Augustine was cognizant of their potential significance for future students of human nature. They were really incidental observations made as he wrestled with his personal problems of guilt and the conquest of sin. In this sense they were by-products of his quest for salvation as he reviewed his life experiences. This direct concern with personal experience was already prominent in the work of Plotinus. In fact, as Brett (1912, p. 49) pointed out, "The Neoplatonic line of thought is significant because it represents the idea of experience." Both Plotinus and St. Augustine have a place in the history of psychology by virtue of what their reflections upon the inner life of experience brought to light.

Philosophy Versus Theology

What St. Augustine and other medieval scholars had to say about mental life, as already suggested, was not the product of a disinterested quest for understanding in the sense in which such a quest had colored the science of classical Greece. Instead the quest had to do with means of furthering religious and moral objectives as determined by Church authority. Scriptural teachings were regarded as the foundation of such authority. Revelation thus supplied medieval man with what he accepted as a true account of the world's creation and the role God expected him to play. For the common man, of course, this meant revelation or Scripture as interpreted by the Church. Church law was the equivalent of divine law. There were two sources of knowledge: revelation and reason, or what later came to be distinguished in terms of the subject matter of theology as contrasted with that of philosophy. In St. Augustine's time, as indicated by F. C. Copleston (1961, p. 15), such a separation of subject matter had not yet emerged and did not do so until the thirteenth century. In the preceding centuries both faith and reason had been regarded as dependable sources of knowledge.

Even after the emergence of theology as a separate discipline distinct from philosophy, both fields continued to be viewed as dependable sources of knowledge. Medieval scholars referred to both as "sciences" in terms of the root meaning of "science" as pertaining to established knowledge in the sense of the Latin word "*scientia*," from "*scire*," to know. In the very early years of the Church there was recognition of a distinction between secular knowledge as embodied in the teachings of pagan philosophers and sacred knowledge as supplied by revelation. Some of the early Church fathers discouraged study of philosophy as being in conflict with a Christian way of life. It was the kind of fear of secular knowledge that even today prompts some religionists to be uneasy about the impact of Darwinian teachings on the religious faith of students exposed to such teachings. By the time of St. Augustine this distrust of philosophy and the use of reason had lessened. In this connection, Crombie (1959, p. 15) has supplied a clarifying interpretation:

St. Augustine himself in his searching and comprehensive philosophical inquiries had invited men to examine the rational basis of their faith. But . . . knowledge continued to be considered of very secondary importance during the early Middle Ages. The primary interest in natural facts was to find illustrations for the truths of morality and religion. The study of nature was not expected to lead to hypotheses and generalisations of science but to provide vivid symbols of moral realities. The moon was the image of the Church reflecting the divine light, the wind an image of the spirit, the sapphire bore a resemblance to divine contemplation, and the number eleven, which "transgressed" ten, representing the commandments, stood itself for sin.

Concern with the nature of numbers was by no means restricted to the latter kind of fanciful regard for the meaning of an individual number like the number eleven. In one of his books St. Augustine concerned himself with the nature of numerical relations by way of showing that, as he expressed it, "the truth of number is present to all who reason." This is clearly exemplified in the following excerpt from a portion of the book as cited in McKeon's edition (1957, pp. 35–36):

. . . if I have perceived numbers by the sense of the body, I have not thereby been able by the sense of the body to perceive also the nature of the separation and combination of numbers. For by this light of the mind I refute him who would report a false sum when he computes whether in adding or subtracting. And I do not know how long anything I touch by a bodily sense will persist, . . . but seven and three are ten, and not only now, but always; nor have seven and three in any way at any time not been ten, nor will seven and three at any time not be ten. I have said, therefore that this incorruptible truth of number is common to me and anyone at all who reasons.

Recognition of numerical relations as absolute or "incorruptible" truths was due to the Neoplatonic notion of eternal ideas. This, in turn, was a reflection of Plato's concept of universal forms presumed to exist independently of any physical object.

Realism Versus Nominalism

As suggested by the rationalistic implications of the Platonic tradition, the process of knowing resulting from stimulations of a sense organ by a physical object was held to arouse the relevant universal form in line with the essential constitution of the human mind. A given person is judged as friendly or beautiful in terms of some ideal of friendliness or beauty. Ideals like these would exemplify Platonic universals. So would concepts like circularity, motherhood, truth, loyalty, humanity, and other abstract terms. During the medieval period a controversy developed regarding the origin and nature of such ideals and general concepts. Those who thought of them in Platonic fashion as universals having an existence in some abstract realm came to be called *realists* in the language of scholastic philosophy. According to this language, *universalia sunt realia* and exist *ante rem*, prior to the concrete individual event. A contemporary analogue to this mode of conceptualization is to be found in references by Jungian psychologists to generic archetypes of the collective unconscious.

By the twelfth century the views of medieval realists began to be questioned by those who denied the prior and independent existence of general ideas or abstract concepts. They attributed such ideas or concepts to perceived likenesses and differences among the events of everyday experience. For example, they held that our concept of triangularity is a consequence of hearing the name "triangle" applied to a multiplicity of three-sided figures which, taken individually, may differ from one another in size, color, and shape, since some are scalene, others equilateral, and still others isosceles. Despite such differences, they all have the common characteristic of being three-sided. It is this common characteristic which comes to be abstracted from the multiplicity of experienced triangular shapes. The word "triangle" is the *name* given to this abstraction. In other words, what the realists regarded as universals came to be viewed as products of learning for which language provided appropriate names; hence the opponents of the realists were known as *nominalists*.

This realist-nominalist controversy became particularly acute as a result of the writings of William of Occam (c. 1285–1349), a British scholastic who belonged to the Franciscan order. As a nominalist, he contended that existence is restricted to that which is directly perceived in experience with individual objects like chairs, houses, flowers, knives, and so on. As a consequence of such experience, we come to learn the meaning of abstract nouns like "furniture," "shelter," "botany," and "cutlery." Moreover, nominalists also held that what St. Augustine had called the "incorruptible truths of number" come into being as a result of experience with concrete arithmetical relations. They are not given innately or prior to the relevant learning experiences. William of Occam's nominalism is thus a scholastic seedbed of what eventually grew into British empiricism and associationistic psychology.

Nominalism, Conceptualism, and Logic

In his advocacy of nominalism and empiricism, William of Occam did not spurn all rationalistic principles. His opposition to the views of medieval realists expressed rejection of Platonic universals as metaphysical entities but not rejection of universals as terms in logical propositions. This is brought out by Copleston (1961, pp. 118–135), in a chapter devoted to the work of Occam in which, among other suggestions, he states that instead of just referring to Occam as a nominalist it might be better to call him a conceptualist.

As a conceptualist, Occam was concerned with the anlaysis of logical propositions. In doing so, he endorsed the principles of deductive reasoning as presented in Aristotelian syllogisms, but he was careful to distinguish between the classes of terms to be found in syllogisms. The one class, known as "terms of first intention," has to do with words designating objects or persons directly, while the other class, dealing with "terms of second intention," has to do with generic or conceptual terms. A word like "ornithology" belongs to the latter class, but a word like "sparrow" belongs to the former. Similarly, a word like "botany" is a second-intention term as contrasted with a word like "carnation" or "lily." The latter, as first-intention terms, refer to real entities, while the former has reference to a conceptual formulation rather than to an existing physical entity. Incidentally, as was mentioned in Chapter 4, this scholastic emphasis on intentionalism came to influence nineteenth-century psychology as a result of the importance attached to the concept by Brentano.

The preceding distinctions have to do with the nature of terms employed by logicians. Occam did not regard logic as a "real science" but as a "rational science." In terms of this distinction, a real science is one that comes to grips with things, in the sense that its propositions are rooted in terms of first intention. A rational science, on the other hand, concerned with relations among terms, deals with categories, classes, hypothetical contingencies, logical abstractions, and kindred second-intention affairs.

Both logic and mathematics are more rational than real in terms of the distinction made by Occam. The symbols and words employed in the construction of syllogisms and mathematical equations may deal with the purely imaginary and be altogether divorced from any directly specifiable physical objects or events. In propositions like "All x is y or $2x=4y$," it is fatuous to insist upon concrete, individual, physical referents for *x* and *y*. To seek such referents is akin to undertaking a search for royal flesh-and-blood referents for the king of diamonds and king of clubs. Because of the absence of such tangible referents for the symbols of pure mathematics, Bertrand Russell once formulated a quasi-humorous definition of mathematics as "the subject in which we never know what we are talking about, nor whether what we are saying is true."

As a nominalist, it should now be evident, Occam called attention to the part played by language in symbolizing the kind of abstractions viewed as Platonic universals by medieval realists. For him, words like "beauty" and "circularity" served as symbols for or names of *concepts* derived from the *perception* of aesthetically pleasing objects as well as objects characterized by a circular form. Thus he was setting the stage for a shift from the purely metaphysical consideration of universals to what was to develop into a more distinctively psychological consideration of their status as conceptual abstractions. Instead of being regarded as *a priori* endowments they were viewed as products of experience involving perception, language, and the process of concept-formation. In brief, by implication Occam brought the problem of universals into an empirically oriented psychology of learning and thinking; hence his place in the history of psychology.

Occam's Razor and Lloyd Morgan's Canon

One other respect in which Occam might be said to have had at least an indirect influence on the history of psychology has to do with a principle or canon of scientific theorizing conventionally known as *Occam's razor*. According to this principle, a good scientific theory or explanation avoids the introduction of unnecessary assumptions. The metaphoric reference to a razor is a reminder of the recommendation to amputate superfluous theoretic appendages. In terms of a rather free translation of the canon attributed to Occam, explanatory entities or factors are not to be increased beyond necessity.[5] Actually, the idea in question was not original with Occam. As De Wulf (1922, p. 110) has pointed out, the principle was already familiar to some of Occam's scholastic predecessors. Nevertheless, tradition has linked it with his name as if he were the originator.

The principle of parsimony is, of course, a synonym for Occam's canon; for it too is intended to guard against extravagance in the formulation of scientific explanations. Allegiance to this principle is supposed to facilitate choice among rival explanations by giving preference to the one involving the smallest number of assumptions needed in order to account for the

---

[5] *Essentia non sunt multiplicanda praeter necessitatem* constitutes the conventional Latin version of Occam's canon. Another version regarded as the one employed by Occam is to the effect that "it is vain to do with more what can be done with fewer."

problem under consideration. All other factors being equal, a simple hypothesis is thus viewed as scientifically more acceptable than a complex one.

Apart from its bearing on the logic of scientific thinking in general, Occam's canon came to have a specific influence on psychology as a result of its application to the work of pioneer animal psychologists. This took place in the 1890s, at a time when C. Lloyd Morgan, a British psychologist, proposed the establishment of a science of *comparative psychology,* by means of which the *behavior* of different animal phyla was to be subjected to controlled investigation. Comparative psychology was to do for animal behavior what comparative anatomy had done for the bodily structure of different animal phyla. Prior to that time there was a dearth of controlled laboratory or field studies. Instead there had been reports of casual observations of chance activities of animals as noted by owners of pets, zoo attendants, hunters, veterinarians, and others having contact with animals. Many of these reports attributed distinctively human characteristics to the animals often suggestive of ability to think and reason. Such reports or anecdotes were welcomed by proponents of the doctrine of evolution as a means of rebutting those of its opponents who regarded thinking and reasoning as exclusively human endowments. Darwin himself had accepted them as dependable sources of scientific evidence.

Morgan was among the first to question the validity of this kind of evidence. He urged that animal behavior be studied as an independent science and not just as a means of undergirding Darwinian teachings. Planned observation was to replace casual observation and experimental evidence was to replace anecdotal evidence. In particular, he warned against the tendency to explain animal behavior in terms of human characteristics when infrahuman ones would suffice. This warning constituted an application of the principle of parsimony to the study of animal behavior. It was a derivative of Occam's canon, and psychologists commonly refer to it as Lloyd Morgan's canon. As worded by Morgan (1894, p. 53), the canon placed this stricture on the interpretation of animal behavior:

> In no case may we interpret an action as the outcome of the exercise of a higher psychical faculty, if it can be interpreted as the outcome of the exercise of one which stands lower in the psychological scale.

As the field of animal psychology developed, this admonition of Morgan's served its intended function of guarding against unwarranted anthropomorphic interpretations. Actually, in terms of its wording, his canon makes no explicit mention of such interpretations. This is to be inferred not only from the context in which it occurs but also from the use of the words "higher" and "lower" with respect to the "psychological scale." The reference to a scale is not to be taken literally in the sense of an arrangement of psychological functions in quantitatively determined steps from low to high.

Instead it referred to commonly accepted judgments of the place of particular mental processes relative to one another when rated in terms of some hierarchical scheme. Thus, olfactory discrimination of two odors would be rated as lower in the psychological scale than auditory discrimination of two melodies. Recognizing a grammatical error would be rated as higher than recognizing a coat as wearing apparel. Ability to reason is given a higher rating than rote memory just as skilled action is rated higher than reflex action.

The fact that psychologists talk about "higher thought processes" is another indication of the sense in which Morgan referred to a psychological scale. For him, such thought processes were not to be invoked as explanations of animal behavior if "lower" processes would serve as well. The continuing relevance for animal psychologists of Morgan's warning about attributing such higher cognitive functions to animals is implied by what H. Harlow (1959, p. 478) has to conclude in connection with his experimental investigations of learning in the rhesus monkey:

> The monkey possesses learning capacities far in excess of those of any other infrahuman primate, abilities comparable to those of low-level human imbeciles. The monkey's learning capabilities can give us little or no information concerning human language, and only incomplete information relating to thinking.

A conclusion like the foregoing means that the scope of animal psychology can never be extended far enough to include the totality of human psychology. The limitation is not just one of degree, just as the difference between "low-level human imbeciles" and high-level Newtons and Shakespeares is not just a difference in amount of intelligence as measured by some psychometric instrument. Intensive study of imbeciles would not enable one to account for the creative work of genius by some far-ranging extrapolation of the results of such study.

Recognition of levels of functioning is, of course, very old in the history of psychology. As related in earlier chapters, it was already manifest in the psychology of Plato and in the writings of Aristotle. Plato, it will be recalled, provided for a rational soul along with a higher and lower irrational soul. A broad division of Aristotle's referred to nutritive, sensitive, and rational souls in terms of which the nutritive was attributed to plants, the nutritive and sensitive to animals, and all three to human beings.

Aristotle did not influence medieval thinking until the rise of scholasticism. By the time of Occam and the nominalist-realist controversy, the schoolmen were already engaged in Aristotelian studies and the Church was shifting from exclusive dependence on St. Augustine's Neoplatonism to what eventually became endorsement of the Aristotelianism of St. Thomas Aquinas. All this belongs to the closing centuries of the medieval period and merits a separate chapter.

References

Armstrong, A. H. *Plotinus.* New York: Collier Books, 1962.

Augustine, A. *The Confessions of Saint Augustine.* (Translated by E. P. Pusey.) New York: The Modern Library, 1949.

Bakan, D. *Sigmund Freud and the Jewish Mystical Tradition.* New York: D. Van Nostrand Company, 1958.

Boring, E. G. *A History of Experimental Psychology.* New York: Appleton-Century-Crofts, 1950.

Brett, G. S. *A History of Psychology,* Vol. I. London: George Allen and Unwin, 1912.

Brett, G. S. *A History of Psychology,* Vol. II. London: George Allen and Unwin, 1912.

Cohen, J. *Humanistic Psychology.* New York: Collier Books, 1962.

Copleston, F. C. *Medieval Philosophy.* New York: Harper and Brothers (Torch Books ed.), 1961.

Crombie, A. C. *Medieval and Early Modern Science,* Vol. 1. Garden City, New York: Doubleday and Company, 1959.

De Wulf, M. *Philosophy and Science in the Middle Ages.* Princeton, New Jersey: Princeton University Press, 1922.

Frankel, C. *The Case for Modern Man.* New York: Harper and Brothers, 1956.

Fremantle, A. "The Age of Belief," in *The Great Ages of Western Philosophy,* Vol. I. Boston: Houghton Mifflin Company, 1962.

Gerard, R. W. "What Is Memory?" *Scientific American,* 1953, *198,* 118–125.

Harlow, H. "The Development of Learning in the Rhesus Monkey," *American Scientist,* 1959, *47,* 459–479.

James, W. *Human Immortality: Two Supposed Objections to the Doctrine.* Boston: Houghton Mifflin Company, 1898.

James, W. *The Varieties of Religious Experience.* New York: Longmans, Green and Company, 1902.

Jones, E. *The Life and Work of Sigmund Freud,* Vol. III. New York: Basic Books, 1957. (See Chapter 13, "Religion," and Chapter 14, "Occultism.")

Jung, C. G. *Modern Man in Search of a Soul.* New York: Harcourt, Brace and Company, 1933.

Jung, C. G. *Psychology and Religion.* New Haven: Yale University Press, 1938.

Klemm, O. *A History of Psychology.* New York: Charles Scribner's Sons, 1914.

MacKenna, S., *Plotinus: The Enneads.* (Translated by S. MacKenna.) 2nd. ed. (Revised by B. S. Page.) New York: Pantheon Books, 1957. Reprinted by permission of Random House, Inc., and Faber and Faber Ltd.

McKeon, R. (ed.). *Selections from Medieval Philosophers,* Vol. I. New York: Charles Scribner's Sons, 1957.

Morgan, C. L. *An Introduction to Comparative Psychology.* London: Scott, 1894.

Oliver, W. D., and Landfield, A. W. "Reflexivity: An Unfaced Issue of Psychology," *Journal of Individual Psychology,* 1962, *18,* 114–124.

Perry, R. B. *The Thought and Character of William James.* New York: George Braziller, 1954.

Reeves, J. W. *Body and Mind in Western Thought.* Harmondsworth, Middlesex: Penguin Books, 1958.

Russell, B. *A History of Western Philosophy*. New York: Simon and Schuster, 1945.

Wechsler, D. "Engrams, Memory Storage, and Mnemonic Coding," *American Psychologist,* 1963, *18,* 149–153.

Woodrow, H. "Time Perception," in *Handbook of Experimental Psychology*. S. S. Stevens (ed.). New York: John Wiley and Sons, 1951.

7

The Later Medieval Background

HISTORIANS NOTE MARKED DIFFERENCES in comparing the so-called Dark Ages with the later centuries of the medieval period. In general, the earlier period dating from the fall of the Roman Empire to about the eleventh or twelfth century lacked exposure to new ideas and the intellectual ferment engendered by such exposure. Aside from the Neoplatonism of Plotinus, very little was known of the Greek philosophic heritage. Even by the beginning of the eleventh century, scholars of medieval Europe were largely ignorant of the works of Plato and Aristotle. They were limited to Plato's *Timaeus* and two of Aristotle's treatises on logic. None of the other writings of these Greek philosophers were available to them. That is why, as was mentioned in the previous chapter, for some eight hundred years the predominant philosophic orientation stemmed from St. Augustine's Neoplatonism.

A narrowed intellecutal horizon was the consequence of being deprived of access to the major works of Greek philosophers. Furthermore, as will be recalled, knowledge of Hellenistic science as it had developed in Alexandria was not transmitted to the European world during the centuries of the Dark Ages. There was ignorance of the achievements of men like Eratosthenes, Herophilus, and Erasistratus. Institutions of learning in the form of universities had not yet come into existence. However, with the rise of scholasticism and the concomitant establishment of monastic schools and universities, some of the "darkness" of the Dark Ages began to be lifted. These changes took place in the closing centuries of the medieval period and paved the way for the emergence of the Renaissance and the beginnings of modern science. It is thus an important transitional period calling for separate consideration.

Influence of Arabian Scholarship

To understand why the Dark Ages gave way to the changes just mentioned, it is necessary to review some facts of medieval history. One of these facts

160

has to do with the rise of Islamic civilization. In many ways the Arabs had a better grasp of philosophy, mathematics, and science than their European contemporaries of the earlier medieval period. As a consequence of their trading contacts with the Hindus, for example, they became familiar with Hindu arithmetic, which eventually developed into what are ordinarily designated as Arabic numerals.

They also became familiar with the writings of Aristotle and translated them into Arabic, with the result that their philosophers were conversant with Greek philosophic and scientific ideas long before Christian scholars had been exposed to them. In fact, the West obtained its introduction to these ideas from Latin translations of the Arabic texts rather from direct translation into Latin of the original Greek. Moreover, these Latin versions did not appear until the thirteenth century as a result of the work of schoolmen who had acquired a knowledge of Arabic.

Toledo in Spain was an important center for this work of translation by the schoolmen. They were able to meet there by the thirteenth century because by that time Toledo was no longer under Muslim sovereignty. It had been wrested from the Arabs in 1085 and became the seat of an archbishopric in the Kingdom of Castile. However, for more than three hundred years prior to 1085, as part of the Iberian Peninsula, it had been dominated by the effects of the Moorish conquest of the peninsula. These effects included the emergence and spread of Islamic interpretations of Aristotle's philosophy along with indigenous developments in arithmetic and algebra. After Muslim sovereignty was replaced by that of Western Christendom, these interpretations and developments aroused the interest of some of the schoolmen. In this way Arabian scholarship came to influence the thinking of the West.

Another way in which Western Europe was influenced by contact with Islamic civilization came as a result of the Crusades. These took place between the eleventh and the fourteenth centuries and undoubtedly are to be included among the factors responsible for the changes in outlook serving to differentiate the earlier from the later medieval periods. The Fourth Crusade, which resulted in the capture of Constantinople in 1204, merits particular consideration because the city had long been associated with Greek studies. Students of ancient history report that the site of the city was settled by Greek colonists as early as the seventh century B.C. and became the Greek city of Byzantium. Some ten centuries later Constantine the Great made the city his capital and changed its name to Constantinople. When the Crusaders captured it they converted it into a tiny state called the Latin Empire of Constantinople. This gave scholars among them access to Greek manuscripts which were translated into Latin. Subsequently these Latin translations were compared with those prepared in Toledo from Arabic translations of the Greek texts. As might be expected, these translations often failed to agree, and controversies arose regarding which ones were correct. The discussion of disputed passages thus precipitated had something to do with promoting scholastic interest in the study of Greek philosophy.

Medieval Education and the Rise of Scholasticism

Throughout the Middle Ages, learning and teaching took place under Church auspices. The leading teachers were monks or friars. Schools developed as part of the activity of monasteries and cathedrals, and in due course became organized into universities with the encouragement of ecclesiastical or royal authority. Probably the first university in Europe came into being at Salerno in Italy, where instruction in medicine was already taking place in the early medieval period. By the eleventh century it had gained a reputation as the leading center for medical training. Other medieval universities began to be founded at about that time and in the next two centuries. Both the University of Bologna and the University of Paris came to be known as leading institutions by the twelfth century, with the former recognized for the prestige of its professors of law and the latter for its eminence as a school of theology.

In large measure, universities came into being to meet the demand for professional training in the fields of medicine, law, and theology. Since Latin was the language of instruction, students could wander from country to country to attend lectures at different universities without being concerned about language barriers.

Such student migrations were also facilitated by the substantial uniformity in the curriculum comprising the so-called liberal arts. As organized in medieval universities, this eventually led to the introduction of academic degrees to signify different levels of academic achievement. Seven branches of learning were designated as liberal arts: grammar, logic, rhetoric, arithmetic, music, geometry, and astronomy. The first three, called the *trivium*, centering on linguistic attainments, led to the baccalaureate degree, while the last four, known as the *quadrivium*, led to the master's degree. The latter degree qualified its possessor for a license to teach, with the license being granted by a cathedral church.

Scholasticism was an outgrowth of the efforts of these medieval university teachers to reconcile revelation and Church doctrine with the demands of reason. The scope of reason was very much widened for them when the translations of hitherto unknown works by Greek and Arab philosophers were placed at their disposal. These works included Aristotle's *De Anima*, so that psychological issues along with formal logic were brought within the scope of reason. The endeavor to reconcile the requirements of faith with the philosophy of Aristotle was complicated by Islamic interpretations of Aristotle stemming from his Arabian translators and commentators. The two outstanding Aristotelians among the Islamic philosophers were Avicenna (980–1037) and Averroës (1126–1198), who were physicians as well as philosophers. Scholastic interpretation of Aristotle was also influenced by the works of another medieval physician and philosopher, Maimonides (1135–

1204), who as a rabbi was especially concerned with the problem of reconciling the religious tradition of Judaism with the rationalism of Aristotle. His more distinctively psychological views will be considered in a later section.

As was mentioned in Chapter 6, the doctrines of Aristotle met with official Church opposition when first introduced by the scholastics. In large measure this opposition was precipitated by some theological teachings linked to the Aristotelianism of Averroës. According to one of Averroës' views, the individual soul is identical with the *anima mundi,* or world soul, and thus personal immortality is called into question. Averroës also sponsored what came to be known as the "double truth" principle. In terms of this principle, reason and faith constitute two sources of truth, and what faith decrees as true may be false in the light of reason, just as what reason finds to be true might be false in the light of faith. A teaching of this sort was regarded as a dangerous threat to the dogmas of religious orthodoxy. As a result, Averroism was stigmatized as heresy and the study of Aristotle was interdicted for a time.

One of the chief concerns of St. Thomas Aquinas (1225?–1274) was to distinguish between Aristotelianism and Averroism. By the middle of the thirteenth century, he and other scholastics ventured to defend Aristotle as divorced from Islamic heresies. It was at about this time that a definite distinction was made between theology and philosophy. The distinction hinged upon the origin of knowledge or the source of "truth." Three sources were recognized: revelation, sensory experience, and reason. Revelation was held to belong to the field of theology, while the two other sources were left to the domain of philosophy.

In general, an effort was made to reduce conflict between philosophic "truths" and the dogmas of theology by striving to demonstrate the reasonableness of such dogmas. When this could not be accomplished, as was the case with Trinitarian doctrines and belief in miracles, then St. Thomas placed his trust in faith as a safer guide than reason. This Thomistic inclination to favor dogma when it clashed with reason was not characteristic of all scholastics. In fact, such contemporaries and near contemporaries as Roger Bacon (1214–1294), John Duns Scotus (1265–1308), and William of Occam (1300–1349) were often at odds with St. Thomas and more inclined to subordinate dogma to rational considerations.[1]

Contrary to a prevalent modern belief, scholastics did not settle their differences by blind appeal to the authority of Plato, Aristotle, or the Bible.

---

[1] In modern times Thomistic interpretations of Aristotelian views have won Church endorsement over rival scholastic interpretations. However, such endorsement did not take place until 1879, when Pope Leo XIII issued an encyclical stressing the value of St. Thomas as supplying the true source of Catholic philosophy. This encyclical initiated the neoscholastic orientation of present-day Catholic philosophers and psychologists. It thus brought about a revival of scholarly interest in scholastic teachings.

R. McKeon (1957, p. xv), an eminent student of scholastic philosophy, has this to say on the scholastic method of dealing with this issue:

> The method indicates the relative place of authority and reason in the solution of philosophical problems. A philosopher must be careful to have examined the solutions to problems which the wise men of the past have found before presuming a resolution of his own. But the common criticism that scholastic problems were solved by reference only to authority is without foundation: a good scholastic was one who could find authority for either side of a question and who was convinced further that truth could be discovered best by examining the interplay of such possible contradictory statements. Authority was only the reason of past thinkers solidified in brief statement, and if reason could not be found for it, the opinion could not be held. Authority, as one of the scholastics remarked, has a nose of wax: it may be turned in any direction whatsoever unless it is fortified by reason. . . . But whatever the metaphysics or theology of the writer, his appeal to authority was literally an appeal to what authors in the past said on the subject: to be free from authority was to be unaware of the history of the problem discussed. . . . The constant appeal to authority in a medieval work does not shackle the imagination and enslave the reason; rather it permits the author . . . to mount the shoulders of the ancients that he may see further than he could with his own unaided vision and at his own stature.

That appeal to authority was not sufficient to elicit acceptance of given conclusions is suggested by the vigor of scholastic disputations. The teachings of St. Thomas Aquinas, for example, even though they were buttressed by citations from "authoritative" writings, were often subjected to adverse criticism by scholastic contemporaries. As a member of the Dominican order, known as the Black Friars, he failed to overawe members of the Franciscan order, known as the Gray Friars. The Franciscans were especially prominent at the University of Oxford, while the Dominicans were more closely affiliated with the University of Paris.

Roger Bacon and the Emergence of Critical Scholarship

Rivalry between the orders was pronounced, and the stand taken on theological or philosophical questions by members of one group often became the occasion for sharp debate by adherents of the rival group. For example, as was mentioned in Chapter 2, the Franciscan Roger Bacon was especially critical of blind appeal to authority and of undue preoccupation with the subtleties of formal logic. Also, he questioned the accuracy of the translations of Greek and Arabic works being cited by Dominicans and others in support of given opinions. To ensure dependable knowledge of the Bible, he urged that it be studied in the original Hebrew and Greek. His vast if unsystematic learning ranged over such varied fields as geography, mathematics, alchemy, physics, astronomy, linguistics, magic, and astrology. Columbus is said to have been influenced by Bacon's work on geography, in which the possibility of circumnavigating the globe is suggested. Bacon was among the first to note that light travels faster than sound. He also described the anatomy of the eye and its connection with the optic nerve, and urged others to confirm his description by dissecting the eyes of animals.

Historians sometimes credit him with being the first writer to introduce the phrase "experimental science." They also call attention to his disparagement of deductive reasoning and his preference for knowledge based upon observation and measurement. In the light of such an orientation, he foresaw possible technological developments in the way of flying machines, suspension bridges, and locomotives.

He stands out as different from most of his scholastic contemporaries in his distrust of their confidence in dogmatic theology and scholastic dialectics as the dual sources of dependable teaching. As a polemicist he was not very successful in winning support for his views. Even the head of his order felt constrained to lodge charges of insubordination against him. Because of his interest in and endorsement of alchemy, astrology, and magic along with his attacks on the views of rival schoolmen, he was suspected of heresy. Twice he was punished by imprisonment, and he died an obscure man whose fame is entirely posthumous.

Whether he really succeeded in speeding recognition of the shortcomings of scholastic methodology and the advent of what was to become the methodology of science is hard to determine. He failed with his contemporaries, and the eventual endorsement of many of his criticisms of what they endorsed was not necessarily a direct consequence of his efforts. In short, it is difficult to trace a straight line of influence from his thirteenth-century proscientific ardor to the beginnings of genuine scientific accomplishment some four hundred years later. Nowadays it is easy to question the extent of his devotion to the methods of science in view of his apparent belief in the reality of magic and the pronouncements of astrologers. On the other hand, F. H. Garrison (1929, p. 165) has suggested that Bacon "approved of astrology and other modes of superstition on account of their psychotherapeutic effect." Nevertheless students of his writings do not report any explicit repudiation of the pseudosciences in question.

In many ways Bacon seems to have been more influenced by the writings of Arabic philosophers than by the writings of his scholastic contemporaries; but he did not hesitate to call attention to what he regarded as false in the teaching of any writer, whether ancient Greek and pagan, medieval and Christian, or medieval and Muslim. Thus, despite his high regard for Aristotle, Bacon did not have an uncritical acceptance of whatever might be quoted from some Aristotelian text.

Nor was he the only medievalist to exhibit such independence. For example, even so ardent a follower of Aristotle as Maimonides was not a blind follower. In his famous *The Guide for the Preplexed* (1881 ed., Vol. II, p. 86) he refers to the "absurdities" involved in Aristotle's theory of creation, and in another passage (Vol. II, p. 72) he voices his disapproval of those philosophers who believe "it wrong to differ from Aristotle, or to think that he was ignorant or mistaken in anything."

It is thus advisable to be wary of generalizations to the effect that men of the scholastic period were altogether unmindful of the demands of critical scholarship and for the most part engaged in slavish worship of authority as they indulged in logic-chopping disputes about trivial questions. Such negative generalizations ought to be qualified by recognition of the positive contributions to the development of critical scholarship growing out of medieval disputes. As has just been indicated, some of the medieval scholars stressed the need to guard against belief in the infallibility of even the most revered authority. They also had occasion to emphasize the importance of going back to original sources and to be alert to the possibility of erroneous translations of such sources.

In addition, they had to come to grips with the problem of judging among conflicting teachings, contradictory doctrines, and the claims of rival schoolmen. Tackling such a problem involves epistemological considerations in the way of determining the true from the false, the probable from the improbable, and fact from conjecture. It also involves the relation of theory to proof or of evidence to conclusion drawn from evidence. This, in turn, requires utilization of the canons of logic by participants in the give-and-take of controversy. With increasing sensitivity to the demands of logic, there is likely to come increasing sensitivity to the niceties of language and thus greater precision in the use of language. What was said in the previous chapter about the medieval concern with the question of nominalism as well as what was said about Occam's razor may serve as reminders of this scholastic interest in logic and language.

Interest in the nature of proof, the mobilization of evidence, canons of logic, and precision of language had been a concern of Greek philosophers. When their writings became known to the scholastics, this interest and concern was reflected in theological disputes and philosophic debates. But the efforts of some scholastics to justify confidence in the truth of religious dogmas in the light of Greek rationalism were strenuous but futile. The futility became evident as an increasing number of the dogmas were relegated to the domain of faith in the sense of not being amenable to rational proof.

Often in the course of these medieval disputes, a member of one order such as the Dominicans would present what appeared to be a way of bringing a particular theological tenet into harmony with an Aristotelian outlook only to have a member of a rival order such as the Franciscans call attention to the weakness of the argument. In retrospect one might say that it became more and more evident that medieval theology could not be brought into line with the philosophy of Aristotle—a philosophy that had developed long before Christianity and whose principles were thus not formulated as a means of coping with problems of scholastic theology. Application of these principles to dogmas of the Church failed to transform articles of faith into demonstrations of rationally justified conclusions. Faith in bodily resurrection or the existence of angels, for example, had to remain matters of faith, since Aristotelian modes of thought were not equal to the task of transforming them into matters of conviction-inducing proof. In brief, the scholastic effort to bring Church doctrine within the orbit of rational proof was not a success.

The failure in question was very likely one of the factors contributing to loss of confidence in the scholastic method as the new interests of the dawning Renaissance marked the decline of medieval interest in subjecting the canons of the Church to the canons of Aristotelian logic. However, to revert to an earlier point, this failure is not to be construed as a complete setback in man's quest for knowledge about himself and his place in the universe. The scholastic controversies may be viewed as learning experiences that not only clarified the distinction between reason and faith but also promoted increased understanding of the nature of critical scholarship in the pursuit of knowledge. As already indicated, this kind of scholarship prompted some philosophers of the medieval period to warn against automatic endorsement of all that some recognized authority has written. Accordingly, the common notion that scholasticism hindered intellectual progress is only partly correct and overlooks the positive implications of what has just been designated as learning experiences incident to scholastic controversies.

It is well to recall that universities came into existence during this late medieval period and that they were scholastic institutions. Mention has already been made of the first universities of continental Europe. The first British universities also came into existence during this period, with Oxford achieving university status by about 1160 and Cambridge being similarly recognized by about 1230. It is also well to recall that, despite Church control of medieval universities, instruction was not restricted to theological subjects. In addition to the liberal arts there was training in law and medicine. Furthermore, with the gradual acquisition of Greek, Arabic, and Hebrew writings there was a broadening of intellectual horizons and, as previously mentioned, the beginnings of what in the course of time came to be recognized as standard precautions to be observed in critical study of ancient texts. Translations of these texts had to be examined with respect to their fidelity to the original. Even the original manuscripts, being hand-written copies of other manuscripts, could not always be accepted as flawless copies of the author's writings. All this paved the way for postmedieval attention to the demands of critical scholarship.

Medieval Science and Technology

During this scholastic period there were also developments which paved the way for the development of postmedieval interest in science and technology.

Incidentally, A. C. Crombie (1959, Vol. 1, p. 15) has called attention to a difference in attitude toward study of natural phenomena during this period as contrasted with the earlier medieval period. In the earlier period there was little of the direct concern with such phenomena that had been manifested by Greek and Alexandrian philosophers. In fact, some of the early Church fathers were opposed to the study of the kinds of questions that had given rise to Greek science because they viewed such study as incompatible with devotion to their ideal of the Christian life.

On the other hand, such study was seemingly encouraged or at least tolerated by St. Augustine in his use of Neoplatonic principles as a means of giving rational support to religious faith. However, this toleration did not result in active interest in the exploration of nature as an independent study. Instead, the study of nature was valued as a means of enhancing moral and religious principles by providing examples and symbols of such principles. Aesop's fables might serve as an illustration of the way in which accounts of animal behavior were employed to inculcate ethical ideals. Similarly, natural phenomena sometimes served as a means to explain the meaning of religious concepts. Simple analogies were introduced. The concept of spirit was rendered less abstract by reference to wind as a natural phenomenon, and the moon shining in reflected light served to suggest divine light reflected by the Church.

By the twelfth century, these moralizing and homiletic tendencies had been replaced by an increasing tendency to consider natural events in the spirit of scientific curiosity. During this scholastic period, with the intellectual stimulus provided by study of newly discovered ancient Greek texts as well as by the works of Arabic writers on scientific subjects, theology ceased to be the exclusive field of active investigation. There was an awakened interest in scientific and technological issues along with interest in general scholarship as such. Because of such an awakening, historians sometimes refer to it as the "twelfth-century Renaissance." In the words of I. B. Cohen (in L. White [ed.], 1956, p. 161), a well-known specialist in the history of science:

> Cultural historians have often viewed the "Renaissance" or rebirth of knowledge as a phenomenon of the fifteenth and sixteenth centuries. From the point of view of the history of science, we would place any such renaissance earlier, preferring to accept what the late Charles Homer Haskins called the "twelfth-century Renaissance," a period in which a frantic activity on the part of European scholars made available the classics of Greek science with their Arabic emendations. Perhaps the word *renaissance* is misleading here, because this may—in a genuine sense—be accounted the birth of science on the European continent rather than a rebirth. The history of science has shown not only the preservation of Greek science in the Islamic world and the changes that occurred there in the individual fields of scientific activity, but also the eventual dissemination of this knowledge in Europe. Symptoms of this influence are such Arabic words in our technical language as algebra, algorithm, alkali, elixir, or the star names Algo and Aldebaran.

The preceding words of Arabic derivation are reminders of the scope of Islamic contributions to the scientific outlook of the late medieval period. These contributions are discussed in more or less detail in the histories of such separate sciences as chemistry, astronomy, optics, and mathematics. As has been mentioned, the contributions to mathematics were not really original with the Arabs, since the Arabian mathematicians had obtained their grasp of arithmetic and algebra from Hindu sources. What are ordinarily called Arabic numerals might thus more accurately, in terms of origin, be called Hindu numerals. According to Crombie (1959, Vol. 1, pp. 50–51), the Arabs had become familiar with these numerals by the ninth century in the course of their business contacts with Hindu traders.

The introduction of the Arabic system into Western Europe was gradual. It began in the twelfth century but knowledge of it was not widely diffused until the thirteenth century. This diffusion was aided by the work of a Spanish Jew, Rabbi ben Ezra, who supplied a detailed explanation of the system as a whole and the use of the special symbol zero. The latter symbol constituted a real innovation to those whose knowledge of computation was restricted to the manipulation of Roman numerals, which had no symbol for zero. In Roman numerals "nine hundred," for example, is written "DCCCC" as contrasted with the Arabic notation of "900." Writing numbers in the latter notation is obviously easier than in the Roman. However, it took several centuries before the Roman system was replaced by the Arabic. According to D. E. Smith and J. Ginsburg (1956, p. 451), two historians of mathematics, Roman numerals continued to be used in commercial book-keeping until the eighteenth century largely because addition and subtraction are easier when Roman numerals are used. Armed with a few facts like "V plus V equals X" and "CCC plus CC equals D," one is ready to add and subtract. There is no need to "carry," as can be noted in the following examples:

ADDITION		SUBTRACTION	
DCV	(605)	DCV	(605)
CV	(105)	CV	(105)
DCCX	(710)	D	(500)

At one time Roman numerals were regarded as preferable for banking transactions since it is more difficult to change their form. A single stroke suffices to transform the Arabic zero into a 6 or a 9, hence furthering the possible falsifications of records by accident or design. Nevertheless, the Arabic system is far less cumbersome than the Roman in operations of division and multiplication, and eventually it displaced the Roman.

In view of the importance of measurement in the progress of science, this assimilation of the Arabic system by men of learning during the scholastic period might well be viewed as another positive contribution of the scholastics to that which was to develop into the methodology of science. Furthermore, more than a system of numerals was assimilated: Islamic mathematicians had also been familiar with other Hindu computational innovations, knowledge of which they transmitted to Western Europe during this late medieval period. These Hindu innovations included such varied arithmetic and algebraic operations as those necessary for manipulating fractions, extracting square and cube roots, solving equations of different degrees of complexity, handling both geometric and arithmetic progressions, dealing with permutations and combinations, and using tables of sines to facilitate solution of trigonometrical problems (Crombie, 1959, Vol. 1, p. 49).

Appreciation of the Islamic mathematical contributions and their value for science was especially manifest in the work of Robert Grosseteste (c. 1168–1253), one of the most learned men of his time. As head of the Franciscan movement at Oxford and also as Bishop of Lincoln, he was one of the leading ecclesiastics of the period. In addition to his theological training, his education at Paris and Oxford had enabled him to become familiar with the fields of law and medicine. One of his biographers, H. W. C. Davis (1910), refers to his being "proficient" in the natural sciences as well. This is in line with the estimate supplied by Roger Bacon, who, as a younger member of the Oxford Franciscans, was directly influenced by the teachings of Grosseteste and came to regard him as "the first mathematician and physicist of his age." Indeed, it now seems likely that Bacon's advocacy of experimental methods and inductive observational procedures, with his corresponding disparagement of reliance on the dogmas of tradition, were outgrowths of what had already been urged by Grosseteste.

In 1214, Grosseteste became Chancellor of Oxford. By this time he had become familiar with newly translated works of Aristotle and thus with what at the time was regarded as the "new science of Aristotle." As a result of his influence, medieval Oxford came to have an abiding interest in the "new science" and in logic and mathematics as well. Nor was the study of lanugages overlooked, especially in terms of the bearing of such study on Biblical scholarship. For Grosseteste, there was no basic incompatibility between the implications of such scholarship for Catholic theology as well as for Aristotelian philosophy. Like Albertus Magnus and St. Thomas Aquinas, who came later, he succeeded in promoting a reconciliation between the Church and Aristotle.

At this stage of Church history, there was no drastic conflict between the Church and science such as was to develop later in the days of Bruno and Galileo. As already explained, with recognition of theology and philosophy as separate disciplines three sources of knowledge had won scholastic approval; namely, revelation, sensory experience, and reason. The first source became the province of theology and the other two belonged to philosophy. Many of the scholastics were both theologians and philosophers, and with some of them, as was the case with Bishop Grosseteste, their philosophic interests turned to mathematics and natural science.

Within the field of mathematics, which was not likely to clash with dogmatic theology, many questions of science could be raised without coming into conflict with the Church. For example, Grosseteste became interested in the phenomenon of tidal changes and noted the relationship between such changes and the phases of the moon. He was also one of the first medieval students of optics and called attention to the use of lenses both for the purpose of magnifying small objects and for bringing distant objects within the field of distinct vision. Work of this sort was followed by the invention of spectacles by some anonymous Italian toward the end of the thirteenth century.

According to Crombie (1959, Vol. 1, p. 102), Grosseteste's primary interest in optics was "to emphasise the value of the experimental and mathematical methods." An instance of this value was shown by the way in which Grossesteste endeavored to account for the shape of the rainbow by attributing it to the refraction of light by a cloud serving as a large spherical lens. He also concerned himself with the question of the transmission of light and sound and proposed a theory of their propagation in terms of pulses or waves moving in rectilinear fashion. His work demonstrates that what we call a scientific outlook may be traced back to this late medieval period and is not to be regarded as a product *de novo* of the century of Galileo and Newton.

Without going into detail, let us consider the scope of this scientific outlook in the scholastic period. It embraced more than the fields of optics and mathematics. There were debates about the Aristotelian and Ptolemaic systems of astronomy, a field of more than theoretical interest. Here, for the Church, there was the practical need to prepare calendars in order to predict the dates of such holidays as Easter. Solar and stellar observations were also of practical importance for navigators in determining latitude and longitude. In making such determinations, medieval navigators were aided by the use of the compass, an invention that had resulted from prior investigation of magnetism. By the end of the thirteenth century, both Arab and Christian navigators are known to have employed compasses with pivoted needles in the Mediterranean (Crombie, 1959, Vol. 1, p. 120). In addition to the investigation of magnetic phenomena there was scholastic investigation of mechanical phenomena such as gravitational effects as measured by changes in velocity when different weights are adjusted to the arms of a lever as well as investigation of the resultant of simultaneous velocities propelling an object in contradictory directions (Crombie, 1959, Vol. 1, pp. 114–119). Nor were the subjects of geology, chemistry, zoology, and botany neglected. Along with many fantastic theories there were significant observations that paved the way for the formulation of more useful theories by students of these subjects in later centuries.

The medieval period was also characterized by technological achievements of a kind involving the application of scientific principles whose nature came to be better understood with postmedieval scientific developments. However, these technological achievements were not without influence on such developments. The sturdiness and magnificence of medieval cathedrals reflect principles of construction now stressed by architectural engineers, just as medieval metalwork involves principles germane to the fields of mining and metallurgy. Medieval alchemists devised glass containers for their investigations and thus prepared the way for the later use of glass apparatus by those responsible for the emergence of chemistry as a separate science. Incidentally, the manufacture of glass was not a medieval discovery, since glassmaking was known even before the Christian era; but medieval artisans helped to improve the art as evidenced by the introduction of stained glass and the elegance of Venetian glass. Modern geography with its dependence on maps owes much to the pioneering labors of medieval cartographers. Moreover, modern industrial chemistry can trace some of its beginnings to medieval skills in preparing paints and varnishes, fixing dyes, tanning leather, distilling alcohol, making ink, controlling fermentation, and other processes of direct concern to chemical engineers and industrial chemists. The empirical knowledge accumulated by medieval artisans and craftsmen laid the foundations for what was to become the tested knowledge of modern applied chemistry.

By way of summary it should now be evident that, contrary to popular opinion, the medieval world was not entirely devoid of scholarly, scientific, and technological insights and achievements. To view the scholastic period as just an age of stultifying theological disputes and uncritical dependence on authority is to overlook these insights and achievements. It is a distorted view because it fails to note the constructive implications for science of medieval interest in logic, mathematics, astronomy, optics, and mechanics, as well as the constructive implications for technology of medieval alchemists, builders, artisans, and craftsmen.

The foregoing summary of scholastic contributions to science, scholarship, and technology is more directly related to the early stages of what was to develop into the modern scientific outlook in general than to the methodology of a scientific psychology in particular. As we have seen, the dream of the latter kind of psychology was not realized until the nineteenth century. The founding fathers of experimental psychology based their notions on laboratory work on the model of laboratory work in physics and physiology. In turn, such work in physics and physiology can be traced back to its roots in Arabic and scholastic concern with problems of mathematics, optics, medicine, logic, and other topics mentioned in the preceding section.

Only in this very indirect fashion can these late medieval developments be said to have influenced the nineteenth-century establishment of a laboratory psychology. Nevertheless, some isolated medieval findings, especially in the field of optics, might be regarded as furnishing a more direct kind of influence. For example, in view of the extent to which the founding fathers of laboratory psychology concerned themselves with the psychophysiology of vision, they might have regarded themselves as indebted to the Spanish-Arabian philosopher and physician Averroës (1126–1198) for their knowledge of the function of the retina. As pointed out by Crombie (1959, Vol. 1, p. 102), Averroës was the first to recognize "that the retina rather than the lens is the sensitive organ of the eye." Interestingly, this recognition did not meet with the immediate endorsement of other medieval students of optics. What is a commonplace fact for the modern student was a subject for controversy in earlier times. Similarly, it was not always "obvious" that the brain is the essential organ for cognitive experience. These are examples of how what one generation accepts as self-evident fact is sometimes the product of evidence mobilized in connection with what had been a controversial issue in previous generations. In this sense the science of the present is indebted to the science of the past.

The Psychology of St. Thomas Aquinas

Does a truism like the foregoing also hold good for psychology? In the strict sense of science, it might be argued there was no *science* of psychology prior to the days of Wilhelm Wundt. A proponent of such a viewpoint might grant there had been a vast tradition of mental philosophy, but might feel constrained to disparage the value of this tradition for the establishment of a scientific psychology striving to emulate physics as an experimental science. At best he might grant some value to the help supplied by the associationist tradition along with other empirically grounded teachings of philosopher-psychologists. He would very likely be more skeptical of the value for a scientific psychology of the rationalistic tradition of philosopher-psychologists. He might be even still more skeptical of the value of scholastic psychology.

Whether such skepticism is justified depends upon what one regards as scholastic psychology. A good portion of it was very much influenced by Aristotle's *De Anima,* and, as we have noted in Chapter 4, much of what Aristotle taught can be regarded as an anticipation of what came to be incorporated into systems of modern psychology. In many ways his general outlook was naturalistic and biological rather than dogmatic and theological. Despite scholastic allegiance to dogmatic theology, there was no widespread repudiation of Aristotle's general outlook. Consequently it might be well to consider, at least in broad outline, the kind of psychology that scholasticism bequeathed to postmedieval psychology. For present purposes it will suffice to consider the views of St. Thomas Aquinas, the most influential of medieval students of psychology.

Thomas Gilby, a British Dominican friar, is one of the outstanding present-day students of the writings of St. Thomas Aquinas. These writings cover a wide array of subjects: theology, Biblical exegesis, commentaries on Aristotle and other philosophers, and discussions of ethics, logic, and other topics. They include large books and smaller monographs. The total, Gilby reports, comes to close to one hundred works. Fortunately, for present purposes, convenient access to some of the key ideas in these works is available in a collection of excerpts that Gilby has selected and translated (1960). In what follows, unless otherwise noted, all references to Aquinas are taken from this collection of excerpts.

Although primarily influenced by Aristotle's views of human nature, those of Aquinas were not just unmodified duplications of these views. This calls for special emphasis because some have held that once scholastic philosophers accepted the authority of Aristotle they would brook no deviation from his teachings. In fact, as quoted by W. C. Gibson (1958, p. 241), with reference to this point it was alleged by one writer: "A philosopher needed only to *know* Aristotle by heart; to *understand* him was a secondary consideration; to *contradict* him was blasphemy." Such blind worship of authority was certainly not endorsed by Aquinas especially with respect to psychological issues. He made this explicit by writing (Gilby, 1960, p. 7), "In the field of human science the argument from authority is weakest." Despite Aquinas' respect for Aristotle,[2] he rejected the Aristotelian view of the soul by regarding the soul not only as the substantial form of the body, but also as being an immortal entity. To view it as immortal is to regard it as separable from the body. Aquinas is very definite about this (Gilby, 1960, p. 205):

> The human soul communicates to bodily matter its own existence. Both make up one thing, so much so that the existence of the whole compound is also the existence of the soul. . . . The human soul keeps its existence when the body breaks up.

In taking this stand, Aquinas was writing as a Christian theologian and not as an Aristotelian psychologist. As G. S. Brett (1912, Vol. II, p. 113) has indicated, the issue is not of direct psychological importance. The dogmas of theology are irrelevant for a study of mental life. Nevertheless, if the term "soul" is employed as a convenient designation for mental functions like perceiving, thinking, wishing, and willing, then the issue of the soul's dependence on the body may not be irrelevant. In maintaining that the soul is separable

---

[2] This should not be regarded as the expression of a preference for Aristotle as contrasted with other Greek philosophers. The reference to respect for Aristotle is the equivalent of a respect for philosophy. F. Copleston (1963, Vol. III, p. 239) is especially clarifying when he states: "If we speak . . . of the attempt of St. Thomas to reconcile Aristotelianism with Christian theology, one will realize the nature of the situation better if one makes the experiment of substituting the word 'philosophy' for the word 'Aristotelianism.' When some of the theologians in the thirteenth century adopted a hostile attitude to Aristotle and regarded his philosophy as being in many respects an intellectual menace, they were rejecting independent philosophy in the name of Christian faith. And when St. Thomas adopted in great measure the Aristotelian system, he was giving a charter to philosophy. He should not be regarded as burdening Christian thought with the system of a particular Greek philosopher. The deeper significance of his actions was that he recognized the rights and position of philosophy as a rational study distinct from theology."

ST. THOMAS AQUINAS (1225?–1274)

from the body, Aquinas was sponsoring a dualistic approach to mental life that in more or less disguised form has influenced psychological theorizing ever since.

In reality it is somewhat misleading to say that Aquinas regarded the soul as entirely separable from the body as an autonomous entity. He was too much of an Aristotelian not to realize the importance of sense organs and visceral structures for the arousal of sensation and appetite. In his treatment of the soul's faculties or functions he makes a distinction between "the body-soul compound" and "the spiritual soul," with the former more definitely linked to bodily structures than the latter (Gilby, 1960, p. 214). The body-soul compound includes the traditional five senses and their derivatives in the way of images, memories, and the Aristotelian commonsense. It also includes appetitive tendencies as exemplified by hunger, thirst, lust, and similar affective-conative dispositions. By way of contrast, Aquinas restricted the functions of the spiritual soul to acts of reasoning and to acts of volition. Apparently he was struck by the absence of any obvious bodily basis for thinking and decision-making in the way in which vision is a function of the eye and hunger a function of the stomach. In his own formulation (Gilby, 1960, p. 196):

> The principle of intellectual activity, which we term the human soul, is a bodiless and completely substantial principle.
>
> This principle, also termed mind or intellect, can act without the body having an intrinsic part of the activity. . . .
>
> We can pass the statement that the human soul understands, though it would be more accurate to say that the man understands through his soul. . . .
>
> Intellectual activity requires a body, not as an organ through which it operates, but in order that an object may be provided.

Passages like the foregoing along with others render it very likely that Aquinas' dichotomy of a body-soul compound, as contrasted with the spiritual soul or intellect, was not altogether a product of theological considerations.

Thomistic Dualism

The dichotomy in question with its dualistic implications has troubled many psychologists for many centuries. Some have blamed Descartes (1596–1650) for having introduced it at the inception of the modern scientific era because he viewed animals as machinelike automata devoid of reason and regarded man as its exclusive possessor. This was tantamount to accounting for animal behavior in terms of bodily machinery but maintaining that mind or reason was somewhat independent of such machinery. What Aquinas called the spiritual soul was similarly independent, and as the basis for reason and acts of volitional choice was also viewed as an exclusively human endowment. This is brought out in the following passage (Gilby, 1960, p. 230):

Wonderful instances of sagacity are manifested in the behaviour of animals such as bees, spiders, and dogs. On coming to a crossing, a hound hunting a stag will cast about to discover whether the quarry has taken the first or second trail, and if he does not pick up the scent on either, being thus assured, he takes the third without sniffing about, as though arguing by the principle of exclusion.

Animals act like this because they are naturally adjusted to complicated processes. We call them keen and clever, but *this does not imply that they have reason and choice,* as appears from the fact that animals of the same breed behave in similar fashion. [Italics not in the original.]

Cartesian dualism in its essentials is thus the same as the much earlier Thomistic dualism. A dualistic orientation has often been viewed with misgivings as being a metaphysical hindrance to the progress of scientific psychology. However, it is possible to argue that without one kind of dualism such progress would be seriously impeded. This is a dualism which accepts the need for and legitimacy of investigating *all* psychological phenomena: those that are now known to be functions of specifiable bodily structures as well as those for which bodily concomitants are only vaguely specifiable. Visual and other sensory phenomena would exemplify the former group, while the latter group would include references to cognitive and volitional factors involved in planning a career, formulating and verifying hypotheses, composing a symphony, detecting fallacies in an argument, or, in brief, engaging in any kind of creative work.

To refer to such work as brain work does little to enhance one's understanding of how it is accomplished. There still is no way for the brain physiologist to supply a clarifying account of what goes on in the brain of a person solving a crossword puzzle as contrasted with what goes on when the same person is planning an experiment or taking an intelligence test. More is known about the psychology of thinking than the physiology of thinking.

This kind of knowledge has grown in virtual independence of concomitant progress in knowledge of brain mechanism involved. What J. P. Guilford (1962) has called "the structure of the intellect," a product of factor-analytic studies of intelligence, has resulted in the differentiation and definition of sixty distinct intellectual abilities. Whether this involves sixty separate cortical patterns has not been determined. The detection of the sixty abilities is a psychological achievement in its own right and was accomplished without the collaboration of brain physiologists. Moreover, the abilities in question are designated by psychological terms rather than by words germane to brain anatomy and physiology. Even if there should be eventual discovery of the cerebral concomitants of each of these abilities, the psychological terms would not be displaced by a physiological vocabulary. Both descriptive volcabularies would be needed to do justice to the two sets of findings. As was mentioned in Chapter 2 in connection with the views of Penfield and Roberts, recourse to such a dual vocabulary or what they termed the "language of busy common sense" is not to be stigmatized as unscientific because it is the language of dualism.

The language of dualism has very different connotations when employed by a modern psychologist than it had when employed by Aquinas. It is a far cry from what a phrase like "intellectual activity" suggests to a contemporary factor analyst and what the same phrase meant to Aquinas. For him, as shown in the following passage (Gilby, 1960, p. 199), it implied an Aristotelian entelechy:

> We should assert that the mind, the principle of intellectual activity, is the form of the human body. The body's first animating principle is the soul. And since life is manifested by various activities in the various grades of living things, that which is the first principle of these vital activities is the soul. For by the soul primarily we take nourishment, feel, walk about, and also understand. Call it mind or intellective soul, this principle is the form of the body. If anyone wishes to deny this, let him explain how otherwise he can attribute the activity of understanding to the individual man. Everybody experiences in himself that it is veritably himself who understands.

Psychology as a Natural Science

In appealing to what "everybody experiences" as support for the latter conclusion, Aquinas was acknowledging the value of self-observation as a means of securing knowledge of mental life. For him, such observation was part of his method of psychological investigation. He regarded psychology as the study of human nature and as capable of being classified as a natural science. In his own words (Gilby, 1960, p. 193): "Psychology is part of natural philosophy and physical science." In commenting on this question of method, Gilby introduced this clarifying footnote (Gilby, 1960, p. 193):

> St. Thomas works with two apparently irreconcilable principles; first, that man is a material and animal substance; second, that his single soul, composing a natural unity with his body, is spiritual. The contrasted themes run throughout his teaching: it was this part of it his contemporaries found most contentious. He has a clear scheme of the specific abilities of man, but his faculty-psychology does not lose sight of the single wholeness of the organism: "actions come from the complete substance," this saying is frequently noted. The appropriate method of inquiry is introspection, but it is based on, and controlled by, external data.

Despite his theological convictions regarding the immortality of the spiritual soul, the veridicality of Biblical miracles, and the existence of God, Aquinas was able to conceive of a wholly naturalistic approach to and interpretation of the universe. He discusses this in the following excerpt (Gilby, 1960, p. 48), in which the opening sentence reflects an anticipation of the law of parsimony as it was to be embodied in Occam's razor a century later:

Moreover, explanations should be economical. It seems that everything that appears in the world can be accounted for on the supposition that God does not exist. Natural processes can be resolved into physical determination, and design can be resolved solely into the factors of human reason or will. There is no need then to postulate the existence of God.

Taken out of context, a passage like the preceding one might be misconstrued as an endorsement of atheism. Aquinas, of course, would have been vehement in his repudiation of such an interpretation. As a religious philosopher he worked out what he regarded as convincing proofs of God's existence; hence the passage in question is not to be construed as a vitiation of these proofs. What it seems to mean is that, in his opinion, it is possible for the scientist to investigate nature without feeling constrained to account for the phenomena being studied in terms of supernatural magic or divine interference with the operation of observed or inferred cause-and-effect relationships. Support for this interpretation of the passage is to be found in what Aquinas has to say about the nature of a scientific explanation and the role played by hypotheses in scientific work. According to him (Gilby, 1960, p. 18):

> Explanation is of two kinds. One goes to the root of the matter, as in natural science when a sufficient proof is advanced to show that the velocity of astronomical motion is constant. The other is less radical, but lays down an *hypothesis* and shows that the observed effects are in accord with the supposition, as when astronomy employs a system of eccentrics and epicycles to justify our observations about the motions of the heavenly bodies. It does not carry complete conviction, because another hypothesis might also serve. [Italics added.]

Additional support for the interpretation in question is supplied by the fact that Aquinas recognized the importance of accurate observation and experiment in the scientific enterprise. Nor was the importance of critical thinking in evaluating the significance of observational data overlooked. What was to become the seventeenth-century conflict between empiricists and rationalists is thus not only anticipated but also resolved by noting the operation of both kinds of attitudes in the work of scientific investigators. Aquinas discusses such work as a cognitive venture undertaken for the purpose of enhancing one's understanding or knowledge. In doing so he considers the process of knowing in these paragraphs (Gilby, 1960, p. 22):

> Let us pause at two periods in knowing, one at the start and the other at the finish, corresponding respectively with the apprehending and the judging. The beginning or principle of every scientific inquiry lies in the senses, and all our intellectual apprehension is abstracted from their data. The boundary or term, however, is not so invariable, for sometimes it is reached in the senses, sometimes in the imagination, sometimes in the pure reason.

When the properties disclosed in sensibility adequately express the nature of a thing then the judgement of the mind should subscribe to the witness of the senses. The natural sciences operate at this stage, for they deal with truths whose existence and meaning involve sensible matter. Therefore their findings should be checked by *sense-observation* and *experiment,* and they lapse into error when this *empiricism* is neglected.

Secondly comes the class of mathematical truths. Their meaning is *independent* of sensible matter, though they exist in it, and judgement about them does not depend on sense-perception to the same extent. [Italics supplied.]

It should now be evident that Aquinas both understood and endorsed the pursuit of knowledge in terms of the naturalistic outlook and methodology of science. As mentioned earlier, for him this outlook has no need "to postulate the existence of God." His understanding of the naturalistic orientation of science was not merely due to his study of Aristotle but was also influenced by familiarity with the scientific work of scholastic contemporaries like Grosseteste and Bacon. Monks and friars whose studies of natural phenomena dealt with topics like magnetism, optics, and mechanics were demonstrating the nature and value of scientific method. Their studies did not have to be conducted in secret because of Church opposition, for such opposition was concerned with heresy and, as indicated by the views of Aquinas, the methodology of science as such was not deemed to be heretical.

The medieval Inquisition as an official Church agency for ferreting out heresy began its operations around 1230. Like Aquinas, most of the inquisitors were Dominicans and were very likely familiar with his writings. Despite Aquinas' repeated endorsement of so many of the views of a pagan philosopher like Aristotle and his approval of experimental science, his religious orthodoxy was not challenged.

How is this to be reconciled with the Inquisition's later prosecution of others for their scientific views? Such prosecution reflected a clash between theology and science or, in the opinion of some, between religion and science. It would be more accurate to say that it was a clash between certain theological or religious convictions and some particular scientific conclusions. The clash did not involve a wholesale indictment of the methodology of science and the naturalistic viewpoint of science.

Only when specific interpretations of science were in conflict with revelation or Church doctrine was there an indictment in the offing. There was no opposition to the scientific study of optics, magnetism, mathematics, metallurgy, and other subjects having no bearing on religious faith as such. Moreover, Aquinas was cognizant of possible conflict between faith and some results of science. In case of conflict his theology prevailed over his science: faith or dogma was deemed superior to the evidence of reason, as shown by the following excerpts from his writings (Gilby, 1960, pp. 30–32):

Christian theology issues from the light of faith, philosophy from the natural light of reason. Philosophical truths cannot be opposed to the truths of faith, they fall short indeed, yet they also admit common analogies; and some moreover are foreshadowings, for nature is the preface to grace. . . .

There are two classes of science: some enlarge on principles evident to the natural light of the reason while others develop principles taken from elsewhere. In this last way Christian theology proceeds from the principles of the high knowledge enjoyed by the blessed. As musical theory accepts principles delivered by mathematics so Christian theology believes principles divinely revealed. . . . From doctrines held by faith the knowledge of other truths can be developed by discourse from principles to conclusion. The truths of faith are the first principles, as it were, of the science of Christian theology, the others are like conclusions. Christian theology is nobler than divine metaphysics for it derives from higher principles.

Thomistic Preternaturalism and Parapsychology

Excerpts like the foregoing indicate that in endorsing the naturalistic science of Aristotle, Aquinas was not rejecting or questioning what he called "the science of Christian theology." His devotion to the Church and to theology prevented him from sponsoring an unqualified naturalism. In fact, his naturalism was colored by a preternaturalism in the sense of recognizing the existence of forces or influences differing from what are ordinarily attributed to the everyday world and which verge on the supernatural. To believe in demons, good spirits, and the reality of miraculous cures is to entertain preternatural beliefs. That Aquinas entertained such beliefs can be noted in his discussion of two kinds of "mysterious forces": (1) those natural ones responsible for action at a distance like the influence of the moon on tides and the effect of a magnet on iron particles, and (2) those preternatural ones responsible for what Aquinas called "enchantments" and attributed to "spiritual substances." To cite a portion of this discussion (Gilby, 1960, pp. 15–16):

> The heavenly bodies and purely spiritual substances are the principles of observed phenomena resulting, not from any settled active form in the material bodies concerned, but from the motions these receive from above; the ebb and flow of tides is from the moon's influence, not from the inherent properties of water; similarly *enchantments* may be produced by *demons,* and sometimes, I believe, by *good spirits.* That the shadow of the apostle Peter or the touch of holy relics should heal sickness is through no inherent virtue, but by the application of divine power turning these bodily influences to such an effect.
>
> Clearly every mysterious operation of nature, is not *preternatural* after this fashion. Many are regular and constant, whereas not every saintly relic is endowed with healing power, but only some and then only on occasion; nor are all fetishes harmful, nor does all water ebb and flow. Some mysterious forces seem to belong to all bodies of the same kind, thus every magnet attracts iron. Consequently we are left to suppose that they must result from some intrinsic principle common to all things of that kind. Moreover, preternatural phenomena are not uniform, an evident sign that they do not derive from an inborn and permanent quality, but from the activation of a superior power. . . . [Italics added.]

From the foregoing quotation it is evident that Aquinas regarded preter-natural phenomena as relatively of rare occurrence, unpredictable, and due to a "superior power." The latter power was conceived of as being either benevolent when attributed to a good spirit or malevolent when attributed to a demon. Conceptualizations of this kind might readily be dismissed as unscientific, superstitious nonsense devoid of psychological interest except as an example of primitive, animistic thinking.

One might well wonder whether this segment of Thomistic philosophy merits inclusion in a history of psychology. This segment is obviously antithetic to the effort of psychology to establish itself as a scientific enterprise governed by the canons of critical thinking as contrasted with the canons of a dogmatic theology. Nevertheless, it is not altogether unrelated to the total sweep of the history of psychology and to certain aspects of present-day psychology.

Throughout the ages there have been persistent reports of events allegedly not explicable in terms of known scientific principles. These so-called occult phenomena are the same as those which Aquinas called preternatural phenomena. They have to do with the folklore of haunted houses and poltergeists as well as belief in mental telepathy, clairvoyance, telekinesis, and kindred topics belonging to what used to be called the field of psychical research and is currently referred to as parapsychology.

As a separate field deserving of investigation by the methods of natural science, psychical research came into being in the 1880s. Despite the adjective "psychical," very few psychologists became members of the official societies sponsoring such research. Instead the membership was made up of engineers, physicists, astronomers, chemists, physiologists, and medical men along with a few psychologists like William James and William McDougall. For the most part, academic psychology kept itself aloof from such investigations. At best, psychical research was regarded as tangential or peripheral to scientific psychology. The selection of a term like "parapsychology" as a more suitable designation for the field of psychical research emphasized this peripheral status. It also served to lessen resistance to such research by elimination of "psychical" with its troublesome connotation of preternatural factors. This connotation was definitely implied in a book entitled *The Case For and Against Psychical Belief* (C. Murchison [ed.]) published in 1927 and consisting of papers delivered at a symposium sponsored by Clark University in 1926. It was a pioneer venture in being the first academic sponsorship of such a symposium. By way of guarding against any possible misinterpretation of the meaning of this sponsorship as implying endorsement of belief in a spirit world, this frank disclaimer was printed in the *Preface* to the volume:

> We want it distinctly understood that Clark University, in promoting this sym-posium, is by no means assuming the role of friend to psychical research and its

various adherents. Clark University is assuming only the role of parliamentarian in the controversy. At this moment it is well to announce that the members of the Clark University Department of Psychology are most decidedly not yet convinced of the validity of the psychical interpretations based upon the subject matter of psychical research. Being scientists, we guarantee fair play in the conduct of this symposium. If there is a spirit world we also, being human beings, are interested in learning about it.

During the decades since the Clark symposium, parapsychology has been especially concerned with the experimental investigation of extrasensory perception. The chief center for such investigation has been the Parapsychology Laboratory of Duke University. No other American university has established such a laboratory. Furthermore despite its many division, the American Psychological Association has no Division of Parapsychology. Of the more than twenty thousand members of the Association, as Gardner Murphy (1958, p. 75) has pointed out, only thirty to forty members are engaged in parapsychological studies. He also points out (p. 69) that surveys of the membership's opinions on the subject of extrasensory perception reveal a somewhat guarded attitude. Some five per cent are convinced of the reality of the phenomenon as convincingly demonstrated. From twenty-five to thrity-five per cent view it as a "likely possibility" and most of the psychologists polled consider research on the problem to be a "legitimate scientific under-taking." Nevertheless, as was just suggested, very few of them engage in this kind of research. As yet it has not been possible to bring the alleged fact of telepathy or extrasensory perception into line with what is known about the psychophysiology of ordinary perception. Very likely this failure is partly responsible for the general reluctance to undertake such research. In the absence of a sound physical theory to account for telepathy there is a persistent undercurrent of skepticism when evidence in support of a belief in extrasensory perception is being evaluated. Murphy has the follow-ing to say about this (1958, p. 74):

> In my experience there is an interesting paradox here. Psychologists who are bothered with the approach are bothered not by the psychological principles, which in one form or another are commonplace, but because a physical transmis-sion system is not provided. The physicists, on the other hand, with whom we have shared such problems, seem to be less troubled by such gaps.

It may well be that the paradox in question is related to what, as previously noted, Aquinas recognized as two kinds of "mysterious forces." One kind had to do with familiar physical phenomena involving action at a distance as illustrated by gravitational, tidal, and magnetic phenomena. The other kind, regarded by Aquinas as preternatural, was attributed to "spiritual substances" that he assumed to exercise occasional and somewhat unpredict-able modifications of the course of natural events. For Aquinas, this distinc-

tion between the natural and the preternatural constituted a frank acknowledgment of the metaphysics of dualism.

In general, the present-day scientific psychologist is on guard against entertaining beliefs that might be construed as endorsement of such metaphysical
dualism. Extrasensory perception involves the concept of action at a distance.
This, being a familiar concept to the physicist, may render him relatively
less skeptical about the reality of the perception in question. He may be able
to assimilate it to other instances of natural phenomena characterized by
action at a distance without being bothered by the specter of metaphysical
dualism. On the other hand, the psychologist is likely to be reaction-sensitive
to such a specter. As a consequence, should he regard the notion of extrasensory perception as having dualistic or preternatural implications, he would
be more troubled by the notion than physicists seem to be.

The preceding suggested explanation for the way in which physicists and
psychologists differ in their reactions to the experimental studies of extrasensory perception involves considerations now known to influence many
fields of psychological inquiry. They are by no means restricted to a peripheral
field like parapsychology, for they concern the effect of any psychologist's
beliefs or expectations on his experimental results and his interpretations of
the results.

An impressive group of studies is now at hand showing that unconscious
bias on the part of the experimenter can affect the experimental outcome.
R. Rosenthal (1963) has supplied an informative survey of these studies.
By way of example it may suffice to mention two of them in each of which
the experimenters investigated the behavior of rats. Both maze learning
and Skinner-box problems were employed in the investigations. The object
of the experiments was to determine the possible influence of experimenter
bias on the results. To accomplish this in each investigation, half of the
experimenters were given to understand that the rats being used had been
bred for brightness and the other half were told that their rats were the
product of a dull strain. In terms of the results, those who believed their
animals to be dull secured poorer learning measures than those convinced
of the brightness of their animals. The obtained differences were statistically
significant. Moreover, as one of the planners of these experiments, Rosenthal
(1963, p. 270) has the following comment regarding the outcome:

> At the conclusion of one of these studies, we told all E's of the nature of the
> experiment which had lasted the entire quarter. Their reaction was most interesting.
> When E's who had run "dull" rats were told that their S's were really not dull at
> all, their uniform reaction was: "How very interestingly you took in those other
> E's—our rat, however, was obviously *really* dull."

Bias in the sense of positive or negative attitudes toward the outcome of
an experiment has also been found to influence the study of extrasensory
perception. This was demonstrated by G. R. Schmeidler and Gardner

Murphy (1946) in a series of experiments in which the subjects were required to indicate the design to be found on each of a stack of well-concealed and randomly assorted cards of a kind conventionally employed in studies of extrasensory perception. As a group, those subjects who believed in extrasensory perception achieved scores above chance expectation, while the group skeptical of the outcome scored somewhat below chance. The magnitudes of the difference above and below chance were small but nevertheless were indicative of divergent trends.

In the present context, one would be well advised to suspend judgment regarding the existence and nature of extrasensory perception and related phenomena. What is of more immediate concern is to note the historical linkage between what Aquinas classified as *preternatural* forces and what contemporary parapsychologists refer to as *paranormal* phenomena. Both terms denote belief in the occurrence of some psychological events which cannot be explained in terms of currently recognized scientific principles. However, they have slightly different connotations in the sense that for Aquinas the term "preternatural" suggests supernatural suspension of or interference with the uniformity of natural law, while the term "paranormal" has no such supernatural connotation for the modern parapsychologist. Instead he operates on the assumption that eventually the concept of natural law will have to be enlarged so as to bring paranormal events within its scope.

Preternaturalism in the Twentieth Century

At this point it might be in order to ask whether there is justification for devoting so much attention to this thirteenth-century distinction between natural and preternatural events. Has it any bearing on twentieth-century psychology, or is it just a matter of antiquarian interest? Should it not be dismissed as a medieval vagary altogether at variance with the presuppositions of a scientific psychology? The majority of psychologists would undoubtedly answer the latter question in the affirmative and yet there might be some negative answers, since the teachings of Aquinas continue to influence the outlook of many Catholic psychologists.

By way of demonstrating the nature of this influence, the work of Thomas Verner Moore merits consideration. His professional training has given him a diversified background so that he has degrees in both medicine and psychology and has contributed to the literature of experimental psychology as well as that of mental hygiene and psychopathology. Moreover, as a Benedictine monk he is well grounded in Catholic tradition. His writings reflect familiarity with and respect for scientific method as applied to psychological issues. Both he and his students are sensitive to the need for laboratory studies, control experiments, and the refinements of modern statistical checks.

Like other Catholic psychologists, he is able to undertake and sponsor such allegiance to strict standards of scientific method quite confident of the approval of his theological superiors. The activity in question would be regarded as consistent with investigation of what Aquinas considered to be the domain of natural law. In this sense, contrary to popular opinion in some circles, there never has been official interdiction by the Church of the methods of science. Men like Mendel and Pasteur were able to conduct their experiments without fear of censure, and the same is true of many lesser men working in the laboratories of Catholic universities. They are not troubled by the shadow of Galileo's unfortunate experience. No Catholic astronomer of today need hesitate to endorse a heliocentric theory; there would be no charges of heresy and no threats of excommunication. The Church has learned to accommodate itself to the findings of the laboratory and the observatory.

The Church's accommodation to the findings of scientific psychology is evident in the writings of Moore and other Catholic psychologists.[3] As was already indicated, it is easy for them to deal with such findings as having to do with what Aquinas recognized and endorsed as natural law. However, this does not mean that they necessarily repudiate what Aquinas also recognized as being of preternatural significance. For example, in discussing the psychology of depressed patients, Moore (1948, pp. 160–161) makes a distinction between melancholy "due to purely natural causes" and the kind which he regards as influenced by "supernatural" factors. In clarification he supplies an account of the depression suffered by St. John of the Cross, who had referred to his suffering as "the dark night of the soul." In this connection Moore states:

> In the "dark night" the soul is not in a state of negligence and lukewarmness, but on the contrary is ever turning to God with a certain heedfulness. The darkness is sometimes associated with a fear of having offended God that has no ground in anything that the person has done, and so there is a certain resemblance to the familiar picture of anxious depression. St. John says that the condition may "be intensified by melancholia or some other abnormal condition, as it often is." But

---

3 Interest in and endorsement of experimental psychology by Catholic psychologists has been evident for many decades. Its nature and wide scope was already manifest back in the 1920s in a massive two-volume work by J. Fröbes, a German Jesuit. Unfortunately, these volumes have never been translated. In more than 1,200 pages of text, one finds scholarly accounts of theoretic and experimental contributions by American, British, French, German, and other psychologists to all phases of psychology, both normal and abnormal. The volumes reflect vast erudition and keen appreciation of the methodology of science. A less ambitious account of experimental psychology is to be found in the work of another Jesuit, J. Lindworsky (1931). The original in German was also published in the 1920s. As a result of Harry De Silva's translation (1931), American psychologists came to know more about Lindworsky's contributions than those of Fröbes.

For those interested in this entire question of possible conflict between the Church and the psychology as science, the following book by two Catholic psychologists will prove an informative survey of relevant issues: H. Misiak, and V. M. Staudt, *Catholics in Psychology—A Historical Survey* (New York: Mc-Graw-Hill Book Company, 1954).

when melancholy is due to purely *natural* causes, rather than to the divine action purifying and sanctifying the soul, the torment that the mind experiences is present indeed, but there is lacking that quiet firm desire of subjecting oneself to the divine will, no matter what one may have to suffer, which is characteristic of the *supernatural* process of purification that takes place in the "dark night of the soul." [Italics added.]

It should thus be evident that for Moore this "supernatural process of purification" emerges from the depressed patient's readiness to turn "to God with a certain heedfulness." In his distress, as Freud once indicated, the patient may turn to God as a "magic helper." However, long before Freud Aquinas had reached a similar conclusion worded as follows (Gilby, 1960, p. 56):

Man's natural reason tells him that he is under a higher power because of the deficiences he feels in himself crying out for care and comfort. Whatever that higher may be, it is what all men term God.

In the modern era some patients may regard the psychoanalyst as a "higher power" or "magic helper." It has even been alleged that unwittingly some psychoanalysts come to attribute such magic powers to themselves. At all events, as J. Marmor (1953) has suggested, it would be well for psychotherapists to guard against such unrealistic self-aggrandizing tendencies. Failure to do so may give rise to what has been called the God complex. Once such a complex has emerged, it is likely to be reinforced by the adulation of neurotic patients in quest of a secular magic helper. In some ways the quest is akin to what Aquinas recognized as the longing "for care and comfort" to assuage felt "deficiencies" in the way of anxiety, guilt, or feelings of unworthiness. He perceived such feelings as pains or penalties incident to violation of moral precepts when he wrote (Gilby, 1960, p. 174): "Guilt and penalty are not the main divisions of evil in general, but of the special evil arising from a moral issue." This is in line with the notion common among religionists to the effect that sin calls for payment. The pangs of conscience belong to the *wages* of sin. As indicated in the following passage, Aquinas (Gilby, 1960, p. 176) regarded the suffering of the sinner as divinely ordained:

When we read, *God made not death,* the sense is that he does not will death for its own sake. Nevertheless, the demands of justice are bound up with the order of the universe, and they require that sinners should be punished. Thus God is the author of the evil of penalty. . . .

This kind of interpretation has induced many conscience-stricken individuals to seek relief from their suffering by appealing to religious leaders for help in their longing for absolution or atonement. Words like "sin," "absolution," and "atonement" belong to the vocabulary of theology and are somewhat alien to the psychologist's professional vocabulary. Of these three words, "sin" is the only one to be included in the most recent dictionary of psychological terms (English and English, 1958) and is there (p. 503) defined quasi-theologically as "conduct that violates what the offender believes to be a supernaturally ordained moral code."

From the Medieval Concept of Sin to Modern Psychotherapy

In the light of the preceding definition, one might well question the relevance for twentieth-century psychology of what Aquinas had to say about sin and sinners in the thirteenth century. At best, one might argue, the topic belongs to the restricted field of those concerned with the psychology of religion. However, to do so is to overlook its relevance for contemporary clinical psychology, in the sense that increasingly in recent years clinicians have begun to note a possible relationship between many neuroses and what may be the patient's quest for punishment in expiation for feelings of sinfulness or guilt. O. H. Mowrer (1963, p. 577), for example, is quite explicit about this:

> There is a growing indication that in so-called neurosis we are dealing, not with a mere "guilt complex," but with *real* guilt. And if this be the case, it is highly probable that persons undergoing "treatment" will interpret the financial cost and other associated sacrifices as repayment for past misconduct—and, therefore, a means of recovering the case and zest in "social situations" and the interpersonal confidence and "security" which are always impaired by "sin."

From the context it is clear that Mowrer intends the foregoing as a directive for psychotherapists. He reminds his fellow therapists of the need to consider personality disorders as being, in large measure, consequences of an impaired sense of ethical responsibility. The goal of psychotherapy is not to be reached without correcting such impairment. Irresponsibility must be eliminated. In this connection he concludes his article with these sentences:

> And the only way for persons to *cease* being irresponsible (and hence sick) is for them to become responsible: i.e., to be meticulously honest, reliable, generous, cooperative, "moral." We psychologists and psychiatrists have been putting great emphasis upon the patient's emotions, his feelings, rather than his actions. That, again, is what the patient has been doing; so it is not surprising that we are often not very helpful to him. Now we are coming to see that the way to *feel better* is to *be better*, in the ethical and interpersonal sense of the term.

Just how a psychotherapist is to get his patient "to be better" is not explained by Mowrer. The article was more concerned with directing attention to the crucial importance of ethical considerations in terms of enhanced moral responsibility than with the practical problem of promoting such enhancement. Disposition of the latter problem would require a separate article, and might have been distracting in the Mowrer article. For him, it was more important to concentrate on theoretic justification for his stand that successful psychotherapy must focus on the centrality of moral responsibility.

Such a stand calls for special justification because in some respects it is at variance with two convictions long held by many psychotherapists. In accordance with one of these convictions, for a psychotherapist to dwell on the moral implications of his patient's behavior is to militate against the success of the psychotherapy. In the light of this conviction, therapists are urged to be nonjudgmental and to maintain an attitude of noncensorious acceptance of whatever the patient tells about himself and his conduct—or misconduct. Sometimes this emphasis on ethical neutrality is reinforced by endowing it with the halo of science, with the argument that questions of ethics have to do with differentiating good conduct from bad conduct and thus introducing standards of value into one's deliberations. One is then reminded that science is supposed to be value-free and that consequently concern with ethical values is to be stigmatized as unscientific.

However, the impact of this contention is weakened by the realization that pure science can never really be altogether value-free since its success hinges on such values as clear thinking, accurate observation, honest reporting, readiness to admit error, and whatever else is needed to safeguard the pursuit of truth. With respect to laboratory work involving animal experimentation, scientists strive to protect their animal subjects from needless suffering, antivivisectionists to the contrary notwithstanding. This effort, of course, constitutes recognition of freedom from pain as a value. Similarly, in an applied science like medicine, preservation of health is a sovereign value. Furthermore, in other applied sciences economic values are rarely an insignificant consideration. Under the circumstances, the indictment of psychotherapists as unscientific because of an interest in their patients' moral values is difficult to sustain. So much for the first conviction of those disposed to question the soundness of Mowrer's thesis.

The second conviction has to do with another aspect of Mowrer's thesis. This aspect is not only at variance with customary assumptions of psychotherapists but is also contrary both to popular beliefs and to prevalent psychiatric teachings regarding the relationship of mental disorder to personal responsibility. According to these assumptions, beliefs, or teachings, the misconduct or antisocial behavior of psychiatric patients is a consequence of neurosis, psychosis, or personality disorder. Because of their "illness" they are not to be held fully responsible for their acts. By implication the "illness" is the cause of their acts. This interpretation is also applicable to a criminal court case resulting in a verdict of not guilty by reason of insanity, meaning that the defendant was adjudged to be "irresponsible."

With respect to "irresponsibility," Mowrer questions views that make it a consequence of mental disorder. Actually he does not have anything to say about the validity of insanity as a defense in criminal proceedings. We introduced this forensic example for the purpose of expository clarification of the conventional view. Whether Mowrer would also question the court's endorsement of the conventional view is brought in rather incidentally and is not the subject of extended elaboration. Nevertheless, even if fragmentary, it is clear-cut and explicit when he writes (p. 579):

> What I have said here about private practice, as the *cause* rather than the cure for personality disorder, is part of a larger, and apparently growing, conception which holds, not that people are "irresponsible" because they are "sick," but that they are sick—sick of themselves and of life—because they are irresponsible, unreliable, "phony."...

To be a "phony" is to be lacking in integrity—to be a bluffer and pretender. By regarding personality disorders to be a result of such moral inadequacy, the stage is set for their recognition and correction by suitably trained non-medical specialists. In other words, the disorders in question are not to be equated with the concept of disease. They are not products of infection, disturbed body chemistry, brain pathology, or malnutrition. They involve biosocial rather than biophysical factors. If this be so, their consideration is more germane to a field like psychology than to that of traditional medicine. This, in brief, is one of the broader implications of Mowrer's thesis.

It might appear as if devoting so much space to a current discussion of the nature of personality disorders is an unwarranted digression in a chapter concerned with the later medieval period. Although it constitutes a digression, it is not unwarranted, for it paves the way for consideration of what in some respects may be regarded as a medieval interest in the kinds of problems mentioned by Mowrer. Put more directly: personality disorder as a function of moral inadequacy was already recognized by Maimonides in the twelfth century. What he published in the 1160s is thus not unrelated to what Mowrer published in the 1960s.

Maimonides and Medieval Psychology

As mentioned early in the present chapter, Maimonides (1135–1204) was among the first medieval scholars to immerse himself in the writings of Aristotle. He was also acquainted with the views of Plato, the Stoics, and the works of contemporary Islamic philosophers. As a practicing physician he possessed professional knowledge of medieval medicine. Moreover, being a rabbi as well, he was a profound student of the Bible and the Talmud. In fact, his detailed commentaries on these sacred texts continue to be consulted. As with Aquinas, his erudition was vast, and also as with Aquinas, his reputation and influence grew with the passage of time. Just as the prestige of Aquinas among Catholic scholars increased in the centuries following his death, so the posthumous prestige of Maimonides among Jewish scholars has risen through the centuries. Incidentally, Aquinas was influenced by the writings of Maimonides and, as noted by Gilby (1960, p. 89), he "always speaks with respect" of his Jewish philosophical predecessor.

Aquinas was born some twenty years after the death of Maimonides. However, in some ways the general drift of scholastic assimilation of Aristotle's psychology is so well summarized by Maimonides that discussion of his teachings will serve to furnish a helpful outline of psychology as viewed by the schoolmen. Such an outline constitutes a convenient means of introducing a summarizing review of the chief trends of medieval psychology; hence the desirability of disregarding chronological sequence.

Preceding references to what Maimonides outlined with respect to the psychology of Aristotle and also with respect to his views of personality disorders as a function of moral inadequacy are not to be construed as references to a separate psychological text in the sense in which Aristotle's *De Anima* is to be so classified. Maimonides failed to consider psychology as a separate field of inquiry in the way in which one might write a treatise on logic or geometry. Instead his psychological teachings are to be found in a treatise primarily concerned with problems of ethics. The treatise consists of eight chapters and was first published in 1168.[4] Written in Arabic, it was intended as an introduction to a section of the Talmud concerned with rabbinic teachings, maxims, sayings, and admonitions calculated to promote ethical well-being. English versions of this Talmudic treatise are usually entitled *Ethics of the Fathers*. Maimonides had no such clarifying title for his introductory monograph to the latter treatise: it is designated as *Eight Chapters* without further elaboration by way of a clarifying subtitle. However, the English translation by J. I. Gorfinkle (1912) is more clarifying: *The Eight Chapters of Maimonides on Ethics—A Psychological and Ethical Treatise.*

Through the centuries the work has aroused the interest of students in many countries as successive translations from the Arabic original rescued it from oblivion. Shortly after publication it was translated into Hebrew and in the course of time it became available in Latin, German, French, Dutch, and English versions. In addition it has been the subject of a large number of critical commentaries. That it merits a place in the history of medieval psychology is indicated by the way in which the work has been characterized in some of these commentaries. Thus (Gorfinkle, 1912, p. 10) it has been variously designated as a "complete system of psychology and ethics," as "the psychological foundation of ethics in general and in particular," as an "ethico-psychological treatise," and as "the celebrated eight chapters on psychology."

---

[4] That the treatise merits consideration in a discussion of the history of psychology during the medieval period was first brought to my attention by Dr. David Winston. I am indebted to his wide scholarship for this important and valued suggestion.

At the very beginning of the first chapter this relationship between psychology and ethics is suggested by reference to "improvement of moral qualities" as a means of "healing the soul." In his opening two paragraphs, as shown in the following quotation (Gorfinkle, 1912, pp. 36–37), Maimonides not only suggests this but also suggests the need for mental-health specialists:

> Know that the human soul is one, but that it has many diversified activities. Some of these activities have, indeed, been called souls, which has given rise to the opinion that man has many souls, as was the belief of the physicians, with the result that the most distinguished of them states in the introduction to his book that there are three souls, the physical, the vital, and the psychical. These activities are called *faculties* and *parts,* so that the phrase "parts of the soul," frequently employed by philosophers, is commonly used. By the world "parts," however, they do not intend to imply that the soul is divided into parts as are bodies, but they merely enumerate the different activities of the soul as being parts of a whole, the union of which makes up the soul.
>
> Thou knowest that the improvement of the moral qualities is brought about by the healing of the soul and its activities. Therefore, just as the physician, who endeavors to cure the human body, must have a perfect knowledge of it in its entirety and its individual parts, just as he must know what causes sickness that it may be avoided, and must also be acquainted with the means by which a patient may be cured, so, likewise, he who tries to cure the soul, wishing to improve the moral qualities, must have a knowledge of the soul in its totality and its parts, must know how to prevent it from becoming diseased, and how to maintain its health.

Some of the key ideas in these introductory paragraphs have their analogues in twentieth-century psychology. For example, the initial reference to "the human soul as one" may be considered to be somewhat related to the concept of an integrated personality. Similarly, the idea of curing the sick soul by doing something about the patient's morals may be construed as an anticipation of the modern psychotherapist's concern with superego factors. It is also well to note that the term "faculty" as a designation for an activity or a *part* of the soul is so qualified as to render what it connotes different from the negative connotation now associated with the term "faculty psychology." For Maimonides, the faculties are not independent powers conceived of as autonomous entities. To paraphrase his formulation: the soul is not divided into separate parts or faculties as are material bodies. He thus avoids the fallacy of reification implicit in the faculty psychology of some early nineteenth-century psychologists for whom faculties were discrete "powers" of the mind. By regarding faculties as "activities of the soul," he is setting the stage for a *process* psychology rather than a faculty psychology.

Although based upon the *De Anima,* the psychological views of Maimonides are not just duplicates of those of Aristotle. This is exemplified by his list of faculties which excludes Aristotle's faculty of motion and, contrary to Aristotle, allows for an imaginative faculty.[5] In other respects his list is like Aristotle's and endows the soul with these faculties: the nutritive, the sensitive, the imaginative, the appetitive, and the rational.

Factor Analysis and Faculty Psychology

Maimonides outlines the characteristics and interrelationships of these five faculties as aspects of the unitary soul. Apparently his concept of a faculty has much in common with the concept of a factor as the latter term is employed by modern factor analysts. This is not to imply that he had any inkling of factor analysis as a statistical technique, but rather to suggest that his notion of a faculty is congruent with the logic implicit in the notion of a factor.

Eysenck (1953) pointed out that long before the mathematics of factor analysis had been developed, its *logical* basis was already operative in the thinking of physicians. By way of illustration, he mentioned the way in which the concept of the syndrome of a disease like tuberculosis emerged through the centuries. Even before the existence of the tubercle bacillus was suspected, there was knowledge of phthisis or consumption as a disease. It was identified by such symptoms as loss of weight, respiratory distress, blood in the sputum, depleted energy reserves, and other symptoms whose concurrence came to be regarded as the syndrome of consumption. The fact of this concurrence of symptoms called for explanation; for, in the words of Eysenck (1953, p. 111): "No symptom by itself is decisive (none is factorially pure), but the syndrome (factor) suggests one underlying cause which gives rise to the various symptoms, and which may sometime be identified." Eventually, with the discovery of the offending bacillus, this cause was identified. It became the essential factor in the syndrome. Without its presence the disease could not develop; but even when it was present the disease was not an inevitable consequence. The bacillus was a necessary but not a sufficient cause; hence accessory factors along with the essential one had to be included in the final account of the etiology of the syndrome. The logic of those engaged in this quest for relevant factors was not different from the logic of psychologists in search of the factors responsible for intelligent behavior, creative thinking, linguistic skills, musical competence, or any other distinctive phase of human achievement.

What Maimonides had to say about faculties of the soul can now be considered in the light of what was just said about the logic of factor analysis. By way of illustration, his discussion of the nutritive faculty is particularly clarifying, for he enumerates "seven faculties" as constitutive of this single faculty. To revert to the preceding analogy: if eating be viewed as a "syndrome" of behavior, then food might be called the essential factor, and

---

[5] Maimonides regards motion as a function of the appetitive faculty. We move toward things we desire and away from things we long to avoid.

what the following quotation (Gorfinkle, 1912, p. 40) lists as "seven faculties" might be classified as accessory factors:

> Returning to our subject of the faculties of the soul, let me say that the nutritive faculty consists of (1) the power of attracting nourishment to the body, (2) the retention of the same, (3) its digestion (assimilation), (4) the repulsion of superfluities, (5) growth, (6) procreation,[6] and (7) the differentiation of the nutritive juices that are necessary for sustenance from those which are to be expelled. The detailed discussion of these seven faculties—the means of which and how they perform their functions . . . belongs to the science of medicine, and need not be taken up here.

Maimonides also avoids "detailed discussion" of some of the other faculties. In his *Eight Chapters* he tends to confine himself to those psychological topics which he regards as having implications for ethics.[7] Thus he glosses over the faculty of sensation by merely listing the names of the five senses without further elaboration such as one finds in Aristotle. He defines imagination quite briefly as "that faculty which retains impressions perceptible to the mind, after they have ceased to affect directly the senses which conceived them." Its role in fantasy production is illustrated by showing how fragments of these retained impressions may be combined into such "impossibilities" as "an iron ship floating in the air" or "an animal with a thousand eyes."

Nature of Appetitive and Reasoning Faculties

Like his Greek predecessors, Maimonides makes no provision for a faculty of emotion. This is not an oversight. Instead it is due to the fact that the concept of faculty as "an activity of the soul" was restricted to mental functions amenable to a modicum of direct control. Within limits one can choose what to touch or hear or look at or imagine or think about; but emotion is not subject to choice in this sense. One is overwhelmed by fear or anger or joy. Such emotions sweep over the individual in spite of himself as events prove threatening or frustrating or gratifying. They are functions of antecedent wishes or desires. A football victory brings joy to

---

6 Including procreation in this list may seem strange upon first thought. What is intended here is a reminder of the need for food in order to nourish the developing fetus. Maimonides is merely availing himself of Aristotle's analysis of the "nutritive faculty" as discussed in the *De Anima*, where it is pointed out that "nutrition and reproduction are due to one and the same faculty." Aristotle clarifies this by describing "the process of nutrition" as "the agent in generation, i.e., not the generation of the individual fed but the reproduction of another like it." (Cf. R. McKeon [ed.], 1957, Vol. I, pp. 182–183).

7 More elaboration of some of the systemic implications of psychological topics is to be found in his *The Guide of the Perplexed* (translated by M. Friedlander, 1881).

partisans of the winning team, gloom to partisans of the losers, and leaves the neutral spectators unmoved. Emotions hinge upon success or failure in realizing one's hopes, ambitions, strivings, or endeavors. In technical language, they may be described as functions of conation or what Maimonides called the appetitive faculty. He recognized this dependence on conation by referring to the faculty in these words (Gorfinkle, 1912, pp. 42–43):

> The *appetitive* is that faculty by which a man desires, or loathes a thing, and from which there arise the following activities: the pursuit of an object or flight from it, inclination and avoidance, anger and affection, fear and courage, cruelty and compassion, love and hate, and many other similar psychic qualities.

In agreement with Aristotle, Maimonides regarded reason or the rational faculty as unique to human beings. In outlining its functions he made a distinction between reason applied to "practical" affairs as contrasted with reason concerned with "theoretical" ones. The former has to do with mechanical or technological problems, while the latter, being "speculative" or more abstract, comes to grips with "the sciences in general." The distinction in question may not be unrelated to the distinction between mechanical and abstract intelligence recognized by E. L. Thorndike and others early in the present century. However, Maimonides limits the scope of the mechanical function of reason to the manual skills needed by artisans and technicians or surgeons. Such skills are one manifestation of the practical reason. Another way in which the practical reason can manifest itself is in working out a fruitful attack on a mechanical problem. One may be devoid of surgical skill and yet be able to suggest an appropriate maneuver for the solution of a surgical problem. An architect can plan a house, foresee certain consequences, know the kind of building materials to select, and be able to direct the work of the carpenters and other artisans even though he lacks their mechanical skills. He would possess what Maimonides called the "intellectual power" to cope with a series of practical problems. At all events, this seems to be the meaning of the closing sentence in the following quotation (Gorfinkle, 1912, pp. 43–44):

> *Reason,* that faculty peculiar to man, enables him to understand, reflect, acquire knowledge of the sciences, and to discriminate between proper and improper actions. Its functions are partly *practical* and partly *speculative* (theoretical), the *practical* being, in turn, either *mechanical* or *intellectual.* By means of the *speculative* power, man knows things as they really are, and which, by their nature are not subject to change. These are called the sciences in general. The mechanical power is that by which the arts, such as architecture, agriculture, medicine, and navigation are acquired. The intellectual power is that by which one, when he intends to do an act, reflects upon what he has premeditated, considers the possibility of performing it, and, if he thinks it possible, decides how it should be done.

In his further discussion of reason, Maimonides anticipated an issue that became the subject of heated controversy in the seventeenth century. This, as mentioned in Chapter 1, p. 10, is often called the empiricist-rationalist controversy. Had Maimonides been engaged in the debates, he would have sided with the rationalists by maintaining that some knowledge, such as the axioms of geometry, is innate. He actually employs the word "inborn" in this connection and contrasts it with "the acquired intellect."

Constitutional, Humoral, and Cerebral Influences

This recognition of "inborn" factors did not extend to an endorsement of the doctrine of original sin. In fact, there is a definite statement (Gorfinkle, 1912, p. 58) to the effect that "no man is born with an innate virtue or vice." This is qualified, however, by recognition of individual differences in constitutional predispositions to certain modes of behavior; for later on he has this to say (p. 85):

> It is impossible for man to be born endowed by nature from his very birth with either virtue or vice, just as it is impossible that he should be born skilled by nature in any particular art. It is possible, however, that through natural causes he may from birth be so constituted as to have a predilection for a particular virtue or vice, so that he will more readily practise it than any other.

By way of illustration of such constitutional predispositions, Maimonides mentions temperamental differences in the way of courageous versus craven attitudes and of cognitive differences in terms of speed of learning, ease of understanding, and excellence of memory. Such differences are attributed to inherent differences in the relative preponderance of one of the four humors, whose psychophysiological significance had come to be stressed since the time of Galen. Thus, difficulties in learning and remembering, Maimonides pointed out, are due to the fact that the brain of the "phlegmatic man" has too much humidity as contrasted with the dryness of the efficient learner's brain. Similarly, the person whose blood is "warmer than is necessary" will have less difficulty learning to behave courageously than one "the temperament of whose heart is colder than it should be."

However, Maimonides does not regard such humoral differences as insuperable biochemical barriers to personal improvement. He is careful to state that the "phlegmatic man" if properly instructed can make intellectual progress even though the learning will be difficult for him. He is also confident about doing something for the man "naturally inclined towards cowardice and fear." By means of "proper training" along with "great exertion" one can "without doubt" change him into "a brave man." A man's future is thus not predestined by his humoral equipment. The final outcome is contingent upon what he learns and experiences in the course of his life. Both nature and nurture are significant sources of influence. This, in short, is the stand taken by Maimonides as expressed in the idiom of today's psychology.

What we have here is an essentially naturalistic approach to psychology— an effort to understand mental life in terms of biological and experiential influences. Man's fate, Maimonides contended, is not governed by the stars. There is vehement repudiation of "the absurd ideas of astrologers" and what they falsely assert. Of course in the light of modern teachings his medieval acceptance of Galenic teachings also belongs to the realm of "absurd ideas." Nevertheless, in terms of the broad underlying conceptual framework responsible for such acceptance there is a naturalistic orientation; for the notion of behavior being affected by humors or fluids in the body is not altogether absurd. As a concept such a notion might be classified as an early, admittedly crude beginning of what eventually became the modern recognition of a relationship between temperament and endocrine juices and between brain functions and neurochemistry. In other words, in the long-range perspective of history there may be an ideational thread linking medieval talk about black bile, phlegm, blood, and yellow bile and modern talk about thyroxin, nor-adrenin, serotonin, and acetylcholine.

What was just referred to as a naturalistic orientation is also reflected by what Maimonides has to say about learning and memory. As mentioned on a previous page, he points out (Gorfinkle, 1912, p. 85) that a man "whose brain matter is clear and not overloaded with fluids, finds it much easier to learn, remember, and understand things that the phlegmatic man whose brain is encumbered with a great deal of humidity." Even though this is manifestly crude physiological psychology, it merits considera- tion as additional evidence in support of what was previously referred to regarding medieval endorsement of Aristotle's teachings. This endorsement was not altogether devoid of a modicum of independent thinking. In the present instance, for example, there is a rejection of Aristotle's dictum con- cerning the function of the brain. As will be recalled, Aristotle failed to recognize its importance for psychology by thinking of it as a kind of thermo- static mechanism serving to prevent the body from becoming overheated. This, of course, is crude physiology. It is not only crude but wrong. Con- sequently, in referring to the brain as the organ which enables one "to learn, remember, and understand things," Maimonides was thus not only sponsor- ing a more correct teaching but also demonstrating a resistance to uncritical, blanket endorsement of Aristotle.

"Diseases of the Soul" and Their Cure

Much of what Maimonides has to say about the "diseases of the soul" and their cure involves endorsement of Aristotle's principle of the golden mean. As mentioned in Chapter 4, pp. 93–95, this principle has to do with the cultivation of virtue by way of enhancing praiseworthy character development. The gist of Aristotle's thought is summarized as follows by Maimonides (Gorfinkle, 1912, pp. 54–55):

> Good deeds are such as are equibalanced, maintaining the mean between two equally bad extremes, the *too much* and the *too little*. Virtues are psychic conditions and dispositions which are mid-way between two reprehensible extremes, one of which is characterized by an exaggeration, the other by a deficiency. To illustrate, abstemiousness is a disposition which adopts a mid-course between inordinate passion and total insensibility to pleasure. Abstemiousness, then, is a proper rule of conduct, and psychic disposition which gives rise to it is an ethical quality; but inordinate passion, the extreme of excess, and total insensibility to enjoyment, the extreme of deficiency, are both absolutely pernicious.

Such extremes are classified as "moral imperfections" and are symptomatic of the sick soul; hence "those whose souls become ill should consult the sages, the moral physicians," for help in order to be "restored to their normal condition" (Gorfinkle, 1912, p. 52). It should now be evident that what Mowrer regards as the core of functional mental disorder has much in common with this twelfth-century teaching. Both Maimonides and Mowrer equate mental disease with moral inadequacy and mental health with moral excellence. Moreover, in stressing the importance of personal responsibility for one's acts of moral choice, Mowrer might have found support in this statement by Maimonides (Gorfinkle, 1912, p. 91):

> Man has become the only being in the world who possesses a characteristic which no other being has in common with him. What is this characteristic? It is that by and of himself man can distinguish between good and evil, and do that which he pleases, with absolutely no restraint.

This ability to "distinguish between good and evil" is not a reference to an innate sense of right and wrong. On the contrary, Maimonides is careful to add, just because man is free to do "just as he chooses, it becomes necessary to teach him the ways of righteousness. . . . "

Maimonides also refers to the cure of the sick soul in the context of teaching. The "moral physician" acting as psychotherapist must do something about his patient's immoral behavior by inducing or teaching him to change his habits. To achieve the golden mean, the patient is first persuaded to overcompensate for his moral defect and then taught to compensate for the overcompensation. The suggestion comes from Aristotle, but the following example is supplied by Maimonides (Gorfinkle, 1912, p. 59):

> Let us take . . . the case of a man in whose soul there has developed a disposition of great avarice on account of which he deprives himself of every comfort in life, and which, by the way, is one of the most detestable of defects, and an immoral

act. . . . If we wish to cure this sick man, we must not command him merely to practice deeds of generosity, for that would be as ineffective as a physician trying to cure a patient consumed by a burning fever by administering mild medicines, which treatment would be inefficacious. We must, however, induce him to squander so often, and to repeat his acts of profusion so continuously until that propensity which was the cause of his avarice has totally disappeared. Then, when he reaches the point where he is about to become a squanderer, we must teach him to moderate his profusion, and tell him to continue with deeds of generosity, and to watch out with due care lest he relapse either into lavishness or niggardliness.

In the language of current psychiatry, the preceding example refers to a personality disorder. In his discussion of the disorder, Maimonides employs a medical rather than a theological vocabulary. He refers to the man as "sick" and needing to be cured and thus reveals a naturalistic approach to the problem. There is no talk about demonic possession, exorcism, talismans, magic incantations, or other "medieval" notions. Furthermore, despite the medical vocabulary employed, the problem is viewed as a psychological one involving, as it does, a treatment technique for transforming an avaricious "disposition" into a generous propensity by means of induced behavioral changes. The "moral physician" has to try to "cure" his patient by suitable application of principles of learning as involved in the transformation of attitudes responsible for maladaptive behavior; hence his psychotherapy suggests learning theory rather than medical theory.

This interpretation is neither forced nor farfetched. It is merely expressing, what is implicit in the writings of Maimonides in the parlance of today's psychology. In brief, we moderns may be catching up with and elaborating some of the insights of medieval Maimonides when (1) we regard personality disorder as rooted in a disturbed ethical value system; and (2) when we view psychotherapy, not as a quasi-mystical relationship, but as a means of helping patients *learn* to overcome neurotic hindrances to personal efficency as ethically mature, responsible adults.

Medievalism and the Judeo-Christian Tradition

A dominant theme in the writings of Maimonides has to do with the importance of reason or intellectual growth in promoting human welfare. In one passage (1881 ed., Vol. III, p. 294) he urges those who "desire to attain human perfection" to think of the intellect as the ruling power of a king. For him it "is greater than any earthly king." In metaphoric language he glorifies its sovereignty: "The king that cleaves to us and embraces us is the Intellect that influences us, and forms the link between us and God." Moreover, the concept of God is even more dominant in his thinking than that of reason.

This is another way of saying that, for him, reason was not enough to guide the quest for the good life. It had to be reason as influenced by "perfect faith" in God's teachings as revealed to Moses and the Prophets and as embodied in Bible and Talmud. Both revelation and reason were held to be sources of truth and enlightenment. Maimonides also held that, properly interpreted, almost all of what is revealed in the sacred books will command itself to reason. However, to achieve proper interpretation it is important to make a distinction between the literal and figurative meaning of many passages. Unless this is done a reader will be needlessly "perplexed." The object in writing his *The Guide of the Perplexed* was to dissipate such perplexity. In his own words (1881 ed., Vol. I, pp. 6–7):

> The object of this treatise is to enlighten a religious man who has been trained to believe in the truth of our holy Law, who conscientiously fulfils his moral and religious duties, and at the same time has been successful in his philosophical studies. Human reason has impelled him to abide within its sphere; and on the other hand, he is disturbed by the literal interpretation of the Law, and by ideas formed by himself or received from others, in connection with those homonymous, metaphorical, or hybrid expressions. Hence he is lost in perplexity and anxiety. . . .
>
> This work has also a second object in view. It seeks to explain certain obscure figures which occur in the Prophets, and are not distinctly characterised as being figures. Ignorant and superficial readers take them in a literal, not in a figurative sense. Even well-informed persons are bewildered if they treat these passages in their literal signification, but they are entirely relieved of their perplexity when we explain the figure, or merely suggest that the terms are figurative.

In line with the latter suggestion, one finds that with reference to the story of creation as found in Genesis Maimonides is disposed to regard its language as allegorical, figurative, and metaphorical. There is no need to regard it as a literal account. Instead it is better to realize that creation "has been treated in metaphors in order that the uneducated may comprehend it according to the measure of their faculties and the feebleness of their apprehension, while educated persons may take it in a different sense" (1881 ed., Vol. I, p. 12).

Despite such interpretative freedom Maimonides himself insists upon a literal interpretation of the opening sentence of the Bible referring to the world's *beginning* by God's creative act. One reason for considering it here is that it constitutes an especially clear instance of medieval resistance to the authority of Aristotle. In opposition to Aristotle's view of the "eternity of the universe," Maimonides held "that the theory of the Creation, as taught in Scripture, contains nothing that is impossible; and that all those philosophical arguments which seem to disprove our view contain weak points which make them inconclusive, and render the attack on our view untenable" (1881 ed., Vol. II, p. 76).

A second reason for introducing it is to call attention to its relationship to medieval dogmatism. In other words, Maimonides in his advocacy of the doctrine of Creation raised questions which he answered by dogmatic references to the inscrutable will of God rather than in terms of his announced intention to remove perplexity by an appeal to reason. The conflict between the latter doctrine and Aristotle's view had momentous consequences. There was a threat to the foundations of religion in acceptance of this view. As Maimonides saw it (1881 ed., Vol. II, p. 119):

> If we were to acept the Eternity of the Universe as taught by Aristotle, that everything in the Universe is the result of fixed laws, that Nature does not change, and that there is nothing supernatural, we should necessarily be in opposition to the foundation of our religion, we should disbelieve all miracles and signs, and certainly reject all hopes and fears derived from Scripture, unless the miracles are also explained figuratively.

Under the circumstances Maimonides concludes that in this instance "we take the text of the Bible literally, and say that it teaches us a truth which we cannot prove." At this point it seems that reason abdicates and faith takes over. At all events, he proceeds to justify endorsement of belief in Creation in this arbitrary fashion (1881 ed., Vol. II, pp. 119–120):

> Accepting the Creation, we find that miracles are possible, that Revelation is possible, and that every difficulty in this question is removed. We might be asked, Why has God inspired a certain person and not another? . . . Why has He commanded this, and forbidden that? . . . and why has He not made the commandments and the prohibitions part of our nature, if it was His object that we should live in accordance with them? We answer to all these questions: He willed it so; or His wisdom decided so.

It should be evident that this is tantamount to substituting dogma for evidence. Actually, whenever he can, Maimonides does introduce what he deems to be sound reasons for particular Biblical injunctions. Nevertheless, as the preceding quotation indicates, in the last analysis these injunctions are to be obeyed even in the absence of rational justification for them. This is justification by faith rather than reason. In general, this solution to the problem of conflict between religious tradition and the findings of science was like the one proposed by Aquinas a generation later. Both Maimonides and Aquinas endorsed a scientific or naturalistic approach to the study of mind and matter, and yet they both were reluctant to permit such study to displace or usurp the claims of revelation. It was this Judaeo-Christian "solution" which medievalism bequeathed to the postmedieval world. Unfortunately, in some respects it proved to be a burdensome legacy for science in general and for scientific psychology in particular.

References

Brett, G. S. *A History of Psychology,* Vol. II. London: George Allen and Unwin, Ltd., 1912.

Cohen, I. B. "History of Science: The Imagination of Nature," in L. White (ed.). *Frontiers of Knowledge in the Study of Man.* New York: Harper and Brothers, 1956.

Copleston, F. C. *A History of Philosophy,* Vol. III. Garden City, New York: Doubleway and Company, Image Books, 1963.

Crombie, A. C. *Medieval and Early Modern Science,* Vol. 1, 2nd ed. Garden City, New York: Doubleday and Company, 1959.

Davis, H. W. C. "Robert Grosseteste," in *Encyclopaedia Britannica,* Vol. VII, 11th ed., 1910.

English, H. B., and English, A. C. *A Comprehensive Dictionary of Psychological and Psychoanalytical Terms.* New York: Longmans, Green and Company, 1958.

Eysenck, H. J. "The Logical Basis of Factor Analysis," *American Psychology,* 1953, *8,* 105–114.

Fröbes, J. *Lehrbuch der Experimentellen Psychologie,* Vols. I and II. Freiburg: Herder and Company, 1923.

Garrison, F. H. *An Introduction to the History of Medicine,* 4th ed. Philadelphia: W. B. Saunders Company, 1929.

Gibson, W. C. *Young Endeavor.* Springfield, Illinois: Charles C. Thomas, 1958.

Gilby, T. *Saint Thomas Aquinas–Philosophical Texts.* (Translated by Thomas Gilby.) New York and London: Oxford University Press, 1960.

Gorfinkle, J. I. *The Eight Chapters of Maimonides on Ethics—A Psychological and Ethical Treatise.* New York: Columbia University Press, 1912.

Guilford, J. P. "An Informational View of Mind," *Journal of Psychological Researches,* 1962, *6,* 1–10.

Lindworsky, J. *Experimental Psychology.* (Translated by H. De Silva.) New York: The Macmillan Company, 1931.

McKeon, R. (ed.). *Selections from Medieval Philosophers,* Vol. I. New York: Charles Scribner's Sons, 1957.

Maimonides, M. *The Guide of the Perplexed.* (Translated by M. Friedlander.) New York: Hebrew Publishing Company, 1881.

Marmor, J. "The Feeling of Superiority: An Occupational Hazard in the Practice of Psychoanalysis," *American Journal of Psychiatry,* 1953, *110,* 370–376.

Moore, T. V. *The Driving Forces of Human Nature.* New York: Grune and Stratton, 1948.

Mowrer, O. H. "Payment of Repayment?" *American Psychologist,* 1963, *18,* 577–580.

Murchison, C. (ed.). *The Case For and Against Psychical Belief.* Worcester: Clark University Press, 1927.

Murphy, G. "Trends in the Study of Extrasensory Perception," *American Psychologist.* 1958, *13,* 69–76.

Rosenthal, R. "On the Social Psychology of the Psychological Experiment: The Experimenter's Hypothesis as Unintended Determinant of Experimental Results," *American Scientist,* 1963, *51,* 268–283.

Schmeidler, G. R., and Murphy, G. "The Influence of Belief and Disbelief in ESP upon Individual Scoring Levels," *Journal of Experimental Psychology,* 1946, *36,* 271–276.

Smith, D. E., and Ginsburg, J. "From Numbers to Numerals and from Numerals to Computation," in J. R. Newman (ed.). *The World of Mathematics,* Vol. I. New York: Simon and Schuster, 1956.

PART  III

ON HISTORICAL SIGNIFICANCE AND PSYCHOLOGY'S KEY PROBLEMS

8

History as Selective Perception: Some Crucial Problems

THOSE ACCUSTOMED TO THINK OF HISTORY as being a fairly straightforward chronological narrative will probably regard the subject matter of this chapter as well as that of the immediately succeeding ones as a drastic deviation from an anticipated time sequence. After chapters devoted to the earlier and later medieval periods of psychology's history, one would be justified in expecting the next ones to deal with the Renaissance and early modern periods. Instead, however, there will be a rather extensive interpolation of material belonging both to the recent past of psychology as well as to its continuing contemporary trends before a treatment of its postmedieval history. In a way such interpolation constitutes an elaborate digression, but one which it is hoped will pave the way for easier and enriched understanding of the significance of salient postmedieval developments.

The acquisition of historical perspective is not just a routine affair of fixing names, dates, and important events in orderly chronological sequence. Often it calls for departure from such a sequence by the advisability of pointing out the relationship between some current problem and some remote historical episode. The preceding chapters were replete with such departures; hence there is no need to clarify this point by the introduction of specific examples. Still, what may require clarification in connection with this matter of historical perspective is the need for such a perspective for the student of psychology. One might ask: Is a perspective of this kind essential for genuine understanding of the nature of psychology as science? E. B. Titchener (1867–1927), pupil of Wundt and leading psychologist at Cornell University for some thirty-five years, in one of his last treatises answered the question as follows (1929, p. 83): [1]

---

[1] The passage being quoted is taken from Titchener's *Systematic Psychology: Prolegomena*, a posthumous volume prepared for publication by Professor A. P. Weld. The book was published in 1929, but the chapter containing this passage had been completed in 1923.

There is . . . no science which stands in greater need than psychology of historical perspective and historical commentary. For the titular problems with which psychology as science has to grapple have in large measure come down to it from a pre-scientific past. Our text-books speak of the psychology of perception and the psychology of thought, and seek to safeguard themselves by the formal announcement that psychology, of course, has nothing to do with a theory of knowledge: whereas the terms of their exposition are filled full of philosophical reference, and will be assimilated by the ordinary reader, if not to a living philosophy, at any rate to so much of dead philosophy as common sense embalms. We cannot undo our past; but we can prevent the evils which flow from the ignoring of it. Historical perspective, combined with a working conception of science at large, must guide the steps and will assure the progress of those who would rightly comprehend the facts and laws of mind.

Some of these "titular problems," to use Titchener's phrase, have already been alluded to in incidental fashion. The present chapter, along with Chapters 9 and 10, will deal with such problems more directly and in some detail. Before they are introduced, however, it seems desirable to justify the break with chronological sequence entailed by their consideration at this point. Such justification involves an understanding of the nature of history as a scholarly enterprise. This is almost like asking what historians are trying to accomplish or what is the purpose of history. To deal with such questions exhaustively would require a separate volume. Fortunately, for present purposes it will be sufficient to deal with them in outline.

The Nature of the Historian's Task

Some of the issues about to be discussed might well have been introduced in the very first chapter, for they have to do with the nature of the historian's task as he undertakes to supply an account of men and events of bygone eras. However, in some ways they lend themselves to more facile exposition in the light of what has already been included in the preceding chapters. In the main the latter chapters were devoted to discussions of the bearing of Greek and medieval philosophy and science on the early modern science that was to lead to the gradual emergence of the foundations of modern psychology. These discussions were not at all complete. Only relatively few of the many men who might have been mentioned were referred to in these discussions. More were excluded than were included. Furthermore, the scope of the discussions was largely restricted to the occidental world. Almost no mention was made of ancient oriental views of the nature of man, even though there are records of early Hindu, Zoroastrian, Buddhist, and Confucian teachings regarding topics which some would deem to be of psychological relevance. Can such neglect be justified? On what basis is the historian to decide what to include and what to exclude? Is it possible to write the history of any subject without being confronted with this problem of selection? These are crucial questions.

As a matter of fact, no two histories of a particular subject concern themselves with precisely the same topics or treat a given topic in identical fashion. With respect to psychology some histories will devote little or no space to the views of Plato or Aristotle or Plotinus or St. Augustine or Aquinas or Maimonides, while others, like the present one, may consider their views at length. Some will have a great deal to say about the history of intelligence testing while others may ignore the topic. The same holds true for other topics like space perception, theories of color vision, cortical localization, psychophysics, defense mechanisms, eidetic imagery, hypnosis, conditioning, and all the other topics likely to be included in a textbook of general psychology. Each such topic has a history, and yet its history is not necessarily to be found in a history of psychology. Quite obviously, historians differ among themselves in reaching decisions concerned with the inclusion or exclusion of given past events.

Although history deals with the past, not every past event is of historical significance. In fact, as a little reflection will show, only relatively few such events come to be endowed with this kind of significance. For example, within the past ten years lectures on psychology were delivered in hundreds of classrooms, psychological experiments were performed in hundreds of laboratories, psychological tests were administered in hundreds of clinics, and thousands of psychological books and articles were published.[2] Each of these lectures, experiments, tests, and publications in point of time is now a past event; but this does not mean that a future historian of psychology will not be doing justice to his subject unless he familiarizes himself with each one. Moreover, what is being said here regarding the history of psychology holds true for any kind of history, whether of Norway or architecture or botany. Every historian, irrespective of the nature and scope of his subject, is thus confronted with this problem of selection. The mere fact that an event lies in the past is not enough to justify its inclusion in a history. But what criteria should be employed? How shall we determine which events to discuss and which events to ignore?

The latter question becomes increasingly acute the closer one comes to the modern period, when writings of psychological import increase in bulk until it becomes impossible for any one person to cope with the avalanche of publications. This is especially true of twentieth-century psychology but is also valid in lesser degree for the preceding centuries, particularly those

---

2 According to a recent estimate made under the auspices of the American Psychological Association, there are about a thousand journals of direct or indirect interest to psychologists. Furthermore, some four hundred institutions have separate technical reports of psychological relevance. As yet there has been no estimate of the average annual output of books likely to command the professional attention of psychologists.

following the medieval period. For this reason, by way of introduction to the history of postmedieval psychology, it seems advisable to consider this broader question in some detail even though it entails what some might regard as an elaboration of the obvious. In this instance, exploration of the "obvious" may prove revealing.

What Constitutes Historical Knowledge?

Concern with the nature of historical knowledge is sometimes regarded as more the province of a special branch of philosophy known as the philosophy of history than as a concern of professional historians. This state of affairs is akin to the relationship between the philosophy of science on the one hand and the work in individual scientific specialties on the other. In general, historians write their books without giving explicit attention to the presuppositions of their historical inquiries. They seem content to let the results speak for themselves, just as scientists publish their laboratory findings without bothering to explain what they happen to regard as the nature of scientific knowledge. As the historian Fritz Stern (1956, p. 14) has stated: "History is deeply imbedded in philosophy and . . . the historian senses this, even when he refuses to deal with it explicitly." By way of additional clarification Stern referred to an address by a British historian who admitted to his audience that he was going to avoid what he described as "the fundamental problem of the nature of historical knowledge" and then added: "I am in good company if I evade a master problem of this kind, since nearly all English historians have evaded it."

One aspect of this "master problem" has to do with the accuracy of a historian's account of a given episode in history. In terms of military history, will British and French historians upon examining relevant documents write substantially equivalent descriptions of the Battle of Waterloo? Will German and French historians agree on the causes of the Franco-Prussian War? In terms of religious history, do Catholic and Protestant historians agree in their reports of the causes and consequences of the Reformation? Of course well-trained historians strive to eliminate personal bias in their evaluation of historical records and to adhere to the canons of scholarly or scientific objectivity.

According to Leopold von Ranke (1795–1886), distinguished for his efforts to safeguard and enhance the standards of historical scholarship, the task of the historian (Stern, 1956, p. 57) is "to show what actually happened" ("*wie es eigentlich gewesen ist*"). This objective of "telling it like it was" is laudable but in a literal sense almost impossible of achievement. Among other suggestions, Ranke urged that historians strive to obtain their data from documents giving the reports of eyewitnesses. However, as every psychologist knows, eyewitnesses may disagree on what took place and may be in error even when they agree. This has been demonstrated in laboratory studies of perceptual accuracy and, more tragically, in studies of court cases involving what turned out to be miscarriages of justice. Back in 1932, for example, Edwin M. Borchard, a member of the faculty of the Yale Law School, wrote a book in which he presented accounts of sixty-five "criminal prosecutions and convictions of completely innocent people." In twenty-nine of the cases, mistaken identification by eyewitnesses was solely responsible for the convictions. Moreover, what merits special emphasis is the fact that in one of these cases seventeen witnesses identified the wrong man as the one who had been passing forged checks. It should thus be obvious that Ranke's advice to historians will not guarantee freedom from error and bias. Documentary reports of eyewitnesses must still be subjected to the historian's critical scrutiny and evaluated in terms of what is known of the fallibility of human testimony. What eyewitnesses have to report regarding what took place as they observed a stage magician's performance may be very different from what the magician himself would report were he to be persuaded to reveal what actually occurred on the stage. He is in a better position to describe "what actually happened" than the eyewitnesses.

The difficulty or impossibility of writing history in accordance with Ranke's standards of strict objectivity so as to present a trustworthy account of the past with "absolute" accuracy is such that Charles A. Beard (1874–1948) once referred to such standards as a "noble dream." He even cited instances of Ranke's failure to make the dream come true. For example, according to Beard (quoted in Stern, 1956, p. 318):

> Ranke could write history, certainly, with a majestic air of impartiality and say that he had written as it actually had been. For example, he could write of popes in a manner pleasing to both Catholics and Protestants of the upper classes. He doubtless believed that he was telling this history of the popes as it actually had been. Did he realize his claim? There is stark validity in the Jesuit objection that Ranke avoided the chief actuality of the story: Was the papacy actually what it affirmed itself to be, "an institution of the Son of God made man," or was it a combination of false claims, craft, and manmade power? How could Ranke avoid that question and yet even claim to be writing history as it actually was?

In place of Ranke's notion of historical absolutism, Beard advocated historical relativism by recognizing the selective nature of the historian's task. Confronted with a mass of documents and reports to be found in historical archives, he has to decide which ones contain data relevant to the kind of history he is writing. His viewpoint determines selection of some items and rejection of others. Such selectivity or choice introduces a subjective factor into his scholarly endeavors. In the words of the historian, H. Holborn (quoted in Stern, 1956, p. 25): "The central problems of a historical methodology or epistemology hinge upon the fact that an objective knowledge of the past can only be obtained through the subjective experience of the scholar."

What this means can be demonstrated by considering the historian's responsibility in undertaking to write a biography such as the life of Lincoln or Alexander Hamilton or John Stuart Mill. A multiplicity of questions confront the biographer: what shall he include with respect to his subject's ancestry, preschool years, food preferences and aversions, favorite toys, childhood anxieties, schoolboy fights, church attendance, sermons heard, newspapers and books read, high-school friends, childhood illnesses, adolescent day-dreams, etc., etc.? The finished biography will be a reflection of what the biographer regarded as significantly related to the man's character development and achievements. Had the man himself been prevailed upon to write his memoirs, the resulting autobiography would likely have included items ignored by the biographer and ignored items which had been included. How a man sees his own life in retrospect may thus be very different from the way his biographer sees it. Both accounts may be factual, but will differ in the list of facts chosen as well as in evaluation of their import. The facts as such can be classified as objective, but the determinants of their choice and evaluation are subjective. This applies to all historical writing and renders the writing of history and biography more art than science.

Is History a Science?

Whether history as such is to be regarded as a science has sometimes been questioned. There are no laws of history as there are laws of physics, chemistry, or astronomy. Historical episodes are treated as unique events and not so much as representatives of a class of similar events. The Rosetta stone, to cite a simple example, in the eyes of the historians is more than a specimen for a petrologist. With its parallel Greek and ancient Egyptian inscriptions, its discovery in 1799 supplied a key that made possible the deciphering of Egyptian writing; hence its historical importance. To appreciate the significance of voyages of discovery, the historian has to study each one separately. Knowledge of the route taken by Magellan does not supply information regarding the voyages of the Cabots or Columbus. Each such voyage in historical perspective has to be studied in its own right. The same applies to the individual careers of historical personages like Julius Caesar, Abraham Lincoln, or Charlemagne. No two historically eminent scientists reflect identical biographies. The life of Darwin was different from that of Pasteur and that of Priestley from that of Lavoisier.

The historian does not present the world with laws or formulas by which eminence is to be achieved, discoveries made, political success attained, or military and economic disaster prevented. At best it might be said that, despite the uniqueness of each historical episode, study of a series of similar episodes may provide suggestions or principles to guide further action. Thus a study of financial panics may enable the economic historian to suggest ways of warding off future panics, just as the study of highway accidents results in suggestions for improving highway safety. War departments engage military historians on the assumption that knowledge of the history of specific campaigns may have some bearing on military strategy of the future. However, as the historian R. Hofstadter (quoted in Stern, 1956, p. 360) has pointed out, such examples of the possible practical lessons that history might be said to teach are not so much examples of scientific laws as they are instances of the way in which historical analysis of given kinds of societal experience may give rise to "workable tools for the performance of certain tasks." A striking instance is supplied by Hofstadter: following the 1923 Tokyo earthquake, the government of Japan cabled Charles A. Beard for help. The cable read, "Bring your knowledge of disaster."

Mainfestly, the Japanese officials believed that a scholarly historian like Beard would be familiar with the administrative tasks incident to facilitating recovery from the devastation wrought by an earthquake. In effect the cable stated that a historian might be expected to know how other communities had dealt with the consequences of such a catastrophe, since the pages of history are replete with accounts of the ravages of war, plague, hurricanes, floods, and kindred upheavals. From this viewpoint it seems appropriate to expect a historian to have special "knowledge of disaster."

However, from another viewpoint it might be regarded as a questionable expectation. The issue under consideration has to do with the effects of disaster on human behavior, consequently, might it not be more appropriate to call on a psychologist for help? To put this a little differently: can the historian understand the behavior of the human beings whose lives he studies without turning to the psychologist for guidance and clarification? Can one understand the motives of a Savonarola or a Cromwell or a Thomas Jefferson or any other key historical personage without preliminary study of the psychology of motivation as presented in our textbooks? If so, does this not make psychology a prerequisite or foundation for historical studies? This broad question was once considered by the philosopher W. Windelband (1848–1915) and answered in the negative with particular reference to the possible dependence of history on technical psychology. As he saw it (1921, p. 280):

This is not at all true of scientific psychology, which as to its method belongs to the natural sciences, and in its content is an inquiry, apart from its value, into the uniform movements of the psychic elements. Its theories are no nearer to the interest of historical research than those of other sciences are. The psychology which the historian uses is a very different thing. It is the psychology of daily life: the practical psychology of a knowledge and understanding of men, the psychology of the poet and the great statesman—the psychology that cannot be taught and learned, but it is a gift of intuitive intelligence, and in its highest form a genius for judging contemporary life and posterity. This sort of psychology is an art, not a science.

Is History Idiographic or Nomothetic?

Windelband's distinction between "scientific psychology" on the one hand and the "practical psychology of a knowledge and understanding of men" on the other has come to influence contemporary psychology. It is reflected in present-day discussions of *idiographic* as opposed to *nomothetic* approaches to psychological problems. These terms were originally proposed by Windelband as convenient designations for the distinction in question. According to him, nomothetic sciences seek general laws applicable to a multiplicity of individual events. Laws descriptive of the acceleration of falling objects, of planetary motion, of the reflection and refraction of light, of the expansion of gases, or of electrical and chemical uniformities are all nomothetic. Such laws belong to natural sciences like physics, chemistry, and astronomy. To a large extent they are products of experimental observations and laboratory measurements. They have to do with what is sometimes referred to as the impersonal forces of nature. In other words, nomothetic thinking views a single event like an earthquake or an object like an insect as an instance of a class of events or objects investigated by such special branches of natural science as seismology and entomology.

By way of contrast, Windelband pointed out, idiographic thinking seeks understanding of the single episode, not as an example of some scientific or natural law, but as something *sui generis*. Events and persons studied by the historian exemplify the idiographic approach. John Calvin is studied as one who exerted a unique influence on Protestant theology and not as a convenient representative of the whole class of Protestant reformers. Similarly, the invention of the steam engine may be examined as a special event by economic historians and not as a means of demonstrating the influence of any invention on the world of industry and commerce. Should they consider this invention along with others for the purpose of noting the effect of inventions in general on unemployment or on wages or consumer spending or some other phase of economics, then their approach would not be idiographic. Their investigation would exemplify a nomothetic interest in the possible existence of economic trends sufficiently uniform and consistent to be designated as *laws* of economics. In this sense the economic interpretation of history by Marx and Engels can be classified as nomothetic.

The same holds true of Kant's effort to note steady progression of man as a species from his prehistoric animal origins through successive epochs of development governed by reason in the service of increasing ethical insight into what enhances civilized living. Hegel's well-known philosophy of history may also be classified as a nomothetic enterprise. The same may be said of all efforts to find some underlying purpose in world history of a kind which Tennyson once put in poetic form in referring to "one God, one law, one element; one far-off divine event toward which the whole creation moves." It also applies to the broad generalization first suggested by the French statesman and economist Turgot (1727–1781) and then elaborated by the French philosopher and pioneer sociologist Auguste Comte (1798–1857). Man's historical development, Comte taught, is marked by an initial stage of theological or mystical dependence on beliefs in gods and magical, supernatural forces. This was followed by an intermediate stage of confidence in *meta-physical* speculation and this, in turn, gave way to the *positivistic* outlook rooted in the controlled observations associated with a scientific orientation toward the world.

None of these attempts to interpret history nomothetically have been very successful. At best some of them may be regarded as provocative working hypotheses which, despite *a priori* plausibility, have had to be rejected either because of a dearth of supporting evidence or an abundance of negative evidence or both. This means that there are no scientific laws of history in the same sense in which there are scientific laws of thermodynamics and laws of planetary motion; hence history is not to be classified as a natural science. Instead it belongs to what the German philosopher Wilhelm Dilthey (1833–1911) referred to as the *Geisteswissenschaften.* According to M. Apel (1930, pp. 51–52), in Dilthey's phrasing the latter word refers to "all the sciences concerned with the investigation of historico-social reality." Taken very literally, the word may be translated by the phrase "mental sciences," but it also connotes what is suggested by phrases like "social sciences" or "humanistic sciences." In the opinion of men like Windelband and Dilthey, psychology is to supply the foundation for the *Geisteswissenschaften.* However, this was not to be the "scientific" laboratory psychology sponsored by Dilthey's nineteenth-century psychological colleagues. This kind of psychology with its natural-science orientation, Dilthey maintained, has little relevance for the historian in quest of a psychological background by means of which to understand the behavior of men involved in the episodes of history.

What was needed was a different kind of psychology that Dilthey regarded as having to do with man as influenced by and influencing social institutions, with his strivings and values in the world of business, trade, religion, government, education, art, music, law, and whatever else belongs to the concept of culture or the notion of civilized living.[3] As already indicated, this different kind of psychology was not the psychology of the textbooks but what Windelband aptly designated as the "practical psychology of a knowledge and understanding of men." It is the sort of psychology employed by dramatists, novelists, and biographers in their efforts to portray character. It is also exemplified by the commonsense psychology of politicians seeking votes, clergymen comforting the bereaved, a host catering to the comfort of his guests, or a teacher helping a puzzled child grasp the mystery of negative numbers.

---

3 Dilthey's negative attitude toward the "new" laboratory psychology and his positive attitude toward *geisteswissenschaftliche* psychology did not go unchallenged. For example, Hermann Ebbinghaus took issue with Dilthey in a lengthy article published in 1896.

Is Education Idiographic or Nomothetic?

This reference to a common classroom situation serves as a reminder of the fact that William James (1842–1910) also took a stand on the issue under consideration. Independently of Dilthey, but also in the 1890s, he raised questions about the aid that might be rendered to another profession by knowledge of the findings of the "new" psychology. Dilthey, it will be recalled, had considered this theme with reference to the subject of history. James, on the other hand, turned his attention to the relationship between the "new" psychology and the subject of education. He presented his views in a series of *Talks to Teachers,* prepared for the teachers of Cambridge. In his very first lecture, entitled "Psychology and the Teaching Art," he cautioned the teachers not to expect too much from the "new" psychology. It may prove clarifying to note the following excerpts from this lecture (1923 ed., pp. 5–8):

> Psychology ought certainly to give the teacher radical help. And yet I confess that, acquainted as I am with the height of some of your expectations, I feel a little anxious lest, at the end of these simple talks of mine, not a few of you may experience some disappointment at the net results. In other words, I am not sure that you may not be indulging fancies that are just a shade exaggerated. That would not be altogether astonishing, for we have been having something like a "boom" in psychology in this country. Laboratories and professorships have been founded, and reviews established. The air has been full of rumors. The editors of educational journals and the arrangers of conventions have had to show themselves enterprising and on a level with the novelties of the day. . . . The "new psychology" has thus become a term to conjure up portentous ideas withal; and you teachers, docile and receptive and aspiring as many of you are, have been plunged in an atmosphere of the vague talk about our science, which to a great extent has been more mystifying than enlightening. Altogether it does seem as if there were a certain fatality of mystification laid upon the teachers of our day. The matter of their profession . . . has to be frothed up for them in journals and institutes, till its outlines often threaten to be lost in a kind of vast uncertainty. Where the disciples are not independent and critical-minded enough . . . we are pretty sure to miss accuracy and balance and measure in those who get a license to lay down the law to them from above.
>
> As regards this subject of psychology, now, I wish at the very threshold to do what I can to dispel the mystification. So I say at once that in my humble opinion there *is* no "new psychology" worthy of the name. . . .
>
> I say moreover that you make a great, a very great mistake, if you think that psychology, being the science of the mind's laws, is something from which you can deduce definite programs and schemes and methods of instruction for immediate schoolroom use. Psychology is a science, and teaching is an art; and sciences never generate arts directly out of themselves. An intermediate inventive mind must make the application, by using its originality.

James then proceeded to illustrate his thesis by pointing out that knowledge of the science of logic will not ensure sound reasoning any more than knowledge of a textbook of ethics will promote right conduct. At best, James indicated, such knowledge will render one more sensitive to the possible occurrence of fallacious reasoning or deviations from standards of right conduct. In other words, all that a science can do is to reveal the principles in terms of which a given art is to be practiced, but just how the applications are to be made must be left to the ingenuity of the individual practitioner. The same principles may consequently be put to work in individually unique but equally effective ways. James made this point in his lecture when he stated, "Many diverse methods of teaching may equally well agree with psychological laws." He then went on to say (1923, p. 9):

> To know psychology, therefore, is absolutely no guarantee that we shall be good teachers. To advance to that result, we must have an additional endowment altogether, a happy tact and ingenuity to tell us what definite things to say and do when the pupil is before us. That ingenuity in meeting and pursuing the pupil, that tact for the concrete situation, though they are the alpha and omega of the teacher's art, are things to which psychology cannot help us in the least.

Commonsense Psychology Versus Scientific Psychology

It should thus be evident that James, like Dilthey, reacted in negative fashion to the scientific psychology of the 1890s with specific reference to having it serve as a foundation for the professional work of historians and educators. By implication they both appeared to recognize the existence of a kind of psychology which differs from the psychology of the textbooks and which reflects knowledge of human nature emerging as a result of dealings with human beings in thousands of different settings—settings ranging from early childhood in the setting of the family and the neighborhood playground on through all the shifting ones of the school years and the subsequent ones devoted to the adult's business and vocational affairs, club and church memberships, parental responsibilities, and whatever else makes demands on the time and energy of the mature citizen. In the course of years one is bound to learn a great deal about human beings as one observes them and interacts with them. For this reason, everybody might be said to know something about psychology as reflected in gossip about the vagaries of the family next door, in character portrayal by novelists and biographers, and in the human scenes of stage and screen.

This sort of psychology is much older than the scientific psychology of the laboratory, just as psychological novels and plays were in existence long before formal textbooks of psychology as science had come into being. Writers of such plays and novels have to know human nature if what they have to say is to be understood. They have to possess what Windelband called a "practical psychology of knowledge and understanding of men." Because of this, as exemplified by authors like Shakespeare or Dostoevski, they succeed in revealing their psychological insights by what they have their characters say and do in a variety of settings. To accomplish this they must avail themselves of what James referred to as the "happy tact and ingenuity" which enable one to know "what definite things to say and do" when confronted with different concrete situations.

This need for "tact and ingenuity" is not restricted to the work of novelists and dramatists but also applies to the work of historians. In fact, there is an echo of Dilthey's thesis of the 1890s in contemporary historical scholarship. Just a few years ago, for instance, the historian Fritz Stern had this to say about the historian's efforts to explain past events (1956, p. 30):

> In explaining the past there are no hard and fast rules. It is a matter of degree, of historical tact. Often the great historian, at least in our age, will be content with a suggestive tentativeness, knowing that the complexity of history is in itself an expression of the great and unpredictable variety of man.

What Stern finds troublesome and challenging in the "complexity of history" in general is also applicable to the "complexity" of psychology's history. Here too something in the way of "historical tact" must serve not only in the selection of men and events to write about, but also in the effort to account for particular developments at given times and places. These tasks become more arduous the closer one comes to the modern period. The term "modern period" in the history of psychology is customarily employed to refer to the last eighty to a hundred years, or the years during which psychology ceased to be mental philosophy and sought to establish itself as an autonomous scientific discipline. The "new" psychology to which William James referred had to do with this discipline—with psychology conceived of as the product of rigorously controlled empirical studies buttressed by laboratory evidence—or, where such evidence was lacking, by critical evaluation of data supplied by field observations of biologists and anthropologists. The result was a psychology striving to be nomothetic in the sense in which physics and chemistry were nomothetic. Just as physics had its laws of thermodynamics and laws of electricity, so the "new" psychology was to have its laws of mental life.

This "new" psychology was to be a *scientific* psychology in contradistinction to the *philosophical* psychology of previous generations. It was a deliberately planned innovation undertaken by the founding fathers of the "new" psychology. In many ways their efforts to initiate a scientific psychology are to be regarded as having ushered in the beginning of what eventually developed into the burgeoning complexity of twentieth-century psychology with its rival schools, diverse branches, proliferation of journals, and active representatives functioning in hospitals, clinics, army camp, courts, prisons, schools, as well as in the world of business and industry.

Within less than a hundred years, what had started as a pioneering venture to apply the methodology of science to the problems of the older mental philosophy was transformed from a small academic beginning to a vast professional enterprise. A century ago there was neither a journal of experimental psychology nor an association of psychologists. Today there are more journals than can be enumerated by the average psychologist. They are printed in Japanese as well as in the major European languages. No one person can possibly keep up with more than a very small fraction of the total number being published. Furthermore, any one psychologist is not likely to belong to more than a very small fraction of the total number of psychological associations in existence. In the United States, in addition to a national organization, there are associations in virtually every state and in many of the larger cities. Similar associations are to be found all over the world and on every continent, and at periodic intervals their representatives assemble at international congresses. In terms of publication costs for journals and books, membership dues in national and regional associations, and money involved in research projects as well as money earned by those rendering psychological services, psychology might be said to have become big business.

The Methods of Science and Psychology's Growth

How is one to account for this almost spectacularly rapid development of psychological activity within the span of three generations? Part of the answer, as previously suggested, is to be found in the changed outlook introduced by those late nineteenth-century philosopher-psychologists who championed the "new" psychology's devotion to the methods of science as contrasted with the "old" psychology's exclusive dependence on the teachings of empiricists and rationalists. The introduction of the methods of science made for a changed outlook, not so much because of problems being solved, but rather because of new questions being raised. There is always new business on the scientific agenda. Investigation of a given problem tends to reveal derivatives of that problem that in turn demand separate investigation. Still different problems may emerge from the latter investigations, and as the work progresses through successive investigations, a given field of inquiry branches out into many separate fields, some of which are far removed from the initial investigation viewed as the instigator of the chain.

By way of illustration it suffices to mention the introduction by the French psychologist Alfred Binet (1857–1911) of a method for measuring individual differences in intelligence. This pioneer venture in mental testing was published in 1905. In succeeding years there was a burst of activity as more and more questions were introduced about the nature of intelligence, new techniques of measurement were proposed, and the scope of mental testing was extended far beyond the circumscribed boundaries of Binet's initial venture. It is a far cry from his testing of French children to current work with tests for superior adults by means of factorially pure psychometric devices. It is also a far cry from his use of tests as a means of estimating mental age to the modern elaboration of the whole testing movement with its achievement tests, interest tests, projective tests, culture-free tests, and group tests, not to mention tests for musical aptitude, artistic talent, creative thinking, frustration tolerance, social maturity, and motor skill. Nor should one overlook the use of inventories and attitude scales for detecting neurotic trends, feelings of insecurity, ethnocentric inclinations, and other personality variables. In fact, by this time there are so many different tests, inventories, and attitude scales available and so many new ones are being devised that it is impossible for the most expert psychometrist to be practiced in the use of more than a very few of them or even to be superficially familiar with all of them.

It should now be evident how introduction of the methods of science transformed the psychological teachings of a handful of mental philosophers into the multifaceted enterprise with its thousands of workers that twentieth-century psychology has become. It should also be evident by this time why in writing about the long past of psychology it was deemed necessary to devote so much space to a discussion of the history of science in general. In other words, to revert to the central issue of this chapter, one of the criteria employed in the choice of topics for inclusion in this history has to do with the relevance of a given topic for an understanding of the methodology of science. Incidentally, it is advisable to note that the latter phrase is not to be construed as referring to a *single* method, for there is no one scientific method; hence it would be more accurate to refer to the *methodologies* of science.[4]

Each separate field of science has to work out its own controls and its own techniques as germane to its own problems. The "new" psychology

---

[4] Just what different methodologies should have in common to merit the accolade of being called "scientific procedures" is not easy to specify. They all ought to reflect a basic regard for the nature of valid proof for the conclusions reached. It is as if all scientists in all fields keep asking, "What is the evidence?" This is almost a truism. Still, a truism of this sort is not sufficient to establish the scientific status of every human undertaking dominated by cautious evaluation of evidence. Courtroom activity is almost routinely characterized by such evaluation, and yet one would hesitate to call it *scientific* activity. Determining the guilt or innocence of a defendant is not a scientific project, even though there be scrupulous adherence to rules of evidence. This suggests that, contrary to a widely held teaching, science may involve more than a matter of method

involved far more than the transfer of the methods of experimental physics to the psychological laboratory, for the problems of the psychologist were different from those of the physicist. This is not a reference to problems pertaining to the adaptation or design of suitable laboratory apparatus, but to basic issues regarding psychology's involvement in man's age-old quest for understanding himself.

William James and the "Persistent Riddles of Psychology"

Whether the "new" psychology at its inception was promoting this kind of self-understanding became a moot question. As we have seen, William James in his lectures to the Cambridge teachers took a dim view of the help they might secure from the "new" psychology. He once referred to it disparagingly as a "brass-instrument psychology" and wrote that its use of the experimental "method taxes patience to the utmost, and could hardly have arisen in a country whose natives could be *bored*" (1890, Vol. I, p. 192). Evidently he found these pioneer experimental reports dull reading. That he dutifully waded through them is reflected in the pages of his classic *Principles of Psychology*. This impressive two-volume work was published in 1890 after twelve years of labor and won instant acclaim. Virtually all of the founding fathers of American psychology were familiar with its contents. In this sense they were all students of James. Even the student of today would profit by familarizing himself with the *Principles*. It would be especially valuable experience for the student of the history of psychology, since its pages are replete with discussions of the older mental philosophers as well as of the newer experimental psychologists. The work thus marks the transition from philosophical to scientific psychology and concerns itself with critical issues stemming from psychology's philosophic heritage. These are issues that continue to have a bearing on contemporary psychology and consequently might be said to influence the historian in deciding on what events of the past are to be endowed with historical significance.

Consideration of the issues is itself related to an important event in the history of American psychology. This has to do with a double celebration occurring in the year 1942 and marking the centenary of the birth of William James along with the semicentenary of the founding of the American

---

and should include consideration of the kind of problem to which the method is applied. A distinguished American physicist, the late P. W. Bridgman (1882–1961), referred to this problem in an article cited by James Bryant Conant in his volume entitled *On Understanding Science* (1951, p. 116):

I am not one of those who hold that there is a scientific method as such. The scientific method, as far as it is a method, is nothing more than doing one's damnedest with one's mind, no holds barred. What primarily distinguishes science from other intellectual enterprises in which the right answer has to be obtained is not the method but the subject matter.

Psychological Association in 1892. Unfortunately, because of wartime travel restrictions the scheduled annual meeting of the Association had to be canceled, and the members could not meet to hear the papers that had been prepared for the occasion. Instead the entire January, 1943, issue of the *Psychological Review* was devoted to the papers in question. In a sense this made it a triple celebration, for that issue marked the beginning of the fiftieth year of the journal's existence.

In preparation for his tribute to the memory of William James, Gordon Allport evidently reread the *Principles* and was struck by certain contradictions in what James had to say in the course of his treatment of given topics. Allport's article deals with these contradictions as products of some of psychology's pivotal problems. They have to do with cardinal issues that lie embedded in psychology's philosophic past and continue to have relevance for psychology's scientific present. As a consequence they may be thought of as guidelines for a perplexed historian trying to find his way through the complex maze of events having either a direct or indirect bearing on the long history of psychology. As persistent problems of psychology they run through the warp and woof of the pattern of its history; hence their usefulness as criteria to aid in discriminating the historically relevant from the irrelevant. They are broad enough in their implications to encompass the major criteria governing the historian's selective perception. In his article Allport refers to them as "the persistent riddles of psychology" likely to puzzle every psychologist in the course of his professional endeavors.

These "riddles" deal with complex questions for which there are no assured answers. Seen from one viewpoint one set of answers seems plausible, but from a different and equally tenable viewpoint another set of answers may seem equally plausible. The result is apparent contradiction or inconsistency, especially if one discusses them in terms of such divergent viewpoints. This lack of agreement makes them paradoxical and productive of thought provoking reflection. At least William James wrestled with each of them in earnest if ambivalent fashion. In Allport's wording, they may be called "the productive paradoxes of William James." Before considering their paradoxical nature, it is well to come to grips with them by paraphrasing Allport's formulation in interrogative form.

There are six basic questions to be raised:

(1) How is mind or consciousness or life as it is experienced related to its physiological substrate? This is the mind-body problem, or the *psychophysical* problem.

(2) With reference to method, are the objective techniques of natural science suitable means of dealing with the subjective aspects of mental life? Can such objective procedures do justice to phenomenal events in their sensory immediacy, as positivists propose? This may be called the problem of *positivism.*

WILLIAM JAMES (1842–1910)

(3) How is one to account for personality integration or the way in which diverse experiences or divergent impulses come to be assimilated by the individual as *his* experiences and impulses? What is the nature of this sense of personal belongingness or relative unity and persistence all through the years of one's identification of a central core of selfhood? This is the puzzle of the *self*.

(4) How can we reconcile our endorsement of determinism in our "scientific" thinking and theorizing with our daily behavior in which we act as if there is freedom of choice? Is behavior predestined or has man a modicum of volitional freedom? In brief, this is the problem of *free will*.

(5) Why is it that from one viewpoint the old laws of association seem to serve as satisfactory explanation for the facts of learning, memory, and mental organization in general, and yet from another viewpoint they seem unsatisfactory? Here we have the vexing problem of *association*.

(6) How does it come about that despite careful analysis of the facts of consciousness and behavior, the uniqueness and distinctiveness of each individual personality still eludes us? This is the problem of *individuality*.

Almost every modern textbook of general psychology contains some discussion of topics related to each of the foregoing six areas of inquiry. The discussions may employ a different descriptive vocabulary but it is nevertheless relatively easy to recognize them as variants or derivatives of the six problem areas. Twentieth-century psychology, viewed historically, thus reveals some continuity with its roots in the philosophical psychology of preceding centuries.

James was especially influential in providing such continuity for the emergence and subsequent development of scientific psychology in America. The first generation of American psychologists, as has been mentioned, were all influenced by his teachings. He himself was as much philosopher as psychologist. With respect to both professional roles he was largely self-taught and was not the possessor of graduate degrees in either philosophy or psychology. In fact, he never had a course in either subject. This is revealed in a letter James wrote in 1902, part of which is quoted by Ralph Barton Perry (1954, p. 78):

> I originally studied medicine in order to be a physiologist, but I drifted into psychology and philosophy from a sort of fatality. I never had any philosophic instruction, the first lecture on psychology I ever heard being the first I ever gave.

James's eminence both as philosopher and psychologist was a result of his private study of the literature of both fields as an independent thinker of rare sensitivity and profundity of insight. The originality of his work as a creative thinker may in part be attributed to this independence. He was free to think things through by himself. There was neither the need to remain loyal to the views of a revered professor nor an antecedent indoctrination by some academic sponsor of a special school, system, or movement.

Eclecticism Versus System-Making in Psychology

Even though he was a leader of American psychology during the years around the turn of the century, James was not a leader in the sense of heading a new school or system. One cannot refer to his psychological views as a *system* in the way in which it is meaningful to talk about Wundt's system or that of Brentano. There is no central, unifying theme running through the twenty-eight chapters of the *Principles.* Instead each chapter is concerned with a special topic and elaborated with respect to that topic so that its contents can be understood without preliminary study of preceding chapters. For example, a student would be able to follow the discussion of the nature of memory as presented in the sixteenth chapter without having to refer to any of the earlier ones. He would find the discussion to be a well-organized, systematic account of memory as a separate mental process considered in the abstract. The same would hold true for other chapters devoted to such topics as habit, attention, instinct, and emotion.

Even though James has been called an "unsystematic" psychologist,[5] his treatment of individual topics is by no means unsystematic in the sense of being disorganized or devoid of a clarifying sequential arrangement of sub-topics related to the main topic. What he failed to do was to select one aspect of mental life as the foundation for all the other aspects. This is what those who establish systems of psychology tend to do. They organize their systems around one feature of mental life that strikes them as fundamental, with other features being presented as related to or functions of that prime feature. Rival systems come into being as different system-builders select different foundation stones for their psychological structures. Thus we have the voluntaristic system of Wundt with its emphasis on will, the act psychology of Brentano stressing the basic importance of the intentionalism of psychical acts, the structuralistic psychology of Titchener glorifying sensation as the key to mental life, the psychoanalytic psychology of Freud elevating the unconscious wish to similar status, the hormic psychology of McDougall

---

[5] The charge of being unsystematic stems from the apparent absence of an obvious unifying plan of organization running through the two volumes of the *Principles.* Gardner Murphy (1949, p. 195), for example, after referring to James as "the *un-*systematic psychologist par excellence," explains this by calling attention to an absence of "structural unity" in the way in which the different chapters of the *Principles* are brought together. According to Titchener (1929, p. 182), however, James repudiated the charge. In fact, Titchener himself regards the charge as unjustified. In his view, James "gives us a work on the principles of knowledge, written from a psychologistic standpoint. If his volumes are read with this interpretation in mind, the critical charge of lack of plan . . . will be found groundless."

organized around the concept of instinct or innate propensity, the behavioristic system of Watson with its focus on reflexes and conditioning, and still other systems based upon such varied central ideas as that of the principle of association or the concept of self or the notion of a Gestalt. As was indicated in Chapter 1, page 11, this explains why we have schools or systems of psychology.

Moreover, to revert to what has just been said about the lack of a neatly articulated system in the work of James, although he devotes space to almost every one of the key ideas just enumerated, he was not disposed to regard any one of them as being the key to unlock the mysteries of psychology as a whole. As a result, his treatment of individual topics is more eclectic than syncretistic.[6] Instead of striving for a finished system, he is more concerned with enhancing understanding of a given subject by noting what seems to be validly established regarding its characteristics and functions, calling attention to its historical antecedents, exposing erroneous ideas to which it may have given currency, and, where relevant data are not yet available, urging suspension of judgment.

This kind of flexibility of approach eliminates one of the chief hazards of premature system-building; namely, the inclination to welcome evidence consistent with the system and to overlook or be resistant to opposing evidence. The system-builder becomes a champion of one set of explanatory principles or of a single explanatory principle. He assembles facts in line with his favorite explanation and is likely either to ignore those at variance with the explanation, or else in Procrustean fashion he distorts them to fit the system. Such ardent partisanship carried to extremes is more in keeping with the founding of a cult than the promotion of a science.

A frequent consequence of such partisan commitments is to make the system paramount and facts a secondary consideration. It characterizes the *modus operandi* of medical cultists, champions of political parties, and zealous religious leaders. Therapeutic systems, political systems, and theological systems come into existence as a result. The outcome may be a well-articulated, consistent, unified group of teachings but hardly a *science*. Vegetarianism and chiropractic are not sciences. Nor do we have Democratic, Republican, or Communistic sciences. Neither Judaism nor Catholicism nor Buddhism is to be classified as a science. The same holds true for the various schools or systems of philosophy; hence one does not refer to a science of realism or a science of idealism.

---

6 Eclecticism is not to be confused with syncretism. The eclectic, in his recognition and selection of evidence calculated to aid in the understanding of particular problems, is on the alert for possible weaknesses or contradictions in the evidence mobilized. He strives to bring as much order as he can in the body of data being examined and, in principle, is ever ready to modify conclusions to accord with new evidence. His theorizing is not a haphazard affair in which incompatible notions are put together more or less indiscriminately in *syncretistic* fashion. Syncretism, in contrast, by uncritically lumping contradictory ideas together, produces spurious theorizing and system-making.

As a matter of fact, the various systems of psychology are not ordinarily designated as sciences. Thus one does not speak of the science of behaviorism or the science of Gestalt psychology or the science of associationism. This in itself suggests that a given system fails to encompass the whole of psychology. At best a system constitutes a view of psychology as seen from a fixed single perspective even though the vastness and complexity of the total field calls for a panoramic view. The latter kind of view is, of course, the equivalent of many perspectives.

The introduction of new systems was particularly frequent during the early decades of the present century. In addition to structuralism and functionalism, the graduate student soon found himself having to study about configurationism, rival systems of behaviorism, and rival psychoanalytic psychologies, along with such systems as personalistic psychology, hormic psychology, organismic psychology, and several others.[7] Strangely enough, such proliferation of systems took place during a period when many psychologists were priding themselves on their emancipation from philosophy and on their devotion to the methods of science. This devotion reflected their admiration of such sciences as physics and physiology. And yet neither of the latter disciples had spawned schools or systems as had been true of philosophy. In other words, when it came to system-making the model for the psychologists seemed to be philosophy rather than physics.

Schools or systems of psychology, as mentioned earlier, tend to overstress the significance of a single concept or principle, whether it be that of sensation or motivation or instinct or reflex or feelings of inferiority. The given concept or principle is then regarded as the foundation of or key to psychology as a whole. This is not characteristic of physics viewed as a model science. The graduate student of physics is not confronted with a variety of systems of physics, one deriving all explanations in the light of thermodynamics, another based exclusively on hydrodynamics, and a third reducing everything to electromagnetic factors. Instead each physical law, principle, or concept becomes operative in a relevant context. The wave theory of light is not used to account for water waves, nor is Pascal's law made the basis for an entire system by striving to apply it to phenomena of light, sound, and magnetism. Moreover, this state of affairs holds true for other natural sciences like chemistry, botany, and physiology. Each such science has several laws or principles to handle the particular sets of phenomena constituting the science in question. One does not find separate schools of each science based upon one master law or one key principle.

---

[7] The multiplication of psychological systems during these early decades is indicated by the titles of two volumes one of which was published in 1928 and the other in 1930. Both were edited by Carl Murchison. The first was called *Psychologies of 1925* and the second was called *Psychologies of 1930*. Incidentally, there were no cognate volumes with titles like *Chemistries of 1925* or *Physiologies of 1930*.

The intensive utilization of a single key principle by the sponsors of a system of psychology has made for divisiveness in psychology as different system-builders employ different key principles. Although this tendency has engendered endless controversy and may have interfered with the promotion of a single science of psychology, it has not been altogether futile. In some ways it may actually have had a constructive influence by bringing the significance of the given key principle into sharp relief. In this manner concepts like conditioning, Gestalt, unconscious motivation, instinct, sensation, organism, person, self, and others serving as key principles have been widely explored and often have been the means of calling attention to hitherto unknown or overlooked factual data. In this respect, system-making has been an asset to psychology. However, it has been a liability to the extent that it has made for divisiveness, cultistic zeal, and blindness to valid findings at variance with the system.

A "Paradoxical" Approach to History

The electicism of James enabled him to be free to subject any theory, doctrine, or principle to judicious evaluation irrespective of its source. It thus served as a safeguard against what has just been described as the cultistic zeal and blindness of those identified with a system like loyal party members. The very broadness and flexibility of his outlook made for a readiness to consider the complexity of controversial issues even at the risk of having to endorse seemingly contradictory views. As a result, in Allport's phrase, he sometimes "landed squarely in the middle of a paradox." Needless to add, James failed to dispose of the paradoxical nature of such complex issues by playing down or arbitrarily ignoring incompatible data in the interests of a finished system. Not having such a system, he had to leave the issues unresolved and in the process to leave himself open to the charge of inconsistency. In some instances the difficulty may have been analogous to the kind of situation in the history of physics in which available evidence induced endorsement of both the wave and the corpuscular theories of light despite the inconsistency involved.

Because such paradoxes are concerned with persistent problems of psychology, they are especially helpful to the historian in search of criteria by means of which to differentiate the historically significant from the insignificant. In other words, whatever has influenced the development of one of these key problems may call for the professional attention of the historian. In their persistence they go back to psychology's philosophic past and extend into psychology's scientific present. By using them as selective criteria, the historian can more easily trace important trends leading to the present.

To a certain degree the paradoxes or riddles of psychology with which James wrestled can be regarded as products of a clash between the views of the older mental philosophers and those of the advocates of the "new" laboratory psychology in the 1890s. His eclecticism facilitated the transition from the old to the new. In his dual role of philosopher and psychologist he was admirably equipped to effect this transition. His eminence in both fields is indicated by the fact that American philosophers and psychologists elevated him to the presidency of their respective professional associations. In fact, James is the only man who was twice elected president of the American Psychological Association, once in 1894 and again in 1904. Furthermore, when the members of that society voted on the relative eminence of distinguished psychologists, they agreed in according William James the highest rank. This also happened twice, once early in the century and again in the 1920s when M. A. Tinker (1927) and his associates polled another generation of American psychologists.

Discussion of the nature and implications of these "productive paradoxes" will pave the way for readier understanding of psychology's postmedieval philosophic past, going back to the seventeenth and eighteenth centuries and including about the first half of the nineteenth century. Accordingly, the next two chapters are to be viewed as preparation for easier exposition of the history of the latter centuries. This exposition will thus be postponed until later chapters. However, this does not apply to the problem of association and to the problem of individuality. These problems will lend themselves to easier exposition in the later chapters. The other four paradoxes will be elaborated upon in some detail in the two following chapters even though this means skipping from the immediate postmedieval period to the time of William James and, in part, to contemporary times. Sometimes a forward look helps to make a backward glance more revealing. As Alfred North Whitehead (1948, p. 3) once put it: "There are two ways of reading history, forwards and backwards. In the history of thought, we require both methods."

References

Allport, G. "The Productive Paradoxes of William James," *Psychological Review*, 1943, *50*, 95–120.

Apel, M. *Philosophisches Wörterbuch*. Leipzig: Walter de Gruyter and Company. 1930.

Borchard, E. M. *Convicting the Innocent*. New Haven: Yale University Press, 1932.

Conant, J. B. *On Understanding Science—An Historical Approach*. New York: New American Library, 1951.

Ebbinghaus, H. "Ueber erklärende und beschreibende Psychologie," *Zeitschrift für Psychologie*, 1896, *9*, 161–205.

James, W. *Principles of Psychology*. Vol. I. New York: Henry Holt and Company, 1890.

James, W. *Talks to Teachers*. New York: Henry Holt and Company, 1923. (First published in 1899.)

Murchison, C. (ed.). *Psychologies of 1925*. Worcester: Clark University Press, 1928.

Murchison, C. (ed.). *Psychologies of 1930*. Worcester: Clark University Press. 1930.

Murphy, G. *Historical Introduction to Modern Psychology*. New York: Harcourt, Brace and Company, 1949.

Perry, R. B. *The Thought and Character of William James*. New York: George Braziller, 1954.

Stern, F. (ed.). *The Varieties of History*. New York: Meridian Books, 1956.

Tinker, M. A., Thuma, B. D., and Farnsworth, P. R. "The Rating of Psychologists," *American Journal of Psychology*, 1927, *38,* 453–455.

Titchener, E. B. *Systematic Psychology: Prolegomena*. New York: The Macmillan Company, 1929.

Whitehead, A. N. *Science and the Modern World*. New York: Mentor Books, 1948. (First published in 1925 by The Macmillan Company, New York.)

Windelband, W. *An Introduction to Philosophy*. London: T. Fisher Unwin, 1921.

9

The Mind-Body Problem and the Challenge of Positivism

THE PERENNIAL NATURE of the mind-body problem in the history of psychology is revealed by recurrent references to it age after age from ancient Greek times to the present. Just when it emerged as a problem in the history of man is difficult to determine. To recognize it as a problem calls for a certain level of sophistication. This topic was mentioned at the beginning of Chapter, 1 in connection with Aristotle's disparagement of the pre-Socratics as unphilosophical thinkers because of their exclusive preoccupation with physical nature.

The distinction between body and soul or mind and matter, it may be recalled, was not made until the time of the Pythagoreans around the close of the fifth century B.C. Because of this, it may also be recalled, Brett wrote, "The origin of Western Psychology was in the study of the organism and not in speculations about a supernatural soul." The young child exemplifies this same pre-Socratic tendency in being aware of and interested in its body before asking questions about minds or souls. Even an older child may not realize that asking questions is different from anything else he does even though his parents may rejoice in his questions as evidence of a developing mind. Here unlike the child, the parents would be reflecting the influence of a mind-body dichotomy. Recognition of such a dichotomy, as just indicated, calls for a certain level of sophistication. As Brett once put it (in Murchison, 1930, p. 54), "We live before we study life, think before we analyze thoughts, and, in general, act before we reflect."

By the time of Socrates and Plato, such study, analysis, and reflection had become well-established philosophic practices. Interest in the nature of mental life had become an integral part of Greek philosophy. The notion of a cleavage between mental life and the bodily organism was already manifest in Plato's concept of a separate realm of universal ideas, in his doctrine of reminiscence, as well as in his mystical belief in reminiscence. Both he and

Aristotle, as has been discussed in Chapter 3, p. 49, had something to say about the bodily locus of mind, with Plato selecting the head and Aristotle, following an earlier teaching of Empedocles, selecting the heart. All such theorizing was, of course, little better than vague speculation; but it does suggest an incipient recognition of what in later centuries developed into explicit recognition of the psychophysical riddle: how is the mind as known to psychologists related to the body as known to physiologists? Both physiological psychologists and neurophysiologists are engaged in the search for clues which might help to solve the riddle. That it remains unsolved was already indicated on page 29, where reference was made to the following conclusion of two contemporary neuropathologists: "We have at present no basis for a scientific explanation of the *brain-mind relationship*."

Toward the end of the nineteenth century, when James was writing his *Principles,* he was in a position to consider the chief theories of the mind-brain relationship as formulated by that time. In fact, no really new theories of this relationship have been proposed since then, so that present-day references to the problem deal with one or more of the theories James had at his disposal some seventy or eighty years ago. Although he considers each one in some detail and with characteristic persuasiveness, he failed to endorse any of them without reservation and qualification. Allport (1943, pp. 97–99) regards his evaluation of the proposed solutions as inconsistent. If James had a final preference, it is virtually impossible to determine it with assurance. It was as if he himself lacked any assured means of arriving at a confident verdict.

Metaphysics and Empirical Science

Moreover, as has just been suggested, there is no way of settling the problem even today. As yet the rival psychophysical views do not lend themselves to experimental investigation. They are not amenable to the kind of formulation that results in testable hypotheses. Dealing as they do with the ultimate nature of existence, they belong to the realm of metaphysics rather than to that of empirical science. This is not to say that they are now devoid of influence on the outlook of the scientific psychologist. In terms of an implicit faith or temperamental bias, he is likely to find himself having preferences with respect to the metaphysical options. Those whom James called tough-minded are apt to have different preferences from the tender-minded. Such preferences tend to color one's psychologizing. Without being a professional metaphysician, every psychologist is influenced by metaphysical consideration—by his hunches or beliefs regarding the ultimate nature of the universe. This is true even of those who pride themselves on their lack of interest in metaphysics. Sometimes this lack of interest may be a consequence of an erroneous notion to the effect that metaphysics is restricted to idle speculation about the vague, the abstruse, the supernatural, or possibly with that which verges on the superstitious. This is altogether at variance with what James had to say regarding the nature of metaphysics, with specific reference to its implications for psychology. The following excerpt from the *Principles* is particularly pertinent in the present context (1890, Vol. I, p. 145):

> Metaphysics means nothing but an unusually obstinate effort to think clearly. The fundamental conceptions of psychology are practically very clear to us, but theoretically they are very confused, and one easily makes the obscurest assumptions in this science without realizing, until challenged, what internal difficulties they involve.

This brief passage does not mean that James was arguing in defense of a metaphysical psychology. In fact, on the last page (p. 189) of the same chapter he suggests as the "wisest course" for the time being the adoption of a "psychophysic formula" which will help to keep psychology "positivistic and non-metaphysical" and in accord with "a psychology which contents itself with verifiable laws, and seeks only to be clear, and to avoid unsafe hypotheses." However, in order to be non-metaphysical one must know enough about metaphysics in order to recognize a metaphysical assumption. This is equivalent to the difference between being able to ignore something and being ignorant of something.

To appreciate the difficulty James had in finding a satisfactory "psychophysic formula," it is advisable to take note of the choices he had at his disposal. These constituted the chief theories of the mind-body relationship which have colored the history of psychology.[1] To the extent that they all either affirm or deny a fundamental difference between what is attributed to mind and what is regarded as body, they involve metaphysical considerations. Stated a little differently: both monistic as well as dualistic theories imply metaphysical commitments.[2] Incidentally, it is well to realize that, contrary to a not uncommon belief, monism is no more scientific than dualism. Science as such is neutral with reference to such ultimate issues, with the result that in expressing a preference for either monistic or dualistic doctrines

---

[1] Only very few of the many theories of this relationship have been taken seriously by professional psychologists. Accordingly, there is no need to catalogue the entire list of variants of the few being considered in this chapter. A complete list would number close to thirty.

[2] Classifying these theories as either monistic or dualistic is not a very old philosophic enterprise. The term "monism" itself was unknown 300 years ago. It was introduced by Christian von Wolff (1679–1754). Furthermore, the monism-dualism dichotomy does not provide for all the metaphysical options. It fails to allow for *pluralism*. As will be explained in the last section of this chapter, James became an advocate of pluralism. For the time being, it is enough to note that the pluralist attributes more than one or two fundamental elements to ultimate reality. In the kind of pluralism sponsored by James, these fundamental elements are not classifiable as being either mental or physical. Instead they are to be regarded as neutral ultimates.

one is giving expression to a metaphysical and not a scientific preference. As yet nobody has succeeded in proposing a valid criterion by means of which the scientist *qua* scientist can decide to advocate monism rather than dualism or vice versa.[3]

Epiphenomenalism Versus Idealism

One of the frequently mentioned monistic formulations is that known as *epiphenomenalism*. This is commonly classified among the so-called mechanistic or materialistic theories. Its advocates regard consciousness as an epiphenomenon or mere by-product or incidental concomitant of neural and bodily changes, with no causal influences on these changes. In somewhat tenuous form, there are early beginnings of this view in the atomistic teachings of Democritus. Less tenuous forms of the theory are implicit in most behavioristic systems of psychology. This holds true in the sense that most ardent champions of behaviorism would probably agree with the statement James (1890, Vol. I, p. 134) attributes to a "most intelligent biologist": "It is high time for scientific men to protest the recognition of any such thing as consciousness in a scientific investigation."

This biologist was evidently stressing science as concerned with the investigation of cause-and-effect relationships. To account for the reflex or automatic withdrawal of the hand from a hot stove, one investigates the structural integrity of the reflex mechanism involved. For the epiphenomenalist it is not the pain that accounts for the withdrawal but the effect of the heat on the nerves and muscles responsible for the flexion reflex. The pain as a conscious phenomenon, he would maintain, is devoid of any causal efficacy. For him, scientific explanations of human and animal behavior are never strengthened by references to feelings or ideas or beliefs or other affairs of consciousness. In terms of a famous simile, suggested by the English metaphysician W. K. Clifford (1845–1879) and mentioned by James, for the psychologist to endow mind with causal influence on behavior would be akin to having an engineer suggest that the friendship between a locomotive engineer and the conductor and not the iron coupling is the bond uniting engine to the car it is pulling. At best the epiphenomenalist regards man as a conscious automaton or a machine that happens to be alive.

James found it impossible to accept epiphenomenalism as a tenable theory. He found it "quite inconceivable that consciousness should have *nothing to do* with a business which it so faithfully attends (1890, Vol. I,

---

3 Psychologists may nevertheless express a preference. E. G. Boring, for example, takes a definite stand in this blunt formulation (1963, p. 14): "While there is no possibility of disproving or proving dualism, the exposition of the present book is based on the assumption that it is scientifically more useful to consider that all psychological data are of the same kind and that consciousness is a physiological event." On a later page (p. 17) he indicates that this is the "faith" of "a hard-headed monist."

p. 136). With reference to causal efficacy, he felt constrained to endorse the commonsense view that "feelings and ideas are causes" (p. 137). The final sentence of his discussion devoted to "reasons for the theory" turns out to be an emphatic indictment of the theory:

> My conclusion is that to urge the automation-theory upon us, as it is now urged on purely *a priori* and *quasi*-metaphysical grounds, is an *unwarrantable impertinence in the present state of psychology.*

A monistic rival to the automation theory as sponsored by the epiphenomenalists is that of *idealism.* Just as epiphenomenalism represents a physicalist metaphysics, so idealism represents a mentalistic metaphysics. Both are monistic theories in the sense of trying to circumvent the dualistic implications of the mind-body dichotomy. The one theory purports to accomplish this by converting mind into body, while the other purports to eliminate body by converting it into mind. For the one, matter is the only basic reality; for the other, what is commonly called "matter" becomes a congeries of sensations. As a result, ultimate reality is conceived of in terms of consciousness or such inferred derivatives as self or spirit.

In the words of Bishop George Berkeley (1685–1753), a famous advocate of idealism, existence is contingent upon perception: *to be is to be perceived.* This postulate was mentioned in Chapter 6, p. 134, in connection with the closely similar views of Plotinus, and there is no need to elaborate upon it at this point. It is enough to note it as one of several forms of spiritistic monism such as objective idealism, monadism, or panpsychism. Their detailed consideration is not of direct relevance for the history of psychology. James touches upon some of these idealistic forms of monism but fails to endorse any of them as useful for a psychology striving to be "positivistic and non-metaphysical."

Psychophysical Parallelism Versus Interactionism

Actually James failed to write a "non-metaphysical" psychology. Writing at a time when the "new" psychology was still close to its philosophical moorings, he did not find it easy to eschew metaphysical considerations. In particular, as has already been evident, he was unable to ignore the mind-body problem. By way of paving the way for his presentation of psychology as a natural science, he devoted two whole chapters to the latter problem. Even though he held that as a natural scientist the psychologist need not trouble himself about "ultimate puzzles" (1890, Vol. I, p. 184), he continued to be troubled by the psychophysical puzzle. He was definitely more drawn to a dualistic solution than to a monistic one. Nevertheless he failed to find one altogether to his liking and worthy of unqualified endorsement. His choice wavered between two of the more influential dualistic proposals: *psychophysical parallelism* on the one hand and *interactionism* on the other.

Since each of these theories is of historical importance, each one calls for a word of explanation.

Psychophysical parallelism is sometimes confused with the closely related *double-aspect* theory. According to double aspectism, there is a fundamental underlying identity between neural events and conscious events. Experience described from the introspective aspect can also be described from the aspect of the brain physiologist. The resulting descriptive differences will merely reflect the differences in viewpoint, just as the description of a sphere seen from its interior will differ from that of an external observer. The *same* sphere will be concave seen from the former aspect and convex when viewed from the latter aspect; hence the underlying identity of the sphere.

As contrasted with double aspectism, psychophysical parallelism does not view mind and body as identical with or as attributes of some unknown or unknowable *tertium quid*. Instead it assumes nothing about a causal relationship between a series of conscious events and concomitant brain events. Its advocates limit themselves to the contention that for every conscious event there is a corresponding or parallel brain event. Unlike double aspectism, it is not an identity hypothesis, it neither affirms nor denies such identity. Instead, in terms of its significance for the kind of naturalistic scientific psychology being urged by James and the sponsors of the "new" psychology, it supplied justification for the study of consciousness or immediate experience as an independent scientific venture, with the study of parallel brain changes being a separate venture. To cite a simple example: the character of color blindness can be investigated by finding out how the world of color is experienced by the victim of such blindness without the necessity of investigating the physiology of color blindness.

This example might serve to suggest what James called "empirical parallelism." He endorsed such "empirical parallelism" as the "wisest course" for psychology to follow and one to which he intended to adhere in writing the *Principles,* even though he also recognized it as "only a provisional halting-place, and things must some day be more thoroughly thought out" (1890, Vol. 1, p. 182). James did not succeed in abiding by his intention to present psychology in accordance with a parallelistic standpoint. At least some of his critics have accused him of inconsistency because of passages in which he seems to be endorsing an *interactionistic* standpoint.

Interactionism reflects the commonsense belief that mind influences the body's functions just as bodily activities may affect mind. As a separate theory of the mind-body relationship, it was brought into sharp focus by the theorizing of Descartes (1596–1650) and will be discussed at greater length in Chapter 11. For the time being, it is enough to note its emphasis on a reciprocal causal relationship between body and mind. Present-day references to psychosomatic medicine suggest endorsement of interactionism in some medical circles. James also endorsed it on occasion. He rejected epiphenomenalism along with the automation theory because, as he saw it, consciousness has a positive function in regulating behavior and is not to be dismissed as a superfluous by-product of brain activity. Although acknowledging his inability to demonstrate *how* it exercises an influence on such activity, he nevertheless was convinced that it does. Consider the following quotation by way of illustration (1890, Vol. I, pp. 141–142):

> Now let consciousness only be what it seems to itself, and it will help an instable brain to compass its proper ends. The movements of the brain *per se* yield the means of attaining these ends mechanically, but only out of a lot of other ends, . . . which are not the proper ones of the animal, but often quite opposed. The brain is an instrument of possibilities, but of no certainties. But the consciousness, with its own ends present to it, and knowing also well which possibilities lead thereto and which away, will, if endowed with causal efficacy, reinforce the favorable possibilities and repress the unfavorable or indifferent ones. The nerve-currents, coursing through the cells and fibres, must in this case be supposed strengthened by the fact of their awaking one consciousness and dampened by awaking another. *How* such reaction of the consciousness upon the currents may occur must remain at present unsolved: it is enough for my purpose to have shown that it may not uselessly exist, and that the matter is less simple than the brain-automatists hold.

By regarding consciousness as "endowed with causal efficacy," as he did in the preceding quotation, James seems to have deserted parallelism in favor of interactionism. If, as is commonly maintained, parallelism fails to provide for this kind of causal efficacy, then James may justifiably be accused of having been inconsistent in endorsing incompatible theories. However, if parallelism can be construed so as to provide for causal efficacy, then the charge of inconsistency would not be justified.

In this connection it may prove helpful to realize that as working or heuristic theories, parallelism and double aspectism are not altogether irreconcilable. They both agree on the concurrence of mental and bodily operations. Unlike epiphenomenalism, they both acknowledge the functional significance of consciousness or immediate experience. Moreover, both theories have a common origin in the thinking of Spinoza (1632–1677), whose place in the history of psychology will be discussed in Chapter 13. At this point it is enough to record his initial sponsorship of double aspectism in the guise of psychophysical parallelism. Since he was a rationalist, the role of reason in the regulation of human affairs was included in this sponsorship. This is tantamount to saying that reason was endowed with causal efficacy in his mind-body theory.

An excellent summary of his view is to be found in the work of H. A. Wolfson, a noted student of Spinoza's philosophy. With reference to the paradox of arguing that even though mind and body do not influence one another, mind can nevertheless succeed in exercising control over the "affections" of the body, Wolfson has this to say (1934, Vol. II, pp. 265–266):

Justification for this assertion is found in the view that there is a parallelism be-tween mind and body, that the mind is the idea or form of the body, and further-more that the mind has knowledge of its body and through it of other bodies. From all this it follows that . . . "the order and connection of the affections of the body is according to the order and connection in the mind of the thoughts and ideas of things." The result of this is that the mind, which in its own sphere is inde-pendent of the body, deriving as it does its power of thinking from the attribute of thought, can harmonize the order and connection of the bodily affection with the order and connection of its own ideas. Reason, then, can guide and control the body and even dictate to it.

Whether this analysis resolves the paradox is open to question. There is no explanation of the mechanism by means of which reason exercises control of the body. The fact of such control is acknowledged, but the question of *how* is not raised. James, in wrestling with the problem some two hundred-odd years after Spinoza, did raise the question and, as indicated on a previous page, found it unanswerable. Moreover, like Spinoza he too acknowledged the fact of mental control of bodily functions. Such acknowledgment is in accord with interactionistic theorizing. For this reason he was charged with inconsistency in advocating interactionism in one chapter and parallelism in another.

Spinoza does not seem to have been similarly criticized. It might be that his double-aspect version of parallelism, with its notion of an underlying identity, warded off criticism by suggesting the kind of convergent parallelism illustrated by the way in which prolonged parallel lines seem to converge and meet at a distant point. This is obviously a vague conjecture and hardly a satisfactory solution to the mind-body puzzle. But there is still no satisfactory solution.

Some psychologists, weary of the futile debates, refuse to concern them-selves with the problem. In the words of J. W. Reeves (1934, p. 22) they "would put aside all questions about body and mind as philosophically senseless and scientifically a waste of time." Others, on the other hand, continue the search for a clarifying formulation. In a current text, edited by S. Koch, for example, one finds whole chapters devoted to the problem, with one chapter concerned with "Brain and Mind" and another entitled "How Man Looks at His Own Brain: An Adventure Shared by Psychology and Neurophysiology."

Critique of the Mind-Matter Dichotomy

A chapter heading like the second one cited from Koch reflects the psycho-physical riddle by suggesting that psychology belongs to one realm of being and neurophysiology to another. This means two separate worlds: one the province of mind and the other the province of material bodies. It is the kind of dichotomy seemingly endorsed by those who conceive of so-called mental *disease* as a condition whose occurrence need not necessarily involve pathology of the brain. It is as if they believe that a given patient may have a sick mind despite a healthy brain. This is the sort of belief that has induced the psychiatrist T. J. Szasz to characterize the concept of *mental* illness as a myth (1960 and 1961).

The notion of two separate worlds of mind and matter has also been called a myth. In his book dealing with a critical analysis of *The Concept of Mind* (1949), Professor G. Ryle refers to this notion as "Descartes' Myth."[4] Ryle is not a psychologist. He is Professor of Metaphysical Philosophy at Oxford. Since, as mentioned earlier, the mind-body problem is really a metaphysical problem, it is entirely appropriate for it to engage the attention of a professional metaphysician. Incidentally, Ryle's trenchant analyses of psychological concepts serve to confirm what James said about metaphysics as meaning "nothing but an unusually obstinate effort to think clearly." However, it would constitute too much of a digression to elaborate upon what Ryle has to say about such psychological concepts as emotion, volition, and intellect. For our present purposes it is sufficient to note that his central thesis is concerned with exploding what he designates as "the two-worlds myth." This refers to the dichotomy of an inner, private world of consciousness and an outer, public world of objects in space. It involves the reification of mind as an autonomous entity capable of separate existence. As a Cartesian myth, Ryle says, it holds that a person's body and mind "are ordinarily harnessed together, but after the death of the body his mind may continue to exist and function" (1949, p. 11). This view equates the concept of mind with the concept of soul or what Ryle stigmatizes as the "ghost" governing the machinery of the body. Accordingly, it follows that (1949, p. 20):

> As thus presented, minds are not merely ghosts harnessed to machines, they are themselves just spectral machines. Though the human body is an engine, it is not quite an ordinary engine, since some of its workings are governed by another engine inside it—this interior governor-engine being one of a very special sort. It is invisible, inaudible and it has no size or weight. It cannot be taken to bits and the laws it obeys are not those known to ordinary engineers. Nothing is known of how it governs the bodily engine.

---

4 Ryle does not employ the term "myth" as a synonym for a fairy story. Instead he views a myth as "the presentation of facts belonging to one category in the idioms appropriate to another. To explode a myth is accordingly not to deny the facts but to re-allocate them" (1949, p. 8). Furthermore, he concedes that "myths often do a lot of theoretical good, while they are still new" (p. 23). In his view, the new Cartesian myth of hidden or "occult" mental forces "was a scientific improvement on the old myth of Final Causes." A more modern instance is to be found in the current view of those who refer to the "myth of mental illness." For them, the medical concept of illness is not germane to the psychological concept of personality disorder. Nevertheless, they would doubtless regard the myth of mental illness as an advance over the prior myth of demonic possession.

The Cartesian formulation, it must be granted, does lend itself to a *reductio ad absurdum* of this sort. It is easy to lampoon Descartes' view of the pineal body as the organ of interaction between body and mind, for it may readily induce one to conjure up a picture of a ghost-like homunculus transacting business with the cells of the pineal body. For some psychologists, all dualistic formulations are anathema because of possible connotations of ghosts or souls. Just as biologists are reluctant to be known as vitalists, so many psychologists do not relish being classified as mentalists. In the case of biologists, the reluctance signifies a conviction or a faith in the adequacy of physiochemical principles to account for the nature of life. Similarly, the nondualistic psychologists believe that eventually these same principles will suffice to account for the nature of mind. Such convictions, faiths, or beliefs are more matters of metaphysics than of science. Both the problems of biology and of psychology can be investigated without prior commitment to some belief about the *ultimate* nature of life and mind.

Moreover, for psychologists to employ a dualistic vocabulary by referring to tastes, smells, pains, anxieties, dreams, thoughts, hunger, and other items of consciousness on the one hand as well as to sense organs, brains, muscles, glands, stimuli, and physical objects on the other does not commit them to endorsement of vitalism or a belief in unique mind stuff or souls or ghosts. As a dualist or pluralist, James was very definite about this. For him this was "the language of common sense" (1890, Vol. I, p. 144). As he saw it (p. 401), "for psychological purposes" there is no need to postulate "an unchanging metaphysical entity like the Soul, or a principle like the pure Ego," and to do so would carry one "beyond the psychological or naturalistic point of view."

By the psychological point of view, James was referring, among other things, to efforts to supply a systematic account of mental life in terms of direct experience or by means of accurate descriptions of the characteristics of consciousness. This is the phenomenological point of view. It accumulates its data by means of introspective reports and hence is subjective in orientation. The subjectivity of introspection has been contrasted with the objectivity allegedly characteristic of observations made by physicists, chemists, astronomers, and other natural scientists. The latter observations are regarded as public while the introspective ones are said to be private. Despite this, as has just been indicated, James referred to the psychological point of view as "naturalistic." This was in keeping with late-nineteenth-century efforts to develop the "new" psychology as a natural science. The methodology of physics was taken over by the pioneer experimental psychologists, but the transfer proved troublesome. It became necessary to justify dependence on introspective methods as scientifically respectable. Their privacy was seemingly in conflict with the public nature of procedures in the laboratories of natural scientists. The big problem was to reconcile the subjectivity of psychological data with the alleged objectivity of physical data. This, it will be recalled, was listed as the problem of *positivism*. It belongs to the persistent problems of psychology and calls for separate discussion.

Positivism's Repudiation of Subjective Data

As mentioned earlier, the term "positivism" was introduced by the French sociologist Auguste Comte a little over a hundred years ago. It referred to his view that the progress of science is handicapped by the introduction of theological and metaphysical notions. According to Comte, questions of the ultimate nature of reality are to play no part in a scientific enterprise. Instead there is to be exclusive dependence on factual data unembellished by unverifiable *a priori* assumptions. To obtain assured or positive knowledge, the investigator must restrict himself to the certainties of observed facts and to logically justified inferences from such facts. This, in. brief, constitutes the standpoint of positivism.

At one time in his thinking about psychology, James was an advocate of this standpoint. At all events, as Perry (1954, p. 194) has shown, he once referred to the "strictly positivistic point of view" of the *Principles* as the only respect in which the work was original. This endorsement of positivism is not to be construed as an unqualified endorsement of Comte. In fact, according to Perry (p. 129), James had once criticized some positivists as being arbitrary and narrow in the kind of positivism they advocated.

Unlike Comte's positivism, that of James was not curbed by the possible metaphysical implications of psychological issues, as is evidenced by his willingness to investigate the paranormal experiences reported by those engaged in psychical research. It was also shown by his readiness to give serious attention to the nature of religious and mystical experiences. In fact, all human experience was grist to his psychological mill. He kept all doors open in the sense of being prepared to welcome whatever might shed light on the nature of such experience. What was welcomed was subjected to critical scrutiny and ejected if found to be untenable because of being factually unwarranted or devoid of psychological significance. He was a positivist in terms of his loyalty to the importance of factual support for given conclusions, but not in his support of Comte's concept of positivism. His opposition to the latter concept was very explicit, for Comte had been vehement in repudiating the validity of introspective reports. James quotes a long passage from Comte in which, among other matters, one finds these sentences (1890, Vol. I, p. 188):

> I limit myself to pointing out the principal consideration which proves clearly that this pretended direct contemplation of the mind by itself is a pure illusion. . . . The thinker cannot divide himself into two, of whom one reasons whilst the other observes him reason. The organ observed and the organ observing being, in this

case, identical, how could observation take place? This pretended psychological method is then radically null and void.

This indictment of introspective observation is by no means outmoded. A large part of Ryle's book is devoted to a similar indictment. He refers to such observation as a "supposed species of perception" (1949, p. 163) and as one of the psychologically baneful consequences of the "Descartes' myth" in terms of which there is supposed to be an inner "occult" world of mental life as contrasted with an outer world of physical existence. In Ryle's view (1949, p. 14), the "myth" has given currency to a belief in the existence of "immediate data of consciousness" capable of being both perceived and introspected. To quote his own formulation:

> Besides being currently supplied with these alleged immediate data of consciousness, a person is also generally supposed to be able to exercise from time to time a special kind of perception, namely inner perception, or introspection. He can take a (non-optical) "look" at what is passing in his mind. . . . This self-observation is also commonly supposed to be immune from illusion, confusion or doubt. A mind's reports of its own affairs have a certainty superior to the best that is possessed by its reports of matters in the physical world. Sense-perceptions can, but consciousness and introspection cannot, be mistaken or confused.

The issues involved here obviously belong to one of psychology's persistent problems, for Ryle's mid-twentieth-century indictment echoes the mid-nineteenth-century one of Comte. Moreover, had Ryle informed himself of what James had written about the fallibility of introspection, he might have softened his indictment. At all events, neither James nor many other advocates of introspective procedures ever maintained that consciousness and introspection are immune to error and confusion. In fact, James (1890, Vol. I, pp. 191–192) expresses his opinion on the subject by giving it the following italicized emphasis in concluding:

> . . . *introspection is difficult and fallible; and that the difficulty is simply that of all observation of whatever kind.* Something is before us; we do our best to tell what it is, but in spite of our good will we may go astray, and give a description more applicable to some other sort of thing. The only safeguard is in the final consensus of our farther knowledge about the thing in question, later views correcting earlier ones, until at last the harmony of a consistent system is reached. Such a system, gradually worked out, is the best guarantee the psychologist can give for the soundness of any particular psychologic observation which he may report.

Ryle and James are at one in their repudiation of psychologies based upon appeals either to a personal soul or to independent mental faculties. Actually, as Ryle points out (1949, p. 319), his book is more concerned with philosophical psychology than with scientific psychology. Hence he does not bother to supply a formal definition either of mind or of psychology. His chief concern is to expose the "myth" of two worlds: the inner world of consciousness and an outer realm of physical being. That is why he refers to the "alleged" data of consciousness. He recognizes that the general drift of his views is in line with behavioristic views, but he regards the mechanistic trend of early behaviorism as a mistake.

The Dread of Mechanistic Explanations

At the risk of a slight digression, it may prove clarifying to consider what Ryle has to say about the not uncommon tendency to glorify the laws of mechanics as some sort of ideal paradigm of science. He calls this "the bogy of mechanism" which induces people to regard the laws of mechanics as "the ultimate laws of nature" and to hope for or dread the day when fields like biology, psychology, and sociology will be "reduced" to the sovereignty of mechanical law. In commenting on this he writes (1949, p. 76):

> I have spoken of Mechanism as a bogy. The fear that theoretically minded persons have felt lest everything found should turn out to be explicable by mechanical laws is a baseless fear. And it is baseless not because the contingency which they dread happens not to be impending, but because it makes no sense to speak of such a contingency. Physicists may one day have found the answers to all physical questions, but not all questions are physical questions. The laws that they have found and will find may, in one sense of the metaphorical verb, govern everything that happens, but they do not ordain everything that happens. Indeed they do not ordain anything that happens. Laws of nature are not fiats.

By way of dissipating the "bogy" Ryle calls attention to a fallacy responsible for the popular dread of mechanistic explanations.[5] People mistakenly interpret the universality of the laws of physics to mean that all of nature functions like a machine or a collection of different kinds of machine. Our concept of a machine is based upon familiarity with man-made contrivances like lawnmowers, typewriters, and dynamos. Machines are affairs of nuts and bolts and wires and wheels and cams. It is virtually impossible to locate anything in a state of inanimate nature that constitutes a machine in this sense. Planetary orbits in terms of their clocklike regularity might be said to resemble

---

[5] Ryle overlooks one other reason for this popular dread. This has to do with the *materialistic* implications of mechanistic concepts. People confuse the ethical with the metaphysical connotation of the word "materialism." One may be a materialist in the metaphysical sense and still be a zealous follower of Emerson's ideal of "plain living and high thinking." On the other hand, one may repudiate materialism or physicalism as metaphysical ultimates and yet regard the accumulation of wealth and the acquisition of material comforts as central personal values. The latter person would be a materialist in the ethical sense but not in the metaphysical sense. In the interest of clear thinking, it is imperative to keep these two meanings of the word separate and distinct.

machines because of their dependable periodicity. But apart from the solar system it is hard to find nonliving analogues to machines in the world of lifeless nature. Machines embody principles of mechanics, but, as Ryle puts it (1949, p. 82), "Inventing machines is not copying things found in inanimate Nature."

For many people, the notion of mechanical laws as applicable to human behavior is an unwelcome notion because they take it to mean the equivalent of regarding man as a mechanical robot. As they see it, such a notion deprives man of reasoning, planning, choosing, evaluating, and in general regulating his conduct as an intelligent responsible being. This too belongs to "the bogy of mechanism." Recognition of the bearing of laws of physics in the regulation of human activity does not make man the helpless shuttlecock of impersonal forces. It does not make him the victim of a bleak determinism without the freedom to be creative and responsible.

Instead, as Ryle suggests, the limitations imposed by mechanical laws are comparable to the limitations imposed by the rules governing games like chess, cricket, or baseball. The rules leave the players free to work out their own maneuvers, plan novel strategy, and adapt their tactics to the changing pattern of the game. There is plenty of opportunity for spontaneity and creative planning. In fact, no two games of baseball, bridge, or badminton are likely to be precisely alike even though they are governed by the same set of rules applicable to each kind of game. Analogously, writers are governed by laws of grammar and rules for spelling and punctuation without a crippling interference with their freedom of expression. Two journalists who are given the same assignment and are subject to the same grammatical laws are not likely to hand their editor identically worded reports. Being subject to the laws does not make them stereotyped writing robots. Seen in this light, the not uncommon aversion to so-called mechanistic explanations of some phases of human behavior appears to be the product of a misinterpretation of the nature and consequences of such explanations.

The Subjective-Objective Dichotomy

There is no need to continue with this digression. Instead it is advisable to revert to a consideration of Ryle's own "bogy" with respect to consciousness and introspection. In his skepticism about the reliability of introspective data along with his reference to the "alleged" data of consciousness, he is taking a stand in line with Comte's positivism. This positivistic orientation is also in line with the stand taken by behavioristic psychologists. Both positivists in philosophy and behaviorists in psychology tend to view the scientific enterprise as an affair of objective procedures with sedulous avoidance of metaphysical broodings and subjective data. For them, the ideal scientific psychologists are to be concerned with what their human and animal subjects *do* rather that with what they might be experiencing. Overt actions rather than covert perceptions, thoughts, dreams, and feelings are to constitute the basis for psychology as science.

As has just been indicated, for objectivists the fundamentals of psychology are to be established by finding answers to this question: What is the organism—man or animal—*doing?* For subjectivists, on the other hand, the equivalent question reads: What is the organism—man or animal—*experiencing?* Since the time of Wundt and James, both objectivists and subjectivists have regarded their respective orientations as indispensable for a scientific psychology. They both have stressed the importance of experimental controls in the conduct of psychological investigations. Both have recognized loyalty to factually established data as the *sine qua non* of science. In terms of such loyalty, both might be regarded as sensitive to the importance of evidence cited in support of what is submitted as fact. But here one comes to the parting of the ways, with the subjectivists regarding the results of controlled introspection as having this kind of support whereas objectivists question their validity.

This subjective-objective dichotomy constitutes one of the crucial problems in the history of psychology, particularly its recent history. It is reflected in the way in which the field of psychology is defined. The contrast is readily brought out by comparing the definition introduced by James with that introduced by some contemporary psychologists. On the first page of his *Principles,* James defined psychology as "the Science of Mental Life, both of its phenomena and of their conditions." He then added that phenomena "are such things as we call feelings, desires, cognitions, reasonings, decisions, and the like." Moreover, in connection with his discussion of methods of investigating such phenomena, there is an emphatic endorsement of introspective observation. His introductory paragraph is both explicit and challenging (1890, Vol. I, p. 185):

> *Introspective Observation is what we have to rely on first and foremost and always.* The word introspection need hardly be defined—it means, of course, the looking into our own minds and reporting what we there discover. *Every one agrees that we there discover states of consciousness.* So far as I know, the existence of such states has never been doubted by any critic, however sceptical in other respects he may have been. That we have *cogitations* of some sort is the *inconcussum* in a world most of whose other facts have at some time tottered in the breath of philosophic doubt. All people unhesitatingly believe that they feel themselves thinking, and that they distinguish the mental state as an inward activity or passion, from all the objects with which it may cognitively deal. *I regard this belief as the most fundamental of all the postulates of Psychology,* and shall discard all curious inquiries about its certainty as too metaphysical for the scope of this book.

Not many decades later, it became evident that this whole subjective orientation was being questioned. With the rise of the *reflexology* of Vladimir

M. Bekhterev (1857–1927) in Russia and of the behaviorism of John B. Watson (1878–1958), many psychologists began to have misgivings about the use of words like "mind," "consciousness," "images," "thoughts," "ideas" and whatever else impressed them as products of introspective observation. In their view, psychology was no longer to be defined as the science of mental life or the science of consciousness or the science of experience. For them, what James had said about the primacy and reliability of the introspective discovery of states of consciousness as the "most fundamental of all the postulates of Psychology" could no longer be reconciled with a psychology defined as the science of behavior. No longer could they accept Titchener's view of mind (1917, p. 9) as "the sum-total of human experience considered as dependent upon the experiencing person." No longer could they accept his view of animal psychology's goal to be the determination of the probable nature of animal consciousness. This was to be based upon the emphatic use of analogy: from a dog's cringing posture one might infer the existence of an inner state of self-abasing fear. According to Titchener (1927, pp. 31–32), when experiment is employed "the animal is thus made, so to say, to observe, to introspect; it attends to certain stimuli, and registers its experience by gesture" and the psychologist "observes the gesture, and transcribes the animal consciousness in the light of his own introspection."

As has been stated, in place of this preoccupation with human and animal consciousness or experience, there was increasing concern with psychology defined as the science of behavior. By 1940, for example, Robert S. Woodworth maintained that "psychology can be defined as the *science of the activities* of the individual" (1940, p. 3). To cite one more example: in a contemporary text E. R. Hilgard (1957) makes a point of classifying psychology with the "behavioral sciences" and defines it "as the science that studies the *behavior* of man and other animals." Furthermore, following behavioristic precedent, he differentiates introspective observations from introspective reports. The latter are accepted as objective means of inferring something about the former. Such reports, regarded as "verbal behavior," lead to inferences which make it "possible to study both conscious and unconscious processes without sacrificing the objectivity of the data of psychological science" (1957, p. 21).

All this emphasis upon objectivity for the purpose of enhancing the scientific status of psychology was in accord with the spirit of positivism. This spirit involved more than the avoidance of metaphysical interpretations. On the positive side it stressed the importance of accurate observation of facts in the scientific enterprise. Rigorous adherence to the canons of logic was to govern inferences derived from such facts. Loyalty to fact was to be the hallmark of all scientific concepts and conclusions.

In part the behavioristic attack on introspection as a valid observational procedure was an expression of this positivistic tradition. An introspective description of a conscious phenomenon was deemed too subjective to be admissible as an established fact for science. For instance, a laboratory subject might respond to a high-pitched auditory stimulus by a grimace and an aversive shift of his head and trunk along with a verbal statement like "That's an unpleasant squeak and reminds me of the way I felt as a schoolboy when the teacher's chalk slipped as she was writing on the blackboard." There is no way for the laboratory worker to observe the unpleasantness or the memory of the classroom experience; hence as conscious events they would be classified as too subjective for acceptance as scientific data. Only what he as a laboratory investigator could observe for himself would merit such acceptance. In the present instance this would include noting the grimace, the shift of the head, and the words uttered. The last would be called a "verbal report" rather than an introspective description. To ask what it is a report *of* is to introduce a troublesome question if one's standards of scientific rigor demand the exclusion of references to phenomenal events or what some would regard as the private world of personal awareness.

In terms of such an exclusion, a hard-boiled objectivist would have difficulty specifying what he takes as the referents of the words in the verbal report. Strictly, as a consistent positivist and objectivist, he ought to regard verbal reports as the meaningless consequences of laryngeal reactions to his laboratory stimuli. Actually no behavioristic psychologist has been so strict and objective in his use of verbal reports. Were this not the case it would be a matter of indifference whether the report were given in English, Chinese, Polish, or some obscure African dialect. Instead the report is taken seriously as a means of communication. The objectivist wants to understand the words of his experimental subject—even words like "pleasantness," "feeling," "me," "headache," and similar subjective terms. Despite the use of objective methods, he thus finds himself lured back into a subjective realm; namely, to subjective states mentioned in the verbal report. In the last analysis he is forced to come to grips with such states. Allport had this in mind when he formulated the riddle of positivism by asking (1943, p. 96), "Are the objective methods you by preference employ suited to the subjective facts that are your ultimate data?"

It is not always possible to establish a sharp line of distinction between the subjective and the objective. By way of simple illustration, one might be asked whether perception of the words on this page is an objective or a subjective process. What the literate person perceives will differ from the perception of one who has never learned to read. The fact that all literate people who are familiar with English can *see* each word as a word would seem to make the reading an objective affair. However, since illiterates or those unfamiliar with English would differ from one another in their reports of what they see on the page, then for them the diverse perceptions would appear to be more subjective than objective. Only by teaching them to read English can their discrepant perceptions be transformed into agreement with respect to what is being perceived. In this instance, then, making things objective means making changes in the subject or observer. In other instances, as in staining the cells of a fragment of brain tissue, making something objective involves a change in the object being scrutinized.

The complexity of the subjective-objective dichotomy was not necessarily disposed of by Comte's positivism. Contrary to what is sometimes presented as his central teaching, for him positivism included recognition of the importance of theorizing in the work of the scientist and was not limited to stressing the importance of collecting facts or "objective" data. Philipp Frank (1957, p. 15) has made this clear by quoting the following from Comte's book on positivism:

> If, on the one hand, every positive theory must necessarily be based on observations, it is equally sensible, on the other hand, that in order to carry out observations our minds need some theory. If, in contemplating the phenomena, we did not attach them to some principles, it would not be possible to combine these isolated observations and to draw from them any conclusions. Moreover, we would not even be able to fix them in our minds. Ordinarily these facts would remain unnoticed beneath our eyes.

Is the preceding paragraph to be classified as an objective account of psychological events? In writing it, was Comte abiding by his positivistic repudiation of self-observation as a source of valid information? Is it not evident that what he has to say about "our minds" being guided by theory in order to "to fix" items of "isolated observations" is a product of self-observation? If this be granted, then it would seem that even the father of positivism availed himself of introspective or subjective data.

Are Scientific Data Completely Objective?

Back in 1944, the *Psychological Review* published an article by the philosopher P. Crissman with this arresting title: "Are Psychological Data and Methods Subjective?" Even though more than twenty years have elapsed since the article was written, it continues to have relevance for the contemporary psychological scene; now as then, psychologists are likely to regard an affirmative answer to Crissman's question as a reflection on the status of psychology as a science. This is particularly true of those who prefer to think of psychology as a natural science like physics or biology.

By way of introduction, Crissman considers the obvious relationship between the dependence of scientific concepts on perceptual data. All sciences must deal with such data as observations made by individual investigators. As events in the experience of each investigator, they may be called subjective. This inference is clearly indicated by Crissman in these words (1944, pp. 162–163):

> For every science, psychology included, concerns itself with some domain of perceptual data. If the data and methods of psychology are subjective, then, in

varying degree, so also are those of the other empirical sciences and for the same reason. The case is much the same if we turn to scientific concepts and laws. If by "subjective" it be meant that these depend for their existence upon the person having them, then, as Pratt[6] points out, "all science is subjective. Objective knowledge . . . can mean nothing more than the cancellation of idiosyncracies by the process of pooling, sifting, and weighing all the bits of individual subjectivities. The result is still subjective, for there is none other available. . . ." Yet this is but to say that scientific methods and laws are formulated by human inquirers and possess neither meaning nor existence apart from operations instituted by some investigator. This is as true of physics as it is of psychology.

From one viewpoint, the antithesis between subjectivity and objectivity seems to be a question of verifiability. Events, concepts, or interpretations capable of verification are thus to be classified as objective, while those refractory to verification are to be deemed subjective. In terms of this distinction, a statement to the effect that the negative afterimage of yellow is blue can be regarded as a statement of objective fact, even though the phenomenon in question occurs within the privacy of the observer's visual experience. However, the existence and nature of afterimages can be verified by other observers who subject themselves to the same kind of visual stimulation. Similarly, despite the subjectivity or privacy involved in noting the phenomenon of the blind spot, the readiness with which any observer can check on its existence for himself renders the phenomenon an objective psychological fact.

All facts, in other words, are not necessarily facts of material or physical existence. It is easy to cite examples by noting the immediate recognition of the factual status of innumerable logical, mathematical, grammatical, and other relationships. Thus it is a fact that the opposite of induction is deduction and that 10 is the square foot of 100 and that words like "participle," "gerund," and "verb" are grammatical terms. Such recognition is a function of one's possession of the requisite concepts belonging to the fields of logic, mathematics, and grammar, respectively. The recognition is a matter of ideational rather than sensory perception, and hence some people might be inclined to classify both the facts and the recognition as subjective. However, with respect to their verifiability as facts they may also be classified as objective.

The concept of a scientific fact thus has both subjective and objective implications. Some scientific facts are more objective than others, as can be noted by considering three meanings of the term "fact" as suggested by Crissman (1944, p. 163). In the *first* group of meanings the notion of fact has to do with matters of direct sensory perception as exemplified by many common laboratory observations embodied in statements like "The litmus paper is now blue," or "The dial on the indicator has moved to number

---

6 Pratt's views will be considered later in this chapter.

16," or "The thermometer reading is 104." As facts of perceptual discrimination, such observations are not to be confused with the bearing they have on particular hypotheses or interpretations for whose sake the observations were made. Such interpretations refer to the *second* group of meanings and refer to what the investigator regards as the significance of perceived items. Facts in this sense take the form of such propositions as "This is an alkaline solution," or "This barometer reading means rain," or "The patient has a fever." Facts of this kind hinge upon judgment and may, of course, turn out to be in error. With reference to the judgment of the patient's fever, for example, if the thermometer was wrongly calibrated, the clinician's interpretation of the reading as an indication of fever would be contrary to fact. To perceive whales as fishes because of their aquatic habitat would constitute another error of judgment. In this instance the perceived data are subsumed under the wrong concept. Finally, in the *third* group of meanings for the word "fact," one is concerned with broad generalizations applicable to a whole class of objects or events. Most so-called scientific laws are facts in this sense, so that a psychologist, thinking of Weber's law, might say, "It is a fact that a just perceptible difference bears a constant ratio to the standard stimulus." Similarly, in terms of Boyle's law, a physicist would regard it as a fact that with temperature held constant a given amount of gas varies in volume inversely as the pressure, just as a neurologist in citing the Bell-Magendie law would regard it as a fact that the anterior roots of the spinal nerves are motor and posterior roots are sensory.

It should thus be obvious that in science facts are the outcome of diligent effort and involve more than the passive consequences of sensory stimulation. As was mentioned in an earlier chapter, their establishment, as Aristotle suggested, marks the difference between having an experience and observing an experience. Both objective and subjective factors are involved in such establishment; hence with respect to the three meanings of the term "fact," Crissman reaches this conclusion (1944, p. 163):

A hypothesis is made true, is verified, and thereby in turn itself becomes a fact, when, as an experimental operation, it leads to the discovery or institution of facts in the first two senses. For purposes of science, all facts may be described as "constructs"; they are not brute "givens" parading before awareness for anyone to read who runs.

The preceding conclusion had already been arrived at by James some fifty years earlier, where it is so well formulated as to constitute a clarifying extension of Crissman's formulation. In the last chapter of the *Principles,* in connection with a discussion of the "effects of experience" on the work of the scientist, James introduced this paragraph (1890, Vol. II, pp. 636–637):

The most persistent outer relations which science believes in are never matters of experience at all, but have to be disengaged from under experience by a process of elimination, that is, by ignoring conditions which are always present. The *elementary* laws of mechanics, physics, and chemistry are all of this sort. The principle of uniformity in nature is of this sort; it has to be sought under and in spite of the most rebellious appearances; and our conviction of its truth is far more like a religious faith than like an assent to a demonstration. The only cohesions which experience in the literal sense of the word produces in our mind are . . . the proximate laws of nature, and habitudes of concrete things, that heat melts ice, that salt preserves meat, that fish die out of water, and the like. Such "empirical truths" as these we admitted to form an enormous part of human wisdom. The "scientific" truths have to harmonize with these, or be given up as useless; but they arise in the mind in no such passive associative way as that in which the simpler truths arise. Even those experiences which are used to prove a scientific truth are for the most part artificial experiences of the laboratory gained after the truth itself has been conjectured. Instead of experiences engendering the "inner relations," the inner relations are what engender the experiences here.

From Empiricism to Science to Technology

The distinction that James made between "empirical truths" and "scientific truths" has far-reaching implications. Both kinds of truth can be regarded as referring to established fact, and thus the distinction has nothing to do with one set of truths being more factual than the other. Empirical truths are the results of casual everyday experiences and embody the fund of commonsense information every child acquires in the course of growing up. They are more products of direct sensory observation than of effortful study or systematic reflection. That birds fly, dogs eat meat, ice is cold, people get angry, candy is sweet, rocks are hard, and a thousand and one similar bits of information are shared by all. As bits of information they are facts without being scientific truths. As information they enable one to come to terms with commonplace situations and to dispose of practical problems. They are to be classified as instances of Crissman's first group of facts. Moreover, many facts belonging to his second group are also to be viewed as empirical truths. More than simple sensory observation is involved with reference to this second group. As will be recalled, this grouping refers to judgments and interpretations of observational data. The examples cited by James of the fact that salt preserves meat and that fish cannot live without water are serviceable instances of this grouping. In order to transform such empirical truths into scientific ones, it is necessary to be able to account for the observed changes in the light of an appropriate body of principles. To explain why or how salt preserves meat calls for knowledge of the chemistry and bacteriology of putrefaction. Similarly, without knowledge of the respiratory equipment of fish it is impossible to explain why an aquatic habitat is essential.

As was mentioned in Chapter 7, medieval craftsmen amassed a vast amount of useful information in various fields of technology. For the most part, however, these technological advances were not the result of deliberate application of scientific principles, any more than a housewife's ability to prepare hard-boiled eggs demonstrates a knowledge of the chemistry of colloids. The advances were more the result of an accumulation of empirical as contrasted with scientific facts, just as the housewife's culinary skill may increase with years of cooking experience despite her ignorance of cooking as a science.

By the thirteenth century, however, philosophers like Roger Bacon began to show an interest in the practical application of scientific principles (see Chapter 7, pp. 164–165). In the course of time this meant that the plausibility or intelligibility of such abstractly formulated principles was not sufficient to establish their validity. They had to be made to square with the facts of experience. The emergence of modern science in the seventeenth century reflected this shift from a purely philosophic interest in scientific principles to an interest in the practical or technological consequences of such principles, Philipp Frank has called attention to the nature of this shift in this way (1957, pp. 28–29):

> From about the year 1600 . . . science became more pretentious; it wanted to derive practical mechanics from theoretical mechanics. . . . Man had become aware that statements derived from intelligible and beautiful principles could account only in a very vague way for observed facts. The union between science and philosophy was possible only during a period of separation between science and technology. Modern science was born when technology became scientific. The union of science and technology was responsible for the separation between science and philosophy.

Can it also be said that modern scientific psychology was born when applied psychology or psychotechnology became scientific? In one sense this question might be answered in the negative; for the founding fathers of the "new" or scientific psychology were not enamored of an applied psychology. They were content to rely on their pioneering laboratory experiments for the establishment of their principles of a scientific psychology. According to Titchener (1929, pp. 66–67), one of their devoted followers, there is a sharp cleavage between pure science and technology:

> For the great difference between science and technology is a difference of initial attitude. The scientific man follows his method whithersoever it may take him. . . . The technologist moves in another universe; he seeks the attainment of some determinate end, which is his sole and obsessing care; and he therefore takes no heed of anything that he cannot put to use as means toward that end. The special "problems" about which the science of a given period is busy are problems set by the logic of the scientific system, and not by any consideration of utility. . . . Technology, on the other hand, exists only in virtue of its special and practical problem. . . .

In subsequent paragraphs Titchener observed that technology would "stagnate" without the help of science and this impels the technologist "to talk things out with his scientific colleague"; but Titchener did not make this a reciprocal relationship by maintaining that science would "stagnate" without recourse to the proving ground of technology. In his view, virtually irreconcilable temperamental differences account for those whose interest in science is primarily utilitarian as contrasted with those whose devotion to science is altogether independent of its practical applications.

The latter nonutilitarian outlook, being far less common than the utilitarian one, is perplexing for many people. By way of clarification, Titchener cites the comment of a distinguished chemist: "For my own part, I must say that science to me generally ceases to be interesting as it becomes useful." It is altogether likely that this remark also reflects Titchener's attitude toward psychology as science.[7] At all events, the kind of "new" psychology he sponsored was decidedly remote from the concerns of those in quest of a practical psychology to be placed at the disposal of efficiency engineers, personnel administrators, sales managers, advertising consultants, and others engaged in regulating, controlling, influencing, or supervising human affairs. Because of this remoteness, as was mentioned in Chapter 8, James in his lecture to the teachers warned them of the futility of expecting any help from the "new" psychology in their work as educators. The "scientific facts" coming to light in the Wundtian laboratories had no obvious bearing on the "empirical facts" of the classroom. This was true in the 1890s when the laboratory approach to psychological problems was still in its early beginnings.

If this approach be viewed as marking the birth of a scientific psychology, then what Philipp Frank said about modern science emerging from a scientific technology would not seem to be confirmed in the case of psychology. Still, this might be an unwarranted or premature conclusion because of a failure to grasp the full import of the stated relationship between modern science and technology. For one thing, by employing a qualifying adjective like "modern," Frank indicates the existence of science prior to 1600. As a tradition, what was to develop into twentieth-century science has roots going back through the late medieval period to the Hellenistic and ancient Greek ages. All this has already been outlined in previous chapters. It is also advisable to observe that Frank is careful to note that the year 1600 marks the approximate time when changes leading to the "birth" of modern science became manifest. This was a gradual process extending over

---

[7] Titchener was not unmindful of the possible practical applications of the "new" psychology. For example, in connection with his discussion of experimental studies of association, he reported (1929, p. 382): "The rules discovered in the laboratory have already been applied, with success, to certain practical problems."

many decades and not a sudden "delivery" marked by instantaneous umbilical severance from philosophy. Physics and chemistry continued to belong to natural philosophy after the year 1600, just as psychology continued to be taught in departments of philosophy after the year 1879.

Separation of individual fields of science from philosophy was more in the nature of a slow transition than a sudden birth. In the course of this transition, the impact of science on practical affairs became increasingly evident. The validity of newly discovered laws of physics was not restricted to laboratory confirmation but received additional confirmation when their application to technological problems proved spectacularly successful. The prestige of science in the eyes of the common man is largely due to this success as he thinks of things like steam engines, turbines, electric lights, locomotives, radios, antitoxins, refrigerators, and so on as products of science. He may be ignorant of the meaning of Einstein's formula, $E = mc^2$, and yet be overawed by the reality of atomic bombs. What he may fail to realize is that the practical achievements of science were preceded by a long history of painstaking thought and investigation having no immediate or obvious utilitarian value. Without the accumulation of the fruits of such "non-utilitarian" theorizing and experimentation, technological progress would have been very much retarded.

This is another way of saying that, in general, pure science contributes more to applied science than the latter contributes to the former. However, an important contribution made by applied science is that of putting the findings of pure science to a pragmatic test. In the process of becoming scientific, technology is checking on such findings by putting them to work. This, it seems, is all that Frank meant by calling attention to the emergence of modern science in a setting of technological achievement. A disciple of Comte might well regard such achievement as the culmination of scientific endeavor viewed as a positivistic enterprise. After all, there is nothing vague, abstruse, or metaphysical about a suspension bridge or a helicopter.

Opposition to Applied Psychology

At the time Titchener voiced his misgivings about an applied psychology, experimental physics has been in existence for well over three hundred years and its findings were being utilized by hydraulic engineers, electrical engineers, civil engineers, and other technologists. On the other hand, experimental psychology had been in existence for only forty to fifty years and its findings were hardly the equivalent of the laws and principles of physics operative in the world of engineering. Under the circumstances, Titchener may have been justified in his stand. In his day, chronologically considered, experimental psychology was still very young as compared with experimental physics. In fact, not until the year 2179 will it be as advanced in years as physics was in the year 1900.

In part, Titchener's misgivings about applied psychology were a recognition of the danger to scientific progress when the search for basic principles is subordinated to the solution of practical problems. Success in disposing of such problems does not necessarily result in enhanced scientific understanding. Preliterate man learned how to build a fire and to shoot arrows without such success giving him a knowledge of the chemistry of combustion or the principles of ballistics. Cattle breeding was carried on long before there was a science of genetics. Generations before there was a subject like animal psychology, animal trainers were successful in getting horses and dogs to obey commands and perform tricks. Learning theory was not a product of their success, any more than it was a product of the success of many generations of teachers whose pupils were taught to read and to write and to cipher. Not until educational psychology became a branch of applied psychology did such pedagogic success become the object of scientific investigation. Moreover, such investigation developed out of the prior existence of the beginnings of an experimental psychology. The prescientific philosophical psychologies did not prompt the emergence of applied psychologies. Titchener had this in mind when he wrote (1929, p. 259):

> It is worth remembering too that, despite all the psychological systems from Aristotle down, it is only since the appearance of experimental psychology and its attainment of impersonal results that the special technologies of mind have sprung into vigorous being.

In calling attention to this relationship between the antecedent rise of an experimental psychology and the later emergence of the "special technologies," Titchener was not trying to defend the pursuit of pure science in terms of its potential practical applications. For him, such a defense was not needed. He was more concerned with safeguarding its purity against the lure of premature efforts to find uses for its findings. Furthermore, he had reason to believe that the foundations of the "new" experimental psychology needed strengthening before psychologists would be justified in becoming practitioners. He saw these foundations being weakened by the claims of sponsors of rival systems of psychology. Advocates of the system of functional psychology were stressing the problem-solving function of consciousness, behaviorists were ignoring consciousness and concentrating on unconditioned and conditioned reflexes, the Gestalt psychologists were attacking what they stigmatized as the atomism of Tichener's kind of psychology.

The Questioning of Basic Concepts

These divergent systems appeared on the psychological scene during the first two decades of this century. Its leaders were influenced by the Leipzig tradition, at least to the extent of recognizing the importance of experimental evidence in support of psychological theorizing. Thus they all agreed in regarding psychology as an experimental science and in promoting laboratory research. Unfortunately, despite the accumulation of an enormous amount of laboratory data, the systematic cleavages persisted. There was failure to reach agreement on the interpretation of the meaning of what was being reported by the laboratory investigators.

In part this failure was due to increasing controversy regarding some of the fundamental concepts of psychology. This sort of controversy had already occurred during the prescientific period, and it did not abate during the transition from philosophical to scientific psychology. Indeed, as laboratory protocols of introspective observations became more and more involved in subtle and often contradictory descriptions of conscious content, there may have been an *increase* in controversy. There were debates about levels of attention, differences between sensory and motor reaction times, the number and nature of elementary feeling states, and how sensations were to be differentiated from images. In addition, the complexity of color vision gave rise to rival theoretic formulations. The polemic atmosphere was also thickened by arguments about the adequacy of different theories of hearing. It began to appear that Comte may have been correct in questioning the reliability of introspection as an observational technique. The "immediate experience" of which introspection was supposed to supply an accurate description turned out to be a strained and artificial experience. The conscious elements into which experience was being analyzed were neither obvious nor immediate, but products of abstraction from what James had called the stream of consciousness. In fact, he once stated that he failed to "see how any one with a sense for the facts can possibly call our systems immediate results of 'experience' in the ordinary sense" (1890, Vol. II, p. 636). Nor would Titchener have denied this. He once wrote (1927, p. 128) that "we never have a perception," since consciousness "is a shifting tangle of processes, themselves inconstant, and the perception is a little bit of pattern raveled out from the tangle and *artificially* fixed for scientific scrutiny" [Italics supplied].

The need to be on the alert for the artificiality of some conventional psychological concepts had already been noted by John Dewey in an article on the reflex arc that was first published in 1896 (W. Dennis [ed.], 1948). Dewey warned against making "rigid distinctions between sensations, thoughts and acts" as concomitants of afferent, central, and efferent segments of the reflex arc. Such segments are artificial abstractions from the "organic unity" of the arc. In terms of such a unity, "sensation as stimulus does not mean any particular physical *existence*." It never occurs as a separate, static entity.

A similar statement applies to the concept of consciousness itself. This was strikingly emphasized in the title of a famous essay by James, namely "Does Consciousness Exist?" (R. B. Perry [ed.], 1912). The question was answered negatively with respect to any notion of its existence in terms of special mind stuff or any particular substance. Instead, James viewed consciousness as a metaphysically "neutral" relational *process* of awareness. It was the sort of question which gave currency to the observation that psychology first lost its soul, then it lost its mind, and now it has lost consciousness. Nevertheless, in terms of James's concept of "neutral" or "pure" experience, all was not lost.

However, even the concept of experience did not escape critical scrutiny. E. G. Boring (1963, p. 154) had occasion to expose its ambiguity by asking:

> *Is experience real?* In any strict sense the author's answer is, No. Experience, the metaphysical Dator of data, is prior to reality. However, there is a certain ambiguity about the words experience and reality which suggests the ground of the present difficulty. Objects are real. Now we do not experience objects as such. They are constructs or inferences derived from the data of experience. Nevertheless they do seem to be in experience because their inferential nature does not appear immediately in introspection—"unconscious inference," Helmholtz therefore called it. Hence experience seems to contain the reals, which are nevertheless recognized as derived from experience. The layman recognizes this paradox when, convinced that reality is an artificial construct derived from experience, he finds that such derived reality seems unreal. The psychologist recognizes it when, in introspection, he suddenly realizes that what he is describing as experience is, after all, an inferential construct like all other objects and not the great Dator of data.

Nor did this mark the end of psychological iconoclasm. By the 1920s, shortly after William McDougall had elaborated a closely knit system of psychology based upon the concept of instinct as part of man's hereditary endowment, the idea of instinct as well as that of heredity began to be questioned with respect to their relevance for psychology. Journal articles appeared with titles like "Are There Any Instincts?" (K. Dunlap, 1919) or "A Psychology without Heredity" (Z. Y. Kuo, 1924). In other words, within a span of about thirty years the psychological world was goaded into critical examination of the existential status and relevance of some of its basic concepts—concepts like consciousness, sensation, perception, reflex, experience, and now instinct and heredity! Something more than the careless use of language seemed to be involved. Scientific psychology, despite its nominal allegiance to the principles of positivism, was having difficulty with its technical concepts.

Psychologists Turn to Operationism

At this juncture, psychology followed historical precedent by turning to physics to find out how the physicist was dealing with the problem of formulating acceptable definitions for his scientific concepts. Meanwhile developments in the world of physics had occasioned a reassessment of its "old foundations," or as Whitehead put it in a book now more than forty years old (1948, p. 18; first published in 1925):

> The old foundations of scientific thought are becoming unintelligible. Time, space, matter, material, ether, electricity, mechanism, organism, configuration, structure, pattern, function, all require reinterpretation. What is the sense of talking about a mechanical explanation when you do not know what you mean by mechanics?

One approach to such reinterpretation was suggested by P. W. Bridgman in his *The Logic of Modern Physics,* which appeared in 1927. Within the next few years psychologists became familiar with his proposal of *operationism* as a means of clarifying the meaning of scientific concepts. In brief, by way of reminder, Bridgman stressed the importance of giving due consideration to the procedures used or the operations performed when engaged in scientific work. Concepts like length, time, or weight, he suggested, are to be defined in the light of what the scientist does when measuring linearity, duration, or heaviness.

By way of illustration, it will suffice to consider the concept of length. An operational definition of length is far more complex than its commonsense formulation as the distance separating two points. Nor will the nature of such a definition be disposed of by a hasty reminder of the everyday use of rulers and tape measures. What a physicist *does* in specifying the "operational meaning" of length involves factors not ordinarily included in commonsense or dictionary definitions. Philipp Frank has listed such factors in the following account (1957, pp. 311–312):

> A concept (*e.g.,* "length") has an operational meaning if we can give an "operational definition" of that concept. This means that we have to describe a set of physical operations, which we must carry out, in order to assign in every individual case a uniquely determinate value to the concept (*e.g.,* to the length of an individual piece of iron). We know that the "length" depends on the temperature, pressure, electric charge, and other physical properties. Since Einstein's theory of relativity, we know that the length of a body will "alter" with its speed. Hence, the description of the operation by which we measure a length contains also the operation by which we keep temperature, pressure, speed, etc., constant. Or, in other words, the operational definition of length contains, strictly speaking, also the operational definitions of temperature, pressure, speed, etc. In order to know how to measure a length while keeping other factors, such as pressure, temperature, speed, etc., constant we must know a great many physical laws. Hence, every operational definition of an individual quantity like "length" must be taken "with a grain of salt," and is to be understood as an approximate definition. In other words, only under "favorable" circumstances can a set of operations be described which would provide unambiguously an operational definition of a single quantity like "length" or "time distance."

It should thus be obvious that operational definitions do not eliminate "subjective" or "observational" factors. As just indicated, in determining the length of an iron bar in the precision laboratory the physicist has to be mindful of a whole series of pointer readings by means of which he checks on pressure, temperature, and other variables known to influence the metal. Merely watching the physicist's "operations" is not likely to enable an unsophisticated laboratory visitor to understand what the physicist means by the concept of length. As Frank suggests, to gain such understanding the visitor must have some familiarity with the nature of the variables being controlled or, to put this in another way, he must share the physicist's knowledge of "a great many physical laws." The knowledge determines the operations to be employed. Possessed of this knowledge, the visitor, along with other physicists similarly informed, could engage in the specified operations and presumably arrive at the same conclusion regarding the length of the bar. By specifying what is to be done, everybody executing the appropriate maneuvers, in theory at least, would share the same concept of length; hence operationism has been regarded as enhancing the *public* nature of the scientific enterprise and enhancing its objectivity by reducing or possibly eliminating subjective factors.

Does Operationism Eliminate Subjectivity?

However, Bridgman himself has not endorsed this interpretation of operationism. On one occasion, as a participant in a symposium on the subject of operationism he commented, as follows (1945, pp. 281–284):

> Several of the contributors have referred to science as of necessity being public in character; I believe on the other hand that simple inspection of what one does in any scientific enterprise will show that the *most important part of science is private* . . . [italics supplied].
>
> The question with regard to the public or private character of science is only part of the larger question of public versus private in general. . . . An analysis of what I do discloses that in situations in which I am concerned with distinctions between mine and thine my operations are patently dual in character. The operations which justify me in saying, "My tooth aches," are different from those which justify me in saying, "Your tooth aches." The operations which justify me in saying, "The toothache which I now have feels like the one which I had last week" are recognizably not the same as those which might justify me in making a similar statement about your toothaches. . . . In general, the operations by which I know what I am thinking about are different from the operations by which I convince myself of what you are thinking about. The question never arises, "Am I deliberately deceiving myself with regard to what I am thinking about?" but the question often arises as to whether you are deliberately deceiving me with regard to what you are thinking about. . . .
>
> The extent to which any discipline suffers by its failure to recognize and insist on the social and the private modes of individual behavior depends on

the subject matter. In physics the question hardly presents itself. But in psychology it seems to me that we do want to deal with topics which demand a clear recognition of the operational duality with which at present we are constrained to deal with all questions of me and thee. To assume that this operational duality may be ignored assumes the result of what is at present only a program for the future. In the light of present accomplishment this assumption seems to me exceedingly hazardous. Until it has been shown that the program has reasonable prospects of being carried through the operational approach demands that we make our reports and do our thinking in the freshest terms of which we are capable. . . . Among other things this demands that I make my reports always in the first person and in language which reproduces the structure of my universe. Since one aspect of the structure of my universe is the operational difference between mine and thine, I must make my report in a language which recognizes this operational duality. Since such a language does not at present exist, one must be devised. For the present it will probably be sufficient never to use such words as thought or feeling without qualification, but always to qualify, as "my thought," "your thought," or "my feeling," "your feeling." It may be that eventually we shall be able to take account of the operational dichotomy in the universe of each one of us in some simpler way. But until that time, it seems to me that by ignoring the dichotomy psychology is engaging in an unnecessary gamble, and is probably riding for a fall.

By maintaining that "the most important part of science is private," Bridgman was calling attention to the *personal* nature of the scientist's observations and the scientific reports to which they give rise. In Bridgman's view, the latter reflect or "reproduce" the structure of the scientist's universe and what a fellow scientist has to report regarding *his* observations of the same events suggests the structure of *his* universe. This, in the language of Bridgman, constitutes an "operational dichotomy." Actually, the issue involved has a rather venerable philosophic history. What philosophers have designated as "the egocentric predicament" is a reference to such a dichotomy by indicating the difficulty in ever eliminating the distinction between "your" pains, impressions, and ideas on the one hand as contrasted with "my" pains, impressions, and ideas on the other. To introduce an extreme example: what vision is for the sighted individual can never become the subject of direct acquaintance for a congenitally blind person. The latter may learn *about* the world of color, but he can never learn what it is like in terms of sensory immediacy.

As understood by Bridgman, operationism does not eliminate subjectivity from the realm of scientific discourse, as is indicated by his reference to the "operations" involved in comparing a present toothache with one experienced last week. In the language of traditional psychology, such "operations" would be regarded as introspective procedures. In other words, Bridgman's "operational dichotomy" provides for introspection as an acceptable scientific "operation" despite its privacy and subjectivity. This concession merits explicit emphasis because it is at variance with the somewhat widely held view of operationism as being restricted to the specifiable and overt maneuvers incident to arriving at a scientific determination. The operations or maneuvers are then regarded as the basis for related scientific concepts. Such concepts are then said to be amenable to operational definition. Thus an operational definition of the concept of time would call for attention to particular techniques employed in its measurement, whether by means of sundials, watches, chronoscopes, or calendars or whether expressed in hours, minutes, milliseconds, centuries, or light-years. The subjective experience of duration as such is not included in this kind of operational definition. Nor may it be necessary in order to understand the temporal aspects of work in physics and astronomy. However, to omit it from a study of the psychology of time would be as fatuous as staging Hamlet without the Prince.

Can Intelligence Be Defined Operationally?

For analogous reasons, the attempt to clarify the meaning of a concept like intelligence by exclusive dependence on an operational definition such as "intelligence is what intelligence tests measure" has been unenlightening. To understand the meaning of a measure of intelligence, one must know how the validity of a given test of intelligence was established. After all, different purported tests of intelligence do not yield identical results when administered to the same group of individuals. The person scoring highest on one test may rank tenth on another test and vice versa. Such discrepancies are especially likely to occur if the one test's validity was established by using high-school grades as the criterion and that of the other was based upon ratings for intelligence supplied by army officers.[8] Discrepancies are also likely to result when one set of measures of intelligence is obtained by employing a test composed of a battery of items selected by means of factor analysis as compared with measures given by a test the items of which had not been subjected to factor-analytic screening.

One additional aspect of this operational definition of intelligence merits consideration. This has to do with what some might regard as the nomothetic implications of the definition. With some plausibility, they might call attention to the fact that measurement of intelligence has resulted in more or less dependable generalizations or laws governing its distribution in the general population as well as in more or less dependable predictions regarding the significance of individual measures as indicators of future accomplishment in educational and vocational endeavor. Thus, particular I.Q. levels are viewed as having a bearing on probable fitness for college work or probable success in law, engineering, or some other profession. Educational and

---

[8] Establishing the validity of psychological tests is more complex than is indicated by this simple illustration. At present there are at least four different kinds of validation procedures: concurrent, predictive, content, and construct validations, respectively. For details, the article by Cronbach and Meehl (1955) is to be consulted.

vocational counselors administer intelligence tests as a routine procedure to facilitate this kind of guidance. If studies have shown an I.Q. of about 115 to be the minimum level for meeting the academic challenge of college work, then counselors feel justified in discouraging clients having I.Q.'s in the 90's from considering college training in their plans for the future. Such guidance represents a nomothetic application of intelligence-test results.

However, the well-trained, conscientious counselor might well consider the results from the idiographic viewpoint before making specific suggestions to an individual client. He would realize that two clients having the same final scores on the same test resulting in identical I.Q.'s ought not to be regarded as being identical in intelligence. Inspection of test results shows that the same I.Q. may emerge even though individual items are not answered in the same way. In the one case there may be relatively high scores on vocabulary items and poor ones on arithmetic items, while this relationship may be reversed in another case with the final outcome symbolized by the same I.Q. Psychological counselors have to evaluate such differences in component scores to determine what they signify in terms of the special strengths, weaknesses, and interests of their clients under the circumstances. This kind of individualized guidance is more idiographic than nomothetic. In practice, or course, more than intelligence-test results are involved in the counseling relationship. The counselor may find himself evaluating the client's temperamental characteristics, mannerisms, ambitions, financial resources, range of interests, and other factors believed to influence vocational success.

Even if we assume the adequacy of the operational definition of intelligence, it should thus be evident that the clinical use of tests in terms of such a definition involves consideration of numerous variables whose nature and relevance the definition fails to reveal. In many respects the situation is comparable to what Frank had to say about the multiplicity of factors to be considered in formulating satisfactory operational definitions of such physical dimensions as "time distance" or "length."

Operationism and Behavioristic Psychology

In the symposium to which Bridgman contributed, one of the participants, B. F. Skinner, ventured to formulate a rigorous definition of operationism. According to Skinner (1945, p. 270):

> Operationism may be defined as the practice of talking about (1) one's observations, (2) the manipulative and calculational procedures involved in making them, (3) the logical and mathematical steps which intervene between earlier and later statements, and (4) *nothing else.*

In developing the implications of this formulation, Skinner indicates very definitely that he does not question the existence of subjective or private phenomena. In his view, "The problem of privacy cannot be wholly solved by instrumental invasion." By this he means there is no way for the victim of an aching tooth to make the specific *quale* of the ache or even the actual existence of the ache known to another person, especially one who himself has never had a toothache. There may be a successful malingerer who, like a competent actor, is able to simulate the overt expression of pain, but such expression is not the pain. In fact, neither malingerer nor actor is really in pain despite their behavior. Skinner maintains that the intrinsic privacy of pain and other subjective phenomena renders them refractory to direct inspection by others. Without such shared inspection there can be no verification, and without verification there can be no science. What can be verified in the present instance is the verbal expression "My tooth aches." However, the alleged ache as the stimulus responsible for the expression is not verifiable, since it is a private affair inaccessible to public scrutiny. This, in brief, as indicated in the following sentences, seems to be Skinner's contention (1945, p. 272):

> We must know the characteristics of verbal responses to private stimuli in order to approach the operational analysis of the subjective term.
>
> The response "My tooth aches" is partly under the control of a state of affairs to which the speaker alone is able to react, since no one else can establish the required connection with the tooth in question. There is nothing mysterious or metaphysical about this; the simple fact is that each speaker possesses a small but important private world of stimuli. So far as we know, his reactions to these are quite like his reactions to external events. Nevertheless the privacy gives rise to two problems. The first difficulty is that we cannot, as in the case of public stimuli, account for the verbal responses by pointing to a controlling stimulus. Our practice is to infer the private event, but this is opposed to the direction of inquiry in a science of behavior in which we are to predict response through, among other things, an independent knowledge of the stimulus.

By "independent knowledge," Skinner is obviously referring to that which the scientific investigator can check on directly. It has to do with the "observation" Skinner includes in his definition of operationism. A somewhat captious critic might ask for an operational definition of the word "observation" as used in this context. To qualify the term, as Skinner does, by referring to "manipulative and calculational procedures" along with "logical and manipulative steps" is helpful but fails to dispose of the sensory immediacy and subjectivity of the observational process. Furthermore, the inclusion of *logical* steps in the definition brings inner cognitive events within the scope of this effort to render the concept of operationism presumably independent of what in ordinary language would be classified as essentially mental or subjective.

One reason for mentioning something so obvious is that as a radical behaviorist, Skinner would prefer to eschew references to the mental and subjective. In the history of psychology, behaviorism as a separate school arose as a protest against the practice of having observers in the psychological laboratory describe changes in awareness resulting from or as a reaction to stimulation provided by the experimenter. Such description was termed *introspection,* although for the most part it was more akin to inspection as contrasted with the popular connotation of introspection as involving morbid brooding or the prolonged ruminations of the fictional characters in psychological novels. At all events, these so-called introspective procedures were viewed as scientifically legitimate by the founding fathers of modern laboratory psychology, and from about the 1870s to 1913 there was a steady stream of published reports based on such reports.

In the latter year, however, John B. Watson questioned the validity of such procedures in a famous article that outlined "Psychology as a Behaviorist Views It." In place of the prior view of psychology as a study of mental processes or of consciousness, Watson suggested a different view. Instead of asking the introspectionist's question, "What is the organism experiencing?" Watson raised a behaviorist's question, "What is the organism doing?" In retrospect it can now be seen that Watson, without using the term, was advocating what Bridgman later called an operational approach. For Watson, this meant the elimination of subjective terminology from the behaviorist's professional vocabulary. There were to be no references to sensations, images, perceptions, thoughts, ideals, intentions, and similar introspectively observable phenomena. Such a mentalistic vocabulary was to be replaced by exclusive dependence upon events controlled and observed by the experimenter: the stimuli he introduced and the reactions they produced. There was to be no concern with introspectively reportable events intervening between stimulation and reaction. Consciousness or subjectivism was taboo.

Can Behaviorism Dispense with Phenomenalism?

In brief, Skinner's operationism is to be viewed as belonging to this Watsonian tradition, which in turn is to be viewed as an elaboration of the *physicalist* tradition already evident in the teachings of Democritus. According to the latter tradition as it relates to psychology, the outlook and language of the physicist are to govern the study of human and animal behavior. Physicalism is thus to be contrasted with *phenomenalism* in the sense that phenomenalism refers to descriptions of what is directly experienced or directly observed. In practice, of course, the physicalist has to avail himself of such direct experience and direct observation. Operational procedures cannot circumvent or eliminate this phase of scientific investigation. This is what Bridgman meant by the previously cited statement to the effect that "the most important part of science is private." What this involves is revealingly elaborated in the following passage from C. C. Pratt's contribution to the symposium (1945, pp. 262–263):

Every scientific observation starts life as a bit of private experience. Someone has to report somehow what he observed somewhere. This statement is no less true of physics than it is of psychology. The star in the sky, as reported by an astronomer, is no more objective and public than is the hue of an after-image as reported by a psychologist. Whether any private experience can ever be the same for two people is a question to which there is no satisfactory answer. Whatever the answer, it has to be taken for granted, and on faith. The great majority of mankind, including scientists and even philosophers, have always taken it for granted, and on faith. The great majority of mankind, including scientists and even philosophers, have always taken it for granted that the world looks pretty much the same to all normal people. The reasonableness of this assumption is repeatedly confirmed by pragmatic test, *viz.*, in practice the assumption almost always works. The view that two people can have the same experience nevertheless remains an article of faith, and can no more be proved by operationism than it has ever been proved or disproved by any of the great arguments of philosophy. The escape from solipsism can only be made by a leap of animal faith. Most sciences have made the jump without much trouble, and often without knowing it. Only psychology stumbled and fell, for reasons which are today fairly obvious.

The separation of the natural sciences from philosophy was accomplished for the most part without any dispute over questions of ontology. The problems of solipsism, if sensed at all by natural scientists, was left behind as a purely domestic quarrel among philosophers. The founders of modern psychology, on the other hand, fastened the problem of solipsism into the very center of their definitions. Once psychology was defined as experience dependent on an experiencing individual, the groundwork was laid for ontological polemics which have not yet wholly disappeared from the introductory chapters to psychology. The revolt of behaviorism only made matters worse, for in trying to pour out the polluted waters of mentalism, the behaviorist nearly lost the very infant he was trying to save. Mentalism is the starting point of all sciences, and is inescapably polluted by privacy. The initial data of behaviorism are no more public than are the data of introspection. Someone has to report the behavior of a rat in a maze. Someone has to report the appearance of red on a screen. Both reports intend experiences which are equally private. Their acceptance within the public domain of science is based either on pragmatism or faith, or both.

It is well to note the significance of Pratt's view of the way in which the natural sciences achieved their independence from their philosophic origins as contrasted with psychology's efforts to achieve similar independence. Pioneer physicists and chemists were far less self-conscious than pioneer psychologists regarding their status as scientists. They made their laboratory observations without brooding over the metaphysical implications of the observational process. Chemists reported on the chromatic and olfactory characteristics of reagents without worrying whether the redness and pungency they noted in a particular compound was precisely identical with the redness and pungency other chemists attributed to the same compound. Such a solipsistic issue was ignored.

Psychologists, on the other hand, in their early efforts to subject the study of mental life to laboratory controls, were not content to adopt similar matter-of-fact attitudes toward what was being reported by their laboratory observers. Having regarded the study of mental life as concerned with consciousness or the nature of experience, they were concerned with the problem of establishing the trustworthiness of introspective reports. It was as if they were asking whether what you experience when you touch a cake of ice is identical with what I experience when I touch a cake of ice. Even though we both use the word "cold" in describing the experience, are we justified in equating identity of descriptive word with identity of sensation? This, of course, illustrates what philosophers have called the egocentric predicament or the problem of solipsism. By defining psychology as the study of behavior, the behaviorists endeavored to circumvent this problem. And yet, as Pratt pointed out, "The initial data of behaviorism are no more public than are the data of introspection."

Moreover, the introduction of operational definitions does not eliminate the factor of privacy inherent in every observation or in every perception. In general, this seems to have bothered psychologists more than chemists, geologists, biologists, and other natural scientists. At all events, as natural scientists they do not seem to have been troubled about the admissibility of phenomena like pain into the universe of scientific discourse. They do not devote symposia to discussion of the meaning of a sentence like "I have a toothache." Incidentally, neither the dentist nor his patient has to wait for an operational definition of the word "toothache" before understanding its meaning. For the patient, the ache or pain is a vividly real experience the existence of which is no more to be questioned than that of the dentist standing before him. Classifying it as "subjective" or "private" does not remove it from the realm of reality to the limbo of the nonexistent. In fact, in ordinary language one way of stressing the reality of a phenomenon is to call it "painfully real." For the behaviorist to shunt out or disregard pain and other subjective phenomena as not amenable to scientific control or as making for a "mentalistic" psychology is a viewpoint hard to reconcile with what has already been referred to as the inherently subjective status of all observation for the individual observer.

The fact that a group of people agree in their description of an experience does not eliminate this subjective aspect. In other words, this so-called *consensual validation* is more a means of establishing the probable reality of a common experience than a means of demonstrating it to be independent of the subjective impressions of each individual contributing to the consensus. By the way of example, the effect of tear gas on crowd behavior might be considered. After dispersion of the crowd, every individual member of the group would undoubtedly attribute his flight to the respiratory distress induced by the gas, but this distress remains an individualized, internal, private, or subjective phenomenon despite the consensus. It is not an externalized, public, or objective phenomenon observable by a behavioristic follower of Skinner's equipped with a gas mask.

Is such a follower under the given circumstances capable of *understanding* the flight of the crowd? As a psychologist is he justified in restricting his report to what he observes; namely, the discharge of the gas and the subsequent flight? He might even engage in a systematic study of the relationship between weak and strong concentrations of the gas in its bearing on crowd behavior and thus come into possession of data enabling him to predict and control the reaction of a crowd to any given concentration. Would such an outcome conform to one's concept of the psychologist's scientific role? Is prediction and control devoid of understanding satisfactory science? Can science rest content with manipulative success and ignore intermediate factors involved in the success?

To put this a little differently: is psychology as a science to be restricted to the technological *how* of behavior to the exclusion of the *why* of behavior? In terms of the present example, the *why* would involve the recognition of the respiratory distress as a phenomenal event, but for an extreme behaviorist such recognition would be scientifically unwarranted since he is unable to confirm its existence in the direct way in which he can note the stimulus of the gas and the response of the crowd's flight. He might even stigmatize references to the respiratory distress and similar conscious phenomena as *mentalistic* references. Like physicalism, the doctrine of mentalism reflects a metaphysical attitude adopted by those seriously concerned with such a doctrine. Behaviorists in general are likely to prefer a physicalist standpoint. As just implied and as discussed earlier, for them the adjective "mentalistic" has a negative or nonscientific connotation. This seems to be ascribable to the fact that in common speech "mental" and "physical" are antithetic terms that to many people suggest a mind-body dualism. The facts of consciousness viewed as mental events are thus regarded as incompatible with a behavioristic orientation, not only because of their privacy or subjectivity but also because of their alleged non-naturalistic status. It is this latter factor that renders this aspect of behaviorism more a matter of metaphysics than of science. One upshot of this repudiation of conscious phenomena or of facts commonly regarded as mental in nature has been a kind of slot-machine psychology restricted to the study of the relation between the input of stimuli and the correlated output of reactions, with minimal reference to intermediate events. This kind of stimulus-response psychology purged of mentalistic data was presumed to safeguard the membership of psychology in the family of natural sciences; but in the opinion of many persons the result has been an impoverished psychology.

Concluding Comments

In general, it should now be evident, behavioristic psychologists because of their physicalist orientation tend, at least by implication, to endorse the metaphysics of epiphenomenalism. In their methodology they come closer to the restricting positivism of Comte than to the liberating positivism of James. Initially the behaviorist methodology was developed in connection with studies of animal behavior, which in itself fostered the natural-science outlook of biologists.

In studying animal behavior there was no need to introduce the outlook of those who view psychology as a social science. As we have seen in Chapter 8, animal psychology does not constitute what Dilthey called a *Geisteswissenschaft*. The behavior of rats, dogs, and chimpanzees can be studied in complete disregard of distinctively human concerns. Animals do not worry about job security, social prestige, accident prevention, income taxes, the hazards of war, and corruption in government. They have no religious conflicts or anxieties about divorce, lung cancer, old age, family friction, and whatever else prompts people to consult priests, lawyers, physicians, psychotherapists, and marriage counselors. All such conflicts and anxieties are alien to the animal laboratory, but the student of human behavior is forced to come to grips with them. He cannot dismiss them as irrelevant epiphenomena or dispose of them within the framework of biological physicalism. He has to wrestle with the problem of personality—with the difference between man as an organism and man as a person. The result will be a humanistic psychology more influenced by the methods and concepts of the social sciences than those of natural sciences like physics, chemistry, and geology.

A humanistic psychology is broader in scope than a conventional behavioristic psychology. In fact, it has to be broad enough to encompass relevant contributions of all schools of psychology. However, in dealing with its problems it cannot profitably restrict itself to physics as the model science for scientific guidance. To the extent that its problems are not exclusively physical problems, it must develop its own methods of attack on these problems. Nor need it make a fetish of operational definitions by way of exorcising the egocentric predicament and mentalistic ghosts. The latter phrase is a reminder of what Ryle had to say about Descartes' dualism as a "myth" which harnesses a spectral or ghostly mind to the machinery of the body. This sort of interpretation of the mind-body dichotomy seems to be a result of regarding minds and bodies as separate entities requiring distinctive locations in time and space. After all, one may adopt a neutral attitude with respect to metaphysical ultimates and view the mind-body dichotomy as a convenient conceptual scheme of classification. Since it is conceptual, there is no need to look for a precise spatial location for the scheme, any more than there is to wonder about the location of a baseball player's home runs when he is not hitting them.

As an approach, humanistic psychology is pluralistic rather than dualistic in the sense of recognizing the need for more than two categories of classification, since it is fatuous to assume that all that exists in the world is either mental or physical. It is also fatuous to assume that being conscious of a physical object is tantamount to attributing two separate existences to the object. Morris Raphael Cohen once disposed of this issue in these words (1949, p. 97):

> The question, how can the same entity be both in space and in consciousness, can be readily answered if we remember that the same thing can be in a number of different classes which are not mutually exclusive. A man may be in this room, in our association, and in a state of weariness, just as a man may be both bankrupt and the author of a number of books on how to succeed in life.

James would have endorsed this quotation, since it illustrates his own pluralistic solution to the psychophysical riddle. He reached this solution many years after writing the *Principles*. In some ways it may appear to be a paradoxical solution, for, as Perry has indicated (1954, p. 332), it "is designed to emphasize *both* plurality and unity." In its emphasis on unity it is monistic in viewpoint, so that, despite its simultaneous advocacy of a pluralistic viewpoint, it represents a neutral monism. The word "neutral" serves to describe a late development in James's thought as a result of which he came to regard mind as "a peculiar type of relationship among terms which in themselves are neither physical or mental" (Perry, 1954, p. 333).

Just how to resolve the paradox of the pluralism of such a neutral monism may not be immediately obvious. Moreover, the entire issue may appear to be more metaphysical than psychological in its implications. In reality, however, it is not more metaphysical than the psychological concept of an integrated personality. To describe a personality as *integrated* is to describe it as *unified*. This, in turn, raises the question, What requires such unification? The answer, of course, calls for a listing of all the diverse and often contradictory desires, interests, purposes, distractions, and loyalties in which human beings find themselves enmeshed. Throughout life they are having to cope with such a *plurality* of pushes and pulls. Failure to maintain a modicum of control over them results in the disintegration of the psychotic self, just as successful maintenance of control suggests a modicum of volitional freedom exercised by a unified self.

These references to personality integration and to volitional freedom may serve as reminders of two of the "productive paradoxes of Williams James" mentioned in the previous chapter. Like the problem of positivism and the mind-body problem discussed in the present chapter they belong to psychology's persistent problems. Both their persistence as well as their paradoxical nature will be reserved for discussion in the next chapter.

References

Allport, G. "The Productive Paradoxes of William James," *Psychological Review,* 1943, *50,* 95–120.

Boring, E. G. *The Physical Dimensions of Consciousness.* New York: Dover Publications, 1963. (First published in 1933 by The Century Company, New York.)

Brett, G. S. "Associationism and 'Act' Psychology," in C. Murchison (ed.). *Psychologies of 1930.* Worcester: Clark University Press, 1930.

Bridgman, P. W. *The Logic of Modern Physics.* New York: The Macmillan Company, 1927.

Bridgman, P. W. "Rejoinders and Second Thoughts," *Psychological Review,* 1945, *52,* 281–284.

Cohen, M. R. *Studies in Philosophy and Science.* New York: Henry Holt and Company, 1949.

Crissman, P. "Are Psychological Data and Methods Subjective?" *Psychological Review,* 1944, *51,* 162–176.

Cronbach, L. J., and Meehl, P. E. "Construct Validity in Psychological Tests," *Psychological Bulletin,* 1955, *52,* 281–302.

Dewey, J. "The Reflex Arc Concept in Psychology," in W. Dennis (ed.). *Readings in the History of Psychology.* New York: Appleton-Century-Crofts, 1948.

Dunlap, K. "Are There Any Instincts?" *Journal of Abnormal Psychology,* 1919, *14,* 35–50.

Frank, P. *Philosophy of Science.* Englewood Cliffs, New Jersey: Prentice-Hall, 1957.

Hilgard, E. R. *Introduction to Psychology,* 2nd ed. New York: Harcourt, Brace and Company, 1957.

James, W. "Does Consciousness Exist?" in R. B. Perry (ed.). *Essays in Radical Empiricism.* New York: Longmans, Green and Company, 1912.

James, W. *Principles of Psychology,* Vol. I. New York: Henry Holt and Company, 1890.

James, W. *Principles of Psychology,* Vol. II. New York: Henry Holt and Company, 1890.

Koch, S. (ed.). *Psychology: A Study of Science.* Study II. *Empirical Substructure and Relations with Other Sciences.* Vol. 4. *Biologically Oriented Fields: Their Place in Psychology and in Biological Science.* New York: McGraw-Hill, 1962.

Kuo, Z. Y. "A Psychology without Heredity," *Psychological Review,* 1924, *31,* 427–451.

Perry, R. B. *The Thought and Character of William James.* New York: George Braziller, 1954.

Pratt, C. C. "Operationism in Psychology," *Psychological Review,* 1945, *52,* 262–269.

Reeves, J. W. *Body and Mind in Western Thought.* Harmondsworth, Middlesex: Penguin Books, 1934.

Ryle, G. *The Concept of Mind.* New York: Barnes and Noble, 1949.

Skinner, B. F. "The Operational Analysis of Psychological Terms," *Psychological Review,* 1945, *52,* 270–277.

Szasz, T. J. "The Myth of Mental Illness," *American Psychologist,* 1960, *15,* 113–118.

Szasz, T. J. "Naming and the Myth of Mental Illness," *American Psychologist,* 1961, *16,* 59–65.

Titchener, E. B. *Experimental Psychology, Student's Manual,* Vol. I. New York: The Macmillan Company, 1927.

Titchener, E. B. *Systematic Psychology: Prolegomena.* New York: The Macmillan Company, 1929.

Titchener, E. B. *A Text-Book of Psychology.* New York: The Macmillan Company, 1917.

Watson, J. B. "Psychology as a Behaviorist Views It," *Psychological Review,* 1913, *20,* 158–177.

Whitehead, A. N. *Science and the Modern World.* New York: Mentor Books, 1948. (First published in 1925 by The Macmillan Company, New York.)

Wolfson, H. A. *The Philosophy of Spinoza,* Vol. II. Cambridge: Harvard University Press, 1934.

Woodworth, R. S. *Psychology,* 4th ed. New York: Henry Holt and Company, 1940.

10

Problems of Selfhood and Volitional Freedom

THE PRESENT CHAPTER will be concerned with two more of psychology's persistent problems: those centering on the concept of the self and those having to do with the perennial controversy of determinism versus free will. Both sets of problems, though reaching back to psychology's philosophic past, also stretch into its scientific present. To explore them in detail would require separate volumes. As a result the ensuing account will be more like a full outline than an unabridged inquiry.

Like the problems discussed in the preceding chapter, those now under consideration are difficult and complex. It is easy to lose one's bearings in the maze of their psychological and metaphysical implications. To avoid doing this, some preliminary orientation is needed. An indirect but revealing way to obtain such orientation is to set these and related problems within the framework of familiar grammatical categories. This approach may seem strange and farfetched, but its relevance will soon be evident.

Mental Functions and Grammatical Categories

There is a close relationship between ordinary language and some of psychology's persistent problems. This is so because language has come into existence as a means of giving symbolic expression to what man deems to be significant for him in the course of everyday experience. In the history of civilization, language emerged long before there was an inkling of psychology as a subject of separate study. Moreover, grammar, viewed as the anatomy of language, came into existence long after written language had come into being. The resulting categories of grammar may thus be regarded as indications of the classes of experience that man came to embody in his speech forms. Just as anatomy reveals the nature of the body's organization so grammar might be said to reflect the organization of mental life as it is experienced.

Back in 1916 the psychiatrist E. E. Southard called attention to the way in which grammatical categories are implicit in the thinking of a psychiatrist as he examines a patient. The resulting case history, with its references to disorientation with respect to person, place, and time, suggests trouble in the accurate use of pronouns, adverbs, and tenses as the patient was asked questions like these: Do you know who you are? Can you tell me where you are? What month is it? The senile patient may confuse past with present and thus employ the wrong tense as he tells about himself. The grammatical distinction between active and passive voice is involved in the delusions of those patients who are convinced that their "bad" thoughts will place a "curse" on others and that their imaginary enemies can place a "curse" on them by the magic of thought. Other grammatical distinctions refer to still other psychological characteristics. Thus the optative mood may indicate wishful thinking, just as the indicative mood comes closer to realistic thinking. It is also evident that prepositions serve as indicators of still other psychological concepts. Both attitude and emotion are suggested by our readiness to do things *for* our friends, *to* our enemies, *with* our children, and *against* the opposition. Similarly, adverbs serve as indicators of the psychological importance of time and place in the business of living as we agree to buy *now* and pay *later* as well as to be *where* we promised to be *when* the time comes. It is also relevant to note the role of adjectives, as indicators of distinctions made in the course of daily routine as we employ words like "neat," "huge," "crimson," "honest," "vacillating," "throbbing," "smooth," "rugged," and thousands of others descriptive of objects and persons. In addition to adjectives as descriptive of qualitative distinctions, man has introduced verbs—hundreds of them—to designate whatever he chances to find important in the way of action or mode of being. As a result, in his comments about himself and his world he tells what he has built, sought, heard, planned, neglected, endured, improvised, and conquered.

The parts of speech just listed were brought to light by noting the function of each separate word employed in the construction of sentences. Such syntactical analysis revealed the anatomy of language as simple and complex sentences were dissected. From this grammatical viewpoint the isolated words may be classified as the structural units of language, with sentences being classified as functional units. Moreover, from a psychological viewpoint sentences may be considered to be the symbolic expressions of the units of thought or the units of experience or the units of behavior, depending on what one prefers to stress as the hallmark of the distinctively mental. At all events, only a most captious critic would be disposed to question the psychological relevance of man viewed as a thinking, experiencing, and behaving organism. All these three aspects of psychology may be compressed in a single appropriately italicized sentence like this one: "As I *thought* about your proposition I became more *worried* about the costs and am now *writing* this letter to let you know of my reluctance to participate in the venture."

The preceding sentence, with its references to thought, worry, and writing, will readily be recognized as embodying the equivalent of allusions to classical psychology's references to cognition, feeling, and will as the three broad classes of mental function. This tripartite scheme is not different from Freudian preoccupation with ego, id, and superego functions, respectively. It is well to be reminded that these functions are not discrete faculties. Their consideration as separate and distinct can only take place by an act of abstraction from the unified complexity of mental life. This unified interrelationship is implicit in the sentence under consideration, in which disposition of a business proposition was the outcome of the interplay of ideational, affective, and volitional factors. The conjoint operation of these three sets of factors constituted the single *act* of dealing with the proposition.[1] Such an interpretation of the psychological import of the sentence is likely to be sanctioned by most psychologists irrespective of their systematic preferences.

What Is the Referent of the Word "I"?

However, one neglected feature of the sentence is refractory to such nonpartisan interpretation. This has to do with the psychological import of the word "I" in the phrases "I thought" and "I became worried." Deciding on the referent of the personal pronoun with precision and certainty is not easy. It involves what Gordon Allport (1943, p. 96) called the "riddle of the *Self*." This persistent problem in the history of psychology, as formulated by Allport, confronts the psychologist with this question: "How do you account for such integration and unity as the human personality manifests?" This is akin to asking how the multiplicity of experienced events that shape human life from childhood to old age comes to be organized into the kind of autobiographical pattern that gives rise to books entitled *My Life Story* or *My Defeats and Triumphs*. The pronominal adjective "my" in such titles suggests personal belongingness, as if to say that what happened to "me" at age seven is the possession of the same "me" at age seventy. Despite drastic tissue changes during the intervening decades so that the man's body is no longer the same body, the man nevertheless claims ownership of childhood impressions. He even identifies pictures in the family album of a little boy of seven as a picture of himself even though there may be little resemblance between his present bewhiskered, corpulent body and the frail little boy in the picture.

The existence of a permanent core to one's being in the form of selfhood has long been taken for granted by commonsense psychology. The Bible

---

[1] This is an allusion to Brentano's act psychology, discussed in Chapter 4.

is replete with references to the continuity of the self. To cite just one passage by way of illustration:

> And Job again took up his parable, and said: Oh that I were as in the months of old, as in the days when God watched over me; When His lamp shined above my head, and by His light I walked through darkness: As I was in the days of my youth . . .

The familiar Greek apothegm "Know thyself" is another ancient reference to the central core of selfhood. St. Augustine made the reference even more explicit when he wrote (B. Rand [ed.], 1912) "that all minds know and are certain concerning themselves. . . . Yet who ever doubts that he himself lives, and remembers, and understands, and wills, and thinks, and knows, and judges?"

It is well to realize that for commonsense psychology neither mind nor self is viewed as an autonomous, insubstantial entity. In commenting on the fact that "for commonsense mind is essentially embodied," the British psychologist G. F. Stout (1860–1944) had this to say (1931, pp. 154–155):

> Mind and body are not primarily apprehended as distinct *things*; mental processes are not taken apart from bodily in such wise as to raise questions concerning the way in which they are combined with each other. What we are primarily aware of is the individual unity of an embodied Self. It is this which is signified by the personal pronouns "I," "you," and "he." Consider the phrases: I see the moon, I hear a bird, I handle a knife, I walk from this place to that, I feel a wound, I am in prison. We cannot, at any rate without a radical change of meaning, substitute for the personal pronoun in these statements either "my body" or "my mind!" I cannot say "My body sees a bird" or "My mind sees a bird!" Such language does violence to Common Sense, though it may be appropriate to some materialistic or spiritualistic theory. I may indeed say "My body walks" or "My body handles a knife." But if I do so it is because I intend to indicate that it is not I but only body that is implicated. It is true also that there are cases in which "I" and "my body" may be used interchangeably. But when this is so, "I" has no longer its proper and primary, but only a transferred and derivative meaning. I may say indifferently that "I" or "my body" will sometime be mouldering in the grave. But I readily recognize that the dead and buried body will not really be I. I continue to speak of it as "I" or even as "my body" only because it is thought of as connected by a continuous history with my present individual experience as an embodied self. The position of Common Sense is that there is no self or mind where there is no individual experience; and that individual experience includes body and mind in one.

For many pious individuals, this notion of the self as embodied is so strong that their religious faith in immortality involves faith in the miracle of bodily resurrection. What they fantasy is not eventual reunion with departed bodiless souls but with resurrected ensouled bodies. They do not feel impelled to explain how this is to be accomplished, any more than they feel impelled to inquire into the physiology of digestion or the biochemistry of enzymes. In similar fashion they take the reality of mind and self for granted without becoming embroiled in psychophysical perplexities. Never having been exposed to a Cartesian mind-body cleavage, they never think to ask how an inextended self and an extended body can influence one another. As Stout suggested, when they hear a friend say "I believe" or "I feel sick" or "I remember," there is no puzzling uncertainty about the meaning of the word "I" in such phrases. If questioned about the meaning, they might well reply, "My friend is conscious of himself as believing something, or feeling sick or remembering something."

Constituents of the Self

The latter kind of reply might have troubled William James. For him, "the consciousness of self" constituted a knotty psychological problem. In fact, the longest chapter in the *Principles* is the one concerned with this problem, and the next longest is the one dealing with the concept of volition, with 110 pages being devoted to the former problem and 106 to the latter one. Both of these sets of problems, it will be recalled, are included in Allport's group of "persistent riddles of psychology." Each of them involves a cluster or, as just indicated, a set of related issues. Those pertaining to volition will be considered in a later section. For the present, discussion will be limited to the other set of issues.

Like Plotinus (see p. 128), James was impressed by the way in which the vicissitudes of individual experience and the vagaries of individual impulse become organized into the semblance of unity. In part, as he saw it, the self functions as a unifying agency. In the idiom of current psychology, this has to do with personality integration. For James, in other words, the concept of self is the equivalent of what the modern psychologist subsumes under the concept of personality. There is no separate chapter in the *Principles* devoted to the subject of personality. However, toward the end of the chapter dealing with "The Consciousness of Self," the word "personality" is used repeatedly in connection with the descriptions of what James designated as the "perversions of personality" (Vol. I, p. 399) observed in cases of multiple personality. The latter cases are, of course, dramatic instance of failure to achieve unity of the self.

From an empirical standpoint, James pointed out, the notion of self comes to embrace whatever one values as an important personal possession, including health, friends, honor, property, family, bodily skills, business acumen, erudition, social standing, church membership, and whatever else a person may regard pridefully or importantly as *his*. In the words of James (1890, Vol. I, p. 291):

In its wildest possible sense . . . a man's Self is the sum total of all he CAN call his, not only his body and his psychic powers, but his clothes and his house, his wife and children, his ancestors and friends, his reputation and works, his lands and horses, and yacht and bank-account.

In considerable detail, James elaborated the implications of this emphasis on the self as a possessive phenomenon by noting the constituents of the self and the kinds of emotional reactions and behavioral consequences prompted by these constituents. He listed four constituents: (1) *material* ones, or those having to do with cravings of the body, desire for personal adornment, acquisitive impulses, domestic comforts, etc., (2) *social* ones, or those pertaining to longings for status and prestige, to fostering friendships, to being admired, etc., (3) *spiritual* ones, or those involved in the pursuit of intellectual goals, in ethical and religious aspirations, etc., and finally, (4) the pure ego, or the sense of personal identity. The first three constituents, James pointed out, belong together, while the fourth one, the pure ego, is to be considered separately; for its existence and nature is more problematic than that of the other three. As he saw it, the first three are more amenable to empirical verification and consequently lend themselves to more confident discussion of their characteristics.

Among these characteristics he noted both motivational and emotional factors. The former are indicated by actions in the interest of self-protection, enhancement of personal welfare, and improvement of spiritual well-being. The latter affective or emotional factors are exemplified by anxieties about illness, finances, loss of reputation, and any threat to personal security as well as by such positive self-feelings as pride of accomplishment, feelings of superiority, and the glow of righteousness.

Some Anticipations of Contemporary Issues

What James meant by the "pure ego" will be considered later. In the present context there are some more things to say about the tridimensional empirical self mentioned in the previous paragraph. That sketchy account of the material, social, and spiritual aspects of the self fails to do justice to the full account, to which James devoted close to forty pages that belong among the classics of psychological exposition. For example, here is the famous description of rivalry among components of the self (1890, Vol. I, pp. 309–310):

I am often confronted by the necessity of standing by one of my empirical selves and relinquishing the rest. Not that I would not, if I could, be both handsome and fat and well dressed, and a great athlete, and make a million a year, be a wit, a *bon-vivant*, and a lady-killer, as well as a philosopher, a philanthropist, statesman, warrior, and African explorer, as well as a "tone-poet" and saint. But the thing is simply impossible. The millionaire's work would run counter to the saint's; the *bon-vivant* and the philanthropist would trip each other up; the philosopher and the lady-killer could not well keep house in the same tenement of clay. Such different characters may conceivably at the outset of life be alike *possible* to a man. But to make any of them actual, the rest must more or less be suppressed. So the seeker of his truest, strongest, deepest self must review the list carefully, and pick out the one on which to stake his salvation. All other selves thereupon become unreal, but the fortunes of this self are real. Its failures are real failures, its triumphs real triumphs, carrying shame and gladness with them.

The student of the 1960s reading these forty pages nearly eighty years after they first were published may find some striking anticipations of subsequent psychological developments. In one passage, for instance, one can note a foreshadowing not only of the current concept of an ego ideal but also of considerations that prompted the emergence of social psychology as a separate field early in the present century.[2] This is the passage in question (Vol. I, p. 315):

In each kind of self, material, social, and spiritual, men distinguish between the immediate and actual, and the remote and potential, between the narrower and the wider view, to the detriment of the former and advantage of the latter. . . .
     Of all these wider, more potential selves, *the potential social self* is the most interesting, by reason of certain apparent paradoxes to which it leads in conduct, and by reason of its connection with our moral and religious life. When for motives of honor and conscience I brave the condemnation of my own family, club, and "set"; when, as a protestant, I turn Catholic; as a Catholic, a free-thinker; as a "regular practitioner," homoeopath, or what not, I am always inwardly strengthened in my course and steeled against the loss of my actual social self by the thought of other and better *possible* social judges than those whose verdict goes against me now. The ideal social self which I thus seek in appealing to their decision may be very remote: it may be represented as barely possible. . . . Yet still the emotion that beckons me on is indubitably the pursuit of an ideal social self, of a self that is at least *worthy* of approving recognition by the highest *possible* judging companion, if such companion there be.

---

2 Just when social psychology came into existence may be subject to debate. There are nineteenth-century studies that may be classified either as contributions to social psychology or as antecedents of social psychology. As early as the 1860s there was German interest in what was called *Völkerpsychologie,* or folk psychology; but this seems to have been more anthropological than psychological in nature and scope. Toward the end of the century there were French studies of crowd behavior and of the significance of social imitation. These were more clearly of direct interest to social psychologists. However, not until the present century did social psychology become a distinctive branch of the psychological tree. William McDougall's *Introduction to Social Psychology* (1908) is sometimes regarded as marking the birth of social psychology.
     For details regarding the history of social psychology, see the book by F. B. Karpf (1932) and the chapter in Lindzey by Allport (1943).

In addition to his early recognition of the concept of an ego ideal, James also anticipated later recognition of the concept of ego involvement in aspiration and achievement. It was not until 1930, with the publication of F. Hoppe's monograph on success and failure, that the importance of aspiration levels engaged the attention of experimentalists. The closely related concept of achievement motives as investigated by D. C. McClelland and his students (1961) was a somewhat later development. Nevertheless, the concepts in question had already been glimpsed by James. In the next quotation, his references to "self-esteem" suggest ego involvement, just as his use of the word "pretensions" is the equivalent of Hoppe's notion of levels of aspiration. This interpretation is borne out by what James had to say about a man's struggle to *achieve* self-appointed goals, with consequent feelings of elation or humiliation depending on his success or failure. According to James (Vol. I, pp. 310–311):

> . . . we have the paradox of a man shamed to death because he is only the second pugilist or the second oarsman in the world. That he is able to beat the whole population of the globe minus one is nothing; he has "pitted" himself to beat that one; and as long as he doesn't do that nothing else counts. He is to his own regard as if he were not, indeed he *is* not.
>   . . . So our self-feeling in this world depends entirely on what we *back* ourselves to be and do. It is determined by the ratio of our actualities to our supposed potentialities; a fraction of which our pretensions are the denominator and the numerator our success:

$$\text{thus, Self-esteem} = \frac{\text{Success.}}{\text{Pretensions}} \text{ Such a fraction may be increased as well by}$$

> diminishing the denominator as by increasing the numerator. To give up pretensions is as blessed a relief as to get them gratified; and where disappointment is incessant and the struggle unending, this is what men will always do.

What James had to say about the social self and the struggle to bolster self-esteem by progress toward chosen goals is also consistent with the general drift of the teachings of Alfred Adler (1870–1937).[3] Like James, Adler was concerned with the unity of selfhood, with individual efforts to ward off the sting of failure, with man as a social being, and with the psychological consequences of feelings of inferiority. Some of these Adlerian teachings are clearly expressed in the following excerpts from Adler's own account of the development of his system of *individual psychology* (C. Murchison [ed.], 1930, pp. 398–399):

---

[3] An excellent account of these teachings in the form of extracts from Adler's writings, along with illuminating editorial comment, is to be found in the volume edited by Heinz and Rowena Ansbacher (1956).

Now I began to see clearly in every psychical phenomenon the *striving for superiority.* . . . It is an intrinsic necessity of life itself. It lies at the root of all solutions of life's problems, and is manifested in the way we meet these problems. All our functions follow its direction; rightly or wrongly they strive for conquest, surety, increase. The impetus from minus to plus is never-ending. . . .

And therewith I recognized a further premise of my scientific proceeding, one which agreed with the formulations of older philosophers, but conflicted with the standpoint of modern psychology: *the unity of the personality.* . . . As Kant has said, we can never understand a person if we do not presuppose his unity. Individual psychology can add to that: this unity . . . is the work of the individual, which must always continue in the way it once found toward victory.

That James would have endorsed Adler's notion of the striving for superiority as "an intrinsic necessity of life itself" is altogether likely. In fact, when these sentences from the *Principles* (Vol. I, p. 318) are taken out of context, the unwary student might be inclined to attribute them to Adler:

We know how little it matters to us whether *some* man, a man taken at large and in the abstract, prove a failure or succeed in life,—he may be hanged for aught we care,—but we know the utter momentousness and terribleness of the alternative when the man is the one whose name we ourselves bear. *I* must not be a failure, is the very loudest of the voices that clamor in each of our breasts: let fail who may, *I* at least must succeed

The Genesis of Selfhood and the Concept of Proprium

James was very interested in determining the nature of this "I," or what he also called "Number One." His discussion of the problem is a lengthy one and takes the question of self-love as its point of departure. What do people mean, James suggests, when they say of a person, "Jones loves himself" or that Jones is satisfied with himself? Are they referring to the material self or the social self or the spiritual self or all three selves? James also wondered what Jones might mean if he were to say, "I must look out for Number One."

In considering these issues, James traced the selfishness they involve back to the infant's complete dependence on others for food and protection. To put this paradoxically: although selfhood is not to be attributed to very young babies, they are nevertheless altogether selfish in their infantile cravings for attention to their creature comforts. Their self-interest is thus an interest in a full stomach and freedom from pain and discomfort, along with whatever caters to bodily needs; hence the eager excitement shown by hungry babies at the sight of the milk bottle. Genetically, this might be the kind of experience leading to the consciousness of self. By extension this sort of experience comes to include adults who feed and play with the child, the toys it receives, the crib in which it sleeps, and whatever else it comes to regard as its own. Self-love, James pointed out, is "always love for something" and not love for one's existence as a conscious being taken in the abstract. To quote him directly (Vol. I, pp. 319 and 324):

> To have a self I can *care for,* nature must first present me with some *object* interesting enough to make me instinctively wish to appropriate it for its *own* sake, and out of it to manufacture one of those material, social, or spiritual selves . . .
>
> The words ME . . . and SELF, so far as they arouse feeling and connote emotional worth, are OBJECTIVE designations, meaning ALL THE THINGS which have the power to produce in a stream of consciousness excitement of a certain peculiar sort. . . .
>
> *My own body and what ministers to its needs are thus the primitive object, instinctively determined, of my egoistic interests. Other objects may become interesting derivatively* through association with any of these things, either as means or as habitual concomitants; *and so in a thousand ways the primitive sphere of the egoistic emotions may enlarge* and change its boundaries.

As just indicated, James found the genesis of selfhood in the kind of objects one *appropriates* and calls one's own. The student of Latin might well regard this last phrase as tautological; for the word "appropriate" in terms of its etymology suggests "one's own," from the root *"proprius,"* meaning just that. The same root accounts for the word "property." Possessiveness, or a sense of ownership, is an essential characteristic of everyday allusions to the self in phrases like "my child," "my idea," "my headache," "my friend," "my diet," "my theory," "my lawyer," "my club," "my joke," and "my mistake." These countless uses of the word "my" reflect the wide range and diversity of items which come to belong to the self or which people claim as their "property," not merely in terms of land and material goods, but also in terms, ideas, feelings, motives, and purposes.

For this reason, Allport (1955, pp. 41–56) has introduced the term "proprium" as a convenient, neutral designation for all that one owns in the way of distinctive psychological possessions—all that makes for the uniqueness of individual personality organization; the unified fusion of the individual's central core of values, strivings, hopes, and beliefs. To really know a person is thus to have understanding of his proprium, in the sense in which well-written biographies are revelatory of personal values, idiosyncrasies, hopes and disappointments, and whatever serves to stamp one person as different from another, from his literary style to what Adler called his life style.

The Concept of Pure Ego and the Meaning of Personal Identity

The concept of proprium has much in common with what James called the empirical self. Both the former and the latter concepts have to do with one's objects of devotion, personal interests, intimate possessions, and ardent loyalties. In brief, both terms include all that James referred to as material, social, and spiritual selves as constituents of the empirical self. The qualifying word "empirical" refers to the self as a product of experience. This phase of selfhood lends itself to readily accepted exposition.

However, what is refractory to such exposition is the possible existence of a nonempirical phase of selfhood. James, it will be recalled, contrasted the empirical self with what he called *the pure ego*. In doing so, he was in search of the referent for the pronoun "I" in sentences like "I think," or "I believe," or "I know." In effect he was asking, "Who or what is doing the thinking or believing or knowing?" The answer, he suggested, must have something to do with "the sense of personal identity," or with whatever enables people to differentiate between what they attribute to themselves and what is alien or attributable to others.

There is a characteristic "warmth and intimacy" about matters identified or acknowledged as one's very own. This holds true of the stream of organic sensations coming from visceral and muscular structures. In fact, when such sensations become overwhelming, as happens to victims of stage fright, the experience in question is described as being *self*-conscious. Consciousness of self becomes distressingly obtrusive under such circumstances.

Evidently such interoceptive and proprioceptive sensations belong to the matrix of selfhood.[4] They belong to the privacy of the individual and are accepted as such. Such acceptance, as Allport once suggested (1955, p. 43), can be illustrated by means of a fantasied experiment in which the subject first thinks of swallowing his own saliva as it chances to accumulate in his mouth and then notes how he would react if requested to drink this same saliva from a glass. Calm acceptance as contrasted with aversion or disgust would be the usual reactions to the two proposals. In the first instance the saliva still belongs to the "self," while in the second it has been transformed into an ejected and alien substance and has ceased to belong to the "empirical me."

In his discussion of what he described as the "feeling" of personal identity James mentioned the "warmth and intimacy" of our familiar background of organic sensations. He noted that "the whole cubic mass of our body

---

[4] The interoceptive sensations are products of changes occurring in visceral organs like heart, lungs, and digestive tract, while the proprioceptive ones indicate changes in muscles, joints, and tendons. Incidentally, the significance of the root *"proprius"* in the latter term should not be overlooked.

. . . gives us an unceasing sense of personal existence." Familiar thoughts and familiar surroundings also contribute to this same store of reminders of an abiding focal center of selfhood despite the vicissitudes of experience and the ravages of time.

Even though there be marked changes in our belongings, our friends, and our bodies as the years mount up, recognition does not fail us. Our once sparkling new car may now be scarred and battered, but we continue to regard it as "the *same* old car." Similarly, our boyhood friend with whom we have "chummed" some forty years, although now bald, bearded, and no longer boyish, is still thought of as "the *same* old Joe." The intervening years may have brought about drastic changes in our own bodily contours, in our posture, and in the texture of our skin, but to us "it's the *same* old body."

This notion of sameness in spite of the drastic changes is what the psychologist refers to as *object constancy* or as *perceptual constancy.*[5] Long before these terms had come into vogue, the phenomenon had been noted by Ernst Mach (1838–1916), an Austrian physicist and psychologist as well as a mathematician. In his psychology he sponsored a radical sensationism by reducing all existence to sensory impressions. A familiar object like a table, he pointed out, is nothing but a cluster of recurrent sensory impressions that one continues to recognize as constituents of the table even though they may fail to recur as duplicates of previous impressions. This is his own account of the phenomenon (B. Rand [ed.], 1912, p. 598):

> My table is now brightly, now dimly lighted. Its temperature varies. It may receive an ink stain. One of its legs may be broken. It may be repaired, polished, and replaced part by part. But for me, amid all its changes, it remains the table at which I daily write.

This is an excellent instance of object constancy. For Mach, it was as if no changes had taken place, for he continued to call it his table and continued to use it as his place of daily work. In other words, his *reactions* to the

---

[5] The examples of constancy just introduced are, of course, not good examples of constancy as studied under laboratory conditions. In the laboratory studies, there are *measured* changes in stimulating factors that subjects are found to disregard in their perceptual reactions. They respond to the object as a whole rather than to discrete sensory qualities. In this sense the examples introduced are illustrative of the constancy phenomenon, but they are not good examples of the careful experimental work that has characterized investigation of constancy as involved in the perception of brightness, color, size, and shape. An excellent survey of this work is supplied by C. E. Osgood (1953, pp. 271–285). Incidentally, Osgood regards the perceptual or judgmental distortion inherent in the use of social stereotypes as an example of perceptual constancy. The prejudiced person who harbors fixed ideas about the characteristics of Negroes, Jews, Catholics, or atheists, as the case may be, judges the individual member of any one of these groups in terms of what he attributes to the group and fails to perceive unique traits at variance with his stereotyped expectations; hence the *constancy* of his judgments.

table remained constant despite the shifting sensory impressions. Behavior-ally—what he called it and how he used it—there was no change all through the years. In this sense it remained as the same old table. There was never any question about its "identity." Similar considerations may help to account for the sense of personal identity as we react to our own bodily sensations and memories by employing the same pronoun "I" or "me" and refer to ourselves by the same proper name when asked to identify ourselves. Mach referred to some of these self-identifying factors in this way (Rand [ed.], 1912, p. 599):

> As relatively permanent, there is exhibited . . . that complex of memories, moods, and feelings, joined to a particular body (the human body), which is denominated the "I" or "Ego." I may be engaged upon this or that subject, I may be quiet or animated, excited or ill-humored. Yet, pathological cases apart, enough durable features remain to identify the ego.

The pathological cases to which Mach alluded are, of course, those rel-atively rare instances of fugue states and of multiple personality in which there is almost complete loss of the sense of personal identity. Their occur-rence serves to emphasize the importance of this question of enduring self-recognition as a normal phenomenon. It is not a meaningless question or one that psychologists can justifiably ignore by classifying it as metaphysical. It has metaphysical implications that James considered in his philosophical moods, but in his more "psychological" moods he welcomed Mach's kind of analysis of the "meaning of personal identity" because it renders "the Self an empirical and verifiable thing." Moreover, even more clearly than Mach, he brought out the relevance of the pathological cases for enhanced understanding of the normal phenomenon. To cite a portion of Jame's account (Vol. I, p. 336):

> If a man wakes up some fine day unable to recall any of his past experiences, so that he has to learn his biography afresh, or if he only recalls the facts of it in a cold abstract way as things that he is sure once happened; or if, without this loss of memory, his bodily and spiritual habits all change during the night, each organ giving a different tone, and the act of thought becoming aware of itself in a different way: he *feels,* and he *says,* that he is a changed person. He disowns his former me, gives himself a new name, identifies his present life with nothing from out of the older time. . . .
>
> This description of personal identity will be recognized by the instructed reader as the ordinary doctrine professed by the empirical school. Associationists in England and France, Herbartians in Germany, all describe the Self as an ag-gregate of which each part, as to its *being,* is a separate fact. So far so good, then; thus much is true whatever farther things may be true; and it is to the imperish-able glory of Hume and Herbart and their successors to have taken so much of the meaning of personal identity out of the clouds and made of the Self an empirical and verifiable thing.

By regarding the self as a "verifiable thing," James intended to rule out nonempirical speculations concerning its nature and thus safeguard the scientific respectability of the concept. For him, it was not to be equated with the concept of a substantial soul even though, as he noted (Vol. I, p. 344), the latter concept has such illustrious supporters as Plato, Aristotle, Hobbes, Descartes, Locke, Berkeley, and Kant. In his view, the soul theory is entirely superfluous as a means of "accounting for the actually verified facts of conscious experience," and consequently "no one can be compelled to subscribe to it for definite scientific reasons" (Vol. I, p. 348). In a closing passage he was most explicit about this (Vol. I, p. 350):

> My final conclusion, then, about the substantial Soul is that it explains nothing and guarantees nothing. . . . I therefore feel entirely free to discard the word Soul from the rest of this book. If I ever use it, it will be in the vaguest and most popular way. The reader who finds any comfort in the idea of a Soul, is, however, perfectly free to continue to believe in it; for our reasonings have not established the non-existence of the Soul; they have only proved its superfluity for scientific purposes.

Are Ego and Self Identical or Different?

It should now be clear why modern psychology has become a psychology without a soul. Except for radical behaviorists and rigorous positivists, it still accepts concepts like ego and self. In fact, the self concept has been made the central focus of some systems of psychology, as in the work of Calkins early in the present century (1905) as well as in the mid-century work (1949) of Snygg and Combs. Contemporary books and articles are replete with reference to terms like "ego" and "self." Babies have self-demand schedules and adults have their self-regarding sentiments. Some happenings are said to be ego-syntonic while others are called ego-dystonic. There are ego ideals along with self ideals; but, interestingly enough, although there are innumerable allusions to self-actualization, no psychologists ever use a term like ego actualization. Why this should be the case will be considered shortly.

For the present it is more important to dwell on this increasing psychological endorsement of the concepts of ego and self in recent decades. Both experimental work and clinical studies reflect this endorsement. The relevant literature is much too vast to be cited here. It is sufficient to note that by the 1940s there were experimental studies dealing with the effects of ego involvement on confidence (Klein and Schoenfeld, 1941) and on forgetting (R. Wallen, 1942), and clinicians were talking about ego strength and ego defensiveness. By the 1950s, personality theorists were devoting whole chapters to the role of self and ego as factors in personality organization. Even a casual perusal of current journals and books indicates that the psychology of the 1960s seems to have assimilated both concepts, at least in terms of the frequency with which one comes across references to them in a variety of contexts.

However, despite the frequency of usage, there is still no unequivocal definition available for each of these terms. One psychologist's ego is sometimes found to be another psychologist's self, and vice versa. Under the circumstances, ego and self may seem to be precisely synonymous. Apparently such equivalence of usage would have been endorsed by James. At all events, in his discussion of the "pure self or inner principle of personal unity" he was solely concerned with "theories of the Ego" (Vol. I, p. 342). Later psychologists, while recognizing the terms as synonymous, did not regard them as precise equivalents of one another. This becomes evident by consulting various dictionaries of psychology. In H. C. Warren's dictionary, now more than thirty years old, the ego (1934, p. 89) is defined as "the individual's conception of himself," while the self (p. 244) refers to "an individual regarded as conscious of his own continuing identity and of his relation to the environment." About twenty years later, J. Drever made the ego somewhat more dynamic by defining it (1952, p. 78) as "an individual's experience of himself, or his conception of himself, or the dynamic unity which is the individual." Like Warren, he viewed the factor of identity as more distinctive of the self; for he suggested that the term "self" (p. 258) "usually" means the ego or personality "regarded as an agent, conscious of his own continuing identity."

In the most recent psychological dictionary, the one compiled by English and English (1958), the terms in question are subjected to much more detailed analysis. With reference to the ego, they mention four different meanings. One is the familiar psychoanalytic notion of the ego as the sum of those psychological functions which keep the individual in touch with the realities of the external world;[6] but this restricted meaning is not of direct concern in the present context. Instead a less familiar notion of the ego ought to be considered; for according to this view the ego is defined as:

> . . . that which is postulated as the "center" to which all a person's psychological activities and qualities are referred. This meaning is often used by those who believe that the ego is unknowable, that it is a mere formal or logical necessity.

---

[6] In psychoanalysis viewed as a system of psychology, the ego is not differentiated from the self. In fact, the term "self" is not used as a distinctive psychoanalytic concept. Of course in psychoanalytic theory, both id impulses and superego functions are differentiated from what is attributed to the ego. Accordingly, one might infer that the latter impulses and functions along with those of the ego constitute the psychoanalytic equivalent of the concept of self.

By describing the ego or the "I" as an "unknowable center" of psychological activity the preceding definition is hardly clarifying. By implication in this context, the term "center" suggests a vague, unverifiable metaphysical entity. Incidentally, that the everyday use of the pronoun "I" may connote metaphysical preferences was once pointed out by Titchener (1917, pp. 545–546):

> Conversation bristles with I and me and mine. . . . It is impossible to avoid the words, and indeed there is no reason for their avoidance; . . . Our everyday speech embodies a personal metaphysics, as it embodies also the metaphysical view of interaction between mind and body. So we all of us talk as if we accepted these theories; but when it comes to technical discussion, we make it clear, in the same theory-ridden terms, whether we do or do not.

Two additional definitions of the ego introduced by English and English are less obviously metaphysical. Both definitions differentiate the ego from the self. In one the ego has to do with "psychological processes that are oriented toward the self" as reflected in adjectives like "egoistic," "egotistical," and "egocentric." In the other the ego becomes "that aspect of the total *self* constituted by one's conception of what one is and what one desires to become." Both of these definitions made the ego subordinate to or less comprehensive than the self. The self might be said to include the ego as indicated by the definitions the authors introduce in their discussion of the term. They present seven different formulations but there is no need to consider each one since some of them overlap to a considerable extent or echo the definitions already considered. Accordingly, only the following three will be introduced (English and English, 1958, p. 485):

> A. In line with the self psychology of Calkins the term self is defined as "that aspect or part of the person or organism which carries out psychic, mental, or psychological acts; the agent for *behavior* (as distinguished from physiological activities)."
> B. In terms of the technical as opposed to the popular meaning of sentiment the self may be regarded as "a *sentiment* composed not only of a special object of experience, the psychological me, . . . but of the feelings and strivings organized about that object; an organization of personal activity oriented with reference to a complex object called the me."
> C. The concept of self may be viewed as identical with the concept of *personality* if self be defined as "the complex organization of characteristics making up the individual."

The Self and Personality Theory

This last definition indicates that for contemporary psychology problems of the self have become personality problems. It is altogether likely this transition was already implicit in some of James's theorizing. This appears to be the case even though he rarely employed the word "personality." In fact, in his long chapter on "The Consciousness of Self" it is not until the last thirty pages, concerned with the "mutations of the self," that "personality" is introduced. He refers to "alterations of the present self" (Vol. I, p. 375) as "the phenomenon of *alternating personality*" (Vol. I, p. 379). And later, in connection with his account of the famous Ansel Bourne case of alternating personality, he refers to the reinstatement of Bourne's "normal personality" (Vol. I, p. 391). This is the equivalent of referring to Bourne's "normal self."

In other words, in terms of historical perspective, contemporary discussions of the nature of personality may be viewed as elaborations of issues many of which James had already considered in his chapter dealing with the nature of the self. In this sense, "self" and "personality" may be regarded as synonymous and interchangeable terms.

Following World War I, there was a gradual increase in the frequency with which the word "personality" occurred in psychological texts as a substitute for the word "self." Where the older texts had chapters or sections devoted to the concept of self, the later ones considered the same concept under the caption of personality. Moreover, this shift took place during the years when there was mounting interest in tests and measurements of all sorts of psychological functions; hence twentieth-century efforts to devise tests for the functions James attributed to the self have come to be called personality tests rather than tests of the self. In effect, though, all so-called personality tests are tests of the self to the extent that they are concerned with assessing aspects of "the complex organization of characteristics making up the individual." For similar reasons, all theories of personality are theories of the self.

Calling them "personality theories" in accordance with current practice is not just due to the caprice of fashion. The word "personality," even though regarded as a synonym for the word "self," has a different connotation. It serves as a reminder that man as a *person* is different from man as an *organism*. Historically considered, this twentieth-century interest in man as a person owes much to the personalistic psychology of William Stern (1871–1938).[7] With respect to ultimate metaphysical questions, Stern advocated a neutral stand for psychologists. For him, the concept of person was "psychophysically neutral" and consequently not subject to involvement

---

[7] This refers to Stern's contribution to systematic psychology. In addition, he made contributions to the study of auditory sensations with the invention of Stern's tone-variators, to psychometrics with his suggestion that individual differences in intelligence be expressed by means of intelligence quotients, and to the development of differential psychology as a separate field of psychology. His studies of the reliability of testimony constitute contributions to forensic psychology, just as his investigations of the psychology of children give him a place in the history of educational psychology.

in the mind-body controversies. He defined psychology (1938, pp. 70–71) as "the science of the person as having experience or as capable of having experience."

Psychology was to be based upon the independent science of personalistics, which was to supply the foundation for all special fields of science concerned with man as a person, not only psychology but biology, physiology, and pathology as well.[8] In considering the scope of psychology in this group of special fields, Stern was not disposed to stress consciousness as the *sine qua non* of psychological study. This was implicit in his definition of person. After defining the term "person" as a "living whole, individual, unique, striving towards goals, self-contained and yet open to the surrounding world, and capable of having experience,"[9] he added the following explanation (1938, p. 70):

> Except for the criterion of "experiencing," which was purposely placed at the end, the specifications throughout are *psychophysically neutral*. Into the totality of the person are interwoven both his physical and psychical aspects. Goal-directed activity is manifested in breathing as well as in thinking and striving. Independence of and exposure to the environment apply both to bodily functions and to conscious phenomena.
>
> The attribute "capable of having experience" is distinct from all the others in that it is *non-compulsory*. Every person *must* be at all times and in all respects a totality possessing life, individual uniqueness, goal-directed activity, independence of and openness to the world, *but not always consciousness*. Even at times when nothing is being "experienced" the person exists, while the loss of any one of the other attributes would suspend existence.

Stern's recognition of goal-directed activity as a factor in the concept of person served to emphasize the importance of motivation for adequate understanding of this concept. He showed how this is related to volitional acts involving "the self as a total personality" (1938, p. 412). The nature of such volitional acts will be considered in a later section. At this point it is more relevant to note that almost all personality theories have been and are

---

[8] In this connection, emphasis on the centrality of the concept of person for psychology has been questioned just because various sciences are engaged in the study of persons. For example, according to I. Chein (1943, p. 98): "Psychology is concerned with behavior and its conditions, not with persons. It is true that only organisms behave and that we are apt to be most interested in a particular organism, man. But so are other sciences interested in man, who represents a point of convergence of many sciences. Granted a primary interest in man, each individual science can make its best contribution to this study by not confusing its subject matter with its ultimate objective." It is somewhat paradoxical that Chein approves of having psychology concern itself with personality but not with persons. What Stern called *personalistics* may serve to resolve the paradox.

[9] The German original reads somewhat more smoothly and is worth quoting: *"Die Person ist eine individuelle, eigenartige Ganzheit, welche zielstrebig wirkt, selbstbezogen und weltoffen ist, fähig ist zu erleben."*

concerned with the impact of motivation on personality development or, what amounts to the same thing, on self-development. In psychoanalytic theorizing one comes across the oft-mentioned clash between imperious cravings of the id as opposed to the ethically sanctioned motives of the superego. This, as mentioned in Chapter 3, was already noted by Plato as a conflict between man's higher and lower "irrational souls" and, of course, can also be noted in everyday allusions to the antithesis between noble and ignoble impulses or good and evil motives as expressions of a better or a baser self.

Moreover, the majority of personality theorists also link motivational factors as determinants of behavior with the concept of self or ego. Although all of them provide for such determinants in the theorizing, some of them do so with little or no reference to the latter concepts. In other words, there are a few theories of personality which disregard the question of a motivated self or a motivated ego. By stressing motivated behavior, they have little or no need for auxiliary concepts like an ego or a self as clarifying intervening variables. However, this is true of only a minority of current personality theories. In fact, as Hall and Lindzey (1957, p. 545) have pointed out, of some thirteen theories they subjected to critical examination, ten "make prominent use of the ego or self concept" and only three fail to do so.[10]

This preponderance of current opinion in favor of a self concept is not to be construed as a final disposition of the question of either the need for or validity of the concept. Questions of a scientific nature are to be settled not by majority vote, but by evaluation of the evidence. To examine this evidence in exhaustive fashion would call for a separate volume. For present purposes it is enough to call attention to the lack of agreement among personality theorists regarding the nature and relevance of the self concept. It serves as a reminder of the status of the concept as belonging to the array of psychology's persistent problems.

Neurology and the Self Concept

The problem of the self concept is not just one of psychology's persistent problems; it is also one of neurology's. This is so because, as a little reflection shows, it is so directly related to questions of brain physiology. It is part of the larger question of the mind-body relationship. Both brain physiologists and physiological psychologists are likely to be troubled if asked to discuss the neurological concomitants of consciousness of self or to account for cases of multiple personality in terms of underlying alternating brain changes.

Nor are they likely to welcome questions about the neurophysiology of so-called ego functions. To revert to the grammatical distinctions mentioned at the beginning of this chapter: when a person says, "I'm ready to admit I

---

10 The personality theories dispensing with self and ego concepts are those of Miller and Dollard, of Eysenck, and of Sheldon.

was wrong" is there a neurological referent for the word "I?" In fact, it might not be easy to indicate the nature of the psychological referent. By hypothesis, the person in question, in thinking over a stand he had taken, is now prepared to think differently. Under the circumstances the word "I" refers to himself as a thinker. However, to equate "I" or the ego with a thinker may be a tricky formulation if it connotes an independent entity or a separate agent or a ghostlike homunculus.

James wrestled with this issue and struggled to find the answer by close observation of his own experiences as a thinker. As a result he found no reason to attribute the thinking to an independent transcendent or "non-phenomenal" agent. In the stream of thinking he found each "passing thought" to be the thinker. A few excerpts from his long discussion may render this conclusion less mystifying. In the following, the first part is taken from the latter portion of his discussion of the sense of personal identity (1890, Vol. I, pp. 339–340) and the final sentence is taken from the end of his discussion (p. 342):

> Each pulse of cognitive consciousness, each Thought, dies away and is replaced by another. The other, among the things it knows, knows its own predecessor, and finding it "warm," . . . greets it, saying: "Thou art *mine,* and part of the same self with me." Each later Thought, knowing and including thus the thoughts which went before, is the final receptacle—and appropriating them is the final owner—of all that they contain and own. Each Thought is thus born an owner, and dies owned, transmitting whatever it realized as its Self to its own later proprietor. As Kant says, it is as if elastic balls were to have not only motion but knowledge of it, and a first ball were to transmit both up into *its* consciousness and passed them to a third, until the last ball held all that the other balls had held, and realized it as its own. It is this trick which the nascent thought has of immediately taking up the expiring thought and "adopting" it, which is the foundation of the appropriation of most of the remoter constituents of the self. Who owns the last self owns the self before the last, for what possesses the possessor possesses the possessed. . . . The passing Thought then seems to be the Thinker; and though there may be another non-phenomenal Thinker behind that, so far we do not seem to need him to express the facts.

The preceding passage was written nearly eighty years ago. It disposes of the thought process without any reference to the neurology of thinking. As a product of introspective or retrospective observation, it equates the "I" as thinker with the passing thought and dispenses with the hypothetical construct of a "non-phenomenal Thinker." The majority of modern psychologists who have dealt with problems of ego and self have also dispensed with such a construct.[11] Furthermore, many modern psychologists ignore these problems

---

[11] In addition to previously mentioned articles support for this conclusion is to be found in a classic paper by Allport (1943) as well as in critiques of this paper in articles by Chein (1944) and P. Bertocci (1945).

entirely and thus dispense both with the problems and the construct. For example, in the 1,400 pages of a mid-century *Handbook of Experimental Psychology* (S. S. Stevens [ed.], 1949), containing chapters by more than thirty psychologists, there are no references to the concepts of ego and self, not even in the chapter devoted to experimental studies of cognitive or thought processes. Here too there was no mention of a "Thinker"—phenomenal or otherwise.

In general, these problems are not of direct interest to those whose experimental work takes place in animal laboratories or whose work with human subjects involves a predominantly behavioristic orientation. They are apt to dismiss such problems as being metaphysical or unscientific vestiges of psychology's philosophic heritage. They have more confidence in laboratory reports than in clinical reports, and for related reasons are more likely to classify psychology as a natural science than as a social science. In their experimental investigations they prefer the language of physics, mathematics, and neurophysiology to that of the phenomenologist's description of the characteristics of consciousness or that of a clinician's account of his patient's anxieties and conflicts. Words like "mental," "consciousness," "ego," and "self" are viewed with a cold eye as having dualistic implications; hence their reluctance to include such words in the vocabulary of science.

As has been suggested in Chapter 9, this fear of dualism may be construed as a fear of ghosts in the sense that terms like "consciousness" or "ego" may reinstate the idea of a soul. James too was warding off such an idea when he found no need to assume the existence of a "non-phenomenal Thinker." In other words, it is possible to employ the language of dualism —or even of pluralism—without becoming enmeshed in metaphysical ultimates. As William Stern urged, by remaining psychophysically neutral the psychologist can be free to investigate all phases of experience without being inhibited by troublesome metaphysical issues.

As matters stand, the mind-body problem has not yet been solved, metaphysical monism to the contrary notwithstanding. If it had been, there would be no continuing justification for the existence of two medical specialties like neurology and psychiatry. As yet there is no one-to-one correspondence between the facts of psychopathology and the findings of neuropathologists. The conceptual framework and professional vocabulary of psychiatry are different from those of neurology. When the psychiatrist refers to a patient's paranoid thinking or weak ego defenses, there is no way of specifying what these diagnoses mean neurologically in terms of cortical patterns. Analogously, when the psychologist talks about habit strength or figural aftereffects or cognitive dissonance, he is employing technical terms for which there are no specifiable cortical equivalents, but that is no reason to impugn the scientific respectability of such terms. A similar statement can be made to apply to terms like "self" and "ego."

This entire discussion might appear to be a superfluous review of issues important in the days of William James but having little relevance for the psychologists of today. In reality these are not dead issues. They have to do with *persistent* problems that continue to plague both psychologists and neurologists. For example, in an article published early in 1964 the eminent British neurologist F. M. R. Walshe took both psychologists and neurologists to task for some of their "current ideas." Among the views of psychologists to which he objected, he mentioned one sponsored by K. S. Lashley and a closely related one endorsed by D. O. Hebb. According to the quotations he cited from their writings, they both were advocates of a physicalistic psychology; for Lashley had declared it as his "faith," to which he believed all students of brain functions subscribe, "that the phenomena of behavior and of mind are ultimately describable in the concepts of the mathematical and physical sciences," while Hebb had formulated "the working assumption of the biological psychologist" as maintaining "that mind and consciousness, thought and perception, feelings and emotions, all consist of nothing but the transmission of messages—nerve impulses—in and through the paths of the nervous system" (Walshe, 1964, p. 199). With reference to Lashley's faith and Hebb's assumption, Walshe raised these two questions (p. 204):

(a) Is life nothing but a pattern of processes exemplifying the known laws of chemistry and physics?
(b) Is the ever-changing flux of all those aspects of mental life enumerated in the quotation from Hebb "nothing but" the physical and chemical activity of the neurons?

By way of setting the stage for disposition of these questions, Walshe called attention to what James had written about the psychologist's need for a knowledge of physiology in general and of neurology in particular. He introduced some quotations from the *Principles* showing the stand James had taken and voiced his approval in this fashion (p. 203):

William James recognized that the psychologist must remain subsidiarily aware of the biological and physical processes the integrity of which is essential to "mental life," but that while he may relate these to psychology, he cannot blend them with it without creating confusion. The physiologist, in his turn, studying these processes has to appreciate that while they *condition* mental life, they do not provide a complete account of it.

That Walshe also consulted the writings of psychologists who came after James is evident from the following statement (pp. 201–202):

Every manual of psychology, and here I do not include clinical psychology, has set out arguments about the brain-mind relationship, but none of them has proved generally acceptable or adequate, with the result that many believe the problem to belong, not to the natural sciences, but to metaphysics.

. . . this view excites the scorn of mechanistic biologists, who seem to have embarked upon their intellectual adventures with return tickets that take them no further than the border where the natural sciences and metaphysics meet. Beyond this, they are persuaded, lies only a desert of arid logomachies with which it is not necessary or even respectable for a scientist to concern himself.

As might be anticipated from the foregoing, Walshe was emphatic in giving negative answers to the two questions prompted by the views of Lashley and Hebb. For him, neither the facts of life nor the facts of mind are reducible to "nothing but" whatever falls within the scope of physics and chemistry. In Walshe's own words (p. 215):

Whatever we can learn from the separate disciplines of psychology and physiology of the phenomena of mind and of life, which together make up the unity of the human person, neither science can account for the nature of the mind-brain relationship, or tell us how consciousness in its infinite variety comes to be associated with material bodies.

The key phrase in the preceding sentence is "unity of the human person." As a neurologist, Walshe, interestingly enough, does not regard the unity in question as being exclusively dependent upon or reducible to what his eminent predecessor C. S. Sherrington, called "the integrative action of the nervous system" (1906). Such "integrative action" is related to but not identical with the dynamics of personality integration. At least this is clearly implied by Walshe's refusal to have the facts of mental life transmuted into neurological facts either by an act of faith or by some kind of metaphysical magic. It is also implied that ignorance of the neurological concomitants of psychological facts is no reason to regard such facts as scientifically suspect.

There is no reason to regard a neurological description or explanation as more scientific than a psychological one. It is entirely legitimate for the psychologist to study the nature of intelligence and its development from infancy to maturity without having to wait for the collaboration of a neurologist. The same holds true for any other aspect of mental development— including the emergence of a child's recognition of the difference between "I" and "you" or "myself" and "yourself." This conclusion is in harmony with that reached by Ladd and Woodworth years ago in one of the closing chapters of their text in physiological psychology (1911, pp. 666–667):

The life of consciousness is a never ceasing change of states. Yet the result of this change of states is an orderly history, a true development. Such development is not merely the expression of the evolution of the material basis of some of these mental states. For it does not follow precisely the same order or the same laws as govern the material evolution; and some of its most important factors cannot be regarded as having any physical correlate, or as evolved from other factors which have such a correlate. *The development of Mind can only be regarded as the progressive manifestation in consciousness of the life of a real being which, although taking its start and direction from the action of the physical elements of the body, proceeds to unfold powers that are sui generis, according to laws of its own.*

What the preceding paragraph means is that mental activity can be studied independently of its neurological substratum. Despite impressive advances made in fields like electroencephalography, neuropathology, and neurochemistry, it is not yet possible to supply a neurological description of this kind of activity. In the words of R. W. Sperry, a contemporary neurophysiologist (1952, p. 312): "Present-day science is quite at a loss even to begin to describe the neural events involved in the simplest forms of mental activity." Under the circumstances, for psychologists to describe complex forms of such activity in terms of self-actualization or ego involvement is scientifically legitimate even though nothing is known about the neurology of the self or a brain center for the ego. There is no justification for restricting "scientific" explanations to the world of test tubes, galvanometers, and tissue culture. If one has to do one's scientific thinking within such physiochemical limitations, then, as was once indicated by the psychopathologist K. Jaspers (1923, pp. 13–14), psychiatrists and psychologists would have "to stop thinking" about mental activity.[12]

Concluding Comments

There is thus no reason to be troubled about the scientific respectability of the concepts of self and ego. Both concepts can readily be brought within the scope of a scientific psychology. As should be evident by this time, their implications in some respects color the entire history of psychology, from the days when the Greeks made "know thyself" a psychological imperative on up to the concern of current personality theorists with "man's search for himself" or his "quest for identity." Moreover, as should also be evident, many of these current discussions of the concepts are elaborations of what James had already touched upon in his long chapter on "the consciousness of self."

One issue which James failed to resolve by way of a clear-cut differentiation had to do with the concepts of self and ego.[13] As mentioned earlier,

---

[12] Here Jaspers was echoing a statement made by Pierre Janet (1859–1947), as Jaspers made clear in this sentence: *"Was aber die Neigung angeht, das Psychologische in somatische Vorgänge phantastischer oder realer Art zu übersetzen, gilt zu Recht was Janet sagt: wenn man immer anatomisch denken muss, muss man resignieren und nichts denken, wenn as sich um Psychiatrie handelt."*

[13] It is altogether likely, as already suggested, that James did not believe there is a distinction to be made. If so, there are psychologists today who would agree with him. For instance, Allport (1961, p. 111) is quite explicit about this when he states, "Since no clear and consistent distinction has been made between *ego* and *self*, we shall need to treat them as equivalent."

even in modern times there are some writers who employ the word "ego" to indicate what other writers refer to as the "self" and vice versa. Traces of this ambiguity or inconsistency may have been detected in the list of formal definitions of "self" and "ego" reviewed on a previous page. In general, however, the trend of these definitions was in the direction of regarding the self as a broader concept in the sense of having the ego classified as a constituent of the self rather than having this relationship reversed. Stated a little differently, it makes for greater clarity to think of the ego as part of the self instead of viewing the self as subordinate to the ego.

This way of distinguishing between the terms was anticipated on an earlier page when attention was called to the fact that whereas there are frequent references to the notion of self-actualization, there are no comparable references to the notion of ego actualization. In this connection, we may note that Shakespeare did not have Polonius urge Laertes to be true to his ego. Instead the admonition took the form of "to thine own self be true." The appeal was to what James would have called Laertes' spiritual self—to his central values as a man of principle. His respect for himself was contingent upon loyalty to what he expected of himself as a man of principle.

From this viewpoint the ego has to do with safeguarding the well-being of the self, with reacting to its troubles, with making judgments about its integrity, with defending it against threat, and with planning for its enhancement. What this means is that as a reflective being man is capable of passing judgment on himself—on his conduct, health, reputation, financial status, job security, family welfare, social standing, and whatever else belongs to his scheme of values or what was previously called his *proprium*. In other words, figuratively speaking, the ego functions as judge and guardian of the proprium. Expressed less figuratively, this is tantamount to recognizing the existence of two sets of reaction tendencies: those involved in the execution of plans and the realization of personal objectives on the one hand and those which signify a readiness to evaluate the outcome in terms of success or failure on the other. The evaluating reactions constitute ego activities while the other set of reaction tendencies constitute activities of the self.

The everyday world is replete with examples of this distinction. It is noted in golfers berating themselves for a poor shot, in housewives making sure the roast is not overdone, in a physician checking on the accuracy of a diagnosis, in a parent's pride in a son's academic achievements, in the riveter's worry about the stability of a girder, and in the million and one other situations involving questions of quality control, efficiency of performance, and estimates of cost, excellence, progress, and success.

In his daily struggles, man not only copes with problems but also judges or evaluates his efforts in terms of right and wrong, success and failure, gains and losses, and similar value dichotomies. For obvious reasons he is also sensitive to the evaluations of others, as instanced by chagrin and disappointment when scolded and his high spirits when praised. In brief, to put it metaphorically, the ego functions as the vigilant guardian of the excellence, stability, and integrity of the proprium or self. The egotist or man of conceit endows himself with an inflated level of excellence, while the victim of feelings of inferiority suffers from a deflated level. An optimal level is exemplified by the man of genuine modesty.

This suggested distinction between ego and self is not to be construed as meaning two sets of independent autonomous mental activities. Instead they are to be viewed as conjoint, interrelated activities. They reflect mind or the person as being what William Stern (1938, p. 73) called a *unitas multiplex* or manifold unity. In the light of this unity, ego activities are embedded in the self or are constituents of the self. Self, in other words, is the more comprehensive concept. To introduce a crude, but possibly clarifying analogy: if the totality of events governing a courtroom trial be compared with the self, then the role of the judge would be comparable to the functions of the ego. The judge is a constituent of the trial—a necessary factor in the trial. This is very different from the absurdity of regarding the trial as a constituent of the judge, or what amounts to confusing a part—even a necessary part—with the whole.

There is much more that might be said about the riddle of the self. However, enough has been said to indicate the widespread ramifications of the concept by way of showing why it has been and continues to be a persistent problem. It would be pretentious and unrealistic to regard the present discussion as having accomplished more than this. Incidentally, this conclusion taken by itself might serve as a final example of what was maintained about the ego's critical or evaluative function. There is no need to elaborate upon this. Instead it will be more profitable to "give up" on the riddle of the self and turn to the somewhat related riddle of the will.

The Myth of Will Power

The problem of the self is related to the problem of volition because every so-called volitional act involves the self. In terms of popular psychology, such acts are attributed to volition or will regarded as an independent mental faculty governing our actions and determining our choices. Such a view is a relic of the outmoded faculty psychology. There is no "will" as a separate entity that exercises executive functions. Spinoza (1632–1677) noted this in his contention that there is no will apart from individual acts of willing. In this denial of will as a genuine entity, as H. A. Wolfson (1934, p. 166) indicates, Spinoza was directly influenced by Aristotle.

Taken by itself the issue is trivial, but as a convenient way of demonstrating the inherent weakness of faculty psychology it merits more than passing notice. In other words, Spinoza's rejection of will as a power or faculty is based on considerations that have resulted in psychology's rejection of memory, attention, imagination, reasoning, and other so-called mental faculties conceived of as independent mental agencies endowing man with the "power" to remember, attend, imagine, and reason. Instead of being "powers" they are *concepts* derived from discrete and often altogether unrelated mental operations. As concepts they have no causal or dynamic influence whatsoever, any more than the concept of color in the abstract is responsible for recognition of particular colors like yellow, green, and scarlet. The concept emerged from the multiplicity of experiences with specific colors and had no antecedent existence as a "faculty" of color. Analogously, the concept of volition has come into being as an abstraction from a multiplicity of individual acts of self-assertion in the face of some sort of opposing circumstances. It is the self that does the willing, not the concept of will.

This reference to the self as the source of volitional control might serve as a reminder of the earlier discussion of such control in connection with the Pelagian controversy (see pp. 142–144). By way of clarifying St. Augustine's opposition to the free-will teaching of Pelagius, it was pointed out that it is not will that determines character, but character that determines will. This might now be paraphrased by saying it is not will that determines self or personality, but self or personality that determines will.

Justification for this paraphrase requires recognition of the significance of character in personality assessment, as indicated by routine business requests for character references. Such requests call for a description or evaluation of personality traits like loyalty, conscientiousness, selfishness, considerateness, and similar ethicosocial traits. Knowledge of such traits supplies information concerning the kinds of choices an applicant is likely to make, the sympathies and antipathies he is likely to display, and the effect he is likely to have on those who have dealings with him. One upshot of such knowledge of behavioral trends might well be knowledge of the applicant's volitional trends, as reflected in descriptions of him as a person of good will or in case of a negative evaluation as being a malevolent character. The organization of such trends is an expression of the whole self and not, to emphasize a point already made, the expression of a separate faculty of volition; hence what popular psychology attributes to strength of will is descriptively misleading. It would be more accurate to talk about strength of character or strong-willed characters.

The Free Will-Determinism Controversy

The problem of the psychology of volition is not just a single problem but a whole group of problems, all of which center around the question of the control of action. In the history of philosophy the question gave rise to the free will-determinism controversy. Allport, it will be recalled, was alluding to this controversy when he classified "the riddle of free will" as one of psychology's persistent problems by reminding his fellow psychologists that despite their "postulate of strict determinism" they "half-believe, and nearly always act on the hypothesis of indeterminism" (1943, p. 97). The same controversy has taken theological form in connection with the doctrine of predestination, with advocates of that doctrine arguing that since God is omniscient and thus knows both past and future, the life and destiny of every creature must be foreordained.

Specialists in ethics and jurisprudence have also become embroiled in the controversy by having to consider whether man is to be held responsible for his actions if he is not "free" to resist temptation, to obey the law, to choose the good, and to eschew evil. The feeble-minded and the insane are thus absolved from legal responsibility for their criminal acts because of their presumed inability to tell the difference between right and wrong or to understand the nature and consequences of their acts.

This common principle of law has obvious psychological implications by making control of behavior a function of adequate knowledge. As a fragment of psychological insight, it is reminiscent of the story of Adam and Eve: not until they had knowledge of good and evil were they capable of sinning, of feeling guilt, or making a moral choice. However, the Biblical account was hardly the beginning of a systematic discussion of the problem of volitional control. It is altogether likely that the problem was not clearly formulated until the time of Plato. At all events from the days of Plato, with his recognition of the dependence of will on the possession of appropriate information, to the days of Schopenhauer (1788–1860), with his subordination of the intellect to the primacy of will, the problem engaged the attention of many generations of philosophers. Detailed consideration of their views belongs to the history of philosophy rather than to the history of psychology. In later contexts there will be incidental mention of a few of those which had a more direct bearing on the psychology of volition.

Impulse, Reason, and Self-Control

In some ways the study of volition has been as fraught with difficulty as the study of the self. This, as suggested earlier, is reflected in the fact that the two longest chapters in James's *Principles of Psychology* are those concerned with the self and with will, respectively. Now, nearly eight decades after those chapters were written, textbooks of general psychology rarely have separate chapters devoted to these subjects. This is more the result of a changed perspective than a loss of interest in the topics as such. As has been mentioned, the issues which James perceived as related to the concept of selfhood have now been brought within the scope of personality theory. Analogously, many of the problems he discussed in his chapter on will are now being discussed in chapters on motivation.

The shift in perspective from volition to motivation serves as a reminder of the need to consider two sets of factors in dealing with the question of the determinants involved in behavior control. One set has to do with ability to foresee immediate and remote consequences of a given course of action, and the other has to do with the urgency of impulse or craving instigating such action. What is ordinarily regarded as irresponsible behavior may be the result of ignorance, stupidity, or delusion, or else it may be the effect of irrepressible impulse.

In other words, control of behavior is a function of ideational and motivational factors. The victim of so-called kleptomania *knows* that stealing is wrong but is overwhelmed by his compulsion to steal. Alcoholics are aware of the baneful outcome of an alcoholic debauch and yet find themselves impelled to yield to an imperious craving. Like drug addicts, they are not "free" to control their indulgence. They are dominated by an irresistible craving. Incidentally, in some states the law governing the question of insanity as a defense in criminal trials provides for an "irresistible impulse test" as an exculpating criterion.[14] This test constitutes a supplement to the previously mentioned criterion pertaining to knowledge of the difference between right and wrong. The latter criterion constitutes recognition of the ideational or cognitive aspect of self-control while the former criterion is an acknowledgment of the relevance of the motivational aspect.

These two criteria are also implicit in the traditional psychological distinction between voluntary and involuntary actions. This distinction was made by Aristotle when he held that personal responsibility is restricted to voluntary behavior. In physiological terms, voluntary behavior is regarded as a function of the striped musculature, while involuntary action is associated with smooth muscle tissue and other visceral structures. Man can learn to raise and lower his arm voluntarily but he cannot learn to raise and lower his blood pressure voluntarily, hence he is held responsible for what he does with his arms but not for what happens to his blood pressure. His arm movements are controlled by the cerebrospinal nervous system, while his blood pressure is regulated by the autonomic nervous system. In general, cerebrospinal functions are more amenable to direct voluntary control than those of the autonomic. The latter functions, it will be recalled, have to do with digestion, respiration, circulation, and other metabolic activities. They have to do with our hungers, thirsts, lusts, angers, fears, jealousies, and other strong emotions.

These body cravings and strong emotions impel to action and thus constitute motivational goads to overt behavior. The greater their intensity the more difficult they are to control. An enraged individual is powerless to convert his rage into affectionate serenity by a simple act of will, just as a person with food lodged in his windpipe is not "free" not to gasp for air if he so choose. The victim of the overwhelming rage is compelled to deal with his rage just as the choking man has to attend to his respiratory distress. Attention to the autonomic upheaval is an involuntary imperative. There is

---

14 See the article by J. Hall (1945) for the relationship of this test to the question of the way in which courts evaluate the relevance of mental disorder as a mitigating or exculpating consideration in deciding issues of criminal responsibility.

no question of choice or freedom to do otherwise. Nobody would think of asking whether the choking man is "responsible" for his gagging and coughing. Even the most ardent champion of the doctrine of man's volitional freedom would concede that man's autonomic imperatives set limits to such freedom. As imperatives they compel attention and, as just mentioned, the attention in question is involuntary.

In classical psychology, such involuntary attention has been contrasted with voluntary attention. Involuntary attention is unlearned, spontaneous, and effortless, while voluntary attention is a product of effortful learning. One does not have to learn to pay attention to the sound of a sudden loud explosion. It occasions an unforced, involuntary startle reaction and is common to animals, young infants, and sophisticated adults. On the other hand, the automotive apprentice has to *learn* to pay attention to the sound of the automobile engine and the young medical student may have to force himself to listen to the rhythm of patient's breathing, just as the high-school student may find it hard to pay attention to what his foreign-language teacher is saying about French phonetics. In all such situations, attention is forced and the result of a deliberate intention to focus on the task in hand. It is not uncommon for people to say, "It takes will power to give this kind of attention."

This is a recognition of an intimate relationship between volition and the process of attention. In fact, James maintained (1890, Vol. I, p. 447) that "volition is nothing but attention." Of course he was referring to the familiar *active* process by means of which there is a self-initiated shift from a continuing activity to a different activity. It is illustrated by the shift from idle daydreaming to concentrated study of a difficult text, and by any situation in which there is a shift from relaxed leisure-time pursuits to the demands of duty. It calls for the ability to shunt out or disregard competing distractions and to maintain an attitude of readiness to observe and deal with the task to be accomplished.

The colloquial phrase "getting down to business" is an obvious allusion to active attention as a volitional process. A pinch hitter waiting for the next pitch has to give this kind of attention to his surroundings. He must disregard the distracting shouts coming from the crowd and limit his perceptual set to the business of laying down a bunt as his manager instructed. To carry out the instruction he has to adjust his grip on the bat as well as his bodily posture to facilitate his execution of the maneuver as he watches or attends to the approaching ball. Depending on the nature of the pitch, he has to decide whether or not to move his bat. Under the circumstances, both the arrest or inhibition of the impulse to swing as well as the decision to swing involve volitional factors. As he might describe it later: "I decided to let the first pitch go by because it looked too high to me and then when the next pitch looked just right I decided to go for it." His decision-making thus reflects his volitional control.[15] His competence as a batter depends on his ability to make the correct decision and to get his muscles to carry out the decision.

Development and Initiation of Voluntary Action

Stripped of some of its complexities, the psychology of volition may consequently be reduced to an investigation of how intentional action occurs or how one succeds in doing what he sets out to do. This is tantamount to asking what initiates a voluntary act such as extending the arm or holding one's breath or, when serving as a subject in a psychological experiment, pressing a telegraph key the instant a signal is given. All such acts call for muscular control; without such control the "will" to move a given muscle group proves futile. For this reason, many of the pioneer experimental studies of volition called for consideration of the psychological factors involved in the execution of simple movements, as exemplified by reaction time studies. From the start there was general agreement that unlearned, involuntary reflex or automatic movements preceded the emergence or acquisition of voluntary ones, for as early as 1811 Charles Bell (1774–1842) had noted (W. Dennis [ed.], 1948, p. 117):

> Instinctive motions are the operations of the same organs, the brain and nerves and muscles, which minister to reason and volition in our mature years. When the young of any animal turns to the nipple, directed by the sense of smelling, the same operations are performed, and through the same means, as afterwards when we make an effort to avoid what is noxious, or desire and move towards what is agreeable.

Years later James gave italicized endorsement to this view in the following statement (1890, Vol. II, pp. 487–488):

> When a particular movement, having once occurred in a random, reflex, or involuntary way, has left an image of itself in the memory, then the movement can be desired again, proposed as an end, and deliberately willed. But it is impossible to see how it could be willed before.
> *A supply of ideas of the various movements that are possible left in the memory by experiences of their involuntary performance is thus the first prerequisite of the voluntary life.*

By implication the preceding statement was in accord with Bell's conclusion (Dennis, p. 124) to the effect that "the will is expressed through the

---

15 In psychopathology, marked inability to initiate action as result of trouble in "making up one's mind" regarding alternative courses of action is classified as a disturbance of volition. The symptom is called *abulia,* from the Greek, meaning "loss of will or determination."

medium of the nerves of motion." For James, volitional activation of such nerves was dependent on the sensory consequences of their prior involuntary activation. He recognized these consequences to be sensory impressions localized in the moving muscles and their skeletal attachments, as well as other sensory impressions incident to a given movement. For example, in shaking its rattle a baby has kinesthetic[16] sensations aroused by the arm's movement as well as concurrent tactual, visual, and auditory ones since the moving rattle is being gripped, seen, and heard at the same time. James referred to the kinesthetic impressions as *resident* consequences of muscular activity in contradistinction to the *remote* concurrent sensory impressions.

In the course of experience, both resident and remote impressions come to add to the "supply of ideas" needed for voluntary control. In terms of this *ideomotor theory,* any one of these ideas of movement may suffice to activate the corresponding muscles or at least arouse an incipient tendency to such activation. Thus, merely thinking of an accordion may induce the muscular set needed to demonstrate the bellows-like action of the instrument. Moreover, the thought of the instrument may involve remote impressions of its sound or appearance as well as resident kinesthetic impressions. Any single impression from the total complex of impressions may suffice to initiate the incipient or actual movement of the arm muscles.

James regarded this total complex, made up of both resident and remote sensory impressions, as the source of kinesthetic ideas. This usage goes beyond the current restriction of the term "kinesthesis" to proprioceptive sensations, or those which James in some contexts called "resident" sensations. It is necessary to be mindful of this extension of the ordinary meaning of the term, in order to grasp the full meaning of a central thesis that James embodied in this passage (1890, Vol. II, pp. 492–493):

> We may consequently set it down as certain that, *whether or no there be anything else in the mind when we consciously will a certain act, a mental conception made up of memory-images of these sensations, defining which special act it is, must be there.*
>
> Now is there anything else in the mind when we will to do an act? . . . My first thesis . . . is, that *there need be nothing else,* and that *in perfectly simple voluntary acts there is nothing else in the mind but the kinaesthetic idea, thus defined, of what the act is to be.*

---

[16] The term "kinesthesis" as a technical designation for "muscle sense" was introduced into psychology about a hundred years ago by the British neurologist H. C. Bastian (1837–1915). Recognition of the existence of "muscle sense" goes back to the early nineteenth century. For example, the Scottish philosopher, Thomas Brown (1778–1820), had stressed the importance of what he called "muscular sense" in his lectures which were published in 1820. For details see D. S. Robinson (1961, pp. 191 and 195).

Kinesthesis Versus Feelings of Innervation

In 1890, this was a bold stand to take. It was contrary to what James called "a powerful tradition in Psychology" according to which more than "kinesthetic ideas" are needed to initiate the volitional process. The additional factor was regarded as a conscious accompaniment of neural impulses being transmitted from the motor area of the cortex to particular muscle groups about to be brought into play. Wundt called this alleged conscious accompaniment a *feeling of innervation*. Such a feeling was viewed as a guiding or directional factor by means of which volitional control was placed at one's disposal. Presumably the intention to flex the toes of the left foot aroused a different feeling of innervation from the one induced by the intention to flex the fingers of the right hand.

In denying the existence of such feelings, James was opposing a generally accepted teaching. According to him, it was defended "most explicitly" by men like "Bain, Wundt, Helmholtz, and Mach." To oppose men of such eminence was a formidable undertaking. More than twenty-five pages of the chapter on will are devoted to considering the evidence against the prevalent teaching. Since it has long been a discredited notion—Wundt himself subsequently repudiated his earlier belief in the existence of feelings of innervation—there is no need to summarize the many arguments adduced by James in the course of his attack.

Actually, as James made clear, there is not even introspective evidence to support the claims of those who ventured to describe their feelings of innervation. In each instance upon closer analysis the description is found to be a reference to resident or remote sensory impressions or memories of such impressions. The impressions are always of peripheral origin and thus products of afferent neural action. There are no sensory impressions intrinsic to the efferent segments of such action. Even to assume their possible existence plunges one into the ideational muddle of trying to conceive of neural output being the same as neural input. All this is so obvious today that in retrospect it seems astonishing that belief in the existence of feelings of innervation had such scientifically eminent nineteenth-century support and that James felt constrained to devote a fourth of his long chapter to demonstrate the nonexistence of these feelings.

Still, on second thought, it is no more astonishing than retrospective judgment of now discredited theories, principles, and beliefs that previous generations of scientific leaders espoused as valid. There were times when such leaders accounted for combustion in terms of the phlogiston theory, believed in the inheritance of acquired characteristics, endorsed the theory of spontaneous generation, conceived of the atom as indivisible, advocated the superiority of Nordics, and attributed general paresis to excessive travel because sailors and salesmen seemed especially vulnerable to what was later

found to be a consequence of syphilitic infection. Once again, to repeat
what was stressed in Chapter 4 (see pp. 71–73), it is well not to be overawed
by the prestige of scientific leaders and thus confuse eminence with evidence.

Increase of Control with Decrease of Cues

Once James had found the evidence in support of the belief in volitional
control as a function of feelings of innervation too weak to sustain the belief,
he was left with what he had regarded as "certain" in the exercise of such
control; namely, the role of resident and remote sensations or their memory
images as the guiding factors. In his subsequent elaboration of this thesis he
anticipated the later doctrine of the school of functional psychology, to the
effect that the function of consciousness is to facilitate learning and problem-
solving.

By way of illustration, it is enough to recall the difficulty a young boy has
in learning to tie his shoelaces. His whole body is likely to be involved in the
struggle as he concentrates on trying to get his fingers to manipulate the
laces. He has to keep watching the laces as well as his twisting fingers. The
effort brings facial muscles and trunk muscles into play. At this stage he
might be said to be vividly conscious of a mass of kinesthetic, tactual, and
visual impressions.

Months later, however, with mastery of the requisite muscular control
established, the laces can be tied in a semiautomatic fashion. Visual
guidance is no longer needed and the maneuver is largely restricted to adroit
finger movements. Minimal or subconscious kinesthetic cues govern the latter
movements. No longer must the boy be vividly conscious of the task in hand.
According to the functionalists, the child's "consciousness" is now left free to
consider other matters.

This shift from preoccupation with a multiplicity of cues at the beginning
of learning to progressively fewer ones as mastery is approached is characteristic of all learning when carried through from the stage of the novice to
that of the expert. All one has to do by way of confirmation is to compare
novices and experts in activities as diverse as golf, cooking, typing, swimming, playing the violin, learning a foreign language, or playing chess. An
increase in skill is paralleled by a decrease in cues needed for volitional
control. As a precursor of functional psychology, James put it this way
(1890, Vol. II, pp. 518–519):

> *There can be no doubt whatever that the mental cue may be either an image of
> the resident or of the remote kind.* Although, at the outset of our learning a
> movement, it would seem that the resident feelings must come strongly before
> consciousness . . . later this need not be the case. The rule, in fact, would seem
> to be that they tend to lapse more and more from consciousness, and that the
> more practised we become in a movement, the more "remote" do the ideas become
> which form its mental cue. What we are *interested* in is what sticks in our

consciousness; everything else we get rid of as quickly as we can. Our resident feelings of movement have no substantive interest for us at all, as a rule. Such an an end is generally an outer impression on the eye or ear, or sometimes on the skin, nose, or palate. Now let the idea of the end associate itself definitely with the right motor innervation, and the thought of the innervation's *resident* effects will become as great an encumbrance as we formerly concluded that the feeling of the innervation itself would be. The mind does not need it; the end alone is enough.

Woodworth on the Cause of a Voluntary Movement

Early in the present century, R. S. Woodworth (see *Selected Papers,* 1939) had quoted a portion of the preceding paragraph in a famous paper entitled "The Cause of a Voluntary Movement." He regarded the description given by James as "more faithful to the sum total of facts than other authors" but not altogether in accord with his own experimental observations. The latter were results obtained under two different conditions: those involved in the acquisition of voluntary control of a new or unfamiliar movement as contrasted with those involved in the execution of well-established familiar ones. Familiar movements consisted of "willing" to open the mouth, to flex the fingers, to wink the eye, to open a pair of scissors, to grip a dynamometer, etc. As instances of unfamiliar movements, Woodworth referred to learning to wiggle one's ears and to move the big toe without having the other toes move at the same time, and to the way in which babies learn to gain voluntary control of their initially random bodily maneuvers.

In particular he was concerned with the question of the alleged importance of kinesthetic imagery in the control of bodily movement. This question is not to be confused with the importance of kinesthetic sensations or afferent impulses incident to action already in progress. Loss of such a stream of resident *sensations* disrupts coordinated muscular activity. However, this is different from loss or absence of the corresponding kinesthetic *imagery*. Moreover, even if a victim of *locomotor ataxia* were to retain vivid kinesthetic imagery of the way his legs felt before his illness, he would still be unable to walk smoothly by substituting the imagery for the vanished sensations. Woodworth was not concerned with such pathological cases. His subjects were healthy adults, and most of them had a good deal of training in psychology and thus were able to report on the conscious antecedents of voluntary movement. In the majority of instances, voluntary movements were executed without any prior kinesthetic imagery; and in the minority of cases in which such imagery occurred, the resulting kinesthetic sensations generally astonished the subjects because they were so different from the anticipated imagery.

As a result, Woodworth held it "safe to conclude that the kinesthetic image is not the exclusive, nor even the typical cue to voluntary movement" (1939, p. 38). This conclusion applies to familiar movements as well as to the mastery of unfamiliar ones. With respect to learning control of unfamiliar movements Woodworth had this to say (1939, pp. 40–41):

> The most important work in this direction is that of Bair, who taught several persons to move their ears at will; he recorded the movements by suitable apparatus, and at the same time determined as far as possible by what process the voluntary control was established. One important fact which he discovered was that familiarity with the feeling of the ear in motion, afforded by repeatedly exciting by electricity the muscle that moves it, was not of itself sufficient to give a person the power to make the movement at will. . . . It is true that the electrical excitation of the muscle was of some help, since persons who had this preliminary passive exercise learned the movement a little more rapidly than other persons; but this difference is sufficiently explained by the greater certainty with which such persons would recognize the right movement when by good luck they made it themselves in the midst of their unsuccessful attempts. A prompt recognition of success is a prime necessity in learning any performance. . . . I infer from the results of Bair, combined with my own, that even in first getting control over a particular movement, at least in the case of adults, the kinesthetic image of that movement is neither a necessary nor a sufficient condition.

In very many of his cases, Woodworth found the execution of the intended act to be devoid of any imagery whatsoever—neither resident nor remote. The "naked thought" of the act itself sufficed to initiate the requisite movement. It was as if instigating cues had been reduced to zero. In the final sections of his paper, Woodworth refers to the "whole determination of an act" persisting even though attention to it has lapsed which he took to mean that "the nervous system may become set or adjusted for a certain act, and remain so for a time without the continuance of clear consciousness of the act, the complete determination being effected in a subsequent moment" (1939, p. 58).

This is virtually the same conclusion reached by N. Ach[17] at about the same time in his investigation of volitional acts. For Ach, such acts were also "imageless" and were attributed to what he called *determining tendencies.* Although Woodworth and Ach conducted their investigations independently of one another, they came close to wording their respective conclusions in equivalent language. Woodworth, as just indicated, found the "whole determination of an act" to be due to a neural set while Ach referred to this as a "determining tendency."

Motivation Versus Causation of Acts

In the light of the foregoing section, volitional control depends upon the ability to initiate appropriate determining tendencies, and this ability, in

---

[17] Ach was a member of the so-called Würzburg school in Germany. His first studies of volition were published in German in 1905; some have been translated by D. Rapaport (1951, pp. 15–38). Relevant bibliographic references are supplied by Rapaport.

turn, depends upon choice of goals or objectives. A pitcher is confronted with such a choice in deciding whether or not to walk the batter. If he decides to issue a walk, he usually has no trouble in pitching wide of the plate. On the other hand, should he decide to try for a strikeout, the resulting determining tendency will entail more precise muscular control. What he intended to be a fast ball on the outside corner may result in a wild pitch that strikes the batter. Under the circumstances, the outcome was at variance with his intention: the injury to the batter is regarded as an accident and the pitcher is absolved of responsibility for the accident, as would not be the case had the pitch been a "bean ball" instead of a wild pitch. This is an illustration of the ordinary distinction between intentional and unintentional acts. It is not the same as a distinction between caused and uncaused acts in the sense in which the concept of causation has been introduced in the controversy over free will versus determinism. All acts may be caused or determined, but not all acts are motivated. Thus the pitcher was motivated to get the ball over the outside corner, but factors beyond his control *caused* the wild pitch.

Failure to make this distinction between motivation and causation has resulted in some questionable psychological theorizing. For example, some psychoanalysts in their espousal of determinism as a scientific doctrine regard everything a patient says or does as an expression of conscious or unconscious motives. Should he be late for his appointment, the lateness is viewed as having motivational significance even if it was caused by a traffic tie-up due to a highway accident. Moreover, should the driver of the car involved in the accident happen to be undergoing analysis, *his* psychoanalyst might attribute the accident to an unconscious self-destructive motive. In reality the accident may have been caused by the need to swerve suddenly in order to avoid hitting a dog or by the blowout of a defective new tire. Such an accident is caused but is not motivated. To salvage the suicide hypothesis, one would have to go to the ridiculous extreme of postulating the unconscious purchase of a defective tire. A police report of the accident would indicate that the driver was not responsible or that the accident was unavoidable.

However, had it been due to the driver's intoxication, he would have been held culpable and subject to legal action on the ground of being responsible for the decision to drive when in no condition to control the car. By implication he would thus be adjudged a "free" agent who was under no compulsion to drive and who could have decided otherwise. In a sense the court is holding him responsible for having made the wrong decision, and in doing so is endowing him with a modicum of volitional freedom.

Would a court psychologist agree with this interpretation? Might he not, as a devotee of science and hence an advocate of determinism, regard volitional freedom as incompatible with a scientific psychology? Such a psychology, he might contend, regards all behavior as a consequence of antecedent causes, so that what a man does today is the result of the countless influences that formed his character plus the immediate situation to which he is responding. He might even argue that, ideally, if we had complete knowledge of *all* these formative influences, we could predict what the man is going to do tomorrow when confronted with other situations.

An argument of this kind reflects an uncompromising determinism: all that happens is due to what has happened. There is no place for luck, supernatural intervention, or control of one's destiny. Man deludes himself if he believes himself to be free to choose between good and evil. Whatever made the good man good determines his choices, just as whatever made the evil man evil determines *his* choices. This makes all so-called free choices forced choices; or tropistic resultants of impinging causal antecedents. This view of scientific determinism is like Calvinistic predestination minus the mystery of salvation by God's grace. An advocate of such radical determinism would be expected to believe that *everything* in the world is predestined with fatalistic inevitability, from the most trivial to the most momentous occurrence, all through the centuries of the past as well as those of the future. To be consistent, he would have to hold that the relentless sweep of causation foreordains the school marks of children yet unborn, the campaign promises of future candidates, the outcome of all football games to be played next year, and the attendance at each of the games. No individual acts of will can be expected to alter these predicted outcomes, for such acts would be included in the totality of causal influences.

Fatalistic Determinism Versus Contingent Determinism

Very few if any working scientists express their endorsement of determinism in such extreme form. In their daily work they act as if their laboratory research might have some as yet unpredictable result and is not a steady march of developments leading to foredoomed failure or inevitable success. They may also talk about wanting to be "free" from administrative interference with their research projects and to be "free" to pursue their own research interests. They do not seem to behave like helplessly passive robots buffeted by the winds of an inexorable destiny. They may pride themselves on being independent thinkers and insist on being "free" to teach the truth as they see it. On occasion they may refer to the "responsibility" of scientists to safeguard this kind of freedom. A stand of this kind suggests belief in volitional control and is difficult to reconcile with belief in a fatalistic determinism.

If questioned about their stand on the free will-determinism controversy, virtually all modern psychologists would classify themselves as determinists, especially when discussing the status of psychology as a science. Ever since psychology ceased to be a branch of philosophy and became increasingly experimental, there has been sensitivity about this status. The founding fathers of the "new" experimental psychology were zealous in their efforts to win recognition as the founders of a science. As indicated in previous chapters, they were readily drawn into debates about the dependability of introspective reports and the adequacy of their experimental controls. For the most part, physics was regarded as the model science: just as its progress was signalized by the successive discoveries of physical laws, so, it was hoped, application of the methodology of physics to problems of psychology would lead to the formulation of laws of mental life.

The quest for law was seen as the *sine qua non* of scientific endeavor. Once a scientific law is discovered, it becomes increasingly possible to predict what will occur under conditions governed by that law. The more law the more determinism, in the sense of knowing what will occur; hence tables predicting ebb and flood tides and the times of sunrise and sunset as well as the times of a future solar or lunar eclipse. In emulation of the outlook and methodology of physics, the "new" psychology was thought of as a natural science. This attitude became even more explicit with the rise of the still "newer" behavioristic psychology around 1912. In a challenging paper launching this "newer" psychology, Watson stated the issue very definitely: (1913, p. 158):

> Psychology as the behaviorist views it is a purely objective experimental branch of natural science. Its theoretical goal is the prediction and control of behavior.

Upon first inspection, this appears to be a blunt endorsement of determinism. The goal of the behaviorist is to establish laws of behavior by means of which to predict what men and animals will do under given circumstances Without determinism, attainment of such a goal would be impossible. However, Watson's additional goal of controlling behavior indicates that his determinism was not a fatalistic determinism. By suitable intervention, he expected to be able to change behavior. In fact, in a later publication he went on record as saying that given complete control of environmental factors, he was prepared to take any normal baby and "guarantee" to "train him to become any type of specialist I might select—doctor, lawyer, artist, merchant-chief and yes, even beggar-man and thief, regardless of his talents, penchants, tendencies, abilities, vocation, and race of his ancestors" (quoted in E. G. Boring, 1957, pp. 82–85).

This is tantamount to saying that his act of selecting a particular vocational goal for the infant will shift what would otherwise have been the direction of the child's development. As experimenter he was to be "free" to choose the direction, and by implication the training was to be such as to force compliance on the part of the child. Watson, once in possession of the laws of behavior, could thus govern the child's destiny. The destiny would be determined but not predetermined. In place of a fatalistic determinism we have a contingent determinism.

Actually, of course, Watson, never having mastered all the laws of behavior and never having achieved full control of any infant's environment, was never in a position to make good on his "guarantee." In some respects it was more an idle boast than the formulation of a testable hypothesis, or else it may have been intended to be a dramatic means of teaching the relationship between tested knowledge and effective control. In the light of such a teaching, man ceases to be the impotent victim of the forces of nature; but he is given to understand that, as his knowledge of these forces increases, he can harness them to facilitate progress toward his chosen goals.

As he chooses a particular goal he may feel it to be a "free" choice, but it may mean no more than the absence of coercion. A determinist would hold that his choice was the more or less inevitable resultant of the interaction of his knowledge, his values, and his expectations. Nor would the advocate of free will claim to be absolutely free in his choices. He would grant the limitations imposed by the constraints of his ethical principles as well as by the rules of the game, so to speak. A bridge player, for example, is not free to make any bid, but is restricted to those falling within the scope of the game's regulations. Since fractional bids are ruled out, no player is free to bid two and a half spades. Nor is he free to bid eight of any suit or to take a card back once it has been played. His personal integrity would render it impossible for him to cheat, thus further restricting the scope of his freedom. All this means is that his alleged freedom to bid and to play a specific card is a relative freedom.

Moreover, what is true of bridge is true of all phases of civilized living to the extent that business, education, government, religion, family life, industry, sports, and other social institutions are enmeshed in a network of rules and conventions. All choices have to be made within the restricting boundaries of such rules and conventions.

Determinism and Freedom of Choice

It is the existence of choice in human affairs which accounts for feelings of volitional freedom. However, choices are not uncaused. They are determined by our motives and interests as well as by knowledge of what to expect as consequences of a particular choice. Thus the novice bridge player, being only moderately motivated and having no knowledge of fine points of the game, will blunder in his choices as contrasted with the way in which a veteran expert would play the same hand. The expert's superior knowledge makes for more intelligent choices and fewer stupid plays. In one sense the novice has more volitional freedom than the expert, for there are more incorrect ways of playing a hand than correct ways. The novice is confronted with a multiplicity of options that the expert need never consider; hence he is less restricted in his range of choices than the expert.

In other words, when it comes to making mistakes the novice is more "free" than the expert. A truism like this serves as a reminder of the fact that effective volitional control is partly a function of ability to make intelligent choices. This, in turn, involves knowledge of probable immediate and remote consequences of proposed courses of action. Very often there are too many unpredictable variables to be considered, so that what appears to be an intelligent choice may turn out to be a blunder.

In choosing a career it is impossible to have detailed advance knowledge of all one is going to encounter in a given field of endeavor. For example, a young man may find himself fascinated by the idea of becoming a concert violinist and equally fascinated by the prospect of becoming a professor of mathematics. After consulting with his school's vocational-guidance specialists, he learns what he already suspected; namely, that he has both the interests and aptitudes justifying a choice of either career. It might well be that his dilemma is rendered more acute by his mother urging the choice of one career and his father more enthusiastic about the other.

Like Buridan's famous donkey standing between equally attractive bundles of hay, the young man may find it difficult to resolve the dilemma. By hypothesis the irresolute donkey's inability to make a choice was supposed to have resulted in death by starvation, but our hero, being a man and not a donkey, is not likely to make an ass of himself by remaining permanently immobilized. Eventually he will bestir himself and embark on one of the alternative careers despite no advance knowledge of future determinants of his successes and failures. However, at the close of life in writing his autobiography, these determinants may be subject to recognition and evaluation as he reviews the high points of his career. In *retrospect* they may stand out as significant causal influences resulting in definite consequences as required by the theory of determinism. They may even be viewed as instances of underlying psychological laws, but even if this should be the case, there would be little likelihood of making *prospective* use of such laws so as to enable prodigies to write finished autobiographies at the threshold of their careers. James had this in mind when he wrote that (1890, Vol. I, p. 576):

> However closely psychical changes may conform to law, it is safe to say that individual histories and biographies will never be written in advance no matter how "evolved" psychology may become.

As James implied, all biographies are retrospective accounts of individual careers. As histories they purport to reveal the factors that account for what the subject of the biography accomplished in some field of human endeavor. Among such factors, mention is often made of ancestry, parental traits, childhood experiences, schooling, health, recreational pursuits, religious background, friendships, and whatever else the biographer regards as having had some bearing on the course of his subject's career. Special attention will be given to the way in which his hero faced personal crises and disposed of difficult questions involving momentous decisions. Such crises and questions are sometimes viewed as especially revelatory of the hero's character, especially if they entail a choice between loyalty to an austere moral principle as opposed to endorsement of a prestige-enhancing but ethically dubious course of action.

Spinoza was confronted with such a crucial issue in 1673 when he had to decide whether or not to become professor of philosophy at the University of Heidelberg. The invitation to teach there assured him of complete freedom of expression concerning all aspects of philosophy except those which might raise doubts about the state's established religion. As a result of this one limitation placed on the philosopher's freedom of thought, he found it impossible to accept the invitation.

In Spinoza's philosophy there was neither chance in the physical world nor free will in the mental realm. Accordingly, he would not have attributed his rejection of the invitation to freedom of choice on his part. Instead it was forced upon him with deterministic inevitability by the drift of his personal ideals. Given such ideals, it was literally impossible for him to act otherwise, just as men of integrity find it impossible to bear false witness no matter what financial inducements are introduced. Analogously, denial of free will means that less conscientious men might find it impossible to resist the lure of such inducements. This makes choice more a function of character than of volition. To put it in another way: *it is not will that determines character, but character that determines will.*

Determinism and Ethics

From this viewpoint of Spinoza's, it seems as if the virtuous man cannot help being virtuous and as if the sinful cannot help sinning. Needless to add, critics of his teachings were more troubled by the latter implication than by the former. By implication James may be included among such critics, even though he fails to mention Spinoza in his discussion of the free-will issue. This is clearly indicated in the following excerpts from this discussion (James, 1890, Vol. II, pp. 572–574):

> My own belief is that the question of free-will is insoluble on strictly psychologic grounds. After a certain amount of effort of attention has been given to an idea, it is manifestly impossible to tell whether either more or less of it *might* have been given or not. To tell that, we should have to ascend to the antecedents of the effort, and defining them with mathematical exactitude, prove, by laws of which we have not at present even an inkling, that the only amount of sequent effort which could possibly comport with them was the precise amount which actually came. . . . We are thrown back therefore upon the crude evidences of introspection on the one hand, with all its liabilities to deception, and, on the other hand, upon *a priori* postulates and probabilities. He who loves to balance nice doubts need be in no hurry to decide the point. . . . But if our speculative delights be less keen, . . . then, taking the risk of error on our head, we must project upon one of the alternative views the attribute of reality for us; we must so fill our mind with the idea of it that it becomes our settled creed. The present writer does this for the alternative of freedom, but since the grounds of his opinion are ethical

rather than psychological, he prefers to exclude them from the present book.

. . . But when scientific and moral postulates war thus with each other and objective proof is not to be had, the only course is voluntary choice, for scepticism itself, if systematic, is also voluntary choice. . . . Freedom's first deed should be to affirm itself. We ought never to hope for any other method of getting at the truth if indeterminism be a fact. Doubt of this particular truth will probably be open to the end of time, and the utmost that a believer in free-will can *ever* do will be to show that the deterministic arguments are not coercive. That they are seductive, I am the last to deny; nor do I deny that effort may be needed to keep the faith in freedom, when they press upon it, upright in the mind.

From the foregoing it appears that James regarded the arguments advanced by determinists as more persuasive than those advanced by indeterminists. He viewed the former arguments as more "seductive" or persuasive than the latter, even though they are not altogether "coercive" or compelling. Moreover, he also granted that resisting the force of these arguments calls for more effort than does meeting those of the defenders of free will. He sided with the defenders because of moral rather than scientific or psychological considerations.

He took determinism to mean that the evil acts of evil men are inevitable and not subject to change. Instead he preferred to endorse (Vol. II, p. 573) "the postulate that *what ought to be can be, and that bad acts cannot be fated, but that good ones must be possible in their place.*" Evidently, as suggested by his use of the word "fated," he was thinking of a fatalistic determinism and not of a contingent determinism; for, as will be recalled, contingent determinism holds that within limits behavior can be changed, but it is opposed to interpretations of such change as being "free" in the sense of being uncaused or unmotivated.

It regards change as a product of learning to exercise control in the light of knowledge of relevant cause-and-effect relationships. The more knowledge the more control; hence man's quest for means of rehabilitating delinquents and alcoholics, for the conquest of disease, for the elimination of war, for the reduction of group prejudice, and, in short, for the promotion of the good life. But this is a quest for the determinants or causes of the evils in question, not a quest for the emancipation of volition. Medical control of yellow fever, malaria, poliomyelitis, and other diseases is a product of increased medical knowledge of the causes of disease. Free will as such is not enough to yield such control. In fact, in the absence of the requisite knowledge the physician is not "free" to exercise effective control, no matter how intense his will to help his patients. With such knowledge, he can save the lives of patients who would have been "fated" to die had they been born in earlier centuries.

A deterministic outlook is thus not necessarily the equivalent of a fatalistic outlook. Furthermore, it is significant that Spinoza, despite his denial of free will, nevertheless in his *Ethics* glorified the *homo liber,* the free man

(Wolfson, 1934, Vol. II, p. 255). His free man was not a servant to his lusts, but was guided by the light of reason. In the psychology of Spinoza freedom of the intellect had to do with man's ability to learn, to profit by experience, to reason, and to progress from ignorance to knowledge and from knowledge to understanding and from understanding to wisdom. His glorification of the free man, as Wolfson indicates, corresponded "to the Stoic apotheosis of the wise man" and with "the saying of the rabbis that the sage is the only man who can be called free."

Determinism and the Contemporary Scene

In the light of the foregoing account of the free will-determinism controversy, it might seem pointless for the contemporary psychologist to continue with the debate. So many generations of philosophers have engaged in the debate, with the arguments pro and con considered in each generation, that further discussion might seem futile. Nevertheless, it continues to belong to psychology's persistent problems as indicated by recurrent references to it through all the years of the past on up to the present. For example, in 1957, in an article entitled "When Is Human Behavior Predetermined?" E. G. Boring dealt with some contemporary aspects of the problem. Among these he mentioned the difference between what classical or Newtonian physics had to say about the concept of causality and what the modern physicist, brought up in an age of electronics, has to say about the same concept. The well-known uncertainty principle of Werner Heisenberg (1901–   ) serves as a convenient reminder of this difference. The nature of physical causation can no longer be disposed of by theories based upon the impact of colliding billiard balls, the action of levers, the influence of inclined planes, and similar mechanical relationships. In fact, as Boring made evident, the current scientific fashion is to lay less stress on theories and more on models. He clarified what this shift in emphasis means by noting (1957, p. 191):

> The theory claims to be true, even though we all know that assurance about the validity of these claims varies greatly from theory to theory and from time to time for the same theory. The theory is an *as,* whereas the model is an *as-if.* The theory is indicative; the model, subjunctive. The model is a pattern to be abandoned easily at the demand of progress. Thus science is less than the whole of wisdom, and the wise teacher of science, being also a human being, will not seek to try to make those other human beings who come under his tutelage less wise or less free than himself.

From the context it seems that Boring, as an advocate of determinism, is thinking of it as a model, but neglects to indicate the precise form it is to take. He regards the wise man's wisdom as different from the scientist's factual knowledge, since, in his view, wise choices or intelligent preferences belong to the world of value and not to the world of science. He restricts the job of the scientist to impersonal factual description uncontaminated by value judgments. This restriction, he adds, makes science "something less than the one way to truth." By implication this suggests the existence of both scientific and nonscientific truths as a perplexing inference. What Boring seems to overlook is the fact that truth as such is a value which the scientist prefers to falsehood just as he prefers a rigorous proof to a sloppy one and clear descriptions to vague ones. To regard science as value-free is thus a dubious assumption.

Boring's double-truth view results in a qualified determinism which leaves a man a modicum of freedom. He is refreshingly frank about this when he writes (1957, p. 195):

> Causal determinism is the scientific model. It works enormously well. There are places in science where it breaks down, but they are not many. On the other hand, there are, in the process of living all the situations in which values are called for and in which the scientific model itself fails. In such cases we get along best with the truncated causality model which we call freedom. . . .
>
> Freedom is a negative concept, a truncated causality, but it is part of the warp of language. To get rid of this concept would change the whole of our civilization. Yet we need not attempt that, for causality is only the form of a model, and freedom is also a model and we can use our models at will without letting them dominate us.

This leaves the psychologist as scientist with two incompatible models, to which he has to reconcile himself despite the contradiction involved. As Boring recognized, the free will-determinism controversy belongs to Kant's list of *antinomies*. By the latter term, Kant was referring to mutually contradictory or antithetic propositions each of which is difficult or impossible to refute. By way of illustration, Kant mentioned our notions of time as applied to the idea of the beginning of the world, since everything must have a beginning. As opposed to this we also entertain the proposition of time as infinite and a world that has always existed. With respect to causality, as Kant pointed out, there is the proposition that some events are due to natural law while others are a product of freedom. Antithetic to this proposition is the conviction that all causality must conform to the laws of nature. Boring's concept of truncated freedom is more in line with the former proposition than with the latter.

In some ways, antinomies are a part of everyday life. On the one hand we hold that parallel lines can never meet, and yet as we view a long stretch of straight railroad tracks their visual convergence is an undeniable fact. In planning a trip around the world we recognize the earth as a globe and every segment of its surface as part of a curve. Nevertheless, in planning to build a house on a small segment of this surface we recognize the segment as flat and uncurved. We come away from a physics lecture convinced that all solid so-called material objects consist of electrons whirling around pro-tons in submicroscopic orbits. However, as we drive home with friends this conviction is displaced by an equally strong conviction in the solidity of the car and the flesh-and-blood reality of our friends. We may find it impossible to think of ourselves as nothing but a congeries of electronic orbits as we chat with our friends about an incidental remark made by our physics professor when he said, "Heisenberg's principle of uncertainty doesn't mean that something like free will has come to play a part in the thinking of the scientist." In the ensuing discussion we may find ourselves siding with the professor as strict determinists and opponents of free will. And yet a moment later, should the driver startle us by the dangerous maneuver of passing a car on the crest of a hill, our ensuing indignant protest would suggest a less strict determinism as we censure the driver for his violation of a cardinal rule of safe driving. Our censure implies, not that the violation was the inevitable consequence of uncontrollable determinants, but that the driver was "free" to abide by the rule. In other words, determinism holds sway, in our scientific theorizing, but when dealing with practical affairs of a routine nature we often talk and act as if freedom of choice, even if truncated, is not to be denied.

Despite the antiquity of the problem and despite its metaphysical over-tones, it continues to be a challenge to every generation of psychologists. As recently as 1964 the *American Psychologist* contained a relatively long article on "Determinism-Freedom in Contemporary Psychology" by L. Immergluck, in which the author argues persuasively in behalf of determinism and yet acknowledges that not all present-day psychologists are to be classified as determinists.

Like the problem of the self, the problem of free will has not yet been settled either by argument or by experiment. Incidentally, in recent years the self concept has been the subject of an increasing number of experimental studies. R. C. Wylie, in her book, *The Self Concept* (1961), in which these studies are reviewed, appends a bibliography of more than 450 articles, the vast majority of which were published during the 1950s.

The concept of determinism has not had a comparable impact on experi-mental psychology. There have been many laboratory studies involving acts of choice and expressions of preference as well as of free association as contrasted with controlled association, but in general such studies have not been designed to get at the question of man's possible volitional freedom. It may never be possible to work out an experimental design by means of which to dispose of the question in decisive fashion. James, it will be recalled, reached this conclusion long ago when he wrote that "the question of free-will is insoluble on strictly psychologic grounds." As a Kantian antinomy, free will may be refractory to solution on any other grounds as well. Even so, should the question be raised at a scientific meeting, there would be little disposition to advocate suspension of judgment. Virtually all the scientists present would voice their belief or conviction in the ineluctable sovereignty of cause-and-effect relationships in the world of science. Paradoxically, though, they might also hold this endorsement of determinism to have been the result of a "free" decision—one prompted by evidence and not by external coercion. In the last analysis, freedom to pursue truth in the light of available evidence is the kind of freedom that both determinists and indeterminists can join forces in endorsing and in welcoming. Without such freedom there can be no science.

References

Adler, A. "Individual Psychology," in C. Murchison (ed.). *Psychologies of 1930.* Worcester: Clark University Press, 1930.

Allport, G. *Becoming—Basic Considerations for a Psychology of Personality.* New Haven: Yale University Press, 1955.

Allport, G. "The Ego in Contemporary Psychology," *Psychological Review,* 1943, *50,* 451–479.

Allport, G. "Historical Background of Modern Social Psychology," in G. Lindzey (ed.). *A Handbook of Social Psychology.* Cambridge, Mass.: Addison-Wesley, 1954.

Allport, G. *Pattern and Growth in Personality.* New York: Holt, Rinehart and Winston, 1961.

Allport, G. "The Productive Paradoxes of William James," *Psychological Review,* 1943, *50, 95*–120.

Ansbacher, H. L., and Ansbacher, R. R. (eds.). *The Individual Psychology of Alfred Adler.* New York: Basic Books, 1956.

Augustine, A. "On the Trinity" in B. Rand (ed.). *The Classical Psychologists.* Boston: Houghton Mifflin Company, 1912.

Bell, C. "Idea of a New Anatomy of the Brain," in W. Dennis (ed.). *Readings in the History of Psychology.* New York: Appleton-Century Crofts, 1948.

Bertocci, P. "The Psychological Self, the Ego, and Personality," *Psychological Review,* 1945, *52, 91*–99.

Bible. Job 29:1–4.

Boring, E. G. "When Is Human Behavior Predetermined?" *Scientific Monthly,* 1957, *84,* 189–196.

Calkins, M. W. *Introduction to Psychology.* New York: The Macmillan Company, 1905.

Chein, I. "The Awareness of the Self and the Structure of the Ego," *Psychological Review,* 1944, *51,* 304–314.

Chein, I. "Personality and Typology," *Journal of Social Psychology,* 1943, *18,* 89–109.

Drever, J. *A Dictionary of Psychology.* Harmondsworth, Middlesex: Penguin Books, 1952.

English, H. B., and English, A. C. *A Comprehensive Dictionary of Psychological and Psychoanalytical Terms.* New York: Longmans, Green and Company, 1958.

Hall, C. S., and Lindzey, G. *Theories of Personality.* New York: John Wiley and Sons, 1957, Chapter XII.

Hall, J. "Mental Diseases and Criminal Responsibility," *Columbia Law Review,* 1945, *45,* 677–715.

Hoppe, F. "Erfolg und Miserfolg," *Psychologische Forschung,* 1930, *14,* 1–62.

Immergluck, L. "Determinism-Freedom in Contemporary Psychology," *American Psychologist*, 1964, *19*, 270–281.

James, W. *Principles of Psychology*, Vol. I. New York: Henry Holt and Company, 1890.

James, W. *Principles of Psychology*, Vol. II. New York: Henry Holt and Company, 1890.

Jaspers, K. *Allgemeine Psychopathologie*, 3rd ed. Berlin: Julius Spranger, 1923.

Karpf, F. B. *American Social Psychology, Its Origins, Developments and European Background*. New York: McGraw-Hill Book Company, 1932.

Klein, G. S., and Schoenfeld, N. "The Influence of Ego-Involvement on Confidence," *Journal of Abnormal and Social Psychology*, 1941, *36*, 249–258.

Ladd, G. T., and Woodworth, R. S. *Elements of Physiological Psychology*. New York: Charles Scribner's Sons, 1911.

McClelland, D. C. *The Achieving Society*. New York: D. Van Nostrand Company, 1961.

McDougall, W. *Introduction to Social Psychology*. New York: Charles Scribner's Sons, 1908.

Mach, E. "Contributions to the Analysis of Sensations," in B. Rand (ed.). *The Classical Psychologists*. Boston: Houghton Mifflin Company, 1912.

Osgood, C. E. *Method and Theory in Experimental Psychology*. New York: Oxford University Press, 1953.

Rapaport, D. *Organization and Pathology of Thought*. New York: Columbia University Press, 1951.

Robinson, D. S. *The Story of Scottish Philosophy*. New York: Exposition Press, 1961.

Sherrington, C. S. *The Integrative Action of the Nervous System*. New Haven: Yale University Press, 1906.

Snygg, D., and Combs, A. W. *Individual Behavior*. New York: Harper and Brothers, 1949.

Southard, E. E. "On the Application of Grammatical Categories to the Analysis of Delusions," *Philosophical Review*, 1916, *25*, 196–227.

Sperry, R. W. "Neurology and the Mind-Brain Problem," *American Scientist*, 1952, *40*, 291–312.

Stern, W. *General Psychology from the Personalistic Standpoint*. (Translated by H. D. Spoerl.) New York: The Macmillan Company, 1938.

Stevens, S. S. (ed.). *Handbook of Experimental Psychology*. New York: John Wiley and Sons, 1951.

Stout, G. F. *Mind and Matter*. Cambridge, England: Cambridge University Press, 1931.

Titchener, E. B. *A Text-Book of Psychology*. New York: The Macmillan Company, 1917.

Wallen, R. "Ego-Involvement as a Determinant of Selective Forgetting," *Journal of Abnormal and Social Psychology*, 1942, *37*, 20–39.

Walshe, F. M. R. "Current Ideas in Neurology and Neuropsychology: A Study in Contrasts," *Perspectives in Biology and Medicine*, 1964, *VII*, 199–218.

Warren, H. C. *Dictionary of Psychology*. Boston: Houghton Mifflin Company, 1934.

Watson, J. B. "Psychology as a Behaviorist Views It," *Psychological Review*, 1913, *20*, 158–177.

Wolfson, H. A. *The Philosophy of Spinoza*, Vol. II. Cambridge: Harvard University Press, 1934.

Woodworth, R. S. "The Cause of a Voluntary Movement," in *Psychological Issues— Selected Papers of Robert S. Woodworth*. New York: Columbia University Press, 1939.

Wylie, R. C. *The Self Concept—A Critical Survey of Pertinent Research Literature*. Lincoln: University of Nebraska Press, 1961.

PART IV

FROM THE RENAISSANCE TO THE MODERN PERIOD

11

The Seventeenth-Century Psychology
of Hobbes and Descartes

CENTURIES VARY IN IMPORTANCE with the extent to which men and events of a given period come to influence the history of subsequent periods. With respect to Western civilization, for example, the centuries from 1500 to 1700 probably are far more important than any preceding span of two hundred years. As Whitehead wrote (1948, p. 6): "Although in the year 1500 Europe knew less than Archimedes who died in the year 212 B.C., yet in the year 1700, Newton's *Principia* had been written and the world was well started on the modern epoch."

This span of two hundred years marks the beginning of the "modern epoch," not only for science but also for literature, religion, geography, government, and philosophy, and for psychology as mental philosophy. These were the centuries of the Elizabethan era, of the Reformation, of Puritanism, of most of the great voyages of discovery, of political upheaval in the days of Cromwell, and of the founding fathers of modern philosophy. Even the modern English language dates from about the year 1500. Experimental physics as well as subjects like analytic geometry and calculus came into vogue during these centuries. So did statistics in the pioneering work of men like John Graunt (1620–1674) and Jacob Bernoulli (1654–1705). Moreover, with the invention and construction of microscopes and telescopes around the year 1600, scientific imagination was quickened by exciting discoveries. It was an age of turbulent change, of new perspectives, of broadened intellectual horizons, of novel insights, and of controversy in philosophy, religion, and government. The mind of modern man was in the making. This is especially true of the modern scientific mind as becomes evident by a review of the notable achievements in the world of science that date from this period.

Seventeenth-Century Scientific Achievements

The foundations of modern astronomy, physics, and physiology were established during the seventeenth and eighteenth centuries. It is enough to recall a few of the outstanding innovators and their accomplishments to appreciate the nature and magnitude of their labors. They came from different countries and had different backgrounds, for science knows no national boundaries. Its international character is reflected in the fact that the foundations in question were the product of Polish, Danish, German, Italian, British, Dutch, and French investigators.

In astronomy we have the heliocentric theory advanced in the year of his death by the Polish astronomer Copernicus (1473–1543), followed by the careful recording of planetary and stellar movements by the Danish astronomer Tycho Brahe (1546–1601). Brahe was assisted in this work by the German Johannes Kepler (1571–1630). Later Kepler succeeded in giving mathematical formulation to the kind of data assembled by Brahe in the three laws now known as Kepler's laws.[1] Although Brahe questioned the heliocentric theory, it obtained impressive confirmation in the discoveries of the Italian physicist and astronomer Galileo (1564–1642). His discoveries included the existence of sunspots, rotation of the sun on its axis, the satellites of Jupiter, the moon's reflected light, the isochronism of the pendulum, the velocity of falling bodies, the parabolic course of projectiles, and other laws of bodies in motion. It is important to note that what Galileo studied was not the movement of bodies as such, but *changes* in their motion. Study of these changes was continued by Isaac Newton (1642–1727) in England and culminated in his law of universal gravitation as well as in his three laws of motion.[2] His *Principia Mathematica,* first published in 1687, ranks as one of the epoch-making books in the history of science. As a result of his demonstration of the relationship between white light and colors of the spectrum, he contributed to the later development of psycho-

---

[1] Kepler's laws have to do with planetary orbits. The first law calls attention to the elliptical nature of the orbits when the center of the sun is taken as one of the foci. According to the second law, the radius vector of each planet moves over equal areas in equal times. The third law refers to the time it takes for a planet to complete its circuit around the sun: the square of this time is proportional to the cube of the planet's mean distance from the sun.

[2] By way of reminder, these three laws stated:

I. "Every body continues in its state of rest, or uniform motion in a straight line, except so far as it may be compelled by force to change that state."
II. "Change of motion is proportional to force applied, and takes place in the direction of the straight line in which the force acts."
III. "To every action there is always an equal and contrary reaction; or, the mutual actions of any two bodies are always equal, and oppositely directed."

logical theories of color vision. Nor should his advocacy of the emission or corpuscular theory of light be overlooked.

During the same period, the Dutch physicist and mathematician Christian Huygens (1629–1695) advanced the rival wave theory of light. Huygens is also noted for his discovery of the rings of Saturn as well as for his invention of the pendulum clock. The chief French contribution to the mathematics and science of the period is to be found in the work of René Descartes (1596–1650). Incidentally, according to Whitehead (1948, p. 47), the outcome of the "combined labours" of Galileo, Newton, Huygens, and Descartes "has some right to be considered the greatest single intellectual success which mankind has achieved."

Astronomy and mathematics were not the only fields of science to have made dramatic progress between the years 1500 and 1700. For example, the chief impetus to the emergence of modern anatomic studies dates from the publication in 1543 of the famous *De Fabrica Humani Corporis* by the Fleming Andreas Vesalius (1514–1564). Another pioneering contribution to the history of biology stems from this period with the construction of microscopes by Anton van Leeuwenhoek (1632–1723) of Holland. Some of the very many instruments he put together enlarged objects by 270 times. As a result of his microscopic studies he was the first man to observe protozoa and bacteria and one of the first to describe red blood cells.[3] He was also the first to describe spermatozoa as well as the first to note the striped appearance of voluntary muscle tissue. As reported by F. H. Garrison (1929, pp. 254–255), all this labor, which resulted in the writing of more than four hundred scientific papers, was avocational or leisure-time work, since Leeuwenhoek supported himself as a draper and by serving as a janitor in the city hall of Delft. One of his most important contributions was related to what Garrison (1929, p. 248) called "the most momentous event in medical history since Galen's time." This was the publication in 1628 by William Harvey (1578–1657) of the experimental evidence in support of his thesis that the heart acts as a muscular force pump in the dynamics of the circulation of the blood. What was lacking in the chain of evidence was a demonstration of the way in which arterial blood gets into the venous system. The missing evidence was supplied by Leeuwenhoek's account of the capillary linkage between arteries and veins.

Many more names might be added to this list of outstanding seventeenth-century scientific pioneers. It is enough to recall just a few by way of indicating the range of the expanding scientific horizon. There was William Gilbert (1540–1603), whose *De Magnete* of the year 1600 brought the study of magnetic phenomena under scientific control, and who introduced the word "electricity" into our vocabulary following his discovery of frictional electricity by rubbing amber. ("*Electrum*" is Latin for "amber.") Then there was Robert

---

[3] They were first described by Jan Swammerdam (1637–1680), also of Holland.

Boyle (1627–1691), who first called attention to the difference between a chemical element and a compound as well as between a chemical reaction and a physical change. He is the same Boyle whose name is familiar in connection with the law governing volumetric changes in gases under pressure. His contemporary Marcello Malpighi (1628–1694), father of histology and distinguished embryologist, has a place in the history of the sense organs for having been the first to demonstrate that the papillae of the tongue are the receptors for taste. Thomas Willis (1620–1675) is another contemporary whose achievements have some relevance for the history of psychology. In the decade of the 1660s he wrote books on the anatomy of the nervous system, on nervous diseases and on hysteria. In commenting on these, Garrison (1929, pp. 262–264) points out they contain the first account of the eleventh cranial nerve as well as excellent clinical descriptions of conditions like general paralysis, along with probably the first demonstration of the condition now known as *paracusis,* in which the hard of hearing are said to hear better when tested in a noisy room. In the case mentioned by Willis, a deaf woman was unable to hear unless exposed to the background noise of a beating drum.

These names suffice as reminders of the exciting vistas opened up by the end of the seventeenth century for astronomers, mathematicians, physicists, chemists, and biologists. This means that the science of today has important historical roots in the seventeenth-century science. Does a similar statement apply to the psychology of today? Does it also have historical taproots in the seventeenth century? Were any exciting psychological vistas opened up by seventeenth-century philosopher-psychologists? To find the answers it is necesary to review the psychological teachings of men like Hobbes, Locke, Descartes, Spinoza, and Leibnitz. Hobbes, as the earliest of these five, merits first consideration.

Introduction to Hobbes as Philosopher-Psychologist

Thomas Hobbes (1588–1679) lived a long life through turbulent times. At the time of his birth, England was being threatened by the approach of the Spanish Armada. In fact, he jokingly attributed his premature birth to the effect of the threat on his mother and the consequent congenital origin of his timid nature. His timidity did not deter him from engaging in intellectual controversy and in attacking popular beliefs and established institutions. However, it probably did account for his chronic fear of death and his abhorrence of violence, revolution, riots, mob rule, and rebellion.

As a contemporary of Oliver Cromwell, he lived at a time when England was in the throes of political upheaval. The Puritans were insisting on the rights of private conscience and the rising mercantile class was demanding more influence in governmental affairs. As was mildly demonstrated by the Gunpowder Plot of 1605, with its plan to end anti-Catholic legislation by blowing up the Houses of Parliament on the day James I was scheduled to be there, violence and bitterness marked the struggle for religious freedom during the ensuing decades. Near the middle of the century the struggle between Parliament and Charles I became increasingly acute, culminating in the execution of the king on January 30, 1649. It was anything but a congenial era for a man like Hobbes, whose longing for personal safety, protection, and the security of a strong, stable government made him an exile in France from 1641 to 1652.

He gave expression to his longing in his most important work, published in 1651, which ensured him a place in the history of philosophy, the history of political theory, and the history of psychology. Ordinarily the book is called *Leviathan,* but its full title is *LEVIATHAN Or the Matter, Forme and Power of a COMMONWEALTH Ecclesiastical and Civil.* Like Plato's *Republic,* it is concerned with the problem of safeguarding human welfare by having an ideal society in an ideal state. Hobbes regarded an absolute monarchy as the best way of realizing such an ideal. For him, the resulting commonwealth ruled by an absolute monarch was like a huge "artificial man" whose activities could be compared to the parts of the human body. This body politic was the "great Leviathan" akin to the huge aquatic animal mentioned in the Bible. The sovereign was like an artificial soul presiding over and giving life to the body politic, and the various administrative officials had duties that Hobbes compared with the functions of nerves, muscles, and joints in the human body. In order to govern the commonwealth efficiently, the sovereign must be acquainted with the nature of his subjects. This, Hobbes pointed out, does not call for knowledge of individual characteristics of particular men, but a just knowledge of mankind in general. Accordingly, he devoted the first portion of his book to a discussion of human nature. What he has to say about psychology is brought out in the 125 pages of this portion, in which he lays the foundations of later British psychology. These pages reflect a basic empirical orientation and the beginnings of what was to become associational psychology. As a consequence, Hobbes has sometimes been referred to as the father of modern psychology.

Both chronologically and actually, the psychological views of Hobbes are postmedieval in the sense of being antimetaphysical and antischolastic. As H. Höffding (1900, Vol. I, p. 264) stated, "in the sphere of mental science" Hobbes "effected a breach with scholasticism similar to that instituted by Copernicus in astronomy, Galileo in physics, and Harvey in physiology." His repudiation of scholastic philosophy was strongly influenced by his admiration of the nature of geometric proof, with its formulation of clear definitions and ordered reasoning to definite conclusions. He had discovered Euclid in 1628 at the age of forty and from then on employed the logic of geometry as the paradigm of the right use of reason. Wrong use of reason makes for error, so that man's privileged position as the only rational animal is not an unmixed blessing; for, as Hobbes pointed out in his *Leviathan* (M. Oakeshott [ed.], 1962, p. 43):

. . . this privilege is allayed by another; and that is, by the privilege of absurdity; to which no living creature is subject, but man only. And of men, those are of all most subject to it, that profess philosophy. For it is most true that Cicero saith of them somewhere; that there can be nothing so absurd, but may be found in the books of philosophers. And the reason is manifest. For there is not one of them that begins his ratiocinations from the definitions, or explications of the names they are to use; which is a method that hath been used only in geometry; whose conclusions have thereby been made indisputable.

Study of geometry made Hobbes sensitive to the importance of language for the promotion of thought, or what he sometimes called "reckoning." He called attention to the need for clear understanding of what words signify or stand for if one is to avoid becoming "entangled in words." This is indispensable for "a man that seeketh precise truth" by thinking for himself instead of blindly accepting what he hears or reads. Hobbes concluded (Oakeshott, pp. 36–37):

. . . therefore in geometry . . . men begin at settling the significations of their words; which settling of significations they call *definitions*, and place them in the beginning of their reckoning.

By this it appears how necessary it is for any man that aspires to true knowledge, to examine the definitions of former authors; and either to correct them where they are negligently set down, or to make them himself. . . . So that in the right definition of names lies the first use of speech; which is the acquisition of science: and in wrong, or no definitions, lies the first abuse; from which proceed all false and senseless tenets; which make those men that take their instruction from the authority of books, and not from their own meditation, to be as much below the condition of ignorant men, as men endued with true science are above it. For between true science and erroneous doctrines, ignorance is in the middle. . . . Nature itself cannot err; and as men abound in copiousness of language, so they become more wise, or more mad than ordinary. Nor is it possible without letters for any man to become either excellently wise, or, unless his memory be hurt by disease or ill constitution of organs, excellently foolish. For words are wise men's counters, they do but reckon by them; but they are the money of fools, that value them by the authority of an Aristotle, a Cicero, or a Thomas, or any other doctor whatsoever, if but a man.

Just as Hobbes was impressed by the implications of Euclid's use of language in presenting geometric proofs, so he was forcibly impressed by Galileo's studies of motion whether of a pendulum, a falling body, or a moving planet. In fact, he visited Galileo in 1636 and came away preoccupied with the importance of motion in the world of science. It dawned on him that motion is characteristic of human behavior and that such behavior might be brought within the scope of the kind of explanation Galileo had employed in his studies of physical objects and heavenly bodies as subject to inertia and the laws of motion. Hobbes began to see man as an engine or a machine in the world of nature. To quote him directly (p. 19):

> Nature, the art whereby God hath made and governs the world, is by the *art* of man, . . . so in this also imitated, that it can make an artificial animal. For seeing life is but a motion of limbs, the beginning whereof is in some principle part within; why may we not say, that all automata (engines that move themselves by springs and wheels as doth a watch) have an artificial life? For what is the *heart,* but a *spring;* and the *nerves,* but so many *strings;* and the *joints,* but so many *wheels,* giving motion to the whole body, such as was intended by the artificer?

Motion as the Key to Sensation and Imagery

In developing this mechanical view of nature and of man's place in it, Hobbes anticipated several distinctions of importance in later psychology. In his discussion of sensation, for example, he noted the difference between contact and distance receptors by referring to taste and touch as aroused by objects "immediately" and vision, audition, and olfaction being aroused "mediately." In this context he also glimpsed what in nineteenth-century psychology came to be known as the theory of *specific energy of nerves.* This theory asserts that, irrespective of the nature of the stimulus applied, each sensory nerve gives rise to a characteristic quality of sensation. Thus, arousal of the optic nerve by pressure will result in a visual sensation, just as mechanical stimulation of the auditory nerve will result in the sensation of sound. To put this more technically: an inadequate stimulus capable of arousing a sensory nerve elicits the kind of sensation characteristic of arousal by the adequate stimulus. Hobbes referred to adequate stimulation by listing light as the normal stimulus for vision, sound for that of hearing, and so on for the other special qualities of sensation. In this connection he wrote (pp. 21–22):

> All which qualities, called *sensible,* are in the object, that causeth them, but so many motions of the matter, by which it presseth our organs diversely. Neither in us that are pressed, are they any thing else, but divers motions; for motion produceth nothing but motion. . . . And as pressing, rubbing, or striking the eye makes us fancy a light; and pressing the ear, produceth a din; so do the bodies also we see, or hear, produce the same by their strong, though unobserved action. . . . So that sense, in all cases, is nothing else but original fancy, caused . . . by the pressure, that is, by the motion of external things upon our eyes, ears, and other organs thereunto ordained.

By the term "fancy" in the preceding quotation, Hobbes meant "appearance" or "image" or "phenomenon." He makes this clear in his discussion of imagination, in which he points out that these terms are not to be restricted

to visual events but are applicable to all the other senses as well, thus providing for auditory, olfactory, and other forms of imagery. All forms of
imagery are attributed to the persistence of motion until it is blocked by
opposing factors, as illustrated by ripples in a pond after the wind has died
down and by the way a sensation of light continues after the light is ex-
tinguished. There is a gradual cessation of the induced motion; hence for
Hobbes, imagery is designated as *decaying sense.* With the lapse of time
this becomes the basis for memory; for, as Hobbes maintained (p. 24):

> This *decaying sense,* when we would express the thing itself, I mean *fancy* itself,
> we call *imagination* . . . : but when we would express the decay, and signify
> that the sense is fading, old and past, it is called *memory.* So that imagination
> and memory are but one thing, which for divers considerations hath divers
> names.

The close relationship between memory and imagination enabled Hobbes
to call attention to the well-known distinction between reproductive and
productive or creative imagination. Hobbes referred to the former as *simple*
and the latter as *compounded* imagination. He explained the difference
by referring to the recall in imaginal terms of the previously experienced
separate impressions of a man and a horse as instances of simple imagination and the creation of a hybrid centaur as an example of compounded
imagination.

Consideration of dream imagery also enabled Hobbes to anticipate issues
of importance for later scientific psychology. He attributed the content of
dream imagery to prior waking experiences that were reactivated either as
total units or in fragments of such units during sleep. Because of the "be-
numbed" condition of the sleeper's "brain and nerves," such reactivation,
Hobbes maintained, cannot very easily be induced by the motion of external stimuli. Instead, the arousal is due to the "agitation of the inward
parts of man's body" as a consequence of disturbance of the body's humors
by heat or cold. The resulting dream imagery can be as vivid and realistic
as a waking sensation or perception.

Because of this vividness of dreams, Hobbes raised the question of the
difference between sensation and image and declared "that it is a hard
matter, and by many thought impossible, to distinguish between sense and
dreaming." Under the circumstances he suggested a distinction in terms of
the mode of arousal, with sensations coming from an external source of
motion and images from an internal source; or, as he worded it, "the motion
when we are awake beginning at one end, and when we dream at another"
(p. 26). More than two hundred years later Oswald Külpe (1862–1915), one
of the leaders of the then "new" experimental psychology, came to grips with the
same problem and reached what is substantially the same conclusion: according
to Külpe, sensations are peripherally aroused images and images are centrally
aroused sensations.

On Free Versus Controlled Association

In addition to analyzing the mode of arousal of images and ideas, Hobbes was concerned with their sequential pattern in the course of dreaming and reflecting. This had to do with what was later termed *ideational association* and is responsible for listing him among the first of the long line of British associationists. Actually, Hobbes never employed the word "association." Instead he referred to the "succession of one thought to another" or to a "train of thoughts." He noted the relevance of the principle of contiguity in experience as a determinant of such a succession or train, by pointing out that even though one may be unable to predict what one "shall imagine next," this much is certain: "it shall be something that succeeded the same before, at one time or another."

Nor did the difference between free and controlled association escape him. This is clearly evident in the distinction he made between "train of thoughts unguided" as contrasted with "train of thoughts regulated." With reference to the former he explained (pp. 28–29):

> . . . the thoughts are said to wander, and seem impertinent to one another as in a dream. Such are commonly the thoughts of men, that are not only without company, but also without care of anything; though even then their thoughts are as busy as at other times, but without harmony . . . And yet in this wild ranging of the mind, a man may oft times perceive the way of it, and the dependence of one thought upon another. For in a discourse of our present civil war, what could seem more impertinent, than to ask, as one did, what was the value of a Roman penny? Yet the coherence to me was manifest enough. For the thought of the war, introduced the thought of the delivering up the king to his enemies; the thought of that, brought up the thought of the delivering up of Christ; and that again the thought of the thirty pence, which was the price of that treason; and thence easily followed the malicious question, and all this in a moment of time; for thought is quick.

On the other hand, controlled association, or the "train of thoughts regulated," is more a matter of focalized thinking as *"regulated* by some desire and design." It is governed by a goal-idea instigated by a felt need, and its operation can be noted in the way people react when some object has been lost. They think back to the time and place when the object was last seen and then try to recall the course of their subsequent moves in order "to find some certain, and limited time and place, in which to begin a method of seeking." It is also illustrated by situations calling for an anticipation of the probable consequences of a proposed course of action. This, Hobbes said, calls for *prudence* on the part of a man who "desires to know the event of an action; and then he thinketh of some like action past, and the events thereof one after another; supposing like events will follow like actions."

From Wishful Thinking to Mental Derangement

Strong desire or passion may interfere with clear thinking and prudent judgment. The implications of this truism are discussed in some detail by Hobbes. For example, he came close to the concept of *wishful thinking* when he stated (p. 62): "Thoughts are to the desires, as scouts, and spies, to range abroad, and find the way to the things desired." Moreover, in his view, mental derangement is the result of intensification of desire in the form of "passion, whose violence, or continuance, maketh madness" and which "is either great *vain-glory* . . . or great *dejection* of mind." Comparable disturbances may be observed in the "behaviors in men that have drunk too much" and whose loss of control releases their "domineering passions." In this connection Hobbes was reminded of the difference between the thoughts to which men give public expression and those private ones they would hesitate to reveal. For Hobbes, this inner world of inhibited ideation is akin to the disordered thinking of the insane. To quote him directly (p. 64):

> For, I believe, the most sober men, when they walk alone without care and employ-
> ment of the mind, would be unwilling the vanity and extravagance of their
> thoughts at that time should be publicly seen; which is a confession, that passions
> unguided, are for the most part mere madness.

Hobbes accounted for insanity or madness in terms of emotional upheaval or "passions unguided." This theory was in opposition to those who attributed insanity to the agency of alien spirits or demons in control of the victim's body. It is true, Hobbes indicated, that the doctrine of demonic possession seems to have Biblical support; but the passages in question are not to be taken literally and were not intended to be other than hortatory appeals. This was a bold stand to take in the seventeenth century and reflects the importance Hobbes attached to the task of safeguarding the freedom of science from interference by the Church or by religious zealots. Accordingly, he ventured to point out (pp. 66–67):

> For they that see any strange, and unusual ability, or defect, in a man's mind;
> unless they see withal, from what cause it may probably proceed, can hardly
> think it natural; and if not natural, they must needs think it supernatural; and
> then what can it be, but that either God or the Devil is in him? . . .
>   The Scripture was written to show unto men the kingdom of God, and to
> prepare their minds to become his obedient subjects; leaving the world and the
> philosophy thereof, to the disputation of men, for the exercising of their natural
> reason. . . .
>   And whereas our Saviour (Matt. xii. 43) speaketh of an unclean spirit, that
> having gone out of a man, wandereth through dry places, seeking rest, and

finding none, and returning into the same man, with seven other spirits worse than himself; it is manifestly a parable, alluding to a man, that after a little endeavour to quit his lusts, is vanquished by the strength of them; and becomes seven times worse than he was. So that I see nothing at all in the Scripture, that requireth a belief, that demoniacs were any other thing but madmen.

Hobbes as Determinist, Positivist, and Nominalist

From the preceding excerpts it is evident that Hobbes had little patience with those who believed that the course of natural events can be altered by the intervention of supernatural agencies. He was a determinist who held science to be "the knowledge of consequences, and dependence of one fact upon another" in strict accord with fixed causal relationships. As a determinist, he ruled out belief in freedom of the will in a forthright statement (p. 43) to the effect that were a man to talk to him of "a *free will*; or any *free,* but free from being hindered by opposition," he would regard the talk as being "without meaning, that is to say, absurd."

In his effort to keep science free from theological opposition Hobbes took a position that foreshadowed the positivism of Comte. He was vehement in his repudiation of medieval theology and its support of Aristotelian teachings. In his view (p. 181): "Scarce anything can be more absurdly said in natural philosophy, than that which now is called *Aristotle's* Metaphysics; nor more repugnant to government, that much of that he hath said in his *Politics*; nor more ignorantly, than a great part of his *Ethics*."[4]

As a nominalist he regarded talk about the real existence of "substantial forms," essences and other abstractions or universals as so much "jargon." He warned against the error of regarding such abstractions as "entities" instead of realizing that they are "names" or words by which we "register to ourselves, and make manifest to others, the thoughts and conceptions of our minds" (p. 484).

This dislike of vague metaphysical abstractions is also reflected in his treatment of emotion and motivation. Whenever possible, in line with his conviction of Galilean motion as a key scientific concept, the treatment

---

[4] Whether Hobbes intended this denunciation to be a wholesale indictment of Aristotle's philosophy is hard to say. It may be that he was deliberately restricting his disparaging comments to the three works mentioned. If so, then one might infer that he was more favorably disposed toward other works by Aristotle. His failure to impugn the *De Anima,* Aristotle's chief psychological treatise, is especially noteworthy. In fact, much of what he has to say about psychology implies endorsement of what is to be found in the *De Anima* and other writings by Aristotle. As will be indicated in a subsequent footnote, the theory of humor sponsored by Hobbes is foreshadowed in Aristotle's *Poetics*. It is hard to reconcile Hobbes's negative view of "men that take their instruction from the authority of books" (Oakeshott, p. 37), with G. S. Brett's conclusion (*Encyclopaedia Britannica,* 14th ed., 1929, article "Psychology, History of"). "In general Hobbes drew upon Aristotle for much of his material and some of his most striking phrases owe their origin to his knowledge of the original Aristotelian language."

stresses the approach-avoidance dichotomy, or motion toward or away from given situations. Even imagined situations, Hobbes suggests, are not devoid of motion; for "imagination is the first internal beginning of all voluntary motion." By this he meant that ideationally aroused tensions are actually incipient motions experienced as "*in*tensions," or what he called "endeavour" and which he defined (p. 97) as the "small beginnings of motion, within the body of man, before they appear in walking, speaking, striking, and other visible actions." It follows that *appetite* or *desire* refers to "endeavour" or motions "toward something," while *aversion* refers to "endeavour" or motions away from something.

For Hobbes, the common words descriptive of emotional life, like "joy," "dejection," "hope," and "anger," all refer to changes induced by relative success or failure, as anticipated or realized, in coping with desires and aversions. He introduced definitions of a long list of such words. For example, he defined "fear" as an "aversion, with opinion of hurt from the object" and "courage" as "the same, with hope of avoiding that hurt by resistance." Many of his definitions show keen psychological insight. By way of illustration, what he had to say about the psychology of laughter merits explicit mention, for it constitutes an early attempt to formulate a theory of humor.[5]

The Psychology of Laughter and Hobbes's Theory of Humor

Hobbes used the word "passion" as a generic term for emotion; thus he referred to laughter as caused by a "passion." In his general account of the "passions," he came close to recognizing emotional expression as a separate psychological problem when he called attention to the question of the "best

---

[5] Hobbes's theory as discussed on the next few pages is an *early* attempt to formulate a theory of humor, not so much because it appeared in the seventeenth century as because the crux of his theory had already been advanced by both Plato and Aristotle. In the *Philebus* of Plato (II. N. Fowler translation, 1952, p. 339), there is reference to the feeling of superiority occasioned by ludicrous situations so that "when we laugh at the ridiculous qualities of our friends, we mix pleasure with pain, since we mix it with envy." Moreover, Hobbes might have been less severe in his indictment of Aristotle had he read Aristotle's *Poetics,* since it contains an explanation of the comic or the ridiculous like the one advanced by Hobbes. According to Aristotle (W. D. Ross [ed.], 1929, p. 330), "The ridiculous may be defined as a mistake or deformity not productive of pain or harm to others; the mask, for instance, that excites laughter, is something ugly or distorted without causing pain." Some elaboration of these and other theories of humor is to be found in a book on aesthetics by E. F. Carritt (1923, pp. 301–336). Among the theories of humor mentioned by Carritt are those of Hegel, (1770–1831), Henry Bergson (1859–1941), Theodor Lipps (1851–1914), and Benedetto Croce (1866–1952). There is no mention of Freud's theory of wit and humor, although Freud had published on the subject in 1905 and the first edition of Carritt's book appeared in 1914. Freud's 1905 book is entitled *Wit and Its Relation to the Unconscious* (A. A. Brill [ed.], 1938). Freud returned to a consideration of the topic in his 1928 article on *Humour (Collected Works,* Vol. V, 1959, pp. 215–221). More than twenty-five years later (1957) the psychoanalyst M. Grotjahn devoted a book to the same topic.

signs of passions" and found them to be "motions of the body" and changes "in the countenance" (Oakeshott, p. 55).[6] Laughter, Hobbes said, is to be contrasted with weeping, and both involve "sudden motions" in the sense of being reactions to the unexpected. With the factor of suddenness eliminated, there will be neither laughter nor weeping; "for no man laughs at old jests or weeps for an old calamity." In other words, with reference to laughter there must be something novel or unanticipated in the provocative situation, especially something which precipitates feelings of superiority or self-enhancing "glory"; for, according to Hobbes (p. 52):

> *Sudden glory*, is the passion which maketh those *grimaces* called LAUGHTER; and is caused either by some sudden act of their own, that pleaseth them; or by the apprehension of some deformed thing in another, by comparision whereof they suddenly applaud themselves. And it is incident most to them, that are conscious of the fewest abilities in themselves; who are forced to keep themselves in their own favour, by observing the imperfections of other men. And therefore much laughter at the defects of others, is a sign of pusillanimity. For of great minds, one of the proper works is, to help and free others from scorn; and compare themselves only with the most able.

It is easy to find jokes and to cite humorous situations which seem to illustrate this theory of "sudden glory." For instance, laughter aroused by so-called moron stories and by "boners" culled from examination papers might, according to Hobbes, be an indication of delight at one's superiority to morons and ignorant students. The same explanation might hold for laughter at malapropisms like "She's a very confined lady" instead of "She's a very refined lady," or "He has hardening of the artilleries" in place of "hardening of the arteries." We laugh, Hobbes might have said, as we suddenly realize that we know better than to make such blunders.

He might also have argued that something akin to self-congratulatory delight is involved in perceiving the point of a joke. We can think of ourselves as "superior" to those who fail to understand the joke. Such feelings of superiority might also be aroused by dialect stories involving foreigners or members of minority groups in the form of jokes about Scots, Negroes, Irishmen, Jews, Italians, or Swedes. Many such stories have to do with alleged weaknesses of the members of such groups in the way of stinginess, laziness, drunkenness, greed, stupidity, and awkwardness. Telling them in dialect reveals a language defect and thus the hearer is reminded of his own freedom from such defect. In this sense, as Hobbes maintained, in laughing at such stories we are laughing "at the defects of others." In doing so we are holding them up to ridicule or what Hobbes called "scorn." Furthermore, he observed that only the weak or "pusillanimous" exhibit such laughter as

---

[6] The full implications of this question were not realized until the 1870s, with the publication of Darwin's *Expression of the Emotions in Man and Animals.*

they compare themselves with the less fortunate or less well endowed. Those who are well endowed with "great minds" have no need to bolster self-esteem by looking down on others. Instead they "compare themselves only with the most able."

Whether possessors of "great minds" find anything to laugh at is not a question which Hobbes considered. By implication their "sudden glory" would be restricted to "some sudden act of their own, that pleaseth them." Just what kind of act this might be is not mentioned. It certainly is not an act involving "apprehension of some deformed thing in another." Consequently, Hobbes did not intend his theory to account for all kinds of laughter. In fact, it is doubtful whether all laughter-provoking situations can be subsumed under a single all-embracing theory.

What Hobbes did do was to initiate interest in the psychology of humor on the part of twentieth-century psychologists. R. S. Woodworth (1918, pp. 77–80), for example, referred to Hobbes as having formulated one of the "most noteworthy" theories of humor. In particular he endorsed what Hobbes had to say about the importance of suddenness as a factor in mirth-provoking situations and gave qualified endorsement to the other factor of feelings of self-glorifying superiority. With reference to the latter factor, he noted its presence in very many instances of wit and humor as well as in many practical jokes. Such a joke, Woodworth indicated, while not usually appreciated by the victim, nevertheless constitutes "about the most effective stimulus to laughter with the untutored man" in that the victim is placed "in a position of temporary inferiority." Often, though, by way of qualification it is well to note that the sight of such inferiority "may awaken pity or disgust, instead of laughter." Unlike "untutored" men, those Hobbes designated as "great minds" are not apt to be amused by coarse practical jokes.

Whether "untutored" young children laugh at the childish equivalents of adult practical jokes is a different question. In one study of preschool children, G. F. Ding and A. T. Jersild (1932) found little if any evidence of laughter induced by feelings of superiority or what amounts to derisive laughter. In another study of preschool children by M. C. Jones (1926), such feelings were not listed among the factors provocative of laughter. Instead Jones found laughter to be an accompaniment of joyous excitement in social interaction with other children as they romped with one another or teased and chased one another. She also mentioned laughter as a result of being tickled. This too calls for recognition of the social factor involved in laughter, since self-stimulation of so-called ticklish spots fails to elicit laughter.[7] The same factor is to be noted in man's readiness to share jokes

---

[7] The term "ticklish spots" is a reference to the obvious fact that some cutaneous areas are more responsive than others when subjected to this kind of stimulation. Areas plentifully supplied with pain and touch receptors may be especially sensitive; for,

and amusing situations with others as well as in his willingness to pay for entertainment provided by clowns and comedians. Moreover, unlike the court jester of old with the restricted audience of the royal household, the modern comedian may arouse the laughter of thousands who have tuned in on his televised performance.

Besides being a universal phenomenon, laughter is unique to man. He is as much a laughing animal as he is a rational or a talking animal. Just how laughter as an involuntary act emerged in the evolutionary scheme of things and in what respect it has survival value are somewhat moot biological issues. Nevertheless, as we have noted, the psychology of laughter as reflected in theories of humor has been and continues to be explored independently of the latter biological issues.[8]

From Feral Man to Civilized Man

Biology as a separate science had not yet come into existence in the seventeenth century, so that it would be unreasonable to expect Hobbes to have concerned himself with the kinds of biological issues just mentioned. His scientific orientation was a reflection of seventeenth-century physics and its preoccupation with mechanics and motion. In line with this orientation, Hobbes had a sketchy view of the body as a mechanical affair and a somewhat less sketchy view of mind as an affair of motion. Because of this, Brett in his 1929 *Britannica* article referred to Hobbes as "essentially a behaviorist who lacked the necessary knowledge of biology and was compelled to employ the methods of a mechanistic age." For Hobbes, man's "appetites and aversions" were the equivalents of modern behavioristic approach-avoidance movements. He regarded some of these as innate and others as products of experience (Oakeshott, p. 48):

---

according to C. H. Best and N. B. Taylor (1945, pp. 800–801), "The tickling sensation appears to be due to the summed effects of stimulating both touch and pain endings." Still, this anatomic fact fails to account for the failure of self-stimulation of the sensitive zones in question. For tickling to provoke laughter, another person must serve as instigator and the act must be playful. Similar stimulation incident to bodily contact in the course of a serious fight is not apt to provoke laughter. Furthermore, laughter due to tickling is not expressive of genuine mirth; it is more like the excited laughter of people undergoing such "safe" dangers as riding on a roller coaster. Analogously, in being tickled there in recognition of the attack by the probing fingers as a sham attack. This is what makes the attack a playful maneuver.

[8] Many of these studies are especially concerned with the relationship between humor and personality factors. References to some of these experimental studies are to be found in the article by W. E. O'Connell (1960) dealing with the psychology of humor as contrasted with the psychology of wit. A later article by E. M. Hetherington and M. P. Wray (1964), concerned with "Aggression, Need for Social Approval and Humor Preferences," may also prove of interest in this connection. Incidentally, aggression or hostility as a factor in many mirth-provoking situations has long been recognized. Aristotle's provocative definition of wit as "well-bred insolence" (W. D. Ross [ed.], 1938, p. 325) serves as a good example of such long-standing recognition.

Of appetites and aversions, some are born with men; as appetite of food, appetite of excretion, and exoneration, which may also and more properly be called aversions, from somewhat they feel in their bodies; and some other appetites, not many. The rest, which are appetites of particular things, proceed from experience, and trial of their effects upon themselves or other men.

In making this distinction between innate and experiential factors, Hobbes recognized an issue that eventually engaged the attention of professional psychologists in the modern period for whom the distinction became the focus of the nature-nurture controversy. The problems involved are far more complex than Hobbes ever suspected. They call for more than an inventory of the newborn baby's reflex equipment and spontaneous "appetites and aversions." They involve study of genetic factors, of prenatal nutritional and circulatory influences, and of postnatal maturational development, along with study and control of the multiplicity of environmental factors likely to have a bearing on the kind of person a young child is to become.

It is important to remember that the child is born into a social environment as well as a physical or geographic environment, and that right from the start he is exposed to the folkways of his people as well as to the world of animate and inanimate objects. To determine what E. L. Thorndike (1919, Vol. I) called his "original nature" is not easy, since the concept of original nature is tantamount to asking what a person would be like had he never been exposed to any social or cultural influences. Apart from direct studies of the newborn child, it is virtually impossible to investigate the course of his later development under culture-free circumstances. In books concerned with mental development and child psychology,[9] there are accounts of many research studies in which efforts have been made to subject such circumstances to a modicum of experimental control. The control is usually rather indirect and has taken the form, for example, of comparing the personality characteristics of identical twins who had been separated in early childhood and reared in very different kinds of homes. This, of course, is not the same as studying personality development of children never exposed to a home environment and growing up like "nature boy."

From time to time there have been reports of abandoned children left to fend for themselves in the wilds of nature and who, like Romulus and Remus, came under the protective care of wolves or bears. As early as the fourteenth century there was mention of such a wild or *feral* child. By the middle of the eighteenth century, Linnaeus (1707–1778) made provision for the possibility of having such a child reach adulthood by suggesting *Homo ferus* as the appropriate scientific designation for such an adult.

---

[9] For an account of mental development, see H. Werner, *Comparative Psychology of Mental Development* (1957). An excellent introduction to the nature and scope of child psychology is supplied by the volume edited by L. Carmichael (2nd ed., 1954).

He predicted that such an adult would be mute and hairy, and would walk and run on all fours like an animal. Although no such adults have ever been discovered, there have been about thirty instances of feral children like the famous "wild boy of Aveyron" reported by J. M. G. Itard (1894) and elsewhere in the literature.[10]

Unfortunately, the reports of the behavior of these feral children, while suggestive, are not altogether reliable and leave many important questions unanswered. For the most part those responsible for the original reports were not trained investigators of child psychology; hence the absence of uniformity in the kinds of traits and episodes observed and the consequent lack of trustworthy comparative data. However, what they do demonstrate, as might be expected, is the crucial importance of culture and association with people for the emergence of "mind" or *human* behavior as contrasted with animal behavior.

Lacking a cultural tradition and human associates, the feral child is more like an animal than a human being. Despite normal receptors and an intact nervous system, such a child will have no language, no ideas of right and wrong, no notions of fair play, no plans for the future, and no ideas of money, of cooking, of games, of sanitation, of family life, of education, of churches, of courts, of libraries, of governments, and whatever else shapes the pattern of life in an ordered, civilized community. Growing up in such a community shapes the mind of the growing child as it becomes increasingly familiar with the folkways of its people. What it thinks, how it thinks, the language it employs, the ideas and ideals it comes to cherish, the skills it acquires, and the controls it comes to exercise are all, to a very large degree, products of interaction with other persons. The child's mind or personality can thus be viewed as a product of such social interaction.

From this viewpoint, the social setting provided by one's cultural heritage becomes the matrix of mind and the separate fields of psychology appear as areas of investigation marked off from or abstracted from social psychology as the foundation for the separate fields. This statement is not to be construed as meaning that social psychology was cultivated as a separate field before the other fields emerged. Actually, as is well known, social psychology did not begin to thrive until early in the present century. However, now that it and the other fields have been well established, their interrelationships can be envisaged in the form of a tree with social psychology as the trunk and the separate fields as branches of the tree. Whether the field of animal psychology constitutes a branch of this metaphoric tree is open to question. To the extent that animal behavior is uninfluenced by some hypothetical analogue to the cultural heritage of human beings, animal psychology is not one of the tree's branches. Possibly, though, in view of the

---

[10] See the book by J. A. L. Singh and R. M. Zingg entitled *Wolf-Children and Feral Man* (1939) and the article by W. Dennis on "The Significance of Feral Man" (1941).

group behavior of swarms of bees, monkey colonies, and flocks of pigeons, there may be justification for regarding animal behavior as sufficiently influenced by social interaction to qualify animal psychology for inclusion among the tree's branches—or twigs. The issue is not momentous and its final disposition may be left to individual preference.

At this juncture it is more important to note that the psychology of feral man may have more in common with animal psychology than with human psychology, and that the humanization of feral man is a product of socializing influences. Hobbes was among the first to glimpse this fact. Because of this, Gardner Murphy (1949, p. 22) referred to Hobbes as "the first 'social psychologist' among the moderns, and the principles which he laid down were epoch-making both for social and for individual psychology."

Hobbes's Central Thesis

Hobbes was much troubled by the disrupting effects of war on the behavior of those engaged in combat. In fact, his position as a pioneer social psychologist is largely the result of his reflections upon the brutalizing consequences of war. For example, in the course of these reflections he wrote (Oakeshott, p. 100):

> Whatsoever therefore is consequent to a time of war, where every man is enemy to every man; the same is consequent to the time, wherein men live without other security, than what their own strength, and their own invention shall furnish them withal. In such condition, there is no place for industry; because the fruit thereof is uncertain: and consequently no culture of the earth; no navigation, nor use of the commodities that may be imported by sea; no commodious building; no instruments of moving and removing, such things as require much force; no knowledge of the face of the earth; no account of time; no arts; no letters; no society; and which is worst of all, continual fear, and danger of violent death; and the life of man, solitary, poor, nasty, brutish, and short.

This kind of psychological teaching served as the foundation for Hobbes's political philosophy.[11] Without governmental controls there can be no safety for anybody. Driven by his constant fear of attack by equally fear-driven savage men, each individual would be impelled to struggle for survival by readiness to attack and the outcome would be a constant state of reciprocal hostility by amoral, predatory beings. In fact, in terms of Hobbes's mechanistic psychology they might be described as sentient robots on the rampage. Nevertheless, by implication Hobbes endowed these robots with the rudi-

---

[11] The teaching in question was not original with Hobbes. Aristotle had incorporated similar views in his *Politics*. As mentioned in Chapter 4, Aristotle had concluded that man growing up in ignorance of law and justice would be "the most savage of animals, and the most full of lust and gluttony."

ments of intelligence, for he assumed that in the dim past some of them decided to do something about a mode of anarchic existence that they finally realized was intolerable. Obviously, without possession of ability to reflect upon the nature of such existence they could never have perceived it as dooming each of them to a "solitary, poor, nasty, brutish, and short" life. At all events, Hobbes assumed that they possessed this ability and reached this conclusion. He also conjectured that they then conferred and decided to unite and subordinate themselves to the authority of a single leader or group of leaders who, in exchange for their loyalty and devotion, would protect them and safeguard their interests. According to Hobbes (p. 132):

> This is more than consent, or concord; it is a real unity of them all, in one and the same person, made by covenant of every man with every man, in such manner, as if every man should say to every man, *I authorize and give up my right of governing myself, to this man, or to this assembly of men, on this condition, that thou give up thy right to him, and authorize all his actions in like manner.* This done, the multitude so united in one person, is called a COMMONWEALTH, in Latin CIVITAS. . . . And in him consisteth the essence of the commonwealth; which to define it, is *one person, of whose acts a great multitude, by mutual covenants one with another, have made themselves every one the author, to the end he may use the strength and means of them all, as he shall think expedient, for their peace and common defence.*

The preceding quotation sums up what for Hobbes was the central thesis of the *Leviathan.* His survey of man's psychology was introduced by way of preparation for readier understanding and endorsement of this thesis; namely, that governments have come into existence by virtue of "mutual covenants" or social contracts in terms of which one man, chosen as leader or chief or king, is to *represent* the needs and rights and interests of those involved in the contractual relationship. In order to promote their own welfare the individuals participating in the covenant have voluntarily delegated authority to govern to a single person, and the person selected is to rule not by divine right but by consent of the governed.

Paradoxically, by introducing this principle of representative government, the political philosopher and royalist Hobbes was giving democratic sanction to a king's absolute authority. Since, by hypothesis, the king was presumed to act in behalf of his subjects and was serving as their agent, to rebel against him would be tantamount to fighting against one's own interests or like attacking one's own protector. In rather oblique fashion Hobbes was thus giving voice to his condemnation of the execution of Charles I. Furthermore, by his repudiation of the principle of rule by divine right he was giving voice to his opposition to the Church. As he saw it, the king was to be the dominant governmental authority, and in a clash between him and a bishop or other Church dignitary the royal will was to prevail, just as it was to prevail in case of conflict between king and any subject.[12]

Hobbes devoted many pages to a discussion of the administration of his ideal commonwealth both in terms of its secular as well as its ecclesiastical affairs, but these are more matters of administrative law and political theory than of direct psychological concern. For our purposes it is enough to note his recognition of the psychological factors operative in political events and administrative control of human behavior. There is a historical linkage between this recognition on the part of Hobbes and interest in such events and such control by some twentieth-century psychologists.[13]

The Outlook of Seventeenth-Century "Experimental Philosophy"

An important outcome of scientific endeavor, as Hobbes understood it, is to give man control over his affairs, since he evidently intended to have his discussion of the nature of man regarded as *science* rather than philosophy. At all events in the early portion of his discussion "Of Man" he introduced the following definition of science (p. 45):

> *Science* is the knowledge of consequences, and dependence of one fact upon another: by which, out of that we can presently do, we know how to do something else when we will, or the like another time; because when we see how any thing comes about, upon what causes, and by what manner; when the like causes come into our power, we see how to make it produce the like effects.

In some ways, the preceding definition reflects the climate of opinion that made the seventeenth century so important in the history of science. In contradistinction to traditional philosophy, the new outlook was even referred to as "experimental philosophy." The new outlook is clearly indicated in a passage cited by A. C. Crombie (1964, p. 108) from a work entitled *Experimental Philosophy* written in the 1660s by Henry Power, a member of the Royal Society who was both a medical man and a naturalist. This is the passage:

---

[12] Just how Hobbes would have disposed of a conflict in which the sovereign orders a subject to bring an accusation against himself is hard to say. The protection against self-incrimination guaranteed by the Fifth Amendment of the U.S. Constitution was already insisted upon by Hobbes when he wrote (p. 110): *"No man obliged to accuse himself. A covenant to accuse oneself, without assurance of pardon, is . . . invalid."*

[13] The relevant studies studies include consideration of personality factors as determinants of political attitudes characterizing those affiliated with radical, conservative, liberal, or fascist movements. Examples of such studies are to be found in *The Authoritarian Personality*, by T. W. Adorno *et al.* (1950), and in H. J. Eysenck's *The Psychology of Politics* (1954). A fictional treatment of administrative control of society by conditioning techniques has been worked out by B. F. Skinner in his well-known novel *Walden Two* (1948).

THOMAS HOBBES (1588–1679)

RENÉ DESCARTES (1596–1650)

These are the days that must lay a new Foundation of a more magnificent Philosophy, never to be overthrown: that will Empirically and Sensibly canvass the *Phaenomena* of Nature, deducing the causes of things from such Originals in Nature, as we observe are producible by Art, and the infallible demonstration of Mechanicks: and certainly, this is the way and no other, to build a true and permanent Philosophy. . . . And he that will give a satisfactory Account of those *Phaenomena,* must be an Artificer, indeed, and one well skill'd in the Wheelwork and Internal Contrivance of such Anatomical Engines.

Hobbes was enamored of this empirically oriented mechanistic thinking. It was evident in his admiration of Galileo's experimental work, in his glorification of motion as a key concept, and in his employment of mechanical analogies in referring to the heart as a spring, to joints as wheels, and to nerves as strings. His empiricism was reflected in his repudiation of scholastic metaphysics, in his nominalism, in his endorsement of positivism, and in his distrust of supernaturalistic theology.[14] It was also reflected in his noting the difference between "thoughts regulated" and "thoughts unguided," in his theory of humor, in the distinctions he made between sensation and image, between native and acquired reactions, and between simple and compound imagination. Because of these and other psychological observations, as previously suggested, Hobbes can be said to have made pioneering contributions to what eventually became the independent fields of developmental, social, and behavioristic psychology, respectively. Moreover, in view of the general empirical drift of these observations, Hobbes can be said to have paved the way for the rise of British empiricism as a distinct movement in the history of psychology. Its empirical character is especially evident in the work of John Locke, who along with Hobbes is to be listed as one of the founding fathers of the movement. However, before we consider Locke's psychological views it might be well to introduce those of Descartes. Not only was Locke influenced by Descartes, but the kind of empiricism he sponsored will be better understood by contrasting it with Cartesian rationalism.

Nature and Scope of Cartesian Rationalism

René Descartes (1596–1650) was a man of many parts whose relentlessly probing intellectual curiosity was rewarded by findings that have given him a secure place in the histories of mathematics, of psychology, of

---

14 Hobbes was tremendously concerned with theological and religious issues. As R. S. Peters has pointed out, "It is seldom realized that over half of *Leviathan* deals with religious matters." According to Hobbes, religion is more like a system of law that a system of truth, and in law the sovereign rather than a Pope is to be the final arbiter of disputes.

philosophy, and of science. He was so frail as a child that his formal schooling was deferred until he was eight, when he was enrolled as a pupil in a Jesuit school. While there, because of his delicate health, he was permitted to rest in bed long after his fellow students had arisen. Such prolonged morning rest became a lifelong habit. This was not a habit of sleeping late but rather a habit of devoting the morning hours to solitary meditation. Quiet for such meditation was an imperative need for him, and to get away from the distracting interruptions of friendly visitors or social obligations he sometimes sought refuge in the anonymity of army life and at other times in the obscurity of some residence remote from Paris. In fact, he spent some twenty years in Holland, where he did most of his writing and studying. Even there he guarded his privacy by periodically changing his residence and concealing the new address by having his letters sent to an intermediary.

It would be misleading to interpret these references to rationalism, to meditative morning hours in bed, and to an imperative need for privacy as the description of a philosopher wholly absorbed in solitary contemplation. The thinking of Descartes was not divorced from a knowledge of the scientific developments taking place at the time. He was conversant with the work of men like Galileo and Harvey, carried on an active correspondence with other scholars, and, despite his liking for solitude, cultivated friendships with Dutch philosophers.

His studies were not restricted to metaphysics and mathematics but included anatomy, optics, botany, astronomy, physics, and chemistry. For him, study entailed more than just reading about such subjects. He was an independent investigator and had recourse to firsthand observation and experiment. For example, to advance his botanical knowledge he cultivated his own garden of specimen plants, and to advance his knowledge of anatomy he would study the results of animal dissections at slaughterhouses and also arranged to have separate organs delivered to his lodgings for more careful examination. In this way he was able to check on the nature of the retinal image by removing the fundus of the eye and substituting a fragment of eggshell or paper to serve as a screen upon which the projected retinal image could be observed.

The chief reason for calling attention to Descartes as an independent investigator and experimenter is to guard against a possible misconception of the customary rationalist-empiricist antithesis. According to one traditional connotation of this antithesis, the rationalist, as suggested in Chapter 1, is more the armchair philosophizing psychologist, while the empiricist is more the tough-minded investigator grubbing for factual evidence. In the light of this distinction the empiricist is apt to be seen as subordinating theory to fact, while the rationalist may appear to ignore facts at variance with his theory. Consequently, empiricism is regarded as more in line with the activities of the working scientist than is rationalism. And yet here at the beginning of the early modern period, in both science and philosophy we have Descartes, the rationalist, grubbing for facts and performing experiments and Hobbes and Locke, representing the fountainhead of British empiricism, relying on casual observation for their facts and never undertaking any experimental work.

How is this paradox to be resolved? Actually it is paradoxical only if rationalism and empiricism are viewed as inherently incompatible or mutually exclusive antithetic concepts. However, in scientific achievement such is not the case. Induction and deduction as logical concepts are antithetic, and yet the working scientist may avail himself of both inductive and deductive procedures in the course of his investigations. Sometimes he proceeds inductively as accumulating data suggest a possible explanatory generalization or theory. He is then exemplifying the empiricist's presumed neglect of theory until he has collected enough facts upon which to base a theory. On the other hand, at other times he may proceed deductively by first formulating a theory or hypothesis and then embarking on a search for relevant factual data in terms of which the hypothesis is either confirmed or rejected. In doing so, he might be said to be exemplifying the rationalist's presumed neglect of isolated facts until he has some theoretic orientation to govern his search.

This, of course, is the well-known *hypothetico-deductive method.*[15] Obviously, though, in order to formulate promising hypotheses the deductive investigator must have prior familiarity with some facts related to his problem, just as the inductive investigator must, at the very least, have an incipient plan to direct his search for facts. The nature of his problem will suggest such an incipient plan; hence as empiricists botanists will search for botanical facts, geologists for geological facts, and psychologists for psychological facts. It should thus be clear that, broadly considered, both induction and deduction are part and parcel of the methods of science. This is virtually the equivalent of recognizing the successful scientist as being both an empiricist and a rationalist.

Under the circumstances one may question the not uncommon tendency to regard those classified as empiricists in the history of psychology as being more "scientific" than those classified as rationalists. In fact, to revert to the case of Descartes, it is easy, despite the historians' reference to him as a rationalist, to demonstrate him to have been more of a scientist than some of his empiricist contemporaries. In his work on optics, for example, he compared the eye to a camera obscura and attributed its accommodation to distance to changes in the shape of the lens. Furthermore, according to F. H. Garrison (1924, p. 258), Descartes introduced "the first experiment in

---

15 In the history of science this method became increasingly fruitful as experimental work became increasingly mathematical. In the words of H. Reichenbach (1951, p. 100): "What made modern science powerful was the invention of the *hypothetico-deductive method,* the method that constructs an explanation in the form of a mathematical hypothesis from which the observed facts are deducible."

reflex action—the familiar one of making a person bat his eyes by aiming a mock blow at them—with the correct explanation of the phenomenon." Descartes regarded this as an automatic process: an afferent impulse reaches the brain and is switched or reflected back to the periphery without the intervention of consciousness. In this emphasis on motion and mechanics he, like Hobbes, was in accord with the climate of prevalent scientific opinion. Like Hobbes, he had also come to distrust the teachings of philosophers. This can be noted in the following passage in which Descartes explains what prompted his solitary quest for "certain knowledge" and in addition reveals an early recognition of the importance of cultural factors for mental development (Rawlings translation, pp. 19–20):

But having learned while I was at college that nothing so strange and so incredible can be imagined that it has not been put forward by one or another of the philosophers; and having noticed since then, while travelling, that all those whose sentiments are most contrary to ours are not on that account either barbarians or savages, but that many employ as much reason as we, or more; and having considered how the same man, being reared from infancy by French people or by Germans, becomes different from what he would be if he had always lived among Chinese or cannibals; and how even to the fashion of our clothes the same thing which has pleased us these ten years, and perhaps will please us again before another ten are out, now appears strange and ridiculous,—so that it is much rather custom and example which persuade us, than any certain knowledge, though as regards the truths which are difficult to discover the majority of voices is not a proof which is of any value, because it is much more likely that one man alone would meet with them than a whole nation,—I could not pick out any one whose opinions seemed to me worthy to be preferred to those of others, and I was, as it were, obliged to undertake to guide myself.

From Cartesian Doubt to Cartesian Dualism

Had Descartes been exposed to twentieth-century advertising, a slogan like "Fifty Million Frenchmen can't be wrong" would have left him unimpressed. For him, truth was not to be established by majority vote—certainly not with respect to a truth "difficult to discover." It is even conceivable that he might have questioned current psychological confidence in so-called *consensual validation* as a dependable criterion of truth or reality. His contemporary, Galileo, would have been ill advised to win support for his heliocentric teaching by an appeal to this criterion. The consensus of the learned elite as well as the "common sense" of the masses would have opposed this teaching. Under the circumstances, to paraphrase Descartes, Galileo was obliged to guide himself in his quest for truth.

Long before the need for such guidance had been recognized by Socrates. After all, the purpose of persistent Socratic prodding was to induce self-examination of the foundations of belief and conviction. Descartes followed this Socratic precedent by being his own gadfly as he goaded himself with relentless self-questioning probings in order to find a solid foundation for knowledge. St. Augustine had also followed this Socratic example (see p. 139) and in doing so arrived at a conclusion very much like the one reached by Descartes so many centuries later. Both St. Augustine and Descartes initiated their self-probings by adopting an attitude of skeptical distrust of everything. Nothing was to be accepted and everything was to be doubted. Descartes explained that this was not a sham attitude when he acknowledged (Rawlings, p. 34):

> . . . I meanwhile eradicated from my mind all the errors which had formerly been able to slip into it. Not that I imitated the sceptics, who doubt only in order to doubt, and affect to be always uncertain, for, on the contrary, my only purpose was to assure myself, and to reject shifting earth and sand in order to find rock or clay.

In this search for rock-bottom certainty, Descartes found himself questioning the evidence of his senses, the nature of geometrical proofs, and the trustworthiness of logic. Moreover, realizing that waking thoughts can also occur in dreams, he proceeded to operate on the assumption that every thought that he had ever entertained might be as chimerical as a dream. However, he reacted to this assumption with the following realization (Rawlings, pp. 38–39):

> But immediately afterwards I observed, that while I thus desired everything to be false, I, who thought, must of necessity be something; and remarking that this truth, *I think, therefore I am,* was so firm and so assured that all the most extravagant suppositions of the sceptics were unable to shake it, I judged that I could unhesitatingly accept it as the first principle of the philosophy I was seeking.
>   Then, examining attentively what I was, and seeing that I could feign that I had no body, and that there was no world or any place where I was, but that nevertheless I could not feign that I did not exist, and that, on the contrary, from the fact that I thought to doubt of the truth of other things, it followed very evidently that I was; while if I had only ceased to think, although all else which I had previously imagined had been true, I had no reason to believe that I might have been, therefore I knew that I was a substance whose essence or nature is only to think, and which, in order to be, has no need of any place, and depends on no material thing; so that this I, that is to say, the soul by which I am what I am, is entirely distinct from the body, and even easier to know than the body, and although the body were not, the soul would not cease to be all that it is.

In regarding mind or soul as "entirely distinct from the body," Descartes was in effect setting the stage for a psychology divorced from physics and physiology especially a purely descriptive or phenomenological psychology. Incidentally, E. B. Titchener had this in mind when he wrote (1917, p. 40): "Reference to the body does not add one iota to the data of psychology, to the sum of introspections." Descartes, by implication, had reached the same conclusion in his efforts to deal with the following age-old question (Rawlings, pp. 132–133):

> But what, then, am I? *A thing which thinks.* What is a thing which thinks? It is a thing which doubts, understands, conceives, affirms, denies, wills, wills not, which also imagines, and feels. . . . Is there, besides, any of these attributes which can be distinguished from my thought, or which can be said to be separated from myself? For it is so self-evident that it is I who doubt, understand, and desire, that there is no need to add here anything to explain it.

Quite evidently Descartes was employing "think" as a word indicative of the whole cognitive enterprise and not in the restricted sense of reasoning. That thinking occurs was his answer to the question "What am I?" which implies the existence of a separate agent as thinker. Actually, though, Descartes failed to demonstrate the existence of a thinker. His use of the pronoun "I" was a matter of grammatical convenience rather than a demonstration of an independent entity separate and distinct from thoughts as such. It would have been more accurate if more awkward had he stated that doubting, understanding, conceiving, affirming, and denying occur. This would have been tantamount to saying that mind exists because thoughts occur or that without cognition there can be no mind.

Differentiating Mind from Matter

As a sponsor of dualism, Descartes was concerned with the task of differentiating between mind and matter. To accomplish this he raised the question of what is involved in classifying wax as a material substance (Rawlings, pp. 135–137). For the sake of illustration he selected a piece of wax just removed from the hive and characterized by a flowery fragrance, a definite form, color, and size, along with plasticity, hardness, and coldness. It possesses "all the things which can distinctly indicate a body." However, when the wax is brought close to fire, drastic changes take place: the wax is melted, the fragrance vanishes, color and form change, and the cold solid becomes a warm liquid. Is it still the same wax despite these changes? Descartes maintained that it would be the same wax, but in doing so introduced a distinction between what Locke later designated as the difference between primary and secondary qualities of sensation. As understood by Locke, primary qualities are inherent in or essential to perceived objects, while secondary qualities are alien to the object and resident in the percipient. Sweetness is not in the sugar any more than pain is in a hot object with which one has chanced to come into contact.

In anticipating the Lockean distinction, Descartes pointed out that the wax as a material object cannot be anything experienced as sensation, "since all the things which come under taste, smell, sight, touch, and hearing are changed, and yet the same wax remains." In effect he was asking what is left to characterize the waxness of the wax, so to speak, after discarding what naïve commonsense mistakenly attributes to it on the basis of experienced sensory qualities? There is nothing there, Descartes held, except "something extended, flexible, and mutable." In using a vague term like "something" he was confessing his inability to specify the precise nature of this "extended" matter or substance. He raised the issue himself by asking (p. 137):

> What, now, is this extension? Is it not also unknown? For it becomes greater when the wax melts, greater again when it boils, and greater still as the heat increases; and I should not conceive clearly and truthfully what the wax is, if I did not consider that this piece which we are contemplating is capable of receiving, as regards extension, more variety than I have ever imagined of it. I say this morsel of wax in particular, for as regards wax in general it is yet more evident. But what is this morsel of wax which cannot be comprehended except by the understanding or by the mind? Certainly it is the same that I see, and touch, and imagine; in short, it is the same that I believed it to be to begin with. Now what is to be especially noticed here, is that its perception is not a seeing, nor a touching, nor an imagining, and never has been so, although it appeared so before, but only an inspection of the mind, which may be imperfect and confused, as it was before, or very clear and distinct, as it is now, according as my attention is directed more or less to the things which are in it and of which it is composed.

In terms of the foregoing analysis, Descartes concluded that matter or body as "something extended, flexible, and mutable" could not be apprehended directly. Instead it was inferred from experienced secondary qualities. Analogously, the "I" of the "I think" was inferred from the experienced thoughts. Both the existence of matter as well as of soul or "I" was thus a product of inferential thinking and not the result of immediate sensory impression.

For Descartes, all perception was characterized by such inferential factors. He noted, for example, that so commonplace an event as seeing men walking on the street is not devoid of such factors, since all one actually sees are moving clothes—and clothes are not men. The clothes might conceal automata, "artificial machines which moved only by springs." Nevertheless, Descartes held, "I judge that these are men; and thus I comprehend by the mere power of judging which resides in my mind, what I believe I see with my eyes" (p. 138). Similarly, he might have added, when we see a person weeping we judge or infer him to be sad or troubled. The sadness or trouble as a concept can never be observed directly.

Now inferences or judgments may be in error. How can one determine their truth? Descartes suggested a principle or criterion of truth to serve as guide; namely, "All the things which we conceive very clearly and very distinctly are true" (p. 143). He recognized too that it is not always easy to determine what things are so conceived. Nevertheless, the criterion served to convince him of the truth of his concept of matter as extended and mind or thinking as inextended.

In terms of this distinction, matter is that which occupies space while thought is that which proceeds in a temporal sequence. The dualism involved in this distinction did not seem to trouble Descartes. He faced the issue in this way (p. 209):

> . . . I know with certainty that I exist, and that nevertheless I do not notice that anything else necessarily belongs to my nature or to my essence, except that I am a thing which thinks, I conclude indeed that my essence consists in this alone, —that I am a thing which thinks, or a substance whose essence or nature is only to think. And although . . . I have a body to which I am very straitly conjoined, nevertheless, because on the one hand I have a clear and distinct idea of myself, inasmuch as I am only a thing which thinks, and not extended, and on the other I have a distinct idea of the body, inasmuch as it is only an extended and non-thinking thing, it is certain that I, that is to say my mind, by which I am what I am, is entirely and truly distinct from my body and can be or exist without it.

Despite the latter conclusion regarding the existence of mind in independence of the body, Descartes granted that "the whole mind appears united to the whole body" (p. 221). However, this factor of wholeness revealed a difference between mind and body in addition to the dichotomy of extended and inextended substances; for "the mind is entirely indivisible," while the body "is always divisible." What Descartes was thus stressing is the *unity* of mental life. In willing, feeling, or perceiving, he pointed out, there are no separate faculties or parts being activated. On the contrary, "it is the same mind which exerts itself wholly to will, and wholly to feel and to perceive." In this respect "the mind or soul of man is entirely different from the body." After all, he suggested, parts of the body like teeth or feet might be separated from the body without impairing cognitive functions. Unlike the mind, all material objects, the body included, are divisible into parts. Even the smallest object can be thought of as split into still smaller fragments.

Descartes on Brain Physiology

One tiny part of the body that came to interest Descartes was the conarium, or pineal body, located near the thalamus in the approximate geometric center of the brain. Descartes did not know that it is constituted of glandular rather than neural tissue.[16] He regarded its central position as strategically ideal for the location of a general receiving station for the sum total of sensory impulses belonging to the Aristotelian commonsense. In his own formulation (pp. 221–222):

> I also observe that the mind does not directly receive the impression from every part of the body, but only from the brain, or perhaps even from one of the smallest parts of the brain,—to wit, that which exercises the faculty called common sense, which, every time it is disposed in the same way, makes the mind feel the same thing, although, nevertheless, the other parts of the body may be diversely disposed, as testified by the infinity of experiments which it is not necessary to recall here.

The preceding passage and others like it in the writings of Descartes indicate why he is ordinarily viewed as the sponsor of an interactionist theory of the mind-body relationship. But even the fragment just cited fails to establish him as an unqalified interactionist. In the first place, he does not seem to have been altogether convinced of the role of the pineal body, for he said that *perhaps* this part of the brain receives the impressions. In the second place, his allusion to the "infinity of experiments" had to do with his more fundamental view of the body as an automatic machine. In the case of animals, even though he knew them to be equipped with brains and pineal bodies, he refused to endow them with minds. Instead he accounted for their activity in terms of automatic reflexes controlled by the flow of "animal spirits." As a concept, the latter phrase was probably not very different in meaning from what a phrase like "neural impulses" suggests to a person ignorant of anatomy and physiology. Descartes, who was by no means ignorant of gross anatomy, has this to say about the physiology of animal spirits (p. 63):

> And lastly, what is most remarkable in all this is the generation of animal spirits, which are like a very subtle wind, or rather a very pure and very lively flame, which, continually mounting in great abundance from the heart to the brain, flows from thence through the nerves in the muscles, and gives motion to all the members. . . .

In other passages Descartes refers to animal spirits flowing from the periphery to the "spinal marrow" and then back to the periphery, thus completing the reflex circuit. This reflex equipment renders animals akin to

---

16 Neither did he know anything about the innervation of the pineal body. Not until the present era with the introduction of the electron microscope was this worked out. It now appears that there are no nerve connections between the brain and the pineal gland. Instead its neutral linkage is with a portion of the autonomic nervous system. For details and relevant bibliography see R. J. Wurtman, and J. Axelrod, "The Pineal Gland," *Scientific American*, 1965, *213*, 50–60, 124.

automatic machines. In fact, Descartes ventured to argue that if machines were to be constructed to behave and look like monkeys or "some other irrational animal," there would be no way of differentiating such machines from their animal counterparts. Although he lived centuries before the age of digital computers, he nevertheless entertained the notion of machines manufactured to resemble human bodies and to duplicate human actions "as far as should be morally possible." If this were done, however, the mechanical men would not be confused with real men.

According to Descartes, even though a machine could conceivably be equipped to make speech sounds, "it is not conceivable that it would arrange them variously, so as to respond to the meaning of everything that should be said in its presence, as the most stupid men are able to do." This is one differentiating factor. Another one would become manifest as the machine tried to reason. There would be rigid restriction to utilization of information introduced by the machine's inventor; hence this would not be the flexible use of knowledge needed for effective reasoning about a diversity of problems. In short, Descartes concluded (p. 67): "by these two means we can know . . . the difference between men and beasts" as meaning "not only that animals have less reason than men, but they have none at all."

Differentiating Animal Souls from Human Souls

Just what Descartes intended when he referred to animals as automata altogether devoid of reason is open to question. His reference to the hypothetical mechanical monkey as virtually identical with a real-life monkey would suggest a concept of animals as being complex machines in the sense of being lifeless contrivances like clocks or guns. Descartes granted that some animals can do some things better than human beings, but not because of different or superior intelligence, because they have no intelligence. Whatever they do he attributed to "nature acting in them according to the arrangement of their organs; just as we see that a clock, which is composed only of wheels and springs, can count the hours and measure time more accurately than we with all our wisdom." Despite this he never maintained that, in contrast to real machines, animals are incapable of suffering pain, feeling hungry, or being conscious. Although he operated on animals, he never justified vivisection by arguing that mindless animal machines may be dismembered without compunction. He even endowed animals with souls, as shown in a passage like the following (p. 69):

I also enlarged somewhat on the subject of the soul, because it is one of the most important; for after the error of those who deny God . . . there is none more likely to divert weak minds from the narrow path of virtue than that of imagining the soul of beasts is of the same nature as ours, and that consequently we have nothing more to fear or to hope, after this life, than have flies and ants. . . .

The chief difference between the animal soul and the human soul, Descartes explained, is that the latter is immortal and the former dies with the body. Moreover, to the extent that he employed the word "soul" as a synonym for "mind," the souls of animals were regarded as being non-rational and unintelligent. Precisely what the function of the animal soul might be is not made clear. By implication, unlike the human soul, it is united with the animal's body. At all events, in commenting on the difference between the two kinds of soul he maintained (p. 69) that the human soul "is of a nature entirely independent of the body, and consequently not liable to die with body." And yet, as has been mentioned, on a later page he seemed to contradict himself when he wrote that "the whole mind appears united to the whole body." The contradiction is not to be disposed of by regarding this wording as meaning an *apparent* union of mind and body; for in discussing awareness of organic sensations he dealt with the same issue in this unambiguous way (p. 213):

> Nature also teaches me by these feelings of pain, hunger, thirst, etc. that I am not only lodged in my body like a pilot in his boat, but also that I am so blended and intermixed therewith, and so very narrowly conjoined to it, that I am but one with it. For were this not so, when my body is wounded, I should not on that account feel any pain, I who am only a thing which thinks, but I should perceive the wound merely by the understanding, as a pilot perceives by sight if anything in his vessel gets broken. And when my body needs to drink or to eat, I should know merely that alone, without being warned of it by confused feelings of hunger and thirst. For in truth all these sensations of hunger, thirst, pain, etc., are only certain confused modes of thought, which spring from and depend on the union of the mind with the body, as if on the blending of the two.

It is obviously difficult to reconcile the latter statement to the "union of the mind with the body" as a "blending of the two" with the former statement regarding the human soul's complete independence of the body. Moreover, it is to be noted that the soul as "blended" with the body, having to do with sensations of hunger, thirst, and pain, was described as involving "certain confused modes of thought." Since animals also behave as if they experience hunger, thirst, and pain, it seems likely that when Descartes referred to the animal soul he came close to attributing "certain confused modes of thought" to animals. If so, the consciousness—at least in the sense of "confused" thinking—becomes an attribute of animals and their status as machinelike automata is to be questioned. As a consequence, Descartes himself seems to have been either "confused" or manifestly inconsistent. When he was viewing mind as "inextended" substance it became "independent" of the body, but when he was considering the role of organic sensations it was viewed as "blended" with the body. If it is "blended," there is no need to account for mind-body interaction in terms of the pineal body as a mediating mechanism.

Greek Sources of Res Cogitans

From another viewpoint it is probably unfair to use words like "confused" and "inconsistent" in connection with what Descartes had to say about the human soul as contrasted with the animal soul. Such adverse criticism is unfair in the sense of expecting a seventeenth-century writer to be in possession of twentieth-century knowledge. It would be just as unfair to indict Descartes for using the word "soul" as a synonym for "mind." In some respects his reference to soul—both human and animal—is not very different from Aristotelian usage. For example, when he referred to the "I" as a "thing which thinks" (*res cogitans*) he came close to duplicating a phrase in the *De Anima* in which Aristotle stated, "By mind I mean that whereby the soul thinks and judges" (R. McKeon [ed.], 1947, p. 218). And when Descartes mentioned the soul of animals he was also following an Aristotelian precedent, for Aristotle pointed out that both "discrimination" and the initiation of "local movement" are functions of the animal soul (McKeon, p. 226). It may be recalled that Aristotle even attributed a soul to plants: this was the vegetative or nutritive soul. As the basis for the ingestion of food and water, the nutritive soul was common to all living creatures. The animal soul was common to animals and men, but the rational soul was unique to human beings.

In the light of this reminder of Aristotle's tripartite scheme of levels of biological function, it is clear that the Cartesian scheme was essentially Aristotelian. There was a difference, though, in the physiological speculations underlying the two schemes. Aristotle had failed to recognize the brain as the organic basis for cognitive functions, but by the time of Descartes such recognition was commonplace. Descartes thus accounted for sensorimotor functions by regarding the ventricles of the brain as the central receiving station for "animal spirits" transmitting sensory impressions and as the point of origin for the motor nerves conveying "animal spirits" to the muscles. All perceptions of the outside world, of internal sensations of hunger, thirst, and other bodily cravings, along with regulation of appropriate motor reactions, were consequently viewed as products of cerebral involvement. Such involvement as applied to the Cartesian animal soul is common to men and animals. However—and this is a crucial difference—when considering the mind as a "thinking thing," Descartes viewed it as independent of cerebral concomitants. By way of explaining this distinction, G. S. Brett (1912, Vol. II, p. 205) introduced the following statement:

> One cardinal feature in the work of Descartes is the definition of mind as essentially a thinking thing, *res cogitans*. Upon this basis, remembering that the mind is a substance, we expect to hear what it is that the mind thinks. This

question Descartes undertakes to answer by a method which is partly introspective, partly dogmatic and scholastic. He asserts, dogmatically, that the
mind can function without the aid of the brain. "I have often shown," he says,
"that the mind can work independently of the brain; for clearly there can be
no use of the brain for pure intelligence, but only for imagination and sensation."
. . . This is a clear statement that the mind has activities that are nothing but
its own motions, the *actus purus* of earlier writers. The operations of the mind
when it thinks are ideas; so the pure activities will be ideas that have no
dependence upon the world of objects either for their origin or for their truth.
These are the so-called innate ideas. As these ideas do not originate from causes
external to us, they arise in the form of memories, and experience is only
the occasion for our consciousness of their existence. This view of the innate is
as old as Plato, and Descartes seems to have adopted this theory at first without
much serious reflection. But objections and criticisms caused him to shift his
ground. He declared that he meant by innate ideas no more than an indefinite
potentiality of thought: the ideas exist only potentially and become actual
in the course of experience.

Mind as if Independent of Brain

It should now be evident that for Descartes, some mental functions were
dependent on the brain while others, those classified as acts of pure intelligence, were independent of the brain. The former, as "blended" with the
body, were not unique to man but characteristic of all mammals. On the
other hand, the latter intellectual functions were exclusively characteristic
of man. In the case of the "blended" functions like vision, hearing, eating,
drinking, breathing, and running, obvious bodily organs were operative and
their structural linkage to the nervous system could be traced. However,
in the case of intellectual functions like solving mathematical problems or
formulating a scientific law, no immediately observable organ is operative.
Even Aristotle had failed to note the relationship between such functions
and the brain as the relevant bodily organ.

Moreover, while all contemporary mental specialists recognize this relationship, many of them proceed with their professional work *as if* the functions
studied were independent of the brain. Thus, tests of intelligence are constructed without bothering to relate each subtest to a distinctive cortical
process. Social attitudes are measured even though nothing is known about
presumed differences in the brains of those classified as radicals and those
listed as conservatives. Psychoanalysts listen to their freely associating
patients without speculating about the neurology of free association. They
talk about Oedipal conflicts, transference, repression, and defense mechanisms even though neither they nor anybody else can clarify such talk in
terms of specifiable brain functions. If challenged, they would be unable
to describe what goes on in their own brains when entertaining the ideas
symbolized by their technical vocabulary.

In short, a vast amount of contemporary psychological activity, for all practical purposes, is proceeding as if there were tacit endorsement of the Cartesian claim to the effect that "the mind can work independently of the brain." Irrespective of their metaphysical presuppositions, those engaged in such activity tend to ignore the neurological concomitants of their psychological investigations and thus give the appearance of operating in terms of a dualistic philosophy.

From Interactionism to Occasionalism

Descartes certainly acted in terms of a dualistic philosophy. As mentioned in Chapter 9, his theory of the mind-body relationship, the interactionist theory, is definitely dualistic. Whether it is just as definitely interactionistic is open to question. On the one hand, he viewed animal behavior and human physiology in terms of a monistic, mechanical physics, while on the other he discussed thinking in terms of an autonomous idealism. Such thinking was independent of animal spirits coursing through the brain, while bodily activity was dependent upon the direction taken by animal spirits as determined by the structural arrangements of sense organs, nervous system, and muscles. Such arrangements sufficed to account for the behavior of animals. As physiological automata, animals were entirely subject to the impact of mechanical forces; hence no theory of mind-body interaction was needed to account for their behavior.

However, in the light of his introspective observations, Descartes noted that the thought or idea of doing something could result in the execution of an appropriate movement. The intention to write a letter can influence the muscles of the fingers. To account for such influence, Descartes introduced the vague notion of ideas guiding the direction of animal spirits leaving the pineal body. Just how inextended ideas can influence an extended body was never explained. Consequently his interactionism met with critical opposition.

His Cartesian successors rejected this part of his teachings and proposed a different theory of the mind-body relationship. This theory, known as *occasionalism* and a forerunner of parallelism, was first formulated by Arnold Geulincx (1624–1669) of Belgium and then amplified by the French philosopher Nicolas Malebranche (1638–1715). As a result, occasionalism may be called the Geulincx-Malebranche theory and both men are to be regarded as expositors of Cartesian teachings, although they differed from Descartes in their rejection of interactionism. In doing so they brought the dualism of Descartes into sharper focus by denying any causal relationship between mind and body. Even though the body seems to respond to the mind's intentions, they held that this is not a consequence of the intentions. What *appears* to be cause and effect is really independent concurrence.

To explain such concurrence, Geulincx introduced an analogy known as the example of the "two clocks." According to this example, two perfectly synchronized clocks might impress the naïve observer as being causally related, since the chimes of the one would ring out whenever the hands of the other announced the hour. This would be a consequence of the clockmaker's arrangement of the respective mechanisms so that the lapse of sixty minutes would be the *occasion* for one of the clocks to strike the hour.

Analogously, God, as creator of mind and body, had so arranged the laws governing mental and bodily events as to have an occurrence like the idea of signing one's name be the occasion for the corresponding finger movements. It was as if God had intervened to bring about such *apparent* interaction, while in reality there is no such interaction; for soul and body operate independently of one another. Mind or the rational soul functions in accordance with mental laws and body in accordance with physical laws.

Furthermore, since bodily changes are strictly determined, the corresponding mental changes must also be determined. Such determinism rendered it impossible to reconcile the theory of occasionalism with Church doctrine concerning man's freedom to resist Satan's temptations in favor of obedience to divine commands. However, this determinism as an expression of lawfulness inherent in the universe of mind and matter was not at all in conflict with the views of Spinoza, for whom God was the symbol of such lawfulness.

The analogy or theory of the "two clocks" as proposed by Geulincx was also introduced by Leibnitz (1646–1716) in his advocacy of psychophysical parallelism. As a theory it ruled out any interaction between mind and body and thus made it appear possible or legitimate to study mental life as detached from or independent of organic events. By implication it might be said to have provided for the eventual emergence of psychology as a separate science as distinct from physiology as a separate science. Both consciousness and behavior might thus be investigated without at the same time being concerned with the complexities of brain physiology. Though related, the two fields of psychology and brain physiology could be cultivated independently of one another, just as the fields of history and geography, also somewhat related, call for independent study. As a result historians are not geographers any more than psychologists are brain physiologists and vice versa. This situation might be construed as one of the outcomes of the doctrine of parallelism or the theory of the "two clocks."

Man as Machine Versus Man as Organism

In some ways the analogy of the "two clocks" as a means of illustrating noncausal concurrence is misleading when applied to the mind-body relationship. Unlike clocks, minds and bodies are not found as discrete entities. The two clocks keeping uniform time may be located in different rooms, but such spatial separation of minds and brains is obviously absurd. It is also misleading to regard the nature of psychophysiology as analogous to the operation of synchronous clocks. Recourse to mechanics for purposes of scientific explanation was particularly frequent in the age of Descartes. It may be recalled that Hobbes compared the nerves to strings and the heart to a spring. And Descartes, it may also be recalled, considered the possibility of regarding men as automata or "artificial machines which moved only by springs." He accounted for circulation and reflex action in terms of mechanics and conceived of animal behavior in similar terms. In fact, he once compared the perfectly healthy animal to a perfect clock. As an automaton, the animal was viewed as a machine functioning in accordance with the principles of physics.

The same principles applied to the regulation of man's body except that, being endowed with an immortal soul, man's body, Descartes held, is amenable to voluntary control. As has been mentioned, in this respect he likened the human body to a boat and the soul to the pilot of the boat. This simile makes the soul an independent agent capable of regulating the machinery of the body in accordance with the interactionist's teaching. However, strictly considered, it is not in accord with interactionism, for interactionism has to do with the mind-body relationship and not with a soul-body interaction. This is not just a specious distinction. For Descartes, mind was the *res cogitans* and, as cognition, mind was also akin to Aristotle's recognition of reason as the hallmark of the rational soul. Consequently, Aristotle and Descartes were in essential agreement regarding the nature of mind; but they differed with reference to the nature of the soul. Brett (1912, Vol. II, p. 212) clarified the issue in this way:

> The mind is for Descartes what the reason was for Aristotle. The two part company most clearly on the question of the *soul,* not the mind. What Aristotle would have described in terms of the principle of life, Descartes attempts to describe mechanically. It is very doubtful whether Descartes had the advantage in that point. . . . As time progresses it becomes more certain that Aristotle's concept of the organism must be preferred to the Cartesian machine and operator.

Aristotle's concept of the organism was based upon a distinction between the animate and the inanimate, or between the living and the lifeless. He defined soul as "the form of a natural body having life potentially within it" (McKeon, 1947, p. 172). To understand the meaning of the word "form" in this context—to get at the "essence" or the organic body—one must note the transformation from potentiality to actuality. By way of example, Aristotle stated if an ax "were a natural body" instead of a man-made artifact and if it also had "the power of setting itself in movement and arresting itself," then its soul or essence or form would be "cutting."

A similar criterion applies to an isolated part of the living body as illustrated by supposing a detached eye to be a living animal. In terms of this supposition (McKeon, p. 173), "sight would have been its soul, for sight is the substance or essence of the eye" and "when seeing is removed the eye is no longer an eye, except in name—it is no more a real eye than the eye of a statue or of a painted figure." In other words, Aristotle regarded the human soul as a biological concept and not as a theological concept or a *deus ex machina,* as Descartes seemed to suggest.

Even though, as was mentioned earlier, Descartes referred to the souls of animals, he failed to clarify what the function of the animal soul might be. He was definite in making it a mortal rather than an immortal soul. The human soul was just as definitely described as being "entirely independent of the body" and thus capable of survival after death. Evidence in support of this distinction between animal and human souls was conspicious by its absence.

Whether Descartes was really convinced of the validity of the distinction has been questioned by some students of his writings. They suggest that, as a cautious man anxious to safeguard his peace and privacy and one who was also mindful of Galileo's fate, he took pains to keep his published views of the nature of the soul in line with the dogmas of the Church. If this be so, then the seeming inconsistency in his views about the nature of human and animal souls was more of a self-protective maneuver than a product of confused thinking.

Unlike Aristotle, Descartes failed to differentiate the animate from the inanimate. In line with the scientific outlook of his age, he regarded movement or mechanical motion as fundamental in the world of nature. Biological phenomena were viewed as mechanical events. In essence the underlying outlook was a dim forerunner of the tropistic theory of J. Loeb (1912) as formulated early in the present century. According to the tropistic theory, both the growth of plants and the movements of living organisms are mechanically determined and forced orientations toward or away from sunlight or food or the soil, much as the motion of the needle of a magnet is deflected by surrounding magnetic influences. Thus Loeb regarded his theory as supplying a "mechanistic conception of life." In commenting on Loeb's theory, E. Nordenskiöld, a specialist in the history of biology, had this to say (1928, p. 606):

Indeed, in the opinion of Loeb, there exist no structural conditions whatever; there is hardly any question of the organism's possessing a chemical composition of its own; all that takes place in the organism is the result of outside impulses, the result being that no discrimination whatever is made between one life phenomenon and another, whether it is a question of sea-urchins, insects, or frogs. The goal to be attained is . . . a mechanical explanation of life, but just because of this exclusive interest for external influences the explanation proves to be essentially negative—a denial of the existence of any operating forces other than the said external influences. . . . Loeb is without doubt a brilliant experimentalist, and as such he deserves mention among the pioneers, though among biological thinkers he can claim no place.

What Descartes and Loeb had in common was this physicalist approach to biology. In terms of such an approach biology becomes a branch of physics, and the current distinction between life sciences and physical sciences is hard to justify. Instead of referring to animal psychology, it would be more in accord with this approach to refer to *animal physics*. The latter phrase would be compatible with the Cartesian tendency to regard the animal as an automaton. Moreover, in line with Descartes' nonbiological orientation, mind became virtually independent of an organic matrix. This was not true of sensation nor of imagination as a derivative of sensation, but it did apply to cognition conceived of as "pure intelligence." To repeat this in the words of Descartes: "I have often shown that the mind can work independently of the brain; for clearly there can be no use of the brain for pure intelligence, but only for imagination and sensation."

A distinction of this sort was more scholastic than Aristotelian. Descartes may have owed this scholastic notion of "pure intelligence" to his early education at a Jesuit institution, just as his familiarity with seventeenth-century physics undoubtedly accounts for his failure to differentiate the living organism from inert material objects because he regarded them both as indifferently subject to the laws of physics. Pure intelligence or cognition as inextended substance was not subject to such laws. It belonged to a different world from the world of extended substance. This made for a dualism of mind and matter of a kind already evident in the philosophy of Plato. For Descartes, the two worlds were almost completely independent of one another. Except for the bridge supplied by the pineal body, the severance was complete. Soon the occasionalist disciples of Descartes made the severance complete by eliminating the bridge.

The resulting parallelism as a conceptual scheme rendered it reasonable to advocate study of the one world without reference to the other. By implication, psychology belonged to one realm and physics to an independent realm. In metaphoric language it might be said that what God had joined together Descartes had split asunder, and undoing or understanding the cleavage became one of the persistent problems for subsequent generations of psychologists.

Descartes as Fountainhead of Behavior Theory and Cognitive Theory

Two trends in later psychology can be traced back to this Cartesian cleavage. The one trend stems from the Cartesian view of animals as physiological automata governed by the laws of physics, and the other from the

Cartesian *res cogitans* as something inextended and *sui generis*. The former trend is reflected in some current predominantly physicalist behavior theories, while the latter trend is reflected in the work of many current cognitive theorists. Martin Scheerer (1901–1962), for example, was one of the leading cognitive theorists among modern psychologists. To honor his memory, his colleagues prepared a series of papers on the subject of cognition which were published as a *Festschrift*. Particularly relevant in the present context is the following observation introduced by MacLeod in his review of the *Festschrift* (1964, p. 246):

> Most of the contributors to the Scheerer volume would probably reject the Cartesian dualism in its cruder formulations. It might not be unfair, however, to regard modern cognitive psychology as a renewed insistence that the nature of *res cogitans* is still a challenge to science; in mid-twentieth century, however, a challenge, which can be met with the weapons of the laboratory, the clinic, and the calculating machine.

Needless to add, long before the modern era "the nature of *res cogitans* constituted a challenge to younger contemporaries of Descartes like Spinoza and Locke. That Spinoza was influenced by Descartes is indicated by the fact that the only work published under his own name during his lifetime was Spinoza's *Principles of Cartesian Philosophy* (H. E. Wedeck translation, 1961), first printed in 1663. That Cartesian principles had a direct influence on Locke's psychological views is suggested by the divergent stand taken by Descartes and Locke on the question of the role of experience in shaping man's understanding of himself and his world. Descartes, as mentioned earlier, endorsed a modified Platonic view of the nature of human understanding, to the effect that there is an innate predisposition to accord with inherent categories of understanding. Locke, on the other hand, as an ardent empiricist denied the existence of such inborn predispositions. He repudiated the notion of innate ideas and made sensory experience the sole foundation of knowledge except as modified by reflection upon such experience. In doing so he was endorsing this old Latin maxim. *nihil est in intellectu, quod non prius fuerit in sensu*, meaning there is nothing in the realm of ideas which did not originate from sensory impressions. Descartes refused to endorse this maxim. This is clear from what he wrote regarding the origin of ideas of God or of mind or soul (Rawlings, pp. 43–44):

> But that which leads many to persuade themselves that there is difficulty in knowing what their soul is, is that they never raise their minds above things of the senses, and that they are so accustomed to consider nothing except by imagining it,—which is a mode of thinking specially applicable to material things,—that all which is not imaginable seems to them unintelligible. This is

sufficiently shown by the maxim which the philosophers hold in the schools,— *that there is nothing in the understanding which has not first been in the senses,* [17] where, nevertheless, it is certain that ideas of God and of the soul have never been, and it seems to me that those who desire to understand them with their imagination, do exactly as if they wished to use their eyes in order to hear sounds or smell odours, except that there is still this difference— that the sense of sight does not less assure us of the truth of its objects than does the sense of smell or of hearing, while neither our imagination nor our senses can ever assure us of anything if our understanding does not intervene.

The preceding reference to the intervention of "our understanding" suggests that for Descartes the development of mind involved more than the impact of sensory impressions on a *tabula rasa* or an intellectual vacuum. In his view, the ideas man comes to entertain are of threefold origin: some are innate, others are of external origin, and still others are products of creative imagination. He was quite explicit about this when he maintained that some ideas (Rawlings, pp. 146–147) "appear to me to be born with me, others to be foreign and to come from without, and others to be made and invented by myself." In other words, while granting the importance of experience in the acquisition of knowledge, Descartes also acknowledged the importance of inborn sources of knowledge.

This contention, as mentioned in Chapter 1, pp. 10–13, was a key issue in the empiricist-rationalist controversy. It is also related to another issue considered in the same chapter (pp. 14–15); namely, Jung's concept of racial archetypes and Freud's notion of some ideas having their roots in phylogenetic inheritance. This Cartesian concept of innate ideas merits careful attention because of its recurrence in the history of psychology. It is not to be disposed of as an outmoded concept altogether devoid of potential scientific respectability. In fact, some modern psychologists have deemed it necessary to explain their experimental results by an appeal to such a concept. [18] For the time being it will be sufficient to explain just what Descartes meant by the concept.

In holding that he was born with some ideas, Descartes did not mean that

---

[17] Italics not in the original.

[18] This is particularly true if the concept be broadly interpreted so as to include genetically determined *Anlagen* responsible for the facilitation of specific modes of adaptive behavior. The maze-learning performances of Robert Tryon's "bright" rats serve as an example of such behavior. For a review of the latter work along with related studies by other experimentalists, see C. S. Hall's chapter on "The Genetics of Behavior" in S. S. Stevens (ed.), 1951. It might also prove clarifying to consider the work of A. Michotte (1963) in this connection; for he seems to have endorsed the Cartesian concept by attributing readiness to perceive causal relationships to an unlearned *Anlage* or inherent predisposition. Incidentally, A. C. Ewing would question this. For him, the idea of causation is neither innate nor a product of sense-experience. In his view, even "if we deny that all ideas are derivable from sense-experience, we still need not hold the doctrine of innate ideas" (1962, p. 49).

such ideas are present at birth as explicit facts of consciousness. He regarded them as latent in the *res cogitans,* or "thinking substance," and as made manifest in the course of or by experience although not derived from experience. Among such ideas he included as self-evident truths "clear and distinct" ideas of the self as a thinking being, the idea of God as a "sovereignly perfect being," inherent notions of space and time, and the impact of geometric axioms. Such ideas, Descartes held, do not originate in experiences. Instead they are expressions of what man as a rational being endowed with an intellect brings to experience. This Cartesian principle was challenged by John Locke. As will be brought out in the next chapter, the nature of the challenge and its systematic elaboration marked a turning point in the history of psychology.

References

Adorno, T. W., Frenkel-Brunswick, E., Levinson, D. J., and Sandford, R. N. *The Authoritarian Personality.* New York: Harper and Brothers, 1950.

Best, C. H., and Taylor, N. B. *The Physiological Basis of Medical Practice,* 4th ed. Baltimore: The Williams and Wilkins Company, 1945.

Brett, G. S. *A History of Psychology,* Vol. II. London: George Allen and Unwin, 1912.

Brett, G. S. "History of Psychology," in *Encyclopaedia Britannica,* Vol. 18, 14th ed., 1929,

Carmichael, L. *Manual of Child Psychology,* 2nd ed. New York: John Wiley and Sons, 1954.

Carritt, E. F. *The Theory of Beauty,* 2nd ed. London: Methuen and Company, 1923.

Crombie, A. C. "Early Concepts of the Senses and the Mind," *Scientific American,* 1964, *210,* 108–116.

Dennis, W. "The Significance of Feral Man," *American Journal of Psychology,* 1941, *54,* 425–432.

Descartes, R. *Discourse on Method and Metaphysical Meditations.* (Translated by G. B. Rawlings.) London: The Walter Scott Publishing Company. (No date.)

Ding, G. F., and Jersild, A. T. "A Study of the Laughing and Smiling of Preschool Children," *Journal of General Psychology,* 1932, *40,* 452–472.

Ewing, A. C. *The Fundamental Questions of Philosophy.* New York: Collier Books, 1962.

Eysenck, H. J. *The Psychology of Politics.* London: Methuen and Company, 1954.

Freud, S. "Humour," *Collected Papers,* Vol. V. New York: Basic Books, 1959.

Freud, S. "Wit and Its Relation to the Unconscious," in A. A. Brill (ed.). *The Basic Writings of Sigmund Freud.* New York: The Modern Library, 1938, pp. 633–803.

Garrison, F. H. *An Introduction to the History of Medicine,* 4th ed. Philadelphia: W. B. Saunders Company, 1929. (Reprinted 1960.)

Grotjahn, M. *Beyond Laughter.* New York: McGraw-Hill and Company, 1957.

Hall, C. S. "The Genetics of Behavior," in S. S. Stevens (ed.). *Handbook of Experimental Psychology.* New York: John Wiley and Sons, 1951.

Hetherington, E. M., and Wray, N. P. "Aggression, Need for Social Approval, and Humor Preferences," *Journal of Abnormal and Social Psychology,* 1964, *68,* 685–689.

Hobbes, T. *Leviathan: Or the Matter, Forme and Power of a Commonwealth, Ecclesiastical and Civil.* M. Oakeshott (ed.). New York: Collier Books, 1962.

Höffding, H. *History of Modern Philosophy,* Vol. I. New York: The Macmillan Company, 1900.

Itard, J. M. G. *The Wild Boy of Aveyron.* (Translated by G. and M. Humphrey.) New York: The Century Company, 1932. (Originally published in 1894.)

Jones, M. C. "The Development of Early Behavior Patterns in Young Children," *Pedagogical Seminary,* 1926, *33,* 537–585.

Loeb, J. *The Mechanistic Concept of Life.* Chicago: The University of Chicago Press, 1912.

McKeon, R. (ed.). *Introduction to Aristotle.* New York: The Modern Library, 1947. "De Anima," pp. 145-235.

MacLeod, R. B. "Tribute to a Cognitivist," *Contemporary Psychology,* 1964, *IX,* 245–246.

Michotte, A. *The Perception of Causality.* New York: Basic Books, 1963.

Murphy, G. *Historical Introduction to Modern Psychology,* rev. ed. New York: Harcourt, Brace and Company, 1949.

Nordenskiöld, E. *The History of Biology.* (Translated by L. B. Eyre.) New York: The Tudor Publishing Company, 1928.

O'Connell, W. E. "The Adaptive Functions of Wit and Humor," *Journal of Abnormal and Social Psychology,* 1960, *61,* 263–270.

Plato. *Philebus.* (Translated by H. N. Fowler.) Loeb Classical Library. Cambridge: Harvard University Press, 1952.

Reichenbach, H. *The Rise of Scientific Philosophy.* Berkeley: University of California Press, 1951.

Ross, W. D. (ed.). *Aristotle—Selections.* New York: Charles Scribner's Sons, 1938.

Singh, J. A. L., and Zingg, R. M. *Wolf-Children and Feral Man.* New York: Harper and Brothers, 1939.

Skinner, B. F. *Walden Two.* New York: The Macmillan Company, 1948.

Spinoza, B. *Principles of Cartesian Philosophy.* (Translated by H. B. Wedeck.) New York: Philosophical Library, 1961.

Thorndike, E. L. *Educational Psychology,* Vol. I. *The Original Nature of Man.* New York: Teachers College, Columbia University, 1919.

Titchener, E. B. *A Text-Book of Psychology.* New York: The Macmillan Company, 1917.

Werner, H. *Comparative Psychology of Mental Development.* New York: International Universities Press, 1957.

Whitehead, A. N. *Science and the Modern World.* New York: Mentor Books, 1948. (First published in 1925 by The Macmillan Company, New York.)

Woodworth, R. S. *Dynamic Psychology.* New York: Columbia University Press, 1918.

12

John Locke's Essay: Its Scope and Significance

JOHN LOCKE (1632–1704) was a versatile man of many interests. Although trained as a physician, he never engaged in extensive medical practice. He was a protégé of the first Earl of Shaftesbury (1621–1683) and served him both as physician and as adviser with reference to the earl's activities in political and governmental affairs. He also served as tutor to the earl's grandson.[1] This assignment undoubtedly influenced Locke's views on education as embodied in his treatise entitled *Some Thoughts Concerning Education* (1693), a work in which he deplored having pupils indulge in burdensome rote memory. Instead he urged the importance of making learning exciting by reducing drudgery and increasing significant understanding in line with the child's interests. Another early assignment obtained through Shaftesbury's influence enabled Locke to serve as secretary to the Board of Trade and become familiar with business and commercial affairs. The resulting interest in economics was reflected in the later publication of his *Observations on Silver Money* (1695).

Religion was still another of Locke's interests. Unlike the skeptical Hobbes, he was personally devout and in his writing defended what he termed the "reasonableness" of Christianity. He was especially aroused by the warring religious sects of his time: the major rift between Protestantism and Catholicism as well as the minor rifts between the Puritans and other Protestant groups. The upshot of his arousal was his *Essay Concerning Toleration* (1666), one of the first pleas for recognition of the right of

---

[1] This grandson, the third Earl of Shaftesbury (1671–1713), as a philosopher was particularly concerned with problems of ethics. It was he who introduced the term "moral sense" as the presumed foundation for the genesis of conscience. According to some theorists, psychopaths are victims of a congenital absence of or defect in such a "moral sense." This gives the earl a niche in the history of psychology.

361

freedom of worship. It was the kind of right later included among those listed in the Bill of Rights of the Constitution of the United States.[2] Nor was this the only respect in which he influenced eighteenth-century political philosophy. In his *Two Treatises of Government* (1690) he, like Hobbes before him, repudiated the doctrine of divine right of kings. However, in opposition to the views of the royalist Hobbes, the king, as representative of the people, was not endowed either with absolute authority or with the right to expect complete subservience and obedience from his subjects. According to Locke, should a king's rule become tyrannical and inimical to the welfare of his subjects, then they would be justified in rebelling. Justification for both the American and French Revolutions was rooted in this Lockean principle. It was as if the philosopher's pen had given power to the revolutionist's sword.

It should thus be evident that one comes across Locke's name in histories of political theory as well as in the histories of other subjects like education, economics, and theology. Still, his chief claim to fame is to be found in what he had to say in his famous *Essay Concerning Human Understanding.* As a contribution to theory of knowledge, this work won him a place in the history of philosophy, and as a contribution to British empiricism it won him a place in the history of psychology. It was first published in 1690, when Locke was close to sixty. In fact, most of his publications appeared in the decade of the 1690s.[3] The *Essay* had actually been started some twenty years earlier and was the product of intermittent effort during the intervening years. It commanded immediate attention and ran into several editions prior to the death of Locke in 1704. Its success as a philosophical and psychological classic is indicated by the fact that there have been some forty editions of the *Essay* since 1704, not counting its frequent translation into other languages. Accordingly, consideration of its contents ought to prove elightening.

The Essay's Origin and Purpose

The *Essay* was started as the result of a chance circumstance. As Locke explained (J. A. St. John [ed.], 1901, Vol. I, pp. 2–5), he and a few friends were engaged in a discussion of a topic unrelated to the subject of the *Essay* when they found themselves deadlocked by irreconcilable differences of opinion. It then occurred to him that such a clash of opinion

---

[2] This constitutional provision was broader in scope than Locke's original plea, for Locke had misgivings about extending toleration to include Catholics and atheists. In his view Catholics were subject to divided loyalty as a result of the "foreign" authority of Rome and atheists were deemed to be poor moral risks because of their lack of loyalty to a Supreme Being.

[3] Had Locke been a twentieth-century university professor, this retarded publication record might have terminated his teaching career.

could be avoided if discussion were restricted to "*objects* our understandings . . . were fitted to deal with." His friends agreed and he undertook to dispose of the issue.

At first he believed a single sheet of paper would suffice to record all he might have to say on the subject. But as he added more and more observations the projected single sheet became many sheets, and in the ensuing years what had been planned as a brief communication for the edification of a small circle of friends grew into a bulky treatise to be offered to a larger reading public in the hope that it might be "useful to others." He disclaimed any other intention than to be "useful" in the sense of paving the way for adequate understanding of the teaching of eminent men of science by an analysis of the nature of human understanding. The *Essay* was to be a modest preparation for the promotion of science rather than a contribution to science as such; for as it appeared to Locke (St. John, Vol. I, p. 7):

> The commonwealth of learning is not at this time without master-builders, whose mighty designs in advancing the sciences will leave lasting monuments to the admiration of posterity: but everyone must not hope to be a Boyle or a Sydenham; and in an age that produces such masters as the great Huygenius, and the incomparable Mr. Newton, with some other of that strain, it is ambition enough to be employed as a under-laborer in clearing the ground a little, and removing some of the rubbish that lies in the way to knowledge; which certainly had been very much more advanced in the world, if the endeavors of ingenious and industrious men had not been much cumbered with the learned but frivolous use of uncouth, affected, or unintelligible terms introduced into the sciences, and there made an art of, to that degree that philosophy, which is nothing but the true knowledge of things, was thought unfit or uncapable to be brought into well-bred company and polite conversation.

Definition and Development of Ideas

To arrive at the "true knowledge of things," Locke undertook to investigate the origin and development of *ideas*. He defined the word "idea" as the term which (St. John, Vol. I, p. 134) "serves best to stand for whatsoever is the *object* of the understanding when a man thinks" and "whatever is meant by phantasm, notion, species, or whatever it is which the mind can be employed about in thinking. . . . " This broad usage apparently failed to restrict the term to conscious content having a symbolic function. Instead it also included all sensory impressions to which attention might be directed—the nonsymbolic along with the symbolic. As a consequence, sensations and perceptions, along with concepts, schemes, intentions, hopes, and moods when dealt with as cognitive objects were all to be classified as ideas. Locke was quite definite about such a broad usage, and in this oft cited passage he made it the basis for one of the crucial questions raised in the *Essay* (Vol. I, p. 207):

Every man being conscious to himself that he thinks, and that which his mind is applied about whilst thinking being the ideas that are there, it is past doubt that men have in their minds several ideas, such as are those expressed by the words whiteness, hardness, sweetness, thinking, motion, man, elephant, army, drunkenness, and others: it is in the first then to be inquired, how he comes by them?

Before considering Locke's answer to the latter question, it is advisable to note his seeming failure to distinguish between percepts and concepts in the preceding passage. The perception of a man or an elephant and the concept of thinking are both listed as ideas. This, as already suggested, is at variance with the ordinary meaning of the word "idea" as a designation for that which refers to or represents something other than an immediate sensory presentation. The victim of a toothache does not describe his distress as an idea of a toothache. Similarly, when we see a man on the street or an elephant at the zoo we do not find ourselves saying, "I have an idea of a man" or "I have an idea of an elephant."

Ideation has to do with the aftereffects of such sensory impressions by means of which we can think about them *in absentia,* so to speak. This was a distinction that David Hume (1711–1776) introduced in the 1730s in his effort to "restore the word, idea, to its original sense from which Mr. *Locke* had perverted it, in making it stand for all our perceptions (C. W. Hendel [ed.], 1927, p. 10). This issue is important because Locke and his empiricist successors made the word *idea* a key concept in what developed into associationistic psychology. In fact, as will be brought out later, the phrase "association of ideas" was first employed by Locke.

Under the circumstances it seems desirable to follow Hume's suggestion and consider the "original sense" of the word "idea." The very concept of mind is intimately related to the meaning of this word. In its derivation, as discussed by H. A. Wolfson (1934, pp. 46–48), it goes back to Aristotle's theory of perception. What the intellectual soul or mind entertains in the act of perception, Aristotle held, is just the *form* of external objects. To employ Aristotle's example: in perceiving a stone "it is not the stone which is in the soul, but the form of the stone." As employed here, the word "form" is a translation of the Greek word "eidos," which through the Latin became the English word "idea." Furthermore, as noted by Wolfson, both Descartes and Spinoza reflected the Aristotelian origin of the term; for Descartes wrote that "idea is a word by which I understand the form of any thought," while Spinoza understood the word to refer to "a conception of the mind which the mind forms because it is a thinking thing."

In the light of this examination of the "original sense" of the term, Hume's indictment of Locke may not be justified. This is not to deny the merit of Hume's distinction between impressions and ideas, but merely to question having the distinction classified as involving *restoration* of the root meaning of the word "idea." It would be more accurate to regard it as a clarifying elaboration of the "original sense." Locke used the word as inclusive of *all* mental content and not in the later more restricted meaning of mental content when representative or symbolic of something else, as exemplified by having Euclid represent geometry or having John Bull symbolize England.

Actually, as can be perceived in any unabridged dictionary, the term "idea" has many more meanings and this fact alone accounts for the difficulty of isolating one of these as the only correct usage for technical psychology. For present purposes it is enough to realize that Locke was not concerned with such a technical issue. Instead he was interested in the broad question of the origin of knowledge or of the heterogeneous array of facts, beliefs, concepts, convictions, notions, and items of information and misinformation that man comes to entertain as a result of possessing a mind. He employed the word "idea" as an unrestricted designation for any of the terms included in such an array of terms. So considered, the stage is set for dealing with Locke's fundamental thesis, which he formulated as follows (St. John, Vol. I, 1901, pp. 205–206):

> *All Ideas come from Sensation or Reflection.*[4]—Let us then suppose the mind to be, as we say, white paper, void of all characters, without any ideas; how comes it to be furnished? Whence comes it by that vast store which the busy and boundless fancy of man has painted on it with an almost endless variety? Whence has it all the materials of reason and knowledge? To this I answer in one word, from experience; in that all our knowledge is founded, and from that it ultimately derives itself. Our observation employed about external sensible objects, or about the internal operations of our minds, perceived and reflected on by ourselves, is that which supplies our understandings with all the materials of thinking. These two are the fountains of knowledge from whence all the ideas we have or can naturally have do spring.

Locke's Indebtedness to Aristotle

In referring to the mind as white paper Locke was reverting to the *tabula rasa* concept of Aristotle. His indebtedness to Aristotle for this concept is shown by another figure of speech in which the analogy of the white paper is changed to that of an empty cabinet. For example, in one passage (St. John, 1901, Vol. I, p. 142) there is a reference to the senses as

---

[4] As a topic sentence this is reminiscent of the stand taken by Socrates in his dialogue with Thaetetus as quoted in Chapter 1. In that passage Socrates refers to sensation and reflection as sources of knowledge or "true opinion." The similarity of language is so striking as to suggest the possibility of Locke's having been influenced by earlier reading of the dialogue. If so, this would be another instance of what is sometimes referred to as unconscious plagiarism.

admitting particular ideas and furnishing "the yet empty cabinet." In commenting on this passage in a footnote, J. A. St. John, editor of this edition of the *Essay,* calls attention to what a Greek scholar has pointed out regarding the meaning of the Greek word *"grammateio"* which Aristotle used and which has sometimes been translated as a "sheet of unwritten paper." Instead it refers to a waxed tablet, and especially significant in the present context, it also had the meaning of "a cabinet." This serves as a reminder of what was mentioned in Chapter 4 regarding Aristotle's relationship to the kind of psychology sponsored by Locke and the other British empiricists.

British empiricism, as elaborated in terms of the implications of Locke's emphasis on sensory experience as the source of "reason and knowledge," is also of Aristotelian lineage. In fact, Locke's entire *Essay* may be regarded as a long sermon based on this text from the *De Anima* (R. McKeon [ed.], 1947, p. 225): "No one can learn or understand anything in the absence of sense." This, as mentioned at the close of the previous chapter, became familiar to scholastic philosophers as they came across the Latin equivalent of this text: *"Nihil est in intellectu, quod non prius fuerit in sensu,"* meaning, "There is nothing in the understanding which was not initially in the sensorium."

St. Thomas Aquinas had given expression and endorsement to this teaching. Furthermore, its acceptance by other medieval schoolmen is indicated by the fact that Descartes, in questioning the teaching, referred to it as "the maxim which the philosophers hold in the schools." What he questioned was the maxim's exclusion of innate determinants of understanding and knowledge. In so doing he was attacking what he regarded as a *medieval* doctrine. Descartes, it may be recalled, recognized three sources of ideas: some ideas are innate, others are products of sensory experience, and still others are the outcome of creative imagination. Locke was especially concerned with this question of innate ideas and was vehement in his denial of their existence. In this respect his *Essay* was an attack on Descartes and not, as sometimes believed, an attack on scholastic thinking.

In upholding the *"nihil est in intellectu"* maxim, then, Locke was supporting an Aristotelian doctrine that had won scholastic endorsement. Seen in this light, British empiricism was not so much an advance over medieval thinking as a revival of a principle already known to and advocated by Aquinas and his contempories.

No Innate Ideas but Some Prenatal Ones

Although Locke ruled out innate ideas, he did not regard the newborn child as altogether devoid of ideas, since he referred to its *tabula rasa* as having been "inscribed" by prenatal experiences. In terms of Locke's other metaphor, the "empty cabinet" of the mind was already minimally furnished at birth. His evidence for such congenital ideas was more conjcctural than empirical, but nevertheless he was not in doubt about their existence when he wrote (St. John, Vol. I, p. 254):

> *Children, though they have Ideas in the Womb, have none innate.*—Therefore I doubt not but children, by the exercise of their senses about objects that affect them in the womb, receive some few ideas before they are born, as the unavoidable effects either of the bodies that environ them, or else of those wants or diseases they suffer; amongst which (if one may conjecture concerning things not very capable of examination) I think the ideas of hunger and warmth are two, which probably are some of the first that children have, and which they scarce ever part with again.

Such a view of congenital ideas would have justified Locke in adding a corollary to his definition of "idea" to the effect that it is the term which "serves best to stand for whatsoever is the object of understanding" when a fetus thinks. At all events, by implication he seems to have endowed the unborn child with understanding and with the capacity to think. This is the equivalent of endowing it with consciousness rather than with the capacity to reason, for Locke repeatedly refers to "the coming to the use of reason" as a later development. In fact, according to him, it is not until the child begins to "use speech" that it comes "to the use of reason" (St. John, Vol. I, p. 141).

That Locke was attributing consciousness to the fetus by his reference to intrauterine ideas is clear from what he had to say about consciousness as the *sine qua non* of perception. He considered this in connection with one of his many arguments designed to expose the invalidity of the doctrine of innate ideas. In particular he was concerned with the contention of those who held certain laws of thought to be innate. In terms of this contention, the law of identity ordinarily formulated as "*A* is *A*" or "What is, is" can be recognized without formal proof as a self-evident truth. The same would hold for the law of contradiction usually formulated as "*A* is not non-*A* and meaning "It is impossible for the same thing to be and not to be." Locke maintained that these laws could not be innate since "it is evident that all children and idiots have not the least apprehension of them." He understood the doctrine of innate ideas to mean ideas present at birth and independent of sensory impressions. Because of this, he concluded (St. John, Vol. I, p. 137):

> If therefore these two propositions, "Whatsoever is, is," and "it is impossible for the same thing to be and not to be," are by nature imprinted, children cannot be ignorant of them; infants, and all that have souls, must necessarily have them in their understandings, know the truth of them, and assent to it.

The latter conclusion followed from Locke's conviction that having something "imprinted" on the mind cannot take place "without the mind's perceiving it." If innate ideas exist, they must be perceptible; and if perceptible, they must be conscious. Locke put it this way (Vol. I, pp. 136–137):

> To say a notion is imprinted on the mind, and yet at the same time to say that the mind is ignorant of it, and never yet took notice of it, is to make this impression nothing. No proposition can be said to be in the mind which it never yet knew, which it was never yet conscious of.

It should thus be clear why, as stated earlier, Locke in assuming the existence of prenatal ideas was attributing consciousness to the unborn child. In effect he was assuming that perceptual learning occurs before birth. This, of course, is a decidedly questionable assumption and Locke presented no evidence in its support.[5] He failed to ask whether maturation of the unborn child's brain cortex has advanced far enough to justify such an assumption. As a matter of fact, he excluded consideration of physiological questions as being at variance with his "design" for the *Essay*. This was made explicit and clear in the introductory chapter in these words (Vol. I, pp. 128–129):

> I shall not at present meddle with the physical consideration of the mind, or trouble myself to examine wherein its essence consists, or by what motions of our spirits or alterations of our bodies we come to have any sensation by our organs, or any ideas in our understandings; and whether those ideas do in their formation, any or all of them, depend on matter or not. These are speculations which, however curious and entertaining, I shall decline, as lying out of my way in the design I am now upon.

In resolving to ignore physiological speculations, Locke avoided becoming embroiled in a mind-body controversy. Despite his medical background, he proceeded to discuss psychological issues as if they were unrelated to the neurophysiological implications of such a background. In doing so, he was setting a precedent for the eventual emergence of psychology regarded as a separate field of study—a relatively autonomous field—rather than as an outgrowth of brain physiology. For the most part, until well along in the last third of the nineteenth century Locke's associationistic successors followed this precedent of refusing to "meddle with the physical consideration of the mind." They also followed him in his denial of innate ideas, in his affirmation of the *tabula rasa* concept, and in his espousal of an empiristic approach to psychological problems.

---

[5] It is not easy to supply such evidence. Attempts have been made to establish conditioned reactions in infants both before birth and shortly after birth. In the case of prenatal conditioning the results have been uncertain and contradictory. Postnatal conditioning has been more amenable to experimental control. For details, the summary review by N. L. Munn (L. Carmichael [ed.], pp. 270–349) may prove informative.

Why Locke Objected to Innate Ideas

It may seem strange that Locke could accept the notion of prenatal ideas and yet be vehement in his opposition to the notion of innate ideas. As an empiricist he might have been justified in rejecting both notions. After all, he had no way of demonstrating the existence of experienced ideas prior to birth, any more than he could find evidence for innate ones after birth.

As mentioned before, he was very literal in his interpretation of the word "innate" as meaning "present at birth." He seemed to overlook the broader connotations of the word as a designation for all genetically determined characteristics, not all of which are manifest in the newborn child. Huntington's chorea, for example, is definitely inherited and yet many years elapse before its first symptoms appear. To cite a nonpathological example: the musical aptitude of operatic stars, although attributable to genetic factors, is not likely to be detected in very early infancy.

Of course Locke was not concerned with such broader implications of genetic determination as a concept. His arguments were restricted to disposing of the Cartesian doctrine of ideas as innate. In doing so, he was not prompted by considerations that might induce a modern geneticist to oppose such a doctrine because of lack of empirical evidence in its favor. Instead his opposition was due to the way in which adherence to the doctrine tended to curtail frank criticism of ideas held to be innate. To say that man is born with an idea of God or with knowledge of the difference between right and wrong is to substitute dogmatic assertion in place of evidence in support of specific conclusions regarding the existence and nature of God or the ethical status of particular acts.

As Locke viewed it, appeal to ideas as innate readily becomes a defense for prejudices and vested interests. Those entertaining such prejudices or having such interests find it difficult to justify themselves in the light of reason and tend to ward off opposition by claiming inborn sanctions for their convictions. To call an idea innate was to render it inviolable and immune from criticism; hence one of Locke's purposes was to abolish such immunity by demonstrating the nonexistence of innate ideas.

For him, every idea, notion, belief, or conviction was a product of experience and thus subject to critical examination with respect to its validity. It had to commend itself to reason in terms of supporting evidence. To argue that it is one of the "truths *imprinted* upon the soul" prior to experience is sheer nonsense. This follows, it will be recalled, from Locke's contention that to have an idea in the mind is to be aware of that idea. Consequently, if there are inborn ideas, then children and savages should be conscious of them. However, they are manifestly ignorant of such alleged innate ideas as the axioms of geometry or the law of contradiction.

Locke devoted many pages to his polemic against innate ideas. He went into great detail and hammered away at his central thesis with repeated blows as he demolished what he regarded as a possible argument of the opposition. More than seventy closely printed pages are devoted to this task. This indicates how important it seemed to Locke to dispose of the opposition and how prevalent the belief in innate ideas had become. There is no need to review all of his arguments, which are scattered and repetitious. A single excerpt will serve as a sample of the general drift of his attack. In connection with what was just mentioned regarding the ideational impoverishment of children and savages Locke had this to say (St. John, Vol. I, p. 153):

But . . . amongst children, idiots, savages, and the grossly illiterate, what general maxims are to be found? What universal principles of knowledge? Their notions are few and narrow, borrowed only from those objects they have had most to do with, and which have made upon their senses the frequentest and strongest impressions. A child knows his nurse and his cradle, and by degrees the play-things of a little more advanced age; and a young savage has, perhaps, his head filled with love and hunting, according to the fashion of his tribe. But he that from a child untaught, or a wild inhabitant of the woods, will expect these abstract maxims and reputed principles of science, will, I fear, find himself mistaken. Such kinds of general propositions are seldom mentioned in the huts of Indians, much less are they to be found in the thoughts of children, or any impressions of them on the minds of naturals. They are the language and business of the schools and academies of learned nations, accustomed to that sort of conversation or learning, where disputes are frequent; these maxims being suited to artificial argumentation and useful for conviction, but not much conducing to the discovery of truth or advancement of knowledge.

The foregoing kind of verbal onslaught is obviously a *reductio ad absurdum*. It was Locke's way of demonstrating the absurdity of belief in the doctrine of innate ideas by showing its implications when pushed to a logical extreme. He did not maintain that any sponsors of the doctrine had actually attributed such inborn "maxims" to "children, idiots, savages, and the grossly illiterate." What he did maintain was that this would be the case if the doctrine were to be taken seriously and applied consistently. Locke himself took it seriously and tried to apply it consistently to different subjects alleged to have roots in inborn ideas. As a result he found no basis for an innate origin for belief in God, for knowledge of arithmetical and other mathematical truths, or for so-called ethical truths. Everything one comes to believe and know is a result of experience and its validity is to be established by analysis of experience. There can be no knowledge apart from experience. This was the upshot of Locke's examination and rejection of the doctrine of innate ideas and accounts for his place in history as one of the pioneer empiricists.

Locke and Descartes as Cognitive Theorists

Locke's entire *Essay* constitutes one of the first very detailed attempts to determine what can be known with certainty as well as how such knowledge originates, in the form of a study of the nature and limits of human understanding. This inquiry, it will be recalled, was his initial purpose in undertaking to write the *Essay*. As such it was primarily epistemological in intent and only secondarily psychological in outcome. This emphasis follows because the effort to establish the origin and limits of knowledge, viewed as a separate human venture, is customarily regarded as the business of epistemologists. In the course of their study they inevitably have to deal with sensory impressions as the raw material of knowledge, and this inevitably entails psychological issues. As a consequence all epistemologists are confronted with problems of psychology, just as all cognitive theorists in contemporary psychology find themselves dealing with problems having epistemological implications.

Both Locke and Descartes may be thought of as pioneer cognitive theorists. They both tackled the fundamental epistemological question of the certainty of human knowledge. In one respect they both went about this work in the same way, by assuming a state of affairs wherein, by hypothesis, the human being might be said to have zero knowledge. Descartes used the method of trying to doubt and discard everything he ever thought he knew. This amounted to an effort to consider his mind *as if* it were a *tabula rasa*. According to his report, as explained in the previous chapter, he succeeded in all respects except one; namely, that awareness of the act of doubting itself could never be doubted. An ineluctable something compelled such awareness. This something was the Cartesian *res cogitans*, or thinking substance.

Analogously, Locke also found it necessary to regard the genesis of mind as involving something different from an unresponsive *tabula rasa*. His references to the latter as akin to a sheet of uninscribed paper or to an empty cabinet were rather misleading when used to explain what Locke himself came to regard as the matrix of mind. To have sensory impressions leaving marks on paper or accumulating in a cabinet is to introduce dubious metaphors under the circumstances. Neither paper nor cabinets can serve as clarifying metaphors unless, unlike real paper and real cabinets, they be endowed with the rudiments of consciousness. Locke seems to have recognized this requirement when he attributed the origin of ideas not only to sensory impressions but also to what he called *reflection*. Sensations of external objects constituted one source of ideas. With respect to reflection, or the second source, Locke wrote as follows (Vol. I, p. 207):

> Secondly, the other fountain, from which experience furnisheth the understanding with ideas, is the perception of the operations of our own mind within us, as it

is employed about the ideas it has got; which operations, when the soul comes to reflect on and consider, do furnish the understanding with another set of ideas, which could not be had from things without; and such are perception, thinking, doubting, believing, reasoning, knowing, willing, and all the different actings of our own minds; which we being conscious of, and observing in ourselves, do from these receive into our understandings as distinct ideas, as we do from bodies affecting our senses. This source of ideas every man has wholly in himself; and though it be not sense, as having nothing to do with external objects, yet it is very like it, and might properly enough be called internal sense. But as I call the other Sensation, so I call this Reflection, the ideas it affords being such only as the mind gets by reflecting on its own operations within itself. . . . These two, I say, viz., external material things, as the objects of sensation; and the operations of our own minds within, as the objects of reflection; are to me the only originals from whence all our ideas take their beginnings.

In this passage Locke made it clear that for him, empiricism involved. more than a *tabula rasa* as the passive recipient of sensory impressions streaming in from the external environment. For him, these impressions are being subjected to the "operations of our own minds." Such operations made reflection an *active* process. It was not the kind of reflection associated with mirrors, requiring the *tabula rasa* to be thought of as having a gleaming, polished surface. Instead it was the kind of reflection associated with what was later called introspective analysis of immediate experience, as well as the kind of reflection involved in less formal self-observation of one's variegated mental activity—observation ranging from casual reverie to effortful self-analysis in the course of which one comes to understand the ordinary meaning of words like "dreaming," "attending," "perceiving," "reasoning," "doubting," and "believing," indicative of what Locke called "different actings of our minds."

What Locke meant by "reflection" is thus not different from what Descartes meant by *res cogitans*, as characteristic of mind in action. Moreover, just as Descartes found it impossible to question the fact of his own existence because, in the very process of trying to question it, he was aware of thinking or doubting, so Locke also arrived at his own version of *cogito, ergo sum* or *dubito, ergo sum*. To quote him directly (1956, pp. 296–297):

Our knowledge of our own existence is intuitive.—As for our own existence, we perceive it so plainly and so certainly that it neither needs nor is capable of any proof. For nothing can be more evident to us than our own existence. I think, I reason, I feel pleasure and pain: can any of these be more evident to me than my own existence? If I doubt of all other things, that very doubt makes me perceive my own existence, and will not suffer me to doubt of that. For if I know I feel pain, it is evident I have as certain perception of my own existence as of the existence of the pain I feel; or if I know I doubt, I have as certain perception of the existence of the thing doubting, as of that thought which I call doubt. Experience, then, convinces us that we have an intuitive knowledge of our own existence, and an internal infallible knowledge that we are. In every act of sensation, reasoning, or thinking, we are conscious to ourselves of our own being, and in this matter come not short of the highest degree of certainty.

The preceding passage is taken from Book IV of the *Essay*. This is the concluding portion of the work and deals with questions of "knowledge and probability." The initial portion, Book I, is concerned with the question of innate ideas, while the intermediate portions, Books II and III, are devoted to the development of ideas and to the nature and significance of language, respectively. Many chapters separate Book I from Book IV, and considering that twenty years elapsed before the *Essay* was completed, the books were probably also separated by many years. As a consequence, by the time Locke set to work on Book IV he may no longer have been vividly aware of the details of the arguments presented in Book I. At all events, it is difficult to reconcile what he said in the passage just cited with his earlier repudiation of innate ideas. For him to regard some knowledge as "intuitive" and "internal" and "infallible" even though not "capable of any proof" may be tantamount to regarding such knowledge as inherent or innate. In this respect, compared with what Descartes had to say about the same issue, the passage in question sounds more Cartesian than Lockean.

In granting that some knowledge is the result of intuition, Locke was changing his earlier contention regarding sensation and reflection as the sole source of our ideas. This twofold source was stressed in Book I of the *Essay*. However, in Book IV he refers to "a threefold knowledge of existence" and illustrates it by attributing knowledge of personal existence to *intuition*, knowledge of God's existence to *demonstration*, and knowledge of the existence of other things to *sensation*. He devotes the entire tenth chapter of Book IV to demonstrating the existence of God, and in the process reveals demonstration to be the equivalent of what he had previously called reflection. Accordingly, he now had modified his original contention to read: all ideas come from sensation or reflection or intuition. As was mentioned at the close of the last chapter, a comparable threefold classification had already been recognized by Descartes when he held that some ideas "appear to be born with me, others to be foreign and to come from without, and others to be made and invented by myself."

No Discrete Mental Faculties

Another respect in which Locke seemed to agree with Descartes concerned the nature of mental faculties. They both denied their independence as discrete functions or operations. As already indicated in Chapter 11, page 346, for Descartes this denial took the form of affirming the mind's unity, since "it is the same mind which exerts itself wholly to will, and wholly to feel and to perceive." Locke's denial took a somewhat different form, but the underlying thought is not altogether different. He disposed of the question in this way (St. John, Vol. I, p. 364):

> *Faculties.*—These powers of the mind, viz., of perceiving, and of preferring, are usually called by another name: . . . that the understandings and will are two faculties of the mind; a word proper enough, if it be used, . . . so as not to breed any confusion in men's thoughts, by being supposed (as I suspect it has been) to stand for some real beings in the soul that performed those actions of understanding and volition. For when we say the will is the commanding and superior faculty of the soul; that it is or is not free; . . . that it follows the dictates of the understanding, &c., . . . yet I suspect, I say, that this way of speaking of faculties has misled many into a confused notion of so many distinct agents in us, which had their several provinces and authorities, and did command, obey, and perform several actions, as so many distinct beings; which has been no small occasion of wrangling, obscurity, and uncertainty, in questions relating to them.

Actually, faculty psychology as a distinct system of psychology did not have an active champion until the 1730s with the publication of the works of Christian Wolff (1679–1754). Subsequent criticism of his faculty doctrine was an elaboration of the kind of objection raised by Descartes and Locke. In general, the objection revealed an appeal to mental faculties to be a question-begging kind of explanation as exemplified by invoking an aquatic faculty to explain swimming or a terpsichorean faculty to explain dancing. This is the equivalent of substituting an impressive label for a genuine explanation, as in saying that some salve will heal a rash because it contains a therapeutic ingredient.

Neither Descartes nor Locke was explicitly cognizant of the question-begging nature of faculty psychology. At best it was implicit in their distrust of the concept of mental faculties. That is why it is preferable to regard the later criticism of the concept as an elaboration of their distrust. What they both glimpsed was the error of making mind a collection of independent agents, forces, or faculties called will, attention, memory, imagination, etc. Descartes seems to have been more aware of this snare than Locke was. His psychology stressed the *unity* of the *res cogitans;* hence no plurality of independent faculties.

However, as will be brought out later, Locke's psychology failed to come to grips with the unified, integrated nature of mind. In fact, as has sometimes been pointed out, his references to the "powers" of the mind may involve little more than substituting the word "power" for the word "faculty." In a chapter entitled "Of Power" (St. John, Vol. I, Chapter XXI), he repeatedly employs terms like "the power of perception," "the power to think," "the power of understanding," "the power of will," or "a power to receive ideas." In doing so he seems to have overlooked what he had to say about a belief in faculties making for "a confused notion of so many distinct agents in us." His "powers" come close to being "distinct agents," so that in place of a faculty psychology we have a power psychology.[6]

For Locke, the mind's "powers" are manifest in what he called reflection. His empiricism is not to be understood as inclusive of these powers in the sense of regarding them as products of experience. In fact, he never discusses the question of their origin and virtually assumes them to belong to the newborn child's original nature. As a result he took it for granted that babies are born with the power to receive sensations, the power to perceive, and all the other powers included in his notion of reflection. They are treated as innate endowments and not as products of experience. In short, Locke's *tabula rasa* analogy applies to the origin of ideas and not to the origin of mind. Mind, with its "powers" of reflection, is not included in the analogy. An empty cabinet or blank paper is obviously incapable of exercising any power or of *doing* anything. It can only be receptive, not reactive, and Locke failed to supplement his *tabula rasa* analogy with a separate one to deal with mind as such.

As we have noted, his fundamental question was epistemological rather than psychological: what is the genesis of knowledge and not what is the genesis of mind. By implication, the "powers" to convert sensory impressions into knowledge were held to be antecedent to such impressions. Leibnitz once called attention to this implication in an oft-cited addition to empiricism's maxim to the effect that there is nothing in the intellect which had not originated in sensory experience. To the maxim's Latin version of "*Nihil est in intellectu, quod non prius fuerit in sensu*" he added the phrase "*nisi intellectus ipse.*" The Leibnitzian version thus held that there is nothing in the intellect which had not first been in the sensorium "except the intellect itself."

That Locke took mind or intellect for granted, as Leibnitz pointed out, is evident from the casual way in which Locke refers to mind as the recipient of ideas without ever discussing the problem of its origin. He seemed to regard its existence as axiomatic. This can be noted in the following sentences culled from different parts of the *Essay* and in which italics are added by way of clarification:

1. External objects furnish the *mind* with ideas of sensible qualities . . . and the *mind* furnished the understanding with ideas of its own operations.

---

[6] Locke ought not to be judged too harshly for this seeming inconsistency. It is not easy to avoid the language of a faculty psychology. Modern textbooks may warn against endorsement of belief in autonomous mental faculties in an introductory chapter and then have later chapters discuss topics like motivation, intelligence, and perception *as if* these were independent or discrete psychological functions. Incidentally, despite his warning about the word "faculties," Locke continued to use the term as a synonym for "powers of the mind."

2. There be other simple ideas which convey themselves into the *mind* by all the ways of sensation and reflection: viz., pleasure or delight, and its opposite, pain or uneasiness; power, existence, unity.

3. Besides the ideas, whether simple or complex, that the *mind* had of things as they are in themselves, there are others it gets from their comparison one with another.

As these quotations suggest, Locke was more concerned with an analysis of ideas than with an analysis of mind. A scholastic familiar with Aristotle's philosophy might have considered these quotations as showing that Locke regarded mind as *a priori* and ideas as *a posteriori*. His fellow scholastics would have understood this distinction to mean the existence of mind as prior to or independent of experience and the existence of ideas as consequences of experience. Analysis of such consequences constitutes the heart of Locke's *Essay* and involves a detailed exposition covering several hundred pages. For our purposes there is no need to do more than sketch some of the salient characteristics of this analysis especially as they came to influence later psychology.

Locke cleared the way for his analysis by devoting the initial chapters of the *Essay* to an attack on the concept of innate ideas. This attack left experience as the exclusive source of all ideas. All the subsequent chapters are concerned with discussions of the ways in which varieties of experience give rise to all that man comes to know and believe about his surroundings, about his fellows, about himself, and even about his God. The exposition proceeds from the simple to the complex, from elements to compounds, and from preschool experiences of the child to abstruse reflections of the adult. It constitutes a panoramic survey of the origin, nature, and limits of human understanding from the standpoint of a seventeenth-century empiricist.

Sensationism and the Classification of Ideas

From the latter standpoint, in the beginning all knowledge originates from *simple* ideas. At a later stage of development, *complex* ideas begin to emerge. Simple ideas are passively aroused as eyes, ears, and other sense organs are stimulated and the gamut of corresponding sensations is brought into being. Complex ideas depend upon a foundation of simple ones for their emergence, for they are products of the mind's operations on simple ideas. By way of provisional example: the sight of domestic animals gives rise to the simple ideas of dogs, cats, and cows, and by subsequent "acts of the mind" one may form such complex ideas as terriers, Maltese cats, and Holsteins or even the complex idea of mammals.

For Locke, possession of such simple and complex ideas was equivalent to perceiving them (St. John, Vol. I, p. 210): "To ask, at what time a man has first any ideas, is to ask when he begins to perceive; *having ideas,* and *perception,* being the same thing." Moreover, Locke made sensation the foundation of all perception. It will be recalled that when he stated that "all ideas come from sensation or reflection," he was making a distinction between sensory impressions of external objects as contrasted with those "internal" ones due to "operations of our minds" which he attributed to "internal sense." In this way he brought his notion of reflection into line, with sensationism as the alpha and omega of his psychology.

The distinction between sensation and reflection enabled Locke to recognize four sources of the simple ideas "we receive from sensation." In the first place there are ideas or sensations "which come into our mind *by one sense only.*" Thus we have ideas of sound from the sense of hearing and of color from the sense of sight. In the second place there are ideas aroused "*by more senses than one.*" The difference in shape between a sphere and a cube can be noted both visually and tactually. A third source of ideas is had "*from reflection only.*" In this way young children learn what it means to forget, to pretend, to be angry, to be thirsty, to be tired, and whatever else might be listed as the consequence of casual self-observation. Finally, there are ideas which come into "the mind *by all the ways of sensation and reflection.*" Such conjoint operation accounts for the acquisition of ideas of time, of death, of cooking, of number, of poverty, of danger, and similar commonplace notions. As commonplace they do not involve any subtle considerations of a kind indulged in by logicians, lexicographers, and metaphysicians. Instead they are *simple* notions of a kind introduced in everyday speech by a question like "What time is it?" Locke would have said that this is different from the *complex idea* raised by a question like "What is time?"

In the case of simple ideas, Locke maintained, the mind is being acted upon, but in the case of complex ideas the mind is reactive and not just receptive. In short, in his view, just as "the mind is wholly passive in the reception of all its simple ideas" so "it exerts several acts of its own" in transforming some simple ideas into complex ones. Although he did not employ the term "association" in this context, he was virtually giving expression to what later associationists recognized as the distinction between passive and active association. This distinction would make simple ideas the outcome of passive association and complex ideas the product of active association.

According to Locke, three kinds of mental acts are chiefly responsible for the acquisition of complex ideas. One consists of the act of *combining* a number of simple ideas into a unitary compound, in what might be termed the act of *synthesizing.* As an instance, Locke cites the idea of man when regarded as a complex idea arising from the fusion of such simple ideas as form, skin color, anatomic characteristics, walking, thinking, talking, and whatever other items come to be included in the concept of man as a distinctive being. A second kind of mental act consists in bringing ideas together without having them merge into unitary wholes or compounds. Instead their ideational juxtaposition forms the basis for making comparisons or noting relationships. All of our *ideas of relations,* Locke pointed out, are obtained by this kind of mental act. He illustrated this by noting that "one single man" may be involved in a multiplicity of relationships such as being a husband, a father, a son-in-law, an enemy, an older brother, a junior partner, a European, a competitor, etc., etc. In the acts of synthesizing and of relating, ideas are being brought together. However, in the third kind of mental act considered by Locke, ideas are sundered or segregated. This is the act of *abstracting,* or separating from a medley of impressions or ideas some distinctive common characteristics which enter into the formation of a concept or what Locke called a *general idea.*[7] Any function or trait shared by all men may thus be isolated for separate consideration. Such isolation or abstraction has given rise to concepts like respiration, mind, gratitude, consciousness, vision, and the concept of "concept" itself.

Locke as Associationist and as Connectionist

As has been mentioned Locke's distinction between simple and complex ideas was the outcome of what was later referred to as the difference between passive and active *association.* In fact, all the preceding distinctions introduced by Locke foreshadow teachings of the later associationists. That is why he and Hobbes are often listed as the founding fathers of British associationism. And yet, strangely enough, in the early editions of the *Essay* Locke fails to refer to ideas as being associated. Instead he refers to ideas as being "united" or being "combined" or "put together" or "compounded" or "joined" but not associated. Not until the publication of the fourth edition of the *Essay* in 1700, when a new chapter entitled "Of the Association of Ideas" was added to Book II, did the word "association" come into prominence. This chapter heading seems to have been the first mention of the phrase which has become so familiar in everyday speech. The phrase itself is not repeated in the chapter itself even though the ten pages of the chapter (St. John, Vol. I, pp. 531–541) are largely, though not exclusively, concerned with ideational association. Words like "association" or "to associate" are conspicuous by their absence. In terms of party labels, Locke does not seem to have been thinking of himself as an associationist. His first use of the word "associate" occurs in the following paragraph, in which the differences between natural and chance "connexions" is being explained (p. 534):

---

[7] In accounting for the acquisition of general ideas by acts of this kind, Locke was following the precedent established by William of Occam, the fourteenth-century British scholastic and early empiricist and defender of nominalism in the medieval realism-nominalism controversy discussed in Chapter 6 (see pp. 153–155). In other words, had Locke engaged in this controversy, he would have sided with the nominalists.

Some of our ideas have a natural correspondence and connexion one with another; it is the office and excellency of our reason to trace these, and hold them together in that union and correspondence which is founded in their peculiar being. Besides this, there is another connexion of ideas wholly owing to chance or custom; ideas, that, in themselves, are not all of kin, come to be so united in some men's minds, that it is very hard to separate them; they always keep in company, and the one no sooner at any times comes into the understanding, but its *associate* [8] appears with it; and they are more than two which are thus united, the whole gang always inseparable, show themselves together.

Throughout the chapter the term "connexion" recurs along with equivalents whereby ideas are "joined" or "annexed," but there is almost no further mention of them being associated. For example, by way of showing how a wrong "connexion" is a "great cause of errors," Locke refers to a child's fear of the dark because a "foolish maid" had implanted the idea of darkness as the abode of "goblins and sprites" so that "darkness shall ever afterwards bring with it those frightful ideas, and they shall be so joined, that he can no more bear the one than the other" (p. 537). Children, Locke pointed out, are especially vulnerable to the establishment of such wrong "connexions," and he cautioned those in charge of their education "diligently to watch, and carefully to prevent the undue connexion of ideas in the minds of young people." Such an "undue connexion" can make for a more or less fixed attitude toward religious beliefs. Locke supplied an example in the form of a rhetorical question: "Let custom from the very early childhood have joined figure and shape to the idea of God, and what absurdities will that mind be liable to about Deity?"

Even though the chapter is called "Of the Association of Ideas," it is not limited to a discussion of ideational association in the restricted sense of one idea being the instigator of another idea. It goes further by showing the connection between an idea and emotion or an aversion or an action. Thus it contains references to what is now referred to as emotional conditioning by citing instances of aversion to reading as a result of distressing childhood experiences at school, and of a man who, after undergoing a successful but painful surgical experience, could not "bear the sight of the operator." There is also a suggestion to the effect that a vessel shaped like a cuspidor, though "ever so clean" and adequate, could not be used as a drinking vessel because of the disgust "annexed" to it. To demonstrate linkage between ideas and action, Locke cited the case of a man who had learned to dance in a room containing "an old trunk" and who subsequently found it difficult to dance unless a similar article was visible on the dance floor.

In terms of the descriptive vocabulary employed, none of the preceding illustrations are cited as examples of association. Instead they are described

---

[8] Italics added.

as instances of the way in which ideational experience comes to be connected or joined to emotions, antipathies, or actions. It seems as if Locke was averse to using the words "association" and "connexion" as precisely equivalent in meaning, with "connexion" broader in scope than "association." All modes of ideational linkage involved "connexions" but not all of them involved associations.

For Locke, the phrase "association of ideas" was limited to thought processes. Although he was also ready to refer to the "connexion" of ideas, he was not ready to refer to the "association" of an idea with an emotion or an idea with an action or of an action with another action. The latter kinds of linkages were called "connexions" rather than associations. At least this is the way in which Locke used the terms and serves to explain his preference for the word "connexion" in a chapter ostensibly devoted to the topic of association.

Locke himself seems to have been unaware of this preference. If he was aware of it, he did not seem to regard it as calling for justification. It is tempting to conjecture that he might have done so had he suspected his future destiny as a pioneer associationist, a destiny he might not have welcomed. In view of what was just said about his preferred descriptive vocabulary, one might hazard the guess that, had he been given the choice, he would have called himself a connectionist rather than an associationist.

Of course, any speculation about how Locke might have classified himself as a psychologist is a rather futile exercise. Since Locke failed to deal with the question directly, there is no way of determining what his answer would have been. One can only make a guess on the basis of the kind of evidence just introduced; namely, that he started to write a chapter entitled "Of the Association of Ideas" and then proceeded to write as if his chapter should have been entitled "Of the Connection of Ideas."

From Locke to Thorndike

The issue might be dismissed as a semantic quibble hardly deserving more than a pedantic footnote and of no obvious historical significance. Why dwell upon it? Why stress something so trivial as Locke's preference for the word "connexion" as contrasted with the word "association"? The preference was expressed back in the year 1700 and might well be ignored as being devoid of historical significance. Nevertheless, to ignore it would be to overlook an interesting example of history repeating itself, for some two hundred years after Locke voiced his preference a leading twentieth-century psychologist, seemingly unconscious of the details of Locke's chapter, wrote a chapter on "The Law of Association" in which he too subordinated the concept of association to the concept of connection.

The psychologist in question was Edward Lee Thorndike (1874–1949), distinguished as a pioneer in the fields of animal psychology, of genetic psychology, and of mental measurement, and especially in the field of educational psychology. In the year 1905 he published an introductory textbook containing the previously mentioned chapter on association in which "the law of association" is discussed as a synonym for "the law of habit-formation." Although Thorndike employs the word "association" far more frequently than Locke did, he follows the Lockean precedent by veering away from initial use of the word to later use of the word "connection." Thus in the main portion of the chapter he writes about "the formation of connections in general" rather than about "the formation of associations in general." His preference for the term "connection" is shown by the way he formulated the laws of association in instances like these (1920 [1905], p. 207):

> 1. The likelihood that any mental state or act will occur in response to any apparent situation is in proportion to the closeness of its connection with the total set of the mind at the time as well as with the apparent situation itself.
> 2. The likelihood that any mental state or act will occur in response to any apparent situation is in proportion to the closeness of its connection with the apparent situation or some element or part thereof.

Some years later the same preference was still emphasized in Thorndike's textbook, *Educational Psychology*. The chapter entitled "Associative Learning in Man" has sentences like the following (1921, p. 138):

> We may roughly distinguish in human learning (1) connection-forming of the common animal type, as when a ten-months-old baby learns to beat a drum, (2) connection-forming involving ideas, as when a two-year old learns to think of his mother upon hearing the word, or to say candy when he thinks of the thing. . . .
> Connection-forming of the common animal type occurs frequently in the acquisitions of early infancy, in "picking up" swimming or skating undirected, in increasing the distance and precision of one's hits in golf or baseball by the mere try, try again method, and in similar unthinking improvement of penmanship, acting, literary style, tact in intercourse, and indeed almost every sort of ability.

By the 1940s Thorndike ceased to regard himself as an associationist. Instead he wanted to be known as a "connectionist." This was not just an insignificant semantic preference but an indication of what in his opinion was a misleading connotation of the concept of association. In particular he questioned the associationist's emphasis on contiguity of impressions as the crucial factor in learning and habit formation. Contiguity does not suffice to ensure the learning of juxtaposed sensory impressions. If it did, then no child would have difficulty in learning to spell correctly, since the separate letters of each word it sees are contiguous as visual impressions. A teacher who calls the roll of her class each morning throughout the semester is having daily contiguous auditory impressions of the alphabetical sequence of names. Despite this, at the end of the term she may not be able to repeat this sequence from memory. The names will not have been connected even though they were adjacent to one another as she glanced at them in her roll book and as she heard them at the beginning of each class period. Their mere existence as contiguous visual and auditory stimuli does not suffice to convert them into associated ideas. For this to happen, she has to *respond* to them.

What Thorndike was repudiating was a passive impressionism, or the notion of associative learning as the equivalent of spongelike assimilation of contiguous items. For learning to take place, there must be a *reaction* to the items.[9] Otherwise one would have a stimulus without a response, input without output, or impression without expression. In less technical jargon, this amounts to saying that one learns by *doing*. In Thorndike's view, this means an active process of establishing effective "connections" or bonds between the doing and its instigators.

In the last decade of Thorndike's long, productive, and influential life as a psychologist, he incorporated this view in what he called "a good simple definition or description of a man's mind" as being "his connection system, adapting the responses of thought, feeling, and action that he makes to the situations that he meets" (1943, p. 22).[10] Such a definition is entirely congruent with Locke's account of the nature and scope of mental "connexions." Thus Thorndike can be said to have made explicit what was already implicit in the writings of Locke.

In one other respect Thorndike's psychology can be regarded as an elaboration of what was already touched upon by Locke. This has to do with the learning process as influenced by rewards and punishments or by the pleasurable or painful consequences of specific acts of behavior. Common-sense psychology has reflected endorsement of such a hedonistic principle from time immemorial; hence praise, honor, and prizes for commendable achievement on the one hand and dispraise, dishonor, and penalties for failure and misconduct on the other. Thorndike was among the first to investigate this hedonistic principle under laboratory conditions in his famous problem-box experiments. He stressed what at one time was called the *hedonic effect* as a crucial factor in the animal's learning to escape from the box. The same factor was noted as operative in human learning and became one of Thorndike's fundamental laws of learning: the one he called the *law of effect*. According to one of his formulations as expressed in terms of

---

[9] Some experimental support for this conclusion is to be found in the curarization study reported by H. F. Harlow and R. Stagner (1933, pp. 283–294). By injection of curare they induced temporary paralysis in their experimental animals so that no *reactions* could be made to electric shocks, flashes of light, and sounds of a buzzer employed as provocative stimuli. The animals that were not curarized soon learned to respond to the light or sound as signals for the unconditioned stimulus of the shock, but such conditioning or learning failed to occur when the paralyzed animals were subjected to the same kind of stimulation.

[10] An excellent account of what Thorndike meant by the term "connection system" is supplied by E. R. Hilgard in Chapter 2 of his *Theories of Learning* (1956).

situation-response connections (S–R bonds), the law reads as follows (1921, p. 71):

> To the situation, "a modifiable connection being made by him between an S and an R and being accompanied or followed by a satisfying state of affairs" man responds, other things being equal, by an increase in the strength of that connection. To a connection similar, save that an *annoying* state of affairs goes with it or follows it, man responds, other things being equal, by a decrease in the strength of the connection.

In addition to hedonic effect, Thorndike recognized other factors as important determiners of what is learned and retained and what makes for improvement in all realms of human endeavor. His law of exercise, for example, stressed the importance of practice: repetition strengthens connections and disuse weakens them. Furthermore, the value of *attentive* repetition was not overlooked; for he noted that "attentive exercise of a function will produce more rapid improvement than exercise of it with attention directed elsewhere" (1921, p. 214).

These Thorndikean principles of learning had already been glimpsed by Locke back in the 1690s. In fact, as mentioned at the beginning of this chapter, he published a treatise on education in 1693. This treatise taken in conjunction with the psychological views embodied in the *Essay* might justify listing him as a founding father—or grandfather—of educational psychology. Had he been endowed with the gift of prophecy, he would have welcomed Thorndike as a disciple, not only for having worked out the systematic implications of connectionism, but also for having elaborated for the benefit of twentieth-century educators and psychologists these foreshadowings of the laws of effect and exercise and their corollaries (St. John, Vol. I, pp. 263–264):

> *Attention, repetition, pleasure and pain, fix ideas.*—Attention and repetition help much to the fixing any ideas in the memory; but those which naturally at first make the deepest and most lasting impression, are those which are accompanied with pleasure or pain. The great business of the senses being to make us take notice of what hurts or advantages the body, it is wisely ordered by nature . . . that pain should accompany the reception of several ideas; which, supplying the place of consideration and reasoning in children, and acting quicker than consideration in grown men, makes both the old and young avoid painful objects with that haste which is necessary for their preservation, and in both settles in the memory a caution for the future.

In referring to pain-avoiding behavior as something "wisely ordered by nature" to promote self-preservation, Locke might be said to have been alluding to what post-Darwinian biologists designated as the survival value of such behavior. This concept of survival value came to influence psychology in the early 1900s with the rise of the school functional psychology[11] and its interest in the adaptive significance of sensations, images, feelings, and other phases of mental life. Of course it is a far cry from Locke's casual hint of the survival value of pleasure-pain mechanisms to the definite biological orientation of early twentieth-century psychology. The gap was bridged by many intermediate developments during the two hundred years separating Locke from Dewey, Angell, Carr, and the other functionalists. It is also a far cry from Locke's passing mention of the impact of algedonic experiences on memory to Thorndike's later interpretation of experimental results in the light of such experiences—results that formed the basis for his law of effect.

What Locke had limited to the fixing of ideas in human memory, Thorndike extended to animals confronted with mazes and problem boxes as well as to human beings confronted with any kind of learning problem. His law of effect inspired a vast amount of research and occasioned much controversy.[12] For some workers, it was not so much a law of learning as a principle of motivation. As they saw it, the pangs of hunger account for the persistence of behavior in maze learning, but not for the animal's ability to discriminate blind alleys from the true path. Analogously, the threat of academic failure and the prospect of academic success may keep the student busy hour after hour on a knotty assignment in calculus and yet such algedonic factors are not revelatory of the solution. They serve as goads to study but not as guides to brilliant insights. Motivation is a necessary but not a sufficient condition of learning; otherwise all problems could be solved by magnifying rewards or intensifying punishments or both.

How motivation is related to learning—especially to learning as persistent, goal-directed behavior—is a difficult question that cannot be disposed of without introduction of some technical issues. These are issues having to do with the neurophysiology of motivation. Even though it involves a digression, it may not be amiss to consider them at least in broad outline.

The Neurophysiology of Motivation

The neurophysiology of motivated, persistent behavior is now being explored by techniques that were unknown when Thorndike formulated his law of effect. In fact, what he called a "satisfying state of affairs" for the experimental animal can be given laboratory demonstration by one of these techniques; namely, the kind of procedure introduced by Walter Rudolf Hess (1883–   ) of Zurich. This involves the implantation of electrodes

---

[11] For an introduction to the chief tenets of this school, see R. S. Woodworth (1948, Chapter 2).

[12] For an account of some of this research, along with a critical discussion of the controversy, see Hilgard (1956, pp. 25–45).

in precisely localized regions of the hypothalamus of the animal in such a way as to render it possible to subject the regions to electrical stimulation. By means of very mild stimulation of some of these regions, Hess induced autonomic changes characteristic of emotion, of digestion, and of other physiological changes. His findings were important enough for him to share the 1949 Nobel prize in medicine.

The Hess technique has since been utilized and extended by many students of neurophysiology in different parts of the world. In the United States, James Olds (1956, pp. 105–116) was able to demonstrate the existence of what he termed "pleasure centers in the brain" by means of the Hess technique. This experiment called for implantation of the electrode in the septal area of the hypothalamus and having the experimental animal placed in a box containing a treadle connected with a source of electricity. By pressing on the treadle with its forepaws, the animal closed the circuit and the current was transmitted to its septal area. Once the animal experienced this effect, it behaved as if obsessed with an insatiable drive to repeat such self-stimulation. Olds reports orgies of self-stimulation at the rate of 5,000 per hour continuing hour after hour. Incidentally, the Hess technique has also been modified so that by implanting a small tube it is possible to stimulate particular brain sites with specific drugs and thus supplement the effects of electrical stimulation by means of chemical stimulation.

In a review of Olds' work, A. E. Fisher (1964, pp. 60–68) has shown that the rat's basic drives are subject to chemical control. Endocrine substances introduced into the hypothalamus have been found to induce maternal behavior in male rats. Acetylcholine is reported to be an activator of drinking, while noradrenalin induces a resumption of eating on the part of the well-fed animal. Electrical as well as chemical stimulation of a different hypothalamic region has been found to suppress feeding.

In brief, the hypothalamus appears to be directly involved in the regulation of drive behavior in animals—in their instinctive approach-avoidance reactions, repetitive and perseverative behavior. Such drive behavior instigates animal learning, but the learning as such—physiologically considered—is more cortical than hypothalamic. Thorndike's law of effect as applied to animal learning is not at variance with the implications of these electrical and biochemical studies. What he termed "a satisfying state of affairs" as contrasted with "an annoying state of affairs" can now be linked to specifiable hypothalamic regions as demonstrated by the provocative experimental work of B. G. Hoebel (1964).

The extent to which these physiological interpretations of the law of effect are applicable to human learning remains to be determined. There is a vast difference between the brain cortex of a human being and that of a rat. Still, it is possible to incorporate this kind of evidence into rather plausible physiological interpretations of human learning. For example, O. H. Mowrer (1950, Chapter 9) has mobilized an impressive amount of evidence to justify his "two factor theory of learning" in terms of which a distinction is made between learning dominated by activation of the autonomic nervous system as contrasted with learning dominated by activation of the cerebrospinal nervous system. The latter is learning of the problem-solving kind involved in the mastery of ideas and acts of skill, while the former has to do with the kind of emotionalized learning associated with the genesis of phobias, the cultivation of likes and dislikes, and the arousal of interests, values, and thrills. There is one kind of learning that leads to mastery of a musical instrument and a different kind of learning that leads to a dislike of Bach and a preference for Mozart, or vice versa.

Locke's Distinction between Primary and Secondary Qualities

After this digressive excursion into twentieth-century psychology, it is time to resume consideration of Locke's seventeenth-century psychology with its emphasis on sensations as the foundation units or building blocks of knowledge. Like his philosophical contemporaries, Locke was especially concerned with the question of the limitations of knowledge. In his view, nothing can be known about the ultimate nature of mind or the ultimate nature of matter. He made this conclusion definite in a passage like this one (St. John, 1901, p. 442):

> Sensation convinces us that there are solid, extended substances; and reflection, that there are thinking ones; experience assures us of the existence of such beings; and that the one hath a power to move body by impulse, the other by thought; this we cannot doubt of. Experience, I say, every moment furnishes us with clear ideas both of the one and the other. But beyond these ideas, as received from their proper sources, our faculties will not reach. If we would inquire farther into their nature, causes, and manner, we perceive not the nature of extension clearer than we do of thinking. . . . so that we are no more able to discover wherein the ideas belonging to body consist, than those belonging to spirit. From whence it seems probable to me that the simple ideas we receive from sensation and reflection are the boundaries of our thoughts; beyond which, the mind, whatever efforts it would make, is not able to advance one jot; nor can it make any discoveries, when it would pry into the nature and hidden causes of those ideas.

Because of the foregoing considerations, Locke concluded that "the substance of spirit is unknown to us, and so is the substance of body equally unknown to us," and that "we know nothing beyond our simple ideas." He was referring to the word "substance" in a strict etymological sense as that which stands under or is the foundation of experienced ideas or perceptions, for the word signifies nothing "but only an uncertain supposition of we know not what, i.e., of something whereof we have no particular distinct positive idea, which we take to be the substratum, or support, of those ideas we do know."

Although Locke ruled out the possibility of ever getting to experience or to know the substantiality or essence either of mind or of matter, he nevertheless accepted the commonsense belief in their existence as two realms of being. He attributed some experienced items to external objects and others to the internal "substratum" of mind. The former were designated as "qualities in bodies" and the latter as "ideas in the mind." He elaborated upon this distinction in the following paragraph (St. John, Vol. I, p. 243):

> Whatsoever the mind perceives in itself, or is the immediate object of perception, thought or understanding that I call *idea;* and the power to produce any idea in our mind, I call *quality* of the subject wherein that power is. Thus a snowball having the power to produce in us the ideas of white, cold, and round, the powers to produce in us as they are in the snowball, I call qualities; and as they are sensations or perceptions in our understandings, I call them ideas; which ideas, if I speak of them sometimes as in the things themselves, I would be understood to mean those qualities in the objects which produce them in us.

By way of clarification, Locke recognized three kinds of qualities in experienced bodies or objects. Those which he called *primary qualities* were deemed to be basically characteristic of the object, just like it, and inseparable from it. He listed extension, solidity, number, shape, and motion or rest as primary in this sense.[13] A flower like a violet is definitely extended, has a degree of softness, a determinate number of petals, and is either motionless or fluttering in the breeze. In addition to these qualities it has a characteristic fragrance and distinctive color. Such fragrance and color, Locke held, are *secondary qualities* or sensations aroused by "insensible particles," so "that a violet by the impulse of such insensible particles of matter . . . causes the ideas of the blue color and sweet scent of that flower to be produced in our minds" (Vol. I, p. 246). The blueness and fragrance are not in the flower but in the percipient; they are nonexistent in the absence of a beholder. On the other hand, according to Locke, the violet's primary qualities are independent of a percipient. He maintained that all primary qualities inhere in their respective objects and "therefore they may be called *real* qualities, because they really exist in those bodies." By implication, secondary qualities are unreal in the sense of being transient sensations rather than enduring, fixed physical characteristics. Their existence or reality vanishes when the corresponding sensations vanish. In the words of Locke, (Vol. I, p. 247): "Let not the eyes see light or colors, nor the ears hear sounds; let the palate not taste, nor the nose smell; and all colors, tastes,

---

13 As was mentioned in Chapter 4, Aristotle's "common sensibles" constitute an anticipation of Locke's notion of "primary qualities." By way of reminder, Aristotle listed motion, rest, form, magnitude, number, and unity as common sensibles, with solidity implied by the recognition of touch as fundamental.

odors, and sounds, as they are such particular ideas, vanish and cease, and are reduced to their causes, i.e., bulk, figure, and motion of parts." Because of their dependence on the sense organs, secondary qualities are to be called *sensible* qualities.

Strangely enough, qualities of the third kind were not called tertiary qualities. Instead they were termed *powers,* since they had to do with the "power" by virtue of which one body changes the qualities of another body. The solidity of a cube of sugar is changed by the dissolving power of water, and the sun has the power to bleach some colored objects. Similarly, fire has the power to convert white paper into gray ash and a block of ice into steam. Changes resulting from blows of a hammer or pestle also illustrate what Locke meant by the "powers" of a body. By way of example he mentioned the effects of pounding an almond, with the result that "the clear white color will be altered into a dirty one, and the sweet taste into an oily one."

Locke's Thermal Illusion

In his analysis of the nature of sensation as characterized by primary and secondary qualities, Locke was not unmindful of neural processes as immediate antecedents of experienced sensations. He regarded sensation not as the direct apprehension of physical events considered in the abstract, but as the result of the influence of such events on the nerves of the percipient. Somewhat in line with the much later nineteenth-century theory of specific energy of nerves, he recognized the nervous system as interposed between the world of physical stimuli and the quality of sensation. Because of such interposition, a given physical situation may give rise to discrepant or contradictory sensory impressions. Locke made this effect clear by reference to a simple demonstration calling for immersion of both hands in a basin of water at a time when one hand is warm and the other is cold. Under the circumstances the water will be experienced as both cold and hot at the same time. The phenomenon in question has sometimes been called *Locke's illusion.*[14] Like Aristotle's illusion, mentioned in Chapter 4, it is another instance of the influence of psychology's philosophic past on its scientific present. Furthermore, in discussing the nature of this thermal phenomenon Locke glimpsed some of its implications for later scientific study of neurophysiology, as is shown by his attempt in the following passage to explain the illusion in terms of seventeenth-century notions of nerves and animal spirits (Vol. I, p. 249):

> . . . we may be able to give an account how the same water, at the same time, may produce the idea of cold by one hand, and of heat by the other; whereas it is impossible that the same water, if those ideas were really in it, should at the same

---

[14] H. C. Warren (1934, p. 315) refers to it as "Locke's cold and warm illusion."

time be both hot and cold. For if we imagine warmth as it is in our hands, to be nothing but a certain sort and degree of motion in the minute particles of our nerves or animal spirits, we may understand how it is possible that the same water may at the same time produce the sensation of heat in one hand, and cold in the other; which yet figure never does, that never producing the idea of a square by one hand which has produced the idea of a globe by another. But if the sensation of heat and cold be nothing but the increase or diminution of the motion of the minute parts of our bodies, caused by the corpuscles of any other body, it is easy to be understood that if that motion be greater in one hand than in the other, if a body be applied to the two hands, which has in its minute particles a greater motion than in those of one of the hands, and a less than in those of the other, it will increase the motion of the one hand, and lessen it in the other, and so cause the sensations of heat and cold that depend thereon.

From one viewpoint, Locke's illusion is more paradoxical than illusory. The sensations of warmth localized in one hand and those of cold in the other are not illusory. What is illusory or at least contradictory is the experience of the same water as both warm and cold at the same time. Locke's explanation in terms of "motion in the minute particles of our nerves" is best regarded as another instance of prevalent seventeenth-century appeal to motion as the substratum of sensation. Hobbes, it will be recalled, had also stressed motion in trying to account for the difference between sensation and image. Of course this emphasis on motion did little more than call attention to presumed neural factors involved in or responsible for sensory phenomena.

Locke failed to account for the qualitative distinction between sensations of warmth and cold. What his thermal illusion accomplished was to set the stage for later investigation of the details of thermal sensitivity. He knew nothing of the existence of separate cutaneous receptors for such sensitivity, of the relevance of temperature gradients, of measuring skin temperature by means of thermocouples, of the difference between radiant and contact stimulation, and whatever else has become important in the modern experimental study of what he classified as the secondary qualities of warm and cold sensations. Nevertheless, his thermal illusion is still a provocative way to initiate the beginner into the complexities of this phase of sensory psychology.[15]

Effect of Sensory Deprivation on Perception

In addition to the thermal illusion, Locke called attention to another problem involving interpretation of sensory data. This problem also continues to be of interest to the contemporary student of sensation and per-

---

[15] For details of modern studies of this phase of sensory psychology, consult the bibliographic references supplied by W. S. Jenkins (1951, pp. 1188–1190).

ception. It has to do with the role of experience in facilitating integration of qualitatively different sensory impressions belonging to the same stimulus object. An orange, for example, can be recognized by vision, by touch, by smell, and by taste. As is altogether obvious, all these sensory data have come to be integrated into a single perceptual complex. What may not be obvious, however, is the need for experience of each constituent sense modality to have it serve as a cue for perceptual recognition. Would the victim of congenital cataract having his first visual impressions following surgery as an adult be able to recognize an orange as an orange by just looking at it? The issue was put to Locke in a letter from his friend William Molyneux (1656–1698), the astronomer and philosopher, in this form (Vol. I, p. 256):

> Suppose a man born blind, and now adult, and taught by touch to distinguish between a cube and a sphere of the same metal, and nighly of the same bigness, so as to tell, when he felt one and the other, which is the cube, which the sphere. Suppose then the cube and sphere placed on a table, and the blind man be made to see: *quaere,* whether by his sight, before he touched them, he could now distinguish and tell which is the globe, which the cube?

Molyneux maintained that the distinction could not be made and Locke was of the same opinion. That this answer is not obvious, Locke pointed out, is indicated by the fact that his friend had rarely obtained this answer when he posed the problem to others. They thought initial sight of cube and sphere would suffice to establish the distinction. Not until they were presented with reasons opposed to this opinion were they ready to agree with Molyneux.

As is obvious, Locke's stand on this issue was that of an empiricist: the congenitally blind cataract patients, without the opportunity to correlate prior tactual experiences with new visual impressions, when once endowed with sight would fail to recognize the visual form of tactually familiar objects. To support this conclusion, Locke contented himself with presenting reasons based upon casual observation of the development of perception. In this instance he was not enough of an empiricist to consider the evidence to be obtained from actual cases of cataract removal, though as a physician he must have known of the existence of the surgery in question. In fact, according to F. H. Garrison (1929, pp. 109 and 186), the operation had already been known during the Graeco-Roman period and spectacles to compensate for the loss of the lens had been recommended by 1623.

It may be that Locke did consider such direct clinical evidence and found it unsatisfactory for his purposes. Recovery from the surgery is a gradual process, and before any visual testing can be undertaken the patient must be fitted with corrective glasses. In the meantime there may have been incidental if blurred visual exploration. There is no abrupt shift from a life of blindness to sudden clear vision; hence the difficulty of settling the problem posed by Locke's friend by an examination of hospitalized cataract patients.[16]

Despite these difficulties, attempts have been made to study the visual world of such patients. In general, the results have confirmed Locke's prediction of their need for special training or learning before recognition of visual forms takes place. They do seem to be able to experience figure-ground discriminations independently of such training. This is to say that if presented with a large square and a large triangle drawn in white chalk on a blackboard, they will report seeing two outlines standing out as figures but will be unable to specify which is a triangle and which is a square. Nor will they be able to distinguish an orange from a banana. In fact, they will learn to recognize the colors of fruit more readily than the form. It may take months before they succeed in recognizing daily associates by sight, and their visual orientation may never equal that of people who enjoyed normal vision from infancy.

In recent decades the problem has been tackled by animal psychologists by methods more amenable to *experimental* control than is possible in *clinical* studies. These methods have nothing to do with removal of cataracts. Instead they require removal of all sources of visual stimulation from the time of birth by rearing the animals in complete darkness for varied periods of time depending on the species being studied. At the expiration of the chosen period, the eyes are exposed to light and the results of the preceding visual deprivation are subjected to systematic investigation. Animals treated in this way have included rats, fishes, birds, rabbits, and chimpanzees. The consequences of such early "blindness" varied from species to species.

In a review of these investigations, F. A. Beach and J. Jaynes (1954, pp. 239–263) report that rats, for example, following their initial exposure to light, require very little visual experience in order to perform as well as normal rats. They soon equal the normal one in judging distance, and in making discriminations based upon differences in size, pattern, or brightness of stimulus objects. On the other hand, rabbits and fishes may require as long as a month before normal visual control is established. For chimpanzees, serious deficiency of visual control was noted. These animals had been reared in darkness from birth for sixteen months. Upon their first entrance to illuminated surroundings, they seemed to be unconscious of them as visually perceptible. Although there was definite response of the pupils to increased brightness of light, other normal eye reflexes were impaired. Thus,

---

[16] For an account of some of these difficulties as well as for references to some of the other studies dealing with Locke's original question, see the article by W. Dennis (1934, pp. 340–351). Additional bibliographic material is supplied by D. O. Hebb (1958, p. 130).

upon the sudden approach of a moving object, the customary blinking reaction failed to be elicited. Furthermore, it was more difficult to establish conditioned reactions involving vision. This was demonstrated by giving the animals a mild electric shock upon touching a certain object. A normal chimpanzee of sixteen months learns to avoid the object after just one or two such painful experiences, but the visually deprived animal can be shocked for many days before it steers clear of the object. In some cases the impairment of visual efficiency of these experimental animals may be a consequence of degenerative changes in the optic nerve and retina. Such changes have been found in some animals after prolonged exposure to darkness in early infancy. Victims of congenital cataract are not likely to be similarly afflicted, since the presence of cataracts does not necessarily result in total exclusion of all vestiges of stimulation by light.

These fragmentary allusions to the twentieth-century experimental attack on the question raised by Molyneux and Locke suffice to reveal its complexities. Their confident seventeenth-century answer to the question was not concerned with such complexities. Nevertheless, the general drift of the modern experimental evidence is in essential agreement with their prediction of the need for special visual experience before cataract patients can learn to recognize objects like spheres and cubes by sight. Whether the prediction holds for all phases of visual discrimination and for all animal species is open to question. The evidence as evaluated by Beach and Jaynes does not justify an unqualified agreement with the prediction in terms of such an extension of its scope. To quote them directly (1954, pp. 242–243):

> The evidence is fragmentary and at points inconclusive, but it does suggest that in at least some species of fishes, birds, lower mammals, and primates absence of the normal amount of visual stimulation during the developmental period may result in inability to respond adaptively to visual cues when such cues first become available to the individual. The defects do not appear to be permanent but seem to disappear with increasing experience in visually directed responses.

Concerning Depth and Distance Perception

Another aspect of perception to which Locke alluded and which also later engaged the attention of experimental psychologists is related to what was just discussed in connection with learning to recognize the difference between spheres and cubes. This aspect is concerned with the psychology of visual depth perception. As applied to Molyneux's original question, it amounts to asking whether postsurgical cataract patients could perceive the hollowness of the inside of a bowl as compared with the convexity of the bottom surface of an adjacent bowl. This is different from asking about recognition of differences in shape as in discriminating circles from squares or other two-diminsional figures. The retinal image of a solid object is two-dimensional but nevertheless results in tridimensional perception. Locke called attention to this phenomenon as a psychological issue by first noting that such judgments of depth often take place unconsciously or, as he worded it, "without our taking notice of it." He then clarified the point by this simple illustration (St. John, Vol. I, p. 255):

> When we set before our eyes a round globe of any uniform color, e.g., gold, alabaster, or jet, it is certain that the idea thereby imprinted in our mind is of a flat circle variously shadowed, with several degrees of light and brightness coming to our eyes. But we having by use been accustomed to perceive what kind of appearance convex bodies are wont to make in us, what alterations are made in the reflections of light by the difference of the sensible figures of bodies, the judgment presently, by an habitual custom, alters the appearances into their causes; so that, from that which truly is variety of shadow or color collecting the figure, it makes it pass for a mark of figure, and frames to itself the perception of a convex figure and an uniform color; when the idea we receive from thence is only a plane variously colored, as is evident in painting.

In the preceding illustration one can detect anticipation of observations that received more explicit emphasis when the problem of visual depth perception became a distinctive psychological challenge. For one thing, Locke noted that the problem involves consideration of devices employed by artists in creating impressions of depth and distance on the flat surface of a canvas. The only one of these devices he mentioned is that of the distribution of light and shade, or what is sometimes listed as *chiaroscuro* when cues to depth perception are being given textbook consideration. Furthermore, in describing this as a judgment based upon "an habitual custom" and occurring "without our taking notice of it," Locke was not only recognizing it as a product of experience, but was also recognizing it as an instance of *unconscious inference*. The latter phrase was first introduced into psychology by Hermann von Helmholtz (1821–1894) in his effort to account for the reciprocal influence of adjacent colors as observed in the phenomenon of color contrast.[17] It assumes that perceptual judgment may occur without

---

[17] For a readily accessible account of Helmholtz's explanation of color contrast, see James (1890, Vol. I, pp. 17–25). The account is rather detailed and includes verbatim excerpts from Helmholtz's *Physiological Optics*. James classifies the theory of Helmholtz as being psychological, in contrast to the rival physiological theory advanced by Ewald Hering (1834–1918). After reviewing the evidence, James decides in favor of Hering's physiological theory. Of course, contrast effects are not restricted to sensations of color. They also influence judgments of size or bulk: a moderately stout man will appear more obese standing next to a cadaverous man than when standing next to a man of average weight. Contrast also influences taste sensations: sweet substances taste sweeter if eaten after one has tasted something bitter. Comparable contrast effects involve other sense modalities. No single theory need apply to all these effects. Some may call for consideration of the conjoint influence of psychological and physiological factors in determining the judgmental outcome.

awareness of an underlying reasoning process presumably responsible for the conclusion reached.

As applied to the globe mentioned by Locke, one judges it to be convex because of the way light is reflected from its surface, and yet there need be no awareness of an inference being drawn from the brightness pattern as such. One is convinced of the globe's convexity without being able to specify the nature of the evidence upon which the conviction is based. At least this is the case with the psychologically unsophisticated observer. All he can say when challenged is that the globe is convex because it "looks" convex. It is as if he is unconscious of the cues involved and the inference he drew from them. What Locke attributed to "an habitual custom" became an "unconscious inference" for Helmholtz.

What Locke had to say about visual perception of space and form was rather fragmentary and incidental. However, it did serve as a point of departure for the more detailed elaboration of the problem by Berkeley, Locke's successor in the development of British empiricism. Indeed, Berkeley's treatment made it an important problem both for philosophy and for psychology, and indirectly it came to influence the thinking of Helmholtz and the other founding fathers of nineteenth-century scientific psychology in Germany. Their interest in space perception, visual illusions, and kindred phenomena may thus, at least in part, be regarded as an outgrowth of questions raised by British empiricists of an earlier generation.

On Concepts of Selfhood and Personal Identity

Still other aspects of later psychology have roots in some of Locke's incidental observations. To note all of them is impossible here. It will suffice to mention one more because it deals with the question of personal identity already considered in earlier chapters as one of psychology's persistent problems. Allport, it will be recalled (see Chapter 8, page 221), referred to it as the "puzzle of the self" and others, such as Calkins and Snygg and Combs (see Chapter 10, page 282), made the concept the focus of their respective self-psychologies. Had the issue come up in his day, Locke might have been willing to classify himself as a self-psychologist. It is enough to quote just a portion of what he had to say on the subject to note the importance he attached to the centrality and persistence of *self* as the hallmark of the concept of "person" (St. John, Vol. I, pp. 466–467):

> . . . to find wherein personal identity consists, we must consider what *person* stands for; which I think, is a thinking intelligent being, that has reason and reflection, and can consider itself, the same thinking thing, in different times and places; which it does only by that consciousness which is inseparable from thinking, and it seems to me essential to it: it being impossible for anyone to perceive, without perceiving that he does perceive. When we see, hear, smell, taste, feel, meditate, or will anything, we know that we do so. Thus it is always as to our

present sensations and perceptions: and by this everyone is to himself that which he calls *self*; it not being considered, in this case, whether the same self be continued in the same or diverse substances. For since consciousness always accompanies thinking, and it is that that makes everyone to be what he calls self, and thereby distinguishes himself from all other thinking things; in this alone consists personal identify, i.e., the sameness of a rational being: and as far as this consciousness can be extended backwards to any past action or thought, so far reaches the identity of that person; it is the same self now it was then; and it is by the same self with this present one that now reflects on it, that that action was done. . . .

For it being the same consciousness that makes a man be himself to himself, personal identity depends on that only, whether it be annexed solely to one individual substance, or can be continued in the succession of several substances. For as far as any intelligent being can repeat the idea of any past action with the same consciousness it had of it at first, and with the same consciousness it has of any present action; so far as it is the same personal self. For it is by the consciousness it has of its present thoughts and actions that it is self to itself now, and so will be the same self, as far as the same consciousness can extend to actions past or to come; and would be by distance of time, or change of substance, no more two persons than a man be two men, by wearing other clothes today than he did yesterday, with a long or short sleep between: the same consciousness uniting those distant actions into the same person, whatever substances contributed to their production.

Compared with what James had to say about the nature of the self, as mentioned in Chapter 10, the foregoing hardly does more than give an inkling of the network of interrelationships implied by concepts like self, identity, consciousness, and person. Locke's recognition of this network in 1690 may be likened to the germ of an idea. By the time of James, two centuries later, this germ had taken solid root and was beginning to send out branches. In succeeding decades these branches extended in different directions and reached out into areas far removed from the boundaries of self and the empirical me as they looked to James.

The issues involved came to interest sociologists, personality theorists, social anthropologists, psychoanalysts, social psychiatrists, and adherents of the many schools of psychotherapy which had come into existence by the 1950s. An increasing list of books and articles dealing with the ramifications of these issues appeared year after year. Some were concerned with man's quest for individualizing identity. Others stressed social forces interfering with this quest by pressures leading to the conformity of the so-called organization man. Still others were concerned with the loneliness apt to be engendered by passive compliance with social expectations of the "crowd." Many of them focused on anxiety as a chronic actual or potential threat to the self and consequently as a key factor in shaping personality development. Moreover, amid the pattern of all these discussions one can often detect consideration of the persistent "riddle" of individuality. This, it may be recalled, was another one of Allport's six "productive paradoxes of William James" (see Chapter 8, page 221). Thus faint beginnings of the later prominence given to these problems of selfhood and individuality may be traced back to Locke. Now, almost three hundred years later, as just indicated, the problems are no longer exclusively psychological. Their prosecution calls for the cooperative effort of investigators representing many different fields of specialization;[18] but to elaborate upon this would constitute too much of a digression. Instead it might be better to call a halt in order to review the many different psychological issues Locke bequeathed directly to his successors and indirectly to us.

Review

The chief reason for devoting so much space to Lockes's *Essay* is not to be found in any one single outstanding psychological discovery revealed in its pages. Nothing like Galileo's epoch-making experiments or Newton's famous laws of motion can be attributed to Locke. Nor did Locke himself attribute great scientific importance to the *Essay*. He regarded it as a preparation for scientific study rather than as a contribution to science per se. This preparation called for understanding and cultivation of the *empirical* method. His importance in the history of psychology is a result of the way in which he applied this method to a vast array of questions having implications for the future science of psychology. Many of his answers to these questions were modified by men who continued his empirical studies during the eighteenth and nineteenth centuries. Seen in this light, he is the fountainhead of the important philosophical and psychological tradition known as British empiricism.

In large measure the "new" psychology of the Wundtian laboratories grew out of this tradition. What was common to the "old" psychology of the tradition and the "new" psychology of the laboratory was the emphasis on experience. Locke's basic thesis was to the effect that "all the materials of reason and knowledge" come from experience, and his entire *Essay* was an elaboration and defense of this thesis. Somewhat analogously, Wundt's basic thesis was to the effect that the scientific study of mind calls for the analysis of "immediate experience." The Lockean tradition was thus a forerunner of the Wundtian innovation. In other words, the empirical observations of Locke facilitated the transition to the experimental observations of Wundt; hence the historical significance of Locke's efforts to account for "human understanding." To repeat: as one of the founding fathers of British empiricism Locke gave direction to a movement that eventually came to have a

---

18 A good example of such cooperative effort is the volume on *Identity and Anxiety*, edited by Stein, Vidich, and White (1960). The detailed bibliographic references supplied by the contributors to the volume serve to indicate the vast scope of the multifaceted interest in the problems.

bearing on the views of the founding fathers of experimental psychology. Moreover, as has been indicated from time to time in this chapter, some of Locke's observations also have a bearing on current psychological issues. By way of general reminder, it might prove helpful to include these observations in the following summary review of the chapter as a whole:

1. The basic purpose of Locke was to determine the nature and limitations of knowledge or to reach the "true knowledge of things" by investigating the origin and development of all ideas—concrete ideas as well as abstract ideas. He defined the word "idea" very broadly as the term that "serves best to stand for whatsoever is the *object* of the understanding when a man thinks."

2. Hume's later criticism of Locke's broad usage of the word "idea" as contrary to the root meaning of the word was not endorsed, even though the value of his distinction between impressions and ideas was recognized.

3. Experience in the form of sensation or reflection constitutes the sole source of ideas and calls for the firm rejection of the doctrine of innate ideas.

4. Locke's references to mind at birth being like white paper or like an empty cabinet were found to be similes already introduced by Aristotle.

5. The repudiation of belief in innate ideas was not as sometimes held, an attack on a scholastic teaching. Instead it was an attack on Descartes, who had defended such a belief.

6. Locke's rejection of belief in innate ideas did not rule out endorsement of a belief in congenital ideas; for he maintained that children "have ideas in the womb." In doing so, he was assuming that perceptual learning occurs before birth and by implication he was attributing consciousness to the unborn child.

7. His polemic against innate ideas was prompted by the conviction that no idea should be exempt from critical analysis and evaluation. To regard a given idea as innate is to substitute dogmatic credence for knowledge subject to proof.

8. By refusing to "meddle with the physical consideration of the mind," Locke avoided becoming involved in the mind-body controversy.

9. Both Locke and Descartes may be classified as pioneer cognitive theorists. The *res cogitans* of Descartes becomes the power of *reflection* for Locke.

10. Locke held that knowledge of personal existence is "intuitive" and "infallible" and not "capable of any proof." It is hard to reconcile this view with his polemic against innate ideas.

11. Both Locke and Descartes seem to have anticipated the opposition to mental faculties by later psychologists. They both refused to regard them as discrete, autonomous mental functions.

12. Locke took mind or intellect for granted; hence his *tabula rasa* analogy, strictly speaking, is not applicable to mind.

13. Locke differentiated *simple* ideas from *complex* ideas on the ground that simple ones are passively aroused while complex ones are a product of "acts of the mind" operating on simple ideas.

14. He recognized four sources of simple ideas:

(a) From one sense modality, resulting in sounds, colors, tastes, and other elementary sensations.

(b) From more than one sense modality, as exemplified by ideas of space and of motion;

(c) From reflection alone, giving rise to awareness of memory, perception, reason and other mental "powers" as ideas of such "powers."

(d) From conjoint action of sensation and reflection, as illustrated by ideas of existence, pleasure, time, death, number, cooking, and similar everyday notions.

15. Three kinds of mental acts account for the acquisition of complex ideas:

(a) Acts of combining or synthesizing several simple ideas into a unitary whole, as in the idea of a city or a man or malaria or grammar.

(b) Acts of combining or connecting simple ideas without having them fuse into integrated wholes, as exemplified by noting the relationship between employer and employee or between uncle and nephew or between synonyms and antonyms.

(c) Acts of isolating or abstracting common characteristics from a mass of impressions or ideas, thus giving rise to formation of general ideas or concepts.

16. Although the preceding distinctions have to do with the concept of association, Locke seemed averse to employing the term even though he was the first to introduce the phrase "association of ideas." In his preference for the term "connection," his psychology was discussed in the light of Thorndike's connectionism.

17. Locke anticipated such later concepts as the law of effect, emotional conditioning, and survival value.

18. A distinction was drawn between primary and secondary qualities, with the primary being intrinsic to or inseparable from a physical object and the secondary being nothing in the object itself except the power to produce sensations. Extension, solidity, number, shape, and motion were listed as primary. All the others, such as smell, color, sound, taste, pain, and temperature, were listed as secondary. Because of their dependence on sense organs they were called *sensible* qualities, in contradistinction to the *real* qualities of the primary group. Incidentally, Locke also called attention to a third group of qualities; namely, the "powers" by virtue of which one object can change the qualities of another object. Thus an acid has the power to change the color of litmus paper.

19. Secondary qualities were illustrated by means of Locke's thermal illusion. The illusion also demonstrated that Locke had an inkling of what eventually was formulated as the nineteenth-century theory of specific energy of nerves.

20. The psychology of space and form perception was considered in terms of clinical and experimental evidence, with the clinical going back to Locke's postsurgical cataract cases and the experimental to modern studies of animals reared in darkness.

21. The network of interrelationships worked out by the social sciences of today, implied by concepts like self, identity, consciousness, and person, was already dimly perceptible to Locke.

Concluding Comments

As indicated in the preceding review, Locke dealt with a wide diversity of seemingly unrelated topics in his *Essay*. At first inspection, aside from the empiristic emphasis, it may be difficult to find a unifying theme running through them. Still, his primary purpose in writing the *Essay* was not so much to champion the empiricist's cause as to establish the nature and limits of man's quest for knowledge. This epistemological quest determined the selection of topics introduced in the long succession of chapters. In this respect the *Essay* of 1690 might be said to resemble James's *Principles* of 1890. The latter classic, with its long succession of chapters, also impressed some readers as being a series of independent studies of discrete psychological topics. It too struck them as being devoid of a central unifying theme. In their eyes, the work lacked the kind of treatment expected of a well-articulated *system* of psychology. However, as indicated in the footnote on page 222 in Chapter 8, E. B. Titchener failed to see it this way. According to him, what endowed the *Principles* with unity and systematic status is the fact that James had presented us with "a work on the principles of knowledge, written from a psychologist's standpoint." In a similar vein, Locke's *Essay* might be described as an account of the principles of knowledge, written from the standpoint of a seventeenth-century philosopher.

Many of the problems discussed by Locke were still being considered by James two centuries later, just as topics introduced by James continue to have significance for the contemporary psychological scene. This is a consequence of the continuity of history. To skip from Locke to James and from James to the present is tantamount to disregarding this continuity. Unless the chronological gaps are filled in by consideration of intermediate developments, the result will be a seriously distorted historical perspective. The psychological tradition stemming from Locke's *Essay* is just one segment of this perspective. As a segment it has been very influential, but there are other segments to be considered. In particular this applies to the psychological teachings of some of Locke's continental contemporaries such as Spinoza and Leibnitz. These will be discussed in the next two chapters. Before we turn to this task, it may be advisable to amplify what was just said regarding the influential nature of the segment of history growing out of Locke's psychological orientation. In the work of his British successors—men like Berkeley, Hume. Hartley, James, and John Stuart Mill, and others—Locke's empiricism, became British associationism. This school, along with Locke's empiricism, had far-reaching consequences. Allport (1955, p. 8) summarized them in this way:

> The Lockean point of view . . . has been and is still dominant in Anglo-American psychology. Its representatives are found in associationism of all types, including environmentalism, behaviorism, stimulus-response (familiarly abbreviated as S-R) psychology, and all other stimulus-oriented psychologies, in animal and genetic psychology, in positivism and operationism, in mathematical models—in short, in most of what today is cherished in our laboratories as truly "scientific" psychology.

The Lockean point of view to which Allport referred is a reminder of what was pointed out earlier in this chapter: that Locke took mind or intellect for granted and was primarily concerned with demonstrating the empirical or sensory origin of its ideas. In effect, he was endorsing what was referred to as the scholastic maxim of *"nihil est in intellectu."* In criticism of this maxim, Leibnitz, it will be recalled, added the telling phrase *"nisi intellectus ipse."* Another important segment of the history of psychology is bound up with the implications of this phrase. If the Lockean segment be thought of as basically empirical and associationistic in orientation, then this other segment may be thought of as more rationalistic, more nativistic, and more activistic in orientation. For obvious reasons, Allport (1955, pp. 12–17) referred to this segment as the Leibnitzian tradition in contradistinction to the other or Lockean tradition. Of course, just as Locke was not exclusively responsible for initiating and giving direction to the Lockean tradition, so Leibnitz is by no means soley responsible for the Leibnitzian tradition.[19] Calling these more or less rival traditions by their names is just a matter of descriptive convenience. And now, as a matter of expository convenience, it is advisable to put off further consideration of this Leibnitzian tradition until a later chapter.

---

[19] With reference to these two traditions and the problems germane to each of them, E. B. Brett long ago had a word of admonition. His warning took this form (1912, Vol. II, p. 302): "This complex of problems is frequently presented as a mere antithesis of Locke and Leibnitz. That formula does justice to neither of these names . . . and therefore it is better to begin by avoiding the errors which might arise from the use of those names; though nothing is gained by obscuring the fact that as the struggle develops English empiricism becomes the archetype of one doctrine and the monadology forms the germ of the other."

References

Allport, G. *Becoming—Basic Considerations for a Psychology of Personality.* New Haven: Yale University Press, 1955.

Aquinas, St. Thomas. *Truth.* (Translated by R. W. Mulligan.) Chicago: Henry Regnery Company, 1956 .

Beach, F. A., and Jaynes, J. "Effects of Early Experiences upon the Behavior of Animals," *Psychological Bulletin,* 1954, *51,* 239–263.

Brett, G. S. *A History of Psychology,* Vol. II. London: George Allen and Unwin, 1912.

Dennis, W. "Congenital Cataract and Unlearned Behavior," *Journal of General Psychology,* 1934, *44,* 340–351.

Fisher, A. E. "Chemical Stimulation of the Brain," *Scientific American,* 1964, *210,* 60–68.

Garrison, F. H. *An Introduction to the History of Medicine,* 4th ed. Philadelphia: W. B. Saunders Company, 1929. (Reprinted 1960.)

Harlow, H. F., and Stagner, R. "Effect of Complete Striate Muscle Paralysis upon the Learning Process," *Journal of Experimental Psychology,* 1933, *16,* 283–294.

Hebb, D. O. *A Textbook of Psychology.* Philadelphia: W. B. Saunders Company, 1958.

Hendel, C. W. (ed.). *Hume—Selections.* New York: Charles Scribner's Sons, 1927.

Hilgard, E. R. *Theories of Learning,* 2nd. ed. New York: Appleton-Century-Crofts, 1956.

Hoebel, B. G. "Hunger and Satiety in Hypothaalmic Regulation of Self-Stimulation," in *Dissertation Abstracts* of Creative Talent Program. Washington, D.C.: American Institutes for Research, 1964.

James, W. *Principles of Psychology,* Vol. I. New York: Henry Holt and Company, 1890.

Jenkins, W. S. "Somesthesis," in S. S. Stevens (ed.). *Handbook of Experimental Psychology.* New York: John Wiley and Sons, 1951, pp. 1172–1190.

Locke, John. *An Essay Concerning Human Understanding.* Chicago: Henry Regnery Company, 1956.

McKeon, R. (ed.). *Introduction to Aristotle.* New York: The Modern Library, 1947. "De Anima," pp. 145–235.

Mowrer, O. H. *Learning Theory and Personality Dynamics.* New York: The Ronald Press Company, 1950.

Munn, N. L. "Learning in Children," in L. Carmichael (ed.). *Manual of Child Psychology.* New York: John Wiley and Sons, 1954, pp. 373 449.

Olds, J. "Pleasure Centers in the Brain," *Scientific American,* 1956, *193,* 105–116.

St. John, J. A. (ed.). *The Philosophical Works of John Locke,* Vol. I. London: George Bell and Sons, 1901.

Stein, M., Vidich, A. J., and White, D. M. (eds.). *Identity and Anxiety—Survival of the Person in Mass Society.* Glencoe, Illinois: The Free Press, 1960.

Thorndike, E. L. *Educational Psychology, Briefer Course.* New York: Teachers College, Columbia University, 1921.

Thorndike, E. L. *The Elements of Psychology,* 2nd. ed. New York: A. G. Seiler, 1920. (First published in 1905.)

Thorndike, E. L. *Man and His Works.* Cambridge: Harvard University Press, 1943.

Warren, H. C. *Dictionary of Psychology.* Boston: Houghton Mifflin Company, 1934.

Wolfson, H. A. *The Philosophy of Spinoza,* Vol. II. Cambridge: Harvard University Press, 1934.

Woodworth, R. S. *Contemporary Schools of Psychology,* rev. ed. New York: The Ronald Press Company, 1948.

13

Spinoza's Hormic Psychology

AS INDICATED FROM TIME TO TIME in previous chapters. modern philosophy, modern science, and modern psychology emerged out of the intellectual ferment of the seventeenth century. The major theories of the mind-body relationship were formulated during this century. Furthermore, some of psychology's major dichotomies discussed in earlier chapters are of seventeenth-century origin—dichotomies like empiricism versus rationalism, atomism versus holism, and empiricism versus nativism.[1] Incidentally, the implications of such dichotomies have not vanished from the current psychological scene. They are reflected in nature-nurture controversies, in the clash between holistic Gestalt doctrines and the more atomistic teachings of associationists and connectionists, and in the views of those who regard man as a rationalizing rather than a rational animal.

Such contemporary issues, historically considered, may be traced back to the time when Hobbes and Locke established the foundations of the British psychological tradition and when Descartes was doing the same for the continental tradition. The latter tradition is by no means exclusively Cartesian. It owes much to the influence of Spinoza and Leibnitz, whose contributions to the seventeenth-century intellectual ferment is not to be minimized. Still, apart from occasional passing references to their work in the preceding chapters, there has been relative neglect of their salient teachings. Such neglect makes for a distorted picture of seventeenth-century psychology. To reduce the distortion, the present chapter will introduce a corrective by viewing psychology through the lenses of Spinoza, and in the next chapter through the spectacles of Leibnitz.

Before we discuss the work of Spinoza, it may be advisable to explain the reason for the order in which the development of seventeenth-century

---

[1] See pp. 13–15 and 91–92.

402

BENEDICTUS SPINOZA (1632–1677)

JOHN LOCKE (1632–1704)

psychology has been and is being presented. More than chronological sequence is the governing consideration. Instead, such sequence has been subordinated to a more basic consideration; namely, the interplay of key viewpoints and concepts as sponsored by these seventeenth-century philosopher-psychologists. Thus, the contrast between the empiricism of Hobbes and the rationalism of Descartes was first introduced by way of setting the stage for subsequent developments. Following this, attention was directed to Locke's empiricism with specific reference to its opposition to Cartesian nativism. Now in the present chapter and the following one, Spinoza will be found to have been influenced by both Hobbes and Descartes as well as by earlier philosophers. As a result of these influences and his reaction to them, Spinoza has become of historical importance to philosophers. Since one of his chief concerns was to discover the laws of mental life, he is also of historical importance to psychologists. To read Spinoza is not easy, but it is a rewarding study, as may become evident in the pages which follow.

Spinoza as Last of the Medievals and First of the Moderns

Baruch Spinoza was born in Amsterdam on November 24, 1632, and died as Benedictus Spinoza in The Hague on February 21, 1677. This change in names from Baruch, Hebrew for "blessed," to its Latin equivalent, Benedictus, is symbolic of the change in the scope of his intellectual horizons. In childhood and early youth, as Baruch, he had immersed himself in study at the Amsterdam school for Jewish boys. Knowledge of Hebrew was essential for mastery of the curriculum. This, according to A. Wolf (1929, p. 231), is known to have included the Old Testament, the Talmud, the Hebrew codes and the works of Ibn Ezra, Maimonides, Crescas, and others. Its mastery undoubtedly resulted in a thorough understanding of the quasi-parochial world view of medieval Jewish philosophers.

It was in early manhood, after Baruch had learned Latin, the language common to the scholars and scientists of the time, that he decided to call himself Benedictus. This, it seems, signalized the transformation of his former world view into one more in accord with the spirit and outlook of seventeenth-century philosophy and science. However, the transformation did not entail elimination of all traces of the earlier outlook. In implicit fashion it continued to leaven the thought of his later years. In fact, H. A. Wolfson, the noted student of Spinoza's writings, has contended that an undercurrent of medieval philosophic lore is to be detected in some of these writings. The explicit mainstream of his thoughts is postmedieval, while the implicit undercurrent is more medieval in its drift. The latter, in Wolfson's opinion, reflects the earlier orientation of the youthful Baruch and the former reveals the later orientation of the mature Benedictus. Consequently, in the words of

Wolfson (1934, Vol. I, p. vii): "Benedictus is the first of the moderns; Baruch is the last of the medievals."

The Metaphysics of Scholastic Science

This raises the question of the nature of the cleavage between the medieval and modern world views: the Baruch view as contrasted with the Benedictus view. It has to do with the difference between the metaphysical presuppositions of scholastic science and those growing out of seventeenth-century science. To appreciate the difference, it is well to recall the significance of the shift from medieval geocentric to modern heliocentric convictions. Such a shift meant far more than a change in lectures on astronomy. It shook the foundations of traditional beliefs about man's place in the universal scheme of things. Its repercussions affected the world of religion as well as the world of science. These were well summarized by the philosopher E. A. Burtt (1954 [1924], pp. 18–20) in his classic *The Metaphysical Foundations of Modern Physical Science:*

> For the Middle Ages man was in every sense the centre of the universe. The whole world of nature was believed to be teleologically subordinate to him and his eternal destiny. Toward this conviction the two great movements which had become united in the medieval synthesis, Greek philosophy and Judeo-Christian theology, had irresistibly led. The prevailing world-view of the period was marked by a deep and persistent assurance that man, with his hopes and ideals, was the all-important, even controlling fact in the universe.
>
> This view underlay medieval physics. The entire world of nature was held not only to exist for man's sake, but to be likewise immediately present and fully intelligible to his mind. Hence the categories in terms of which it was interpreted were not those of time, space, mass, energy, and the like; but substance, essence, matter, form, quality, quantity—categories developed in the attempt to throw into scientific form the facts and relations observed in man's unaided sense-experience of the world and the main uses which he made it serve. Man was believed to be active in his acquisition of knowledge—nature passive. When he observed a distant object, something proceeded from his eye to that object rather than from the object to his eye. And, of course, that which was real about objects was that which could be immediately perceived about them by human senses. Things that appeared different *were* different substance such as ice, water, and steam. . . .
>
> The earth appeared a thing vast, solid, and quiet; the starry heavens seemed like a light, airy, and not too distant sphere moving easily about it. . . . What more natural than to hold that these regular shining lights were made to circle round man's dwelling-place, existed in short for his enjoyment, instruction, and use? The whole universe was a small, finite place, and it was man's place. He occupied the centre; his good was the controlling end of the natural creation.
>
> Finally, the visible universe itself was infinitely smaller than the realm of man. The medieval thinker never forgot that his philosophy was a religious

philosophy, with a firm persuasion of man's immortal destiny. The Unmoved Mover of Aristotle and the personal Father of the Christian had become one. There was an eternal Reason and Love, at once Creator and End of the whole cosmic scheme, with whom man as a reasoning and loving being was essentially akin. In the religious experience was that kinship revealed, and the religious experience to the medieval philosopher was the crowning scientific fact. . . . The world of nature existed that it might be known and enjoyed by man. Man in turn existed that he might "know God and enjoy him forever."

The preceding sketch of the impact of Judeo-Christian tradition on medieval science serves as a satisfactory reminder of Spinoza's intellectual orientation during his Baruch days. This was what made him "the last of the medievals."

Spinoza and the Metaphysics of Emerging Modern Science

In his Benedictus years as "the first of the moderns," Spinoza developed a monistic philosophy essentially in harmony with the metaphysical assumptions implicit in the thinking of many present-day natural scientists. In his view, everything and everybody is subject to the impersonal operation of the forces of nature, in accordance with an ineluctable determinism. Interference with such operation by miracles or supernormal divine intervention is excluded even as a theoretical possibility. Man is no longer regarded as the special object of God's concern. He has no special role to play in a cosmic drama involving God's interest in the salvation of his soul. There is no divine purpose running through the scheme of things. Teleology, in the sense of final causes operative in the universe, was thus ruled out of scientific court.

For Spinoza, man as a finite being was part of Nature, and his distinctively human nature was not to be accounted for by appealing to mystical or supernatural or superstitious influences. He regarded superstition as "the bitter enemy of all true knowledge and true morality" (J. Ratner, [ed.], 1927, p. 48). What he called "true knowledge" was tantamount to getting to know Nature and for him getting to know Nature was equivalent to getting to know God. His God was not a transcendental Being but a symbol of the sum total of fixed principles of order or scientific law in the light of which the universe is viewed as a cosmos and not as a chaos.[2] It was a sophisticated elaboration of what the Psalmist

---

2 At best this is to be regarded as a *possible* interpretation of what Spinoza meant by his concept of God. As Wolfson makes clear, students of Spinoza have not agreed among themselves in their accounts of what the term meant for Spinoza. Moreover, Wolfson found it difficult to dispose of the problem by direct examination of what Spinoza had written about God. To quote Wolfson directly: "When we leave what others have said about Spinoza's God and turn what he himself has said about Him, we find that the matter does not become any clearer" (1934, Vol. I, p. 299).

glimpsed when he wrote, "The heavens declare the glory of God, And the firmament showeth His handiwork." As indicated in the following passage, this amounted to making God and Nature synonymous concepts (Ratner, p. 46):

> Everything takes place by the power of God. Nature herself is the power of God under another name, and our ignorance of the power of God is co-extensive with our ignorance of Nature. It is absolutely folly, therefore, to ascribe an event to the power of God when we know not its natural cause, which is the power of God.

In equating the power of God with Nature, Spinoza was giving expression to his metaphysical concept of God as both extended and thinking substance and as reflected, for example, in Kepler's laws, in Newton's laws, in the laws of chemistry, and in all uniformities of nature—especially those amenable to precise mathematical formulation. At all events, this seems to be one way of clarifying what he seemed to mean by Nature when spelled with a capital "N."

It was different from the ordinary commonsense connotation of the word. In the language of Spinoza, it called for the consideration of all happenings *sub specie aeternitatis*, or from the viewpoint of their essential or eternal aspects or implications. By doing so, one comes closer to understanding God as creative Nature [3] or as inherent in the basic lawfulness of the cosmic scheme of things. Such a God was very different from the anthropomorphic God of the medieval religionist.[4] He was not a God of caprice who could suspend His own laws by performing miracles. It was no more possible for Him to reverse the direction of the rotation of the earth than to construct a triangular quadrilateral. In short, according to the Benedictus view, God's law was natural law and natural law was God's law. Moreover, what merits special emphasis is that this concept

---

[3] The phrase "creative nature" has to do with the medieval term *natura naturans* employed by Spinoza. A discussion of his interpretation of this term is supplied by Wolfson (1934, Vol. I, pp. 251–256).

[4] Actually Spinoza was indebted to some of his medieval predecessors for his repudiation of anthropomorphic concepts of God as well as for his so-called "higher criticism" of the Bible. The shift from the Baruch to the Benedictus outlook was prepared for by these predecessors; for, according to Wolf (1929, pp. 231–232):

> Spinoza was in his twenty-second year when his father died. His studies so far had been mainly Jewish. But he was an independent thinker and he had found more than enough in his Jewish studies to wean him from orthodox theology. In the Biblical commentary by Abraham Ibn Ezra (1092–1167) one meets with many "a word to the wise" directing attention to some inconsistency in Scripture, to the post-Mosaic authorship of parts at least of the so-called "Five Books of Moses," or to the different authorship of the two parts of *Isaiah*. In the *Guide of the Perplexed* of Moses

of the pervasive lawfulness of the universe was inclusive of what Spinoza referred to as "sure mental laws" (Ratner, 1927, p. 47). By implication this suggested the possibility of making the study of mental life a *scientific* study.

Introduction to Spinoza's Psychology

Before discussing Spinoza's specific contributions to the study of mental life, it is well to note his recognition of the importance of a detached, impartial attitude in the conduct of such a study. He resolved to "consider human actions and appetites just as if I were considering lines, planes or bodies" (Ratner, 1927, p. 213). In the light of such an objective attitude, he sought to discover the laws of mental life whose existence was virtually assured by his metaphysics.

Thus, even though two hundred years were to elapse before there was to be a deliberate effort to establish psychology as a science, justification for doing so was already to be found in the metaphysics of Spinoza. This explains why it was deemed advisable to say something about his metaphysical teachings—to his notions of God and Nature—before considering his psychological teachings. Furthermore, in many respects the latter teachings came to be his chief interest in the sense that he was more concerned with the discovery of mental laws than with other laws operative in the universe. This is especially evident in his work on *Ethics,* as Wolfson points out in this comment (1934, Vol II, p. 6):

> But the main object of Spinoza's work, after he had discussed God in the First Part, is, as he himself says, "to consider those things only which may conduct us as it were by the hand to a knowledge of the human mind and its highest happiness." He therefore confines himself to those things "which concern man." His subject is thus the higher phases of human psychology and certain phases of human conduct.

Maimonides (1135–1204) attention is drawn to various crudities in Biblical theology, and to the provisional character of certain Biblical ordinances. In the writings of Gersonides (1288–1344) rationalism encroaches on miracles and prophecy in an attempt to eliminate the element of supernaturalism. Already Maimonides had insisted on interpreting Scripture in such a way as to harmonize it with reason. Gersonides went further than that. He faced the possibility of a conflict between Reason and Revelation, and maintained that, in such an event, the Bible "cannot prevent us from holding that to be true which our reason prompts us to believe." Again the popular conception of the world's creation out of nothing was denied by both Ibn Ezra and Gersonides, who believed in the eternity of matter. Maimonides also repudiated the belief that man is the center of creation, maintaining that each thing exists for its own sake; he also suggested the relativity of good and evil. The Jewish mystics had taught that Nature is animated. Crescas (1340–1410) ascribed extension to God, denied the validity of the conception of final causes (or the explanation of objects and events by reference to their alleged purposes), and, like Ibn Ezra, maintained a thoroughgoing determinism. Here was food enough for thought, and incentive enough for heresy.

Empirical Foundations of Spinoza's Rationalism

Spinoza's psychology has often been contrasted with that of Locke and the other British empiricists. In histories of philosophy he has been classified as a rationalist along with Descartes and Leibnitz. As explained in Chapter 1, empiricists tended to exalt sensory experience as the foundation of mental development, whereas rationalists attributed greater importance to the role of reason. Another way of putting this is to say that although both empiricists and rationalists recognized the importance of sensory data for the acquisition of knowledge, the empiricist derived *all* knowledge from such data while the rationalist regarded *some* knowledge as *a priori* or independent of sensory experience.

Modern defenders of the *a priori* viewpoints, such as A. C. Ewing (1962, pp. 31–58), regard logic and mathematics as fields concerned with propositions the validity of which can be established by taking thought as opposed to direct sensory inspection. If this be so, then all so-called empirical scientists are rationalists to the extent that their scientific work involves mathematical and logical considerations. In contrast, all so-called rationalists in philosophy are empiricists to the extent that they avail themselves of the results of direct sensory experience.

Under the circumstances the conventional classification of Spinoza might be open to question. As a metaphysician he was obviously a rationalist.[5] And yet in much of his philosophy and psychology he eschewed the *a priori* in favor of careful attention to the facts of experience. Because of this, after noting that Spinoza was not a mystic, Wolfson (1934, Vol. I, p. 74) described him as "a hard-headed, clear-minded empiricist, like most of the medievals and like Aristotle."

The empiricism of Spinoza is particularly evident in the frequency with which what he had to say about man turns out to be an anticipation of what generations later came to be recognized as psychological fact or as important for psychological theory. For example, as has been mentioned in Chapter 3, the Freudian concept of unconscious motivation may be viewed as an independent discovery and confirmation of what Spinoza had in mind when he wrote, "men are usually ignorant of the causes of their desires; for . . . we are conscious of our actions and desires, but ignorant of the causes by which we are determined to desire anything" (Ratner, 1927, p. 253). Similarly, Spinoza may also be said to have anticipated the Adlerian concept of feelings of inferiority as spurs to compensatory ambitious striving, for in connection with a reference

---

[5] It is illustrated, for example, by his reference to the *innate* basis for confidence in divine law in a passage in which he declared, "We have shown that the divine law, which renders men truly blessed, and teaches them the true life, is universal to all men; nay, we have so intimately deduced it from human nature that it must be esteemed innate, and, as it were, ingrained in the human mind" (Ratner, 1927, p. 88).

to feelings of despondency and humility he held that they "are very rare, for human nature, considered in itself, struggles against them as much as it can, and hence those who have the most credit for being abject and humble are generally the most ambitious and envious" (Ratner, p. 227).

Another basic feature of Adlerian psychology anticipated by Spinoza has to do with what Adler called *Gemeinschaftsgefühl* or the feeling of belonging to or being identified with or accepted by the community or some social group. Without such affiliation, Adler taught, there can be no healthy personality development and one feels friendless, isolated, rejected, rootless, and alone. What he taught about the importance of *Gemeinschaftsgefühl* may be regarded as an elaboration of what Spinoza compressed into this single sentence (Ratner, p. 289):

> Above all things it is profitable to men to form communities and to unite themselves to one another by bonds which may make all of them as one man; and absolutely, it is profitable for them to do whatever may tend to strengthen their friendships.

Discovery in Psychology as Rediscovery

Such anticipations of Freudian, Adlerian, and other psychological teachings suggest that, owing to psychology's long philosophic past, many seemingly original discoveries in psychology are likely to be rediscoveries. Psychology may still be waiting for its Galileo or its Newton or its Darwin. As E. R. Hilgard has noted (1965, p. 37):

> It is one of the awkwardnesses of psychology as a science that owing to the anticipations of philosophers and thinkers throughout the ages profound discoveries are very rare; the problems of psychology are too close to home to have been neglected, although by the same token the solutions to psychological problems are slow to achieve objective verification because every thinker is his own psychologist and clings strongly to his own interpretations.

This relative absence of strikingly original discoveries in the history of psychology is not to be construed as the absence of genuine progress in man's quest for understanding of his human nature. Although the statement to the effect that all seemingly original discoveries are likely to be rediscoveries holds true for basic ideas or key concepts, it does not for their detailed elaboration. Even though, as was shown in Chapter 4, the notion of configurations or *Gestalten* was already evident to Aristotle, it would be a gross distortion of fact to dismiss the contributions of modern *Gestalt* psychologists as nothing but a rediscovery of what was already known to Aristotle. It would be equally fatuous to equate Spinoza's anticipations of the concepts of the unconscious motivation and of compensation for feelings of inferiority with what Freudians and Adlerians have done with these concepts.

If space permitted, it would be possible to demonstrate that many of Spinoza's views regarding ethics, Biblical interpretation, political administration, and psychology had been anticipated by Aristotle, by medieval rabbis, by Hobbes, and by Descartes, respectively. However, his treatment of these anticipations rendered them more than a mere repetition or precise duplication of these older teachings. By way of illustration, his handling of some Cartesian views will prove helpful. As indicated in Chapter 12, his familiarity with the work of Descartes is shown by the fact that the only book published under his own name in his lifetime was his *Principles of Cartesian Philosophy* (translated by H. E. Wedeck, 1961). This book was not so much an endorsement of these principles as an exposition of their nature for the enlightenment of students.

Spinoza's Theory of Mind

In fact, even though both Spinoza and Descartes have been classified as rationalists, in many respects Spinoza was definitely anti-Cartesian. His opposition was evident in his effort to substitute a monistic metaphysics in place of the dualistic metaphysics of Descartes. As already described in Chapter 9, pp. 233–235, this resulted in his double-aspect theory as an alternative to Cartesian interactionism. His own formulation of this theory took this form (Ratner, p. 352):

> The order and connection of ideas is the same as the order and connection of things, and *vice versa,* the order and connection of things is the same as the order and connection of ideas. Therefore, as the order and connection of ideas in the mind is according to the order and connection of the modifications of the body it follows *vice versa,* that the order and connection of the modifications of the body is according to the order and connection in the mind of the thoughts and ideas of things.

This was very different from the Cartesian view of mind as inextended substance having a separate existence from the extended substance of the body with occasional interaction via the pineal gland. Spinoza denied such separate existence. For him, mind and body constituted an inseparable union. In Spinoza's era this was both a novel and daring contention and prompted Wolfson to conclude (1934, Vol. II, p. 53):

> This must be considered the essential point in Spinoza's theory of mind—its inseparability from the body. It runs counter to the entire trend of the history of philosophy down to his time, for everybody before him, for diverse reasons, insisted upon the separability of mind from body.

Spinoza's Theory of Emotion

Spinoza's recognition of the inherent inseparability of mind and body was strikingly evident in his discussion of emotion. In fact, what William James and Carl Georg Lange (1834–1900), writing in the 1880s, had to say about emotion as bodily commotion is essentially consistent with what Spinoza had to say more than two centuries earlier. What has come to be called the James-Lange theory might thus be regarded as the equivalent of Spinoza's theory. One might even conjecture that had James been reminded of Spinoza's formulation, he would have welcomed it as support for his own formulation. For James, it may be recalled, there can be no emotional experience apart from bodily changes. By way of reminder it may suffice to consider the following excerpt from James's long chapter on emotion (1890, Vol. II, p. 451):

> I now proceed to urge the vital point of my whole theory, which is this: *If we fancy some strong emotion, and then try to abstract from our consciousness of it all the feelings of its bodily symptoms, we find we have nothing left behind,* no "mind-stuff" out of which the emotion can be constituted, and that a cold and neutral state of intellectual perception is all that remains.

In the definition of emotion supplied by Spinoza the bodily symptoms mentioned by James are referred to as "modifications of the body" and our "ideas of these modifications" constitute a reference to what James had described as consciousness of the bodily symptoms. With this in mind the absence of a basic difference in the two views becomes obvious, for Spinoza defined emotion as follows (Ratner, p. 213):

> By emotion I understand the modifications of the body, by which the power of acting of the body itself is increased, diminished, helped, or hindered, together with the ideas of these modifications.

In this definition, to revert to an earlier comment, one can also note Spinoza's empiricism, for it is a fact of experience that the bodily upheaval characteristic of emotion may have facilitating or inhibiting effects on action. Spinoza made this one of his postulates which took this form (Ratner, p. 214): "The human body can be affected in many ways, by which its power of acting is increased or diminished, and also in other ways which make its power of acting neither greater nor less." Spinoza failed to supply specific examples of these many ways, presumably because for him there was no need to illustrate something so obvious as the way in which some fears promote active flight and others result in helpless paralysis. Similarly, anger may result in energetic, well-coordinated fighting behavior, while intense rage may militate against such coordinated efficiency. Both terror and rage may leave their victims speechless and impotent. By means of such commonsense, everyday observations, it is easy to find empirical support for Spinoza's definition.[6] Incidentally, the word for "emotion" employed by Spinoza is the Latin word *"affectus"*; hence the technical meaning in psychology of the word "affection" as a generic term for "feeling" and "emotion" in contradistinction to its more restricted popular meaning of "a liking for somebody."

The Problem of Basic Emotions and the Concept of Basic Conatus

Another aspect of the psychology of emotion considered by Spinoza has to do with the nature and number of primary emotions. Here the question of basic or elementary emotions is involved. It is comparable to the question of elementary gustatory or color sensations or like asking what kinds of emotion can be aroused in the very young infant at the very start of its emotional history.

Spinoza was not the first to consider this issue, for it had also been of interest both to Hobbes and to Descartes. In the *Leviathan*, Hobbes had listed seven "simple passions called appetite, desire, love, aversion, hate, joy, and grief." In his view, as these become combined or modified in the course of experience, more complex emotional patterns come into existence. These give rise to the long list of words to designate the resulting nuances of emotion—words like "jealousy," "contempt," "elation," and "dejection," etc. Hobbes even ventured to define some of the latter words. Following Hobbes, Descartes in his *The Passions of the Soul* argued that the complexity of emotional experience can be accounted for in terms of these six elementary "passions": joy, sadness, wonder, love, hate, and desire.

Spinoza was more parsimonious than either Hobbes or Descartes, since he reduced the list to the three emotions of joy, sorrow, and desire,[7] and concluded that "besides these three" he knew "of no other primary emotion, the others springing from these" (Ratner, p. 217). Both the primary and derived emotions are either direct or indirect functions of

---

[6] The well-known studies of W. B. Cannon (1920) might be cited as giving experimental support to the definition. At least this applies to the dynamogenic effects of emotion—to an increase in the body's "power of acting." In his emergency theory of emotion Cannon neglected to consider instances of a decrease in this power. This was brought out years ago in a provocative paper by C. Kling (1933, pp. 368–380).

[7] These are common English equivalents for the Latin terms employed by Spinoza: *"laetitia"* for "joy," *"tristitia"* for "sorrow," and *"cupiditas"* for "desire." However, his own definitions of these words differed somewhat from the ordinary meaning of their English equivalents.

what Spinoza regarded as "the basic endeavor of all things" to "persevere" in their own being. By this "basic endeavor" or *conatus*, as Wolfson (1939, Vol. II, p. 338) makes clear, Spinoza was referring to the principle or law of self-preservation operative in the universe:

> In its universality this law applies to every individual thing within the universe, man as well as beast, and in a certain sense also to inanimate objects. Each particular thing within the universe, by the eternal necessity of the nature of the universe as a whole of which it is a part, strives to maintain its existence, which is life in the case of living beings and motion in the case of non-living beings.

This reference to self-preservation is not to be interpreted in the restricted meaning of a struggle to maintain life when threatened by danger. Instead it refers to what was previously described in Spinoza's phrase as the *conatus* to persevere in one's own being. It constitutes the source of all striving, longing, ambition, self-expression, or of what Kurt Goldstein (1963 [1940], p. 120) includes in his concept of "coming to terms with the world." Goldstein regards self-actualization as the matrix of all motivation, or as what he calls the "basic drive" which accounts for all human activity. He questions the existence of isolated motives or separate drives in mature, healthy individuals. As isolated phenomena they are products of immaturity when noted in children, or pathology when observed in adults, and of artificial laboratory restrictions when reported by animal psychologists. There thus seems to be a close relationship between Spinoza's "basic *conatus*" and Goldstein's "basic drive" of self-actualization.

Spinoza Opposed to Hedonism

The "basic *conatus*" as described by Spinoza manifests itself in all expressions of striving, wishing, seeking, and desiring. Moreover, as a theory of motivation it is at variance with hedonistic theories, which hold the pursuit of pleasure to be the regnant principle of motivation. Such theories tend to make pleasure the object of human endeavor, as if what is deemed to be pleasurable or good in the abstract determines the direction of endeavor.

Spinoza recognized that nothing is pleasurable or good in the abstract but is always a function of antecedent desire or striving. To cite a commonplace example: To be forced to eat in the absence of hunger may result in nausea or some other nonpleasurable consequence. Food would constitute an evil and not a good for the victim of such coercion. The relativity of good and evil, as expressed by Spinoza, took this form (Ratner, pp. 254–255):

With regard to good and evil, these terms indicate nothing positive in things considered in themselves, nor are they anything else than modes of thought, or notions which we form from the comparison of one thing with another. For one and the same thing may at the same time be both good and evil or indifferent. Music, for example, is good to a melancholy person, bad to one mourning, while to a deaf man it is neither good nor bad. But although things are so, we must retain these words. For since we desire to form for ourselves an idea of man upon which we may look as a model of human nature, it will be of service to us to retain these expressions in the sense I have mentioned.

By *good,* therefore, I understand . . . everything we are certain is a means by which we may approach nearer and nearer to the model of human nature we set before us. By *evil,* on the contrary, I understand everything which we are certain hinders us from reaching that model.

From the foregoing it is clear that Spinoza was sponsoring a goal-directed theory of motivation, in terms of which pleasure and unpleasure as good and evil are envisaged as by-products of success and failure in moving toward or away from desired goals and are not to be confused with or identified with the goals as such. For example, the goal of a conscientious physician is to cure his patient and will be pursued even though it involves a long bedside vigil entailing cancellation of the afternoon's golf and the evening's concert. The model of the ideal physician he has set before himself renders such cancellation inevitable. By hypothesis, neither the pleasures of golf nor of music are permitted to deflect him from the professional task at hand. His desire to safeguard the welfare of his patient rather than a desire for pleasure as such will determine his choice of "good" medical procedures. Both he and his conscientious medical colleagues might, if they were familiar with Spinoza's view of motivation, justify their stand by saying (Ratner, p. 216), "We neither strive for, wish, seek nor desire anything because we think it to be good, but on the contrary, we adjudge a thing to be good because we strive for, wish, seek, or desire it."

Dynamic Psychology in the Making

The preceding quotation reveals the broad extent of Spinoza's concept of conation. It encompasses both motivational as well as emotional factors: both the instigators of overt action as well as the covert "modifications of the body" mentioned in his definition of emotion. Emotion may thus be regarded as the affective aspect of conation and motivation as its effective aspect. For Spinoza, conation as the process of striving toward goals implied being moved as well as moving. In physiological terms this implies activation of the autonomic as well as the cerebrospinal nervous systems.

In regarding desire as a primary emotion as well as the essential characteristic of "basic endeavor" or *conatus,* Spinoza was supplying a hint of what was to emerge along the lines of the dynamic psychologies of the modern period. As just indicated, he used words like "striving," "wishing," and "desiring" as synonymous terms. In other words, long before Freud, he noted the motivational import of the wish. He also noted the existence of wishful thinking and of rationalization long before these ego-defensive maneuvers had been given these descriptive labels. That he recognized them as factors in the dynamics of mental life is evident in the following excerpt from his discussion of hatred and the *endeavors* it generates (Ratner, p. 240):

> If we imagine that we are hated by another without having given him any cause for it, we shall hate him in return. If we imagine that we have given just cause for the hatred, we shall then be affected with shame. This, however, rarely happens; we endeavor to affirm everything, . . . concerning ourselves . . . which we imagine will affect us . . . with joy, and on the contrary, we endeavor to deny everything that will affect . . . ourselves with sorrow.

Furthermore, in connection with his concept of desire as having both conative and affective aspects, Spinoza called attention to another issue which came to have great importance for modern dynamic psychologists; namely, the role of mental conflict in human affairs. Although he failed to employ the actual phrase "mental conflict," he was clearly cognizant of its nature and existence. For example, in one of his explanations of the word "desire" there is this unambiguous reference to the phenomenon of mental conflict (Ratner, p. 218):

> By the word "desire," therefore, I understand all the efforts, impulses, appetites, and volitions of a man, which vary according to his changing disposition, and not unfrequently and so opposed to one another that he is drawn hither and thither, and knows not whither he ought to turn.

On Popular Versus Technical Definitions

This quotation embodies Spinoza's definition of desire as one of the three primary emotions. He not only supplied definitions of joy and sorrow, the two other "primitive or primary emotions," but also of a long series of emotions for which we have names in ordinary speech. Before considering some of these definitions, it is advisable to note that they are not identical with dictionary definitions giving the common meaning of the names in question. Spinoza was well aware of this discrepancy, for as he explained (Ratner, p. 223):

> I am aware that these names in common bear a different meaning. But my object is not to explain the meaning of words but the nature of things, and

to indicate them by words whose customary meaning shall not be altogether opposed to the meaning which I desire to bestow upon them.

Stated a little differently, Spinoza was proposing technical as contrasted with popular definitions of words descriptive of the gamut of emotional states. In doing so, he was establishing a precedent for later scientific psychology when words of everyday usage were retained but given technical definitions somewhat different from although not "altogether opposed to the meaning" they ordinarily suggest. For example, the word "red" as part of our vocabulary of color has both an everyday, popular dictionary meaning as well as a technical meaning. The ordinary dictionary definition will have references to pink, scarlet, ruby, and the color of blood by way of explaining the meaning of the word. On the other hand, a psychological dictionary in its technical definition of the word dispenses with such clarifying references and instead states that red is "a visual sensation typically evoked by stimulation of the normal retina with radiation of wave-lengths within the range of 670 to 760 millimicrons" (H. C. Warren, 1934, p. 226). Without special explanation of the terms employed, the uninitiated would be baffled by such a technical definition. For comparable reasons, without initiation into Spinoza's technical philosophic vocabulary, his definitions of ordinary words like "joy" and "sorrow" are not likely to be understood. He does not use these words as designations for *feelings* of gladness and sadness in accordance with their dictionary definitions. Instead he defines them as follows (Ratner, p. 218):

Joy is man's passage from a less to a greater perfection.
Sorrow is man's passage from a greater to a less perfection.

In these definitions the word "perfection" is a synonym for reality, as Spinoza made clear when he wrote, "By reality and perfection I understand the same thing" (Ratner, p. 156). This does not refer to perfection in the sense of *flawless* accomplishment, for it would be absurd to speak of a "greater" degree of flawlessness. In this context the phrase "greater perfection" as a synonym for "greater reality" suggests progressive accomplishment or coming closer to the *realization* of what one is striving to attain or complete. This makes joy and sorrow functions of the striving or *conatus* toward the *desired* goal; hence, desire, joy, and sorrow as the primary emotions. Support for this interpretation is indicated by the fact that Spinoza employs the word "passage" in his definitions of joy and sorrow. He does not call them feelings. Instead for him they have to do with transitions toward or away from ends to be realized.

Some Derived Emotions Defined

Having specified the nature of the primary or primitive emotions, Spinoza proceeded to supply definitions of emotions derived from them. In some instances he contented himself with the formulated definition and in others he provided an explanation for his formulation. It will suffice to introduce just a few of his definitions by way of illustrating his general approach to the psychology of emotion and conation. He himself did something of this sort, for he explained that his list of emotions is by no means exhaustive. In fact, he held that it was sufficient for his "purpose to have enumerated only those which are of consequence" and, furthermore, "that the emotions can be combined in so many ways, and that so many variations can arise, that no limits can be assigned to their number" (Ratner, p. 234). Among those he regarded as "of consequence" were six he listed in order and then compared in a final explanation. These were courtesy, ambition, luxuriousness, drunkenness, avarice, and lust. They constitute a convenient means of demonstrating his way of disposing of the problem of derived emotions. This is what he had to say about them (Ratner, pp. 230–232):

Courtesy or *moderation* is the desire of doing those things which please men and omitting those which displease them.
Ambition is the immoderate desire of glory.
Explanation.—Ambition is a desire which increases and strengthens all the emotions, and that is the reason why it can hardly be kept under control. For so long as a man is possessed by any desire, he is necessarily at the same time possessed by this. *Every noble man,* says Cicero, *is led by glory, and even the philosophers who write books about despising glory place their names on the title-page.*
Luxuriousness is the immoderate desire or love of good living.
Drunkenness is the immoderate desire and love of drinking.
Avarice is the immoderate desire and love of riches.
Lust is the immoderate desire and love of sexual intercourse.
Explanation —This desire of sexual intercourse is usually called lust, whether it be held within bounds or not. I may add that the five last-mentioned emotions have no contraries, for moderation is a kind of ambition, and I have already observed that temperance, sobriety, and chastity show a power and not a passion of the mind. Even supposing that an avaricious, ambitious, or timid man refrains from an excess of eating, drinking or sexual intercourse, avarice, ambition, and fear are not therefore the opposites of voluptuousness, drunkenness, or lust. For the avaricious man generally desires to swallow as much meat and drink as he can, provided only it belongs to another person. The ambitious man, too, if he hopes he can keep it a secret, will restrain himself in nothing, and if he lives amongst drunkards and libertines, will be more inclined to their

vices just because he is ambitious. The avaricious man, too, does what he does not will; and although, in order to avoid death, he may throw his riches into the sea, he remains avaricious; nor does the lascivious man cease to be lascivious because he is sorry that he cannot gratify his desire. Absolutely, therefore, these emotions have reference not so much to the acts themselves of eating and drinking as to the appetite and love itself. Consequently, nothing can be opposed to these emotions but nobility of soul and strength of mind.[8]

The emotions considered in the preceding quotation suffice to indicate the way in which Spinoza, by regarding each of them as derivatives of *desire,* made them secondary elaborations of one of his three primary emotions. In comparable fashion he defined other emotions as derivatives of the primary emotions of joy and sorrow. As elaborations of joy, for example, he defined "gladness" as "a joy with the accompanying idea of something past, which, unhoped for, has happened," and "self-satisfaction" as "the joy which is produced by contemplating ourselves and our own power of action." Instances of his elaborations of sorrow are supplied by the definition of "remorse" as "sorrow with the accompanying idea of something past, which, unhoped for, has happened" or by the definition of "humility" as "the sorrow which is produced by contemplating our impotence or helplessness." To understand these definitions it is, of course, necessary to restrict the meaning of "joy" and "sorrow" to what, as previously explained, Spinoza meant by relating these terms to his concept of perfection.

Classification of Emotions: A Persistent Problem

In the light of this sketch of Spinoza's analysis of the complexities of emotion, it is evident that he tried to be comprehensive and systematic. In his distinction between primary and derived emotions as well as in his effort to outline an orderly classification of emotions, he was setting a precedent for later approaches to the problem. His successors in the eighteenth and nineteenth centuries were also concerned with the question of elementary emotions and their modification in the course of development. There was little agreement in the resulting accounts. James expressed his disappointment in them in trenchant language (1890, Vol. II, p. 448):

But as far as "scientific psychology" of the emotions goes, I may have been surfeited by too much reading of classic works on the subject, but I should as lief

---

[8] This allusion to "strength of mind" indicates that, despite the monism presupposed by his double-aspect theory, Spinoza lapsed into the language of dualism. He even explains his failure to consider such "external modifications of the body which are observed in the emotions, such as trembling, paleness, sobbing, laughter, and the like, . . . because they belong to the body alone without any relationship to the mind" (Ratner, p. 235).

read verbal descriptions of the shapes of the rocks on a New Hampshire farm as toil through them again. They give one nowhere a central point of view, or a deductive or generative principle. They distinguish and refine and specify *in infinitum* without ever getting on to another logical level.

Since Spinoza antedated the existence of a "scientific psychology," James could not have been including him in this indictment of the "scientific" approach to the psychology of emotion. In fact, there is only a single reference to Spinoza in the two volumes of the *Principles,* and this one has nothing to do with emotion. From the context it appears that the indictment was directed at nineteenth-century efforts to describe and classify emotions in terms of physiological characteristics, biological origins, modes of arousal, range of variations, etc. These efforts did not yet include any direct experimental studies of emotion. At least James failed to mention any such studies,[9] so that his indictment is not to be construed as a criticism of the then new "scientific psychology" as an *experimental* enterprise.

Whether James would have withdrawn his indictment had he lived long enough to witness twentieth-century experimental studies of emotion is open to question. Rather early in the century there was a famous pioneer experimental attack on the question of primary emotions. This was undertaken by John B. Watson and J. J. B. Morgan (1917, pp. 163–174), who observed the emotional reactions of very young babies to a variety of stimulating conditions. In their findings they agreed with Spinoza regarding the number of primary emotions but differed radically from the ones he recognized as primary.

In place of his emotions of desire, joy, and sorrow they reported fear, rage, and love as the sole primitive or unlearned emotional reactions. More definitely, they found fear to be elicited by loud sounds or sudden loss of support, rage to be a response to hampering or restriction of bodily movement, and love when defined as expansive bodily relaxation to be the consequence of gentle stroking of the skin and erogenous zones. Unfortunately, these findings were not confirmed by subsequent studies. Babies failed to react with stereotyped consistency to each of these stimulating conditions. Sudden loss of support, for example, did not always result in a cry of fear. It is to be understood, of course, that Watson and Morgan were not pretending to report on what the babies might have been experiencing. In their use of words like "fear" and "rage," they were exclusively concerned with observable bodily changes.

Similarly, in a later study by K. M. B. Bridges (1932, pp. 324–334) involving developmental changes in emotional expression from birth on through the first two years, modification of overt behavior was the basis for the descriptive vocabulary employed. According to Bridges, there

---

[9] He did mention Gustav Fechner's (1801–1887) experimental studies of aesthetic judgments.

are no specific differentiated emotions manifest at birth. Instead, all one detects is an undifferentiated state of agitation or excitement. If so, then there is a single primary emotion to be called "excitement," from which other emotional patterns are to be differentiated as the infant grows older. At six months, for instance, Bridges noted manifestations of distress, delight, fear, anger, and disgust. By the end of the year, elation and affection were added to the list, to be followed by jealousy at about eighteen months and by joy by the end of the second year. Quite evidently maturation was operative as these differentiations took place. Still, such maturation may also have been influenced by what the infants experienced in the way of social stimulation and random exploratory behavior. Consequently, aside from the pattern of excitement it is difficult to justify classification of those later emerging emotional patterns as definitely primary in the sense of having been uninfluenced by learning experiences.

Emotional development in early infancy is a product of the conjoint influence of maturation and conditioning—of growth and social interac-action.[10] As a result, it has not yet been possible to establish the nature and number of primary emotions by experimentally controlled studies of infant development.

McDougall's Theory of Instincts

Independently of these studies of the emotional reactions of infants, there was another approach to the problem of primary emotions that came into prominence early in the present century. This was an outgrowth of an observation stressed by James in the opening paragraph of his chapter on the emotions, where he introduced this italicized sentence (1890, Vol. II, p. 442): *"Every object that excites an instinct excites an emotion as well."* James failed to elaborate upon the implications of this sentence as an approach to the problem in question. This was left to William McDougall (1871–1938), who, as an ardent admirer of the writings of James, was undoubtedly familiar with this sentence. It may be thought of as an inspiration leading to the system of psychology McDougall came to sponsor.

In this system he elevated the concept of instinctive urges into a pivotal doctrine by regarding them as the driving forces of behavior. He viewed all behavior as a direct or indirect expression of such urges. Because of this emphasis he called his psychology a *hormic* psychology, since "hormic" in terms of its Greek origin suggests that which has to do with an urge to action.

What he meant by hormic psychology was explained in 1908 in his widely circulated *Introduction to Social Psychology*. In it he pointed out that man is

---

[10] The relevance of social interaction for control and understanding of such development is clearly brought out in the monograph by R. A. Spitz and K. M. Wolf (1946).

endowed with some twelve instincts each of which prompts him to pay attention to objects of a certain class, to be emotionally aroused by these objects, and to feel impelled to deal with them in a certain way. For example, the instinct of curiosity prompts a person to pay attention to something novel or strange, to experience the emotion of wonder, and to have an urge to examine or explore the object of his curiosity. In the case of the parental instinct, to cite another example, a helpless and terrified child is likely to arouse the immediate interest of a concerned adult, a characteristic *tender emotion,*[11] along with a desire to protect, comfort, and reassure the youngster. In other words, according to the hormic theory, every instinct involves perceptual, affective, and impulsive features: attention-getting stimuli, specific emotions, and definite strivings or desires.

McDougall did not regard the instincts as stereotyped, mechanical, permanently fixed modes of behavior. Instead, he recognized their modifiability both with respect to mode of arousal as well as mode of response. The instinct of pugnacity may serve as a convenient illustration. Combativeness comes to be touched off by a wide gamut of stimulus situations, from the frustrations of young children to aspersions on the honor of mature adults. We do not learn to be angry, but we do learn what to be angry about. Similarly, the desire to attack or punish the object of our anger is unlearned; but how the desire is to be expressed is a product of experience. It varies in extent from the biting and scratching of the young child to the libel suit of the litigious adult.

As a reaction to interference, such a desire and its concomitant emotion constitute the permanent core of the instinct which does not change from childhood to old age. This applies to the central core of each of the other instincts in McDougall's list. Both babies and adults feel hungry and desire food and with respect to this feeling and desire, there is no change throughout life. What is changed, though, is the kind of food preferred and the manner of getting it into the mouth. Table manners are learned, not instinctive. Most food preferences and aversions are also learned and not instinctive. For this reason it makes sense to speak of a cultivated appetite and nonsense to speak of a cultivated hunger.

Instincts Changed to Propensities

Even though McDougall was explicit in recognizing the modifiability of instinct, this recognition seems to have been overlooked by some of his critics. This applied particularly to those sociologists like L. L. Bernard

---

11 McDougall very likely owes this term to Alexander Bain (1818–1903). At all events, James (1890, Vol. II, p. 458) credits Bain with having introduced the term. Support for this is to be found in the fact that Bain's book on *The Emotions and the Will* has an entire chapter under the heading of "Tender Emotion." A. Bain, *The Emotion and the Will*, 3rd ed (New York: D. Appleton and Company, 1875), Chapter VII.

(1924) and psychologists like K. Dunlap (1919), who had become disenchanted with the concept of instinct as a valid or useful scientific concept. This gave rise to the anti-instinct controversy of the 1920s and much talk about the preponderant importance of environmental influences and learning experiences in shaping the patterns of human behavior. Social forces were played up and instinctive forces were played down. By this time there was uncertainty regarding the meaning of the term "instinct" and some psychologists hesitated to employ it for fear of being misunderstood.

Accordingly, McDougall decided to scrap the term and in a book published in 1932, he introduced the word "propensity" as a designation for the unlearned emotional-impulsive core of human behavior. As had been the case with the discarded term as discussed in the 1908 volume, the new term provided for modification of each propensity as a result of learning and experience. However, this modification was still restricted to the perceptual and response aspects of the propensities. As emotional-impulsive cores they were not subject to modification. As angers, fears, lusts, hungers, fatigues, feelings of tenderness, and other affective states, along with their respective impulses to action, they were presumed to remain the same throughout life. Furthermore, they continued to be viewed as unlearned or native features of man's psychobiological organization.

Still, as a hormic psychologist, McDougall was less concerned with the question of their native or instinctive origin than he was with having these cores or propensities recognized as the sources of man's goal-directed strivings. Man was to be recognized as a creature of endeavor, of aims, and of purposes, not as a complex, purposeless stimulus-response mechanism. Unlike the 1908 volume with its emphasis on instincts, the 1932 volume with its emphasis on propensities was not so much an "introduction to social psychology" as it was "a study of the fundamentals of dynamic psychology." Hormic psychology had become a synonym for dynamic psychology. In fact, shortly before the appearance of the 1932 volume McDougall made this clear in what amounted to a crusading article entitled "The Hormic Psychology" (C. Murchison [ed.], 1930).

The Crusade against Mechanistic Psychology

It was a crusade against mechanistic psychology in behalf of a teleological psychology. By mechanistic psychology McDougall meant a psychology patterned after the conceptual framework of the physical sciences. He was most emphatic about this when he explained (C. Murchison [ed.], p. 4) that hormic psychology is a psychology

> which refuses to be bound and limited by the principles current in the physical sciences; which asserts that active striving towards a goal is a fundamental category of psychology, and is a process of a type that cannot be mechanistically explained or resolved into mechanistic sequences; which leaves it to the future

development of the sciences to decide whether . . . we are to have ultimately one science of nature, or two, the mechanistic and the teleological. For hormic psychology is not afraid to use teleological description and explanation. Rather, it insists that those of our activities which we can at all adequately describe are unmistakably and undeniably teleological, are activities which we undertake in the pursuit of some goal, for the sake of some result which we foresee and desire to achieve.

Extrinsic Versus Intrinsic Teleology

This was a bold stand to take. It ran counter to prevalent opinion regarding the scientific respectability of the concept of teleology. As a concept it had theological connotations stemming from medieval teachings regarding God's purposes in directing the course of mundane events by supernatural intervention. To account for earthquakes or plagues as God's way of punishing man for his sins would illustrate this mode of teleological thinking.

McDougall was explicit in his repudiation of this interpretation of the concept. This was not the kind of teleology he was advocating. His kind had nothing to do with supernatural forces, God's purposes, or Satan's designs. Belief in such forces, purposes, or designs exemplifies what McDougall called *extrinsic* teleology in contradistinction to *intrinsic* teleology. Failure to make this distinction, McDougall maintained, had resulted in confusing the teleology implicit in man's purposive behavior with the teleology of theologians. As a consequence, *all* teleological considerations had come to be viewed as the equivalent of interference with the course of natural events by a *deus ex machina*.

Moreover, since the time of Newton, the physical sciences had been increasingly successful in accounting for natural events by means of measurable cause-and-effect sequences. As mechanists, the physicists explained such sequences without recourse to the concept of purpose. They did their scientific thinking in terms of concepts like mass, momentum, inertia, and acceleration, not in terms of concepts like striving, intending, desiring, needing, and planning. The latter concepts as germane to human behavior have to do with *intrinsic* teleology and this serves to differentiate them from the former concepts.

The behavior of a man walking downhill to a corner for the purpose of mailing a letter does not lend itself to the same kind of explanation as that used by the physicist watching a billiard ball roll down an inclined plane. There is no question of what the ball is trying to accomplish; hence no need for teleology in the mechanistic world of the physicist. It is a world devoid of purpose, or in McDougall's term an "ateleological" world. In his view, mechanistic explanations are *ateleological* explanations, and according to him, there is no other way of defining the word *mechanistic* "than this negative way which defines it by excluding all trace of teleology, all reference to the future; mechanistic means ateleological" (1930, p. 6).

In effect, by equating mechanistic explanations with ateleological explanations, McDougall was expressing his opposition to those who equated scientific psychology with adherence to the principles of physicalism. The language of physics could not be used to explain the fact of purpose in human life. Purpose and all it implies in the way of intentions, aspirations, and strivings looms too large in the life of man to be ignored by psychologists; hence the need for a hormic psychology as a corrective to mechanistic, stimulus-response psychologies. This, in short, was the gist of McDougall's polemic.

By making a distinction between extrinsic and intrinsic teleology, McDougall was making a distinction between unscientific and scientific notions of teleology. Intrinsic teleology brought the fact of intention or purpose into line with what had become scientifically acceptable, non-mystical efforts to account for the dynamics of mental life. As mentioned in Chapter 4, p. 80, Brentano's act psychology constituted one such effort—one that was not without influence on McDougall's thinking.[12] It might even be argued that Brentano's intentional inexistence had become McDougall's intrinsic teleology.

Hormic Psychology Opposed to Hedonistic Psychology

Furthermore, nineteenth-century hedonistic psychology, with its emphasis on pleasure and pain as goads and guides to action, can also be thought of as a psychology whose sponsors had come to recognize the importance and scientific respectability of a concept like teleological causation. As a matter of fact, McDougall thought of it in this way even though he could not give it unqualified endorsement. In particular he objected to it as a general theory of motivated behavior. Hormic psychology was not to be confused with hedonistic psychology. After referring to the "truth" of what hedonism had to say about pain inducing action calculated to promote avoidance or riddance of distress and about pleasure as making for activity likely to initiate or prolong pleasantness, McDougall declared (C. Murchison [ed.], p. 12):

> But it is false if put forward as a general theory of all action. We do seek to prolong pleasant activities and to get rid of pain. But it is not true that all, or indeed any large proportion, of our activities can be explained in this way. Our seeking of a goal, our pursuit of an end, is an activity that commonly incurs pleasure or pain; but these are incidental consequences. Our striving after food, or a mate, or power, knowledge, revenge, or relief of others' suffering is commonly

---

[12] This influence may be attributed to McDougall's familiarity with the writings of G. F. Stout, the British supporter of Brentano's act psychology. In his memorial tribute to McDougall, C. Spearman (1939, p. 175) lists Stout as one from whom McDougall "derived especial benefit" in the course of his psychological studies.

but little influenced by the hedonic effects incident to our striving. The conation is prior to, and not dependent upon, its hedonic accompaniments, though these may and do modify its course.

McDougall held that conation with its affective concomitants, although having its genesis in the instincts or propensities, advances beyond this genesis as psychological maturity is achieved. He did not hold that all adult striving is a direct manifestation of instinctive striving, nor did he hold that all the nuances of adult emotion are direct expressions of the primary emotions characteristic of the activated instincts.

The Concept of Sentiment

The strivings and emotions of the mature adult are far too complex to be amenable to this kind of reductive analysis. Their complexity is an outgrowth of the way in which the conative-affective "cores" of the instincts become organized into more or less enduring dispositions in the course of personality development. Such dispositions or *sentiments*, rather than simple instincts, come to prevail as the chief motivating factors in adult years. What one comes to regard as an important personal value is likely to give rise to a sentiment. Thus a patriot's love of country, a mother's devotion to her child, the religionist's preoccupation with the church, the artisan's zeal for good workmanship, a laborer's pride in his union, a person's anxiety about a sick friend, and a professor's interest[13] in his reputation as a scholar are all instances of what McDougall meant by the term *"sentiment."* They are all instances of matters of vital concern to the persons mentioned.

By way of further clarification, it is well to note that McDougall did not regard love as a simple emotion or as an innate propensity. Instead, it is to be classified as a sentiment. As such it may come to involve many strivings and emotions, depending on provocative circumstances. Thus because of his love for a son, a father may feel lonely when the boy is away at college, angry when the boy neglects his studies, anxious at times of serious illness, elated when he recovers, proud if he should graduate with honors, sad if he should fail to graduate, and, in short, find himself ready to safeguard the boy's welfare at all times. This sentiment obviously involves far more than the tender emotion of the parental instinct although it too may continue to be a latent and sometimes manifest constituent of the array of emotionalized attitudes just enumerated.

Because of his close identification with his son, the father's love for the

---

13 The word "interest" is especially important in the present context: for its etymology suggests "being concerned" or "that which is of advantage or of value to us." It comes from the Latin infinitive *"interese,"* meaning "to be concerned." In the present indicative, the third person singular is *"interest,"* meaning "it concerns"; hence whatever is related to our desires or scheme of values can become an object of interest to us.

boy is very likely to be fused with another sentiment; namely, what McDougall called the sentiment of *self-regard* and what he designated as "the most important of all the sentiments, by reason of its strength and the frequency and far reaching nature of its operations." It has to do with the development of one's reaction-sensitivity to expressions of approval or disapproval, to ego-enhancing compliments and ego-deflating slurs, and to whatever has a bearing on reputation or social status. It has to do with self-respect and self-disparagement and with readiness to defend one's honor or to act as if there is no honor worth defending. In the latter instance, one is resignedly submissive, in the former, actively self-assertive. McDougall referred (1923, p. 427) to these contrasting attitudes as "the two great conative dispositions of self-assertion and submission" and as the "two main tendencies of the sentiment" of self-regard.

The foundation of hormic psychology, it should now be evident, is to be found in the affective-conative nature of the propensities and their subsequent organization into sentiments. Man's conduct is chiefly a function of his sentiments rather than his unmodified instincts or propensities. As "moral sentiments" they determine his notions of right and wrong, of justice and injustice, and become constituents of the master sentiment of self-regard.

And once again it is well to note that the concept of sentiment as used here is not just a way of feeling but also connotes modes of judgment and conation. Feelings are involved, but not the kind suggested by the word "sentimental" in the sense of maudlin, mawkish, insincere emotions. Such adjectives are not applicable to activation of the moral sentiments and the concurrent arousal of feelings like righteous indignation, hatred of cruelty, contempt for deceit, disgust with vulgarity, and love for benevolence, courage, and other virtues. All such feelings or emotions are reflections of character and indicate how their possessor is impelled to act; for character, as defined by McDougall, is "the system of directed conative tendencies" and as exemplified by "the finest type is that which is complex, strongly and harmoniously organized, and directed toward the realization of higher goals or ideals" (1923, p. 417).

What McDougall and Spinoza Have in Common

The preceding hasty review of the essentials of McDougall's hormic psychology might seem out of place in a chapter centering on the psychological contributions of Spinoza. It is a digression, but not an irrelevant one. What makes it relevant is the fact that almost three hundred years before McDougall, Spinoza was already championing a hormic psychology. Mention has already been made of Spinoza's "basic *conatus*" just as attention has been called to McDougall's emphasis of "intrinsic teleology," on conative tendencies, and goal-directed striving. The "basic *conatus*," it may be recalled, referred to the principle of self-preservation. As a principle, H. A. Wolfson has pointed out, it was already mentioned by the Stoics, later by Cicero, and still later by Augustine, Aquinas, and other philosophers of the medieval period. Nor was the principle unknown to postmedieval philosophers. As explained by Wolfson (1934, Vol. II, pp. 196–197):

> At the time of Spinoza the principle of self-preservation became a commonplace of popular wisdom, so much so that in the Hebrew collection of sermons by his teacher Rabbi Saul Levi Morteira one of the sermons begins with the statement that "nature, mother of all created beings, has implanted in them a will and impulse to strive for self-preservation."
>
> Now, . . . self-preservation is spoken of as a sort of wish or will or desire expressed by such terms as *vult, velle, appetit.* These terms may all be traced to the Greek *hormé,* which is used in the passage quoted above. But *hormé* . . . can also be translated by *conatus.* Cicero himself uses *conatus* and *appetitio* as synonymous terms, and considers both of them as Latin equivalents of the Greek *hormé.* Furthermore, according to Hobbes, the term *appetitus* or *cupido,* which he uses as the Latin equivalent of the Greek *hormé,* is a form of *conatus,* so that subsequently, in the following passage, he uses the verb *conor* in connection with the striving for self-preservation: "And in the way to their end, which is principally their own conservation . . . [they] endeavor (*conatur*) to destroy, or subdue one another." From whatever source, therefore, Spinoza has directly drawn his formulation of the principle of self-preservation, there is a historical connection between the term *conatus* and the term *hormé.*

The principle of self-preservation has often been called the *instinct* of self-preservation. However, McDougall failed to list it as a separate instinct. Instead, he provided for it in the sense that his list of instincts can be regarded as an analysis of the factors involved in self-preservation as a concept. His list provides for innate propensities to eat when hungry, to reject disgusting food, to fight when attacked, to flee from danger, etc. All these are obviously necessary impulses if an organism is to survive. Had he been so inclined, McDougall might have lengthened his list by making provisions for the impulse to drink when thirsty, to urinate when the bladder is full, to struggle for air when choking, etc. That he neglected to catalogue these was probably not an oversight. A more plausible explanation would be to assume that he regarded them as too obvious to call for specific enumeration. It was enough for him to have indicated conation as rooted in man's biological equipment. In other words, the conative trends implicit in Spinoza's principle of self-preservation became explicit in McDougall's list of instincts.

In their treatment of the dynamics of self-preservation, Spinoza and McDougall were in substantial agreement regarding pleasure-pain theories of motivation. As already mentioned, they both rejected such theories as contrary to the goal-directed nature of conation. The direct end of man's striving is not pleasure but some object of purpose:[14] food when hungry, water when thirsty, a bed when sleepy. Conation in the form of antecedent desire rather than in the form of anticipated pleasure accounts for motivated behavior. In place of hedonistic formulations, McDougall argued that "conation is prior to, and not dependent upon its hedonic accompaniments," while Spinoza has expressed the same thought by maintaining that "We do not strive for something because we deem it good, but we deem it good because we desire it."

In making desire one of the three primary emotions, Spinoza might be said to have been using it as a generic term to include the conative aspect of all emotions. In this respect his conative psychology was different from McDougall's hormic psychology. In listing desire as an emotion, Spinoza was in agreement with Hobbes and Descartes, both of whom had referred to desire as one of the "passions." Incidentally, the latter word was not used in the current popular sense of rage, overwhelming ardor, or intense excitement, but as a reference to the "emotions of the soul." As explained by Wolfson (1934, Vol. I, pp. 193–194), this meaning of "passion," from the Greek *"pathos,"* is in accord with an Aristotelian usage. It should thus be evident that what Hobbes and Descartes had called a "passion" was synonymous with what Spinoza had called an "emotion."

What may not be evident is their reason for regarding desire as a passion or an emotion. It was not mentioned in McDougall's list of affective-conative cores and yet was singled out by Spinoza as a primary emotion along with joy and sorrow. At first inspection desire in the sense of yearning, wishing, wanting, or craving might appear different from full-fledged emotions like terror, rage, lust, or joyous excitement. And yet, upon closer analysis, as was clear to McDougall, every emotion involves something in the way of desire. In anger we desire to injure or discomfit the opposition, in fear we desire to escape from danger, when hungry we desire food, and when self-assertive we desire to dominate or master. Thus desire inheres in each of the native propensities.

---

14 In connection with the phrase "object of purpose" G. F. Stout, McDougall's older British contemporary, once called attention to an important distinction between such an object and what he described as the "terminus of purpose." According to him (1913, pp. 123–124), conation as goal-directed striving or purposive activity involves two meanings of the *goal* or *end* of the striving. One has to do with obtaining the means of accomplishing the purpose and the other with making effective use of the means. The thirsty traveler seeks water. Finding it is the *object* of his purpose. Not until he quenches his thirst by drinking it will his purpose be accomplished. Elimination of the thirst constitutes the *terminus* of his purpose. In the same way curiosity about the meaning of a strange word may impel one to seek a dictionary. Being the means of satisfying one's curiosity, the dictionary is the immediate *object* of endeavor, while locating and understanding the definition of the strange word mark its *terminus.* Thus Stout's account of motivation is also a nonhedonistic theory. Pleasure as such is neither one of the objects nor one of the termini of purpose or of conation.

Since desire was an inherent characteristic of each propensity considered separately, there was no need for McDougall to regard desire as a separate emotion. On the other hand, Spinoza seems to have considered desire as a manifestation of his notion of "basic endeavor" or *conatus* and hence as operative in all goal-seeking behavior. For him it was a generic term having both affective and conative implications. Its affective ones made it a primary emotion while its conative ones were reflected in his previously quoted definition of desire as "all the efforts, impulses, appetites, and volitions of man." Moreover, it will be recalled that his definitions of joy and sorrow, the two remaining primary emotions, had to do with "man's passage" to or from given degrees of "perfection." These definitions were found to be interpretations of joy and sorrow as marking the transition toward or away from the object of desire.

Seen in this light, Spinoza's three primary emotions constitute a complex unit of motivation or "basic endeavor." This amounts to saying with the Stoics of old that without desire there can be neither joy nor sorrow. It also serves to make Spinoza's psychology a dynamic psychology—a seventeenth-century foreshadowing of the kind of psychology McDougall came to sponsor in the twentieth. As a complex unit of motivation, it is in harmony with McDougall's notion of intrinsic teleology, just as McDougall's rejection of extrinsic teleology is in agreement with Spinoza's denial of final causes. Finally, as has been pointed out, they were in essential agreement in their opposition to the theory of hedonic causation

Despite these points of agreement, there is no evidence to indicate that McDougall was directly influenced by Spinoza. In fact, in his discussion (C. Murchison [ed.], 1930, pp. 33–35) of the "origins of hormic psychology" there is no mention of Spinoza. McDougall recognized Aristotle's psychology as an early form of hormic psychology since it is "thoroughly teleological." However, he found it fell short because, as with "most of the later authors who approximate a hormic psychology, his hormic theory is infected with hedonism."

Apollonian Versus Dionysian Viewpoints

In his evaluation of Aristotle and these "later authors," McDougall's touchstone was the Apollonian-Dionysian dichotomy. This Nietzschean dichotomy, he maintained, makes for a serviceable classification of psychological systems and theories. It is akin to the familiar classic-romantic dichotomy and highlighted the difference between an austere, formal, controlled attitude toward life as contrasted with an attitude of unconstrained spontaneity. Apollo as the Olympian god of light and leader of the Muses was symbolic of the former, and Dionysius as the Olympian god of wine and lusty enjoyment was symbolic of the latter. Accordingly, those adhering to the Apollonian tradition would identify the good life with the intellectual and aesthetic virtues of order, balance, form, symmetry, reasonableness, and avoidance of excess. In contrast, the devotees of the other tradition would pride themselves upon their freedom from such constricting standards and be unashamed of their endorsement of the spirit of the Mardi Gras. As applied to systems of psychology, the antithesis in question is reflected in such contrasts as intellectualism versus voluntarism, the rational versus the instinctual, or the cognitive versus the emotional.

As might be expected, McDougall viewed his hormic psychology as Dionysian and most academic psychology as Apollonian. In historical retrospect he saw the Socratic tradition as Apollonian because it equated virtue with knowledge. On the other hand, as contrasted with Socrates he held "that Aristotle was on the Dionysian side." Apparently this judgment was unduly influenced by what McDougall described as the "thoroughly teleological" nature of Aristotle's psychology. It is impossible to square this with all that Aristotle taught regarding man as a rational being, amenable to logic and steadfast in pursuit of the golden mean. This makes him just as Apollonian as Socrates if not more so. To call him Dionysian is as gross a blunder as calling Hamlet a happy prince.

McDougall took a dim view of Apollonian psychology. It was too intellectualistic, too mechanistic, and too hedonistic. The psychologies of Descartes, Locke, and the British associationists were cited as being guilty of such extremes. The more favored Dionysian view was not evident to him except in the writings of some members of the Scottish school and in the writings of some nineteenth-century continental authors. Among the latter he mentioned Schopenhauer because of his emphasis on "the primacy of will"; Nietzsche because his incidental remarks about psychology "are thoroughly hormic"; and also Freud because his psychology would also be "thoroughly hormic" had it not been "spoilt" by the "hedonist fallacy" of the pleasure principle.[15] It is altogether probable that McDougall would have been even more uncertain of Freud's psychology as being "thoroughly hormic" had he known that Freud was going to substitute what he called the "primacy of the intellect" (see Chapter 3, p. 55) for Schopenhauer's "primacy of will."

Since McDougall failed to consider Spinoza's psychology in his discussion of the "origins of hormic psychology," there is no way of knowing just what he might have thought about it. With its emphasis on "basic *conatus*" he should have welcomed it as being basically hormic in orientation. However, in view of his avowed preference for a Dionysian psychology, it seems probable that his welcome might have been less than enthusiastic; for Spinoza's psychology was definitely Apollonian in spirit. For McDougall to

---

[15] This is somewhat paradoxical. Taken in the abstract, endorsement of the pleasure principle would seem to be more welcome to a Dionysian than to an Apollonian. McDougall might have resolved the paradox by noting the intellectualistic view of hedonism as a consequence of a *reasoned* anticipation of probable pleasure or possible pain.

have found him "on the Dionysian side" is thus difficult to conjecture. In fact, he would have been obligated to call Spinoza an Apollonian for the same reason he advanced in referring to Socrates as Apollonian. In other words, as with Socrates, for Spinoza virtue is to be identified with knowledge. Reason and understanding, according to Spinoza, are essential for the ideal moral life. He was quite explicit on this point (Ratner, 1927, pp. 269–270):

> To act absolutely in conformity with virtue is nothing but acting according to the laws of our own proper nature. But only in so far as we understand do we act. Therefore, to act in conformity with virtue is nothing but acting, living, and preserving our being as reason directs, and doing so from the ground of seeking our own profit.
>
> In so far as a man is determined to action because he has inadequate ideas he suffers, that is to say, he does something which through his essence alone cannot be perceived, that is to say, which does not follow from his virtue. But in so far as he is determined to any action because he understands, he acts, that is to say he does something which is perceived through his essence alone, or which adequately follows from his virtue.
>
> All efforts which we make through reason are nothing but efforts to understand, and the mind, in so far as it uses reason, adjudges nothing as profitable to itself excepting that which conduces to understanding.

Spinoza's Psychology Both Hormic and Apollonian

The foregoing passage expresses one of Spinoza's deep-seated convictions regarding man as a moral being. What he had to say about psychology was a preparation for this teaching, since knowledge of human nature must precede the acquisition of ethical insights. By means of this teaching he hoped to emancipate man from the "human bondage" of uncontrolled impulsiveness. Furthermore (see Chapter 10, pp. 310–312), despite his repudiation of the free-will doctrine and his endorsement of determinism, he held that man is capable of exercising such control.

His determinism was not a fatalistic determinism. Instead, to revert to a distinction made in Chapter 10, pp. 306–308, it was a contingent determinism. It enabled him to regard the man who had learned "to govern or restrain the emotions" as a free man in contradistinction to the man in "bondage" to them. His ideal of the *homo liber* was that of a man who "lives according to the dictates of reason." There are repeated allusions to this ideal throughout Spinoza's *Ethics*. They serve to stamp Spinoza as a rationalist and as Apollonian in outlook and conviction. The following from the Ratner volume will serve as illustrations of such allusions:

> The primary foundation of virtue is the preservation of our being according to the guidance of reason. The man, therefore, who is ignorant of himself is ignorant

of the foundation of all the virtues, and consequently is ignorant of all virtues. Again, to act in conformity with virtue is nothing but acting according to the guidance of reason, and he who acts according to the guidance of reason must necessarily know that he acts according to the guidance of reason (pp. 280–281).

There is no rational life . . . without intelligence and things are good only in so far as they assist man to enjoy that life of the mind which is determined by intelligence. Those things alone, on the other hand, we call evil which hinder man from perfecting his reason and enjoying a rational life (p. 287).

I have finished everything I wish to explain concerning the power of the mind over the emotions and concerning its liberty. From what has been said we see what is the strength of the wise man, and how much he surpasses the ignorant man who is driven forward by lust alone (p. 375).

Expressions like the *power* of mind and *strength* of the wise man which occur in the preceding quotations suggest something dynamic about Spinoza's rationalism. It is as if the "basic endeavor" of his *homo liber* had come to fruition in a *desire* or dominating motive to be governed by reason, to eschew self-deception, and to act in the light of long-range perspectives. In the hormic psychology of McDougall, such a desire so organized and so disposed would constitute a *sentiment* of rationality.

Furthermore, as made clear by Wolfson (1934, Vol. II, p. 218), for Spinoza such a desire would involve active rather than passive emotions. The latter distinction goes back to Aristotle's recognition of a difference between rational desire and irrational desire and the difference between intellectual joy and sensual joy. And as Wolfson also makes clear (Vol. II, pp. 231–232), Spinoza's free man achieves self-mastery by learning how to have reason's active emotions prevail over unreason's passive emotions. However, this does not mean that the free man is the possessor of a free will. There was no room for free will in Spinoza's world of cause and effect and there is no reference to strengthening one's will in his ethical admonitions and exhortations. Instead there are urgings to nurture reason by the acquisition of appropriate knowledge.

Reason, or the life of the intellect, is part of nature and hence subject to Nature's laws. The power of reason is the power of knowledge and the power of active emotions. Without such power man is in bondage to his lusts, hungers, fears, and other passive emotions. The free man is free in the sense of being free from the tyranny of such bondage, but not in the sense of being able to disregard the insights provided by true knowledge— the kind of knowledge which differentiates a man of virtue from a man of vice. In short, Spinoza's hormic psychology recognized the driving force of virtue as well as the driving force of vice. This made his rationalism a dynamic rationalism and not the passive intellectualism McDougall attributed to the Apollonian tradition.

It should now be evident why Spinoza is commonly classified as a rationalist. Nevertheless, as was mentioned earlier in this chapter, he might also be classified as an empiricist. Some justification for this conclusion has already been introduced in connection with his anticipation of the Freudian notion of unconscious motivation and the Adlerian notion of compensation for feelings of inferiority. Additional justification for the conclusion is to be found in other anticipations of the teachings and insights of later psychologists. A few of these are now introduced not only by way of revealing him to have been an empiricist but also, to revert to an earlier phrase, "the first of the moderns."

Rejection of Faculty Psychology

Although Spinoza employed terms like "reason," "emotion," "intellect," and "will," he—like the modern psychologist—warned against the error of regarding such nouns as references to distinct entities or separate faculties. Instead he regarded them as convenient verbal labels for concepts or universals obtained by abstraction from the realities of individual experience. As abstractions they have no real existence, any more than whiteness exists apart from white objects or circularity apart from circular objects. To endow them with real existence involves the fallacy of reification, as it has come to be called. Actually, Spinoza had called attention to this fallacy when he wrote (Ratner, p. 199) that it is "to be observed how easily we are deceived when we confuse universals with individuals, and the entities of reason and abstractions with realities." Recognition of this fallacy was tantamount to exposing faculty psychology as fallacious. And this is what Spinoza did in the following comments about certain alleged faculties (Ratner, pp. 191–193):

> These and the like faculties, therefore, are either altogether fictitious, or else are nothing but metaphysical or universal entities, which we are in the habit of forming from individual cases. The intellect and will, therefore, are related to this or that idea or volition as rockiness is related to this or that rock, or as man is related to Peter or Paul. . . .
>
> In the mind there exists no absolute faculty of willing or not willing. Only individual volitions exist, that is to say, this and that affirmation and this and that negation. . . .
>
> The will and the intellect are nothing but the individual volitions and ideas themselves. But the individual volition and idea are one and the same. Therefore the will and the intellect are one and the same.

Dialectical Nature of Spinoza's Armchair Psychology

Spinoza arrived at this indictment of faculty psychology by questioning an accepted teaching and subjecting it to critical examination in the light of his own experience. To the extent that the indictment squares with current convictions regarding the unscientific status of faculty psychology, it serves as a reminder of the value of such an examination as part of the scientific enterprise. As indicated in Chapter 1, this kind of examination or psychological argument or analysis has often been viewed with a cold eye as armchair psychology and hence to be discouraged as alien to the spirit of science. It will be recalled that, as traditionally understood, armchair conclusions were contrasted with those based upon experimental findings, to the disparagement of the former. Taken strictly, this would mean that almost every psychological teaching prior to about the middle of the nineteenth century is to be viewed askance as armchair psychology. Empiricists like Hobbes and Locke, as well as rationalists like Descartes and Spinoza, did their work as armchair psychologists. Nevertheless, to review what has already been pointed out, they and their philosophical predecessors had not worked in vain. As a result of their armchair observations, experimental psychologists did not have to start from scratch. A vast body of fact and theory, along with a useful descriptive vocabulary and provocative problems, was placed at their disposal.

It is well to be reminded of this heritage in the present context, for many of Spinoza's conclusions are especially revelatory of the value of sound armchair psychology. It is also well to realize that this kind of armchair psychology in the sense of a critical analysis of experience—everyday experience as well as clinical and experimental experience—is an important and necessary component of scientific method. In terms of method, Spinoza was neither clinical nor experimental. His critical analyses might be called *dialectical* as an alternative to the negative connotation still aroused by mention of armchair methods. What he had to say about faculty psychology, as just discussed, is one instance of the potential value of this method. There are still other instances to be considered by way of noting the value of this dialectical method and the soundness of Spinoza's armchair observations.

The dialectical method calls for a questioning attitude and the examination of given beliefs or opinions in the light of their factual support and logical implications for the purpose of determining their validity. One is on the verge of using the method as soon as one questions or wonders about the truth of something apt to be of philosophic or scientific significance. It is a truism that all philosophy and science are grounded in curiosity and wonder and gets under way when the right questions are raised. Most people fail to progress as thinkers because, with curiosity blunted, they fail to wonder and to question. The result is complacency and fixed beliefs immune to challenge. In the words of Spinoza (Ratner, p. 107): "Most people think they sufficiently understand a thing when they have ceased to wonder at it."

Spinoza as Social Psychologist

Among the many things Spinoza wondered about was man's role as a social being, or in that phase of human behavior that had prompted

Aristotle to regard man not only as a rational animal but also as a political animal. Hobbes, it will be remembered, had dealt with this phase in his *Leviathan* and therefore has been considered a pioneering social psychologist. Spinoza, whose curiosity had been aroused by reading Hobbes, dealt with some of the same problems and thus might also be listed among the forerunners of modern social psychology.

Like Hobbes, Spinoza attributed the origin of social organization to a "compact" men enter into to safeguard their security, for "every one wishes to live as far as possible securely beyond the reach of fear, and this would be quite impossible so long as every one did everything he liked, and reason's claim was lowered to a par with those of hatred and anger" (Ratner, p. 300). However, he went beyond Hobbes by not regarding protection against attack the sole reason for the "compact." Gregariousness in the form of cooperative activity results in these other advantages (Ratner, pp. 91–92):

> The formation of society serves not only for defensive purposes, but is also very useful, and, indeed, absolutely necessary, as rendering possible the division of labor. If men did not render mutual assistance to each other, no one would have either the skill or the time to provide for his own sustenance and preservation: for all men are not equally apt for all work, and no one would be capable of preparing all that he individually stood in need of. Strength and time . . . would fail, if every one had in person to plow, to sow, to reap, to grind corn, to cook, to weave, to stitch and perform the other numerous functions required to keep life going; to say nothing of the arts and sciences which are also necessary to the perfection and blessedness of human nature. We see that peoples living in uncivilized barbarism lead a wretched and almost animal life, and even they would not be able to acquire their few rude necessaries without assisting one another to a certain extent.

Spinoza and Hobbes differed from one another in their views of social control. Although they both recognized the need for laws to achieve such control, they were not in agreement with respect to matters of legislation and law enforcement. As indicated in Chapter 13, Hobbes as a royalist was an advocate of authoritarian control by the sovereign, whose will was to prevail because authority had been delegated to him by his subjects. In effect, Hobbes maintained, for subjects to rebel against him was to rebel against themselves.

On the other hand, Spinoza recognized that government might be too repressive and engender rebellion, for he maintained that (Ratner, p. 92) "human nature will not submit to absolute repression" and that "violent governments, as Seneca says, never last long; the moderate governments endure." The ones most likely to endure, he concluded, are the democratic ones; for in his opinion (Ratner, p. 306) "of all forms of government" democracy is "the most natural and the most consonant with individual liberty." Moreover, to win support for a given regime he urged the use of positive reinforcement by having laws (Ratner, p. 93) "so arranged that people should be kept in bounds by the hope of some greatly desired good, rather than by fear, for then every one will do his duty willingly." In general, such a suggestion is in line with current psychological teaching to the effect that reward is superior to punishment as a means of influencing behavior.

Concerning Prejudice, Wishful Thinking, and Rationalization

Spinoza also noted the way in which social attitudes toward whole groups of people may be the result of a single experience with a single member of a given group. Thus a gratifying or rewarding experience with a man from Alaska may induce one to be favorably disposed toward Alaskans as a class, whereas a suspicious attitude toward Alaskans may be induced as a result of having been victimized by an Alaskan confidence man. The underlying principle was summed up by Spinoza in a single sentence (Ratner, p. 238):

> If we have been affected with joy or sorrow by any one who belongs to a class or nation different from our own, and if our joy or sorrow is accompanied with the idea of this person as its cause, under the common name of his class or nation, we shall not love or hate him merely, but the whole of the class or nation to which he belongs.

The principle accounts for many of our likes and dislikes and not just for the origin of group prejudice, and thus enables us (Ratner, p. 237) "to understand why we love or hate certain things from no cause which is known to us, but merely from sympathy or antipathy." Locke, as mentioned in the preceding chapter (see p. 379), accounted for aversions by the same principle. And the contemporary psychologist is alluding to the same principle when he talks about emotional conditioning. For example Allport, in his discussion of racial prejudice as a product of conditioning (1954, p. 314), quotes the same sentence from Spinoza's *Ethics* as a formulation of the governing principle. As he makes clear, in terms of this principle when expressed in modern terminology, ethnic prejudice is very often a result of overgeneralization following a single traumatic experience and as such exemplifies one-trial learning or conditioning.

Spinoza also noted that bias or prejudice as an emotionalized attitude involves wishful thinking. This is clearly evident from his observation to the effect that "we easily believe the things we hope for, and believe with difficulty those we fear, and we think too much of the former and too little of the latter" (Ratner, p. 237). In other words, our wishes or desires may outweigh evidence in the determination of our beliefs. Experimental confirmation of this Spinozistic observation was supplied by F. H. Lund (1925) in his investigation of the psychology of belief; for he found a correlation of

.88 between belief and desire as contrasted with a correlation of .42 between belief and evidence. Metaphorically speaking, when it comes to belief the heart seems twice as strong as the brain and logic has to yield to desire.

Just as the imperiousness of desire makes for wishful thinking, so it makes for rationalization, or the readiness to account for belief and conduct by self-justifying reasons and a concomitant resistance to giving due consideration to self-incriminating ones. As a technical designation for this tendency the term "rationalization" was introduced into psychology by Ernest Jones in 1908. However, the tendency as a common human trait was evident to Spinoza in this previously cited paragraph (Ratner, p. 240):

> If we imagine that we are hated by another without having given him any cause for it, we shall hate him in return. If we imagine that we have given just cause for the hatred, we shall then be affected with shame. This, however, rarely happens; we endeavor to affirm everything, both concerning ourselves and concerning the beloved object which we imagine will affect us or the object with joy, and, on the contrary, we endeavor to deny everything that will affect either it or ourselves with sorrow.

On Projection and the Psychologist's Fallacy

As was just shown, even though Spinoza failed to employ terms like wishful thinking and rationalization, he recognized and understood the nature of the mental processes to which they refer. It might even be said that he recognized and understood the nature of a related mechanism like projection. For example, projection is implied by what Ratner (1927, p. xiv) has described as "Spinoza's psychological law freely expressed in the dictum that Paul's idea of Peter tells us more about Paul than about Peter." By this it is meant that Paul is likely to attribute or read into the character of Peter what he thinks ought to be there rather than what is actually there. If he knows that Peter is an army officer, his idea of Peter will be colored by his notions of army officers. Similarly, should Peter be a Methodist, Paul's notions of Methodism may influence his judgment of Peter.

As Ratner suggests, this dictum of Spinoza's is not very different from what William James warned against as "the psychologist's fallacy." In the words of James (1890, Vol. I, p. 196) this "*great* snare of the psychologist is the *confusion of his own standpoint with that of the mental fact* about which he is making his report." For example, as a result of psychological analysis he is familiar with the cues responsible for judgments of distance —cues like convergence, angular perspective, superposition, etc. Should the psychologist assume that his naive subject in judging distance is aware of these cues as cues, he would be guilty of the psychologist's fallacy. He would be projecting or reading into the subject's perceptual act what he, as psychologist, believes ought to be there. Actually, in "making his report," his experimental subject, never having learned about the cues, would have to content himself with a simple statement like, "I could tell this object was nearer because—well, because it looked nearer."

A skeptic might be justified in questioning what was just said about Spinoza's recognition and understanding of the nature of projection. After all, Spinoza never employed the word "projection." To contend that he had a grasp of the concept from what he had to say about Paul's idea of Peter may seem rather forced. The skeptic might argue that this is reading too much into Spinoza's dictum and constitutes projection on the part of anybody upholding the contention on the basis of this fragment of evidence. However, his skepticism might vanish by inducing him to read Spinoza's comments on the credibility of eyewitnesses and the objectivity of historians (Ratner, p. 115):

> It is very rare for men to relate an event simply as it happened, without adding any element of their own judgment. When they hear or see anything new, they are, unless strictly on their guard, so occupied with their own preconceived opinions that they perceive something quite different from the plain facts seen or heard, especially if such facts surpass the comprehension of the beholder or hearer, and, most of all, if he is interested in their happening in a given way.
>
> Thus men relate in chronicles and histories their own opinions rather than actual events, so that one and the same event is so differently related by two men of different opinions, that it seems like two separate occurrences; and, further, it is very easy from historical chronicles to gather the personal opinions of the historian.

Under the circumstances it thus seems quite obvious that Spinoza was familiar with the distorting effects of projection. His account constitutes an early recognition of selective perception previously discussed in Chapter 8. In the latter chapter attention was called to potential sources of error both in the case of ordinary everyday observation as well as in the case of the historian trying to be meticulously accurate in his description of a given historical episode. In other words, Spinoza was well aware of selective perception as being what James might have called a "great snare" in the historian's professional endeavors; hence, just as James warned against the psychologist's fallacy, so Spinoza in the passage just quoted was warning against the historian's fallacy.

A historian would be guilty of this fallacy if he were to regard Spinoza's rationalism as the equivalent of a nonempirical psychology. Were he to do so, he would be overlooking Spinoza's empirically grounded psychological observations. In the present instance, as should be evident, Spinoza's allusions to projection, wishful thinking, and rationalization exemplify such observations. They were products of his experiences with people and not arbitrary, *a priori* products of a rationalist's metaphysical broodings.

This is not to be construed as a denial of his affiliation with the rationalist tradition. To revert to a previous statement, Spinoza was a rationalist in his espousal of the place of reason in the business of living, in learning to make intelligent choices, and in avoiding bondage to the self-destructive drive of uncontrolled impulsiveness. Reason for him, as expounded in his *Ethics,* was rooted in knowledge and understanding and not in some abstract mental faculty divorced from the realities of everyday living. Without knowledge and understanding of such realities, it is impossible to behave reasonably. In this sense, Spinoza was both a rationalist as well as an empiricist.

Spinoza as Pioneer Mental Hygienist

Spinoza's interest in such psychological issues as reasoned control of behavior, improvement of the intellect, fidelity of report, and the other topics mentioned in the previous section was more than a theoretician's interest. He had a definite interest in promoting human welfare by suggesting ways of promoting mental health. Because of this interest, he might be classified as a pioneer mental hygienist. Wolfson even devotes some ten pages to what he calls "Spinoza's principles of psychotherapy."[16] These principles, Wolfson shows, have to do with the fact that Spinoza thought of the irrational emotions as "a sickness of the mind" (*animi aegritudo*) and that he had some practical suggestions to offer by way of curing or warding off such sickness. Spinoza referred to these suggestions as "remedies [*remedia*] against the emotions." He evidently did not regard them as especially novel or original, for in one of his writings he described them as being what "everyone experiences, but does not accurately observe nor distinctly see." As Wolfson notes (1934, Vol. II, p. 265):

> The remedies offered by him are indeed such as popular wisdom in the past has reduced to the form of proverbs, which are writ large on the pages of copybooks. In our own time they have been garbed in a technical nomenclature and reduced to a science, and are administered in the form of incantations.

There is no need to consider each of these "remedies." It will suffice to mention just one by way of illustration. As a matter of fact, there was incidental reference to one of them on a previous page in connection with the discussion of the achievement of self-mastery by having reason's active emotions displace unreason's passive emotions. The distinction in question, as already pointed out, stems from Aristotle's distinction between rational and irrational desires and consequently refers to the conative aspect of

---

[16] The reference to principles of psychotherapy occurs in the index (1934, Vol. II, p. 386), where the reader is referred to pp. 263–274 for discussion of the principles.

emotion. In anger one desires or strives to discomfit or defeat the opposition, and in fear one desires or strives to flee from a menacing situation. Should there be a clear and distinct idea of the reason for the anger or fear, then, in Spinoza's terminology one would be dealing with an active emotion and with what Aristotle called a rational desire. This follows from Spinoza's identification of a passive emotion with a "confused" or "inadequate" idea and seems to be related to what he had to say about men usually being ignorant of the causes of their desires. In their ignorance they would adduce spurious reasons for their desires and thus reveal their "confusion."

A modern psychotherapist would regard Spinoza's passive emotion as a product of unconscious motivation and the spurious reasons as the rationalized products of wishful thinking. He might also regard the distinction between active and passive emotions and between rational and irrational desires as foreshadowings of his distinction between normal and neurotic emotions and desires. Moreover, he might agree with Spinoza to the extent of describing his neurotic patients as being "confused" about the real nature of their anxieties, hatreds, and loves. Furthermore, to the extent that one of his therapeutic aims is to clear up the confusion by having his patients achieve "insight," he would be endorsing Spinoza's "remedy" for the distress of passive emotions; namely, to "form some clear and distinct conception of the emotion." According to Spinoza (Ratner, p. 353), "Every one has the power, partly at least, if not absolutely, of understanding clearly and distinctly himself and his emotions, and consequently of bringing it to pass that he suffers less from them." This thought is then elaborated upon in the following paragraph (pp. 353–354):

> We have therefore mainly to strive to acquire a clear and distinct knowledge as far as possible of each emotion, so that the mind may be led to pass from the emotion to think those things which it perceives clearly and distinctly, and with which it is entirely satisfied, and to strive also that the emotion may be separated from the thought of an external thought and connected with true thoughts. Thus not only love, hatred, etc., will be destroyed, but also the appetites or desires to which the emotion gives rise cannot be excessive. For it is above everything to be observed that the appetite by which a man is said to act is one and the same appetite as that by which he is said to suffer. For example, we have shown that human nature is so constituted that every one desires that other people should live according to his way of thinking, a desire which in a man who is not guided by reason is a passion which is called ambition, and is not very different from pride: while, on the other hand, in a man who lives according to the dictates of reason it is an action or virtue which is called piety.[17] In the same manner, all the

---

[17] By piety Spinoza means behavior justified by reason. In this context it is behavior that helps others to learn to be guided by the dictates of reason.

appetites or desires are passions only in so far as they arise from inadequate ideas and are classed among the virtues whenever they are excited or begotten by adequate ideas; for all the desires by which we are determined to any action may arise either from adequate or inadequate ideas. To return, therefore, to the point from which we set out: there is no remedy within our power which can be conceived more excellent for the emotions than that which consists in true knowledge of them, since the mind possesses no other power than that of thinking and forming adequate ideas.

Concerning Emotion and Mental Health

It would be wrong to interpret Spinoza's emphasis on the mind's "power" to think and to form "adequate ideas" as a denial of the value and importance of emotion for the "preservation of our being according to the guidance of reason." In fact, he made a distinction between good or healthy emotions on the one hand and evil or unhealthy emotions on the other, as is illustrated by his evaluation of joy and sorrow (Ratner, p. 273):

> Joy is an emotion by which the body's power of action is increased or assisted. Sorrow, on the other hand, is an emotion by which the body's power of action is lessened or restrained, and therefore joy is not directly evil, but good; sorrow, on the other hand, is directly evil.

Moreover, in his view (Ratner, pp. 274–275), hatred and derivatives of hatred like "envy, mockery, contempt, anger, revenge" and kindred emotions were deemed to be evil, while cheerfulness, love, generosity were deemed to be good; hence the man of reason is likely to strive to ward off the former and be eager to welcome the latter.

In some respects this last generalization does not quite reflect Spinoza's thought if it is taken to mean that his ideal man of reason determined the moral worth of actions solely by their emotional consequences. Taken by themselves, they are not to be trusted as guides to action. As Spinoza noted, parents are often arbitrary in their use of praise and blame in training children to think of some actions as wicked and others as good. By dint of repetition this causes "the emotions of sorrow to connect themselves with the former, and those of joy with the latter." Thus, family tradition and custom rather than reason lay the foundation for notions of right and wrong with their concomitant feelings of joy and sorrow. The result, according to Spinoza, is moral relativism (Ratner, p. 225):

> Experience proves this, for custom and religion are not the same everywhere; but, on the contrary, things which are sacred to some are profane to others, and what are honorable with some are disgraceful with others. Education alone, therefore, will determine whether a man will repent of any deed or boast of it.

For the man of reason in quest of moral excellence, Spinoza indicated, his education must go beyond blind adherence to the results of emotional conditioning incident to parental praise and reproof in early childhood. He must subject specific deeds which occasioned such praise or reproof to reasoned analysis to find out why they merit approval or disapproval. The emotions they engender taken by themselves are not enough to establish such merit. Intelligent action requires an understanding of the "causes" of our emotions and desires. Otherwise man will be in bondage to impulsiveness.

To gain control over impulsiveness and understanding of desire, Spinoza urged planning on a reasoned course of action *before* the imperiousness of desire is experienced. Wolfson (1934, Vol. II, p. 272) regards this recommendation along with Spinoza's other suggested "remedies" as an expression of Spinoza's teaching to the effect that "all these remedies are more effective as preventive measures than as cures."

In the present instance, what Spinoza was urging was the desirability of coming to grips with emotional crises by thinking about them when free from the pressure of their demands. To wait until they are upon us is to endanger the rule of reason. Panic, terror, fury, jealousy, and other forms of emotional excitement preclude clear thinking and controlled behavior. By anticipating such crises when calm and untroubled, it is possible to work out intelligent ways of coping with them if and when they occur.

This seems to be what Spinoza meant when he wrote that "so long as we are not agitated by emotions which are contrary to our nature do we possess the power of arranging and connecting the affections of the body according to the order of the intellect." Taking advantage of this power will promote the development of active emotions with clear and distinct ideas of their nature as a replacement for the passive emotions with their confused and inadequate ideational accompaniments. Active emotions are exemplified by the organized behavior of men who have learned how to cope with emergencies, whereas passive emotions are exemplified by men who react to emergencies with disorganized agitation and helpless bewilderment. It is the difference between the impotence of ignorance and knowing what to do and how to do it.

The relation between passive emotions and impotence was pointed out by Spinoza in an important passage in which he regards passive emotions as "signs of mental impotence." The passage is important because it reveals Spinoza's view of the place of emotion in a life governed by rational considerations. It reads as follows (Ratner, p. 276):

> I make a great distinction between mockery (which I have said is bad) and laughter; for laughter and merriment are nothing but joy, and therefore, provided they are not excessive, are in themselves good. Nothing but a gloomy and sad

superstition forbids enjoyment. For why is it more seemly to extinguish hunger and thirst than to drive away melancholy? My reasons and conclusions are these: No God and no human being, except an envious one, is delighted by my impotence or my trouble, or esteems as any virtue in us tears, sighs, fears, and other things of this kind, which are signs of mental impotence; on the contrary, the greater the joy with which we are affected, the greater the perfection to which we pass thereby, that is to say, the more do we necessarily partake of the divine nature. To make use of things, therefore, and to delight in them as much as possible (provided we do not disgust ourselves with them), is the part of a wise man. It is the part of a wise man, I say, to refresh and invigorate himself with moderate and pleasant eating and drinking, with sweet scents and the beauty of green plants, with ornament, with music, with sports, with the theatre, and with all things of this kind which one man can enjoy without hurting another.

It is clear from the foregoing that Spinoza's exaltation of reason and the intellectual virtues was not the exaltation of joyless ratiocination. His rationalism did not call for a regimen of austerity and ascetic self-denial. His ideal man of reason was not a killjoy. Instead, although avoiding the bondage of passive emotions, such a man would value the positive emotions. He would be mindful of the difference between enslaving joys and emancipating joys, having learned "that the joy by which the drunkard is enslaved is altogether different from the joy which is the portion of the philosopher" (Ratner, p. 245). As a wise man, his concept of optimal mental health would include both cognitive and emotional values. It is likely, of course, that as a rationalist he would tend to view the cognitive ones as more important then the emotional ones. On the other hand, one might conceive of rationalists who would regard them as of coordinate importance or even of some who might deem the emotional ones more vital for man's well-being than the cognitive ones. These rationalists might support such a conclusion by arguing that in everyday life we reveal our interest in and solicitude for our friends by inquiring after their feelings rather than their thoughts; for, upon meeting them, we ask "How do you feel?" and not "How do you think?" To complicate matters, some of them may answer by talking about some "painful thoughts" while others may refer to their "injured feelings." The problem is manifestly too complex to be disposed of in easy fashion.

Concerning Cognition and Mental Health

It is also well to realize that the problem under consideration is not to be disposed of by dismissing it as an outmoded philosophical issue. As a matter of fact, it is neither outmoded nor exclusively philosophical. As recently as 1965 J. McV. Hunt subjected the problem to critical study when he raised this question: "Are emotional factors so much more important than cognitive factors in psychological development?" In reviewing the evidence bearing on this question, he noted that following the appearance of Freud's theory of stages of psychosexual development from early infancy onwards, personality theorists tended to give an affirmative answer to the question. Freud's monograph dealing with this theory was published in 1905. This was about the period during which psychologists became increasingly interested in the measurement of intelligence. Before long, many of them began to regard level of intelligence as fixed by genetic determinants. This became the doctrine of the constancy of intelligence quotients. Opposed to such constancy was the flexibility of emotional development in terms of the Freudian theory. For healthy personality development, the child's alleged libidinal needs were to be met as it advanced from stage to stage. The pleasure principle was to govern nursing, weaning, and toilet training if the child's emotional security was to be assured. By hypothesis its intelligence is fixed, but its emotional welfare is amenable to parental control; ergo, cognitive factors are less important than emotional factors.

However, in the light of studies undertaken during the 1940s and 1950s and reviewed by Hunt, this latter conclusion is to be questioned. The evidence is weighty and cumulative and results in this verdict (1965, pp. 87–88):

> Reviews of those relatively objective studies of the effects of the emotional factors pointed up in the theory of psychosexual development have generally tended to depreciate the importance of those factors. Every study finding significant effects can be matched with another which does not. Moreover, the better controlled the study, the less likely is it to have found significant effects. . . .
>
> As I see it, these various lines of evidence combine to indicate that cognitive experience—or, more precisely, the organism's informational interaction with the environment—can be as important for psychological development as emotions based on the fate of instincts, and perhaps it is typically more important.

As already suggested, it is altogether likely that Spinoza would have concurred in the general import of Hunt's verdict. Actually, what he had to say about principles of psychotherapy and about human nature in general did not give rise to the question formulated by Hunt. There is no direct statement to the effect that cognition is more important than emotion. Nevertheless, the entire drift of his psychology is in accord with such a statement. It is consistent with what was previously referred to as his Apollonian viewpoint. Furthermore, centuries before Freud he had already rejected the pleasure principle in favor of a reality principle conceived of in terms of goal-directed striving. Over and over again, it will be recalled, he referred to the importance of "clear and distinct ideas" if such striving was to be successful. Moreover, it will also be recalled, that long before the Freudian era, in effect he had warned against cognitive distortion as a consequence of wishful thinking, prejudice, rationalization, and projection.

To round out this hasty review of Spinoza's anticipation of some of Freud's ideas, mention ought to be made of the deterministic and dynamic character of his hormic psychology. This constitutes another respect in which his seventeenth-century mental philosophy resembles the twentieth-century psychology of Freud. The same applies to the parallel between Freud's concept of unconscious motivation and Spinoza's recognition of our ignorance of the causes of our desires. One might even argue that Spinoza's rationalism—his glorification of Reason—was a foreshadowing of what Freud came to designate as the "primacy of the intellect."

In all the foregoing respects, Freudian teachings are rediscoveries of Spinozistic teachings. For the most part these teachings have to do with causal relationships and with warped thinking, and thus pertain to cognition rather than emotion. As such they are no longer unique to the psychology of Spinoza and Freud. The existence of cognitive distortion as a result of wishful thinking, projection, and similar mechanisms is no longer questioned and no longer unique to a psychoanalytic orientation. The mechanisms in question have become assimilated into general psychology, as a consequence of their having been verified by casual observation in the course of everyday experience once attention was directed to them by description of their nature and by giving each of them a distinctive name. This resulted in confirmation of their existence by psychologists of every persuasion, including non-Freudians as well as anti-Freudians. In fact, by this time they have become part of popular psychology and terms like "rationalization" and "wishful thinking" are readily employed by all educated people.

To say that some Freudian teachings are rediscoveries of the insights of Spinoza is not the same as saying that Spinoza influenced Freud. There is no mention of such influence in the long chapter that Ernest Jones devoted to tracing possible sources of "Freud's theory of mind." He even quotes Freud as having written that "psychoanalysis grew on a narrowly restricted basis" (1953, Vol. I, p. 370). Evidently this basis was not broad enough to include Freud's philosophical predecessors. As was indicated in Chapter 3, Plato also anticipated many Freudian teachings, and yet examination failed to reveal Freud as having been familiar with Plato's writings. In the realm of ideas, history can repeat itself without involving a direct causal relationship between the earlier and the later ideas.

Freud's approach to psychology was different from Spinoza's in basic orientation. Spinoza was familiar with Greek, medieval, and postmedieval psychological views. On the other hand, Freud lacked such familiarity with the heritage of philosophical psychology.[18] According to Jones (1953,

---

[18] This statement ought to be qualified by noting that Freud had familiarized himself with what many of the philosophers had written on the subject of dreams. Freud's long bibliography at the end of the *Traumdeutung* contains references to Kant and Schopenhauer, among others. In addition it contains references to numerous of his contemporary academic psychologists such as Woodworth, Calkins, Titchener, Wundt, and Lipps. Furthermore, as will be considered in a later chapter, he was especially influenced by the writings of Herbart, who had introduced the notion of a dynamic unconscious some forty years before the birth of Freud.

p. 371), he was even "ill-informed in the field of contemporary psychology" and "often admitted his ignorance of it." As a consequence his psychology was more or less an *ad hoc* improvisation to facilitate understanding and treatment of his neurotic patients. His orientation was that of a physician trying to cure sick people. What he discovered in the way of cognitive distortion, defense mechanisms, and emotional fixation was an outgrowth of this orientation. In short, his psychology developed out of his preoccupation with psychopathology. Incidentally, with its emphasis on the imperiousness of id impulses and the driving force of life and death instincts— the relentless dynamism of unconscious strivings—this psychology, like Spinoza's, is a hormic psychology.

However, unlike Freud's, Spinoza's hormic psychology was not an *ad hoc* improvisation. It was rooted in his knowledge of the psychological teachings of philosophers like Aristotle, Aquinas, Maimonides, Hobbes, and Descartes. It was not prompted by the need to cure sick people; but, in line with his philosophical forebears, it was viewed as a necessary prelude to the quest for ideal self-actualization. Stated a little differently, his interest in desire, emotion, cognition, and other psychological topics was related to his more basic interest in a sound philosophy of life. For him this meant a life lived in accordance with rationally grounded ethical ideals; hence most of his psychological views are presented in his *Ethics*. His concern with principles of psychotherapy was less a product of interest in psychopathology and more the result of his interest in promoting realization of the rationalist's ideal of the good life. In terms of this ideal, the concept of mental health implies something more positive than freedom from mental illness. Instead it connotes strength of character and a maturity of outlook which Spinoza might have equated with the moral excellence Plato attributed to Socrates.

Self-Fulfillment as Moral Excellence: Concluding Comments

As suggested in the previous section, cognition was stressed in Spinoza's psychology as a means of arriving at a sound philosophy of life. In this respect his psychology differed from the psychology of Locke. The empiricism of Locke was essentially concerned with an examination of the genesis of our ideas. In this sense it was an epistemological enterprise. In contrast, Spinoza's rationalism was more concerned with establishing the foundations for the good life and was thus more of an ethical enterprise. Like Plato's rationalism, it had more to do with conduct than with behavior.[19] Furthermore, his psychology also resembled that of Plato in its recognition of the importance of conation.[20] In terms of this recognition

---

[19] See pp. 68–69 regarding this distinction

[20] Plato's recognition of conative factors was discussed on page 56.

both psychologies are hormic psychologies. The focus of both psychologies is on the conflict between duty and desire and with the quest for moral excellence. A modern Freudian might prefer to formulate this as a conflict between id and superego and the quest for mental health. The really big problems of psychology are of ancient vintage.

A big problem for Spinoza, it should now be evident, was how to achieve and safeguard moral excellence. The principles of psychotherapy implicit in his psychology can now be seen as principles of right conduct. They involve suggestions for the promotion of enhanced self-respect, keener insight, and the kind of understanding to be acquired by the steady accumulation of clear and distinct ideas. A life lived in accordance with these principles, Spinoza implied, would enable one to meet personal crises and difficult conflicts with a greater likelihood of having active emotions prevail over passive ones. As a result there would also be a greater likelihood of meeting them with courage and disciplined reason provided one concentrates on their essential aspects by viewing them *sub specie aeternitatis.*

As Spinoza saw it, self-fulfillment as the quest for moral excellence is an arduous quest. It calls for critical thinking, self-discipline, and persistent effort. If successful, it leads to nobility of character as the acme of moral excellence. However, in his view, this degree of success is a rare occurrence; for, according to one of his famous aphorisms: "All things excellent are as difficult as they are rare."

Reason with a capital "R" loomed large in Spinoza's scheme of values. But it was not a detached Reason divorced from the realities of everyday living and interest in and concern for human welfare. It was dedicated to the pursuit of truth as manifested in Nature and as indicated by Nature's laws. In some respects devotion to this pursuit was the supreme value for Spinoza. It marked the culmination of man's quest for moral excellence as expressed by the harmonious fusion of cognition and emotion that Spinoza experienced as the "intellectual love of God." What this means is intimated by the *Ethics* he wrote, but is more clearly revealed by the ethics he lived. This explains why Russell once referred to him (1945, p. 569) as "the noblest and most lovable of the great philosophers" and then added, "Intellectually, some others have surpassed him, but ethically he is supreme."

References

Allport, G. *The Nature of Prejudice*. Boston: The Beacon Press, 1954.

Bernard, L. L. *Instinct: A Study of Social Psychology*. New York: Henry Holt and Company, 1924.

Bridges, K. M. B. "Emotional Development in Early Infancy," *Child Development*, 1932, *3*, 324–334.

Burtt, E. A. *The Metaphysical Foundations of Modern Physical Science*, rev. ed. Garden City, New York: Doubleday and Company, 1954. (First published in 1924.) Reprinted in 1967 by Humanities Press, New York.

Cannon, W. B. *Bodily Changes in Pain, Hunger, Fear and Rage*. New York: D. Appleton-Century Company, 1929.

Dunlap, K. "Are There Any Instincts?" *Journal of Abnormal Psychology*, 1919, *14*, 307–311.

Ewing, A. C. *The Fundamental Questions of Philosophy*. New York: Collier Books, 1962.

Goldstein, K. *Human Nature in the Light of Psychopathology*. New York: Schocken Books, 1963. (First published in 1940.)

Hilgard, E. R. Review of *The Act of Creation*, by Arthur Koestler. *Science*, 1965, *147*, 37–38.

Hunt, J. McV. "Traditional Personality Theory in the Light of Recent Evidence," *American Scientist*, 1965, *53*, 80–93.

James, W. *Principles of Psychology*, Vol. I. New York: Henry Holt and Company, 1890.

James, W. *Principles of Psychology*, Vol. II. New York: Henry Holt and Company, 1890.

Jones, E. *The Life and Work of Sigmund Freud*, Vol. I. New York: Basic Books, 1953.

Jones, E. "Rationalization in Everyday Life," *Journal of Abnormal Psychology*, 1908, *3*, 161–169.

Kling, C. "The Role of the Parasympathetics in Emotions," *Psychological Review*, 1933, *40*, 368–380.

Lund, F. H. "The Psychology of Belief," *Journal of Abnormal and Social Psychology*, 1925, *20*, 174–196.

McDougall, W. *The Energies of Men: A Study of the Fundamentals of Dynamic Psychology*. London: Methuen and Company, 1932.

McDougall, W. "The Hormic Psychology," in C. Murchison (ed.). *Psychologies of 1930*. Worcester: Clark University Press, 1930, pp. 3–36.

McDougall, W. *An Introduction to Social Psychology*. London: Methuen and Company, 1908.

McDougall, W. *Outline of Psychology*. New York: Charles Scribner's Sons, 1923.

Ratner, J. (ed.). *The Philosophy of Spinoza—Selected from His Chief Works*. New York: The Modern Library, 1927. Reprinted by permission of the editor.

Russell, B. *A History of Western Philosophy*. New York: Simon and Schuster, 1945.

Spearman, C. "The Life and Work of William McDougall," *Character and Personality*, 1939, *7*, 175–183.

Spinoza, B. *Principles of Cartesian Philosophy*. (Translated by H. E. Wedeck.) New York: The Philosophical Library, 1961.

Spitz, R. A., and Wolf, K. M. "The Smiling Response: A Contribution to the Ontogenesis of Social Relations," *Genetic Psychology Monographs*, 1946, *34*, 57–125.

Stout, G. F. *A Manual of Psychology*, 3rd ed. London: Hinds, Noble and Eldredge, 1913. (First edition published in 1899.)

Warren, H. C. *Dictionary of Psychology*. Boston: Houghton Mifflin Company, 1934.

Watson, J. B., and Morgan, J. J. B. "Emotional Reactions and Psychological Experimentations," *American Journal of Psychology*, 1917, *28*, 163–174.

Wolf, A. "Spinoza, Benedictus de," in *Encyclopaedia Britannica, 21*, 14th ed., 1929, 231–239.

Wolfson, H. A. *The Philosophy of Spinoza*, Vol. I. Cambridge: Harvard University Press, 1934.

Wolfson, H. A. *The Philosophy of Spinoza*, Vol. II. Cambridge: Harvard University Press, 1934.

14

The Rationalism of Leibnitz and the Psychology of Wolff

THE LAST FEW CHAPTERS—those concerned with Hobbes, Descartes, Locke, and Spinoza—had to do with seventeenth-century psychology. This is definitely true of Hobbes, Descartes, and Spinoza, but less definitely true of Locke. His *Essay*, although first published in 1690, appeared in subsequent editions during the next century. In fact, as emphasized in Chapter 12, p. 378, he first employed the phrase "association of ideas" in the fourth edition, which appeared in 1700. Accordingly, his *Essay* marks the transition from the seventeenth-century to eighteenth-century psychology just as James's *Principles* of 1890 marked the transition from nineteenth-century to twentieth-century psychology. The influence of Leibnitz (1646–1716), as a contemporary of Locke, also extended into the eighteenth century. His critical analysis of Locke's *Essay* was first published in 1765, the death of Locke in 1704 having caused Leibnitz to withhold publication. With reference to his place in the history of psychology there is thus sound reason to classify Liebnitz as an eighteenth-century philosopher.

When Spinoza died in 1677, Leibnitz was thirty-one and just at the threshold of his career so that he was in a position to profit by Spinoza's teachings. The extent to which he did so will be considered shortly. For the time being, it is better to continue with consideration of the question of having him classified as a seventeenth- or an eighteenth-century thinker. In some respects, of course, this is not a momentous issue. Still, more than a matter of chronological sequence is involved; for there was a difference in the general orientation of the leading thinkers of the centuries in question. The vestiges of medieval thinking were more evident in the one century than in the other. This was alluded to in the previous chapter by referring to Spinoza as the last of the medievals and the first of the moderns. Emancipation from the medieval outlook, which had gotten under way in Spinoza's century, was completed in the following century. In this connection, G. S. Brett (1912, Vol. II, pp. 327–328) referred to the eighteenth century as "the real end of the medieval period in the history of sciences and of philosophy," and he added that "as such it is the true foundation of the nineteenth century."

Eighteenth-Century Psychology: Preliminary Survey

A preliminary survey of the general sweep of psychological trends during the eighteenth century may serve to outline how these trends became "the true foundation of the nineteenth century." In the first place, it is well to recall that the empirical trend initiated by Hobbes and Locke gathered momentum during the eighteenth century as a result of the work of a succession of British associationists. Key figures in this succession were men like George Berkeley (1685–1753), David Hartley (1705–1757), and David Hume (1711–1776). In basic orientation they followed the Lockean tradition of minimizing the role of innate factors in the genesis of mind or intellect and maximizing the role of experiential factors in the way of sensory impressions. Broadly considered, theirs was an environmentalist orientation.

In the second place, it is well to note a different kind of orientation of the eighteenth-century German philosopher-psychologists as revealed in the work of key figures like Leibnitz, Christian van Wolff (1679–1754), and Kant. In general, theirs was a rationalistic or cognitive orientation in the sense of being an endorsement and development of the concept of *res cogitans* stemming from the Cartesian tradition. In their view, mind or intellect constitutes an innate endowment responsive to sensory impressions rather than just a product of sensory impressions. For them, the growth of ideas was a function of *active* thinking and not the automatic consequence of a *passive* bombardment by sensory impressions.

This contrast between British and German psychology as reflected in eighteenth-century developments is not limited to psychology, but might be said to color the general scientific outlook of British thinkers when compared with German thinkers. J. H. Randall (1963, pp. 53–54) has noted this by contrasting the Newtonian tradition with that of Leibnitz. The former has tended to stress knowledge in terms of sensory data and their relations, whereas the latter has tended to emphasize the relevance of mathematical formulations. According to Randall, with the exception of James Clerk Maxwell, the British man of science has sought clarity in his scientific thinking by recourse to mechanical analogies, while the German "has been satisfied with a world mathematically related in correlated functional series." The empiricist tradition made British science less a matter of abstract concepts and more a matter of ideas amenable to pictorial representation. However, in Randall's view, this British tradition is now breaking down, as he notes in the following paragraph:

Today, it seems that the Newtonian world, the British tradition, is crumbling in science, the very notion of substance, is disappearing from scientific thought. No mechanical model seems possible for the systems of radiation we now handle mathematically with such confidence. The physicists now present us with a world that is literally unimaginable—to the layman, though hardly to the mathematician, it often seems unintelligible as well. Leibnitz is triumphant, Newton is beaten. . . . In the early twenties there used to be on display in departments of physics mechanical models of the "Bohr atom." They have since been quietly removed. But we do not need to dilate here on the relative fertility of these two national traditions; it is enough to use them to illustrate what a national tradition is. One might add Bertrand Russell's observation, that American rats, placed in mazes, dash around madly and finally by accident blunder out; while in the same mazes German rats sit down quietly, figure out the exit, and proceed sedately to it. Even rats have a national tradition—in the laboratories of psychologists.

In terms of the latter metaphor, the twentieth-century German rats are the beneficiaries of the Leibnitzian eighteenth-century rationalist tradition, while the trial-and-error scampering of American rats is a product of the British empiricist tradition. The metaphor also indicates that the outlook of the German rats is closer to that of modern science than the outlook of the American rats. Because of this difference in outlook, Randall mentioned the triumph of Leibnitz over his British rival. To put all this less metaphorically: the teachings of Leibnitz had important consequences for science in general and for psychology in particular. Before considering these teachings and their consequences, it seems desirable to introduce a few biographical details.

Leibnitz: A Biographical Sketch

The city of Leipzig, birthplace of laboratory psychology, was also the birthplace of Gottfried Wilhelm Leibnitz. His father was professor of moral philosophy at the University of Leipzig, where Wundt was destined to introduce an experimental psychology more than two centuries later. Shortly after his father's death in 1652, when Leibnitz was a child of six, he became interested in the books he found in his father's library. By the time he was ten he had become familiar with many of the Greek and Latin classics. His precocity was such that he became a university student at fifteen and received his doctor's degree at twenty.[1] This was at the University of Altdorf, where he was offered a professorship despite his extreme youth. However, he had other plans and rejected the offer.

---

[1] F. G. Boring (1950, p. 178) has a reference to the precocity of Leibnitz based upon the study of genius, by C. M. Cox (1926), in which she placed Leibnitz among the top three of the three hundred geniuses included in her survey. According to her, the Leibnitz I. Q. approximated 185.

In view of his outstanding intellectual accomplishments as a child prodigy, it may not be too speculative to assume that he had solid personal experience upon which to argue years later that intellect is more than and different from the result of an enormous accumulation of Lockean sensations. The *intellectus ipse* to which he referred in his controversy with Locke may well have been his own.

IIis vast erudition, the result of wide reading and persistent study, enabled him to write on law, physics, mathematics, metaphysics, theology, diplomacy, and other subjects. At the age of thirty he invented the infinitesimal calculus, but publication of his work on the subject was delayed until 1684, when he was thirty-eight. In the meantime Newton had completed a manuscript on the same subject that was not published until 1687. Neither one knew of the other's work, and the question of priority became a matter of bitter dispute. Leibnitz also engaged in a dispute with Robert Boyle because of Boyle's skepticism regarding some dogmas of religion. In addition to the calculus, Leibnitz invented a calculating machine that he demonstrated to the British Royal Society. His interest in science induced him to suggest the founding of an Academy of Sciences in Berlin. When this was established in 1700, he became its first president. At one time he became very interested in China and advanced the theory that Chinese might be the original source of all languages. Manifestly, there can be no question about the range and diversity of his intellectual curiosity.

For Leibnitz, all these intellectual activities were avocational pursuits in the sense that they were independent of the work by means of which he supported himself. He earned his living by serving as a diplomat for the Archbishop-Elector of Mainz and later as librarian and privy councillor to the Duke of Brunswick. During his service as a diplomat he spent several years in Paris, where he met some of the leading philosophers. His travels also took him to London and Amsterdam. While in the latter city he came to know Spinoza and engaged in numerous talks with him. In addition he was able to read a manuscript copy of the *Ethics* and to make notes of some of the passages.

According to Bertrand Russell (1945, pp. 580–581), who has made a special study of the life and work of Leibnitz, the consequences of the visit with Spinoza were such as to reveal Leibnitz to have been less than an exemplary character. In Russell's blunt wording, "He was wholly destitute of those higher philosophic virtues that are so notable in Spinoza," and even though his more technical philosophic system was "largely Spinozistic," he failed to acknowledge his indebtedness to Spinoza. Instead he actually "joined in decrying Spinoza, and minimized his contacts with him, saying he had met him once, and Spinoza had told him some good anecdotes about politics."

In addition to what has just been referred to as his more technical philosophic system, Leibnitz sponsored a less technical, more popular one. The former system was never revealed to the public until long after the death of Leibnitz, when later editors gained access to his unpublished manuscripts. Russell describes it as "profound, coherent, largely Spinozistic, and amazingly logical." The other system, the popular one, is described as "orthodox, fantastic, and shallow." It was as if this system was intended to curry favor with people of distinction by having it accord with what Leibnitz thought they wanted to believe, while the other system—the unpublished one—was an expression of what he really believed. It is this other system that accounts for his posthumous reputation as a philosopher-psychologist.

Leibnitz as Philosopher-Psychologist

Before considering the psychologically significant teachings of Leibnitz, it would be well to revert to a point stressed in earlier chapters regarding the role of philosophy in the history of psychology. The preceding reference to Leibnitz as a philosopher-psychologist is not to be interpreted as a disparaging reference. After all, until the turn of the century virtually all psychologists were philosopher-psychologists. Every important one from Plato to Locke and Spinoza and their eighteenth-century successors is important for the history of philosophy as well as for the history of psychology. The same applies to some of the nineteenth-century psychologists. Calling them philosopher-psychologists is not to be construed as meaning that what they had to teach is necessarily scientifically suspect. What it does mean is that, in general, their concern with psychology had no sharply circumscribed boundaries but extended into concern with questions of epistemology, ethics, axiology, and ontology. Their psychology, in other words, was not divorced from metaphysics. This was clearly evident in the psychology of Spinoza as presented in the preceding chapter and will also be evident in the psychology of Leibnitz as considered in the present one. It is consequently pertinent to ask whether this dual role detracts from their status as psychologists. Brett raised this question years ago and his answer continues to have relevance for post-Freudian psychology in this electronic era. It merits direct quotation as follows (1921, Vol. III, pp. 147–148):

> It is an open question whether a psychologist can be an idealist or a realist. He should perhaps be simply a psychologist. But apart from collectors of detail and writers of monographs, history has failed to produce a psychologist who was not a philosopher of some kind; and it is notorious that a rejection of all metaphysics is the most metaphysical of all positions. The fruits of the sciences may be plucked by every chance comer; yet the tree that bears them must strike its roots deep or quickly wither away.

There can be no question that the roots of Leibnitzian doctrines are deeply embedded in metaphysical soil. This is what makes it difficult to bring their psychological implications into line with everyday experience. Leibnitz's entire system is based upon his concept of the *monad,* and there is no easy way of making clear what he meant by this term. It is so abstruse that it cannot be represented pictorially or hinted at by means of familiar analogies. To define it as the ultimate unit of being of which reality is composed approximates a verbal description of the term, but to the metaphysically uninitiated this definition must be more baffling than revealing. And to amplify the description by saying with Leibnitz that each monad is indestructible, uncreatable, and immutable is to plunge the uninitiated deeper into the darkness of a metaphysical morass. In terms of a trite simile, the result might be akin to the frustration of a blind man trying to find a black cat in a dark cavern after the animal has escaped from the cavern. On second thought, the simile is not quite adequate, for the blind man is familiar with the object of his search. To find the referent for the word "monad" is a more elusive quest.

Leibnitz was not the first philosopher to employ the word "monad." It was introduced into philosophy by Giordano Bruno (1548?–1600) to designate the smallest units of which substances are composed. Bruno's monads were both psychical and material or both mental and extended. This was not the case with Leibnitz's monads. His were inextended, purely psychical bits of ideational force or nonspatial units of perceptual energy. He even referred to God as the "monad of monads" and to the human soul as a monad. This suggests why he described monads as indestructible, uncreatable, and immutable, for such adjectives are applicable to the concept of God either as Aristotle's unmoved Mover or as Spinoza's panpsychic Thinker. However, being all-pervasive throughout the universe, Spinoza's God was an extended Thinker, while for Leibnitz the monad of monads was not extended. This may suffice as a first approximation to what Leibnitz was driving at. Its relevance for psychology is admittedly tenuous except that the concept of monad has to do with something psychical.

John Dewey's Critique of Leibnitz

A more immediately obvious way of indicating the relevance of Leibnitzian philosophy for the history of psychology would be to resume consideration of his clash with Locke. As a matter of fact, the work in which Leibnitz voiced his objections to Locke's empiricism was once subjected to critical analysis by John Dewey (1859–1952). This was back in 1888, during the decade following the emergence of the "new" psychology of the laboratory. At that time Dewey was at the threshold of his distinguished career and had already made a name for himself as a psychologist, for he had published a book on psychology in 1886. This, as Boring (1950, p. 552) has noted, was the first textbook written by an American to be concerned with the "new" psychology. In it Dewey urged psychologists to be mindful of the philosophical presuppositions underlying their analyses of mental life. Two years later, Dewey's interest in such presuppositions was manifested by the publication of a book that he entitled *Leibnitz's New Essays Concerning Human Understanding—A Critical Exposition.* The book may be regarded as an examination of Leibnitzian teachings from the standpoint of one of the early exponents of the "new" psychology.

At the time Dewey wrote this book, he was as much a psychologist as a philosopher. Its publication in 1888 was four years before the founding of the American Psychological Association. That Dewey was thought of as a psychologist during these years is indicated by his election to the presidency of the Association in 1899. It is also indicated by his close identification with the psychologists at the University of Chicago who were sponsoring functional psychology in the early 1900s. Furthermore, there is a relationship between what he found in Leibnitz and his later endorsement of functional psychology.

Functional psychology, it will be recalled, was particularly concerned with the adaptive value of the facts of mental life. It reflected the impact of Darwinian teachings on the "new" psychology and thus gave psychology a biological orientation. In doing so, it was making explicit what had already been evident in the monadology of Leibnitz, whose monadology had developed out of biological considerations. In fact, such considerations loomed large in his thinking. Dewey put it this way (1888, p. 34):

> But it is the idea of organism, of life, which is radical to the thought of Leibnitz. (Names of Swammerdam, Malpighi, Leeuwenhoek occur and recur in his writings.) . . . He had already learned to think of the world as organic through and through, and found in the results of biology confirmations, apt illustrations of a truth of which he was already thoroughly convinced.

Leibnitz's notion of the world as a vast organization of heirarchically arranged monads seems to have had its inception in what was being revealed by Leeuwenhoek's microscopes. Drops of water were found to be teeming with life; hence that which appeared lifeless to the naked eye was actually part of an organic realm. This fact, as quoted by A. K. Rogers (1932, 3rd ed., p. 282), induced Leibnitz to write:

> In the smallest particle of matter there is a world of creatures, living beings, animals, entelechies, souls. Each portion of matter may be conceived as like a garden full of plants, and like a pond full of fishes. But each branch of every plant, each member of every animal, each drop of its liquid parts, is also some such garden or pond. Thus there is nothing fallow, nothing sterile, nothing dead in the universe; no chaos, no confusion save in appearance, somewhat as it might appear to be in a pond at a distance, in which one would see a confused movement, and, as it were, a swarming of fish in the pond, without separately distinguishing the fish themselves.

Monads as Conatus

Broadly considered, the biological outlook of Leibnitz was thus consistent with that of the modern physiologist's view of the organism as a complex cooperative enterprise of continuing biochemical activity involving cells, tissues, and organs. Even though Leibnitz lived before the cell theory had been introduced and before histology as a separate study had come into existence, he had a general conception of each tiny unit of the body as a dynamic source of activity harmoniously related to the activity of larger units so as to result in the unified activity of the organism as a whole. According to this conception, it was as if each unit of activity or monad were striving to fulfill a specific function, as would be illustrated by the digestive activity of gastric cells or the oxygenating activity of red blood cells. The initiative for such activity, Leibnitz seems to have held, comes from within the cell or monad. In fact, he appears to have equated his understanding of this activity with Spinoza's notion of *conatus.* E. Nordenskiöld alluded to this in his *History of Biology* in these words (1928, p. 128): "The activity of the monads is not motion, as the atomic theory supposed, for motion is something relative, but their ultimate quality can only be conceived as force—*conatus,* as Leibnitz calls it."

As *conatus,* the monad has to do with striving, desiring, intending, and incitement to action. It is a center of force either potential or actual. Brett (1912, Vol. II, p. 304) refers to it as "pure energy known and interpreted through our own self-consciousness." Leibnitz himself, as quoted by Dewey (1888, p. 54), compared the monad to "that particular something in us which thinks, apperceives and wills, and distinguishes in a way of its own from whatever else thinks and wills." With this as a point of departure he then conceived of degrees of this "particular something" ranging in continuous fashion from the clear vivid consciousness of man as a rational being with his apperceptions to the less vivid consciousness or perceptions of lower animals on down to the simplest microorganisms with their incipient or potential consciousness.

He conceived of nature as dynamic and active. In opposition to Descartes, the essence of the physical world was not a static condition of extension but activity of some sort. Moreover, as Dewey pointed out (1888, p. 30), what he did take over from Descartes was "the idea that nature is to be explained mechanically" and "that this is to be brought about through the application of mathematics." Consequently, he, along with Spinoza, saw the "rational" basis of nature in the fact that all the laws of physics can be formulated as mathematical laws. As a result, Dewey concluded (1888, pp. 41–42):

Nature is thus seen to mean Activity, and Activity is seen to mean Intelligence. . . .
In the applicability of the calculus to the discussion of physical facts,

Leibnitz saw two truths reflected,—that everything that occurs has its reason, its dependent connection upon something else, and that all is continuous and without breaks. While the formal principles of his logic are those of identity and contradiction, his real principles are those of sufficient reason and of continuity. Nature never makes leaps; everything in nature has a sufficient reason why it is as it is: these are the philosophic generalizations which Leibnitz finds hidden in the applicability of mathematics to physical science. Reason finds itself everywhere expressed in nature; and the law of reason is unity in diversity. . . .

The final and fundamental notion . . . by which Leibnitz interprets the laws of physics and mathematics is that of life. This is the regnant category. It is "that higher and metaphysical source" from which the very existence and principle of mechanism flow. The perpetual and ubiquitous presence of motion reveals the pulsations of life; the correlation, the rationality, of these motions indicate the guiding presence of life. This idea is the alpha and omega of his philosophy.

Leibnitz's Psychobiological Perspective

In making the concept of life his chief category, Leibnitz was more biological in his thinking than either Descartes or Spinoza. Like Aristotle, he was struck by the idea of growth as a process of continuous change in which the potential becomes realized in the actual. The egg becomes a chicken and the acorn becomes the oak. In such transformations nature makes no leaps as was noted by Aristotle in his observations of embryological development. Leibnitz regarded such development as an inner-directed process of progressive differentiation resulting in the gradual emergence of limbs and organs. In Dewey's opinion (1888, p. 34) he was thus anticipating the later biological theory of epigenesis in contrast to the older and less credible preformation theory. In this connection, Dewey called attention to the following biological considerations, which came to have marked significance for Leibnitz.

The fact that the individual organs of the organism are responsible for unique operations, each of which contributes to the harmony and efficiency of the functioning of the organism, induced Leibnitz to stress the importance of three factors. One had to do with the life process as a dynamic affair of persisting activity. Another emphasized the unity resulting from the coordinated nature of this activity. The third factor gave prominence to the goal or end indicative of the resulting unity. In brief, from this biological perspective Leibnitz saw the world as a vast organism operating in accordance with inherent lawfulness. He saw it as a cosmos and not as a chaos. In effect he was echoing Spinoza's famous dictum: "The order and connection of ideas is the same as the order and connection of things." This dictum is implicit in his principle of *sufficient reason,*[2] for as explained by Dewey (1888, pp. 242–243), this "is not a principle of the external connection of one finite, or phenomenal, part with another." Instead "it is a principle in the light of which the whole phenomenal world is to be viewed, declaring that its ground and meaning are to be found in reason, in self-conscious intelligence."

Leibnitz's biological perspective might more accurately be called a psychobiological perspective, in the sense that his concept of monads was derived from observations and analyses of mental phenomena. In particular he noted changes in the degree of perceptual clarity ranging from vivid, sharply focalized clearness through barely perceptible blurs to seeming abolition of awareness in deep sleep or comatose states. For him, maximal clearness was obtained in the certainty and distinctness of mathematically demonstrated ideas. Along with Descartes and Spinoza, he was enamored of mathematical proof, which served as a paradigm of the method of rationalism. According to Dewey (1888, p. 28), an adherent of this method was urged to:

> Reduce everything to simple notions. Get clearness; get distinctness. Analyze the complex. Shun the obscure. Discover axioms; employ these axioms in connection with the simple notions, and build up from them. Whatever can be treated in this way is capable of proof. Leibnitz . . . possessed this method in common with Descartes and Spinoza. The certainty and demonstrativeness of mathematics stood out in the clearest contrast to the uncertainty, the obscurity, of all other knowledge.

Atomism Versus Holism

As noted from time to time in previous chapters, the contrast to which Dewey alluded in the foregoing passage was exemplified by the contrast

---

2 This principle, sometimes called the *principle of universal rationality,* is accepted as an implicit postulate by most scientists. It expresses faith in the inherent lawfulness of the universe and assumes that once the relevant facts have been discovered they will suffice to make the subject being investigated understandable in terms of reason; hence the term "sufficient reason."

Leibnitz made a distinction between "truths of reason" and "truths of fact." His principle of sufficient reason applied to truths of fact. Moreover, such truths, being dependent upon appropriate circumstances, are only *contingently* true. (The truth of the fact that water boils at a specified temperature is contingent upon the barometric pressure.) On the other hand, "truths of reason" are not contingent. They qualify as truths provided they are devoid of contradiction as exemplified by an arithmetic truth like 225 is the square of 15. In general, truths of reason are to be tested by the principle of noncontradiction, while truths of fact are to be tested by the principle of sufficient reason.

Long before Leibnitz, the distinction between the two classes of truth had already been suggested by Aquinas. As indicated in Chapter 7, p. 178, Aquinas distinguished truths dependent on "sense-observation" from "mathematical truth" whose "meaning is independent of sensible matter."

between the psychology of an empiricist like Locke and a rationalist like Leibnitz. The Lockean emphasis on sensation resulted in what Dewey (1888, p. 90) described as a "thoroughly atomic theory of mind." In contrast, by implication the Leibnitzian emphasis on intellect makes for a more holistic theory of mind. Holistic theories, as contrasted with atomistic theories, hold that the organism functioning as a dynamic whole has properties or characteristics different from those of its constituent elements. This central tenet of Gestalt psychology, it will be recalled, was already noted by Aristotle when he wrote, "The whole is of necessity prior to the part." (See Chapter 4, p. 92.) With reference to psychology British empiricism was non-holistic by maintaining that the congeries or sensations is prior to the emergence of mind or intellect. Leibnitz, on the other hand, as quoted by Brett (1912, Vol. II, p. 305) recognized the priority of intellect when he wrote, "The intellect is innate to itself." It was in this connection, as mentioned at the close of Chapter 12, that Brett epitomized the clash between atomistic and holistic psychological traditions by referring to empiricism as the "archetype of one doctrine" and Leibnitz's monadology as "the germ of the other." To repeat what was mentioned at the beginning of this chapter: the one tradition tended to attribute the growth of ideas to passive bombardment by sensory impressions, while the other tended to stress the active role of the *res cogitans* in dealing with such impressions.

Both Spinoza and Leibnitz, it should now be evident, set the stage for the emergence of a scientific psychology by their endorsement of holistic views. In the light of their metaphysical views, the outward confusion of phenomenal events becomes ordered and intelligible when conceived of in terms of the universe as a whole. So conceived, the universe is glimpsed as eternal, infinite, and lawful. In Spinoza's phrase, one develops such a faith or conviction by viewing the world *sub specie aeternitatis*. From this viewpoint, as brought out in the previous chapter, Spinoza envisaged the operation of laws of physics as well as what he called "sure mental laws" (see Chapter 13, p. 407).

The Spinozistic viewpoint is reflected in the metaphysics of Leibnitz as elaborated in his monadology, with its emphasis on the universe as interrelated, continuous, and subject to the kind of logical order exemplified by mathematics. The monads were thought of in terms of a linear series arranged in hierarchical order, just as a biologist might think of the world of living creatures in terms of evolutionary development from the simplest virus to the most advanced organism. However, instead of following the biological model by defining the hierarchically arranged series in terms of structure or morphology, Leibnitz followed a psychological model by making degree of consciousness the differentiating characteristic between one level and the succeeding one. The succession was conceived of as a continuous gradation of monads characterized by minimal changes in perceptual clarity from one level to the adjacent one. As a consequence, the monads were thought of as differing from one another in the degree to which they mirror their surroundings.

The end result, metaphysically considered, was like Spinoza's in being a panpsychism. Incidentally, this is truer of Leibnitz's "private" or unpublished beliefs than of his "popular" published writings. In the latter he espoused a theological concept of God, whereas in the former he made God the monad of monads. Spinoza, on the other hand, as Dewey (1888, p. 48) noted, introduced a "scientific" rather than a "theological" idea of God in his panpsychism.

The Mind-Body Dichotomy

That Leibnitz was influenced by Spinoza to a greater extent than he admitted is further indicated by his disposition of the mind-body dichotomy. Histories of the subject usually credit Leibnitz with having first formulated the theory of psychophysical parallelism and Spinoza as having been the first to sponsor the double-aspect theory. The nature of these two theories has already been described in Chapter 9. There is no need to say more about them in the present context except to call attention to what was mentioned in Chapter 9 concerning double aspectism as a form of parallelism. (See p. 233.) By way of reminder, it will suffice to introduce H. A. Wolfson's succinct account of Spinoza's view of the mind-body relationship (1934, Vol II, p 23):

> Since thought and extension . . . are only two aspects of one and the same thing, they form two mutually implicative series, so that "the order and connection of ideas is the same as the order and connection of things." Without acting upon one another, mind and body, by virtue of their being attributes which only appear to be two but in reality are one, are so well co-ordinated that there is a perfect correspondence between their actions.

Leibnitz, like Spinoza, recognized this perfect correspondence between mind and body as a parallelism of mental activities and concomitant brain processes. He differed from Spinoza in substituting a dualistic interpretation for Spinoza's monistic interpretation of the parallelism in question. As has been indicated in Chapter 11, pp. 352–353, he used the occasionalist's analogy of the two synchronized clocks to illustrate his interpretation. This amounted to a rejection of the identity hypothesis implicit in Spinoza's double-aspect theory.

According to Dewey, the analogy of the two clocks is really an inadequate way of clarifying the Leibnitzian version of parallelism. For Leibnitz, matter was not composed of monads any more than thoughts per se are composed of matter. He was explicit about this in writing that monads "are not ingredients or constituents of matter, but only *conditions* of it" (Dewey, 1888, p. 138). He even cautioned against efforts to endow monads with spatial qualities: "To say they are gathered in a point or are scattered in space, is to employ mental fictions, *in trying to imagine what can only be thought*" (Dewey, p. 139). Under the circumstances, as Dewey pointed out (1888, pp. 146–147), he was guilty of violating his own injunction when he employed the analogy of the two clocks. In doing so he was suggesting a pictorial or spatial representation. One can think of the infinity of time even though it is impossible to draw a picture of it.

The issue in question is by no means outmoded. H. Feigl, for example, has considered it in his discussion of the mind-body problem. He seems to regard a Spinozistic monistic identity hypothesis or what he calls the "double-language view" as more tenable than a Leibnitzian dualistic parallelism. A detailed account of his discussion would constitute too much of a digression. For present purposes it is sufficient to note the contemporaneity of this phase of one of psychology's persistent problems.[3] In fact, conceivably Feigl might have had the misleading nature of the analogy of the two clocks in mind when he wrote (1953, p. 626), "The alleged difficulties of the identity view are mainly due to a confusion of pictorial appeals with cognitive meanings."

How Leibnitz Influenced Later Psychology

As an omnivorous reader, Leibnitz was familiar with the history of philosophy. His psychology is drawn from diverse sources including Aristotle, the Stoics, St. Augustine, Descartes, and Spinoza. As a result, in the words of J. M. Baldwin (1913, Vol. I, p. 151), it "has left an indelible mark upon modern thought" and in its psychological view of the world it stands "as the culmination of the rationalism of Descartes and Spinoza." Many later psychological developments may be traced back to this culmination. Moreover, even though empiricism might be said to have had a greater influence on the emergence of experimental psychology than the rationalist tradition, rationalism had some influence on systematic psychology. Be this as it may, it is well to note what Boring (1950, p. 167) had to say about this in connection with the impact of the Leibnitzian tradition on psychology: "The whole psychological family is so intimately

---

[3] The problem under consideration became known as the problem of "imageless thought" early in the present century. It is especially associated with the introspective observation of psychologists connected with the University of Würzburg. They reported the occurrence of thoughts devoid of any specifiable mental content. To paraphrase Leibnitz: they had thoughts which could not be imagined. In having them, they were confirming one of St. Augustine's introspective observations, as mentioned in Chapter 6, p. 141, when he "turned to the nature of the mind" and found "what he was not able to see in the mind."

connected that it is impossible to ignore one branch and yet understand the other in anything like its entirety." To facilitate such understanding, some of the chief features of this Leibnitzian branch ought now to be considered with specific reference to their influence on later psychological developments.

In the first place, Leibnitz might be said to have set the stage for a biologically oriented psychology. In Dewey's phrase, it will be recalled, life was Leibnitz's "regnant category" and the "alpha and omega of his philosophy." Dewey's own contribution to the rise of functional psychology constitutes a reflection of this biological orientation.

Secondly, the *conatus* of the monads made for an *activity* psychology. Brentano's psychical *acts,* Wundt's *processes,* the *transitive* states of James, the *propensities* of McDougall, and the *cathexes* of Freud are all variants of a common recognition of mind as active. There are no fixed entities like perception, memory, desire, and thought. Instead there are activities like perceiving, remembering, desiring, and thinking.

In the third place, the *intellectus ipse* of Leibnitz might be viewed as the matrix of later introspective studies of the thought processes as well as of still later psychometric investigations of the organization of intellect. For Leibnitz, intellect was not a passive derivative of sensory bombardment. In fact, as already mentioned, he once stated in opposition to the Lockean view that "the intellect is innate to itself." This dictum amounted to making it different from a mere receiving station for sensations and a source of reactions to them. In line with the emphasis on activity, intellect was thus viewed as inherently active and not just reactive. It was deemed capable of noting its own operations or of reacting to its own activities. As a result, the stage was set for acceptance and endorsement of introspection as a valid scientific method by the German founding fathers of the "new" psychology.

It is also well to note that the psychophysical parallelism of Spinoza and Leibnitz had an influence in getting the "new" psychology under way. In effect it justified investigation of mental life as an independent venture to be pursued in its own right. There was no theoretic need for these pioneer investigators to regard themselves as responsible for investigating the brain events presumed to run parallel to the ones they were studying. Psychology constituted one field of study and brain physiology was a different and parallel field. The quest for Spinoza's "sure mental laws" could be started without having to wait for the formulation of concomitant cerebral laws.

In addition to activity as a key idea, the monadology also gave prominence to the idea of unity. This meant that mind is not only active but also integrated. Its unity is at variance with a faculty psychology. The so-called faculties are abstractions from a complex, unified whole of ongoing activity. Writing a letter, for example, involves a totality of mental functions: perception, memory, choice, thought, motivation, attention, etc. Such functions operate concurrently and make for a *unitas multiplex*—a manifold unity. Furthermore, this Leibnitzian emphasis on the unity of mind is to be contrasted with associationism's emphasis on sensation as the elementary unit of mental life. This emphasis, as Dewey indicated, results in an atomistic approach to psychology as contrasted with the holistic approach of Leibnitz. The former starts with a plurality of elements to be associated or connected into a unified whole, while the latter starts with a whole from which the constituent parts become differentiated as development proceeds. Consequently, it ought to be obvious that modern Gestalt psychology reflects this Leibnitzian approach.

Finally, one other Leibnitzian principle came to affect psychology of the modern period. This is the principle of *continuity*. As already mentioned, Leibnitz taught that nature never makes leaps. In his hierarchy of monads, there was a gradual transition downward from the maximal perceptual clarity of apperception through lesser degrees of awareness to the minimal level of potential consciousness. Such a continuum of change allows for the later recognition of concepts like subconscious and unconscious ideas, sensory thresholds, subliminal stimulation, and negative sensations. In the language of Leibnitz, negative sensations were called *petites perceptions*. He illustrated them by his oft-cited example of the roar of the ocean as the resultant of myriad waves striking the beach. Each wavelet or drop of water taken by itself would not be heard. As a *petite perception* it would be unconscious, but a mass of wavelets may be barely audible and the breakers themselves can be heard without difficulty. From this viewpoint there is an obvious relationship between the monadology of Leibnitz and the psychophysics of Gustav Fechner (1801–1887). Both men were thinking in terms of the principle of continuity. It is the kind of thinking that is with us today whenever we have recourse to a normal distribution curve.

The monadology belongs to metaphysics. Some might be inclined to relegate it to mythology, but they would have to grant that it has been a very influential myth in the history of psychology. Some of its varied influences were sketched in the preceding paragraphs, but it might be well to note one additional line of influence. This has to do with the knotty problem of unconscious ideas or the existence of unconscious mental events. Those who equate the concept of mind with the concept of consciousness find it difficult to reconcile this concept with that of an unconscious mind. For them it is a manifest contradiction; hence an untenable fiction. On the other hand, many contemporary psychologists and psychiatrists seem to regard the unconscious mind either as verified doctrine or as a necessary and useful fiction. They make it an *as if* construction: certain items of experience, otherwise inexplicable, operate *as if* prompted by hidden mental forces. Execution of posthypnotic suggestions, for example, is attributed to such forces and not to the mechanics of nonconscious brain action. What this means, at least by implication, is endorsement of the metaphysics of panpsychism. This is implicit both in Fechner's psychophysics and Freud's concept of the unconscious. It may be either the monistic panpsychism of Spinoza or the dualistic panpsychism of Leibnitz. This is not the important consideration in the present context. What is important, however, is to realize the subtle way in which metaphysical issues continue to lurk in the background of current psychology. To put this metaphorically: despite our official repudiation of metaphysics, the spirits of Spinoza and Leibnitz have not yet been exorcised.

Leibnitz and the Unity-of-Science Movement

Finally, it might be said that the spirit of Leibnitz is still prevalent in another segment of the modern scientific scene; namely, the unity-of-science movement. The nature of this movement has already been considered in Chapter 2, p. 37. As an active enterprise, it is a twentieth-century product that developed out of the examination of the logical foundations of science by a group of Viennese scholars under the leadership of the philosopher Moritz Schlick (1882–1936). From this original group, known as the "Vienna Circle," the movement spread to other countries and soon became international in scope. It supplied a common meeting ground for philosophers interested in the nature of science as well as for philosophically sophisticated scientists. This community of interests resulted in the emergence of a new orientation within the field of traditional philosophy which came to be thought of as a scientific philosophy.

A fundamental question brought into sharp focus by this new orientation was this: considering the large number of different sciences, what, if anything, might they have in common by virtue of which each one is deemed to be a science? It obviously cannot be the subject matter being investigated. Botany, astronomy, psychology, bacteriology, seismology, and genetics, for example, are manifestly too different from one another to be subsumed under some comprehensive caption inclusive of such varied fields of investigation. With subject matter ruled out, is there any respect in which such differing sciences may nevertheless share something in common? Is there an underlying unity in the family of sciences, or just irreconcilable diversity? This was a crucial question for the scientific philosophers inspired by the Vienna Circle and brought together in their quest for the unity of science. Some of them suggested the unity might be found in the kind of thinking or in the kind of logic characteristic of what has come to be recognized as the methodology of science. In doing so, they were touching upon a theme that had already been considered by Leibnitz almost three centuries before. In fact, S. S. Stevens has regarded Leibnitz as the "father" of the idea of the unity of science to the extent to which any single man may be so regarded; for, according to Stevens (in M. H. Marx [ed.], 1951, pp. 41–42):

> In 1666 the twenty-year-old Leibnitz dreamed his own dream about the unity of science and recorded it in *De Arte Combinatoria*. He himself called it a schoolboy's essay, but in it he proposed to create *"a general method in which all truths of reason would be reduced to a kind of calculation. At the same time this would be a sort of universal language or script, but infinitely different from those projected hitherto; for the symbols and even the words in it would direct the reason; and errors, except those of fact, would be mere mistakes in calculation."*

What the youthful Leibnitz envisioned here was the application of mathematical symbols to logic. His vision became a reality with the appearance of symbolic logic in the nineteenth century. As is well known, symbolic logic helped to remove some of the ambiguities of Aristotelian logic. In short, Leibnitz seems to have glimpsed something in common between the language of mathematics and the language of science. If so, he was foreshadowing the viewpoint of those moderns who view the unity of science as a unity of language. Others, of course, see it as a unity of method and still others as a unity of outlook or attitude. In other words, scientific philosophers have not yet reached agreement in their continuing quest for the unity of science. As an area of disagreement it does not appear to lend itself to the kind of resolution Leibnitz had in mind for the future of disagreements among scientists; for he once prophesied that the time would come when controversy in science would be settled if one of the disputants were to make a suggestion like "let us calculate." He was referring to the kind of calculation embodied in the preceding quotation from his writings, which it is an anticipation of twentieth-century efforts to understand the logic of science clearly enough to render it an explicit logic. Moreover, it is a tribute to the genius of Leibnitz that as early as the 1660s he could cherish the modern faith in an underlying unity amid the bewildering plurality of scientific endeavors.

In general, it is well to guard against a possible misinterpretation of such an underlying unity. Just what it ought to connote may be subject to debate. However, for present purposes the following excerpt from J. Robert Oppenheimer's discussion (1954, pp. 95–96) of the problem may serve as a clarifying introduction to a complex issue:

> This heartening phrase "the unity of science," often tends to evoke a wholly false picture, a picture of a few basic truths, a few critical techniques, methods, and ideas from which all discoveries and understanding of science derive; a sort of central exchange, access to which will illuminate the atoms and the galaxies, the genes and the sense organs. The unity of science is based rather on just such a community as I have described. All parts of it are open to all

GOTTFRIED WILHELM LEIBNITZ (1646–1716)

CHRISTIAN WOLFF (1679–1754)

of us, and this is no formal invitation. The history of science is rich in example of the fruitfulness of bringing two sets of techniques, two sets of ideas, developed in separate contexts for the pursuit of new truth, into touch with one another. The sciences fertilize each other; they grow by contact and by common enterprise. Once again, this means that the scientist may profit from learning about any other science; it does not mean he must learn about them all. It means that the unity is a potential unity, the unity of the things that might be brought together and might throw light one on the other.

The concept of the unity of science as a *potential* unity implies a faith in the universe as potentially intelligible. Without such faith no scientist would be sustained in his research efforts. To elaborate upon this theme would constitute too long a digression. It must suffice to note that with reference to psychology, there is also an implicit faith in the potential unity of all the different branches of psychology. This is tantamount to a belief in a *single* science of psychology despite its seemingly disparate fields of investigation and its history of rival schools or systems of psychology. To paraphrase Oppenheimer: no one can become expert in all these fields and systems, but he may profit from learning about any of them in terms of the light they shed upon one another.

In this sense, the psychology of the empiricist sheds light on the psychology of the rationalist, and vice versa. It is well not to regard these as two irreconcilably antithetic kinds of psychology. Instead it would be better to think of the opposition as akin to the antithesis between induction and deduction. In other words, as mentioned from time to time in earlier chapters, empiricists were not altogether uninfluenced by rationalistic considerations, just as rationalists were not altogether blind to the facts of experience. This was clearly evident in the work of Christian Wolff, Leibnitz's immediate successor in the line of continental rationalists stemming from Descartes.

Christian Wolff as First Academic Psychologist

Not a single one of the seventeenth-century and eighteenth-century philosophers considered in the last few chapters belonged to the academic world. None of them were university professors. This holds true for Hobbes, Descartes, Locke, Spinoza, and Leibnitz. It will also hold true for some to be considered in later chapters, including some important nineteenth-century figures.

What this suggests is that to a significant extent psychology's break with scholastic teachings may be attributed to men whose freedom from university ties rendered them less exposed to the influence of such teachings. As outsiders, so to speak, they were more independent of medieval traditions still current in the academic world of their day. Under the circumstances, Christian Wolff (1679–1754) stands out as the first postmedieval university professor to have played an influential role in the history of psychology, and as a consequence he merits more than passing mention. Incidentally, he did not start his academic career as a philosopher-psychologist but as a mathematician. He served as professor of mathematics at the University of Halle from 1706 to 1711, when he turned to philosophy.

Not long after he began lecturing on philosophy at Halle, Wolff became involved in a bitter controversy regarding free will. His advocacy of determinism aroused the enmity of theologians who were proponents of the free-will doctrine, and who convinced King Frederick William I of Prussia that Wolff's determinism would undermine military discipline by rendering desertion a nonpunishable offense. According to their argument, it would be futile and meaningless to punish the deserter if desertion ceased to be subject to voluntary control and came to be regarded as an irresistible, involuntary, predestined flight. As a result the king was induced to bring about the dismissal of Wolff. However, in 1740 the king's successor, Frederick the Great, arranged for Wolff's return to his Halle professorship. This outcome suggests an interesting paradox: as a determinist Wolff succeeded in striking a blow for *Lehrfreiheit* or academic freedom.

In the course of his academic career Wolff wrote on many subjects: logic, ethics, political philosophy, mathematics, theoretical physics, physiology, and psychology. Furthermore, according to E. Nordenskiöld (1928, pp. 248–249), he was both a "clever mathematician" and "a sound botanist" who "contributed much towards inculcating an interest in natural science in Germany." One may thus conclude that rationalism is neither necessarily alien to the spirit of natural science nor necessarily incompatible with the spirit of empiricism. As already suggested, an investigator may consider a given problem in terms of its deductive or rationalistic implications as well as in terms of its inductive or empirical implications. In doing so he would not be inconsistent or unscientific; for both kinds of procedures are indispensable for the working scientist and, metaphorically speaking, constitute the warp and woof of his pattern of work.[4]

Metaphysical Rationalism Versus Critical Rationalism

In his approach to psychology, Wolff endeavored to incorporate both empirical and rationalistic viewpoints. In fact, he devoted separate volumes to each of these viewpoints: the first one, the *Psychologia Empirica,* appeared in 1732 and the second, the *Psychologia Rationalis,* was published in 1734. As M. Dessoir (1912, p. 135) pointed out, by defining the soul as that "which is conscious of itself and of other things

---

[4] For details, see what H. Reichenbach (1951, pp. 95–104) refers to as "the twofold nature of classical physics: its empirical and its rational aspect."

besides itself," Wolff provided for consideration of both viewpoints in his psychology. His empirical psychology dealt with the facts of inner experiences along with what might be concluded from them directly. On the other hand, his rational psychology was concerned with deductions from the empirical data regarding the essential nature of the soul, and here he went beyond the data as such into metaphysical speculations.[5] This divergence had important consequences for later philosophy and resulted in a distinction between the *metaphysical* rationalism of Wolff and the *critical* rationalism of Kant. The difference between the two kinds of rationalism, according to E. Cassirer (1929, p. 992), involves the following considerations:

> Wolff supplements each form of empirical cognition by a corresponding "rational" form. The propositions, for instance, which in the field of physics result directly from observation and from experiments, must be raised to the rank of genuine cognitions of reason by being deduced from the principles of general ontology and general cosmology. . . .
>
> It is against this rationalism of Wolff that the attack of Kant is directed in the *Critique of Pure Reason.* . . . All that reason can reach, lies within the boundaries of experience itself; it cannot recognize the nature of things in themselves, its sole task in theoretical cognition consists in "spelling phenomena in order to be able to read them as experiences."

Like Wolff, Kant was a university professor. As will be discussed in the next chapter, even though Kant never wrote a separate work on psychology he had some influence on the thinking of later psychologists. As a result of his views, psychological issues engaged the attention of post-Kantian German university professors and thus paved the way for the eventual emergence of psychology as a subject of academic interest. The nonacademic psychology of Locke had been studied and criticized by Leibnitz. As a follower of Leibnitz, Wolff might be said to have introduced the essentials of British empiricism and German rationalism into the beginnings of an academic tradition. This tradition was reinforced by Kant's opposition to Wolff's rationalism. One might think of it as a tradition leading from Wolff to Wundt.

Concerning Faculty Psychology, Monism, and Psychometry

The Wolffian psychological tradition has long been known because of its endorsement of faculty psychology. In fact, R. Müller-Freienfels

---

[5] The rational psychology of Wolff was a branch of metaphysics and not an independent science. However, he regarded the establishment of an empirical psychology as an autonomous venture free from metaphysical considerations. In fact, he was the first to employ the phrase "empirical psychology." It is one of Wolff's "important virtues," as Brett (1912, Vol. II, p. 314) noted, that he "named and defined empirical psychology." For Wolff, empirical and rational psychology were of equal importance.

(1935, p. 293) refers to Wolff as the "father of faculty psychology" who regarded man's faculties or capacities for attending, remembering, perceiving, and so on as more or less independent mental powers. By way of explanation Wolff once compared the faculties to bodily organs like heart, stomach, and lungs. Apparently for Wolff it seemed helpful to think of discrete faculties, just as physiologists may consider circulation, digestion, and respiration as separate activities.

At all events, Wolff did not argue for complete or absolute independence of the faculties. By implication he recognized their interdependence as analogous to that of circulation and respiration and similar physiological functions. Moreover, despite his recognition of separate mental faculties, he also recognized the inherent unity of mental life. For him, this unity was viewed as function of integration mediated by symbols— especially language symbols—as representatives of or surrogates for experience. As explained by Dessoir (1912, p. 135), Wolff referred to the *vis repraesentativa* as the "fundamental power of the soul" or "unifying force" manifested by the various modes of activity conceived of as "faculties of the soul."

Although influenced by Leibnitz, Wolff was by no means a slavish disciple. For example, he disregarded the monadology and substituted the notion of atoms for the concept of monads. In addition, although endorsing parallelism, he did not stress pre-established harmony in terms of the Leibnitzian analogy of the two synchronized clocks. Instead he merely assumed a correspondence between every mental process and a concomitant bodily process, thus sponsoring a dualistic viewpoint rather than a monistic one. In fact, as was mentioned near the beginning of Chapter 9, he invented the term "monism," now in common use as the antonym for dualism.

Wolff also seems to have been responsible for the term "psychometry." This coinage was very likely related to his training as a mathematician. At all events, according to Dessoir (1912, p. 217), "the desire for mathematical treatment had already appeared in Wolff's demand for a 'psychometry.' " This constitutes an early and possibly the first recognition of the *possibility* of mental measurement. At the time, this was not at all an obvious suggestion. About a hundred years were to elapse before initial realization of this possibility came to pass with the pioneer measurements of difference thresholds by Ernest Heinrich Weber (1795–1878) in the 1830s. In retrospect one might hold Kant partly responsible for this delay, since Kant, in opposition to Wolff, maintained that mental phenomena were not subject to measurement. Because he regarded measurement an absolute prerequisite for the development of a science, he held that psychology could never become a science. Of course twentieth-century psychology has answered Wolff's "demand for a psychometry" with a vengeance. Just how Kant might have viewed this state of affairs must remain undetermined.

Wolff's Law of Redintegration

In addition to psychometry, Wolff had another important suggestion to make. This had to do with his emphasis on the *vis repraesentativa* as the mind's power to re-present impressions or experiences. It is another way of referring to ideational association. However, what was original with Wolff was his discovery of *redintegration* as a factor in associative sequences. Brett (1912, Vol. II, p. 313) alludes to this factor as Wolff's law of redintegration to the effect that "when a present perception forms part of a past perception, the whole past perception tends to re-instate itself." This is a variant of Dessoir's (1912, p. 135) version of Wolff's formulation: "Every idea tends to recall to the mind the total idea of which it is a part." The phrase "total idea" is a reference to the sum total of events or impressions suggested by such everyday expressions as "Tell me about the accident," "How was your trip?" or "What was the party like?" Accidents, trips, parties, and similar everyday episodes are not just congeries of discrete sensations. They are structured or organized events or clusters of patterned, integrated impressions. What Wolff noted was the fact that subsequent to the establishment of such clusters of experiences, any one of them might be recalled by reinstatement of any fragment or constitutent part of the original cluster. Thus the sound of thunder may suffice to revive or redintegrate a childhood memory of the day our house was struck by lightning. Similarly, reading the name of a particular ocean liner might bring back memories of our first trip to France or a whiff of certain perfume might serve as a reminder of a party that took place on board ship. The part or fragment functions as a symbol that stands for the antecedent whole. Just what is meant by this concept of an antecedent whole is an issue that was partly responsible for later dissatisfaction with the atomistic implications of traditional British associationism. Wolff's law of redintegration of the "total idea" may be construed as a law of association devoid of such atomistic implications.

Redintegration was brought into twentieth-century psychology as a key concept in the writings of the American H. L. Hollingworth (1880–1957). Interestingly enough, he borrowed the word from the Scottish philosopher Sir William Hamilton (1788–1856) and seems to have overlooked Wolff's prior introduction of the concept. In the preface to one of his books (1926, p. xi), Hollingworth wrote: "The psychology of redintegration is merely that of a new or better associationism, freed from certain impediments of the older associationism." In the same preface he recognized definite anticipations of the concept by Locke, by Berkeley, and by Edmund Burke. He also noted its resemblance to some forms of conditioned reactions as described by the Pavlov school, to Bertrand Russell's notion of "mnemic causation," to what Jacques Loeb called "associative memory," to E. L.

Thorndike's principle of "associative shifting" and to some other variants of such allusions to what he stressed as the redintegrative sequence. He explained this sequence as follows (1926, pp. x–xi):

> A complex antecedent, ABCD, instigates a consequent, XYZ. Thereafter the consequent XYZ, or one belonging to the same class, may be instigated by the detail A, or a detail belonging in the same class, by virtue of the historic participation of A in the situation ABCD. A partial stimulus is substituted for a total antecedent.

As developed by Hollingworth, the concept of redintegration was not restricted to the reactivation of the cognitive or ideational aspects of prior experiences. It was not just an affair of remembering bygone episodes but was enlarged to include the behavioral consequences of such episodes. In terms of the preceding formula, the XYZ consequent might have been a clenched fist, a paralysis of fear, a feeling of guilt, a surge of confidence, a drinking bout, a spending spree, laughter, or any one of the thousands of ways in which people react to the vast gamut of provocative situations. What Hollingworth stressed was that reinstatement of a fragment or a detail of one of these provocative situations might suffice to provoke the reaction previously elicited by the original total situation. Moreover, such reactions did not necessarily entail recall of the instigating situation: A elicits XYZ without any memory of BCD.

By means of this broadened interpretation of the nature of redinte-grative sequences, Hollingworth demonstrated their relevance for en-hanced understanding of mental life—both normal and abnormal. In the 1926 book just quoted, he analyzed thought processes from the redintegrative viewpoint and demonstrated the operation of redintegra-tive sequences in dreams, in making judgments, in ordinary thinking, and in reasoning. In an earlier volume, *Psychology of the Functional Neuroses* (1920), he gave an account of his work with World War I victims of so-called shell shock. Here too the redintegrative formula was employed as a means of explaining the neurotic disabilities under consideration. Final-ly, in a later volume entitled *Psychology: Its Facts and Principles* (1928), he elaborated and organized the principle of redintegration into a systematic general psychology. A principle glimpsed by Wofff in the eighteenth century had opened up an expansive psychological vista in the early decades of the present century.

Wolff's Place in the History of Psychology

By this time it must be evident that Wolff's place in the history of psychology goes beyond his endorsement of a faculty psychology. As suggested earlier, as the first academic psychologist he initiated interest in psychology as part of the German university tradition. In a book on

Contemporary Psychology written by Guido Villa at the turn of the century, this phase of Wolff's influence was particularly stressed in the following passage (1903, pp. 14–14):

> Wolff was the cause of awakening in Germany a decided interest in psychological studies, and we have in that country during the eighteenth century a great number of philosophers who gave those studies their special attention, whether as his disciples or his adversaries, or as striving to conciliate eclectically the different views. . . . Most of these start from the *Empirical Psychology* of Wolff, a work of great merit, which is neither entirely speculative nor entirely experimental in its method. . . . Many important problems were discussed at that time regarding the nature and method of psychology, and, amongst others, the question which was to be taken up again later, as to whether Psychology is to be considered a philosophic science—*i.e.,* a branch of metaphysics—or a physical science. The old-fashioned dogmatists had a leaning toward the former opinion, whereas the younger and more empirical scientists followed the latter view.

These eighteenth-century debates regarding the fundamental nature of psychology are still with us. As recently as 1964, for example, C. R. Rogers (p. 5) was asking:

> What kind of a discipline are we? Do we resemble physics? Oceanography? Religion? Or?
> What is to be the nature of our science and what are the methods of that science to be? Or more deeply, how do we contribute effectively to knowing?
> Can we develop tough, dedicated, persistent, humanistic scientists?
> Do we have the skills actually to promote more effective and creative interpersonal relationships?
> What is to be our view as to what makes life worth living? What is the philosophy of life and living which we will contribute to our culture?

In terms of a broad perspective, questions like the foregoing may be viewed as outgrowths of issues implicit in Wolff's recognition of psychology as neither exclusively empirical nor exclusively rational. As outgrowths they have changed markedly from their Wolffian roots. In particular their rational or philosophic implications are being considered with far less attention to metaphysics than was true in Wolff's time. However, as was true in Wolff's day, we are still concerned with the nature of man's inner life and with the problem of valid methods for its investigation. This too goes back to Wolff; for, as noted by Villa, his school of psychology came to be known as the *psychology of internal experience.* Furthermore, Villa credits Wolff with having introduced "introspection" as the first "real psychological method" for the study of experience. To quote Villa directly (1903, p. 129):

England was the first country in which Psychology acquired an empirical character, although even there it lacked a scientific method. On the Continent, from Descartes to Leibnitz and even later, Metaphysics reigned supreme, and the solution of psychological problems was always made to depend on general philosophical premises, and was not considered of much importance. In order to find a real psychological method, we must come down as late as Christian Augustus Wolff, who is the pioneer of that steady and methodical study which was taken up by the German universities and had so great an influence on the evolution of philosophical thought. [6]

It is thus altogether likely that Wundt's later refinement of introspection as a process governed by laboratory controls and limited to *trained* observers was a nineteenth-century culmination of the "steady and methodical" method initiated by Wolff. Incidentally, Wundt restricted the scope of introspective observations to simple, relatively uncomplicated conscious events—those that presumably were amenable to accurate report. The more complex so-called "higher" thought processes were not to be subjected to introspective observations. As was indicated in Chapter 3, Plato had regarded the rational soul as "higher" or "nobler" than the irrational soul and also divided the latter soul into groups of "higher" and "lower" impulses. Wolff and his followers followed this Platonic precedent by regarding some faculties as higher and others as lower. Cognition, for instance, was deemed to be higher than desire or appetite. Furthermore, each of these faculties, in turn, was divided into higher and lower levels. With respect to cognition, to cite a simple example, the faculty of reason was given a higher status than the faculty of memory. Similarly, with respect to desire, impulsively lustful ones were ranked lower than those indicative of self-discipline. In short, the later Wundtian allusions to higher and lower psychological functions may be viewed as a reflection of this Wolffian tradition. [7]

The Wolffian tradition also influenced Kant, and the Kantian tradition was not without its influence on Wundt's generation. In this way, eighteenth-century rationalists had an effect on the nineteenth-century founding fathers of scientific psychology. Wundt's emphasis on the psychology of feeling as a distinctive problem might serve as an illustration of this indirect effect on the continuity of tradition. Recognition of feeling as a

---

[6] It must be remembered that this was written in the 1890s, when psychology was still being taught by professors of philosophy; hence Villa's reference to "philosophical thought" is to be construed as having to do with the thinking of philosopher-psychologists in German universities from the time of Wolff up to and even beyond the Wundtian period.

[7] As previously discussed, this tradition was also reflected in Lloyd Morgan's canon. See Chapter 6, pp. 155–157.

separate faculty was an indirect product of Wolff's faculty psychology. By way of reminder, as mentioned in a footnote on p. 58, this recognition became explicit in a work by Moses Mendelssohn in 1775, a year after Wolff's death. Brett (1912, Vol. II, p. 319), after referring to Mendelssohn as "a very influential writer in his own day," continued with these sentences:

> Mendelssohn's *Letters on Sensation* (*Briefe ueber die Empfindungen,* 1755) were a popular but effective plea for the feelings and a definite claim to give them an independent position between knowledge and desire. The "three faculty" doctrine, according to which all the activities of the soul come under the heads knowing, feeling and willing, may be regarded as established by this work of Mendelssohn.

The independent position accorded the feelings, it seems evident, came as a result of noting that what Wolff had classified as faculty a desire involved both affective and conative components. Abstracting these components for separate consideration gave rise to the faculties of feeling and willing, respectively. As will be brought out later, this was made explicit by Johann Nikolaus Tetens (1736–1807), one of Wolff's followers, who changed Wolff's bipartite scheme into a tripartite one. This tripartite scheme was accepted by Kant and thus the classic account of mind in terms of the faculties of knowing, feeling, and willing came into fashion.

Despite its repudiation of mental faculties as independent or autonomous powers or functions, current psychology continues to reflect tripartite conceptualizations by a triad like cognition, affection, and volition of a triad like ego, id, and superego. In fantasy one might even think of a triple play from Tetens to Kant to Freud. A more academically disposed fantasy would have the play go from Tetens to Kant to Wundt. In less figurative language, this means that Kant was a key figure in the development of eighteenth-century rationalism. How his rationalism influenced psychology calls for a separate chapter.

References

Baldwin, J. M. *History of Psychology*, Vol. I. New York: G. P. Putnam's Sons, 1913.

Boring, E. G. *A History of Experimental Psychology*, 2nd ed. New York: Appleton-Century-Crofts, 1950.

Brett, G. S. *A History of Psychology*, Vol. II. London: George Allen and Unwin, 1912.

Brett, G. S. *A History of Psychology*, Vol. III. London: George Allen and Unwin, 1921.

Cassirer, E. "Rationalism," in *Encyclopaedia Britannica*, Vol. 18, 14th ed., 1929.

Dessoir, M. *Outlines of the History of Psychology.* (Translated by Donald Fisher.) New York: The Macmillan Company, 1912.

Dewey, J. *Leibnitz's New Essays Concerning Human Understanding—A Critical Exposition.* Chicago: C. C. Griggs and Company, 1888.

Feigl, H. "The Mind-Body Problem in the Development of Logical Empiricism," in H. Feigl and M. Brodbeck (eds.). *Readings in the Philosophy of Science.* New York: Appleton-Century-Crofts, 1953, pp. 612–626.

Hollingworth, H. L. *Psychology: Its Facts and Principles.* New York: D. Appleton and Company, 1928.

Hollingworth, H. L. *Psychology of the Functional Neuroses.* New York: D. Appleton and Company, 1920.

Hollingworth, H. L. *The Psychology of Thought—Approached Through Studies of Sleeping and Dreaming.* New York: D. Appleton and Company, 1926.

Müller-Freienfels, R. *The Evolution of Modern Psychology.* (Translated by W. Beran Wolfe.) New Haven: Yale University Press, 1935.

Nordenskiöld, E. *The History of Biology.* (Translated by L. B. Eyre.) New York: Tudor Publishing Company, 1928.

Oppenheimer, J. R. *Science and the Common Understanding.* New York: Simon and Schuster, 1954.

Randall, J. H. *How Philosophy Uses Its Past.* New York: Columbia University Press, 1963.

Reichenbach, H. *The Rise of Scientific Philosophy.* Berkeley: University of California Press, 1951.

Rogers, A. K. *A Student's History of Philosophy,* 3rd ed. New York: The Macmillan Company, 1932.

Rogers, C. R. "Some Questions and Challenges Facing a Humanistic Psychology," *Journal of Humanistic Psychology,* 1965, *V,* 1–5.

Russell, B. *A History of Western Philosophy.* New York: Simon and Schuster, 1945.

Stevens, S. S. "Psychology and the Science of Science," in M. H. Marx (ed.). *Psychological Theory—Contemporary Readings.* New York: The Macmillan Company, 1951, pp. 21–54.

Villa, G. *Contemporary Psychology.* (Translated by Harold Manacorda.) London: Swan Sonnenschein and Company, 1903.

Wolfson, H. A. *The Philosophy of Spinoza,* Vol. II. Cambridge: Harvard University Press, 1934.

15

The Kantian Background

WHEN PSYCHOLOGISTS THINK of eighteenth-century association-ists like Berkeley, Hume, and Hartley, they think of empiricism. However, when historians think of the eighteenth century they do not refer to it as the age of empiricism. Instead they refer to it as the age of rationalism. For them it marked a period of intellectual and social upheaval cul-minating in the French and American Revolutions. It was a period con-cerned with the rights of man, with liberty of conscience, with freedom from governmental tyranny, and with freedom of worship. It was a period when there was increasing recognition of the right of private judgment and when dogmas of the Church were being questioned. It was the period when there was more and more talk about man's "inalienable rights." It was the time when Alexander Pope declared that "The proper study of mankind is man" and when the common man was inspired by a slogan like "Liberty, Equality, and Fraternity." By the emancipation of his reason he was encouraged to make "the pursuit of happiness" a legitimate and valid quest. Reason was to illuminate this quest; hence the period in question was also known as *the Enlightenment.*

Histories of the period call attention to the way in which Voltaire (1694–1778) satirized religious orthodoxy, ridiculed metaphysics, and exposed the shortcomings of political and social institutions of his day. They also mention similar satirical attacks to be found in the writings of Diderot (1713–1784), the famous French encyclopedist. In addition, they usually refer to Rousseau (1712–1778) and his plea for democratic rule and for educational reform. These three were among key figures of the Enlightenment in France just as Frederick the Great (1712–1786), Lessing (1729–1781), and Goethe (1749–1832) are to be listed among the key figures of the German Enlightenment, or what German historians have come to call the *Aufklärung.*

477

The apotheosis of reason during this age of Enlightenment had its philosophical center of gravity in Germany in the person of Immanuel Kant. Man's critical intellect was to be the chief instrument in the fight for enlightenment, and Kant set himself the task of examining this instrument in order to find out how it works and what it can be expected to accomplish. The age of Enlightenment in Germany was the age of Kant, and the *Aufklärung* and Kant came close to being synonymous terms.

A Brief Biography

Although the former East Prussian capital of Königsberg is now the Soviet naval base of Kaliningrad, visitors to the city seeking places of historical interest will doubtless have their attention called to Kant's tomb as well as to a statue of Kant erected in 1864. It is the city of his birth and death; throughout his long life from 1724 to 1804 he never left the environs of the city. His poverty and frail constitution kept him close to home. The presumed educational advantages of foreign travel were not for him. Neither was there any compensation for this lack by being brought up by highly educated parents in an intellectually stimulating home environment. His mother, a woman of limited education but of sound intelligence, was profoundly religious, and the sincerity of her beliefs made a deep and lasting impression on her son. As an adult he once described her to one of his friends as a "tender mother" whose piety, affection, sweetness, and exemplary virtue were among his lasting memories. Kant's father earned his living as a saddler and, as might be expected, never became a man of means. Although not sharing his wife's religious convictions, he did endorse and identify with her moral earnestness. Such earnestness came to have a tremendous effect on Kant as he was growing up, and in the course of time had much to do with shaping the course of his thinking as a mature philosopher for whom fulfillment of duty became an ethical imperative.

The austerity of Kant's home life was reinforced by his early schooling in an academy governed by Pietist regulations. Pietism, as an evangelical movement, had developed in the latter part of the seventeenth century as a reaction against the institutionalized, authoritarian dogmatism of Lutheran theology. Its originator, Philipp Jakob Spener (1635–1705), stressed the importance of rigorous commitment to the ideal of personal devoutness in accordance with Scriptural teachings. The adjective "Pietist" as a name for the movement was originally a term of derision (as were "Methodist" and "Quaker") which adherents of the movement came to accept as a suitable designation for their way of religious life. As Pietists, they objected to dancing, to the theater, and other relaxing diversions. Like the Calvinists they regarded human nature as inherently wicked, and their educational regimen, as outlined by F. N. Freeman (1944), was designed to root out such wickedness. At frequent intervals, pupils were reminded of their sinful souls and urged to confess their sins. The school day started with religious exercises with prayers at the end of each class period and a final session of prayerful devotions. Sunday was replete with hymn singing, sermon after sermon, and reviews of the catechism. All this evangelical fervor was too much for Kant. He found it extremely distasteful and as a grown man he continued to react negatively to such ritualized emotionalism; hence his aversion to hymns, prayer, and hortatory religiosity. However, his later positive convictions regarding moral law, the obligations of duty, and his famous *categorical imperative*[1] might well have been engendered by what was stirred up by his Pietistic childhood.

Kant attended the local Pietist academy in Königsberg from the age of nine until he was sixteen. He then matriculated at the University of Königsberg, where he soon came under the aegis of the professor of philosophy. The latter was an ardent follower of the teachings of Wolff so that early in his university days Kant became familiar with those teachings. Moreover, Kant's interest was not restricted to philosophy, but included mathematics and science. In fact, upon becoming a member of the faculty at the University of Königsberg in 1755 he spent the next fifteen years lecturing on such diverse subjects as mineralogy, mathematics, logic, metaphysics, physical geography, mechanics, and even the science of fortification. During all these years he failed to achieve promotion to the rank of professor; it was not until 1770 that he received an appointment to the professorship of logic and metaphysics. Within the next few years he became more and more famous, and students from all over Germany flocked to his lectures and by the end of the century his books had aroused interest in every German university. Before long the entire world of philosophy concerned itself with Kantian teachings. They became the subject of commentaries and controversy, arousing both praise and condemnation, and gave rise to a tremendous literature. Kant's impact on philosophy in this respect was like that of Freud on psychology. Their respective teachings commanded attention and could not be ignored. In the course of time there were groups of ardent Kantians, of anti-Kantians, and of neo-Kantians just as there have been groups of ardent Freudians, of anti-Freudians, and of neo-Freudians.

Kant's Rationalism Versus Hume's Empiricism

Kant's philosophy is too complex to lend itself to summary formulation. It will be enough to restrict the present account to some of the ways in which his views came to influence psychology. The leading late nineteenth-

---

[1] This was the injunction to "act as if the maxim from which you act were to become through your will a universal law of nature."

century pioneer sponsors of the "new" scientific psychology in Germany were all professors of philosophy and affected by Kant's views directly or indirectly to varying degrees; hence Kant's significance in the history of psychology.

Although Kant wrote on many subjects, he did not write a separate work on psychology.[2] Nevertheless, his philosophy involves psychological issues since one of his primary problems was concerned with the nature and limits of knowledge. Like the empiricists, he was asking questions about the source of our ideas, how they become organized into concepts, and how they correspond with *reality*. This last word is italicized to direct attention to its importance as a key term in the polemics of the period.

By the time of Kant, Locke's distinction between primary and secondary qualities had been subjected to criticism, first by Berkeley and then by Hume. According to Locke, as mentioned in Chapter 7, primary qualities like extension and solidity were regarded as belonging to and inseparable from the "reality" of physical objects, whereas secondary qualities like color and smell were not held to be genuine attributes of objects. Instead Locke endowed the objects with the mere "power" to arouse such sensations. For him, only primary qualities were *real* and were thus to be differentiated from those he called *sensible* and classified as secondary. This was tantamount to recognizing secondary qualities as mental and primary qualities as physical, in the sense of regarding secondary qualities as subjective in contradistinction to the objective status of primary qualities. To illustrate: Locke would have agreed that the yellowness, sourness, and fragrance of a lemon are subjective impressions and not inherent characteristics of the fruit, as contrasted with its shape and solidity as inalienable and objective characteristics. The existence of such primary qualities was presumably not dependent on a percipient of these qualities.

As will be brought out in greater detail in the next chapter, the Lockean distinction between primary and secondary qualities was called into question by Berkeley, who held that both groups of qualities are products of sensory impressions. In the absence of a percipient of these impressions there would be no warrant for their existence. An inkling of this Berkeleian contention had already been evident in what Plotinus had to say about the meaning of a concept like *matter* (see Chapter 6, p. 134). Plotinus too had equated an object's weight, shape, color, and size with sensory impressions and would have agreed with Berkeley that there never is any direct perception of the presumed physical substratum for these

---

[2] He did write a book on anthropology in 1798 which included discussions of sensation, imagination, feeling, and other psychological topics. Theory of knowledge was not included among these topics. In his view this *Anthropologie,* along with psychology as one of its branches, could never be a science, since what it had to teach was not amenable to mathematical formulation.

impressions. Existence of objects is contingent upon awareness of a complex of sensations; hence Berkeley's famous aphorism: *to be is to be perceived.* Leibnitz with his hierarchy of monads, ranging from subconscious *petites perceptions* to the maximal clearness of apperception, came close to echoing this phrase. Both he and Berkeley identified reality with perception. In effect they were making the notion of matter a derivative of mind in contrast to Locke, who had made mind a derivative of matter. Actually, Berkeley's subjective idealism dispensed with the notion of matter. To account for the persistence of objects in the absence of human percipients, he had an omnipresent divine percipient ensuring their continued existence. In addition, he assumed the existence of a self as a percipient of sensory impressions.

These two Berkeleian assumptions were called into question by Hume, who was unable to find evidence for the existence of a percipient God or a percipient self. In Hume's view, all experience consists of a succession of sensations and images. Neither a self nor a nonsensorial material substance can be detected in this stream of experience. As a consequence, Hume's empiricism amounted to repudiation of belief in the existence of God, of a self, or of a physical world. Existence or reality was limited to the sequential procession of sensations and their derivatives as they chanced to be associated. Hume even reduced causal relationships to such sequences by regarding them as habitual associations. If experience X is usually or invariably followed by experience Y, they become associated and thus one comes to expect this sequence. A flash of lightning is commonly followed by thunder, and as a result of this temporal sequence of sight and sound the visual event comes to be considered a cause of the auditory event. However, according to Hume, all we are dealing with here is association by temporal contiguity: one event succeeds a preceding one just as night follows day. From this viewpoint, a cause is not a force compelling or necessitating a particular effect, instead it is merely the antecedent of an associated consequent, and this is all that experience brings to light. As an empiricist, Hume refused to go beyond experience by an appeal to that which cannot be verified by observation. To go beyond experience is to indulge in metaphysics; hence his skepticism regarding unobservable causal factors, material forces, or spiritual selves. In effect he held that what cannot be experienced cannot be known. This was the empirical challenge that shocked Kant into a re-examination of his prior endorsement of the rationalism of Leibnitz and Wolff. In particular, as Kant himself stated, it was Hume's criticism of the concept of causality which awakened him from his "dogmatic slumbers."

At the risk of begging the question, it is tempting to regard Hume as the *cause* of Kant's subsequent philosophizing, especially as revealed in his three famous *Critiques*; namely, the *Critique of Pure Reason,* which appeared in 1781 after about ten years of laborious writing and was followed in 1785 by the publication of the *Critique of Practical Reason* and of the *Critique of Judgment* in 1790. This last work in large measure is concerned with aesthetic judgment and *feelings* of pleasure associated with objects deemed to be beautiful. In the volume dealing with *Practical Reason,* Kant undertook an analysis of reason as a guide to the *practice* of ethical conduct by the exercise of *volitional* control. The initial volume of the trilogy, the *Critique of Pure Reason,* paved the way for the other two. It is Kant's most important work and has to do with cognition, the nature and limits of the *knowing* process. It is thus evident that, psychologically considered, the three volumes reflect the three "faculties" of knowing, feeling, and willing.

As mentioned at the close of the previous chapter, in employing this tripartite scheme Kant was following the psychology of Tetens rather than that of Wolff. It might be well to note something more about this psychology; since, as Brett (1921) mentioned, "Kant was well acquainted with the work of Tetens and derived from that source the psychological groundwork of his philosophy."

A Note about Johann Nikalaus Tetens

Tetens (1736–1807) was a younger contemporary of Kant. His first academic post was at the University of Rostock, where he lectured on physics and metaphysics from 1760 to 1776, when he transferred to the University of Kiel to become professor of philosophy and mathematics. After thirteen years at Kiel he left academic pursuits to engage in administrative work for the Danish government at Copenhagen. The latter work involved the application of mathematics to financial and actuarial problems. During all these years he published a great deal on a wide range of topics reflecting his diverse scientific, philosophical, and practical interests.[3] There is general agreement among historians that his most important work was his book on human nature and its development.[4] This was published in 1777 and, as noted by Brett (1912, Vol. II, pp. 328–329), it contains "the first clear statement of a purely psychological method."

The method of psychology sponsored by Tetens calls for the observation and analysis of experience as it is experienced with repeated checks of one's observations. It was to be purely empirical and devoid of references to mechanical analogies or to hypothetical neurophysiological correlates of experience. In particular he was objecting to the psychology of the Swiss

---

[3] Villa (1903, p. 15) cites Dessoir as having reported that Tetens had written some sixty-five articles and books.

[4] The book was entitled *Philosophische Versuche über die menschliche Natur und ihre Entwickelung.* Incidentally, during the last third of the eighteenth century there was increasing interest in problems of *Entwickelung.* This was manifested by studies of linguistic origins and development and by theories of cultural change as related to the history of civilization. History as a separate discipline was coming into its own.

naturalist Charles Bonnet (1720–1793),[5] who had ventured to explain thinking and feeling as products of the movements of nerve fibers. In this connection Tetens wrote: "My way is the way of observation, while that of Bonnet was the way of hypothesis." What he objected to was reliance on a speculative neurology as a valid explanation for the facts of experience. Psychology was not to be reduced to physics or to physiology. His objection continued to be voiced by psychologists of the modern period. For example, what Tetens had written in the introduction to his book was echoed by Hollingworth in the preface to his 1928 textbook in statements like the following (pp. vi–vii):

> Since this is a textbook of psychology, it resolutely stands by its title. It has no chapters on neuro-anatomy . . . or the structure of the sense organs. It finds plenty of psychological material at hand. . . .
>
> It is the writer's belief that the preoccupation of psychologists with hypothetical features of neurones, brain centers, synapses, and nerve tracts has impeded rather than advanced science. . . .
>
> It is sometimes maintained that "reference to the nervous system introduces into psychology just that unity and coherence which a strictly descriptive psychology cannot achieve." In reply, it is to be observed that biology did not go outside its own field to find its guiding principle (evolution); neither did physics import from foreign fields its ruling dogma (the conservation of energy). Why should not psychology also find its unity and coherence precisely within the field which it explores?

In their objections to neurological theorizing, neither Tetens nor Hollingworth was pleading for a disembodied psychology. They were not defining psychology as the science of the soul. What they both objected to was subordinating the facts of mental life to neurological or physiological considerations. Tetens did not ignore such considerations when he found them relevant. He took them into account when discussing the relationship between mental development from birth to maturity and concomitant physical development. Such parallelism is not a reductionism. In general, Tetens was definitely more empirical than metaphysical or speculative in his psychology. In fact, Villa (1903, p. 15) refers to his psychology as an attempt to establish "an independent Psychology which should be solely based on observation and on experiments." The attempt failed; it did not begin to succeed until a century later, in the time of Wundt. Furthermore, as Villa indicates, Wundt was not unmindful of the importance of Tetens as one of his predecessors.

There are two respects in which Tetens can be said to have anticipated

---

[5] Bonnet is important in the history of entomology. He was the first to call attention to parthenogenesis among insects.

Wundt. In the first place, like Wolff, he recognized introspection as a distinctive method for psychological investigation; and in the second place, unlike Wolff, he recognized feeling as related to but different from sensation. In doing so, he called attention to what later came to be called the *feeling tone* of sensation. This, it will be recalled, is not identical with the sensation per se. (The redness and fragrance of a carnation are qualitatively distinct visual and olfactory sensations that are not to be confused with their accompanying feelings of pleasantness.) Tetens also noted that sensations, in contradistinction to feelings, have objective reference. (The redness is attributed to the carnation, but the pleasantness is an inner event.) For Tetens, this did not mean that feeling tone occurs apart from sensation. Instead it is an invariable accompaniment of sensation. Nevertheless, though dependent on sensation, feeling tone is not the same as sensation. Furthermore, Tetens did not restrict the phenomenon of feeling to sensation, but regarded it as a characteristic of all conscious processes, in the sense that every memory, perception, or other ideational event involves the pleasantness-unpleasantness continuum to some degree. In view of these considerations, Tetens made feeling a separate mental faculty, and his resulting triad of reason, will, and feeling was adopted by Kant. There is much more that might be said about feeling and other psychological topics as discussed by Tetens, but it seems preferable to resume consideration of Kant's philosophy.

Metaphysics and the Limits of Pure Reason

Like many present-day students, Kant had serious misgivings about the status of metaphysics. In the preface to the first edition of his *Critique of Pure Reason* (T. M. Meyer [ed.], 1928, pp. 1–8) he refers to it as "the battle-field of . . . endless controversies" and as having been under the despotic "dominion of the dogmatists." In fact, he might have been referring to the modern era when he wrote, "At present it is the fashion to despise Metaphysic." He also mentioned the efforts of "the celebrated Locke" to dispose of metaphysical controversies by a study of human understanding with the result that everything has fallen "back into the old rotten dogmatism, and the contempt from which metaphysical science was to have been rescued, remained the same as ever." In the preface to the second edition he attributed the deplorable state of metaphysics to the fact that its method "has hitherto consisted in groping only, and what is worst, in groping among mere concepts" (Meyer, p. 13). Accordingly, a chief purpose of his critique of pure reason was "to deprive metaphysic, once for all of its pernicious influence, by closing up the sources of its errors" (Meyer, p. 23).[6]

---

[6] This effort to strengthen the status of metaphysics by disposing of its errors has not vanished from modern philosophy. J. H. Randall, for example, has written (1958) a provocative chapter on "The Nature of Metaphysics: Its Function, Criteria, and Method." He regards metaphysics as a "specific scientific inquiry, with a definite field

A major source of error responsible for the futility of metaphysical debate, according to Kant, is the failure to understand the nature and limits of pure reason. Such failure leads to the "loquacious shallowness" of dogmatic metaphysics or to "that scepticism which makes short work with the whole of metaphysics" (Meyer, pp. 25–26). The *Critique* was intended to correct this failure and thus do away with the shallowness as well as the skepticism. It was "to form a necessary preparation in support of a thoroughly scientific system of metaphysics."

Moreover, since Hume's empiricism had resulted in a skepticism that made metaphysics "a mere delusion of reason" (Meyer, p. 40), Kant found it necessary to begin by examining the validity of what empiricists had to say about the origin of knowledge. He agreed with Locke and other empiricists that all knowledge has its beginning in experience. Without the antecedent arousal by sensory impressions there would be no knowledge. Kant did not question this basic tenet of the empiricists. He agreed that all knowledge begins with sensory experience, but in granting this he was making it a necessary but not a sufficient condition for intellectual development. In his view, "Although all our knowledge begins with experience, it does not follow that it arises from experience" (Meyer, p. 26).

For Kant, in other words, sensory impressions are just the "raw material" of knowledge which has to be dealt with "by our own faculty of knowledge." The latter faculty is obviously the same as the *intellectus ipse* of Leibnitz. This means that Kant endorsed the rationalism of Leibnitz rather than the empiricism of Locke. He voiced his endorsement in this way: "Leibnitz *intellectualized* the phenomena just as Locke altogether *sensualized* the concepts of understanding, i.e., regarded them as nothing but empirical or abstracted concepts of reflection."[7]

To grasp the full implications of this distinction between intellectualization and sensualization, it is necessary to understand what Kant meant by differentiating *a priori* knowledge from *a posteriori* knowledge. The latter refers to knowledge that follows from or is dependent upon experience, while *a priori* knowledge may be either entirely or partly independent of experience. When entirely independent in the sense of being altogether free from any empirical admixture Kant called the *a priori* knowledge in question *pure*.

A few simple examples will help to clarify these Kantian distinctions. Such experienced facts as the wetness of water, the coldness of ice, the heaviness of marble, and the sweetness of sugar are manifestly instances of *a posteriori* knowledge. With this knowledge one can predict what a baby will experience the first time it deals with water, ice, marble, or sugar. That is, *prior* to the baby's experience one has knowledge of what that

and subject-matter of its own, a science that like any other is cumulative and progressive, a science that has in fact during the past half-century made remarkable progress. Metaphysics is the science of existence as existence" (1958, p. 123).

[7] Quoted by E. Cassirer (1929, p. 993) from the *Critique of Pure Reason*.

experience will be. However, this is not wholly *a priori*, since it is contingent upon what had initially been learned from sensory experience. As a consequence this is not to be classified as pure *a priori* knowledge. Similarly, to cite one of Kant's own examples (Meyer, p. 18), the proposition "that every change has its cause, is a proposition *a priori*, but not pure; because change is a concept which can only be derived from experience." Pure *a priori* knowledge, though related to experience, is not derived from experience. Our recognition of the truth of the propositions of mathematics, Kant maintained, is an example of this kind of knowledge. The propositions are both universally as well as necessarily true so that universality and necessity are the governing criteria of this kind of knowledge. For instance, the commutative law $a + b = b + a$ holds true everywhere and at all times and is thus universally true. It admits of no exceptions; hence it is also necessarily true. A Kantian rationalist might add that our reason tells us that it always has been true and always will be true. If so, then some knowledge transcends or goes beyond and is independent of experience.

It was in connection with his discussion of pure *a priori* knowledge that Kant took issue with Hume's view of cause-and-effect relationships as a product of experienced associations by temporal contiguity. In opposition to Hume, he held that our conviction of some cause being responsible for every change is not of empirical origin but is an *a priori* proposition, because "the concept of cause contains so clearly the concept of the necessity of its connection with an effect, and of the strict universality of the rule, that it would be destroyed altogether if we attempted to derive it, as Hume does . . ." (Meyer, p. 29).

Kant regarded his analysis of pure reason as characteristic of what he called his *transcendental* philosophy in the sense that his investigations went beyond the world of subjective events as immediately experienced. In doing so he thought of himself as an objective investigator. At least this is clearly indicated by the fact that he once stated: "Tetens investigates the concepts of pure reason merely subjectively . . .; I objectively; the former analysis is empirical, the latter transcendental."[8] He identified his investigation of the nature of pure reason with the work of Copernicus (Meyer, p. 14). Just as Copernicus had revolutionized astronomy by his then novel assumption of the astronomer "turning around, and the stars to be at rest," so Kant believed he had introduced a rewarding innovation by assuming that "objects must conform to our mode of cognition" instead of having cognition conform to objects. In effect he was maintaining that sensory impressions do not impinge upon a Lockean *tabula rasa* and by dint of repetition give rise to understanding in accordance with empiricist teachings. As he viewed it, there are "rules of understanding" of nonexperiential origin which govern experience. To quote him directly (Meyer, p. 15):

---

[8] Quoted by Dessoir (1912, p. 149).

"Experience, as a kind of knowledge, requires understanding, and I must therefore, even before objects are given to me, presuppose the rules of the understanding as existing within me *a priori,* these rules being expressed in concepts *a priori*, to which all objects of experience must necessarily conform, and with which they must agree. . . ."

Apperception and the Rules of Understanding

Pure reason, Kant held, functions in accordance with the rules of understanding. The rules and the reason are virtually synonymous terms. Knowledge or understanding increases by the activation of these rules as applied to mental content or sensory phenomena. Such activation brings order and meaning and significance into what would otherwise be a chaotic, confused congeries of sensory impressions. That which is activated is not a product of such impressions, as the philosophy of empiricism seems to suggest. Instead the impressions as they occur are occasions for its activation. The result is *organized* experience and the unity of consciousness. Dessoir (1912, p. 151) supplied this clarifying account:

> Kant finds the characteristic thing about the soul, not in its possession of certain contents, but in its ordinary activity, in connecting and separating, in identifying and distinguishing. These operations, by which the mind brings unity into a manifold, do not inhere in simple or compound ideas. They are rather something completely novel and decisive, to which Kant applies the Leibnitzian expression "apperception"; they are rooted in the logical unity of consciousness which lies at the basis of everything.

As a technical term, "apperception" has become obsolete. Current introductory texts are not likely to mention it. From the time of Kant until the early decades of the present century, however, it was a well-known psychological term. All students of the Wundtian psychology were familiar with it. Even though the term is outmoded, the process to which it referred has not vanished. It is necessary to say something about this process in order to understand Kant's rationalism. As used by Kant, apperception is closely related to active attention. To focus on some item of experience so as to perceive it with maximal clearness is to "apperceive" the item. In the course of doing so, one is likely to judge the characteristics of the item and to note how it is related to and differs from other items. By way of illustration, the word "apperception" itself may serve as such an item. One who just chanced to see the word without dwelling upon it and without actually taking note of it can be said to have *perceived* it. On the other hand, one who was struck by the word's strangeness and puzzled over it long enough to recognize it as a psychological term can be said to have *apperceived* it. In doing so, he *judged* it to belong to the general *category* of psychological terms.

As used by Leibnitz, Kant, and psychologists of Wundt's generation, apperception is a more active and more focalized conscious process than passive perception. It is more effortful than perception and calls for logical thinking, in that the perceived item is being judged in terms of relevant categories. To think of barium as a chemical, of elephants as mammals, and of baptism as a religious rite is to think in terms of relevant categories. Without the process of judgment and without categories, there can be no reasoning or logical thinking. Because of this, Kant was particularly concerned with an analysis of the concept of judgment and its relationship to what he called the "pure concepts of the understanding, or of the categories." The meaning of this relationship depends upon Kant's analysis of the psychology of judgment.

Analytic Versus Synthetic Judgments

Many judgments when verbalized take the form of simple declarative sentences indicating some connection between subject and predicate. They consist of propositions like "All fathers are men" or "All children need vitamins." The latter sentence is obviously more informative than the one about fathers. It required considerable research before the need for vitamins was discovered; just knowing the meaning of the word "children" as a concept was not sufficient to prompt the discovery. However, knowing the meaning of the word "fathers" is enough to suggest or imply their maleness. The sentences under consideration thus illustrate Kant's famous distinction between analytic and synthetic judgments. In analytic ones the predicate fails to enlarge the meaning of the subject, so that the relationship between subject and predicate is virtually tautological. In the case of synthetic judgments the predicate adds something new to the subject. Kant called them "expanding" judgments in contradistinction to the "illustrating" analytic judgments. In his view (Meyer, p. 34) it should thus be evident:

1. That our knowledge is in no way extended by analytical judgments, but that all they effect is to put the concepts which we possess into better order and render them more intelligible.
2. That in synthetical judgments I must have besides the concept of the subject something else (X) on which the understanding relies in order to know that a predicate, not contained in the concept, nevertheless belongs to it.

Kant was enough of an empiricist to regard *all* analytic judgments as products of experience—as *a posteriori*. This would also apply to many but not all synthetic judgments. There are some, he maintained, that are not *a posteriori*. He called these synthetic judgments *a priori*. As a rationalist, he found these judgments to involve concepts that were not derivatives of experience. By way of example, he pointed out that all mathematical judgments are "*a priori,* and not empirical, because they carry along with them necessity, which can never be deduced from experience" (Meyer, p. 36). We have an intuitive conviction, he suggested, that $7+5$ *must* equal 12, has always equaled 12, and will always equal 12. In entertaining such a conviction of what always has been and always will be, we are going beyond experience and are dealing with *a priori* knowledge. Reason rather than experienced sensation is the source of such knowledge.[9] This may suffice as a reminder of the drift of Kant's rationalism as related to the process of judgment. At all events, enough has been said about the latter process to serve as an introduction to the previously mentioned relationship between this process and the Kantian categories of understanding.

Cognition and the Kantian Categories

A fundamental question for Locke as well as for Kant might be said to have taken this form: What determines the nature of human understanding? Locke sought the answer by viewing experience as the fountainhead of knowledge, while Kant looked for it by examining the way in which reason deals with experience. Moreover, in agreement with Berkeley and Hume, he was unable to endorse the Lockean distinction between primary and secondary sensory qualities. This meant denial of primary qualities as the source of knowledge of the intrinsic characteristics of perceived objects. Consequently, there is no possibility of ever finding out what they are like independently of being perceived as sensory phenomena. As contrasted with the latter *phenomenal* realm, he assumed the existence of a *noumenal* realm. Knowledge of the intrinsic or inner being of perceived objects was relegated to this permanently inaccessible noumenal realm. Apart from its presumed existence, there is nothing more that can be said about it.

In the Kantian scheme of things, the phenomenal world—the world of appearance—is the only world man can ever know or understand or think about. With the human mind at work its sensory phenomena can be perceived, apperceived, and judged. Knowledge and understanding are thus products of the ways in which the mind works. These ways are *a priori* or inherent in the structure of the human mind. They are not the results of experience, but ways of dealing with experience. By their means, the items of experience are judged and classified in ways that Kant reduced to tabular

---

9 For modern evaluations of this and other Kantian teachings by a scientific philosopher, see Reichenbach (1951, Chapers 5, 6, and 8). His basic position is reflected in this excerpt from his Chapter 8, p. 125:

The principles which Kant had considered to be indispensable to science and nonanalytic in their nature have been recognized as holding only to a limited degree. Important laws of classical physics were found to apply only to the phenomena occurring in our ordinary environment. For astronomical and for submicroscopic dimensions they had to be replaced by laws of the new physics, and this fact alone makes it obvious that they were empirical laws and not laws forced on us by reason itself.

form. Thus, on one page of the *Critique* (Meyer, p. 63) he supplied a table of judgments and on another (p. 66) he introduced a table of categories. At the risk of a slight exaggeration, one might say that the central core of his "critical" analysis of "pure reason" is compressed in these two tables, which thus merit more than passing mention. They sum up what was previously referred to as Kant's rules of understanding. Their relationship to one another will be more readily perceptible by listing them side by side: [10]

TABLE OF JUDGMENTS	CORRESPONDING CATEGORIES
I. *Quantity*	I. *Of Quantity*
1. Universal	1. Totality
2. Particular	2. Plurality
3. Singular	3. Unity
II. *Quality*	II. *Of Quality*
1. Affirmative	1. Reality
2. Negative	2. Negation
3. Infinite	3. Limitation
III. *Relation*	III. *Of Relation*
1. Categorical	1. Inherence and Substantiality
2. Hypothetical	2. Causality and Dependence
3. Disjunctive	3. Reciprocity between the Active and the Passive
IV. *Modality*	IV. *Of Modality*
1. Problematic	1. Possibility and Impossibility
2. Assertory	2. Existence and Nonexistence
3. Apodictic	3. Necessity and Contingency

The foregoing neat arrangement of four forms of judgment with corresponding categories and precisely three divisions under each major caption outlines Kant's application of formal logic to the psychology of thinking. Under the first major caption, that of *Quantity,* he was concerned with the logic of quantitative judgments as embodied in a sentence like "*All* dogs are mammals, *some* dogs are St. Bernards, and Rover is the *sole* or only St. Bernard in our town." Actually, Kant failed to supply such concrete instances of the terms listed in his two tables. He was just concerned with the "logical use of the understanding in general" in order to arrive at the "logical function of the understanding." To accomplish this purpose, he explained, "consideration of the contents of any judgment" was disregarded in order to fix "attention on the mere form of the understanding." The result was the list of barren abstractions just cited. As given they supply form without content. To render them meaningful, it might prove helpful

---

[10] The listing is not a precise duplication of the tables as presented in the text of the *Critique*. For example, under *Quantity* an obvious error in the listing has been corrected. In addition, a few minor changes in word endings have been introduced.

to introduce such illustrative content by a hasty review of the list with Rover in mind.

The first category, that of Quantity, was just illustrated by substituting the simple words "all," "some," and "only" for Kant's more technical equivalents. To illustrate the second triad of terms, those having to do with Quality, it may suffice to note that Rover is *affirmed* to be a thoroughbred, not sick (*negative*), and possessed of *infinite* loyalty to his master. Moreover, with reference to the third caption, of Relation, Rover has the characteristics which "inhere" in or constitute the essence or *substantiality* of the concept of dog. His barking is one of these distinctive characteristics. According to his owner, "*If* a stranger approaches, then Rover barks." In addition to the latter *hypothetical* relation, the owner also mentions this *disjunctive* one: Rover either waits passively to be fed in the kennel or prowls actively for food in the neighborhood. His prowling can also be used to explain the meaning of the terms subsumed under the caption of Modality. For instance, whether he will prowl tonight is *problematic* in the sense that he may or may not do so. However, should he be chained to his kennel, it will be impossible for him to prowl and one can then *assert* the nonexistence of prowling tonight. In fact, with a strong chain and *contingent* upon having the gate locked, the owner may give voice to an *apodictic* or most certain judgment to the effect that of *necessity* Rover will not prowl tonight.

Concerning Aristotle's Realism and Kant's Critical Idealism

Kant's list of categories, it can now be seen, was intended to reveal the fundamental ways in which experience is ordered or classified by the human mind. The categories amount to predicates in terms of which the subjects or items of experience are fitted into or subsumed under appropriate concepts. To say that Rover is a dog is to include him in the concept of dog. On the other hand, to say that he is not a Great Dane is to exclude him from the concept of Great Danes. This means that the Kantian categories provide for both affirmative and negative predicates. In this as well as in other respects, they differ from Aristotle's famous list of ten categories. The Greek terms in Aristotle's list are usually translated as follows: [11]

1. Substance	6. Time
2. Quantity	7. Position (or situation)
3. Quality	8. State (or condition)
4. Relation	9. Activity
5. Place	10. Passitivity (or being acted on)

---

[11] For the original Greek and their Latin equivalents, see the *Britannica* article on "Category" by Abraham Wolf (1929, p. 28).

There is some obvious overlap in the two lists: the first four and the last two in Aristotle's list are included in Kant's. However, Kant's category of Modality is absent from Aristotle's list while Aristotle's references to Time and Place are missing from Kant's list. In part the discrepancy in the two lists is due to a difference in fundamental viewpoint. Aristotle's categories had to do with basic ways of describing or classifying what he took to be the real world—the world of commonsense experience. On the other hand, in view of his distinction between noumenal and phenomenal realms, Kant's categories had nothing to do with the "real" world, i.e., the noumenal realm. Instead his categories had to do with ways in which man can *think* about events belonging to the phenomenal realm. In place of Aristotle's categories as modes of *being,* Kant's categories became modes of *thinking.* In dealing with *being*—with events as they "really" are— Kant's category of Modality is less applicable than it is when the structure of events is attributed to the molding influence of cognition; hence the absence of Modality from Aristotle's list.

In general Aristotle's orientation was more that of the realist and empiricist, whereas Kant's orientation became known as that of the *critical* idealist. According to this orientation, what we understand by and of the external world is predominantly the outcome of the organizing influence of the Kantian categories on the world of *appearance.* In Kant's words as quoted by P. Frank (1957, p. 56): "By sensuous intuition we can know objects as they *appear* to us (to our senses), not as they are in themselves, and this assumption is absolutely necessary if synthetical propositions *a priori* be granted as possible." As interpreted and explained by Frank in the same passage, this was something new:

> This new idea has been given by Kant and his school the name of "critical idealism." The word "idealism" denotes a world view according to which the results of our sense observations are not pictures of real objects. These objects may not exist at all, or may be very different from the way they appear to us. The first view which denies the reality of the world of our experience is called plain "idealism." The Kantian view asserts that the external world exists in itself, but appears to us in a way that is determined by the nature of our minds. This view is called "critical idealism."

Kant's critical idealism is not to be regarded as restricting the "nature of our minds" to the roles played by his twelve categories of understanding. Its nature was also characterized by two additional features which differentiated his list of categories from those recognized by Aristotle. Comparison of the two lists will show that Kant failed to include Aristotle's categories of Place, Time, and Position. This was not an oversight on Kant's part. The facts of time and space in everyday experience are much too obvious to have been overlooked. Indeed, for Kant they constituted the *a priori* groundwork for all experience. He regarded this as an axiomatic principle which he formulated in this way (Meyer, p. 112). "All phenomena contain, so far as their form is concerned, an intuition[12] in space and time, which forms the *a priori* foundation of all of them." Without this there can be no experience of anything; for, as Kant explained, "Phenomena are not things in themselves," and their apprehension "is possible only through pure intuition of space and time." This is tantamount to saying that it is impossible to think of an object or of anything as being unrelated to a spatio-temporal continuum. Whatever occurs must happen some place at some time. In Kant's scheme of things this is an *a priori* psychological necessity. By making it *a priori* he paved the way for later *nativistic* theories of space perception.

Psychology Loses Its Soul

Still other later psychological developments were influenced by Kantian teachings. As a consequence of one of these teachings, for example, the stage was set for the emergence of definitions of psychology that made no reference to a soul. Thus in the post-Kantian era, psychology ceased to be defined as the science of the soul even though the root meaning of "psyche" was still recognized as a reference to the soul concept. In his *Rational Psychology,* Wolff had endorsed this concept by viewing mental phenomena as manifestations of a substantial soul. However, as a result of Kant's critique of this Wolffiian endorsement, psychology lost its soul. All observation, Kant pointed out, is observation of phenomena. There never is observation of a soul's substantiality any more than there is observation of a material substance as a thing-in-itself; i.e., as something stripped of all phenomenal characteristics. Kant was as much opposed to what he called a "baseless spiritualism" as he was to a "soulless materialism."

In the quest for dependable knowledge, man must rest content with evidence based upon mental processes as he experiences them. To go beyond such evidence is to indulge in "fruitless speculation." It is futile, Kant maintained, to attempt to decide whether one's personal existence confirms the metaphysics of materialism or the metaphysics of spiritualism. He disposed of this issue in the following manner (Meyer, p. 179):

> . . . so far as I think myself, it is really impossible by that simple self-conscious-ness to determine the manner in which I exist, whether as substance or as an

---

12 The word "intuition" is the customary translation of what Kant called *Anschauung.* It is not an altogether satisfactory translation and yet there is no precise English equivalent. The German word connotes a nonsensory awareness or spatiotemporal ordering of phenomenal events. Taken in the abstract as thing-in-themselves, the world of objects lacks such ordering. Kant's *Anschauungsformen* impose such ordering on objects as an inevitable *a priori* psychological imperative.

accident. Thus, if *materialism* was inadequate to explain my existence, *spiritualism* is equally insufficient for that purpose, and the conclusion is, that, in no way whatsoever can we know anything of the nature of our soul, so far as the possibility of its separate existence is concerned.

In taking this stand, Kant was neither a materialist nor a spiritualist. This stand was a forerunner of the one adopted by Stern so many years later when, as mentioned in Chapter 10, William Stern wrote his "psychophysically neutral" psychology. It was a stand that enabled Wundt and the other founding fathers of the "new" psychology to win readier acceptance for their definition of this psychology as the study of consciousness or the study of immediate experience. Thanks to Kant, there was little need for them to explain why psychology had ceased to be the science of the soul. Mental phenomena—the facts of consciousness—were to be studied in their own right by means of controlled introspection without reference to the metaphysics of spiritualism. Moreover, they felt no obligation to justify the resulting subjectivism involved in this proposal for an experimentally controlled psychology. Kant's critical idealism had rendered such justification unnecessary. It had also rendered it unnecessary for them to be concerned with the metaphysics of materialism. This meant there was no felt need to reduce all mental phenomena to neural correlates. Mind was not just an epiphenomenon of a "material" brain. The resulting "new" psychology was dualistic in the sense that psychophysical parallelism is dualistic.[13] After all, Kant had shown that it is possible to discuss topics like reasoning, judgment, understanding, and the nature of space and time as "subjective" experiences or as genuine phenomena without bothering about their ultimate noumenal implications. It is true, of course, that for Kant discussion of such topics in terms of their bearing on the categories of understanding was an affair of logic and that Kant did not regard logic as part of psychology. However, this Kantian contention was disregarded by the founding fathers. In their view, logical thinking as a cognitive enterprise—as a phenomenal experience—was as much part of psychology as any other kind of experience.

Kant's Influence on Later Psychology

Furthermore, they had to disregard Kantian teaching in one other respect; namely, in their contention that mind or consciousness could be subjected to experimental investigation. This contention marked a definite break with Kant; for, as summarized by Farrell (A. C. Crombie [ed.], 1963, p. 562):

Kant had argued that the mind could not be investigated in the proper scientific way. His chief grounds reduced to: (i) that mathematics is not really applicable

---

[13] This description of the "new" psychology as dualistic is not to be interpreted as disparaging. Taken in the abstract, a dualistic view of the mind-body relationship is no less "scientific" than a monistic one. Contrary to a prevalent belief, neurophysiologists and specialists in brain physiology are not necessarily committed to monistic interpreta-

to the manifold of inner sense, as this has one dimension only, namely, time; and (ii) that the items in the inner sense cannot be separated and connected again at pleasure, and cannot, therefore, be subject to experiment. This argument cast its forbidding shadow well into the nineteenth century.

In arguing this way, Kant was thinking of the possibility of having psychology become a natural science. The work in which he introduced the argument was published in 1786. Its German title can be translated as "Metaphysical Presuppositions of Natural Science." Under the circumstances it is quite evident that he was not considering the possibility of having psychology develop into a social science. He lived too early to entertain this possibility. Instead, by implication, he seems to have been thinking of a possible mental mechanics or a mental chemistry. Dessoir (1912, pp. 164–165) quotes him as having written that psychology can "disentangle the manifold of inner observation only by mere analysis of thoughts, but cannot retain it as separated and put the components together again." Such analysis without synthesis, he held, could not get very far. At best it might establish empirical laws like the laws of association. Nevertheless, Dessoir credits Kant with having introduced "essential advances" into psychology. In particular he mentions a nativistic factor in space perception as well as what Johannes Peter Müller (1801–1858) was to formulate as his "law of specific nerve energics."

According to Dessoir, these Kantian anticipations of later psychological developments were not as important or as influential as Kant's critical study of what came to be designated as the higher thought processes. This study marked a shift from (a) consideration of simple sensations as the foundation of cognition to (b) sensations as derivative abstractions from cognition as an organized process. It was a shift that recognized the priority of "higher" organized wholes as related to their "lower" constituent parts. It made Kant's account of cognition compatible with views brought into prominence by Gestalt psychologists early in the present century. In this respect he might be thought of as having paved the way for the eventual emergence of the Gestalt viewpoint in German psychology. Dessoir (1912, p. 165) suggested this role when he maintained: [14]

. . . the psychology which turns its attention especially toward relations, form-qualities, complexes, etc. may rightly credit itself with origin from Kant; and no less closely connected with him are the attempts to understand the actual

---

tions. The distinguished British neurologist W. R. Brain has disposed of the issue in this way (1965, p. 196):

To investigate what activity of the neurons in the brain is involved in thought, speech, memory, or feeling is a scientific activity, but, as science, it does not logically involve any particular view of the nature of the mind, or of the relationship between mind and brain. Sherrington, one of the greatest neurophysiologists, was himself a dualist, who did not identify the mind and the brain.

---

[14] Dessoir wrote this just at the time Gestalt psychology was getting under way in Germany. The German edition of his *Outlines of the History of Psychology* was published

life of consciousness as, so to speak, a symbolic representation of fundamental logical conditions. . . . Kant had made possible a psychology "von oben" without himself having put it in operation.

In general, rationalism tackled problems "von oben" while empiricism tackled them "von unten." In other words, the former approach was holistic and the latter atomistic. To revert to an earlier point: in terms of logic the holistic approach was more deductive while the atomistic approach was more inductive. Actually, of course, both kinds of approach are important in the methodologies of science, so that the successful working scientist has to be both a hard-headed empiricist as well as a clear-headed rationalist.

With reference to the history of psychology, it should now be evident that the psychology of today has its roots in the empiricism of men like Locke as well as in the rationalism of men like Kant. This is true even though Locke's *Essay* was more directly devoted to psychological issues than were Kant's three *Critiques*. As Dessoir noted (1912, p. 166):

> Kant, unfortunately, devoted no special work to psychology. However, his occasional changes in the traditional material, and especially his whole mode of attack, gave significant directions for a reshaping of the science.

As previously intimated, one of the "significant directions" alluded to by Dessoir refers to the fact that Kant aroused interest in the higher thought processes. In the post-Kantian era, cognition could no longer be disposed of in terms of the compounding of Lockean sensations. Kant's analysis of the categories of understanding, along with what he had to say about the nature of judgment, had to be reckoned with by the "new" psychology. This was the case even though Kant was more concerned with the logic of thinking than with the psychology of thinking. His table of judgments with their corresponding categories can be considered as a schematic elaboration of Leibnitz's *intellectus ipse*. Along with the spatiotemporal intuitions or *Anschauungen*, it outlines Kant's notion of the structure of intellect, summarizing his view of the way in which man succeeds in organizing or coping with the stream of phenomenal events. One might also think of Kant's table as a logician's detailed elaboration of what was implicit in Locke's notion of *reflection*. Its neat arrangement

---

in 1911 and Wertheimer's pioneer contribution to the Gestalt movement appeared in 1912. It is thus hardly likely that Dessoir could have been referring to the movement launched by Max Wertheimer (1880–1943). Nevertheless, the passage in question does reflect the Gestalt viewpoint. Incidentally, there is no referenc to Brentano or to Wundt in Dessoir's *Outlines*, although he does mention James and has a bibliographic reference to the 1901 publication of *Die moderne Psychologie* by Edward von Hartmann (1842–1906). Why he overlooked Brentano and Wundt in his history is a baffling question. The omission of their names is a good example of what was pointed out in Chapter 8 regarding history as selective perception.

of four categories with precisely three subheadings under each category is almost too neat, and understandably has caused critics of Kant to question the extent to which his scheme dovetails with psychological reality. His entire structure of twelve categories might well be an artifact.

On the other hand, to use a current phrase, it might be a *hypothetical construct*.[15] If so, then the twelve categories might be construed as a foreshadowing of the kind of conceptualization characteristic of contemporary factor analysis. Kant's scheme, theoretically considered, is as much a proposed version for "the structure of intellect" as the one J. P. Guilford presented in his 1956 monograph entitled "The Structure of Intellect." Of course Kant's version is devoid of any statistical support and it is a far cry from his twelve "factors" to the more than fifty that Guilford came to recognize.[16] Kant lived long before correlation studies had come into existence. His own misgivings regarding the possibility of ever introducing measurement into psychology rendered the very thought of such studies alien to his psychological theorizing.

Conceivably, a modern factor analyst might subject Kant's scheme to factorial study by means of suitably selected items presumably indicative of each of the twelve "factors." What the outcome would be is impossible to forecast. None of the twelve might turn out to be factorially pure, or one or more of them might be. The twelve might well be more complex than Kant suspected, and each of the categories thus be the resultant of groups of unit factors just as Guilford (1961, p. 11) found the "products" of cognitive "operations" to comprise "the six categories of factors known at present." It is also of interest to note that just as Kant's views were found to be in line with the holistic orientation of Gestalt psychology, so Guilford (1961, p. 19) interprets his factorial approach as "useful to the Gestalt psychologist."

This is not to say that all factor analysts would agree with Guilford's general interpretations. As is well known, the precise meaning of factors continues to be a controversial issue.[17] As a consequence, the end products of factor analysis are subject to varying interpretations; but this is of relatively minor importance in the present context. It is more important to recognize Kant's "rules of understanding" as an early approach to what has become the factor-analytic approach to the structure of intellect. This means that the problem of its structure when viewed as a problem may be considered to be an outgrowth of psychology's Kantian heritage.

---

[15] For the meaning of this term see the article by K. MacCorquodale and P. E. Meehl (1948).

[16] In a later paper, Guilford (1961, p. 6) wrote that "theoretically, there should be ... about 120 instead of the 55 presently recognized."

[17] The controversy has resulted in very many books and articles. A list of relevant references is to be found in J. R. Royce's paper on "Factors as Theoretical Constructs" (1963) and in R. W. Coan's paper on "Facts, Factors, and Artifacts" (1964).

A Summary Review

This Kantian heritage as considered up to this point can be summarized as follows:

1. Although Kant never wrote a separate book on psychology, he did not neglect psychological issues in his philosophy. The psychology he employed was more influenced by the work of Tetens than that of Wolff. Tetens has stressed a tripartite scheme involving thinking, feeling, and willing as essential aspects of mind. Kant's three *Critiques* reflect a similar scheme.

2. Sensory impressions constitute the "raw material" of knowledge that has to be dealt with by the intellect. In Kant's words: "Although all our knowledge begins with experience, it does not follow that it arises from experience."

3. *A priori* knowledge as partly or wholly independent of experience is to be differentiated from *a posteriori* knowledge. The former kind of knowledge is a product of the inherent organization of the intellect by means of which it deals with the raw material; hence objects must conform to the modes of cognition. By *a priori* knowledge Kant was not endorsing a doctrine of innate ideas in the sense of attributing such knowledge to the newborn infant. He was referring to the mind of the reflective adult. Analogously, those who speak of "native" intelligence in connection with the interpretation of I.Q. data are not attributing full-fledged intelligence to the newborn baby. Instead they are thinking of a genetically determined potential development. In the language of Kant, it would be an *a priori* development.

4. The operations of the intellect make for organized experience as revealed by the unity of consciousness. Cognitive activity in terms of apperception or controlled attention is the fundamental operation responsible for the emergence of this unity.

5. Apperception involves judgment and judgment involves general concepts or categories. Without judgment and without categories there can be no logical thinking. To speak of man as a rational animal is to speak of him as a categorizing animal. All abstract thinking is a function of judgments made in the light of relevant categories of understanding.

6. In connection with the psychology of judgment, Kant noted the difference between analytic and synthetic judgments. The former are elaborations of the obvious and verge on the tautological, while the latter reveal something new. In an analytic proposition the predicate merely *illustrates* the subject. On the other hand, the predicate of a synthetic proposition *expands* the meaning of the subject. A sentence like "All spinsters are unmarried" is analytic in this sense as contrasted with a synthetic sentence like "Duckbills are egg-laying aquatic mammals." All analytical judg-

ments are *a posteriori*. So are many synthetic ones; but some, like the truths of pure mathematics, are *a priori*.

7. It is also well to recall another characteristic Kantian distinction; namely, the difference between the *phenomenal* world and the *noumenal* world, or the world of perceived objects and events and the world as existing in and of itself independently of being apprehended by a sentient being. Accordingly, by hypothesis the noumenal world is not open to inspection, investigation, or profitable speculation. In the very nature of things, such activities are restricted to the phenomenal world. It is the world of immediate experience and as such is neither spiritual nor material. Such psychophysical neutrality set the stage for later definitions of psychology as the science concerned with immediate experience and psychology ceased to be the science of the soul. At best the notion of soul was tacitly relegated to an inaccessible noumenal realm.

8. Experience is not just the result of passively received sensory impressions; such impressions must conform to "the rules of understanding," and these rules are not products of experience. They are *a priori* ways of dealing with the impressions. Without their operation there can be neither knowledge nor understanding.

9. Kant's table of twelve judgments with their corresponding categories supplies a schematic outline of the rules of understanding. The list of categories shows the different ways in which experience is ordered or classified by the human mind. It has more to do with the logic of thinking than with the psychology of thinking.

10. In comparing Kant's list of twelve categories with Aristotle's list of ten categories, it was pointed out that Aristotle's list reflected the orientation of an empiricist and a realist while that of Kant reflected his critical idealism. Aristotle was interested in modes of being—in classifying things as they actually are. In contrast Kant was primarily interested in modes of logical thinking. It was also pointed out that Aristotle's categories of time and place are missing from Kant's list.

11. For Kant, Space and Time constituted the *a priori* foundation for the apprehension of experience. Every event involves a spatiotemporal intuition or *Anschauung*. This characteristic Kantian teaching was compatible with later *nativistic* theories of space perception.

12. Kant's general approach to cognitive functions was holistic rather than atomistic. What the founders of the "new" psychology came to designate as "the higher thought processes" had to do with these cognitive functions, just as what came to be known as Gestalt psychology had something to do with Kant's holistic approach.

13. It was suggested that, broadly considered, Kant's effort to account for cognition in terms of the operations of his twelve categories of understanding might have something in common with twentieth-century efforts to account for the structure of intellect by factor-analytic methods. What is

common to Kant and the factor analysts is recognition of the problem as a problem and not their respective modes of tackling the problem. This is tantamount to saying that the quest for rules of understanding has the same objective as the quest for knowledge of the structure of the intellect.

A Paradox and Its Resolution

The foregoing summary indicates, at least in broad outline, ways in which Kant influenced the thinking of some of his psychologizing successors. Interestingly enough, despite Kant's verdict to the effect that psychology could never become a science, a few of these successors ignored this verdict and began to write about psychology as if it might become a science. For example, this was especially true of Johann Friedrich Herbart (1776–1841), Kant's immediate successor at Königsberg. One of his books was actually entitled *Psychology as Science*. By the time of Wundt, two or three generations after Kant, the dream of a scientific psychology no longer seemed chimerical. The dream was first entertained by German philosophers rather than British empiricists. They and not the British were the first to convert empirical observations into experimental observations. Laboratory psychology was their innovation. In view of Kant's enormous prestige and in view of his predominantly rationalistic orientation, this appears to be a paradoxical development. British empiricists rather than post-Kantian philosophers should have been the pioneer experimental psychologists.

The paradox in question can be resolved by reconsidering the nature of Kant's rationalism. His strictures with respect to psychology as science were overshadowed by his recognition of the inherent lawfulness of mental life. Like Spinoza, he seemed convinced of the existence of "sure mental laws." What he called "the rules of understanding" were equivalent to *laws* of understanding. His "rules" of logic were equated with the "rules" of nature. This was evident in his *Introduction to Logic,* a little volume based upon his lectures and first published in 1800. The opening paragraphs of the book reveal Kant's conviction of the lawfulness of mental life. There can be no doubt about this particularly if one substitutes the word "law" for Kant's use of the word "rule" in the following quotation (1963 ed., pp. 1–2):

> Everything in nature, whether in the animate or inanimate world, takes place *according to rules,* although we do not always know these rules. Water falls according to laws of gravity, and in animals locomotion also takes place according to rules. The fish in the water, the bird in the air, moves according to rules. All nature, indeed, is nothing but a combination of phenomena which follow rules; and *nowhere* is there *any irregularity.* When we think we find any such, we can only say that the rules are unknown.

The exercise of our own faculties takes place also according to rules, which we follow at first *unconsciously,* until by a long-continued use of our faculties we attain the knowledge of them, and at last make them so familiar, that it costs us much trouble to think of them *in abstracto.* Thus, *ex, gr.* general grammar is the form of language in general. One may speak, however, without knowing grammar, and he who speaks without knowing it has really a grammar, and speaks according to rules of which, however, he is not aware.

Now, like all our faculties, the *understanding,* in particular, is governed in its actions by rules which we can investigate. Nay, the understanding is to be regarded as the source and faculty of conceiving rules in general. For just as the sensibility is the faculty of intuitions, so the understanding is the faculty of thinking, that is, of bringing the ideas of sense under rules. It desires, therefore, to seek for rules, and is satisfied when it has found them. We ask, then, since the understanding is the source of rules, What rules does it follow itself? For there can be no doubt that we cannot think or use our understanding otherwise than according to certain rules. Now these rules, again, we may make a separate object of thought, that is, we can conceive them, *without their application,* or *in abstracto.*

In thus giving expression to a firm faith in the underlying lawfulness of mental events and in mind as belonging to the order of nature, Kant provided a climate of opinion readily conducive to the emergence of faith in the promise of a scientific psychology. Without such faith, the search for principles of psychology or laws of mental life would be meaningless and quixotic. Rationalism as a philosophical outlook is grounded in such faith. Having given this faith explicit formulation and unqualified endorsement, Kant might be said to have been the unwitting instigator of the kind of thinking which eventually resulted in having scientific psychology get under way in Germany. In some respects this may have been his most important contribution to psychology. In this connection it is well to recognize that in reality he was an advocate of *empirical* psychology. This is evident from what he had to say about the role of opinion in the acquisition of knowledge (1963 ed., pp. 57–58):

In all our knowledge we begin for the most part from opinion. Sometimes we have an obscure presentiment of the truth; a thing seems to us to contain marks of truth; we *suspect* the truth even before we recognize it with definite certainty.

Now what is the proper sphere of mere opinion? Not in any sciences that contain *a priori* cognitions; therefore not in mathematics, nor in metaphysics, nor in ethics, but only in *empirical* branches of knowledge, in physics, psychology, and the like. For it is in itself absurd to have an opinion *a priori.* And in fact nothing could be more ridiculous than, *ex, gr.* in mathematics, to have a mere opinion. In this science, as also in metaphysics and ethics, the rule holds— *either we know, or we do not know.* It is, therefore, only the objects of empirical knowledge that can be matters of opinion—a knowledge that in *itself* indeed is possible, but only *for us* impossible from the empirical limitations and conditions of our faculty of experience, and the particular degree of this faculty that we possess, and which depends on these conditions. Thus, for instance, the Ether of modern physicists is a mere matter of opinion. For in the case of this, as well as every opinion generally, whatever it may be, I perceive that the opposite might possibly admit of proof. My assent, then, in this case is both objectively and subjectively inadequate; although considered in itself, it may be complete.

Taken strictly, the latter quotation fails to reveal Kant as an *advocate* of empirical psychology. It merely demonstrates his readiness to classify psychology as an empirical subject. His advocacy is brought out in other contexts. In one passage, for example, he refers to Locke as "amongst the greatest and most meritorious reformers of philosophy in our times" (Reichenbach, 1951, p. 23), and in another passage he includes Hume in a list of writers "one should read" in order to learn to write clearly without "pedantry and dilettantism" so as to give "evidence of much insight into science" (1963 ed., pp. 37–38).

It should thus be manifest that Kant was by no means opposed to empiricism. As has just been indicated, he was actually an admirer of British empiricists like Locke and Hume. Furthermore, as was also just indicated, in his view psychology had to be studied as an empirical discipline. In short, his rationalism is not to be construed as antithetic to the development of psychology as an empirical science. His approval of British empiricism, along with what was previously alluded to as his faith in the underlying lawfulness of mental events, made for an outlook or an intellectual tradition in the light of which the nineteenth-century founding fathers of the "new" psychology could glimpse the possibility of developing a *science* of empirical psychology. This was in line with their Kantian background. What was not in line with this background was their plan to make psychology an *experimental* science. As has been mentioned, to envision this possibility they had to disregard Kant's negative pronouncements concerning the idea of an experimental psychology. They had good reason to defy the prestige and authority of Kant in this respect. In fact, they could have justified their defiance by quoting Kant to the following effect (1963 ed., p. 67):

Reason is an active principle which ought not to borrow anything from mere authority of others—nay, not even from experience, in cases where the *pure* use of reason is concerned. But the indolence of very many persons makes them prefer to tread in the footsteps of others rather than to exert their own understandings. Such persons can never be anything but copies of others, and if all men were of this sort the world would for ever remain in one and the same place.

References

Brain, W. R. "Science and Antiscience," *Science,* 1965, *148,* 192–198.

Brett, G. S. *A History of Psychology,* Vol. II. London: George Allen and Unwin, 1912.

Brett, G. S. "History of Psychology," in *Encyclopaedia Britannica,* Vol. 18, 14th ed., 1929.

Cassirer. E. "Rationalism," in *Encyclopaedia Britannica,* Vol. 18, 14th ed., 1929.

Coan, R. W. "Facts, Factors, and Artifacts," *Psychological Review,* 1964, *71,* 123–140.

Dessoir, M. *Outlines of the History of Psychology.* (Translated by Donald Fisher.) New York: The Macmillan Company, 1912.

Farrell, B. A. "Clinical and Objective Psychology: A Problem of Scientific Method," in A. C. Crombie (ed.). *Scientific Change.* New York: Basic Books, 1963.

Frank, P. *Philosophy of Science.* Englewood Cliffs, New Jersey: Prentice-Hall, 1957.

Freeman, F. N. "Education and Concepts of Human Nature." In *Education and Society,* by Members of the Faculties of the University of California. Berkeley: University of California Press, 1944, pp. 23–36.

Guilford, J. P. "Factorial Angles to Psychology," *Psychological Review,* 1961, *68,* 1–20.

Guilford, J. P. "The Structure of Intellect," *Psychological Bulletin,* 1956, *53,* 267–293.

Hollingworth, H. L. *Psychology: Its Facts and Principles.* New York: D. Appleton and Company, 1928.

Kant, I. *Introduction to Logic.* (Translated by T. K. Abbott.) New York: Philosophical Library, 1963. (First published in 1800.)

MacCorquodale, K., and Meehl, P. E. "On the Distinction Between Hypothetical Constructs and Intervening Variables," *Psychological Review,* 1948, *55,* 95–109.

Meyer, T. M. (ed.). *Kant: Selections.* New York. Charles Scribner's Sons, 1929.

Randall, J. H. *Nature and Historical Experience.* New York: Columbia University Press, 1958.

Reichenbach, H. *The Rise of Scientific Philosophy.* Berkeley: University of California Press, 1951.

Royce, J. R. "Factors as Theoretical Constructs," *American Psychologist,* 1963, *18,* 522–528.

Villa, G. *Contemporary Psychology.* (Translated by Harold Manacorda.) London: Swan Sonnenschein and Company, 1903.

Wolf, A. "Category," in *Encyclopaedia Britannica,* Vol. 5, 14th ed., 1929.

16

The Berkeleian Background

AS NOTED IN CHAPTER 15, Kant was influenced not only by the Leibnitz-Wolff-Tetens continental tradition but also by the British empiricist tradition. He was especially affected by the way in which the latter tradition was reflected in the writings of Hume. Furthermore, just as Kant had reacted against Hume, so Hume has reacted against Berkeley, and Berkeley, in turn, had reacted against Locke. The incidental allusions to this series of reactions introduced on previous pages must now be given more direct consideration in order to appreciate the nature and drift of British associationism.

These eighteenth-century philosopher-psychologists, along with their nineteenth-century British and Scottish successors, brought psychological issues into greater prominence and sharper focus. In this sense they were initiating the kind of outlook that eventually resulted in having psychology viewed not as mental philosophy but as science; hence their importance in the history of psychology. This is not to regard them as exclusively responsible for the change in question, because the notion of psychology as science was not entirely a product of British empiricism. It was also a derivative of continental rationalism with its faith in the existence of "sure mental laws." The latter influence, stemming from Descartes and his rationalistic successors, has been traced in the last three chapters through its eighteenth-century developments. However, the former influence, stemming from Hobbes and Locke, has not yet been considered in the light of its eighteenth-century developments; hence the present chapter and the one to follow.

Crosscurrents of Affiliation

Devoting separate chapters or sections of chapters to empiricists on the one hand and to rationalists on the other is a matter of expository conveni-

GEORGE BERKELEY (1685–1753)

IMMANUEL KANT (1724–1804)

ence. It is not to be interpreted as indicative of a mutually exclusive antithesis making for two irreconcilable orientations. In some respects, individual empiricists were more in accord with particular views of individual rationalists than they were with other empiricists. For example, Hobbs and Locke were both empiricists, and yet Hobbes sided with royalists in his political philosophy, while Locke was a champion of democracy. In taking this stand Locke as an empiricist was in agreement with the political philosophy of a rationalist like Spinoza.

Similar crosscurrents of affiliation are to be noted in the attitudes toward religion, with Hobbes and Spinoza in basic agreement regarding Biblical miracles and the veridicality of revelation. Like Hobbes and Spinoza, Kant was unable to endorse any form of religious orthodoxy. In this regard he differed from his fellow rationalist Leibnitz, who, at least in his popular writings, urged support of a conventional theology. This was in opposition to the stand taken by Locke, who in his espousal of Unitarianism was obviously heterodox in his theology. The same can be said about the anticlerical Hobbes with his distrust of the Puritanism of Cromwell and his repudiation of whatever verged on a belief in the supernatural. Such repudiation was in line with Hobbes's commitment to the teachings of Galileo regarding the physics of motion. His psychological views, it will be recalled, were markedly influenced by these teachings. However, Berkeley, his eighteenth-century empiricist successor and an active member of the Anglican communion, rejected such physicalist interpretations of mental life in favor of a teaching less at variance with the spiritual implications of church doctrine. In fact, he employed his empiricism to justify such implications;[1] but this support of church doctrine is not what accounts for his place in a history of psychology. What accounts for it is more directly related to what he had to say about experience in general and visual experience in particular. Some of his views have already been alluded to in incidental fashion in Chapters 6 and 15. It is time to consider them more directly and in greater detail in the light of his life and work.

Berkeley: A Biographical Sketch

George Berkeley was born in Ireland in 1685 and died in England in 1753. He is described as having been a very bright, imaginative, and thoughtful youngster who, even as a youth, began to wonder about the existence of what is ordinarily called the material world. After attending the Kilkenny School ("The Eton of Ireland"), where he received a grounding

---

[1] It might be more accurate to say that Berkeley appealed to reason rather than experience in support of such implications. In the preface to one of his books (1913 ed., p. 5) he declared, "As it was my intention to convince Sceptics and Infidels by reason, so it has been my endeavour strictly to observe the most rigid laws of reasoning."

in the classics and in mathematics, he matriculated at Trinity College, Dublin, in 1700. There he was able to pursue his interest in philosophy, as a result of which he became conversant with the teachings of Descartes and the views of Locke. In particular he must have been struck by the Cartesian definition of matter as extended substance and the Lockean identification of matter with primary qualities of sensation. By way of reaction, he had a sudden inspiration by means of which he expected to undermine belief in material substance and thus transform psychophysical parallelism into a spiritual monism by his defence of subjective idealism. Just how he tried to accomplish this will be considered shortly.

At the age of twenty-two he became a Fellow of Trinity College and in 1709 he was ordained as a priest in the Anglican Church. These were the years in which he wrote his three most important works. The first one, entitled *An Essay Towards a New Theory of Vision,* was published in 1709. A year later he became the author of *A Treatise Concerning the Principles of Human Knowledge.* This was followed in 1713 by his third book, *Three Dialogues Between Hylas and Philonous,* a semipopular exposition of his reasons for denying the reality of material substance. With these three publications he had won a place for himself in histories of philosophy and in histories of psychology while he was still in his twenties. They all are concerned with his analysis of the nature of sensory processes. According to A. K. Rogers (1915, p. 347), he almost lost his life as a result of this interest in the subject of sensation. During his college days he had witnessed an execution by hanging and became curious about the sensation of strangling. To satisfy this curiosity, he persuaded some friends to suspend him from an overhead support and lost consciousness before he could be cut down. Maybe this dramatic incident helped to convince him that one ceases to be when all sensation ceases.

Shortly after graduating from Trinity, Berkeley became a member of the faculty as a teacher of Greek. This career was interrupted by a trip to London in 1713, where he met Swift and other famous writers of the period. Following this sojourn, he journeyed to Italy as secretary and chaplain to a British official assigned to diplomatic duty in Sicily. He returned to England when the diplomat was recalled. Subsequently he went back to Europe as tutor to the son of a church dignitary. In 1720, when England was in the throes of the financial panic precipitated by the scandal of the South Sea Bubble, Berkeley had completed a third trip to the continent. The next few years saw him back in Dublin and active at Trinity, first as University Preacher and then as Dean and incumbent of the Hebrew lectureship.

It is of interest to note that his academic appointments did not include a professorship in philosophy, even though he made his mark in history as a philosopher and not as a specialist in Greek and Hebrew. His work at Trinity had nothing to do with British empiricism. It took a long time before British universities extended official recognition to the teachings of British associationists. As a consequence, Berkeley is not an exception to what was mentioned in an earlier chapter regarding the nonacademic status of British psychology from Hobbes to Bain.

In a way Berkeley did receive posthumous university recognition; for the city of Berkeley,[2] noted as the location of the University of California, is named for him. This was in appreciation of his poem entitled *Destiny of America,* which contains the famous line "Westward the course of empire takes its way." The poem was an expression of Berkeley's disillusionment with conditions in Europe and his compensatory dreams of a finer civilization developing in America. He even planned for a university to be established in the Bermudas and obtained a charter for it from George I and began to solicit funds for its establishment. In conjunction with this plan, he decided to travel to America. Shortly after his marriage he set sail with his bride and landed at Newport, Rhode Island, in 1728. He lived in Rhode Island for about three years, working on his plans for the Bermuda institution and waiting for the financial backing he had been promised. However, the promise was not kept and the dream was never to become a reality.

He returned to England for a few years, and then in 1734 he left for Ireland to assume his duties as the newly appointed Bishop of Cloyne. In addition to attending to his diocesan responsibilities, he found time to write about the allegedly great health-promoting benefit to be derived from drinking tar water. With this departure from philosophic and ecclesiastical pursuits, he left a dubious mark on the history of medicine and prompted F. H. Garrison to refer to "the lucubrations of Bishop Berkeley on the virtues of tar-water" as evidence of the fact that eighteenth-century "English clergymen dabbled in therapeutics" (1929, p. 393). He continued to serve as bishop for almost twenty years. Toward the end of this period, despite the use of tar water, his health failed. He died in England in 1753.

Berkeley's "New Principle"

In an earlier paragraph, reference was made to Berkeley's sudden inspiration regarding the nonexistence of material substance. He himself called this inspiration a "new Principle" of human knowledge.[3] As a principle it equated reality with sensory experience and made knowledge a function of such experience. This amounted to holding that mind is to be identified with reality, on the implicit assumption that the term "mind" has to do with

---

[2] It is customary to pronounce the name of the philosopher as if it were spelled "Barkley" and to refer to the city as if it were spelled "Birkley."

[3] The "new Principle" was first mentioned in what Berkeley called his *Common Place Book.* This personal diary, in which he noted what he deemed to be important ideas, was not discovered until 1871. Although it contains an entry regarding the "new Principle," there is no definite elaboration of what it meant to the youthful Berkeley.

sensation and perception. The simplest exposition of his "new Principle" is to be found in his *Three Dialogues between Hylas and Philonous,* in which he employs the Socratic method by having Philonous in the role of Berkeley goad the skeptical Hylas into an examination of his everyday beliefs and convictions. The following excerpt will illustrate his method (1913 ed, pp. 12–13):

> *Phil.* This point then is agreed between us—that *sensible things are those only which are immediately perceived by sense.* You will further inform me, whether we immediately perceive by sight anything beside light, and colours, and figures; or by hearing, anything but sounds; by the palate, anything beside tastes; by the smell, beside odours; or by the touch, more than tangible qualities.
> *Hyl.* We do not.
> *Phil.* It seems, therefore, that if you take away all sensible qualities, there remains nothing sensible?
> *Hyl.* I grant it.

At one point in the dialogue, Philonous also forces Hylas to grant that the same object cannot be both hot and cold at the same time. He then refers to Locke's thermal illusion by asking, "Suppose now one of your hands hot, and the other cold, and that they are both at once put into the same vessel of water, in an intermediate state; will not the water seem cold to one hand, and warm to the other?" Accordingly, Hylas has to concede that "heat and cold are only sensations existing in our minds," just as the pain occasioned by contact with burning coal is not in the coal. He further concedes that smells "cannot exist in any but a perceiving substance or mind." Consideration of the phenomenon of color induces Hylas to be less yielding. He makes a distinction between apparent colors and real colors by defining the former as those which disappear when brought closer to the eye while real colors persist under close examination. By way of rejoinder, Philonous shows that under still closer examination by means of a microscope, the "real" color is changed. Philonous then tries to clinch the argument with this comment (pp. 27–28):

> Even our own eyes do not always represent objects to us after the same manner. In the *jaundice* every one knows that all things seem yellow. Is it not therefore highly probable those animals in whose eyes we discern a very different texture from that of ours, and whose bodies abound with different humours, do not see the same colours in every object that we do? From all which, should it not seem to follow that all colours are equally apparent, and that none of those which we perceive are really inherent in any outward object?

Hylas is now willing to admit that all colors are "equally apparent, and that there is no such thing as colour really inhering in external bodies." However, in line with Locke's distinction between primary and secondary qualities, he continues the colloquy in this way (p. 31):

I frankly own, *Philonous,* that it is vain to stand out any longer. Colours, sounds, tastes, in a word all those termed *secondary qualities,* have no existence without the mind. But, by this acknowledgement I must not be supposed to derogate anything from the reality of Matter or external objects; seeing it is no more than several philosophers maintain, who nevertheless are the farthest imaginable from denying Matter. For the clearer understanding of this, you must know sensible qualities are divided by philosophers into *primary* and *secondary.* The former are Extension, Figure, Solidity, Gravity, Motion, and Rest. And these they hold exist really in bodies. The latter are those above enumerated. . . . But all this, I doubt not you are apprised of. For my part, I have been a long time sensible there was such an opinion current among philosophers, but was never thoroughly convinced of its truth until now.

By appropriate questioning Philonous soon induces Hylas to admit that whatever arguments are cogent with reference to secondary qualities are just as conclusive when applied to the primary ones. Extension and solidity are just as much dependent on a perceiving subject as are color and smell. There is no justification for the Lockean distinction. Having acknowledged this, Hylas nevertheless has trouble with a teaching that reduces external objects to what Philonous describes as "sensations in the soul." Hylas finds it "necessary to suppose a material *substratum* without which they cannot be conceived to exist." This notion of a substratum is akin to what Kant came to call "the thing-in-itself." As might be expected, Philonous cannot accept belief in a substratum. He challenges Hylas to show by which of his senses he became aware of the existence of a material substratum. The upshot of the ensuing discussion takes this form (pp. 46–47) :

Phil. . . . You tell me Matter supports or stands under accidents. How! is it as your legs support your body?
Hyl. No; that is the literal sense.
Phil. Pray let me know any sense, literal or not literal, that you understand it in. . . .
Hyl. I declare I know not what to say. I once thought I understood well enough what was meant by Matter's supporting accidents. But now, the more I think of it the less can I comprehend it; in short I find that I know nothing of it.
Phil. It seems then you have no idea at all, neither relative nor positive, of Matter; you know neither what it is in itself, nor what relation it bears to accidents?
Hyl. I acknowledge it.

Existence Equated with Perceptibility

In thus denying the reality or existence of matter, Berkeley was taking issue with Locke, in that Locke's primary qualities were presumed to inhere in a corporeal substratum. They had to do with material objects. It will be recalled that he had defined the word "idea" as "the term which . . . stands best for whatsoever is the object of the understanding when a man thinks." For Locke, objects having primary qualities continued to have those qualities even in the absence of a perceiving or thinking being. This is what Berkeley denied. What he affirmed about the objects of human knowledge can be gleaned from the following excerpts from his *Principles of Human Knowledge* (1910 ed., pp. 113–114):

> It is evident to any one who takes a survey of the objects of human knowledge, that they are *ideas* actually (1) imprinted on the senses, or else such as are (2) perceived by attending to the passions and operations of the mind, or lastly, ideas (3) formed by help of memory and imagination. . . . But besides all that endless variety of ideas or objects of knowledge, there is likewise something which knows or perceives them, and exercises operations, as willing, imagining, remembering about them. This perceiving, active being is what I call *mind, spirit, soul,* or *myself.* By which words I do not denote any one of my ideas, but a thing entirely distinct from them, *wherein they exist,* or which is the same thing, whereby they are perceived; for the existence of an idea consists in being perceived. . . . That neither our thoughts nor passions, nor ideas formed by the imagination, exist *without* the mind, is what *every body will allow.* And (to me) it seems no less evident that the various sensations or ideas imprinted on the sense, however blended or combined together (that is, whatever objects they compose), cannot exist otherwise than *in* a mind perceiving them. I think an intuitive knowledge may be obtained of this, by any one that shall attend to *what is meant by the term exist,* when applied to sensible things. The table I write on, I say, exists, that is, I see and feel it; and if I were out of my study I should say it existed, meaning thereby that if I was in my study I might perceive it, or that some other spirit actually does perceive it. There was an odour, that is, it was smelled; there was a sound, that is to say, it was heard; a colour or figure, and it was perceived by sight or touch. This is all that I can understand by these and the like expressions. For as to what is said of the absolute existence of unthinking things without any relation to their being perceived, that seems perfectly unintelligible. Their *esse* is *percipi,* nor is it possible they should have any existence, out of the minds or thinking things which perceive them.

By equating existence with perception, Berkeley made everything in the world ideational. He employed the term "idea" in a broad sense to include immediately experienced sensory events as well as events merely recalled or imagined. However, he called attention to this difference between them (1910 ed., p. 127):

> The ideas of sense are more strong, lively, and *distinct* than those of the imagination; they have likewise a steadiness, order, and coherence, and are not excited at random, as those which are the effects of human wills often are, but in a regular train or series, the admirable connexion whereof sufficiently testifies

the wisdom and benevolence of its author. Now *the set rules or established methods, wherein the mind we depend on excites in us the ideas of sense, are called the laws of nature;* and these we learn by experience, which teaches us that such and such ideas are attended with such and such other ideas, in the ordinary course of things.

In thus recognizing the "laws of nature," Berkeley was affirming the existence of what are ordinarily called the laws of physics. Just what role he assigned to physics as a science is problematic. For him, with his denial of the existence of material substance, physics could not be the science of matter. Instead it would have to be a science dealing with ideas or sensations of sound, heat, light, color, motion, solidity, and fluidity. In effect Berkeley made physics "mentalistic," since for him it would be meaningless to have a science dealing with nonexistent *material* substances.

Bertrand Russell (1945, p. 658) touched upon this issue in his chapter on Berkeley by noting the difficulty of formulating satisfactory definitions of the words "mind" and "matter." As a first approximation, in line with his principle of mnemic causation, he suggested that a "mental" event is "one which remembers or is remembered." He also suggested that "matter" might be defined as "what satifies the equations of physics." Should there be nothing to satisfy these equations, then "either physics or the concept 'matter' is a mistake." Moreover, Russell added that if the concept of substance is rejected, then the concept of "matter" will have to be retained as a "logical construction."

The Esse of Mind Is Not Percipi

Berkeley was not altogether consistent in equating existence with perceptibility. He held to a belief in the existence of spiritual substance even though, in his words, spirit "cannot of itself be perceived." In his view, spirit is the "cause of ideas" and is considered to be "an incorporeal active substance" of which it can be said that (1910 ed., p. 126):

A spirit is one simple, undivided, active being; as it perceives ideas, it is called *understanding,* and as it produces or otherwise operates about them, it is called the *will.* Hence there can be no idea formed of a soul or spirit: for all ideas whatever, being passive and inert, they cannot represent unto us, by way of image or *likeness,* that which acts. A little attention will make it plain to any one, that to have an idea which shall be like that active principle of motion and change of ideas, is absolutely impossible. Such is the nature of *spirit,* or that which acts, that it cannot be of itself perceived *but only by the effects which it produceth.* . . . [Words like] *understanding, mind, soul, spirit,* do not stand for different ideas, or in truth, for any idea at all, but for something which is very different from ideas, and which being an agent cannot be like unto, or represented by, any idea whatsoever. Though it must be owned at the same time, that we have some notion of soul, spirit, and the operations of the mind, such as willing, loving, hating, inasmuch as we know or understand the meaning of those words.

It should thus be evident that Berkeley was ready to admit the existence of mind even though it could not be perceived. As an active agent or process, it was refractory to any kind of ideational representation. Its existence was inferred from effects produced. He was careful to avoid saying that we have an *idea* of mind. Instead he referred to having "some notion" of mind. In other words, just as Russell had made the concept of matter a logical construction, so in effect Berkeley was arguing that if the concept of a spiritual agent is rejected, then the concept of "mind" will have to be retained as a logical construction. In acknowledging the existence of mind or spirit as an active agent, he was no longer restricting *esse* to *percipi.* He was now saying that "to be" is "to be perceived or to be inferred." Even though he was prepared to *infer* the existence of other minds and of God, he balked at inferring the existence of what commonsense calls *material* substances. Their "materiality" was reduced to qualities of perceptible sensations and as such they had no independent existence in a non-ideational realm.[4] Had he been altogether consistent, he might have argued that just as we have "some notion" of mind so we have "some notion" of body or matter. He could accept the nonperceptible Cartesian *res cogitans,* but not the Cartesian *res extensa* having independent thinghood.

Realism or Thinghood Versus Atomistic Idealism

As a word, "thinghood" refers to objects as definite entities. Common objects like chairs, trees, pencils, cabbages, and shoes have thinghood in this sense. They are readily perceptible as real *things.* Such a statement, some would say, is the standpoint of a naïve realist. It is opposed to Berkeley's subjective idealism and to the stand taken by the empiricists in general. For them as for Berkeley, "things" were reduced to congeries of sensations. The atomism involved in such a reduction should not be overlooked. It has often been regarded as an invalid account of the perception of objects and as a weakness of the empirical or associationist tradition in psychology. The physicist C. E. Weizsäcker has given trenchant expression to this weakness in connection with his criticism of what he

---

[4] This denial of the existence of matter struck Samuel Johnson as absurd. Boswell has this to say about it (G. B. Hill [ed.], 1887, p. 545):

> After we came out of the church, we stood talking for some time together of Bishop Berkeley's ingenious sophistry to prove the non-existence of matter, and that every thing in the universe is merely ideal. I observed, that though we are satisfied his doctrine is not true, it is impossible to refute it. I shall never forget the alacrity with which Johnson answered, striking his foot with mighty force against a large stone, till he rebounded from it, "I refute it *thus.*"

calls the "radical sensualism" derived from Berkeley's teachings. His objection takes this form (1952, pp. 110–111):

> If only sensations are given us, then only they and, in a derived sense, "bundles of sensations" can really be called "things" or "natural laws"; everything which makes a claim to reality must be reducible to sensations. . . . [However] "Sensations in themselves" are by no means given to our consciousness. On the contrary, our immediate perception is of "things," in which only a new concentration of attention discovers particular sensory elements. We do not see spots of colour, but trees, people, even joy in a man's face—which is not a thing, still less a sensation. It is a mere hypothesis—and presumably a false one —that everything given to our consciousness can be analysed into elementary sensations.

As a physicist, Weizsäcker, like the Gestalt psychologists, was thus objecting to atomistic accounts of ordinary perception. It should be obvious, or course, that the word "atomistic" is not to be taken literally in this context, but as a way of referring to sensations as analogous to the atoms of the physicist. The analogy breaks down in one respect: the atoms cannot be seen, but a sensation like a pain or a color can be brought to awareness. Berkeley's "to be is to be perceived" dictum is not applicable to atomic physics. Weizsäcker makes this clear in his discussion of the concept of perceptibility [5] by noting the difference between classical physics and modern atomic physics. As was suggested at the beginning of Chapter 14, classical physics treated its concepts as if they could be clarified by means of mechanical models, while modern atomic physics is concerned with experimental results not amenable to such clarification. Classical physics tried "to represent the non-perceptible in the image of the perceptible," but this attempt fails when dealing with the mathematics involved in atomic experiments. According to Weizsäcker (1952, p. 32), "We do not immediately perceive the atom itself; it is given us not as object in space and time, but as the result of a series of inferences from our measurements" and it cannot "be described after the pattern of a spatiotemporal object."

Berkeley lived in the age of classical physics; hence his strictures regarding perceptibility were not readily refutable on logical grounds. Just how he might have dealt with the nonperceptible world of atomic physics must remain conjectural. Had his Hylas known about electrons and atomic

---

[5] In a footnote (1952, p. 13) Weizsäcker explained that "perceptibility" is a translation of the German word *Anschaulichkeit,* which the author had "used in the original to describe a quality common to the theories of classical physics: that they describe nature by models formed analogously to things that can be perceived by the senses." This was still the scientific fashion until shortly after the turn of the century. For example, according to J. H. Hildebrand (1965, p. 441), the great German chemist Wilhelm Ostwald (1853–1932) had maintained that "since atoms could not be seen it was not proper even to talk about them."

energy, he could have given Philonous more trouble. Philonous's defense of idealism might have been punctured and Hylas might have found a foothold for his realism. There is no need to pursue these speculations. They have more to do with Berkeley's metaphysics than with his psychology, and especially with the psychology involved in what Berkeley called a "new theory of vision."

Theory of Vision: Introduction

The *Essay Towards a New Theory of Vision* is one of the classics in the history of empiricism and associationism. With its publication in 1709, the youthful Berkeley might be said to have established his reputation as a mature and provocative thinker. What he set out to demonstrate was the *empirical* origin of our ideas of the location, size, and shape of visually perceived objects as well as of objects perceived by touch. In doing so he was taking a stand against *nativistic* theories of space perception. He made his thesis quite definite in these early paragraphs of the *Essay* (1910 ed., p. 13):

> It is, I think, agreed by all, that *distance* of itself, and immediately, cannot be seen. For *distance* being a line directed end-wise to the eye, it projects only one point in the fund of the eye. Which point remains invariably the same, whether the distance be longer or shorter.
>
> I find it also acknowledged, that the estimate we make of the distance of *objects* considerably remote, is rather an act of judgment grounded on *experience* than of *sense*. For example, when I perceive a great number of intermediate *objects,* such as houses, fields, rivers, and the like, which I have experienced to take up a considerable space; thence from a judgment or conclusion, that the *object* I see beyond them is at a great distance. Again, when an object appears faint and small, which, at a near distance, I have experienced to make a vigorous and large appearance; I instantly consider it to be far off. And this, it is evident, is the result of *experience;* without which, from the faintness and littleness, I should not have inferred any thing concerning the distance of *objects.*

In the course of his analysis of visual perception, Berkeley noted many of the criteria influencing our judgments of size and distance. The preceding paragraph, for example, refers to the criteria of interposition and relative size. As a result of experience, one learns the spatial significance of "intermediate objects" and of changes in size as objects recede or approach. A decrease in size comes to mean remoteness, while an increase means nearness. With respect to the latter criterion, Berkeley called attention to what later came to be known as the phenomenon of *perceptual constancy.* He illustrated this by noting (1910 ed., p. 39): "A man placed at ten foot distance, is thought as great, as if he were placed at the distance of only five foot," even though "the visible magnitude" is "far greater at one station than it is at the other."

Aerial Perspective and the Moon Illusion

Another distance cue recognized by Berkeley has come to be known as *aerial* perspective. He referred to this cue in his efforts to account for the famous moon illusion: the horizon moon appears to be much larger than the zenith moon. To account for the illusion, Berkeley called attention to the distorting effects of mist, fog, and similar atomospheric conditions which result in *fainter* visual impressions. Since the diameter of the moon does not change, its fainter appearance at the horizon induces a judgment of increased size. With size constant, the visual angle subtended by the moon must be the same irrespective of the moon's location. However, Berkeley argued, we have learned in terms of experience that distant objects appear fainter than near objects as well as smaller than near objects. For an object to subtend the same visual angle at a great distance from the eye as it does from a nearer distance, the object must be correspondingly enlarged; hence the compensatory enlargement of the *fainter* horizon moon. Berkeley elaborated upon this topic in considerable detail by way of warding off anticipated objections to his explanations, but there is no need to consider his elaboration. Instead, it seems desirable, even at the risk of a slight digression, to say something about the history of the moon illusion.

As a matter of fact, the moon illusion constitutes one of the most persistent of psychology's minor problems and has been the subject of much controversy. Berkeley (1910 cd., p. 57), for example, refers to the "fruitless" explanations by men like Hobbes and Descartes. According to C. E. Osgood (1953, p. 248), this controversy was started by Ptolemy as far back as A.D. 150 and has continued down through the centuries. Both Helmholtz and James considered the problem. The latter, in general, endorsed Berkeley's explanation in this way (1890, Vol. II, pp. 92–93):

> The well-known increased *apparent size of the moon on the horizon* is a result of association and probability. It is seen through vaporous air, and looks dimmer and duskier than when it rides on high; and it is seen over fields, trees, hedges, streams and the like, which break up the intervening space and make us the better to realize the latter's extent. Both these causes make the moon seem more distant from us when it is low; and as its visual angle grows no less, we deem that it must be a larger body, and we so perceive it. It looks particularly enormous when it comes up directly behind some well-known large object, as a house or tree, distant enough to subtend an angle no larger than that of the moon itself.

A twentieth-century reconsideration of the problem was introduced by E. G. Boring (1943). He and his associates subjected the problem to experimental study over a period of several years. They found that the illusion appears to be a function of binocular vision, since the illusion fails to occur if the observer keeps a patch over one eye for a protracted period, also, it is not invariably experienced by people who have lost an eye. Moreover, the horizon moon, when viewed through a tube, shrinks in size. The illusion also vanished when the horizon moon is viewed with the head inverted by lying on one's back and having the head bent over the edge of some support. This would duplicate the view obtained by standing on one's head or by bending over so as to view the horizon moon between one's legs. When one resumes an erect position, the illusion is again experienced. Because of this fact and for other reasons, Boring concluded (1943, p. 56) that the illusion "depends upon the physiological properties of the observer and not upon physical factors external to him—not upon refraction, nor upon atmospheric haze which might make the horizon look more distant than the zenith." By suitable controls, Boring demonstrated that the "physiological properties" in question have to do with eye movements and not with associated movements of head, neck, and trunk. The position of the eyes when the head is inverted, with resulting shrinkage of the horizon moon, is different from their position when the head is erect. Why the size of the horizon moon should change as the eyes are raised or lowered is a perplexing question. As Boring concedes, no satisfactory explanation has yet been proposed and "we are forced to leave the problem . . . without ultimate solution."

Boring was not the first to call attention to the change in visual dimensions when a scene is viewed with inverted head, for James mentioned the phenomenon in his chapter on space perception in the section dealing with the third dimension. He reported that the phenomenon can be noted by viewing the distant horizon from the top of a hill first with the head erect and then with the head inverted. The result "will be a startling increase in the perspective, a most sensible recession of the maximum distance; and as you raise the head you can actually see the horizon-line again draw near" (1890, Vol. II, p. 213). James did not say anything about the moon illusion in this connection. It is nevertheless quite obvious that the recession of the horizon line reported by James and the shrinkage of the moon reported by Boring are consistent reports. Furthermore, the reports are also in agreement regarding the absence of a satisfactory explanation for the phenomenon. As James points out in a footnote, the phenomenon fails to occur when the visual field is inverted by means of mirrors or prisms while the head is in an erect position. It is solely a consequence of vision with head inverted. Retinal disparity, James indicates, is not a relevant factor, since the enhancement of depth effect is also experienced by one-eyed observers. In view of these considerations, he concluded (1890, Vol. II, p. 213) "that anyone who can explain the exaggeration of the depth sensation in this case will at the same time throw much light on its normal constitution."

Convergence and Accommodation

In preparation for his work on visual perception, Berkeley had familiarized himself with principles of optics. As a result he was able to give due consideration to some of these principles as he developed his own theory. He was particularly concerned with the difference between distinct vision and blurred or what he called "confused" vision. To account for the difference, he had recourse to this dioptric explanation (1910 ed., p. 26):

> First, any radiating point is then distinctly seen, when the rays proceeding from it are, by the refractive power of the crystalline, accurately reunited in the retina. . . . But if they are reunited, either before they are at the retina, or after they have passed it, then there is confused vision.

In a succeeding paragraph, Berkeley qualified the latter reference to confused vision by making a distinction between confused vision and faint vision. He did this by calling attention to the three conventional diagrams showing light rays coming to a focus (1) on the retina, (2) in front of the retina, and (3) in back of the retina. Reference to the diagrams, he pointed out, "may show us the difference between confused and faint vision." He thus suggested that faint visual impressions become signs of remoteness and confused visual impressions become signs of nearness.

As an empiricist, Berkeley attributed judgments of distance based upon such signs to *experience* and not to any native predispositions. He made this especially clear in a passage dealing with the significance of convergence (1910 ed., p. 16):

> Not that there is any natural or necessary connexion between the sensation we perceive by the turn of the eyes, and greater or lesser distance. But because the mind has by constant *experience* found the different sensations corresponding to the different dispositions of the eyes, to be attended each with a different degree of distance in the *object*: there has grown an habitual or customary connexion, between those two sorts of *ideas*.

By the phrase "customary connexion," Berkeley meant an acquired association. The word "ideas" was italicized in the preceding passage to stress what Berkeley deemed particularly important; namely, that the association in question was between sensory impressions and the idea of distance and not between degree of convergence and judgment of distance. He stressed this because in doing so he was contradicting those writers on optics who had argued that the perception of space involves awareness of angular changes incident to convergence as well as awareness of refractive changes incident to rays coming to a focus in front or in back of the retina.

In effect Berkeley was saying that what opticians know about the nature of visual perception is not to be confused with what is actually experienced by the ordinary observer. He voiced his opposition in this trenchant passage (1910 ed., pp. 15–16):

> I appeal to any one's experience, whether, upon sight of an *object,* he computes its distance by the bigness of the *angle* made by the meeting of the two *optic axes*? Or whether he ever thinks of the greater or lesser divergency of the rays, which arrive from any point of his *pupil?* Nay, whether it be not perfectly impossible for him to perceive by sense the various angles wherewith the rays, according to their greater or lesser divergence, do fall on his eye. Every one is himself the best judge of what he perceives, and what not. In vain shall the *mathematicians* in the world tell me, that I perceive certain *lines* and *angles* which introduce into my mind the various *ideas* of *distance*; so long as I myself am conscious of no such thing.[6]

Berkeley clarified the preceding statement in his discussion of convergence. There is a greater degree of convergence in near vision as an object is brought closer to the eye; but one is not directly aware of such convergent changes. One may be aware of resulting blurred vision if the eyes remain relaxed or else aware of sensations of tension as the blurring is prevented "by straining the eye" and objects are "esteemed so much the nearer" when increased effort is required to render vision distinct (1910 ed., p. 19). This is obviously a reference to accommodative effort; but Berkeley has nothing to say about the mechanism of accommodation.[7] Nor does he say anything about the extent to which felt differences of strain function as cues to distance. Actually, of course, they are not operative for distances greater than about sixty feet; hence other cues must be involved in judging relative distances beyond this range. For Berkeley, it sufficed to call attention to a difference in sensations of effort or strain as the eyes shift from convergent to parallel axes or vice versa; for this "brings the idea of greater or lesser distance into the mind."

---

[6] In taking this stand Berkeley was anticipating what, as explained in Chapter 13, William James was to call "the psychologist's fallacy."

[7] The fact that the lens changes its shape in near vision was already known in Berkeley's time. According to F. H. Garrison (1929, pp. 260–261), Christoph Scheiner, a Jesuit astronomer, had demonstrated these changes by means of his famous pinhole experiment as early as 1619 and their existence was confirmed by Descartes in 1637. The relationship of these changes to the ciliary muscle was not worked out until the nineteenth century. Helmholtz advanced the most widely accepted theory to account for this relationship by assuming that contraction of the ciliary muscle induces anterior bulging of the lens by a forward pull on the lens capsule. Ernest G. Clarke, a British ophthalmologist, has expressed some reservations about this theory in comparison with the rival theory of M. H. E. Tscherning. In his opinion (1914, p. 4), "all physiological proof is on the side of the Helmholtz theory, but there is no doubt that on the clinical side Tscherning's arguments assume a very strong position."

Height as a Distance Cue

In connection with the moon illusion, Berkeley had noted the relevance of a factor in addition to that of aerial perspective. This had to do with a change in the apparent size of an object when viewed at a given distance directly in front of the observer as contrasted with the same distance directly above the observer: there is a tendency to judge a vertically placed object as being more remote than when it is viewed horizontally. Berkeley accounted for this phenomenon in the following way (1910 ed., pp. 44–55):

> The reason whereof is, that we are rarely accustomed to view objects at a great height; our concerns lie among things situated rather before than above us; and accordingly our eyes are not placed on the top of our heads, but in such a position as is most convenient for us to see distant objects standing in our way, and this situation of them being a circumstance which usually attends the vision of distant objects, we may from hence account for . . . an object's appearing of different magnitude, even with respect to its horizontal dimension, on the top of a steeple, for example, a hundred feet high, to one standing below, from what it would if placed at a hundred feet distance on a level with the eye.

What Berkeley had noted in this observation is not unrelated to the familiar vertical-horizontal illusion as exemplified by the fact that a vertical line ten inches long will appear longer than a ten-inch horizontal line. This illusion causes a geometrically perfect square to look less like a perfect square than one drawn with slightly shorter vertical lines or else with slightly longer horizontal lines. Artists are mindful of such visual effects when they create impressions of a third dimension on a two-dimensional surface. They realize that objects painted in the upper part of the canvas will seem more distant than objects located in the lower part.

Visual Space as Related to Tactual Experience

Berkeley regarded all visual impressions of depth and distance as products of tactual experience. Our knowledge of the height, breadth, and nearness of objects, he maintained, is based upon the results of tactual manipulation. Such manipulation, in turn, is preceded by reaching for or walking toward objects in order to establish contact. The reaching and the walking and the touching give meaning to words like "near," "far," "up," "down," "thin," "thick," "smooth," "rough," "wet," "dry," "light," "heavy," and whatever else a congenitally blind person comes to know about his surroundings in terms of distance, shape, and other characteristics of objects. Without contact receptors, distance receptors would virtually cease to supply cues to distance, depth, and other spatial characteristics.

For Berkeley, spatiality has to be learned; it is not an innate idea as was implied by Descartes when he defined matter or body as extended substance. In his "new theory of vision" he was opposing this Cartesian implication by arguing that matter as such can never be perceived. As previously mentioned, in developing this theory he had studied works on optics current in his day. In particular he refers to a work on dioptrics by "the ingenious Mr. Molyneux" who, it may be recalled, aroused Locke's interest in the post-surgical experience of cataract patients (see Chapter 12, pp. 389–392). Although Berkeley fails to mention Locke's disposition of the original question posed by Molyneux until later in the book, he must have been reminded of the question, for he first alludes to it in the following way (1910 ed., pp. 30–31).[8]

> . . . it is a manifest consequence that a man born blind, being made to see, would, at first, have no idea of distance by sight; the sun and stars, the remotest objects as well as the nearer, would all seem to be in his eye, rather in his mind. The objects intromitted by sight, would seem to him (as in truth they are) no other than a new set of thoughts or sensations, each whereof is as near to him, as the perceptions of pain or pleasure, or the most inward passions of his soul. For our judging objects perceived by sight to be at any distance, or without the mind, is . . . entirely the effect of experience, which one in those circumstances could not yet have attained to.

On page 50 he elaborated upon this point as follows:

> Hence it is evident, one in those circumstances would judge his thumb, with which he might hide a tower, or hinder its being seen, equal to that tower, or his hand, the interposition whereof might conceal the firmament from his view, equal to the firmament: how great an inequality soever there may, in our apprehensions, seem to be betwixt those two things, because of the customary and close connexion that has grown up in our minds between the objects of sight and touch, whereby the very different and distinct ideas of those two senses are so blended and confounded together, as to be mistaken for one and the same thing; out of which prejudice we cannot easily extricate ourselves.

In further support of his conclusion regarding tactual manipulation as fundamental to the development of visual perception, Berkeley introduced the subject of retinal inversion. He pointed out that knowledge of such inversion is restricted to students of optics and consequently there is no awareness of its existence by others. We react to objects and not to retinal images, and these reactions involve eye-hand coordinations. Our notions of spatial position are established by reaching for objects; hence, the blind and

---

[8] More than forty pages later he quotes the entire passage from Locke's *Essay* concerned with "Mr. Molyneux's problem" regarding initial visual recognition of a cube and a sphere solely on the basis of prior tactual knowledge of the difference in form.

the sighted make the same movement when asked to touch the top or bottom of some object like a box. What is "perceivable by touch," Berkeley maintained, governs judgment of spatial location, and thus he was "certain that a man actually blind, and who had continued so from his birth, would by the sense of feeling attain to have ideas of upper and lower." In terms of this analysis, the problem of retinal inversion became a pseudo-problem.

However, experimental confirmation for Berkeley's analysis was not obtained until the 1890s, when G. M. Stratton (1896 and 1897) published the results of his famous experiment dealing with the behavioral consequences of a reversed visual system. By means of an appropriate optical instrument, he was able to transform the customary up-down and right-left relations of his retinal image. After an initial period of confusion during which his visual world appeared to be upside down, he learned to compensate by suitable modification of his motor responses to the transposed visual cues. Once these responses were established, his visual world ceased to appear confused and unnatural. His experience was akin to that of the microscopist who becomes accustomed to the reversed and inverted nature of his microscopic field.[9]

Locke's Primary Qualities Really Secondary

What is revealed by a microscope, Berkeley noted, can be altogether at variance with what is experienced tactually, for "what seems smooth and round to the touch, may to sight, if viewed through a microscope, seem quite otherwise" (1910 ed., p. 61). In this connection he pointed out that tactual judgments of magnitude or extent are not necessarily confirmed by visual judgments. He even applied this to the perception of number: five patches of color on a canvas will not yield five separate cutaneous impressions. Furthermore, in the course of his discussion of number he disagreed with those who, like Locke, listed number as one of the primary qualities of the external world. As he saw it, number "is entirely a creature of the mind" and not something "fixed and settled, really existing in things themselves." The numerical designation for our ideas is a function of our purposes or intentions. To show what he meant by this he noted that we sometimes refer to a chimney as a single unit or to a window as a single unit and yet, even though a house has many windows and several chimneys, we nevertheless refer to the house as *one* house just as we refer to a grouping of very many houses as a city. Accordingly, he concluded (1910 ed., p. 63):

---

[9] Interest in the kind of problem investigated by Stratton in the 1890s has continued to engage the attention of investigators in all the succeeding decades. References to these later studies along with a re-evaluation of Stratton's findings are to be found in a 1965 article by C. S. Harris.

In these and the like instances, it is evident the *unit* constantly relates to the particular draughts the mind makes of its ideas, to which it affixes names, and wherein it includes more or less, as best suits its own ends or purposes. Whatever therefore the mind considers as one, that is a unit. Every combination of ideas is considered as one thing by the mind, and in token thereof is marked by one name. Now, this naming and combining together of ideas is perfectly arbitrary, and done by the mind in such sort, as experience shows it to be the most convenient: without which, our ideas have never been collected into such sundry distinct combinations as they now are.

It should thus be evident that in making number a product of mental activity Berkeley was voicing his opposition to the classification of number as a *primary* quality in the Lockean sense of being something "inseparable from a body." In fact, he questioned the validity of Locke's basic distinction between primary and secondary qualities. For him *all* qualities of sensation conform to Locke's category of secondary qualities. All of them—sounds, tastes, motions, forms, pains, colors—as experienced are equally perceptual in nature; hence equally ideational or mental in nature. Experience failed to reveal a "body" separate and distinct from Locke's primary qualities. In his unqualified reliance on experience Berkeley might be said to have been more empirical than Locke.

Some Anticipations of Later Psychology

In his examination of the nature of sensory experience, Berkeley made several observations which anticipated later developments of scientific psychology. For example, in his discussion of the size of objects he noted the obvious distinction between the "tangible and visible magnitude" depending on whether size is based upon cutaneous or retinal impressions. In this connection he anticipated the later nineteenth-century concept of the *limen* or sensory threshold when he wrote: "There is a *minimum tangible,* and a *minimum visible*, beyond which sense cannot perceive" (1910 ed., p. 36). Furthermore, as already mentioned, he also anticipated the concept of *perceptual constancy* by noting the fact that our impression of a man's height does not always change with changes in the size of the retinal image. When standing ten feet away, the man seems no taller than when standing fifteen feet away.

Still another instance of an anticipation of later psychology is to be found in Berkeley's recognition of the difference between distance receptors and contact receptors. His recognition of eye and ear as distance receptors, for example, is quite explicit in this passage (1910 ed., p. 33):

From what we have shown it is a manifest consequence, that the ideas of space, outness, and things placed at a distance, are not, strictly speaking, the object of sight; they are not otherwise perceived by the eye than by the ear. Sitting in my study I hear a coach drive along the street; I look through the casement and see it; I walk out and enter into it; thus, common speech would incline one to think, I heard, saw, and touched the same thing, to wit, the coach. It is nevertheless certain, the ideas intromitted by each sense are widely different, and distinct from each other; but having been observed constantly to go together, they are spoken of as one and the same thing. By the variation of the noise I perceive the different distances of the coach, and know that it approaches before I look out. Thus by the ear I perceive distance, just after the same manner as I do by the eye.

Berkeley's List of Spatial Cues Not Exhaustive

From one viewpoint Berkeley's enumeration of the cues operative in the perception of size and distance can be regarded as having set the stage for what was to become an important problem for the founding fathers of scientific psychology. In their accounts of space perception they took note of the cues mentioned by Berkeley—cues like aerial perspective, accommodative strain, interposition, and so on. Incidentally, although Berkeley was familiar with Locke's *Essay,* he failed to include Locke's reference to the distribution of light and shade in his list of cues. This may have been an oversight for, as mentioned in Chapter 12, even long before the time of Locke artists had obtained depth and distance effects by introducing highlights and shadows into their paintings. Accordingly, it is unlikely that Berkeley had never read about or noted this. He may have regarded it as unnecessary to introduce an exhaustive list of these cues in order to defend his "new theory of vision"; for chiaroscuro was not the only cue he failed to list. He also had nothing to say about *relative movement* as a criterion of distance. This too is so commonplace as an experience as hardly to have escaped his notice. When riding in his coach he must have observed the way in which distant objects like the moon seemed to move in the same direction as the coach while near objects like trees seemed to move in the opposite direction.

In addition to his neglect of the criteria of chiaroscuro and relative movement he also failed to elaborate upon the significance of binocular as contrasted with uniocular vision. As an empiricist he did note "that the judgment we make of the distance of an object, viewed with both eyes, is entirely the result of experience" (1910 ed., p. 17). This was a reference to convergence. Fixation on an object very close to the eyes involves marked convergence which decreases as the object recedes. When the object is about sixty feet away the optic axes are parallel and convergence ceases to be a factor in judging distances beyond this point. Consequently it can function as a cue for relative nearness of objects, but not for relative remoteness of objects viewed by non-converging eyes. However, Berkeley failed to mention this restricted nature of the influence of convergence.

He also failed to say anything about the influence of retinal disparity in binocular vision. It is hard to account for this failure since he had familiarized himself with works on optics current in his day. Moreover, as C. F. Osgood (1953, p. 248) has indicated, the fact of retinal disparity had been known for centuries. As early as 300 B.C. Euclid had already observed this fact of a difference in visual impressions made by each eye when both are focussed on the same scene or object. Around A.D. 150 Galen called attention to the same observation and so did Leonardo da Vinci in the fifteenth century.

Under the circumstances it seems strange that so keen a student of visual experience as Berkeley, writing in the eighteenth century, neglected to say anything about retinal disparity. His neglect might have been due to the absence of evidence indicative of the role of such disparity in enhancing the perception of depth. Such evidence was not available until Charles Wheatstone (1802–1875), the English physicist, invented the stereoscope in 1838. However, what was available to Berkeley was evidence pertaining to *diplopia* as a function of binocular vision. It was available not only because Aristotle had noted the doubling incident to displacement of the focus of one eye,[10] but also because the problem of *single* vision despite *two* retinal impressions had been studied in the seventeenth century and resulted in the commonly accepted solution to the problem in terms of the concept of the *horopter* as related to identical points of retinal stimulation.

Under conditions of binocular vision the horopter is the locus of all points in the visual field whose images fall upon corresponding points of the two retinas. This results in single vision. In cases of muscular imbalance, when both eyes cannot be fixated on a common point of regard, non-corresponding retinal areas are stimulated and the result is double vision.[11] The outward indication of such imbalance is evident in the ocular deviation seen in strabismus. Spectacles for the correction of the latter condition, F. H. Garrison (1929, p. 203) notes, had already been introduced by the 1550s.

Accordingly, it seems safe to assume that Berkeley had come across discussions of strabismus and diplopia in the course of his studies of optics. There is even a bare hint of knowledge of the horopter when with reference to "defects" of the "visive faculty" he states that "in respect of the extent or number of visible points that are at once perceivable by it" he finds it

---

[10] It was available to him in the sense that Aristotle's writings were available to him. Moreover, as mentioned in Chapter 4, Aristotle called attention not only to diplopia but also to the illusion of relative movement and neither of these visual phenomena were mentioned by Berkeley.

[11] This is an oversimplification. Sometimes the result will be a distortion of distance judgments rather than double vision. A careful analysis of this whole problem of the relation of the horopter to single vision is supplied by C. H. Graham (1951).

"narrow and limited to a certain degree" (1910 ed., p. 52). However, there is no elaboration of this in terms of double vision even though in an ensuing passage he refers to "the divers perceptions of sight and touch" (1910 ed., p. 53) as exemplified by the lack of correspondence between what an object looks like when viewed through a microscope as compared with what it feels like to the touch. The microscope, he points out, "presents us with a new scene of visible objects, quite different from what we behold with the naked eye"; hence the lack of correspondence. He then adds that "objects perceived by the eye alone" do "have a certain connection with tangible objects." In line with his subjective idealism he might have said their visible existence is confirmed by tangible impressions. But this does not apply to diplopia: one of the double images lacks a corresponding tactual impression. What appears to exist visually ceases to exist tactually. This complicates the notion of existence as expressed in Berkeley's "to be is to be perceived" dictum. Maybe he ignored the phenomenon of double vision in order to avoid such complication.

After all, his main purpose was to demonstrate the *experiential* foundation of visual judgments of the distance, size, and spatial location of objects. This is what induced him to regard his theory as a *new* theory opposed to the *old* theory of the "writers of optics" who had accounted for visual perception in terms of "optic angles" and "optic axes." Although never experienced directly, the latter were nevertheless assumed to enter into judgments of distance "by a kind of natural geometry." Berkeley questioned this assumption because the ordinary person is ignorant of optical measurements and not because he questioned the validity of laws based upon such measurements. Those "unskillful in optics" never base their judgments of distance upon such laws. To endow them with "a kind of natural geometry" is tantamount to endowing them with an innate, rationalistic foundation for making such judgments.

In other words, Berkeley's theory was an empiricist's answer to the nativism implicit in the rationalist's theory of space perception. According to him, distance as such cannot be perceived directly and immediately. A light ray, he indicated, can impinge on only a single point of the retina no matter whether it comes from a near object or a distant object; hence the difference in distance cannot be seen. Furthermore, the retina being a two-dimensional surface renders it difficult to account for the direct tridimensional visual perception of depth or volume of objects. This suggests that, genetically considered, all early visual impressions are flat or two-dimensional and that subsequent visual impressions of depth or solidity are products of experience. In effect Berkeley ruled out reliance on the Cartesian notion of matter as extended substance, on Lockean primary qualities, and on Kantian *a priori* spatial intuitions. His new theory of vision had constituted an empiricist's challenge to the psychology of nativists and rationalists.

From Berkeley to William James

Quite unwittingly Berkeley had set the stage for what was to become a central problem for the new nineteenth-century psychology of the laboratories. James, in his chapter dealing with this problem of space perception, credited Berkeley with having started "the scientific study of the subject," though he qualified this by noting that Descartes merits prior credit. By the time of James the subject had become so important for psychology that his chapter on "The Perception of Space" is the longest one in the *Principles.* More than ten per cent of its pages are devoted to this topic.[12] What James had to say about Berkeley's central thesis merits more than passing mention. Even though he later came to sponsor what he called "radical empiricism" James could not endorse Berkeley's empiricism as reflected in the "New Theory of Vision." In particular he objected to having the visual apprehension of distance derived from some nonvisual experience. With considerable vehemence he noted (1890, Vol. II, p. 212):

> According to Berkeley this experience was tactile. His whole treatment of the subject was excessively vague,—no shame to him, as a breaker of fresh ground, —but as it has been adopted and enthusiastically hugged in all its vagueness by nearly the whole line of British psychologists who have succeeded him, it will be well for us to begin our study of vision by refuting his notion that depth cannot possibly be perceived in terms of purely visual feeling.

This opposition to Berkeley's theory of vision was not prompted by opposition to Berkeley's idealism, for as late as 1894, according to Ralph Barton Perry (1954, p. 273), James "still professed idealism of the Berkeleian type." Instead it was a product of a specific objection to a theory which derived ideas of space from non-spatial sensations. Mere association of non-spatial impressions, James maintained, cannot give rise to notions of distance, depth, volume, or extensity. In the final analysis, he wrote, there are only these three possible theories of space perception (1890, Vol. II, pp. 271–272):

> Either (1) there is no spatial *quality* of sensation at all, and space is a mere symbol of succession; or (2) there is an *extensive quality given* immediately in certain particular sensations; or, finally, (3) there is a *quality produced* out of the inward resources of the mind, to envelop sensations which, as given originally,

---

[12] The whole subject of vision continues to be an important one for psychologists of the modern period. More than twelve per cent of the pages of the Stevens' *Handbook of Experimental Psychology* has to do with vision. Incidentally, at the close of his chapter on space perception James reported: "The literature of the question is in all languages very voluminous" (1890, Vol. II, p. 282).

are not spatial, but which, on being cast into the spatial form, become united and orderly. This last is the Kantian view.

James devoted the major portion of his chapter to an exposition of the second type of theory: extensity or voluminousness is a constituent feature of almost every kind of sense modality. With respect to hearing, he pointed out, the rumble of thunder bulks larger than the squeak of a slate-pencil.[13] The cutaneous senses are replete with comparable examples, as shown by the differences between the restricted pain of a pinprick on the finger as contrasted with the more diffused pain of a sunburned back or the difference in extensity of a feeling of warmth when the hand is dipped into the bath water as compared with the feeling aroused by having the whole body immersed in the same water. Nor is this factor of relative diffuseness entirely absent from the sensations of smell and taste. Some of them, James wrote, appear to be less diffuse than others. There are smells, for example, that may be limited to a corner of the room and others that fill the room, just as there are tastes that affect the tip of the tongue and others that seem to engulf the mouth.

Extensity [14] as an attribute of sensation is thus not necessarily limited to a flat, two-dimensional spread but may also involve impressions of depth. James illustrated this effect by citing some examples introduced by Ewald Hering (1834–1918). Hering noted the difference between surface colors and volumic colors as revealed by comparing a cube made of transparent green glass with an opaque cube painted green. Both a flame and a red-hot poker, Hering indicated, look luminous all the way through.[15] James also called attention to the familiar experience of exploring a dental cavity with the tongue and feeling it to be "quite monstrous."

For James, voluminousness, depth, and distance were not, as Berkeley taught, altogether products of initially nonspatial sensory impressions. He made this clear in two italicized sentences: *"The measurement of distance is, as Berkeley said, a result of suggestion and experience. But visual*

---

[13] In opposition to James, empiricists have attributed a difference of this kind to experience. Instead of regarding it as a native endowment, they account for it as a consequence of associating voluminous sounds with large, bulky objects and less voluminous ones with smaller objects. By way of illustration they mention the difference in sounds produced by bass violins and brass drums as contrasted with those of violins and snare drums.

[14] According to James, James Ward (1843–1925), the Cambridge University philosopher-psychologist, is the man who first used the term "extensity" as "an element in each sensation just as intensity is" (1890, Vol. II, pp. 135–136).

[15] Early in the present century David Katz initiated a series of studies in line with these distinctions. His resulting phenomenological observations account for the well-known current references to three kinds of colors: surface colors, film colors, and volumic colors.

experience alone is adequate to produce it, and this he erroneously denied" (1890, Vol. II, p. 215). By way of evidence against Berkeley's dependence on tactual experience as the foundation for the development of visual space, James referred to an 1838 report of a girl of fourteen who, even though born without arms or legs, was able to make correct estimates of the size and distance of objects in her visual field. The anecdotal nature of such quasi-clinical evidence renders it suggestive rather than coercive, and James relegated it to a footnote (Vol. II, p. 214). He was more concerned with the kind of evidence already mentioned in connection with what he had to say about vision with the head inverted and about the diffuseness of sensory impressions in general.

In opposition to Berkeley and the other empiricists, James, though not denying the role of secondary criteria of space perception, insisted upon the role of inborn factors as the primary foundation for the perception of space. In doing so he was siding with the nativists, not only as against an eighteenth-century empiricist like Berkeley, but also as against his contemporary nineteenth-century empiricists like Helmholtz and Wundt. After considering the drift of all their arguments, he was still convinced that "we have *native* and fixed optical space-sensations" (Vol. II, p. 237; italics supplied). But this conviction was not shared by all students of the question at the close of the last century. Their twentieth-century successors continued to consider the issue and broadened its scope.

Space Perception in Animals and in Infants

One way in which it was broadened was to investigate space perception in animals. Neither Berkeley nor James had raised questions about this. They failed to ask how it comes about that birds can swoop down from a great height to a bit of food or how squirrels gauge distances as they make spectacular leaps from branch to branch. Nor did they ask about the visual acuity of newly hatched chicks as they peck at grains of corn. The latter question was subjected to experimental study by several investigators,[16] following an initial study by F. S. Breed in 1911.

As formulated by E. C. Tolman (1932, p. 314), the results demonstrated that chicks possess "a very considerable degree of innate skill (i.e., a skill depending mostly upon maturation) as to how to carry out such pecking." The former question was also subjected to experimental study. For example, the accuracy with which an animal like the rat can gauge distance in jumping from one perch to another was investigated by J. T. Russell (1932). He trained his animals to locate their food by jumping from one raised platform to another. This, in his words, involved "depth discrimination." By means

---

[16] A list of these investigators is supplied by Tolman (1932, p. 314).

of a device attached to the starting platform, he was able to measure the force with which the animal initiated its jump. In the course of the experiment he had the animals make the jumps when the distance separating the platforms was varied and he found a consistent gradation in the force expended. Thus, one rat expended 190 grams of force in jumping across a twenty-centimeter gap and 564 grams when the gap was extended to forty centimeters. The difference in muscular adjustment was inferred to be a consequence of an estimate of the visual difference in the separated distances.

In a subsequent experiment (1934), K. S. Lashley and J. T. Russell employed this technique to find out whether such depth discrimination was innate or a product of learning. They reared one group of rats in darkness and another group in light and then subjected both groups to a series of trials in the jumping situation. The rats reared in the dark, like those reared in light, were found to make appropriate muscular adjustments to varying distances. Consequently, the investigators concluded that rats are innately equipped to perceive depth. With reference to the present chapter, this meant that Berkeley's "new theory of vision" does not apply to rats.

The theory has also been found wanting when applied to other animal species, including human infants. This was demonstrated by E. J. Gibson and R. D. Walk in an ingenious experiment (1960) by means of what they called a "visual cliff." The "cliff" did not entail an actual fall but was made to look as if a fall might occur. A portion of a sheet of heavy glass, elevated some distance above the floor, was partly covered with a board. The remaining portion of the glass was retained as a transparent surface revealing the floor below. Both board and the surface of the lowered floor were given the same appearance by using patterned material having a checkerboard design. As a consequence the board side of the enclosure was solid and substantial while the other side of the enclosure exposing the floor below *looked* precarious. The latter side constituted the "visual cliff," for it seemed to reveal a chasm. In terms of the visual impression aroused, it was as if one were in a room having a solid floor projecting from one wall but failing to reach the opposite wall, with an apparent chasm separating the unfinished part of the floor from the opposite wall.

The experimenters were especially interested in learning whether crawling or toddling infants would react to the cliff as a hazardous place by refusing to move off the solid floor. In other words, would they perceive the depth of the chasm? It is well known, of course, that babies have to be protected from falling off a bed or falling down a flight of stairs. Not until they become sure-footed are they freed from the confines of a crib or a playpen and permitted to negotiate a staircase with restraining gate removed. In the course of becoming sure-footed they have repeated tumbles. It is commonly believed that the tumbles teach the toddlers the hazards of climbing on a box or being on an elevated surface like a bed or sofa. This belief is in accord with Berkeley's empiricism: depth perception is the result of experience and not an innate factor.

Gibson and Walk proceeded to subject this belief to experimental check by exposing infants to the visual-cliff situation. In the actual test the infant was placed on the solid board and the mother urged the child to come to her, when she was standing on the cliff side of the enclosure as well as when she was on the opposite "safe" side. In all, thirty-six babies were tested in this way. They ranged in age from six to fourteen months and thus represented varying levels of locomotor development. Not all of them answered the mother's call from the "safe" side by moving off the board; but of the twenty-seven who did, only three also crawled onto the glass over the chasm. Many of them moved away from the mother when she made her plea from the cliff side. Others, unable to reach her without crossing the chasm, burst into tears. That their reluctance to cross was a function of vision was shown by their behavior. For instance, upon reaching the glass they would look down and then back away to "safety." In some instances they would pat the glass and yet refuse to cross even though the patting presumably supplied tactual evidence of a solid surface separating them from the mother. As a result the experimenters concluded that "most human infants can discriminate depth as soon as they can crawl" (1960, p. 64).[17] However, as the experimenters were careful to point out, this does not prove depth perception in the human infant to be innate.

Nevertheless, a presumption in favor of such an interpretation was supplied by what happened when the young of various animal species were confronted with the visual cliff. Chicks less than twenty-four hours old never hopped off on the chasm side of the board. Similarly, even at the age of one day, no lamb or goat ventured to step on the glass. In the case of rats the results were a little different, for they stepped on the glass after exploring its surface with their vibrissae. When the solid board was raised to render such exploration impossible, they veered away from the cliff.

In addition, the experimenters confirmed the Lashley-Russell finding regarding the rat's depth discrimination by testing dark-reared rats in the visual-cliff situation. In the absence of prior visual experience the dark-reared rats, like the newly hatched chicks, gave evidence of innate depth perception. The same was found to hold true for dark-reared kittens in the sense that maturation and not trial-and-error visual experience accounted for

---

[17] In this connection Gibson and Walk introduced a word of warning. They found that many of the infants in trying to get to the mother on the safe side would lack sufficient motor control to avoid coming into contact with the glass. Had it not been for the glass they would have fallen. Their depth perception was better than their motor control; hence there is still need for parental vigilance to guard crawling infants against falling from heights.

their avoidance of the cliff. Findings of this kind emboldened the investigators to close their report with this statement (1960, p. 71): "From our first few years of work with the visual cliff we are ready to venture the rather broad conclusion that a seeing animal will be able to discriminate depth when its locomotion is adequate, even when locomotion begins at birth. But many experiments remain to be done, especially on the role of different cues and on the effects of different kinds of early visual experience."

Broadly considered, the visual-cliff experiments served to confirm what James had maintained regarding the weakness of Berkeley's theory. They showed the visual recognition of depth to be an intrinsically visual phenomenon and not a derivative of tactual-motor experience as Berkeley had contended. Furthermore, the experimenters also showed that such recognition is mediated by motion parallax as a cue. At least this applied to infant rats and day-old chicks. The relevance of other cues was not established. No attempt was made to find out whether depth perception is a binocular or a uniocular phenomenon or whether it is dependent upon the presence of sharply defined contours in the visual field. That is why Gibson and Walk noted the need for many additional experiments "especially on the role of different cues."

Concerning Stereoscopic Vision and Movement Parallax

One attempt to investigate the role of different cues was made by B. Julesz (1964 and 1965) This had nothing to do with the visual cliff and was not concerned with depth perception in infants or animals. Instead it was restricted to the investigation of depth perception or *stereopsis,* with all uniocular clues like relative size and superposition eliminated. So were all binocular cues with the exception of retinal disparity. This was accomplished by using a computer to provide stimulus material consisting of randomly scattered patterns of dots to be viewed stereoscopically. The resulting stereograms were altogether nonrepresentational and devoid of any familiar contours or geometrical shapes. They had no more meaning than the pattern of a herringbone weave. By shifting identical areas of each of the stereograms horizontally, Julesz introduced some disparity in the distribution of the dots. This change could not be detected by visual scrutiny with one eye, but when viewed with a stereoscope there was a definite impression of a central pattern floating above a background pattern.

To rule out the possible effect of convergence and accommodation, Julesz exposed this stimulus material tachistosopically, with the exposure time too brief for the latter muscular adjustments to occur. The stereoscopic effect still took place. However, as Julesz indicated, this does not mean that such adjustments "do not influence the perception of depth when the presentation time is longer" (1965, p. 46). In the same way, depth perception is influenced by uniocular cues when such cues are present. As Berkeley taught, their influence is a product of experience, but the work of Julesz demonstrates that they are not essential for depth perception. Herein lies its importance, for it constitutes a method for reducing stereopsis to the important cue of disparity. As a cue retinal disparity functions automatically and unconsciously. Ordinarily there is no awareness of retinal discrepancy when the *two* eyes perceive a *single* solid object in the field of view. Boring has supplied the following clarifying account of this phase of stereoscopic perception (1946, pp. 105–106):

> In stereoscopic vision the evidence for depth or solidity lies in that slight disparity of the two retinal images which is furnished by binocular parallax. Given a few constants of the binocular system, the forms and sizes of the two disparate images, and the assignment of one image to the left eye and the other to the right, and you can figure out geometrically by conscious inference what the dimensions in depth are. The visual mechanism, however, makes this inference instantaneously and unconsciously. If the stereograms are photographs, rich in detail, it is as impossible ever to see the disparity between, as it is to be aware of disparity in the binocular observation of a solid object. . . . In the perception the brain reaches a correct inferential conclusion as to the depth of the perceived object, but the process is no more conscious than is the inference of an electronic computer which calculates almost instantly from relevant data a range and elevation and correctly aims a gun.

One can learn to aim at a target with one eye closed by taking advantage of movement parallax. This means that retinal disparity is not essential for the location of spatial position. In fact, some evidence suggests that movement parallax is a significant cue in the spatial orientation of very young infants. This evidence was supplied by T. G. R. Bower (1965), who employed a simple conditioning technique by means of which infants were trained to move their heads when white paper cubes appeared in the visual field. The cubes served as signals for the experimenter to bob up from beneath the crib in peek-a-boo fashion. Twenty-seven infants ranging in age from forty to sixty days were the subjects of this study. Some of them wore a patch over one eye during the experimental sessions while others viewed the cubes binocularly. Bower interpreted the results to mean that motion parallax rather than binocular parallax was a necessary cue for the spatial discrimination he attributed to his infant subjects. If this finding should be confirmed, it might mean that, in terms of developmental sequence, motion parallax appears earlier than retinal disparity in the functioning of visual cues.

Experiments like the foregoing ones reveal that Berkeley was in error when he made touch primary and vision secondary in man's spatial orientation. He was misled by concentrating on the retina as a two-dimensional surface on which two-dimensional images are projected. Consequently, for him the third dimension had to be missing from initial visual impressions of the infant. His difficulty might be compared to that of a person who finds it hard to understand how the flat surface of a mirror can reveal impressions of solid objects seemingly located deep within the mirror. The two-dimensional mirror gives rise to three-dimensional images of depth and distance; hence this hypothetical person's perplexity. Were he then to account for the tridimensionality of mirror images as a derivative of nonoptical factors he would be bringing this analogy into line with Berkeley's theorizing. In this respect he would be duplicating Berkeley's error.

The Importance of Active Movement

Despite this error, Berkeley was not entirely wrong in his theory of space perception. His emphasis on the importance of touch and active movement is not without relevance. After all, the congenitally blind do succeed in becoming oriented in space and the sighted have to establish a multiplicity of eye-hand coordinations. There is thus an obvious relationship between spatial orientation and the striped musculature. What is the nature of this relationship? Would visual experience taken by itself suffice to supply an adequate foundation for spatial orientation? On theoretic grounds Berkeley, with his emphasis on the primacy of touch, would have answered this question in the negative.

As was brought out in Chapter 12, pp. 391–392, one way in which modern psychologists have dealt with the latter question involved rearing animals in darkness. In addition to the effects of such sensory deprivation on animal behavior the effects of early restriction of movement on later behavior has also been subjected to experimental study. In one such study, referred to by R. Held (1965, p. 94), kittens were prevented from walking as soon as their eyes were ready for visual stimulation. In effect they were immobilized in a visual environment. The immobilization made for exposure to a narrow range of visual events. Upon release from confinement they showed manifest impairment of behavior subject to visual control. As Held noted, the impairment might be attributed to impoverished visual stimulation, since the immobilized kittens lacked the diversity of visual impressions available to freely roaming cats. On the other hand, the impairment might have been a consequence of inability to move in response to such visual stimulation as had taken place. Held regarded the latter possibility as the more likely explanation, and he proceeded to subject these alternative explanations to experimental study.

To carry out the experiment, Held and a colleague worked out a device by means of which one kitten could actively explore a circular enclosure while simultaneously exposing another kitten to passive visual inspection of the same scene. The device consisted of something like a seesaw which, instead of moving up and down, could be revolved. Two kittens of about the same age were tested at the same time. One of the kittens was harnessed to one end of the device in such a way that as it walked in circular fashion either to the left or right, the other end of the device moved in the same direction. The second kitten was relatively immobilized in a little gondola suspended from this other end with its head protruding. It was thus possible for this kitten to turn its head and to move its paws inside the gondola. As a result of this arrangement, active exploratory movements of the first kitten were transmitted to the second one as passive movements. To control the character of visual stimulation received by the animals, a uniform pattern of lines was applied to the walls of the circular enclosure. Consequently both kittens were exposed to the same kind of visual stimulation.

In the course of the experiment, ten pairs of kittens were introduced to the enclosure. Eight of these pairs had been reared in darkness for from eight to twelve weeks or until such time as one of them was strong enough to give its "partner" a free ride in the goldola. By way of additional check on factors of possible relevance, the two other pairs were not reared in uninterrupted darkness. Instead, while prevented from walking, they were exposed to visual stimulation coming from a patterned surface for an interval of three hours each day. This took place before they were ready for the revolving device. Then they, like the other eight pairs, were introduced to the device for three hours a day for about ten days. At the close of each training session the kittens were returned to their mothers, who were confined in dark cages. Visual stimulation was thus restricted to the three hours of the training period.

The results confirmed what was implicit in Berkeley's recognition of *active* movement as an important factor in the acquisition of visuomotor control. When the kittens were tested with respect to such control, the active ones showed normal development. However, the passive ones showed defective sensorimotor control. For example, an object brought close to their eyes failed to elicit the normal blinking reaction. To cite another example: when introduced to the visual cliff, they failed to avoid the deep side. On the other hand, the active kittens reacted normally to such hazards. Held did not find the defective coordinations to be irreversible, for after some days of unrestrained activity the passive kittens reacted normally to the hazards in question.

Actually, Held's work with the kittens was just one of a series of experiments concerned with spatial orientation. In the others, he investigated the ways in which human beings adapt to visual distortion. The distortion was produced by means of prisms. In one experiment the effects of passive as opposed to active movement were studied. This was accomplished by having the subject don prism goggles through which he viewed a scene while standing on a wheeled platform pushed around by an associate. The active subject, instead of using such perambulator-like transportation, walked around while wearing the goggles. As might be anticipated, there was adaptation to the visual distortion by the active subject but not by the passive one.

Other experiments involved adaptation to the displacement induced by viewing mirror images through a prism, which involved an effort to locate the corners of a square under conditions of distorted vision. This adaptation was also tested by comparing active and passive modes of behavior. In the active phase the subject was permitted to learn to compensate for the displacement through his own efforts to establish the requisite eye-hand coordination. In the passive phase he was instructed to relax his arm muscles so that the experimenter could guide his hand to the target areas. Again active motion was found to be superior to passive motion in gaining visual control over the spatial distortion.

By means of these and related experiments, Held demonstrated the importance of a sensory feedback from active muscles for the establishment of such control. In less technical language, it might be said that this series of experiments once again demonstrated the importance of the principle of learning by doing. As applied to everyday affairs, these experiments showed the futility or limitations of trying to learn to play the piano by watching pianists or trying to become a surgeon just by viewing operations. In terms of a long-range psychological perspective, this may be regarded as the chief practical implication of Berkeley's "new theory of vision."

The results of Held's kind of experimentation appear to support Berkeley's contention regarding the primacy of active movement and touch in the organization of visual space. Held's results of the 1960s are thus like Stratton's results of the 1890s. They both found that distorted vision is corrected by appropriate corrective motor adjustments. In the development of visuomotor efficiency, such adjustments seem to be primary and vision secondary. If so, it might be more accurate to speak of hand-eye coordinations rather than of eye-hand coordinations. Visual impressions, passively received, fail to establish visuomotor control. In the visual-cliff situation, it may be recalled, Held's immobilized kittens failed to avoid the deep side. Does this mean that they failed to perceive the depth of the deep side? After all, Gibson and Walk found that their kittens did avoid the deep side. However, the latter animals had not been subjected to restricted activity by confinement in a gondola; hence they may be presumed to have had better motor control than Held's animals. Lack of motor control rather than absence of depth perception seems to account for the contradictory findings.

Summary and Tentative Conclusion

In the more than two hundred and fifty years that have elapsed since Berkeley published his empiricist's account of space perception, a mass of evidence bearing on the problem has accumulated. Aspects of the problem not dreamed of by Berkeley have come to light. As was just indicated, ingenious experimental techniques for investigating the problem have come into being. What Berkeley started in 1709 has burgeoned into a major psychological enterprise having many ramifications. Considered in this light, the enterprise serves as a good example of the continuity of history in the history of science: the apparent solution of one problem engenders new problems.

Despite all the effort that has been expended on the problem of space perception from Berkeley's day to the present, it cannot yet be said that the basic issue has been settled to the satisfaction of all active students of the problem. Consensus is still lacking with respect to the basic issue regarding the primary or secondary role of visual data in the genesis of space perception. Some findings lend force to the contention of empiricists, while other findings seem to support the contention of nativists. This state of affairs has been well summarized in an article by C. S. Harris in this way (1965, pp. 441–442):

> Psychologists have traditionally looked to studies of adaptation to distorted vision for clues about the development of visual perception in the infant. The usual, empiricist assumption . . . is that visual space perception is "secondary." It is based on the spatial sensations given by touch, kinesthesis, and position sense. As Dewey (1898) put it: "Ultimately visual perception rests on tactual. . . . Spatial relations are not originally perceived by the eye, but are the result of the association of visual sensations with previous muscular and tactual experiences."
>
> This belief in the primacy of touch is so ingrained that experimental results are sometimes flagrantly misinterpreted in order to support it. Carr (1925), for instance, concluded: "It is thus obvious that the Stratton experiment involves no reconstruction or alteration of tactual . . . space. It is the visual system that is disrupted and then reorganized so as to conform to touch. . . . " Stratton's . . . and Held's findings have been cited over and over as evidence that visual space perception is flexible and therefore must have been acquired through tactile-proprioceptive and motor experience. The reinterpretation of these findings that has been presented here suggests the opposite conclusion. Vision seems to be largely inflexible, whereas the position sense is remarkably labile.
>
> The implication, if one dare draw any, is that the Berkeleyan notion should be turned around. It seems more plausible to assume that proprioceptive perception of parts of the body (and therefore of the locations of touched objects) develops with the help of *innate* visual perception rather than vice versa. A growing number of recent studies support the view that many aspects of visual perception are not influenced by experience and are largely *innate.* [Italics added.]

The preceding conclusion amounts to endorsement of what James had maintained many years ago when, as previously cited, he insisted that "we have native and fixed optical space-sensations." In this respect James, in opposing Berkeley, was siding with the nativists. In other respects, in agreement with Berkeley, he sided with the empiricists. For example, he recognized the importance of past experience in order to account for a curious phenomenon involved in uniocular inspection of the hollow side of an ordinary mask. If such a mask is painted the same way on the inside and the outside, the concavity appears to be convex when the inside is looked at with one eye closed. As James noted, the illusion is present despite parallax and changes in accommodation being in accord with perception of the mask's concavity. Prior experience with human faces counteracts the customary influence of such cues. In the words of James (1890, Vol. II, p. 217): "Our mental knowledge of the fact that human faces are always convex overpowers them, and we directly perceive the nose to be nearer to us than the cheek instead of farther off."

In looking back upon this venerable controversy regarding the nature of space perception, it seems fair to say that the empiricism-nativism dichotomy does not constitute a mutually exclusive antithesis. The complexities of space perception cannot be accounted for by one-sided allegiance to one of these orientations. Cues signifying height, depth, and distance and resulting from experience do not become effective in the absence of an inborn foundation for such experience. Perception of space is not, as Berkeley maintained, something that develops out of a nonspatial *tabula rasa*. His empiricism has to be supplemented by recognition of a core of innate spatial factors upon which experience operates. This seems to be the soundest conclusion to draw in the light of the general trend of available evidence.

Berkeley's Epistemology and His Theory of Objects

It is customary to classify Berkeley as belonging to the tradition of British associationism. As E. B. Titchener put it (1917, p. 374): "All the great names in British psychology, from Hobbes down to Bain, are connected with this doctrine of the association of ideas." He then listed them as Hobbes, Locke, Berkeley, Hume, Hartley, Thomas Brown, James Mill, John Stuart Mill, Bain, and Spencer, with the qualification that the last three are not to be considered "pure associationists." Moreover, if associationism be restricted to the association of *ideas,* then Berkeley was not a pure associationist, since in his theory of space perception he stressed the importance of the linkage between bodily movement and visual impressions.

As a matter of fact, the word "association" is conspicuously absent in Berkeley. Instead one comes across expressions like "one idea may suggest another to the mind," or because of "an habitual connexion" one idea gives rise to another. Such expressions do not differ in meaning from what Locke had called "association of ideas." The latter phrase, it will be recalled, was not at all prominent in Locke's *Essay.*

It is thus altogether likely that neither Locke nor Berkeley regarded themselves as participants in a common psychological enterprise that historians were to label *associationism.* They both thought of their efforts as contributions to philosophy: Locke with his *Essay* dealing with the nature of human understanding and Berkeley with a treatise published in 1710 and entitled *Of the Principles of Human Knowledge* (1910 ed., pp. 113–195). From their viewpoint, this concern with understanding and with knowledge had more to do with epistemology than with psychology. They both lived long before the emergence of psychology as an independent field of study, and it is thus hardly likely that they could have thought of themselves as psychologists. Actually the issue is rather trivial and does not merit more than this passing mention.

There is a more important issue connected with Berkeley's *Principles of Human Knowledge* that merits more extended discussion because, like his theory of vision, it has a bearing on later psychology. The issue takes this form: what is involved in the perception of meaning? Sometimes this question is regarded as having to do with the *theory of objects*. The word "object" in this phrase is employed in the same sense suggested by Locke's definition of idea as "whatsoever is the object of the understanding when a man thinks." Berkeley, as previously quoted, elaborated upon the definition in this way (1910 ed., p. 113):

> It is evident to any one who takes a survey of the objects of human knowledge, that they are either *ideas* actually (1) imprinted on the senses, or else such as are (2) perceived by attending to the passions and operations of the mind, or lastly, ideas (3) formed by the help of memory and imagination, either compounding, dividing, or barely representing those originally perceived in the aforesaid ways ... Thus, for example, a certain colour, taste, smell, figure, and consistence having been observed to go together, are accounted one distinct thing, signified by the name *apple*. Other collections of ideas constitute a stone, a tree, a book, and the like sensible things, which, as they are pleasing or disagreeable, excite the passions of love, hatred, joy, grief, and so forth.

From the foregoing it is clear that Berkeley employed the term "idea" in a loose sense to designate all kinds of mental content. This practice, as explained in Chapter 12, had prompted Hume to object to having the word "stand for all our perceptions" and induced him to try "to restore the word ... to its original sense from which Mr. Locke had perverted it." Hume was objecting to Locke's failure to mention the difference between perceptions and ideas. In the preceding quotation Berkeley was guilty of a similar failure. In effect he was saying that an object like an apple "actually imprinted on the senses" was an idea of an apple. Hume would have called this the perception of an apple rather than an idea of an apple. To close one's eyes and still think of the apple, Hume might have said, is to have an idea of the apple. Consequently he would have endorsed Berkeley's third use of the term, with its reference to "the help of memory and imagination." This third use, with its allusion to imagination "barely representing" what was "originally perceived," not only conforms to Hume's notion of idea but also reflects Berkeley's theory of objects.

This is not to say that Berkeley developed this as an explicit theory; but it is implicit in what he has to say about sensory impressions arousing thoughts of absent objects. Thus in the present instance, hearing the word "apple" suffices to signify the fruit, just as in a previously quoted passage he referred to the sound of wheels as signifying a coach out in the street. Although he was sitting in his study at the time, the sound, he implied, was enough to instigate an image of the coach. The sound *qua* sound *meant* the coach as an object.

Titchener's Context Theory of Meaning

Berkeley's theory of objects can thus be viewed as a theory of meaning. As such it appears to be an anticipation of Titchener's *context* theory of meaning. The term "context" as employed by Titchener went beyond the ordinary usage of the term as a designation for the setting in which words occur, so that the meaning of a given word can change drastically when shifted from one sentence to another. A word like "stole," for example, has one meaning in "He stole ten dollars," a different meaning in "He stole third base," and a still different one in "She wore a beautiful stole." In each of these sentences the word "stole" arouses a different array of images. They constitute the context that determines the meaning of the word and serve to illustrate what Titchener meant by his statement: "Meaning, psychologically, is always context; one mental process is the meaning of another mental process if it is that other's context" (1917, p. 367). However, Titchener was not restricting his theory to this obvious, everyday meaning of context. In fact, he failed to mention it. Instead he was concerned with its less obvious implications, especially as they were related to the psychology of perception in general.

Titchener differentiated pure perceptions from mixed perceptions. Both kinds involve sensations, but the latter kind are supplemented by imaginal concomitants. Stated differently, pure perceptions are restricted to groups of sensations, while mixed perceptions are made up of sensations plus images. A clarifying instance of this distinction was supplied by Titchener. He was once shown a photograph of jerky lines superimposed on a circular background with a request to identify the zigzag scrawl. He perceived it as a photograph, but its meaning or significance eluded him. No relevant images came to mind; hence it was an instance of pure perception. It then occurred to him to glance at the back of the photograph. Here he found a date recorded and the date was that of a big earthquake. Immediately he recognized the photograph as a seismogram. The thought or image of an earthquake supplied the requisite context for the perception of meaning.

Pure perceptions are relatively rare. The vast majority of perceptions are mixed, and they may be supplemented by images from any sense modality, by verbal images, or by kinesthetic factors. The latter factors are likely to come into prominence when we think of the meaning of words like "trombone," "corkscrew," "pirouette," or "accordion." They are also implicit in children's definitions such as "A chair is to sit on" or "A wagon is to pull." Moreover, as Titchener noted (1917, p. 368): "In minds of a certain constitution, it may well be that all conscious meaning is carried by total kinesthetic attitude or by words.'"

Titchener was deliberate in his use of the phrase "conscious meaning," for the qualifying adjective was intended to suggest that meaning need not always be a conscious affair. What started out as a conscious affair may, as a result of practice or habituation, take place in quasi-automatic fashion. According to Titchener, its "meaning may be carried in purely physiological terms." In learning to read a foreign language, for example, the beginner is conscious of translating each foreign word into the corresponding word of his mother tongue. Without such translation the meaning eludes him. Once he has learned to think in the new language, the meaning of a passage is grasped immediately without dependence upon translation. The student who has majored in French knows the meaning of a sentence like "*Je suis malade*" at a glance. He does not have to experience imagery associated with the concept of illness in order to understand the meaning of "*malade.*" [18] Such imagery is latent and could be revived were a child to ask for a definition of the word "illness," but ordinarily there is no need for such revival. Its latency, in Titchener's view, is a matter of brain physiology and serves to exemplify unconscious meaning. This phase of his context theory may consequently be interpreted as consonant with the doctrine of imageless thought. [19] But this phase belongs to twentieth-century psychology and has no bearing on the relationship of the theory to Berkeley's theory of objects.

---

[18] The question of the relevance of imagery for the arousal of meaning was once investigated experimentally by T. V. Moore in 1915, in connection with the claims of members of the Würzburg School regarding what came to be known as *imageless* thought. Moore had his subjects react to a series of words, either seen or heard, under two sets of instructions. One set called for a reaction as soon as the meaning of the word was understood and the other called for a reaction as soon as an image was evoked. The reaction consisted of removing the finger from a depressed telegraph key so that the time of reaction could be measured. For eight of his nine subjects, meaning was experienced in less time than was required for the arousal of imagery. On the average, the time for the reaction to meaning was half a second, while the average for imagery arousal was almost a full second. Moore, in opposition to Titchener's context theory, regarded his results as justifying a structural psychology in which *meaning* is added as a separate element to those recognized by Titchener. This made for four classes of independent elements: Titchener's sensations, images, and feelings plus Moore's meanings. However, Moore's addition never received general acceptance.

[19] Whether Titchener would have endorsed this interpretation is open to question. As is well known, he was very explicit in his opposition to the notion of imageless thought. In his writings on the subject he tended to call attention to obscure organic sensations,

Is the Quest for Meaning Innate?

There is another phase of Titchener's theory that seems to mark a departure from Berkeley's views considered in the light of British empiricism. Titchener's theory of meaning, unlike Berkeley's theory of objects, is not in agreement with a *tabula rasa* concept of mind, for in discussing what he refers to as "the gist" of his theory Titchener appears to be more of a nativist than an empiricist. This "gist" is reduced to the contention "that it takes at least two sensations to make a meaning" and that a single sensation in the abstract, divorced from its context, is devoid of meaning (1917, pp. 368–369).

To appreciate this contention, one might conceive of a hypothetical creature incapable of having any sensory impressions with the sole exception of being sensitive to a single tone. By hypothesis the creature would be unable to relate the tone to anything else. Consequently, as a bare sensation unrelated to any other item, it would lack significance; unless something is signified, there can be no meaning. For the sake of illustration, let it be further assumed that the creature not only *hears* the sound but *sees* the vibrating tuning fork producing the sound. It now has *two* sensory impressions, with the result that sight and sound, as associated impressions, establish the irreducible minimum for the arousal of meaning. On subsequent occasions, and again by hypothesis, the mere sight of the fork would suggest or signify the tone just as the mere sound would come to mean the fork. In the light of this simple example, meaning is revealed as the perception of a relationship: a single item is perceived as pointing to or related to or associated with or as signifying another item.

In all likelihood Titchener would not have objected to the preceding hypothetical case introduced to show why he had maintained that "it takes at least two sensations to make a meaning." However, he would have objected to any intimation that this is the way meanings, genetically considered, are actually engendered. In his view, meanings did not emerge from a matrix of confused, chaotic sensations. He held that there is "no reason to believe that mind began with meaningless sensations, and progressed to

---

kinesthetic tensions, and other sensory features that advocates of imageless thinking had failed to note. For example, he had the latter advocates in mind when he wrote this passage (1917, p. 507):

> Some psychologists maintain, definitely, that there are awarenesses of meaning . . . which cannot be reduced to simpler terms, but must be accepted as non-sensory and imageless components of the higher mental processes. The author believes, on the contrary, that the attitudes so far as they are conscious at all, are always analysable.

And yet, as already noted, on page 369, he had agreed that "meaning may be carried in purely physiological terms." Taken at face value, this seems to be the equivalent of making the latter kind of meaning a "non-sensory and imageless" process.

meaningful perceptions." Instead in line with a nativistic orientation he held "that mind was meaningful from the very outset."[20]

Titchener even referred to the organism's "inherited organization" that governs its responsiveness to a given stimulating situation and he defined a situation as "the meaningful experience of a conscious present" (1917, p. 369). So defined, the word "situation" included both external and internal sources of stimulation: sounds, sights, and smells along with aches, hungers, tensions, and memories. For example, in the visual-cliff situation, it is by virtue of inherited organization that crawling babies avoid the "deep" side of the visual cliff. In the course of their subsequent explorations, with increasing motor control, the youngsters learn to cope with heights as they slide down a banister, jump off a sofa, and climb a tree. What height comes to mean for them varies with the context of each of the latter kinds of situations. This learning illustrates the nub of Titchener's context theory of meaning as well as Berkeley's theory of objects. Objects like banisters, sofas, and trees have come to be *associated* with a variety of bodily maneuvers; hence perception of one of these objects is likely to elicit a specific maneuver based upon what the youngsters have experienced in the course of their exploratory maneuvers.

The Meaning of Perceptual Learning

As has just been implied, the context theory has to do with perceptual learning as viewed from the standpoint of associationistic psychology. Seen in this light, the theory is by no means outmoded. In fact, it serves as a clarifying instance of the continuity of psychology's history in the sense of revealing the philosophic roots of current psychological issues. In part, as J. J. and E. J. Gibson have noted, it harks back to the nativism-empiricism controversy. To quote them directly (1955, p. 32):

> The term "perceptual learning" means different things to different psychologists. To some it implies that human perception is, in large part, learned—that we learn to see depth, for instance, or form, or meaningful objects. In that case the theoretical issue involved is *how much* of perception is learned, and the corresponding controversy is that of nativism or empiricism.

As formulated by the Gibsons, the theoretical issue in question takes this form: "Does all knowledge . . . come through the sense organs or is some knowledge contributed by the mind itself?" In their survey of the answers to this question, they mentioned Locke and Titchener along with contemporary

---

[20] This conclusion is reflected in a broad generalization known as *Bowden's principle*. According to D. Rapaport (1951, p. 665) the principle is formulated as follows: "The mind tends to order all the material presented to it, however disorganized, so as to make it meaningful."

psychologists like Hebb, Hilgard, and others. Moreover, what concerned them especially was the soundness of the traditional associationistic answer, to the effect that perception is enriched by the accumulation of memory images and other effects of past experience having direct or indirect connections with a present sensory impression. Such *enrichment* is the equivalent of what Titchener called context.

As an alternative to this enrichment theory, the Gibsons proposed a theory that makes perceptual learning more a consequence of discriminating attention to the specific details of objects perceived and less a consequence of associated memory images. To illustrate this *specificity* theory, they compared a connoisseur of wines with a person having limited familiarity with them. Confronted with three red wines like burgundy, chianti, and claret the latter person would be unable to tell the difference while the connoisseur, after noting differences in smell and taste, would label each wine correctly. For him the differentiation would be less a function of context and more a function of sensitivity to specific stimulus variables. This, in short, is one way to show how the specificity theory differs from the context or enrichment theory.

The Gibsons also introduced some experimental support for their specificity theory, but for present purposes there is no need to consider this. Furthermore, as might be expected, their theory did not go unchallenged. L. Postman (1955), for example, in a defense of the enrichment or associationistic theory, listed what he regarded as the inadequacies of the specificity theory. By way of rejoinder, the Gibsons listed what they regarded as inadequacies in Postman's defense. The controversy has not yet been settled. Perceptual learning is a complex affair, and eventually a compromise between both theories may have to be formulated in order to account for all phases of perceptual learning.

It may well be that some kinds of perception involve more discriminatory awareness of stimulus variables and that other kinds are more dependent upon reactivation of past experience. Distinguishing between scotch and bourbon is a different perceptual task from perceiving the difference between two quadratic equations. The specificity theory seems to be more applicable to the former task than to the latter; it should be obvious that for a person ignorant of mathematics even protracted inspection of the two equations will not enable him to perceive what is immediately evident to the trained mathematician.

Furthermore, there may be some kinds of perception hard to account for in terms of either of the two rival theories under consideration. For instance, is perceiving the point of a joke just a function of context, or is it a function of differentiated detail? Two people may both get the point of a joke and yet while one of them is amused, the other person is bored. Is perception of beauty in music or painting ascribable to enrichment or differentiation, or may it also involve something unique in the way of aesthetic sensitivity?

By now it should be evident that perceptual learning, like learning in general, embraces a diversity of situations. To subsume all such situations under one comprehensive theory of learning may be a challenging but futile undertaking. Tolman had this in mind when he pointed out that "there is more than one kind of learning" and that "the theory and laws appropriate to one kind may well be different from those appropriate to other kinds" (1949, p. 144). Incidentally, the fact that *perceptual* learning has emerged as a separate problem in contemporary psychology lends support to what Tolman said about there being more than one kind of learning.

Review and Concluding Comments

More than two and a half centuries have elapsed since Berkeley proposed his theory of objects, which has burgeoned into a controversial issue for modern learning theorists. Were he to be resurrected and induced to read what these theorists have incorporated in their chapters on perception and learning, he would be baffled and startled by the enormous changes introduced since his day. He might have trouble recognizing his theory of objects when disguised as a context theory or an enrichment theory. He would be perplexed by references to goal gradients. Wistar rats, tension reduction, T-mazes, and kindred technicalities altogether foreign to his eighteenth-century outlook. He might be disappointed to learn that his "new" theory of vision is now neither novel nor entirely valid. He might even be chagrined to discover that his defense of empiricism has been challenged by modern students who maintain that the "bases" for "the simple rules of space, time, force, and quantity . . . are certainly innate" (Tolman, 1949, p. 153).

In addition, upon examining current textbooks of general psychology in search of aillusions to his "principles of human knowledge," he would find this search futile. This, understandably enough, might puzzle him for a time. Then it might dawn upon him that what he had treated as problems having to do with the acquisition of knowledge and the origin of abstract ideas are now being treated as problems of learning. At first he might view this as an inconsequential verbal preference. However, upon reflection, it ought to strike him as indicative of an important difference. He had limited his essay to human cognition and had ignored problems of animal behavior. Moreover, had it occurred to him to consider the latter problems in a companion essay, he might well have balked at a title like *Principles of Animal Knowledge*. Under the circumstances he would understand why the twentieth-century psychologist, interested in animal nature as well as in human nature, seems to be more preoccupied with principles of learning than with principles of knowledge.

In the light of the foregoing considerations, one might wonder whether Berkeley, were he alive today, would think of himself as having had something to do with shaping the course of events that made twentieth-century psychology what it is. Would he think of himself as a causal link in the long chain of influence that historians trace through successive generations of thinkers and doers? Would he regard modern views of space perception as indirect effects of causes he had set in motion in 1709? It is altogether likely that he would have been troubled by questions of this sort. For him, the nature of causation in general was a troublesome affair. Because of his espousal of idealism, he found all appeals to material causation absurd and meaningless. Existence, he contended, is restricted to the sequential flow of ideas. In his *Principles of Human Knowledge* he recognized this flow as "artfully laid together" and as proceeding "according to rule," but why this should be so was a question that gave him pause. For him, the "rule" governing the connection of ideas had nothing to do with cause-and-effect relationships. Instead it had something to do with "purpose"; for, as he put it, "Since one idea cannot be the cause of another, to what purpose is that connexion?" He disposed of this question by the following reply (1910 ed., pp. 145–146):

> . . . my answer is, *first,* that the connexion of ideas does not imply the relation of *cause* and *effect,* but only of a mark or *sign* with the thing *signified.* The *fire* which I see is not the cause of the pain I suffer upon approaching it, but the mark that forewarns me of it. In like manner, the noise that I hear is not the effect of this or that motion or collision of the ambient bodies, but the sign thereof . . .
>
> Hence it is evident, that those *things* which, *under the notion of a cause co operating or concurring to the production of effects, are altogether inexplicable,* and run us into great absurdities, may be very naturally explained, and have a proper and obvious use assigned them, when they are considered only as marks or signs for our information. And it is the *searching after, and endeavouring to understand those signs . . . instituted by the author of nature,* that ought to be the employment of the natural philosopher, and not the pretending to explain things by corporeal causes; which doctrine seems to have too much estranged the minds of men from that active principle, that supreme and wise spirit, "in whom we live, move, and have our being."

Berkeley's misgivings regarding the concept of causation, it should now be evident, followed from his denial of matter or what he referred to as "corporeal causes" in this quotation. It seems safe to say that he would have objected to Aristotle's endorsement of the notion of a material cause. On the other hand, he might have accepted Aristotle's notion of formal and final causes, since he did not eschew all dependence on the idea of causation. For example, the subtitle to his treatise on *Human Knowledge* is worded as follows, with italics added: "Wherein the *chief causes* of error and difficulty in the sciences, with the grounds of scepticism, atheism, and irreligion, are inquired into" (1910 ed., p. 87). Furthermore, by implication he recognized spirits as causes when he defined a spirit as that which "cannot be of itself perceived *but only by the effects which it produceth*" (p. 126). In the light of this definition he affirmed the existence of a spiritual God as well as a spiritual mind or ego. However, had he been consistent in adhering to his principle of *esse est percipi,* he could not have affirmed the being or reality or existence of anything which cannot be perceived. His theology seems to have interfered with his empirical philosophy.

A more consistent empiricism was worked out by the nontheological Hume, who like Berkeley tackled the knotty problem of causation but, unlike Berkeley, was under no obligation to act as defender of the faith and thus, as will be shown in the next chapter, felt free to sponsor an associationistic psychology without a soul, a self, or an ego.

References

Berkeley, G. *A New Theory of Vision and Other Select Philosophical Writings.* London: J. M. Dent and Sons, 1910.

Berkeley, G. *Three Dialogues Between Hylas and Philonous,* reprinted. Chicago: Open Court Publishing Company, 1913. (First published in 1713.)

Boring, E. G. "The Moon Illusion," *American Journal of Physics,* 1943, *11,* 55–60.

Boring, E. G. "The Perception of Objects," *American Journal of Physics,* 1946, *14,* 99–107.

Bower, T. G. R. "Stimulus Variables Determining Space Perception in Infants," *Science,* 1965, *149,* 88–89.

Breed, F. S. "Development of Certain Instincts and Habits in Chicks," *Behavior Monographs,* 1911, *1,* No. 1.

Clarke, E. G. *Problems in the Accommodation and Refraction of the Eye—A Brief Review of the Work of Donders.* London: Braillière, Tindall and Cox, 1914.

Garrison, F. H. *An Introduction to the History of Medicine,* 4th ed. Philadelphia: W. B. Saunders Company, 1929.

Gibson, E. J., and Walk, R. D. "The Visual Cliff," *Scientific American,* 1960, *202,* 64–71.

Gibson, J. J., and Gibson, E. J. "Perceptual Learning: Differentiation or Enrichment," *Psychological Review,* 1955, *62,* 32–41.

Gibson, J. J., and Gibson, E. J. "What Is Learned in Perceptual Learning? A Reply to Professor Postman," *Psychological Review,* 1955, *62,* 447–450.

Graham, C. H. "Visual Perception," in S. S. Stevens (ed.). *Handbook of Experimental Psychology.* New York: John Wiley and Sons, 1951, 868–920.

Harris, C. S. "Perceptual Adaptation to Inverted, Reversed, and Displaced Vision," *Psychological Review,* 1965, *72,* 419–444.

Held, R. "Plasticity in Sensori-Motor Systems," *Scientific American,* 1965, *213,* 84–94.

Hildebrand, J. H. "Order from Chaos," *Science,* 1965, *150,* 441–450.

Hill, G. B. (ed.). *Boswell's Life of Johnson,* Vol. 1. New York: Bigelow, Brown and Company, 1887.

James, W. *Principles of Psychology,* Vol. II. New York: Henry Holt and Company, 1890.

Julesz, B. "Binocular Depth Perception Without Familiarity Cues," *Science,* 1964, *145,* 356–362.

Julesz, B. "Texture and Visual Perception," *Scientific American,* 1965, *212,* 38–48.

Lashley, K. S., and Russell, J. T. "The Mechanism of Vision. A Preliminary Test of Innate Organization," *Journal of Genetic Psychology,* 1934, *45,* 136–144.

Moore, T. V. "The Temporal Relations of Meaning and Imagery," *Psychological Review,* 1915, *22,* 177–225.

Osgood, C. E. *Method and Theory in Experimental Psychology.* New York: Oxford University Press, 1953.

Perry, R. B. *The Thought and Character of William James.* New York: George Brazilier, 1954.

Postman, L. "Association Theory and Perceptual Learning," *Psychological Review,* 1955, *62,* 438–446.

Rapaport, D. *Organization and Pathology of Thought.* New York: Columbia University Press, 1951.

Rogers, A. K. *A Student's History of Philosophy.* New York: The Macmillan Company, 1915.

Russell, B. *A History of Western Philosophy.* New York: Simon and Schuster, 1945.

Russell, J. T. "Depth Discrimination in the Rat," *Journal of General Psychology,* 1932, *40,* 136–159.

Stratton, G. M. "Some Preliminary Experiments Without Inversion of the Retinal Image," *Psychological Review,* 1896, *3,* 611–617.

Stratton, G. M. "Vision Without Inversion of the Retinal Image," *Psychological Review,* 1897, *4,* 341–360, 463–481.

Titchener, E. B. *A Text-Book of Psychology.* New York: The Macmillan Company, 1917.

Tolman, E. C. *Purposive Behavior in Animals and Man.* New York: Appleton-Century Company, 1932.

Tolman, E. C. "There Is More Than One Kind of Learning," *Psychological Review,* 1949, *56,* 144–155.

Weizsäcker, C. F. *The World View of Physics.* (Translated by Marjorie Greve.) Chicago: University of Chicago Press, 1952.

17

The Humean Background

THE PRESENT CHAPTER, like the preceding one, will be concerned with eighteenth-century British empiricism. Referring to empiricism as British is a venerable historical convention. However, it is well to note that not all participants in the movement were English in the sense in which Hobbes and Locke were English. Berkeley, it will be recalled, came from Ireland, and David Hume was proud of being a Scotsman. Nor was Hume the only Scot to be classified as an empiricist. His nineteenth-century successors, such as James Mill, Sir William Hamilton, and Alexander Bain, were also of Scottish origin.

Psychology in Eighteenth-Century Scotland

By the eighteenth century, Scotland had an established university tradition. Its four leading universities had been in existence for several centuries. The oldest, Saint Andrews, had been founded in 1411. Then came the one at Glasgow in 1450, Aberdeen University in 1494, and the University of Edinburgh in 1582. For a long time, as was true of the beginnings of continental universities, Latin was the language of instruction, and lectures on philosophy were mainly concerned with Aristotle.

An important change was introduced by Francis Hutcheson (1694–1746), professor of moral philosophy at Glasgow. According to Brett (1921, Vol. III, pp. 12–13), he was the first to break with the old pattern by lecturing in English and also by following the precedent of his teacher Gerschom Carmichael, who had introduced consideration of the teaching of Hobbes and Locke into his lectures. Through Carmichael, Brett noted, Scotland came to oppose the political philosophy of Hobbes and to endorse the "mental philosophy" of Locke. This preference resulted in retention of the "best work of antiquity" along with a readiness to adopt what seemed valid in the new work. The intellectual climate in Scotland was thus rendered more independent and more vigorous.

Both the fusion of old and new and the spirit of independent thinking were exemplified in the teachings of Hutcheson. Even though he found himself in agreement with Locke's general treatment of the psychology of understanding, he did not endorse it completely. In particular he supplemented Locke's list of the modalities of sense by retaining Aristotle's notion of a "commonsense." Hutcheson also argued that Locke had overlooked other important senses. As enumerated by one writer,[1] these included a sense by which one perceives one's own mind, a sense of honor making for sensitivity to praise and blame, an aesthetic sense rendering one sensitive to beauty, a sense of the ridiculous, and, finally, a moral sense.

In his professional role as occupant of the chair of moral philosophy, Hutcheson was especially concerned with the nature of the alleged moral sense. In general, he treated the subject along lines laid down by the third Earl of Shaftesbury (1671–1713), the man who had first postulated the existence of a moral sense.[2] Following Shaftesbury, he recognized an aesthetic factor in the activation of the moral sense when he referred to the "moral sense of beauty in actions and affections, by which we perceive virtue or vice, in ourselves or others." He also followed Shaftesbury in making the promotion of the general welfare the touchstone for determining the moral worth of particular actions. This criterion was an anticipation of the ethical standard Jeremy Bentham (1748–1832) came to stress in his utilitarianism. In fact, Hutcheson seems to have been the first to formulate this standard as being the kind of action likely to promote "the greatest happiness of the greatest number."[3] In doing so he was giving expression to a hedonistic theory of motivation having both ethical and psychological implications. As *ethical* hedonism it made concern for the welfare or happiness of others a concern which one *ought* to foster, and as *psychological* hedonism it held that desire for happiness is in fact a regnant human motive. In what H. M. Jones (1953) has called "the glittering generality" of the pursuit of happiness, this theory of motivation influenced the thinking of those who formulated the Declaration of Independence in 1776. By that

---

[1] *See* the unsigned article on the life and work of Hutcheson in *Encyclopaedia Britannica,* 14th ed., 1929.

[2] As mentioned at the beginning of Chapter 12, Locke served as physician to Shaftesbury's grandfather and as tutor to the grandson.

[3] He is mentioned as having been the first to have introduced this phrase in one of his essays published in 1725. In the *Britannica* article cited in Footnote 1, the essay is said to demonstrate Hutcheson's anticipation of "the utilitarianism of Bentham even in the use of the phrase 'the greatest happiness for the greatest number.'" However, this statement is at variance with the *Britannica's* reference to the work of Beccaria (1738–1794), whose famous *On Crimes and Punishment* appeared in 1764. The reference in question contains this statement: "The French translation, by Morellet (1766), contained an anonymous preface by Voltaire. In the preface to this book first appeared the phrase 'the greatest happiness of the greatest number.'"

time—thirty years after the death of Hutcheson—they were regarding the pursuit of happiness as one of the "unalienable rights" with which men "are endowed by their Creator."

Psychological hedonism, as understood by Hutcheson, clashed with the earlier views of Hobbes regarding the driving forces of human nature. Hobbes, it will be recalled, thought of man as inherently selfish, hostile, and predatory, so that in a state of nature his life would be "solitary, poor, nasty, brutish, and short." His was a malevolent picture of feral man. Hutcheson, in contrast, thought of man as harboring benevolent impulses and not just basically selfish ones. He regarded them as expressions of the soul's *sympathetic* sense, concerning which he wrote as follows (D. S. Robinson [ed.], 1961, p. 35):

> Another important determination or sense of the soul we may call the *sympathetic,* different from all the external senses; by which, when we apprehend the state of others, our hearts naturally have a fellow-feeling for them. When we see or know the pain, distress, or misery of any kind which another suffers, and turn our thoughts to it, we feel a strong sense of pity, and a great proneness to relieve, where no contrary passion withholds us. And this without any artful views of advantage to accrue to us from giving relief, or of loss we shall sustain by these sufferings. We see this principle strongly working in children, where there are the fewest distant views of interest; so strongly sometimes, even in some not of the softest mold, at cruel executions, as to occasion fainting and sickness. This principle continues generally during all our lives.

This principle of sympathetic fellow-feeling was stressed by Hutcheson in his theory of morals. As a consequence his theory is usually classified as a "benevolent theory." This theory influenced the thinking of Adam Smith (1723–1790), who of course is best known for his place in the history of economics because of his famous *The Wealth of Nations.*[4] However, the influence of the theory is especially manifest in Smith's *The Theory of Moral Sentiments,* which was published in 1759, or more than fifteen years before his better-known book.

Smith accounted for the origin of moral judgments in terms of man's capacity to sympathize with others. In doing so he paved the way for a naturalistic ethics. The biologist G. G. Simpson had reference to this in an article on naturalistic ethics in which he pointed out that "Adam Smith held that the ethical sense arose in a natural manner" (1966, p. 28). A teaching of this kind is one reason for incidental reference to Smith in a history of

---

[4] The full title of the book is *Inquiry into the Causes of the Wealth of Nations.* It was published in 1776. Incidentally, the phrase "wealth of the nations" is of Biblical origin. It occurs three times in the Book of Isaiah as follows: "The wealth of the nations shall come unto thee" (60:5), "That men may bring unto thee the wealth of the nations" (60:11), and "Ye shall eat the wealth of the nations" (61:6). Whether Smith was influenced by these verses is altogether conjectural.

psychology. A possibly more important reason has to do with the close relationship between Smith and Hume. They both reflected the influence of Hutcheson in their interest in the psychology of moral action. In the case of Smith this interest was directly related to his university work, for he followed Hutcheson as professor of moral philosophy at Glasgow University. Even though he is almost always referred to as an economist, he never occupied a chair of economics. However, as F. S. C. Northrop (1947, pp. 127–128) has pointed out, "He regarded his economic science as essentially connected with moral philosophy."

Smith's moral philosophy and his economics were both affected somewhat by what Hume had to say about the nature of man. Smith had first met Hume on a trip to Edinburgh in 1748, and the acquaintanceship developed into a warm friendship that lasted for more than twenty-five years. Hume was eleven years older than Smith and had written about the nature of man almost twenty years before Smith's book on moral sentiments was published. For this reason it is altogether understandable that during the course of their long friendship, Hume had had considerable influence on Smith's thinking. Moreover, some of Hume's essays dealt with topics like balance of trade, taxation, commerce, money, and similar subjects belonging to the field of economics. For this reason, as well as because of his friendship with Smith, Hume has a place in the history of economics. Moreover, as was mentioned in the previous chapter, there is no question about Hume's views having had a direct impact on Kant and thus having had some bearing on the course of German philosophy.[5] Furthermore, in the words of Northrop, "Bentham's philosophy was determined by that of David Hume" (1947, p. 111). In short, Hume's thinking had consequences not only for the field of psychology but for other fields as well, and thus his importance as an eighteenth-century philosopher-psychologist is evident. In the opinion of V. C. Chappell, "David Hume is probably the greatest philosopher to write in English" (1963, p. vii).

Hume's Life and Work

Hume was born in Edinburgh in 1711. Shortly before his death in 1776 he wrote his own obituary in the form of a brief autobiographical essay entitled "My Own Life" (Northrop, 1947, pp. 3–10). In this he reports that he was an infant when his father died, leaving David's mother to look after an older son and daughter as well as himself. He refers to his mother as "a woman of singular merit, who, though young and handsome, devoted herself entirely to the rearing and educating of her children." Concerning his

---

[5] On occasion it is pointed out that this was not the only link between Kant and Scotland; the family of Kant's father had come to Germany from Scotland some hundred years before Kant's birth.

own education, he has little to say beyond a laconic statement to the effect that he "passed through the ordinary course of education with success." The schooling he received at home enabled him to enter the University of Edinburgh at the age of twelve. While there he presumably read the classics and thus received some grounding in Greek and Roman philosophy. Not very much is known about this period of his life. However, something went wrong; for, despite his precocity and love of learning, he left the university after two or three years without obtaining a degree.

Subsequently, at his family's urging he took up the study of law; but, as he states in his autobiography, he found that he had "an unsurmountable aversion to everything but the pursuits of philosophy and general learning." Instead of studying the law books, as his family assumed he was doing, he was secretly devouring Cicero and Vergil. Finding the study of law so distasteful, he became a "dropout" for the second time. This was in 1734 when he was twenty-three and in poor health which he attributed to his "ardent application" to study.[6] By way of a change, he then decided to engage in a business career by entering the employ of a Bristol merchant. This venture also proved distasteful and, after a few months, he resigned his post with the intention of once again resuming a life of study. To execute the intention, he left for the quiet of a country retreat in France. The place he finally chose was La Flèche, a small town noted as the site of the Jesuit school where Descartes had studied. During the three years of his sojourn in France he worked on his *Treatise of Human Nature.*

Writing the *Treatise* was his first literary venture, and it was with high hopes for its success that he took the manuscript to London in 1737. It was published in 1739 when he was still a young man of twenty-eight. Like the precocious Berkeley, the precocious Hume had written an important book before he was thirty. Unfortunately for Hume's burning desire for recognition as a writer, the *Treatise* failed to arouse much interest when it first appeared. According to Hume, "It fell *dead-born from the press,* without reaching such distinction, as even to excite a murmur from the zealots." Despite this disappointment, he remained undiscouraged and applied himself to writing his *Essays on Moral and Political Subjects,* which were published as a book in 1741 and dealt with economics, government, history, and politics.

Unlike the *Treatise,* the *Essays* commanded immediate attention and

---

[6] His knowledge of philosophy was largely a product of omnivorous reading. In addition to ancient writers, he studied Newton's *Principia,* Hobbes's *Leviathan,* and Locke's *Essay* along with the writings of Bacon, Berkeley, Malebranche, Descartes, Montaigne, and others. As a result of all this self-initiated study he taught himself philosophy just as James taught himself psychology. At this period, Hume was especially concerned with the writings of Locke and Berkeley. In the words of R. Adamson and J. M. Mitchell (*Encyclopaedia Britannica,* 11th ed., 1910): "This time the intensity of his intellectual activity in the area opened up to him by Locke and Berkeley reduced him to a state of physical exhaustion."

brought Hume a modicum of fame and before long he was on terms of friendship with some of the brilliant writers of the period. Hutcheson was one of these friends, and he may have had something to do with Hume's effort to obtain a university post. At all events, it was about this time that Hume applied for the chair of moral philosophy at Edinburgh, but his heterodox views rendered him *persona non grata* to the university. Close to ten years later he tried to secure the professorship of logic at the University of Glasgow, but this attempt also proved vain. He thus failed to become an exception to what was mentioned in an earlier chapter regarding the nonacademic status[7] of all the British associationists from Hobbes up to, but not including, Alexander Bain.

Hume was not always just a cloistered student and writer. There was one period when he spent a year looking after a mentally disturbed young marquis. All that he had to say about this venture is that it paid well. Following this he accepted a position as secretary and aide-de-camp to a General James St. Clair. This appointment involved traveling to different countries and living in different cities. He was with the general for two years and in retrospect he describes them as the only period in his life during which his studies were interrupted; but they were pleasant years passed in pleasant company.

Prior to the interruption of his studies, Hume had undertaken a revision of the *Treatise*. He deemed a revision necessary because, in his view, he had been too impulsive in going to press with the *Treatise*. Its failure, he believed, was due to the way in which it was written and not in what was written. Accordingly, he decided to present his ideas in more persuasive fashion. The first part of the revision was published in 1748 as *Philosophical Essays Concerning Human Understanding,* and in 1758 the final complete revision appeared under the title of *An Enquiry Concerning Human Understanding.* The *Treatise* and the *Enquiry* account for Hume's place in the history of psychology and their contents will be considered shortly.

No sketch of Hume's life would be complete without mentioning his role as historian. Shortly after 1752 he began writing his *History of England* when, as he reports, "the Faculty of Advocates chose me their Librarian, an office from which I received little or no emolument, but which gave me the command of a large library." The *History* proved to be an ambitious undertaking requiring five volumes for its completion, with the last volume appearing in 1761.[8] According to Hume, the scale of the books "much ex-

---

7 "Nonacademic status" is not to be taken in a literal sense, but rather as a reference to the fact that none of the men in question ever became professors of philosophy. Two of them did have academic appointments for a time: Locke as lecturer in Greek at Oxford and Berkeley as lecturer in Hebrew at Trinity.

8 In later editions the work was divided into more than five volumes.

ceeded anything formerly known in England," and he became "not only independent, but opulent." Nor was this just transient popularity; the *History* continued to be viewed as a standard work for many decades after Hume's death. It broadened the outlook of professional historians by including more than a chronicle of military and political events in their perspective. Social, literary, and other phases of a nation's life were woven into the pattern of history. Furthermore, by inquiring into the *causes* of historical change, Hume presented this as a dynamic pattern and the writing of history ceased to be a mere recording of the temporal sequence of battles, wars, and dynasties. This is worth noting because, as will be brought out later, Hume had misgivings about causation as a dynamic factor.

Hume also wrote on the subject of religion and aroused the opposition of the sponsors of orthodoxy. He was no stranger to opposition, for he reported that as a result of his defense of King Charles I in his *History* he "was assailed by one cry of reproach, disapprobation, and even detestation." However, he was neither crushed nor enraged by the hostility his writings provoked. In the closing paragraph of his brief autobiography he alluded to this hostility as he presented a retrospective appraisal of his own character and temperament. He wrote this in 1776 when he was already stricken with what he knew to be a fatal illness. Those who knew him well regarded it as an accurate appraisal. Since he thought of it in terms of his life being finished, what follows was put in the past tense (E. C. Mossner [ed.], 1963, pp. 8–9):

> I was . . . a man of mild disposition, of command of temper, of an open, social, and cheerful humour, capable of attachment, but little susceptible of enmity, great moderation in all my passions. Even my love of literary fame, my ruling passion, never soured my temper notwithstanding my frequent disappointments. . . . In a word, though most men anywise eminent, have found reason to complain of calumny, I never was touched, or even attacked by her baleful tooth: and though I wantonly exposed myself to the rage of both civil and religious factions, they seemed to be disarmed in my behalf of their wonted fury. My friends never had occasion to vindicate any one circumstance of my character and conduct: not but that the zealots, we may well suppose, would have been glad to invent and propagate any story to my disadvantage, but they would never find any which they thought would wear the face of probability. I cannot say there is no vanity in making this funeral oration of myself, but I hope it is not a misplaced one; and this is a matter of fact which is easily cleared and ascertained.

It is hard, if not impossible, to reconcile the preceding self-appraisal with what Hume had written so very many years earlier about the concept of selfhood. The "funeral oration," with its references to "my love" and "my friends" and its frequent repetition of the word "I," might have been written by a self-psychologist. And yet when he was writing as a psychologist Hume was anything but a self-psychologist. As will be brought out later, the kind of psychology he sponsored was at variance with the concept of an active ego or a regnant self.

What Hume Meant by the "Science of Man"

Hume is usually classified as an empirical psychologist along with Hobbes, Locke, and Berkeley. He may even have thought of himself as an experimental psychologist or as an experimental philosopher. This is suggested by the full title of his *Treatise,* which reads as follows: *A Treatise of Human Nature, Being an Attempt to Introduce the Experimental Method of Reasoning into Moral Subjects.* In the introductory chapter he explains that the *Treatise* is concerned with the "science of man," which is to supply "the only solid foundation for the other sciences." Consequently, he adds, it too must be established upon the "solid foundation" of "experience and observation" and by the "application of experimental philosophy."[9] Hume employed the word "experimental" to denote his understanding of scientific reasoning; hence his use of the phrase "experimental method of reasoning." Newton served as a model for this kind of reasoning. In fact, in his youthful enthusiasm, Hume thought the *Treatise* might do for the mental realm what the *Principia* had done for the physical realm. In general, he followed what he took to be the method of science by (1) carefully formulating the specific mental problem to be investigated; (2) tracing the origin of each mental phenomenon to some instigating impression; (3) giving due consideration to alternative modes of explanation; and (4) deliberately attempting to find evidence that might run counter to any conclusions being entertained.

In his effort to establish a "science of man" by experimental procedures, Hume was not anticipating the nineteenth-century innovation of a laboratory psychology. Instead it was to be a science based upon direct observations of human affairs plus critical thinking regarding the significance of such observations. According to Hume's own formulation (V. C. Chappell [ed.], 1963, pp. 13–14):

> We must therefore glean up our experiments in this science from a cautious observation of human life, and take them as they appear in the common course of the world, by man's behaviour in company, in affairs, and in their pleasures. Where experiments of this kind are judiciously collected and compared, we may

---

[9] As noted in Chapter 11, the phrase "experimental philosophy" had already been employed by Henry Power in the seventeenth century. Nor was this unique with him. Locke employed the same phrase in his *Essay* in so casual a manner as to suggest that he did not regard it as an innovation. For instance, in connection with a discussion of knowledge and probability he wrote (1956 ed., p. 263): " . . . I am apt to doubt that, how far soever human industry may advance useful and experimental philosophy in physical things," scientific certitude "will still be out of reach."

hope to establish on them a science, which will not be inferior in certainty, and will be much superior in utility to any other human comprehsneion.

To some extent, of course, virtually all philosophers might contend that what they had to say about the nature of man was based upon "a cautious observation of human life." Hume was not unique in availing himself of such observations. Even rationalists like Descartes and Kant, it should be obvious, did not exclude such observations. Furthermore, it should also be obvious that Hume's "method of reasoning" about experienced observations is a rationalistic procedure. In short, the empiricist-rationalist dichotomy is not to be construed as a rigid, mutually exclusive dichotomy devoid of intermediate gradations. All empiricists had to think or reason and sometimes even speculate, just as rationalists could not keep their reasoning free from empirical considerations. How a given philosopher-psychologist is to be classified in terms of the dichotomy in question is not always easy. It depends on the degree to which he stresses what Locke called sensation as contrasted with what he called reflection. If sensation and perception are the dominant themes, he is placed in the empiricist category. On the other hand, should he subordinate sensation and perception to cognitive functions, he comes to be classified as a rationalist.

How Is Hume to Be Classified?

Just how Hume is to be classified in the light of the preceding criterion is a moot issue. As already indicated, he is usually regarded as an empiricist by historians of psychology in their accounts of the history of associationism. Similarly, in histories of philosophy his work is ordinarily discussed in the chapters concerned with empiricism. However, this traditional or conventional way of classifying his work has not gone unchallenged. For example, C. W. Hendel (1927, p. xiii), after granting Hume's allegiance to "the empirical method of science," added the qualification that sometimes "the rationalist's spirit of speculation descended upon him," especially when he tried to lend added force to his arguments. And Northrop, to cite another example, was even more explicit and emphatic in this respect than Hendel; he came to this conclusion (1947, p. 117): "The truth is that Hume was not an empiricist, but a rationalist, a rationalist who took Locke's theory of ideas for granted and pursued it to its logical consequence."

To say that Hume "took Locke's theory of ideas for granted" is not to be interpreted as meaning an unquestioning endorsement of Locke's views. Hume did his own thinking. As will be brought out later, his account of the difference between simple and complex ideas was not a duplication of Locke's account. Furthermore, to say with Northrop "that Hume was not an empiricist, but a rationalist" is a "truth" which ought to be qualified. Since Hume did not present a tightly knit and altogether consistent system, students of Hume have not agreed on how to characterize his position. As in Biblical exegesis, it is possible to find quotations that justify one interpretation and other quotations that lend support to an opposite interpretation. Nor is this choice limited to the empiricist-rationalist dichotomy. As Chappell has indicated, commentators have classified Hume in various ways as a phenomenalist or an atomist or a sensationalist or a naturalist or an empiricist or in some other way, while there have also been commentators "for whom Hume's thought consists almost entirely of contradictions" (1963, p. lix). Nevertheless, they would all very likely agree with Northrop to the extent of granting that with respect to his psychological views, Hume was greatly indebted to Locke.

Hume Influenced by Locke

That Locke influenced Hume is evident from the fact that both men started their respective psychologies by considering the nature of human understanding. Hume's revision of his *Treatise* was entitled *An Enquiry Concerning Human Understanding* and thus almost duplicated the title of Locke's *Essay*. Moreover, the *Treatise* was divided into three parts, and Book One was called *Of the Understanding*. The second book was called *Of the Passions*; and the third *Of Morals*. This tripartite division reflects a recurrent one in the history of psychology. As mentioned in Chapter 3, it was already implicit in Plato's myth of the charioteer and received explicit formulation in Moses Mendelssohn's "three faculty" doctrine in 1755.[10] Johann Nikolaus Tetens, it may be recalled, also based his psychology on the latter doctrine, with its three key concepts of thinking, feeling, and willing. It was also reflected in Kant's three *Critiques* as well as in Freud's ego, id, and superego. Academic psychologists have reference to the same triad of concepts when they talk about cognition, affection, and volition. Hume's account of human nature in terms of understanding, passions, and morals thus centered around the same three themes. It is well not to be misled by a mere change in descriptive vocabulary. Plato's rational soul, Locke's understanding, and Freud's ego are just alternative ways of alluding to cognition.

Hume's account of the nature of understanding is an elaboration of Locke's account. He begins by making understanding a product of perception and, as noted in Chapter 12, by taking Locke to task for neglecting to distinguish between impressions and ideas. By way of correction he suggested restricting the term "idea" to the "faint images" of recalled impressions, with the "impressions" defined as "all our sensations, passions, and emotions, as they make their first appearance in the soul." He then qualified this definition by noting that the imagery characteristic of ideation need not be

---

[10] There is a Biblical foreshadowing of this doctrine in Deuteronomy 6:5: "And thou shalt love the Lord thy God with all thy heart, and with all thy soul, and with all thy might."

faint but may approximate the vividness of sensory impressions in dreaming and in the delirium of fever. For Hume, then, the imagery of ideation was not the equivalent of what Hobbes had called "decaying sense." In fact, he stated, there are times when sensory impressions are so faint "that we cannot distinguished them from our ideas." In general, however, impressions are more vivid than ideas and there is no difficulty in making a distinction as "every one of himself will readily perceive."

Although Hume, like Locke, made a distinction between simple impressions and ideas as contrasted with complex ones, his account of the distinction differed somewhat from the one introduced by Locke. He based the distinction on two characteristics: (1) separability into parts in the case of complex perceptions, and no analysis into parts in the case of simple ones; and (2) degree of resemblance between given impressions and corresponding ideas.

With respect to complex ideas, Hume observed, there need be no exact correspondence between the instigating impression and the corresponding idea. By way of illustration, he noted the difference between his idea of Paris as contrasted with his impression of the city as he walked its streets. His idea failed to "perfectly represent all its streets and houses in their real and just proportions." On the other hand, with respect to simple ideas, he contended, there is very close resemblance between them and their instigating impressions.[11] The color red, he pointed out, which strikes the eyes in bright light differs only in degree from the idea of red as one chances to think of the color in the darkness of night. In effect he was maintaining that simple ideas are copies of simple impressions but that complex ideas are not facsimiles of complex impressions.

From the example he introduced, it seems that Hume was making his notion of a simple impression the equivalent of an elementary sensation. Thus, the color red *qua* red conforms to his characterization of a simple perception as that which admits "of no distinction nor separation." It is in this respect that his account of a simple idea differs from the account given by Locke. Hume, to cite his own example, regarded perception of an apple as a complex impression or idea, because even though its "colour, taste, and smell are qualities all united together," they are nevertheless "distinguishable from each other." Locke would have called this a simple idea involving "more senses than one."

Hume failed to mention his lack of agreement with Locke's way of differentiating simple from complex perceptions. Instead he seemed content to

---

11 In fact, in connection with a discussion of our impressions of the distances separating "many visible bodies" as compared with our subsequent *ideas* of these distances, he noted that "every idea is derived from some impression which is exactly similar to it" (C. W. Hendel [ed.], 1927, p. 15). This, of course, is contrary to psychological fact. Our memory image of the size of a postage stamp or even of the length of our index finger when outlined on a slip of paper will rarely be found to be "exactly similar" to the dimensions of the perceived stamp or finger.

introduce his own view without explaining his rejection of Locke's view. Under the circumstances there is no indication of just what he had in mind. It is nevertheless evident that he and Locke were not using the same criteria in distinguishing simple from complex perceptions. Locke's criterion consisted of the difference between passive and active observation: all chance impressions give rise to simple ideas, while those due to activation of the "powers" of the mind result in complex ideas. The mere sight of an apple would be a simple perception, but trying to decide whether it is a genuine Gravenstein would involve a Lockean complex perception.

Hume employed a different criterion by restricting simple perceptions to those due to a single sense modality while those due to more than a single sense modality were deemed to be complex. He thus came close to basing his distinction on the somewhat troublesome distinction between sensations and perceptions.[12] His simple impressions or ideas, as previously suggested, were virtually unanalyzable items like a color, a sound, a smell, a pain, or any other unstructured, "meaningless" sensory item. He might be said to have been anticipating the later structural psychologists who regarded so-called pure sensations as the raw material of perception. When structured or organized into complex impressions, Hume might have argued, simple impressions or ideas become perceptions of a landscape or a melody or a garden or an illness. Viewed in this light, Hume's distinction between simple and complex impressions is consistent with one kind of familiar psychological analysis. Locke's distinction in terms of passive and active orientations is also consistent with later psychological developments. The two views are supplementary rather than contradictory.

Why the Treatise Was Written

In writing the *Treatise,* Hume, although obviously influenced by his knowledge of what Locke and Berkeley had written, had a different purpose in mind. As a matter of fact, each of the three men had different purposes in mind in their respective psychological studies. Locke, it will be recalled, undertook to write about the nature of human understanding in order to get at the origin and limits of knowledge. His was an epistemological quest. Berkeley's quest was essentially theological, as is evident from the subtitle of his book on the principles of knowledge, which states that the work will expose "the chief causes of error and difficulty in the sciences, with the

---

12 The distinction is troublesome because of the difficulty of supplying a satisfactory definition for the word "sensation." It has been maintained, for example, that a so-called pure sensation is always embedded in a perceptual setting and never occurs as isolated mental content or as a mental process divorced from concurrent ones. As an abstraction from such a setting, the word "sensation" is a construct rather than a mental something having an independent existence. This is one view. According to another view, genetically considered, sensation precedes perception, and thus all knowledge is a derivative of sensation.

grounds of scepticism, atheism, and irreligion" being given due consideration. For Hume, the quest had to do with understanding man as a moral being mindful of the rights of others as well as his own rights, sensitive to injustice, and ready to judge some acts as good and others as bad.

That his proposed "science of man" was primarily concerned with man viewed as an ethical being is clearly shown by the final sentence of the *Treatise,* in which Hume came to this conclusion: "And thus the most abstract speculations concerning human nature, however cold and unentertaining, become subservient to *practical morality,* and may render this latter science more correct in its precepts and more persuasive in its exhortations" (Chappell, p. 303). To a far greater degree than was true of Locke and Berkeley, Hume's interest in psychological issues reflected a social-science orientation. It was the kind of orientation which, at various periods in his life, induced him to devote himself to questions of economics, of literature, of politics, and of history. Along with Hobbes, he may thus be thought of as a pioneer social psychologist.

Introduction to the Treatise

This social-science orientation is not clearly evident in the early portions of the *Treatise.* As already mentioned, Hume begins his account by taking Locke's *Essay* as his point of departure. However, he fails to make this explicit, just as his subsequent utilization of Berkeleian conclusions is introduced without any mention of Berkeley by name. A reader unfamiliar with the writings of Locke and Berkeley would not recognize Hume's indebtedness to his two philosophic predecessors. Furthermore, in his discussion of ideational association he writes as if there had been no prior consideration of the principles involved. There is no reference to Aristotle; and even though Hume comes close to duplicating Locke's chapter heading by entitling his discussion "Of the Connection or Association of Ideas," Locke's name is conspicuously absent. It may be that Hume expected to appeal to sophisticated readers who would recognize source material without specific bibliographic reminders. He certainly did not try to conceal his indebtedness to Locke, as is shown by his repeated use of Lockean phrases.

In addition to his reinterpretation of Locke's distinction between simple and complex ideas, Hume also modified what Locke had said regarding sensation and reflection as the two sources of all ideas, with sensation having to do with "external sensible objects" and reflection with "the internal operations of our minds." Locke did not question the existence of external objects. For him, the primary qualities of sensation sufficed to establish their existence. Berkeley eliminated this distinction between primary and secondary qualities, made existence a function of perception, and thus undermined belief in the "materiality" of nonperceptible objects. As a student of both Locke and Berkeley, Hume was able to consider the topics of sensation and reflection in the light of their teachings. The influence of Berkeley is shown by

Hume's ascription of the origin of sensations to unknown causes, just as the influence of Locke is revealed by what Hume had to say about sensation and reflection (Chappell, p. 31):

> Impressions may be divided into two kinds, those of Sensation and those of Reflection. The first kind arises in the soul originally, from unknown causes. The second is derived in great measure from our ideas, and that in the following order. An impression first strikes upon the senses and makes us perceive heat or cold, thirst or hunger, pleasure or pain of some kind or other. Of this impression there is a copy taken by the mind, which remains after the impression ceases, and this we call an idea. This idea of pleasure or pain, when it returns upon the soul, produces the new impressions of desire and aversion, hope and fear, which may properly be called impressions of reflection because derived from it. These again are copied by the memory and imagination and become ideas, which perhaps in their turn give rise to other impressions and ideas. . . . The examination of our sensations belongs more to anatomists and natural philosophers than to moralists, and therefore shall not at present be entered upon. And as the impressions of reflection, *viz.,* passions, desires, and emotions, which principally deserve our attention, arise mostly from ideas, it will be necessary to reverse that method which at first sight seems most natural, and in order to explain the nature and principles of the human mind, give a particular account of ideas before we proceed to impressions. For this reason I have chosen to begin with ideas.

The preceding passage supplies almost the first indication that the *Treatise* is to be concerned with problems of morality. Hume barely suggested this in the sentence in which he made examination of the senses the appropriate concern of "anatomists and natural philosophers." By implication, his interest in "the nature and principles of the human mind" was to be different from that of the natural philosophers or those who later came to be called natural scientists. Instead, to revert to an earlier point, his interest was that of the social philosophers, or those who later came to be called social scientists. This marks one of the earliest manifestations of the kind of cleavage with respect to the nature of psychology that became clear-cut by the 1890s in the conflict between those who regarded psychology as a *Naturwissenschaft* in opposition to those who regarded it as a *Geisteswissenschaft*. It is the same conflict which has induced some twentieth-century universities to place psychology with biology in a division of the life sciences, while others place psychology with sociology in a division of social relations.

In line with his social-science orientation, Hume referred to "impressions of reflection" as particularly important or, as he put it, principally deserving of our attention. Later on in the *Treatise* he contrasted them with external impressions by designating them the "internal impressions" of "our passions, emotions, desires, and aversions" (Chappell, p. 52). When reactivated by memory or imagination—mental functions that he seemingly takes for granted—these impressions become ideas. As ideas, they may serve as impressions that give rise to other ideas. In the idiom of a later psychology, Hume was saying that a stimulus gives rise to a response that in turn becomes the stimulus to another response, with the latter serving as a stimulus to a still different response, and so on and on. It is this sequence, instigated by our external and internal impressions. with which Hume chose to begin his discussion of human nature.

Laws of Association as Universal Principles

In the course of his discussion of this sequence of impressions and ideas, Hume was the first to bring the phrase "association of ideas" into prominence. Locke had been the first to use it, but Hume was the first to use the word "associate" repeatedly and so to give currency to the phrase. Indeed, he ignored both Locke's prior use of the phrase and Aristotle's allusions to the concept; the topic is presented as if consideration of the underlying issue were original with Hume. Moreover in one of his later books, Hume referred to the "essential and universal properties of human nature" (Hendel, p. 282). For him, the laws of association are such properties or "universal principles." He makes this clear in the opening paragraph of his discussion of association (Chappell, pp. 33–34) :

> As all simple ideas may be separated by the imagination and may be united again in what form it pleases, nothing would be more unaccountable than the operations of that faculty were it not guided by some universal principles, which render it, in some measure, uniform with itself in all times and places. Were ideas entirely loose and unconnected, chance alone would join them, and it is impossible the same simple ideas should fall regularly into complex ones (as they commonly do) without some bond of union among them, some associating quality by which one idea naturally introduces another. This uniting principle among ideas is not to be considered as an inseparable connection, for that has been already excluded from the imagination; nor yet are we to conclude that without it the mind cannot join two ideas, for nothing is more free than that faculty, but we are only to regard it as a gentle force which commonly prevails, and as the cause why, among other things, languages so nearly correspond to each other, nature in a manner pointing out to every one those simple ideas which are most proper to be united into a complex one. The qualities from which this association arises, and by which the mind is after this manner conveyed from one idea to another, are three, viz., RESEMBLANCE, CONTIGUITY in time or place, and CAUSE and effect.

This marks the first attempt since Aristotle to formulate laws or principles of association. Neither Hobbes nor Locke had given them explicit formulation, although, as was indicated in Chapter II, Hobbes did recognize the relevance of the principle of contiguity. That principle had also been mentioned by Aristotle, along with the principles of similarity and association by contrast. All associationists have agreed on the relevance and importance of contiguity. It has come to be thought of as the primary or fundamental law of association, with the others regarded as secondary or subordinate. There has never, however, been agreement concerning the number of secondary laws. Aristotle and Hume both accepted resemblance or similarity, but Hume had nothing to say about contrast and Aristotle did not mention a law of cause and effect. Eventually, all of these were brought within the scope of the principle of contiguity. The so-called secondary laws such as those of primacy, recency, vividness, and others were not formulated until the early nineteenth century, but this is a minor consideration in the present context. It is more important to note what Hume had to say about association in general and about cause and effect in particular.

On Relations, Modes, and Substances

In referring to association as a "uniting principle among ideas," Hume believed that he was coming to grips with something of major importance. As a principle, it was to do for the mental realm what Newton's law of gravitation had done for the physical realm. According to Hume, it was "a kind of ATTRACTION, which in the mental world will be found to have as extraordinary effects as in the natural, and to show itself in as many and as various forms" (Chappell, pp. 35–36). The attraction was also described as a "gentle force," and among the "various forms" in which it showed itself, none were "more remarkable than those complex ideas" characteristic of ordinary thinking and reasoning. Hume divided these complex ideas into "*relations, modes,* and *substances.*" In doing so he was duplicating Locke's statement to the effect that "complex ideas are either of modes, substances, or relations" (Locke, 1956 ed., p. 77). Still, Hume's explanation of these terms was not a precise duplication of Locke's explanation. This was especially true of the idea of substances; Locke, in accordance with common sense, regarded the word as meaning "*particular* things subsisting by themselves," while Hume, in agreement with Berkeley, made the word stand for the "fiction" that the sensory qualities of objects inhere in "an unknown *something.*" The difference between their views can be noted by comparing Locke's example of lead as a substance with Hume's example of gold as a substance in these two quotations:

(1) Thus, if to substance be joined the simple idea of a certain dull, whitish color, with certain degree of weight, hardness, ductility, and fusibility, we have the idea of lead . . . (Locke, 1956 ed., p. 78).

(2) Thus our idea of gold may at first be a yellow color, weight, malleableness, fusibility, but upon the discovery of its dissolubility in *aqua regia,* we join that to the other qualities, and suppose it to belong to the substance as much as if its idea had from the beginning made a part of the compound one (Chappell, p. 39).

Obviously, Hume chose almost to duplicate Locke's example. Even his use of the word "join," to designate the act of connecting the simple ideas, is the same one Locke had employed.

It seems safe to assume that Hume kept consulting Locke's *Essay* as he was writing the *Treatise*. What he had to say about modes and relations amounts to a paraphrase of what Locke had said. By the term "mode," both he and Locke meant a complex idea which, although dependent on objects, is not a separate entity like a table. Instead it refers to the concept of a *class* of objects like furniture. Modes are categories or general ideas, as illustrated by ideas of gratitude, of conservation, of a dozen, of vertebrates, and of beauty. Furthermore, there is also virtual agreement in their respective accounts of the complex ideas of *relation*. They reserve this term for ideas resulting from the comparison of one idea with another. This involves ideas aroused by expressions like "more than," "later then," "heavier than," "different from," "similar to," "identical with," "superior to," or even "consequence of."

Are Causes Perceived or Inferred?

Of all the relations suggested by the preceding array of common expressions, the one that Hume subjected to the most careful study was that suggested by "consequence of" or some equivalent phrase. One encounters it in a multiplicity of contexts. The daily press reports that "The strike was a consequence of labor agitators" or that "The accident was due to the fog." All such reports imply a direct relationship between given causes and specified effects. Virtually everybody—both the sophisticated and the unsophisticated—takes the existence of such a relationship for granted.

Hume questioned the commonsense interpretation of this relationship. He regarded it as important, by making the principle of cause and effect one of his three principles of association. The other two principles—similarity and contiguity—did not trouble him especially. After all, it is easy to tell by inspection whether one object or item is identical with or resembles another or comes next to another in time or space. The ideas resulting from such sensory impressions make it possible to think or reason about the objects or items even when they have vanished. However, if need be, one can usually trace the ideas back to their original impressions. But with respect to the idea of a cause such tracing is futile. Causes, Hume indicated, are not seen or felt. They are inferred and are not products of direct observation. Hume brought the issue into sharp focus (Chappell, p. 66):

Here then it appears that of those three relations which depend not upon the mere ideas, the only one that can be traced beyond our senses and informs us of existences and objects which we do not see or feel is *causation*. This relation, therefore, we shall endeavor to explain fully before we leave the subject of the understanding.

To begin regularly, we must consider the idea of *causation* and see from what origin it is derived. It is impossible to reason justly without understanding perfectly the idea concerning which we reason, and it is impossible perfectly to understand any idea without tracing it up to its origin, and examining that primary impression from which it arises. The examination of the impression bestows a clearness on the idea, and the examination of the idea bestows a like clearness on all our reasoning.

What Hume proposed was an examination of specific instances of causation in order to find out what they have in common as original sensory impressions giving rise to corresponding ideas. He was asking why some people might say that lightning *causes* thunder, that exhaustion *causes* sleep, or that storms *cause* damage. The events involved have nothing in common to account for the use of the same verb. As a result, Hume turned to an examination of the causal relation itself in his quest for the "origin" of the idea of causation, and he noted two characteristics of the relation in question: *contiguity* and *priority*. By the latter term he meant that causes are always experienced as antecedent or *prior* to their effects. Causation has to do with *temporal* sequence. If Event A is the cause of Event B, then A must precede B in time. To influence B, however, Event A must come into contact with or be *contiguous* with B. In other words, in addition to a temporal aspect, causation has a *spatial* aspect: either directly or indirectly, causes must come into juxtaposition with their effects. By way of example, Hume might have called attention to a familiar phenomenon like sunburn. Rays from the distant sun cause the burn by impinging on the skin, and their radiation occurs prior to the burn.

Needless to add, Hume was astute enough to realize that, taken by themselves, contiguity and priority are not sufficient to establish a causal relationship. Contiguous events may come to be associated without being causally related. Failure to realize this accounts for some superstitious or quasi-magical practices. For instance, a student who chanced to be wearing a bright sweater on the day of a final examination was elated with the A grade he received. After that, he donned the same sweater when reporting for any final examination. Some phobic rituals, along with some beliefs about what presages good luck or bad luck, are the products of this kind of reaction to causally unrelated contiguous happenings with one of them occurring prior to the other. When the prior one reoccurs, it comes to arouse expectation of a recurrence of its erstwhile associate. To entertain such expectation is to confuse mere succession of events with the causation of events. Hume had this sort of confusion in mind when he raised this question (Chappell, p. 68):

Shall we then rest contented with these two relations of contiguity and succession, as affording a complete idea of causation? By no means. An object may be contiguous and prior to another without being considered as its cause. There is a NECESSARY CONNECTION to be taken into consideration and that relation is of much greater importance than any of the other two above-mentioned.

Meaning of "Necessary Connection"

The meaning of a "necessary connection" was not immediately clear to Hume. In the course of his efforts to find an illuminating answer, he considered a variety of possibly related issues. He wondered, for example, why we take it for granted that everything that has a beginning must *necessarily* also have a cause, and how it comes about that we have convictions regarding specific causes *necessarily* having specific effects. He devoted considerable space to discussion of these issues. As a close student of Berkeley's writings, he must have been familiar with Berkeley's disposition of the entire concept of causation as related to some of these issues. Berkeley, as was brought out at the close of the previous chapter, had argued that "the connexion of ideas does not imply the relation of *cause* and *effect,* but only of a mark or *sign* with the thing *signified.*" The fire one sees, he declared, is not the cause of impending pain as one gets too close, but a warning sign of danger.

Without referring to Berkeley's discussion of causation, Hume availed himself of the same illustration in his quest for the meaning of a "necessary connection" between cause and effect. However, his interpretation of the association between fire and suffering was not the same as Berkeley's. Hume regarded it as involving an inference from the sight or impression of fire to the idea of pain. Furthermore, he stressed the point that it is "by EXPERIENCE only that we can infer the existence of one object from that of another." To explain this statement, he added: (Chappell, pp. 78–79):

> Thus we remember to have seen that species of object we call *flame,* and to have felt that species of sensation we call *heat.* We likewise call to mind their constant conjunction in all past instances. Without any further ceremony, we call the one *cause* and the other *effect,* and infer the existence of the one from that of the other. In all those instances from which we learn the conjunction of particular causes and effects, both the causes and the effects have been perceived by the senses, and are remembered. But in all cases wherein we reason concerning them, there is only one perceived or remembered, and the other is supplied in conformity to our past experience.
>
> Thus in advancing we have insensibly discovered a new relation between cause and effect, when we least expected it, and were entirely employed upon another subject. This relation is their CONSTANT CONJUNCTION. Contiguity

and succession are not sufficient to make us pronounce any two objects to be cause and effect, unless we perceive that these two relations are preserved in several instances.

Hume marshaled a great deal of evidence in support of his thesis regarding the nature of the idea of a necessary connection between a cause and its effect. He thought he had presented "this evidence" so persuasively that it "may seduce us unwarily into the conclusion, and make us imagine it contains nothing extraordinary, nor worthy of our curiosity." Consequently, he felt constrained to warn that he had been dealing with "one of the most sublime questions in philosophy, *viz., that concerning the power and efficacy of causes,* where all the sciences seem so much interested" (Chappell, p. 103).

According to Hume, the alleged power or efficacy or energy of a cause is never observed. All that is observed is a temporal sequence in which Event A is always followed by Event B. The key word "always" refers to the *constant conjunction* of A and B. This means that A and B are invariably associated in experience. Their occasional or isolated contiguity or conjunction comes to mean the absence of a necessary connection. Just how often their contiguous relationship must be noted in order to be classified as a *constant* conjunction is a moot issue. Hume's reference to "several instances" of a conjoint relation as sufficient to establish A as the cause of B is too vague to be helpful. Even a hundred instances of a particular contiguous relationship may not suffice to justify calling this an example of a *constant* conjunction. The fact that a hundred Canadians can speak both French and English is not sufficient to establish a conclusion regarding the bilingualism of all Canadians. In brief, Hume's criterion of constant conjunction involves the difficulty or hazard of induction by simple enumeration as discussed in Chapter 2.[13] By way of reminder, it may be enough to recall Bertrand Russell's hypothetical cause of the census taker who blundered when he concluded that *all* the men in a given Welsh village were named William Williams.

---

13 In everyday thinking, as contrasted with rigorous scientific thinking, induction by simple enumeration is a common means of arriving at conclusions regarding people and events. The recall of a few items either in favor of or opposed to a given issue suffices to generate a verdict. In this way, people are ready to take sides on all sorts of questions such as the following: Are Senators more intelligent than Representatives? Can ministers be bribed? Are comic books ever of educational value? Heated arguments may be precipitated by such questions. For the most part, the disputants tend to have recourse to inductive logic. The psychological factors involved are intimately related to problems of effective communication. In recent decades, these problems have been the subject of many experimental studies. The study by C. Gilson and R. P. Abelson (1965) on "The Subjective Use of Inductive Evidence" contains a helpful bibliography of related studies. References to the broader implications of the problem of induction are to be found in a volume by J. J. Katz (1962) entitled *The Problem of Induction and Its Solution.*

Hume, however, was not concerned with this issue. He evidently assumed there would be no question regarding the meaning of what he designated as the constant conjunction of events deemed to be causally related. The issue that concerned him was the ordinary interpretation of the conjunction as meaning that the prior event or *cause* has the power or force or energy to produce or elicit the conjoint successive event known as the *effect*. In his opinion, such an interpretation is not justified. Anything like power or force or energy is never observed. Once a causal relationship has been established, experience of the cause arouses the confident expectation of the associated effect. What is established is thus an ideational relationship, so that, as Hume concluded, a cause may be defined as *"an object precedent and contiguous to another, and so united with it in the imagination that the idea of the one determines the mind to form the idea of the other, and the impression of the one to form a more lively idea of the other"* (Chappell, p. 118).

This conclusion appears to be consistent with Berkeley's notion of a cause as being the sign or mark of an anticipated consequent. Thus on the basis of experience we come to regard dark clouds as a sign of approaching rain, a clenched fist as a mark of imminent attack, and a wagging tail as a sign of the dog's friendliness. These are all common associations that reflect the kind of temporal sequences Hume might have cited as instances of what he meant by a causal relation. There is no reference to force or power in the description of such sequences. Experience has established this kind of relation so that the impression of Event A is followed by the *association* of the idea of Event B. This is the core of Hume's doctrine.

Are Causes Forces or Powers?

But at this juncture Hume seemed to have forgotten what he had written about association being a "gentle force." In terms of his own strictures regarding the need to observe forces or powers in order to be assured of their existence, he should have repudiated any interpretation of association as a force—gentle or otherwise. His failure to do so is of more than transitory interest, not to be dismissed as a minor inconsistency due to failure to remember a preceding reference to the "force" of association. After all, the principle of association was a subject of crucial importance for Hume, since he hoped to have his analysis of the principle become as important for psychology as Newton's study of the principle of gravitation had become for physics.

Under the circumstances, it is hard to believe that he was unmindful of his characterization of the principle as involving a "kind of attraction" or a "gentle force." In the given context, it served his purpose to bring out the parallel between an ordinary phrase like "force of gravitation" and the then novel phrase "force of association." Furthermore, it appears that he had reservations about the phrase even in the latter usage. Instead of designating association as an unambiguous "attraction," he made it a *kind* of attraction; and instead of just calling it a "force," he made it a *gentle* force. Later on in his analysis of causal relations, these reservations became more pronounced as he sought for direct observational confirmation of a force or a power linking causes to consequences. All he could note was their constant conjunction in terms of temporal sequence, just as in re-citing the alphabet B follows A and C follows B and D follows C without this order revealing any force or power of the antecedent letter on the following one. In Hume's terminology it would be descriptively more ac-curate to say that A as a cause *determines* B than to say that A *forces* the emergence of B. In brief, as an empiricist he was reluctant to transcend the limits of direct experience. Forces, powers, or energies, he maintained, are never experienced, because, as he noted (Chappell, p. 107):

> All ideas are derived from and represent impressions. We never have any impres-sion that contains any power or efficacy. We never therefore have any idea of power.

Hume's Influence on Kant and on Nineteenth-Century Science

Just why Hume retained the idea of *causal* sequence is perplexing. For him, the word "cause" had ceased to have its ordinary connotation. Never-theless, he made the connection between cause and effect one of his three principles of association. Having done so, he then had to strip the phrase of its common meaning. This called for a lengthy and somewhat labored discussion, the upshot of which came close to duplicating what Berkeley had said about the connection of ideas not implying "the relation of cause and effect, but only of a mark or sign with the thing signified."

Both Berkeley and Hume attributed the origin of the idea of causal re-lations to experience—to the observation of uniformities in the flow of impressions and ideas. Reasoning in the abstract, independently of experi-ence, Hume insisted, can never give rise to the idea of causation. To argue that it can do so would be the equivalent of considering causation to be an innate idea; and this principle, Hume added, "is now almost universally rejected in the learned world" (Chappell, p. 104). What he could not know or anticipate was how "the learned world" of Kant was to deal with the problem of causation: as stated in Chapter 15, Kant held thinking in terms of cause-and-effect relations to be an inherent characteristic of intellect. For him, this mode of thinking as one of the *a priori* categories was one of the ways in which the understanding is predisposed to bring order into what would otherwise be confusing experience. By calling it *a priori* or antecedent to experience, Kant, in opposition to Hume, held man's readiness to note causal relations to be an innate endowment rather than altogether a product of experience.

A chief reason for devoting space to this eighteenth-century philosophic controversy regarding the nature of causality is that the controversy affected nineteenth-century science. As A. Wolf (1929) has pointed out, leading scientists of the period—men like Helmholtz, Ernst Mach, and Karl Pearson—began to wonder whether it is the business of science to raise questions about the causation of natural phenomena. Mindful of Hume's critique of the principle of causation and Kant's *a priori* disposition of the principle, they suggested eliminating it from the enterprise of science.

Instead of searching for causes, they urged men of science to be on the alert for the kinds of uniformities indicative of *law.* Accordingly, science was to be descriptive rather than explanatory. Newton's laws of motion tell us *how* objects move, not *why* they do. The same applies to the laws of optics, of chemistry, of astronomy, and similar uniform sequences amenable to fairly precise mathematical formulation. This view of science is not concerned with metaphysical issues or with speculation regarding the ultimate nature of being. As a descriptive venture it is tough-minded and positivistic. It is in accord with what G. S. Brett, with keen insight, had to say about Hume, to the effect that Hume's "positivism" accounts for his "success in refining ideas and failure in explaining facts" (1912, Vol. II, p. 271). Moreover, Hume himself seems to have glimpsed the consequences of his positivistic principles for those whose scientific outlook comes to be governed by such principles. This is evident in the following concluding paragraph of the *Enquiry* (Chappell, p. 391):

> When we run over libraries, persuaded of these principles, what havoc must we make? If we take in hand any volume of divinity or school metaphysics, for instance, let us ask: *Does it contain any abstract reasoning concerning quantity or number?* No. *Does it contain any experimental reasoning concerning matter of fact and existence?* No. Commit it then to the flames, for it can contain nothing but sophistry and illusion.

Hume a Rationalist as Well as an Empiricist

The preceding paragraph quite manifestly suggests Hume's positivism as well as his empiricism. What may not be immediately obvious is that it also suggests Hume's rationalism. This is implicit in the distinction he made between abstract reasoning on the one hand and experimental reasoning on the other. He clarified the nature of this distinction in his *Enquiry* when, by implication, he identified abstract reasoning with "relations of ideas" and experimental reasoning with "matters of fact." Algebra, arithmetic, and geometry were cited as examples of sciences concerned with the former kind of reasoning, while the latter kind was said to be concerned with the relation of cause and effect. In the pages devoted to consideration of this distinction (Chappell, pp. 325–330), Hume endorsed both empirical and rational procedures as valid ways of enhancing human understanding. For example, his endorsement of empiricism received this italicized formulation: *"Causes and effects are discoverable, not by reason but by experience."* His endorsement of rationalism was just as forthright in statements to the effect that mathematical truths "are discoverable by the mere operation of thought, without dependence on what is anywhere existent in the universe," or which result in propositions regarded as "either intuitively or demonstratively certain."

It should now be evident that Hume was both an empiricist and a rationalist. This duality is not to be construed as evidence of inconsistency. Instead it is to be construed as a reminder that empiricism and rationalism are not antithetic concepts like past and future or some other dichotomy involving mutually exclusive categories. By way of contrast, the empiricism-rationalism dichotomy when applied to the working scientist reveals him to be both an observer as well as a thinker. His operations are neither exclusively inductive nor exclusively deductive.

Psychological Implications of Hume's Thesis

Hume recognized the interdependence of observation and thinking in everyday affairs as well as in scientific affairs. This is what he wrote about the role of reason in settling questions of fact (Chappell, p. 326):

> All reasonings concerning matter of fact seem to be founded on the relation of *cause* and *effect*. By means of that relation alone can we go beyond the evidence of our memory and senses. . . . A man, finding a watch or any other machine in a desert island, would conclude, that there had once been men in that island. All our reasonings concerning fact are of the same nature. And here it is constantly supposed, that there is a connexion between the present fact and that which is inferred from it.

To understand the significance of the watch on the desert island, Hume's hypothetical man had to perceive it as a sign of a previous visit by a human being. As a perceptual act, this involved reasoning in the sense of deducing or inferring something about the history of the watch. The watch *qua* watch served as a sign or symbol which elicited a conclusion regarding what it signified or symbolized. This, for Hume, meant thinking in terms of the relation of cause and effect. Under the circumstances, the watch symbolized a manufactured article and as such was something caused by human agency; hence the conclusion regarding a person's having once been on the island.

According to Hume's analysis, the connection between cause and effect is thus an outcome of ideational associations. He made this point explicit by maintaining "that the understanding never observes any real connection among objects, and that even the union of cause and effect, when strictly examined, resolves itself into a customary association of ideas" (Chappell, pp. 180–181). This is tantamount to saying that causes are never directly perceived, but arise from "noncausal" impressions and ideas. Moreover, as Russell has pointed out, whether or not a causal relation can ever be perceived is a question to which Hume answered "no" while his opponents said "yes." Viewed as a question of empirical fact, Russell added, "It is not easy to see how evidence can be produced by either side" (1945, p. 669).

In making this statement, Russell was evidently thinking of the general *philosophical* implications of Hume's thesis. Had Russell been thinking of the ways in which the notion of causality might be subjected to experimental study in terms of its *psychological* implications, he might have reached a different conclusion.[14] At all events, experimental psychologists have succeeded in producing evidence that has a bearing on the question of the perceptibility of causation. At the risk of begging the question, one might thus say that Hume's thesis has been a cause of their experimental studies; or, to put it a little differently, what Hume had to say about causation has some bearing on the interpretation of these twentieth-century studies. In terms of historical perspective, this conclusion reveals Hume's relevance for one segment of contemporary psychology; namely, the investigation of this question of the origin and nature of what we come to regard as causal sequence.

Jean Piaget (1896–   ) in Geneva, Switzerland, and Albert Eduard Michotte (1881–1965), in Louvian, Belgium, have been two of the leading investigators of the psychological implications of Hume's thesis. They and their students have amassed a wealth of experimental data related to causality as an experienced phenomenon. It will be impossible to supply more than a bare outline of their findings. In general, Piaget has been more interested in genetic aspects of the problem, while Michotte has been more concerned with phenomenological aspects. This is to say that Piaget has concentrated on studies of the child's emerging and changing notions of the nature of causal interaction, while Michotte has concentrated on studies of stimulus conditions giving rise to impressions of causal efficacy. The difference in emphasis is reflected in the titles of their books. Piaget has written on *The Child's Conception of Causality* (1930) and on *The Child's*

---

14 Although Russell did not allude to such possible *experimental* studies, he did not overlook the psychological implications of the problem. After granting that "Hume is wholly in the right" so far as concerns the physical sciences, he noted the possibility of opposition to Hume's thesis on psychological grounds. This opposition, he suggested, might take the form of arguing that a causal relation can be perceived when sudden pain results in a grimace or when a volitional fiat results in the execution of an intended act.

DAVID HUME (1711–1776)

Edouard Claparède (1873–1940)

Albert Michotte (1881–1965)

Construction of Reality (1955),[15] and Michotte has written on *The Perception of Causality* (1963). All three volumes summarize and systematize the results of many decades of laboratory findings many of which had previously been reported in journal articles.[16]

Piaget and the Question of Causality as a Dynamic Process

A fundamental issue considered by Piaget has to do with the origin of the notion that a cause involves force or energy if it is to be effective in bringing a given effect into being. According to this notion, an antecedent event cannot be the cause of an invariable or inevitable subsequent event unless power of some sort is operative. Thus, although day follows night with Humean regularity, we nevertheless balk at having night referred to as the cause of day—or vice versa. Similarly, it might strike us as odd were we to read that life causes death or infancy causes childhood or calves cause cows or April causes May. Despite the regularity of such sequences, or what Hume would have described as their constant conjunction, we might well hesitate to call them *causal* sequences. The transition from antecedent to consequent is too passive to admit of a causal nexus. Nothing like manifestly active movement seems to be involved, such as occurs when a pull on the trigger causes a gun to discharge or when a kick causes a football to soar over the crossbar.

Piaget noted that children's ideas of causation emerge from such experiences with active events, especially with those they learn to deal with directly. Their idea of causality develops out of experiences in which they find themselves able to make things happen. Shaking a rattle causes a noise, and tugging at a blanket causes a concealed toy to reappear. The notion of cause as a *force* has its origin in such kinesthetically experienced maneuvers.

According to Piaget, the French philosopher Marie François Maine de Biran (1766–1824) deserves credit for his early recognition of the relation between such "inner experience" and the "idea of force." In Piaget's opinion, "The fact that the idea of force owes its existence to inner experience seems to be beyond dispute" (1930, p. 126). By this statement Piaget did not mean differentiation between inner and outer experience by the very

---

[15] The volume concerned with the child's notions of reality was published twenty-five years after the one dealing with the child's notions of causality. The third chapter of the later book is especially relevant in the present context. It discusses "The Development of Causality."

[16] The two volumes by Piaget serve as an introduction to his investigations of the child's emerging notions of causality. These investigations constitute but a small segment of the total range of Piaget's studies of child psychology and related themes. In fact, appropriately enough, R. D. Tuddenham has described these studies by Piaget and his collaborators as "a prodigious program of research and theory building" which has resulted in a tremendous list of publications. The list includes "more than 20 full-length books" and most of the material in the "30 bulky annual volumes of the *Archives de Psychologie;* in all, over 180 major studies covering thousands of pages, of which the barest fraction has been translated into English" (1966, p. 207).

young child. Kinesthetic and organic impressions as "inner" are fused with exteroceptive ones as "outer"; hence in the beginning the child attributes forces to external objects, and only later, with the emergence of selfhood, does "force become gradually withdrawn from external objects and confined within the ego" (1930, p. 132). At this stage, should the child be taken for a stroll on a moonlit evening, he might regard himself as having the power of "making the moon go along" with him on his stroll (1930, p. 73).

This analysis reflects the egocentric nature of the child's view of causality. It is as if he can force the moon to accompany him on his walk. The moon as an external object is doing what he wants it to do. There is still incomplete awareness of self as distinct from the surrounding environment; hence the illusion of control over the moon. Egocentrism accounts for the child's animistic interpretations of natural events, so that it can think of a river as being happy when the ice melts and the river is set free. Inanimate objects are endowed with human characteristics, so that a toy that fails to function may be called "mean" or "stubborn." What Ruskin called "the pathetic fallacy" is related to such animistic thinking.

Piaget on "Types" of Explanation

One way in which Piaget investigated the mind of the child was to make a collection of the kinds of questions a child asks. Having obtained a long list of sentences beginning with "Why?", Piaget proceeded to classify them in terms of what the child seemed to be trying to find out. Most of them suggested a desire to have matters explained such as "Why do things fall?", "Why is coffee black?", "Why do trees have leaves?", "Why haven't little goats any milk?", and "Why do people say 'wicked' instead of 'bad'?" The questions were so diverse that they could not be subsumed under a single category of explanation. Accordingly, Piaget first prepared the following classification of five "types" of explanation characteristic of adult thinking (1952, pp. 180–181):

1. *Causal* explanation, or what Piaget also designated as *mechanical* explanation, involving "causation by spatial contact." *Example*: A bicycle chain revolves because of the structural linkage between it, the pedals, and the gear wheel.

2. *Statistical* explanation, in which events are attributed to *chance*. Piaget regards this kind of explanation as due to "our powerlessness to explain." *Example*: Because of chance, a tossed coin happens to fall head up.

3. *Finalistic* explanations, or commonsense explanations of biological phenomena in terms of a final cause or function subserved. *Example*: An animal has lungs in order to breathe.

4. *Psychological* explanations are those which account for purposive action by an appeal to some *motive*. *Example*: The man bought luggage because he was going on a trip.

5. *Logical* explanations are those which serve to *justify* a given assertion by citing a reason for it. *Example*: A particular X is larger than a particular Y because all X's are larger than Y's.

Piaget recognized that there might be some overlap in the foregoing types of explanation when applied to specific situations. Nevertheless, in general he held them to be "distinct in adult thought and even in ordinary common-sense." His chief purpose in considering them was to show how different they are from the child's quest for explanations.

Precausal Thinking

Before the age of seven or eight, these types of explanation are blurred and indistinct in what children have to say about why things happen. They are not yet ready to think of causal relations or purely logical ones inde-pendently of motives and intentions. For example, a question like "Why do trees have leaves?" might elicit such answers as "Because they make the trees pretty" or "Because God put them there" or "So that people can sit in the shade."

The adult's appeal to mechanical explanations or what Piaget classified as a *causal* explanation is alien to the child's outlook. Where the adult thinks in terms of spatial contact, the child is likely to think in terms of motivation. As a consequence Piaget calls this kind of thinking *precausal.* He defines *precausality* as a "primitive relation in which causation still bears the marks of a quasi-psychological motivation" (1952, p. 181). In this sense, pre-causal thinking is egocentric and results in anthropomorphic interpretations of nature.

By way of clarifying the meaning of precausality, Piaget called attention to the characteristics of children's drawings, since they reveal "one of the most important phenomena of the mental life of the child between the years of 3 and 7." Students of these drawings have noted that they reflect not only what the child *sees* but also what the child *knows* about the object being drawn. Thus in a profile view of a man the figure will have *two eyes* and in an exterior of a house there will also be a schematic indication of the rooms *inside* the house. It is as if the child is unable to divorce what he really knows about the object from the visual impression as such. As a consequence this kind of drawing has been regarded as a product of the child's "intellectual realism." While the child is drawing there is concomitant thinking, and this thinking distorts his vision.

The distortion in question, as interpreted by Piaget, means that the child is confusing physical events with mental events. This is what makes him an intellectual realist in the sense of being engulfed in the confluence of his stream of thinking with the stream of sensory impressions. Intellectual realism refers to a transitional phase of mental development in which the emerging self of the child has not yet been segregated from the not-self;

hence the fusion of thoughts with things. As a consequence, the immature child is unable to deal with situations in terms of their impersonal logical implications or in terms of what the sophisticated adult would call their purely mechanical cause-and-effect relations. The ability to think in terms of such cause-and-effect relations comes later and is an outgrowth of this earlier transitional phase of development. Consequently, Piaget has introduced the term "precausal" to designate the egocentric, autistic, and often animistic nature of this phase of the child's quest for understanding.

From Hume to Claparède to Piaget

Piaget's distinction between causal and precausal thinking is far removed from Hume's critique of causality. Nevertheless, in terms of historical perspective it is possible to see a relationship between the problem of the nature of the concept of causality as formulated by Hume back in the 1700s and Piaget's experimental and clinical studies of that problem some two hundred years later. For many years Piaget has been head of the Institut Jean-Jacques Rousseau in Geneva.[17] This institute was founded by Edouard Claparède (1873–1940) for the study of child psychology and for the study of improved methods of teaching. In fact, what has just been referred to as Piaget's *clinical* study of the child has to do with a method that Claperède had introduced. This way of learning about the child's thought processes consists in keeping a record of the child's questions and answers—spontaneous ones as well as those initiated by the psychologist. The method assumes that the child in talking is giving verbal expression to its thoughts. In Claparède's phrase, this amounts to *"reflexion parlée,"* or thinking aloud.

As Claparède's successor, Piaget might be said to have inherited this method. Moreover, he might also be said to have inherited his interest in causality; for, as indicated by Michotte (1963, p. 261), Claparède had considered the question of causality as early as 1903. At that time Claparède had questioned Hume's conclusion regarding the need for repetition of a "conjoint relation" in order to perceive it as a causal sequence. Instead he held that a "feeling of causality" may be aroused whenever one event seems to touch off another event. An example of what this feeling means is supplied by the report of a boy's panic at the time of the 1965 power failure in New York. The boy had chanced to swing a stick against a street-light stanchion and the city was plunged in darkness at the moment of impact. Feeling that his blow had *caused* the blackout, he rushed home in terror. Even if the report is apocryphal, it serves to illustrate the kind of feeling suggested by a phrase like "feeling of causality." This was the first and only time the boy had experienced a blackout. Nevertheless, Hume to the

---

[17] It is now known as the Institut des Sciences de l'Éducation.

contrary notwithstanding, for the boy there was a necessary connection between the blow and the blackout. Claparède would have referred to this as a "feeling of necessity." In opposition to Hume he had this to say about such a feeling (1963, pp. 261–262):

> My claim is that the feeling of necessity appears at the first encounter of the associated elements. If the child is burned at the stove or is clawed by the cat, he will run away from both, without waiting for repeated experiences to convince him that the stove burns and the cat claws. . . .
>
> If we were not disposed, in meeting an object for the first time, to regard its qualities as necessary attributes, how should we know how to behave when we had to deal with it the second time? . . . .
>
> The necessity of a connexion thus tends to appear at the very start.

The child's initial reaction to the clawing cat was Claparède's way of indicating the beginnings of causal thinking in the child. A single experience of being scratched sufficed to establish an avoidance reaction. The example serves to illustrate Hume's statement to the effect that "Causes and effects are discoverable, not by reason but by experience."

A contemporary learning theorist might well regard the reaction as an instance of one-trial learning. Repetition of experience or practice is not invariably essential for *all* kinds of learning. In the present instance the child is assumed to have learned the clawing hazards of cats as a species on the basis of his first and only encounter with a clawing cat. What Hume would have called a "constant conjunction" between the sight of the cat and the idea of danger had been established by this *single* encounter. Such an outcome is at variance with Hume's meaning of "constant conjunction" as the result of *repeated* instances of what comes to be viewed as a necessary connection between antecedent and consequent. This is the crux of Claparède's criticism of Hume: some causal relationships are established independently of induction based upon a series of similar experiences.[18]

It should now be obvious that Piaget's studies of the child's conception of causality were a continuation of what Claparède had introduced into the work of the Geneva Institut by his criticism of Hume. Moreover, Piaget's distinction between causal and precausal thinking and all that it implies constitutes a provocative elaboration of the latter work. Consequently, to revert to an earlier point, according to one meaning of the word "cause," viewed historically Hume was a cause of the psychological work of

---

[18] Such one-trial causal relationships are often products of traumatic experiences. Contact with a hot stove and an encounter with a clawing cat are manifestly traumatic. Many phobic reactions originate in this way. For example, a woman is reluctant to undertake a trip on a Saturday because her husband died on a Saturday. In her thinking, Saturday may be a cause of misfortune or disaster.

Claparède and Piaget. In a similar sense he was a cause of the psychological work of Michotte, which is considered in the next section.

Michotte on the Functional Significance of Causal Impressions

Michotte devoted more than thirty years to the study of causality as a psychological problem. The results of this study are presented in considerable detail in his *The Perception of Causality* (1963). He was especially concerned with the *functional* significance of this kind of perception. In his view it has to do with man's ability to cope with his surroundings by coming to know how objects affect other objects, how they influence him, and how he can influence them. We learn what objects *are* by finding out what they can *do*. This sequence is what endows causal perception with psychological importance. Because of its role in the regulation of human and animal behavior, it is also of biological importance. The existence of things comes close to being equated with their functional significance. Michotte introduced the following episode to show how this is to be understood (1963, pp. 4–5):

> One of my children, when aged about three or four, once asked me, "What are pictures hung on walls for?" and when I explained, he replied, "Then pictures *aren't anything!*" This is a good illustration of the extent to which, for us, the essence of things consists in what they are able to do.

As noted by Michotte, for a child to know what a thing does or can be made to do is not the same as knowing its functional significance. In the case cited, his child came to know that pictures hang on walls without knowing them as possible objects of aesthetic interest or as reminders of departed relatives or as a means of concealing torn wallpaper. In fact, a single portrait of a beloved grandmother strategically placed over the damaged paper may subserve all three functions, exemplifying aesthetic, mnemonic, and utilitarian functions. It would explain why the picture was placed on the wall. But as the *reason* or justification for its being there, the explanation failed to satisfy the child. He was unable to perceive a relationship between the motionless picture and what his father said the picture was *doing*; hence for him the picture ceased to be something. The effects of the picture on the father left the immature child mystified. Consequently the child could not see the picture as the *cause* of these effects. Apparently the child had already formed some notion of the causal relationship in the light of which the father's explanation was found wanting.

Michotte's researches were concerned with an investigation of the origin and nature of the functional significance of this notion of causal relationships. He was asking whether causality can be perceived. Incidentally, although his book is entitled *The Perception of Causality,* he had reason to question the adequacy of the title. In some respects, as he explains in a footnote

(1963, p. 15), he prefers to use the term "causal impression" in order to "bring out more clearly the idea of an immediate datum." By this he meant the direct rather than the indirect experience of causality.

In his view, it is the kind of experience which the Germans call an *Erlebnis*. There are two words for "experience" in the German language: *Erlebnis* and *Erfahrung*. The latter refers to indirect and the former to direct experience. For the sighted person, the world of color is an *Erlebnis;* but for the congenitally blind, who have been told about color, it can only be an *Erfahrung*. The distinction is the same as that between knowledge of acquaintance and knowledge about. A phrase like "causal impression," Michotte suggested, is more likely to connote an *Erlebnis* or knowledge of acquaintance than is the equivalent phrase "perception of causality." In this sense of causal impression is synonymous with what Claperède called a "feeling of causality."

Michotte's Views Opposed to Those of Hume and Kant

Michotte recognized his view of causality as an *Erlebnis* to be at variance with the views of Hume and Kant. Their approach to the problem, he pointed out (1963, p. 6), was essentially epistemological:

> They were concerned to discover what could justify the characters of necessity and universality in causal relations, and the work of the empiricists was primarily intended to show that these characters could not be derived directly from the data of experience. If matters had rested there, there would have been nothing in their views to cause us any special concern. But Hume has gone further. He has expressly asserted that in perceptual experience we have no direct impression of the influence exerted by one physical event on another. This assertion has been so widely accepted that it can still be regarded today as an almost universal assumption; and is found in very different contexts.

To support the latter conclusion, Michotte (1963, pp. 7–9) compared the statements of various twentieth-century psychologists with the following excerpts from Hume's *Enquiry*:

> It appears that, in single instances of the operation of bodies we never can, by our utmost scrutiny, discover anything but one event following another. . . . So that, upon the whole, there appears not, throughout all nature, any one instance of connexion, which is conceivable by us. All events seem entirely loose and separate. One event follows another; but we never can observe any tye between them. They seem *conjoined*, but never *connected*.
>
> After a repetition of similar instances, the mind is carried by habit, upon the appearance of one event, to expect its usual attendant, and to believe that it will exist. This connexion, therefore, which we *feel* in the mind, this customary transition of the imagination from one object to its usual attendant, is the sentiment or impression, from which we form the idea of power or necessary connexion.

Our idea of power is not copied from any sentiment or consciousness of power within ourselves, when we give rise to animal motion, or apply our limbs to their proper use and office. That their motion follows the command of the will is a matter of common experience, like other natural events. But the power or energy by which this is effected, like that in other natural events, is unknown and inconceivable.

In a footnote to the latter paragraph, Hume granted that the voluntary initiation of bodily activity, although failing to give rise to an "accurate precise idea of power," does enter "very much into the vulgar, inaccurate idea, which is formed of it." In general, since Hume held that the cause of a voluntary movement is unknown,[19] as indicated in Chapter 10, he was giving expression to a conclusion which was later confirmed by the experimental studies of Bair and of Woodworth as well as by Ach's investigation of determining tendencies. The upshot of the latter type of experiment was to the effect that the "naked thought" of a particular act sufficed to initiate its execution. There was no concomitant experience of power or energy, nor necessarily of any resident or remote imagery. This was one of the findings of those who sponsored the doctrine of imageless thinking as advocated by members of the Würzburg School during the first decade of the present century. Incidentally, Michotte had supplied experimental confirmation of some of these findings as early as 1910.

As a result of later experimental work, Michotte came to oppose Hume's reduction of cause-and-effect relations to the consequences of *repeated* instances of associated temporal contiguities. The common notion of a cause as a power or force compelling a specific effect, Hume had argued, is a derivative of such associations and never a product of direct sensory impression. In Hume's own wording, "we never can observe any tye" between a cause and its effect. Michotte had reason to believe that such a "tye" can be observed. He made this clear in a thesis which he presented at an International Congress of Psychology at Yale in 1927. In retrospect he had this to say about it (1963, p. 15):

---

[19] Hume was well aware of the difference between voluntary and involuntary activity and of the need for anatomico-physiological data in order to account for the difference. For example, he raised this question (C. W. Hendel [ed.], 1927, p. 150): "Why has the will an influence over the tongue and fingers, not over the heart or liver?" In the course of dealing with the question, he pointed out "that the immediate object of power in voluntary motion, is not the member itself which is moved, but certain muscles, and nerves, and animal spirits, and, perhaps, something still more minute and more unknown, through which the motion is successively propagated, ere it reach the member itself whose motion is the immediate object of volition" (Hendel, p. 151). In effect he was anticipating what Russell had said about efforts to explain such voluntary control of action "by the laws of habit and association." Eventually, Russell maintained (1945, p. 669), "These laws themselves, in their accurate form, will be elaborate statements as to nervous tissue—primarily its physiology, then its chemisty, and ultimately its physics."

The thesis which I put forward at the Yale conference was in direct disagreement with all the theories of the traditional kind . . . since I expressed the opinion that certain physical events give an immediate causal impression, and that one can "see" an object *act* on another object, *produce* in it certain changes, and *modify* it in one way or another. I quoted various examples in this connexion, e.g. that of a hammer driving a nail into a plank, and that of a knife cutting a slice of bread. The question that arises is this: when we observe these operations, is our perception limited to the impression of two movements spatially and temporally co-ordinated, such as the advance of the knife and the cutting of the bread? Or rather do we directly perceive the action as such—do we see the knife actually cut the bread? The answer does not seem to me to admit of any doubt.

Michotte's Laboratory Studies of Causality

The impression of causality aroused by the preceding kind of everyday observations paved the way for Michotte's laboratory studies of causality. These were too numerous and too complex to lend themselves to easy summary. Exhaustive treatment is out of the question. However, even a cursory account may suffice for present purposes. All of the experiments were based upon two fundamental ones: one had to do with what Michotte called the *Launching Effect* (*l'effet lancement*) and the other with what he called the *Entraining Effect* (*l'effet entrainment*). Each of these experiments is given detailed treatment in Michotte's book, but it is possible to understand their general nature in the following accounts without reference to the technical details:

A. *The Launching-Effect Experiment.* This involved a small red square and a small black one separated from one another by a short distance. The subject is instructed to focus on the red square. Then the black one is made to move toward the red one at a uniform speed until it just touches the red one. At the instant of contact the black one stops moving and the red one is set in motion either at the same rate of speed or at a reduced rate. The distance traversed by the red square is varied in accordance with the rate: the slower the speed, the shorter the distance.

Variations of procedure were tried on several hundred subjects of "all ages." The results, Michotte reports, with just one or two exceptions were invariably the same: the black square is seen as having bumped the red one and *launching* or sending it off into motion. One square *makes* the other one *go* or *shoves it forward* or *gives it a push* or *sets it in motion*. The observers employed such varying descriptive phrases, but the meaning for all of them was the same. They saw the black square as the cause of what they perceived as the induced motion of the red one. Michotte adds, "The same experiment has been tried hundreds of times on some subjects, and their impression of causality remained unaffected."

B. *The Entraining-Effect Experiment.* Like the previous experiment, this one also involved two differently colored squares and having one move toward the other. In this type of experiment, however, the black square continues to move at the same rate of speed after coming into contact with the red one, with the result that both squares are perceived to be moving with the same speed and the observer has the impression of a black-red rectangle in which the black part is *carrying* or *entraining* the red part. Here too, as in the launching type of experiment, the impression of causality is immediate and clear-cut: the black square is *making* the red one *go forward* or *taking it with it* or *pushing it ahead.*

It is obvious that these two kinds of experimental results are at variance both with what Berkeley said about a cause being a mere symbol of what may be expected to follow and with what Hume said about it in terms of temporal contiguity and the *repetition* of experienced contiguities. Instead, as Michotte has expressed it (1963, p. 21):

> In the case of these two experiments the production of movement is thus *directly experienced.* There is no question of an interpretation, nor of a "significance" superimposed on the impression of movement; in other words, what is actually "given" is not a mere representation or a symbol of causality. In the same way as stroboscopic movement is not, psychologically speaking, the "symbol" of a movement, but *is* a phenomenal movement, so the causality perceived here *is* a phenomenal causality.

Cause as Phenomenon Versus Cause as a Concept

The perception of what Michotte referred to as phenomenal causality was not just a product of the launching and entraining experiments. These two experiments were elaborated in a variety of ingenious ways and served to reveal both quantitative and qualitative aspects of the problems being investigated. Close to ninety such experiments were described, but to say more about them would constitute too much of a digression. Their number suffices to indicate the thoroughness with which Michotte has considered these problems. For present purposes it is enough to consider the bearing of Michotte's findings on Hume's skepticism regarding causality as an immediate sensory phenomenon.

It will be recalled that what Hume questioned in particular was the existence or reality of causes as forces or powers necessitating specific consequences. Prior to his time, as A. C. Ewing has noted, it had been taken for granted as an *a priori* principle and a "necessary presupposition of science" that every change is attributable to a cause. However, Ewing regards it as a misinterpretation of Hume to equate his skepticism with rejection of the principle, since Hume "merely raised philosophical difficulties which he thought made it impossible to justify or defend it" (1962, pp.

171–172). According to Hume, there is no empirical basis for the principle. To repeat what he said about this: "One event follows another; but we never can observe any tye between them."

Moreover, his skepticism regarding the notion of causality was not just an eighteenth-century vagary. It has also been voiced in the present century. As mentioned on a previous page, Russell judged Hume to be "wholly in the right" with reference to cause as a useful notion for the worker in any of the physical sciences. At one time Russell even urged elimination of the word "cause" from the vocabulary of philosophers because it "is so inextricably bound up with misleading associations." He then went on to say that "the reason why physics has ceased to look for causes is that, in fact, there are no such things," and that "The law of causality . . . is a relic of a bygone age" (H. Feigl and M. Brodbeck [eds.], 1953, p. 387). From the context it is obvious that Russell was particularly concerned with the relevance of the notion of causality in the study of gravitational astronomy. Under the circumstances, he was really endorsing the stand of men like Mach and Helmholtz, who, as already noted, had also urged elimination of the quest for causes from the work of the physicist. In this respect they too might have said that Hume was "wholly in the right."

It is well to note Michotte's view of this phase of Hume's critique of the notion of causality. As he saw it, Hume was not wholly in the wrong. By implication, Michotte was in agreement with Russell's endorsement of Hume's strictures regarding causality as a universal physical principle. As shown in the previously cited passage, he conceded that he was not objecting to what empiricists had to say about the impossibility of deriving "the necessity and universality in causal relations" from the data of experience. What Michotte did object to was Hume's contention regarding the absence of any direct impression of a causal relationship in perceptual experience. Michotte's experiments were designed to demonstrate the occurrence of such impressions as unambiguously observable happenings. Hume to the contrary notwithstanding, phenomenologically considered, Michotte's subjects *saw* one physical object *cause* the movement of another object. In this respect Michotte's psychology seemed to clash with Hume's philosophy. Whether it constitutes an irreconcilable clash is difficult to determine. In a critical essay appended to Michotte's book, T. R. Miles has this to say about it (1963, pp. 414–415):

It is dangerous, . . . in my opinion, to be too dogmatic as to what is the correct interpretation of Hume. It is always possible, as Kant has pointed out, to understand a philosopher better than he understands himself; and as a result it is very easy to make the move from "This is what so-and-so might have said or ought to have said" to "This is what so-and-so really meant." Nowadays we think of Hume as a philosopher; and it may well be that from our point of view we feel like saying that Hume "ought" to have been discussing conceptual matters, not phenomenological ones. This "ought" is dangerous, however, since there can be no doubt that Hume's formulations are so worded that at least they *seem* like phenomenology; he certainly *seems* to be denying that a causal impression in Michotte's sense ever occurs, and this is the interpretation put on him not only by Michotte but by many other psychologists in the same tradition such as Claparède and Köhler. From the point of view of modern psychology, however, disputes as to the correct interpretation of Hume cannot be regarded as of major importance. Moreover, we should remember that the distinction between conceptual and phenomenological issues was one which Hume never made, and the situation created by Michotte in which visual stimuli are studied in isolation was one which Hume never considered. What he would have said if these points had been put to him can be no more than a matter of historical speculation. In the absence of any means of questioning him it is at least not unreasonable to interpret him phenomenologically; and Michotte insists that it is only in so far as Hume is talking phenomenology that there is any serious disagreement between them.

Finally, there is the problem of the psychological origin of the idea of causality. On this issue Michotte seems to me to be on particularly strong ground. Not only is there a *prima facie* case in his favour from the very fact that, unlike Hume, he performed systematic experiments; in addition he has clearly shown that habit and expectation are not the crucial factors in giving rise to a causal impression. If the stimulus-conditions are right, according to Michotte, the causal impression occurs (provided there is sufficient degree of maturation) almost invariably the first time off, whereas if the stimulus-conditions are wrong it does not occur however often the experiment is repeated. Hume's appeal to habit and expectation is thus psychologically incorrect.

Possible Shortcomings of Hume's Thesis

It should now be evident that Michotte's launching and entraining experiments demonstrated immediate and direct causal impressions. Such impressions were not based upon induction following the kind of repetition of experience which Hume regarded as giving rise to "a customary association of ideas." Instead on the basis of a single experience there was a perception of induced movement as one object came into contact with another object. Moreover, in this respect the Michotte experiments revealed Hume to have been in error when he maintained that "the understanding never observes any real connection among objects."

Hume might also be said to have been mistaken in making the causal relation one of invariable temporal sequence by maintaining that a cause *always* precedes its effect. As a little reflection will show, sometimes the relation is a concurrent one. Driving an automobile causes the consumption of gasoline, but the mounting miles and dwindling fuel take place concurrently. Similarly, there is a synchronous relationship between friction of the moving parts of the engine and reduced efficiency. Still, this is a relatively minor oversight on Hume's part. He would have had little trouble in reconciling such synchronous affairs with his fundamental thesis by arguing that they too are the outcome of "a customary association of ideas" indicative of a "necessary connection" between the concurrent phenomena. He might have held their concurrence to be the limiting case of temporal priority in the sense that when the interval between a cause and its effect becomes smaller and smaller, simultaneity of occurrence is approached.

After all, Hume might have pointed out, the interval separating a cause from its effect may vary all the way from years to these limiting instances of synchronous operation. Thus years elapse between the hereditary "cause" of Huntington's chorea and its "effects" as an affliction of adult life. And months separate the spring planting from the fall harvest. Actually a long series of intermediate changes serves to link such widely separated events, with each one being an effect of the immediately preceding one. By harvest time no seeds are present to "cause" the harvest. Only in retrospect can one note a causal relation between last spring's seeds and this fall's harvest. Such a relation, Hume would have insisted, is the result of experience with many plantings and is not a product of *a priori* reasoning regarding any *necessary* effects to be expected from seeds.

In short, the causal relation is rooted in experience. We *learn* what to expect and what follows from what, so that we come to anticipate given consequences from given experienced events. To express this in Hume's words: "Causes and effects are discovered, not by reason but by experience," or, as he also expressed it, "The union of cause and effect, when strictly examined, resolves itself into a customary association of ideas." The ideational associations in question, he argued, were not products of *reasoning* from cause to effect. In arguing this way he was definitely an empiricist in his psychology. His empiricism and antirationalism—at least with respect to causality—are clearly indicated by the following passage, in which he considered an issue mentioned earlier in this chapter in connection with Claparède's reference to a "feeling of causality" (Hendel, pp. 130–131):

It is certain that the most ignorant and stupid peasants—nay infants, nay even brute beasts—improve by experience, and learn the qualities of natural objects, by observing the effects which result from them. When a child has felt the sensation of pain from touching the flame of a candle, he will be careful not to put his hand near any candle; but will expect a similar effect from a cause which is similar in its sensible qualities and appearance. If you assert, therefore, that the understanding of the child is led into this conclusion by any process of argument or ratiocination, I may justly require you to produce that argument; nor have you any pretence to refuse so equitable a demand. You cannot say that the argument is abstruse, and may possibly escape your enquiry; since you confess that it is obvious to the capacity of a mere infant. If you hesitate, therefore, or if, after reflection, you produce any intricate or profound argument, you, in a manner, give up the question, and confess that it is not reasoning which engages us to suppose the past resembling the future, and to expect similar effects from causes which are, to appearance, similar.

A contemporary Humean would say the child had been conditioned to avoid the flame. This is another way of saying that an *association* had been established between the sight of a candle and the flexion reflex. Claparède would have attributed a "feeling of causality" to the child. The term "feeling" would make the episode a conditioned emotional reaction; thus, in line with Hume's contention, the reaction would not be a product of *reasoning* from cause to effect. However, Hume came close to arguing that a single painful experience sufficed to establish this causal relation. He even attributed this kind of learning to "brute beasts." This suggests that he must have been familiar with the commonplace observation of the speed with which a whipped dog learns to cringe at the sight of the whip. The chimpanzee, as mentioned in Chapter 12, learns to avoid a pain-inducing object after just one or two painful encounters.

In other words, the infants and "brute beasts" to which Hume referred, contrary to what he said in other contexts, did seem to perceive a causal relation without having had to be exposed to "several instances" of the "constant conjunction" of the cause and the experienced effect. To revert to one of his other phrases; they did seem to observe a "tye" between cause and effect. In this respect the example of learning from painful experiences appears to contradict Hume's basic thesis to the effect that "contiguity and succession are not sufficient to make us pronounce any two objects to be cause and effect, unless we perceive that these two relations are preserved in several instances."

Inductive Versus Experiential Aspects of Causality

Hume does not seem to have been aware of any inconsistency between the burnt-child example and his general thesis regarding the inductive foundation of causal beliefs and convictions. The oversight is very likely due to the fact that the example was introduced not to illustrate this inductive aspect of the thesis but to clinch the experiential aspect. He was intent on proving that knowledge of causal relations can never be the result of *a priori* reasoning. Such knowledge, he was ready to affirm, may even be acquired by creatures incapable of reasoning; hence his reference to stupid peasants, infants, and children learning "the qualities of natural objects, by observing the effects which result from them." The burnt-child example was intended to demonstrate that not reason but experience enables the child to find out that fire burns. Understandably in the circumstances, Hume ignored the question of how often this kind of experience must occur before the child "will be careful not to put his hand near any candle." Had he been dwelling on this question, he might have realized the difficulty of reconciling the answer with what he had to say about the *inductive* aspect of his general thesis in the following paragraph (Hendel, p. 155):

Even after one instance or experiment where we have observed a particular event to follow upon another, we are not entitled to form a general rule, or foretell what will happen in like cases; it being justly esteemed an unpardonable temerity to judge of the whole course of nature from one single experiment, however accurate or certain. But when one particular species of event has always, in all instances, been conjoined with another, we make no longer any scruple of foretelling one upon the appearance of the other, and of employing that reasoning, which can alone assure us of any matter of fact or existence. We then call the one object, *Cause*; and other, *Effect*. We suppose that there is some connexion between them; some power in the one, by which it infallibly produces the other, and operates with the greatest certainty and strongest necessity.

In the light of the preceding contention, the child, following a single experience of being burned by the candle, should not be able to "foretell what will happen in like cases." Hume failed to indicate just how often the experience must recur before the child will be persuaded that the flame "always" causes pain. His reference to "all instances" is obviously not to be taken literally. He means either several or many instances. Furthermore, it is important to realize that his allusion to forming "a general rule" had to do with very ordinary kinds of learning such as learning about the sensory characteristics of everyday objects. For example, he mentioned the taste of eggs in connection with a discussion of how it comes about that "from causes which appear *similar* we expect similar effects" (Hendel, p. 127). Nevertheless, despite the fact that eggs look alike, we learn *not* to expect "the same taste and relish in all of them." Presumably tasting an egg for the first time does not suffice to inform the child of the taste of *all* eggs. This appears to be the gist of Hume's argument.

Upon reflection, however, it is a rather weak argument; for it overlooks the effect of initial gustatory impressions on the child. A single dose of castor oil suffices to arouse resistance to the administration of a subsequent dose, just as an initial experience with candy makes for eager acceptance of future offers of candy. The child acts as if it expects the one substance to continue to be unpleasant and the other to be pleasant. Similarly, just one experience of eating an egg may be enough to let the child know whether to expect eggs to have a pleasant or an unpleasant taste. In terms of expectations aroused, the child does not expect eggs to taste like grapes or ice cream. Each new item of food introduced into the child's diet may thus be said to be a cause of anticipated effects with reference to the kind of taste to be expected. The child expects an apple to taste like an apple even though it comes to experience differences in the taste as it bites into different varieties of apples. Despite these differences, each bite confirms the expectation of the taste of an apple. Analogously, although its initial experience with a piece of candy is not a sample of the wide variety of candies in the world, experience with this wide variety is not a prerequisite for the child's having "a general rule" about liking candy. This, of course, is not the same as saying the child likes all varieties to the same degree. Establishment of preferences depends on subsequent experiences with these varieties, but the later existence of such preferences does not invalidate the early rule of liking candy in general. From this viewpoint, Hume's argument concerning eggs as the cause of a particular gustatory effect is not altogether convincing; but there is another phase of the argument to be considered.

Does Empiricism Suffice as a Basis for Science?

This other phase has to do with expectation based upon established cause-and-effect relations. Expectations refer to the future—to that which has not yet occurred. Is an empiricist justified in entertaining expectations? If so, then he might be said to be transcending experience, since the future has not yet been experienced. Predicting the future assumes the uniformity of nature in the sense of expecting known causes to produce experienced effects. Hume's reference to the taste of eggs was partly for the purpose of introducing this issue. In short, he was asking whether we can be sure that tomorrow's egg which has the same appearance as yesterday's egg will have the same taste. Our expectation of a pleasant taste would be nullified by a rotten egg. Ordinarily, Hume pointed out, we expect similar effects from causes which *appear* similar, and yet in this instance similar-appearing causes result in different effects. In the course of a somewhat lengthy discussion of the larger implications of this seemingly obvious point, Hume reached this thought-provoking conclusion (Hendel, pp. 129–130):

> For all inferences from experience suppose, as their foundation, that the future will resemble the past, and that similar powers will be conjoined with similar sensible qualities. If there be any suspicion that the course of nature may change, and that the past may be no rule for the future, all experience becomes useless, and can give rise to no inference or conclusion. It is impossible, therefore, that any arguments from experience can prove this resemblance of the past to the future; since all the arguments are founded on the supposition of that resemblance. Let the course of things be allowed hitherto ever so regular; that alone, without some new argument or inference, proves not that, for the future, it will continue so. In vain do you pretend to have learned the nature of bodies from your past experience. Their secret nature, and consequently all their effects and influence, may change, without any change in their sensible qualities. . . . What logic, what process of argument secures you against this supposition? . . . Can I do better than propose the difficulty to the public, even though, perhaps, I have small hopes of obtaining a solution?

Hume raised the latter question in a section having to do with what he called his "sceptical doubts." What he doubted in particular is the empiricist's reliance on induction as the basis for confident causal predictions. As Hume indicated, in terms of abstract logic the principle of induction cannot be established as valid by an inductive inference from a series of specific instances of inductive reasoning. This would be begging the question and thus amount to arguing in a circle. What is required for satisfactory proof is some principle which in itself is not based upon induction. In the absence of such a principle, as Russell has noted, Hume can be said to have undermined the empirical foundation of science; for, according to Russell (1945, p. 674):

> To this extent, Hume has proved that pure empiricism is not a sufficient basis for science. But if this one principle is admitted, everything else can proceed in accordance with the theory that all our knowledge is based on experience. It must be granted that this is a serious departure from pure empiricism, and that those who are not empiricists may ask why, if one departure is allowed, others are to be forbidden. These, however, are questions not directly raised by Hume's arguments. What these arguments prove—and I do not think the proof can be controverted—is that induction is an independent logical principle, incapable of being inferred either from experience or from other logical principles, and that without this principle science is impossible.

Three Kinds of Argument

Hume also concerned himself with the question of proof by argument. He objected to Locke's disposition of the question because Locke had divided all arguments into *two* classes: those which purport to *demonstrate* something as true and those which establish something as *probably* true. On the basis, Hume declared, "We must say, that it is only probable all men must die, or that the sun will rise to-morrow" (Hendel, p. 143). Hume was not enough of a skeptic to endorse this kind of probabilism. By implication he was saying that although we cannot *demonstrate* that all men must die or that the sun will rise tomorrow, we can *prove* that this must happen. This is suggested by his recognition of *three* kinds of argument: demonstrations, probabilities, and proofs; and by proofs he meant "such arguments from experience as leave no room for doubt or opposition."[20]

He introduced this threefold division in connection with a discussion of probability. By way of introduction, he employed the conventional example of rolling dice by noting that if a die has one number on two sides and a different number on the other four sides, then it is more probable that the

---

[20] This reference to demonstrations, probabilities, and proofs is taken from the *Enquiry*. In the corresponding section of the *Treatise* Hume referred to "knowledge" instead of to "demonstrations" and then explained (V. C. Chappell [ed.], 1963, p. 98):

> By knowledge, I mean the assurance arising from the comparison of ideas. By proofs, those arguments which are derived from the relation of cause and effect and which are entirely free from doubt and uncertainty. By probability, that evidence which is still attended with uncertainty.

latter number will turn up. Moreover, he observed, confidence in the outcome to be expected would be very much increased were one to have a die
with a thousand sides with all sides except one having the same figure. Under
these conditions prediction would just fall short of certainty. To achieve
certainty, all the sides would have to be marked with the same figure: thus
if each side has five dots, no other number can possibly turn up. This
conclusion is not based upon induction in the sense of requiring a long series of
trials in order to give it empirical confirmation. Even the most ardent
empiricist would agree with the rationalist that such a conclusion is independent of experience. They would both agree that there is no *chance* of
any other outcome. In rolling ordinary dice, the outcome is said to be due to
chance. For Hume, this use of the word "chance" means ignorance of the
causes of the outcome and not some quasi-magical, uncaused, fortuitous
influences. To quote him directly (Hendel, p. 143):

> Though there be no such thing as *Chance* in the world; our ignorance of the real
> cause of any event has the same influence on the understanding, and begets a
> like species of belief or opinion.

On the basis of experience, Hume argued, we become familiar with the
causes of events. As in the case of rolling dice, we learn that some outcomes
are more probable than others; but in ordinary affairs, determination of the
probable outcome is not amenable to *a priori* deductive analysis of the
numerical factors involved. Instead it is a product of a series of experiences
as a result of which, by implicit induction, some causes come to be regarded
as more probable determinants of given effects than other causes. There
even are instances of conviction in the inevitability rather than the mere
probability of a specific effect. This happens, Hume pointed out, when a
given cause always results in the same effect and no exception to this
sequence of events has ever been found. As examples he noted that "fire
has always burned, and water suffocated every human being," and that
"the production of motion by impulse and gravity is an universal law, which
has hitherto admitted of no exceptions."

In other instances, however, it is impossible to be certain of the results.
A drug may have different effects on different patients and even on the same
patient at different times. Sometimes the cumulative experience of many
physicians is needed to establish all the possible effects of some new medica-
tion, and hence will be regarded as more probable. This, in brief, serves
to suggest the drift of Hume's teaching regarding the inductive or empirical
foundation of our knowledge of cause and effect.

The Problem of Induction

By means of this teaching, Hume believed that he had solved or at least
shed light on the problem of induction. He seems to have been less con-

cerned with the logic than with the psychology of induction.[21] In terms of his empirical approach, inductive thinking was viewed from the standpoint of associationistic psychology. Hume was especially concerned with demonstrating that such thinking gives rise to knowledge of causal relations. His chief interest was in the *origin* of this kind of knowledge rather than in its *validity*. The latter question has more to do with theory of knowledge or epistemology than with psychology. For him, the psychological aspect loomed so large that he subsumed perception of cause-and-effect relations under a separate principle of association. As already mentioned, he recognized three such principles: similarity, contiguity, and cause and effect. Incidentally, Hume is the only associationist to have listed cause and effect as a separate principle. The others would have regarded the "constant conjunction" which Hume attributed to causality as an instance of contiguity.

It is hard to believe such an obvious relationship could have eluded Hume's keen mind. Nevertheless he failed to call attention to it. His silence may have been deliberate in order to bring the issue of causality into bold relief. As he saw it, he was dealing with a momentous issue in novel fashion; hence it merited special emphasis and separate consideration. In this connection it is well to recall that he had referred to it as "one of the most sublime questions in philosophy, viz., that concerning the power and efficacy of causes, where all the sciences seem so much interested."

In retrospect it can be seen that Hume was justified in stressing the importance of his critique of inductive thinking as related to the perception of causality. As already indicated, he influenced the thinking of men like Mach, Helmholtz, Pearson, Russell, Claperède, and Michotte. Nor has he been overlooked by contemporary students of the problem of induction. For example, Jerrold J. Katz's book on *The Problem of Induction and Its Solution* (1962) begins by referring to Hume as having been the first to have recognized the problem as a problem. It is not to be dismissed as an outmoded eighteenth-century vagary of the skeptical Hume. On the contrary, as a persistent problem it continues to engage the attention of twentieth-century specialists in the related fields of logic, probability theory, and philosophy of science. It cuts across all these fields especially when considered in terms of its epistemological implications.

Those who regard the problem as fundamentally a problem for epistemology, Katz notes, have objected to what they interpret as Hume's psychological approach to the problem. They view this approach as a retreat to *psychologism* and consequently as avoidance of relevant epistemological issues. This follows because the term *psychologism* refers to a

---

21 The problem of induction is intimately related to the theory of probability, and its adequate treatment would call for an excursion into the field of logic. As C. S. Peirce once put it (J. R. Newman [ed.], 1956, Vol. 2, p. 1334): "The theory of probabilities is simply the science of logic quantitatively treated." He showed how this is to be understood in his paper on "The Probability of Induction" (Newman, Vol. 2, pp. 1341–1354).

contention to the effect that psychology constitutes the basis for all knowledge from knowledge of the sensory characteristics of commonplace objects to knowledge of abstruse philosophic teachings and knowledge of abstract scientific laws. From the standpoint of psychologism the principles of aesthetics, logic, and ethics would be traced to subjective origins as derivatives of experienced contiguities. Similarly, investigations of the genesis of religion, law, custom, and other social institutions were presumed to be rooted in such experienced contiguities. In other words, from this standpoint psychology is viewed as the basis of all science.

According to Katz, critics of Hume have charged him with sponsoring an untenable psychologism (1962, pp. 119–121). They even stigmatize it as "the fallacy of psychologism." The fallacy consists in judging or evaluating the end results of a process or movement by its origins or beginnings. The end result may be incommensurable with its origins in the way in which oak trees are different from acorns. Analogously, the dignity or worth of man is not to be judged by reference to his biological origins from infra-human species. Similarly, the scientific status of chemistry is not to be questioned because of its historical antecedents in the pseudo-science of alchemy. Furthermore, even though chemistry depends on man's psychological ability to perceive and analyze, this fact does not make chemistry a branch of psychology. To argue that it does would be another instance of the fallacy of psychologism. In short, to put this metaphorically, events are to be judged by their fruits and not by their roots. A sinful parent may have a virtuous child. As Katz implies, should he also have a criminal son, the parent's sinfulness would not exonerate the son from responsibility for criminal behavior. By way of illustrating the fallacy of psychologism Katz alluded to the student of psychoanalysis who ventured to defend himself in court by telling the judge that not he but his parent ought to be on trial. Instead of justifying his deed he explains how it originated.

Katz maintains that Hume's treatment of the problem of induction did not entail the fallacy of psychologism. Hume did not attempt to justify induction as a certain basis for predicting the future; hence he is to be exonerated of the charge in question. Seen in "correct perspective," Katz contends, all that Hume attempted was to show was the way in which anticipation of future events comes to be established. This is different from trying to prove the soundness of predictions implicit in such anticipations.

It is well to recall that Hume had attributed inductive conclusions to the "constant conjunction" of given experienced events. He had argued that if event A is invariably followed by event B, then we come to expect or to predict the advent of B whenever A is experienced. Thus the sudden appearance of dark clouds arouses the expectation of rain and the dinner bell arouses the anticipation of food. An epileptic patient expects a seizure to follow the aura just as the malaria patient expects a fever to follow the chill. Anticipation or expectation of given consequences, Hume had argued, is a product of repeated conjoint experiences. The more frequent the occurrence of such experiences the stronger one's faith in the anticipated outcome. Faith is involved because all expectations or anticipations rest upon the unprovable assumption that future contiguities will duplicate past contiguities. Even though event B has followed event A a thousand times there is no way of demonstrating that it will follow A in the future until the future becomes the present. Hume did not venture to demonstrate this; for he never undertook to specify how often A and B must be experienced as a recurrent sequence before their conjunction may be judged to be *constant*. Nor did he argue that a feeling or conviction of constancy was tantamount to *proof* of constancy in the future. His argument had to do with the psychology and not with the logic of induction. Katz expressed this succinctly in his defense of Hume in this way (1962, p. 121):

> We are simply creatures so constructed as to be involuntarily conditioned by a constant conjunction of two events. Whenever the first appears, we involuntarily expect the second to appear also. Thus, if Hume's account of human psychology is true, this is no more a matter to which criticism and justification are relevant than is the feeling of pain when one is burned.

Hume's Distinction between Causation and Motivation

This mention of the pain of a burn serves as a reminder of an important distinction Hume introduced. It has to do with the difference between causes and motives as psychological phenomena. Although they both involve the conjunction of antecedents and consequents, they are not identical. Motives are causes that touch off voluntary actions as opposed to causes of involuntary reactions. Hume called attention to this distinction when he noted that the "conjunction between motives and voluntary action is as regular and uniform as that between the cause and effect in any part of nature" (Hendel, p. 168). This amounts to saying that all motives are causes, but not all causes are motives. Reflexes are not motivated responses. In the present example, the burn can be said to have caused the flexion reflex. Withdrawal of the hand from a hot object is involuntary. As such it is unlearned and automatic, like the pupillary dilatation in bright light or the flow of saliva when chewing.

Reactions of this sort are not products of motives or desires or intentions. Pavlovians would classify them as unconditioned reactions. Even after they have become conditioned reactions by being linked to extraneous stimuli, their involuntary status remains unchanged. The conditioned stimuli in these instances are causes and not motives for the conditioned responses. A human subject in such a conditioning experiment would not say, "I was motivated to dilate my pupil" or "I had a motive in activating my salivary glands."

He might not even be aware of the conditioned reactions in question. They are segmental reactions, of interest to the experimenter but not to the subject. What interests the subject is the symbolic import of the conditioned stimulus. In the case of the conventional conditioning paradigm dealing with Pavlov's drooling dog, the animal can be described as responding to the signal of the bell as if he expects to be fed. The drooling is an involuntary concomitant of this expectation. For the dog the bell means food, even though it means drooling from the experimenter's viewpoint. In terms of the dog's expectation, the conditioned reaction is in accord with Hume's account of a causal reaction: as a result of experiencing several instances of the "constant conjunction" of conditioned and unconditioned stimuli, the dog comes to expect to be fed when the bell rings. Hume would have considered the sound of the bell as the *cause* of the dog's expectation.

From Hume to Pavlov

As a matter of fact, Hume came close to a description of a conditioned reaction in connection with an account of what he called "a reasoning" in animals which "is not in itself different, nor founded on different principles, from that which appears in human nature." By way of explaining what he meant by this kind of animal reasoning or judgment, Hume introduced the following two considerations concerning the animals (Hendel, p. 52):

> It is necessary in the first place, that there be some impression immediately present to their memory or senses, in order to be the foundation of their judgment. From the tone of voice the dog infers his master's anger, and foresees his own punishment. From a certain sensation affecting his smell, he judges his game not to be far distant from him.
>
> Secondly, the inference he draws from the present impression is built on experience, and on his observation of the conjunction of objects in past instances. As you vary this experience, he varies his reasoning. Make a beating follow upon one sign or motion for some time, and afterwards upon another; and he will successively draw different conclusions according to his most recent experience.

Some moderns may object to the preceding references to reasoning, judging, and inferring on the part of animals, as being anthropomorphic interpretations of animal behavior.[22] It is likely that the skeptical Hume did not intend his use of these terms to mean that the cognitive functions to which they refer are precisely like those of a sophisticated human being. Accordingly, one may conjecture that he was using these terms in the sense of *as if* constructions meaning that the dog, for example, behaves *as if* he

---

[22] On the other hand, those contemporary psychologists who have found it expedient to attribute "insight" to chimpanzees or "hypotheses" to rats may have little reason to quarrel with Hume's descriptive vocabulary.

infers something from his master's tone of voice. Students of Pavlov's writings may recall Pavlov's references to a dog's *cortical analyzers.* This too is more plausibly regarded as an *as if* construction. In any event, if one can accept the notion of the dog's cortex analyzing something, why balk at the idea of having the dog judge something? Objection to Hume's choice of descriptive or explanatory terms ought not obscure recognition of his associationistic account of the dog's learning as virtually the equivalent of showing how the animal's behavior was modified by conditioning.

The underlying conceptualization is essentially the same in both accounts despite differences in descriptive vocabulary. This point was already suggested in Chapter 12 in connection with a discussion of Locke's anticipation of the concept of emotional conditioning. In this respect Hume's associationism constitutes an elaboration of Locke's connectionism. Furthermore, it is well to recall that both men were concerned with the effects of experience on the development of understanding. "Understanding" is not to be rigidly restricted to meaning the development of intellect or ideational growth as divorced from the behavioral consequences of such development, as the phrase "association of ideas" ordinarily connotes. Hume's dog, it is clearly implied, *behaved* differently as he drew "different conclusions" from his experiences.

From this viewpoint, the psychology of the associationists is a psychology of learning that readily lends itself to formulations in terms of theories of conditioning. As a laboratory technique, conditioning may be described as experimental associationism. From Hume to Pavlov may not be such a giant step, once the conceptual identity of association and conditioning is recognized. The signals that Hume's dog obeyed are equivalent to the stimuli to which Pavlov's dog reacted. Furthermore, according to the distinction Hume made, both the signals and the stimuli are to be classified as causes and not as motives of the responses they elicit.

Hume's Confidence in "Principles of Human Nature"

Because he questioned so many commonly accepted notions, Hume came to be regarded as a skeptic. However, despite his skepticism, he had faith in the underlying regularity or uniformity of nature. He noted that, unlike philosophers, "the vulgar" often "attribute the uncertainty of events" to failure of causes to operate in an expected manner. They fail to allow for "the secret operation of contrary causes." In the case of medicine, he noted, a given drug fails to have its customary effect; but the physician, who knows that "a human body is a mighty complicated machine," is not surprised by such failure. Irregularity in the therapeutic efficacy of the drug does not shake his conviction that some cause or causes are responsible for the irregularity. The situation, Hume went on to say, is comparable to the seeming irregularity of the weather. Even though a predicted change in the weather fails to occur, the meteorologist does not regard this result as meaning a fortuitous or uncaused event. He would agree with Hume that "the irregular events, which outwardly discover themselves, can be no proof that the laws of nature are not observed with the greatest regularity in its internal operations and government" (Hendel, p. 167).

With reference to seeming irregularities in human behavior, Hume also refused to regard them as evidence for the absence or suspension of lawful governing principles. Our inability to account for such irregularity is due to ignorance of the responsible factors. To illustrate, Hume mentioned an unexpectedly peevish remark from a man ordinarily thought of as being amiable and pleasant. His irritability is at variance with one's judgment of the man's disposition. However, those who know him better *explain* that his peevishness is caused by a toothache. We understand the causal relation between a toothache and irritability in the light of our own experience. Guided by experience, we become familiar with psychological principles, or what Hume called "the principles of human nature" and elaborated upon as follows (Hendel, p. 164);

> By means of this guide, we mount up to the knowledge of men's inclinations and motives, from their actions, expressions, and even gestures; and again descend to the interpretation of their actions from our knowledge of their motives and inclinations. The general observations treasured up by a course of experience, give us the clue to human nature, and teach us to unravel all its intricacies. Pretexts and appearances no longer deceive us. Public declarations pass for the specious colouring of a cause. And though virtue and honour be allowed their proper weight and authority, that perfect disinterestedness, so often pretended to, is never expected in multitudes and parties; seldom in their leaders; and scarcely even in individuals of any rank or station. But were there no uniformity in human actions, and were every experiment which we could form of this kind irregular and anomalous, it were impossible to collect any general observations concerning mankind; and no experience, however accurately digested by reflection, would ever serve to any purpose. Why is the aged husbandman more skilful in his calling than the young beginner but because there is a certain uniformity in the operation of the sun, rain, and earth towards the production of vegetables; and experience teaches the old practitioner the rules by which this operation is governed and directed.

Like Spinoza before him, Hume was thus giving expression to a faith in the existence of "sure mental laws." As such they are products of experienced cause-and-effect contiguities which we come to regard as *necessarily* associated. This, after all, is the crux of Hume's teaching; namely, apart from the invariable *conjunction* of sequential events and the resulting *inference* from one event to the other, there is no other basis for our notion of a *necessary* connection between a cause and its effect. In the course of experience we come to perceive a vast array of such connections, so that thinking in terms of causal relationships constitutes an everyday phenomenon. It even appears to spring from what Hume once referred to as "the essential and universal properties of human nature" (Hendel, p. 282). If so, then in this respect Hume and Kant might be in essential agreement, with Hume finding a readiness in man to perceive such connections and with Kant attributing such readiness to a form or category "in which the understanding spontaneously orders its experiences."

It is true, of course, that for Kant such readiness was deemed to be an *a priori* endowment, whereas Hume failed to commit himself on this point in explicit fashion. Still, in view of what he had to say about the ease with which simple causal connections come to be perceived by the "most ignorant and stupid peasants" as well as by infants and "brute beasts," it is hard to believe that he would have attributed the readiness *per se* to experience. Since in a different context he did acknowledge the existence of "essential and universal properties of human nature," one may hazard the guess that had this question of the origin of the readiness as such been raised in his day, he would have disposed of it by calling it one of these essential properties.

Conscious and Unconscious Motivation and Dream Analysis

Among the "essential and universal properties of human nature" to which Hume directed his attention were those concerned with the motivation of behavior As was mentioned at the beginning of this chapter, both Hume and Adam Smith endorsed Hutcheson's "benevolent theory" of motivation. The antithesis of this theory is not so much a "malevolent theory" as a theory of exclusive self-interest of the sort that Hobbes had sponsored. Adherents of the self-interest theory maintain that *all* conduct is prompted by selfish motives. They attribute heroic actions to a desire for the joy of being lauded as a hero. Similarly, seemingly unselfish generous behavior is attributed to a longing for social approval or fear of disapproval. According to the self-interest theory, altruism in the sense of unselfish concern for the welfare of others turns out to be a form of egoism. In opposition to this view, adherents of the benevolent theory tend to attribute interest in and solicitude for the welfare of others to an inherent readiness to respond to human suffering and human need. For Hume, as shown in the following passage (Hendel, p. 249), such readiness was deemed to be instinctive:

> The social virtues of humanity and benevolence exert their influence immediately by a direct tendency or instinct, which chiefly keeps in view the simple object, moving the affections, and comprehends not any scheme or system, nor the consequence from the concurrence, imitation, or example of others. A parent flies to the relief of his child; transported by that natural sympathy which actuates him, and which affords no leisure to reflect on the sentiments or conduct of the rest of mankind in like circumstances. A generous man cheerfully embraces

an opportunity of serving his friend; because he then feels himself under the dominion of the beneficent affections, nor is he concerned whether any other person in the universe were ever actuated by such noble motives, or will ever afterwards prove their influence. In all these cases the social passions have in view a single individual object, and pursue the safety or happiness alone of the person loved and esteemed. With this they are satisfied: in this they acquiesce.

From the foregoing excerpt it appears evident that Hume did not sponsor a hedonistic theory of motivation. In terms of the example cited, a parent rushes to the aid of his troubled child because of a spontaneous desire to aid and not because of a generalized impulse to seek pleasure and to avoid distress. As indicated in Chapter 13, pleasure and distress are by-products of goal-directed striving and not ends in themselves. To repeat Spinoza's succinct formulation of this point: "We do not strive for something because we deem it good, but we deem it good because we desire it." Without mentioning Spinoza, Hume made the same point in this way (Hendel, pp. 247–248):

There are bodily wants or appetites acknowledged by every one, which necessarily precede all sensual enjoyment, and carry us directly to seek possession of the object. Thus, hunger and thirst have eating and drinking for their end; and from the gratification of these appetites arises a pleasure, which may become the object of another species of desire or inclination that is secondary and interested. In the same manner there are mental passions by which we are impelled immediately to seek particular objects, such as fame or power, or vengeance without any regard to interest; and when these objects are attained a pleasing enjoyment ensues, as the consequence of our indulged affections. Nature must, by the internal frame and constitution of the mind, give an original propensity to fame, ere we reap any pleasure from that acquisition, or pursue it from motives of self-love, and desire of happiness. If I have no vanity, I take no delight in praise: if I be void of ambition, power gives me no enjoyment: if I be not angry, the punishment of an adversary is totally indifferent to me.

Another respect in which Hume and Spinoza were in agreement has to do with the subject of unconscious motivation. Even though neither employed that phrase,[23] there can be no doubt about their recognition of the phenomenon. As may be recalled, this was quite clear to Spinoza when he wrote, "Men are usually ignorant of the causes of their desires." It is also revealed in this statement by Hume (Hendel, p. 246): "Our predominant motive or intention is, indeed, frequently concealed from ourselves when it is mingled and confounded with other motives which the mind, from vanity or self-conceit, is desirous of supposing more prevalent."

Furthermore, in the spirit of a pre-Freudian Freudian, Hume also enter-

---

[23] Spinoza and Hume were not alone in this pre-Freudian recognition of the unconscious. There were many others, as L. L. Whyte has shown in his book dealing with *The Unconscious before Freud* (1960).

tained the notion of bringing concealed motives to light by means of dream analysis.[24] Evidently he was not alone in suggesting this, for he refers to it as the recommendation of "several moralists" (Chappell, pp. 153–154):

> Several moralists have recommended it as an excellent method of becoming acquainted with our own hearts and knowing our progress in virtue to recollect our dreams in a morning, and examine them with the same rigor that we would our most serious and most deliberate actions. Our character is the same throughout, say they, and appears best where artifice, fear, and policy have no place, and men can neither be hypocrites with themselves nor others. The generosity or baseness of our temper, our meekness or cruelty, our courage or pusillanimity, influence the fictions of the imagination with the most unbounded liberty, and discover themselves in the most glaring colors.

Hume's Theory of Objects

By referring to dreams as "fictions of the imagination," Hume was evidently recognizing the commonsense distinction between the veridical nature of waking perceptions and the unreal nature of dreams. Like Berkeley, he was skeptical of Locke's notion of primary qualities having existence independently of being perceived or as being characteristic of what commonsense designates as a substance. His endorsement of Berkeley's principle of *esse est percipi* took this form (Hendel, p. 21):

> We may observe . . . that nothing is ever really present with the mind but its perceptions . . . and that external objects become known to us only by those perceptions they occasion. To hate, to love, to think, to feel, to see; all this is nothing but to perceive.
>
> Now since nothing is ever present to the mind but perceptions, and since all ideas are derived from something antecedently present to the mind; it follows, that it is impossible for us so much as to conceive or form an idea of any thing specifically different from ideas and impressions.

For Hume, in short, the stuff of which dreams are made is the same as the stuff of which all other experiences are made; namely, ideas and impressions. To regard this stuff as related to some nonperceptible, underlying something in the form of a material or spiritual substance was meaningless to the skeptical Hume. This is what he had to say about it (Hendel, p. 82):

> We have no perfect idea of anything but a perception. A substance is entirely different from a perception. We have, therefore, no idea of a substance. . . .

---

[24] This serves as a reminder of what was mentioned in Chapter 13 concerning the frequency with which discoveries in psychology turn out to be rediscoveries.

What possibility then of answering that question, *whether perceptions inhere in a material or immaterial substance,* when we do not so much as understand the meaning of the question?

Hume contended that it is a "fallacy" to believe in the continued existence of objects as perceptible entities distinct from and independent of perception. Many of his arguments in support of this contention were the same as those mentioned in the previous chapter in connection with Berkeley's theory of objects, and there is no need to review Hume's version of them. One of his arguments, however, merits consideration because it comes close to being an anticipation of the theory of *specific energy of nerves.* It is based upon a consideration of diplopia as shown in the following excerpt from a section entitled "Of Scepticism with Regard to the Senses" (Hendel, p. 65):

When we press one eye with a finger, we immediately perceive all the objects to become double, and one half of them to be removed from their common and natural position. But as we do not attribute a continued existence to both these perceptions, and as they are both of the same nature, we clearly perceive, that all our perceptions are dependent on our organs, and the disposition of our nerves and animal spirits. This opinion is confirmed by the seeming increase and diminution of objects, according to their distance; by the apparent alterations in their figure; by the changes in their colour and other qualities from our sickness and distempers; and by an infinite number of other experiments of the same kind; from all which we learn, that our sensible perceptions are not possest of any distinct or independent existence.

Although Hume's theory of objects was the same as Berkeley's, his interpretation of this theory was not the same. Berkeley used the theory as a sponsor of subjective idealism or as a defender of the primacy of the spirit and an opponent of materialism. On the other hand, as was just shown, Hume regarded it as meaningless to talk about a spiritual substance or a material substance. For him, impressions and ideas are what they are just as they are experienced and it is futile to ask whether they "inhere in a material or immaterial substance." With respect to this metaphysical issue, he was psychophysically neutral and consequently is not to be classified as a Berkeleian idealist.

Concerning Personal Identity

Hume differed from Berkeley with reference to another and somewhat related issue. This has to do with the question of a self. Berkeley, it will be recalled, after equating existence with perceptibility, had argued that there is "something" which does the perceiving and that "this perceiving, active being is what I call *mind, spirit, soul,* or *myself.*" Furthermore, he defined spirit as that which "cannot be of itself perceived *but only by the effects which it produceth.*" Had he been consistent, he might have used the same logic to account for the existence of matter as the substratum of perceived objects. Hume was more consistent in his adherence to the principle of "to be is to be perceived." In a section concerned with the question of "personal identity," he asked how sensations, emotions, and all other items of experience might be regarded as belonging to or connected with a self, and then supplied this answer (Chappell, pp. 84–85):

> For my part, when I enter most intimately into what I call *myself,* I always stumble on some particular perception or other, of heat or cold, light or shade, love or hatred, pain or pleasure. I never can catch *myself* at any time without a perception, and never can observe any thing but the perception. When my perceptions are removed for any time, as by sound sleep; so long am I insensible of *myself,* and may truly be said not to exist. . . . If any one upon serious and unprejudiced reflexion, thinks he has a different notion of *himself,* I must confess I can reason no longer with him. All I can allow him is, that he may be in the right as well as I, and that we are essentially different in this particular. He may, perhaps, perceive something simple and continued, which he calls *himself*; though I am certain there is no such principle in me,.
>
> But setting aside some metaphysicians of this kind, I may venture to affirm of the rest of mankind, that they are nothing but a bundle[25] or collection of different perceptions, which succeed each other with an inconceivable rapidity, and are in a perpetual flux and movement. Our eyes cannot turn in their sockets without varying our perceptions. Our thought is still more variable than our sight; and all our other senses and faculties contribute to this change; nor is there any single power of the soul, which remains unalterably the same, perhaps for one moment. The mind is a kind of theatre,[26] where several perceptions successively make their appearance; pass, re-pass, glide away, and mingle in an infinite variety of postures and situations. There is properly no *simplicity* in it at one time, nor *identity* in different; whatever natural propension we may have to imagine that simplicity and identity. The comparison of the theatre must not mislead us. They are the successive perceptions only, that constitute the mind; nor have we the most distant notion of the place, where these scenes are represented, or of the materials, of which it is composed.

---

[25] This allusion to mind as a *bundle* of different perceptions has a familiar ring for the contemporary psychologist because of one of the chief objections to association psychology as voiced by sponsors of Gestalt psychology. This objection takes the form of stigmatizing associationists as advocates of a "bundle hypothesis." However, Gestaltists were not the first to raise this criticism. More than twenty years before the rise of Gestalt psychology, James had already referred to "protests against Hume's 'bundle' theory of mind" (1890, Vol. I, pp. 369–370).

[26] The same figure of speech was employed by James. In connection with his account of Herbart's notion of an idea as a "permanently existing entity" James wrote: "So far as it succeeds in occupying the theatre of consciousness, it crowds out another idea previously there" (1890, Vol. I, p. 603).

It is thus evident that Hume could not agree with Berkeley's assumption of a spiritual "something" which functions as a percipient of perceptions. For Berkeley, this "something" plus its perceptions constitutes mind. Hume, on the other hand, restricted the constitution of mind to the flux of successive perceptions. Furthermore, for him, "Every distinct perception, which enters into the composition of the mind, is a distinct existence, and is different, and distinguishable, and separable from every other perception, either contemporary or successive." This makes mind a congeries of discrete perceptions. Notwithstanding their discreteness, Hume regarded the individual perceptions as united in some way. In effect, he was asking how they are brought together so as to identify them as belonging to the same mind or the same person. He wondered "whether it be something that really binds our several perceptions together, or only associates their ideas in the imagination." He rejected the former explanation in favor of the latter by attributing the mind's semblance of unity to his three principles of association (Chappell, pp. 88–89):

> These are the uniting principles in the ideal world, and without them every distinct object is separable by the mind, and may be separately considered, and appears not to have any more connexion with any other object, than if disjoined by the greatest difference and remoteness. It is, therefore, on some of these three relations of resemblance, contiguity and causation, that identity depends; and as the very essence of these relations consists in their producing an easy transition of ideas; it follows, that our notions of personal identity, proceed entirely from the smooth and uninterrupted progress of the thought along a train of connected ideas.

Hume was thus accounting for personal identity in terms of the way in which individual perceptions come to be related to one another as causally connected, or as similar, or as contiguous in time or place. On the whole, this makes for a passive associationism: a "bundle" of perceptions becomes the equivalent of a mind. It is a *passive* affair because for Hume there is no activity of a self or ego or personal agent to choose and select from among the multiplicity of perceptions that happen to become linked together in each "bundle." The passivity is also suggested by Hume's other metaphor according to which, as he said, "The mind is a kind of theatre." By implication, perceptions move across the stage of their own accord, and, as Hume also said, "we" have no notion of the origin of the "scenes" they represent nor of the "materials" of which the "theatre" as the equivalent of "mind" is composed. The result is a question-begging and perplexing trope. It is question-begging because, with the elimination of the concept of an active self or ego, there is no referent for the "we" to which Hume alludes; and it is perplexing because, in terms of the theatrical analogy, the plays produced do not have an audience: there is no provision for spectators to enjoy the performances; the shows play before empty houses.

With perceptions as the actors there is nobody to perceive them unless the "theatre" itself as the equivalent of mind is endowed with perceptual sensitivity, but this would be tantamount to recognition of the concept of a percipient self.

Now, as mentioned earlier, Hume reported that when he entered "most intimately" into what he called *himself,* all he could find was a specific impression of some sort in the way of being cold or seeing a light or having a pain. He could never perceive a separate or independent self; hence he concluded there is no such self. All he could perceive were perceptions; and when they ceased, as in sleep, he ceased to exist. Had he cared to paraphrase Descartes, he might have written, "I perceive, therefore I am." For him the "I" in the latter sentence would have been another perception. In his efforts to identify himself as a self, all he could locate was some item of mental content.

This result is reminiscent of what was mentioned in Chapter 12 in connection with what James had to say in his discussion of the sense of "personal identity," in which he concluded that "the passing thought" serves as the "thinker." Like Hume, he too failed to observe a separate process or entity or configuration or however else one might choose to call Berkeley's "something" which is presumed to perceive and to think and to choose. James, however, unlike Hume, though dispensing with a nonphenomenal or transcendental self or thinker, nevertheless endowed each successive nascent thought with the functions ordinarily associated with the concept of a self. In fact, after quoting at considerable length from what he referred to as Hume's "famous chapter on Personal Identity" and calling it a "good piece of introspective work," James wrote that Hume "proceeds to pour out the child with the bath, and to fly to as great an extreme as the substantialist philosophers" (1890, Vol. I, p. 352). He endorsed the introspective report as confirmation of his own finding with respect to the answer to a question like "What do I experience when I am most intimately aware of myself?"

Both Hume and James found nothing but "different perceptions," as Hume put it; but they differed in their interpretations of this finding. For Hume, this meant just a sequence of diverse perceptions whose very diversity precluded recognition of a unifying focus. In the metaphor of James, this failure to perceive a unifying focus in the way of self because of undue preoccupation with the diversity was tantamount to pouring out the baby with the bath. He found this to be just as one-sided and distorted as an interpretation as that of those whose preoccupation with the unity of mind resulted in failure to perceive the diversity so obvious to Hume. James viewed mind as a *unitas multiplex*—a manifold unity—and consequently objected both to those who made "the Self nothing but Unity" as well as to those like Hume, who reduced it to "nothing but Diversity."[27] This

---

27 This unity-diversity antithesis is really another of psychology's persistent problems. It has been brought into consideration in a variety of contexts as indicated by such

explains why he concluded that "Hume is at bottom as much of a meta-physician as Thomas Aquinas" (1890, Vol. I, p. 353) .

Solipsism and Hume's Idea of the Self

James might also have written that Hume is as much of a metaphysician as Berkeley. They both gave expression to opinions concerning the nature of *substance* as that which, metaphysically considered, is presumed to underlie phenomena as they are perceived either as their physical substratum to render them durable or as their spiritual substratum to render them perceptible. Berkeley accepted the latter meaning of substance but rejected the former meaning, while Hume refused to endorse either meaning. In other words, just as Berkeley had eliminated the concept of material sub-stance from physics so Hume had eliminated the concept of spiritual substance from psychology. Hume did this by questioning the existence of self as a nonperceptible something. He argued that since all ideas are products of antecedent impressions, then if the idea of self is valid, it too ought to be traceable to antecedent impressions or to that which can be perceived. When he tried to do this, as he reported, by entering "most intimately" into what he called *himself,* he could never perceive a self. All he perceived were sensory impressions of a particular sort like being cold or in pain or in some emotional state; hence his conclusion: "I never catch *myself* at any time without a perception, and never can observe anything but the perception." Being unable to locate a perceptible self as something existing independently of those perceptions, he held that there is no empirical justification for the idea of such a self.

The only self Hume could locate turned out to be a bundle of perceptions and not an independent spiritual something as Berkeley would have it. In short, he refuted Berkeley's conclusion by using Berkeley's argument to the effect that existence means perceptibility. An independent self is not perceptible; ergo its nonexistence. Stated a little differently, in the absence of a perception of self there can be no idea of self.

Does this necessarily follow? Can one have an idea of something in the absence of prior perception of the something in question? After all, a man can have an idea of his own spinal cord without having to wait for X-ray demonstration of its perceptibility. His idea is an inference from his knowledge of anatomy. Similarly, the historian can have an idea of Oliver Cromwell without ever having perceived him. All such inferred or derived ideas constitute knowledge *about* a subject as contrasted with

---

controversial issues as the following:

(a) Is there a unifying *G*-factor in intelligence or just a multiplicity of *S*-factors?

(b) Is there a sound basis for referring to a man's memory, or should one just talk about his specific levels of retentiveness as shown by his scores on memory tests for numbers, faces, music, poetry, jokes, news items, and other kinds of material?

(c) Does the brain function as an integrated whole as a unity of component functions, or are the latter functions localized in different cortical centers?

knowledge of acquaintance. To deny the validity of such knowledge would render it impossible to have science of any kind. As a denial it amounts to saying, "I can only know what I experience or perceive directly at first-hand."

This would be the standpoint of a *solipsist,* one who maintains that all knowledge is restricted to what he alone can experience. This is evident from the word's derivation from the Latin *solus,* "alone," and *ipse,* "self." As a theory of knowledge it equates existence or reality with the self. With his misgivings about the concept of self, Hume could not have been a solipsist. In fact, for anyone to take solipsism seriously is tantamount to committing cognitive suicide, for it rules out all knowledge *about* a subject and is thus limited to direct acquaintance with the subject. Accordingly, to revert to the previous examples, a solipsist would question his possession of a spinal cord and he could never convince himself that there ever was a Cromwell or any other historical personage whom he had not met in person.

To resume consideration of Hume's analysis of the concept of self, it should now be evident that in seeming to say there can be no idea of a self without a prior impression or perception of a self he was not talking like a solipsist. Instead he seems to have been primarily concerned with exposing the weakness of Berkeley's argument in behalf of the idea of a transcendental self. What he said in the process of doing so can be interpreted as an argument in behalf of the idea of an empirical self.

What James had called Hume's "good piece of introspective work" had to do with the problem of personal identity. In doing this "work," Hume was trying to observe the experience of being "most intimately" aware of what he called himself. This means that he did have an idea of self. His problem was to find out what kinds of impressions had given rise to this idea, for he operated on the principle that all ideas are products of antecedent impressions or perceptions. He never denied having an idea of self. His introspective work traced this idea back to an array of particular perceptions. As he said, he could never catch himself without a perception. As a consequence, it is incorrect to interpret Hume's psychology as having done away with the idea of a self. For James to have made such an interpretation by saying that Hume poured "out the child with the bath" may have been unfair to Hume.[28]

Actually, Hume was quite explicit in his affirmation of the existence of what James came to designate as the empirical self. For example, in Hume's section on personal identity he pointed out that the self of today is the same self of yesterday and of previous days as a result of our memory of the

---

[28] He was unfair if he meant that Hume had denied having had an *idea* of a self. On the other hand, if all he meant was that Hume had failed to provide for an *active* self in the sense in which James referred to the passing thought by designating it as "the thinker," then, of course, he was not unfair.

past, and then he concluded that "memory does not so much *produce* as *discover* personal identity" (Hendel, p. 91). It is obviously impossible to *discover* something which has no existence. Another example of this affirmation of a self is to be found in the Appendix to the *Treatise,* in which Hume returned to the problem of personal identity by showing what he believed "forms the self." Once again he introduced introspective evidence as follows (Hendel, p. 104):

> When I turn my reflection on *myself,* I never can perceive this *self* without some one or more perceptions; nor can I ever perceive any thing but the perceptions. It is the composition of these, therefore, which forms the self.

As mentioned earlier, in thus equating the idea of self with the kinds of perceptions he noted when he reflected upon the notion of self, Hume came close to providing a variant of the Cartesian formula by, in effect, changing it to read, "I perceive, therefore I am." Incidentally, he probably might also have been ready to endorse the original formula, for at one point in the *Treatise* he made "mind" synonymous with the "thinking principle" (Hendel, p. 89). He employed this "thinking principle" in arriving at his conclusion regarding the self as the focus of personal identity with memories of earlier perceptions serving to make for continuity of self.

A simple analogy may help to clarify the nature of this way of getting at Hume's meaning of the idea of self. Let it be assumed that some contemporary Hume begins to wonder about his idea of London and then begins to "enter most intimately" into what he calls his idea of London. One may safely predict he will "always stumble on some particular" memory of what he had perceived on previous visits. There will be reactivation of impressions of the Thames, of Hyde Park, of Buckingham Palace, of Baker Street, of Charing Cross station, and of many other characteristic London scenes he had chanced to perceive. As a Humean, he would then conclude that it is "the composition" of these perceptions which "forms" his idea of London. In short, in terms of this analogy Hume can be said to have sponsored a context theory of the meaning of self.[29] This, in Humean terminology, makes the self a "bundle" of perceptions and not, as Berkeley held, an independent entity or spiritual "thing."[30]

Summary Review

Although Hume was influenced by the teachings of Locke and Berkeley, he reacted to these teachings in independent fashion and did not hesitate

---

[29] See p. 539 for an explanation of the context theory.

[30] Some of Hume's critics regarded this as a complete repudiation of the idea of the self. Instead it is only a repudiation of the idea of a trascendental self. It should be evident that Hume did not reject the idea of an empirical self.

to reject some of them, modify others, and introduce some of his own. The result, as brought out in this chapter, was an array of more or less distinctively Humean interpretations of psychological issues that may be outlined as follows:

1. Hume regarded his *Treatise of Human Nature* as concerned with the "science of man" which, in turn, was to supply a "solid foundation for the other sciences." Methodologically, this called for study based upon "experience and observation" as well as for the "application of experimental philosophy."

2. The *Treatise* was divided into three parts concerned with understanding, the passions, and morals, respectively. This may be compared with other familiar tripartite schemes like cognition, affection, and volition or ego, id, and superego.

3. The psychology of the *Treatise* was intended to supply a foundation for "practical morality" and thus may be viewed as having paved the way for a social psychology.

4. Hume was the first since Aristotle to formulate the laws of association. He regarded them as "universal principles" and recognized three: (a) resemblance, (b) contiguity in time or place, and (c) cause and effect.

5. Hume expected that his principle of association would be as important for psychology as Newton's principle of gravitation was for physics.

6. He followed Locke in referring to complex ideas as having to do with relations, modes, or substances; but he did not accept Locke's explanation of substances as "*particular* things subsisting by themselves." Instead he agreed with Berkeley to the effect that "substance" can only mean the cluster of sensory qualities characteristic of objects; hence rejection of Locke's distinction between primary and secondary qualities.

7. He subjected the commonsense notion of causality to critical analysis and stressed these points: (a) causes are inferred and not observed; (b) are not forces or powers; (c) are the result of the "constant conjunction" of experienced temporal contiguities.

8. His analysis of the concept of causality had marked influence on the thinking of Kant in philosophy, on Mach and Helmholtz in physics, and on Claparède, Michotte, and Piaget in psychology. In philosophy, Kant had made causality one of the *a priori* categories of understanding. Mach and Helmholtz had suggested dispensing with consideration of the causes of natural phenomena. The relevance of the concept of causality in psychology was indicated by Claparède's discussion of a "feeling of causality" as well as by Michotte's launching-effect and entraining-effect experiments. It was also indicated by Piaget's studies of precausal thinking, intellectual realism, and "types" of explanation listed as causal or mechanical, statistical, finalistic, psychological, and logical.

9. Hume's work is difficult to classify. He was not just an empiricist, for in

some ways he was also a rationalist, a positivist, a sensationalist, and a phenomenalist.

10. Possible shortcomings of Hume's thesis have to do with his failure to consider synchronous causation as well as by his failure to note the contradiction between what he had to say about young children learning to avoid a flame after a *single* painful experience and his emphasis on the need for "several instances" of given experiences in order to establish a causal relationship.

11. Because of the difficulty of proving the validity of the principle of induction in terms of abstract logic, Hume's thesis has been said to have undermined the empirical foundation of science.

12. According to Hume, questions are to be settled by three kinds of argument: by means of demonstrations, by consideration of probabilities, and by proofs or "such arguments from experience as leave no room for doubt or opposition."

13. Induction viewed as an outgrowth of Hume's account of the causal relationship has become an important problem both in logic and in philosophy of science.

14. Hume recognized a difference between causation and motivation.

15. In his discussion of reasoning in animals, Hume came close to Pavlov's principle of conditioned reactions. There is no essential difference between psychological connections attributed to association and those attributed to conditioning.

16. Hume had confidence in "principles of human nature" and thus in the possibility of a science of psychology.

17. With respect to motivation Hume (a) endorsed the "benevolent" theory; (b) opposed hedonism; (c) recognized unconscious factors by noting that "our predominant motive is frequently concealed from ourselves"; and (d) also recognized dream analysis as a means of bringing concealed motives to light.

18. Hume followed Berkeley in his theory of objects, but differed from Berkeley in his interpretation of the theory. He was psychophysically neutral and not a Berkeleian idealist. His account foreshadows what came to be called the theory of *specific energy of nerves*.

19. In connection with his discussion of the problem of personal identity, Hume provided for acceptance of an empirical self. He attributed such unity as seems to characterize the self to the operation of the laws of association. For him, mind appears to be a congeries of discrete perceptions. Hume could not agree with Berkeley's assumption of a substantial or transcendental self. He was more consistent than Berkeley in his adherence to the principle of "to be is to be perceived."

20. Hume's theory of the self amounts to a context theory.

Concluding Comments

The youthful Hume was grievously disappointed by the lack of interest aroused by the *Treatise* upon its publication. As he said, "it fell dead-born from the press." Had he been able to see into the future, he would have had no reason for complaint, on the score of having been ignored, for his writings have been subjected to careful study by professional philosophers from the time of Kant on up to the present. There have been successive editions of his works and many critical essays dealing with his works. Virtually every history of philosophy devotes considerable space to Hume. To compile a complete bibliography of all that has been written about him in different languages would constitute a laborious undertaking. Whether Hume would have been pleased with what the commentators said about him is another question. Some see Hume as fundamentally an empiricist and others as a rationalist, while still others find it difficult to classify him as the sponsor of any consistently systematic viewpoint. Similarly, his teachings with respect to specific topics have won the endorsement of some critics and the disapproval of others.

Hume's intention was to have his study of "human nature" become a "science of man" that was to supply "the only solid foundation for the other sciences" (Hendel, p. 6). This ambition can hardly be said to have been realized. Critics have had little trouble in locating contradictions in various sections of the *Treatise* and the *Inquiry*. Nor have they had difficulty in finding weaknesses in some of Hume's arguments and conclusions. Hume himself, had he lived to read such adverse comments, might have regarded them as fulfillments of his own prediction. As shown in the following passage, he anticipated hostile reviews and was not unmindful of the possibility of "error and absurdity" in his reasoning (Chappell, p. 185):

> When I look abroad, I foresee on every side dispute, contradiction, anger. calumny, and detraction. When I turn my eye inward, I find nothing but doubt and ignorance. . . . Every step I take is with hesitation, and every new reflection makes me dread error and absurdity in my reasoning.

His misgivings about his work extended to a candid acknowledgment of dissatisfaction with what he had written about the nature of personal identity. He added an Appendix to the *Treatise* in which he confessed an inability to correct what, in retrospect, he recognized as an inadequate exposition of the nature of the *self* as given in the body of the *Treatise*. In doing so, as shown in the following excerpt, he virtually admitted that his principles of association failed to explain the nature of the consciousness of self (Chappell, pp. 310–311):

Most philosophers seem inclined to think that personal identity *arises* from consciousness, and consciousness is nothing but a reflected thought or perception. The present philosophy, therefore, has so far a promising aspect. But all my hopes vanish when I come to explain the principles that unite our successive perceptions in our thought or consciousness. I cannot discover any theory which gives me satisfaction on this head.

In short there are two principles which I cannot render consistent, nor is it in my power to renounce either of them, *viz., that all our distinct perceptions are distinct existences,* and *that the mind never perceives any real connection among distinct existences.* Did our perceptions either inhere in something simple and individual, or did the mind perceive some real connection among them, there would be no difficulty in the case. For my part, I must plead the privilege of a skeptic, and confess that this difficulty is too hard for my understanding. I pretend not, however, to pronounce it absolutely insuperable. Others, perhaps, or myself, upon more mature reflections, may discover some hypothesis that will reconcile those contradictions.

Hume, it should now be evident, was concerned with some of the persistent problems of psychology as outlined in Chapter 8. As just indicated, he was obviously troubled by the problem of the *Self* and by the difficulty of accounting for the unity or *individuality* of selfhood by means of his principles of *association.* In addition, the *psychophysical* problem was an especially acute one for him, since in his view, as he put it, "the essence of the mind" is "equally unknown to us with that of external bodies." By implication this would make the venerable mind-body puzzle either meaningless or hopelessly baffling; for, according to Hume, it would be the equivalent of asking about the relationship between a nonperceptible or unknown "internal" mind and a nonperceptible or unknown "external" body.

The complacency of the average reader in Hume's time was also likely to have been disturbed by Hume's disposition of the cause-and-effect relationship. In summary, this denied the perceptibility of a cause and reduced the relationship to an accustomed temporal sequence involving the "necessary conjunction" of antecedent and consequent with no awareness of a "tye" between them. Although Hume was convinced of the "solid proof and reasoning" he had mobilized in support of this doctrine, he believed that "with the generality of readers the biass of the mind will prevail, and give them a prejudice against the present doctrine" (Hendel, p. 51). In some ways this was his most influential doctrine, for, as has been brought out in the present chapter, it not only induced some nineteenth-century scientists to dispense with causal explanations but also came to have a bearing on twentieth-century critiques of the logic of induction as well as on contemporary psychological studies of the origin and nature of the causal relationship.

In brief, the skeptical Hume with his probing questions served as a Socratic gadfly to goad others into an examination of their customary beliefs. This has been indicated in the account of Kant's reaction to Hume as presented in Chapter 15, when mention was made of what Kant had said about having been awakened from his "dogmatic slumbers" by reading Hume. Furthermore, as will be considered in Chapter 19, Hume shocked some of his Scottish compatriots into vigorous defense of common beliefs and intellectual traditions which they deemed to have been threatened by Hume's skepticism. Accordingly, in retrospect one might even hold that Hume's place in the history of psychology has more to do with the questions he raised than with the answers he proposed. Even those who rejected his answers respected his questions. Kant, it may be recalled, paid tribute to Hume by including him in a list of authors, he said, "one should read" because they write clearly without "pedantry and dilettantism" and who give "evidence of much insight into science."

What Kant wrote constitutes a tribute to Hume as a philosopher. Those who knew Hume personally were ready to pay tribute to him as a man. An especially moving personal tribute was paid to him in this eulogy written by Adam Smith in 1777 and quoted by E. C. Mossner as follows (1963, pp. xix–xx):

> Thus died our most excellent, and never-to-be-forgotten friend, concerning whose philosophical opinions men will no doubt judge variously, every one approving or condemning them according as they happen to coincide, or disagree with his own; but concerning whose character and conduct there scarse be a difference of opinion. His temper, indeed, seemed to be more happily balanced, if I may be allowed such an expression, than that perhaps of any other man I have ever known. . . . The extreme gentleness of his nature never weakened either the firmness of his mind, or the steadiness of his resolutions . . . And that gaiety of temper, so agreeable in society, but which is so often accompanied with frivolous and superficial qualities, was in him certainly attended with the most severe application, the most extensive learning, the greatest depth of thought, and a capacity in every respect the most comprehensive. Upon the whole, I have always considered him, both in his lifetime, and since his death, as approaching as nearly to the idea of a perfectly wise and virtuous man, as perhaps the nature of human frailty will admit.

References

Adamson, R., and Mitchell, J. M. "Hume, David," in *Encyclopaedia Britannica,* Vol. 13, 11th ed., 1910.

Brett, G. S. *A History of Psychology,* Vols. II and III. London: George Allen and Unwin, 1912, 1921.

Chappell, V. C. (ed.). *The Philosophy of David Hume.* New York: The Modern Library, 1963. © by Random House, Inc.

Ewing, A. C. *The Fundamental Questions of Philosophy.* New York: Collier Books, 1962.

Gilson, C., and Abelson, R. P. "The Subjective Use of Inductive Evidence," *Journal of Personality and Social Psychology,* 1965, *2,* 301–310.

Hendel, C. W. (ed.). *Hume—Selections.* New York: Charles Scribner's Sons, 1927.

Hutcheson, F. "Concerning the Finer Powers of Perception," in D. S. Robinson (ed.). *The Story of Scottish Philosophy.* New York: Exposition Press, 1961.

James, W. *Principles of Psychology,* Vol. I. New York: Henry Holt and Company, 1890.

Jones, H. M. *The Pursuit of Happiness.* Cambridge: Harvard University Press, 1953.

Katz, J. J. *The Problem of Induction and Its Solution.* Chicago: University of Chicago Press, 1962.

Locke, J. *An Essay Concerning Human Understanding.* Chicago: Henry Regnery Company, 1956.

Michotte, A. *The Perception of Causality.* (Translated by T. R. Miles and Elaine Miles.) New York: Basic Books, 1963.

Mossner, E. C. (ed.). *An Enquiry Concerning Human Understanding and Other Essays* (by David Hume). New York: Washington Square Press, 1963.

Northrop, F. S. C. *The Meeting of East and West–An Inquiry Concerning World Understanding.* New York: The Macmillan Company, 1947.

Peirce, C. S. "The Probability of Induction," in J. R. Newman (ed.). *The World of Mathematics,* Vol. 2. New York: Simon and Schuster, 1956, pp. 1341–1354.

Peirce, C. S. "The Red and the Black," in J. R. Newman (ed.). *The World of Mathematics,* Vol. 2. New York: Simon and Schuster, 1956.

Piaget, J. *The Child's Conception of Causality.* (Translated by Marjorie Gabain.) London: Routledge and Kegan Paul, 1930.

Piaget, J. *The Child's Construction of Reality.* (Translated by Margaret Cook.) London: Routledge and Kegan Paul, 1955.

Piaget, J. *The Language and Thought of the Child.* (Translated by Marjorie Gabain.) London: Routledge and Kegan Paul, 1952.

Russell, B. *A History of Western Philosophy.* New York: Simon and Schuster, 1945.

Russell, B. "On the Notion of Cause, with Applications to the Free-Will Problem," in H. Feigl and M. Brodbeck (eds.). *Readings in the Philosophy of Science.* New York: Appleton-Century-Crofts, 1953, pp. 387–407.

Simpson, G. G. "Naturalistic Ethics and the Social Sciences," *American Psychologist,* 1966, *21,* 27–36.

Tuddenham, R. D. "Jean Piaget and the World of the Child," *American Psychologist,* 1966, *21,* 207–217.

Whyte, L. L. *The Unconscious before Freud.* New York: Basic Books, 1960.

Wolf, A. "Causality," in *Encyclopaedia Britannica,* Vol. 5, 14th ed., 1929.

18

Empiricism Becomes
Associationism

IN TERMS OF A BROAD historical perspective, it can be argued, the main philosophical foundations of scientific psychology have now been outlined. The founding fathers of that psychology as professors of philosophy did not start with a psychological *tabula rasa*. They had a rich and diversified legacy stemming from mental philosophy upon which to build. As summarized in the earlier chapters, this heritage dealing with psychology's long past went back to Plato and Aristotle in ancient times, to St. Augustine in the fourth and fifth centuries, to Aquinas in medieval times, and to Descartes, Hobbes, Locke, Spinoza, Leibnitz, Berkeley, Hume, and Kant in later periods. In different ways these thinkers had been dealing with topics of psychological import. In one sense it might be said that all of them had been engaged in trying to understand the nature of human understanding. All of them had been dealing with aspects of human nature.

In the course of all these centuries of thinking, observation, and speculation, the major areas of concern for a scientific psychology had been brought up for consideration. There is no need to list them all. By way of reminder it suffices to mention interest in the origin of ideas, in the cause of illusions, in the perception of space and time, in the difference between sensation and image, in conation and motivation, in the self-object dichotomy, in the mind-body dichotomy, in concept formation, and in conditioning or association.

This last-mentioned topic has become the problem of learning in current psychology and as such has come to have a different frame of reference from what it had when associationism was being developed under philosophic auspices. A similar statement might be made with reference to all the other topics just mentioned. In many instances the changed descriptive vocabulary and the transformed laboratory or clinical setting of many of these topics had made for a scientific superstructure that obscures their underlying philosophic foundations. As has been repeatedly suggested in the previous chapters, however, when early interests in these topics are viewed as anticipations of later developments, their bearing on these developments becomes less obscure. Thus, contemporary studies of depth perception and spatial orientation were seen as outgrowths of Berkeley's "new theory of vision." Similarly, twentieth-century investigations of the perception of causality and related themes were found to be more or less technical elaborations of an issue that Hume has brought into sharp focus. To cite one more still older instance: in broad outline Plato's tripartite psychology, with its allusions to wishful dreaming, was seen to be a foreshadowing of Freud's tripartite psychology and his concern with the dream as revelatory of man's wishes.

In other words, to use an arboreal metaphor, the main philosophic roots of the various branches of modern psychology can be traced to the key figures already considered in earlier chapters from the one dealing with Plato to the last one dealing with Hume. With the exception of William James, those who came after him are not key figures as philosopher-psychologists. Consequently, the men who will be mentioned from now on as precursors of scientific psychology may be viewed as stars of the second magnitude,[1] or, to revert to the arboreal metaphor, as those who cultivated psychology's philosophic rootlets as offshoots from the main roots. A convenient way of showing what this means is to sketch some of the ways in which the topic of association came to be regarded by those who came after Hume. To change the metaphor: if what Aristotle, Hobbes, Locke, Berkeley, and Hume had to say about association be compressed

---

[1] This implies that those whose views have already been considered are stars of the first magnitude. Their eminence was suggested either by the amount of space devoted to consideration of their teachings or else by inclusion of their names in chapter headings. Furthermore, the majority of those to be singled out in terms of these criteria are to be considered as stars of the first magnitude not only as philosophic precursors of scientific psychology but also as men of outstanding literary accomplishment. This is so because their names are to be found included in a list of the authors of "The 100 Greatest Books Selected by 100 Qualified Persons," to use the title of an article by Daniel Starch published in 1942. In his study, Starch had a hundred experts from different fields of learning express their judgment of books worthy of being called great. They were instructed to "regard greatness as whatever you think it should mean," with the proviso that it was to include "influence on mankind and civilization of an enduring character." The final list expressed the pooled judgments of all these experts. They represented the major areas of academic specialization such as literature, history, physics, astronomy, economics, philosophy, linguistics, and journalism. The eminence of the judges is indicated by the fact that psychology was represented by Terman, Thorndike, and Woodworth. Incidentally, the judgment was restricted to books published prior to 1900. For present purposes it is enough to note that among the works given this accolade of distinction were the writings of Aristotle, Aquinas, Descartes, Hume, James, Kant, Locke, Plato, Spinoza, and St. Augustine. With reference to the previously mentioned two criteria of eminence, Hobbes, Leibnitz, and Berkeley are thus not stars of the first magnitude in terms of having written one of "the 100 Greatest Books." Their eminence is restricted to their impact on the history of philosophy.

into a single text, then what Hume's successors had to contribute to clarification of the topic may be thought of as a series of commentaries on this text. In terms of chronological sequence, the first of these successors to be considered is David Hartley, a contemporary of Hume.

Hartley's Role as Associationist

As noted in the previous chapter, Hume was the first to give prominence to Locke's initial but incidental use of the phrase "association of ideas." David Hartley (1705–1757) did more than this. He made the principle involved the keystone of a psychological system. From this viewpoint, he might be said to have spearheaded the establishment of associationistic psychology as an explicit or definite school of psychology. In Boring's apt wording, although Hartley had predecessors who dealt with the fact of association, "there is not the least doubt that Hartley prepared it for its *ism*" (1950, p. 194). This means that association as a principle can be traced back to Aristotle, but that associationism as a school or system begins with Hartley.

Hartley himself does not seem to have realized this. In the preface to his major psychological work he explained, "I cannot be called a system-maker, since I did not first form a system, and then suit the facts to it, but was carried on by a train of thoughts from one thing to another, frequently without any express design, or even any previous suspicion of the consequence that might rise" (1749, Vol. 1, p. iv).[2] This sounds as if his resulting associationism were a product of free association.

This major work has a rather formidable title: *Observations on Man, His Frame, His Duty and His Expectations.* It is divided into two parts, with a separate volume devoted to each part. According to the subtitle, the first part contains "observations of the frame of the human body and mind and on their mutual connections and influences," while the second part contains "observations on the duty and expectations of mankind." In terms of the history of psychology, this second part is far less important than the first. In general, Part II reflects Hartley's theology, whereas Part I reveals his role in psychology as a link in the chain of British empiricists.

Hartley's Three Fields of Interest

Like almost all the British empiricists, Hartley was not a university professor. His psychology as presented in his *Observations* was a nonacademic development of leisure-time writing and reflection. He wrote it over a span of some eighteen years during such time as he could spare from his work as a practicing physician. In this respect he resembles Locke, for Locke

---

[2] However, on the same page he wrote: "I have in one Part or other of these Papers, alleged all that I know material, in *Support of my System* [Italics added.]".

had also studied medicine and had also made the writing of his psychology an avocational pursuit so that twenty years were required for completion of the *Essay*. Hartley's interest in psychology, however, was much more intimately related to his interest in religion than was the case with Locke. As a matter of fact, Hartley had studied for the ministry before he shifted to medicine, and medicine seems to have been his second choice as a vocation. According to Boring (1950, p. 195), his "insurmountable objection to the doctrine of eternal punishment" prevented his ordination, since as a man of good conscience he found it impossible to sign "the required Thirty-nine Articles" that included the doctrine.[3] But this refusal did not entail his alienation from the Church. A perusal of the second part of the *Observations* reveals Hartley as a zealous champion of scriptural authority and seriously concerned with theological teachings. This volume, for example, has chapters on "The Being and Attributes of God," on "The Truth of the Christian Religion," on "The Terms of Salvation," and similar topics. He thought it probable that "the Soul will remain in a State of Inactivity, though perhaps not of Insensibility, from Death to the Resurrection."

It should thus be clear why, as already suggested, this second part has little to do with Hartley's associationism. Had he restricted his writing to this second volume, he would have been ignored by historians of psychology. What he had to say about man's duty and expectations was not among the factors that came to influence the thinking of the founding fathers of scientific psychology. His importance in the history of psychology is entirely a result of what he had to say in the first volume, in which his "Observations on Man" were more influenced by his medical training than by his theological studies.[4] All further quotations of Hartley in this chapter are from the first volume.

Hartley Not Influenced by Hume

In lists of names of those responsible for the rise of associationistic psychology, David Hartley usually follows David Hume. Actually, Hartley was six years older than Hume, who outlived him by almost twenty years. Thus, chronologically considered, Hume was Hartley's successor. However,

---

[3] Years later, Hartley seems to have been able to bring his thinking into line with Anglican orthodoxy with reference to this issue. At all events, in the preface to his *Observations,* written in December, 1748, he declared: "I do most firmly believe, upon the authority of the scriptures, that the future punishment of the wicked will be exceedingly great both in degree and duration, *i.e.* infinite and eternal, in that real and practical sense to which alone our conceptions extend" (1749, Vol. I, p. vi).

[4] This does not imply complete exclusion of theological considerations from the first part. For example, Hartley devoted several pages toward the end of the volume to what he termed *Theopathy*. He defined this as "all those pleasures and pains, which the contemplation of God, and his attitudes, and of our relation to him raises up in the minds of different persons, or in that of the same person at different times" (p. 486). There are also incidental allusions to impiety, to immortality, and to God as "the cause of causes, the one only source of all power" (p. 508).

DAVID HARTLEY (1705–1757)

in terms of making their respective psychological views known, Hume preceded Hartley, whose *Observations* was not published until 1749, a year
after the appearance of Hume's *Enquiry* and about ten years after the
Treatise. There is nothing in the *Observations* to suggest familiarity with
either of Hume's books. Apart from a common interest in the principle
of association, along with identical initials, the two Davids had little in
common. Temperamentally and in general philosophic outlook, the two
men were very different. Hume was restlessly ambitious, chronically self-
disparaging, critical of all theological dogma, and ready to voice his "sceptical doubts" about a variety of commonly cherished teachings. By contrast
Hartley was self-assured in his work as physician and writer, at peace with
himself and his God, confident of his orthodoxy, and genuinely concerned
about the welfare and salvation of others. It seems safe to say that Hartley
did not get his associationism from Hume.

Indeed, according to Hartley (p. iii), it was a clergyman who was responsible for arousing his initial interest in the subject of association:

> About eighteen years ago I was informed that the Rev. Mr. Gay . . . asserted the
> possibility of deducing all our intellectual pleasures and pains from association.
> This put me upon considering the power of association. Mr. Gay published his
> sentiments on this matter, about the same time, in a Dissertation on the funda-
> mental Principle of Virtue, prefixed to Mr. Archdeacon Law's Translation of
> Archbishop King's Origin of Evil.

Hartley as "Originator" of Physiological Psychology

Hartley is important in the history of psychology for the same reason
that Descartes is important. In some respects he might be described as
a British Cartesian. In the first place, like Descartes, he was a dualist in
his psychology in his clear-cut distinction between body and mind. As he
saw it, "man consists of two parts, body and mind," with the former to be
studied "as the other parts of the external world" and the latter having to do
with "that substance, agent, principle," or kindred something "to which we
refer the sensations, ideas, pleasures, pains, and voluntary motions." In
the second place, also like Descartes, he tackled the problem of the mind-
body relationship. Both men may consequently be regarded as pioneer
physiological psychologists.[5] They both tried to account for mind as a func-

---

[5] A French physician, Pierre Cabanis (1757–1808), is also to be listed as a pioneer
in this respect. G. S. Brett in *A History of Psychology* states: "Cabanis has been
deservedly called the founder of the modern physiological psychology" (1912, Vol. I,
p. 376). On p. 279, however, in a discussion of Hartley's period, he had declared: "The
possibilities of a physiological psychology were at the time wholly unsuspected, Hartley
takes his place as the originator of this branch of science." Unfortunately, Brett failed
to indicate just how the originator of a movement differs from the founder of a
movement.

tion of neural action and brain process. In doing so, they differed from Locke, Berkeley, Hume, and Kant, all of whom had ignored or dodged the problem. Locke, it may be recalled, had stated that he was not going to "meddle with the physical consideration of the mind," and Hume was ready to delegate the problem to "anatomists and natural philosophers." Hartley was the first British psychologist to face the problem.

In dealing with the problem, Hartley availed himself of three bodies of data. From his medical studies he had knowledge of the gross anatomy of the nervous system as this had been developed by the early part of the eighteenth century. His reading of Newton's *Principia* and *Optics* supplied him with a "doctrine of *vibrations*" to account for neural activity as correlated with mental activity. For Hartley, mental activity was synonymous with association; and, as he put it, he obtained his knowledge of association from "what Mr. Locke, and other ingenious persons since his time have delivered concerning the influence of *association* over our opinions and affections, and its use in explaining those things in an accurate and precise way, which are commonly referred to as the power of habit and custom . . ." (1749, Vol. I, p. 5). Just who these "other ingenious persons" were was never made explicit. Hartley has a relatively extensive discussion of vision but does not mention Berkeley by name. As has been noted, he has nothing to say about Hume. It may be that he was thinking of Nicolas de Malebranche (1638–1715) the occasionalist, and of Leibnitz (1646–1716) the parallelist, as exponents of mind-body theories. At all events, he refers to both of these writers in the last part of the first volume (p. 511) in connection with a discussion of the "mechanism of the human mind." They both came after the time of Locke and both might qualify as "ingenious persons."

The Scope of Hartley's Psychology

The scope of what Hartley observed in his *Observations* is indicated by the fact that each "'observation" is cast in the form of a *Proposition,* of which there are ninety-nine in the first volume and ninety-five in the second. Moreover, each proposition, after first being presented in succinct formulation, is subjected to careful elaboration that may run from just a page or two to twenty or more pages. The ninety-five in the second volume, which have to do with Hartley's theology rather than his psychology, may be disregarded. His psychology is to be found in the first volume, in which the doctrine of vibrations, combined with the principle of association, is applied to sensory and muscular phenomena in general and to each of the special senses in particular. It is also applied to language functions, to ideation, memory, imagination, dreams, and even to "the desires of the sexes towards each other." This dual approach marks the first attempt to apply the principle of association to so wide a range of psychological topics in such systematic form; hence Hartley's significance as the sponsor of a systematic psychology in the sense in which functionalism, behaviorism, configurationism, and other "schools" of psychology came to be classified as "systems" of psychology.

Neural Damage Correlated with Psychological Impairment

Many conventional introductions to general psychology have devoted the initial sections or chapters to a description of the nervous system. The writers might be said to have been following a precedent set by Hartley; for the first of his ninety-five Propositions, along with its commentary, reads [6] as follows (pp. 7–8):

> *The white medullary Substance of the Brain, spinal Marrow, and the Nerves proceeding from them, is the immediate Instrument of Sensation and Motion.*
>
> Under the word *brain,* in these *observations,* I comprehend all that lies within the cavity of the skull, *i.e.,* the *cerebrum, . . .* the *cerebellum,* and the *medulla oblongata.*
>
> This proposition seems to be sufficiently proved in the writings of physicians and anatomists; from the structure and functions of the several organs of the human body; from experiments on living animals; from the symptoms of diseases, and from dissections of morbid bodies. Sensibility, and the power of motion, seem to be conveyed to all the parts, in their natural state, from the brain and spinal marrow, along the nerves . . When the nerves of any part are cut, tied, or compressed in any considerable degree, the functions of that part are either entirely destroyed, or much impaired. When the spinal marrow is compressed by a dislocation of the *vertebrae* of the back, all the parts, whose nerves arise below the places of dislocation, become paralytic. When any considerable injury is done to the medullary substance of the brain, sensation, voluntary motion, memory, and intellect, are either entirely lost, or much impaired; and if the injury be very great, this extends immediately to the vital motions also, viz. to those of the heart, and the organs of respiration, so as to occasion death. . . . In dissections after apoplexies, palsies, epilepsies, and other distempers affecting the sensations and motions, it is usual to find some great disorder in the brain from preternatural tumors, from blood, matter, or serum, lying upon the brain, or in its ventricles, etc. This may suffice as general evidence for the present.

---

[6] In the first edition (1749), *all* nouns are capitalized, as in the italicized proposition as printed here. This edition also deviated from modern orthography by using the eighteenth-century type for the letter "s," which looks so much like the letter "f" that at first glance the word *association* seems to be spelled *affociation.* In later editions such as the fourth (1801), although the page numbering of the first edition is retained, modern orthography has been introduced. All nouns are no longer capitalized. To facilitate ease of reading, all subsequent quotations will be presented in this later orthography.

Hartley was evidently drawing on his medical background to set the stage for his vibrational associationism. In the preceding quotation he summarized the kind of evidence an experienced physician might mobilize to demonstrate neural integrity as the foundation for sensory efficiency and muscular control. In effect, he was calling attention to cranial and spinal nerves as the structural linkage between central nervous system and sensorimotor functions.[7] In terms of a later terminology, he was making the peripheral nervous system responsible for incoming sensory and outgoing motor impulses coming into and going out of spinal cord and brain. However, he regarded the brain as solely involved in ideation or, in his words, as the "immediate instrument by which ideas are presented to the mind" and, consequently, as having to do with "the faculties of memory, attention, imagination," and so on. He recognized "mental disorders" as due to brain damage because "all injuries done to" the brain "affect the trains of ideas proportionably" and "these cannot be restored to their natural course, till such injuries be repaired (pp. 8–9).

Hartley's Doctrine of Vibrations

The doctrine of vibrations by means of which Hartley proposed to account for the neurophysiology of sensation, motion, and ideation was based upon considerations supplied by Newton. An important consideration had to do with the structural characteristics of nerves. The distinguished Dutch physician Hermann Boerhaave (1668–1738), Hartley noted, had thought of the nerves as tubes, a notion in harmony with the notion of animal spirits coursing through definite channels. According to Hartley, Newton, in opposition to Boerhaave, thought of the nerves as "solid capillaments." The latter phrase connotes continuous, closely packed, hairlike filaments and as such made it easier to conceive of the transmission of vibrations. Continuity of structure was attributed to these capillaments, with the result that "there is no part of the medullary substance separated from the rest, but all make one continuous white body," and thus "the whole brain, spinal marrow, and nerves" are interconnected (p. 16).

Hartley was explicit in his advocacy of a theory of vibrations to account for the action of the nervous system. He was clear about the advocacy but unclear about the precise mechanism of neural transmission. In proposition V he maintained, "The vibrations . . . are excited, propagated, and

---

[7] He had a general understanding of afferent and efferent functions of the peripheral nervous system, even though he was ignorant or uncertain of many neuroanatomic details. In considering the various sensory modalities, he referred to the cranial nerves by number. For example, in connection with taste he stated that there is "some evidence, that the fifth pair, not the ninth, supplies the tongue with sensory nerves" (p. 152). And with respect to auditory sensations he wrote: "The immediate organ of hearing appears to be the soft portion of the seventh pair of nerves distributed in the *cochlea,* and the semicircular canals" (p. 223).

kept up, partly by the aether, *i.e.* by a very subtle and elastic fluid and partly by the uniformity, continuity, softness, and active powers of the medullary substance of the brain, spinal marrow, and nerves" (p. 13). He credited Newton with having advanced the idea of "the existence of this aether" and then confessed, "I am not satisfied, that I understand him perfectly on this subject." Nevertheless, he was willing to assume the existence of aether as an all-pervasive medium having something to do with neural transmission and thus reached this conclusion: "We are to conceive, that when external objects are impressed on the sensory nerves, they excite vibrations in the aether residing in the pores of these nerves" (p. 21). But he also conceived this phenomenon to involve vibratory action of the medullary substance of the nerves. He compared this vibratory action to the oscillation of a pendulum and thought of it as a back-and-forth motion of the "infinitesimal, medullary particles."

To conceive of the vibrations as an agitation of strands of nerves as if they might move like strings of a violin struck him as "highly absurd" (p. 12). In short, to account for the vibratory transmission of the nerve impulse, he seemed to find it necessary to assume conjoint involvement of molecular neural particles and Newton's aether. The precise nature of this conjoint activity was left vague. There is a hint to the effect that the neural activity exercises an indirect influence on what Hartley called "the pulses of the aether." He mentioned this in connection with a discussion of four ways in which the neural vibrations differ from one another· in "degree, kind, place, and line of direction." Differences in degree, he explained, account for differences in intensity as sensory impressions are stronger or weaker and induce changes in the amplitude of vibration. The changes in question "affect the medullary particles more or less vigorously, either directly and immediately, or mediately, by generating a greater or less degree of condensation in the pulses of the aether" (p. 31). Evidently the latter "pulses" were deemed to be different from the neural "pulses."

What Hartley meant by this exposition is hard to determine. His reference to *kind* of vibration is easier to understand. As opposed to amplitude, it had to do with frequency of vibration and thus was to provide for the neural concomitant of qualitative differences in sensation. His allusion to *place* had to do with changes resulting from having the vibrations reaching one brain region rather than another. Hartley thus seemed to have an inkling of what was to become the knotty problem of cortical localization. If so, he understood the problem to be related to what he designated as the "line of direction" taken by the vibrations, for he explained that "they differ in the line of direction, according as they enter by different external nerves." In this sense the optic nerve differs from the auditory nerve in its "line of direction." Accordingly, it appears that Hartley, as a pioneering physiological psychologist, had a glimpse of the problem of the functional specificity of neural pathways.

Two Kinds of Vibrations

In his neurological scheme of things, Hartley postulated two kinds of vibrations of the "infinitesimal, medullary particles." By calling them "infinitesimal," he was regarding them as too minute to be observed or to be subjected to some kind of indirect measurement of a kind that Anders Jonas Ångström (1814–1874) was to introduce a century later when wavelengths came to be measured in millionths of a millimeter. Under the circumstances, all Hartley could do was to speculate about his hypothesized vibrations. Like a settler opening up new territory, he had to rest content with crude makeshifts.[8] On the one hand he had to account for the neurology of sensation and motion, and on the other for the neurology of ideas. As impressions, sensations are mediated by cranial and spinal nerves; and as images, ideas are functions of brain activity. This distinction seemed obvious to Hartley from his knowledge of anatomy and his knowledge of the results of nerve and brain injury.

He also realized that memory images are usually fainter than their corresponding original sensory impressions. This fading effect suggested a difference in their respective neurological counterparts: one kind of infinitesimal vibrations propagated along the nerves and a different kind of still more minute vibrations characteristic of brain activity. He called the former *vibrations* and the latter *vibratiuncles* in the following Proposition (p. 58):

> *sensory vibrations, by being often repeated, beget in the medullary substance of the brain, a disposition to diminutive vibrations, which may also be called vibratiuncles and miniatures, corresponding to themselves respectively.*
>
> This correspondence of the diminutive vibrations to the original sensory ones, consists in this, that they agree in kind, place, and line of direction; and differ only in being more feeble, *i.e.* in degree.

In modern terminology, these vibrations and vibratiuncles might be regarded as hypothetical constructs that Hartley introduced in order to account for the perseverative effects of sensory stimulation. He was struck by the fact that the effects of stimulation continue after cessation of the stimulation, or, as he worded it: "The sensations remain in the mind for a short time after the sensible objects are removed" (p. 9). By way of example, he quoted Newton to the effect that a circle of fire is perceived when a burning coal is "nimbly moved round in a circle" and also that the sensation of white is obtained when the spectral colors are presented in rapid succession. Both of these phenomena have to do with the persistence

---

[8] These crude makeshifts have been drastically transformed by Hartley's neurological successors. In the two centuries since his time, the "territory" presents a very different picture. For a survey of the scene as it looked in the middle of the twentieth century, see Frank Brink's chapter in S. S. Stevens's *Handbook of Experimental Psychology* (1951).

of the positive afterimage. The fact that sometimes a tune keeps obtruding itself long after the orchestra stopped playing is a familiar instance of the kind of perseverative phenomenon Hartley had in mind. Hartley would have attributed the obsessive reactivation of the melody to his hypothetical construct of perseverating "miniature" vibrations in the brain as the cerebral counterpart of the experienced melody. This is a rather cumbersome way of putting it, but Hartley's parallelism renders simpler formulation less than adequate.

Hartley's Truncated Parallelism

It is difficult to deal with Hartley's parallelism because, upon examination, it seems to be an uncertain parallelism. The uncertainty is due to Hartley's failure to commit himself regarding the terminus or termini of the parallel streams of ideational processes and their concomitant miniature vibrations. The result is a truncated parallelism. He is definite about the latter physical vibrations coursing along the medullary substance of the brain, but vague about the course of mental processes as sensations give rise to their corresponding ideas. The Proposition in question reads as follows (p. 46):

> *sensations, by being often repeated, leave certain vestiges, types, or images, of themselves, which may be called,* simple ideas of sensation.

What is striking about the latter formulation is Hartley's failure to say anything about the locus of the "certain vestiges." Since he had localized their corresponding vibratiuncles in the brain, one might have expected him to have localized the vestiges in the "mind" or "soul" or even the "unconscious." Instead he just had their antecedent sensations "leave" them in an unspecified realm. This does not seem to have been an oversight. A more likely explanation is to be found in the fact that Hartley had misgivings about the adequacy of his parallelistic theorizing. As indicated in the following cumbersome passage, he had trouble finding a suitable word to designate the nature of the relationship between brain events and concomitant mental events (pp. 32–33):

> . . . if that species of motion which we term vibrations, can be shown by probable arguments, to attend upon all sensations, ideas, and motions, and to be proportional to them, then we are at liberty either to make vibrations the exponent of sensations, ideas, and motions, or these the exponents of vibrations, as best suits the inquiry; however impossible it may be to discover in what way vibrations cause, or are connected with sensations, or ideas; *i.e.* though vibrations be of a corporeal, sensations and ideas of a mental nature.

Describing sensations and ideas as "exponents" of vibrations, or vice versa, seemed to bother Hartley, for he followed the preceding statement

by consideration of a supposition which amounted to endorsement of interactionism. Just as Descartes had made the pineal body the "mechanism"
of psychophysical interaction, so Hartley attributed the same function to
what he referred to as "an infinitesimal elementary body" in this statement
(p. 34):

> If we suppose an infinitesimal elementary body to be intermediate between
> the soul and gross body, which appears to be no improbable supposition,
> then the changes in our sensations, ideas, and motions, may correspond to the
> changes made in the medullary substance, only as far as these correspond to
> the changes made in the elementary body. And if these last changes have some
> other source besides the vibrations in the medullary substance, some peculiar
> original properties, for instance, of the elementary body, then vibrations will not
> be adequate exponents of sensations, ideas, and motions.

It should now be evident why Hartley's parallelism was previously
described as a truncated parallelism and why he had nothing to say about
the realm to which the "vestiges" of sensation are to be allocated. It is as
if he could not decide whether to place them in the brain, in the soul, or
in the "elementary body" assumed to be "intermediate between the soul
and gross body."

The Problem of "Vestiges"

The issue is not to be dismissed as an inconsequential eighteenth-century
vagary of a medically trained associationist whose interest in theology
engendered a murky dualism. If this were the case, there would be no
justification for devoting space to the issue. In reality it has to do with a
problem that has implications for physiology, for biology, and for psychology in general and for associationism in particular. This is the problem
of the nature of the memory process, or, in broader terms, of the nature of
human and animal learning by means of which today's behavior is what it is
because of what was experienced yesterday or last year or even earlier.

In effect, Hartley was tackling this momentous question: How does it come
about that the consequences of experience are preserved long after the
experiences themselves have become history? All he could propose in the
way of an answer was to say that experiences as sensory impressions must
"leave" something of themselves. What was left was described by vague
terms like "vestiges, types, or images." Just where and how the latter aftereffects of experiences were deposited or retained was a question that Hartley
ignored. At all events, he failed to raise the question. It is difficult to believe
that it failed to occur to him.[9] He may have ignored it because he found it
too baffling.

---

[9] It is difficult to believe this because he really was concerned with the locus of
psychological events. As mentioned earlier, for example, he had something to say
about the "place" and "line of direction" of the diminutive vibrations.

Even if Hartley could not decide whether the "vestiges" of experience were to be localized in the brain or in the mind, some of his successors were ready to render a decision. For instance, the German psychologist Friedrich Beneke (1798–1854) took a definite stand with respect to this issue in a volume published in 1832 and entitled *A Textbook of Psychology as a Natural Science.*[10] According to J. T. Merz (1965, p. 209), Beneke was greatly influenced by the "English thinkers of the Associational school" and was especially interested in the application of psychological principles to learning and teaching. He might thus be classified as a pioneer educational psychologist. As such he was, of course, concerned with the problem of retaining or remembering that which has been taught. He did not refer to the "vestiges" left by experience. Instead he referred to "traces" resulting from sensory impressions.

As an opponent of faculty psychology, Beneke did not think of these traces as impressions made on an independent faculty of memory, as the common phrase "memory traces" might suggest. Neither did he make them neural traces or brain traces. Instead, as Gardner Murphy has noted (1949, p. 97), Beneke dispensed with such possible physiological considerations and "insisted on the right of psychology to treat of its laws without recourse to the data of another science." Beneke thus conceived of traces as belonging to the realm of the mind. In view of his educational interests, he might have illustrated this by saying that the recall of material learned in secondary school can take place years after graduation because of "traces" left in the mind. This is another way of referring to Hartley's "vestiges" of experience, but not at all more clarifying as a descriptive term.[11] As a matter of fact, long before Beneke, Hartley had made incidental use of the word "trace" as a synonym for the "vestige" of a sensory impression.

Another term for Hartley's "vestiges" was introduced by the biologist Richard Semon (1859–1918). Unlike Beneke, he had no reluctance to regard them as localized in the brain; he took it for granted that learning must entail some kind of structural or biochemical modification of brain tissue. For a man of seventy to recall what he had learned in school decades earlier must mean a recording or a storing of the effects of the learning during the intervening years. Consequently, Semon proposed the term "engram" to designate an hypothesized change in brain tissue to account for the retention of what has been learned or experienced. (Presumably the recall

---

[10] Because of failure to gain access to this book, what is being said about it is based upon secondary sources except for a brief selection included in B. Rand's *Classical Psychologists* (1912).

[11] This should not be interpreted as meaning that Beneke's notion of "traces" has been eliminated from modern psychology. Students of the memory process continue to employ the term. For example, in a 1966 article dealing with short-term memory, L. R. Peterson in referring to the work of two students of the memory process wrote this sentence: "Their objective was to see if a single presentation leaves any lasting trace."

of the formula for picric acid involves a different engram from the one involved in the recall of the difference between a gerund and a participle.)

Engrams have never been observed and their existence is purely conjectural. Had Semon been familiar with the term, he might have called them *intervening variables*. Incidentally, Semon regarded engrams as falling within the scope of a broader concept which he called *mneme*. By the latter term he was designating a universal tendency of all living forms—trees, worms, protozoa, and men—to be influenced by what *has happened* to them as well as by what *is happening* to them. In Semon's phrase, as quoted by W. Stern (1938, p. 189), all life is "historically conditioned," so that the past has a bearing on the present.[12]

To say that the past has a bearing on the present is a commonplace observation. It applies to physical events as well as to mental events. A particular automobile accident, for example, may be attributed to the blowout of an old tire. In this instance what had happened to the tire long before the accident is presumed to be a cause of the present accident and as such would be classified as a physical cause. Similarly, for a car to skid on an icy road would be classified as a physical event. If, however, on a subsequent occasion the driver were to reduce his speed at the sight of an icy road, his action would constitute a mental event. By hypothesis his memory of the previous mishap would call for reduced speed. Bertrand Russell, influenced by Semon's notion of mneme, would have classified this as an instance of *mnemic causation*. In *The Analysis of Mind* (1921), Russell made such mnemic causation the distinctive hallmark of a mental event. Whenever behavior is modified or influenced by reminders of a previous experience, mnemic causation is being brought into play. The reminders are signs, signals, or symbols of what has been experienced or is about to be experienced. Ability to respond to them as surrogates for experience is the *sine qua non* of a mental reaction. In the case at hand, the mere sight of the icy road, being a symbolic reminder of the dangerous skid, serves as the mnemic cause of pressure on the brake pedal.

What Russell attributed to mnemic causation others have attributed to *associative memory*. The latter phrase means substantially the same as the former one: the sight of an icy road being associated with the memory of an earlier accident suffices to make the driver cautious. Unless the earlier accident had left some sort of record of itself, there would be neither mnemic causation nor associative memory. Learning by experience—the basic tenet of associationism—presupposes such a record. Beneke's traces, Semon's engrams, and Hartley's vestiges are just different ways of referring to such a record.

In the final analysis, it seems futile to regard one of these terms as being

---

[12] For elaboration of Semon's concept of mneme, see Chapter X of the volume by Stern (1938) and Chapter V in E. Rignano's *Biological Memory* (1926).

descriptively more accurate than the other two. This follows because the neurophysiology of memory has not yet revealed a neural equivalent of the serpentine markings to be found in the grooves of a phonograph record. R. W. Gerard, a neurophysiologist who has concerned himself with this problem, has referred to such markings indiscriminately as "neural traces" and as "memory traces" and has been candid enough to write that "the nature of trace is almost a pure guess" (1953, p. 121). In this connection, one of the questions he raised was reminiscent of Hartley's approach to the problem, for Gerard asked, "Are memories marks placed on violin strings or are they wave trains playing over those strings?" This query suggests that Hartley's eighteenth-century vibrational neurology is not altogether alien to the conjectures of a twentieth-century neurophysiologist.

Hartley as Pioneer Psychophysiologist

Just as psychiatrists differ from neurologists, so psychophysiologists differ from neurophysiologists. The existence of such areas of specialization reflects implicit recognition of the conventional mind-body dichotomy. Although there is considerable overlap in the problems encountered by workers in these fields of endeavor, an underlying difference in orientation accounts for their separation into distinct specialties.

In general, the neurophysiologist may be said to concern himself with investigations of the functions of the structural characteristics of the nervous system. He takes his point of departure from such characteristics by asking, for example, what is the function of the red nucleus or of the cerebellum or of the thalamus or of some spinal tract or any other apparently distinct neural structure.

In contrast, the psychophysiologist takes his point of departure from what he happens to regard as distinctively characteristic of mental life and then proceeds to try to determine the cerebral or neurophysiological correlates of such characteristics. He asks, for example, about the bodily concomitants of attention, of anger, of visual imagery, of laughter, of idle daydreaming, of reasoning, of feeling tired, of writing and talking, and of the thousand and one other experiences and activities he notes in himself and others. His knowledge of the existence of these experiences and activities far exceeds his knowledge of their concomitant brain physiology. Indeed, more is known about the psychology of thinking than about the neurology of thinking, and about the psychology of prejudice than about the neurology of prejudice. We know that fallacious thinking occurs even though we cannot yet say anything about the neurology of logical blunders. All this is so obvious that citing more examples would amount to listing tedious truisms.

The chief reason for considering the subject is to set the stage for an exposition of Hartley's mode of procedure. He began with what he took to be the facts of sensation, of perception, and of associated ideas. This was his point of departure from which he embarked upon his speculative neurologizing.

The issue is important because of its bearing on Hartley's associationism. For example, his Proposition X deals with the psychology of association, while his Proposition XI deals with the presumed neurology of association. Each of these calls for some clarification; hence they will be treated under separate headings.

The Psychology of Association

Proposition X reads as follows (p. 65):

Any sensation A, B, C, *etc., by being associated with one another a sufficient number of times, gets such power over the corresponding ideas* a, b, c, *etc., that any one of the sensations* A, *when impressed alone, shall be able to excite in the mind,* b, c, *etc., the ideas of the rest.*

Sensations may be said to be associated together, when their impressions are either made precisely at the same instant of time, or in the contiguous successive instants. We may therefore distinguish association into two sorts, the synchronous, and the successive.

The influence of association over our ideas, opinions, and affections, is so great and obvious, as scarcely to have escaped the notice of any writer who has treated of these, though the word *association,* in the particular sense here affixed to it, was first brought into use by Mr. Locke. But all that has been delivered by the ancients and moderns, concerning the power of habit, custom, example, education, authority, party-prejudice, the manner of learning the manual and liberal arts, etc., goes upon this doctrine as its foundation, and may be considered as the detail of it, in various circumstances.

From the preceding formulation it seems evident that Hartley, unlike Hume, had no reservations regarding association as something dynamic; hence his use of the word "power." He also differed from Hume in his recognition that this "power" is exercised on simultaneous as well as on successive events. To cite a simple example: a violinist's idea of his instrument would be the resultant of simultaneous or concurrent visual, tactual, auditory, and kinesthetic sensations. According to Hartley, they would be *synchronously* associated into a unified impression of the violin. However, the violinist's mastery of a new musical composition would entail the temporal succession of the notes being played in sequential association. Similarly, recognition of a familiar word would exemplify synchronous association, while reading a series of paragraphs would involve successive association.

It is also well to note the broad scope of Hartley's associationism. By implication its "power" accounts for the habit of smoking, for the custom of tipping waiters, for the influence of a good example, for the effect of classroom drills, for the genesis of attitudes, and for learning in general. As a concept it is thus not restricted to ideational affairs as suggested by a literal interpretation of the phrase "association of ideas." In fact, Hartley was careful to include the learning of "manual" arts in his elaboration of the diversity of situations to be explained in terms of the doctrine of association. From this viewpoint, learning to upholster a sofa is just as much a matter of associative learning as memorizing a speech. Both kinds of activity call for making appropriate connections, between successive muscular adjustments in the one case or between a sequence of words in the other case.

The Neurology of Association

Having sketched the psychology of association, Hartley then considered the neurology of association. In doing so, as already indicated, he was moving from the familiar to the unfamiliar or from the known to the unknown. Under the circumstances, Proposition XI, despite its dogmatic tone, is to be regarded as more conjectural than Proposition X.

Proposition XI reads as follows (p. 67):

> *Any vibrations, A, B, C, etc., by being associated together a sufficient number of times, get such a power over a, b, c, etc., the corresponding miniature vibrations, that any of the vibrations A, when impressed alone, shall be able to excite b, c, etc., the miniatures of the rest.*

Hartley went into considerable detail in trying to show how such a cluster of associated vibrations may be presumed to gain control over the corresponding cluster of miniature vibrations. What he did was to translate his analysis of a particular "observation" into some neural or cerebral vibration as the concomitant of each constituent fragment into which the observed experience had been analyzed.

As he conceived it, "all sensations and vibrations are infinitely divisible" and their "infinitesimal parts" are held together by association. He introduced the idea of a horse as a case in point. In his view, "We could have no proper idea of a horse, unless the particular ideas of the head, neck, body, legs, and tail, peculiar to this animal stuck to each in the fancy, from frequent joint impression" (p. 70). Taken literally, of course, these "parts" of the horse are hardly "infinitesimal." However, as seems evident from other examples employed by Hartley, he would have pointed out that any one of these "parts" involves still smaller ones. Thus the head contains eyes, ears, mouth, and nose, and each of these smaller "parts" can be analyzed into still smaller ones. All these infinitely divisible ideational "parts" would have to have their vibrational counterparts to give rise to the complex idea of the whole horse. Furthermore, as expressed in Proposition X, let *A* symbolize the vibration corresponding to the "sensation" of the horse's hoof; then *A* occurring by itself may suffice to excite all the miniature vibrations corresponding to the rest of the horse, with the result that the percipient of the hoof will find himself thinking of a horse and not just of the hoof. The hoof as part of the horse is associated with all the other parts; hence association accounts for the arousal of the idea of the whole animal.

The "parts" into which Hartley analyzed experiences were also referred to as "simple ideas of sensation," and their linkage to one another by association resulted in "clusters and combinations" that, he reported, will finally "coalesce into one complex idea, by the approach and comixture of the several compounding parts." By way of example he mentioned the "coalescence of letters into syllables and words" as leading to complex ideas symbolized by or associated with the words.

A Critique of Associationism

At this juncture it might be well to digress in order to give some consideration to a long-deferred issue: the adequacy of association as an explanatory principle. This, as mentioned in Chapter 8, constitutes one of the "persistent riddles of psychology." As formulated in that chapter, the "riddle" takes this form:

Why is it that from one viewpoint the old laws of association seem to serve as a satisfactory explanation for the facts of learning, memory, and mental organization in general and yet from another viewpoint they seem unsatisfactory?

Although the question was raised in the earlier chapter, it was deemed advisable to postpone discussion of its implications. This time has now arrived; since, as outlined in the present chapter, with Hartley the empiricist tradition culminated in association psychology as a system. Under the circumstances it seems appropriate to come to grips with the long-deferred question by asking, "In what respects is association 'unsatisfactory' as a psychological principle?" To answer this question, a convenient point of departure is supplied by Hartley's example of associations involved in one's idea of a horse.

As an advocate of associationism, Hartley maintained that one's idea of a horse is a product of experience. In this sense all associationists are empiricists. This generalization, however, is not to be construed as meaning that all empiricists are associationists in accordance with Hartley's concept of association. To put it a little differently: it is possible to reject the latter concept and still accept experience as the indispensable foundation for the acquisition of knowledge and skills. Both associationists and antiassociationists can thus be viewed as basing such acquisition on experience. They part company when venturing to explain how this acquisition takes place. Those who agree with Hartley would explain it in terms of the summation of the constituent parts into which a given experience has been analyzed. Each part involves a particular idea, so that knowledge of an experienced object results in a collection or cluster of such associated ideas. This cluster is what Hume called a "bundle" of ideas.

As applied to Hartley's horse, the "bundle" would contain all the constituent features of the animal that, in Hartley's phrasing, have become "stuck to each other in the fancy, from frequent joint impression." The idea of the whole horse is thus the resultant of getting the parts of the animal to stick together "in the fancy." By implication, perception of the parts is prior in time to perception of the whole, and only "frequent joint impression" of these parts will be followed by perception of the whole animal. To paraphrase Euclid: the whole animal is equal to the sum of its parts or, as Hartley put it, the parts have "coalesced" into the whole animal.

Apparently, despite his recognition of synchronous association, Hartley was not ready to account for the "complex" idea of a horse in terms of such simultaneity of impressions. Those who rejected the "bundle" theory of perception, however, held that the whole is different from the sum of its parts and that its perception precedes recognition of the parts as constituent features of the whole. Such recognition comes later as a process of differentiation from the perceived whole. For example, a baby gets to recognize its mother long before it becomes cognizant of specific features having to do with posture, gait, eye color, shape of nose, height, weight, and such other details as might interest a portrait painter or the chief of a missing-persons bureau at police headquarters. Similarly, these critics of Hartley's associationism would argue that the baby's acquisition of language precedes awareness of isolated speech sounds as described by phoneticians. The baby learns to call for its mother without knowing anything about the constituent syllables or letters employed in writing the word "mother." Furthermore, when just a few years old, the child can be taught to recognize the word by its visual appearance without bothering about the individual letters that Hartley might have said have been "stuck" together to form the word.

The issue under consideration was already touched upon in Chapter 3, in the course of explaining the difference between holism and atomistic analysis. It was pointed out that analysis of a perception into a cluster of associated sensations may be descriptively accurate and yet be misleading if it should then be assumed the individual sensations as mental elements had first to be brought together in order to synthesize a perception. This would be akin to arguing that in the history of a child's perceptual development it will be unable to perceive an orange as an orange until it has had prior awareness of each of the sensations—visual, tactual, olfactory, and gustatory—into which the perception of the fruit can be analyzed. For associationists to argue this way by reducing experience to component sensations involves them in what Brett said about this (1912, Vol. I, p. 85):

> The fallacy of sensationalism lies in its persistent habit of constructing the history of mind backward; it finds in sensation the last product of analysis, and then makes it the first element of construction.

Somewhat related to the fallacy mentioned by Brett is an objection to the Hartleyean kind of perceptual analysis as voiced by G. F. Stout (1860–1944) back in the 1890s. According to him, "it is quite false to regard an association as merely an aggregate of disparate units," since "the *form* of the new idea is quite as important as the elements which it comprises" (1896, Vol. II, p. 47). The word "SAW" is made up of the same "units" as the word "WAS," and yet the perceptual difference in the resulting form or pattern is of coordinate importance with identity of these units. Similarly, an aggregate of separate musical notes may be arranged to yield different melodic forms or patterns. The character or identity of each note changes as it becomes an integral part of a different melody, just as the meaning of a word may change drastically in different contexts.

Associationists, Stout argued, seem to have overlooked this phenomenon; they seem "to assume that the parts that go to form the whole retain their identity unimpaired" when as a matter of fact "each part or element is *ipso facto* modified by the very fact of its entering into such combination." That form may be altogether independent of component parts was made evident by a simple example Stout introduced in a later volume (1913, p. 151) when he called attention to the way in which round stones can be piled up to form a pyramid. The resulting pyramidal shape of the "associated" stones has nothing to do with the spherical form of the individual parts.[13] In the language of Gestalt psychology, the pyramid as a whole is different from the sum of its parts.

Just how Hartley might have answered such objections to his associationism must remain conjectural. He never had to face them, for they were all raised long after his time. In his day it seemed obvious that association served as a regnant principle of explanation. He might have reminded his critics that all understanding depends upon knowledge of how things are connected or associated and such knowledge comes with experience. Once the child has learned the alphabet, he can connect the letters into words. And when he hears the letters "H-I-J," the "power" of association will induce him to think of the letter K. Knowledge of the letters is the foundation for reading, just as knowledge of numbers is the prelude to multiplication, division, and subtraction. His education proceeds by mastery of simple

---

[13] Stout was not alone in stressing the importance of form perception. One of his Austrian contemporaries, Christian von Ehrenfels (1859–1932), introduced the term *"Gestaltqualität,"* or form quality, to designate what he regarded as a factor in perception that is different from and not reducible to its instigating sensory elements. His views did not constitute as much of a break with associationistic psychology as those of Stout. Both men reflected the influence of Brentano's act psychology and they both, working independently of one another, were writing about the perception of form in the 1890s. As a result of his interest in and development of the topic, von Ehrenfels became the leader of a movement known as the *Austrian School* or the *School of Gestaltqualität.* Stout was not a member of this school. Neither were those who, starting around the year 1912, launched the not altogether unrelated movement of Gestalt psychology.

things before complex ones can be understood. Simple ideas precede complex ones in mental development, and the transition is from the concrete to the abstract, from the elementary to the advanced, and from the particular to the general.

All this suggests advancing from parts to wholes and from elements to compounds and not vice versa. It seemed self-evident to the associationists that there could be no understanding of the whole without prior knowledge of its constituent parts; thus the idea of "regiment" presupposes the idea of "soldier" and the idea of "library" presupposes the idea of "books." Accordingly, given the associationists' *tabula rasa* view of the genesis of mind, they had sound reasons for describing its growth as starting with sensations as elementary units that in the course of experience become associated into percepts and then, with still more experience, give rise to concepts. Similarly, they could describe the growth of motor control as a process of associating or combining simple reflexes into increasingly complex coordinated acts of skill. Without this capacity to form associations, Hartley might have argued, it would be impossible for man to develop a mind and to achieve muscular control. And had he known about the "riddle of association," he might have cited these considerations to show that "association seems to serve as a satisfactory explanation for the facts of learning, memory, and mental organization in general."

Summary Review

Instead of continuing with such speculation about "observations" that Hartley might have made, it seems preferable to resume consideration of "observations" he really did make. It is just a little more than two hundred years since he published his *Observations on Man*. One of its chief values as a contribution to the history of psychology is that it shows what the field of psychology looked like two centuries ago. Stated more accurately, it shows what the field looked like to a thoughtful, pious, scholarly eighteenth-century physician. He cultivated the field as an avocational pursuit over a period of eighteen years as time from his busy medical practice permitted. Some of his "observations" were a direct result of his medical orientation and his work with patients. The point was already made at the beginning of this chapter. By way of reminder and summary these other points were made in the rest of the chapter:

1. Empiricism's implicit reliance on the principle of association became explicit in the work of Hartley. With him, empiricism became associationism and thus gave association psychology systematic status.

2. He was not influenced by the writings of Hume.

3. Three sources of influence entered into the development of his psychology: (a) appreciation of the "power of association" came from the

Reverend Mr. Gay, from Locke, and "other ingenious persons"; (b) knowledge of man's "frame" with particular reference to the structure and functions of the nervous system was a product of his medical studies; and (c) familiarity with the ether hypothesis and the concept of vibrations came from his studies of Newton.

4. In close to a hundred Propositions, the principle of association is applied to a wide range of topics: the special senses, memory, dreams, language, likes and dislikes, sexual desire, and so on.

5. Hartley was not only a pioneer *systematic* associationist but also a pioneer physiological psychologist, as is indicated by (a) his general interest in the question of the bodily concomitants of mental functions; (b) his recognition of a direct relationship between neuropathology and psychopathology; (c) his anticipation of the problem of the specificity of neural pathways as well as the problem of cortical localization; and (d) his theory of vibrations in afferent nerves as correlates of sensation and vibratiuncles in the brain as correlates of images and ideas.

6. He was the first to emphasize the difference between synchronous or concurrent associations and successive or sequential ones.

7. His concept of association was not restricted to ideational association but extended to include acquisition of motor skills, cultivation of food preferences, adoption of customs, and the formation of habits and attitudes; hence to all learning.

8. Despite his interest in physiological psychology, Hartley was more of a parallelist than an interactionist. His parallelism, however, was found to be truncated.

9. Hartley's parallelism is shown by his formulation of separate and distinct Propositions to account for the *psychology* of association on the one hand and for the *neurology* of association on the other.

10. He raised the question of how the effects of experience are preserved and suggested they must leave "vestiges" of themselves as the basis for subsequent recall. This suggestion was congruent with Beneke's later reference to memory "traces" as well as to Semon's still later notion of "engrams."

11. With reference to what was mentioned in Chapter 8 regarding the adequacy of association as an explanatory principle, it was deemed advisable to introduce a brief critique of associationism by way of outlining later objections to the doctrine and also by way of conjecturing what Hartley might have argued in defense of the doctrine.

Concluding Comment

The section dealing with a critique of associationism neglected to mention what some critics would consider a serious shortcoming of the doctrine. In some ways this is just as well, for the issue is sufficiently important to merit separate consideration in this concluding section.

The issue has to do with the notion of vestiges, traces, or engrams as residues of experienced sensory impressions.[14] According to associationism, such residues account for retention of what has been experienced. There are two ways in which this conventional teaching may be interpreted: (1) the impression leaves some sort of neural or ideational facsimile of itself; or (2) the significance or meaning of the impression is retained despite the absence of any residual duplicate of the instigating impression. A child may be taught to recite the Lord's Prayer in Latin just as an exercise in rote memory. There need be no understanding of the meaning of any of the words, and yet after a sufficient number of repetitions the youngster can demonstrate verbatim recall of the prayer. Such a performance seems to be in harmony with the engram type of theory. On the other hand, after having an interesting story read to him, the child may be asked to tell the story in his own words and succeed in giving the gist of the story without slavish adherence to the original wording.

An especially striking instance of such freedom from dependence on the original wording has been supplied by W. Stern (1938, p. 205). He referred to an article by J. Ronjat, a French linguist whose wife was German and whose son thus grew up in a bilingual household. From early infancy the mother and nursemaid spoke German to the boy, while the father always talked to him in French. Once, when the boy was two and a half years old, the father asked him to leave the room and go to the nursemaid because the room was too cold. His exact words were, "*Ne reste pas ici, il fait trop froid*" ("Don't stay here, it is too cold"). When the child reached the nursemaid, he said "*Papas Zimmer ist zu kalt*" ("Papa's room is too cold"). What he had translated was not a German version of the individual words he had heard. Whether he had even noticed them as individual words is open to question. If so, then the words as words had not been associated. Instead he had grasped the *meaning* of the whole sentence. This is what he retained and this is what he put into his own words. Instances of this sort, Stern wrote, "conclusively disprove the 'trace' theory of the mnemic process."

What Ronjat's little boy demonstrated was that the mnemic process is not something like the process of cutting a phonograph record of a speech in which the sound of each word leaves an imprint of itself on the *tabula rasa* of the record. Terms like "trace" or "vestige" or "engram" are descriptively appropriate when applied to the imprint. It would also be descriptively correct to regard each imprint as *associated* or connected with the adjacent imprint,

---

[14] The issue is far more complicated than Hartley could possibly have suspected. As shown in a 1966 article by J. L. McGaugh, it is being subjected to provocative experimental study by some contemporary psychologists. Its complexity is suggested by the fact that, as McGaugh points out, "there may be three memory trace systems": one to provide for immediate memory, another for longer-lasting short-term memory, and one for the still longer instances of relatively permanent memory. Under the circumstances, should this supposition be verified, McGaugh concludes: "Any search for *the* engram or *the* basis of memory is not going to be successful."

so that the entire series of imprints results in a facsimile of the speech. Moreover, if each separate imprint were viewed as analogous to what the associationists called an *idea,* then the speech as recorded, in accordance with the trace or engram theory, would be the mechanical equivalent of the association of ideas. But the little boy failed to act as if each separate word of his father's request had been separately recorded; hence there was no series of separate ideas to be associated.

Instead there was *understanding* of the import or significance of the request as formulated in French by the father and as expressed in German by the little boy. Neither Hartley's vestiges nor Beneke's traces nor Semon's engrams can account for this result. What the boy expressed in German was not a "facsimile" or translation of what he had heard in French. Consequently there is no need to puzzle over a mysterious transformation of French engrams into German ones or of French ideas into German ones. The incident merits this amount of attention because it leads to this question: In understanding the *meaning* of his father's request, was the boy associating ideas, or—to put it very simply—was he just dealing with a cold room? Another way of putting this is to ask whether, strictly speaking, it is ever sound psychology to say that our "ideas" are associated.

The first man to raise this question was Thomas Reid (1710–1796) of Scotland. Reid launched a movement which became known as the *Scottish School.* As head of the movement, Reid was opposed to some phases of British empiricism and to Hartley's vibrational associationism, but his main target was Hume rather than Hartley. Despite this opposition, the British psychological tradition continued to flourish, particularly as a result of the work of James Mill (1773–1836). Mill endorsed many of Hartley's teachings, and in some ways they served as the foundation for Mill's early nineteenth-century continuation of the British tradition. It seems advisable to put off further consideration of this tradition until the chapter after next and to devote the next chapter to the movement initiated by Reid, in order to find out what he had against empiricism in general and to the notion of ideational association in particular.

References

Boring, E. G. *A History of Experimental Psychology,* 2nd ed. New York: Appleton-Century-Crofts, 1950.

Brett, G. S. *A History of Psychology,* Vol. I. London: George Allen and Unwin, 1912.

Brink, F. "Excitation and Conduction in the Neuron," in S. S. Stevens (ed.). *Handbook of Experimental Psychology.* New York: John Wiley and Sons, 1951, pp. 50–93.

Gerard, R. W. "What Is Memory?" *Scientific American,* 1953, *199,* 118–126.

Hartley, D. *Observations on Man, His Frame, His Duty and His Expectations,* 2 vols. Bath and London: James Leake and Wm. Frederick, 1749.

McGaugh, J. L. "Time-Dependent Processes in Memory Storage," *Science,* 1966, *153,* 1351–1358.

Merz, J. T. *A History of European Thought in the Nineteenth Century,* Vol. III. New York: Dover Publications, 1965. (First published in 1912.)

Murphy, G. *Historical Introduction to Modern Psychology,* rev. ed. New York: Harcourt, Brace and Company, 1949.

Peterson, L. R. "Short-Term Memory," *Scientific American,* 1966, *215,* 90–95.

Rand, B. (ed.). *The Classical Psychologists.* Boston: Houghton Mifflin Company, 1912.

Rignano, E. *Biological Memory.* (Translated by E. W. MacBride.) New York: Harcourt, Brace and Company, 1926.

Russell, B. *The Analysis of Mind.* New York: The Macmillan Company, 1921.

Starch, D. "The 100 Greatest Books Selected by 100 Qualified Persons," *Journal of Applied Psychology,* 1942, *26,* 257–267.

Stern, W. *General Psychology from the Personalistic Standpoint.* (Translated by H. D. Spoerl.) New York: The Macmillan Company, 1938.

Stout, G. F. *Analytic Psychology,* Vol. II. London: Swan Sonnenschein, 1896.

Stout, G. F. *A Manual of Psychology,* 3rd. ed. London: Hinds, Noble and Eldredge, 1913. (First edition published in 1899.)

19

The Scottish School and
Its "Faculties"

SOME CRITICISMS OF association psychology were outlined in the previous chapter. Most of these, it will be recalled, were raised by twentieth-century critics, men who thought of themselves as scientific psychologists rather than philosophical psychologists. They were preceded, however, by a group of philosophical psychologists whose objections to the teachings sponsored by the associationists were first voiced by Thomas Reid (1710–1796) of Scotland and continued by his nineteenth-century Scottish successors Dugald Stewart (1753–1828), Thomas Brown (1778–1820), and Sir William Hamilton (1788–1856). All these men, unlike the associationists they opposed, were university professors in Scotland; and the movement they represented is commonly referred to as the *Scottish School* of psychology.

The fact that Reid and his successors were university professors means that in some respects their orientation was different from the outlook of the nonacademic associationists. As professors, they had obligations of which the nonacademic scholar is relieved. To some extent this applies to all teachers in every generation, but it applied to Reid's generation with more than customary stringency as a result of Hume's iconoclastic views. The situation was well summarized by J. T. Merz (1965, Vol. III, pp. 222–223):

. . . the position of an official teacher imposes upon him obligations which the unofficial and extramural scholar has never to face. These demands, which the position of a university professor officially imposes, made themselves felt when the Scotch universities took up the teaching of moral and mental philosophy in the eighteenth century; they were accentuated when that crisis of thought had to be faced, which was marked by the writings of David Hume.

The crisis was especially acute for Reid because in addition to his university responsibilities, as an ordained minister he had responsibilities to his church. As a staunch Scotch Presbyterian he was troubled by Hume's skepticism, or what is more accurately to be described as Hume's agnosticism.[1] Such agnosticism challenged the philosophical foundations of Reid's religion; hence, like Kant, he might have given Hume credit for having goaded him into a critical examination of these foundations. In fact, he came close to acknowledging this indebtedness in the preface to one of his books, where he explained that he "never thought of calling in question the principles commonly received with regard to the human understanding, until the *Treatiste of Human Nature* was published in 1739" and that "the ingenious author of that treatise . . . hath built a system of skepticism which leaves no ground to believe any one thing rather than its contrary" (*Inquiry*, 1814, pp. iv–v). Furthermore, he added, there appeared to be no flaw in Hume's reasoning and the skeptical conclusions seemed to follow from the premises upon which they were based. Accordingly, he deemed it necessary to question these premises or else "to admit" the conclusions. His own philosophy was a product of this questioning.

Reid's Philosophy of Commonsense

Reid had received his first instruction in philosophy at the University of Aberdeen and upon graduation he became librarian at the university's Marischal College. Later he was the pastor of a church not far from Aberdeen. In 1752 he returned to that city to serve as professor of philosophy at King's College, after having won recognition as a philosopher when his first scholarly work appeared in the *Transactions* of the Royal Society. This was an examination and denial of a thesis he had come across in the course of his reading, to the effect that degrees of merit and virtue are amenable to quantitative treatment. Incidentally, he was well qualified to deal with the issue, since he had devoted himself to mathematical studies during the decade he had served as Marischal College librarian.

Reid's first definitely psychological work was published in 1764 under the title of *Inquiry into the Human Mind, on the Principles of Common Sense*. In that year he succeeded Adam Smith as professor of moral philosophy at the University of Glasgow. His next work of psychological relevance was undertaken after his retirement from Glasgow at the age of seventy-one and resulted in the publication of his essays on the *Intellectual*

---

1 Hume had called himself a skeptic with reference to the dogmas of theology and traditional philosophy. However, it was not so much a matter of denial regarding these dogmas as just not knowing whether or not they are true. In short, Hume was not denying the existence of God, or material substance, or a spiritual soul. For him, the referents of such terms are unknown or even unknowable. Had he known the word he would have called himself an "agnostic," but this word did not exist until Thomas Huxley introduced it around 1870. Furthermore, had he lived in the days of Auguste Comte, he might have called himself a "positivist."

Powers of Man in 1785 when he was seventy-five along with a companion volume three years later entitled *Essays on the Active Powers of the Human Mind.*

The movement started by Reid has come to be called the *Scottish School* because all his followers were connected with Scottish universities. Occasionally it is referred to as the *Common Sense School* because of the stress Reid placed upon what he regarded as the "principles of common sense." This was not the same as Aristotle's allusion to commonsense. Nor was it precisely synonymous with the popular meaning of commonsense as sound practical judgment in disposing of everyday problems having "obvious" solutions. There was a slight suggestion of the latter meaning when Reid lodged a protest in the name of commonsense against the Berkeley-Hume denial of the reality of material substance; but it had still other meanings for him. In fact, he failed to restrict the phrase to a single, sharply delimited meaning amenable to clear-cut formulation. In the words of Noah Porter (1811–1892),[2] one of his more sympathetic critics, "his conception of common sense was indefinite and inconsistently conceived" (D. S. Robinson, [ed.], 1961, p. 119); and G. S. Brett, a less sympathetic critic, found his use of "common sense" so vague as to have rendered "it impossible for anyone to say exactly what that was" (1921, Vol. III, p. 15).[3]

Reid objected not only to the Berkeley-Hume denial of a material world but also to the Descartes-Locke efforts to prove the existence of such a world. One of his views of commonsense can be glimpsed by noting what he had to say about such efforts (D. S. Robinson [ed.], 1961, pp. 139–141):

> Descartes . . . and Locke have . . . employed their genius and skill to prove the existence of a material world; and with very bad success. Poor untaught mortals

---

[2] Noah Porter was a keen student of the Scottish philosophers. As an educator and philosopher he belongs to the history of American philosophical psychology. After his graduation from Yale in 1831 he first became a Congregational minister and then was appointed professor of moral philosophy at Yale in 1846. His interest in psychology is reflected in his volume *The Human Intellect, with an Introduction upon Psychology and the Human Soul,* published in 1868. His chief claim to fame, however, is connected with the fact that he served as president of Yale from 1871 to 1886. Incidentally, many years later the Yale trustees appointed a more experimentally minded psychologist as president in the person of James Rowland Angell (1869–1949), who served from 1921 to 1937.

[3] In his *Essays on the Intellectual Powers,* Reid devoted one essay to the subject of commonsense. In it he argues that to believe "there can be any opposition between reason and common sense" would be absurd (A. D. Woozley [ed.], 1914, p. 338). Furthermore, he maintained, they always go together in the conduct of daily affairs. He equated commonsense with sound judgment in holding that (Woozley, pp. 330–331):

> A man of sense is a man of judgment. Good sense is good judgment. Nonsense is what is evidently contrary to right judgment. Common sense is that degree of judgment which is common to men with whom we can converse and transact business.

THOMAS REID (1710–1796)

DUGALD STEWART (1753–1828)

believe undoubtedly that there is a sun, moon and stars; an earth, which we inhabit; country, friend, and relations, which we enjoy; land, houses, and movables which we possess. But philosophers pitying the credulity of the vulgar, resolve to have no faith, but what is founded upon reason. They apply to philosophy to furnish them with reasons for the belief of these things which all mankind have believed, without being able to give any reason for it. And surely one would expect, that, in matters of such importance, the proof would not be difficult: but it is the most difficult thing in the world. For these . . . great men, with the best good will, have not been able, from all the treasures of philosophy, to draw one argument that is fit to convince a man that can reason, of the existence of any one thing without him. . . .[4]

It may be observed, that the defeats and blemishes in the received philosophy concerning the mind, which have most exposed it to contempt and ridicule of sensible men, have chiefly been owing to this—that the votaries of this Philosophy, from a natural prejudice in her favour, have endeavoured to extend jurisdiction beyond its just limits, and to call to her the dictates of Common Sense. But these decline this jurisdiction; they disdain the trial of reasoning, and dis own its authority; they neither claim its aid, nor dread its attacks.

In this unequal contest betwixt Common Sense and Philosophy, the latter will always come off both with dishonour and less; nor can she ever thrive till this rivalship is dropt, these encroachments given up, and a cordial friendship restored: for, in reality, Common Sense holds nothing of Philosophy, nor needs her aid. But, on the other hand, Philosophy . . . has no other root but the principles of Common Sense; it grows out of them, and draws its nourishment from them. Severed from this root, its honours wither, its sap is dried up, it dies and rots.

Evidently Reid recognized the possibility of conflict between the convictions of commonsense and the teachings of philosophy. He even maintained that in the event of a conflict, philosophy ought to submit to the guidance of commonsense. In his view, philosophic doubts regarding the existence of material substances and the inherent spirituality of mind were akin to "clouds and phantoms" that philosophy ought to be able to dispel. Should

---

[4] By the phrase "without him," Reid meant having independent existence in an external realm and continuing to exist in the absence of a percipient being. For Reir, commonsense sufficed to justify both the existence of percipient beings as well as a world of external objects. Merz (Vol. III, 1965) has a revealing comment on this phase of Reid's psychology:

Reid . . . appeals to common sense against the skepticism of Hume, as immediately revealing to us two facts: the existence of an external world, and that of the soul. These two principles are elements of our original nature as it came from the hands of the Creator. Every sensation which I receive brings with it the belief in an external object and of myself, the experiencing subject. Reid, in fact, appealed to . . . the data of consciousness, and in doing so, he opened up and cultivated the great field of observation of the phenomena of the inner world. He has been blamed for multiplying too much the number of these immediate data, but he and his followers have the merit of taking due note of the breadth and fullness of the human mind, of its active as well as its intellectual powers, and of encountering the one-sided intellectualism and the exclusiveness of those who would find the solution of the philosophical or psychological problem in a single principle.

philosophy lack the power to do so, so much the worse for philosophy. Exposure of such weakness, Reid added, would compel him to proclaim, "I despise Philosophy, and renounce its guidance—let my soul dwell with Common Sense." (Robinson [ed.], 1961, p. 140.)

Commonsense as Understood by Stewart

Just what kind of guidance Reid expected to receive from commonsense is difficult to specify. At the risk of begging the question, one might guess that he expected a person of ordinary commonsense to understand what he had in mind. Unfortunately, as we have noted, his use of the phrase was too inconsistent and vague to justify such an expectation. Even Dugald Stewart (1753–1828), professor of moral philosophy at the University of Edinburgh for close to thirty-five years and Reid's disciple and successor as head of the Scottish School, had reason to complain, "The phrase *Common Sense* . . . has been occasionally employed without a due attention to precision" (Robinson, p. 170). Stewart acknowledged this vagueness in connection with an effort to answer "objections to Reid's philosophy of common sense." According to one of these objections, for example, Reid's renunciation of the guidance of philosophy in favor of commonsense had been interpreted as meaning disparagement of conclusions arrived at by critical thinking when such conclusions fail to square with commonly accepted beliefs. This disparagement would be tantamount to trying to settle controversial scientific issues by majority vote of the scientifically unsophisticated masses. Stewart regarded this conclusion as a misinterpretation of Reid's meaning, and he tried to dispose of the objection by the following explanation (Robinson, p. 172):

> To speak . . . of appealing from the conclusions of philosophy to common sense, had the appearance, to title-page readers, of appealing from the verdict of the learned to the voice of the multitude; or of attempting to silence free discussion, by a reference to some arbitrary and undefinable standard, distinct from any of the intellectual powers hitherto enumerated by logicians. Whatever countenance may be supposed to have been given by some writers to such an interpretation of this doctrine, I may venture to assert, that none is afforded by the works of Dr. Reid. The standard to which he appeals is neither the creed of a particular sect, nor the inward light of enthusiastic presumption, but that constitution of human nature without which all the business of the world would immediately cease; and the substance of his argument amounts merely to this, that those essential laws of belief, to which skeptics have objected when considered in connexion with our scientific reasonings, are implied in every step we take as active beings; and if called in question by any man in his practical concerns, would expose him universally to the charge of insanity.

This last statement concerning insanity is not to be dismissed as rhetorical exaggeration. Had Stewart cared to elaborate upon it, he might have pointed out that the issues raised in a philosophic setting by men like Descartes, Berkeley, and Hume have very serious implications when raised in a psychiatric setting by ordinary patients. For a patient to express doubt about his personal existence or to deny the existence of his stomach or the outside world suggests mental breakdown to his psychiatrist. The patient is described as out of touch with "reality" and as harboring a *nihilistic* delusion. In other words, Stewart's allusion to insanity can be interpreted as an oblique way of suggesting that Reid's commonsense view of reality conforms to the psychiatric view.

Reid's concept of reality, Stewart indicated, is subject to misunderstanding when referred to as based upon the "principles of common sense." The "truths" Reid desired to suggest by the phrase, in Stewart's opinion, would be less subject to misunderstanding if they were called "fundamental laws of human belief" and given explicit formulation. By way of illustration, Stewart formulated some of them in the form of these italicized propositions (Robinson, p. 170):

> *I am the same person today that I was yesterday; The material world has an existence independent of that of percipient beings; There are other intelligent beings in the universe beside myself; The future course of nature will resemble the past.* Such truths no man but a philosopher ever thinks of stating to himself in words, but all our conduct and all our reasonings proceed on the supposition that that they are admitted. The belief of them is essential for the preservation of our animal existence; and it is accordingly coeval with the first operations of the intellect.

Reid's Distinction between Sensation and Perception

In thus explaining Reid's commonsense in terms of fundamental laws of belief, Stewart was making explicit what was implicit in Reid's psychology. Reid himself had already come close to equating his principles of common-sense with principles of belief. For example, in discussing imagination as contrasted with sensation and memory, he had concluded (*Inquiry*, 1814, p. 43):

> Sensation and memory . . . are simple, original, and perfectly distinct operations of the mind, and both of them are original principles of belief. Imagination is distinct from both, but is no principle of belief. Sensation implies the present existence of its object, memory its past existence, but imagination views its object naked, and without any belief of its existence or non-existence, and is therefore what the schools call *Simple Apprehension*.

Subsequently Reid no longer maintained that "sensation implies the present existence of its object." Instead he reserved the term "perception" to designate existence of an object and limited the word "sensation" to sensory impressions devoid of objective reference. In doing so, he was calling attention to an important distinction.[5] By way of illustration, he introduced the hypothetical case of a person who had never had any olfactory experience whatsoever and then, as his very first such experience, "finds himself affected" by the smell of a rose. By hypothesis he has not yet seen the flower, so that he has no way of connecting the smell with any external object or with any other kind of odor. As pure *sensation,* in Reid's words, the odor would have "no similitude to anything else, so as to admit of a comparison; and, therefore, he can conclude nothing from it, unless, perhaps, that there must be some unknown cause for it" (*Inquiry,* 1814, p. 38). Later when the person has become familiar with the flower as the "cause" of the odor, he will *perceive* it as the odor of a rose.

What initially had been a "meaningless" sensation now has objective reference. Perception, as understood by Reid, always has to do with an external object. In waking life, he pointed out, we perceive surrounding objects, remember objects or scenes formerly perceived, and imagine some that have never been perceived. These distinctions are readily made under ordinary circumstances. To the anticipated objection that mistakes occur in dreams or in a delirium, he had this to say (*Inquiry,* 1814, p. 47):

> I know it is said, that, in a delirium, or in dreaming, men are apt to mistake one for the other. But does it follow from this, that men who are neither dreaming nor in a delirium cannot distinguish them? I cannot tell: neither can I tell how a man knows that he exists. But, if any man seriously doubts whether he is in a delirium, I think it highly probable that he is, and that it is time to seek for a cure, which I am persuaded he will not find in the whole system of logic.

The preceding comment about the man's need for a "cure" justifies Stewart's later interpretation of Reid's notion of commonsense as related to a sane outlook, so that one lacking this kind of commonsense might be adjudged insane. If challenged, Stewart might have cited the above passage in support of what he had gleaned in the way of a psychiatric implication from Reid's notion. Still, this is a rather trivial issue. It is more important to revert to consideration of Reid's recognition of objective reference as the hallmark of perception.

---

[5] Merz refers to Reid's deep "psychological insight" in making this distinction and shows how it differs from the sensationalism of association psychology, in the following clarifying explanation of Reid's view of the problem (1965, Vol. III, p. 241):

> According to his view, single sensations or ideas were not the original given components but these consisted of perceptions, *i.e.* of single elements already joined together. He thus may be considered as the first psychologist who maintained that the thinking process in the adult intelligent person is not the putting together of loose material, but that the beginning of this synthesis is afforded already in our perceptions. The single sensation is itself a mental abstraction, and as such never given in experience alone.

For Reid, "Ideas" Are Never Associated

Objective reference, as understood by Reid, involves what might be regarded as his most original contribution to psychology. It has to do with the nature of ideational association. As noted at the close of the previous chapter, Reid was the first man to ask whether "ideas" are ever associated. In his view, the "existence of ideas" as Hume had defined ideas is open to question. This was one of Hume's premises that Reid set out to examine in his *Inquiry*. He announced this as his intention in the following prefatory statement (1814, pp. vi–vii):

For my own satisfaction, I entered into a serious examination of the principles upon which the skeptical system is built; and was not a little surprised to find, that, it leans with its whole weight upon a hypothesis, which is ancient indeed, and hath been very generally received by philosophers, but of which I could find no solid proof. The hypothesis I mean, is, that nothing is perceived but what is in the mind which perceives it: That we do not really perceive things that are external, but only certain images and pictures of them imprinted upon the mind, which are called *impressions and ideas*.

In the course of his "examination," Reid came to regard a phrase like "association of ideas" as psychological fiction. In a strongly worded indictment he maintained (1814, pp. 41–42):

. . . that no solid proof has ever been advanced of the existence of ideas; that they are a mere fiction and hypothesis, contrived to solve the phenomena of the human understanding; that they do not at all answer to this end; and this hypothesis, of ideas or images in the mind, or in the sensorium, is the parent of those many paradoxes so shocking to common sense, and of that skepticism which disgrace our philosophy of mind, and have brought upon it the ridicule and contempt of sensible man.

In the course of his elaboration of this indictment, Reid seems to have been especially opposed to association viewed as the passive or mechanical linkage of elementary units in the form of sensations and "ideas." Instead he seemed to be taking a stand in favor of the view that Franz Brentano (1838–1917) was to champion almost a century later in his *Psychology from the Empirical Standpoint* (1874). As explained in Chapter 4, Brentano's act psychology, with its emphasis on intentionality as an active process involving objective or transcendent reference, was also at variance with the empiricism of British associationists. At all events, there is a suggestion of Brentano's concept of a psychical act in Reid's recognition of transcendent reference as the essential characteristic of mental activity, even though his descriptive vocabulary is very different from that of Brentano. In his account of Reid's work, Brett, as shown in the following quotation (1921, Vol. III, p. 16), alluded to this verbal divergence by noting the way in which Reid accounted for mental activity in terms of an "inductive principle" (italics added):

> The association of ideas, both name and thing, is rejected in favour of an "inductive principle." Reid was both *original and right in thinking that "ideas" are not associated,* but his own exposition of "experience" is equivalent to the process called by others association; if, as is probable, Reid meant to assert the activity of the mind in "experience," as opposed to "association," his distinction may be reckoned valuable. That this was the case might be argued from the fact that Reid shifted the emphasis from interrelation of ideas to judgment, from mechanical union to something like a creative synthesis.

Brett's distinction between mechanical union and creative synthesis involves the difference between uncomprehending rote memory and original thinking. Reciting a list of memorized nonsense syllables, counting from one to ten, repeating the doggerel of some nursery rhymes, and reciting the alphabet are mechanical activities virtually devoid of meaning. Young children can readily master any one of these activities. Long before they have any notion of the concept of number, they can be taught to count from one to ten. In fact, they can be taught to count in French, Swedish, or any other language. The counting is an automatic laryngeal habit akin to the recitation of the Lord's Prayer in Latin by a person ignorant of Latin. Establishment of such laryngeal habits as an associated sequence of speech movements does not call for transcendent reference; hence there need be no understanding of what is being said.

Mechanical activities or automatic performances conform to the contiguity principle of the associationists. What Reid questioned, however, as pointed out by Brett, was the application of this principle to instances of genuine thinking. In effect Reid held that planning an experiment, inventing a machine, and analyzing the cogency of an argument are not activities that can be explained by reference to the contiguity of associated ideas.

Independently of Reid, the same stand was taken by William James many decades later in the early part of his chapter on association in the *Principles.* His indictment of this phase of associationism is so clearly expressed that it helps to clarify what Reid was driving at in his less clearly formulated indictment. This is the way James put it (1890, Vol. I, pp. 553–554):

> But the whole historic doctrine of psychological association is tainted with one huge error—that of the construction of our thoughts out of the compounding of themselves together of immutable and incessantly recurring "simple ideas." It is the cohesion of these which the "principles of association" are considered to account for. . . . [As already indicated] there are abundant reasons for

treating the doctrine of simple ideas or psychic atoms as mythological; and, in all that follows, our problem will be to keep whatever truths the associationist doctrine has caught sight of without weighing it down with the untenable incumbrance that the association is between "ideas."

Association, so far as the word stands for an *effect, is between* THINGS THOUGHT OF—*it is* THINGS, *not ideas which are associated in the mind.* We ought to talk of the association of *objects,* not of the association of *ideas.* And so far as association stand for a *cause,* it is between *processes in the brain* —it is these which, by being associated in certain ways, determine what successive objects shall be thought.

Had it occurred to Reid and James, they might have quoted Locke's definition of idea in support of their respective views; for Locke, it will be recalled, had defined an idea as "whatever is the *object* of understanding when a man thinks" (italics added). Taken at its face value, this definition ought to make the association of ideas, as James contended, the equivalent of the association of objects. Unfortunately, Locke's conversion of objects into congeries of simple ideas shifted the emphasis from thinking about thinking to preoccupation with the problem of connecting these simple ideas or psychic atoms, as James called them, in order to form objects.

Locke's primary qualities were supposed to be a kind of external nucleus around which the secondary qualities were projected for the eventual construction of the world of objects. However, with Berkeley's elimination of primary qualities by making *all* qualities secondary or mental, Locke's original object of understanding lost its objectivity and empiricists became bogged down in talk about association of ideas instead of association of objects. In the process, they overlooked or neglected the pointing function of ideas: that they point to or intend objects and thus have transcendent reference. But Reid, Brentano, and James did not overlook this attribute as they dispensed with what Reid had stigmatized as the "fiction" of simple ideas along with what James had regarded as the mythology of psychic atoms. To transform the reality of a world of objects into such fictions was to contradict what Reid called "commonsense."

Reid Not Opposed to Empiricism

Reid warned against acceptance of any psychological doctrine just because it has the backing of some authority either ancient or modern. His warning took this form (Woozley, p. 34):

Let us . . . lay down as a fundamental principle in our inquiries into the structure of the mind and its operations—that no regard is due to the conjectures or hypotheses of philosophers, however ancient, however generally received. Let us accustom ourselves to try every opinion by the touchstone of fact and experience.

In terms of this "fundamental principle," Reid's attack on British associationists is not to be construed as opposition to empiricism.[6] Thus, in accordance with his commonsense psychology, he would not have denied the role of experience in establishing such familiar connections as the one between the sight of a lemon and its sour taste or that between the sound of a violin and the thought of the instrument or that between the sight of a word like "boat" and the vessel symbolized.

Reid did not refer to such connections as associations. Instead he established a precedent followed by his successors in the Scottish School of substituting the word "suggestion" for the word "association." Interestingly, he may have been influenced by Berkeley in this choice; as mentioned in Chapter 16, Berkeley also preferred a descriptive phrase like "one idea may suggest another to the mind." He even used an illustration that Berkeley had introduced in elaborating upon the implications of being able to *hear* a coach being driven on the street while sitting in his study. Under the circumstances, although Reid made no mention of Berkeley in this connection, something akin to unconscious plagiarism may have been operative when he wrote the following (*Inquiry*, pp. 63–64):

> I beg leave to make use of the word *suggestion*, because I know not one more proper, to express a power of the mind, which seems entirely to have escaped the notice of philosophers, and to which we owe many of our simple notions which are neither impressions nor ideas, as well as many original principles of belief. I shall endeavour to illustrate, by an example, what I understand by this word. We all know, that a certain kind of sound suggests immediately to the mind, a coach passing in the street; and not only produces the imagination, but the belief, that a coach is passing. Yet there is here no comparing of ideas, no perception of agreements or disagreements, to produce this belief; nor is there the least similitude between the sound we hear and the coach we imagine and believe to be passing.

---

[6] He was opposed to the atomistic aspects of their empiricism as indicated by their emphasis on single sensations as the genetic foundation of knowledge. However, in his opposition he was not denying the role of experience as essential for cognitive development. Woozley, in the introduction to his edition of the *Intellectual Powers of Man*, has put it this way (1914, pp. xxxviii–xxxiv):

> Reid was anti-empiricist only in the sense that he held the empiricist psychology to be faulty—that by viewing our experience as made up of simple elements which our minds compound into various types of complex it gave a false account of what we are conscious of as happening, and that it led to a philosophy the procedure of which was synthetic but the material of which was too oversimplified for synthesis to produce true conclusions. Fundamentally this interpretation of empiricism seems fair: although Locke sometimes spoke as though ideas would be experientially complex, and although Hume admitted complex impressions, yet they concentrated their attention almost wholly on what they took to be the *simple* data of experience, and on the question what knowledge could be built up from them.

It is true that this suggestion is not natural and original; it is the result of *experience and habit* [italics added]. But I think it appears, from what hath been said, that there are natural suggestions: particularly, that sensation suggests the notion of present existence, and the belief that what we perceive or feel does now exist; that memory suggests the notion of past existence, and the belief that what we remember did exist in time past; and that our sensations and thoughts do also suggest the notion of a mind, and the belief of its existence, and of its relation to our thoughts. By a like natural principle it is, that a beginning of existence, or any change in nature, suggests to us the notion of a cause and complete our belief of its existence.

Belief in Causality Not a Product of Experience

As indicated in the latter paragraph, Reid's "natural suggestions" were opposed to those due to "experience and habit." By also calling them "original principles of belief," he made them native endowments and not products of learning. As such, it appears, they were to be included in his notion of commonsense. The information, knowledge, or convictions they supplied were thus not effects of sensory impressions or the results of philosophic reflections.

In particular, Reid regarded confidence in the principle that any change is necessarily due to some cause as an instance of one of these "natural suggestions." This conviction, of course, constituted one of his chief objections to Hume's disposition of the causal relationship. Belief in the principle of causation, Reid maintained, is indispensably necessary for the conduct of daily life. All prudent action depends upon it and to disregard it would be madness. Nevertheless, he added, a philosopher like Hume, who acted in accordance with this belief in his daily life, had seen fit to question its validity by reducing it to a matter of temporal contiguity based upon *experience.* It cannot be a product of experience, Reid contended, for the following reasons (D. S. Robinson [ed.], 1961, pp. 138–139):

First—*Because it is a necessary truth, and has always been received as a necessary truth. Experience gives no information of what is necessary or of what must be.*

We may know from experience, what is, or what was, and from that may probably conclude what shall be in like circumstances; but, with regard to what must necessarily be, experience is perfectly silent. . . .

[Furthermore] if we had experience, ever so constant, that every change in nature we have observed, actually had a cause, this might afford ground to believe, that, for the future, it shall be so; but no ground to believe that it must be so; and cannot be otherwise.

Another reason to show that this principle is not learned from experience is— *That experience does not show us a cause of one in a hundred of those changes which we observe, and therefore can never teach us that there must be a cause of all.*

Of all the paradoxes this author has advanced, there is not one more shocking to the human understanding than this, That things may begin to exist without a cause. This would put an end to all speculation, as well as to all the business of life. The employment of speculative men, since the beginning of the world, has been to investigate the causes of things. What pity is it, they never thought of putting the previous question, Whether things have a cause or not? This question has at last been stated; and what is there so ridiculous as not to be maintained by some philosopher?

The preceding defense of the principle of causation serves to illustrate what Reid referred to as "the experimental method of reasoning" that Hume had professed to employ. He noted that Hume had introduced the phrase and he approved of Hume's "very laudable attempt" to use the method. In his opinion, however, Hume had failed to adhere to one rule required by the method: "that conclusions established by induction ought never to exclude exceptions, if any such should afterwards appear from observation or experiment" (D. S. Robinson [ed.], p. 135). In other words, in the passage just quoted, Reid believed that he had found exceptions to Hume's conclusion regarding experience as the sole foundation for belief in the causal relationship. In addition, to revert to an earlier point, the passage also serves as an example of the way in which Reid appealed to "common-sense" as the arbiter of philosophic controversy.[7]

Concerning Reid's Respect for Hume

Just how Hume might have reacted to Reid's disparaging comments can never be determined. They were published in 1785, almost a decade after the death of Hume, so that Hume never had an opportunity to defend himself against the charge of having raised a "ridiculous" question. He might not even have anticipated Reid's vehement opposition to his work as a philosopher. More accurately, Hume had reason to expect opposition, but not the kind of condescending disparagement implied by Reid's use of the word "ridiculous." At all events, he would have had reason to anticipate Reid's high regard for him as a philosopher even though they differed on

---

[7] Once again, by way of final comment on this issue, it is well to realize that by appealing to "commonsense," Reid was not elevating popular beliefs above the reasoned conclusions of critical thinking. For him, "commonsense" involved judgment as more fundamental than the simple impressions of Locke and Hume. As Pringle-Pattison, one of Reid's Scottish successors, pointed out in the *Encyclopaedia Britannica* (11th ed., 1910):

The unit of knowledge is not an isolated impression but a judgment; and in such a judgment is contained, even initially, the reference both to a permanent subject and to a permanent world of thought; and, implied in these, such judgments, for example, as those of existence, substance, cause and effect. Such principles are not derived from sensation, but are "suggested" on occasion of sensation, in such a way as to

specific issues. Hume could have justified such anticipation by citing excerpts from a letter Reid had sent to him on March 18, 1763. Here are a few of Reid's words of commendation (quoted in Robinson, 1961, p. 133):

> . . . I shall always avow myself your disciple in metaphysics. I have learned more from your writings in this kind, than from all others put together. Your system appears to me not only coherent in all its parts, but likewise justly deduced from principles commonly received among philosophers; principles which I never thought of calling in question, until the conclusions you draw from them in the *Treatise of Human Nature* made me suspect them. . . . I agree with you . . . that if this system shall ever be demolished, you have a just claim to a great share of the praise, both because you have made it a distinct and determined mark to be aimed at, and have furnished proper artillery for the purpose.
>
> . . . A little philosophical society here . . . is much indebted to you for its entertainment . . . you are brought oftener than any other man to the bar, accused and defended with great zeal, but without bitterness. If you write no more in morals, politics, or metaphysics, I am afraid we shall be at a loss for subjects.

These words of deferential regard for Hume's standing as a philosopher were not an expression of a youthful scholar's understandable respect for a venerable senior colleague. At the time the letter was written Reid was no longer youthful nor had Hume become venerable: Reid was fifty-three and Hume was fifty-two. Hume's reputation as a philosopher had already been established. On the other hand, at the time Reid was writing to Hume, he was just getting his work on the *Principles of Common Sense* ready for publication. In fact, he had submitted portions of it to Hume for critical appraisal. According to Dugald Stewart, he did this because "he was anxious, before taking the field as a controversial writer, to guard against the danger of misapprehending or misrepresenting the meaning of his adversary" (Robinson, 1961, p. 130). This suggests some uneasiness about the outcome of his clash with Hume. For the next twenty years, however, Reid continued to lecture on his philosophy of commonsense; and presumably as his confidence in that philosophy increased, he became less anxious about the soundness of his criticisms of Hume.

---

constitute the necessary conditions of our having perceptive experience at all. Thus, we do not start with "ideas," and afterwards refer them to objects; we are never restricted to our own minds, but are from the first immediately related to a permanent world. Reid has a variety of names for the principles which, by their presence, lift us out of subjectivity into perception. He calls them "natural judgments," "natural suggestions," "principles of our nature," "first principles," "principles of commonsense." The last designation . . . was undoubtedly unfortunate, and has conveyed to many a false impression of Scottish philosophy. It has been understood as if Reid had merely appealed from the reasoned conclusions of philosophers to the unreasoned beliefs of common life. . . . Reid everywhere unites commonsense and reason, making the former "only another name for one branch or degree of reason." Reason, as judging of things self-evident, is called commonsense to distinguish it from ratiocination or reasoning.

Mental Powers: Fact or Fiction?

Reid became especially critical of Hume's denial of *cause* as a force or power. As may be recalled, Hume had contended that "we never have any impression that contains any power or efficacy." Reid subjected this contention to careful analysis during his many years of lecturing, an analysis that culminated in the publication of his *Essays on the Intellectual Powers of Man* in 1785. To show the weakness of one of Hume's arguments, Reid called attention to Hume's inconsistency in demanding a definition for the term "power" but not requiring definitions for words like "pride" and "humility." He made this clear in the following critique of Hume's formulation of the problem (Robinson, 1961, pp. 135–136):

> He begins with observing, "That the terms *efficacy, agency, power, force, energy,* are all nearly synonymous; and, therefore, it is an absurdity to employ any of them in defining the rest. By this observation," says he, "we reject at once the vulgar definitions which philosophers have given of *power* and *efficacy.*"
>
> Surely this author was not ignorant that there are many things of which we have a clear and distinct conception, which are so simple in their nature, that they cannot be defined any other way than by synonymous words. It is true that this is not a logical definition; but that there is, as he affirms, an absurdity in using it, when no better can be had, I cannot perceive.
>
> He might here have applied to *power* and *efficiency,* what he says, in another place, of *pride* and *humility.* "The passions of *pride* and *humility,*" he says, "being simple and uniform impressions, it is impossible we can ever give a just definition of them. As the words are of general use, and the things they represent the most common of any, every one, of himself, will be able to form a just notion of them without danger of mistake."

Under the circumstances, in frank opposition to Hume, Reid had no hesitation in using the word "power" in discussing psychological affairs. Nevertheless, as if mindful of the need to justify his use of the term, he explained why it, along with other psychological terms, could not be reduced to a satisfactory verbal definition. What he proposed instead might be construed as an approach to the modern concept of an operational definition.[8] At all events, he was careful to point out that the concept of mind has to do with activities and not with entities. He wrote, "The mind is active in its various ways of thinking; and, for this reason, they are called its operations,

---

[8] "Support for this interpretation is to be found in Chapter 9 in connection with what was referred to as the subjective aspect of operational definitions. By way of reminder P. W. Bridgman, the man who first formulated the concept of operational definitions, had recognized this when he wrote that "the most important part of science is private" and that "the operations by which I know what I am thinking about are different from the operations by which I convince myself of what you are thinking about."

and are expressed by active verbs" (Woozley, p. 5). Reid also noted that execution of an operation like walking or measuring or talking *implies* the power to walk or to measure or to talk, but that possession of these powers does not imply their execution. A silent man may continue to have the power to speak, just as a sleeping one still has the power to walk or to measure.

Since power, as such, can only be inferred from acts or performances, Hume was not in error when he reported failure to observe power directly; but this did not justify his reluctance to draw the inference.[9] This seems to be one of Reid's objections to Hume's refusal to grant the validity of common references to physical and mental powers. The only way to establish the possession of such powers, Reid held, is by some operational test. Having an *idea* of power, he noted, is not the equivalent of having power. In this connection he wrote (*Essays,* 1819, Vol. III, p. 8):

> I am conscious that I have a *conception* or *idea* of power, but, strictly speaking, I am not conscious that I have *power*. . . . Thus, a man who is struck with a palsy in the night commonly knows not that he has lost the power of speech till he attempts to speak; he knows not whether he can move his hands till he makes the trial; and if, without making the trial, he consults his consciousness ever so attentively, it will give him no information whether he has lost these powers, or still retains them.

Faculties Different from Habits

For Reid, a phrase like "powers of the mind" was synonymous with a phrase like "faculties of the mind." However, he suggested reserving the word "faculty" for inherent powers in the sense of being "original and natural" as contrasted with "other powers, which are acquired by use, exercise, or study, which are not called faculties, but *habits*." In addition, he noted that "There must be something in the constitution of the mind necessary to our being able to acquire habits—and this is commonly called *capacity*" (Woozley, p. 6). Thus, in terms of these distinctions, it would be correct to speak of a man's capacity to learn chess or hockey or architecture and incorrect to refer to such skills as faculties. Moreover, once these skills are acquired, their exercise might well involve memory, judgment, and perception as well as the other "powers" Reid recognized as faculties. All "powers"—both original ones and acquired ones—are ways of functioning, or what Reid described as "*operations* of the mind." As ways of functioning or operating, in effect, he was recognizing them as *processes* and not as

---

[9] If Hume's strictures were to be accepted, then contemporary animal psychologists would no longer be justified in attributing "habit strength" to their rats and clinical psychologists would no longer be justified in talking about the "ego strength" of their clients.

independent things or objects. For him, these processes constitute *mind,* since he defined mind as "that which thinks" and is capable of having different kinds of thoughts "such as seeing, hearing, remembering, deliberating, resolving, loving, hating, and many other kinds of thought" (Woozley, p. 4). Such operations or processes are not found in an inert object or a material thing "which moves only as it is moved, and acts only by being acted upon." Reid then added (Woozley, p. 5):

> But the mind is, from its very nature, a living and active being. Everything we know of it implies life and active energy; and the reason why all its modes of thinking are called its operations is that in all, or in most of them, it is not merely passive, as body is, but is really and properly active.

Intellectual and Active Powers as Faculties

In thus stressing mind as active, Reid was opposing a passive associationism. His distinction between "intellectual powers" on the one hand and "active powers" on the other was not intended to suggest that the former are less "operational" than the latter. As "powers" they were both viewed as dynamic in the sense of requiring effort. A weary physician has trouble thinking clearly about perplexing diagnostic possibilities, just as a weary surgeon may have trouble executing delicate surgical maneuvers. The one may refer to his "speculations" about diagnostic possibilities as "hard work" and the other may also call his efforts to suture torn ligaments "hard work." Reid would have said the diagnostician had been employing his "speculative powers" and the surgeon his "active powers." This follows from what he had to say about the difference between the two kinds of powers (*Essays,* Vol. III, 1819, p. 14):

> The term active power is used, I conceive, to distinguish it from speculative powers. As all languages distinguish action from speculation, the same distinction is applied to the powers by which they are produced. The powers of seeing, hearing, remembering, distinguishing, judging, reasoning, are speculative powers; the power of executing any work of art or labour is active power.

Reid's recognition of the "original and natural" powers of the mind as "faculties of the mind" has resulted in his psychology's being called a faculty psychology. Such a designation, as is common knowledge, has come to have a negative connotation. Faculty psychology is usually regarded as a misleading or spurious kind of psychology because, so it is alleged, it tries to explain mental events by the kind of question-begging procedure immortalized by Molière's specialist who attributed the sleep-inducing effect of opium to the soporific principle. In terms of this kind of faculty psychology, it is popularly maintained that the alcoholic drinks to excess because he lacks will power and that his ingenious excuses for his drinking reflect the power of his imagination. This is the equivalent of attributing causal efficacy to the faculty in question and amounts to a tautology like saying, "I can remember what I heard at the meeting *because* I have a powerful memory" or "He doesn't pay attention *because* he can't concentrate."

Critics of Reid have accused him of sponsoring this kind of tautological faculty psychology. For example, H. C. Warren (1934, p. 102) has referred to Reid as a "typical" exponent of a faculty psychology, defined as a "system of psychology, based upon the classification of mental processes and performances under a small number of generic powers, called *faculties,* which are treated as entities, causes, or principles of explanation for the facts themselves." Similarly, Boring has alluded to Reid's faculties as indicative of the kind of popular psychology indulged in by those who contend "that imitation is explained by referring it to an instinct of imitation, or a good memory depends on having a good faculty of memory." In Boring's phrase (1950, p. 207), "such naming is word magic."

Whether these criticisms of Reid's brand of faculty psychology are justified is open to question. He seems to have been aware of naming as word magic when he had this to say about the faculty of memory (Woozley, p. 197):

> I find in my mind a distinct conception and a firm belief of a series of past events, but how this is produced I know not. I call it memory, but this is only giving a name to it—it is not an account of its cause, I believe most firmly that I distinctly remember, but I can give no reason of this belief. It is the inspiration of the Almighty that gives me this understanding.

Reid did not regard this last statement as an explanation for the phenomenon of memory. It was his way of saying that we are so made that we can remember, just as we are made to exercise other original powers such as hearing, reasoning, judging, and so on. Furthermore, contrary to Warren's view of faculties as entities, Reid, as previously noted, viewed powers or faculties as ways of functioning and not as independent "things." He recognized some of them as mechanical and instinctive, such as an infant's breathing, crying, sucking, and swallowing. Others such as imitative behavior, he regarded as partly though not entirely instinctive.

Faculties and the Instinct Controversy

In this connection, Reid noted man's disposition "to imitate what he approves" and his readiness, when interested in mastering an art, to copy or be influenced by the example of those expert in the art. In such cases, "however, the imitation is intended and willed, and therefore cannot be said to be instinctive" (*Essays,* Vol. III, 1819, p. 133). On the other hand, he held "instinctive imitation" to be largely responsible for the resemblance between a child's speech mannerisms and gestures and those of its parents.

Whether such appeals to an instinct of imitation are sound psychology has been a controversial issue ever since the concept of instinct was called into question back in the 1920s.[10] Among animal psychologists, the issue took the form of experiments designed to find out whether untrained animals can profit by observing the successful food-getting maneuvers of trained animals. In general, they seemed to profit only to a very limited degree. For example, in the case of the problem box, some of them learned the location of the bolts or releasing mechanisms, but not how to work them. As one of the investigators expressed it, "The monkey learns by monkeying; he never apes." Reid's instinct of imitation thus failed to get experimental confirmation, and imitation became suspect as a satisfactory principle of explanation.

Later laboratory studies, however, provided rather impressive evidence indicative of imitative behavior in infant monkeys. As reported in a paper by H. F. and M. Harlow (1966, p. 250), the infant monkey does "ape" its mother's behavior:

> The rhesus infant follows maternal behavior and within the limits of its capabilities matches the mother's action. The infant follows the mother's peregrinations: when the mother explores a physical object, so does the infant; when the mother is startled or frightened, the infant clings to the mother's body and observes. Such primitive *imitation* [italic added] has been described . . . as matched-dependent behaviors. These behaviors enable the infant to profit from maternal experience so that its own exploratory behavior is not blind and the dangers inherent in untutored exploration are minimized.

Reid might have classified such imitative behavior of the rhesus infant as akin to one of the "active powers" or "faculties" he attributed to human beings. As evidence, he might have argued, it seems to support belief in some kinds of imitative behavior as instinctive. Of course, in his day there was no need to be defensive about endorsement of the concept of instinct. The legitimacy of the concept was not questioned, and it was accepted as self-evident that animals are governed by instinct. Nor did nineteenth-century biologists hesitate to account for the spider's web and the bee's honeycomb by reference to the concept. Furthermore, up until the close of the World War I era, psychologists also recognized the scientific respectability of the concept. The textbooks of the period usually contained whole chapters devoted to the instinct doctrine. Then, in the postwar period of the 1920s, as mentioned in Chapter 9, psychologists began to have misgivings about the existence of instincts and the explanatory value of the concept. The instinct doctrine became the instinct hypothesis—and for many of them it

---

[10] The shortcomings of efforts to account for imitative behavior by appeals to an instinct of imitation are clearly presented in an article by J. Peterson (1922).

came to be an untenable hypothesis. Textbooks devoted less space to the subject of instinct, and the word "instinct" became taboo in scientific psychology. Animals now had *drives* but no instincts. In observance of the taboo, the word "propensity" was also proposed as a suitable substitute for instinct.

This disposition of the instinct controversy, viewed in retrospect, can now be seen as a reflection of the empiricist standpoint. Experience, learning, environmental forces, training, educational influences, and similar nonhereditary factors were played up and nativistic factors were played down. Even a phrase like "native intelligence," in vogue during the early years of the mental-testing movement, did not go unchallenged. By the middle of the century, however, a reaction had set in and allusions to hereditary influences met with less skepticism.

For present purposes it will suffice to introduce just one example of such lessened resistance to the notion of intelligence as a *native* endowment—an example from Karl Lashley indicative of forthright endorsement of the notion rather than of mere reduction of resistance to the notion. As an endorsement or a teaching, as L. Carmichael has noted, it constitutes one of the last of Lashley's many contributions to psychology. Lashley died in 1958, and in a memorial tribute to him, Carmichael called attention to this teaching. It had to do with Lashley's interpretation of experiments which suggested that chimpanzees are capable of insight. Lashley saw a relationship between the chimpanzee's "innate" manipulation of simple tools and man's manipulation of ideas. Moreover, as a sort of last bequest to his fellow psychologists, Lashley seemed to be urging them not to permit their preoccupation with the concept of intelligence to shunt out consideration of the role of instincts. At all events, as quoted by Carmichael (1958, p. 1411), this is what Lashley had to say about the chimpanzee's insightful behavior:

> The insight is the immediate, one-trial learning to use the innate manipulative acts in the manner discovered by chance, and the generalization of the acts to other, similar situations . . . an extension of the same concepts to the manipulation of ideas may well lead to the conclusion that man has failed to identify his own *instincts* because he calls them intelligence [italics added].

It is tempting to dwell upon the implications of this last statement by asking, "Precisely what instincts did Lashley have in mind when he stated that what others call intelligence he identifies as instincts?" In view of the context in which the statement was made, he was evidently thinking of intelligence as a mode of insightful, problem-solving behavior. By equating this behavior with instinct, he must have regarded it as in some way related to man's original biological endowment. If so, then he was not only making an oblique reference to *native* intelligence but was also stating that its nativistic characteristics were being overlooked. Metaphorically speaking, it was as if he had found Locke's empiricism in need of the *intellectus* of Leibnitz as a corrective. He seemed to regard this *intellectus* as complex in the sense that he identified it not with a single instinct but with "instincts." Since he failed to elaborate, there is no way of knowing what "instincts" he had in mind. It may be that some of them might have been identical with or related to the "intellectual powers" that Reid had described as "instinctive." This is a relatively minor issue, however. It is more important, in view of the instinct controversy, to note this implicit agreement between the "instincts" Lashley identified with intelligence and the "instinctive" intellectual powers Reid regarded as "original and natural." For both of them, the concept of native intelligence was meaningful and valid.

Commonsense as a Synonym for Intelligence

Actually, Reid did not refer to native intelligence in so many words. What was just mentioned as his endorsement of the concept was based upon his recognition of some "intellectual powers" as "original and natural." Furthermore, despite his conviction of the importance of the concept of commonsense, he failed to list commonsense as one of these intellectual powers. He seems to have taken it for granted that commonsense would be understood to be the outcome or resultant of the effective functioning of these powers. As he saw it, to act in accordance with the principles of commonsense was to behave intelligently and rationally. This made commonsense a synonym for intelligence, and his list of powers can thus be considered to be what he took to be the components of intelligence.

If this interpretation is correct, then Reid's approach to the problem, broadly considered, was not unlike the approach of those psychologists of the modern period who first ventured to construct tests of intelligence. They, too, had to decide what "powers" or abilities are essential for intelligent behavior. Their decision was reflected in the kinds of items they selected for inclusion in their array of test items.

A bewildering diversity of tasks came to be incorporated in the tests devised by different investigators. To catalogue them all would result in a tediously long list. It is enough to mention vocabulary tests, general-information items, memory-span tests, reasoning tests, arithmetic items, tests of reading comprehension, tests of spatial imagination, and tests of ability to detect absurdities.

This proliferation of tests indicated lack of agreement both with respect to what was to be measured and with respect to the measuring devices to be employed. Some psychologists excluded tests that some others included. There is no need to say more about something so obvious. The only reason for calling attention to it is that a similar state of affairs was already evident in connection with Reid's attempt to decide on what to include in his list of intellectual powers. This becomes evident by comparing Reid's list with Dugald Stewart's.

Reid's list of intellectual powers was enlarged by Stewart. While retaining Reid's broad division of faculties into active powers and intellectual powers, Stewart added faculties to each of these divisions so that his final list came to a total of about fifty while Reid's list amounted to about thirty.[11] Their failure to agree on the number and kinds of faculties is a foreshadowing of the disagreements among twentieth-century psychologists regarding the number and kinds of mental functions to be included in tests of intelligence. Indeed, what Reid and Stewart listed as intellectual powers constitutes an early attempt to analyze the concept of intelligence. It was as if they were asking what is involved in Plato's rational soul, in Aristotle's *nous,* or in the *intellectus* of Leibnitz. These are all ways of alluding to cognition; hence their "intellectual powers" may also be called "cognitive powers." As such, they refer to areas of competence deemed to be essential for intelligent behavior.

To speak of "an area of competence" is to introduce a neutral term by means of which to designate any one feature or characteristic of mental life likely to be singled out for separate consideration. Words like perceiving, counting, remembering, attending, concentrating, judging, hearing, reasoning, imagining, analyzing, and comprehending will serve as familiar instances of the wide range of topics to be included within the notion of an area of competence. They refer to activities man is capable of executing; hence Reid and Stewart would have called them "intellectual powers" or "faculties." Since faculty psychology has become a taboo topic, it has become customary to avoid calling them faculties. Instead, depending on circumstances and individual preference, they may be subsumed under some generic term like "cognitive functions," "mental abilities," or "mental processes." If sifted through a correlation matrix, they may be called *factors*—but not faculties![12]

The phrase "area of mental competence" was just introduced to avoid the taboo term "mental faculty." Upon reflection, it seems to be an awkward phrase and a dubious way of circumventing the taboo. It would have been much easier and more direct and less ambiguous to disregard the taboo and talk about "mental faculties." The taboo may have outlived its usefulness. We need a word to designate the group of topics previously referred to as falling within the scope of man's areas of psychological competence—such topics as hearing, judging, attending, and so on. Why be squeamish about

---

[11] The precise number of faculties each of them recognized can be only approximated, because of the way in which they listed some of them. For example, they refer to "hunger and thirst" and thus render it difficult to decide whether this bracketing means one or two active powers. Under intellectual powers Reid includes "size and novelty," a linking not used by Stewart.

[12] The relation between the concept of a mental faculty and the concept of a factor as understood by factor analysis was discussed in Chapter 7. For details see p. 192.

saying that a deaf man has lost the faculty of hearing or that the delirious patient's faculty of judgment is impaired? Such usage would not stamp one as a faculty psychologist in the pejorative connotation of the term, any more than an allusion to "school spirit" connotes a belief in ghosts. It is foolish to permit fear of this sort of misinterpretation to outlaw words like "faculty" and "spirit" from one's working vocabulary. Hobbes had this kind of foolishness in mind when he wrote, "Words are the counters of wise men, and the money of fools."

Reid Not a Wolffian Faculty Psychologist

Although both Reid and Stewart talked about mental faculties, this does not necessarily make them faculty psychologists. As noted in Chapter 14, page 470, the term "faculty psychology" should be reserved for the kind of psychology sponsored by Christian Wolff. For Wolff, the faculties were relatively independent, autonomous mental functions that he compared to such physiological functions as circulation, digestion, and breathing. The latter functions are obviously related to heart, stomach, and lungs as discrete organic structures.

Can analogous separate bodily structures be specified for each of the mental functions that Reid and Stewart recognized as faculties? Those having to do with the faculties of vision, audition, olfaction, and other sensory functions are, of course, linked to their respective receptor structures. But what about faculties like judgment, memory, friendship, attention, and ambition? To recognize them as dependent upon the brain is not the equivalent of ascribing them to specific parts of the brain. But neither Reid nor Stewart had anything to say about the cerebral localization of mental powers or faculties. Furthermore, Reid in particular was disinclined to indulge in speculations about brain events as causes or comcomitants of mental events.[13] For him, Hartley's flights into physiological psychology were just that— flights of fancy. This is what he had to say about Hartley's notions (Woozley, pp. 61–62):

> As to the vibrations and vibratiuncles, whether of an elastic ether or of the infinitesimal particles of the brain and nerves, there may be such things for what we know; and men may rationally inquire whether they can find any evidence of their existence; but while we have no proof of their existence, to apply them to

---

[13] Reid's successor, Stewart, was particularly emphatic in urging psychology's emancipation from anatomic and physiological foundations. His trenchant protest took this form (Robinson, p. 160):

> It has been recommended of late, by a Medical author of great reputation, to those who wish to study the human mind, to begin with preparing themselves for the task by the study of anatomy. I must confess, I cannot perceive the advantages of this order of investigation, as the anatomy of the body does not seem to me more likely to throw light on the philosophy of the mind, than an analysis of the mind to throw light on the physiology of the body.

the solution of phenomena, and to build a system upon them, is what I conceive we call building a castle in the air.

In this criticism Reid was not objecting to Hartley's empiricism. On the contrary, he was finding fault with Hartley for substituting neurological conjectures for experientially verified data. In effect he was warning against confusing speculation—even plausible speculation—with proof. Nor was this just an indirect way of voicing opposition to association psychology; he was just as vehement in giving expression to objections to the physiological psychology of Descartes, as is shown in the following paragraph (Woozley, p. 59):

> The ancients conjectured that the nervous fibres are fine tubes filled with a very subtle spirit, or vapour, which they called *animal spirits*; that the brain is a gland by which the animal spirits are secreted from the finer part of the blood and their continual waste repaired; and that it is by these animal spirits that the nerves perform their functions. Descartes has shown how by these animal spirits going and returning in the nerves, muscular motion, perception, memory, and imagination are effected. All this he has described as distinctly as if he had been an eye-witness of all those operations. But it happens that the tubular structure of the nerves was never perceived by the human eye nor shown by the nicest injections; and all that has been said about animal spirits, through more than fifteen centuries, is mere conjecture.

Under the circumstances, it seems safe to say that had Reid's attention been called to Wolff's teaching regarding the nature of mental faculties, he would have rejected the teaching as "mere conjecture." If this be so, then criticisms directed against Wolff's kind of faculty psychology might not apply to what Reid had to say about mental faculties.

It is well to be reminded of these criticisms because of their bearing on a number of important problems. For the most part these are problems that neither Reid nor Stewart had to consider. Viewed in historical perspective, however, they appear to be outgrowths of the considerations that resulted in the repudiation of the concept of mental faculties. As problems, they have historical roots in the fact that both Reid and Stewart, unlike psychologists of the modern period, were not at all reluctant to refer to mental faculties, and their faculty psychology came to be indicted along with Wolff's psychology; but neither they nor Wolff could have foreseen these problems. As problems, also, they all have to do with mental organization, or the way in which abilities, capacities, skills, traits, aptitudes, habits, attitudes—what Reid and Stewart called "powers"—are structured or interrelated.

A Note on the History of Faculty Psychology

To appreciate the nature and scope of these problems, it is well to consider a segment of the history of faculty psychology by raising this question:

How did the faculty taboo come into being? It appears to have had its origin in an attack launched by an educational theorist, Johann Friedrich Herbart (1776–1841). His interest in education was aroused by his work as a private tutor when still a young man. This interest continued during his mature years when he succeeded Kant as professor of philosophy at Königsberg, and was reflected in publications in which he urged that education be developed along "scientific" lines by taking note of psychological principles. Because of what he envisioned in the light of such a development, Herbart may be thought of as a founding father of applied psychology in general and of educational psychology in particular.

Herbart published a textbook of psychology, *Lehrbuch zur Psychologie*, in 1816. In it he voiced his misgivings regarding what he called "the hypothesis of mental faculties." What he had in mind is well summarized in the following excerpt as quoted by C. Spearman (1927, pp. 36–37):

"Memory and imagination agree in that their superior strength is usually limited in every man to particular kinds of objects. . . . He who easily remembers the technical expressions of a science that interests him often has a bad memory for the novelties of the town." Again, lunatics, he says, frequently show their imagination to be diseased in respect to some "fixed idea," whilst retaining "a very healthy activity, indeed, often the exaltation of genius, for everything not concerned with the fixed idea. . . . The marvel of these things vanishes on discarding the hypothesis of mental faculties."

Spearman also quoted a passage from the 1903 edition of Thorndike's *Educational Psychology* that merits consideration in the present context because it shows that Herbart's plea for a science of pedagogy as well as his criticism of mental faculties had been taken seriously by one of the leaders of the then new field of educational psychology. This is the passage (1927, p. 37):

The science of education should at once rid itself of its conception of the mind as a sort of machine, different parts of which sense, perceive, discriminate, imagine, remember, conceive, associate, reason about, desire, choose, form habits, attend to. . . . There is no power of sense discrimination to be delicate or coarse. . . . There are only the connections between separate sense stimuli and our separate senses and judgments thereof. . . . There is no memory to hold in a uniformly tight and loose grip the experiences of the past. There are only the particular connections between particular mental events and others.

Carried to an extreme degree, this Thorndikean emphasis on learning as a process of establishing *particular* stimulus-response connections might, if taken literally, render teaching a more arduous undertaking than it is. For example, one might wonder whether a youngster who has been taught to say "Four" when his teacher writes 2 plus 2 on the blackboard in white chalk would make the same response if she were to shift to yellow chalk. That learning might entail such extreme specificity of established connections was once indicated in this episode as reported by James (1890, Vol. I, pp. 568–569):

> A father wishes to show to some guests the progress of his rather dull child in Kindergarten instruction. Holding the knife upright on the table, he says, "What do you call that, my boy?" "I calls it *a knife,* I does," is the sturdy reply, from which the child cannot be induced to swerve by any alteration in the form of the question, until the father recollecting that in the Kindergarten a pencil was used, and not a knife, draws a long one from his pocket, holds it in the same way, and then gets the wished-for answer, "I calls it *vertical.*"

Faculties as Useful Descriptive Categories

Actually, of course, early stages of learning are not characterized by sharply delimited or particularized discrimination of initial experiences. Young children are likely to call all grown men "Daddy" and all furry animals "kitty." This indicates overinclusion or overgeneralization. Nor is this restricted to very young children. On the basis of just a few meals in a foreign country, adults are often ready to pass judgment on the country's cuisine. A single unpleasant encounter with an overbearing traffic officer may suffice to establish a negative attitude toward all policemen.

Man is a categorizing animal; hence it is not easy for him to restrict his interpretation of novel events to their Thorndikean particularity. He tends to regard each one as belonging to a class or category of events, and his experience with the single event colors his judgment of the category to which he assigns it. On this basis he permits one rotten apple to tell him something about the other apples in the crate. Single events tend to be viewed as samples or representatives of more inclusive categories. Thus, a dog is viewed as a mammal or as representative of a particular breed, a soldier is classified as belonging to an army or as a member of a regiment, and a fur coat may be considered as a luxury or a necessity depending on circumstances. Terms like mammal, breed, army, regiment, luxury, and necessity are all categories or subcategories indicative of the vast array of classes and subclasses that govern thinking.

Even a word like "thinking" refers to a class of mental events. Moreover, in the course of thinking about thinking, a psychologist may find it helpful to classify his observations of the complexity of the thought process into a variety of subclasses as he notes that thinking includes perceiving, judging, analyzing, combining, conceiving, inferring, remembering, planning, and so on. As suits his convenience, he may give names to these subclasses, and, should he be writing a book about thinking, these names may become chapter headings resulting in separate chapters on such topics as judgment, concept formation, memory, imagination, discrimination, association, and fallacies.

Had such a book about thinking been available to Reid or Stewart, they would not have hesitated to say that it dealt with intellectual faculties. As a descriptive term, the phrase would be a convenient designation for the range of topics dealt with in the book. A term like "cognitive faculties" would serve just as well. In the eighteenth century, it will be recalled, the "three-faculty doctrine" of psychology was reflected in Kant's three *Critiques,* so that terms like "cognitive faculties," "faculties of feeling," and "faculties of willing" were easily understood. The division of mental life into the three broad categories or faculties of cognition, affection, and volition found ready acceptance as helpful *descriptive* designations for man's capacity to know, to feel, and to act.

As descriptive categories, they reflected the tripartite division of philosophy into epistemology, aesthetics, and ethics, respectively. This is another way of saying that as fields of inquiry they have to do with questions of truth, beauty, and goodness, respectively. Their psychological counterparts are concerned with the acquisition of knowledge, with emotional development, and with achieving muscular control. As viewed by physiological psychologists, these counterparts are related to functions of the central nervous system, to activation of the autonomic nervous system, and to involvement of the striped musculature. Furthermore, as mentioned in Chapter 3, p. 52, a tripartite faculty psychology was already glimpsed by Plato in his myth of the charioteer struggling with his spirited horses. And as pointed out in the same chapter, this myth constitutes a foreshadowing of Freud's tripartite scheme of ego, id, and superego functions. The Freudian triad, it will be recalled, is just another way of giving abstract formulation to the implications of three simple expressions: "I know," "I want," and "I ought."

Furthermore, as a moment's reflection will show, in terms of systematic psychology these three expressions have to do with cognition, conation, and conduct. When used as major captions, these three words serve as convenient headings for arrays of topics that come to be included in books on general psychology. The precise terms employed for such captions may differ from text to text, but usually it is not difficult to recognize them either as variants of the "three-faculty doctrine" or as subordinate constituents of these three. Thus the chapter on intelligence will be recognized as having something to do with cognition, the one on motivation as dealing with conation, and the ones on habit formation and conflict as related to conduct or behavior. From this viewpoint it can be argued that the "three-faculty doctrine" and its derivatives have not vanished from twentieth-century psychology. But even in disguised form the doctrine has been stripped of its negative Wolffian connotations. Directly or indirectly, it continues to serve as a matter of descriptive convenience.

It is well to stress this *descriptive* convenience of the word "faculty." The mere fact that a writer alludes to mental faculties in general or to perceptual and memory faculties in particular does not serve to stamp him as a faculty psychologist. Hartley, for example, as mentioned in the previous chapter, had occasion to refer to "faculties of memory, attention, imagination" and others; but this did not make him a sponsor of faculty psychology.[14] And long after the time of Hartley, to cite another example, Binet (1857–1911) wrote that "The mind is unitary, despite the multiplicity of its faculties" (J. Peterson, 1925, p. 263).[15] The faculties to which Binet was referring were those of speech, comprehension, memory, imagination, and judgment. These were mental functions operative in acts of intelligence; and even though he stated that "intelligence considered independently of the phenomena of sensibility, emotion, and will is above all a *faculty* [italics added] of apprehension," this statement did not make Binet a faculty psychologist. Like Reid and Stewart, for descriptive purposes Binet was considering cognitive or intellectual faculties as abstracted from emotional and volitional ones; but this was not to endow them with the stigma of being Wolffian faculties. They had no autonomous existence as independent powers. The mind's *unitas* rendered such secession impossible.

This brings up an important consideration; namely, that the mind's *unitas* is not to be extended to its faculties. A chief objection to faculty psychology, it will be recalled, was that it assumed each faculty to function as an integrated unit. In the case of memory, for example, as Herbart noted, a man may have a good memory for some kinds of facts and a poor memory for other kinds of facts. To overlook this and treat memory as if it functions on all items to be remembered with uniform efficiency is to be guilty of Wolff's error by making memory a unitary faculty. That members of the Scottish School were not thinking of faculties in this way is suggested by the fact that Stewart, for instance, listed memory for colors as different from other kinds of memory. This differentiation is not to be interpreted as meaning that Stewart anticipated Herbart's and Thorndike's criticisms of the educational implications of Wolff's brand of faculty psychology. What it does do, though, is to exonerate Stewart of the charge of being a faculty psychologist.

Concerning Transfer and Retroaction

Around 1900, Herbart's objections to unitary faculties began to influence the experimental work of learning theorists. They raised questions

---

[14] Nor is Hume to be called a faculty psychologist even though he had defined memory as "the faculty by which we repeat our impressions, so as that they retain a considerable degree of their first vivacity, and are somewhat intermediate betwixt an *idea* and an *impression*."

[15] Quoted by Peterson from Binet's 1909 book *Les Idées modernes sur les enfants*.

regarding the extent to which training in a specific kind of mental function would carry over to a different task which seemed to involve the same function. It was held that if memory, for example, is a unitary faculty, then training the memory by memorizing poetry should enhance retention of dates in history, rules of grammar, items of news, chemical formulas, French vocabulary, and whatever else calls for memory. Similarly, if judgment is a unitary faculty, then exercise in judging anything at all should improve judgment of anything else. In general, however, experiments designed to check on these suppositions failed to reveal substantial carry-over from one task to another. Improvement seemed to be restricted to the specific kind of performance exercised during the training sessions, with little if any improvement of presumably related tasks. According to Thorndike, who was a pioneer in starting many of these investigations, learning one task will influence the learning of another task only to the extent that there are identical elements in the two tasks.[16] The process of learning is more a matter of mastering specific skills than of strengthening general faculties like memory, judgment, or attention. There are no such general faculties. Instead there are specific abilities like a good memory for musical scores, good judgment of wines, and pronounced readiness to attend to the financial news. Moreover, the same person who possesses these specific abilities may have a poor memory for his children's birthdays, be unable to judge football plays, and find it difficult to pay attention to real-estate news.

Determining whether a given skill carries over from one learning situation to other situations is usually referred to as the problem of *transfer.* As such it is limited to the influence of present learning on future learning as opposed to the possible effect of present learning on previous learning. The latter possibility is known as the problem of *retroaction.* If study of the geography of China should be found to facilitate the subsequent study of the history of China, we would have an instance of transfer. On the other hand, should the study of China's geography be found to enhance understanding of the preceding study of the geography of India, we would have an example of a retroactive influence.

In the course of the many laboratory studies of transfer and retroaction, it soon became evident that the effect of one kind of learning on another kind could not always be known in the absence of experimental findings. Predictions based upon obvious resemblance of the two kinds of learning sometimes failed to be confirmed. For instance, practice in developing speed and accuracy in canceling two letters of the alphabet such as "J" and "X" did not necessarily carry over to the related task of canceling two other

---

[16] For relevant bibliographic references as well as for a judicious evaluation of Thorndike's investigations along with related studies by other psychologists, see E. R. Hilgard's *Theories of Learning* (1956, pp. 22–47, and references in the index under "'Transfer").

letters such as "B" and "Q." In fact, for some subjects the initial practice with "J" and "X" can interfere with speedy perception of "B" and "Q"; the "habit" of responding to the former letters has a retarding effect on quick reaction to the latter ones. Analogously, for some individuals, practice in playing tennis may militate against the acquisition of skill in ping-pong but will be of decided help when they start to learn badminton. Furthermore, the self-confidence they develop in any of these games may have no effect on their self-confidence as public speakers. Stage fright may still plague them as it does some football heroes when called on to make a speech at the victory banquet. Attitudes engendered by one situation may be specific to that situation; hence the honest cardplayer may cheat on his income tax without compunction. The liberal in politics may be conservative in religion, just as an indulgent father may be a strict employer.

As L. W. Webb suggested back in 1917, these problems of transfer and retroaction lend themselves to clarifying conceptualization in terms of six possible relationships. These can be schematized by letting A stand for an initial kind of learning and having B represent a later kind of learning. Then if A facilitates mastery of B, we have *positive* transfer; if A interferes with the learning of B, we have negative transfer; and if A has no influence on B, we have *zero* transfer. Similarly, if B strengthens A, we have *positive* retroaction; if B weakens A, we have *negative* retroaction or retroactive inhibition; and if B has no effect on A, we have *zero* retroaction.

Many of the experimental studies of transfer revealed either no or negligible improvement from A to B. Such findings resulted in an unwarranted conclusion to the effect that little if any carry-over from one learning situation to another is to be expected. In everyday discussion of the subject, it was not unusual for somebody to deny the occurrence of positive transfer and to cite Thorndike's emphasis on the specificity of learning in support of this contention. Fortunately a corrective to this misinterpretation was introduced by J. E. Coover (1912). He reviewed eighteen experimental studies of transfer dealing with many different kinds of mental functions and found that A resulted in the improvement of B to *some* extent. In addition, even Thorndike showed the possible importance of what appears to be a negligible amount of transfer by arguing (1914, p. 282):

. . . that a very small spread of training may be of very great educational value if it extends over a wide enough field. If a hundred hours of training in being scientific about chemistry produced only one hundreth as much improvement in being scientific about all sorts of facts, it would yet be a very remunerative educational force. If a gain of fifty per cent in justice toward classmates in school affairs increased the general equitableness of a boy's behavior only one-tenth of one per cent, this disciplinary effect would still perhaps be worth more than the specific habits.

In granting that there may be this kind of "spread of training," Thorndike was not retracting what he had stressed concerning the educational importance of teaching specific skills. He was not, even by implication, suggesting that unitary faculties of scientific thinking and of justice were being strengthened by instruction in chemistry and by treating classmates justly. Had he been thinking of such Wolffian faculties, he would not have limited the hypothesized spread to such fractional amounts of transferred improvement. Instead he would have predicted large amounts of improvement. In accordance with the kind of analogy that used to be advanced by proponents of the outmoded faculty psychology, he might have argued that exercise of the two faculties in school should transfer to other situations away from school, just as strengthening arm muscles by lifting weights in the gymnasium will help in doing work outside the gymnasium. Thorndike would never have advanced this argument, because he knew this analogy to be faulty. Mental faculties have no specifiable structural analogues to arm muscles in the sense of having one segment of brain tissue involved in scientific thinking and a different segment operative in behaving justly. To attribute separate mental operations to such circumscribed segments of brain tissue is to make the same mistake the phrenologists made.

Phrenology as a Faculty Psychology

The pseudoscience of phrenology originated in the teachings of Franz Joseph Gall (1758–1828) around the close of the eighteenth century and the early years of the nineteenth century. Although entirely discredited for many decades, it continues to survive along with palmistry and fortune-telling as a form of quackery having an appeal for the ignorant and the gullible. Gall himself, however, was not a quack. He was one of the foremost brain anatomists of his day and had no intention of misleading the public. [17] As a result of observations made during his school days, long before he studied medicine, he became convinced of a relationship between skull contour and character. It seemed plausible to him that a classmate's outstanding ability should be reflected in a specific elevation of the cranium to accommodate enlargement of the brain region presumed to be responsible for the ability in question. By knowing which boy was the best student of mathematics and then noting some cranial protuberance, he was ready to designate the

---

[17] Even those who rejected his phrenological teachings spoke highly of his knowledge of brain anatomy. For example, Pierre Flourens (1794–1867), famous for his experimental studies of the brain by means of the method of extirpation of definite cerebral structures and vehemently opposed to Gall's phrenology, is quoted by Merz (1965, Vol. I, p. 477) as having shown his admiration of Gall's work as brain anatomist in this statement: "*Gall fut un observateur profond, qui nous a ouvert, avec génie, l'étude de l'anatomie et de la physiologie du cerveau.*"

latter as the "bump" of mathematical aptitude. On this basis he proceeded to search for the correlation between particular "bumps" and particular personality traits. Later, as an adult, he extended his observations to the inmates of jails and asylums for the insane as well to the cranial characteristics of friends and prominent people whose traits were matters of public knowledge. By studying composers he expected to locate the "bump" for music, just as he found a "bump" for what he called the "wish to destroy" by examining the heads of murderers. In the course of time he had a list of some twenty-seven faculties with their corresponding "bumps."

In general, it might be said that Gall gave wrong answers to good questions. For one thing, he was raising the question of *individuality*. This, as mentioned in Chapter 8, p. 221, is one of "the persistent riddles of psychology" and is concerned with the problem of accounting for the uniqueness and distinctiveness of each individual personality. By implication Gall thought he had solved this riddle by recognizing variations in the prepotency of the inherited unitary faculties. In doing so, he was raising another question: How is the mind organized, or how account for personality as integrated or for the unified patterning of traits, impulses, and aptitudes? Contemporary references to "the structure of the intellect" are obviously related to this question. Actually, Gall never raised this question in explicit fashion. It is just implicit in his faculty psychology; hence there is no way of knowing how he might have disposed of it. However, there is a way of knowing his answer to another question he did raise in explicit fashion. This is the knotty question of cerebral localization: Does each function revealed by psychological analysis have a specifiable "seat" in the brain? Is there one brain center for speaking, another for imagining, a third for reasoning, a fourth for worrying, and so on, or does the brain function as a unified whole irrespective of the activity being executed? Gall disposed of this question by locating each of the faculties in a different region of the brain. Finally, Gall might be given credit for having raised the question of psychodiagnosis; since, in effect, his phrenological scheme purported to be a way of judging character and personality. It was an early and erroneous way of trying to find answers to the kind of diagnostic questions being considered by contemporary mental-health practitioners when confronted with new patients. In fact, it is the kind of question that obtrudes itself whenever one has to write a letter of recommendation, for such letters also express judgments of character and personality.

Gall based his judgments of character on protuberances of the skull as diagnostic signs of subjacent faculties. Consequently, he referred to his system as *craniology* and not as phrenology. The latter word was introduced by one of Gall's pupils, the anatomist Johann Spurzheim (1776–1832), who had become Gall's collaborator. The word itself was not original with Spurzheim, but had been suggested to him by the naturalist Georg Forster, as a substitite for Gall's *Schädellehre* or craniology.[18] As a substitute it shifts the emphasis from the skull to the mind, since the adjective "phrenic" came to have the meaning of "pertaining to the mind."

To digress for a moment, this meaning of the adjective is of minor historical interest. Its primary meaning, etymologically considered, has to do with a reference to the diaphragm, as indicated by *"phren,"* the Greek word for "midriff." This primary meaning is still preserved in allusions to the innervation of the diaphragm by the phrenic nerve. However, the derived meaning implicit in Spurzheim's phrenology is reminiscent of ancient notions regarding the diaphragm as the locus of mind. After all, *psyche* or spirit as related to breathing has an obvious connection with the diaphragm. When it ceased to move, the ancients concluded that the *psyche* had vanished; hence for them the diaphragm became important as the seat of the soul or mind, just as the heart had become important for Aristotle. By the time of Gall and Spurzheim, the brain had long since usurped the place of diaphragm and heart in this respect, so that a word like "phrenology," while retaining its connotation of mind, was no longer apt to arouse thoughts of the midriff any more than the word "schizophrenia" is apt to suggest a split diaphragm.

As a faculty psychology, phrenology is based upon five principles only one of which merits endorsement: a truism to the effect that the brain is the organ of mind. A second principle assumed the mind to consist of innate, independent, autonomous faculties.[19] Their independence is reflected in a third principle that assumed each faculty to be connected with a separate fragment of brain tissue. A fourth principle postulated a direct relationship between the size of each fragment and the strength of its correlated faculty. According to the fifth principle, the contour of the skull conforms to the hypothesized variations in size of the underlying segments of brain tissue.

In Gall's time, principles like the foregoing impressed many people as plausible teachings, and phrenological demonstrations sometimes seemed to confirm their validity. G. Murphy, (1949, p. 134) cites a report published in 1843 in which a young woman when placed in a hypnotic trance responded appropriately as given "bumps" were stimulated. The surgeon who had induced the trance observed:

---

[18] Gall had been lecturing on craniology for some ten years before Forster suggested the term "phrenology." Gall himself never employed the word. However, his name has become so closely identified with what, strictly speaking, is really Spurzheim's phrenology that it seems futile to try to disassociate Gall's craniology from it. Also, the ordinary dictionary definitions of craniology have nothing to do with Gall's meaning. The latest psychological dictionary by English and English (1958) omits the word entirely, while H. C. Warren's older one (1934, p. 13) has a parenthetic reference to craniology as being a synonym for phrenology "in a historical sense."

[19] This principle applies to Spurzheim's phrenology. Whether it applies to Gall's craniology is open to question.

"Under adhesiveness and friendship" she clasped me, and on stimulating the organ of "combativeness" on the opposite side of the head, with the arm of that side she struck two gentlemen (who, she imagined, were about to attack me) in such a manner as nearly laid one on the floor, whilst with the other arm she held me in the most friendly manner. Under "benevolence" she seemed quite over-whelmed with compassion; under "acquisitiveness" stole greedily all she could lay her hands on, which was retained whilst I excited many other manifestations, but the moment my fingers touched "conscientiousness" she threw all she had stolen on the floor, as if horror-stricken, and burst into a flood of tears.

As might be expected, not all demonstrations were successful and the subject of phrenology became a highly controversial issue. Gall himself was forced to leave Vienna; he moved to Paris, where his doctrine engaged the attention of some of the leading scientists of France but failed to win their approval. On the other hand, he must have won popular acceptance; accord-ing to F. H. Garrison (1929, p. 539), "two medals were struck in his honor in Berlin" and "he died rich in Paris." The popular appeal of phrenology is further indicated by the fact that, as Boring has noted (1950, p. 57), at one time "there were twenty-nine phrenological societies in Great Britain and several journals," one of which managed to survive from 1823 to 1911.

Did Gall Obtain His List of Faculties from Reid and Stewart?

At one point in his illuminating chapter on "Phrenology and the Mind-Body Problem," Boring (1950, p. 53.) also noted that "It was from the lists of Thomas Reid and Dugald Stewart that Gall obtained his analysis of the mind into thirty-seven powers and propensities." As a generalization, this seems to hold good for Spurzheim's list but not for Gall's list. Their collabora-tion did not last very long, and after friction between them developed, Spurzheim broke with Gall in 1813 and published on his own. He was more of a propagandist than Gall and lectured more widely, so that his list came to be better known. Nor was his list of thirty-seven powers just an extension of Gall's twenty-six powers. The two lists are very different. It is easier to detect some resemblances between Stewart's faculties and those of Spurzheim than between those of the latter and Gall's faculties. For exam-ple, Stewart and Spurzheim both include hope as one of their faculties, but Gall fails to include hope in his list. In connection with this fact, A. Macalister, a Cambridge anatomist, noted that hope was "not regarded as primary by Gall, who believed hope to be akin to desire and a function of every faculty which desires" (*Encyclopaedia Britannica,* 14th ed., 1929). Here too, a question arises regarding Gall's acceptance of a belief in unitary facul-ties. At all events, in his treatment of memory he might be said to have anticipated Herbart's criticism of those who made this a unitary faculty; for, according to Gall's list, there are four different kinds of memory: verbal memory, memory for persons, local memory, and memory for languages.[20] By way of contrast, memory of any kind is not one of Spurzheim's thirty-seven faculties, even though both Reid and Stewart recognized memory as one of the "intellectual powers."

Gall's recognition of several kinds of memory indicates that he was ready to subject given faculties to psychological analysis. This point is worth noting because it seems to have been overlooked by James. Actually, it is at variance with what James regarded as a shortcoming of Gall's mode of procedure. He wrote (1890, Vol. I, p. 27) that Gall "took the faculty psychology as his ultimatum on the mental side, and he made no farther psychological analysis." If James had examined Gall's list of faculties directly, he would not have reached this conclusion. It may be that he mistakenly assumed one of Spurzheim's lists to be the same as Gall's list.

Careful comparison of Gall's list of faculties with those of others was made by H. D. Spoerl in the 1930s. He drew up a "comparative table of faculties," giving Reid's list of 1780 in one column, Stewart's list of 1827 in an adjacent column, and Gall's list of 1810 in a third column (1936, p. 222). Having the three parallel columns on a single surface facilitated detection of similarities and differences. In addition to those already mentioned, there are a few worth considering. It is evident that Stewart was not Reid's slavish disciple and was ready to correct his professor. For example, Reid had classified language as one of the active powers, whereas Stewart listed it as one of the intellectual powers. Furthermore, apparently in view of his misgivings concerning ideational association, Reid failed to mention the subject. He also failed to include attention in his list of powers. On the other hand, Stewart regarded attention and association of ideas as separate intellectual powers. In general, he accepted almost all of Reid's powers but added more than fifteen of his own. Among those added were such alleged powers as "propensity to action and repose," "acquired appetite for drugs," "self-confidence," "instinct for construction," "sense of similarity and contrast," and "sense of the ridiculous."

Comparison of Gall's list with Reid's reveals more differences than similarities. That his treatment of memory differed from Reid's has already

---

[20] Contemporary factor-analytic studies more than confirm Gall's belief in several distinct kinds of memory abilities. Just how many there are has not yet been established. According to one estimate, in theory there may be as many as twenty-four "to be expected on the basis" of J. P. Guilford's model of the structure of intellect (S. W. Brown et al., 1966, p. 3). Of these twenty-four, six have to do with semantic information and appear to have been identified. (Semantic information is primarily dependent on the use of words as contrasted with pictures, signs, and numbers.) These six semantic-memory abilities are listed as: (1) memory for isolated items of information; (2) memory for class ideas; (3) memory for meaningful connections between meaninful items of information; (4) memory for the order of information; (5) memory for changes in information; and (6) "memory for arbitrary connections between meaningful items of information" (S. W. Brown et al., 1966, p. 26).

been demonstrated. He also recognized some faculties that are not represented in Reid's list; such as "sentiment of property," "metaphysical depth," "theosophy, religion," "wish to destroy," "educability," "firmness of character," and "mechanical aptitude." His list does not appear to be derived from Reid. Moreover, as previously noted, Spurzheim's later list[21] seems to owe more to Stewart than to Gall.

Under the circumstances, all things considered, it is hard to believe that Gall was indebted to Reid. It is also hard to believe that he was a Wolffian faculty psychologist, as is so frequently stated in textbook discussions of phrenology. Spoerl subjected both of these issues to critical study, and his findings merit direct quotation (1936, pp. 224–225):

> Since Gall has often been accused of uncritically borrowing from the conceptions of others, it is pertinent to examine the charge and the facts concerning it. The comparative table suggests that Gall might have made some use of Reid's work, which was published before Gall's books were written. Yet, it seems that Gall had no knowledge of the Scottish faculty psychology. Two of his French critics, Lélut in 1836 and Garnier in 1839, called attention to the nominal similarity, Garnier constructing a table similar to ours. But Lélut held that Gall did not know of the Scottish work, and Garnier, in concurring, added that Gall's intent was to controvert the "narrow and false psychology of the French philosophers of the 18th century, with which he was alone acquainted." In any event, the charges against Gall are contentions that he borrowed, not from the Scottish faculty psychology, *but from the continental faculty psychology which he expressly repudiated.* This fantastic notion, which may have begun with Johannes Müller, was developed by Wundt, who called Gall's psychology a "caricature of the (Wolffian) theory of faculties," and repeated by James. In explanation of the attitude of Müller, Wundt, and James, it should be stated that they quote not Gall but Spurzheim, whose "psychology" was indeed primitive and a caricature, with the result that "Gall had to suffer for Spurzheim's errors."

In order to set the record straight, it should now be evident, the sentence from Boring cited at the beginning of this section should be changed to read: "It was from the lists of Thomas Reid and Dugald Stewart that *Spurzheim* obtained his analysis of the mind into thirty-seven powers and propensities." This exonerates Gall of the charge of plagiarism—conscious or otherwise—as well as of the charge of having been the advocate of an untenable faculty psychology. Furthermore, Spurzheim's advocacy of this kind of psychology should not be charged to the Scottish School. As already suggested, Reid was mindful of the word magic involved in a tautological "explanation" to the effect that we can remember events because we have a faculty of memory. In general, it will be recalled, he was not likely to

---

[21] For Spurzheim's later list, see Boring (1950, p. 55).

confuse conjecture with evidence. Thus, he acted like a Humean positivist in rejecting the Cartesian notion of animal spirits coursing through tubular nerves and in rejecting Hartley's theory of sensation as a product of the vibrations either of neural filaments or of an elastic ether. He warned against the tendency to believe in the validity of a reasonable or favored hypothesis in the absence of confirmation of its validity. His warning, as presented in his *Essays on the Active Powers of the Human Mind,* took this form (1819, Vol. III, p. 118):

> Men who are fond of a hypothesis, commonly seek no other proof of its truth, but that it serves to account for the appearances which it is brought to explain. This is a very slippery kind of proof in every part of philosophy, and never to be trusted, but least of all, when the appearances to be accounted for are human actions.

The warning was first printed back in the 1780s, but it continues to have relevance for modern psychology. Support for many of the conclusions reached by psychoanalysts and clinical psychologists rests on what Reid designated as a "very slippery kind of proof." E. R. Hilgard had something of this sort in mind when he echoed Reid's warning by noting (1956, p. 80), "The difference between plausibility and proof is one of the differences that hounds psychological science," especially with reference to its clinical problems. Obviously, this observation is not to be restricted to clinical issues. Sensitivity to the "difference between plausibility and proof" ought to characterize one's approach to any issue involving evaluation of evidence. Moreover, as Reid pointed out, the principle is particularly important in trying to account for human actions; hence its relevance for a scientific psychology. Had Spurzheim been mindful of the principle, the faculties he borrowed from the Scottish School might have had a very different history and the pseudoscience of phrenology might have been stillborn.

The development of phrenology was not the only way in which history was affected by the Scottish School. In retrospect this development is to be judged as more of a hindrance than an aid to the eventual emergence of psychology as a science. A more constructive setting for this emergence was supplied by the work of Thomas Brown, the third member of the Scottish School.

Thomas Brown (1778–1820): A Brief Biography

With Thomas Brown, psychology moved into the nineteenth century. He was twenty-two in the year 1800 and his professional career lay ahead of him. The choice of a career must have troubled him, for he first studied law and then decided on medicine and obtained his medical degree at the University of Edinburgh in 1803. In collaboration with another physician he started a successful practice, but seems to have found other pursuits more alluring. Literature in general and poetry in particular were among his strong interests. In fact, some of his own poetry was published. He was further distracted from medical work by preoccupation with problems of philosophy. In this respect he was like Hartley, who combined an interest in medicine with an interest in philosophical psychology. Hartley, however, resolved the conflict by continuing with medicine and making philosophy an avocational pursuit. Brown did not follow this precedent. He longed for an academic appointment and made two unsuccessful attempts to obtain a professorship. Finally, in 1808, Dugald Stewart was unable to continue with his university duties because of illness and Brown was invited to substitute for him. He continued to lecture after Stewart's return and in 1810 became Stewart's colleague as associate professor of moral philosophy.

Despite his youth, Brown was emboldened to try for a professorship in philosophy on the basis of his first important publication. This consisted of an effort to *demonstrate* that Hume's views of the causal relationship are not necessarily incompatible with religious orthodoxy. He was only twenty-six when this book was published, and thus his precocity is reminiscent of Berkeley and Hume. This book, entitled *An Inquiry into the Relation of Cause and Effect,* aroused sufficient interest to justify three editions within about a decade and established Brown's reputation as a philosopher. He died at the relatively early age of forty-two and during the ten years of his professorship he did not write another book. Following his death, however, his lectures on psychology were published under the title *Lectures on the Philosophy of the Human Mind.* This work was even more of a success than his earlier book, running to nineteen editions following the first edition in 1820.

The work consists of a hundred lectures presented in the form in which they were delivered; they were not based on notes taken by his students as sometimes happens in the case of posthumous publications. Each one had been written out with evident concern not only for content but also for stylistic elegance. As a result they are replete with rather ornate passages obviously prepared for oral delivery. They are also replete with quotations from many sources that indicated the wide extent of Brown's reading.

Even a cursory sampling of these lectures suffices to show that Brown was an independent thinker not apt to be overawed by the eminence of authors he chanced to quote. For example, he took issue with some of Reid's doctrines and even of some which had won the endorsement of Stewart. The fact that Stewart was twenty-five years his senior, his former teacher, and his departmental colleague did not deter him from voicing his disagreement if he deemed a given teaching to be in error. Such rugged individualism, indeed, was characteristic of the members of the Scottish School. As Brett put it (1921, Vol III, p. 15): "Dugald Stewart corrects

Reid, Brown corrects Stewart, and Hamilton corrects everybody."[22] Stewart's "correction" of Reid's list of powers has already been mentioned. So has his modification of Reid's notion of commonsense. Brown's divergence from Reid was even more striking. One of his contemporaries, according to Noah Porter, even characterized it as "an open revolt against the authority of Reid" (D. S. Robinson [ed.], 1961, p. 192). This statement, however, may not be fair to Brown. It suggests animus against Reid and warped thinking due to such animus. On *a priori* grounds, there is no more reason to say that Brown was in open revolt against the authority of Reid than there would be to say that Reid had been in open revolt against the authority of Hume. In their polemics, members of the Scottish School, as independent thinkers, were not governed by any need to be loyal to any fixed principles of the school. There were no such fixed principles akin to the orthodoxy of a church or the platform of a political party. The doubts they entertained and the questions they raised were more the product of inquiring minds than an expression of disgruntled rebelliousness. A consideration of Brown's stand on some key issues will help to confirm this. It will be especially helpful to begin by considering what he had to say about the nature of consciousness.

The Nature of Consciousness

Brown devoted a portion of one lecture[23] to the subject of consciousness (1822, Vol. I, pp. 169–177). What concerned him particularly was the fact that Reid had included consciousness in his list of the intellectual powers. Consciousness, Reid explained, although not definable, is considered to be "an operation of the understanding" that deals with all mental events at the instant of their occurrence. This refers to doubts, pains, hopes, thoughts, emotions, "and all the actions and operations of our own minds." In brief, any such mental process while present becomes an object of consciousness by virtue of the "power" Reid attributed to consciousness. According to Brown, in thus making a distinction between consciousness on the one hand and the objects of consciousness on the other, Reid had introduced a decidedly questionable distinction. Reid's objects of consciousness referred to all that Brown meant by being conscious. To suffer pain, to be perplexed, to feel angry, to hear a noise, to see a star, to remember a quotation, and so on are all ways of being conscious. Brown contended that there is no other way. It is true, he conceded, that one may employ the word "consciousness" as a generic term under which all

---

[22] He might have added that, in turn, John Stuart Mill corrects Hamilton.

[23] More accurately, a portion of each of two lectures was devoted to the subject of consciousness. The last part of Lecture XI and the first part of Lecture XII dealt with the subject.

Thomas Brown (1778–1820)

SIR WILLIAM HAMILTON (1788–1856)

these specific ways of being conscious may be subsumed, but this generic term is just a matter of verbal convenience and not an additional way of being conscious, as Reid had seemed to maintain. Reid's mistake, Brown argued, was tantamount to confusing an abstract term like "mammal" with the individual animals classified as mammals. It was akin to maintaining that there are individual conscious states like thoughts, emotions, perceptions, feelings, and also a general one like consciousness. In Brown's opinion, Reid had confused consciousness in the abstract with specific instances of awareness. To dispose of such confusion, he brought his lecture to a close with the following statement of his own position (1822, Vol. I, p. 177):

> Consciousness, then, I conclude, in its simplest acceptation, when it is understood as regarding the present only, is no distinct power of the mind, or name of a distinct class of feelings, but is only a general term for all our feelings, of whatever species they may be—sensations, thoughts, desires; in short, all those states or affections of mind, in which the phenomena of mind consist; and when it expresses more than this, it is only the remembrance of some former state of the mind, and a feeling of the past and the present states of one sentient substance. The term is very conveniently used for the purpose of abbreviation, when we speak of the whole variety of our feelings, in the same manner as any other general term is used, to express briefly the multitude of individuals that agree in possessing some common property of which we speak; when the enumeration of these, by description and name, would be as wearisome to the patience, as it would be oppressive to the memory. But still, when we speak of the evidence of consciousness, we mean nothing more than the evidence implied in the mere existence of our sensations, thoughts, desires—which is utterly impossible for us to believe to be and not to be; or, in other words, impossible for us to feel and not to feel at the same moment.

Sir William Hamilton (1788–1856) also lectured on the subject of consciousness at Edinburgh, where he was appointed to the chair of logic and metaphysics in 1836. As in the case of Brown, his lectures were published posthumously, appearing in 1859 under the title *Lectures on Metaphysics and Logic*. In the eleventh lecture, concerned with the nature of consciousness, Hamilton takes issue with Brown. He was more conversant with the history of philosophy than Brown or the other members of the Scottish School. Noah Porter rated him "the most learned student of his time" and added, "No writer had so completely mastered the works of the Aristotelian commentators, of the schoolmen and their successors" (Robinson, p. 215).

As might be expected, Hamilton was thoroughly conversant with the works of his Scottish predecessors: Reid, Stewart, and Brown. Furthermore, his knowledge of Kant enabled him to interpret his countrymen's works in the light of some characteristic Kantian teachings. Hamilton's psychology, Porter noted, although largely based upon Reid's approach and terminology, was also influenced by Kant to a considerable extent.

According to Hamilton, the term "consciousness" was first employed by Descartes.[24] It is implicit in the Cartesian *cogito*. Hamilton regarded it as futile to attempt to make this term explicit by a formal definition of consciousness. As is evident in the following excerpt from his lecture, it is in this connection that he took issue with Brown (Robinson, pp. 232–233):

> Consciousness cannot be defined—we may be ourselves fully aware what consciousness is, but we cannot, without confusion, convey to others a definition of what we ourselves clearly apprehend. The reason is plain. Consciousness lies at the root of all knowledge. Consciousness is itself the one highest source of all comprehensibility and illustration—how, then, can we find aught else by which consciousness may be illustrated or comprehended? To accomplish this, it would be necessary to have a second consciousness, through which we might be conscious of the mode in which the first consciousness was possible. Many philosophers— and among others Dr. Brown—have defined consciousness as *feeling*. But how do they define feeling? They define, and must define it, as something of which we are conscious; for a feeling of which we are not conscious, is no feeling at all. Here, therefore, they are guilty of a logical see-saw, or circle. They define consciousness by feeling, and feeling by consciousness—that is, they explain the same by the same, and thus leave us in the end no wiser than we were in the beginning.

Inspection of the previously cited excerpt from Brown's lecture will show that, strictly speaking, he did not introduce the term "feeling" in a formal definition of consciousness, as Hamilton implied. He used it as "a general term" to designate what in the days of Wundt came to be called "mental content" or "conscious content." Furthermore, Hamilton's statement regarding "a second consciousness" seems to be another way of alluding to the duplication that Brown had mentioned in connection with his criticism of Reid; namely, conscious content in the way of specific items of experience plus an additional observing consciousness. In this respect Brown and Hamilton appear to be in agreement. It also seems safe to say that they were not in fundamental disagreement regarding the futility of the search for an unambiguously clear and rigorous definition of consciousness. The hopelessness of such a quest, however, is not necessarily an insuperable hindrance to scientific progress. At one time biology was defined as the science of life even though the term "life" was refractory to precise definition. Analogously, there was a time when some people defined psychology as a science of consciousness and managed to amass a considerable

---

[24] For a brief account of pre-Cartesian allusions to what in retrospect might be construed as having something to do with the concept of consciousness, see O. Klemm's *History of Psychology* (1914, pp. 166–172). In substantial agreement with Hamilton, Klemm stated (p. 169): "The discovery of consciousness as a fundamental psychical fact was not made before Descartes."

body of significant data despite the absence of a satisfactory definition of consciousness.[25]

Consciousness, Hamilton stated, can be analyzed even though it cannot be defined. To accomplish this analysis, he first called attention to consciousness as related to knowledge, feeling, and desire (Robinson, pp. 233–234):

> The knowledge, the feeling, the desire, are possible only under conditions of being known, and being known by me. For if I did not know that I knew, I would not know—if I did not know that I felt, I would not feel—if I did not know that I desired, I would not desire. Now this knowledge, which I, the subject, have of these modifications of my being, and through which knowledge alone these modifications are possible, is what we call *consciousness*. The expression *I know that I know, I know that I feel, I know that I desire* are thus translated by *I am conscious that I know, I am conscious that I feel, I am conscious that I desire*. . . . Consciousness, thus in its simplicity, necessary involves three things—(1) A recognizing or knowing subject; (2) A recognized or known modification; and (3) A recognition or knowledge by the subject of the modification.

It is important to note that Hamilton's reference to three modes of recognition has to do with a single act or process of being conscious. They pertain to consciousness, not to consciousnesses. In opposition to Brown, this restriction appears to be Hamilton's justification for Reid's notion of consciousness as an intellectual power. He was stressing consciousness as a transitive relationship that might be exemplified by a simple sentence like "I have a toothache." In this instance the toothache would illustrate the modification mentioned by Hamilton: for it to be recognized as an ache, there must be a perceiving or knowing subject. But unless the ache is noted or perceived, there will be no consciousness of its existence. This, in ultrasimple terms, seems to be what Hamilton was driving at. Whether Brown would have accepted this sort of elaboration of the implications of the Cartesian *cogito* must remain conjectural. At all events both Brown and Hamilton, in their efforts to clarify the concept of consciousness, paved the way for later laboratory efforts to determine the precise nature of the varieties of conscious content.

In general, Brown was more influential as a psychologist than Hamilton. After all, Brown lectured on psychological topics, while Hamilton's lectures dealt with problems of metaphysics and logic. This is not intended as disparagement of Hamilton's work, nor does it mean that his writings were devoid of psychological relevance. The brief account of his analysis of the concept of consciousness just introduced is an obvious instance of such

---

[25] The difficulty of finding a satisfactory definition of consciousness is discussed by English and English in *A Dictionary of Psychological Terms*. They even suggest having the word eliminated from psychology as a technical term and having it replaced by some other in technical reports. They added, however, this is not to be construed as complete and permanent banishment from psychology, because "some of its informal usages are probably unavoidable—even by psychologists" (1958, p. 113).

relevance. There is no need to introduce additional examples.[26] Instead it seems preferable to resume consideration of Brown's teachings.

"On Power, Cause, and Effect"

This caption was the title of one of Brown's lectures in which he expressed approval of Hume's notions of power and of the meaning of causality. He evidently deemed it unwise, however, to express his indebtedness to Hume, since there is no mention of Hume at any point in the lecture. Very likely, knowing that the skeptical Hume *was persona non grata* in orthodox circles, he expected to win readier agreement with these notions by presenting them as his own.[27] If so, it was a strategic maneuver calculated to avoid resistance by association.

In the lecture (Vol. I, pp. 98–112) he duplicated Hume's formulation by defining a cause as "the immediate invariable antecedent in any sequence" and the effect as its "immediate invariable consequent." In line with this emphasis on temporal contiguity he designated power as meaning "immediate invariable antecedence" because, as he went on to explain (1822, Vol. I, pp. 102–103):

> Power is nothing more than the relation of one object or event as antecedent to another object or event. . . . To take an example, . . . when a spark falls upon gunpowder, and kindles it into explosion, every one ascribes to the spark the *power* of kindling the inflammable mass. But let any one ask himself, what it is which he means by the term, and without contenting himself with a few phrases that signify nothing, *reflect,* before he gives his answer, and he will find, that he means nothing more than that, in all similar circumstances, the explosion of gunpowder will be the immediate and uniform consequence of the application of a spark.

---

[26] One such example would have to do with Hamilton's influence on British associationism. As will be brought out in the next chapter, John Stuart Mill was an important associationist. He subjected Hamilton's lectures to careful analysis and thus through Hamilton became familiar with the views of the Scottish School. Another example would involve discussion of Hamilton's principle of redintegration. This principle, as mentioned in Chapter 14, was borrowed from Hamilton by H. L. Hollingworth and served as the basis for the development of Hollingworth's redintegrative psychology. Finally, to cite a third example, Hamilton was one of the first to consider the problem of attention span; the question of the number of distinct items that can be perceived when they are presented simultaneously for a fraction of a second.

[27] He could present them as his own without having his orthodoxy impugned. Many of his lectures were concerned with an exposition and defense of religious themes. In one of them he held philosophical considerations to be secondary to "the primary and essential interests of religion and morality" (1822, Vol. I, p. 412). In others he lectured on "The Existence of the Deity" and the "Immortality of the Soul." The very last topic of the very last lecture is concerned with the "Cultivation of Religious Happiness." Furthermore, six of the lectures in Vol. III have to do with man's "Duties." In other words, his *Philosophy of the Human Mind* reflects the same ethico-religious orientation as Hartley's *Observations on Man.*

Brown also explained that power cannot exist independently of a substance, just as the *form* of an object must coexist with the "elementary atoms" constituting the object. In this connection he warned against the fallacy of reification, which occurs when Aristotelian forms are treated as if they and the formed material actually belong to separate realms of existence. He summarized the relation between form and power in a single sentence (1822, Vol. I, p. 100):

> The *form* of bodies is the relation of their elements to each other in space,—the power of bodies is their relation to each other in *time*; and both form and power, if considered separately from the number of elementary corpuscles, and from the changes that arise successively are equally abstractions of the mind, and nothing more.

In addition to warning against the fallacy of reification, Brown warned against the seductiveness of word magic in the same lecture. He did this by quoting a passage from Malebranche (1638–1715) reminiscent of Molière's famous quip about the soporific principle in opium.[28] As noted in an earlier section, members of the Scottish School have been accused of succumbing to word magic by sponsoring a tautological faculty psychology. That Reid did not endorse this kind of faculty psychology has already been indicated. It is also well to note that Brown, by his approval of the following quotation, was even more explicit than Reid in his repudiation of word magic (1822, Vol. I, p. 110):

> "What is there," says Malebranche, "which Aristotle cannot at once propose and resolve, by his fine words of genus, species, act, power, nature, form, faculties, qualities, causa per se, causa per accidens?" His followers find it very difficult to comprehend that these words signify nothing; and that we are not more learned than we were before, when they tell us, in their best manner, that fire melts metals, because it has a solvent faculty; and that some unfortunate epicure, or glutton digests ill, because he has a weak digestion.

In thus warning against the errors of reification and word magic in his lecture on causality, Brown was setting the stage for presentation of his interpretation of scientific method. He developed this in the following lecture on the subject "Hypothesis and Theory." This was a long discourse on the importance of distinguishing the *how* of events from the *why* of events. Among other points, he mentioned Newton's failure to *prove* the existence of ether as well as Torricelli's successful experiment undertaken to *prove* that air has weight. It is especially striking to note that Brown dealt with

---

[28] Malebranche and Molière were contemporaries.

such issues because of what he described as the "application of the laws of physical inquiry to the study of mind." In short, as a philosopher he was thinking of an experimental psychology. He was lecturing at a time when physics was still natural philosophy and psychology was still mental philosophy. As a consequence his students found nothing strange in having him refer to the *experiments* of philosophers, as he did when he stated that "to make experiments, at random, is not to philosophize; it becomes philosophy, only when the experiments are made with a certain view; and to make them, with any particular view, is to suppose the presence of something, the operation of which they will tend either to prove or disprove" (1822, Vol. I, p. 120). Had he written a century later, he might have expressed the same thought by saying that an experiment "becomes science only when it is so planned as either to prove or disprove some testable hypothesis." Justification for this surmise is to be found in Brown's own formulation of what he regarded as the upshot of his long chapter on hypothesis and theory. It merits verbatim quotation because it amounts to an early nineteenth-century formulation of twentieth-century principles of scientific theorizing (1822, Vol. I, p. 128):

> The practical conclusion to be drawn from all this very long discussion is, that we should use hypotheses to suggest and direct inquiry, not to terminate or supersede it; and that, in theorizing,—as the chance of error, in the application of a general law, diminishes, in proportion to the number of analogous cases, in which it is observed to hold,—we should not form any general proposition, till after as wide an induction, as it is possible for us to make; and, in the subsequent application of it to particulars, should never content ourselves, in any new circumstances, with the mere probability, however high, which this applica-cation of it affords; while it is possible for us to verify, or disprove it, by actual experiment.

It should now be evident that in his analysis of the concepts of causality and power Brown, like Hume, recognized the importance of these concepts for scientific understanding. Even though he failed to mention Hume in this connection, he obviously had taken Hume's account as his point of departure for elaboration of these concepts. As previously noted, because he was in substantial agreement with Hume on these issues, he found it expedient to avoid having them presented as elaborations of Humean teachings. On the other hand, when considering some issue in which he found himself in disagreement with Hume, he presented it as being a refutation of a Humean teaching.

With reference to causality, both Hume and Brown regarded the causal relationship as a matter of invariable sequence. As they saw it, the scientific quest for such a sequence meant finding out what goes with what and what follows from what. It meant finding out why Event A is always followed by Event B, why Event X reminds us of Event Y, and why Event Alpha sometimes reminds us of Event Beta and at other times of Event Delta or even of Omega or Zeta. This last contingency, as will soon be shown, was of particular interest to Brown. He would have treated it and these other schematic relations as references to laws of suggestion. For Hume, of course, they would have been references to the laws of association. As Brown saw it, this was not just a trivial difference of opinion regarding preferred terminology. He had serious misgivings about the concept of association in general and of association of ideas in particular. In fact, he argued that the concept of suggestion ought to replace the concept of association and that his principles of suggestion supplied a more accurate account of the psychological factors involved in what others attribute to the principles of association. Under the circumstances, had he been asked to classify himself, he would have preferred to call himself a suggestionist rather than an associationist, just as about a century later, as mentioned in Chapter 12, Thorndike called himself a connectionist rather than an associationist.

Brown's Concept of Suggestion

The previous sentence may serve as a convenient introduction to the present topic. It was written as an answer to this question: How, in terms of systematic psychology, would Brown have classified himself? This was the very first time the question had been raised; but once raised, it was followed by the word *"suggestionist"* as the answer. The answer, in turn, was followed by the thought of Thorndike's classification of his own systematic position. For the present writer, this was something altogether novel. Never before had he perceived this analogy between Brown and Thorndike and their respective reactions to the concept of association. There had been no prior linkage of Brown and Thorndike. They had never been *associated* before; hence the instigating question did not activate an established connection. Instead it *suggested* or gave rise to a new connection.

Perception of analogies, Brown held, is more a matter of suggestion than of association. It involves the perception of relations hitherto unnoticed as exemplified by the introduction of clarifying metaphors and similes. Brown's avocational interest in poetry enabled him to quote from Latin and English classics by way of specific illustration of the way in which "poetic genius" makes use of metaphor as it "breathes its own spirit into every thing surrounding it." Thus, one comes across metaphoric expressions to the effect that "zephyrs *laugh*,—the sky *smiles*,—the forest *frowns*" and kindred *suggestions* of nature as animated. They have to do with resemblances noted by the poet, or what associationists would attribute to the principle of association by similarity. In a lecture concerned with *resemblance* as one of his *primary laws of suggestion,* Brown alludes to the latter principle in the following passage dealing with metaphors and similes as analogies (1822, Vol. II, pp. 14–15):

It is the *metaphor* which forms the essence of the language of poetry; and it is to that peculiar mode of association which we are now considering,—the suggestion of objects by their analogous objects,—that the metaphor owes its birth. . . . The metaphor expresses with rapidity the analogy, as it rises in immediate suggestion, and identifies it, as it were, with the object or emotion which it describes; the *simile* presents, not the analogy merely, but the two analogous objects, and traces their resemblance to each other with the formality of regular comparison. The *metaphor,* therefore, is the figure of passion, the *simile* the figure of calm description.

In the foregoing passage Brown was implying that metaphor is to poetry as simile is to prose. He evidently did not intend this to mean the complete absence of similes in the language of poetry, for in a later passage he referred to the "comparisons of objects with objects which constitute the similes and metaphors of poetry" (1822, Vol. II, p. 89). Nor is the prose of novels completely devoid of metaphoric language. Accordingly, Brown was referring to the more frequent occurrence of metaphors in giving expression to emotion and sentiment as contrasted with the more frequent use of similes in the dispassionate description of impersonal events. The analogies and comparisons introduced in scientific writing, for example, are more likely to be clarifying similes than stirring metaphors.[29] A scientific model is virtually a simile in which the less well-known Phenomenon X is said to be like or to resemble the more familiar or better-known Phenomenon Y.

Stumbling on an apt scientific model is akin to the emergence of a fruitful working hypothesis. As occurrences, Brown would have said, they arise as suggestions and not as associations. By way of illustration he might have cited this excerpt from one of his lectures (1822, Vol. II, p. 22):

When the crucible of the chemist presents to him some new result, and his first astonishment is over, there arise in his mind the ideas of products, or operations, in some respects analogous, by the comparison of which he discovers some new element, or combination of elements, and perhaps, changes altogether the aspect of his science. A Newton sees an apple fall to the ground,—and he discovers the system of the universe. In these cases, the principle of analogy, whether its

---

[29] This is not to be interpreted as meaning that metaphors are rarely clarifying or that similes may not be prompted by strong emotion. The statement as formulated refers to scientific *writing* and not to the inner life of the scientist and the excitement that may affect him as he dwells on the significance of what he is about to write. Brown was not the first to be concerned with this issue. In an article, for example, the philosopher Scott Buchanan mentions Greek efforts to differentiate creative poetry from scientific and philosophic speculation. In this connection he recalled a comment Aristotle made in the *Poetics* to the effect that "the mastery of metaphor is a sign of genius" and that "metaphors are often the seeds from which worlds grow in the human mind" (1966, p. 24).

operation be direct or indirect, is too forcible, and too extensive in its sway, to admit of much dispute. It is sufficient to know, that by the *suggestions* [italics added] which it has afforded to those . . . series of minds, which spread from age to age the progress of improvement over all the . . . generations of mankind, we have risen to a degree of empire over nature, which, compared with our original imbecility, is a greater advance in the scale of being, than that fabulous apotheosis which the ancient world conferred on its barbarous heroes.

This excerpt comes close to explaining why Brown attached such importance to the concept of suggestion. In his view, the novel insights of the world's scientific heroes are *original* suggestions responsible for progress in science.[30] Without such suggestions there can be no creative thinking and, as Brown saw it, creative thinking is different from uninspired thinking dominated by *associative* memory. The latter kind of thinking tends to be stereotyped and routinized. It follows traditional patterns of established *associations*. Brown did not deny the existence of such patterns, and his announced preference for the term "suggestion" was not intended as a substitute for the term "association" in all contexts. He himself had no hesitation in speaking of association. For example, in one lecture he granted that, given certain qualifications, he would "make no objection to the term association" (1822, Vol. II, p. 94) and in a later lecture he referred to "our knowledge of the general principles of association" (1822, Vol. III, p. 25).

The former concession was made in a lecture entitled "Reasons for Preferring the Term Suggestion to the Phrase Association of Ideas." Incidentally, although Reid had expressed the same preference, Brown failed to call attention to this fact. Instead he presented the topic as if the issue had never received consideration. He may have deemed it unnecessary to mention Reid, because his reasons for the preference were somewhat different from Reid's.

There is no need to list all of Brown's reasons for objecting to what he called "the unfortunate phrase *association of ideas.*" It will suffice to mention just one, which was related to his three primary laws of suggestion: the laws of contiguity, contrast, and resemblance. It was Brown's "belief" that these "varieties of suggestion might all be found to be reducible to one general tendency of succession, according to the mere order of former proximity or coexistence" (1822, Vol. II, p. 89). The existence of the "unfortunate phrase" renders such reduction difficult, however, because it restricts the search for the relevant proximate or coexistent factors to those

---

[30] For a contemporary elaboration of the role of analogies in scientific thinking, an article by H. A. Simon and A. Newell on scientific models may be consulted. They point out that "in principle" there is no fundamental difference between analogies and theories. "All theories are analogies, and all analogies are theories" (1963, p. 103).

which give rise to ideas.[31] A restriction of this sort, Brown maintained, makes it impossible to account for all thoughts by tracing them back to such factors. To illustrate the difficulty Brown once again resorted to examples from the field of poetry, as shown in this statement (1822, Vol. II, pp. 89–90):

> In cases of the more shadowy resemblance of analogy, . . . as in those comparisons of objects with objects which constitute the similes and metaphors of poetry,—though there may never have been in the mind any proximity of the very images compared, there may have been a proximity of each to an emotion of some sort, which as common to both, might render each capable of indirectly suggesting the other. When, for example, the whiteness of untrodden snow brings to our mind the innocence of an unpolluted heart,—or a fine morning spring the cheerful freshness of youth,—they may do this only by the influence of a common emotion excited by them.

The preceding examples constitute one of the first occasions when the factor of *emotional congruity*[32] was given explicit recognition as a factor governing the course of ideation. In them Brown was calling attention to a familiar phenomenon that had been overlooked by the associationists. In their preoccupation with associated *ideas,* they had failed to note the influence of emotion and mood on the instigation of thought. Sadness induces sad thoughts, anger precipitates hostile thoughts, and in times of anxiety apprehensive thoughts tend to obtrude themselves. Brown had reference to such commonplace experiences when he noted that not only are objects connected with other objects in the course of thinking but that emotion may also be connected with the sequence of thoughts. This does not constitute an associative connection; for, according to Brown, "our feelings are suggested, and not associated."

This fact was one of the reasons that induced Brown to speak of "association of ideas" as an *unfortunate* phrase. However, he did not call the word *association* an "unfortunate" word. As already mentioned, he sometimes used the word but seemed to limit it to established as opposed to new connections. Apparently he would not have objected to remarks like "I associate Detroit with automobiles" or "I associate Hamlet with Denmark." Of course

---

[31] Brown was unwilling to set any limits to the scope of association as a psychological principle by restricting it to *ideational* association. He was firmly opposed to such restriction, as he made clear in this sentence: "The influence of the associating principle itself extends, not to ideas only, but to every species of affection of which the mind is susceptible" (1822, Vol. I, p. 524).

[32] Emotional congruity is not to be confused with emotional conditioning. The latter refers to the influence of thought on emotion and the former to the influence of emotion on thought. As noted in Chapter 12, emotional conditioning was recognized by Locke, but he was not anticipating Brown's recognition of emotional congruity.

in these instances one might also say that Detroit *suggests* automobiles and that Hamlet *suggests* Denmark. On the other hand, he would have objected to a sentence like "I *associate* your plans for the new house with interesting possibilities." He would have preferred the sentence to read, "Your plans for the new house *suggest* interesting possibilities." By hypothesis, the possibilities in question as *novel* thoughts have to do with ideas that had never been brought up for consideration. In the concluding portion of his lecture, Brown summarized his position with respect to this point in the following way (1822, Vol. II, p. 99):

> . . . it must always be remembered, that the association of ideas denotes as much the successions of ideas of objects which never have existed together before, as the successions of ideas of objects which have been perceived together,—that there are not two separate mental processes, therefore, following perception, and necessary to the succession, *one* by which ideas are primarily associated, and *another* by which they are subsequently suggested,—but that the *association* is, in truth, only another word for the fact of the *suggestion* itself.

From the context, it appears that Brown found his primary principles of contiguity, contrast, and resemblance to be operative both in the case of the initial establishment of an ideational sequence and in the subsequent reactivation of that sequence. In this sense, he argued, the same mental process accounts for both sequences as sequences. Consequently, these primary principles could not account for the emergence of "ideas of objects which never have existed together before." To account for their emergence, Brown supplemented his three primary laws of suggestion with nine secondary laws of suggestion. In some respects his formulation of these secondary laws constitutes his most important contribution to psychology. Associationists came to endorse most of them as secondary laws of *association*. As might be expected, they never shared Brown's preference for the word "suggestion" but accepted suggestion and association as synonymous terms. As a result, Brown's laws are commonly called laws of association. The fact that these laws are also commonly classified as being either primary or secondary is obviously based upon Brown's original classification and thus constitutes a specific way in which he influenced psychology of the early modern period.

Brown's Primary Laws of Association

Brown's three primary laws or principles of contiguity, resemblance, and contrast had already been recognized by Aristotle. Whether Brown was indebted to Aristotle for these principles is difficult to determine. He discusses them without any mention of Aristotle, and it is conceivable that he was unaware of having received an Aristotelian teaching. In his discussion of association he does mention Hume's principles of resemblance, contiguity, and causation. Consequently, two of his three primary principles were obviously related to his study of Hume's writings. In fact, he was explicit in his criticism of Hume's own failure to note that causation as viewed by Hume was the same as Hume's view of contiguity. Brown's criticism took this form: "To speak of *resemblance, contiguity,* and *causation,* as three distinct classes, is, with Mr. Hume's view of causation, and, indeed with every view of it, as if a mathematician should divide lines into *straight, curved,* and *circular*" (1822, Vol. II, p. 10).

Since Hume had also neglected to mention Aristotle's prior allusions to the principles of contiguity and resemblance, Brown could not have been reminded of Aristotle's priority by his study of Hume. Nevertheless, it is hard to believe that Brown's views of the principles of association were altogether uninfluenced by familiarity with Aristotle's account of association. As mentioned in Chapter 4, pp. 90–91, Aristotle had recognized frequency and uniqueness as two principles in addition to the principles of contiguity, resemblance, and contrast. The principles of frequency and uniqueness constitute two of Brown's secondary laws and the other three constitute his primary laws.

It is thus evident that Brown accepted all of Aristotle's laws and added some of his own. Just how he came to group some of them as primary and others as secondary can only be conjectured; Brown has nothing to say about his grouping. It may be that dwelling on Aristotle's principles of uniqueness and frequency as contrasted with Hume's failure to recognize these principles had something to do with it. At all events, Brown's distinction between primary and secondary principles is implicit in Aristotle's list of five principles. Recognizing the distinction and making it explicit by detailed elaboration was Brown's own achievement.

The primary laws have to do with the initial formation of associations or connections. These might be between perception and idea, idea and idea, emotion and idea, action and idea, idea and action, idea and impulse, or any other such linkage of discriminable features of mental life being brought together for the first time. Unless they are brought together or made *contiguous,* there will be no linkage. This is not to say that contiguity suffices to establish an association. What it does say is that without contiguity there can be no association. Learning a foreign language, for example, involves vocabulary drill as foreign words are linked to known equivalents. Similarly, learning arithmetic involves being drilled in addition, division, subtraction, and multiplication. In the process of drilling, contiguous items are being presented to the pupil, but, as every teacher knows, the presentation as such is not sufficient to establish the desired associations. Contiguity is a necessary but not a sufficient condition for their establishment. A given pupil may have intoned the multiplication table in class drills many, many times and yet not know the answer to a question like "How much is three times eight?" For such a pupil, contiguity of the experienced items was not enough to supply the correct answer. However, neither Brown nor the British associationists were concerned with such limitations of the principle of contiguity. Their only concern was with its essential role in the acquisition of knowledge and skill. The only reason for mentioning its limitations in the present context is to keep the problem aspect of associationism from being overlooked.

Brown repeatedly mentioned "proximity and coexistence" in his discussion of association. In doing so, he was calling attention to the temporal and spatial modes of contiguity. One event may follow another and thus be contiguous in time, or two events may be concurrent and thus be contiguous in space. Listening to a melody is an example of the former and inspecting a portrait is an instance of the latter. The distinction is the same as Hartley's distinction between successive and simultaneous associations.

Inspection of a portrait may exemplify the principle of resemblance as well as contiguity. In fact, Brown raised an interesting question in this connection. He asked whether a good portrait of a person we know very well is instantly recognized as a result of association. If it is a photographic likeness with faithful reproduction of every feature, those who know the person will not say, "It resembles him." Instead their comment will be, "It looks just like him." The situation is comparable to the instantaneous recognition of a friend we were with yesterday when we meet him again today. His face today is the same face we saw yesterday; hence there is no need for a special principle of association to account for the recognition. At least Brown saw no need for such a principle.

Nevertheless, for descriptive purposes it would be helpful to have a name for the principle in question. Accordingly, it might be called the principle of *identity,* since the factors accounting for today's instantaneous recognition are identical with those of yesterday's recognition. When this principle is operative, there is no question of one experience reminding us of another. We do not say, "Our friend's face today reminds us of the way he looked yesterday." However, upon being introduced to our friend's cousin we might be struck by a *resemblance* between the cousins as we note the same forward thrust of the jaw, the same facial contours, and other *identical* features along with other *nonidentical* ones such as differences in hair color, shape of mouth, and so on. Under the circumstances, the cousin would remind us of our friend as we react to the identical features in a setting of nonidentical ones. Association by similarity or resemblance thus always involves noting likenesses as well as differences. Failure to note the differences results in association by identity, which can have tragic consequences when witnesses of a crime identify an innocent man as the culprit.

Brown also employed the human figure to illustrate the operation of *contrast,* his third primary principle of association. The sight of a midget, he pointed out, suggests a giant. Any extreme departure from a norm is viewed in terms of a contrasting extreme. Health is contrasted with disease, masculine with feminine, affluence with poverty, bravery with cowardice, north with south, and so on. It is as if polar opposites color our judgments either explicitly or implicitly.

As Brown saw it, these three principles of contiguity, resemblance, and contrast constitute inherent ways of dealing with experience. Contiguous items tend to be associated, similarities tend to be noticed, and opposites tend to be suggested because, independently of special training, the mind is predisposed to function in terms of such tendencies. Metaphorically speaking, they are expressions of the warp and woof of cognitive structure. It is in this sense that the principles involved are *primary* principles of association.

Brown's Secondary Laws of Association

To account for the total sweep of associated or suggested events, Brown found it necessary to supplement the three primary laws by nine secondary ones.[33] In doing so, as he noted, he was not pretending "to discover facts that are new, or little observed, but to arrange facts that, separately, are well known" (1822, Vol. II, p. 44). The facts to be arranged were needed in order to deal with this basic question: Since Event A in the course of experience comes to be contiguous to a multiplicity of other events, what determines which one of these many possible associates is likely to be aroused by A on any particular occasion? Thus, if Event A be the thought of a dog, then in view of the hundreds of experiences connected with the word "dog," what factors will govern the arousal of one of these connections rather than any other? This is the same as asking why some experiences of a given class of events are more likely to be recalled than others.

Brown answered the latter question by *first* nothing the importance of the factor of *duration* of a given experience.[34] It is obvious that we are less likely to remember a stray dog who chanced to pass us on the street last year than the dog we owned as a pet for ten years during our childhood. This differentiation illustrates the first of Brown's secondary laws, which he referred to in the following way (1822, Vol. II, p. 44):

---

[33] These nine laws are to be found in the *Readings in the History of Psychology* edited by W. Dennis (1948, pp. 125–128) and in *A Source Book in the History of Psychology* edited by R. J. Herrnstein and E. G. Boring (1965, pp. 355–363).

[34] He also noted the importance of duration or the time factor in judgments of extent. To demonstrate this factor, he suggested performing a simple experiment by moving the hand along the edge of a book or table with eyes closed and varying the speed of movement from slow to moderate to rapid. Under these conditions, the length of the edge traversed will be found to vary with the speed of movement. Brown also suggested having the same maneuver carried out passively by having an associate move one's arm along the edge at different rates (1822, Vol. I, pp. 337–378).

Every one must be conscious, that innumerable objects pass before him, which are slightly observed at the time, but which form no permanent associations in the mind. The longer we dwell on objects, the more fully do we rely on our future remembrance of them.

A _second_ factor of influence on the permanence of memory has to do with what Brown described in terms of the liveliness of original experience. This is sometimes referred to as the law of vividness or of intensity. The dog whose barking rescued the sleeping family from a fire is not likely to be forgotten. Whatever engenders strong emotion tends to be remembered. Brown had this to say about this factor (1822, Vol. II, p. 45) :

> We remember for a whole lifetime, the occasions of great joy or sorrow; we forget the occasions of innumerable slight pleasures or pains, which occur to us every hour. That strong feeling of interest and curiosity, which we call attention, not only leads us to dwell longer on the consideration of certain objects, but also gives more vivacity to the objects on which we dwell,—and in both these ways tend . . . to _fix_ them, more strongly, in the mind.

The _third_ factor listed by Brown is the factor of _frequency_. This is too obvious to require extended comment. Everybody knows that repetition facilitates retention and that several readings are generally required for verbatim recall of a poem or a paragraph.

Brown's _fourth_ factor also reflects the commonplace observation that recent happenings are more likely to be remembered than less recent ones. It is easier to recall the joke we heard five minutes ago than one we heard five weeks ago. It may be possible to repeat this last sentence immediately after reading it and yet be impossible to do so five minutes from now. However, this law of recency is not without its exception. As Brown noted:

> There is, indeed, one very striking exception to this law, in the case of old age: for events, which happened in youth, are then remembered, when events of the year preceding are forgotten. Yet, even the case of extreme age,—when the time is not extended so far back,—the general law still holds; the events, which happened a few _hours_ before, are remembered, when there is total forgetfulness of what happened a few days before.[35]

---

[35] Brown's conclusion with respect to the influence of age on the recency factor was later modified as a result of laboratory studies governed by _measurements_ of the strength of associations as well as by control of relevant time intervals. For example, something in the way of a principle of diminishing returns was found to be operative in what has come to be known as _Jost's Law_. According to this law, repetition or frequency is more effective in strengthening older associations than more recent ones, even though both sets of associations are of equal initial strength. As a principle it accounts for the fact that, in general, spaced learning requires fewer repetitions than unspaced learning.

The *fifth* factor mentioned by Brown refers to the *uniqueness* of experience. Brown did not employ this descriptive word, but it seems to be a satisfactory one to indicate what he meant when he wrote that "our successive feelings are associated more closely, as *each has coexisted less with other feelings.*" By way of example, he noted the difference in memories aroused by a song rendered by several people as contrasted with a song we have never heard except from one person. In the latter instance, hearing the song on a subsequent occasion will serve as a reminder of that person. Similarly, the student with only a single grade of A in his four years at college is likely to remember this particular experience when the subject of A grades is mentioned, as contrasted with memories aroused in the student who had received many A grades. What was relatively commonplace for the latter student was *unique* for the former; hence the difference in associative memory.

As a *sixth* factory affecting the primary laws, Brown called attention to *original constitutional differences,* both those referring "to the mind itself" as well as those referring to "varieties of bodily temperament." This is an obvious reference to individual differences in native endowment, by virtue of which those having an aptitude for music are likely to differ from those having an aptitude for mathematics, just as those inherently predisposed to be cheerful have different associations from those inherently predisposed to be fearful, irascible, lethargic, or whatever else is to be attributed to the biochemistry of temperament.

Brown recognized that temperamentally cheerful people are not invariably cheerful and that temperamentally irascible people are not invariably angry. The optimist may have his moments of discouragement, just as the pessimist may have his moments of confident hope. A transient mood will color the drift of induced associations. This observation accounted for Brown's *seventh* factor, that a "momentary feeling of joy or sorrow" will "have the power of modifying our suggestions" in accordance with the emotion in question. As a matter of descriptive convenience, this factor is often referred to as association due to *emotional congruity.* Brown was among the first to recognize the phenomenon even though he failed to employ the phrase. Similarly, he was one of the first to recognize the phenomenon of *projection* even though he failed to use the term. He made this evident in the following elaboration of one of the effects of this seventh factor (1822, Vol. II, p. 51):

It is in this way that every passion, which has one fixed object,—such as love, jealousy, revenge, derives *nourishment* from *itself,* suggesting images that give it, in return, new force and liveliness. We see, *in every thing,* what we feel *in ourselves;* and the thoughts which external things seem to suggest, are thus, in part at least, suggested by the permanent emotion within.

In addition to fluctuations of mood, Brown recognized fluctuations in physiological status as determiners of the course of associations. His *eighth* factor dealt with such bodily changes. Had the term been in existence in his time, he might have conceived of this factor as a *homeostatic disturbance*. In extreme form, such a disturbance is exemplified by the delirium of fever or by the confused thinking of the alcoholic. In less extreme form, as Brown pointed out, one has only to recall "how different are the trains of thought in *health* and in *sickness,*—after a *temperate meal*, and after a *luxurious excess!*"

With reference to the *ninth* factor, Brown noted that "trains of thought" are also influenced by "general tendencies produced by prior habits." The latter phrase is an allusion to habitual attitudes and habitual modes of speech associated with given professions, vocations, and dominant fields of interest. A given scene viewed by an engineer, an artist, an economist, and a geologist is not likely to affect each of these men in precisely the same way. Their reports of what they saw will be colored by their professional habits. Thus, if the scene chanced to be a new bridge, the engineer may stress its structural characteristics, the artist its symmetry, the economist its effect on business, and the geologist the solidity of its foundations. Their respective interests will have determined the trend of their thinking. Accordingly, this ninth factor may be designated as the factor of *prevailing interest*.

This list of secondary laws of association has turned out to be fairly complete.[36] It serves as another instance of what was mentioned in Chapter 1 as sound armchair psychology. Furthermore, the factors listed by Brown in terms of association psychology came to influence twentieth-century psychology in terms of learning theory. In other words, his laws of suggestion or association are to be thought of as laws of learning. As such they are also to be thought of as concerned with principles of teaching. Even though Brown failed to espouse a definite theory of learning or to formulate specific principles of teaching, he may be regarded as having set the stage for the later elaboration of his laws of association into their implications for learning theory in general and for educational psychology in particular. This in itself was a major achievement.

Concerning "Muscular Feelings" and Mental Chemistry

Brown's distinction between the primary and secondary laws along with his systematic account of the latter laws, in terms of its relevance for

---

[36] A later addition to the list, for example, is the law of *primacy*. This is the counterpart of the law of *recency* and holds that initial or early phases of learning are more readily fixed or retained than intermediate phases.

later psychology, was justly classified as a major achievement. This was not the only respect in which he influenced later psychology; he also influenced it by making the important distinction between cutaneous sensations and those resulting from variations in muscular tension, or what he called "muscular feelings." These "feelings" are, of course, now known as *kinesthetic* sensations; but the term "kinesthesis" was unknown in Brown's time. In fact, it remained unknown until the 1880s, when it was introduced by Henry Charlton Bastian (1837–1915), one of the founding fathers of British neurology. However, that the phenomenon of kinesthesis was noted by Brown decades before Bastian supplied the technical label is clearly evident in the following excerpt from one of Brown's lectures (1822, Vol. I, pp. 244–245):

> According as the body is hard or soft, rough or smooth,—that is to say, according as it resists in various degrees, the progress of our effort of contraction,—the muscular feeling, which arises from the variously impeded effort, will vary in proportion; and we call hard, soft, rough, smooth, that which produces one or the other of the varieties of these muscular feelings of resistance,—as we term sweet or bitter, blue or yellow, that which produces either of these sensations of taste or vision. With the feeling of resistance, there is, indeed, in every case, combined, a certain tactual feeling, because we must touch whatever we attempt to grasp; but it is not of this mere tactual feeling we think, when we term bodies hard or soft,—it is of the greater or less resistance which they afford to our muscular contraction.

In retrospect it is hard to believe that kinesthetic sensitivity has been overlooked until Brown called attention to its existence.[37] Even today there is no term for it in common speech as there is for vision, hearing, and the other special senses. And yet it is of coordinate importance with them for the management of our daily affairs. In some respects it may be said to be of greater importance; for without kinesthesis there would be no muscular control—no walking, talking, standing, sitting, painting, singing, dancing, chewing, exercising, playing, or any kind of activity whatsoever. Brown's "muscular feelings"[38] are indispensable for the execution of any skilled movement.

---

[37] Whether Brown was the first to call attention to such sensitivity is hard to determine. It had not been overlooked by Hartley and was also mentioned by Erasmus Darwin (1731–1832), the grandfather of Charles Darwin and a noted naturalist.

[38] Brown's reference to "muscular feelings" is now best regarded as a first approximation to a phenomenon that is more complex than Brown realized. It is not just a muscular phenomenon, since it also involves the tendons and the joints. In Brown's day, nothing was known about the kinesthetic receptor structures. Not until the latter half of the nineteenth century, with the advance of histological techniques, were such structures as Pacinian corpuscles, muscle spindles, and Golgi tendon organs discovered and described. Needless to add, Brown lived too early to know anything about the neurology of kinesthesis.

Brown's discovery of "muscular feelings" was a result of his acumen as an introspectionist. This is not to be construed as a reference to the kind of systematic introspection under laboratory control that Wundt came to advocate so many years later. Instead it is a convenient way of referring to the kind of casual but critical analysis of experience that Brown seemed to advocate. His list of secondary laws of association may be viewed as a product of such analysis. In his view there can be no "science of mind" without analysis of the complexity of experience. He even argued that just as the chemist has to analyze compounds into their constituent elements, so the "intellectual inquirer" has to do the same with the events of mental life. His argument took this form (1822, Vol. I, pp. 151–152):

> In the mind of man, all is in a state of constant and ever-varying complexity, and a single sentiment may be the slow result of innumerable feelings. There is not a single pleasure, or pain, or thought, or emotion, that may not,—by the influence of that associating principle, which is afterwards to come under our consideration,—be so connected with *other* pleasures, or pains, or thoughts, or emotions, as to form with them, forever after, an union the most intimate. The complex, or seemingly complex, phenomena of thought, which result from the constant operation of this principle of the mind, it is the labour of the *intellectual inquirer* to *analyze*, as it is the labour of the *chemist* to reduce the compound bodies, on which he operates, however close 'and intimate their combination may be, to their constituent elements.

This plea for a mental chemistry was not just a transitory notion. Brown took it very seriously and reverted to it several times in the course of his lectures. For example, he once reminded his students (1822, Vol. I, p. 240):

> The science of mind, as it is a science of analysis, I have more than once compared to *chemistry,* and pointed out to you, and illustrated, its various circumstances of resemblance. In this too, we may hope the analogy will hold,—that, as the innumerable aggregates, in the one science, have been reduced and simplified, · the innumerable complex of feelings in the other will admit of a corresponding reduction and simplification.

Concluding Comment

More than 150 years have elapsed since Brown gave expression to the hope that his chemical analogy would hold for the eventual establishment of "the science of mind." Of course nothing as impressive as Mendeleev's periodic table of the chemical elements has come to be paralleled by the results of psychological analysis. In this sense, Brown's analogy has not held. Nevertheless, it might be argued that Wundt and his pupils did succeed in reducing the complexities of immediate experience into constituent elements of sensation, simple feelings, and their attributes and that, if arranged in tabular form, the result would be a crude analogue to Mendeleev's table. It would be a crude analogue because there would be no psychological equivalent to the periodic law.

Whether it is a helpful analogy in other respects is a moot question having too many ramifications to be considered in the present context. For the time being it is enough to note Brown's early introduction of the analogy. Some decades later it was also used by John Stuart Mill, who, like Brown, endorsed the notion of a "mental chemistry." In doing so he was offering an alternative to the "mental mechanics" sponsored by his father, James Mill. Thus the father, Brown's contemporary, conceived of associations or mental connections in terms of a physical analogy, while the son added a chemical analogy.[39] Their respective views on the subject belong to the history of British associationism rather than to the history of the Scottish School. They are more directly related to Hartley than to the movement started by Reid.

This last statement serves as a reminder of the fact that at its inception under Reid's aegis the Scottish School was clashing with the teachings of Hume and Hartley. However, as may be recalled, Brown was able to endorse some of Hume's teachings. After all, Reid was almost seventy when Brown was born, and hence Brown had no obligation to play the role of disciple to a revered leader. Brown's membership in the Scottish School was more a matter of academic affiliation than of party loyalty. As a result, being free to do his own thinking, the psychology he came to espouse can be said to have had more in common with the British tradition than with Reid's opposition to that tradition. In short, his secondary laws and his mental chemistry are more consonant with nineteenth-century British associationism than with Reid's eighteenth-century Scottish "commonsense" psychology. It is also well to add that Brown referred to an "intellectual physics" as well as to a mental chemistry. Both of these analogies came to influence nineteenth-century associationism. In fact, as will be brought out in the next chapter, John Stuart Mill, who was especially impressed by the notion of a mental chemistry, was familiar with Brown's lectures and acknowledged his indebtedness to Brown for the notion in question.

---

[39] It would be more accurate to say that John Stuart Mill made the chemical analogy explicit. As will be explained in the next chapter, the analogy was already implicit in the writings of James Mill even though he did not actually call it an instance of mental chemistry.

References

Boring, E. G. *A History of Experimental Psychology,* 2nd ed. New York: Appleton-Century-Crofts, 1950.

Brett, G. S. *A History of Psychology,* Vol. III. London: George Allen and Unwin, 1921.

Brown, S. W., Guilford, J. P., and Hoepfner, R. "A Factor Analysis of Semantic Memory Abilities," *Reports from the Psychological Laboratory,* No. 37. Los Angeles: University of Southern California, 1966.

Brown, T. *Lectures on the Philosophy of the Human Mind,* 3 vols. Andover: Mark Newman, 1822.

Buchanan, S. "World Order," *Center Diary: 15.* The Fund for Republic (November–December, 1966), pp. 23–34.

Carmichael, L. "Karl Spencer Lashley, Experimental Psychologist," *Science,* 1958, *129,* 1410–1412.

Coover, J. E. "Formal Discipline from the Standpoint of Experimental Psychology," *Psychological Monographs,* 1912, No. 87.

Dennis, W. (ed.). *Readings in the History of Psychology.* New York: Appleton-Century-Crofts, 1948.

English, H. B., and English, A. V. *A Comprehensive Dictionary of Psychological and Psychoanalytical Terms.* New York: Longmans, Green and Company, 1958.

Garrison, F. H. *An Introduction to the History of Medicine,* 4th ed. Philadelphia: W. B. Saunders Company, 1929. (Reprinted 1960.)

Hamilton, W. "The Nature of Consciousness," in D. S. Robinson (ed.). *The Story of Scottish Philosophy.* New York: Exposition Press, 1961, pp. 228–236.

Harlow, H. F., and Harlow, M. "Learning to Love," *American Scientist,* 1966, *54,* 244–272.

Herrnstein, R. J., and Boring, E. G. (eds.). *A Source Book in the History of Psychology.* Cambridge: Harvard University Press, 1965.

Hilgard, E. R. *Theories of Learning,* 2nd ed. New York: Appleton-Century-Crofts, 1956.

James, W. *Principles of Psychology,* Vol. I. New York: Henry Holt and Company, 1890.

Klemm, O. *A History of Psychology.* (Translated by E. C. Wilm and R. Pintner.) New York: Charles Scribner's Sons, 1914.

Macalister, A. "Phrenology," in *Encyclopaedia Britannica,* 14th ed., 1929.

Merz, J. T. *A History of European Thought in the Nineteenth Century,* 4 vols., rev. ed. New York: Dover Publications, 1965. (First published between 1904 and 1912.)

Murphy, G. *Historical Introduction to Modern Psychology,* rev. ed. New York: Harcourt, Brace and Company, 1949.

Peterson, J. *Early Conceptions and Tests of Intelligence.* Yonkers, New York: World Book Company, 1925.

Peterson, J. "Imitation and Mental Adjustment," *Journal of Abnormal and Social Psychology,* 1922, *17,* 1–15.

Porter, N. Four chapters in D. S. Robinson (ed.). *The Story of Scottish Philosophy.* New York: Exposition Press, 1961: "Thomas Reid—The Man and His Work," pp. 118–150; "Dugald Stuart—The Man and His Work," pp. 151–189; "Thomas Brown—The Man and His Work," pp. 190–197, "Sir William Hamilton—The Man and His Work," pp. 214–220.

Pringle-Pattison, A. S. "Thomas Reid," in *Encyclopaedia Britannica,* 11th ed., 1910.

Reid, T. *Essays on the Powers of the Human Mind.* Vol. III. Edinburgh: Bell and Bradfute, 1819. (Reprint of *Essays on the Active Powers of the Human Mind,* first published in 1788.)

Reid, T. *An Inquiry into the Human Mind, on the Principles of Common Sense,* 7th ed. Edinburgh: Bell and Bradfute, 1814. (First published in 1764.)

Simon, H. A., and Newell, A. "The Use and Limitations of Models," in M. H. Marx (ed.). *Theories in Contemporary Psychology.* New York: The Macmillan Company, 1963, pp. 89–104.

Spearman, C. *The Abilities of Man—Their Nature and Measurement.* New York: The Macmillan Company, 1927.

Spoerl, H. D. "Faculties versus Traits: Gall's Solution," *Character and Personality,* 1936, *4,* 216–231.

Thorndike, E. L. *Educational Psychology, Briefer Course.* New York: Teachers College, Columbia University, 1914.

Warren, H. C. *Dictionary of Psychology.* Boston: Houghton Mifflin Company, 1934.

Webb, L. W. "Transfer of Training and Retroaction," *Psychological Monographs,* 1917, No. 104.

Woozley, A. D. *Reid's Essays on the Intellectual Powers of Man.* (Edited and abridged by Woozley.) London: Macmillan and Company, 1914.

20

The Millean Backgrounds

WITH THE PUBLICATION OF the first edition of Brown's *Lectures* in 1820, the Scottish School became part of early nineteenth-century psychology. It might be more in accord with fact to say that it became part of nineteenth-century mental philosophy, for psychology in the sense of a post-Wundtian autonomous field of investigation was a late nineteenth-century development. The lectures, it will be recalled, were concerned with the *philosophy* of the human mind. Although they dealt with many issues that subsequently became the subject of laboratory study, there was virtually no reference to the possibility of such study. The very notion of a psychological laboratory would have seemed fantastic at the time.

Even the notion of a *physiological* laboratory might have seemed strange in the early 1880s. Johannes Purkinje (1787–1869), who became professor of physiology at the University of Breslau in 1823, struggled for years to secure laboratory facilities for his experimental work. As E. Nordenskiöld noted in his *History of Biology* (1928, p. 380), Purkinje had to "overcome the opposition of his superiors and colleagues" before a physiological institute was placed at his disposal. This took place in 1840 and constituted the first such institute in Germany. During the preceding years, Purkinje had to perform his experimental work at home. Nor would he have found a physiological laboratory in the United States during these years. According to F. H. Garrison (1960, p. 537), it was not until 1871 that such a laboratory came into existence.[1] This was the

---

[1] It was founded by Henry Pickering Bowditch (1842–1921). He had spent two years studying physiology at Leipzig, and upon his return to assume an assistant professorship in physiology at Harvard he established the laboratory and equipped it with apparatus he had purchased in Germany at his own expense. Both William James and G. Stanley Hall were influenced by his teachings. In fact, James mentions several of Bowditch's experimental findings in the *Principles* (1890, Vol. I, p. 87, and Vol. II, p. 247 and p. 520).

same decade during which laboratory psychology had its official beginnings; hence, chronologically considered, experimental physiology as an ongoing American enterprise is not much older than experimental psychology.

Despite his medical training Brown discussed psychological problems with little attention to their physiological implications. In this respect he differed from Hartley whose medical background was obviously related to his doctrine of neural vibrations as correlates of mental processes. In general, the members of the Scottish School ignored the psychophysical riddle or the mind-brain puzzle. Reid, Stewart, and Brown were in agreement in rejecting Hartley's proposed solution. They failed to understand how the soft, moist, pulpy nature of nerves and brain could vibrate like the strings of a violin. Their disposition of the basic problem was well summarized by Stewart when he wrote that "the anatomy of the body does not seem to be more likely to throw light on the philosophy of the mind, than an analysis of the mind to throw light on the physiology of the body" (D. S. Robinson [ed.], 1961, p. 160).

In thus ignoring the subject of physiological psychology, these Scottish philosopher-psychologists were following the precedent of Locke, who had also decided not to "meddle" with the subject. Anyway, not enough was known around the year 1800 to have warranted fruitful speculation about the details of psychophysiology. The subject of histology had just come into being around 1801 with the pioneer descriptions of the body's tissues by Marie François Xavier Bichat (1771–1802). It was not until the 1830s that the basic cellular structure of all plant and animal tissues was established.[2] Furthermore, as mentioned in the preceding chapter, brain anatomy and brain physiology had their significant beginnings in the work of men like Gall and Flourens. Moreover, it was not until 1811 that Sir Charles Bell (1774–1842) supplied the first experimental evidence regarding the motor functions of the anterior spinal nerve roots.[3] All the specialized branches of biology such as paleontology, embryology, comparative anatomy, and neurology got under way in the early decades of the nineteenth century. Interestingly enough, they could not have been referred to as branches of biology prior to 1800, for the word "biology," as indicated by Nordenskiöld (1928, p. 320), was first introduced by Lamarck (1744–1829) in a book published in 1802.

---

[2] This was due to the combined efforts of the botanist Matthias Jakob Schleiden (1804–1881) and the anatomist Theodor Schwann (1810–1882). For details see F. H. Garrison (1960, pp. 454–455).

[3] At the time, Bell failed to differentiate the posterior roots as sensory and the anterior ones as motor. According to Garrison, "conclusive experimental proof" for this differentiation was supplied by François Magendie in 1822 and subsequently confirmed by Johannes Müller (Garrison, 1960, pp. 446–447). By 1826, Garrison added, Bell had come to a correct interpretation of his original experiment. This explains why the phenomenon in question is often referred to as the Bell-Magendie Law.

Under the circumstances it should be easy to understand why biological considerations in general and physiological ones in particular failed to engage the sustained attention of members of the Scottish School and their immediate British successors of the nineteenth century. The first of these successors was James Mill, who in turn was followed by his son, John Stuart Mill, in the line of British associationists. In the work of these two men the Scottish School of psychology had a direct influence on British empiricism. The father was especially influenced by the teachings of Brown and the son by the teachings of Hamilton. In fact, as will be brought out in the next section, James Mill was more Scottish than English in terms of his background.

James Mill: Biographical Sketch

James Mill (1773–1836) was a man of many parts. As a writer he contributed to such varied fields as history, political economy, psychology, philosophy, education, and penology. Never a member of any university faculty, he was not a professor of any of these subjects. Nor can he be said to have majored in any of them as a university student. His books and essays dealing with these topics were the fruits of individual study and reflection. They were not the results of identification with a learned father, for his father was a small tradesman. In this respect, his own background was very different from that of his distinguished son, since John Stuart Mill's precocity and erudition were intimately related to identification with *his* father.

A native of Scotland, the elder Mill spent the first thirty years of his life there. Although all of his formal schooling was Scottish, historians of psychology list him with the British associationists and not as a member of the Scottish School. He attended the University of Edinburgh and became familiar with the outlook of the Scottish School as presented in Dugald Stewart's lectures on philosophy. These must have struck him as memorable, for years later he still recalled Stewart's eloquence. At Edinburgh he won distinction not as a student of philosophy but as a student of Greek. He also studied theology and became a preacher at twenty-five. However, this proved to be an unfortunate choice of vocation. His sermons failed to inspire his congregation and after a time he tried to support himself by tutoring. In 1802 he went to London and began his career as a writer. Three years later, at the age of thirty-two, he married and in the succeeding years found himself burdened financially by a family of four sons and five daughters. John Stuart Mill, born in 1806, was the eldest child. His advent may have prompted the start of Mill's most ambitious and most famous literary undertaking, his *History of India*. John Stuart Mill was about six months old when his father began the history and he was a boy of twelve by the time it was published. It resulted in Mill's being appointed to a position with the East India Company which at long last afforded him a modicum of freedom from monetary concerns as his salary rose with successive promotions during the seventeen years he remained as an official of the company.

During the twelve years he was writing the *History of India,* Mill was also writing articles for various periodicals and he continued to do so after the work was published. Many of them were concerned with the explanation of the principles of utilitarianism and their application to different social and political problems. His endorsement of these principles stemmed from his long and close friendship with Jeremy Bentham (1748–1832), whom he had first met in 1808.

As a social philosophy, utilitarianism has both ethical and psychological implications in terms of its seeming hedonistic emphasis on the pursuit of happiness and the pleasurable gratification of desire.[4] As an ethical theory, it holds that man *ought* to promote his own and the general welfare by maximizing pleasure, and as a psychological theory it holds that satisfaction of desire is man's regnant motive. As explained in Chapter 12, Thorndike's law of hedonic effect illustrates this kind of motivational theory. James Mill's endorsement of utilitarianism thus seems to reflect an implicit theory of motivation, though in his one work on psychology this was not stressed as an explicit theory. As will be evident in the next few sections, his approach to psychology did not involve recognition of motivation as a key problem.

Introduction to James Mill's Psychology

Although James Mill had been introduced to psychological issues during his student days by attending the lectures of Dugald Stewart, he was much more directly influenced by Hartley's teachings during his adult years. Both he and John Stuart Mill had much to do with weaving these teachings into the pattern of nineteenth-century British psychology. Of course, there was not complete acceptance of all of Hartley's "observations." James Mill rejected some of them, retained others, and added some of his own. A similar statement applies to John Stuart's reaction to his father's psychological views. In fact, John Stuart never wrote a separate book on the subject of psychology per se. His father did that with the publication in 1829 of his *Analysis of the Phenomena of the Human Mind.* This work in two volumes had been started in 1822 and was in the nature of an avocational pursuit; as John Stuart Mill explained in his *Autobiography* (1882, p. 69), his

---

[4] Utilitarianism is usually regarded as a hedonistic doctrine because it holds that the purpose of action is or should be the promotion of the greatest happiness of the greatest number. However, as will be indicated in a later section in connection with John Stuart Mill's endorsement of the doctrine, it may be possible to interpret it as nonhedonistic.

JAMES MILL (1773–1836)

JOHN STUART MILL (1806–1873)

father "could only command the concentration of thought necessary for this work, during the complete leisure of his holiday of a month or six weeks annually."

A new edition of the work was published in 1869. This one was edited by John Stuart Mill and is replete with critical and explanatory notes many of which serve to reveal ways in which he differed from his father and constitute an important source of information regarding John Stuart Mill's own psychological views. In addition to contributing his own notes, John Stuart Mill as editor had Alexander Bain supply comments based upon later developments of association psychology. He also enlisted the aid of Andrew Findlater (1810–1885), a specialist in philology, and of George Grote (1794–1871), a specialist in Greek history and philosophy. The new edition of his father's work was thus subjected to the critical scrutiny of four different scholars. In the preface to this edition John Stuart Mill recommended that the "real student" first read what his father had written without paying any attention to the notes and then, upon a second reading, begin to take the notes into consideration. By this procedure, he indicated, the student "will be in a better position for profiting by any aid the notes may afford, and will be in less danger of accepting, without due examination, the opinion of the last comer as the best" (1869, p. xxi).

It was thus evident that both he and his collaborators regarded the book as worthy of careful study even though forty years had elapsed since its first appearance. During the intervening years Bain himself had written an associationistic psychology. Nevertheless, he seemingly regarded the earlier work of James Mill on the same subject as important enough for him to contribute critical notes to the new edition of this earlier work. Furthermore, even though John Stuart Mill's own notes revealed how he had come to question some of his father's interpretations, he was by no means ready to take issue with the general drift of his father's associationism. He could still endorse what he took to be the purpose of his father's book, which he formulated as follows (1869, p. x):

> It is an attempt to reach the simplest elements which by their combination generate the manifold complexity of our mental states, and to assign the laws of those elements, and the elementary laws of their combination, from which laws, the subordinate ones which govern the compound states are consequences and corollaries.

This way of conceiving of the problem of psychology, he acknowledged, was not original with his father. He mentioned Aristotle's interest in analysis of mental phenomena and the contributions of Hobbes and Locke. Neither Berkeley nor Hume was mentioned in this context. Hartley, however, was singled out for special commendation along with Aristotle, Hobbes, and Locke in this way (1869, pp. x–xi):

These three philosophers have all left their names identified with the great fundamental law of Association of Ideas; yet none of them saw far enough to perceive that it is through this law that Experience operates in moulding our thoughts and forming our thinking powers. Dr. Hartley was the man of genius who first clearly discerned that this is the key to the explanation of the more complex mental phenomena, though he, too, was indebted to an otherwise forgotten thinker, Mr. Gay. Dr. Hartley's treatise . . . goes over the whole field of the mental phenomena, both intellectual and emotional, and points out the way in which, as he thinks, sensations, ideas of sensation, and association, generate and account for the principle complications of our mental nature. If this doctrine is destined to be accepted as, in the main, the true theory of Mind, to Hartley will always belong the glory of having originated it. But his book made scarcely any impression upon the thought of his age.

John Stuart Mill then explained why Hartley failed to be appreciated during his own lifetime. One reason was that he complicated his presentation with his doctrine of neural vibrations. Interestingly, Mill did not characterize the doctrine as irrelevant or wrong or misleading. Instead he called it a "premature hypothesis respecting the physical mechanism of sensation and thought" with which Hartley had "incumbered his theory of Association." He failed to indicate in what sense Hartley's excursion into neurophysiological theorizing was premature. It might be that he believed that not enough was known about brain physiology to justify such theorizing, or else that he deemed it more important to win support for associationistic psychology per se before venturing to speculate about the "physical" concomitants of this psychology. Mill had another reason to account for Hartley's failure to win support for his theory: the lack of solid proofs for his "observations" and the interpretations to be derived from them. It was as if Hartley had become so familiar with them that he seemed to think a few hints would suffice to render his conclusions obvious to others. He neglected to provide the intermediate links in his chain of reasoning.

An additional reason for delay in recognizing the importance of Hartley's contribution, according to John Stuart Mill, was the fact that publication of his *Observations* "so nearly coincided with the commencement of the reaction against the Experience psychology, provoked by the hardy skepticism of Hume." For all these reasons, he concluded, Hartley's teaching had suffered from general neglect until, with the publication of his father's book, it was given "an importance that it can never again lose." Consequently, his father is to be credited with the "honour . . . of being the reviver and second founder of the Association Psychology."[5]

---

[5] In effect John Stuart Mill was contending that the psychological importance of the principle of association was not realized until Hartley appeared on the scene. Although it had been recognized as a principle from the days of Aristotle, he believed that its

The Problem of Psychological Analysis

From the title of his book, it was clear that James Mill was primarily concerned with the *analysis* of mental phenomena. In writing the preface to the new edition of the book some forty years later, John Stuart Mill deemed it advisable to elaborate upon the subject of scientific analysis. He pointed out, for example, that there are two kinds of analyses: (1) those pertaining to the order or sequence of natural phenomena; and (2) those having to do with the structure or composition of the phenomena themselves. To illustrate the first kind of analysis, he mentioned Newton's law of gravitation as the outcome of an analysis of the motion of the planets so that "a great number of the successions which take place in the material world were shown to be particular cases of a law of causation pervading all Nature" (1869, p. vi). The second kind of analysis, he suggested, is illustrated by chemical analysis of water into hydrogen and oxygen. At the time this was written, close to 1870, both physics and chemistry were sufficiently advanced to render this distinction between the two kinds of analysis fairly obvious to the sophisticated reader. What may not have been so obvious at the time was the following contention (1869, p. vii):

> Both these processes are as largely applicable, and as much required, in the investigation of mental phenomena as of material. And in the one case as in the other, the advance of scientific knowledge may be measured by the progress made in resolving complex facts into simpler ones.

To show what he meant by this contention, John Stuart Mill then proceeded to quote at some length from one of Brown's *Lectures*. This was one of the lectures in which, as mentioned at the close of the previous chapter, Brown had referred to both "a chemistry of the mind" as well as to an "intellectual physics." In one part of the lecture Brown had referred to what he called the "associating principle" as follows (1869, pp. viii–ix):

> The complex . . . phenomena of thought, which result from the constant operation of this principle of the mind, it is the labour of the intellectual inquirer to analyse, as it is the labour of the chemist to reduce the compound bodies on which he operates, however close and intimate their combination may be, to their constituent elements . . . and as, in chemistry, it often happens that the qualities of the separate ingredients of a compound body are not recognizable by us in the apparently different qualities of the compound itself,—so in this spontaneous *chemistry of the mind* [italics added], the compound sentiment that results from the association of former feelings has, in many cases, on first consideration,

---

explanatory value had not been appreciated by any of Hartley's empiricist predecessors. Moreover, in his view, his father had been the first to appreciate Hartley; hence each was called a "founder" of "the Association Psychology."

so little resemblance to these constituents of it, as formerly existing in their elementary state, that it requires the most attentive reflection to separate, and evolve
distinctly to others, the assemblages which even a few years may have
produced.

Brown then concluded that it is "scarcely possible to advance even a single
step, in *intellectual physics* [italics added], without the necessity of performing some sort of analysis, by which we reduce to simpler elements some
complex feeling that seems to us virtually to involve them." The "explanations" given by Brown in the quoted passage, John Stuart Mill maintained,
serve to "define and characterize the task which was proposed to himself"
by his father in undertaking his analysis of the human mind. This analysis,
it thus appears, was to call for an "intellectual physics" as well as for a
"chemistry of the mind." James Mill was ready to employ both kinds of
analysis, as suggested by Brown's references to a mental physics and a
mental chemistry. In terms of the chemical analogy, James Mill, for example,
accounted for the emergence of the sensation of white when the seven
spectral colors are presented on a revolving surface in rapid succession. To
quote him directly (1869, p. 91):

> By the rapidity of the succession, the several sensations cease to be distin-
> guishable; they run, as it were, together, and a new sensation, compounded of
> all the seven, but apparently a simple one is the result. Ideas, also, which have
> been so often conjoined, that whenever one exists in the mind, the others
> immediately exist along with it, seem to run into one another, to coalesce, as it
> were, and out of many to form one idea; which idea, however in reality complex,
> appears to be no less simple, than any one of those of which it is compounded.

There are not many such applications of Brown's mental chemistry in
Mill's *Analysis of Mind*. For the most part Mill cited instances of a more
distinctively *mechanical* juxtaposition of sensations and ideas; but the
chemical analogy was by no means altogether alien to his thinking. In
Brett's apt phrase, "James Mill coquetted with chemistry" (1921, Vol. III,
p. 204). This ideational flirtation was undoubtedly the result of his having
been introduced to Brown's notion of a "chemistry of the mind." He was
familiar with Brown's *Lectures* and referred to them from time to time. In
fact, he introduced his chapter on "The Association of Ideas" with an
approving quotation from the *Lectures*.

In terms of its broader implications, the issue is rather trivial. After all,
it might be asked, "Why is it important to find out whether James Mill
entertained the concept of a mental chemistry back in the 1820s?" It
would not be at all important were it not that the issue has been introduced
in several textbooks[6] in a manner that is at variance with the historical facts

---

[6] The following histories of psychology are to be considered in this connection:

as noted in the previously cited excerpts from John Stuart Mill's preface. For these textbooks to list James Mill as altogether unmindful of the chemical analogy and his son as the first to have suggested the use of this analogy is at variance with the preface as well as with Brown's lectures. As has just been indicated, Brown was the first to propose the idea of a mental chemistry in contradistinction to a mental physics or a mental mechanics when he referred to a "chemistry of the mind" and to an "intellectual physics."

Both kinds of analyses, John Stuart Mill believed, characterized what his father had written about the nature of mind. If so, then fifty years before the first psychological laboratory had come into existence, by his recourse to physical and chemical analogies, James Mill might be said to have given his empirical associationism an orientation seemingly congruent with the outlook of the natural scientist. From this viewpoint, the way was being prepared for the orientation of those founding fathers of scientific psychology who looked to physics as the model science. The resulting shift from an empirical associationism to an experimental associationism was more in the nature of a transition than an abrupt innovation.

The Sensationism of James Mill

In presenting his empirical associationism James Mill reflected the teachings of Locke, Hartley, and Brown to a greater degree than those of Hobbes, Berkeley, or Hume or those of the continental philosopher-psychologists considered in previous chapters. He was especially influenced by Hartley, but not by Hartley's vibrational neurophysiology. Apparently, like Locke, James Mill did not care to "meddle with the physical consideration of the mind." In fact, in one editorial note John Stuart Mill refers to his father's "unwillingness to admit the possibility that ideas as well as sensations may be directly affected by material conditions" and in some instances, he noted, such unwillingness resulted in "the author's usual acuteness of discernment" being "blunted" (1869, p. 104). Furthermore, from the context it is evident that James Mill did not agree with Hartley's parallelism. He was prepared to endorse interactionism to the extent of noting the effect mental states can have on organic functions, but not on a reciprocal effect of the latter functions on mental states. Thus, to cite one of his examples, although he was willing to grant that anxiety may provoke digestive disturbances, he seemed unwilling to reverse the process. Both John Stuart Mill and Bain called attention to this as one of James Mill's "shortcomings."

---

(1) Gardner Murphy wrote that the "most celebrated" of John Stuart Mill's doctrines is "mental chemistry," which is to be contrasted with James Mill's purely "mechanical conceptions" (1949, p. 107).

(2) In the volume by J. C. Flugel this statement is made: "For the rigid mechanical scheme of interaction between unitary ideas, in terms of which James Mill has described the working of the mind, J. S. Mill substituted a 'chemical' conception . . . " (1964, p. 63).

In his general approach to the analysis of mind James Mill began with the topic of sensation. This, of course, was entirely consistent with his endorsement of the empiricism of Locke and Hartley. His opening chapter is devoted to a hasty presentation of the traditional five senses along with three additional ones. The latter included sensations in the alimentary canal as experienced by victims of indigestion and was thus an allusion to what later came to be designated as organic or visceral or interoceptive sensations. He also recognized "muscular sensations, or those feelings which accompany the action of muscles," as qualitatively distinct from other departments of sense. These "muscular sensations," or what Henry Charlton Bastian (1837–1915) was later to call kinesthetic sensations, James Mill pointed out, had been overlooked until writers like Hartley, Erasmus Darwin, and Brown had called attention to them. Mill referred to his third group of sensations as "sensations of disorganization." By this phrase he was referring to any threat to bodily integrity as experienced in sensations of a painful sort due to inflammation, disease, or "lacerations, cuts, bruises, burnings" and so forth. At best, one might say that his "sensations of disorganization" have survived in later references to *nociceptive* sensations.

Fewer than fifty pages are concerned with these eight classes of sensation, so that of necessity each one was disposed of in rather superficial fashion. The one point of possible interest worth mentioning is the fact that in his presentation he first introduced the topic of olfactory sensations. This had nothing to do with the olfactory nerve being the first of the cranial nerves, since his second topic had to do with hearing, or what neurologists would designate as the eighth cranial nerve. Instead, as Bain explained in the following paragraph (1869, p. 7), Mill's choice of an initial topic was reminiscent of Condillac:

> The author, like Condillac,[7] selected Smell to begin with, as being a remarkably simple and characteristic feeling; he has found another expository advantage in

---

[7] Étienne Bonnot de Condillac (1715–1780) was an influential French philosopher who, despite being the head of a monastery, preferred the empiricism of Locke to the rationalism of Descartes and Leibnitz. As a result of his writings, Locke's views became familiar to French thinkers. In one respect Condillac was even more empirical than Locke, for instead of endowing the newborn child with capacity for both sensation and reflection in accordance with Locke's assumption, he argued that sensation alone would suffice to account for the genesis of mind. To show how this could be accomplished, he introduced a Pygmalion-like example of a sentient statue animated by a soul capable of experiencing sensations of smell, but initially deprived of all other modalities of sense. He did this because he regarded smell as contributing less to the acquisition of knowledge than any of the other senses. By hypothesis, accordingly, his statue would start with zero knowledge and lack even the vestige of any Cartesian innate ideas. The first impression to be made on its unblemished *tabula rasa* might be the smell of a rose. Being sentient, the statue would have to be conscious of this smell; and to be conscious of it means noticing it, and to notice something is the equivalent of paying *attention* to it. With the introduction of a second kind of smell, the statue could compare it with

it, by disturbing our routine mode of regarding the intellect as principally made up of sensations of sight. It has a startling effect on the reader, to suggest a mental life consisting wholly of smells and ideas of smells.

Ideas as "Copies" of Sensations

After his hasty consideration of smell and the other seven classes of sensation, James Mill introduced the topic of ideas. He employed the word "feeling" as a generic term to include both sensations and ideas. For him, ideas refer to the effects of sensation or that which remains after the object or cause of sensation is no longer activating a sense organ. To look at a horse is to have a sensation of the horse, but to continue "seeing" the animal with eyes closed is to have an idea of the horse. The idea, Mill stated, is thus "a copy, an image," or "sometimes a representation, or trace of the sensation." In summary (1869, p. 52):

> We have two classes of feelings: one, that which exists when the object of sense is present; another, that which exists after the object of sense has ceased to be present. The one class of feelings I call SENSATIONS: the other class of feelings I call IDEAS.

It is to be noted that in terms of this classificatory scheme, there is no special provision for affective phenomena in the way of feelings of pleasantness, sadness, malaise, elation, and whatever else is descriptive of man's life of emotion. In general, Mill ignored noncognitive aspects of experience. It is also well to note his failure to make a distinction between afterimages and ideas as well as between sensation and perception. For him, the sight of a horse was just as much a sensation as a sour taste. In fact, he may have been borrowing Hartley's horse when he introduced his version of ideational association in this way (1869, p. 70):

---

the first kind. This would involve attending to two items at the same time and give rise to *judgment*. Some smells would be pleasant and others unpleasant, and thus desire and aversion as the foundation for preference and *motivation* would come into being. Recurrence of particular smells would enable the statue to recognize them as having been experienced, and such recognition of a past event as having taken place is the same as having a *memory* of something. Moreover, in the process of comparing past smells with present ones, the statue would be *associating* them. If this olfactory being were now to be supplied with tactual sensations, it would be able to learn about external objects and, of course, with the subsequent addition of other kinds of sensory experience, Condillac maintained that his statue would soon be in possession of a human mind. Being an abbot, he was probably inhibited from falling in love with his eighteenth-century Galatea, but both he and his followers could be proud of what they took to be her successful demonstration of a Lockean approach to the origin of mind. What they failed to realize was the spurious nature of the demonstration. The *intellectus ipse* of Leibnitz or the reflections of Locke had unconsciously been taken for granted rather than derived as passive resultants of sensory experience.

I see a horse: that is a sensation. Immediately I think of his master: that is an idea. The idea of his master makes me think of his office; he is a minister of state: that is another idea. The idea of a minister of state makes me think of public affairs; and I am led into a train of political ideas; when I am summoned to dinner. This is a new sensation, followed by the idea of dinner, and of the company with whom I am to partake it. The sight of the company and of the food are other sensations: these suggest ideas without end; other sensations perpetually intervene, suggesting other ideas: and so the process goes on.

That Mill may have had Hartley's horse in mind in this passage is suggested by the fact that he next stressed Hartley's recognition of the difference between synchronous and successive associations, with the former reflecting spatial coexistence and the latter accounting for temporal sequence. In particular, Mill called attention to the influence of *frequency* as a significant factor governing the formation of specific groupings or patterns of constituent sensations. He illustrated this in the case of synchronous associations by noting the simultaneity of the taste and sight of roast beef as frequent experiences and the sight of a man being stabbed by a knife as a rare experience. Similarly, with reference to successive associations he mentioned lightning being followed by thunder as an instance of a frequent sequence, as contrasted with the rarity of the sight of hemlock being followed by the taste of hemlock.

The common objects with which one is surrounded in daily life thus come, because of frequency of experience, to have relatively fixed arrays of sensation; hence the table looks hard and the pillow looks soft and we expect fire to be warm and snow to be cold. Frequent associations have become familiar and expected sensations. Furthermore, Mill contended, "Our ideas spring, or exist, in the order in which the sensations existed, of which they are copies." The following elaboration of this contention by reference to James Mill's ideas of stone, a flower, a bird, and a man serves as a good example of what has been responsible for the characterization of his associationism as a kind of mental mechanics (1869, pp. 79–80):

From a stone I have had, synchronically, the sensation of colour, the sensation of hardness, the sensation of shape, and size, the sensation of weight. When the idea of one of these occasions occurs, the ideas of all of them occur. They exist in my mind synchronically; and their synchronical existence is called the idea of the stone; which, it is thus plain, is not a single idea, but a number of ideas in a particular state of combination.

Thus, again, I have smelt a rose, and looked at it, and handled a rose, synchronically; accordingly the name rose suggests to me all these ideas synchronically; and this combination of these simple ideas is called my idea of the rose.

My idea of an animal is still more complex. The word thrush, for example, not only suggests an idea of a particular colour and shape, and size, but of a song, and flight, and nestling, and eggs, and callow young, and others.

My idea of a man is the most complex of all; including not only colour, and shape, and voice, but the whole class of events in which I have observed him either the agent or the patient.

Mill's Failure to Distinguish Sensations from Perceptions

From the foregoing examples of James Mill's idea of things like stones, flowers, and birds it seems evident that he was alluding to the *meaning* each of these things came to have for him. If so, then as discussed in Chapter 16, he was sponsoring a context theory of meaning. For him, the meaning of the word "stone" was supplied by the context of associated "ideas" of its hardness, size, shape, and other "copies" of contiguous "sensations." Quotation marks are needed in the latter sentence because Mill failed to differentiate between sensations and perceptions. Accordingly, for him the song of a bird was just as much a sensation as the hardness of a stone, and recognition of a horse as a horse was the sensation and not the perception of a horse.

This broad usage of the term "sensations" to include *perceptions* renders interpretation of Mill's examples rather difficult. His analysis of each example of an "idea" results in the "idea" becoming a combination of simple "ideas." In the case of the rose, as he suggested, its color, fragrance, and texture are concurrently experienced as it is being handled and looked at. It is the *combination* of these characteristics—to use a neutral term—that constitutes the rose. What is not clear is whether Mill regarded such a combination as the product of a cluster of unified sensations given *ab initio* as *in* association or whether they come to *be* associated in the course of experience. If the former is what he meant, then he would have been justified in describing initial exposure to a rose as a perceptual process. On the other hand, if he had the latter possibility in mind, then the initial exposure would be more of a sensory process involving discrete sensations not yet combined or associated into the unified pattern of impressions one learns to call a rose.

In general, it seems that Mill was ready to endorse both of these possible interpretations, with perceptual apprehension characterizing initial exposure to simple impressions but with repetition of experience required for perception of complex impressions. To illustrate in terms of his examples: the idea of furniture, being a complex idea, could only be the consequence of repeated simple ideas, while the idea of a violin in terms of its appearance and sound might well follow a single experience with the instrument. With reference to the latter example, Mill had this to say (1869 p. 78):

Of those sensations which occurred synchronically, the ideas also spring up synchronically. I have seen a violin, and heard the tones of the violin, synchronically. If I think of the tones of the violin, the visible appearance of the violin at the same time occurs to me.

Memory Images and the Arrangement of Associations

In terms of a later descriptive phrase, Mill was maintaining that his *memory image* of the violin involved some sort of reinstatement of visual and auditory impressions. He had two points to make with respect to memory images: (1) they are derivatives of sensations and not of objects, and (2) they are "copies" of sensations. To quote his own formulation of these two points (1869, p. 78):

> Our ideas spring up, or exist, in the order in which the sensations existed, of which they are copies.
> This is the general law of the "Association of Ideas"; by which term, let it be remembered, nothing is here meant to be expressed, but the order of occurrence.

According to Mill, association was thus to be restricted to the spatial and temporal order of the items constitutive of any given experience. This is one interpretation.[8] Recollection of how the family had been posed for a group picture would exemplify Mill's notion of a spatial occurrence, while recall of the words of the national anthem would illustrate what he meant by a temporal occurrence. In both cases the arrangement of the recalled items would be a consequence of the arrangement of the sensations of which the items were copies. Ideas, he wrote, "derive their order from that of sensations" and "are not derived from objects." In fact, Mill was so convinced of this as an empirical fact that he thought it might be used as a courtroom test of the credibility of witnesses (1869, p. 81):

> Of witnesses in courts of justice it has been remarked, that eye-witnesses, and ear-witnesses, always tell their story in the chronological order; in other words,

---

[8] This is Boring's interpretation of the preceding quotation. He takes it to mean that "association is . . . not a power, nor a force, nor a cause; it is simply a matter of concurrence or contiguity" (1950, p. 224). Possibly this is a correct interpretation of what Mill intended to have excluded from consideration in the given context. The troublesome phrase—troublesome because of its ambiguity—is Mill's qualification to the effect that "nothing is here meant" except the order of occurrence. This might be the equivalent of saying, "For the time being or for present purposes, all that we mean by association is the matter of order or sequence," or else it might be tantamount to saying, "Let it be understood that what is being said here applies to association in general." Boring seems to have accepted the latter meaning; hence his conclusion regarding Mill's unwillingness to consider association as a force or power. The former meaning, however, is more likely indicative of Mill's intention. At all events, much later in his book he does refer to the "power" by which a name calls up its associated referent and also to "the irresistible laws of association" (1869, pp. 264–266). On the assumption that what is irresistible is overpowering, Mill, in opposition to Boring's interpretation, did conceive of association as a *force* and not just an arrangement of connected items and not "simply a matter of concurrence or contiguity."

the ideas occur to them in the order in which the sensations occurred; on the other hand, that witnesses, who are inventing, rarely adhere to the chronological order.

Mill's emphasis on the order of ideas as a reinstatement of the order of instigating impressions is not entirely justified. It applies to instances of stereotyped rote memory as saying the Lord's Prayer, counting from one to a hundred, or reciting the alphabet. If, however, one were to be asked to summarize the news after spending an hour reading the Sunday paper, it would be exceedingly rare for a person to recall the individual items of news in the order in which they had been read. Sometimes the last item read, being the most recent in experience, would be the first one to be recalled. At other times the most dramatic item would head the list of items. In general, the reader's personal interests rather than chronological order is likely to determine the sequence of recalled items. What happened in the world of sports or in the world of finance or in the cartoon world is more likely to have a bearing on the recall of different individual readers even if, by chance, they happened to have read the paper in the same order.

In this connection, one more instance from everyday life might be mentioned in order to note what happens when a group of people are actually confronted with the same sequence of items. The words of an ordinary college lecture constitute such a sequence, and yet no experienced lecturer expects his students, even bright and alert students, to duplicate the original sequence of topics on an examination restricted to the content of the particular lecture. Had Mill read many examination papers, he would hardly have concluded that "our ideas spring up . . . in the order in which the sensations existed." Nor would he have described most of the papers as "copies" of the lecture.

Concerning Ideas as "Copies"

Mill's notion of ideas as copies of sensations or perceptions is thus not to be taken literally as meaning that a memory image is a facsimile or photographic duplicate of instigating sensory impressions. Whether he was using the word "copy" in this literal sense is hard to determine. Although he failed to qualify his use of the word with reference to successive ideas, his reference to "synchronical ideas" did suggest endorsement of a copy theory of the memory image. He stated: "Of those sensations which occurred synchronically, the ideas also spring up synchronically." If he intended this to mean ideational or imaginal reproduction of *all* original sensations, then the statement is contrary to psychological fact.

Innumerable classroom demonstrations of incidental memory have shown the absence of a precise duplication of a simple perceptual experience in the form of a memory image of that experience. This holds true even of experiences undergone hundreds of times. For example, most people succeed in getting a memory image of a postage stamp or a penny or the face of a watch and yet, when induced to draw pictures of these common objects with utmost fidelity to original perceptions, the pictures rarely conform to the original. The precise size of the coin or stamp is not reproduced, and details of wording are only crudely approximated. Sometimes there is trouble deciding whether Lincoln's head on the penny faces right or left, and the date may be left out entirely or wrongly placed. The size of the postage stamp may be overestimated or underestimated. Such errors of omission and commission are not due to lack of artistic skill; their existence is ordinarily not realized until the drawings are compared with the objects of which they were supposed to be copies.

Mill's copy theory has also been found wanting when subjected to experimental study. J. J. Gibson (1929), for instance, presented a series of simple but unconventional "meaningless" geometrical forms to his subjects to find out whether they would be duplicated from memory. Their general tendency was to draw something meaningful in place of the "nonsense" figures. Furthermore, F. C. Bartlett (1932, pp. 180–181) has demonstrated that meaningful figures such as an outline drawing of a cat are subject to transformation in the memory image. Had experimental findings such as these been available to Mill, he might have been constrained to write, "Of those sensations which occurred synchronically, very few if any also spring up synchronically as perfect copies of the original."

It may be, of course, that Mill did not intend to have his use of the word "copy" interpreted as a photographic duplication of an original sensory impression. Had the issue been brought up, he might have guarded against such possible misinterpretation by making a distinction between an occurrence per se and how it happens to be perceived. The sight of a horse as a perception, he might have explained, it is not necessarily precisely an identical perception for all viewers. Some may notice a brand on the animal's flank while others may fail to notice it. The length of the tail may be observed by one person and ignored by another. What the artist sees would be different from what a veterinarian sees, just as what a little child sees would differ from what a horse trader sees. The resulting *ideas* these different viewers have as they think about the horse on the following day might be "copies" of what they had noticed the previous day. As memory images these "copies" would differ from one another, and it might well be that no one of them would be a precise facsimile of a Kodachrome picture of the animal. Despite these differences, these "copies" of what had been noticed would serve as surrogates or symbols of the horse as suggested by Mill's notion of an *idea* of a horse.

This interpretation of his copy theory of ideas might have struck Mill as obviously in accordance with what he meant, for it really goes back to Aristotle's distinction between having and observing an experience. In his student days at the University of Edinburgh, Mill had won honors as a

Greek scholar and he was widely read in the Greek classics. Accordingly, it is probable that he was familiar with this Aristotelian distinction and expected sophisticated readers in his day to share his familiarity and thus to know enough not to misunderstand what he meant by referring to an idea as the "copy" of an experience. Moreover, the fact that neither Bain nor John Stuart Mill bothered to write an editorial note either by way of protest or by way of explanation for this use of the word "copy" lends support to this conclusion. Had they expected the word to be taken literally, as sophisticated critics they would have introduced a clarifying comment, as they did repeatedly in the course of their editorial work.

Scope and Limitations of Association

James Mill is also liable to be misunderstood by too literal an interpretation of his use of the phrase "association of ideas." Although the phrase is the heading for an important chapter, the material included in the chapter is not limited to a consideration of ideational association in the restricted sense of meaning the linkage between one idea and another idea. Instead he applied what he referred to as "the great law of association" to a variety of nonideational phenomena: to emotional factors, to visceral disturbances, and to muscular control. He applied the law to emotional factors by this example of a conditioned emotional reaction: "The spot on which a tender maiden parted with her lover when he embarked on the voyage from which he never returned, cannot afterwards be seen by her without an agony of grief" (1869, p. 87). With respect to the law's bearing on visceral changes, he mentioned the association between anxiety and indigestion as well as the way in which the receipt of shocking news can affect the rate of breathing.

In calling attention to association as important for the acquisition of motor control, James Mill anticipated a cardinal teaching of the later functional psychologists. He did this by noting that mastery of a musical instrument requires the beginner to learn to connect each successive note with the "key or string which he is to touch, and the finger he is to touch it with" (1869, p. 89). Then, as the beginner becomes more proficient by regular practice, the movements of the fingers become so associated that an entire series of such associated movements "at last becomes so strong, that it is performed with the greatest rapidity, without an effort, and almost without consciousness." For Mill, in short, association came to connote far more than a sequence of connected ideas. As a principle it was made to account for the acquisition of skill as well as for the development of knowledge, and for the emergence of likes and dislikes as well as for digestive, respiratory, and other autonomic changes.

Despite his glorification of association as a sovereign psychological principle, Mill recognized its limitations. There are some experiences, he held, which can never be brought together in association and others which, when once united in association, can never be separated. He described the indissoluble kind of union as follows (1869, p. 93):

> Some ideas are by frequency and strength of association so closely combined, that they cannot be separated. If one exists, the other exists along with it, in spite of whatever effort we make to disjoin them. For example, it is not in our power to think of colour, without thinking of extension; or of solidity, without figure.

That such indissolubility of association occurs may be granted, even though Mill's explanation for its occurrence is far from satisfactory. As an explanation it reveals what has come to be viewed as one of the weaknesses of traditional associationism: its atomistic reductionism. It is the kind of reductionism or psychological analysis that James could have cited as an instance of the psychologist's fallacy. As an adult reflecting upon his experience of a colored surface or a solid figure, Mill noted what he deemed to be simple ideas of color on the one hand and its spatiality on the other, and of the figure's solidity on the one hand and its shape on the other. For him, such simple ideas were the constituent units or "atoms" of the experiences in question. Having detected these units by analysis of the experiences, he then assumed their initial occurrence as simple ideas in the course of mental development. This was akin to arguing that the infant first notices color and then extensity before learning to associate them in what is to become an indissoluble union, and arguing in the same way with respect to the simple ideas of shape and solidity. To argue this way is to endow the child with the psychologist's sophistication and to assume that it has to combine these simple ideas before it can perceive its blue blanket as both blue and extended in space and its nursing bottle as both solid and bottle-shaped. Mill seems to have failed to consider a more plausible hypothesis to the effect that some associations are indissoluble because they were never separated in the first place. [9]

Mill thus neglected to entertain the kind of holistic hypothesis which Gestalt psychologists came to favor and which reflected their opposition to the associationist's atomistic reductionism. Moreover, more than twenty years before the rise of Gestalt psychology, James had already given expression to such opposition, as was considered in a previous chapter. The follow-

---

[9] Some support for this hypothesis is provided by recent experimentation showing that even newborn infants pay attention to a patterned visual stimulus. This, as the experimenters suggest, is to be regarded "not simply as an interesting but isolated piece of behavior; rather it can be appreciated as part of the great complex of regulatory and adaptive mechanisms that one observes in normal individuals from the moment of birth" (G. Stechler et al., 1966, p. 1248).

ing sentence from James merits repetition in the present context: "But the whole historic doctrine of psychological association is tainted with one huge error—that of the construction of our thoughts out of the compounding of themselves together of immutable and incessantly recurring simple ideas" (1890, Vol. I, p. 553).

As has been intimated, Mill also maintained that there are ideas "which it is not in our power to combine" by association (1869, p. 97). In theory it ought to be impossible to cite examples of this inability, for in the very process of thinking of an example ideas are being combined. Nevertheless, Mill did venture to supply illustrations by noting the impossibility of associating the taste of sugar with the idea of asafoetida or the "idea of pleasure with the word pain." These are decidedly dubious examples. They suggest the impossibility of experiencing antithetic ideas and as such are at variance with Aristotle's recognition of *contrast* as a principle of association. Moreover, in the days when mothers forced their children to wear a little bag of asafoetida as a protection against illness, it would have been easy to establish the "impossible" association simply by rewarding each child with a piece of candy on mornings the ill-smelling bag was accepted without protest. Furthermore, had the phenomenon of masochism been known to Mill, he probably would not have deemed it impossible for the idea of pleasure to be associated with the word "pain."

Even contradictory ideas can be combined or associated, as Kant demonstrated when he introduced his famous *antinomies*.[10] In fact, in an ordinary paired-associate experiment any two ideas, no matter how bizarre or irrelevant, can be brought into juxtaposition. As a result an experimental subject can be taught to respond with the word "sweet" when he hears the word "asafoetida" and with "ecstasy" when the stimulus word is "pain." Had these considerations been brought to Mill's attention, he might have reached a different conclusion, to the effect that "it is in our power to bring any experienced ideas into association with one another—even bizarre, contradictory, or arbitrarily connected ideas."

Concerning Dissociation, Noegenesis, and Memory

Mill actually recognized the existence of arbitrary combinations in the stream of ideation. He mentioned this in the course of a discussion on the classification of ideas in which he reached the following conclusion (1869, pp. 137–138):

---

[10] By "antinomies," Kant was referring to situations in which one is confronted by equally plausible but irreconcilably contradictory propositions. For example, the proposition of complete volitional freedom conflicts with the proposition that the will, like everything else, is determined. This is one antinomy. Another is the conviction of the infinity of space and time as opposed to the conviction that everything must have a beginning.

We may thus distinguish three classes of ideas: 1. simple ideas, the copies of single sensations: 2. complex ideas, copied directly from sensations: 3. complex ideas, derived indeed from the senses, but put together in *arbitrary* combinations [italics added].

As examples of such arbitrary combinations, he cited the idea of a centaur and the idea of a mountain of gold. Unlike the ideas belonging to the first two classes, these arbitrary combinations are not just memory images or reproductions of sensory impressions. Instead they are products of what are sometimes called acts of creative imagination. Something novel is brought into being as transposition of memory images. In the case of a centaur the head of man is transposed to the neck of a horse, and in the case of a mountain of gold a mass of the metal is transposed to a hollow mountain. The transpositions obviously result in new associations or, to use Mill's phrase, in arbitrary combinations.

What Mill failed to note was that such transpositions involve *dissociation* as well as association. To form the centaur in imagination, the heads of man and beast have to be separated from their respective torsos; and to form the mountain of gold, the mass of rock has to be removed from the memory image of the contours of a mountain. Creation of a new pattern requires the breakup of the old. Such breakup or dissociation is of coordinate importance for creative thinking as association itself; and creative thinking, while dependent on experience, goes beyond experience by the discovery or formation of something novel or original. It is the kind of thinking that Charles Edward Spearman (1863–1945) described as *noegenetic* in his book dealing with the principles of cognition (1923).

Noegenesis has to do with the emergence of new knowledge, the perception of novel relations, and the replacement of routine thinking by novel insights. Mill neglected to elaborate upon such noegenetic implications of what he alluded to as ideas "put together in arbitrary combinations." He and other associationists were too preoccupied with ideas as a product of remembered experiences to consider the origin of new ideas. Spearman regarded this preoccupation with memory as one of the shortcomings or weaknesses of an exclusively associationistic psychology. It was too passive in orientation to do justice to the active intellect of an original thinker.

In some ways this interest in the topic of memory followed from the associationist's repudiation of nativistic interpretations. As an empiricist, his inclination was to question such interpretations in favor of those which stressed the relevance of sensory impressions for mental development. It was as if he regarded sensation as the matrix of mind, since for him all ideas are derivatives of sensation. Moreover, in his view the emergence of mind is a function of *remembered* sensations and ideas. This general outcome of the associationist's empiricism is clearly evident in Mill's psychology. In the following discussion, for example, he not only reveals his interest in associative memory but also his recognition of the difference between knowledge of acquaintance and knowledge-about (1869, p. 328): [11]

There are two cases of Memory. One is, when we remember sensations. The other is, when we remember ideas. The first is, when we remember what we have seen, felt, heard, tasted or smelt. The second is, when we remember what we have thought, without the intervention of the senses. I remember to have seen and heard George III, when making a speech at the opening of his Parliament. This is a case of sensation. I remember my conception of the Emperor Napoleon and his audience when I read the account of his first address to the French chambers. This is a case of ideas.

In the course of his account of the psychology of memory, Mill called attention to, among other things, the origin of a curious spatial metaphor to be noted on occasions when people are listing a series of reasons in support of some thesis they are trying to defend. Should there be three reasons, they are apt to refer to them by successive references to the first place, the second place, and the third place, even though there is no manifest referent for the word "place" in the given context. According to Mill, this practice originated as a mnemonic device employed by "ancient orators and rhetoricians." The orator, having decided on the sequence of topics or arguments he planned to develop in the course of his speech, would associate each one with a different object in the room. Or else, he would select a different part of the room as the imaginary locus for each topic, with the first one placed on the floor, the second on the ceiling, the third in one corner, the fourth in another, and so on. In this way, as Mill indicated, "the orator made a choice of a set of objects, sufficient in number to answer his purpose" (1869, p. 324). His subsequent references to the different "places" served as reminders of specific topics he had linked to each of them. This ancient mnemonic device has vanished, but its verbal surrogates have survived in everyday talk.

On the Strength of Associations and the Problem of Similarity

In developing his associationism, Mill did not follow Brown by making a distinction between primary and secondary laws of association. It may be that he had not yet read Brown's *Lectures* at the time he was writing

---

[11] This difference, as explained in Chapter 17, is reflected in the fact that the German language has two words for experience: *"Erlebnis"* for knowledge of acquaintance and *"Erfahrung"* for knowledge-about,

this part of his *Analysis*.[12] However, in connection with his discussion of variations in the strength of associations, Mill did allude to three principles that Brown had classified as secondary. These had to do with the factors of frequency, recency, and vividness or what Brown had called liveliness. Mill's recognition of the frequency factor was discussed on an earlier page, and its influence on the strength of associations is too obvious to require more than passing mention. What may not be immediately obvious is the possibility of making the recency factor the equivalent of the vividness factor. This is what Mill did by noting that recent associations tend to be more vivid than remote ones. He mentioned this as one of the "three cases of vividness," with the other two being fairly obvious "cases." One of these two "cases" refers to the greater vividness of actual experiences as contrasted with mere "ideas" of these experiences. The other group of "cases" has to do with the difference in vividness of emotional as compared with nonemotional experiences. In accordance with this analysis, Mill believed that he had reduced the "causes of strength in association" to (1) "the vividness of the associated feelings" and (2) "the frequency of the association" (1869, p. 83).

Mill also believed that he had reduced the factor of resemblance or similarity to a special case of frequency. To establish this, he pointed out (1869, pp. 110–111):

> When we see a tree, we generally see more than one; when we see an ox, we generally see more oxen than one; a sheep, more sheep than one; a man, more men than one. From this observation, I think, we may refer resemblance to the law of frequency, of which it seems to form only a particular case.

John Stuart Mill was unable to endorse this effort to reduce resemblance to a special case of frequency. In an editorial note he stated that it is "perhaps the least successful attempt at a generalization and simplification of the laws of mental phenomena" (1869, p. 112). As an explanation, he noted, it cannot account for the fact that the sight of a portrait reminds us of the original. Nor does it serve to explain the not uncommon experience of seeing a stranger for the first time and immediately being struck by his resemblance to a person we met a long time ago, with no prior contiguity to connect the sight of the stranger with the memory of the person. This fact prompted John Stuart Mill to comment as follows (1869, pp. 112–113):

---

[12] That this is a possibility is indicated by a statement in John Stuart Mill's *Autobiography* with reference to his own reading during the years his father was writing the *Analysis*. After listing the books he had read, he added, "Brown's *Lectures* I did not read until two or three years later, nor at that time had my father himself read them" (1882, p. 69). The time in question was the period from 1822, when the *Analysis* was started, to 1829, when it was published. Since Brown is mentioned in the book, James Mill must have read the *Lectures after* the writing had gotten under way.

The attempt to resolve association by resemblance into association by contiguity must perforce be unsuccessful, inasmuch as there never could have been association by contiguity without a previous association by resemblance. . . . There is thus a law of association anterior to, and presupposed by, the law of contiguity: namely, that a sensation tends to recall what is called the idea of itself, that is the rememberance of a sensation like itself, if such has been previously experienced. This is implied in what we call recognizing a sensation, as one which has been felt before; more correctly, as undistinguishably resembling one which has been felt before.

In short, in opposition to his father, John Stuart Mill regarded association by similarity as a separate law not reducible to the law of contiguity. Furthermore, by calling attention to the "undistinguishably resembling" factors involved in association by similarity, he was referring to the principle of *identity* mentioned in the previous chapter; namely, that to say one thing is *like* another thing is tantamount to saying it is identical with it in some respects and different from it in other respects. By way of illustration, it might be asked in what way are the words DEFT, FIRST, and STUN alike or similar? The answer comes to light as soon as one detects the *identical* factor of three letters in alphabetical sequence in each of the three *different* words: EFT, RST, and STU, respectively. Association by similarity always involves this kind of recognition of identity in an alien setting.

James Mill: A Son's Tribute

The preceding objection to his father's effort to classify similarity as a special case of frequency is not to be construed as representative of the son's basic attitude toward James Mill's associationism. Objections to specific teachings were relatively rare, and on the whole he was not merely in agreement with the general drift of the *Analysis* but decidedly enthusiastic in his evaluation of the book. Because of it, he maintained, James Mill "will be known to posterity as one of the greatest names in that most important branch of speculation, on which all the moral and political sciences ultimately rest, and will mark one of the essential stages in its progress" (1882, p. 204). And with specific reference to his father's associationism he had this to say (1882, p. 108):

In psychology, his fundamental doctrine was the formation of all human character by circumstances, through the universal Principle of Association, and the consequent unlimited possibility of improving the moral and intellectual condition of mankind by education. Of all his doctrines none was more important than this, or needs more to be insisted on: unfortunately there is none which is more contradictory to the prevailing tendencies of speculation, both in his time and since.

Mill failed to enlarge upon the "prevailing tendencies" that he regarded as militating against successful application of his father's important doctrine. He evidently had two sets of tendencies in mind: those prevalent around 1830, when the *Analysis* first appeared, and those prevalent around 1870, when the *Autobiography* was being written. Calling them "tendencies of speculation" was Mill's way of referring to modes of thinking or differing climates of opinion. From the context it is clear that he was thinking of them as not conductive to endorsement of the associationist's empiricism. In general, empiricism is to be contrasted with rationalism as well as with nativism. Consequently, one may hazard the guess that he was thinking of post-Kantian rationalism as antithetic to his father's doctrine in the 1830s and of post-Darwinian nativism being the antithetic tendency in the 1870s. Both tendencies are calculated to set limits to what can be accomplished by education, since both are opposed to the *tabula rasa* implications of the empiricist tradition. It must be remembered that in terms of the heredity-environment dichotomy, empiricists are inclined to lend greater weight to environmental influences, whereas rationalists are more likely to dwell on the importance of innate influences. The concept of *native* intelligence is more in accord with the rationalist tradition than with the empiricist tradition.

As will be brought out shortly, James Mill had good reason to think of "unlimited" possibilities for intellectual improvement by means of education. Had the question of intelligence as native come up in his day, he most probably would have sided with the environmentalists. And John Stuart Mill would have taken the same stand. As indicated in the previous quotation, he too believed in the "unlimited" possibilities of education. What he knew of his father's life and what he had experienced in his own education seemed to justify such a belief.

From John Stuart Mill's early childhood until his adolescent years, his father was the only teacher he ever had. It seems safe to say that he would have attributed his own richness of intellect, moral earnestness, and solicitude for the welfare of the common man to the molding influence of this paternal teaching rather than to exceptional native endowment. In writing his autobiography he has nothing to say about his ancestors except to refer to his paternal grandfather as a petty tradesman.

In one respect it is a most unusual autobiography. Although page after page is concerned with his father's views, accomplishments, and personality traits, there is not a single reference to his mother. It is as if she never existed and as if, being motherless, he had to look to his father for guidance. In retrospect, as a mature adult, he must have thought of this as forceful and persuasive guidance; for in tribute to the memory of his father he wrote: "In the power of influencing by mere force of mind and character, the convictions and purposes of others, and in the strenuous exertion of that power to promote freedom and progress, he left, as far as my knowledge extends, no equal among men, and but one among women" (1882, p.

205).[13] Furthermore, in another passage, after acknowledging that Bentham "is a much greater name in history" than his father, he added (1882, pp. 101–102):

> But my father exercised a far greater personal ascendancy. . . . I have never known any man who could do such ample justice to his best thoughts in colloquial discussion. His perfect command over his great mental resources, the terseness and expressiveness of his language and the moral earnestness as well as intellectual force of his delivery, made him one of the most striking of all argumentative conversers: and he was full of anecdote, a hearty laugher, and when with people whom he liked, a most lively and amusing companion.

The Education of John Stuart Mill Viewed as Experimental Pedagogy

During childhood John Stuart Mill had little reason to regard his father as a "lively and amusing companion." He was anything but that to his son. Instead he was a serious-minded tutor, firm disciplinarian, and exhorting moralist. He was all of these because in his role as father he was rearing his son in accordance with his belief in the pedagogic implications of association psychology. As noted in the preceding section, this involved his conviction in man's *unlimited* capacity for intellectual and moral growth by education. When John Stuart Mill was still an infant, this may have been more a faith than a conviction on James Mill's part. If so, then in planning for the education of his son he might be said to have subjected his faith to experimental test. In terms of the eventual outcome of the test, this faith became a conviction concerning the soundness and importance of his associationistic educational philosophy.

As a mature adult, in looking back upon his life, John Stuart Mill found himself sharing his father's conviction regarding man's unlimited capacity for mental and moral improvement. This, as his father's most important doctrine, called for wider dissemination and prompted him to undertake the writing of his autobiography. Unlike Saint Augustine's *Confessions*, it was not to be the story of a guilt-ridden youth's quest for salvation. Nor was it to be the self-aggrandizing memoir of a famous man. Actually, Mill thought of his life as "uneventful" and explained his reasons for writing about it in the opening paragraph of the *Autobiography*:

> I do not for a moment imagine that any part of what I have to relate, can be interesting to the public as a narrative, or as being connected with myself. But

---

13 This one woman was Harriet Taylor, who became his wife in 1851 and whose character, intellect, and understanding answered Mill's deepest emotional needs. His love for her was a reverential love not far removed from worship. Following her death he wrote. "Her memory is to me a religion, and her approbation the standard by which, summing up as it does all worthiness, I endeavor to regulate my life" (1882, p. 251).

I have thought that in an age in which education, and its improvement, are the subject of more, if not of profounder study than of any former period of English history, it may be useful that there should be some record of an education which was unusual and remarkable, and which, whatever else it may have done, has proved how much more than is commonly supposed may be taught, and well taught, in those early years which, in the common modes of what is called instruction, are little better than wasted.

At its inception the *Autobiography* was thus to be in the nature of an impersonal report of a successfully executed educational experiment. The laboratory was home, James Mill the experimenter, and John Stuart Mill the subject. Viewed as an experimental report, it becomes clear why there is no mention of his mother in the *Autobiography*. She had nothing to do with the experimental venture; hence she could be ignored in the final report. Presumably, for the same reason, apart from acknowledging their existence, there is almost no mention of his siblings. One never even learns their names or anything about them as individuals. He does refer to "sisters and brothers" whom he tutored without indicating how many there were or whether any of them were his favorites as playmates, or if he engaged in any kind of childish activity with them. From the standpiont of his own intellectual development, they ceased to be siblings and became pupils; hence, aside from the tutorial relationship, there was no reason to mention them.

The first chapter of the *Autobiography* supplies an account of the staggeringly impressive amount of intellectual progress John Stuart Mill made during his boyhood. He may have had an infancy, but he certainly had no childhood in the sense of carefree interludes of play with other children. He reports having no recollection of the time when he started to study Greek, but adds that according to what he was told, he was three. By the time he was seven he had read six of Plato's dialogues and had begun the study of Latin. Thus in his eighth year, when he received his first Latin lesson, he had already been reading Greek some four years. With neither a Greek-English nor a Latin-English dictionary available, he had to ask his father for the meaning of every new word. Since he did his studying while seated at the same table where his father was absorbed in his writing, these repeated interruptions might have taxed the father's patience. Instead as reported by the son, although his father was "one of the most impatient of men," he yielded to these incessant interruptions and despite them succeeded in writing "several volumes of his History and all else he had to write during those years."

Not only did John Stuart Mill have to study Latin as a child of eight; he also had to teach it to his younger sister and then in succeeding years to other siblings. He found this a burdensome task, for his father held him responsible for lack of progress on the part of his pupils. In looking back upon this phase of his childhood, he had serious misgivings about this kind of juvenile teacher-pupil relationship. Although it increased the "teacher's" retention of the lessons being taught and may have been of some value in forcing him to try "to explain difficulties to others," it is not to be encouraged as sound educational policy. The teaching is inefficient and is not likely to promote amicable sibling relationships. At least this is the way it looked to the "teacher" in retrospect once he had reached adulthood.

The daily routine was not restricted to receiving and giving instruction and to the study of books assigned as required reading. There was also leisure devoted to private reading chiefly in the fields of history and government. It is difficult to supply an adequate summary of the vast range of subject matter with which John Stuart Mill had become familiar by the time he was twelve years old. His list of books studied and skills acquired in the four years from eight to twelve is more than the equivalent of what is symbolized by the average M.A. degree. In Greek he had read the *Iliad* and the *Odyssey,* Aristotle's *Rhetoric,* and some of the plays by the leading Greek dramatists. His Latin studies included Virgil, Horace, Ovid, and Cicero. Among the classics of English literature which he read during these four years he mentioned the writings of Shakespeare, Milton, Dryden, Scott, Burns, Spenser, and others. In mathematics under his father's tutelage he reports having learned "elementary geometry and algebra thoroughly," and "the differential calculus and other portions of the higher mathematics far from thoroughly."

Concerning Formal Logic and Mill's "Advanced" Education

The foregoing list of names and subjects will serve to supply a general notion of the nature and scope of the educational progress of John Stuart Mill by the time he was twelve. By implication this was deemed to be preparatory for later work, since he wrote that "from about the age of twelve" he "entered into another and more advanced stage" of his education. It was as if the previous work was intended to give him a background for sound thinking and penetratingly clear critical analysis and evaluation.

At this "more advanced" level, he was initiated in the fundamentals of valid reasoning. He began to think about thinking as, again under his father's guidance, he studied treatises on logic by Aristotle, by some of the scholastics, and by later logicians. His father had great confidence in the educational value of training in the syllogistic logic, and on the basis of his own experience he came to agree with his father. His comment on this issue merits direct quotation (1882, p. 19):

My own consciousness and experience ultimately led me to appreciate quite as highly as he did, the value of an early practical familiarity with the school logic. I know nothing, in my education, to which I think myself more indebted for whatever capacity of thinking I have attained. The first intellectual operation in which I arrived at any proficiency, was dissecting a bad argument, and finding in what part the fallacy lay: and though whatever capacity of this sort I attained was

due to the fact that it was an intellectual exercise in which I was most persever-
ingly drilled by my father, yet it is also true that the school logic, and the mental
habits acquired in studying it, were among the principal instruments of this
drilling. I am persuaded that nothing, in modern education, tends so much,
when properly used, to form exact thinkers, who attach a precise meaning to
words and propositions, and are imposed on by vague, loose, or ambiguous terms.

Manifestly Mill believed that there is a substantial amount of positive
transfer from training in formal logic to improvement in ability to reason
correctly about everyday problems and routine personal difficulties. He
even urged that such training be introduced at an early stage of education.
Furthermore, he regarded his training as having greater educational value
than training in mathematics, because mathematics is not concerned with
"the real difficulties" of correct reasoning. In addition to the educational
value of logic, he stressed the educational benefits to be derived from the
study of Plato (1882, pp. 21–22):

> There is no author to whom my father thought himself more indebted for his own
> mental culture, than Plato, or whom he more frequently recommended to young
> students. I can bear similar testimony in regard to myself. The Socratic method,
> of which the Platonic dialogues are the chief example, is unsurpassed as a
> discipline for correcting the errors, and clearing up the confusions incident to
> the *intellectus sibi permissus,* the understanding which has made up all its
> bundles of associations under the guidance of popular phraseology. The close,
> searching elenchus by which the man of vague generalities is constrained to
> express his meaning to himself in definite terms, or to confess that he does not
> know what he is talking about; the perpetual testing of all general statements
> by particular instances; the siege in form which is laid to the meaning of large
> abstract terms, by fixing upon some still larger class-name which includes that and
> more, and dividing down to the thing sought—marking out its limits and defini-
> tions by a series of accurately drawn distinctions between it and each of the
> cognate objects which are successively parted off from it—all this, as an education
> for precise thinking is inestimable, and all this, even at that age, took such hold
> of me that it became part of my own mind.

As a boy, in morning walks with his father, John Stuart Mill received
this kind of "education for precise thinking." He came to appreciate the
educational significance of the "school logic" implicit in the Socratic
questions raised by his father. Their walks were occasions for Platonic
dialogues with the themes based upon what he had been reading or studying
the day before. Presumably it was in this way that he obtained what he
referred to as the "early practical familiarity with the school of logic."

For him, logic was not just an academic subject enshrined in a college
text but an intrinsic part of his being or, as he said, part of his own mind.
From being an "advanced" phase of his education during his adolescent
years it became one of his central interests for many succeeding years. His

first major work dealt with the subject of logic.[14] He started this in 1830, when he was twenty-four, but the work was not published until 1843. How it developed during these intervening years calls for a brief explanation, since it has something to do with Mill's place in the history of psychology.

Mill's Logic: Its Development, Scope, and Influence

In his account of the development of his *Logic,* John Stuart Mill reports that when he began to write in 1830, he first wrote about the logical distinctions involved in giving names to things and actions and about the significance of logical propositions with a view "towards clearing up the theory of logic generally" (1882, p. 159). He soon found himself struggling with the thorny problem of induction. Since he regarded induction as "a process for finding the causes of effects," he proceeded to consider the operations by means of which cause-and-effect relationships are established in physical science. He seems to have spent about two years in working on what became the early chapters of the book, and it was not until 1837 that he took it up again. His explanation for the delay is of more than passing interest (1882, pp. 207–208):

I had not touched my pen on the subject for five years, having been stopped and brought to a halt on the threshold of Induction. I had gradually discovered that what was mainly wanting, to overcome the difficulties of that branch of the subject, was a comprehensive, and, at the same time, accurate view of the whole circle of physical science, which I feared it would take me a long course of study to acquire; since I knew not of any book, or other guide, that would spread out before me the generalities and processes of the sciences, and I apprehended that I should have no choice but to extract them for myself, as best I could, from the details.

At about this time, Mill adds, a book dealing with the history of the inductive sciences was published and he found it to supply many of the details he needed. However, he was unable to endorse most of its philosophy. In addition to using this book, he obtained help from a treatise on "natural philosophy" that he now studied for the second time. After devoting much effort to think through the logical implications of the scienti-

---

[14] Like his father, John Stuart Mill wrote on a variety of subjects both in books and in essays. For example, he wrote on political economy, on the emancipation of women, on religion, on Comte's positivism, on utilitarianism, on representative government, and other topics. Consequently, he can be studied as a philosopher, as a psychologist, as a logician, as social reformer, as educational theorist, and as pioneer social scientist and critic of scientific method. For a list of important writings by and about him see the source material cited by Max Lerner in the *Essential Works of John Stuart Mill,* which he edited (1961, pp. 433–434).

fic work discussed in these books, he was ready to resume his writing. He was unable to do this until he had become familiar with the work of the Keplers, the Newtons, and the Daltons of science. By analysis of their procedures he endeavored to determine the essential characteristics of scientific data, scientific evidence, scientific conclusions, and whatever else can be regarded as belonging to the *logic* of science. He studied physics, chemistry, astronomy, and related subjects primarily in order to understand the nature of science as a cognitive enterprise. His book, as he planned it, was to include an elaboration of the logical implications of this enterprise. Among other considerations, it was to supply an answer to a question like "What does it mean to think or reason scientifically?" This objective was reflected in the title he selected for the completed work. He called it *A System of Logic Ratiocinative and Inductive—Being a Connected View of the Principles of Evidence and the Methods of Scientific Evidence.*

Mill's objective actually went beyond the goal of supplying an explication of the logic implicit in the *methods* of science. As indicated by his use of the phrase "methods of scientific evidence," he was well aware of the futility of trying to restrict the methodology of science to a single mode of procedure. Accordingly, it would be misleading to speak of *the* scientific method as if all problems in all fields of science are to be tackled in the same way. As Mill saw it, however, all knowledge based upon the methods of science is rooted in experience and is never to be considered a derivative of "innate principles." Mill employed the latter phrase in connection with a passage in the *Autobiography* dealing with his misgivings about popular acceptance of his *Logic* as well as with his chief purpose in writing it. A few excerpts from this passage will serve to make this clear (1882, pp. 224–225):

A treatise . . . on a matter so abstract could not be expected to be popular; it could only be a book for students, and students on such subjects were not only (at least in England) few, but addicted chiefly to the opposite school of metaphysics, the ontological and "innate principles" school. . . . I have never indulged the illusion that the book had made any considerable impression on philosophical opinion. The German, or *a priori* view of human knowledge, and of the knowing faculties, is likely for some time longer . . . to predominate among those who occupy themselves with such inquiries, both here and on the Continent. But the "System of Logic" supplies what was much wanted, a textbook of the opposite doctrine—that which derives all knowledge from experience, and all moral and intellectual qualities principally from the direction given to the associations. . . . The notion that truths external to the mind may be known by intuition or consciousness, independently of observation and experience, is, I am persuaded . . . the great intellectual support of false doctrines and bad institutions.

Although Mill did not refer to Kant by name in the foregoing passage, it is very likely that Kant was included in his disparaging allusion to the "*a priori* view of human knowledge."[15] If he intended this to mean a rejection of empirical evidence by Kant, then, as noted at the close of Chapter 15, his criticism of Kant in this respect is not warranted. It may be recalled that Kant also wrote a treatise on logic in which he classified "physics, psychology, and the like" as belonging to "*empirical* branches of knowledge." Kant's rationalism, despite its *a priori* overtones, is thus not irreconcilably antithetic to Mill's empiricism. Moreover, as will be brought out in a later section, Mill's empiricism was by no means devoid of rationalistic overtones.

This is a matter of minor importance. It is of more immediate importance to note that in their respective treatises on logic both Kant and Mill had something to do with the rise of a scientific psychology. For Kant, as mentioned on page 501, his own confidence in the underlying lawfulness of mental events and in mind as belonging to the order of nature established a climate of opinion favorable to the notion of getting at such lawfulness by the methods of science. For Mill, his influence on the emergence of a scientific psychology involved more than the establishment of a favorable climate of opinion. He was more explicit and more detailed in his espousal of a scientific psychology. This came as a direct result of his systematic examination of the logical foundations of the methods developed by workers in established sciences like astronomy and physics and then considering the possible applicability of such methods to less well-established fields of investigation. Among the latter he considered both psychology and sociology. In fact, he was one of the first to make a distinction between the physical and the social sciences. He even raised questions regarding the kind of evidence relied upon by historians in their efforts to formulate "laws" of history. In addition to this question of the status of history as a science, he considered the status of ethics and public administration as sciences. Nor did the question of the difference between a science and an art escape his analytic probling.

All this serves to outline the vast scope of topics dealt with in Mill's *Logic*. Even though written more than a century ago, much of what it contains is by no means outmoded. The modern reader will still find many of its chapters timely, illuminating, and insightful. This observation applies with particular force to the modern student of psychology—especially to the student of the history of psychology in his efforts to find out how modern psychology underwent the metamorphosis from mental philosophy to scientific psychology.

---

15 It is hard to believe that Mill was unmindful of Kant as the outstanding German exponent of *a priori* doctrines. With reference to the 1840s, when Mill was working on his *Logic*, J. T. Merz wrote, "It is not likely that Mill had at that time any knowledge at first hand of Kant's 'Critique of Pure Reason'" (1965, Vol. III, p. 377). Nevertheless, it seems safe to assume that he knew *about* the *Critique* and its salient teachings.

This development, of course, was not due to the efforts of a single man. However, as stated repeatedly in previous chapters, Wilhelm Wundt was a key figure among those responsible for the transformation in question. His was the first psychological laboratory brought into being as an official undertaking under university auspices. In this sense scientific psychology as a deliberately initiated movement was made in Germany. Interest in Mill's *Logic* on the part of German scholars came rather early; as noted by Merz, a German translation was published in 1849. The famous chemist Justus von Liebig (1803–1873), the man who established the first chemistry laboratory as an adjunct of university instruction in chemistry, was especially influential in having the translation made.[16] It was in this way that Wundt became familiar with Mill's views. That he was influenced by these views is shown by the following quotations from Merz (1965, Vol. III, p. 375):

> It is interesting to note what Prof. Wundt himself says regarding Mill. "If the historian of science in the nineteenth century should wish to name the philosophical works which during and shortly after the middle of the century had the greatest influence, he will certainly have to place Mill's 'Logic' in the first rank. This only slightly original work has hardly had any important influence on the development of philosophy. It was first recommended by Liebig to the German scientific world, which at the time possessed few philosophical interests, and was frequently consulted when philosophical questions had perforce to be considered. Thus also the labours of Helmholtz . . . moved decidedly under the sign of Mill's 'Logic.' "

Since Helmholtz, like Wundt, is one of the founding fathers of scientific psychology, the fact that he too was impressed by Mill's *Logic* is an additional reason for thinking of Mill as one who facilitated the birth of psychology as science. A closer examination of the *Logic* will show how this came about.

Mill on Psychology as Science

Mill's discussion of psychology as science was not introduced until the latter part of his *Logic*. All the preceding parts served as background for this discussion. Apparently he deemed it necessary to lay a detailed groundwork for understanding the logic of scientific thinking in general before considering the "logic of the moral sciences" or those sciences having something to do with psychology. To appreciate what laying this ground-

---

[16] It may be of incidental interest to note that Mill was familiar with some of Liebig's experimental work. In fact, in one chapter of the *Logic* concerned with supplying concrete examples of Mill's four experimental methods, he cited Liebig's studies of the lethal effects of metallic poisons (1875, Vol. I, Book III, Ch. IX).

work entailed, it is necessary to say something more about the organization of the *Logic*.

Mill divided his *Logic* into six books, with each book containing a varying number of chapters depending on the complexity of the topic being discussed. Thus, Book I, dealing with "Names and Propositions," contains eight chapters; Book II, on "Reasoning," has seven; Book III, on "Induction," has twenty-five; Book IV, on "Operations Subsidiary to Induction," has eight; Book V, on "Fallacies," has seven; and Book VI, on "The Logic of the Moral Sciences," has twelve. Of these sixty-seven chapters, only five or six in the very last book are directly concerned with the status of psychology as a science.

Incidentally, Mill's early misgivings regarding the popular acceptance of the *Logic* turned out to be unwarranted. From its original publication in 1843 as a two-volume work until shortly after Mill's death in 1873, there were nine editions of the two volumes.[17] This ninth edition (1875) thus embodies all changes Mill introduced during the intervening thirty years; hence, unless otherwise noted, whatever is being said about the *Logic* in the present chapter is based upon Volume II of this edition.

Like Aristotle, Mill recognized establishment of a *science* of human nature to be a formidable undertaking. He considered it to be "the most complex and most difficult subject of study on which the human mind can be engaged" (p. 418). This sounds like an echo of Aristotle's famous statement to the effect that "To attain any assured knowledge about the soul is one of the most difficult things in the world." Unlike Aristotle, however, Mill had post-Newtonian concepts of the nature of scientific knowledge at his disposal. It was the kind of knowledge that had given rise to laws of physics and laws of astronomy as precise formulations of underlying uniformities of results to be expected under given conditions. As Mill understood it, the quest for such uniformities is the *sine qua non* for the establishment of a science.

In other words, unless there are laws of human nature there can be no *science* of psychology. To expect them to equal the precision and predictability of the laws of physics, Mill pointed out, would be chimerical. Nevertheless, he maintained, despite lesser degrees of precision and less certain predictions, it would still be possible to establish a science. One can have a science even though it is not an *exact* science. In its early stages of development, Mill noted, astronomy was not an exact science. Similarly, he added, meteorology is to be classified as a science even though its predictions of tomorrow's weather are notoriously fallible. There are too many fluctuat-

---

[17] The two volumes are now available in a single volume based upon the eighth edition and published in London by Longmans, Green and Company in 1961. Compressing the work into a single volume required rather fine print and two columns per page.

ing variables to be taken into account to make weather predictions as precise as predictions of planetary motion. On the other hand, when it comes to predicting high tide and low tide, with fewer variables to consider, the resulting predictions will be more dependable. Even so, allowance will have to be made for changes in wind velocity, changes in the ocean floor, and contour of the shoreline so that tidal predictions will not be fulfilled with complete accuracy at all times in all places; hence, published tide tables are best regarded as *approximations* of what is likely to occur. Viewed as a science, tidology, or the study of tides, is more exact than meteorology and less exact than astronomy. Mill regarded it as being intermediate in character between an advanced science and a very imperfect one. According to him, psychology has this kind of "intermediate" status (pp. 432–433):

> The science of human nature is of this description. It falls far short of the standard of exactness now realized in Astronomy; but there is no reason that it should not be as much a science as Tidology is, or as Astronomy was when its calculations had only mastered the main phenomena, but not the perturbations.

As if in anticipation of what laboratory psychology was to become, Mill urged that the science of human nature avail itself of the methods so successfully employed in the physical sciences. Only by "consciously and deliberately" applying such methods to its "difficult inquires" can psychology be rescued "from Empiricism" (p. 418). This, of course, is a pejorative use of the word "empiricism" and suggests an uncritical reliance on experience in the sense in which the empiric in medicine is uncritical. Experience per se, unchecked by the safeguards of scientific medicine, gives rise to quackery. By implication, Mill was suggesting that the empiric in psychology may be deluding himself as well as others.[18] Scientific psychology as envisaged by Mill was to guard against such self-delusion.

In his discussion of psychology as science Mill anticipated several later conclusions reached by those who shaped the foundations of modern psychology and related fields of investigation—fields like neurology, physiology, psychiatry, sociology, anthropology, and physiological psychology. There are dualistic implications to be detected in the very existence of such

---

[18] This is not to be interpreted as meaning that Mill was referring to the fraudulent employment of empirical observations as connoted by the quackery of medical empirics. What he had in mind was reliance on *unexamined* empirical observations. By way of illustration, he called attention to an "empirical law" to the effect that the young are impetuous and the old are cautious (p. 449). Until such an empirical law is *explained* in terms of causal factors such as ignorance of consequences and lack of experience, it will be misunderstood; "for it is not because of their youth that the young are impetuous, nor because of their age that the old are cautious." Under given circumstances young people may be cautious and old people impetuous. "The really scientific truths . . . are not these empirical laws, but the causal laws which explain them."

diverse fields. They are reflected in such correlated specialties as psycho-pathology and neuropathology or psychiatry and neurology or psychology and brain physiology. Writing in the 1840s, long before these specialties had come into existence, Mill in a chapter concerned with the "laws of mind" had this to say about such dualistic implications (pp. 436–437):

> The immediate antecedent of a sensation is a state of the body, but the sensation itself is a state of mind. If the word means anything, it means that which feels. Whatever opinion we hold respecting the fundamental identity or diversity of matter and mind, in any case the distinction between mental and physical facts, between the internal and external world, will always remain, as a matter of classification: and in that classification, sensations, like all other feelings, must be ranked as mental phenomena. The mechanism of their production, both in the body itself and in what is called outward nature, is all that can with any propriety be classed as physical. . . .
>
> All states of mind are immediately caused either by other states of mind, or by states of body. When a state of mind is produced by a state of mind, I call the law concerned in the case, a law of Mind. When a state of mind is produced directly by a state of body, the law is a law of Body, and belongs to physical science.

Mill realized that this recognition of laws of the mind as distinguished from laws of the body would be subject to controversy. He especially expected objections to be raised by those physiologists who attribute all mental states to concomitant neural states. Such physiologists would account for the familiar fact that one thought recalls another by referring to an association between two states of the brain rather than two states of the mind. This sort of disposition of the psychophysical problem, Mill argued, would make psychology a branch of physiology. It would make experience or consciousness a byproduct or epiphenomenon of brain action. This, Mill noted, was a conclusion arrived at by the positivist, Comte, who "not only denies to Psychology . . . the character of a science, but places it, in the chimerical nature of its objects and pretensions, almost on a par with astrology" (p. 438). In terms of general orientation, Comte was thus fore-shadowing the "objectivism" of twentieth-century behaviorists who questioned the scientific status of "mentalistic" interpretations.

In opposition to Comte, Mill set out to provide for an autonomous science of psychology related to but independent of physiology. His general orientation was that of an associationistic empiricist. As an empiricist he was sponsoring the kind of psychology men like James Ward and G. F. Stout were later to define as "the science of individual experience." This kind of orientation is at variance with Comtean positivism and behavioristic objectivism. In brief, according to the one orientation the psychologist is asking, "What is the organism experiencing?" whereas according to the other he is asking, "What is the organism doing?"

These antithetic orientations did not really clash until the early decades of the present century. As just indicated, Mill's opposition to Comte was a foreshadowing of this clash. In their day, laboratory psychology had not yet come into being. When it was launched by Wundt and his followers some forty years after Mill had completed his *Logic,* it turned out to be Mill's kind of experiential psychology rather than Comte's kind of positivistic psychology. As a deliberate effort to launch a *scientific* psychology with an avowed "mentalistic" orientation, it reflected the following justification for such an orientation as presented by Mill in answer to Comte's refusal to endow psychology with "the character of a science" (pp. 438–439):

> But, after all has been said which can be said, it remains incontestable that there exist uniformities of succession among states of mind, and that these can be ascertained by observation and experiment. Further, that every mental state has a nervous state for its immediate antecedent and proximate cause, though extremely probable, cannot hitherto be said to be proved, in the conclusive manner in which this can be proved of sensations; and even were it certain yet every one must admit that we are wholly ignorant of the characteristics of these nervous states; we know not, and at present have no means of knowing, in what respect one of them differs from another; and our mode of studying their successions or coexistences must be by observing the successions and coexistences of the mental states, of which they are supposed to be the generators or causes. The successions, therefore, which obtain among mental phenomena, do not admit of being deduced from the physiological laws of our nervous organization: and all real knowledge of them must continue, for a long time at least, if not always, to be sought in the direct study, by observation and experiment, of the mental succession themselves. Since therefore the order of our mental phenomena must be studied in those phenomena, and not inferred from the laws of any phenomena more general, there is a distinct and separate Science of Mind.
>
> The relations, indeed, of that science to the science of physiology must never be overlooked or undervalued. It must by no means be forgotten that the laws of mind may be derivative laws resulting from laws of animal life, and that their truth therefore may ultimately depend on physical conditions; and the influence of physiological states or physiological changes in altering or counteracting the mental successions, is one of the most important departments of psychological study. But, on the other hand, to reject the resource of psychological analysis, and construct the theory of the mind solely on such data as physiology at present affords, seems to me as great an error in principle, and an even more serious one in practice. Imperfect as is the science of mind, I do not scruple to affirm, that it is in a considerably more advanced state than the portion of physiology which corresponds to it; and to discard the former for the latter appears to me an infringement of the true canons of inductive philosophy, which must produce, and which does produce, erroneous conclusions in some very important departments of the science of human nature.

To revert to a point made at the close of the previous section, it should now be clear why Wundt held that "the historian of science in the nineteenth century" would have to place Mill's *Logic* in the first rank among works having had the "greatest influence" on the science of the second half of the century. Wundt was referring to its influence on science in general as suggested by his references to Liebig and Helmholtz. However, in view of what Mill had to say about psychology in the preceding quotation, it may well be that Wundt was not unmindful of his influence on psychology in particular.

Wundt could have cited the entire quotation as an expression of his own views of psychology as science. This applies particularly to Mill's emphasis on analysis of experience by "observation and experiment"[19] as an undertaking to be pursued in its own right and not as an offshoot of neurology. Psychology was not to be ancillary to physiology. This implied endorsement of psychophysical parallelism in a pragmatic rather than a metaphysical sense. By avoiding metaphysical commitments, both Mill and Wundt were helping to liberate psychology from its ties to mental philosophy, just as physics as an autonomous science has succeeded in divorcing itself from natural philosophy. John Stuart Mill is thus to be listed among those who helped to bring about the emergence of psychology as a science. He was not a direct founding father as were the men of Wundt's generation, but in his indirect influence he was a founding grandfather.

Mill on the Metaphysics of Mind and Matter

The previous statement regarding Mill's avoidance of metaphysical commitments does not mean that he ignored metaphysical issues. In the very early part of his *Logic*, he devoted one section to consideration of the concept of body and another to the concept of mind.[20] Unlike Descartes, who had tackled the same problem, he failed to commit himself to a differentiation

---

[19] Mill devoted a whole chapter to the subject of "observation and experiment" (1875, Vol. I, Book III, Ch. VII). In it he considered situations in which experiment has advantages over observation and others in which observation has advantages over experiment. In this context he was using the term "experiment" as a reference to controlled observations of any kind and not just to those restricted to laboratory isolation of factors to be observed. He referred to the latter as "artificial" experiments. In envisaging a psychology based upon "observation and experiment," he does not seem to have been thinking of a laboratory for the conduct of such "artificial" experiments. This was Wundt's innovation. What Mill had in mind was the application of his "four experimental methods" to psychological problems. These, as is well known, consisted of (1) the method of agreement, (2) the method of difference, (3) the method of concomitant variations, and (4) the method of residues. The "non-artificial" utilization of one or more of these methods was regarded as experimental work by Mill. In this sense Kepler's laws of planetary motion and Darwin's field observations belong to experimental science. Under the circumstances Mill would have had no hesitation in classifying many contemporary nonlaboratory correlational studies in psychology and sociology as experimental studies.

[20] See Vol. I, Book I, in which the seventh paragraph is concerned with the meaning of "body" and the eighth paragraph is concerned with the meaning of "mind."

in terms of extended and inextended substances. Instead he suggested having the word "body" stand for the "unknown" cause of sensations and the word "mind" stand for the "unknown" percipient not only of sensations "but of all our other feelings." He then added: "As body is understood to be the mysterious something which excites mind to feel, so mind is the mysterious something which feels and thinks." This left the concepts of body and mind, taken in the abstract, both unknown and mysterious. What is known and presumably not so mysterious is sensation.

Interestingly enough, toward the end of his *Logic* in returning to consideration of the topic of sensation, Mill stated that sensation belongs to "the province of Physiology." Accordingly he was regarding sensation as more distinctively a function of body than of mind.[21] Support for this interpretation can be found in the amount of space that textbooks of physiology devote to visual, auditory, olfactory, and other sensations. One can also hold with Franz Brentano, as mentioned in Chapter 4, page 81, that sensation belongs to the province of physics, supporting this contention by pointing to chapters on light and sound in textbooks of physics. Others, of course, are quite certain of the place of sensation within the province of psychology. Only radical behaviorists, uneasy about the "mentalistic"[22] connotation of the concept of sensation, would restrict it to the realms of physiology and physics. Neutral outsiders would have little difficulty in recognizing the stimulus aspect of sensation as being essentially physical in nature, the receptor and neural aspect as being fundamentally physiological in nature, and the qualitatively unique experiential aspect as being predominantly psychological in nature.

There can be no satisfactory complete account of sensation without due consideration of all three aspects; hence it is futile to argue about the relative importance of these aspects or about the scientific "province" to which the topic of sensation is to be allocated. To say more about this would be to dwell upon the obvious.

What may not be so obvious is Mill's disposition of the concept of matter

---

[21] This is not to be construed as meaning the exclusion of sensation from the province of psychology. In Mill's words, sensations, in their status as "feelings," "like all other feelings must be ranked as mental phenomena." With reference to their causal antecedents, however, they may be classified as physical events. Mill argued that the cause of every sensation is to be found in the nervous system; "whether this affection originate in the action of some external object, or in some pathological condition of the nervous organization itself. The laws of this portion of our nature—varieties of our sensations, and the physical conditions on which they proximately depend—manifestly belong to the province of Physiology" (p. 437).

[22] The question of "mentalism" seems to be a persistent problem for psychologists and keeps cropping up for reconsideration. A clarifying contemporary review of the salient issue involved in the problem is supplied by E. Stotland's article on "Mentalism Revisited" (1966).

or physical substance. His views on this topic are not to be found in his *Logic* but in a later work concerned with a critique of Sir William Hamilton's teachings. This is a very detailed study published in 1865 in two volumes. As a source of his own psychology it is as important as the *Logic* and as his notes on his father's book on *Analysis of the Phenomena of the Human Mind*. Since he never wrote a separate book on psychology as such his own psychology has to be gleaned from these other sources.

His failure to devote a separate volume to the subject is not to be interpreted as a lack of sustained interest in the subject nor as failure to appreciate its importance. His interest is reflected in the amount of space devoted to psychological issues in the three sources just mentioned. Furthermore, his appreciation of the importance of psychology is given explicit recognition at the very beginning of his examination of Hamilton's philosophy by a statement to the effect that "A true Psychology is the indispensable scientific basis of Morals, of Politics, of the science and art of Education" (1865, Vol. I, p. 10). Determining the nature of this "true Psychology" was thus an important issue for Mill. Presumably, by implication, this meant differentiating it from the "true Physics." At all events, it was in connection with his dissatisfaction with Sir William Hamilton's philosophy that he presented his own explanation for the origin of our ordinary conviction regarding the *physical* existence of external objects.

Mill realized that in terms of Berkeley's subjective idealism there is no way of establishing the existence of external objects independently of their being perceived. Actually, as noted in Chapter 6, page 134, this Berkeleian notion had been anticipated by Plotinus in the third century when in discussing the concept of matter he concluded that we must "refuse to it all that we find in things of sense." Then, it may be recalled, Plotinus decided that if matter is to refer to an "underlying substratum" it will have to be defined "as a Potentiality and nothing more." In thus defining it, he was foreshadowing Mill's famous definition of matter as the "permanent possibility of sensation."

For Mill, the issue regarding the nature of matter was not so much a metaphysical question or even a physicochemical question. He was primarily concerned with it as a psychological issue having to do with the origin of our belief in the existence of an external world of ordinary objects like tables, trees, paper, dogs, and people. In opposition to those like Sir William Hamilton who attributed such a belief to an intuitive or unlearned conviction, Mill attributed the belief to the effects of experience and not to an innate endowment. He voiced his opposition in a long chapter of sixty pages (1865, Ch. XI).[23] An excerpt from the latter part of this chapter will

[23] Excerpts from this chapter are to be found in the *Source Book* edited by Herrnstein and Boring (1965, pp. 182–188).

738 FROM THE RENAISSANCE TO THE MODERN PERIOD

serve to show the kind of evidence Mill introduced in support of his position. After many pages of argument he went on to say (1865, pp. 243–246):

> Matter, then, may be defined, a Permanent Possibility of Sensation. If I am asked, whether I believe in matter, I ask whether the questioner accepts this definition of it. If he does, I believe in matter: and so do all Berkeleians. In any other sense than this, I do not. But I affirm with confidence, that this conception of Matter includes the whole meaning attached to it by the common world, apart from philosophical, and sometimes from theological, theories. The reliance of mankind on the real existence of visible and tangible objects, means reliance on the reality and permanence of Possibilities of visual and tactual sensations, when no such sensations are actually experienced. We are warranted in believing that this is the meaning of Matter in the minds of many of its most esteemed metaphysical champions, though they themselves would not admit as much: for example, Reid, Stewart, and Brown. For these three philosophers alleged that all mankind, including Berkeley and Hume, really believed in Matter, inasmuch as unless they did, they would not have turned aside to save themselves from running against a post. Now, all which this manoeuvre really proved is, that they believed in Permanent Possibilities of Sensation. We have therefore the sanctions of these eminent defenders of the existence of matter, for affirming, that to believe in Permanent Possibilities of Sensation *is* believing Matter. It is hardly necessary . . . to mention Dr. Johnson . . . who resorts to *argumentum baculum* of knocking a stick against the ground. Sir William Hamilton . . . never reasons in this manner. He never supposes that a disbeliever in what he means by Matter, ought in consistency to act in any different mode from those who believe in it. He knew that the belief on which all the practical consequences depend, is the belief in Permanent Possibilities of Sensation, and that if nobody believed in a material universe in any other sense, life would go on exactly as it now does. He, however, did believe in more than this, but, I think, only because it had never occurred to him that mere Possibilities of Sensation could to our artificialized consciousness, present the character of objectivity which, as we have now shown, they not only can, but unless the known laws of the human mind were suspended, must necessarily present. . . .
>
> The belief in such permanent possibilities seems to me to include all that is essential or characteristic in the belief in substance. I believe that Calcutta exists, though I do not perceive it, and that it would still exist if every percipient inhabitant were suddenly to leave the place, or be struck dead. But when I analyze the belief all I find in it is, that were these events to take place, the Permanent Possibility of Sensation which I call Calcutta would still remain; that if I were suddenly transported to the banks of the Hoogly, I should still have the sensations which, if now present, would lead me to affirm that Calcutta exists here and now.

In thus holding that matter or body consists of "permanent possibilities of sensation," Mill was no longer holding to the position he had taken many decades earlier in his *Logic*. In that work he had defined "body" as the "unknown" and "mysterious" cause of sensations. This might be construed as the equivalent of Kant's noumenal realm—the unknowable world of "things in themselves." This appears to have been the something "more" which, according to Mill, Sir William Hamilton had added to the "permanent possibilities of sensation." As an issue it suggests the futile and meaningless kind of question posed by those who wonder about what thunder sounds like when there is nobody around to hear it or what an apple looks like when nobody sees it. Conceivably, questions of this kind might have been raised by those whom Mill regarded as opposed to his empiricism. He numbered Sir William Hamilton among such opponents, and, as he explained in his *Autobiography,* his chief reason for subjecting Hamilton's philosophy to such careful analysis was to expose its weaknesses and the "almost incredible multitude of inconsistencies which showed themselves on comparing different passages with one another" (1882, p. 276).

At the time Mill undertook this analysis, more than twenty years had elapsed since the completion of his *Logic* and he was in a position to formulate a new definition of matter without mentioning the old one given in the *Logic.* It may be that he had forgotten about it. At all events, he was silent on the subject as he presented his detailed exposition and vigorous defense of the new definition. The upshot of this exposition was to account for belief in external objects in terms of experience and association. This, as a belief or conviction in "the permanent possibilities of sensation," was at variance with those philosophers who accounted for such belief or conviction by an appeal to intuition or innate endowment. Mill saw himself as identified with one school of philosophy and Sir William Hamilton as identified with an opposing school. This was not just a matter of academic rivalry. For Mill, the difference between the two schools was likely to be fraught with momentous consequences, which he explained as follows (1882, pp. 273–275):

> Now, the difference between these two schools of philosophy, that of Intuition, and that of Experience and Association, is not a mere matter of speculation; it is full of practical consequences, and lies at the foundation of all the greatest differences of practical opinion in an age of progress. The practical reformer has continually to demand that changes be made in things which are supported by powerful and widely-spread feelings, or to question the apparent necessity and indefeasibleness of established facts; and it is often an indispensable part of his argument to show, how those powerful feelings had their origin, and how those facts came to seem necessary and indefeasible. There is, therefore, a natural hostility between him and a philosophy which discourages the explanation of feelings and moral facts by circumstances and association, and prefers to treat them as ultimate elements of human nature; a philosophy which . . . deems intuition to be the voice of Nature and of God, speaking with an authority higher than that of reason. In particular, I have long felt that the prevailing tendency to regard all the marked distinctions of human character as innate, and in the main indelible, and to ignore the irresistible proofs that by far the

greater part of those differences, whether between individuals, races, or sexes, are such as not only might but naturally would be produced by differences in circumstances, is one of the chief hindrances to the rational treatment of great social questions, and one of the greatest stumbling blocks to human improvement. . . . My father's Analysis of the Mind, my own Logic, and Professor Bain's great treatise, had attempted to re-introduce a better mode of philosophizing, latterly with quite as much success as could be expected; but I had for some time felt that the mere contrast of the two philosophies was not enough, that there ought to be a hand-to-hand fight between them, that controversial as well as expository writings were needed, and that the time was come when such controversy would be useful.

The clash between the outlook of Mill and that of Sir William Hamilton thus belongs in the general setting of the perennial nature-nurture conflict. As a social reformer and as one interested in the reduction of human distress, Mill, as he said, found advocacy of nativism "one of the greatest stumbling blocks" toward achievement of improvement in the human condition. His attack on Sir William Hamilton's philosophy was for the purpose of removing this stumbling block.

On Mill's Opposition to Nativism

As an empiricist and associationist, Mill, in line with a *tabula rasa* orientation, regarded individual differences in character, ability, and intelligence as predominantly products of training, experience, and education. In his view, as noted in the preceding excerpt, "all the marked distinctions of human character" are not innate and indelible but are the consequences of differences in circumstances to which people are exposed. In terms of later arguments regarding the relative importance of heredity versus environment, he would have sided with the environmentalists. Similarly, were he living in the modern era, he would be vehemently opposed to those who attribute inferior school work of Negro children to innate inferiority.[24] Instead he would have attributed the inferiority in question to inferior schooling and to cultural deprivation. In doing so, he would have been voicing his allegiance to the school of Experience and Association as contrasted with what he had called the school of Intuition.

In thus aligning himself with the school of Experience and Association against the school of Intuition, Mill was identifying with the Lockean tradition rather than with the tradition of Leibnitz and Kant. Broadly considered, the latter tradition is reminiscent of terms like *res cogitans, intellectus ipse,* categories of understanding, the *a priori,* and innate ideas, whereas the former tradition is reminiscent of terms like *tabula rasa,* sensory impres-

---

[24] For a recent study that purports to supply "scientific" evidence in support of this kind of hereditarian conclusion, see A. M. Shuey, *The Testing of Negro Intelligence* (1966).

sions, empiricism, conditioning, learning, and stimulus-response connections. In short, as just pointed out, intuitionists tended to lend more weight to factors of heredity and nature as contrasted with the associationist's emphasis on factors of environment and nurture.

The entire drift of the educational regimen to which John Stuart Mill had been subjected was calculated to promote his affiliation with the associationist tradition and his alienation from the *a priori* or intuitionist tradition. It never dawned on him that his educational progress was unusual and that it was indicative of exceptional intellectual endowment. He found himself falling short of his father's expectations, so that, as he reports, "If I thought anything about myself, it was that I was rather backward in my studies." His father made a deliberate effort to prevent him from hearing himself praised for his accomplishments, and he had little opportunity to compare them with those of other boys since, in accordance with his father's intentions, contact with other boys was kept to a minimum. It was not until his fourteenth year, when he was about to embark on a protracted absence from home, that his father broached the subject of what he might be tempted to regard as superior attainments. He was told to expect to discover as he got to know other people that they had not been taught what he had been taught. He was also told to expect to hear himself complimented upon his store of knowledge; but then his father pointed out (1882, pp. 34–35):

> That whatever I knew more than others, could not be ascribed to any merit in me, but the very unusual advantage which had fallen to my lot, of having a father who was able to teach me, and willing to give the necessary trouble and time; that it was no matter of praise to me, if I knew more than those who had not had a similar advantage, but the deepest disgrace to me if I did not. I have a distinct rememberance, that the suggestion thus for the first time made to me, that I knew more than other youths who were considered well educated, was to me a piece of information, to which, as to all other things which my father told me, I gave implicit credence, but which did not at all impress me as a personal matter. I felt no disposition to glorify myself upon the circumstance that there were other persons who did not know what I knew; nor had I ever flattered myself that my acquirements, whatever they might be, were any merit of mine: but, now when my attention was called to the subject, I felt that what my father had said respecting my peculiar advantages was exactly the truth and common sense of the matter, and it fixed my opinion and feeling from that time forward.

The youthful John Stuart Mill was thus convinced that intellectual achievement was entirely a matter of opportunity, of educational advantages, and rare teachers like his father. Apparently he was given to believe that his father could have secured the same results with any other pupil; hence, as he concluded, the final outcome would not be due to "any merit" of the pupil. Evidently he was not thinking of some pupils as bright and others as dull, or at least not as inherently bright or dull.

He was born just about a century before Binet constructed the first intelligence test, which some came to regard as a measure of *native* intelligence. Had Mill been clairvoyant, he might have been startled to find out what was going to be said about his native intelligence as symbolized by the intelligence quotient. He would have found himself classified as one of the most gifted children in a group of gifted children who became eminent adults and whose childhood histories were sufficiently well known to enable their I.Q.'s to be approximated on the basis of their histories. Had he consulted the report by C. M. Cox (1926, pp. 707–709), he would have discovered that she had rated him as having had a childhood I.Q. of 190. This was a higher estimate than for any other philosopher in her group. Leibnitz came close with an estimated I.Q. of 185 and Hume came next with a rating of 155, followed by Descartes with 150 and Francis Bacon with 145. Even as rough approximations, these estimates point to individual differences in native endowment among intellectually gifted children.

Recognition of differences in intellectual endowment that comes to be influenced by experience is more in accord with the intuitionist's than with the associationist's outlook. As a boy of fourteen, John Stuart Mill does not seem to have suspected the existence of such differences in intellectual endowment. If he had, he might not have been so ready to give his father sole credit for his outstanding record as a precocious student. At the time, both he and his father appeared to be endorsing a *tabula rasa* interpretation of the genesis of mind. However, as an adult no longer overawed by his father's teachings, he seems to have modified this interpretation. There are a few references to man's "natural sagacity" in the *Logic*, in one of which Mill opposes "natural sagacity" to "acquired" sagacity. Such opposition suggests the "natural" as innate and unlearned and the "acquired" as a product of experience and learning. As a descriptive phrase, "natural sagacity" may thus be taken as a synonym for a phrase like "native intelligence." According to one passage in which Mill referred to natural sagacity, such sagacity is taken to be a prerequisite for the eventual acquisition of scientific knowledge and the construction of the theories and methods of science. This is the passage (1875, p. 417):

Principles of Evidence and Theories of Method are not to be constructed *a priori*. The laws of our rational faculty, like those of every other natural agency, are only learnt by seeing the agent at work. The earlier achievements of science were made without the conscious observance of any Scientific Method; and we should never have known by what process truth is to be ascertained, if we had not previously ascertained many truths. But it was only the easier problems which could be thus resolved: *natural sagacity* [italics added], when it tried its strength against the more difficult ones, either failed altogether, or if it succeeded here and there in obtaining a solution, had no sure means of convincing others that its solution was correct. In scientific investigation, as in all other works of human skill, the way of obtaining the end is seen as it were instinctively, by superior minds in some comparatively simple case, and is then, by judicious generalization, adapted to the variety of complex cases. We learn to do a thing in difficult circumstances, by attending to the manner in which we have spontaneously done the same thing in easier ones.

The preceding passage was written some twenty years before Mill undertook the examination of Sir William Hamilton's philosophy. He had not yet come to consider the conflict between the standpoint of intuitionists and that of associationists. He thus had no reason to be on guard against possible agreement with a standpoint he was to oppose many years later. Actually, such agreement appears to be expressed in the quoted passage even though it fails to mention the word "intuition." Nevertheless, if intuition be defined as the direct or unmediated knowledge[25] of something, then Mill was referring to an intuitive process in his allusions to the resolution of some problems by "natural sagacity" and to what "superior minds" can do "instinctively" or "spontaneously." This meaning of "intuition" is not to be confused with its other meaning as some sort of supernormal, ineffable knowledge mystics talk about. Instead it is to be restricted to the immediate unreflective apprehension of the significance of experienced events. The perception of causality by Michotte's experimental observers as discussed in Chapter 17 is an instance of this kind of apprehension. Had Mill known about these experiments, he might have attributed such perception to natural sagacity as an instinctive or spontaneous process. He might well have been ready to make this concession to the intuitionists, just as he might well have been willing to attribute some of the superiority of "superior minds" to native endowment. His opposition to nativism when viewed in terms of the nature-nurture dichotomy is thus to be interpreted as a conviction of nurture as relatively of far greater influence for the shaping of character, without, however, the complete exclusion of nativistic influences.

Ethology as the Science of Character Formation

That Mill, as just suggested, had definite convictions about influences that determine character development is a statement of fact and not just a plausible conjecture. In fact, toward the end of the *Logic* he devoted a whole chapter to the subject (1875, pp. 448–463).[26] The chapter is entitled "Of Ethology[27] or the Science of the Formation of Character." From the context it is clear that he was not thinking of character in the restricted moralistic

---

25 So defined, it approximates the meaning of *unmittelbare Erkenntnis,* which is the German equivalent of the English word "intuition."

26 Parts of this chapter are included among the selections in the *Readings in the History of Psychology* edited by W. Dennis (1948, pp. 174–177).

27 Mill's use of the term "ethology" is different from its current use by zoologists as a designation for comparative studies of the ecology of animal behavior.

sense employers have in mind when they request letters of recommendation. He was employing the word in its broader, more neutral, non-evaluative connotation as suggested by conventional references to the Japanese character, the adolescent character, the character of London police, the character of modern plays, the character of Queen Elizabeth or any other public figure. Such references have to do with individual and group differences. Mill recognized that determining the nature, amount, and origin of these differences is an important but exceedingly difficult undertaking.

In outline he seemed to foresee that the undertaking would involve what was later to become known as an *idiographic* approach. As already considered (see page 212), the latter term was introduced by Wilhelm Windelband to refer to the study of the single case and the unique event or that which is *sui generis*. Windelband contrasted this approach with *nomothetic* studies, or those sciences concerned with general laws or impersonal uniformities, such as the laws of planetary motion or the laws of chemistry. In terms of this distinction, physics calls for the nomothetic approach, whereas biography calls for the idiographic approach. As applied to psychology, it seems safe to classify physiological psychology as a nomothetic study, in contrast to the idiographic implications to be found in a field like the psychology of personality.

According to Windelband, getting to understand an individual personality called for what he called an "intuitive intelligence" that cannot be learned or taught. In his view, such intelligence is to be found in the gifted poet and great statesman by virtue of which they gain revealing insights into the life of man. Their insights are not the results of a mastery of nomothetic abstractions to be found in textbooks of psychology. Instead their insights are the fruits of idiographic observations of concrete individuals, experienced in the course of everyday dealings with their fellow human beings. In short, Windelband recognized two kinds of psychology: (1) nomothetic psychology as the *science* of human nature or of mental life; and (2) idiographic psychology as the *art* of understanding people in their individual uinqueness.

The issue is of more than passing historical interest. It is intimately related to if not identical with one of the six key problems of psychology as outlined in Chapter 8. This is the problem of *individuality,* or the problem of accounting for the idiosyncratic distinctiveness of human nature. No two people are ever precisely alike in all respects. Even identical twins have distinctive personalities.[28] Were they to attend the same schools and be in the same classes, their examination papers would not be identical in wording. Moreover, were they both to become novelists, their literary styles, even though conceivably similar, would nevertheless be unique for each twin. In

---

[28] An excellent survey of the large number of studies concerned with the likenesses and differences to be found in twins—both identical and fraternal twins—has been supplied by Helen L. Koch (1966).

terms of Windelband's proposal, investigation of such uniqueness would call for an idiographic approach.

More than sixty years before Windelband had introduced his proposal for two kinds of psychology, Mill had made a similar proposal. He suggested having psychology deal with general or universal laws of human nature and ethology deal with that which is unique to individualized human nature. Unlike Windelband, he did not think of psychology as a science and ethology as an art. For him, both were to be regarded as sciences, with the laws of ethology being derived from those of psychology. He was quite definite about this when he reached this conclusion (1875, pp. 457–458):

> The laws of the formation of character are, in short, derivative laws, resulting from the general laws of mind, and are to be obtained by deducing them from those general laws by supposing any given set of circumstances, and then considering what, according to the laws of mind, will be the influence of those circumstances on the formation of character.
>
> A science is thus formed, to which I would propose to give the name of Ethology, or the Science of Character, from *ethos* a word more nearly corresponding to the term *character,* as I here use it, than any other word in the same language. The name is perhaps etymologically applicable to the entire science of our mental and moral nature; but if, as is usual and convenient, we employ the name Psychology for the science of the elementary laws of mind, Ethology will serve for the ulterior science which determines the kind of character produced in conformity to those general laws by any set of circumstances, physical and moral. According to this definition, Ethology is the science which corresponds to the art of education, in the widest sense of the term, including the formation of national or collective character, as well as individual. It would indeed be vain to expect (however completely the laws of the formation of character be ascertained) that we could know so accurately the circumstances of any given case as to be able positively to predict the character that would be produced in that case. But we must remember that a degree of knowledge far short of the power of actual prediction is often of much practical value. There may be great power of influencing phenomena, with a very imperfect knowledge of the causes by which they are in any given instance determined. It is enough that we know that certain means have a *tendency* to produce a given effect, and that others have a tendency to frustrate it. When the circumstances of an individual or of a nation are in any considerable degree under our control, we may, by our knowledge of tendencies, be enabled to shape those circumstances in a manner much more favourable to the ends we desire than the shape they would themselves assume. This is the limit of our power, but within this limit the power is a most important one.

Mill's proposal regarding ethology as a separate field of investigation was just left in the form of a proposal. He failed to elaborate upon it by means of specific examples to illustrate the difference between the field of psychology on the one hand and the field of ethology on the other hand. He evidently thought his reference to the molding influence of education on character would suffice to indicate the difference. From the context, it is clear that he was using the word "education" in its widest connotation, as the sum total of cultural influences affecting human development. In this sense he had repeatedly referred to psychology as a "moral science," meaning a science having to do with conduct as contrasted with behavior. In terms of this distinction, animal psychology would not be a moral science. Actually, of course, the phrase "moral science" is now as obsolete as Mill's use of the word "ethology." However, the phrase is of some historical interest; for, to revert to an earlier point (see page 213), Wilhelm Dilthey's term *"Geisteswissenschaft"* came to be the German translation of Mill's phrase. Later writers, in trying to find a suitable English rendering for Dilthey's term, failed to revive Mill's phrase. Instead it was variously rendered as "cultural science," "social science," or possibly "humanistic science." As Dilthey used it, the contrasting term was "natural science." Under *"Geisteswissenschaften"* he included such diverse subjects as economics, sociology, and history as contrasted with natural sciences like chemistry, astronomy, and physics. In other words, Mill's distinction between psychology and ethology foreshadowed the later debates between those who listed psychology as a natural science and those who classified it as a social science. This is not unrelated to still later debates between those who regard what they term "personology" as a distinct branch of psychology and those who question the "scientific" status and need for such a separate branch. All personologists are psychologists, but not all psychologists are personologists. Along with books and journals on psychology there are also books and journals concerned with personality. The former deal with topics more or less common to all men, while the latter deal with topics presumably related to man's *individuality*.

The Problem of Individuality

It is almost a truism to note that some things apply to all men, other things to some men, and still others just to individual men. All men need sleep, some men speak Danish, and only one man wrote *Hamlet* and *Othello*. Human nature may thus be studied in terms of its universal, parochial, and individual characteristics, respectively. Mill had this in mind when he distinguished between ethology as the study of the parochial and individual characteristics and psychology as the study of universal ones.

Independently of Mill, something of a comparable sort was noted by one of his contemporaries, James Clerk-Maxwell (1831–1879), the distinguished Scottish physicist. As quoted by Merz, Clerk-Maxwell called attention to two ways of obtaining knowledge of human events; namely, the statistical and the "dynamical." The statistical is too familiar to require more than a few words of explanation. The knowledge accumulated in actuarial tables will serve as a convenient reminder. By reference to the tables, it is possible to calculate the chances per specified units of population of the occurrence of particular events. Within the limits specified by the tables, it is thus possible to predict the probable incidence of suicide, divorce, academic success, crop failure, or heart failure. But this is different from predicting which particular *individuals* are going to commit suicide, be divorced, succeed at college, be ruined as farmers, or suffer heart attacks. To make such predictions, Clerk-Maxwell stated "students of human nature" have to avail themselves of the following "dynamical" method (Merz, 1965, Vol. I, p. 125):

> They observe individual men, ascertain their history, analyze their motives, and compare their expectation of what they will do with their actual conduct. This may be called the dynamical method as applied to man. However imperfect the dynamical study of man may be in practice, it evidently is the only perfect method in principle, and its shortcomings arise from the limitation of our powers rather than from a faulty method of procedure. If we betake ourselves to the statistical method, we do so confessing that we are unable to follow the details of each individual case, and expecting that the effects of widespread causes, though very different in each individual, will produce an average result of the whole nation, from a study of which we may estimate the character and propensities of an imaginary being called the Mean Man.

Had the terms been in existence in his day, Clerk-Maxwell might have alluded to the statistical method as a nomothetic procedure and his "dynamical" method as an idiographic procedure. The one procedure, as he indicated, gives "imaginary" results in the form of averages or generalized abstractions, while the other supplies individualized accounts of actual people. His imaginary "Mean Man" is the same man whom economists used to enshrine as Economic Man. This abstract creature, assumed to be both prudent and rational, was then described in accordance with the theoretic consequences deduced from the operation of the principles of supply and demand, marginal utility, and other laws of economics. However, the laws as formulated did not render it possible to predict the economic behavior of individual men without personal knowledge of each one. The miserly might deny their families necessities and the socially ambitious might spend too much on prestige-enhancing luxuries, and thus the dynamics of individual behavior might be at variance with the statistics of group averages. This, in brief, is what both Mill and Clerk-Maxwell were driving at in their allusions to ethology and "dynamical" methods, respectively.

The problem of individuality as touched upon by Mill and Clerk-Maxwell was ignored or glossed over by the founding fathers of laboratory psychology. Clerk-Maxwell died in 1879, the year in which Wundt established the Leipzig laboratory, and Mill had died six years earlier. Consequently, neither men had anything to do with the initiation of laboratory psychology. Moreover, the kind of psychology that Wundt sponsored was general rather than individual. Wundt was not a personologist. Psychological measurements made in his laboratory could be used to illustrate what Clerk-Maxwell meant by "the Mean Man." As noted in Chapter 8, it was this kind of psychology as based upon such measurements to which Dilthey objected and which, in oppostion to Dilthey, Hermann Ebbinghaus defended.

This Dilthey-Ebbinghaus controversy took place in the 1890s. The issues involved are troublesome, complex, and persistent. They continued to be debated in the 1960s. For example, in 1962 R. R. Holt published an article entitled "Individuality and Generalization in the Psychology of Personality," in which he presents an informative historical review of the issues, and argues vigorously not only against Dilthey's psychology as a *Geisteswissenschaft* but also against Windelband's recognition of an *idiographic* psychology. Holt even urged getting rid of the latter adjective, along with its correlative "nomothetic" in the following withering indictment (p. 402):

> Today Windelband's terms continue to appear in psychological writing but largely as pretentious jargon, mouth-filling polysyllables to awe the uninitiated, but never as essential concepts to make any scientifically vital point. . . .
>   The idiographic point of view is an artistic one that strives for a nonscientific goal; the nomothetic, a caricature of science that bears little resemblance to anything that exists today. Since no useful purpose is served by retaining these mischievous and difficult terms, they had best disappear from our scientific vocabularies.

In general, as might be expected from the foregoing, Holt champions the viewpoint of those for whom psychology as science is to reflect the impersonal outlook of the natural scientist. This outlook is concerned with the discovery of generalized uniformities, with prediction and control, and with what lends itself to summarized exposition by means of curves and equations. It is not concerned with the individual *qua* individual, but only as a member of the human species. To venture to *understand* individuals in the sense of *Verstehen*[29] as unique personalities, Holt makes clear, is not the job of the scientific psychologist. As he sees it, such understanding entails the "romantic" outlook of the artist, the novelist, the biographer, and personologists who have recourse to such nonscientific methods as empathy and intuition. Unlike the "objective" outlook of the

---

[29] This qualification is necessary because the connotation of the English word "understanding" does not quite reflect the connotation of the German word *"Verstehen."* In some respects the German word *"begreifen"* comes closer to a translation of the English word understanding. It suggests understanding something in the sense of comprehending it. All sciences involve understanding in this sense, but not all sciences involve understanding in the restricted psychological sense of *Verstehen*. In the former sense one is referring to a *goal* of science, whereas in the latter one is alluding to a

scientist, the outlook of the romantic personologist, with his interest in meanings and values, is a "subjective" outlook. In terms of these strictures, Mill's proposed science of ethology would hardly qualify as science. Whether he would have endorsed these strictures is a separate question that need not be considered in the present context. It is more important to note that his proposal of the two kinds of psychology continues to be a subject of controversy in contemporary psychology.

Without going into great detail, it might be well to say something more about the controversy in question. Despite Holt's cogent arguments, the issue of individuality as a problem for scientific psychology has not yet been eliminated from the arena of current debate. In fact, the article by Holt is followed by an article by Gordon Allport which, although written without prior access to the Holt article, may nevertheless be viewed as a rejoinder. It presents cogent arguments in behalf of the need for and scientific legitimacy of psychological studies of the uniqueness of individual personality. Incidentally, Holt and Allport agree in one respect: they both advocate avoidance of the words *"idiographic"* and *"nomothetic."* But Allport's reasons for doing so are different from Holt's; as Allport explains (1962, p. 409):

> It would serve no good purpose here to review the long-standing debate between partisans of the nomothetic and idiographic methods, between champions of explanation and understanding Indeed, to insure more rapid progress I think it best to avoid traditional terms altogether. For the purposes of our present discussion I shall speak of "dimensional" and "morphogenic" procedures. Let me explain the latter term.
>
> The science of molecular biology shows us that life-substances are identical across species. The building blocks of life—vegetable and animal—turn out to be strikingly uniform in terms of nucleic acids, protein molecules, and enzymatic reactions. Yet an antelope differs from an ash tree, a man from an antelope, and one man is very unlike another. The challenge of morphogenesis (accounting for pattern) grows more rather than less acute as we discover the commonalities of life. Yet biologists admit that morphogenic biology lags far behind molecular (or dimensional) biology. So too does morphogenic psychology lag far behind dimensional psychology.

In contrasting dimensional (nomothetic) with morphogenic (idiographic) objectives, Allport, unlike Holt, was not regarding the former as the foun-

---

method of reaching comprehension. As a method it calls for empathic participation in order to understand a segment of human or animal behavior. Such empathic participation is not required in order to understand Boyle's Law or Mendel's Law, the laws of thermodynamics, or similar scientific laws. However, the sponsors of the psychology of *Verstehen* hold that empathic participation is indispensably necessary to understand the grief of a mourner, the loneliness of a stranger, a parent's love for a child, or a starving animal's quest for food. A critique of this meaning of understanding is supplied by T. Abel in his article on "The Operation Called Verstehen" (1953).

dations for a scientific psychology and the latter as the basis for a variety of nonscientific literary or artistic exercises. Allport deemed both to be objectives falling within the purview of psychology as science. The objectives in question, Allport noted, were the same as those mentioned by John Stuart Mill when he "proposed that we distinguish sharply between psychology, the science of mind-in-general, and ethology, a science of character" concerned with tracing "the operation of psychological laws in specifically individual combinations—such as the pattern of the single person or of a single culture or nation" (1962, p. 407).

Research in psychology was not to be restricted to the problem of finding out how and why people are alike or what they have in common. The problem of finding out how and why they differ from one another or what makes them distinctive personalities was regarded as being of coordinate importance. Moreover, even though research involving dimensional methods is more advanced than morphogenic research, this does not justify abandoning or despairing of the morphogenic quest. In a brief review, Allport called attention to several morphogenic and semi-morphogenic methods introduced in recent decades indicative of progress in dealing with problems Mill would have classified as ethological problems. Finally, had Mill been conversant with these methods, it seems safe to say that he would have considered them no less scientific than the more familiar dimensional methods of traditional general psychology.

Some support for the foregoing conjecture regarding the scientific status of morphogenic or idiographic methods comes from the field of genetics. In a recent article, the geneticist T. Dobzhansky has made it clear that the focus of research in genetics centers on the fact of the individuality of organisms. If all members of a given species were precisely alike, there would be nothing for the geneticist to investigate. It is the fact of their differences from one another that arouses his professional curiosity. In reviewing the evidence bearing upon the genetic basis for such differences, Dobzhansky restricted himself to evidence from the laboratories of geneticists, with the list of references appended to his article being limited to works by biologists and geneticists. Works by psychologists on the subject of individual differences are not mentioned. Nevertheless, it almost seems as if he might have had both the article by Holt and the one by Allport in mind when he disposed of their conflicting views in these two illuminating paragraphs (1967, p. 41):

One of the assertions which have gained acceptance by dint of frequent repetition is that science is competent to deal only with what recurs, returns, repeats itself. To study something scientifically, this something must be made representative of a class, group, or assemblage. A single *Drosophila* is of no interest whatsoever. A fly may merit some attention only if it is taken as a representative of its species. An individual person may, to be sure, merit attention. However, it is allegedly not in the province of science, but of insight, empathy, art, and literature to study and understand a person in his uniqueness.

I wish to challenge this view. Individuality, uniqueness, is not outside the competence of science. It may, in fact it must, be understood scientifically. In particular, the science of genetics investigates individuality and its causes. The singularity of the human self becomes comprehensible in the light of genetics. You may, of course, object that what science comprehends is not really a singularity but a plurality of singularities. However, an artist, no less than a biologist, becomes aware of the plurality because he has observed some singularities.

How Mill Conceived of Individuality

Although Mill was keenly aware of this fact of singularity or individuality, he would have been puzzled by reading that it "becomes comprehensible in the light of genetics." In his day, genetics as a separate branch of biology had not yet come into existence. Terms like DNA, RNA, and chromosomes would have mystified him. Of course, he was not unmindful of heredity as a general phenomenon. His use of a phrase like "natural sagacity" is indicative of such recognition. As an empiricist, however, he was more disposed to account for individuality as the product of education and personal effort in coping with the challenges of daily life. For him, character was not just the passive resultant of a multiplicity of educational experiences. Man is not only acted upon by such experiences but can also react to them. According to Mill, even though a man's character is "in the ultimate resort, formed for him," this "is not inconsistent with its being, in part, formed by him as one of the intermediate agents." Then Mill added, "We are exactly as capable of making our own character, if we will, as others are of making it for us" (1875, Vol. II, p. 426).

In the *Logic,* from which the preceding statements were quoted, there is very little elaboration of this recognition of self-determination as a factor in character development. Such elaboration can be found in Mill's famous essay *On Liberty.* This was published in 1859, some sixteen years after the first edition of the *Logic* appeared. A central theme running through the essay is the importance of freedom to nurture one's own individuality. For example, Mill wrote that "It is only the cultivation of individuality which produces, or can produce, well-developed human beings," and that "Whatever crushes individuality is despotism, by whatever name it may be called, and whether it professes to be enforcing the will of God or the injunctions of men" (M. Lerner [ed.], 1961, p. 312). Regimented conformity or robotlike obedience was anathema to him. He voiced this in an eloquent passage which seems timely in this age of increasing automation when the digital computer impresses some as a promising analogue to human problem-solving in general and to brain-action in particular (Lerner, pp. 307–308):

He who lets the world, or his own portion of it, choose his plan of life for him, has no need of any other faculty than the ape-like one of imitation. He who chooses his plan for himself employs all his faculties. He must use observation to see, reasoning and judgment to foresee, activity to gather materials for decision, discrimination to decide, and when he has decided, firmness and self-control to hold to his deliberate decision. And these qualities he requires and exercises exactly in proportion as the part of his conduct which he determines according to his own judgment and feelings is a large one. It is possible that he might be guided in some good path, and kept out of harm's way, without any of these things. But what will be his comparative worth as a human being? It really is of importance, not only what men do, but also what manner of men are that do it. Among the works of man, which human life is rightly employed in perfecting and beautifying, the first in importance surely is man himself. Supposing it were possible to get houses built, corn grown, battles fought, causes tried, and even churches erected and prayers said, by machinery—by automatons in human form—it would be a considerable loss to exchange for these automatons even the men and women who at present inhabit the more civilized parts of the world, and who assuredly are but starved specimens of what nature can and will produce. Human nature is not a machine to be built after a model, and set to do exactly the work prescribed for it, but a tree which requires to grow and develop itself on all sides, according to the tendency of the inward forces which make it a living thing.

Mill's recourse to an arboreal metaphor when thinking about the individuality of human nature marks a departure from the allusions to a mental mechanics and a mental chemistry that historians tend to associate with the Millean background. The metaphor in question, with its reference to the inward forces of a living thing, is more definitely biological in scope, and is in harmony with Allport's later stress on individualized morphogenic patterns. In fact, Mill foreshadowed this emphasis when he wrote (Lerner, p. 315):

There is no reason that all human existences should be constructed on some one or some small number of patterns. If a person possesses any tolerable amount of common sense and experience, his own mode of laying out his existence is the best, not because it is the best in itself, but because it is his own mode.

Concerning Functional Autonomy

There is one other respect in which Mill anticipated one of Allport's teachings. This has to do with the subject of motivation, or what Allport came to designate as the *functional autonomy* of *motives* (1937). As a doctrine it allowed for a diversity of motivational patterns in place of a restricted number of motives or instinctual urges common to all men. It dealt with the acquisition of new motives and new interests and their variation from person to person, and thus with the motivational aspect of individuality. In brief, the doctrine held that any means employed for the purpose of gratifying some motive might become a motive in its own right. The man who engages in business in order to make money may continue in business long after he has accumulated more millions than he can possibly spend; hence, business as a means has become an independent or autonomous drive. Analogously, the man who takes up golf under protest and only as a means of losing weight may later find himself an avid golfer even though his trim figure suggests elimination of the original motive.

These instances of functional autonomy manifested by the businessman and by the golfer were introduced by R. S. Woodworth as examples of acquired motives close to twenty years before Allport wrote his paper on the functional autonomy of motives. This technical designation for the process was original with Allport; but, as Allport recognized, Woodworth was the first to call attention to the process itself. For Woodworth, any motive was called a *drive,* and any means or instrumental act involved in the satisfaction of a drive was called a *mechanism.* His view of the relationship between drives and mechanisms was described as follows (1918, p. 104):

> In short, the power of acquiring new mechanisms possessed by the human mind is at the same time a power of acquiring new drives; for every mechanism, when at the stage of its development when it has reached a degree of effectiveness without having yet become entirely automatic, is itself a drive capable of motivating activities that lie beyond its immediate scope. The primal forces of hunger, fear, sex, and the rest, continue in force, but do not by any means, even with their combinations, account for the sum total of drives actuating the experienced individual.

For the past thirty or more years this Woodworth-Allport thesis has given rise to a large number of experimental studies.[30] For purposes of descriptive convenience, it is customary to refer to them as studies of functional autonomy. Rarely, if ever, are they spoken of as studies of the conversion of mechanisms into drives. As a result, Woodworth's earlier recognition of the problem tends to be overlooked in favor of Allport's later formulation of the problem as the problem of the functional autonomy of motives. In considering the history of the problem, it is not unusual to have it traced back to 1937, when Allport's formulation appeared, instead of to 1918, when Woodworth's formulation appeared.

It is possible to go still further back into the past and trace initial pres-

---

[30] A list of most of these studies along with a brilliant re-evaluation of the concept of functional autonomy is to be found in a paper by John P. Seward (1962). In it Seward expresses the hope that as a result of these studies we may be on the verge of solving "one mystery of mind: the persistence and individuality of human motives."

entation of the problem to the year 1863, with the publication of John Stuart Mill's *Utilitarianism*.[31] Although the essay contains no technical equivalents of terms like "drives and mechanisms" or "functional autonomy," there can be no question that Mill was dealing with the central issue now designated by such terms. This is clearly evident in the following paragraph, in which he was discussing the genesis of man's love of money or of fame or of power or other "cases" of love of something for its own sake (Lerner, p. 223):

> In these cases the means have become a part of the end, a more important part of it than any of the things which they are means to. What was once desired as an instrument for the attainment of happiness, has come to be desired for its own sake. In being desired for its own sake, it is, however, desired as *part* of happiness. The person is made, or thinks he would be made, happy by its mere possession; and is made unhappy by failure to obtain it. . . . Life would be a poor thing, very ill provided with sources of happiness, if there were not this provision of nature, by which things, originally indifferent, but conducive to, or otherwise associated with, the satisfaction of our primitive desires, become in themselves sources of pleasure more valuable than the primitive pleasures, both in permanency, in the space of human existence that they are capable of covering, and even in intensity.

Hedonism Versus Self-Actualization

As indicated by the last sentence, Mill differentiates primitive desires and pleasures from acquired ones. In terms of his utilitarian doctrine, the acquired ones were deemed "more valuable" than the primitive ones. He regarded this doctrine as supplying the foundation for a theory of morals and as sponsoring what he called Greatest Happiness Principle. It might possibly be classified as a hedonistic principle; for, as explained by Mill, happiness is desired as an end, and other things are desirable to the extent that they serve as means to that end. To a demand for proof in support of this principle, Mill had this to say (Lerner, p. 221):

> The only proof capable of being given that an object is visible, is that people actually see it. The only proof that sound is audible, is that people hear it: and so of the other sources of our experience. In like manner, I apprehend, the sole evidence it is possible to produce that anything is desirable, is that people do actually desire it. . . . No reason can be given why the general happiness is desirable, except that each person, so far as he believes it attainable, desires his

---

[31] It may be of incidental interest to note that Mill wrote that he had "reason for believing himself to be the first person who brought the word utilitarian into use" (Lerner, p. 194). He was careful to add that he had come across it in an earlier somewhat neglected publication.

own happiness. . . . Happiness has made out its title as *one* of the ends of conduct, and consequently one of the criteria of morality.

The "proof" that Mill presented in the preceding quotation has been questioned by Bertrand Russell (1945, p. 778). He finds it "so fallacious that it is hard to understand" how Mill could have deemed it valid. It is fallacious, Russell maintained, to argue that because the only things perceptible are things perceived, "the only things desirable are things desired." According to Russell, what Mill failed to realize is that things are visible or audible if they *can* be seen or heard, while things are desirable if they *ought* to be desired.

Russell's objection to Mill's argument is sound, provided Mill intended his use of the word "desirable" to be restricted to its implications for a theory of ethics.[32] It may be, however, that Mill was using the word in the sense of craving, yearning, wishing for, or simply wanting something. In this sense children desire candy, politicians desire votes, and football coaches desire touchdowns. Those harboring such desires are not likely to raise troublesome ethical questions by asking whether they *ought* to have candy or votes or touchdowns. As a psychological phenomenon, desire in the sense of "I want" can occur independently of desire in the sense of "I ought." Moreover, from the viewpoint of mental development the notion of ethical obligation is always a later development in the transition from childhood to maturity. If Mill had considerations of this kind in mind, Russell's charge of fallacious reasoning is not justified.

In the paragraph cited, Mill did not make happiness the exclusive end of conduct. He stressed the fact of its being just *one* of the ends. In a subsequent passage he explained (Lerner, p. 222):

The ingredients of happiness are very various, and each of them is desirable in itself, and not merely when considered as swelling the aggregate. The principle of utility does not mean that any given pleasure, as music for instance, or any given exemption from pain, as for example health, are to be looked upon as means to a collective something termed happiness, and to be desired on that account. They are desired and desirable in and for themselves; besides being means, they are a part of the end. Virtue, according to the utilitarian doctrine, is not naturally and originally part of the end, but it is capable of becoming so; and in those who love it disinterestedly it has become so, and is desired and cherished, not as a means to happiness, but as part of their happiness.

Mill's account of the way love of virtue comes into being is another instance of functional autonomy: what had been desired as a means to an end is now desired for its own sake. If, as Mill indicated, this disinterested

---

[32] It must be granted that the context does suggest such restriction.

love of virtue has now become part of happiness, does this mean that the man of virtue is prompted to behave virtuously because to do so affords him pleasure or makes him happy? This amounts to asking whether Mill, in his advocacy of the Greatest Happiness Principle, was endorsing a hedonistic theory of motivation. If so, then he was sponsoring a decidedly questionable theory. It is questionable because it assumes that pleasure is the cause of desire, and this, as Russell says, "is usually untrue" (1945, p. 779). It is untrue because pleasure is a consequence and not a cause of desire. In Spinoza's pithy statement mentioned in Chapter 13: "We do not strive for something because we deem it good, but we deem it good because we desire it." A seasick passenger is never tempted by food.

Although Mill's *Utilitarianism* is replete with references to pleasure and happiness, there is no separate discussion of hedonism as a theory of motivation. Consequently, there is no immediately obvious way of deciding whether or not he would have endorsed the theory. However, there are views expressed which suggest that he would have had misgivings about the soundness of the theory. He certainly was not an advocate of a life of sybaritic self-indulgence. Nor did he regard a state of cowlike complacency as his idea of the good life. Gratification of "primitive" desires was not enough to establish a utilitarian community, even if the members of such a hypothetical community were to declare themselves satisfied or happy with their mode of life. Mill might have voiced his objections to such a community in the following famous oft-quoted passage (Lerner, p. 197):

> It is better to be a human being dissatisfied than a pig satisfied; better to be Socrates dissatisfied than a fool satisfied. And if the fool, or the pig, are of a different opinion, it is because they only know their own side of the question. The other party to the comparison knows both sides.

If hedonism merely calls for the establishment of a satisfying, pleasurable, pain-free state of affairs, then Mill's glorification of a *dissatisfied* Socrates is at variance with a hedonistic psychology of motivation. His Greatest Happiness Principle may not be a hedonistic principle. At all events, the idealized Socrates does not appear to have made the pursuit of happiness his fundamental endeavor or basic *conatus*. Just what guiding purpose Mill would have attributed to Socrates cannot be inferred from the preceding quotation. However, from something he wrote in his essay on *Liberty* it seems likely that he would have characterized it as self-development. He alluded to self-development in one paragraph of the essay following an account of the Calvinistic view of man as sinful and his need to seek redemption by ascetic self-denial and humble submission to the will of God. This is the paragraph (Lerner, p. 311):

> There is a different type of human excellence from the Calvinistic; a conception of humanity as having its nature bestowed on it for other purposes than merely

to be abnegated. "Pagan self-assertion" is one of the elements of human worth as well as "Christian self-denial." There is a Greek ideal of *self-development* [italics added], which the Platonic and Christian ideal of self-government blends with, but does not supersede. It may be better to be a John Knox than an Alcibiades, but it is better to be a Pericles than either; nor would a Pericles, if we had one in these days, be without any good which belonged to John Knox.

For Mill, as he made evident in the succeeding paragraph, self-development is opposed to regimented uniformity. It calls for cultivation of distinctive personalities sensitive to "high thoughts and elevated feelings." As Mill saw it, individuality is to be the end-result of self-development. "In proportion to the development of his individuality, each person becomes more valuable to himself, and is therefore capable of being more valuable to others." This is different from a hedonistic pursuit of happiness, and stamps Mill as a forerunner of those contemporary psychologists who prefer self-actualizing personalities to well-adjusted personalities.

Concluding Comment

As has been brought out in this chapter, for a man who never wrote a book on psychology John Stuart Mill had a great deal to contribute to the subject. As a philosopher, he was especially interested in the methods of science and the nature of scientific evidence. A good portion of his *Logic* was concerned with such matters. It will be recalled that following the German translation of the *Logic,* both Wundt and Helmholtz, among others, were influenced by Mill's thinking. In this way, he might be said to have had something to do with the emergence of psychology as science. His death in 1873 occurred just a few years before Wundt brought laboratory psychology into existence. In some respects Mill might be called the last of the philosophical psychologists. Those who came after him belonged to Wundt's generation, many of whom, despite being professors of philosophy, were thinking of psychology as science and not just as mental philosophy The Millean backgrounds, along with the other philosophic backgrounds outlined in the previous chapters, paved the way for this "new" psychology; but the new psychology continued to have roots in the old psychology, as will be evident in the next chapter.

Actually, of course, this relationship between scientific psychology and its philosophic heritage has been noted from time to time, not only with reference to the work of James Mill and John Stuart Mill in the present chapter but also in connection with the long line of their predecessors. This is what characterizes the continuity of history, and constitutes one of the chief values of the study of history. As Santayana once observed, "Those who cannot remember the past are condemned to repeat it."

References

Abel, T. "The Operation Called Verstehen," in H. Feigl and M. Brodbeck (eds.). *Readings in the Philosophy of Science.* New York: Appleton-Century-Crofts, 1953, pp. 677–687.

Allport, G. W. "The Functional Anatomy of Motives," *American Journal of Psychology,* 1937, *50,* 141–156.

Allport, G. W. "The General and the Unique in Psychological Science," *Journal of Personality,* 1962, *30,* 405–422.

Bartlett, F. C. *Remembering.* Cambridge: Cambridge University Press, 1932.

Boring, E. G. *A History of Experimental Psychology,* 2nd ed. New York: Appleton-Century-Crofts, 1950.

Brett, G. S. *A History of Psychology,* Vol. III. London: George Allen and Unwin, 1921.

Cox, C. M. *Genetic Studies of Genius: Early Traits of Three Hundred Geniuses.* Stanford: Stanford University Press, 1926.

Dennis, W. (ed.). *Readings in the History of Psychology.* New York: Appleton-Century-Crofts, 1948.

Dobzhansky, T. "Of Flies and Men," *American Psychologist,* 1967, *22,* 41–48.

Flugel, J. C. *A Hundred Years of Psychology, 1833–1933.* New York: Basic Books, 1964.

Garrison, F. H. *An Introduction to the History of Medicine,* 4th ed. Philadelphia: W. B. Saunders Company, 1929. (Reprinted 1960.)

Gibson, J. J. "The Reproduction of Visually Perceived Forms," *Journal of Experimental Psychology,* 1929, *12,* 1–39.

Herrnstein, R. J., and Boring, E. G. (eds.). *A Source Book in the History of Psychology.* Cambridge: Harvard University Press, 1965.

Holt, R. R. "Individuality and Generalization in the Psychology of Personality," *Journal of Personality,* 1962, *30,* 377–404.

James, W. *Principles of Psychology,* 2 vols. New York: Henry Holt and Company, 1890.

Koch, H. L. *Twins and Twin Relations.* Chicago: University of Chicago Press, 1966.

Lerner, M. (ed.). *Essential Works of John Stuart Mill.* New York: Bantam Books, 1961. © 1961 by Bantam Books, Inc.

Merz, J. T. *A History of European Thought in the Nineteenth Century,* 4 vols. New York: Dover Publications, 1965. (First published between 1904 and 1912.)

Mill, J. *Analysis of the Phenomena of the Human Mind.* A new edition illustrative and critical by Alexander Bain, Andrew Findlater, and George Grote. Edited with additional notes by John Stuart Mill, 2 vols. London: Longmans, Green, Reader and Dyer, 1869.

Mill, J. S. *Autobiography,* 7th ed. London: Longmans, Green and Dyer, 1882. (First published in 1873.)

Mill, J. S. *An Examination of Sir William Hamilton's Philosophy and of the Principal Philosophical Questions Discussed in His Writings,* 2 vols. Boston: William V. Spencer, 1865.

Mill, J. S. *A System of Logic—Ratiocinative and Inductive—Being a Connected View* of the *Principles of Evidence and the Methods of Scientific Investigation,* 2 vols., 9th ed. London: Longmans, Green, Reader and Dyer, 1875. (First published in 1843.)

Murphy, G. *Historical Introduction to Modern Psychology,* rev. ed. New York: Harcourt, Brace and Company, 1949.

Nordenskiöld, E. *The History of Biology.* (Translated by L. B. Eyre.) New York: Tudor Publishing Company, 1928.

Russell, B. *A History of Western Philosophy.* New York: Simon and Schuster, 1945.

Seward, J. P. "The Structure of Functional Autonomy," *American Psychologist,* 1962, *18,* 703–710.

Shuey, A. M. *The Testing of Negro Intelligence,* 2nd ed. New York: Social Science Press, 1966.

Spearman, C. E. *The Nature of "Intelligence" and the Principles of Cognition.* London: Macmillan and Company, 1923.

Stechler, G., Bradford, C., and Levy, H. "Attention in the Newborn: Effect on Motility and Skin Potential," *Science,* 1966, *151,* 1246–1248.

Stewart, D. "Four Objections to Reid's Philosophy of Common Sense Answered," in D. S. Robinson (ed.). *The Story of Scottish Philosophy.* New York: Exposition Press, 1961, pp. 151–179.

Stotland, E. "Mentalism Revisited," *Journal of General Psychology,* 1966, *75,* 229–241.

Woodworth, R. S. *Dynamic Psychology.* New York: Columbia University Press, 1918.

21

The Scientific Foreground:
Herbart and Lotze

IN GENERAL, THE PRECEDING CHAPTERS were concerned with tracing what Ebbinghaus had called the "long past" of psychology, in which he was contrasting its long philosophic past with its short scientific history. More than fifty years have been added to the short history Ebbinghaus had in mind, but even this lengthened span is short when contrasted with psychology's philosophic backgrounds. These backgrounds extend through the centuries from Plato to John Stuart Mill, while scientific psychology covers only the decades from Wilhelm Wundt to the present day. The centuries shaped psychology's variegated philosophic background, while the decades were marked by the emergence of psychology's scientific foreground.

This and the following two chapters will call attention to some of the important characteristics of this foreground as the setting for later developments. The chief objective will be to facilitate understanding of the transition from the old orientation of psychology as envisaged by philosophers to the new orientation of those nineteenth-century pioneers who, without rejecting or ignoring the past, set the stage for the shift from psychology as mental philosophy to psychology as science.

Herbart and the Transition to Psychology as Science

In introductory courses in psychology, students are often told that scientific psychology dates from 1879 when Wundt established his laboratory at the University of Leipzig. Strictly speaking, this is more a matter of descriptive convenience than an accurate recording of the birth of scientific psychology. Actually it is somewhat misleading to think of scientific psychology as having been born at a definite time and place. As should be clear by this time, it grew out of its philosophic roots just as the specialized natural sciences grew out of natural philosophy. Moreover, no one man is to be regarded as the first to have conceived of psychology as science. Wundt may well have been one of the first, if not the very first, to think of it as a laboratory science,[1] but this is not the precise equivalent of thinking of it as a science. Not all sciences are necessarily laboratory sciences. Neither is any kind of laboratory activity sufficient to establish a science. If it were, then alchemy would have been a science.

As mentioned in the previous chapter, John Stuart Mill, with his suggestions of psychology as a general science of mind and of ethology as a special science of character, had thus been proposing a scientific psychology long before 1879. And Wundt, it will be recalled, was familiar with the German translation of the *Logic* in which Mill had introduced this proposal.

Furthermore, some fifteen years before the *Logic* was published, Johann Friedrich Herbart (1776–1841) had already been sponsoring the idea of a scientific psychology. This was reflected in the title of one of his books: *Psychologie als Wissenschaft* or *Psychology as Science*.[2] He did not intend this to be a psychology altogether emancipated from philosophical presuppositions, because the psychology he was advocating was to be based upon metaphysics as well as upon experience and mathematics. As Kant's successor at Königsberg, Herbart was widely known and Wundt was undoubtedly influenced by his teachings. Consequently Herbart, like Mill, is to be listed as one of the forerunners of what was to emerge as the "new" psychology of Wundt's era

They were forerunners with respect to endowing psychology with the status of a science although not with respect to making it a laboratory science. Furthermore, as noted on page 662, Herbart succeeded in paving the way for efforts to establish a *science* of education, with the result that histories of education usually refer to him as "the father of scientific pedagogy." In thus launching what was to develop into the field of educational psychology, Herbart may be classified as a pioneer applied psychologist. In more ways than one, his advocacy of psychology as science in the 1820s foreshadowed the severance of psychology from its philosophic moorings. In Boring's apt formulation, "What Herbart gave to psychology was status" (1950, p. 252). It was to be a discipline in its own right and not just a

---

[1] Wundt established the first formal laboratory for psychological experiments, but it was preceded by a small informal one that William James had introduced at Harvard.

[2] Herbart's use of the word *"Wissenschaft"* is not to be regarded as having precisely the same meaning as the word "science" had for Mill. There is no exact English equivalent for the German *"Wissenschaften,"* which came to include all the fields of study falling within the scope of the German university system. Thus theology, jurisprudence, medicine, and philosophy were regarded as *Wissenschaften*. As products of critical scholarship, they were all presumed to contribute to the sum total of human knowledge. Church history, Biblical criticism, philology, and metaphysics when studied in accordance with the canons of such scholarship were classified as "sciences" in the sense of being *Wissenschaften*. Under the circumstances, scientific psychology as envisaged by Mill was not identical with Herbart's *Psychologie als Wissenschaft*.

branch of philosophy or an offshoot of brain physiology. Moreover, as a discipline it was to be based upon experience as well as upon mathematics and metaphysics.

Herbartian Ideas and Their Apperception

In basing psychology upon experience, Herbart was advocating an empirical psychology. His empiricism is shown by his use of familiar, everyday happenings to illustrate salient aspects of mental life. For example, the nature of attention was made clear by reference to a trained musician's reaction to a false note and by reference to the changed behavior of school children when the teacher introduces an interesting anecdote in the midst of a monotonous academic exercise. Another example had to do with the perception of time. To show the meaning of the experience of "empty time," James (1890, Vol. I, p. 626) quoted the following from Herbart's *Psychology as Science*: [3]

> Empty time is most strongly perceived when it comes as a *pause* in music or in speech. Suppose a preacher in the pulpit, a professor at his desk, to stick still in the midst of his discourse; or let a composer (as is sometimes purposely done) make all his instruments stop at once; we await every instant the resumption of the performance, and, in this awaiting, perceive, more than in any other possible way, the empty time.

Presumably the preceding allusions to preacher, professor, and composer were readily understood. In ordinary language, one would say the printed words gave rise to three ideas. Herbart would have talked about three *Vorstellungen*. Students of German will recognize the latter noun as related to the verb "*vorstellen*," which means "to introduce" or "to present"; hence the three ideas in question can be designated as three presentations. Discussion of Herbart's psychology will be facilitated by calling attention to the fact that the word "*Vorstellung*" also refers to the presentation of a theatrical performance.

Metaphorically speaking, it is as if Herbart were considering the play of ideas on the stage of awareness. Something is always going on. Ideas come and go, and having gone may recur, just as actors move from the center of the stage to the side or disappear into the wings and then return. Influenced by Leibnitz,[4] Herbart noted the difference between vague or

---

[3] Herbart's *Psychologie als Wissenschaft* has not been translated. The excerpt cited was translated by James.

[4] Herbart's metaphysics is somewhat reminiscent of the metaphysics of Leibnitz. In place of monads as ultimate units of being, Herbart assumed the existence of what he called "Reals." Each "Real" was regarded as simple and immutable. As such it preserves its identity, and in Herbart's scheme of things accounts for what Kant had called the

marginal ideas and those which stand out with maximal clearness in the spotlight or center of consciousness, so to speak. The marginal ones are dimly perceived, while the central ones were said to be *apperceived*. Apperception, as focused perception of a given presentation, rivets attention on that presentation.

The notion of apperception, as developed by Herbart, became especially important in his "scientific pedagogy." For a presentation to be clearly grasped, readily understood, or *apperceived,* Herbart pointed out, it is necessary to possess familiarity with the context of the presentation. "Context" in this sense refers to a background of relevant information. A phrase like "no trump" is meaningless to one ignorant of bridge, just as the word "chukker" is meaningless to one ignorant of polo. Without some knowledge of the games in question, such terms will continue to be meaningless. Similarly, without special training or preparation it is impossible to understand a financial report, to interpret X-ray photographs, to read Chinese, or solve quadratic equations. The special training or preparation would constitute a context of relevant experience in terms of which the foregoing presentations would cease to be baffling.

It was in this connection that Herbart introduced his celebrated phrase "apperceptive mass" as a designation for such a context of experience. Herbartian teachers were urged to be mindful of the importance of taking the apperceptive mass into account in preparing their lesson plans. Teaching was to proceed from the known to the unknown. Without an apperceptive mass of the known, there could be no ready assimilation or apperception of the unknown. Although these Herbartian terms are now outmoded, their educational implications have not become obsolete. There is a vestige

---

thing-in-itself. As such, it can never be known and must remain as the inaccessible, inferred concomitant of experience. For Herbart, the soul is a "Real" and the entire universe a vast manifold of "Reals."

This phase of Herbart's teaching is obviously not a contribution to empirical psychology. Logical positivists would doubtless question it as a contribution to philosophy. However, this is not to be taken as disparagement of Herbart's standing as a philosopher or as a challenging thinker. According to James Ward (1929), Herbart merits this encomium: "His criticisms are worth more than his contributions; indeed for exactness and penetration of thought he is on a level with Hume and Kant." Furthermore, with specific reference to Herbart's metaphysics, Brett had this to say (1921, Vol. III, p. 62):

> Metaphysics he regarded as indispensable, because, sooner or later, the limit of the demonstrable is reached and the mind strains after some hypothesis whose guarantee is the system which makes it possible. This width of comprehension and depth of insight make Herbart one of the truly great thinkers known to history.

In one sense it might be argued that Herbart's recognition of psychology's dependence on metaphysics is not an altogether outmoded notion. At all events, even the present-day psychologist may find himself toying with metaphysical connotations when challenged to explain what he means by the word "reality" in phrases like "adjustment to reality" or "flight from reality." To justify repudiation of metaphysics in itself involves something in the way of a metaphysical orientation.

of Herbartian psychology in every university catalogue which specifies that Course X is a prerequisite for Course Y.

Herbart's Psychology Influenced by Leibnitz

Herbart is often remembered not only for his notion of apperception but also for his opposition to faculty psychology. The basis for his opposition was discussed in Chapter 19, page 662, and need not be repeated at this point. It is altogether likely that his rejection of mental faculties, along with his elaboration of the concept of apperception, is an outgrowth of Leibnitzian teachings.[5] He was indebted to Leibnitz for the notion of apperception as well as for the notion of mind as *unified* and for ideation as an *active* process.

For Herbart, "ideas" were not inert entities but active forces. Despite the multiplicity of such dynamic "ideas" in ceaseless flux, there is an underlying unity that, in terms of Herbart's metaphysics, reflected the integrating function of the soul. In other words, like Leibnitz and others, Herbart conceived of mind as a *unitas multiplex*. He posited a "soul" to account for the *unitas*, or what modern psychologists allude to when they speak of personality as *integrated*. It would be a mistake to equate Herbart's soul with a ghost or anything except some unknown integrating activity; as Brett noted (1921, Vol. III, p. 43), Herbart wrote that "the simple nature of the soul is wholly unknown, it is an object neither of speculative nor of empirical psychology." Apparently, as an unknown it served Herbart as a convenient fiction or construct. Similarly, chemists once attributed combustion to the unknown phlogiston and physicists once posited the existence of an unknown luminiferous ether. As an unknown, the soul could never be experienced or, as just stated, could never be brought within the purview of empirical psychology. Since man can be conscious of or know himself, Herbart's soul was not the same as the concept of Self. What James had called the "empirical self" would have been recognized by Herbart as an apperceiving process falling within the scope of psychology as science.

In developing his views of psychology as science, Herbart, to revert to a previous metaphor, viewed consciousness as a stage occupied by constantly moving presentations or *Vorstellungen*. These presentations never remain stationary.[6] As idea-forces, they keep moving in a steady flow as

---

[5] As was noted in Chapter 14, Leibnitz conceived of a continuous transition from the subliminal *petites perceptions* to the maximal supraliminal clarity of apperception.

[6] It must be understood that Herbart's *Vorstellungen* have to do with the sequence of thoughts or ideas and not with sensory impressions considered in the abstract. A *persistent* pain as a sensory impression is stationary in its persistence, but the ideational presentations aroused by the pain do not cease coming and going. Similarly, it is impossible to focus on something like this dollar sign ($) and while staring at it to think of nothing except the bare visual phenomenon stripped of its symbolic import.

one presentation gives way to another in the kind of succession James came to describe as "the stream of consciousness." This is not to be interpreted as meaning that consciousness is a fluid medium in which presentations float along like corpuscles in the blood stream. There is no fluid medium. The stream is just a stream of ideational processes.

Conflict and Coalescence among Ideas

The stream of ideation as described by Herbart was rather complex and dramatic. It was not a calm flow of successive presentations, but instead was an interplay or struggle among competing idea-forces striving for ascendancy, so to speak. In this dynamic interplay of presentations, Herbart noted some as being in harmony with or congruous with others, just as he noted some as being antagonistic to or in conflict with others. He referred to the *Selbsterhaltung* of each presentation, which, taken literally, means the self-preservation of each one. This amounts to saying that ideas maintain their identity in the sense that the idea of a tree is not to be confused with the idea of the sky. A dictionary supplies a list of such identifiable or *selbsterhaltende* ideas to the extent of their verbal communicability.

Herbart also noted the loss of identity as two or more ideas merge or fuse to form a different idea. Some congruous ideas may combine or fuse rather readily. Thus, the idea of red may fuse with the idea of yellow to give the idea of orange. Calling this kind of combination of ideas a *fusion* is a translation of Herbart's term *"Verschmelzung."* It can also be translated by the word "coalescence." The latter word, it may be recalled, was employed by James Mill in referring to ideas which "coalesce" so as to form one idea out of many. Mill and Herbart were in agreement in their recognition of such fusion or coalescence of ideas. They were also in agreement in their recognition of ideas that combine without losing their identity. The idea of furniture, for example, although constituting a single idea resulting from the assimilation of separate presentations of chairs, tables, and so on, is capable of being analyzed into these constituent presentations. An even clearer instance of such preservation or identity of parts despite their union into a new idea was supplied by Mill when he formed the idea of a centaur by imagining the substitution of a man's head for the head of a horse.

Apperception also involved coalescence in the sense that the apperceptive mass was conceived to be the outcome of merging of convergent and related ideas. For example, Herbart would have noted increases in a pupil's arithmetic apperceptive mass as he learns to add, substract, multiply, divide, and to deal with square and cube roots. Given this ideational equipment, the pupil will then be able to "apperceive" what is common to the following series of terms confronting him for the first time:

$$50 + 14, \ 4^3, \ 95 - 31, \text{ and } \sqrt{4096}.$$

This example of a schoolboy doing his arithmetic homework can be used as an introduction to one of Herbart's most provocative teachings; namely, the nature and disposition of antagonistic ideas. Let it be assumed that while concentrating on the solution of a problem in arithmetic the boy is distracted by hearing his brother say, "I'm going ice skating."[7] As an avid skater he might now find himself eager to join his brother; but to dwell on the idea of skating is to shunt out the arithmetic idea.[8] It is impossible to entertain both sets of ideas at the same time: one has to yield to the other. Since Herbart conceived of presentations as idea-forces, he would have predicted that the less forceful idea would yield to the more forceful idea. The process of yielding, as he described it, involved the inhibition, or *Hemmung,* of the former by the latter. Or he might have said that the less forceful idea is repressed, or *verdrängt.* Both terms suggest one idea being pushed away or displaced by another stronger idea.

It is especially important to note that by attributing strength to an idea, Herbart was conceiving of cognition as a dynamic process. That is why his ideas are to be described as idea-forces or as energized ideas. Furthermore, even though he was writing at a time when conservation of energy had not yet become a universal law of physics,[9] he wrote as if this law was applicable to the realm of ideas. This is so because, as he saw it, displaced or repressed weaker ideas are not destroyed. They are banished from awareness, but in due time may once again make their presence known. In terms of the preceding example: dwelling on the prospect of ice skating may have inhibited consideration of the arithmetic problem, and yet after a time there will be renewed consideration of the problem. Its renewal is contingent upon the removal or weakening of the counteracting idea-forces. In the interim, as Herbart held, it must continue to exist as a potentially conscious idea.

---

[7] This example is an oversimplification of Herbart's views and fails to include considerations Herbart would have regarded as important. These considerations are being disregarded as a matter of expository convenience. Their inclusion would have involved discussion of Herbartian speculations concerning the outcome of clashes between antagonistic ideas of equal strength as contrasted with those of unequal strength. It was in connection with such speculations that Herbart ventured to show how mathematics could aid in predicting the outcome of the clashes by assigning arbitrary degrees of force to hypothetical ideas and treating the assumed interaction of the statics and dynamics of the forces algebraically. There was no empirical testing of the predicted outcomes, and his followers were not impressed by this early attempt to apply quantitative methods to psychological data.

[8] This too is an oversimplification. Actually, the boy could have been *thinking* about going skating and about doing his arithmetic. In other words, it is possible to entertain a pair of antagonistic ideas simultaneously. Hamlet did it in his "to be or not to be" soliloquy, and judges do it in debating the guilt or innocence of defendants.

[9] It was not promulgated as a universal law until the 1840s.

Was Freud Indebted to Herbart?

This notion of potential consciousness marks the introduction of the paradox[10] of unconscious consciousness. At all events this means that long before the advent of Freud those who read Herbartian psychology were already familiar with the notion of unconscious mental forces. Long after the advent of Freud, students of the history of psychoanalysis raised the question of Freud's indebtedness to Herbart for such characteristic notions as intrapsychic conflict, repression, and a dynamic unconscious. One of these students, Ernst Kris, believed that Freud had found a "stimulus" in Herbart's psychology. In the introductory section of a book entitled *The Origins of Psychoanalysis*, Kris wrote: "It was the stimulus provided by Herbart's mechanistic psychology that caused Freud to be the first to replace Herbart's mechanistic psychology of association with a new one" (1954, p. 47).

How is this sentence to be interpreted? In view of Herbart's conception of an apperceptive mass as a constellation of *associated* ideas and Freud's reliance on free *association* of ideas, both men were sponsoring some sort of association psychology. Both men stressed the importance of conflict, but differed with respect to the kind of conflict deemed to be of importance. For Herbart it was a conflict of ideas, and for Freud it was a conflict of motives or urges. Apparently Kris regarded the former as a "mechanistic" conflict and the latter as a dynamic one. By implication this would make Herbart the sponsor of a "mechanistic" unconscious and Freud the sponsor of a dynamic unconscious.

If this is a correct interpretation of what Kris had in mind, it is at variance with an account of Herbartian influences on Freud's psychology as presented by Ernest Jones, since Jones considered Herbart's unconscious to be a dynamic unconscious. As a summary of the history of the issues in volved, Jones's account is particularly clarifying and merits being quoted *in extenso* (1953, Vol. I, pp. 371–374):

> It was a Polish psychologist, Luis von Karpinska, who first called attention to the resemblance between some of Freud's fundamental ideas and those promulgated by Herbart seventy years previously. . . . The one Karpinska especially dwells on

---

[10] Followers of Herbart would probably have approved of the word "paradox" in this connection. His critics might have preferred a reference to the inherent *contradiction* of unconscious consciousness. James was one of these critics. He objected to Herbart's notion of each idea being "a permanently existing entity" and went on to say: "I must confess that to my mind there is something almost hideous in the glib Herbartian jargon about *Vorstellungsmassen* and their *Hemmungen* and *Hemmungssummen*, and *sinken* and *erheben* and *schweben*, and *Verschmelzungen* and *Complexionen*" (1890, Vol. I, p. 603).

is Herbart's conception of the unconscious which was the only *dynamic* one before Freud's [italics added]. According to it, unconscious mental processes are dominated by a constant conflict which Herbart describes in terms of ideas of varying intensity—a notion which Freud later replaced by a conflict of affects; with Herbart ideas are always primary to affects, as in the later James-Lange theory. The conflict Herbart describes is partly intrapsychical but more characteristically between those of one person and of another. The latter are treated as disturbing, or aggressive, elements which evoke "self-preservative" efforts on the part of the subject. Mental life is throughout dualistic, as Freud also always conceived it. Herbart actually describes an idea as "*verdrängt*" when it is unable to reach consciousness because of some opposing idea or when it has been driven out of consciousness by one! He conceives of two thresholds in the mind, which correspond topographically with the position of Freud's two censorships. One, the "static threshold," is where an inhibited idea is robbed of its activity and can enter consciousness only when the inhibition is lifted; it is, therefore, not unlike a "suppressed" idea in the pre-conscious. At another level is what he calls the "mechanistic threshold" where wholly repressed ideas are still in a state of rebellious activity directed against those in consciousness and succeed in producing indirect effects, e.g., "object-less feelings of oppression (*Beklemmung*)." "Science knows more than what is actually experienced [in consciousness] only because what is experienced is unthinkable without examining what is concealed. One must be able to recognize from what is experienced the traces of what is stirring and acting 'behind the curtains'!"

All this is very interesting, but there is more. People vary in the way in which the body responds to affects (Freud's somatic compliance), which Herbart calls the "physiological resonance"; this leads to a "condensation of the affects in the nervous system." Mental processes are characterized by a "striving for equilibrium" (Freud's constancy principle). "Ideas" are indestructible and are never lost. Nor do they ever exist alone, only in chains of ideas that are so interwoven with one another as to form networks. Affects arise only when the equilibrium is disturbed through an excessive quantity of intensity being present in the ideas. Consciousness of self (the ego) comes about when active ideas are inhibited (frustrated?). . . .

Notions such as those just described could have filtered through to Freud from many sources, but those echoes from the past are nonetheless noteworthy. It is not very likely that Freud would ever have had reason to make a study of Herbart's writings, though it is of course possible. We do not even know if Meynert[11] did, but his published works make it certain that he was very familiar with Herbartian psychology, on which his own was based and of which his was an extension and modification. He must in any case have had access to it through the full exposition of it by Griesenger,[12] of whose writings Meynert thought highly and which Freud probably also read.

---

11 This is a reference to Theodor Meynert (1833–1892) who served as professor of neurology and psychiatry at the University of Vienna. Freud was closely associated with Meynert in his student days and later, upon graduation, as a worker in Meynert's laboratory.

12 Wilhelm Griesinger (1817–1868) published a widely known textbook on psychiatry

In connection with his efforts to show how many of "Freud's ideas can be ultimately traced to Herbart," Jones indicates that Freud was exposed to Herbartian psychology even before he entered the university. This was due to the introduction of a *Textbook on Empirical Psychology* by one Gustaf Lindner during Freud's senior year at the *Gymnasium.* The book in question, published in 1858, was written as an introduction to the psychology of Herbart. Among other things, Jones noted, the book contains this sentence: "A result of the fusion of ideas proves that ideas which were once in consciousness and for any reason have been repressed (*verdrängt*) out of it are not lost, but in certain circumstances may return" (1953, Vol. I, p. 374).

All things considered, there can thus be no question of Freud's indebtedness to Herbart for the fundamentals of his psychological orientation. However, Freud's later elaboration of these fundamentals in the development of his distinctively psychoanalytic approach to problems of psychopathology came to include many non-Herbartian innovations. His views of psychosexual development, of latent and manifest dream content, of the psychopathology of everyday life, of a death instinct, of the id as a caldron of seething excitement, of a tyrannical superego, and similar views are not to be traced to Herbart. As suggested in Chapter 13, page 446, they were more or less *ad hoc* improvisations to facilitate understanding of the neurotic character. As provocative suggestions or challenging hypotheses, they account for the recognition accorded Freud as an *original* thinker. For Jones and others to have traced some of Freud's key ideas back to a Herbartian foundation does not make the psychoanalytic superstructure Herbartian rather than Freudian.

Was Freud Influenced by Academic Psychology?

Whether Freud himself was aware of his indebtedness to Herbart is difficult to determine. In his own account of the origins of the psychoanalytic

---

in the 1840s. It is hard to understand why Jones was constrained to write that Freud "probably" read Griesinger when some twenty pages earlier Jones had written this sentence: "Freud himself repeatedly refers to a sentence of Griesinger's which called attention to the wish-fulfillment feature common to dreams and psychoses, a remarkable piece of insight" (1953, Vol. I, p. 353). This insight reflected Griesinger's recognition of unconscious mental processes, as is evident in this brief passage which L. L. Whyte (1960, pp. 160–161) culled from the 1965 English translation of Griesinger's textbook: "There is in intelligence an actual, though to us an unconscious, life and movement; we recognize it however by its results, which often suddenly make their appearance from some unexpected source. A constant activity reigns over this almost, if not wholly, darkened sphere, which is much greater and more characteristic for the individuality than the small number of impressions which pass into the state of consciousness."

movement (1959, Vol. I), there is no mention of Herbart. Neither is there any mention of Griesinger or Lindner and their Herbartian teachings.

Moreover, as was noted in Chapter 3, page 58, with reference to the doctrine of repression, Freud definitely disavowed having been influenced by anything he had read or heard. He was emphatic on his point: "The doctrine of repression quite certainly came to me independently of any other source: I know of no outside impression which might have suggested it to me. . . ." Then he added that the doctrine in question "is the foundation-stone on which the whole structure of psychoanalysis rests, the most essential part of it . . ." (1959, Vol. I, pp. 297–298).

It is tempting to conjecture that Freud's inability to recall Herbart's prior references to *Verdrängung* may have been due to wish-fulfilling repression. Just what he might have said had some colleague called his attention to Herbartian allusions to repression and a dynamic unconscious must also remain a matter of fruitless conjecture. As a matter of fact he failed to discuss the origin of the latter concept so that there is no way of knowing whether, as with the concept of repression, he would have thought of it as having come to him "independently of any other source." It seems likely that earlier exposure to Herbartian teachings had something to do with his later readiness to welcome the advent of both concepts.

Freud's failure to mention the unconscious specifically was probably not an oversight, for acceptance of the doctrine of repression presupposes endorsement of the concept of unconscious mental activity. On the other hand, such endorsement does not necessarily presuppose recognition of repression. In fact, as Whyte has demonstrated, many writers preceded Freud in appealing to the notion of an unconscious in order to account for aspects of mental life unrelated to repression. One of these writers was the distinguished British psychiatrist Henry Maudsley (1835–1918), whose *Physiology and Pathology of the Mind* was published in 1867. According to Whyte, the volume contains this sentence: "The most important part of mental action, the essential process on which thinking depends, is unconscious mental activity." Whyte adds (1960, p. 162) that in 1874 "Brentano published in Vienna a detailed examination of Maudsley's views." At that time, Freud was in close association with Brentano. In fact, as was mentioned on page 59, between 1874 and 1876 Freud had taken six of Brentano's courses at the University of Vienna. It is thus possible that through Brentano, Freud's attention was called to Maudsley's views of unconscious mental activity.[13]

If this is so, then the not uncommon opinion to the effect that psychoanalysis developed independently of academic psychology may be con-

---

[13] That Freud later informed himself of Maudsley's views is suggested by a reference to Maudsley's *Pathology of Mind* in the bibliography appended to the first edition of the *Traumdeutung*.

trary to fact. To a greater extent than he realized, Freud's espousal of the doctrines of repression and unconscious mental activity appears to have had roots in what he had learned in his student days from academicians like Herbart and Brentano. Furthermore, although the evidence is more tenuous, it may be that Freud's endorsement of psychophysical parallelism may also be traced to a Herbartian stand that, in turn, can be traced to a Leibnitzian stand.[14]

Both Herbart and Freud Viewed "Psychology as Science"

Like Herbart's early nineteenth-century presentation of his "psychology as science," Freud's early twentieth-century presentation of psychoanalysis also claimed to be a contribution to psychology as science. With reference to Freud's claim, it is well to make a distinction between psychoanalysis as a technique of psychotherapy and psychoanalysis as a segment of scientific psychology. One may have misgivings about its effectiveness as a treatment procedure[15] and still be favorably disposed toward some aspects of its theoretic orientation and many of its clinical observations. Freud himself had something of this sort in mind when he stated: "The future will probably attribute far greater importance to psychoanalysis as the science of the unconscious than as a therapeutic procedure" (1929, Vol. 18, p. 673).

Neither Herbart nor Freud was thinking of psychology as an *experimental* science; they regarded it as an *empirical* science. Herbart made this explicit by stating that as a science it was to be based upon experience, and Freud was almost as explicit in his recurrent appeals to clinical experience.

To say that both Herbart and Freud envisaged psychology as a nonexperimental empirical science is not to say that their teachings had no bearing on experimental psychology. They both had something to do with the emergence of two groups of experimental studies, those belonging to the field of learning and those belonging to the field of motivation.

As fields of investigation, in some respects these two are particularly characteristic of psychology's development during the present century. Unlike the textbooks of the preceding centuries, virtually every introductory

---

[14] As reported by Jones (1953, Vol. I, pp. 367–368), Freud "proclaimed himself an adherent of the doctrine of psychophysical parallelism" as early as 1891 in his monograph on *Aphasia,* in which Freud had stated that "the psychical is a process parallel to the physiological."

[15] Establishing the efficacy of any technique of psychotherapy is fraught with difficulties. Of the more than thirty-odd procedures that have been introduced at various times, not one, in terms of controlled investigations of results achieved, has established itself to be incontestably superior to all the others. For a summary of the difficulties involved and a review of some of the investigations, see H. J. Eysenck's study of "The Effects of Psychotherapy" (1965). The major variables to be considered in evaluating such effects are outlined and examined in a paper by G. L. Paul (1967).

textbook of psychology published within the last four or five decades has chapters on learning as well as on motivation. Herbart, in his role as the father of scientific psychology, aroused interest in the systematic study of the nature of the learning process. This is especially true of those who brought educational psychology into being as a separate branch of psychology. Consequently, to the extent that educational psychologists have become engrossed in the experimental investigation of learning and teaching, they might, at least in part, trace their current preoccupation with this kind of investigation back to the impetus of Herbart's scientific pedagogy. For example, as noted in Chapter 19, pp. 665–668, the many laboratory studies of transfer and retroaction, along with critiques of the doctrine of formal discipline, might all be said to have been inspired by Herbart's rejection of mental faculties as independent and autonomous abilities. This suggests a provocative paradox: that experimental work in psychology was influenced by someone who had never even heard of experimental psychology. Despite the lapse of close to a hundred years, there is a connection between the teachings of a nonexperimentalist like Herbart and the introduction of laboratory studies of the learning process by an experimentalist like Thorndike.

Unlike Herbart, Freud had heard of experimental psychology, and yet he developed his psychoanalytic psychology as a nonexperimental exploration of the vagaries of motivation. That the subject of motivation served as the matrix for this development is clear from what he himself once wrote about the founding of psychoanalysis. In a statement possibly reminiscent of his early exposure to Herbartian psychology, Freud declared (1929, Vol. 18, p. 673):

> . . . psychoanalysis derives all mental processes (apart from the reception of external stimuli) from the interplay of forces, which assist or inhibit one another, enter into compromises, etc. All of these forces are originally in the nature of *instincts*, that is to say, they have an organic origin.

In general, Freud's psychological horizon was an outgrowth of this interest in instinctual forces as goads to action. Had he written an introduction to psychology, it would have been very different from the conventional introductions written by professors of psychology. Despite his medical training, there would have been no chapter on the nervous system and no chapters on the sense organs. Topics like color vision, reaction time, maze learning, laws of association, conditioning, and mental measurement would have been ignored. Instead his exposition would have been replete with discussions of the dynamics of wishing, intending, wanting, resisting, and whatever else has to do with the life of motivation both conscious and unconscious. In line with his endorsement of determinism, these wishes and intentions would have been treated as "psychic causes" both of man's dreams as well as man's actions. In fact, as Woodworth once pointed out, there is a direct relationship between this emphasis on psychic causation and Freud's basic orientation toward psychology as science. Woodworth had this to say about it (1948, p. 173):

> A "psychic cause," according to Freud, is a wish, motive, intention. Such a cause has to work through the bodily mechanisms, including brain structures and connections, but these belong to physiology rather than psychology. Freud apparently relegated to physiology all studies of conditioned responses and of factors favorable or unfavorable to efficiency of learning and accuracy of perception. For him, motivation was practically the whole field of psychology.

On Early Opposition to Freud

This nonexperimental motivational psychology of Freud's was not regarded as a contribution to scientific psychology in the early decades of the present century. At least it was not so regarded by eminent academic psychologists. Titchener, for example, failed to mention Freud either in his *Text-Book* of 1917 or in his *Systematic Psychology* of 1929. This omission was not due to unfamiliarity with psychoanalytic principles, for Titchener had met Freud and had listened to the talks given by Freud and Jung in 1909 at Clark University in Worcester in conjunction with the institution's celebration of its twentieth anniversary

This first official recognition of the psychoanalytic movement by an American university was initiated by G. Stanley Hall (1844–1924), president of Clark University and one of the founding fathers of American psychology. Apparently he hoped to win a favorable reception for Freud's views, but this hope was not realized during his lifetime. His disappointment is suggested by a comment made by J. McKeen Cattell in 1927 when he had this to say about Hall's interests in insanity and other aspects of psychopathology (1943, pp. 63–64):

> These interests were maintained and in the last conversation I had with him in his lonely house at Worcester he wanted especially to know why orthodox American psychologists cared so little for Freud and psychoanalysis. He showed me a mass of publications and notes he had collected on the subject.

As Hall noted, relatively few American psychologists of the time were ready to endorse Freudian teachings. Woodworth called attention to this situation in the opening paragraph of his 1917 critique of Freudian psychology (p. 174):

> A number of psychologists, as Holt, Watson, Wells, and Lay, have espoused the Freudian teaching to a greater or less extent, though usually with considerable

independence of judgment. The majority, however, while keeping silence in the journals, are probably to be counted as skeptics. For myself I am very skeptical. I admit that a good deal of stimulus can be derived from the work of the psychoanalysts toward a study of neglected topics in psychology; and I rather expect that many germs of truth will, in the course of time, be found in the teachings of this school; but their methods, considered as means of demonstrating psychological facts, seem to me excessively rough and ready, and their conclusions one-sided and exaggerated.

The body of the critique is not concerned with psychoanalysis as a mode of treatment, but with psychoanalysis as a means of discovering facts about mental life and as a technique for arriving at valid psychological conclusions. In Woodworth's incisive criticisms, very few of these facts and conclusions were found to have been the products of sound scientific methodology. The general drift of his indictment is well summarized in the closing sentences of the article, in which he had this to say about Freudian theory (1917, p. 194):

> It is not void of scientific value, but so obsessed is it with a few elements in the complex human personality that it gives us a narrow and one-sided psychology, utterly lacking in perspective.
>
> Nor can the success of the treatment—regarding which I do not pretend to judge—be used as weighty evidence in favor of the theory. The "pragmatic argument" will not work in this case. We have a number of other treatments, all more or less successful in treating neurotic cases, and each one purporting to be based on a different theory. If the psychoanalytic treatment could be rigidly deduced from the Freudian theory and from no other known theory, or even if the practice had originated as a deduction from the theory, this argument would have weight. As a matter of history, however, the treatment grew up first, and the theory was then developed as a sort of rationalization of the treatment. The theory is extended far beyond the needs of the practitioner. The psychology of the Freudians, and also their views on history, mythology, and the world in general are not essential to the practice, but are to be regarded as products of the decorative art.

This critique was not calculated to win support among American psychologists for Freudian theorizing. It was published during the decade when, as Boring pointed out in the first edition of his *History of Experimental Psychology* (1929, p. 494), Freud was "beginning to be discovered" by American psychology. Incidentally, in this first edition not a single paragraph is devoted to a consideration of Freudian theory. As will be brought out shortly, this virtual neglect of Freud in the 1929 edition contrasts drastically with what Boring has to say about him in the 1950 edition. There is also a contrast between Woodworth's negative attitude toward Freud's work as it looked to him around 1917 and the more positive attitude to which he gave expression many years later in his general survey of the psychoanalytic school. Although still critical of many of the school's teachings regarding personality in general and motivation in particular,[16] Woodworth paid tribute to Freud as an original and fearless thinker "whose important place in the history of psychology is amply assured" (1948, p. 192).

On Later Recognition of Freud

In the course of time, Boring also became convinced of Freud's assured place in the history of psychology. As has been noted, the first edition of Boring's *History* virtually ignores the subject of Freud and the dynamic psychology he sponsored. There is no reference to *The Interpretation of Dreams* or to any of Freud's other writings. Aside from passing mention of Freud's name in connection with the work of Herbart and also with that of Hall at Clark University and Charcot in Paris, this 1929 edition has nothing to say about Freud as a psychologist. Furthermore, there is no chapter on dynamic psychology in this edition. All is changed, however, with the publication of the second edition in 1950, with its long Chapter 26 on dynamic psychology. This chapter contains a separate section dealing with psychoanalysis, in which Freud is credited with having "put the dynamic conception of psychology where psychologists could see it and take it," and in which the prediction is made that for the next three hundred years Freud's name is likely to be included in every volume claiming to be "a general history of psychology." Boring is thus convinced of Freud's posthumous greatness.

In the final pages of his *History,* Boring resumed consideration of Freud's greatness. This was in connection with his retrospective assessment of psychology's history as it looked to him around 1950 as compared with his outlook in the late 1920s. The intervening years had brought about a change in his judgment. In 1929 he had concluded that "there have been no great psychologists." By 1950, however, he felt constrained to note that, although psychologists had not accepted Freud as one of their own for many years, he is now "seen as the greatest originator of all, the agent of the *Zeitgeist* who accomplished the invasion of psychology by the principle of the unconscious process" (p. 743). And he added: "Judged by the

---

[16] Woodworth was especially interested in the psychology of motivation. In his auto-biography he reports having told Thorndike, when they both were still youthful psychologists, of his intention to develop what he called the subject of *motivology* (C. Murchison [ed.], 1932, p. 366). Woodworth and Freud thus had a common interest in the dynamics of dreaming. In fact, one of Woodworth's earliest papers was his 1897 article on the rapidity of dreams, and Freud lists this article in the bibliography of the *Traumdeutung*. Freud also had a copy of Woodworth's *Dynamic Psychology* (1918) in his waiting room. This volume presented the first systematic exposition of his "motivology," and it marked the first time the phrase "dynamic psychology" had been used in the title of a book.

criterion of their persistent posthumous importance, there are at least four very great men in psychology's history: Darwin, Helmholtz, James and Freud." Just what is implied by selection of these four names involves a variety of considerations, some of which may not be obvious. To elaborate upon these implications at this point would involve too much of a digression; hence they will be taken up later.

The Importance of Göttingen in Psychology's History

In some ways, proceeding from Herbart's ideational dynamics to Freud's motivational dynamics and then to Freud's eminence was somewhat of a digression. It entailed neglect of the period separating the age of Herbart from that of Freud. There was even failure to note that toward the close of his life Herbart was no longer at Königsberg but had assumed the professorship of philosophy at the University of Göttingen. He went there in 1833 and finished his career there in 1841. This is worth noting because Göttingen is almost as important as Leipzig in the history of psychology. In part this is due to the character of Göttingen as a university and in greater measure to the psychological contributions of the men who came after Herbart. The first of these was Rudolf Hermann Lotze who occupied the Göttingen chair from 1844 to 1881, and who was succeeded by the distinguished experimentalist George Elias Müller whose professorship extended from 1881 to 1921. The Göttingen chair is thus obviously an important one and merits more than passing mention. But before discussing the work of the occupants of this chair, it is advisable to introduce a few comments concerning the university itself.

When Herbart went to Göttingen, the university had been in existence about one hundred years, having been established in 1734. This made it a relatively late arrival on the German academic scene,[17] but one which marked the inauguration of a new departure in university education by deliberate encouragement of critical thinking in an atmosphere of intellectual freedom. In a long chapter entitled "On the Growth and Diffusion of the Critical Spirit," J. T. Merz introduced the following summary of Göttingen's key role in fostering this spirit (1965, Vol. III, pp. 129–130):

> Criticism . . . became in the hands of the great Göttingen professors and their pupils an academic method and an instrument of education. For it was mainly under influences coming from Göttingen that a change in the higher education of Germany took place. This consisted in taking the leadership in the learned schools out of the hands of theological and placing it in the hands of classical teachers. Under the enlightened guidance of these the German gymnasium

---

[17] Some of the German universities were established in the fourteenth and fifteenth centuries; Heidelberg in 1386 and Leipzig in 1409 serve as illustrations.

JOHANN FRIEDRICH HERBART (1776–1841)

Rudolf Hermann Lotze (1817–1881)

attained its great influence, which has lasted for nearly a century.[18] The mental discipline and intellectual atmosphere at these schools during that period was really owing to the workings of the critical spirit in the wider sense of the word; of free inquiry, based upon methodical study: it took the place of the theological spirit, which had ruled before but has had in the end largely to give way to the ruling of the scientific spirit in the narrower sense of the word that is synonymous with the term exact or mathematical.

Herbart's proposal for a mathematical psychology was thus in keeping with this "narrower sense" of science while his simultaneous proposal for a metaphysical psychology suggested the broader sense of science as *Wissenschaft*. His mathematics was not based upon actual measurements of the rise and fall and conflict of Herbartian ideas. As speculative quantitative psychology, it was not taken seriously by the next generation of pioneering experimental psychologists or even by Herbart's nonexperimental followers. It may be, however, that his abortive effort had the effect of arousing some interest in the possibility of changing it into a successful effort by the introduction of genuine psychological measurements.[19]

In arguing for a psychology based upon mathematics, Herbart was opposing Kant's dictum concerning the impossibility of establishing psychology as a science; for, according to Kant, a genuine science must be grounded in mathematics, and mind is not amenable to measurement. By challenging this dictum, Herbart may have encouraged others to try to do what Kant had said could not be done. Thus in voicing his objection to a Kantian teaching while still occupying Kant's chair at Königsberg, Herbart was giving expression to the kind of academic freedom which Göttingen had brought into German university life and which made him a welcome occupant of the Göttingen chair. The same kind of freedom of inquiry was exhibited by Lotze, his successor to this chair. Lotze, as will soon be evident, also had something to do with fostering the notion of psychology as science.

Summary of Important Developments

Rudolf Hermann Lotze was born in 1817 and died in 1881. Within this span of years the forces that culminated in the founding of laboratory psy-

---

[18] Merz wrote this early in the present century. Had he been writing this some decades later, he would have had occasion to write about the end of this "great influence" with the advent of Nazism.

[19] The psychophysical measurements of Gustav Theodor Fechner (1801–1887), along with his notions of threshold differences and subliminal or unconscious negative sensations, are in line with Herbartian teachings. Furthermore, as noted by Gardner Murphy (1949, p. 180), when Ebbinghaus started his quantitative studies of memory in the 1880s he was influenced by Herbart's mathematical formulae, which he "almost alone of all psychologists took rather seriously."

chology gained momentum. These were the years when mental philosophy was being transformed into the beginnings of what was to develop into an independent science of psychology by the turn of the century. Many men had a share in this transformation. They came from different countries and represented different callings. Some were astronomers, some logicians, and some physicians.

For present purposes, it will suffice to list a few of the important themes these men brought into the forum of science. Thus mention might be made of G. L. Fechner's psychophysics, Darwin's doctrine of evolution, F. W. Bessel's concept of the personal equation, Sir Francis Galton's studies of heredity, E. H. Weber's work on tactual sensitivity, Ewald Hering's theory of color vision, Helmholtz's theories of vision and hearing, the rod-cone duplicity theory of Johannes von Kries, Ramón y Cajal's discovery of the synapse, Ernst Mach's analysis of sensations, F. C. Donder's reaction-time studies, Emil Du Bois-Reymond's investigations of electrophysiology, and Jean Charcot's studies of hysteria. These and kindred studies all came to have a direct or indirect bearing on the emergence of the "new" scientific psychology of the Wundtian era. And all these studies loomed up on the scientific horizon during the forty years separating the death of Herbart from that of Lotze—the years from 1841 to 1881. They were the years of Lotze's active career at Göttingen, in the course of which he came to grips with crucial issues embedded in these exciting studies.

Hermann Lotze: A Biographical Sketch

Lotze was well prepared to cope with these issues in terms of their implications for a scientific psychology. This was because he possessed training both in physiology and in philosophy. His training in physiology was connected with his work as a medical student, since at that time physiology was not yet divorced from the medical curriculum. While at the University of Leipzig, where he pursued these medical studies, he also engaged in the study of philosophy, earning a degree in medicine as well as a doctorate in philosophy. He had acquired both degrees by 1839, when he was twenty-two. He must have created a favorable impression on his examiners; despite his youth, he received a dual appointment as *Dozent* or lecturer in the faculty of philosophy as well as in the faculty of medicine. Within the next five years his publications won him still greater academic distinction, as is evidenced by his call to Göttingen in 1844 to succeed Herbart as professor of philosophy. He thus was launched on his professorial career as a young man of twenty-seven, and in his next thirty-seven years at Göttingen he made it a distinguished career.

Lotze was a man of many parts: poet, physician, physiologist, logician, aesthete, philosopher, and psychologist. The range of his books and articles can be suggested by supplying English translations of some of them. In addition to a volume of poems, he was the author of a work entitled *General*

Pathology and Therapy as Mechanical Natural Sciences, another on *Metaphysics,* a *History of Aesthetics in Germany,* a *System of Philosophy,* and his famous *Medical Psychology or Physiology of the "Seele."* The latter book was published in 1852 and was his most important work on psychology. His lectures on psychology were published after his death in a volume translated by G. T. Ladd under the title *Outlines of Psychology* (1886).

Lotze's Concept of a Cognitive Soul

Just how to classify Lotze's psychology is not easy. He thought of it as a *Wissenschaft,* or scientific psychology, even though it was not an experimental psychology. It was neither Herbartian nor associationistic. In terms of its metaphysics it was both realistic and idealistic. And somewhat paradoxically, although Lotze was opposed to vitalism, his endorsement of mechanism did not entail exclusion of the concept of soul; for his psychology was endowed with a soul not in the sense of an immortal ghost, but in the sense of a phase of man's being enabling him to think, to feel, to decide, to act, to suffer, to enjoy, and to be persuaded that he possesses a mind.[20]

In general, his *Ideal-Realismus,* along with his retention of the soul concept, echoes the metaphysics of Locke's empiricism. Locke's primary qualities, it may be recalled, were attributed to "material" or "real" objects, whereas his secondary qualities belonged to the realm of ideas. Furthermore, after stating that "our idea of *soul,* as an immaterial spirit, is of a substance that thinks and has a power of exciting motion in body by writing and thought," Locke went on to compare the ideas of body and spirit in this pre-Lotzean fashion (J. A. St. John [ed.], 1901, Vol. I, pp. 442–443):

> . . . in short, the idea we have of spirit, compared with the idea we have of body, stands thus: the substance of spirit is unknown to us, and so is the substance of body equally unknown to us; two primary qualities or properties of body, viz., solid coherent parts and impulse, we have distinct clear ideas of; so likewise we know and have distinct clear ideas of two primary qualities or properties of spirit, viz., thinking, and a power of action, i.e. a power of beginning or stopping several thoughts or motions. We have also the ideas of several qualities inherent in bodies, and have the clear distinct ideas of them; which qualities are but the various

---

[20] This explanation would have been unnecessary if the English word "mind" had a precise German equivalent. Actually there is no one German word by means of which to translate such common English phrases as "he is out of his mind," "bear this in mind," and "make up your mind." Moreover, no one of them would allude to the German word for "soul," any more than the word "soul" could be substituted for the English phrases in question by saying "make up your soul" or "he is out of his soul." The subtitle of Lotze's *Medical Psychology* is *"Physiologie der Seele"* the literal translation of which is "Physiology of the Soul." However, it would be more in keeping with the contents of the volume to translate the subtitle as "Physiology of Mind." Evidently Brett accepted a literal translation, for he wrote. "The distinctive feature of Lotze's psychology is the retention of the concept of 'soul' " (1921, Vol. III, p. 141).

modifications of the extension of cohering solid parts and their motions. We have
likewise the ideas of several modes of thinking, viz., believing, doubting, intending, fearing, hoping; all of which are but the several modes of thinking. We
have also the ideas of willing, and moving the body consequent to it, and with
the body itself too; for . . . spirit is capable of motion.

For Locke, the word "soul" as a designation of "the several modes of thinking" was the equivalent of the Cartesian *res cogitans*. The latter, in turn, may
be regarded as a variant of the Aristotelian *"nous"* and the Platonic rational
soul. In retaining the concept of soul in his physiological psychology of 1850,
Lotze was thus following a venerable psychological tradition. In line with
this tradition, he was dealing with a *cognitive* rather than a theological soul.
From the standpoint of physiology, he viewed the soul as the percipient of
afferent neural impulses and the source of efferent ones.

Concerning Psychology and Metaphysics

In trying to make his psychology a scientific psychology, Lotze did not
dodge metaphysical issues. His problem might be compared to that of some
contemporary student of so-called "ego psychology" when challenged to
describe the physiology or neurology of the ego. In striving to meet the
challenge, such a student might find his concept of ego embedded in a metaphysical setting that he had overlooked or evaded prior to the challenge.
With this discovery, he might disclaim responsibility on the ground that as
a scientific psychologist he leaves metaphysical issues like the ideality or the
reality of the ego to philosophers. Were he to take this stand, he would be at
odds with a stand taken by Brett as revealed in this statement (1921, Vol.
III, pp. 147–148):

> It is an open question whether a psychologist can be an idealist or a realist. He
> should perhaps be simply a psychologist. But apart from collectors of detail
> and writers of monographs, history has failed to produce a psychologist who was
> not a philosopher of some kind; and it is notorious that a rejection of all meta-
> physics is the most metaphysical of all positions. The fruits of the sciences may
> be plucked by every chance comer; yet the tree that bears them must strike its
> roots deep or quickly wither away. *Lotze's psychology has not perished yet.*
> [italics added]. For that reason, if for no other, it deserved a careful valuation,
> root and branch. The central problem is the question of method. Is psychology
> a branch of physiology, or a department of metaphysics? To call it a science
> is ambiguous. If by science we mean a natural science, what is the meaning of
> nature? Is there one nature for science and another for philosophy? Is metaphysics
> necessarily the antithesis of science? The answer depends on the most funda-
> mental of all sciences—the science of categories, terms, or classification. A new
> point of view, as opposed to a discovery of detail, is essentially a reform of
> the categories.

Lotze Opposed to a "Materialistic" Psychology

In writing his *Medical Psychology,* Lotze was attacking what at the time had become an influential and widely accepted teaching regarding the "scientific" status of mind or soul. It was classified as a "materialistic" teaching because it equated or identified mental events with brain metabolism. As a teaching, it bothered Lotze as much as it had distressed Fechner. The physiologists and philosophers[21] who sponsored it had given currency to a slogan like "No thought without phosphorus" (*"Ohne Phosphor kein Gedanke"*), since chemists had found phosphorus to be an ingredient of brain tissue. Foods rich in phosphorus were consequently believed to enhance cognitive functions. This emphasis on diet gave rise to another slogan involving a pun on the German expressions for "to be" and "to eat" and which took the form of *"Der Mensch ist was er isst,"* meaning "Man is what he eats." Still another way in which the teaching became popularized was to maintain that the soul or mind is a product of brain metabolism or that the brain produces ideas just as the kidneys produce urine and the liver produces bile. In short, according to the teaching, mental events as experienced are mere epiphenomenal by-products of brain activity akin to the smoke pouring from the chimney of a busy factory.[22]

In opposition to the latter teaching, Lotze argued that mental events as experienced—the world of inner experience—is not to be confused with the outer world of physical events. The distinction in question is somewhat related to Fechner's distinction between inner and outer psychophysics. Thus both Lotze and Fechner conceived of stimuli and resulting afferent neural currents as physical events. Light waves do not change the color of the optic nerve into green or blue or yellow as stimuli are changed. Instead the sensations of color are consequences of transformations occurring at the central terminus of the optic nerve. Although the nature of this transformation from the physical neural process to the mental process of sensation is unknown, Lotze regarded the sequence of steps from stimuli to neural currents to sensation as empirically established. For him, the neural current *qua* motion is a physical event while the color *qua* sensation is a mental event. Both kinds of events are equally real as happenings and

---

[21] The following are some of the more prominent names associated with this so-called materialistic teaching: Pierre Cabanis (1757–1808), Ludwig Feuerbach (1804–1872), Karl Vogt (1817–1895), and Jacob Moleschott (1822–1893).

[22] The dependence of mental efficiency on optimal conditions of brain metabolism does not necessarily entail endorsement of epiphenomenalism. Linus Pauling (1968), for example, has presented both experimental and clinical evidence of such dependence without implying that psychological phenomena are mere by-products of biochemistry.

the former as a "materialistic" physical event does not make the latter an inconsequential chimerical event. The world of sensation or of inner experience is not a superfluous duplication of the stimulus world as described by the physicist. In the words of Lotze: "Sensations are phenomena in us which, although they are the consequences of external stimuli, are not copies of them" (1886, p. 26).

Ideas Not Copies of Stimuli

Now, if sensations, perceptions, and ideas are not copies of external stimuli, it would be wrong to describe them as if they were copies. Analogously, it would be wrong to describe the recall or memory of an experience as a copy or duplicate of that experience. As noted in Chapter 6, page 133, Plotinus had called attention to such an error when he asked, "And what is there pleasant in the memory of pleasure? What is it to recall yesterday's excellent dinner?" The only reason for mentioning something so obvious is that Lotze deemed it advisable to raise the issue. And what makes it important is that in doing so he was exposing a Herbartian error. Herbart had treated presentations as if they were copies or reinstatements of external events. Thus, he regarded contrasting ideas as being in conflict, just as if they were the counterparts of physical forces. On the other hand, Lotze held that opposites like right and left or fast and slow or heavy and light, as presentations or *ideas,* are not opposed to each other as if they were identical with corresponding physical activity. He made this clear in a single sentence as follows (1886, p. 33):

> Ideas in general, never are, of themselves, that which they *signify*:[23] the idea of what is red is not a red idea; the idea of what is triangular is not triangular; the idea of what is choleric is not choleric.

In accordance with the foregoing theme, Lotze might have added that ideas of an hour or a week or a century are not themselves durational. And neither are ideas of a mile or an acre or a globe themselves spatial. They are neither elongated nor spread out nor spherical. Nevertheless they signify or point to positions in space—both visual as well as cutaneous space. How this is brought about calls for consideration of Lotze's celebrated notion of *local signs.*

---

[23] Lotze had already alluded to this distinction in the following way (1886, p. 28):

> The idea of the brightest radiance does not shine, that of the intensest noise does not sound, that of the greatest torture produces no pain . . . the idea quite accurately represents the radiance, the sound, or the pain, which it does not actually reproduce.

With reference to statements like the foregoing, Titchener wrote that he "believes that such statements betray a form of the stimulus-error" (1917, p. 398).

The Concept of Local Signs

Lotze introduced the notion of local signs to account for some familiar, everyday experiences whose psychophysiological implications are apt to be overlooked under ordinary circumstances. Although people readily refer to specific areas of the body in talking about the location of experienced pains, pressures, itches, and other cutaneous impressions, they rarely ask themselves questions like "How do I know where it hurts?" or "How can I tell that my left arm feels warmer than the right arm?" Such questions, if raised, would be calling attention to a problem that has become closely connected with the name of Lotze. The problem is not concerned with qualitative differences among the modalities of cutaneous sensation such as touch, pressure, warmth, pain, and so on. Instead it is restricted to the determination of the factors by means of which the locus of a given cutaneous stimulus is known.

A simple hypothetical example will serve to explain the problem as Lotze viewed it. Suppose a spot on the right thumb and the homologous spot on the left thumb were to be subjected to precisely identical tactual stimuli, then how does it happen that a blindfolded subject would have no difficulty in discriminating between the right and left loci even though, by hypothesis, the two cutaneous impressions are qualitatively, temporally, and intensively identical? To answer this question Lotze assumed there must be some sign or indication of the locality being stimulated. He referred to this as a *Lokalzeichen*. This word ought to be translated "locality sign" in order to supply an accurate rendition of Lotze's intention. However, the less accurate term "local sign" has been sanctioned by long usage and need not be given up provided the connotation of *locality* is retained.

Lotze referred to local signs as "accessory impressions" accompanying each qualitatively distinct sensation of touch or warmth or pain or color. With reference to the retina, for example, he indicated that seeing one red dot in a particular place and other red dots in different places involves stimulation of different retinal spots a, b, c which give rise to the sensation of color, and that there are "accessory impressions" a', b', and c' which are "independent of the nature of the color seen, and dependent merely on the nature of the place excited" (1886, p. 52). Similarly, as applied to cutaneous sensitivity, stimulation of the skin surface involves accessory impressions of the locality being stimulated along with accompanying sensations of touch, warmth, or pain, as the case may be.

Incidentally, some evidence in support of Lotze's belief in the existence of such cutaneous local signs is suggested by well-known neurological reports of impaired cutaneous localization. Thus, in a condition known as *dyschiria*, the examining neurologist finds that his patient has trouble pointing to the exact spot that has just been touched while the patient's eyes are closed.

If the tip of the right thumb has been touched, the patient may point to the wrist or to another finger on the same hand. In another condition known as *allochiria,* the error of localization is less random than it is in dyschiria, since the patient experiences the stimulus as if it had been applied to the corresponding spot on the opposite half of the body. Stimulation of the right thumb, for example, is localized in the left thumb, and a tap on the left shoulder is localized on the right shoulder. Such findings suggest spinal-cord pathology to the neurologist and they would have suggested local-sign pathology to Lotze.

Local signs as accessory impressions give rise to ideas of space, but the ideas themselves as *ideas* are not spatial. Lotze linked these impressions to motor adjustments and accompanying kinesthetic changes by comparing them with the "feeling of the same kind as that by which we are, when in the dark, informed of the position of our limbs" (1886, p. 56).[24] He also, of course, recognized the conjoint action of visual and cutaneous impressions as a common occurrence. In this connection he noted: "Although we easily perceive the stimuli on the various points of the skin as generally different in place, their disposition on definite points in space on the body very often involves associations between them and the images of vision" (R. J. Herrnstein and E. G. Boring [eds.], 1965, p. 138).

Establishing such associations comes with experience; hence empiricists could approve of Lotze's theory of space perception. On the other hand, the fact that he also recognized spatial perception as "an original, *a priori* property of the nature of the mind" was calculated to win the approval of nativists. This does not imply inconsistency on Lotze's part. What it does imply is that the differences between nativists and empiricists are not irreconcilable. The perception of space is neither entirely a product of native propensities nor the exclusive result of postnatal experience. In general, however, Lotze's notion of local signs was interpreted as lending more support to the empiricists than to those who regarded space perception as an unlearned native endowment akin to a Kantian *Anschauung.*

From Local Signs as Unconscious Cues to Theory of the Unconscious

In designating the local sign as an "accessory impression," Lotze was not assuming actual awareness of the impression. Instead he was regarding it as an implicit determinant of a spatial judgment in the way in which a symbol can point to what it symbolizes without awareness of the symbol as symbol. A familiar instance of this process is supplied by judgments of mood on the basis of facial expression. People judge one another as "looking"

---

[24] The implications of this observation were elaborated and reviewed in the light of later experimental studies in an article by Peterson on "Local Signs as Orientation Tendencies" (1926). The article is especially valuable as an introduction to the kind of experimental work prompted by Lotze's concept of local signs.

sad or mean or kind without being able to specify the precise facial clues giving rise to the judgments. The clues are implicit while the judgments are explicit. To refer to them as implicit is tantamount to calling them subconscious or unconscious. As impressions or ideas, Lotze observed, such clues are not "always" noticed. Moreover, in agreement with Herbart, he was ready to relegate such unnoticed ideas to an unconscious realm. For example, at the close of a discussion concerned with the appearance and disappearance of ideas or images, he had this to say (1886, p. 29):

> From the foregoing facts we conclude, that meantime our ideas have not been wholly lost, but have been transformed into some kind of "unconscious states" of which we, of course, can give no description, and for which we employ the self-contradictory but convenient name of "unconscious ideas," in order to indicate that they have originated from ideas, and under certain conditions, can become such again.

In his acceptance of the notion of unconscious ideas, Lotze[25] was thus following a Herbartian precedent. It is worth noting that he did so even though, unlike Herbart, he was mindful of the physiological aspects of psychology. Under the circumstances one might have expected him to substitute a hypothetical neural process for the Herbartian unconscious ideas. After all, as Lotze noted, "no description" can be given of unconscious ideas. This makes their existence hypothetical. Had the term been in vogue in their day, both Lotze and Herbart might have called their notion of unconscious ideas a hypothetical construct. Since they were engaged in trying to make psychology a science in its own right, they evidently had no misgivings regarding the scientific respectability of the notion.

Such misgivings, however, were voiced by their later successors among the founding fathers of the "new" scientific psychology. For example, in a famous passage dealing with the alleged distinction between conscious and unconscious mental states, James wrote: "It is the sovereign means for believing what one likes in psychology, and of turning what might become a science into a tumbling-ground for whimsies" (1890, Vol. I, p. 163). He then devoted several pages to consideration of so-called proofs for the existence of unconscious mental states along with separate rebuttals of each of ten proofs. Most of these proofs James found to be "pure mythology." And Titchener, a follower of Wundt[26] and an ardent champion of the "new"

---

[25] This conclusion seems justified in the light of the excerpt from Lotze's lectures as just cited in which he refers to "unconscious states" as "unconscious ideas." Evidently O. Klemm overlooked this lecture; for he wrote that "the doctrine of the unconscious... was rejected by the leading English psychologists, J. S. Mill, Bain, and Spencer, and by H. Lotze in Germany" (1914, p. 175).

[26] At one time Wundt endorsed Helmholtz's concept of unconscious inference, but later he disavowed belief in unconscious mental processes.

psychology's scientific status, also regarded the notion of unconscious ideas as a myth or fiction. In his view, the recall of forgotten ideas is to be explained in terms of some bodily process and not in terms of some intercurrent unconscious mental process; bodily processes never cease, while sleep interferes with the continuity of consciousness. As a psychophysical parallelist, Titchener did not regard the bodily or neural process as the *cause* of the concomitant mental process. Instead he was careful to note that "reference to the body does not add one iota to the data of psychology."[27] He added (1917, p. 40):

> It does furnish us with an explanatory principle for psychology; it does enable us to systematise our introspective data. Indeed, if we refuse to explain mind by body, we must accept the one or the other of two, equally unsatisfactory alternatives: we must either rest content with a simple description of mental experience, or must invent an unconscious mind to give coherence and continuity to the conscious. Both courses have been tried. But, if we take the first, we never arrive at a science of psychology; and if we take the second, we voluntarily leave the sphere of fact for the sphere of fiction.

Both James and Titchener were in agreement in their refusal to accept the hypothesis of an unconscious mind. They were especially concerned because, as they saw it, the hypothesis is not consonant with psychology's scientific aspirations. And yet men like Herbart and Lotze, who had also cherished such aspirations for psychology, had been willing to endorse the notion of unconscious mental states. It would be easy to list the names of many other students of mental life who came to follow this precedent to some extent, just as it would be easy to list others who refused to follow it. Furthermore, in the post-Freudian era, belief in an unconscious mind came to be both commonplace and unquestioned in some circles.

The whole issue is difficult to settle because those who reject the concept of an unconscious mind as well as those who endorse the concept may do so for different reasons. Actually, without separate and individual inquiry there is no way of knowing precisely what is being rejected or what is being endorsed. The term "unconscious" is fraught with ambiguity. It lacks a clear, fixed, and consistent meaning. Back in 1942, in a survey of the literature, J. G. Miller reported sixteen different ways of being unconscious. According to English and English, there may even be more. At all events, after noting that "Unconscious is one of the most troublesome terms in the psychological disciplines," they added the following by way of explanation (1958, p. 469):

> It is said that there are no less than 39 distinct meanings of unconscious; it is certain that no author limits himself consistently to one. And nearly all meanings

---

27 The dualistic implications of this sentence were noted in Chapter 11 in connection with the discussion of Cartesian doubt. See page 344.

are closely linked to debatable theories. Any user of the term therefore risks suggesting agreement with theories that he may deplore.

In short, with so many possible meanings, some may be in accord with fact while others doubtless belong in the "sphere of fiction" as Titchener suggested. Unless critical discrimination is exercised, the careless use of the word "unconscious" may transform the field of psychology into "a tumbling-ground for whimsies," as James suggested. Nevertheless, to revert to Lotze's early reference to unconscious ideas, his use of the word does not appear to have been careless. In the excerpt quoted at the beginning of this section, he showed due caution by noting the term as being self-contradictory and as being introduced just to indicate the fact of the potential reinstatement of experienced ideas after they have ceased to be experienced. He seemed to be reluctant to use the term even in this restricted sense, as if mindful of its misleading connotations. This attitude was in keeping with his mid-nineteenth-century effort to bring psychology within the orbit of science. Lotze's critical approach to psychological problems was conducive to the emergence of an experimental attack on these problems. This catalytic effect is reflected by the influence he had on his pupils as well as on those who were influenced by his writings.

Lotze's Influence on Scientific Psychology

In breadth of outlook, sensitivity to human needs, and understanding of and devotion to the spirit of science, Lotze might be said to resemble William James. Although neither man was an experimentalist, they both were mindful of the importance of experimental evidence. Both men were keen introspectionists and critical thinkers. They both recognized the relevance for psychology of clinical reports of abnormal mental states. Further, neither was reluctant to face metaphysical difficulties and to call attention to them. For all these reasons, they were influential figures in the history of psychology, especially in that they both were teachers of men whose subsequent careers had an impact on this history.

The careers of two of Lotze's students stand out as particularly good illustrations of his influence as a champion of psychology as science. Moreover, in terms of experimental psychology they accomplished more than their teacher. One of them, Carl Stumpf (1848–1936), belongs to the first generation of experimental psychologists. Under his leadership the laboratory at the University of Berlin gained increasing importance as a center of experimental studies, particularly in connection with the psychology of acoustics and music. The other distinguished student was Georg Elias Müller (1850–1934), who, as Lotze's successor at Göttingen, developed the Göttingen laboratory into a rival of the Leipzig laboratory as a center of the "new" experimental psychology. His many studies of psychophysics and of the psychology of memory served as impressive demonstrations of the fruitfulness and the exciting promise of laboratory psychology. Needless to add, both he and Stumpf in the course of their long professorships had students who as second-generation experimental psychologists extended the range of problems being subjected to experimental investigation.[28] Thus, even though he was not himself an experimentalist, Lotze may be said to have inspired experimental work both directly and indirectly, and he belongs in any list of pioneering scientific psychologists. In fact, George Trumbull Ladd (1842–1921), who launched experimental psychology at Yale, paid tribute to Lotze as a scientific psychologist in the introduction to his translation of Lotze's *Outlines of Psychology*. This was in the 1880s, some five years after the death of Lotze. Among other things, Ladd had this to say about Lotze (1886, pp. vi and vii):

> He may fitly be called a born psychologist. He had the delicate tact, the reflective insight, the subtlety in analysis of mental states, which psychology demands for its successful cultivation. Moreover, his training was of that comprehensive kind which alone makes it possible to look upon the many-sided human mind from all of its many sides. . . . He was thoroughly versed in the sciences of human physiology and human pathology. His early lecture courses included these subjects. While a young man at Leipzig, we find him offering instruction in "pastoral medicine," therapeutics, "juridical medicine," and the functions and diseases of the nervous system. . . . He was thoroughly acquainted with all that modern science has done for the study of mind by opening the approaches to it from the experimental and physiological points of view.

Concluding Comments

This praise by Ladd is a tribute to Lotze's success in winning support for a scientific psychology. As Ladd put it, Lotze understood what might be accomplished "for the study of mind" by means of experimental and physiological "approaches." Herbart's vision of psychology as science did not include these approaches. In this respect, Lotze enlarged the scope of what was to be included within the purview of a scientific psychology. Furthermore, Herbart and Lotze both included consideration of metaphysical implications in their views of psychology as science. It was in this connection that, as mentioned earlier, Brett maintained, "Lotze's psychology has not perished yet." Brett evidently regarded sensitivity to and understanding of metaphysical implications as important for the progress of scientific psychology. Others, of course, have taken an opposite stand by making a disregard of metaphysical implications essential or advantageous for the advance of psychology as science. The controversy involves complex

---

[28] Informative biographical sketches of the life and work of Stumpf and Müller, along with the names of their more distinguished students, are supplied by Boring (1950, pp. 362–383).

issues the elaboration of which would entail too much of a digression. In the present context it is enough to call attention to the existence of the controversy and to note that its resolution depends on one's philosophy of science as well as on what one takes to be a metaphysical issue. To be intelligently antimetaphysical requires some knowledge of metaphysics.

As was explained at the beginning of this chapter, the decades of the nineteenth century were marked by increasing recognition of the prospects for a scientific psychology. As contrasted with the previous chapters and their surveys of psychology's philosophic backgrounds, consideration of the latter prospects made the present chapter more of a survey of psychology's scientific foreground as it developed during the earlier decades of the century. This called for particular emphasis on the work of Herbart and Lotze as key figures in this development. Since they had written on the subject of psychology as science, linking their names with this development during the period in question was largely a matter of expository convenience. During the later decades of the century there were others who wrote on the same subject. To consider all of them is out of the question. However, by way of rounding out this survey of psychology's scientific foreground it will again be convenient to focus on the work of two men as points of departure for such a survey. These men, Alexander Bain and Wilhelm Wundt, each in his own way helped to lay the foundations for scientific psychology as an autonomous enterprise that gained momentum in the closing decades of the nineteenth century and became a full-fledged reality in the early decades of the present century. How this came about will be considered in the next two chapters.

References

Boring, E. G. *A History of Experimental Psychology.* New York: The Century Company, 1929.

Boring, E. G. *A History of Experimental Psychology,* rev. ed. New York: Appleton-Century-Crofts, 1950.

Brett, G. S. *A History of Psychology,* Vol. III. London: George Allen and Unwin, 1921.

Cattell, J. McK. "The Founding of the Association and of the Hopkins and Clark Laboratories," *Psychological Review,* 1943, *50,* 61–64. (From an address delivered in 1927.)

English, H. B. and A. C. *A Comprehensive Dictionary of Psychological and Psychoanalytical Terms.* New York: Longmans, Green and Company, 1958.

Eysenck, H. J. "The Effects of Psychotherapy," *International Journal of Psychiatry,* 1965, *1,* 101–142.

Freud, S. "On the History of the Psycho-Analytic Movement," (Translated by Joan Riviere.) In *The Collected Papers of Sigmund Freud.* New York: Basic Books, 1959, I, 287–359.

Freud, S. "Psychoanalysis: Freudian School," in *Encyclopaedia Britannica*, 14th ed., 1929.

James, W. *Principles of Psychology*, 2 vols. New York: Henry Holt and Company, 1890.

Jones, E. *The Life and Work of Sigmund Freud*, Vol. 1. New York: Basic Books, 1953.

Klemm, O. *A History of Psychology*. (Translated by E. C. Wilm and R. Pintner.) New York: Charles Scribner's Sons, 1914.

Kris, E. "Introduction," in S. Freud, *The Origins of Psycho-Analysis—Letters to Wilhelm Fliess, Drafts and Notes: 1887–1902*. (Translated by E. Mosbacher and J. Strachey.) New York: Basic Books, 1954, pp. 3–47.

Lotze, R. H. "On Local Signs in Their Relation to the Perception of Space," in R. J. Herrnstein and E. G. Boring (eds.). *A Source Book in the History of Psychology*. Cambridge: Harvard University Press, 1965, pp. 135–140.

Lotze, R. H. *Outlines of Psychology*. (Translated by G. T. Ladd.) Boston: Ginn and Company, 1886.

Merz, J. T. *A History of European Thought in the Nineteenth Century*, 4 vols., rev. ed. New York: Dover Publications, 1965. (First published between 1904 and 1912.)

Miller, J. G. *Unconsciousness*. New York: John Wiley and Sons, 1942.

Murchison, C. (ed.). *A History of Psychology in Autobiography*, Vol. II. Worcester, Mass.: Clark University Press, 1932.

Murphy, G. *Historical Introduction to Modern Psychology*, rev. ed. New York: Harcourt, Brace and Company, 1949.

Paul, G. L. "Strategy of Outcome in Psychotherapy," *Journal of Consulting Psychology*, 1967, *31*, 109–118.

Pauling, L. "Orthomolecular Psychiatry," *Science*, 1968, *160*, 265–271.

Peterson, J. "Local Signs as Orientation Tendencies," *Psychological Review*, 1926, *33*, 218–236.

St. John, J. A. (ed.). *The Philosophical Works of John Locke*, Vol. I. London: George Bell and Sons, 1901.

Titchener, E. B. *A Text-Book of Psychology*. New York: The Macmillan Company, 1917.

Ward, J. "Johann Friedrich Herbart," in *Encyclopaedia Britannica*, 14th ed., 1929.

Whyte, L. L. *The Unconscious before Freud*. New York: Basic Books, 1960.

Woodworth, R. S. *Contemporary Schools of Psychology*, rev. ed. New York: The Ronald Press, 1948.

Woodworth, R. S. *Dynamic Psychology*. New York: Columbia University Press, 1918.

Woodworth, R. S. "Note on the Rapidity of Dreams," *Psychological Review*, 1897, *4*, 524–526.

Woodworth, R. S. "Some Criticism of the Freudian Psychology," *Journal of Abnormal Psychology*, 1917, *12*, 174–194.

22

Bain and the Scientific Foreground

BOTH THE PRESENT CHAPTER and the next and final one may be considered to be continuations of Chapter 21. As indicated by the chapter headings, all three have more to do with psychology's quest for scientific status than with its philosophic backgrounds. For the most part they are concerned with a reorientation in the outlook of the nineteenth-century founding fathers of modern psychology, so that mental philosophy of earlier centuries became the scientific psychology of the twentieth century. Furthermore, just as the preceding chapter took the work of Herbart and Lotze as points of departure for discussion of this reorientation, so the present chapter will continue the discussion by considering the work of Alexander Bain, while the following chapter will conclude the discussion by considering the work of Wilhelm Wundt.

All these men—Herbart, Lotze, Bain, and Wundt—had one thing in common: they were all interested in having psychology become a science even though they differed in their proposals for bringing this about. For example, in their thinking about psychology as science, both Lotze and Wundt had taken physiological considerations into account, but this was not true of Herbart's prospectus for a psychology as science. Herbart was not trained in medicine, whereas both Lotze and Wundt had medical degrees. Before Lotze there was Hartley's eighteenth-century physiological psychology of neural vibrations and, as noted in Chapter 18, this interest in psychophysiology was attributed to Hartley's medical background. On the other hand, James Mill, who lacked medical training, was able to endorse Hartley's associationism and to disregard Hartley's physiology.

For the most part, those nineteenth-century investigators who concerned themselves with the physiological aspects of mental life had received medical training. This was true not only of Lotze and Wundt but also of Weber, Fechner, Johannes Müller, Helmholtz, and William James. Thomas Brown was a conspicuous exception. Despite his medical background, he paid scant attention to problems of physiological psychology.[1] Bain is to be listed as an exception for a different reason. Even though he lacked medical training, he deemed knowledge of the nervous system to be important for the student of psychology. In some ways he was more of a psychologist than any of his Scottish or British predecessors or even than men like Herbart and Lotze. This is true even though, as will soon be evident, his interests were not restricted to psychology.

Alexander Bain: A Brief Biography

Bain was born in Aberdeen in 1818 and died there in 1903. His life thus spanned all the years leading up to and following the emergence of the "new" scientific psychology. And he had a share in establishing its foundations.

Unlike John Stuart Mill, Bain was not the son of a learned man. His father, an impecunious weaver, was barely able to support his family of five children. Bain's formal schooling was curtailed by the need to contribute to the meager family income. He too worked as a weaver.[2] When he was not busy at the loom, however, a driving intellectual curiosity made for the introduction of a self-imposed regimen of private study. He read widely and studied assiduously, and in the course of years managed to master several fields of mathematics, teach himself some Latin, and obtain a grounding in works of metaphysics and philosophy. This preparation enabled him to matriculate with a scholarship at Marischal College, Aberdeen, in 1836 and to graduate with honors four years later.

When he was only twenty-two his first article as a contributor to the *Westminster Review* was accepted for publication. At about this time he met John Stuart Mill and they became lifelong friends. As may be recalled, years later he collaborated with Mill in editing the new edition of James Mill's *Analysis of the Phenomena of the Human Mind.* Years before, he had already helped Mill with the revision of his *System of Logic.*

It was not until 1860 that Bain obtained a satisfactory university appointment. In that year a new chair of logic and English was established at the University of Aberdeen and Bain obtained the post. As will be explained in the next section, this was after he had written the first edition of his chief

---

[1] Incidentally, this also applies to Freud. Even though he had specialized in neurology as a young physician and had engaged in neurological research, he developed his psychoanalytic psychology as a field of inquiry virtually independent of or unrelated to neurophysiology. In fact, he did not regard medical training as a *sine qua non* for the psychoanalytic practitioner.

[2] Years later, after he had won a name for himself as a philosopher, his youthful occupation as a weaver prompted some wag to make him the subject of this bilingual pun: *Wee-vir, rex philosophorum.*

psychological work.[3] Following his appointment to the new chair he wrote several books on English grammar. He also wrote a *Manual of Rhetoric* as well as a book on logic. Among his other publications mention might be made of *The Study of Character, Including an Estimate of Phrenology,* of a work entitled *Mind and Body,* of another on *Education as a Science,* and of one called *John Stuart Mill: a Criticism, with Personal Recollections.* In addition he wrote a biography of James Mill.

With some justification, Bain might thus be called a biographer, a grammarian, a rhetorician, a logician, and an educator, as well as a psychologist. Even though he contributed to many fields other than psychology, it is as a psychologist that he made his most important contribution. Of the long line of Scottish thinkers who contributed to the history of psychology, Bain's contribution, as the culmination of this long line, was probably the most influential. What he had to say about psychology has some bearing on the transition from psychology as a branch of philosophy to psychology as an independent scientific venture.

Bain as Psychologist

Bain's work on psychology, like the *Principles* of James, called for two volumes. Unlike James, Bain gave each volume its own title even though both volumes were concerned with the total field of psychology as it looked to Bain. The first volume, called *The Senses and the Intellect,* was started in 1851 and published in 1855. The second volume, entitled *The Emotions and the Will,* appeared in 1859. These volumes were revised in succeeding decades, with the fourth and last revision of the second volume being published in 1899. This is worth noting because the forty years from 1859 to 1899 were years when psychology and related disciplines had to come to terms with the doctrine of evolution.

The year 1859 is noteworthy in the history of human thought as the year when Darwin's epoch-making book, *The Origin of Species,* first appeared and made evolution the focus of a heated controversy. This accounts for a significant difference between the first edition of Bain's psychology and the later ones, which were among the first books to consider psychological issues in the light of Darwinian teachings.[4]

---

[3] At the time this first edition was published in 1859, Bain listed himself on the title page as "EXAMINER IN LOGIC AND MORAL PHILOSOPHY IN THE UNIVERSITY OF LONDON." In subsequent editions he was listed as "PROFESSOR OF LOGIC IN THE UNIVERSITY OF ABERDEEN."

[4] Incidentally Darwin was familiar with both of Bain's volumes of psychology. He consulted them in connection with his *The Expression of the Emotions in Man and Animals,* which appeared in 1872. Bain had considered the problem in the early editions of his psychology and Darwin has some six references to Bain's views. Then in later editions Bain reconsidered his views in the light of Darwin's book.

Like Lotze's *Medical Psychology* of 1852, Bain's first edition of the 1850s was planned as a physiological psychology. Thus the same decade was marked by the publication of two works, one German and one English, each of which purported to consider mind as dependent on the nervous system. Although Lotze's book was published some three years earlier than Bain's initial volume, there is no evidence to indicate that Bain had patterned his book on Lotze's.[5] His was an independent undertaking and in some ways more explicitly physiological than Lotze's. In successive editions he made changes in the chapter on the nervous system in accordance with new findings as reported since the preceding edition had appeared. In the preface to the 1855 edition he wrote (p. iv): "Conceiving that the time has now come when many of the striking discoveries of Physiologists relative to the nervous system should find a recognized place in the Science of Mind, I have devoted a separate chapter to the Physiology of the Brain and Nerves." Then in the next edition (1864) he pointed out that the "explanations of the Nervous system and the Senses have been amended according to the best recent authorities on Physiology." Similarly, the preface to the 1868 edition explains that the "sketch of the Nervous system, and the Physiological references generally, have been compared with the statements given in the newest works."

Psychology to Be a Branch of Science

Bain's purpose in writing his treatise on psychology was to present it as a scientific psychology. He made this quite explicit on p. iii of the preface dated June, 1855, where he stated that he was "endeavouring to present in a methodical form all the important facts and doctrines bearing upon mind, *considered as a branch of science*" [italics added]. He also alluded to the "high scientific character" which "the subject of Mind" might attain. It was not to be a metaphysical psychology such as Herbart sponsored in his presentation of psychology as science. In a comment on Herbart, Bain implied that he regarded metaphysical considerations either as irrelevant or as a possible hindrance to the work of the scientific psychologist. It was a guarded

---

5 Boring (1950, p. 238) believed that Bain was not even familiar with Lotze's book:

It is almost certain that Bain did not know this book of Lotze's; he never spoke German, and it is doubtful if he read it. It is also probable that he did not know Johannes Müller's psychological physiology. He rarely mentioned German sources.

The foregoing opinion appears to have been based upon the first edition of Bain's treatises. At all events, the third edition does refer to Lotze and other German sources. For example, in a footnote of this edition Bain had this to say about the local-sign theory (1868, p. 397):

It is maintained in Germany by Lotze, Wundt, and others, upon the evidence of experiments, that the tactile sensations of the two hands, and of the skin everywhere,

comment to the effect that the "metaphysical point of view did not prevent Herbart from cultivating empirical psychology" (p. 671). This is an obvious plea for a psychology divorced from metaphysical preoccupations. Moreover, in its equally obvious endorsement of empirical psychology it reveals Bain's agreement with Herbart's proposal to base scientific psychology on experience.

Herbart's proposal for a scientific psychology was written some thirty years before Bain's proposal. In the meantime there had been progress in experimental physiology. Consequently, unlike Herbart, Bain could think of scientific psychology as being both empirical and experimental. These terms do not refer to antithetic or even divergent ways of obtaining data for a scientific psychology. As so zealous a champion of experimental psychology as Titchener put it: "For all experimental psychology is in the broad sense empirical, and a psychology which is in the narrow sense empirical may still have recourse to experiment" (1929, p. 8).

Bain evidently intended his treatise to be the foundation for the eventual realization of a psychology having "high scientific character." As he saw it, to attain this status, psychology was to avail itself of experimental findings as well as of empirical observations. The experimental findings he introduced in the early editions by way of illustration were taken from the reports of anatomists, physiologists, physicists, and chemists. These data were not cited to demonstrate the need for psychological laboratories. In the idiom of journalism, Bain did not scoop Wundt; completion of the treatise in 1859 was not a foreshadowing of events at Leipzig in 1879.

Bain's plans for a scientific psychology did not seem to envisage having psychologists embark upon laboratory work on their own. Instead they were to be mindful of the possible relevance of the experimental results of others as a means of enhancing their own activities as empirical psychologists. They were to be experimentally minded without being experimentalists, just as architects may keep abreast of relevant developments in structural engineering without being engineers. Bain's scientific psychology was not projected as a basically experimental psychology, but as a basically empirical psychology interpreted in the light of ancillary experimental findings. To show what this implied, it may prove clarifying

---

are *qualitatively* different, and that this difference of quality assists us greatly in learning to discriminate the several qualities.

Furthermore, on p. 264 he has a long quotation from Müller on antagonistic muscles, and he cites additional quotations from Müller on pp. 296–299. Other German authors cited in this volume are Kant, Herbart, Weber, Helmholtz, and Du Bois-Reymond (1818–1896). It is not easy to determine changes in source material in the different editions, since the volume in question lacks an index and the index in the first edition omits all mention of authors cited. Boring's failure to come across these German sources in Bain's later editions is thus readily understandable. To wade through both volumes of all four editions might be more of a pedantic than a scholarly undertaking. Each volume contains more than six hundred pages.

to cite a few examples of empirical observations and of experimental findings that Bain introduced.

From Empiricism to Science

Reliance upon empirical observations is not unique to psychology. Virtually every science develops out of such observations either directly or indirectly. Had man failed to note differences among insects, there would be no entomology. Without prior observation of mountains and rock formations, there would be no geology. Analogous statements can be made about the genesis of astronomy, botany, physiology, genetics, mechanics, and so on. It is a truism to say that they all got their start as a result of raising questions about everyday observations. One does not have to study meteorology to find out about the existence of rain, snow, fog, sleet, and sunshine. Neither does one have to study psychology to know that people fight, get hungry, feel sad, experience joy, undergo fatigue, make choices, write prose, form friendships, build houses, play games, have jobs, loaf, and read and pray. One knows these things as a result of commonplace experiences. They constitute empirical knowledge. Bain's treatise is replete with references to this kind of knowledge. The following will serve as examples that Bain introduced in different parts of the treatise:

> [1] The feeling of "warmth" is identified as belonging to effects that have no connexion with heat; we hear of warm colors and warm affections.
> [2] The lachrymal effusion is an accompaniment of grief, but there are also tears of joy. In the extreme of merriment, the eye is moistened and suffused.
> [3] The movements of animals afford many other varieties [of movement]; in quadrupeds, the walk, trot, canter, gallop, shamble; in birds, numerous characteristic modes of flight; the darting of the bat, the frog's leap, the serpent's undulation, the crawl of the sluggish snail.

Empirical observations like these are not enough to establish a science. For them to become *scientific* observations, they must give rise to systematic as opposed to casual observations. They become systematic to the extent that they constitute answers to a series of related questions. The questions have to do with the what and how, and often with the why, of the instigating empirical observation. For example, the feeling of warmth referred to by Bain is familiar to everybody as a phase of cutaneous experience, but only a very, very few people were prompted to raise the kind of questions the answers to which became the laws of thermodynamics.

Similarly, not many people have reacted to the experience as a psychological issue by asking questions like the following: How many different qualities of cutaneous sensation are there? Does each different kind such as warmth and cold and touch involve a different kind of receptor? Is the entire skin surface equally sensitive to warmth? By how much must the temperature of the skin be raised or lowered for a change to be detected? Does a single sensory nerve mediate all cutaneous sensations, or is there a separate one for thermal sensations and for each of the other skin sensations? Is a given segment of the skin uniformly sensitive to all modalities of cutaneous sensation, or are there discrete spots of specialized sensitivity? Are all vertebrates equipped with the same kind of cutaneous receptors? What induces the sensation of tickle and how is it related to laughter?

Obtaining answers to such an array of questions is a major undertaking. Some of them require microscopic examination of subcutaneous tissues and others call for exploratory stimulation of the skin surface with a variety of stimuli. Some of the questions will entail recourse to measurement and calibrated instruments. Many of them will involve preliminary training of subjects to prepare them for recognition of the sensory phenomena under investigation. The entire project may necessitate collaboration with specialists in neurology, histology, physics, and dermatology. In short, haphazard empirical observations will have to be supplemented by systematic experimental observations for successful prosecution of such a project. It was the gradual and increasing recognition of this need for controlled systematic observations that marked the transition from empirical to scientific psychology. Bain is one of the founding fathers who recognized this need. In addition to noting facts derived from empirical observations, his treatise called attention to facts based upon experimental observations. Here are a few of them as formulated by Bain:

[1] A beheaded frog, whose hind foot is touched with an acid, makes efforts with the other hind foot to wipe the acid away. If a drop is placed on the back, on one side, the animal uses the leg on that side to relieve itself of the sting; but if by cutting the nerve that leg is rendered powerless, the other leg is stimulated to remove the acid. These actions have the essential character of voluntary actions, and yet they proceed from no higher a centre than the spinal cord. . . . The appearances would betoken that the pain is felt, or that the animal is conscious.

[2] The researches of Helmholtz and others seem to establish the fact that the differences of sounds as regards Sweetness, . Timbre, and Vowel Quality, are owing to the combination of the principle tone of each with a number of *over-tones*; which combinations are susceptible of great variety.

[3] It is a singular fact, discovered by Weber, in connexion with the sense of temperature, that when two substances of the same weight, but of different temperatures, are estimated by the sense of touch or of pressure, the colder appears the heavier.

[4] The experiments of Du Bois-Reymond, show that there is a community of nature between the nerve force and common electricity. Electric currents are constantly maintained in the nerves and muscles, their character being changed during sensation and muscular contraction.

From the preceding examples, it should be clear that the experimental findings Bain incorporated into his psychology were reports of experiments

conducted by physiologists and physicists. They were experiments having
implications for psychology rather than distinctively psychological experiments. By taking them into account, the scientific status of empirical psychology was to be enhanced. This is different, however, from advocating its
enhancement by means of an experimental psychology. Bain was not
thinking of this possibility in the 1850s and 1860s. Like Hartley before him,
he was thinking of a neurological setting for associationism, but his was
a different neurology from Hartley's vibrational neurology of 1749. He had
the advantage of being able to base his neurological theorizing on the
electrophysiological experiments of Du Bois-Reymond, whereas a century
earlier Hartley had to content himself with a mythological neurology of
undulating "medullary particles." In this respect Bain's physiological
psychology was less speculative than Hartley's. In addition to profiting from
the work of Du Bois-Reymond, it reflected the experimental findings of such
men as Sir Charles Bell (1774–1842), Marshall Hall (1790–1857),
Pierre Jean Marie Flourens (1794–1867), and Charles Edouard Brown-
Séquard (1817?–1894). It was not an elementary presentation for
popular consumption.

Bain's Physiological Psychology

Even though Bain's account of the gross anatomy of the nervous system
was written more than one hundred years ago, it would not require drastic
changes to approximate a contemporary introduction to the subject. Much
of the descriptive detail, with illustrative outline drawings, is taken directly
from *Elements of Anatomy* (1828), by Jones Quain. There is no avoidance
of technical terms, and conventional Latin nomenclature is employed with
minimal attention to possible English equivalents. Thus, there are blunt
introductions to terms like *"medulla oblongata," "pons Varolii," "medul-
lated fibres,"* and *"corpora striata."* Along with such references to
cerebrospinal structures there were others to the principal parts of the
sympathetic system. Nor are spinal and cranial nerves overlooked. Bain
listed nine and not twelve pairs of cranial nerves, although admitting that
some of them can be further subdivided.[6]

After compressing his description of neural structures into some twenty
pages, Bain devoted about the same amount of space to consideration of
the function of each of these structures. For example, with reference to the
spinal cord he noted the ventral horn as efferent and the dorsal as afferent

---

[6] Knowledge of the cranial nerves goes back to Galen (131–201 A.D.), but he too
failed to account for all twelve. He listed seven and grouped some together
which are listed separately today. According to C. Singer (1957, p. 56), he grouped
the ninth, tenth, and eleventh together as the "sixth pair of nerves" and the seventh
and eighth as the "fifth pair of nerves."

in function, with resulting control of trunk and extremities through the medium of the spinal nerves. He called particular attention to the maintenance of muscle tone as a factor in the regulation of bodily movement. In general, he based his interpretation of a structure's function by appealing to the results of extirpation experiments on animals. Often the interpretation was reinforced by specific reference to the innervation of the extirpated structure. The following quotation will serve to illustrate this mode of interpretation (1868, p. 44):

> The cerebral ganglion named the *Corpora Quadrigemina* is associated with the power of sight. Its destruction produces blindness, and also a permanent dilatation and immobility of the eye. The destruction of one side causes loss of vision on the opposite side; but the irritation of one side will produce contraction of both pupils. The partial removal of the ganglion is attended with partial and temporary blindness, debility of the muscles on the opposite side of the body, and sometimes giddiness and slight rotatory movements. The anatomical connexions with the optic nerve also point to the conclusion that the principal track of visual impressions to the brain is by the *corpora quadrigemina*. [7]

With the exception of what Bain had to say about the functions of the cerebral hemispheres, there is no need to devote space to his conclusions regarding the functions of other divisions of the nervous system such as the cerebellum and the medulla. However, as a mid-nineteenth-century view of the problem of cortical localization, his conclusions regarding the cerebral hemispheres merit consideration.

The Problem of Cortical Localization

Localization of function is a venerable and persistent problem in the history of neurology. As a problem it had already been considered by Galen.[8] At all events his writings, as reviewed by F. H. Garrison, suggest an early effort to account for the cerebral locus of mental functions. Galen held that the forebrain has to do with imagination, the midbrain with cogitation, and the hindbrain with memory (1929, p. 113). This proposal warrants listing Galen among the earliest physiological psychologists despite

---

[7] This account of the function of the corpora quadrigemina is not in accord with later findings. For one thing, only a portion of the structure—the superior colliculus—has to do with the visual pathway. The other portion—the inferior colliculus—belongs to the auditory pathway. Both portions are reported to be important for the regulation of reflex adjustments rather than for the mediation of visual and auditory sensations as such. For details see C. H. Best and N. B. Taylor (1945, p. 1025).

[8] For a history of the problem see Chapter IV of W. Riese's *History of Neurology* (1959). This chapter has a separate section (pp. 79–85) entitled "Galen on Cerebral Localization."

the arbitrary guesswork upon which these localizations are based.[9] His localizations appear to have been prompted by the realization that man's intellect enables him to imagine the future, to think about the present, and to remember the past; hence the designation of three brain areas.

Similarly, the localizations that Gall proposed centuries later in his craniology were prompted by the need to assign each of the many phrenological faculties to a particular brain area. Both Gall and Galen followed the same procedure of first noting some psychological characteristic and then linking it to some more or less circumscribed segment of brain tissue. This is different from first noting the segment and then considering its probable psychological correlate. The latter procedure was followed by those neurologists who traced the course of cranial nerves from receptor and effector to cortical terminus and then designated such termini by terms like "visual area," "auditory center," "motor area," and so on. They even prepared diagrams to show the locations of these areas.[10] These diagrams of what came to be called the "new phrenology" often appeared in textbooks of introductory psychology as ostensible evidence of psychology's scientific progress.

Localization of function as viewed by the sponsors of the "new phrenology" failed to win the support of all nineteenth-century brain physiologists. Those who questioned the doctrine of specific localization emphasized the *unity* of mental life as correlated with the nervous system as a system, with emphasis on the fact that directly or indirectly every part of the brain is linked to every other part. The architectonics of the system, they argued, thus renders it impossible for any part to function in isolation.

The issues involved in the controversy are far too complex to be elaborated upon without too much of a digression. It will suffice to restrict their consideration to the overriding issue of antithetic interpretations of brain action.

On the one hand, there are indications of possible autonomous functioning of a given brain area, such as the visual area. On the other hand, from another viewpoint, all areas or centers are so interdependent that such hypothesized autonomy of any one of them is impossible. Those who accept the latter viewpoint stress the underlying unity of brain action, while advocates of the former viewpoint stress the importance of localized activity.

---

[9] Not all of Galen's teachings were the result of such arbitrary guesswork. Many of them were the result of animal dissections and acute clinical observations. Among his accomplishments, as noted by Garrison, was the fact that he was "the first to describe the cranial nerves and the sympathetic system," the first to supply a valid account of the mechanism of breathing, and the first to introduce experimental transections of the spinal cord. For these and additional accomplishments Garrison called Galen "the first and foremost contributor to *experimental physiology* before Harvey, and the first experimental neurologist" (1929, p. 115).

[10] These diagrams of nineteenth-century neurologists have been likened to maps, since

This oversimplified statement of the rival interpretations is accurate enough to facilitate understanding of Bain's stand on the overriding issue. He was definitely opposed to the "new phrenology," as is clear from the following paragraph (1868, p. 46):

> The attempt to localize the mental functions in special portions of the central mass has been thwarted by observations of a remarkable kind. The phrenologists noticed cases where the destruction or disease of one hemisphere was unaccompanied with the entire loss of any function; the inference being that the hemispheres were duplicates performing the same office, like the two eyes, or the two halves of the nostrils. But cases have been recorded of disease of large portions of the brain in both hemispheres at once, without apparent loss of function; which would require us to extend still farther the supposition of a plurality of nervous tracks for a single mental aptitude.

Aside from its repudiation of belief in a fixed correspondence between certain bits of brain tissue and given psychological functions, the preceding paragraph is rather vague. It fails to suggest a clear-cut alternative to the repudiated belief. Stated a little differently, it fails to show how the brain is related to what Bain had in mind when he wrote that it "may be considered as associated with the most complicated of the mental functions, namely, those related to Intelligence" (1868, p. 45). This is another way of saying that he had failed to solve the psychophysical riddle.

Bain's failure might be attributed to the fact that he had been considering the problem of cerebral localization long before psychological evidence bearing on the problem was available. After all, in the 1850s there had not been any experimental studies of the psychological effects of brain injury of a kind that had been undertaken by the 1950s.

Would Bain have arrived at a different conclusion had he had access to the vast number of such studies that have accumulated in recent decades? In a critical survey of many of these studies, V. Meyer, like Bain, was unable to settle the issue. For the most part, Meyer's survey was limited to studies involving human subjects, since, as he pointed out, animal studies "are of limited value in determining cerebral functions and their localization in man" (H. J. Eysenck [ed.], 1960, p. 529). After consulting more than

---

they purport to show the location of a given psychological function just as the geographer's map shows the location of a city or a river. Henry Head (1861–1940), the distinguished British neurologist, had little patience with this kind of hypothetical geography of the brain. He expressed his disapproval by referring to those who prepared such maps as "diagram makers." His own investigations made him especially distrustful of diagrams assigning different locations for reading, writing, calculating, speaking, and other language functions. Although more than forty years have elapsed since Head published his account of these investigations, many portions of it continue to merit the attention of contemporary psychologists. This applies particularly to Volume I of his study of aphasia (1926).

250 reports of relevant studies, Meyer reached this conclusion (1960, pp. 557–558):

> The evidence presented does not enable this survey to be concluded with a clear-cut statement of definite principles with regard to brain functioning and organization. Neither the strictly "departmental" nor the strictly "unitary" views in their present form have been conclusively supported by experimental data. One finds the greatest support for the theory of "regional equipotentiality" in many psychological functions, but no one has conclusively and precisely established the dependence of any function on any brain region.

Bain as Psychophysical Parallelist

The statement to the effect that Bain had failed to solve the psychophysical problem does not mean he had failed to consider it. What he had to say about it is hinted at in his previously cited comment about intelligence being "associated" with the brain. Taken out of context, this is hardly a revealing statement. On earlier pages, however, Bain had mentioned the increase in richness of the convolutions along with increase in brain weight when the brains of the intellectually well endowed are compared with the appearance and weight of the brains of idiots. He also mentioned the decrease both in neural complexity and concomitant "mental endowment" as one descends "in the animal scale" and studies mammals, birds, reptiles, and still simpler creatures (1868, p. 12).

In referring to the concomitance as "associated," Bain was employing a neutral term to indicate the nature of the relationship in question. All that the term suggests is that one series of events is accompanied by another series of events. As applied to the mind-body problem, this means endorsement of psychophysical parallelism.

There is every reason to regard Bain as a sponsor of a parallelistic psychology. One of his admirers, William Leslie Davidson, even declared, "He was the originator of the theory of psychophysical parallelism, which is so widely used as a working basis by modern psychologists" (*Encyclopaedia Britannica*, 11th ed., 1910, article on "Alexander Bain"). On the face of it, this appears to be contrary to fact. For the general theory, Leibnitz was the originator. And Hartley, it may be recalled, had preceded Bain in at least coming close to an application of the theory to psychology in the form of a truncated parallelism (see pp. 623–624). Davidson must have been familiar with the views of Leibnitz and Hartley. He had occupied Bain's chair at Aberdeen as professor of logic and metaphysics and consequently is not apt to have overlooked the metaphysical implications of Leibnitz's concept of pre-established harmony. That Davidson was familiar with Hartley's psychology is evident from an article of his that appeared in *Mind* in 1904.

This was a year after Bain's death, and the article is in the nature of a memorial tribute. The following excerpt from this article, as quoted by Merz (1965, Vol. III, p. 214), not only serves to demonstrate his knowledge of Hartley's work but also serves as a reminder of a significant trend in psychology's history; namely, the tendency for psychological theorizing to change with changes in the prevailing climate of scientific opinion:

> Be it noted that Prof. Bain was, as most British philosophers have been, under the influence of the leading scientific conceptions of the moment. It may be affirmed generally that the advance in psychology in our land has very much followed the advance in physical research. The theory of sound, for instance, was the outstanding physical theory in the time of Hartley. Consequently, he proceeded to interpret mind according to the analogy, and represent the nervous process as simply propagations of vibrations as in sound. Chemistry, in like manner, came to the front in the days of Mill. Consequently the process of Association was interpreted in terms thereof—it was set forth as kind of mental chemistry. So, in Dr. Bain's time, physiology was attracting much attention, and the work of Johannes Müller, in particular, was greatly in evidence, and there was also an awakened interest in biology. Hence the physiological reference became prominent, and the method of natural history pointed the way to Dr. Bain's mode of procedure.[11]

The "mode of procedure" employed by Bain called for examination of psychological issues in the light of their physiological implications on the assumption that every mental process is accompanied by a neural process. At one time, before the words "psychosis" and "neurosis" had acquired their current psychiatric meanings, this assumption was expressed in a catch phrase: *no psychosis without neurosis.* As a phrase it epitomizes the standpoint of psychophysical parallelism that Bain had adopted. In maintaining that Bain was the *originator* of this standpoint, Davidson, it should now be evident, was not thereby necessarily revealing ignorance of the metaphysics of Leibnitz and the psychology of Hartley. Leibnitz never came to grips with the physiological aspects of parallelism; and Hartley's parallelism, as already noted, turned out to be a truncated affair. In the sense of having been the first to try to write a psychology in accordance with the

---

11 At the time Davidson was writing this article, psychological theorizing was reflecting the impact of the doctrine of evolution. Somewhat later, with advances in anthropology and sociology, there was an increasing recognition of the importance of cultural influences and social tradition on personality development and a lessened confidence in the importance of instincts and heredity in accounting for such development. Still later, with advances in electronics and the introduction of computers, the professional vocabulary of psychologists began to include references to imput, feedback, "bits," "communication theory," and similar terms altogether alien to a precybernetic psychology.

theory, Bain might be called an "originator."[12] This is why Davidson in his 1910 article on Bain also described him as having been "the first in Great Britain during the nineteenth century to apply physiology, in a thoroughgoing fashion to the elucidation of mental states."

Does Knowledge of Mind Equal Knowledge of Brain?

Actually Bain was not as thoroughgoing in his application of physiology as Davidson implied. A thoroughgoing psychophysical parallelism would require a specific neurophysiological description as the concomitant of every kind of mental state. Otherwise the "elucidation" Davidson attributed to Bain would not occur. To say there is no psychosis without neurosis is not the same as being able to demonstrate the neurosis that is believed to parallel a given psychosis. In other words, to continue with this obsolete but convenient catch phrase, Bain referred to many mental states or psychoses without any mention of their associated neuroses. A conspicuous instance of this failure is supplied by Bain's treatment of the principle of association. This failure merits special emphasis because Bain's psychology may be regarded as the culmination of British associationism. He devoted more space to a discussion of contiguity and similarity—his two key principles—than any of his predecessors. The chapter dealing with the principle of contiguity covers close to one hundred and thirty pages, and that on similarity almost ninety pages. To summarize their contents is unnecessary. It will be enough to introduce his formulation of the "law of contiguity" as a means of illustrating the failure under consideration.

For Bain, all mental development or learning of any kind involves the operation of the law of contiguity. By basing his formulation of the law so as to include Sir William Hamilton's principle of redintegration, he was able to reveal its broad scope as the foundation of "mental science." His general statement of the law took this form (1868, p. 327):

> Actions, Sensations, and States of Feeling, occurring together or in close succession, tend to grow together, or cohere, in such a way that, when any one of them is

---

[12] This means that Davidson had as much justification for calling Bain an "originator" in this respect as John Stuart Mill had for calling Hartley the "founder" of association psychology and for calling his father its "second founder."

According to Herrnstein and Boring, Fechner was as much an "originator" in this respect as Bain. They have this to say about Bain's parallelism (1965, p. 593):

> He believed . . . that the parallel courses of mind and body are really but one stream that can be observed objectively as matter or subjectively as mind. Like Fechner, then, he was a metaphysical monist and an epistemological dualist.

Since epistemology is a branch of metaphysics, the latter sentence may prove troublesome. It would be less perplexing to say that Bain was an *ontological* monist and an epistemological dualist. Whether Bain would have approved of this as a correct characterization of his metaphysical position is hard to say. As will be brought out shortly, he advocated having psychology as science steer clear of metaphysical issues.

afterwards presented to the mind, the others are apt to be brought up in idea.

Although his entire long chapter on contiguity is devoted to elaboration of this law by rather detailed examples of its operation in daily life, there is no discussion of the neurophysiology of the law. One never learns about brain changes taking place when actions and states of feeling "cohere" or when something is "brought up in idea." Such changes should have been considered in Bain's treatise if it really deserved to be called a "thoroughgoing" physiological psychology. The neurological correlate of contiguity— his fundamental psychological principle—failed to be mentioned, and it is this failure that consequently stands out as a conspicuous example of failure to demonstrate the neurological process presumed to parallel an important psychological process.

Upon reconsideration, the foregoing argument appears to be little more than an elaboration of the obvious. Possibly it ought to be dismissed as a needlessly labored tour de force. It would have been easier and more direct to have stated that knowledge of brain physiology had not advanced to a level equal to the task of accounting for *all* psychological events with detailed specificity. It would be easy, for instance, to demonstrate that one man might know Swedish, be a bridge expert, and be ignorant of chemistry, while another man might know Chinese, be a chess champion, and be ignorant of bridge. Despite such striking differences in their respective kinds of knowledge and skill, no brain physiologist could detect these differences if he were to subject their brains to postmortem examination. This is just as true today as it was when Bain wrote his treatise and when Davidson wrote about the treatise. As sophisticated scholars, they must have realized that more is known about the psychology of thinking than about the neurophysiology of thinking. As a professor of logic and metaphysics, Davidson must have known that neither Bain nor anybody else could describe what went on his brain as he shifted from thinking about Plato's universals to thinking about Aristotle's syllogisms. If this be so, then what induced him to credit Bain with having applied "physiology in a thoroughgoing fashion to the elucidation of mental states?"

There is no way of knowing just how Davidson would have answered the question. Nevertheless it is possible to think of a plausible answer, since it might well be that the phrase "thoroughgoing fashion" as employed by Davidson was not intended to be taken literally as meaning giving due attention to the physiological concomitant of *every* mental state. Instead Davidson might have used the phrase to suggest a consistent readiness on Bain's part to consider such concomitants in the light of available physiological evidence, so that he had to be content with rather vague descriptions in some cases and complete silence in others. Thus, Bain's reference to the cerebral hemispheres as being "associated" with intelligence did not admit of any more "thoroughgoing" statement by way of showing how the cerebral tissues of bright people differ from those of stupid people. Similarly, although he could give accurate descriptions of contiguous associations, lack of evidence forced him to be silent on the subject of their neural equivalents.

This conjecture that Davidson in his use of the word "thoroughgoing" meant a *consistent* readiness might be a somewhat forced interpretation, an instance of reading more into a text than the author intended. In that case, it ought to be dismissed as unwarranted conjecture. It may, however, be neither a forced interpretation nor an unwarranted conjecture. At all events, in the same paragraph in which Davidson paid tribute to Bain for having been *thoroughgoing* with respect to the physiological aspects of psychology, he also wrote that Bain had *"consistently* advocated the introspective method in psychological investigation" (italics added). This is not very different from saying that Bain had been thoroughgoing in his advocacy of the introspective method.

Introspection as an Epistemological Issue

Bain's physiological psychology, it can now be seen, was also an introspective psychology. Endorsement of the scientific adequacy of introspection as a method thus rendered it unnecessary to supplement every introspective observation with some sort of physiological inference. The law of association by contiguity could be called a scientific law even though nothing was known about a parallel law of neural contiguity.

This concern with methodology, Davidson pointed out in his *Britannica* article, "gave scientific character" to Bain's work. Then he added: "In line with this, too, is his demand that psychology shall be cleared of metaphysics; and to his lead is no doubt due in great measure the position that psychology has now acquired as a distinct positive science." This meant that Bain was urging disengagement from metaphysical considerations for the establishment and advance of psychology as science. In doing so, he was differing from Herbart and Lotze, both of whom had included such considerations in their sponsorship of psychology as science. Accordingly, it is of more than passing interest to note that Davidson, the professor of metaphysics, appeared to approve of Bain's rejection of metaphysics and regarded such rejection as having enhanced psychology's status as a science. Since metaphysics is a branch of philosophy, this approval may be interpreted as approval of having psychology emancipate itself from its philosophic moorings. It meant approval of the effort to transform mental philosophy into an independent scientific psychology.

At the time Davidson was expressing approval of Bain's rejection of metaphysics, the validity of introspective observations had not yet been called into question. Its validity did not become the subject of serious controversy until the second decade of the present century with the rise of the behavioristic movement. Had Davidson anticipated this controversy, he might not have been so ready with his endorsement of Bain's position. This is so because the controversy involves an epistemological issue: Does the method of intro-spective observation supply scientific psychology with trustworthy data? To deal with this question is to deal with a metaphysical issue, since episte-mology is a branch of metaphysics. All arguments regarding the soundness of given scientific methods are thus embedded in an epistemological setting. To this extent they may be characterized as being metaphysical arguments, in one of the technical meanings of metaphysics. This, of course, is different from calling them ontological arguments. In short, both those who endorse introspection as a scientific method and those who oppose it are taking a metaphysical position, even though they may not realize it. In this restricted sense, Herbart may have been justified in what he had to say about the relationship between metaphysics and psychology as science.

From Bain's Treatise to Twentieth-Century Textbooks

Some twenty years after the publication of the first volume of Bain's treatise, Wundt's famous work on physiological psychology was completed. This was in 1874 and foreshadowed the later founding of the Leipzig laboratory in 1879. As a textbook of psychology it bore some resemblance to Bain's treatise, despite many differences. Both books stressed psychology as a science. They both reflected the viewpoint of psychophysical paral-lelism, and both presented this in terms of physiological findings along with introspective observations. In each case the student was introduced to a description of the nervous system before being introduced to consideration of more distinctively psychological issues. He was given to understand that such preliminary grounding in neuroanatomy would facilitate his subsequent grasp of the latter issues.

Many of the introductory textbooks of psychology written during the first few decades of the present century followed this general pattern of organiza-tion. A short introductory chapter would be followed by one or more chapters dealing with the nervous system as implicit preparation for the later chapters concerned with topics the reader had come to expect in a book on psychol-ogy—topics like perception, memory, reasoning, motivation, personality, and so on. Often, too, these topics would be discussed without any mention of concurrent cerebral changes. The chapter on reasoning, for example, would have nothing to say about the neurology of deductive thinking as con-trasted with inductive thinking. It was as if the chapter on the nervous sys-tem, with its references to neurones, myelin sheaths, and Brodmann's areas had nothing to do with the psychology of reasoning. Not very much has changed in this respect since James wrote his chapter on reasoning for the *Principles*. James devotes almost fifty pages to the topic but devotes a single paragraph to physiology of the topic, the upshot of which is a confession of ignorance along with a readiness to "bequeath the problem to abler hands than our own" (1890, Vol. II, p. 366).

As a matter of fact, James followed the precedent of Bain and Wundt in devoting the early chapters of the *Principles* to consideration of the nervous system and its functions. Chapter II deals with "The Functions of the Brain," and the next chapter is devoted to "Some General Conditions of Brain-Activity." Of the subsequent chapters there are some which have occasion to revert to these early chapters and others which ignore them. Like Bain and Wundt, James made an effort to introduce physiological considerations— even speculative ones—whenever possible. Often it did not seem to be possible and no such considerations would be introduced. In general, in this respect the *Principles* may be viewed as a late nineteenth-century transition to the previously mentioned pattern of textbook organization characteristic of so many of the textbooks written as introductions to scientific psychology during the early decades of the present century. The work by James is transitional in the sense that he was consulting the writings of both Bain and Wundt while working on the *Principles*. In fact, there are about twenty-five references to Bain and about thirty references to Wundt in the *Principles*. As a result of the prestige and influence of James, the neurological model that Bain had introduced in the 1850s came to be taken for granted as an acceptable textbook model for twentieth-century psychology.[13]

Virtually every early twentieth-century introductory textbook of psychology assured the reader that he was about to embark on the *scientific* study of mental life. This expectation was reinforced by more or less detailed descriptions of neuroanatomy and the structure of eye, ear, and other receptors. As introductions to psychology as a science, these books were following the general pattern already evident in Bain's neurological model of the 1850s.

Beginning about 1920, a reaction set in as the value for psychology of neurophysiological theories and concepts began to be questioned. Some were arguing for "purely behavioral" psychology while others were arguing for a "purely phenomenological" psychology. Disenchantment with the neurological model was also evident in the writings of psychoanalysts. They had nothing to say about the neural correlates of repression, of the superego,

---

[13] This applies to very many of the introductory textbooks written a generation ago as well as to some current ones. However, there were exceptions even in the early years of the present century. For example, although Titchener's textbook reflected hearty endorsement of Wundt's experimentally controlled introspective observations, it did not reflect endorsement of Wundt's physiological approach to the subject. There are no pictures of the brain and nerve cells and other neural structures as there are in Wundt's textbook. Neither are there brief verbal accounts of such structures. To understand the reason for these omissions, it is necessary only to recall this sentence from Titchener's textbook: "Reference to the body does not add one iota to the data of psychology, to the sum of introspections" (1917, p. 40).

of latent content, of sublimation, or of any other distinctively Freudian notion. Although most of them had received medical training, like John Locke they seemed to prefer not to "meddle with the physical consideration of the mind." All these departures from the Bain-Wundt-James neurological introductions to psychology gave rise to debate concerning an appropriate or satisfactory scientific model for psychology as science. In short, what Bain had started in the 1850s became the subject of controversy by the 1950s.

Concerning Bain's Influence

During the latter half of the nineteenth century, Bain's volumes on *The Senses and the Intellect* and *The Emotions and the Will* were widely read by British students of psychology. Until about 1900 his treatise was the standard text in England. Then it was replaced by Stout's *Manual of Psychology*. Each of Bain's volumes covers close to 700 pages and a digest of their contents is thus out of the question. They are replete with examples from everyday life, many of which may have some interest for the contemporary student. For instance, this is the way in which one approach to a theory of laughter was introduced (*The Emotions and the Will*, 1859, pp. 282–283):

It is commonly said that the ludicrous is caused by *incongruity;* that it always implies the concurrence of at least *two* things or qualities, that have some sort of oppositeness of nature in them. But the question comes, what kind of incongruity or oppositeness is it that inevitably causes laughter? A decrepit man under a heavy burden, five loaves and two fishes among a multitude, and an unfitness and gross disproportion; an instrument out of tune, a fly in the ointment, snow in May, Archimedes studying geometry in a siege, and all discordant things; a wolf in sheep's clothing, a breach of bargain, and falsehood in general; the multitude taking the law in their own hands, and everything of the nature of disorder; a corpse at a feast, parental cruelty, filial ingratitude, and whatever is unnatural; the entire catalogue of vanities given by Solomon,—are all incongruous, but they cause feelings of pain, anger, sadness, loathing, rather than mirth.

By way of additional illustration of Bain's apt use of concrete examples, the following excerpt from his discussion of the enjoyment of "muscular feelings" merits direct quotation (1868, p. 90):

In horse exercise, there is a large amount of the ingredient of activity. The rider is saved a part of the exhaustion caused in walking, and has yet exercise enough for the stimulus of the bodily functions, and for muscular pleasures.

The rocking chair, introduced by the Americans, who seem specially attentive to the luxuries of muscular sensibility, is another mode of gaining pleasure from movement. Anciently, furniture was adapted for the pleasures of repose solely, but now the boy's rocking horse has its representative among the appurtenances of grown men.

Some of Bain's insights and suggestions had a direct influence on later psychology. That James took some of them into account when writing the *Principles* has already been mentioned. Mention has also been made of Darwin's references to Bain's rather detailed descriptions of emotional expression and of Bain's subsequent critique of Darwin's three theories of emotional expression. Later efforts to explain why we blush, weep, laugh, tremble, frown, and undergo all the other kinds of bodily change incident to emotional upheaval have their historical roots in questions raised by Bain and Darwin. Incidentally, Bain is responsible for the term "tender emotion" as a designation for the emotional state aroused by "the helplessness of infancy, of age, and of the sick bed" (1859, p. 98). As mentioned in Chapter 13, (page 421), McDougall made this term familiar to twentieth-century psychologists by making it the affective concomitant of the parental instinct.

A more important respect in which Bain influenced the vocabulary of later psychology has to do with the phrase "trial and error" learning. Although Bain failed to employ the word "learning" in any of his chapter headings, he nevertheless introduced the topic in his chapter on "Constructive Association." One of his illustrations of such constructive association had to do with motor learning as exemplified by swimming. The beginner, Bain pointed out, usually starts with previously acquired voluntary control of arm and leg movements. His immediate task is to introduce a new combination of these movements. After repeated attempts he hits upon the "happy combination" and proceeds to practice it. After a more detailed account of the foregoing steps, Bain introduced this summary statement (1868, p. 572):

> In the full detail of Constructiveness, we shall have to exemplify these three main conditions: —namely, (1) a previous command of the elements entering into the combination; (2) a sense of the effect to be produced; and (3) a voluntary process of *trial and error* [italics added] continued until the desired effect is actually produced.

Another one of his illustrations had to do with verbal learning as in learning to find the requisite combination of words to express a complex thought. According to Bain, this would also entail constructive association, which he described as follows (1868, p. 574):

> It would thus appear, that the first condition of verbal combinations for the expression of meaning, is a sufficient abundance of already formed combinations to choose from; in other words, the effect depends on the previous acquisitions, and on the associating forces whereby old forms are revived for the new occasion. If a complex meaning has to be expressed, every part of this meaning will revive by contiguity and similarity, some former idea of an identical or like nature, and

ALEXANDER BAIN (1818–1903)

HAYIM STEINTHAL (1823–1899)

MORITZ LAZARUS (1824–1903)

the language therewith associated; and out of the mixed assemblage of foregone phrases, the volition must combine a whole into the requisite unity, by *trial and error* [italics added]. The more abundant and choice the material supplied from the past by the forces of intellectual recovery, the better will be the combination that it is possible for the mind to form by the selecting effort.

Bain thus appears to have been the first to describe both motor and verbal learning as a process of trial and error maneuvering. In doing so he might be said to have anticipated Thorndike's theory of learning as expressed in the law of effect. He actually used the word "effect" in the previously quoted summary of three phases of motor learning when he referred to "a sense of the effect to be produced." And in connection with his discussion of verbal learning he again alluded to the importance of this phase of the learning process. This is evident from what he had to say about the common experience of trying to find the right combination of words to express what one has in mind (1868, p. 574):

When there is not a sufficiency of forms within reach of the present recollection, the process of intellectual recovery must be plied to bring up others, until the desired combination is attained. A voluntary effort is quite equal to the task of cutting down and making up, choosing and rejecting, sorting and re-sorting; *the feeling of the end to be served* is the criterion to judge by, and when this is satisfied, the volition ceases, the stimulus being no longer present. In all difficult operations for purposes or ends, the rule of "trial and error" is the grand and final resort.

Originally the law of effect was known as the law of hedonic effect. In one of Thorndike's formulations, this hedonic aspect was preserved by using "satisfyingness" and "annoyingness" as synonyms for positive and negative reinforcement, respectively. The hedonic aspect was not overlooked by Bain, as is obvious from his references to a *desired* combination and to a *feeling* of the end being sought as the criterion to be *satisfied.* It is thus evident that Bain was describing trial and error learning in terms of hedonic effects. Accordingly, he may be thought of as a nineteenth-century Thorndike, or, if one prefers, Thorndike may be classified as a twentieth-century Bain turned experimentalist. In other words, Thorndike's famous description of a cat's maneuvers in the problem box is reminiscent of Bain's description of trial and error as "the grand and final resort" when confronted with "difficult operations."

A Note on the Chronology of the First Journals of Psychology

No summary of Bain's influence on psychology would be complete without mention of his role in starting one of the first journals of psychology. No science is likely to flourish without a journal, and Bain in his concern with psychology as science must have been well aware of this truism. At all events, according to Davidson (1910), as a result of Bain's initiative and financial backing a journal of psychology came into existence in 1876, when the first issue of *Mind* was published.[14] George Croom Robertson (1842–1892), a former student of Bain's and professor of mind and logic at the University of London, accepted the editorship of the new journal. As editor he gave somewhat more prominence to reports of psychological import than to articles dealing with more distinctively philosophical aspects of mind, though these were not excluded. Important articles of the former sort were contributed by men like Ribot, Ward, and Stout. (Incidentally, Stout succeeded Robertson as editor following Robertson's death in 1892.) William James also contributed an important article in the 1880s dealing with the initial formulation of his famous theory of emotion.

For many years *Mind* was the only British psychological journal. Then in 1904 another one, the *British Journal of Psychology,* was started with James Ward and W. H. R. Rivers as editors. During the intervening years other journals in other countries had begun publication. In Germany the work of the Leipzig laboratory was being reported in *Philosophische Studien,*[15] which Wundt had founded in 1881. Work from other German laboratories found an outlet in the *Zeitschrift für Psychologie und Physiologie der Sinnesorgane.* The latter journal was launched in 1890 under the auspices of Hermann Ebbinghaus and Arthur König. In 1895 Alfred Binet and Henri Beaunis founded *L'anneé psychologique,* France's first psychological journal, or the second if Ribot's *Revue* of 1876 be taken as the first. The first similar publication in the United States dates from 1887 with the appearance of the *American Journal of Psychology,* under the editorship of G. Stanley Hall. This was followed by the *Psychological Review,* the initial volume of which dates from 1894, with J. Mark Baldwin as editor. The field of abnormal psychology was represented by its own journal as early as 1905, when Morton Prince founded the *Journal of Abnormal Psychology.* In subsequent decades other fields of psychology followed this precedent by establishing their own journals to deal with problems of child psychology, animal behaviour, experimental procedures, personality, educational psychology, and other areas of specialization. Before long there were so many journals and bulletins in so many languages that a separate monthly,

---

[14] The year 1876 was also the year when Théodule Ribot (1839–1916) started the *Revue Philosophique de la France et de l'Etranger.* Ribot, as a close student of German and English psychology of the period, did not restrict the new journal to a review of philosophy. In fact, as noted by Merz (1965, Vol. III, p. 274), it began by "favouring the new psychology" in the early issues.

[15] In some ways this was a misleading title since the "Studien" reported in the journal tended to be more in line with the new psychology of the laboratory as contrasted with nonexperimental mental philosophy. In fact, Bain's journal, *Mind,* contained more "philosophical studies" than Wundt's journal.

Psychological Abstracts, was needed just to list the contents of this steady flow of periodicals. Thus, in considerably less than a century after Bain had promoted the first issue of *Mind* in 1876, there were more psychological journals in existence than any one person was likely to know by name. And unless he knew Russian, Polish, Japanese, German, and other languages he would have trouble in merely reading a list of all their names.

One reason for selecting the year 1876 as a point of departure in considering the subsequent mushrooming of psychological journals is that Bain is sometimes said to have launched the very first of these journals. Boring, for example, has maintained "that Bain founded *Mind,* the first psychological journal in any country" (1950, p. 236). Taken literally, this statement is to be questioned. It would be more in accord with fact to characterize *Mind* as one of the first rather than *the* first. Actually, a psychological journal was started by two of Bain's German contemporaries as early as 1859. This was the *Zeitschrift für Völkerpsychologie und Sprachwissenschaft.* As suggested by the title, it had to do with folkways, customs, ethnology, comparative philology, and what has now become the special interest of students of psycholinguistics. This *Zeitschrift* was founded by Hayim Steinthal (1823–1899) and his brother-in-law, Moritz Lazarus (1824–1903). They both were Herbartians in their approach to psychological and educational issues.

Steinthal was one of the leading authorities on comparative linguistics and lectured on philology and mythology at the University of Berlin. Among his writings was a book on the history of *Sprachwissenschaft,* or science of language, another on the classification of languages, and still another on some phases of African Negro languages. In the 1850s he spent three years in Paris studying Chinese and was thus able to add knowledge of one Oriental language to the knowledge of Greek, Latin, and Hebrew acquired in his youth. His co-editor, Lazarus, had majored in history and philosophy at the University of Berlin, where he obtained his doctorate in 1850. For some years he lectured on psychology at the University of Bern in Switzerland and later, from 1873 to 1896, he served as professor of philosophy at Berlin.

The journal started by Steinthal and Lazarus was relatively successful. By 1890 it had grown to twenty volumes so that their notion of *Völkerpsychologie* must have become increasingly familiar to their readers during the intervening years. In general, their notion might considered an early recognition of the importance of culture and group tradition in molding character, determining family organization, establishing religious rituals, setting standards of conduct, and preserving a people's social institutions from one generation to the next. Titchener referred to it as having to do with the "products of the collective life of mind" (1929, p. 103). And he had occasion to consider it in connection with a critique of Wundt's psychology; for the concept of *Völkerpsychologie* came to have great significance in Wundt's view of psychology as science. To consider it in the present chapter constitutes a digression. Consequently, its further consideration will be put off until the next chapter. But first it seems desirable to conclude the present chapter with a review of the salient features of Bain's career as a psychologist.

Summary Review

The following enumeration will serve as a digest of these salient features:

1. The successive editions of Bain's *The Senses and the Intellect* and *The Emotions and the Will* were intended to supply the basis for a psychology having "high scientific character."

2. In this connection the physiological foundations of mental life were deemed to be important; hence Bain's outline sketch of neuroanatomy, structure of the sense organs, and so on.

3. Attention was called to the psychological significance of experimental observations reported by men like Bell, Flourens, Weber, Du Bois-Reymond, and Helmholtz.

4. Bain objected to theories of cortical localization as expressed in the "new phrenology" or schematized in what Henry Head later dubbed the work of the "diagram makers."

5. With reference to the mind-body problem, Bain favored psychophysical parallelism as a working hypothesis.

6. British associationism culminated in the work of Bain and is reflected in his detailed elaboration of his two key principles: contiguity and similarity.

7. His law of contiguity was comprehensive in formulation so as to include the principle of redintegration and also to provide for more than ideational association by recognizing connections between ideas and actions, sensations and feelings, or between any discriminable items of experience.

8. Presumably to facilitate the emancipation of scientific psychology from its philosophic moorings Bain urged the avoidance of metaphysical entanglements.

9. The organization of his introduction to psychology served as a model for later textbooks.

10. Along with Darwin, Bain was one of the first to deal with the psychology of emotional expression.

11. Modern psychology is indebted to Bain for terms like "tender emotion" and "trial and error" learning.

12. In discussing problem solving by means of trial and error, Bain anticipated Thorndike's law of effect.

13. As a result of Bain's initiative and financial backing, the very first English journal of psychology came into being when Croom Robertson edited the initial number of *Mind* in 1876.

References

Bain, A. *The Emotions and the Will*. London: John W. Parker and Sons, 1859.

Bain, A. *The Senses and the Intellect,* 3rd ed. London: Longmans, Green and Company, 1868.

Best, C. H., and Taylor, N. B. *The Physiological Basis of Medical Practice,* 4th ed. Baltimore: The Williams and Wilkins Company, 1945.

Boring, E. G. *A History of Experimental Psychology,* 2nd ed. New York: Appleton-Century-Crofts, 1950.

Darwin, C. *The Expression of the Emotions in Man and Animals*. Chicago: University of Chicago Press, 1965. (First published in 1872.)

Davidson, W. L. "Alexander Bain," in *Encyclopaedia Britannica,* 11th ed., 1910.

Garrison, F. H. *An Introduction to the History of Medicine,* 4th ed. Philadelphia: W. B. Saunders Company, 1929. (Reprinted 1960.)

Head, H. *Aphasia and Kindred Disorders of Speech,* 2 vols. Cambridge, England: Cambridge University Press, 1926.

Herrnstein, R. J., and Boring, E. G. (eds.). *A Source Book in the History of Psychology*. Cambridge: Harvard University Press, 1965.

James, W. *Principles of Psychology,* 2 vols. New York: Henry Holt and Company, 1890.

Merz, J. T. *A History of European Thought in the Nineteenth Century,* 4 vols., rev. ed. New York: Dover Publications, 1965. (First published between 1904 and 1912.)

Meyer, V. "Psychological Effects of Brain Damage," in H. J. Eysenck (ed.). *Handbook of Abnormal Psychology*. New York: Basic Books, 1960, pp. 529–565.

Riese, W. *A History of Neurology*. New York: MD Publications, 1959.

Singer, C. *A Short History of Anatomy and Physiology from the Greeks to Harvey,* 2nd ed. New York: Dover Publications, 1957. (First published in 1925.)

Titchener, E. B. *Systematic Psychology: Prolegomena*. New York: The Macmillan Company, 1929.

Titchener, E. B. *A Text-Book of Psychology*. New York: The Macmillan Company, 1917.

23

Wundt and the Scientific Foreground

THERE HAVE BEEN incidental references to Wilhelm Wundt in many of the preceding chapters. Almost as if in anticipation of this final chapter, there was mention of Wundt in the very first chapter as "the greatest psychologist." That tribute, it may be recalled, was paid to Wundt by E. W. Scripture in the preface to his book on *The New Psychology*. At the time—this was in the 1890s—Scripture was at Yale, where he had started the psychological laboratory shortly after his return from Leipzig with a doctorate obtained under Wundt. Scripture's "new" psychology was the psychology of Wundt's laboratory, with its emphasis on the introduction of experimental methods in the study of mental life. This was an exciting innovation. At long last, psychology was to cease to be mental philosophy and was to emulate physics, which long before had ceased being natural philosophy. Scripture's tribute to Wundt as "the greatest psychologist" was an outgrowth of his Leipzig training. His hopes for the "new" psychology's future were a reflection of this training.

Scripture's tribute was very likely exaggerated. To avoid invidious comparisons and futile debate, it might have been better if he had called Wundt one of the greatest psychologists. In terms of impact on the history of psychology, it indeed seems safe to regard Wundt as one of the greatest. In fact, more than twenty years after Scripture had given expression to his tribute, E. B. Titchener, another of Wundt's doctoral students, gave eloquent testimony to this effect. According to Titchener (1921, p. 177), Wundt's fame will endure because "he established a new point of view and from it surveyed the whole scientific and philosophical domain. In this sense I am prepared to say that Wundt is the founder not of experimental psychology alone, but of psychology."

There is thus no question about Wundt's key role in promoting the idea of psychology as an experimental science. It was this phase of Wundt's teaching which Scripture had called the "new psychology" and which induced him to stigmatize nonexperimental psychology as "armchair psychology." In doing so, however, he disregarded another phase of Wundt's teaching, one that dealt with the quest for and acceptance of certain kinds of data even though they are not products of laboratory observations. The data of *Völkerpsychologie* mentioned at the close of the preceding chapter is a case in point. As will be brought out shortly, these data came to loom large in Wundt's view of psychology as science or *Wissenschaft*. The latter word, as explained in Chapter 21, has a somewhat different connotation from the English word "science" when used in the restricted sense of laboratory science or experimental science. Philology, archaeology, economics, sociology, and the history of medicine would not be sciences in this restricted sense, instead they would be *Wissenschaften*. Even though Wundt was the "founder" of experimental psychology, he was prepared to sponsor psychology as a *Wissenschaft* in terms of this broader connotation of the concept of science. This seeming paradox may be better understood when presented in the light of his professional background, out of which his sponsorship of a scientific psychology eventually emerged as the salient foreground.

Wundt's Professional Background

Wundt was born long before anybody had thought of psychology as a career, and he died when the choice of such a career had already become rather commonplace. This is another way of saying that he lived a long life. He was born near Mannheim, Baden, on August 16, 1832, and died near Leipzig, Saxony, on August 31, 1920, at the age of eighty-eight. His life thus began a decade before the birth of William James and lasted a decade longer. Whereas much is known about the early life of James and about his parents, comparable information about Wundt is meager. James has been the subject of several long biographies of interest to the general reading public[1] but the few books or chapters concerned with Wundt's life are not likely to arouse such interest. Wundt's biography has to be largely restricted to an account of his writings, because so little is known about his personal life, especially during his formative years. As for his father, we know little about him except that he was a Lutheran minister. This is in striking contrast to what has been written about the father of William James, the elder Henry, and also about his mother. Wundt's mother, like the mother of John Stuart Mill, has been overlooked by historians.

As Titchener said of Wundt, "We know nothing of the family life of his parents or of his schooldays" (1921, p. 162). More is known about his

---

[1] One of the most recent and most detailed biographies is the one written by Gay Wilson Allen and published in 1967 by Viking under the title *William James*.

university days. At the age of nineteen he enrolled at the University of Tübingen, where his uncle was professor of anatomy. This uncle may have acted as his nephew's academic adviser, since at this time Wundt showed more interest in pathological anatomy than in physiology. His interest in the latter field came to predominate within a year, when he had definitely decided on a career in medicine. This decision was prompted by the death of his father and the consequent need to select a profession likely to provide for his financial security. Actually, the prospect of active medical practice seems to have had less appeal for him than the prospect of studying the sciences embraced by the medical curriculum. In particular he found himself drawn to physiology as an academic subject, and at the end of his first year he transferred from Tübingen to the medical school at Heidelberg intent upon becoming a physiologist. With the exception of the second semester of his senior year, all of his medical studies were pursued at Heidelberg. This exception was an important one, for the semester was spent at Berlin and brought him into contact with Johannes Müller and other outstanding scientists of the day. Upon Wundt's return to Heidelberg in 1856 he received his medical degree, and the following year he was appointed *Privatdozent,* or instructor in physiology, and his academic career was launched.[2]

Even though Wundt had begun to publish the results of his research while still a medical student and had continued to do so at an impressive rate following his graduation, he failed to achieve the rank of full professor during his seventeen years as member of the Heidelberg medical faculty. For seven years from 1857 to 1864 he remained as *Privatdozent.* In the latter year he was promoted to the rank of *ausserordentlicher Professor,* or university lecturer, and remained at this rank for the next ten years. Then in 1874—he was forty-two at the time—he left Heidelberg to accept appointment to the professorship of inductive philosophy at the University of Zürich. He left Switzerland the following year and returned to Germany as professor of philosophy at the University of Leipzig, where he continued to serve for the next forty-two years until his retirement in 1917. It was his work during these four decades that gave him his assured place in the history of psychology.

By the beginning of his Leipzig professorship, Wundt had already shifted the focus of his scientific interests from physiology to psychology. As will be brought out in later sections, these were the decades when he became the

---

[2] Wundt's training and involvement in physiology are definitely established. What is not established is the source of his training in philosophy. Although he had a doctorate in philosophy, it is not known whether this was an earned degree, when it was conferred, or by what university. Titchener, who was well qualified to know about such matters, was constrained to write, "I do not know where or when the doctorate in philosophy was taken; I have been told that it was an honorary degree" (1921, p. 162).

Nestor of scientific psychology in general and of experimental psychology in particular. However, before considering the nature of his psychological activities both before and during these decades, it seems desirable to supplement this summary of his professional background by the addition of a personality sketch. This is akin to noting how he impressed those who came to know him as a person and not just in his role as professor and the author of a steady stream of technical articles and books.

Wundt as a Person

One of Wundt's contemporaries, Harald Höffding (1843–1931), lectured on Wundt's work as psychologist and philosopher at the University of Copenhagen in the fall of 1902. This was the opening lecture of a series dealing with some leading philosophers of the time.[3] Höffding, it should be noted, was the foremost Danish philosopher-psychologist at the turn of the century and thus well qualified to subject Wundt's writings to critical analysis and evaluation. A few of his comments about some phases of these writings will be mentioned in later sections. For the time being, it is more pertinent to call attention to what Höffding had to say about Wundt's personality which, as he stated, failed to be revealed in the writings themselves. Höffding added that those who had occasion to come into personal contact with him were affected by his "gentle warmth, manifest cordiality, and quiet enthusiasm for things intellectual" (1905, p. 7).

From the fact that Wundt wrote so much at such great length, one might have expected him to have been prone to dominate the conversation at informal social gatherings. Also, in view of the polemical nature of many of his writings, one might also have expected his talk at such gatherings to have been punctuated by eristic monologues. According to Titchener, who had been in close personal contact with Wundt, such expectations would not have been realized. This is what he had to say about Wundt as a person (1921, pp. 175–176):

> In personal intercourse he was unassuming, cordial, tolerant; by no means given to monologue; showing frequent flashes of a pleasant, wholly academic humor. There was no trace, as one sat with him in his study, of the roaring lion of controversy or the somewhat Olympian arbiter of science and philosophy. He disliked public ceremonies, and could not be persuaded even to attend a psychological congress, though when occasion demanded his public appearance he played his part with dignity and success. He also disliked traveling, and his

---

[3] These lectures were delivered in Danish. They were subsequently published in a German translation in 1905, and still later, in 1915, in an English translation. The present account is based on the German translation, since the one in English was not readily available. Incidentally, the last lecture of Höffding's series was devoted to William James.

holiday excursions never took him far afield. . . . Wundt lived the simple family life of the old southwest German tradition, a retiring, sheltered life, which was probably the one condition under which his tremendous self-appointed task could have been accomplished.

This "tremendous self-appointed task" marked a turning point in psychology's history. If successful, it meant that finally psychology was to cease to be a branch of philosophy and by adopting the methodology of science was to win recognition for itself as a member of the family of sciences. In the words of Höffding (1905, p. 12), "Psychology was to take its place among the special sciences . . . and was not to be counted as philosophy." The idea of this self-imposed task occurred to Wundt back in the 1860s during his Heidelberg days, when he was still thinking of himself as a physiologist. Its execution proved to be a complex undertaking spread over the more than four decades of his work at Leipzig after he had begun to think of himself as a psychologist while serving as a professor of philosophy. This duality of interests involved no conflict of interests. Like Herbart before him, Wundt could advance the cause of a scientific psychology and, without being inconsistent, could also be loyal to the cause of philosophy. In fact, he wrote books on philosophy as well as on psychology. This suggests that he thought of himself as being both a psychologist and a philosopher.

Wundt Both Philosopher and Psychologist

Wundt was still at Heidelberg when he wrote the first edition of what proved to be his most important psychological work. This was his *Grundzüge der Physiologischen Psychologie*. The nature of this work on physiological psychology will be discussed in a later section. For the present it is more relevant to note that Wundt was thinking of Herbart when he started the book. In the foreword to this first edition, which he wrote in March, 1874,[4] he expressed his high regard for Herbart as psychologist and as philosopher. This regard was to be stressed by way of offsetting the effects

---

[4] As noted in Chapter 4, Brentano's *Psychology from an Empirical Standpoint* was also published in 1874. Titchener once referred to both books as being of "first-rate importance for the development of modern psychology." He acknowledged psychology's debt to both authors for all that they did to promote "her place among the sciences." Moreover, despite marked differences in their views of psychology, Titchener noted the following points of agreement (1929, p. 6):

They agree that psychology holds a place of high importance in the fellowship of the sciences, and that it is logically prior to natural science. They agree that it may dispense with the concept of substance and confine itself to an account of phenomena. They reject the unconscious as a principle of psychological explanation. They define the unity of consciousness in substantially the same terms. So far there is agreement: and though the agreement is largely of a formal kind, and though a good deal of it has a negative ground in the reaction against Herbart, it serves nevertheless to mark out a common universe of discourse.

of the "polemic attacks" he had directed against Herbart. Moreover, he added, "Next to Kant I am most indebted to Herbart for the elaboration of my own philosophical views" (1902, Vol. I, p. vii).

For Wundt, the latter views continued to be important. His role as the champion of scientific psychology did not call for repudiation of his role as a philosopher. For him, the shift from mental philosophy to scientific psychology was not the equivalent of a complete rejection of psychology's philosophical heritage. In this respect he was like Herbart, Bain, and James, who also thought of themselves as philosophers as well as psychologists.

Wundt's students conducted their psychological experiments under the aegis of the philosophical faculty. Later on, as noted in Chapter 2, page 26, a generation of students began to enroll for the study of psychology in bifurcated Departments of Philosophy and Psychology. The bifurcation suggested a division of labor along with community of interest rather than two completely sundered academic households. To change the metaphor; the bifurcation was akin to an interlocutory divorce, with the final decree being signalized by the still later appearance of separate Departments of Psychology.

Whether Wundt would have been enthusiastic about the divorce is hard to say. The fact that he had his students publish their experimental findings as *Philosophische Studien* suggests no manifest intention to plan for one.[5] The issue is not a momentous one and need not be pursued. It will be more profitable to trace the emergence of his philosophical and psychological interests as shown in the chronology of his many publications. It will be enough to consider just a few of them, for there were far too many to list completely.

Wundt published his first paper in 1853 while still a medical student at Heidelberg. He was just twenty-one at the time. His last publication appeared in 1920, the year of his death. During the intervening years he kept writing articles, publishing new books, and revising earlier ones until the total output for one man in one lifetime reached staggering proportions. It is hard to believe that any one person has ever read everything that Wundt wrote. Boring once amused himself by calculating that Wundt wrote at the rate of "about one word every two minutes, day and night, for the entire sixty-eight years" from 1853 to 1920 (1929, p. 345).

An inspection of a list of Wundt's books arranged in chronological order reveals a change following the 1874 edition of the *Grundzüge*: those prior to and including 1874 dealt with physiology and psychology, and not until after 1874 did he write on logic, ethics, and philosophy. This division suggests that his concern with the latter fields were outgrowths of his ground-

---

[5] He might have entertained the notion years later. At all events, after the *Philosophische Studien* had appeared for some twenty years, Wundt started a new series in 1905, which was called *Psychologische Studien*.

ing in the former fields. Stated differently, he seems to have been first a physiologist and psychologist and then a philosopher, rather than a philosopher first and then a physiological psychologist. In this respect he and William James resembled one another. They both started as medically trained physiologists[6] whose books on philosophy came after they had written on psychology. It is thus likely that their psychology was less of a philosophical psychology than would have been the case had the sequence been reversed.

Concerning Wundt's Beiträge

Wundt's initial emphasis on a physiological approach to psychology was already evident some thirteen years before he joined the Leipzig faculty. This was marked by the publication in 1862 of a volume dealing with contributions or *Beiträge* to a theory of sensory perception.[7] The work as a whole has never been translated into English. In Titchener's opinion, the major portion of the book is not of psychological significance. However, he regarded the introduction,[8] dealing with the "methods in psychology," as "of solid and enduring interest" (1921, p. 163). Although written at a time when Wundt was still immersed in physiological studies, it foreshadows his preoccupation with psychological studies and is thus of more than passing interest for several reasons.

For one thing, Wundt was already thinking of an experimental psychology. In fact, as Titchener pointed out, it was in the *Beiträge* that the phrase "experimental psychology" appeared in print for the first time (1929, p. 5). It took the following form (T. Shipley [ed.], 1961, p. 70):

> The importance which experimentation will eventually have in psychology can hardly be visualized to its full extent as yet. We do have, surely, many noteworthy beginnings in the field of psychological investigations, but as a coherent science, *experimental psychology* still awaits its foundations [italics added].

---

[6] Wundt spent many semesters working in Helmholtz's physiological laboratory at Heidelberg, and James worked in Bowditch's laboratory at Harvard during the 1870s. In fact, according to Ralph Barton Perry, in the "autumn of 1875 James announced a graduate course on 'The Relations between Physiology and Psychology'" (1954, p. 142). This was some three years before he began to work on the *Principles*.

[7] The book was entitled *Beiträge zur Theorie der Sinneswahrnehmung*. As a result of its publication, Wundt's work on sensory perception became widely known. For example, James heard about it when he was in Berlin in 1867. In a letter to his father written from there he stated. "I think now of going to Heidelberg. There are two professors there, Helmholtz and Wundt, who are strong on the physiology of the senses, and I hope I shall be well enough to do some work in their laboratory" (Perry, 1954, p. 85).

[8] A translation of this introduction is now available in Shipley's *Classics in Psychology* (1961).

The idea of an experimental psychology was not original with Wundt. As was explained in Chapter 20, he was directly influenced by John Stuart Mill's *Logic* in his thinking about the methodology of science. Titchener called attention to this influence in his memorial tribute to Wundt when he stated that he had "no doubt of Wundt's indebtedness to Mill" (1921, p. 165), and then he added this important proviso: "Where John Mill theorized, Wundt performed; and the spirit of his performance has spread over the civilized world" (1921, p. 173).

Scientific psychology as it came to be envisaged by Wundt was not an exclusively experimental psychology. In his view, only the simpler mental process could be subjected to laboratory investigation. The more complex ones—the so-called higher thought processes—would have to be investigated by means of the methods germane to *Vökerpsychologie* as sketched at the close of the previous chapter in connection with the work of Steinthal and Lazarus. Although Wundt did not make this distinction explicit until the 1890s, he already had an inkling of it in the 1860s when he wrote the *Beiträge*. Writing as a young physiologist, he recognized that *Völkerpsychologie* "still offers a rich, open field, in which great preliminary works are already in existence, on linguistics, cultural history and the history of morals, but which as yet have hardly been utilized in the service of psychology" (T. Shipley [ed.], 1961, p. 55). Years later, as an old psychologist, starting in the year 1900 he managed to write ten volumes on the subject of *Völkerpsychologie* before his death in 1920.

In laying the groundwork for what was to develop into the "new" scientific psychology, Wundt also recognized the potential value of statistics for the future psychologist. By way of example, he mentioned the application of statistical methods for the investigation of "the more remote causes of suicide, by furnishing information concerning its occurrence according to age, sex, the national character and the occupation of the individual, according to the climate, the weather, the season of the year, and to many other external factors." And then, after mentioning another example, he concluded: "We can learn more psychology from statistical data than from all the philosophers, with the exception of Aristotle" (1961, p. 68).

Like Bain but unlike Herbart, Wundt regarded metaphysics as a hindrance to the promotion of a scientific psychology. As he saw it, metaphysics has more to learn from psychology than psychology has to learn from metaphysics. He was quite definite about this in holding that "psychology does not need metaphysics; but, on the contrary, at least in the entire domain of inner experience, metaphysics is in need of psychology for its firm foundation" (1961, p. 60).

Wundt ended his chapter on "Methods in Psychology" with an approving reference to Fechner's *Elements of Psychophysics,* which had been published in 1860. This was just two years before publication of the *Beträge*; hence it was a timely reference to what might be accomplished for psychology by experimentation and by measurement. Incidentally, Wundt had nothing to say about what Fechner had been trying to accomplish for metaphysics. There was no room for this phase of Fechner's work in his program for a scientific psychology. However, according to Titchener, Wundt was not yet thinking of such a psychology as an independent science. In the *Beiträge* he was writing about psychology from the viewpoint of a physiologist, and in doing so made "the mistake of supposing that psychology is nothing more than an applied logic" (1929, p. 5). But this "mistake" seems to have been corrected by 1874, when the first edition of the *Grundzüge* was published; for in the preface to this edition Wundt explained: "The work which I herewith present to the public attempts to mark off *a new field of science*" (p. v; italics added).

Shortly after the appearance of this edition, Wundt left Heidelberg for Zurich and then, in 1875, left Zurich for Leipzig, where he proceeded to cultivate the "new field of science" for the next forty years. Soon the promise of an experimental psychology as urged in the *Beiträge* became a reality with the founding of the Leipzig laboratory. Succeeding generations of students from different countries journeyed to Leipzig to learn the "new" psychology. They attended Wundt's lectures, worked in his laboratory, and studied his *Grundzüge*. The latter is a far more important work than the *Beiträge* and in large measure accounts for Wundt's eminence as a founding father of the "new" scientific psychology.

Concerning Wundt's Grundzüge

Some of the many students who journeyed to Leipzig to study the "new" psychology under Wundt's aegis became his disciples and upon graduation they followed his example by starting laboratories of their own. Thus many of the early psychological laboratories came into existence as a result of Wundt's influence, and their founders tended to endorse the kind of psychology they had studied in the *Grundzüge*.

That work constituted the standard textbook for Wundt's students. During the many years of Wundt's professorship, however, different generations of students were not studying the same textbook; like Bain's work on psychology the *Grundzüge* changed with successive editions. There were six in all, with the sixth appearing in 1911 in three volumes. The fifth edition, which had been published some nine years earlier, was also a three-volume affair. Only the first edition was limited to a single volume; the second, third, and fourth editions required two volumes. Evidently these editions over a period of close to forty years were major undertakings involving revisions of and additions to each preceding edition.

Unfortunately, none of these editions has ever been published in English translation. At least there is no complete translation of any single volume.

There is a translation by Titchener (1904) of a portion of the first volume of the fifth edition of 1901. Of the nine chapters in the original text, Titchener translated the first six. Consequently, the remaining three chapters and the other two volumes of this edition have never been translated. Translating all of the chapters of this edition would be a formidable task. Volume I contains 553 pages of which only the first 338 are available in English. The indefatigable Wundt kept adding more pages to the next two volumes, with 680 pages in Volume II and 796 pages in Volume III.

Anybody, reasonably conversant with the German language, who reads several pages in any of these volumes will appreciate the magnitude of Titchener's accomplishment and will also understand why he called a halt after the first six chapters. Wundt's sentences are long, involved, and somewhat cumbersome. Simple declarative sentences are conspicuous by their rarity. Titchener found Wundt's "use of connecting particles, of parentheses, of echo clauses" not only complex but "at times extraordinarily complex," and then he went on to say (1904, p. xi):

> Wundt's style has grown with the years;[9] it is his increasing tendency to clothe his ideas in conceptual garb, to write in a sort of shorthand of abstractions. I have never thought of him, for this or for the other reason, obscure; the meaning is always there, and can be found for the searching. But there are many and many passages where a halfway literal English rendering would be unintelligible; where one is forced, in translating, to be concrete without losing generality; and in cases like this the translator's lot is not a happy one.

Titchener's translation was not published until 1904, so that Wundt's nineteenth-century American students had to struggle with the German original. These were men like J. McKeen Cattell, G. Stanley Hall, Howard C. Warren, Charles H. Judd, George M. Stratton, and a few others who belong to the first generation of American laboratory psychologists. The majority of Wundt's students came from Germany, and for them reading the *Grundzüge*, although not easy, entailed less of a struggle than it did for their American fellow students. It is even possible that the young Germans who had studied English as a second language found the *Principles* of

---

[9] Titchener had firsthand acquaintance with these stylistic changes. While still at Oxford he had translated all of the third edition of the *Grundzüge*. After reaching Leipzig in 1890, he spent close to a year in revising this translation. Not until "the late summer of 1891" did he inform Wundt of what he had done. By that time, the fourth edition was already under way and Titchener's "manuscript was never offered to a publisher" (1904, p. x). He then translated the fourth edition, but before he could subject it to a final revision Wundt had already made substantial headway with the fifth edition.

From the foregoing it is obvious that Titchener had a good command of German even before he enrolled at Leipzig. Incidentally, according to Boring, who had been Titchener's assistant at Cornell, Titchener was a great linguist who "spoke well and elegantly in any of four languages, including Latin and Greek" (M. H. Hall, 1967, p. 65).

William James easier reading than the *Grundzüge* of Wilhelm Wundt. Wundt himself may have found this to be the case. At all events, Lincoln Steffens has reported an incident which renders this likely. He had spent the winter semester of 1890–1891 at Leipzig and did some work in Wundt's laboratory. While there he had the following experience (1931, pp. 149–150):

> One day when the good old professor was looking over us and our works, his . . . eye fell upon William James's great book on psychology, just out. . . . He picked up James, . . . and beginning at once to read, started off like a somnambulist for the door.
>
> Then he remembered, turned, and asked my indulgence. "Sie erlauben?" When I "allowed," he went on reading and walking into his own room. The next morning he came back, laid the book on my table, and thanked me.
>
> "You have read it?" I asked, astonished.
>
> "All night long," he answered. "Word for word, every word."
>
> And his familiars told me afterward that this was literally true. He had sat down with the book when he got it from me, read it word by word . . . and finished it the moment he returned it to me. As he was about to leave it with me, I stopped him with a question: What about it?
>
> "Well, and—?" I said, ("*Na, und—*")
>
> "It is literature, it is beautiful," he stammered, "but it is not psychology."

At the time this incident occurred, there was no one-volume edition of the *Principles,* so that Wundt's demonstration of speed reading was probably restricted to Volume I. There are close to seven hundred pages in this volume. If Wundt completed the reading in one sitting lasting twelve hours, he would have had to read at the rate of about one page per minute. Whether one can read "every word" of a page of James's text at this rate is open to question. And to read pages of the *Grundzüge* at this rate is out of the question. The work is neither literature nor beautiful, even if it is psychology—or psychology as Wundt saw it.

On Psychology Versus Psychologies

A phrase like "psychology as Wundt saw it" raises an important issue that Brett once connected with Wundt's approach to psychology as science. The issue, Brett pointed out, involves making a distinction between construct-ing *a* psychology and discovering *the* psychology. By defining psychology as the study of immediate experience, Wundt, as interpreted by Brett, was attempting to set the stage not for Wundt's scientific psychology but for *the* scientific psychology. Brett then went on to say (1921, Vol. III, p. 154):

> The distinction was subtle, but full of significance. The greatest condemnation that can be passed on a science is to make it the peculiar property of an indi-vidual; to speak of a psychology with the addition of its author's name as a sign

of its character is to relegate psychology to the sphere of inventions. If it can be made a science, these distinctions must disappear in the gradual evolution of the one and only psychology.

Another way of expressing this viewpoint is to say that as long as there are psychologies there can be no psychology, or as long as there are physiologies there can be no physiology. Theories may be designated by their sponsors, but not established fields of science like chemistry or astronomy. To refer to *a* psychology as Freud's or Jung's or Kurt Lewin's or John B. Watson's or that of any other leader of a school, system, or cult is not to refer to psychology as an independent field of science being cultivated by many but not owned by anybody. In Brett's apt phrase, a science can never be "the peculiar property of an individual."

It may be true, as Brett implied, that Wundt had no intention of claiming ownership of a psychological domain. If so, he failed; for the outcome of his labors continues to be called Wundt's psychology. But even though it was a failure in this respect, it was a success in arousing interest in and winning support for his efforts to promote psychology as science. Although the kind of experimental psychology Wundt brought into being is outdated, it continues to have historical significance because it supplied the impetus for the kinds of experimental psychology that have come to take its place. As much as any man, he helped to transform philosophical psychology into scientific psychology. The Wundtian orthodoxy is gone, but its devotion to the concepts and methods of science has helped to make contemporary psychology reaction-sensitive to such concepts and methods.

Why Physiological Psychology?

Wundt was uniquely prepared for his effort to transform mental philosophy into scientific psychology, or what he termed physiological psychology. Unlike Bain, he had firsthand laboratory experience; as he explained in the preface of the 1874 edition of the *Grundzüge*, he had repeatedly dissected human and animal brains (1902, p. v). In addition, he had a thorough grounding in the history of philosophy. This meant familiarity with the philosophical backgrounds of modern psychology, as is shown by the fact that the majority of philosophers mentioned in the preceding chapters are referred to from time to time in the pages of the *Grundzüge*. Plato, Aristotle, Hobbes, Descartes, Locke, Leibnitz, Wolff, Kant, and others are all mentioned in connection with various topics. Even though Thomas Reid, Donald Stewart, and Thomas Brown of the Scottish School are not mentioned, Wundt's allusions to the writings of David Hume, James Mill, and Alexander Bain may be regarded as evidence of knowledge of some phases of the Scottish psychological tradition.

In Wundt's opinion, his philosophical predecessors were not interested in psychology for its own sake. Instead, he noted, "Psychological inquiries have, up to the most recent times, been undertaken solely in the interest of philosophy" (1904, p. 2). This prepossesion is what he set out to change by writing a physiological psychology. Wundt's primary objective was to further the interests of psychology and not those of physiology or of philosophy. As he viewed it (1904, pp. 2–3):

> Physiological psychology is . . . first of all *psychology*. It has in view the same principal object upon which all other forms of psychological exposition are directed: *the investigation of conscious processes in the modes of connexion peculiar to them*. It is not a province of physiology; nor does it attempt, as has been mistakenly asserted, to derive or explain the phenomena of the psychical from those of the physical life. . . . As employed in the present work, the adjective "physiological" implies simply that our psychology will avail itself to the full of the means that modern physiology puts at its disposal for the analysis of conscious processes. . . .
>
> Since . . . the experimental modification of the processes of life, as practiced by physiology, oftentimes effects a concomitant change, direct or indirect, in the processes of consciousness, . . . it is clear that physiology is . . . qualified to assist psychology on the side of *method*; thus rendering the same help to psychology that it itself received from physics. In so far as physiological psychology receives assistance from physiology in the elaboration of experimental methods, it may be termed *experimental psychology*. This name suggests, what should not be forgotten, that psychology, in adopting the experimental methods of physiology, does not by any means take them over as they are, and apply them without change to new material. The methods of experimental physiology[10] have been transformed—in some instances, actually remodelled—by psychology itself, to meet the specific requirements of psychological investigation. Psychology has adapted physiological, as physiology adapted physical methods, to its own ends.

The method of experimental physiology that Wundt transferred to the psychological laboratory involved the control of stimulating conditions, careful observation of conscious processes aroused by specific stimuli, and, if necessary, due attention to bodily changes induced by the stimuli. This method called for *trained* observers competent to observe and report accurately. It also called for the use of calibrated instruments to govern the intensity and duration of tones or lights or other stimuli being used, as well as for the measurement of the speed of reaction. What changed an experiment from physiological to psychological was the observation and analysis of consciousness as an "immediate" experience. This was the crux of the experiment as a psychological procedure. In physiological experiments, on the other hand, interest in conscious processes was either nonexistent or

---

10 The text reads "experimental psychology" at this point. Reference to the German original shows this to be a typographical error, as is evident from the context.

secondary to the brain processes activated. This distinction constitutes an oversimplified digest of the difference between a psychological and a physiological experiment as viewed by Wundt.

In Defense of "Psychical Causation"

To safeguard the autonomy of psychology, Wundt warned against having psychology become subordinate to physiology by interpreting the phenomena of consciousness as caused by brain changes. For him, such an interpretation was tantamount to concern with a metaphysical issue, and he was adamant in his conviction that the scientific psychologist *qua* psychologist ought to avoid metaphysical commitments. Moreover, as he made clear in the following paragraphs, he considered that endorsement of the latter interpretation was tantamount to lapsing into a metaphysical commitment (1904, p. 9 and pp. 10-11):

> On this conception, there is no such thing as psychical, but only physical causation, and every causal explanation of mental occurrence must consequently be couched in physiological terms. It is accordingly termed the theory of "psychophysical materialism." . . . Yet after all, the assertion that there is no such thing as psychical causation, and that all psychical connexions must be referred back to physical, is at the present day nothing else than it has always been, a metaphysical assumption. . . .
>
> The effects of such teaching upon psychology cannot but be detrimental. In the first place, it conceals the proper object of psychological investigation behind facts and hypotheses that are borrowed from physiology. Secondly and more especially, it recommends the employment of the experimental methods without the least regard to the psychological point of view, so that for psychology as such their results are generally valueless. Hence the gravest danger that besets the path of our science today comes not from the speculative and empirical dogmas of the older schools, but rather from this materialistic pseudo-science. Antipsychological tendencies can hardly find clearer expression than in the statement that the psychological interpretation of the mental life has no relation whatever to the mental life itself, as manifested in history and in society.

In Defense of Psychophysiology

Wundt also objected to the antiphysiological tendencies of psychologists who "regard as superfluous any reference to the physical organism" and who "have supposed that nothing more is required for a science of mind than the direct apprehension of conscious processes themselves." In opposition to this view, he proposed to have physiology serve the interests of psychology "wherever the occasion seems to demand" recourse to physiological considerations (1904, p 2). The latter qualification indicated recognition of occasions when psychology might dispense with such considerations.

Apparently Wundt did not expect *all* conscious phenomenal and behavioral events to require consideration of their presumed neurological correlates. Neither did he think it necessary for the psychologist "to follow brain anatomy into all the details which it has brought to light concerning the connexions within the brain" (1904, p. 12).

Nevertheless, judging by the amount of space he devoted to the subject, he evidently expected the psychologist to be conversant with many of the details. Close to three hundred pages of the *Grundzüge* have to do with neuroanatomy and neurophysiology. More than a hundred figures illustrative of individual nerve cells, embryonic brains, adult brains, and cross-sections of brain segments are introduced. This is far different from the forty-three pages and five figures Bain had required for his discussion of the nervous system. Both men might be said to have set the fashion for later textbook writers whose introductions to psychology required the student to read about neural structures before coming to grips with more manifestly psychological topics. In doing so, however, the later writers tended to follow Bain rather than Wundt in terms of the amount of space devoted to physiological topics. To consider these topics in Wundtian detail would easily double the size of the average introductory textbook.

This amounts to saying that the neurological part of the *Grundzüge* was the equivalent of a separate volume. It covered the progress of nineteenth-century neurology and surveyed the status of the subject by the turn of the century. Unlike Bain's presentation, it reflected direct laboratory experience with many of the topics, along with direct acquaintance with relevant source material. There are references to Gall's phrenology, to the extirpation experiments of Pierre Flourens, to the cortical-localization studies of G. Fritsch (1839–1927) and E. Hitzig (1838–1907), to Sherrington's investigation of reflexes, to Ramon y Cajal's histological findings, to the neuron theory of Wilhelm von Waldeyer (1836–1921), and even to Freud's 1891 monograph on aphasia. Evidently Wundt expected students of the Leipzig brand of scientific psychology to have more than a dilettantish grasp of neurophysiology. Like some of his twentieth-century academic successors, he may have regarded such emphasis on neurophysiology as one way of impressing students that psychology had now become a scientific enterprise. At the same time, he was intent upon having them understand it to be a psychological and not a physiological enterprise. It was physiology in the service of psychology, and not vice versa.

Concerning Wundt's Grundriss

A somewhat different account of Wundt's view of the interrelation between physiology and psychology is given in his *Grundriss der Psychologie,* published in 1896. An English translation entitled *Outlines of Psychology* was made by Charles H. Judd (1873–1946), one of Wundt's students who brought the gospel of the new experimental psychology back with him to the United States and who, after early teaching posts at Wesleyan and Yale, moved to the University of Chicago, where he won distinction as an educational psychologist. In preparing the translation of the *Grundriss,* which was published in 1897, Judd worked in collaboration with Wundt to ensure its accuracy.

The *Grundriss* differs from the *Grundzüge* in its virtual neglect of physiological considerations. It has no diagrams or illustrations, and there are no verbal descriptions of neural structures, receptors, and other organic features. In this respect it is more distinctively psychological than the *Grundzüge.* As Wundt himself explained in a footnote in the latter work (1904, p. 12):

> In my *Grundriss* . . . in which I have attempted to give an elementary exposition of psychology so far as possible under the exclusive guidance of psychological principles, I have adhered more strictly to the systematic point of view. Hence the *Grundriss* may be regarded in this connexion both as supplement and as introduction to the present work.

As an introduction to Wundt's physiological psychology, the *Grundriss* presents his systematic psychology in outline. He explained that it was written in order to supply his students "with a brief manual to supplement the lectures on Psychology" (1897, p. v). Evidently a familiarity with the lectures is presupposed, for the exposition is terse and often devoid of clarifying concrete examples. Too much is taken for granted to make for ease of comprehension. Thus, it is not at all easy to understand just how Wundt intended to have psychology classified with respect to the family of sciences in general and with respect to physiology in particular. On the one hand, in a passage like the following, he regarded it as "supplementary" to the realm of natural science (1897, p. 16):

> Any particular fact can, strictly speaking, be understood in its full significance only after it has been subjected to the analyses of both natural science and psychology. In this sense, then, physics and physiology are auxiliary to psychology, and the latter is, in turn, supplementary to the natural sciences.

On the other hand, in this next passage he seemed to classify psychology as the basic mental science (1897, p. 16):

> As the science of the universal forms of immediate human experience and their combination in accordance with certain laws, it is the *foundation of the mental sciences.*[11] The subject-matter of these sciences is in all cases the activities

---

[11] The term "mental sciences" was Judd's translation of the word "*Geisteswissenschaften.*"

proceeding from immediate human experiences, and their effects. Since psychology has for its problem the investigation of the forms and laws of these activities, it is at once the most general mental science, and the foundation for all the others, such as philology, history, political economy, jurisprudence, etc.

According to these last two quotations, Wundt regarded psychology as indispensable for the cultivation of social sciences, and as being aided by natural sciences like physics and physiology as well as being a source of help to them. He also regarded psychology as important for the student of philosophy because both epistemology and ethics involve psychological issues. In fact, as he viewed it, psychology supplies the necessary introduction to the latter "two foundations of philosophy." All this is equivalent to saying that psychology is *fundamental* to the social sciences, *supplementary* to natural science, and *introductory* to philosophy. As the champion of the new psychology, Wundt was thus ready to fight for recognition of its importance to related disciplines as well as for its status as science.

Psychology as the Science of Immediate Experience

Wundt was especially insistent upon having psychology given first-class scientific citizenship. He wanted it to be classified as coordinate with and not subordinate to natural science. He saw the status of psychology threatened by those who assigned the investigation of *all* experience to the province of natural science. In his view, however, natural science is concerned with experience as divorced from the immediacy of personal awareness, and not with the totality of experience. It is a vast impersonal conceptual abstraction from *immediate* experience.[12] Furthermore, the study of immediate experience is the special province of psychology and as such cannot occur without an experiencing subject. Natural science eliminates the experiencing subject from consideration. It deals with light waves rather than sensations of color, with lacerated tissues rather than pains, with gastric contractions rather than hunger, and with vibration frequencies rather than tones. Colors, pains, hunger, and tones are directly experienced as familiar conscious events prior to the discovery of their physical and physiological correlates. In other words, without an experiencing subject —Wundt never refers to an ego—there can be no natural science. Subjective phenomena have to do with an experiencing subject. To understand

---

12 The phrase "immediate experience" is a literal translation of what Wundt referred to as *"unmittelbare Erfahrung,"* in contradistinction to *"mittelbare Erfahrung"* or "mediate experience." It is well to note that Wundt did not employ the word *"Erlebnis"* as a designation for experience in this context. The latter German synonym for "experience" restricts experience to knowledge of direct acquaintance, while *"Erfahrung"* goes beyond this by suggesting knowledge about as well. Thus, the congenitally deaf are limited to knowledge about the nature of sound by reading accounts of tones, noises, and related auditory phenomena. For them, the nature of sound can never be an *"Erlebnis."*

and define the nature of such a "subject" is the obligation of psychology. It was this contention which Wundt was ready to defend and which he believed to be threatened by attempts to define the "subject" in the language of natural science. He had this to say about it in a vehement indictment (1897, pp. 17–18):

> Instead of recognizing that an adequate definition of "subject" is possible only as a result of psychological investigations, a finished concept formed exclusively by the natural sciences is here foisted upon psychology. Now, for the natural sciences the subject is identical with the body. Psychology is accordingly defined as the science which has to determine the dependence of immediate experience on the body. This position, which may be designated as "psycho-physical materialism," is epistemologically untenable and psychologically unproductive. Natural science, which purposely abstracts from the subjective component of all experience, is least of all in a position to give a final definition of the subject. A psychology that starts with such a purely physiological definition depends, therefore, not on experience, but, just like the older materialistic psychology, on a metaphysical presupposition. The position is psychologically unproductive because, from the very first, it turns over the causal interpretation of psychical processes to physiology. But physiology has not yet furnished such an interpretation, and never will be able to do so, because of the difference between the manner of regarding phenomena in natural science and in psychology. It is obvious, too, that such a form of psychology which has been turned into a hypothetical brain-mechanics, can never be of any service as a basis for the mental sciences.

Psychology as the "Auxiliary" of Physiology

From the foregoing, it is clear that the *Grundriss,* unlike the *Grundzüge,* presented the student of the 1890s with an introduction to psychology that required no preliminary consideration of the essentials of neuroanatomy and neurophysiology. Presumably the student received an impression of scientific psychology different from the impression he would have received from studying the *Grundzüge.* That work made knowledge of the fundamentals of neurology important for the student of psychology, and many of the early chapters are devoted to a detailed review of these fundamentals.

In contrast, not a single chapter of the *Grundriss* is concerned with even a cursory review of these fundamentals. It was as if Wundt had lost confidence in the value of a neurological approach to the problems of psychology; hence his disparaging reference to "hypothetical brain-mechanics" and his readiness to subordinate neurophysiological data to what he came to regard as the-independent data of psychology. This amounted to holding that a scientific psychology could be developed without recourse to the standpoint of the physiological psychologist. Stated differently, this also amounted to saying that mastery of neurology would not suffice as a substitute for the study of psychology, any more than the well-trained psychologist can take the place of the well-trained neurologist even though there are circumstances when their respective spheres of activity supplement one another. Wundt accounted for the need for such reciprocal supplementation in this way (1897, pp. 10–11):

> Whenever breaks appear in the interconnection of psychical processes, it is allowable to carry on the investigation according to the physical method of considering these same processes, in order to discover whether the lacking coherency can be thus supplied. The same holds for the reverse method of filling up the breaks in the continuity of our physiological knowledge, by means of elements derived from psychological investigation. Only on the basis of such a view, which sets the two forms of knowledge in their true relation, is it possible for psychology to become in the fullest sense an empirical science. Only in this way, too, can physiology become the true supplementary science of psychology, and psychology, on the other hand, the auxiliary of physiology.

Psychology is seen as the "auxiliary" of physiology whenever the physiologist finds it necessary to appeal to the facts of immediate experience in order to explain the function of some specific anatomic structures such as the rods and cones or the taste buds or the organ of Corti. To do so, he refers to what he has experienced in the form of sensations of color or as gustatory sensations or as sounds and tones of varying pitch. Analogously, Wundt held, the psychologist has recourse to physiology in order "to formulate a theory of sleep, dreams, and hypnosis" (1897, p. 274):

Wundt on the Mind-Body Problem

The foregoing allusions to the relation between psychology and physiology reflect Wundt's effort to dispose of the mind-body problem. He even believed that the problem "never would have existed if the case had been correctly stated" (1897, p. 10). His own antimetaphysical formulation of the problem was intended to be such a correct statement.[13] This called for rejection of belief in mind as an immaterial something and of body as a material something. To entertain such beliefs, Wundt indicated, was to transcend experience by invoking unverifiable metaphysical postulates. As scientists, neither the psychologist nor the physiologist has any need for postulates of this sort. They both may rest content with facts of experience without being seduced by futile questions regarding the ultimate, nonexperiential nature of these facts.

Both deal with the same experience from different points of view:

---

[13] Wundt does not seem to have convinced himself that his "correctly stated" formulation had revealed the problem to be a pseudoproblem. Although he treated it as a pseudoproblem in the very early pages of the *Grundriss,* he treated it as a real problem more than three hundred pages later in a section dealing with "the question of the *relation of body and mind*" (1897, p. 316).

the psychologist treats experience subjectively from the viewpoint of the experiencing subject, whereas the physiologist treats experience objectively as divorced from the experiencing subject or as it is dealt with from the viewpoint of a physicist. Wundt thus appears to have eliminated Locke's secondary qualities from consideration by physicists, physiologists, and other natural scientists and restricted them to the world of primary qualities. On the other hand, the psychologist has to include both primary and secondary qualities in his consideration of experience. He deals with "the *total* content of experience in its immediate character" (1897, p. 4), while the natural scientist deals with the partial content of experience in its mediate character. In terms of this distinction, natural science and psychology are "both empirical sciences in the sense that they aim to explain the contents of experience, though from different points of view, still it is obvious that, in consequence of the character of its problem, psychology is the *more strictly empirical*" (1897, p. 6).

Wundt's disposition of the psychophysical relation in terms of a mere difference in viewpoint is reminiscent of Spinoza's double-aspect hypothesis. Wundt himself failed to note this. Instead, as shown in the following quotation, he saw himself as sponsor of psychophysical parallelism (1897, pp. 317–318):

> As a result of this relation, it follows that there must be a necessary relation between all the facts that belong at the same time to both kinds of experience, to the mediate experience of the natural sciences and to the immediate experience of psychology, for they are nothing but components of a single experience which is merely regarded in the two cases from different points of view. Since these facts belong to both spheres, there must be an elementary process on the physical side, corresponding to every such process on the psychical side. This general principle is known as the *principle of psycho-physical parallelism.* [14]

In elaborating upon this principle, Wundt stressed the fact that each side is governed by its own causal laws. Psychical causality is different from physical causality; hence the uniformities of mental life are not the same as the uniformities symbolized by the laws of physics. The causal laws pertaining to psychology reflect qualitative changes as contrasted with the quantitative changes illustrated by the laws of physics. Wundt attributed the former changes to psychical energy and the latter ones to physical energy. In other words, the quantitative effects belonging to physics have

---

[14] In view of what Wundt had to say about psychology as the "auxiliary" of physiology and of the latter as "supplementary" to the former, his endorsement of parallelism ought to be qualified. He appears to have considered it to be an *intermittent* parallelism, since he noted "breaks' in the flow of psychical processes along with "breaks" in the "continuity" of what is known about physiological processes. As Höffding (1905, p. 12) pointed out, parallelism was just a working hypothesis (*Hilfshypothese*) for Wundt and not a "final standpoint."

to do with "objective masses, forces, and energies" and the qualitative effects belonging to psychology have to do with "subjective values and ends" (1897, p. 322). By implication psychological laws are not reducible to physical laws, since each set of laws was regarded as a product of different kinds of energy. Consequently Wundt's parallelism connotes a dualistic interpretation. This means that his effort to free psychology from metaphysical notions was less successful than he seemed to realize.

He also failed to realize that in the very effort to avoid metaphysical commitments, he was concerning himself with metaphysics. For example, he evidently did not regard psychical energy as derived from some mind-stuff or what he called the "concept of mind-substance." He was explicit in rejecting the latter concept. Neither his knowing "subject" nor his concept of mind involved such a concept. The one concept he did adopt was that of "the actuality of mind" because, as he explained (1897, pp. 316–317):

When the concept of actuality is adopted, a question upon which metaphysical systems of psychology have been long divided is immediately disposed of. This is the question of the *relation of body and mind*. So long as body and mind are both regarded as substances, this relation must remain an enigma, however, the two concepts of substance may be defined. If they are like substances, then the different contents of experience as dealt with in the natural sciences and in psychology can no longer be understood, and there is no alternative but to deny the independence of one of these forms of knowledge. If they are unlike substances, their connection is a continual miracle. If we start with the theory of the actuality of mind, we recognize the immediate reality of the phenomena in psychological experience. Our physiological concept of the bodily organism, on the other hand, is nothing but a part of this experience, which we gain, just as we do all the other empirical contents of the natural sciences, by assuming the existence of an object independent of the knowing subject. Certain components of mediate experience may correspond to certain components of immediate experience, without its being necessary for this reason, to reduce the one to the other or to derive one from the other. In fact, such a derivation is absolutely impossible because of the totally different points of view adopted in the two cases.

Parallelism as a Metaphysical Issue

Whether, as Wundt believed, the foregoing defense of parallelism was devoid of metaphysical considerations is open to question. In replacing the "concept of a mind-substance" with the "concept of the actuality of mind," he was merely substituting a dualism of process for the dualism of substance. Moreover, in maintaining that the psychical and the physical are not to be derived the one from the other, he was revealing his endorsement of dualism. In doing so, contrary to his intention, he was giving expression to a metaphysical opinion, since questions of monism versus dualism are commonly classified as metaphysical questions.

Wundt was not alone in venturing to dispose of the mind-body problem in accordance with the principle of psychophysical parallelism; Bain had also believed that he was avoiding a metaphysical commitment in endorsing this principle. Furthermore, as brought out in the previous chapter, Freud is also to be listed as an endorser of psychophysical parallelism. All three men had studied neurology as well as psychology. Both Wundt and Freud, in the course of their medical training and subsequent laboratory work, had been concerned with problems of neurology before they became involved in psychological studies. And Bain, it will be recalled, although not a trained neurologist, had become familiar with the essentials of neurology by independent reading.

Bain, Wundt, and Freud can thus be said to have started their psychological work in the light of a prior interest in brain physiology. If they had found that a grounding in brain physiology sufficed to dispose of the mind-body problem, they would have become sponsors of a monistic epiphenomenalism. Their endorsement of a dualistic parallelism suggests that they failed to find such grounding to be the equivalent of training in psychology.

In the case of Bain's presentation of psychology, the majority of his many chapters made no mention of the neurological data contained in his introductory chapter. In the case of Wundt, his review of psychology as contained in the *Grundriss* failed to include a section on the nervous system. This omission was in striking contrast to the more than three hundred pages devoted to neurological issues in the *Grundzüge*. The *Grundzüge* suggests that knowledge of neurophysiology is essential for the training of a psychologist, while the *Grundriss* is reminiscent of Locke's statement to the effect that psychology can be studied without having to "meddle with the physical consideration of the mind." Finally, in the case of Freud, his endorsement of parallelism made it possible to develop a psychoanalytic psychology without having to "meddle with the physical consideration" of a tyrannical superego, a seething id, or an unresolved Oedipal conflict. Freud's famous and influential *Traumdeutung*, which was published in 1900, discussed the psychology of dreaming but failed to include a chapter on the neurology of dreaming.

It should be evident that by the turn of the century men like Bain, Wundt, and Freud, despite their prior interest in neurology and brain physiology, developed their respective psychologies more or less independently of the latter interest. Their endorsement of parallelism left them free to consider a given problem either from the viewpoint of neurology or from the viewpoint of psychology, as circumstances seemed to warrant. Wundt was particularly emphatic in arguing that this difference in viewpoint did not constitute a difference in scientific status. He was unwilling to regard a neurological account of some segment of experience as more scientific than a corresponding or parallel psychological account of the same segment of experience. Nor could one account be substituted for the other. At best they were supplementary or auxiliary, but never identical.

A simple analogy may help to clarify the stand taken by Wundt and other sponsors of parallelism in their efforts to safeguard the claim of psychology to scientific independence. Their general stand might be compared to the position of a specialist in the physics of sound who also happens to be a talented violinist. By hypothesis he would be having two parallel interests calling for separate cultivation. Were he to concentrate on music by preparing for a recital, he would be neglecting his laboratory research; and were he to concentrate on the research, his violin practice would suffer. Although related, the two fields of endeavor may be pursued independently. One can become an accomplished musician and be well versed in the theory of harmony despite being ignorant of physics, just as one may become a specialist in acoustics without having to graduate from a conservatory.

Had Wundt approved of this analogy, he might have stated that music is to acoustics as psychology is to neurology. In much of his writing, as in the successive editions of the *Grundzüge,* the neurological implications of the latter relationship continued to receive attention. In the successive volumes of Wundt's *Völkerpsychologie,* however, neurological implications tended to be ignored. There, Wundt was foreshadowing a later and still current polarization of attitudes regarding the nature of psychology as science. Those who view psychology as a biological or natural science (*Naturwissenschaft*) reflect the neurological orientation of the *Grundzüge,* whereas those who view psychology as a social science (*Geisteswissenschaft*) reflect the non-neurological orientation of the *Völkerpsychologie.* [15]

These antithetic orientations involve implicit metaphysical considerations whose existence may be overlooked or ignored by those contemporary psychologists who believe a scientific psychology must avoid metaphysical entanglements. In ignoring them, of course, they are following the anti-metaphysical precedent of Bain and Wundt without realizing that the very act of repudiating metaphysics presupposes a knowledge of metaphysics. For example, with reference to the antithetic orientations in question, the implicit metaphysical issue has to do with the monism-dualism dichotomy.

---

[15] At the time Wundt had started writing his *Völkerpsychologie,* or what Titchener called Wundt's "social psychology" (1921, p. 166), he was ready to classify psychology as a *Geisteswissenschaft.* This is evident from a passage that Höffding (1905, p. 11) quoted from Wundt's *Einleitung in die Philosophie,* published in 1901:

The single sciences (Wissenschaften) in the course of their development divided experience among themselves. They can be divided into three groups. Mathematics has to do with numbers, space, and movement. Natural science has to do with natural processes (Naturvorgänge) and natural objects (Naturgegenstände). *Geisteswissenschaft* is divided into psychology, philology, and history.

As Höffding noted, "Psychology had taken its place among the special sciences along with philology and history and was no longer regarded as a branch of philosophy" (1905, p. 12).

The neurological approach to psychology tends to be monistic, while the social-science approach tends to be dualistic. As an advocate of psychophysical parallelism, Wundt by using both approaches was thus not really avoiding a metaphysical commitment.[16]

Metaphysics in Contemporary Psychology

It may not be too much of a digression to note that psychologists of the modern era do not always succeed in avoiding metaphysical commitments despite their efforts to do so. Although they rarely give direct consideration to questions of monism, parallelism, and similar obviously metaphysical issues, they sometimes give them indirect consideration by allusions to concepts like *mentalism* and *physicalism*. Those who define psychology as the science of behavior take a dim view of "mentalistic" reports of conscious contents and of phenomenological descriptions of experience.[17] In calling such reports and descriptions "mentalistic," they are objecting to the animistic connotation they attribute to the doctrine of mentalism. In general, because of this connotation they would object to having psychology defined as the science of mind or consciousness. As they see it, words like "mind" or "consciousness" may be subtle synonyms for the word "soul" and as such may interfere with efforts to keep psychology within the realm of science to the extent that this realm is based upon concepts and methods germane to physics. D. O. Hebb is a contemporary exponent of this viewpoint, as shown in the following quotation (1958, p. 3):

> There are two theories of mind, speaking very generally. One is animistic, a theory that the body is inhabited by an entity—the mind or soul—that is quite different from it, having nothing in common with bodily processes. The second

---

[16] Modern philosophers, especially those who call themselves logical empiricists, have also concerned themselves with these issues. In general, they have tried to divest debates about these issues of metaphysical or ontological interpretations. An informative account of their efforts to bring the mind-body problem within a nonmetaphysical frame of reference has been written by H. Feigl and is included in the *Readings in the Philosophy of Science* edited by Feigl and M. Brodbeck (1953). Had logical empiricism been developed in Wundt's day, he might have joined the movement. His antimetaphysical strictures were certainly in harmony with the stand taken by logical empiricists. By the introduction of a few qualifying sentences, he might have succeeded in avoiding the suggestion of a metaphysical commitment to the extent that logical empiricists have done.

[17] This view is not to be confused with Wundt's view concerning the limitations of introspective observations. He warned against the introspective study of the higher thought processes; hence his objection to the Würzburg studies of judgment and thinking. Instead the view in question goes back to Watson's behavioristic attack on introspection as a method and on analysis of experience or consciousness as a goal. The issues involved continue to be the subject of controversy in current psychology. For details, see the articles by N. Brody and Oppenheim (1966), R. M. Zaner (1967), and M. Henle and G. Baltimore (1967).

theory is physiological or mechanistic; it assumes that mind is a bodily process, an activity of the brain. Modern psychology works with this latter theory only.[18] Both are intellectually respectable (that is, each has support from highly intelligent people, including scientists), and there is certainly no decisive means available of proving one to be right, the other wrong.

As a preliminary approach to the psychophysical problem, this quotation might have received Wundt's endorsement. Furthermore, despite the many decades separating Wundt from Hebb, some of Wundt's other views of psychology as science have not vanished from the current scene as viewed by Hebb. For example, Wundt stressed the independence of psychology as a separate field of study different from although related to neurology. Similarly, according to Hebb, "It will never be possible to substitute neurology for psychology" (1958, p. 265). In this connection he referred to "psychological entities" as being just as "real" as neurological ones; hence it would be wrong to say that "the study of the nerve impulse is a more scientific affair than the study of anxiety or motivation" (1958, p. 264). Moreover, in opposition to some behaviorists[19] he was willing to retain the concept of *consciousness* provided it is not regarded as "an attribute of mind and soul instead of a brain activity" (1958, p. 200). Wundt would have been ready to approve of the latter contention. As he made clear in the *Grundzüge,* the concept of the "actuality of mind" or consciousness is an acceptable scientific concept provided it remains uncontaminated by being linked to the metaphysics of a substantial soul.

Wundt would not have extended his concept of "the actuality of mind" to include the concept of an unconscious mind. This is another respect

---

[18] This statement is not to be taken literally as meaning an active interest in brain physiology by all "modern" psychologists. Many of them—especially the personality theorists—never "work" with physiological theories or neurological models. As yet there is no agreement among them with reference to an ideal theoretical model. An excellent introduction to this problem is to be found in the contributions to a symposium on "Theoretical Models and Personality" published in the *Journal of Personality,* 1951, *20,* 1–42. Hebb's contribution to the symposium supplies an elaboration of, what he means by the statement under consideration. His contribution (pp. 39–55) is entitled "The Role of Neurological Ideas in Psychology."

[19] Hebb prefers the term "behavioristics" as a designation for his approach to psychology. He objects to the term "behaviorism" because it is "often used to mean a particular kind of theory, which when first formulated denied the existence of mental processes entirely; behavioristics refers to a method of studying mental process" (1958, pp. 3–4). Evidently he has reference to John B. Watson as the one who "first formulated" the theory of behaviorism and who "denied the existence of mental processes entirely." Whether Watson actually denied their existence is open to question. His rejection of Wundtian introspections was not necessarily a denial of the existence of mental processes. He had no use for them in his behavioristic scheme of things, but ignoring something is not the same as denying its existence. D. E. Broadhurst (1961, p. 24) has alluded to this distinction in the following summary statement of Watson's proposal to have psychologists study human behavior by methods employed in the study of animal behavior:

in which he and Hebb appear to be in agreement. At all events Hebb, while recognizing the existence of unconscious and subconscious processes, warns against attributing them to "the unconscious" as "constituting an organized and separate agency" or as "a second mind whose contents are not accessible to the first or conscious mind" (1958, p. 203). For Wundt, such a notion of a mind within the mind was an untenable metaphysical assumption concerning which he had this to say (1897, p. 196):

> We can know nothing of an unconscious or, what amounts to the same thing for psychology, a material process which is not immediately perceived but merely assumed hypothetically on the basis of metaphysical presuppositions. Such metaphysical assumptions are obviously merely devices to cover up an incomplete or entirely wanting psychological observation. The psychologist who pays attention to only the termination of the volitional process, will very easily hit upon the thought that the immediate cause of volition is some unconscious or material agent.

Concerning Wundt's Voluntarism

Wundt himself paid a great deal of attention to the volitional process and made it a central feature of his psychology. Although he may be called a *structuralist*, in the light of the emphasis he placed on the structure or composition of mental content as revealed by experimentally controlled introspective analyses, he is also to be classified as a *voluntarist* in terms of his systematic psychology. Both his structuralism and his voluntarism were presented as congruent with the standpoint of empirical psychology, especially when viewed as an explanatory rather than a descriptive psychol-

---

Just as the rat is observed to turn into one alley of a maze rather than another, so one can study the movements of human beings and compare the results of experiments on them with those on other species. In neither case is there any need to drag in conscious experience. This attitude has sometimes been regarded as a denial of the reality of consciousness, but it is hard to find any statement by Watson which goes so far. All he said was that science, being a public process, must ignore private awareness and deal only with those data which are available to everyone.

Actually this issue is not of behavioristic origin. It goes back to 1904, some eight years before Watson's first public announcement of his espousal of behaviorism, when William James raised the issue in his famous essay entitled "Does 'Consciousness' Exist?" As has been noted in Chapter 9, James argued that consciousness does not exist as an entity or as some "aboriginal stuff" composing experience or in which experience is embedded. Instead in line with his doctrine of "radical empiricism" James defended this thesis (1912, p. 25):

Consciousness connotes a kind of external relation, and does not denote a special stuff or way of being. *The peculiarity of our experiences, that they not only are, but are known, which their "conscious" quality is invoked to explain, is better explained by their relations—these relations themselves being experiences—to one another.*

ogy.[20] A descriptive empirical psychology, Wundt noted, runs the risk of developing into a fallacious faculty psychology. It employs descriptive categories like attention, habit, and association, and then proceeds to treat each category as a force by referring to the "power" of attention or the "force" of habit or association. To replace this kind of empirical psychology, Wundt endorsed what he called *explanatory* empirical psychology, which he recognized as having developed along two different lines: either as *intellectualistic* or as *voluntaristic* psychology.[21] Intellectualistic psychology concentrates on the objects of immediate experience, whereas voluntaristic psychology is more concerned with investigating the "subjective rise of all experience."

Wundt objected to the intellectualistic approach, with its emphasis on logic, reason, and association of ideas, as too one-sided in its neglect of the affective and volitional aspects of mental life. In addition, he objected to its tendency to treat ideas as entities rather than as processes. For him, "the actuality of mind" was synonymous with a *process* psychology. After noting that "the psychology of immediate experience . . . tends toward voluntarism," he explained its relation to a process psychology in the following statement (1897, pp. 14–15):

> The concept of *process* excludes the attribution of an objective and more or less permanent character to the contents of psychical experience. Psychical facts are *occurrences* not objects; they take place, like all occurrences, in time and are never the same at a given point as they were the preceding moment. In this sense *volitions* are typical for all psychical processes. Voluntaristic psychology does not by any means assert that volition is the only real form of psychosis, but merely that, with its closely related feelings and emotions, it is just as essential a component of psychological experience as sensations and ideas. . . . In fact, immediate experience shows that there are no ideas which do not arouse in us feelings and impulses of different intensities and, on the other hand, that a feeling or volition is impossible which does not refer to some ideated object.

As just indicated, Wundt regarded feeling as a volitional process. Furthermore, since he thought of emotions as being feelings of greater intensity, both feelings and emotions were deemed to be volitional processes.

---

[20] As indicated in Chapter 2, there is a close relation between the descriptive and explanatory levels of science. See pp. 31–33.

[21] According to Höffding, Wundt acknowledged his indebtedness to Friedrich Paulsen (1846–1908) for this distinction between intellectualistic and voluntaristic psychology. In fact, in his *Einleitung in die Philosophie* of 1892, Paulsen has a chapter entitled "Intellektualistische und Voluntaristische Psychologie" (Höffding, 1905, p. 207). The second edition of Wundt's *Logic* was published a year or two later. In it, Höffding noted, Wundt "designated his conception of psychology as voluntarism, an expression which, according to his own statement, he had borrowed from Friedrich Paulsen who had introduced the term as an antithesis (Gegensatz) to the intellectualism of the older psychology" (1905, p. 20).

What he had in mind was the impulsive or conative aspect of feeling and emotion. An unpleasant feeling occasioned by a disgusting scene results in efforts to get rid of the scene, just as an unpleasant emotion such as fear results in efforts to flee from a terrifying object. Feelings and emotions as affections become volitional processes to the extent that they impel to or result in action of some sort; hence "a feeling may be thought of as the beginning of a volition" (1897, p. 185) and an "emotion . . . together with its result is a *volitional process*" (1897, p. 183).

In terms of this approach, Wundt's voluntarism might be said to have paved the way for the twentieth-century interest in the topic of motivation. Wundt himself recognized a dynamic or motivational psychology as implicit in his voluntarism. This is what he had to say about it (1897, pp. 185–186):

> Those combinations of ideas and feelings which in our subjective apprehension, of the volition are the immediate antecedents of the act, are called *motives* of volition. Every motive may be divided into an ideational and an affective component. The first we may call the *moving reason,* the second the *impelling force* of action. . . . The reason for a criminal murder may be theft, removal of an enemy, or some such idea, the impelling force the feeling of want, hate, revenge or envy.

Wundt also called attention to the fact that volitional acts prompted by the impelling force of emotion result in the elimination of the instigating emotion. Curiosity about the contents of a package vanishes with the opening of the package, and the feeling of hunger disappears after a full meal. According to Wundt, opening the package and ingesting food would be volitional processes having "the special property of *producing the external effect which removes the emotion itself*" (1897, p. 184). Figuratively speaking, emotions commit suicide as a result of their volitional consequences.

Herbart's Cognitive Dynamics Versus Wundt's Voluntaristic Dynamics

As conceived of by Wundt, voluntarism is not to be confused with the popular notion of will power. Such a notion attributes the initiation and control of action to "power" exercised by an autonomous *faculty* of volition. In agreement with Herbart, Wundt objected to this as a fallacious conclusion apt to result from a descriptive psychology that mistakenly regards a purely descriptive category like volition or attention as having explanatory value. Such a descriptive psychology results in tautological propositions to the effect that we can remember things because we have a faculty of memory or can carry out intentions because we have a faculty of volition. An explanatory psychology, Wundt held, is on guard against such propositions. Both he and Herbart, in their sponsorship of a scientific psychology, may thus be said to have rejected descriptive in favor of explanatory psychology.

Furthermore, they both developed dynamic psychologies along different lines: Herbart's was a cognitive or intellectualistic dynamics, and Wundt's was more of an affective or voluntaristic dynamics. They differed in other respects as well. Herbart relegated repressed ideas to the limbo of an unconscious, while Wundt rejected the concept of unconscious consciousness. For Wundt physiological psychology was an important field of investigation, while Herbart ignored physiological considerations. Analogously, educational psychology was important for Herbart but not for Wundt. Furthermore, Wundt's antimetaphysical scientific psychology was avowedly experimental, while Herbart's metaphysical psychology as science was nonexperimental. Finally, two Herbartian concepts that recur in Wundt's psychology are those of apperception and threshold, or limen. Wundt employs both terms in connection with the following account of the difference between the *clearness* as contrasted with the *distinctness* of apperception (1897, pp. 208–209):

> Clearness is the relatively favorable comprehension of the object in itself, distinctness the sharp discrimination from other objects, which is generally connected with clearness. The state which accompanies the clear grasp of any psychical content and is characterized by a special feeling, we call *attention*. The process through which any such content is brought to clear comprehension we call *apperception*. In contrast with this, perception which is not accompanied by a state of attention, we designate *apprehension*. Those contents of consciousness upon which attention is concentrated are spoken of . . . as the *fixation-point of consciousness*. . . . On the other hand, the whole content of consciousness at any given moment is called the *field of consciousness*. When a psychical process passes into an unconscious state we speak of its *sinking below the threshold of consciousness* and when such a process arises we say it *appears above the threshold of consciousness*. These are all figurative expressions and must not be understood literally. They are useful, however, because of the brevity and clearness they permit in the description of conscious processes.

Apperception as the process of bringing an object of interest into the focus or fixation point of consciousness involved active attention, and for Wundt this made apperception a voluntaristic process. Determining the number of words of Latin origin in the previous sentence would involve apperception in this sense. It would also serve to illustrate what Wundt meant by clearness and by the "special feeling" of attention. The phenomena in question might also be illustrated by everyday experiences such as planning a trip, deciding on an investment, or studying a blueprint. However, such illustrations would not have won Wundt's approval as suitable ways of obtaining satisfactory understanding of volition as a psychological process. His objection would have taken this form (1897, pp. 196–197):

> The exact observation of volitional processes is . . . impossible in the case of volitional acts that come naturally in the course of life; the only way in which

a thorough investigation can be made is, therefore, that of *experimental* observation . . . The experiments which serve this purpose are the so-called *reaction-experiments.*

Volitional Aspects of the Reaction Experiments

The reaction experiments, unlike everyday volitional acts, were simple enough to permit trustworthy introspective observation. Being experimental, the observations were made under controlled conditions for specific purposes by trained observers or subjects mindful of the importance of accuracy in the execution of laboratory assignments. Hence Wundtian introspections had nothing in common with the "morbid introspections" of psychiatric patients or the introspective reminiscences to be found in autobiographies. In other words, Wundt was mindful of the need for caution in the use of introspection as a scientific procedure. That is why he restricted its use to the simpler mental functions as contrasted with more complex ones such as the so-called higher thought processes. In the case of the reaction experiments, for example, in which speed of reaction to a given stimulus was being measured, the introspective task might have been limited to observing the mental process immediately preceding the execution of the reaction. The instructions given the subject called for depressing a telegrapher's key the instant a light was flashed, and the time of reaction was measured by a chronoscope in thousandths of a second. This experiment thus involved attention to the stimulus along with voluntary initiation of flexion of the finger poised over the key.

Both the nature of the task and the instructions given the subject were varied in different kinds of reaction-time studies, but there is no need to consider these variations here. It will suffice to employ the given example to show how in Wundt's opinion the reaction experiment served as a means of bringing the volitional process under observational scrutiny.

The time of reaction of a subject to a specific stimulus was found to vary from trial to trial, so that the final determination of his reaction time was expressed as the average of many trials or else as the shortest time in a series of trials. Similarly, a champion sprinter's time varies from race to race, with his shortest time being taken as his record for the given distance.

Various factors were found to influence reaction time. Among them, special importance came to be attached to the preparatory *set* of the subject. Just as a sprinter prepares for the start of a race not merely by getting "ready" but also by getting "set," so the experimental subject had to alert himself. To get "set" means to adopt an attitude likely to promote maximum alertness, as shown by the posture[22] of a crouching sprinter waiting for the sound of the starter's pistol. While waiting, the sprinter may be fixing his attention

---

[22] The close relationship between posture and attitude is reflected in the common phrase "strike an attitude" with its suggestion of a theatrical pose.

either on his tense muscles poised for a quick start or else on his anticipation of the pistol shot. The former suggests concentration on a muscular reaction and the latter suggests concentration on quick apprehension of an expected signal.

The subjects in reaction-time experiments reported similar differences in their preparatory sets. Some gave priority to optimal tension of the reacting finger, while others concentrated on the light signal. As a result of these introspective reports, a distinction was recognized between muscular and sensorial reactions. Since the muscular set seemed to result in quicker reactions than the sensorial set, the latter was taken to be more complex than the former on the assumption that it required a shift of attention from the signal to the movement. In the case of the muscular reaction no such shift would be involved, since attention was already directed upon the movement. As interpreted by Wundt, execution of the muscular reaction would be touched off by *perception* of the light, but the redirection of attention required by the sensorial set made execution of the intended movement follow *apperception* of the light signal.

The volitional factor involved in the reaction experiments becomes obvious in the previous allusion to the execution of an *intended* movement. In fact, as H. C. Warren suggested, instead of referring to the outcome as reaction or response time, it would be more accurate to call it *intentional response time* (1934, p. 224). In accordance with the experimenter's instructions, the subject *intends* to respond with a minimum of delay. This is his *purpose*, and he is well aware of it in the early stages of a long series of reactions. However, in the later stages following repeated presentations of the light stimulus, his reaction becomes more and more automatic until finally it takes place almost like a reflex response without awareness of either intention or purpose. What had started as a volitional process has been transformed into a mechanical process akin to a well-entrenched habit like smoking or swimming or even like the way some people say grace.

Instincts as Lapsed Intelligence

This transition from voluntarism to automatism loomed large in Wundt's psychology. In his view, it even accounted for the origin of reflexes and instincts; since as patterns of behavior, even though mechanically executed, they promote the organism's welfare. In the case of the scratch reflex, for example, it is *as if* the animal intends to remove a source of irritation. The cough reflex serves to dislodge a particle of food from the windpipe. Here too, it is *as if* the coughing is for the purpose of getting rid of respiratory distress. Similarly, in the case of instincts it is *as if* the complex behavior is intended to accomplish something useful or advantageous for the well-being of the individual creature or the species. The spider's web traps edible insects and the bird's nest safeguards the young.

Wundt was not arguing that the animal has any foresight of the ends to be accomplished by such instincts and reflexes. He recognized them as belonging to the organism's genetic endowment, ready to function automatically under appropriate conditions of stimulation. As *native* equipment, they were activated involuntarily rather than intentionally or purposively. To this extent Wundt was a nativist, but in his view of the phylogenetic origin of reflexes and instincts he was an empiricist.

He held that in the distant biological past these automatic patterns of behavior had not yet existed as fixed, stereotyped patterns. Instead they began as quasi-intelligent efforts to cope with crucial needs *experienced* by the remote ancestors of living animal species. The coping was assumed to have been a voluntary process—an affair of intention and purpose. Successful maneuvers kept being repeated and thus gradually required less and less intelligent choice and guidance as they became a matter of routinized habit. In successive generations the offspring of these coping ancestors were presumed to have inherited these habitual mechanisms of behavior.

As a possible explanation for the origin of instinct, this view came to be known as the *lapsed intelligence theory.*[23] Endorsement of this theory obviously meant endorsement of the Lamarckian theory regarding the potential hereditary transmission of some organic changes involved in the acquisition of acts of skill especially those which had become habitual. Wundt's own endorsement of the lapsed intelligence theory took this form (1897, p. 280):

> We may . . . explain the complex instincts as developed forms of originally simple impulses that have gradually differentiated more and more in the course of numberless generations through the gradual accumulation of habits that have been acquired by individuals and then transmitted.

At the time Wundt took this stand, Lamarckianism had already come to be questioned as a result of the experimental work of August Weismann (1834–1914), who by the early 1880s had given explicit formulation to his germ-plasm theory with its denial of the heritability of acquired characters. Since the preceding quotation was written some ten years after publication of Weismann's book on heredity, Wundt should have been familiar with it. James was familiar with it and mentions it with approval in the last chapter of the *Principles* (1890, Vol. II, p. 686). In fairness to Wundt, however, it must be granted that at one time Lamarckianism had won the support of eminent biologists. Darwin, for example, might have been cited by Wundt in support of Lamarck's teaching. In his book on emotional expression, which first appeared in 1872, Darwin's support is evident in a sentence like the following (1965 ed., p. 29):

---

[23] The British philosopher and essayist George Henry Lewes (1817–1878) suggested this term as a designation for this theory of the origin of instincts. In addition to Wundt, men like Lamarck and Spencer advanced the theory.

That some physical change is produced in the nerve-cells or nerves which are habitually used can hardly be doubted, for otherwise it is impossible to understand how *the tendency to certain acquired movements is inherited* [italics added].

By 1882, however, Darwin had ceased to be a Lamarckian. In that year, shortly before the death of Darwin, an English translation of Weismann's articles appeared in a volume entitled *Studies in the Theories of Descent,* to which Darwin contributed a preface. In it, in opposition to Lamarck, he no longer attributed evolutionary change to inherited habits but to random variation of germ-plasm origin. In short, by the 1880s both Darwinism and Weismannism were opposed to Lamarckianism; but a decade later Wundt was still a Lamarckian. And still later, as noted in Chapter 1, page 15, both Freud and Jung referred to phylogenetic inheritance as a product of ancestral experience.

Wundt as Ardent Empiricist

Wundt's continued acceptance of Lamarckian interpretations may have been due to his preference for voluntaristic and empiristic interpretations. The dynamics of reflex action and of instincts could be attributed to the genetic consequences of ancestral experiences. In accordance with this assumption, innate predispositions could be traced back to experiential factors and there was no need to transcend the realm of experience. As Wundt kept repeating, the basic difference to be considered was the distinction between immediate and mediate *experience.* The distinction was a fundamental principle governing his view of psychology as science. He gave it renewed emphasis toward the end of the *Grundriss* in these words (1897, p. 318):

> The psychological principle . . . starts with the assumption that there is only *one* experience, which however, as soon as it becomes the subject of scientific analysis, is, in some of its components, open to *two* different kinds of scientific treatment, which investigates ideated objects in their objective relations to one another, and to an *immediate* form, which investigates the same objects in their directly known character, and in their relations to all the other contents of the experience of the knowing subject.

In some ways this glorification of experience made Wundt, the German, as much if not more of a champion of the spirit of British empiricism than any of the British empiricists. As has just been indicated, he even ventured to account for reflexes and instincts as the results of phylogenetically determined experiences, thus converting nativism into latent empiricism. This made his empiricism more radical than the "radical empiricism" that William James came to sponsor.

James introduced the latter phrase in connection with a philosophic doctrine he came to espouse more than a decade after completion of the *Principles*. He developed this in a series of journal articles that Ralph Barton Perry brought together in a single volume called *Essays in Radical Empiricism* (1912). One of these essays has already been mentioned in a footnote on page 841.

Another of the essays is of particular relevance in the present context because it seems to suggest that in developing his doctrine of radical empiricism James was influenced by Wundt's voluntaristic empiricism. This essay, originally published in 1905, is entitled "The Place of Affectional Facts in a World of Pure Experience." At the beginning of the essay James stated, "There is no thought-stuff different from thing-stuff," and that "pure experience" as "the *materia prima* of everything" can be made to "stand alternately for a 'fact of consciousness' or for a physical reality, according as it is taken in one context or in another" (1912, pp. 137–138). This statement appears to be congruent with what Wundt had said about "*one* experience" being "open to *two* different kinds of scientific treatment," namely, as conscious content and as the mediate basis for the conceptual world of physics.

This apparent agreement between Wundt and James may be coincidental. Taken by itself, it is not sufficient to show that the radical empiricism of James may have been influenced, at least in part, by the voluntaristic empiricism of Wundt. However, support for this interpretation is to be found toward the end of the essay in a passage dealing with "affective values" and reading as follows (1912, pp. 151–152):

> It is by the interest and importance that experiences have for us, by the emotions they excite, and the purposes they subserve, by their affective values, in short, that their consecution in our several conscious streams, as "thoughts" of ours, is mainly ruled. Desire introduces them; interest holds them; fitness fixes their order and connection. I need only to refer for this aspect of our mental life, to Wundt's article "Ueber psychische Causalität," which begins Volume X, of his *Philosophische Studien*.

"Psychical Causality" Related to "Affective Values"

By implication James was thus approving of Wundt's concept of "psychical causality." This, as already explained, differed from his concept of physical causality, which he restricted to quantitative changes resulting from the utilization of physical energy. On the other hand, psychical causality was presumed to account for qualitative changes attributed to psychical energy involved in the realization of "subjective values and ends," or what James had called "affective values." In effect James seems to have regarded radical empiricism as being in accord with Wundt's treatment of experience in the light of a voluntaristic rather than an intellectualistic explanatory psychology. This amounted to a recognition of ideation, thinking, and other cognitive processes as related to the guiding influence of interests, desires, and similar conative factors.

It also amounted to implicit recognition of the significance and validity of Spinoza's emphasis on *conatus* in the instigation, regulation, and understanding of behavior. As mentioned in Chapter 13, page 414, Spinoza had pointed out: "We neither strive for, wish, seek, nor desire anything because we think it to be good, but, on the contrary, we adjudge a thing to be good because we strive for, wish, seek, or desire it." The *conatus* of Spinoza, the "affective values" of James, and the voluntarism of Wundt are different ways of calling attention to the dynamics of mental life as revealed in goal-directed strivings and their associated hopes, fears, yearnings, anxieties, and kindred shifts in feeling in the course of such strivings. All three men—Spinoza, James, and Wundt—might thus be said to have been sponsoring a dynamic psychology long before the term had been introduced. Furthermore, as has just been indicated, Spinoza had included the *wish* as a factor in the dynamics of striving. Students of Latin may detect the same factor in Wundt's voluntarism, since the latter word is derived from "*volo,*" meaning "I wish." And with the advent of Freud, the wish became the keystone of a full-fledged dynamic psychology.[24]

Wishes are obviously linked to preferences, hopes, and desired happenings or to things we value. They have to do with things we like; hence James would have described them as *affective* values just as Wundt would have regarded them as *subjective* values. As values, they involve things we strive to attain and about which we may have strong *feelings.* The close relationship between volitional and affective processes was not overlooked by Wundt. Consequently, an adequate discussion of his voluntarism calls for consideration of his treatment of affective processes as experienced in the life of feeling and emotion.

Concerning Feeling as Different from Sensation

Wundt recognized immediate experience or consciousness as a complex unity whose complexity is nevertheless amenable to analysis, just as a complex substance like sugar or bone is amenable to chemical analysis. Furthermore, just as chemical analysis depends upon recognition of chemical elements, so psychological analysis depends upon recognition of psychical elements. The former procedure reveals the chemical structure of objects, the latter procedure, in the Wundtian approach to psychology,

---

[24] The Freudian wish was probably a product of Freud's own insight and not an elaboration of Spinoza's *conatus* or of Wundt's voluntarism. There is no indication that Freud was familiar with Spinoza's work. Freud does mention Wundt's *Grundzüge* in the bibliography of the *Traumdeutung* and, according to Ernest Jones, he did read Wundt's *Völkerpsychologie*. But this was around 1910, after Freud had already developed his views on the dynamics of wishing (1955, Vol. 2, p. 251).

was intended to reveal the structure of consciousness. For this reason, Wundt's psychology came to be known as *structural* [25] psychology. Moreover, in line with this chemical analogy, Wundt referred to combinations of psychical elements as psychical compounds. The idea of an orange, for example, constitutes such a compound. As a compound, it can be analyzed into its constituent psychical elements in terms of visual, tactual, olfactory, and other sensations or their corresponding images. This would be one group of elements. Another group of elements has to do with the way in which we might be *affected* by the orange as an experienced object— how we feel about it. In contradistinction to the objective status of the former group of elements, the latter group consists of subjective elements. As Wundt explained (1897, p. 29):

> The subjective elements . . . are designated as *affective elements,* or *simple feelings.* We may mention as examples the feelings accompanying sensations of light, sound, taste, smell, hot, cold, or pain, the feeling by the sight of an agreeable or disagreeable object, and the feelings arising in a state of attention or at the moment of a volitional act.

Although, as Wundt stated, feelings *accompany* sensations, this is not to be interpreted as a causal relationship. Feelings are not *caused* by sensations, nor are feelings a species of sensation. Both of these opinions are false for the following reasons (1897, p. 37):

> The first of these opinions is false because affective elements can never be derived from sensations as such, but only from the attitude of the subject so that under different subjective conditions the same sensation may be accompanied by different feelings. The second is untenable because the two classes of elements are distinguished on the one hand by the immediate relation of sensations to objects and of feelings to the subject, and on the other by the fact that the former range between maximal differences, the latter between maximal opposites.

---

[25] Shortly after the turn of the century, structural psychology was often contrasted with functional psychology in a manner comparable to the distinction between anatomy and physiology. Later Titchener, the leading American structuralist, raised objections to both terms and hoped he had rendered them "obsolete" (1929, p. 178). He preferred the term "existential psychology" for the kind of Wundtian psychology he had brought with him from Leipzig and was fostering at Cornell. This early form of existential psychology is not to be confused with current references to existentialism as a philosophy or as a school of psychotheraphy. It has little in common with the teachings of men like Sartre, L. Binswanger, and Rollo May. Instead, for Titchener, the existential approach to psychology was the equivalent of a scientific approach in the sense that the "data of science . . . are bare *existences*" devoid of extrinsic meaning. For Titchener, the "tendency of the scientific man is toward the existential substrate that appears when use and purpose—cosmic significance, artistic value, social utility, personal reference—have been removed" (1929, pp. 32–33). (Italics added.)

The preceding quotation is evidently a summary of arguments Wundt had developed in a lecture and then condensed for inclusion in the *Grundriss*. As a result, the meaning of the condensation may not be immediately obvious. A few clarifying examples may facilitate understanding of what Wundt was driving at. With reference to his first point concerning the absence of a direct causal relationship between sensations and feelings, it is well to recall that a given musical selection may be pleasing as dance music, displeasing at a funeral, distracting when taking an examination, and distressing when one is trying to sleep. The attitude or subjective state of the listener rather than the selection per se determines the affective outcome.

With reference to the second point concerning the difference between sensations as such and feelings as such, it is well to call attention to two considerations. In the first place, sensations are usually localized, while feelings lack such localization. The yellow sensation of an orange is attributed to the surface of the orange and its tart taste to the mucous membrane of the mouth, but the pleasantness of the taste is just in us without being localized in any particular part.[26] The pain of an injured finger is located in the finger, but the unpleasantness of the pain is diffused throughout our being; hence Wundt's conclusion to the effect that sensations are related to objects or things while feelings are related to the experiencing subject.

In connection with the second consideration—the one having to do with maximal differences and maximal opposites—it appears that Wundt was thinking of the ordinary distinction between quantitative and qualitative differences and arguing that the former are more characteristic of sensation and the latter more characteristic of feeling. He may have been thinking of a long series of differently saturated red papers arranged in order from the faintest pink at one extreme to the reddest red at the opposite extreme. Under the circumstances the maximal difference would be a *quantitative* one, as shown by the *amount* of red pigment present in the first and last papers. On the other hand, in the case of feelings, an analogous arrangement obtained by recalling the difference between the feeling of being maximally excited and maximally tranquil is more of a *qualitative* difference. This example will be better understood by turning to one of Wundt's most celebrated theories, his tridimensional theory of feeling.

---

[26] The pleasantness may also be experienced as not entirely independent of the gustatory sensation but as an attribute of the sensation along with other attributes such as intensity and extensity. Such an affective attribute would be called a *feeling tone* of the sensation.

The Tridimensional Theory of Feeling

Just as the chemists of Wundt's era regarded chemical elements as irreducible units of chemical analysis, so Wundt regarded sensations as irreducible units of psychological analysis. As elements, they could not be analyzed into still simpler units, but they could interact with one another to form chemical and psychological compounds, respectively. Analogously, Wundt made a distinction between affective elements and affective compounds. Irreducible affective elements were called *simple* feelings.

It is easier to note and describe the varieties of sensation than the varieties of simple feeling. As Wundt pointed out, there is a paucity of words to refer to the entire gamut of subjective changes incident to the subjective life of feeling and emotion. This is in contrast to the rich descriptive vocabulary by means of which the characteristics of the objective word can be talked about. Words like "mauve," "cerise," and "magenta" serve to designate nuances of visual sensation, just as words like "hiss," "crackle," and "buzz" do the same for auditory sensation. There is no comparable refinement of verbal designations for the nuances of feeling states. However, Wundt viewed it as "a gross psychological mistake" to infer from this impoverished descriptive vocabulary that there are fewer simple feelings than elementary sensations. On the contrary, as he saw it (1897, p. 81):

> The variety of simple affective qualities is exceedingly great, much greater than that of sensations. This is due to two facts. First, every sensation of the many-dimensional systems belongs at once to several series of feelings. Secondly, and this is the chief reason, the different compounds arising from the various combinations of sensations, such as intensive, spacial, and temporal ideas, and also certain stages in the course of emotions and volitions, have corresponding feelings, which are . . . irreducible and must therefore be classed among the simple feelings.

The "many-dimensional systems" of cutaneous, visual, organic, and other sense modalities thus have feelings "belonging" to their myriad individual sensations as attributes or *feeling tones* of these sensations; but Wundt regarded it as a mistake to classify such feeling tones as sensations. Instead he classified them along with other simple feelings within the conceptual framework of three affective dimensions or directions. This framework or manifold of feelings, he maintained, is to provide for "a great variety of most delicately shaded qualities."

As a framework it was a conceptual scheme, just as a map is a conceptual scheme and not a photographic copy of geographic reality. A dot can stand for a city like London with its millions of residents, but the residents as individuals are not symbolized by the dot. As best the dot serves as a reminder of their residence as Londoners. However, thinking of them as Londoners is not the same as thinking of them in terms of their "delicately shaded qualities" of individual personality. The dot conceals more than it reveals.

Wundt's conceptual scheme was like a map or diagram of our feelings, even though he did not actually present a diagram in the *Grundriss*. Nevertheless, as will soon be evident, his verbal description of his scheme is such as to lend itself to diagrammatic representation. For example, he refers to "pleasurable and unpleasurable feelings"[27] as polar opposites of a continuum of change so that these might be shown as the end points of line representative of the continuum. Like the dot on a map these end points would stand for a multiplicity of different things just as a collective noun like "furniture" stands for a multiplicity of different things. Thus the "unpleasurable" end point would stand for every conceivable feeling of unpleasantness, with the understanding that just because each one is unpleasant it is not precisely the same as every other one. Losing a purse is unpleasant and so is the experience of being rebuked or having to listen to dull sermons or riding in an overcrowded subway. The list of such unpleasant feelings can be extended almost indefinitely. Even though they are all unpleasant and so have something in common, they may also be different from one another. This is akin to pointing out that chairs, tables, and beds are different from one another even though they have something in common in being articles of furniture. The analogy is misleading in at least one respect: articles of furniture are *things,* while feelings are *processes,* and being processes, they *proceed* in given directions. Wundt was very explicit about this when he wrote (1897, p. 84):

> We are never to forget . . . that pleasurable and unpleasurable . . . are not names of single affective qualities, but of *directions,* within which an indefinitely large number of simple qualities appear, so that the unpleasurable quality of seriousness is not only to be distinguished from that of a painful touch, of a dissonance, etc., but even the different cases of seriousness itself may vary in quality.

Wundt was also very explicit about having the end points or opposite extremes of the pleasantness-unpleasantness continuum regarded as collective nouns and not as the names of single feelings. Instead he wanted each name "to be looked upon as a collective name including an endless number of feelings differing from one another" (1897, p. 83). Analogously, he might have said, words like "height," "breadth," and "thickness" are collective names which include an endless number of specific dimensions

---

27 This is Judd's translation of what Wundt had called *"Lustgefühle" und Unlustgefühle.* A more literal rendition would be "feelings of pleasure and feelings of displeasure." At all events, it refers to the pleasantness-unpleasantness antithesis.

of an endless number of concrete objects. By means of these three continua of direction, the spatial characteristics of any particular physical object such as a room or a cube of sugar may be specified. Whether Wundt actually had this spatial analogy in mind in developing his theory of feeling is just a matter of conjecture. What is not conjectural is that in thinking about the "directions" taken by affective processes he also found them moving along three dimensions, and this observation resulted in the formulation of his *tridimensional theory of feeling*. It was first presented in the *Grundriss* and took this form (1897, p. 83):

> *Three* . . . chief directions may be distinguished; we will call them the direction of *pleasurable* and *unpleasurable* feelings, that of *arousing* and *subduing* (exciting and depressing) feelings, and finally that of feelings of *strain* and *relaxation*. Any concrete feeling may belong to all these directions or only to two or even only one of them.

Besides the total number of discriminable elementary sensations into which consciousness could be analyzed, Wundt had now recognized an even larger number of countless simple feelings as additional elements. These could fuse with one another and with sensations to produce a wide diversity of psychical compounds. It was as if a chemist had discovered a vast array of hitherto unknown chemical elements. However, unlike such a supposititious chemical discovery, Wundt's finding was not the outcome of experimental investigations. Instead it was largely the result of casual observations of his own affective experiences when subjected to reflective analysis. In this respect the theory was based upon empirical rather than experimental evidence. It might have been mentioned in Chapter 1 as an example of armchair psychology, at least in its inception. Later Wundt sought to get experimental support for the theory by having his laboratory investigate physiological changes incident to affective changes, with the expectation that a definite feeling of pleasantness and an associated shift in respiratory pattern would contrast with the pattern associated with a definite feeling of unpleasantness. Comparable respiratory, cardiac, and other physiological measures were studied as concomitants of the other two dimensions of antithetic groups of feelings.

As might have been anticipated, the findings were inconclusive: occasional results seemed to support the theory while other findings— especially those in other laboratories—argued against the theory. Actually, it is difficult to subject the theory to strict experimental control if such control be regarded as calling for the arousal of two precisely antithetic feelings. To cite a simple instance, how can the experimenter induce feelings of security and of insecurity of equivalent intensity? Precise measurement of feelings and emotions is thus fraught with major technical difficulties. As a consequence, the tridimensional theory became the subject of much controversy. The controversy was never settled to the satisfaction of all participants, and in the course of time what had been a momentous issue ceased to arouse the interest of later generations of psychologists.

But interest in the theory did not subside entirely. Some sixty years after Wundt had first advanced the theory, it was still taken seriously by some investigators. In connection with a famous symposium on *Feelings and Emotions* held in 1948 and published in 1950, two of the papers submitted reflected serious interest in the theory. Interestingly enough, they both found factor analytic support for the theory. In his paper on "Emotions and Sentiments in Recent Psychology,'" the Swedish psychologist John Elmgren made this quite clear (M. L. Reymert [ed.], 1950, p. 143):

> According to general principles we must, even now, following the lines of thought developed by Wundt, feel the necessity of characterizing the phenomena of affective life, from the simplest level to the most complex, as some bipolar structure which has been described by Thurstone and Burt in recent factorial studies. Let us try to revive the Wundtian affective theory by adding more components to it and after that try to make (upon a modern psychophysiological basis) an analysis of what components necessarily must be retained and what eventually might be left out. Starting from this point we may arrive at an objective basis for discussion of further classification of emotional experience.

The second paper in question was submitted by Sir Cyril Burt, the British psychologist mentioned in the preceding quotation. Burt's paper dealt with "The Factorial Study of Emotions," and in connection with the interpretation of some "primary emotional factors" as the equivalent of conative impulses or "forces" he observed (Reymert, p. 540):

> Something of this sort had already been suggested by Wundt, who argued that "the entire system of the feelings can be regarded as a three-dimensional manifold, in which each of the three dimensions includes two opposite dimensions." On this basis any complex state of feeling could in theory be re-resolved into three abstract *Faktoren oder Komponenten,* and these *Gefühls-resultante,* after the analogy of the combination of visual sensations in color mixture, as illustrated by the familiar *Farbenkugel.*[28] Applied to the classification of the emotions, Wundt's tridimensional theory of feeling led to a threefold scheme not unlike that set out above.

Burt's "threefold scheme" provided for a factor of "general emotionality" and for two bipolar factors. The general factor had to do with what

---

[28] Burt's interpolation of the German terms is based upon Wundt's presentation of his theory in the 1910 edition of the *Grundzüge.* The word *"Farbenkugel"* may be translated as "color pyramid" or "color spindle" or more literally as "color sphere." It refers to a tridimensional representation of all chromatic and achromatic sensations along the vertical and horizontal axes of a solid figure. The brightness dimension ranging from light to dark is located along the vertical axis, with the dimensions of hue and saturation indicated by polar coordinates intersecting with the vertical.

McDougall had regarded as a "common fund of emotional energy" and which Burt viewed as analogous to the notion of "general intelligence" advanced by some investigators of the nature of cognition. Just as people are rated as having a given level or degree of intelligence, so they were to be rated with reference to their level or degree of emotional energy. The two bipolar factors, on the other hand, characterized them with respect to *qualitative* rather than intensive aspects of emotional behavior. One of these involved a distinction between *sthenic* or overtly demonstrative emotional expression as contrasted with *asthenic* or more covert and inhibited manifestations of emotion. The distinction in question is seemingly not unrelated to Jung's extroversion-introversion dichotomy.

The second bipolar factor was based upon the common recognition of some emotions as being pleasant or *euphoric* and others as being unpleasant or *dysphoric*. As Burt noted, everyday allusions to the "contrast between the sanguine and the melancholy temperament" or the contrast between optimistic and pessimistic dispositions suggest popular recognition of this factor (1950, p. 541). These contrasts or antitheses, Burt warned, are not to be understood as referring to mutually exclusive distinct types of temperament. Instead, as polarities, they refer to the tail ends of normal distributions in the way in which tall individuals may be contrasted with short ones. Wundt also presented his antithetic feelings as end points of a continuum of change in the sense that pleasantness, for example, may vary in degree from maximal pleasantness to lesser degrees through a neutral feeling to incipient unpleasantness on up to maximal unpleasantness.

Although Wundt employed the term *"Faktoren"* in connection with his discussion of three dimensions of feeling, and thus was using the language of factor analysis, his theory had not been subjected to any statistical check. Indeed, the factor analysis had not yet been developed when the theory was first formulated. Moreover, Burt does not seem to have interpreted his factorial study as direct confirmation of Wundt's theory, and in planning his study does not appear to have had Wundt's theory in mind. It was only after an analysis of the results indicated a "threefold scheme" of emotions that Burt was reminded of Wundt's tridimensional theory of feeling. If feelings are fundamentally different from emotions, then Burt's study fails to lend support to Wundt's theory. Wundt, however, might have reached a different conclusion, in view of what he had to say about the difference between feeling and emotion.

On the Difference between Feeling and Emotion

To call attention to a close relationship between feelings and emotions is to call attention to the obvious. Recognition of the relationship is part of commonsense psychology. The conjunction of the words "feeling" and "emotion" came into existence long before psychologists existed. This suggests early recognition either of two related but different *kinds* of affective experience or of two related but different *degrees* of affective experience. Wundt decided in favor of the latter alternative. He noted that feelings of increasing intensity become emotions. Moreover, the transition is so gradual as to render it impossible to determine the precise moment of change from feeling to emotion. This, to quote him directly, becomes conspicuously evident in connection with feelings of rhythm (1897, pp. 169–170):

> Every feeling of greater intensity passes into an emotion, and the separation between the two depends on a more or less arbitrary abstraction. In the feelings that have a certain particular form of occurrence, that is *feeling of rhythm*, such an abstraction is strictly speaking impossible. The feeling of rhythm is distinguished at most by the small intensity of its moving effect on the subject, which is what gives "emotion" its name. Still even this distinction is by no means fixed, and when the feelings produced by rhythmical impressions become somewhat more intense, as is usually the case, especially when the rhythm is connected with sensational contents that arouse the feelings greatly, they become in fact emotions. Feelings of rhythm are for this reason important aids both in music and poetry for portraying emotions and arousing them in the auditor.

Since feelings differ from emotions only in degree of intensity of affective arousal, Wundt's tridimensional theory is as much a theory of emotion as it is a theory of feeling. In other words, like feelings, emotions may be characterized by all three or just two or even one of the three directions of change recognized by the theory. In extreme anger, for example, there may be feelings of unpleasantness, excitement, and strain. Less extreme anger may not involve any strain and be limited to feelings of annoyance and incipient arousal, while still less extreme anger may be restricted to the single feeling of unpleasant irritation.

As applied both to feelings and emotions, the term "tridimensional," as understood by Wundt, did not refer to the possible concurrent existence of three different affective states. Instead he maintained that at "a given moment only one total feeling is possible, or in other words, all the partial feelings, present at a given moment unite, in every case to form a single total feeling" (1897, p. 168). This fusion of feelings took place in accordance with what Wundt called the principle of *unity of the affective states*. By implication, he invoked the same principle in the following summary statement of two respects in which an emotion may be said to differ from a complex feeling (1897, p. 170):

> An emotion is a *unitary whole* which is distinguished from a composite feeling only through the two characteristics that it has a definite temporal course and that it exercises a more intense present and subsequent effect on the interconnection of psychical processes [italics added].

The phrase "interconnection of psychical processes" is another way of referring to ideational association; hence the latter quotation may be regarded as a reference to the influence of the principle of emotional congruity on the flow of ideas. Had Wundt cared to elaborate upon his statement, he might have said something about the way in which grief engenders sad thoughts or the way in which joy inhibits them. The flow of ideas as a "psychical process" is thus obviously governed by dominant emotions and prevailing moods; but this is not their only effect. Wundt also called attention to their effect on bodily functions.

Emotion as Bodily Commotion

Emotions are expressed by changes in complexion, in posture, in heart action, energy levels, breathing, digestion, and muscular control. Such widespread disruptive effects of strong emotion are common knowledge. Shocking news may result in feelings of weakness or even in loss of consciousness. Terror or violent anger may precipitate a surcharge of energy resulting in frantic efforts to flee or attack. All this renders the subject of emotion as much of a problem for the physiologist as it is for the psychologist. Nor is this truism limited to the subject of emotion. It also applies to the subject of feeling. At least it applies to Wundt's views of the problem, since for him the chief difference between a feeling and an emotion was just a change in the degree of intensity of the aroused affective state. Accordingly, he expected feelings to have some minimal effect on the bodily functions so manifestly, altered by strong emotion. He summarized his view of the problem in this paragraph (1897, pp. 171–172):

> The intensification of the effect which may be observed in the course of an emotion, relates not merely to the psychical contents of the feelings that compose it, but to the *physical* concomitant as well. For single feelings these accompanying phenomena are limited to very slight changes in the innervation of the heart and respiratory organs, which can be demonstrated only by using exact graphic methods. With emotions the case is essentially different. As a result of the summation and alternation of successive affective stimuli there is here not only an intensification of the effect on heart, blood-vessels, and respiration, but the *external muscles* are always affected in an unmistakeable manner. Movements of the oral muscles appear at first (mimetic movements), then movements of the arms and of the whole body (pantomimetic movements). In the case of stronger emotions there may be still more extensive disturbances of innervation, such as trembling, convulsive contractions of the diaphragm and of the facial muscles, and paralytic relaxation of the muscles.

Wundt interpreted these widespread bodily changes as expressions of emotions, with the implication that a distinction is to be made between an emotion as such and its physiological consequences or concomitants. The psychology of emotion was not to be swallowed up by the physiology of emotion. He objected to classification of emotions in terms of patterns of bodily changes by insisting that "the deciding characteristic for the classification of emotions must be psychological" (1897, p. 175).[29] In line with this emphasis on psychology, he relegated the bodily changes to a subordinate place by endowing them with the "important psychological attribute of *intensifying the emotions*" (1897, p. 177). Such intensification was not viewed as lending support to the Jamesian theory of emotion. On the contrary, in an obvious reference to the latter theory Wundt mentioned "the strange theory . . . that emotions are nothing but the results of expressive movements" so that "the emotion of sorrow, for example, is regarded as made up entirely of the sensations that come from the mimetic movements of weeping" (1897, p. 174). This "strange theory" was untenable because it equated emotion with bodily commotion. As Wundt saw it, this was tantamount to confusing an act with its consequences. It was akin to holding that because perplexity is expressed by a frown, therefore the frown and perplexity are identical. The act of perceiving the point of a joke may be associated with laughter, but this does not nullify the ordinary distinction between appreciation of humor and its bodily expression. On occasion people indulge in forced laughter to conceal their failure to understand the point of a joke. These reminders should suffice to explain why Wundt regarded James as having sponsored a "strange theory."

The preceding reminders with their allusions to perplexity, appreciation of humor, and forced laughter may also serve to explain why Wundt was unwilling to have the psychology of emotion reduced to the physiology of emotion. The realm of psychology as a separate field of scientific investigation was not to be usurped by the brain physiologist. Wundt made this clear in the 1874 edition of his *Grundzüge* when he wrote, "Physiological psychology . . . if first of all *psychology*." This stand received additional clarification and emphasis in the 1896 edition of the *Grundriss* when he ventured to formulate laws of psychology as different from the laws of physiology.

---

[29] The classification of emotions is a persistent problem in the history of psychology. It has been touched upon in earlier chapters when attention was called to the classifications proposed by Descartes and by Spinoza in the seventeenth century and by McDougall in the twentieth. An elaborate and provocative classification was proposed in a work published in 1888 by Cardinal Mercier of Belgium (1851–1926). Like Freud, he had studied under Charcot in Paris. Later he became a professor of philosophy at the University of Louvain, where he taught psychology. His classification of feelings and emotions is presented in an interesting and detailed outline on pp. 330–337 of *Introduction to Psychology*, by C. E. Seashore (1866–1949). For a contemporary discussion of some aspects of this problem see the article by Peters on "Affect and Emotion" (M. H. Marx [ed.], 1964).

Wundt on the "Fundamental Laws of Psychical Phenomena"

Titchener wrote, "Wundt's whole thought centres about psychology and that he therefore sees the other sciences always in their elation to psychology" (1929, p. 113). It is entirely likely that Wundt saw a special relation between chemistry and psychology. At all events there is an obvious analogy between his view of the nature of psychological analysis and the ordinary nineteenth-century view of chemical analysis. In place of chemical elements, Wundt referred to psychical elements. In fact, the sequence of topics as presented in the *Grundriss* was somewhat reminiscent of the sequence found in textbooks of chemistry. The sequence went from elements to compounds, from compounds to the "interconnection of psychic compounds," and from the latter to "psychical causality and its laws."

Wundt held that the connection between these elements and compounds can only be understood "through *psychological* analysis in the same way that objective phenomena, such as those of weight, sound, light, heat, etc., or the processes of the nervous system, can be approached only by physical and physiological analysis." He then, as shown in the following paragraph, pointed out that adoption of the principle of parallelism gives rise to two different kinds of causal relations inherent in these two kinds of analysis (1897, p. 320):

> Thus, the principle of psycho-physical parallelism . . . leads necessarily to the recognition of an *independent psychical causality*, which is related at all points with physical causality and can never come into contradiction with it, but is just as different from this physical causality as the point of view adopted in psychology, or that of immediate, subjective experience, is different from the point of view taken in the natural sciences, or that of mediate, objective experience due to abstraction. And just as the nature of physical causality can be revealed to us only in the fundamental *laws of nature,* so the only way that we have of accounting for the characteristics of psychical causality is to abstract certain *fundamental laws of psychical phenomena* from the totality of psychical processes. We may distinguish *two* classes of such laws. The laws of one class show themselves primarily in the processes which condition the rise and immediate interaction of the psychical compounds; we call these the *psychological laws of relation*. Those of the second class are derived laws. They consist in the complex effects that are produced by combinations of the laws of relation within more extensive series of psychical facts; these we shall call the *psychological laws of development*.

All these laws could be subsumed under Wundt's basic concept of psychical causality. This differed from physical causality in being restricted to the phenomenal world of immediate experience—to the continuing flow of ideas and feelings as mental processes. Moreover, to revert to an earlier point, unlike physical causality, psychical causality is a voluntaristic process related to the "affective values" of James and the "basic *conatus*" of Spinoza.

As a voluntaristic process, psychical causality involves what Wundt referred to as "the concepts of value and end" (1897, p. 319). In the German original Wundt employed the word "*Zweck*" for the word "end" in the latter phrase. The German word also means "purpose," as the object or aim of striving; hence it might come closer to Wundt's notion of psychical causality to say that it involved the concepts of "value and purpose." Interest and desire are determinants or causes of the directions taken by the trains of thought, the quest for information, and mental development in general.

Wundt's psychical causality as a voluntaristic process involving the *actuality* of mind can thus be understood as recognition of the underlying *lawfulness* of the ceaseless flow of phenomenal events. His two classes of psychological laws gave direct expression to this lawfulness. Furthermore, in view of the relationship between Wundt's voluntarism and Spinoza's *conatus,* it is tempting to think of Wundt's psychological laws as a nineteenth-century justification for Spinoza's seventeenth-century confidence in the existence of "sure mental laws." Just as Wundt considered psychical causality to be "related at all points with physical causality," so, it may be recalled, Spinoza considered "the order and connection of ideas" to be "the same as the order and connection of things." Both the concepts of causality and of order suggest the kind of dependable regularity that gets to be formulated as a scientific law.

Until such laws are discovered, no field of human endeavor can be said to have achieved full-fledged scientific status. Wundt, of course, was well aware of this truism, and seemed to take it for granted in his effort to win recognition for psychology as an autonomous field of science. His "new" experimentally grounded scientific psychology was not to be an offshoot of physics; hence his distinction between physical causality and "an independent psychical causality."

Wundt was able "to abstract" six "fundamental laws of psychical phenomena" from the "psychical" mode of causality. Three of these were classified as laws of relation and the remaining three were classified as laws of development. Since the latter three presuppose the former three, the laws of relation have to be given prior consideration.

Laws of Relation

Among the laws of relation, the best known is the *law of psychic resultants*. Wundt also referred to this law as the *principle of creative synthesis*. As such it was analogous to the familiar chemical synthesis of two or more elements into a compound whose resultant characteristics are different from those of the constituent elements. Similarly, Wundt's law was illustrated by the results of combining two or more mental elements into a psychical compound. Here too, he noted, the emergent compound is different from the mere sum of the attributes of its component elements. For example, the delight occasioned by a pleasing melody is not to be accounted for by summation of the feeling tone of each constituent note sounded by itself. The affective outcome might even be displeasing were the same notes to be rearranged to form a different melody. This example serves not only to show the meaning of creative synthesis but also to show why, as contrasted with physical causality, Wundt perceived psychical causality as involving values experienced and ends or purposes realized.

The principle of creative synthesis is obviously just another way of referring to what Thomas Brown and John Stuart Mill had called "mental chemistry." Wundt, however, does not seem to have been indebted to them for the concept in general and for its relation to psychical causality in particular. According to his own report, as cited by J. T. Merz (1965, Vol. III, p. 595), Wundt traced the origin of his recognition of the principle to the year 1858 or 1859, when he was conducting his physiological investigations of visual sensations as subsequently published in the *Beiträge*. He was working on a theory of visual perception as influenced by "complex local signs" when, Wundt wrote, he realized that he had "to do with a process which was fully intelligible through its elements, but which was nevertheless, compared with them something new,—a creative synthesis of these elements. And so this simple process of perception seemed to me to throw a clear light on the essence of psychical processes in general, &c."

As a supplement to the law of creative synthesis, Wundt introduced a separate law concerned with the analysis of mental content. He called this the law of *psychic relations*. It is concerned with the problem of meaning or the significance of a particular item of mental content, and it calls attention to the fact that meaning is *related* to context. For example, the word "content" in the previous sentence has a different significance in a sentence like "He is *content* to live on the farm." In turn, its meaning in the latter sentence is different from its meaning in a sentence like "The word 'content' is of Latin origin." To appreciate the difference in the meaning of the word in these last two sample sentences, Wundt would have argued, it is necessary "to apperceive" the key word both clearly and distinctly. The relationship between clearness and distinctness to apperception has already been considered in a previous section (see page 844). As applied to the present instance, it is to be noted that at first inspection the word "content" stands out *clearly* in each sentence, and then, when the process of active attention or "apperceptive analysis" reveals the word to be a verb in the one sentence and a noun in the other, the difference in meaning stands out *distinctly*. This somewhat oversimplified example may suffice as an introduction to Wundt's own presentation of the law in the following paragraph (1897, pp. 323–324):

The law of *psychical relations* supplements that of resultants; it refers not to the relation of the components of a psychical inter-connection to the value of the whole, but rather to their reciprocal relation. The law of resultants thus holds for the synthetic processes of consciousness, the law of relation for the analytic. Every resolution of a conscious content into its single members is an act of relating analysis. Such a resolution takes place in the successive apperception of the parts of a whole which is ideated at first only in a general way, . . . and then in clearly recognized form in the division of aggregate ideas. In the same way, every apperception is an analytic process whose two factors are the emphasizing of one single content and the marking off of this one content from all others. The first of these two partial processes is what produces *clearness,* the second is what produces *distinctness* of apperception. The most complete expression of this law is to be found in the processes of *apperceptive analysis* and the simple *relating* and *comparing* functions upon which it is based. In the latter more especially, we see that the essential content of the law of relations is the principle that every single psychical content receives its significance from the relations in which it stands to other psychical contents.

Wundt did not overlook the fact that his law of relations was just an extension of Weber's earlier findings regarding the relativity of judgment of sensory impressions and as expressed in what came to be known as *Weber's Law.* Stated in nonmathematical terms, Weber's quantitative studies showed that for a given kind of judgmental task, equal *relative* differences are equally perceptible. To state the law another way: for a change in stimulation to be noticed, the stimulus has to be increased or decreased not by an *absolute* amount, but by an amount that is proportional to itself. One individual, for example, may be unable to detect the difference in weight between one pound and a weight of eighteen ounces, but can just barely perceive a weight of twenty ounces to be heavier. This does not mean, though, that he will judge any weight to be heavier if it is increased by four ounces. For him, in terms of Weber's Law, a weight of four pounds would have to be increased to five pounds before the increase could be noticed. This principle of relativity applies to judgments of changes in color, length of lines, severity of pain, loudness of sounds, brightness of lights, and intensity of odors and tastes.[30]

The preceding reference to tastes may be used as a point of departure for considering the third of Wundt's laws of relation; his *law of psychic contrast.* A sweet substance tastes sweeter if eaten immediately after we have tasted a sour substance. Similarly, a cold shower feels colder if preceded by a hot one, and white paper looks whiter against a black background than against a gray background. In each of these instances, the heightened effect is readily recognized as a contrast effect. In subsuming such effects under a separate law of contrast, Wundt appears to have been thinking in terms of the polarities that characterized his tridimensional theory of feeling.

---

[30] Weber's Law does not hold for extremes of stimulation, but does hold for intermediate ranges of stimulation. The same may be said about Fechner's extension of Weber's Law.

Although he regarded contrast as a phenomenon falling within the scope of a separate law, he did not regard the law as altogether independent of the laws of relativity and creative synthesis. He made this clear when he pointed out (1897, p. 325):

> On the one hand, it may be regarded as the application of the general law of relations to the special case where the related psychical contents range between opposites. On the other hand, the fact that under suitable circumstances antithetical processes may intensify each other, while falling under the law of contrast is at the same time a special application of the principle of creative synthesis.

As has just been suggested, the three principles of creative synthesis, relativity and contrast are not necessarily mutually exclusive. Indeed they often operate conjointly. For example, when we say that the pavement looks wet, all three principles are involved in such a commonplace observation. In the first place, Wundt would have referred to this combination of a visual impression with a prior cutaneous sensation as the phenomenon of *complication*, since it involved data from two modalities. Thus the resulting complication of looking wet constitutes the synthesis of two disparate sensory impressions. Furthermore, perceiving the pavement as wet implies having the perception in question *related* to its contrasting appearance when dry. Innumerable complications of this sort are formed in the course of mental development, and Wundt considered some of them along with other aspects of mental growth in connection with his three "psychological laws of development."

Laws of Development

Wundt's laws of development were outgrowths of his laws of relation. That is why each group consisted of three laws. The difference between them may be understood as the difference between three principles taken in the abstract as contrasted with their application to actual situations. This may be compared to the difference between having to learn the principles of safe driving before taking the wheel and then putting the principles to work under actual driving conditions. It may also be compared to the difference between first having to learn the grammar of a foreign language and then having to apply the grammatical rules to the exigencies of conversation and writing. Bearing these comparisons in mind will facilitate understanding of Wundt's laws of development.

The first law of development to be considered is the *law of mental growth.* Wundt regarded it as having to do with the "law of resultants, whose application it is," and as operative in the life of the "normal individual" subject to the "continuity" of mental growth (1897, p. 326). The growth of concepts might serve as a convenient illustration of this law. A preschool child starts to have the beginning of a concept of arithmetic when he learns to count from one to ten. This incipient concept gradually changes during his school years as he learns to multiply, divide, and subtract, and to deal with fractions, percentages, surds, and cube root. It will be further modified when as an adult professor of mathematics he is engaged in writing research papers on number theory. The resultant concept of the sophisticated professor has been drastically transformed from the child's naïve concept.

Wundt's second law of development, the *law of heterogeny of ends,*[31] does not lend itself to such easy exposition. It appears to have been an elaboration of the law of relations, especially as applied to the realm of ethics. It is concerned with moral growth and the development of ethical sensitivity. Consequently, it is to be understood as intimately associated with Wundt's voluntarism and his emphasis on value and purpose as the hallmarks of psychical causality.

Often a survey of the consequences of an act reveals the act to be *related* to a rather wide array of diverse and unanticipated effects. The ends realized go beyond the intended purpose. When Roentgen was experimenting with cathode rays, he had no intention of laying the foundation for the X-ray industry or for radiology as a medical specialty. Einstein could not have foreseen that one of his formulas would lead to the tragedy of Hiroshima. Neither was Fleming able to foresee the "heterogeny of ends" to be realized as a result of his chance discovery of penicillin that paved the way for the related discovery of still other antibiotics, the prosperity of drug firms, changes in the treatment of disease, and the relief of human suffering.

The foregoing examples illustrate one way of interpreting Wundt's concept of heterogeny of ends. However, they are misleading as examples of Wundt's thinking if they are taken to mean that Wundt restricted the operation of the principle to ends resulting from great scientific discoveries. Such a restriction would fail to reflect Wundt's view of the principle as a factor in the mental development of ordinary people making ordinary decisions as they engage in ordinary acts. As he saw it, the principle governs the mental life of all of us and not just of the rare scientific genius. This is what he had to say about it (1897, p. 327):

> The principle of heterogeny of ends in its broadest sense dominates all psychical processes. In the special teleological coloring which has given it its name, it is to be found primarily in the sphere of *volitional processes,* for here the idea of end attended by their affective motives are of chief importance. In the various spheres of applied psychology it is therefore especially *ethics* for which this law is of great importance.

Wundt neglected to supply a concrete instance of the operation of this law. He may have regarded the preceding formulation in the *Grundriss*

---

[31] This is Judd's translation of what Wundt had formulated as *"Heterogonie der Zwecke."* It may also be translated "heterogeny of purpose."

as a sufficient reminder of what had been elaborated upon in his classroom lecture. Without such elaboration, the formulation in question is too abstract to render its meaning obvious. It would have helped had Wundt added a clarifying illustration from everyday life. He might have called attention to the ethical consequences likely to follow if a businessman were to succumb to the temptation of finishing a long and exciting novel by reading until the early hours of the morning. Under the circumstances his purpose is to finish reading the novel. This is what accounts for the "teleological coloring" of his decision to continue reading hour after hour. Waking up feeling tired and irritable was not inherent in this purpose, but it is one of its concomitant "ends."

As a result of his extreme fatigue his efficiency at the office is reduced: employees are scolded, customers handled tactlessly, and business judgment impaired. At the end of the day, when he feels even more wretched because of increased fatigue and his "troubles" at the office, both his wife and children become victims of his low threshold of irritability and poor emotional control. Each incident at the office and each outburst at home is thus one of the "ends" following from the previous night's reading. Being different ends affecting different people, they constitute a *heterogeneous* array of ends. Finally, since this heterogeny of ends has subjected so many persons to unwarranted scolding and criticism, it is by no means devoid of ethical implications. At least this is the way it would have appeared to Wundt in the light of his second law.

Unlike the second law, Wundt's third law of development does not require labored explanation. In general, it has to do with developmental changes associated with different periods of life, starting with infancy and ending with senility. Wundt perceived these changes in terms of his law of contrast, with a given stage of development being followed by a contrasting stage. For this reason he called his third law the *law of development towards opposites* and then added the following clarifying comment (1897, p. 322):

> It has long been recognized that the predominating temperaments of different periods of life present certain contrasts. Thus, the light sanguine excitability of childhood, which is seldom more than superficial, is followed by the . . . more retentive temperament of youth with its frequent touch of melancholy. Then comes manhood with its mature character, generally quick and active in decision and execution, and last of all, old age with its leaning toward comtemplative quiet.

This reference to five ages of man is reminiscent of Shakespeare's more famous and more dramatic account of the seven ages of man. Both references deal with developmental changes which in Wundt's words have "long been recognized." He might have added that, although long recognized, they had not yet been subjected to systematic investigation. This was in the

1890s, when he had just given expression to his three laws of development. Developmental psychology as a separate field of psychology had not yet come into existence.

Concerning Wundt's Folk Psychology

As a matter of fact, Wundt viewed his work on *Völkerpsychologie* as a contribution to developmental psychology. Starting at the turn of the century—in the decade following completion of the *Grundriss*—Wundt wrote ten volumes on this subject of folk psychology. These volumes have never been translated into English. In 1912, however, Wundt published a one-volume survey of the subject that was translated four years later. In the preface, Wundt indicated that one of his purposes in undertaking "investigations in folk psychology" was to find out "whether or not mental development is at all subject law" (1916, p. xiii). This purpose was given special emphasis in the subtitle to the book which explains that the volume presents the "outlines of a Psychological History of the Development of Mankind."

A central thesis of Wundt's folk psychology is to the effect that the mind of the individual is largely a product of social tradition. To quote him directly (1916, p. 2):

> All phenomena with which mental sciences[32] deal are, indeed, creations of the social community. Language, for example, is not the accidental discovery of an individual; it is the product of peoples, and, generally speaking, there are as many different languages as there are originally distinct peoples. The same is true of the beginnings of art, of mythology, and of custom.

As Wundt saw it, folk psychology, although not experimental, was nevertheless an important part of scientific psychology. He restricted experimentation to investigation of the simpler mental processes. The "complex" functions of thought," he held, are not amenable to trustworthy introspective analysis and consequently could not be subjected to laboratory control. The study of folk psychology was intended to compensate for this restriction. Accordingly, he wrote that when it comes to "the analysis of the higher mental processes," folk psychology is found to be "an indispensable supplement to the psychology of individual consciousness" (1916, p. 3). Furthermore, since folk psychology studies the origin and development of social institutions, it is to be thought of as being, "in an important sense of the word, *genetic psychology*" (1916, p. 3).

The genetic viewpoint involves the investigation of the evolution of mental life from its early primitive beginnings to its most advanced stages

---

[32] Reference to the German original shows the phrase "mental sciences" to be a translation of *"Geisteswissenschaften."*

of development. Such an investigation amounts to a study of the history of social institutions and their influence on man's outlook and behavior—on his language, beliefs, customs, taboos, sanctions, and so on. According to Wundt, history is thus brought within the scope of folk psychology. He made this clear in one of the final paragraphs of his book in which he reached the following conclusion (1916, p. 522):

> Now, history is really an account of mental life. As such, it gives consideration to physical factors only in so far as they furnish the indispensable basis of mind. . . . Although the concrete significance of the particular, as such, precludes the historian from disregarding it, everything that is merely particular should be ignored by one who is giving a psychological account of events. The aim, in this latter case, should be that of discovering and determining motives of historical life and its changes, and of interpreting these by reference to the universal laws of mind. Supplementing this aim should be the endeavor to gain, so far as possible, an insight into the laws that are immanent in history itself.

In thus providing for a rapprochement between psychology and history, Wundt was evidently trying to settle a controversy that had arisen some twenty years earlier in connection with Wilhelm Dilthey's attack on the "new" laboratory psychology. As mentioned in Chapter 8, page 213, Dilthey had objected to the natural-science orientation of the latter kind of psychology because of its inability to come to grips with "historico-social reality." Wundt's kind of experimental psychology was too nomothetic in its objectives to be of help to the historian investigating the dynamics of history as influenced by changing social institutions and by men of historical importance. History was classified as a social science or *Geisteswissenschaft* and not as a natural science; hence its alienation from the concerns of the Leipzig laboratory.

By the time Wundt started to write the first volume of his *Völkerpsychologie,* around 1900, he was ready to regard this phase of psychology as a *Geisteswissenschaft.* The resulting ten volumes, it will be recalled, dealt with "a psychological history of the development of mankind." For Wundt, this was a nonexperimental but nevertheless scientific supplement to the work of the laboratory. It was scientific in the same sense in which philology, anthropology, comparative jurisprudence, sociology, economics, history, and other nonlaboratory scholarly disciplines are deemed to be scientific.[33]

By treating *Völkerpsychologie* as a serious scientific enterprise, Wundt

---

[33] The disciplines in question are commonly classified as social sciences. Those who equate the word "science" with the conceptual framework of modern natural science may be disinclined to classify these disciplines as sciences. J. B. Conant, for example, has taken this stand. He even includes psychology among these nonscientific disciplines in his recent article on the subject and, as shown in the following excerpt from the article, finds support for his stand in the history of psychology (1967, p. 325):

had disposed of Dilthey's earlier objections to the "new" psychology. Wundt's "new" psychology had turned out to be both a *Naturwissenschaft* and a *Geisteswissenschaft*. It was almost as if he had anticipated later clashes of opinion among his second- and third-generation psychological descendants between those who argued that psychology is a natural science as contrasted with those who regarded it as a social science. Had he lived another twenty years, he might have ventured to adjudicate the controversy by reminding the quarreling grandchildren that his *Grundzüge* reflected the viewpoint of natural science whereas his *Völkerpsychologie* reflected a social-science viewpoint, and that both viewpoints were needed for the cultivation of a satisfactory and comprehensive scientific psychology.

Summary Review

Wundt wrote so much for so many years on different aspects of psychology that what has been included in the present chapter is to be regarded as an incomplete outline or summary of his long campaign in behalf of a scientific psychology. In the course of his campaign, he laid the foundations for the later emergence of several of modern psychology's many divisions.[34] Thus, he was a founding father not only of experimental psychology, but of general, physiological, social, and genetic or developmental psychologies as well.

By defining psychology as the study of immediate experience, he gave it status as an independent discipline different from established sciences like physics and chemistry which, as he maintained, deal with mediate experience. This was a kind of tour de force by making the physical sciences dependent on psychology, since it was tantamount to arguing that without immediate experience there can be no mediate experience.

In terms of systematic psychology, Wundt was a sponsor of a voluntaristic, process psychology. And with reference to methodology he was a cautious introspectionist: only trained observers reporting on simpler mental processes under conditions of laboratory control could be relied upon to

---

The social sciences are not yet sciences; no *widely accepted* conceptual scheme with posits other than those of common sense has as yet developed. Perhaps some day it will. So I have been assured by friends in economics, sociology, anthropology, and psychology, for half a century. I am beginning to doubt it. The failure, I have come to think, is to be traced to the fact that the instruments used in the natural sciences cannot talk back. Human beings can and do. On this basis, experimentation with animals, even if performed by investigators who label themselves "psychologists," is part of a science, namely biology. Psychology, as an examination of human behavior, like sociology, is in quite another category. I am inclined to think the history of psychology will bear out my rather unusual dissection of a field which for practical reasons many professors have in recent years endeavoured to consider as a closely knit unit.

34 The word "many" is used advisedly. Every few years a new division seems to be

supply trustworthy introspective data. For more complex mental processes or the so-called higher thought processes, he advocated reliance upon the nonintrospective methods of *Völkerpsychologie.*

Scientific psychology as envisaged by Wundt was not an insulated subject having fixed boundaries. He saw it as having potential significance for other subjects and as being fundamental to the social sciences, supplementary to the physical sciences, and even as introductory to philosophy. As an ardent champion of empiricism, he went to the extreme of attributing reflexes and instincts to ancestral experience in accordance with the lapsed-intelligence theory.

Among the key teachings of Wundt, mention has been made of the tridimensional theory of feeling, of more intense feelings as emotions, of psychical causality as the realization of "subjective values and ends," of apperception as a process of active rather than passive attention, and of mind as *actual.* All these teachings were found to be consistent with the conative implications of his voluntarism.

In addition to being a voluntarist, Wundt was a structuralist. From the viewpoint of structuralism, he perceived one of the objectives of psychology to be the determination of the structure of mental content by (1) analyzing experience into its constituent elements, (2) noting how these elements combine to form psychical compounds, (3) investigating the "interconnection" of psychical compounds, and (4) establishing the laws of psychical causality operative in the organization and development of mental content. The latter laws were regarded as related to but different from the laws of physical causality. Wundt recognized six such fundamental laws, with three of them being laws of relation and the other three being laws of development.

Even though he had started his professional career as a physiologist before embarking on his career as a psychologist, Wundt did not regard mind as an epiphenomenal by-product of brain physiology. Instead he adopted the standpoint of a *modified* psychophysical parallelism as best suited to serve the interests of scientific psychology. It was modified to the extent of eliminating notions of spiritual or material entities from the meaning he attributed to the word "psychophysical." His concept of "the actuality of mind" was not an oblique reference to a substantial soul. He also held that a "materialistic" interpretation of the suffix in the word "psychophysical" is "epistemologically untenable and psychologically unproductive." As he saw it, both idealistic as well as materialistic assumptions are to be ruled out of scientific court as unverifiable metaphysical hindrances to the progress of psychology. In many respects his antimetaphysical process psychology,

---

formed. In 1968 the American Psychological Association recognized twenty-nine divisions. Wundt's five divisions are still represented; but in addition there are many he never considered as separate fields. For example, there are divisions of evaluation and measurement, of psychopharmacology, of military psychology, of school psychologists, of clinical psychology, and of consumer psychology.

in terms of basic orientation, adumbrates the following definition of mind which the philosopher Abraham Kaplan once formulated in connection with a discussion of cybernetics (J. R. Newman [ed.], 1956, p. 1308):

> The analysis of mind and individual personality as a structure of certain information processes renders obsolete not only the "mind substance" of the idealist, but mechanistic materialism as well. *Mind is a patterning of information and not spirit, matter, or energy* [italics added].

The Rise and Fall of the New Psychology

By the decade of the 1890s, Wundt might have surveyed the psychological scene with a gratifying sense of personal accomplishment. His campaign in behalf of experimental psychology was manifestly successful. Students he had taught at Leipzig had established laboratories of psychology at various universities both in Germany and in America. They were quoting their Leipzig professor in lectures to their students. His books were being widely circulated and some of them had already appeared in translation. There were repeated references to his work in the new psychological journals being published in Germany, France, and the United States. All this was taking place even before he had started to write the first of his books on *Völkerpsychologie*. The success of his campaign was thus already assured before the latter books were written. Under the circumstances, he had ample reason to think of himself as the leading experimental psychologist of the period. Indeed, as was mentioned on the first page of the present chapter, a Yale professor had accorded him, and not James of Harvard, the accolade of being "the greatest psychologist."

Furthermore, the future of the cause Wundt had championed so zealously now seemed to be secure. An increasing number of universities were replacing their courses in mental philosophy by courses in psychology. Each year witnessed more students enrolling in these courses. Obtaining a doctorate by defending a psychological thesis was ceasing to be a novelty. More and more recipients of these doctoral degrees were calling themselves psychologists. This was taking place both in Europe and in the United States.[35] Before long, there were enough psychologists in existence to warrant the formation of psychological associations.

---

[35] The First American Ph.D. in psychology was granted prior to 1890. According to W. B. Pillsbury, it was in 1886 that Joseph Jastrow (1863–1944) "received the first Ph.D. to be given in America specifically in psychology" (1944, p. 261). This took place at the Johns Hopkins University under the chairmanship of G. Stanley Hall. Jastrow's dissertation dealt with "The Perception of Space by Disparate Senses." In 1888 Jastrow was appointed professor of psychology at the University of Wisconsin. As noted by Pillsbury, "This was one of the first chairs in psychology in America and the first west of the Atlantic seaboard" (1944, p. 262).

Incidentally, some writers list Hall as the first recipient of an American Ph.D. in

What drew them together was not a common endorsement of Wundtian psychology. Even those who were Wundtians did not necessarily agree with all of his teachings. Nevertheless, all of them were in agreement with Wundt in one fundamental respect: that the future of psychology was to be a scientific future, and that wherever possible this was to be an experimental future. The latter qualification is necessary because, as Wundt himself had realized, there are aspects of mental life which are not amenable to laboratory investigation. Moreover, some aspects he had regarded as unsuitable for experimental study were subjected to such study by those who were not bound by his strictures. As early as the 1880s Ebbinghaus had demonstrated this by his ingenious use of nonsense syllables in the experimental investigation of some phases of memory. And shortly after the turn of the century, Oswald Külpe (1862–1915) and his associates at Würzburg had also demonstrated this by their laboratory studies of various so-called higher thought processes. But these and other departures from the Wundtian scientific orthodoxy were undertaken by men who, like Wundt, were intent upon promoting psychology as science.

By the time of his death in 1920, drastic changes had occurred in what he had started in Leipzig around 1880 and had developed in subsequent years. Many of the Leipzig laboratory findings had been assimilated by general psychology and subjected to further refinement, but Wundtian interpretations of such findings had often been disregarded. Wundt's reliance upon introspective reports had been challenged by adherents of the various behavioristic psychologies that had appeared on the scene. Sponsors of applied psychology found Wundt's kind of analyses of immediate experience too remote from the realities of everyday living to make for a

---

psychology. He obtained his degree at Harvard in 1878. However, his thesis was not based on experimental work and was done under the supervision of a physiologist, Henry P. Bowditch, and not under a psychologist. However, James did approve of it. Like Jastrow's, Hall's thesis was on "The Perception of Space."

Because, unlike Jastrow's, Hall's thesis was a nonexperimental treatment of the subject, some would regard it as less definitely psychological. When the issue was put to Boring for adjudication, he replied: "You can have Hall or Jastrow for the first Ph.D., depending on whether you want to regard Hall's Harvard degree as a degree in psychology or in philosophy, in view of the fact that it was not experimental although he did it primarily under a physiologist" (personal communication). Still, some sixteen years before Boring had rendered this verdict, he was co-author of an article in which, among other things, the statement was made that "Hall took the first American Ph.D. in psychology at Harvard in 1878" (1948, p. 531). Actually, since the article was not directly concerned with the issue under consideration, the latter statement is not to be construed as being a contradiction of what Pillsbury had said about Jastrow's Ph.D. having been "specifically in psychology."

Unfortunately, there is no way of finding out how Hall would have disposed of the issue. After all these years there might be no objection were one to indulge in the fantasy of assuming that, had the question been put to Hall, he would have decided that in terms of enhancement of professional standing it is more blessed to have given than to have received the first Ph.D.

serviceable psychology. And leaders of the then new school of Gestalt psychology objected to the "atomistic" nature of a psychology which reduced mind to a congeries of discrete units of sensation that had to be compounded into "bundles" in order to account for *organized* experience.

All such objections to and criticisms of Wundt's psychology were being voiced during the last decade of his life. His Leipzig prescription for a scientific psychology was being replaced by other prescriptions. Consequently, whether he could still have thought of his campaign in behalf of scientific psychology as a successful venture might well be questioned. The new generation of psychologists were ignoring his leadership and disregarding his taboos. Under the circumstances he might have felt like paraphrasing Isaiah by saying, "Psychologists have I trained and guided, but they have rebelled against me."

Had he lived another year, he might have been somewhat reconciled to the outcome of his campaign as appraised by a leading historian of the day. This is what Brett had to say about it in 1921 (Vol. III, pp. 164–165):

> In short, the new psychology of 1880 is now a little old, a little disillusioned, a little wiser and sadder. But no generous student of history would care to emphasize this change of mood as a disparagement of the life-work of Wundt. Progress is itself a kind of critic; but it does not despise the things it must discard.

One thing Wundt's critics never discarded was his faith in psychology as an experimental science. Often their opposition to his teachings was the consequence of the extension and modification of laboratory procedures that had been introduced in his laboratory. In other words, they based their opposition upon *their* experimental findings. Their recourse to chronoscopes, tachistoscopes, plethysmographs, galvanometers, and other instruments had been commonplace as a result of what Wundt had initiated at Leipzig. In large measure they were thus indebted to Wundt for the idea of an experimental attack on psychological problems. Viewed in this light, Wundt had not labored in vain.

Both in terms of what he championed as well as in terms of the opposition he aroused, he had much to do with shaping the course of twentieth-century psychology during its early decades. Had his teachings not been challenging and provocative, they would have been ignored. Even those who came to differ with him had reason to respect him as a psychologist. Unlike Scripture, they very likely would not have called him "the greatest psychologist" but might not have hesitated to call him "a great psychologist."

On "Very Great Men in Psychology's History"

This brings up a question that was merely touched upon in Chapter 21 (see pp. 775–776); Who are the great figures in the history of psychology? As was noted there, Boring had once written, "There have been no great

WILHELM WUNDT (1832–1920)

"Four Very Great Men in Psychology's History"

CHARLES DARWIN (1809–1882)

HERMANN VON HELMHOLTZ (1821-1894)

THE BETTMANN ARCHIVE

WILLIAM JAMES (1842–1910)

SIGMUND FREUD (1856–1939)

THE BETTMANN ARCHIVE

psychologists." This was in the 1929 first edition of his *History of Experimental Psychology*. However, the 1950 second edition stated "There are at least four very great men in psychology's history: Darwin, Helmholtz, James and Freud." Apparently, his quest for "very great" psychologists had not been very successful, since of the four men chosen, James was the only one who had ever been actively identified with the field of psychology. In his career Helmholtz had held professorships of physiology and of physics, but never a professorship of psychology or philosophy. His classic studies of physiological optics and of physiological acoustics have been universally acclaimed as epoch-making contributions to the psychology of vision and of hearing. Despite this, he continued to be thought of as a physiologist and physicist and not as a psychologist. In analogous fashion, some decades later Pavlov continued to be classified as a physiologist despite the tremendous impact of his experimental studies of conditioning on the psychology of the learning process. Similarly, Darwin has never ceased to be classified as a biologist despite the tremendous impact of his work on the orientation of post-Darwinian psychologists. What is more, neither Darwin, Helmholtz, nor Pavlov regarded himself as a psychologist. Furthermore, it seems safe to conjecture that Freud did not think of himself as a psychologist in the way in which he would have thought of men like Wundt, James, and G. Stanley Hall as psychologists. In fact, both he and his orthodox disciples were and continue to be sensitive about their exclusive right to the designation of their professional status as psychoanalysts rather than as psychologists.

There is no reason to quarrel with Boring's choice of these four as great men in psychology's history, but there is reason to dwell on the implications of his choice. Of the four, one was British, another German, and the other two American and Austrian, respectively. This serves as a reminder of the fact that the development of psychology, as is true of every science, was a product of international endeavor. Science is a cooperative venture that ignores geographic boundaries and prefers the free exchange of ideas to their chauvinistic concealment from fellow scientists in other countries. That is why developed sciences have *international* congresses at periodic intervals.[36] Moreover, if by some miracle all those who have had a share in making modern psychology what it is could be resurrected to attend a posthumous international congress, in addition to the four countries just mentioned, there would be representatives from Italy, France, Denmark, Russia, Belgium, Italy, Canada, Spain, Australia, Japan, and other parts of the world.

---

[36] Interest in psychology has become truly international. By 1965 The International Union of Psychological Science numbered twenty-eight member societies, with every continent being represented. In 1966 the American Psychological Association published a monograph of close to four hundred pages on *International Opportunities for Advanced Training and Research in Psychology,* in which more than seventy-five countries were listed as providing such opportunities or hoping to provide them.

Nor would all the delegates be there as representatives of psychology as a profession, for a variety of professional specialties has entered into the making of psychology as it is today. For example, astronomy contributed reaction-time studies and the related notion of the personal equation. Ophthalmology and otology enhanced understanding of the psychology of vision and hearing. Endocrinology has had to be taken into account by students of emotion as well as by students of mental retardation. Progress in fields like biochemistry and electroencephalography have changed the thinking of physiological psychologists. Anthropology and sociology have not been without influence on social psychology. These examples suffice to suggest the extent to which psychology is indebted to workers in other fields for the widening of its horizons as its roots in mental philosophy developed into the many branches of modern scientific psychology. To trace the history of this development in detail would call for a separate volume and the collaboration of experts in each of the branches.

In addition to the foregoing implications of Boring's choice of the four great men, there are other implications to be considered. One of these involves this question: Since the choice was made at the end of a survey of the history of *experimental* psychology, why were nonexperimentalists chosen? If the word "experimental" is restricted to observation of dependent variables under controlled conditions, then Helmholtz was the only outstanding experimentalist among the four. Darwin was more of a field naturalist than a laboratory worker, and James was temperamentally disinclined to undertake laboratory investigations. In fact, Boring characterized him as "a half-hearted experimentalist" who, despite this fact, is undoubtedly "America's foremost psychologist" (1950, pp. 509–510). About the only experiment James conducted is one he reported in a footnote in his chapter on memory. With himself as subject he tried to find out whether retention could be improved by practice in memorizing. Accordingly, he memorized a given number of lines of poetry during a series of practice days and then memorized a different kind of poetry to see if less time would be required to learn a line of the different poetry. He found that it took a little longer, "just the opposite result from that which the popular view would lead one to expect" (1890, Vol. I, pp. 666–668).

Aside from this one rather poorly designed experiment, there is little else to justify calling James an experimentalist—even a half-hearted one. At least he was not an active contributor to the literature of experimental psychology. He was familiar with what experimentalists of the time were doing and the pages of the *Principles* reflect this familiarity; but in general he does not appear to have been enamored of the "new" experimental psychology of the Wundtians. His reference to it as a "brass instrument psychology" was indicative of an unenthusiastic attitude and of misgivings concerning the significance of the experimental findings. Often he could accept the findings as factual data, but not the interpretations given to these findings by the Wundtians.

Although both he and Wundt were concerned with safeguarding the foundations of psychology as science, they went about the task in different ways. Both men were grounded in physiology as a result of their medical training, and both were well grounded in the history of philosophy. Their differences were not due to a difference in erudition or scholarly preparation for the task at hand. It was more of a difference in basic orientation toward that task. For Wundt, in accordance with German academic tradition, fulfillment of the task meant being the leader of a school or the sponsor of a system. Once the framework of the system had been constructed, psychological issues were apt to be interpreted in terms of their congruence with the system. Furthermore, as the sponsor of a school the German professor expected his students to be his disciples and not to deviate from his system. He expected loyalty in this sense. James, on the other hand, approached the task with no such commitment to a system and with no ambition to head a school of psychology and to surround himself with loyal adherents. As a result he could be more flexible in his thinking, more tolerant of dissent, and more ready to examine a given question from a variety of viewpoints.

Of course there were other differences between the two men in terms of personality and direction of interests and, most of all, in style of writing. As shown by excerpts in the present chapter, reading Wundt is a chore, whereas, as shown by excerpts in previous chapters, reading James is a delight. What he brought to psychology was not only literary elegance but also breadth of vision, penetrating insights, freedom from dogmatism, good-humored tolerance of opposition, honest recognition of difficulties and contradictions, an ability to suspend judgment in the absence of satisfactory evidence, and an open mind with respect to new evidence.

All these things considered, it might even be argued that, although he was not a founding father of an *experimental* psychology as was Wundt, James was more influential as the founding father of a *scientific* psychology. Maybe this accounts for the fact that there is a reproduction of a bronze plaque of Wundt as the frontispiece of Boring's *History of Experimental Psychology*—the only picture in the entire book—and yet when it comes to listing psychology's great men at the end of the book, Wundt fails to make the grade while James does. And the book is dedicated not to one of the four but to Titchener, who came closer to being identified with the Wundtian tradition than any other psychologist in the United States.[37] Both the picture and the dedication were appropriately symbolic of the book's chief objec-

---

[37] This does not mean that Titchener was in complete agreement with Wundt. For example, he did not regard the study of value as falling within the province of scientific psychology, as Wundt did in terms of the concept of psychical causality. For Titchener, working out the relationship between existence or experience and value "is the task of philosophy, and not of science; only, the scientific man should remember that his own account of the world . . . gives at best an incomplete and one-sided picture of human experience" (1929, p. 77).

tive; namely, to account for the emergence of psychology as an *experimental* science. Experimental psychology is far more indebted to Wundt and Titchener than it is to James.

Boring's unwillingness to include Wundt in his list of "very great men" is not hard to explain. It must be recalled that his criterion of greatness was "persistent posthumous importance." It is the criterion by means of which a book comes to be regarded as a classic; hence neither Wundt's *Grundzüge* nor his *Grundriss* is a classic in terms of Boring's criterion. That the *Principles* by James deserves to be called a classic is hardly to be questioned. Still, this is not to disparage the historical significance of Wundt's writings. His books, although not classics, were nevertheless markedly influential in their impact on the thinking of the first generation of experimental psychologists.

It is also well to note that the four men were selected because they were deemed to be *very* great. This, of course, suggests lesser degrees of greatness, and assuredly one of these lesser degrees applies to Wundt. As a matter of fact, there are decidedly many more references to Wundt throughout the body of Boring's *History* than to any one of the four, and more space is devoted to Wundt's biography than to the biography of any other man. He stands out as the leading figure in this historical survey of experimental psychology. Even though Boring was reluctant to call him a *very* great figure, he treated him as the most important figure. In effect, he was recognizing him as great, because more than any other man he brought experimental psychology into sharp relief so that it stood out against the background of philosophical psychology.

A Closing Thought: "Wir Sind Alle Epigonen"

To think of experimental psychology as having been projected against a background of mental philosophy is to recognize it as having emerged from its philosophic antecedents. Without these antecedents as progenitors, experimental psychology might never have been born. Wundt was not unmindful of this sort of metaphor. He gave expression to it in a phrase that Merz referred to as "Wundt's well-known dictum: 'Wir Sind Alle Epigonen' " (1965, Vol. III, p. 95). Freely translated, this means we are all the intellectual heirs of preceding generations of thinkers. (The word "*epigone*" is Greek for "successor" or "heir.") In line with the metaphor, the dictum suggests that founding fathers have bequeathed something to epigones as their sons. And if the sons become founding fathers, that which they inherited may be transmitted, often very much modified, to a new generation of epigones.

Wundt's own development as a psychologist reveals the significance of his dictum. He became a founding father of the new experimental psychology by availing himself of his philosophic heritage. The kind of scientific psychology he "bequeathed" to his students at the turn of the century was not entirely a product of his own thinking and unrelated to the work of others. For example, the idea of an experimental psychology was engendered by a passage in John Stuart Mill's *Logic*. Both Weber and Fechner had supplied him with techniques by means of which sensory impressions could be subjected to measurement. He was indebted to physiologists like Johannes Müller and Helmholtz for some of his laboratory apparatus. Many generations of anatomists had contributed to his understanding of the nervous system. Had these men never existed, his *Grundzüge* might never have been written. Furthermore, had chemists not made a distinction between elements and compounds, he might never have thought of making a distinction between psychical elements and psychical compounds. He "inherited" the concept of psychophysical parallelism from Leibnitz, the term "apperception" from Herbart, and the doctrine of local signs from Lotze. His empiricism with its associationistic implications was an outgrowth of his familiarity with the writings of British philosopher-psychologists. Similarly, the writings of Steinthal and Lazarus supplied him with the concept of *Völkerpsychologie*. There is no need to add more examples. These suffice to show how he might have demonstrated the soundness of his dictum by showing the extent to which he was indebted to others for help in his efforts to establish an experimental psychology and to transform mental philosophy into a scientific psychology.

Were Wundt's efforts successful? Certainly not in terms of the survival of the kind of Wundtian experimental psychology that Scripture had welcomed so enthusiastically. And not in terms of contemporary endorsement of Wundt's systematic psychology. Still, in terms of the survival of his underlying faith in the promise of an experimentally oriented scientific psychology he was successful. As his epigones, we still cherish this faith. It accounts for our continuing efforts to fulfill the promise in question.

Another way to put this is to say that in many respects twentieth-century experimental psychology can trace its beginnings back to the Leipzig of 1879. What took place there served as a point of departure for the subsequent introduction of different techniques and new viewpoints. The Wundtian orthodoxy gave way to new attacks on old problems as well as to recognition of hitherto unformulated new ones. Sometimes these changes were prompted by a lack of confidence in Wundt's experimentally controlled introspections. But even those who opposed his views can be said to have been stimulated by his teachings.

As might be expected, before long the experimental psychology of the early decades of the present century ceased to be restricted to the kind of problems that Wundt had sanctioned for experimental investigation. As a result, the experimental psychology of today is very different from what had been going on in the Leipzig laboratory back in the 1880s and 1890s.

Similarly, the social psychology of today is very different from the social psychology of the *Völkerpsychologie*. Contemporary physiological psychology differs from the *Grundzüze,* and no current system of psychology is a duplicate of the system embodied in the *Grundriss.*

Whether *all* the foregoing changes constitute progress is a question which cannot be subjected to experimental investigation. To the extent that it can be answered, it must be answered by reasoned evaluation of relevant considerations. It is the kind of question that confronts the scientist when asked whether a given experimental proposal is too trivial to merit endorsement and financial support. No laboratory procedure will supply the answer, but it can be answered by critical analysis of the scientific implications of the proposal.

This serves as a reminder of something which was already evident to Wundt: that science is not exclusively experimental. For this reason, he did not hesitate to regard his nonexperimental investigations of the so-called higher thought processes as scientific investigations. As investigations, they called for critical thinking; and for appreciation of what this entails, Wundt, like the rest of the scientific community, owed something to a venerable method by means of which Socrates is said to have goaded his pupils into searching examination of their beliefs. Science stagnates when questioning ceases, and it advances when the right questions are raised. This truism is an obvious part of our philosophic heritage.

If publication of the *Grundzüge* in 1874 be taken as the start of Wundt's campaign in behalf of scientific psychology, then scientific psychology will soon be ready for a centenary celebration. In the course of the century, an ever-increasing number of psychologists all over the world have been loyal to the Wundtian tradition in one sense: they have sought to solve the mystery of mind by steadfast adherence to what they believed to be the methods of science. In particular, as a derivative of the Wundtian tradition, their faith in the strategies of the experimental scientist has remained unshaken.

In broad perspective, their quest can be seen as the quest for an understanding of human understanding. This, of course, in large measure had also been the quest of men like Plato, Descartes, Spinoza, Locke, Hume, Kant, and other philosophers. But, unlike these philosophers, in the course of their quest the psychologists of the past century have accumulated increasing masses of experimental, clinical, and sociological data. As a result they surpass their philosophic forebears in knowledge of the human condition. Whether they surpass them in wisdom is not for the historian to judge.

At one time it was expected that with the advent of scientific psychology the relative certainty of tested knowledge would replace the endless debates and controversies of philosophical psychology. This expectation has not been realized as yet.[38] Despite a century of scientific psychology, debate and controversy continue to be reflected in the polemics of countless journal articles. The mystery of mind is still with us. At best, if the current state of psychological affairs were to be expressed in the language of a parliamentary report, the chairman would announce that his committee has found a modicum of progress, but that there is enough unfinished business on the psychological agenda to keep scientific psychologists busy for another few centuries.

---

[38] Some days after completion of this chapter, it was discovered that E. Nagel had given more explicit expression to the conclusion arrived at in this final paragraph. After granting that experimental psychology "has made substantial advances in detailed knowledge of numerous psychological processes," he had this to say (B. J. Wolman and E. Nagel [eds.], 1965, pp. 25–26):

> Nevertheless, the hope shared by many of the founding fathers of experimental psychology that its achievements would soon match those of the older natural sciences has not yet been realized; and the radical separation of psychology from philosophy has not been an unmixed blessing to either discipline. The theories current in psychology are hardly the equals of most of those available in physics and biology either in reliability or range of explanatory power. Indeed, unlike these sciences, psychology is marked by the existence of warring schools, which differ not only in their interpretations of newly gathered empirical data . . . but are also at odds over the "proper" way of studying as well as interpreting phenomena that have long been subjects of investigation. This persistence of divergent schools of psychology makes evident that the achievement of comprehensive and objectively grounded theoretical knowledge is not assured by formally disavowing all "philosophical" preconceptions when conducting inquiries directed toward that end; for such disavowal is no guarantee that insufficiently analyzed if not entirely tacit philosophical assumptions will not control the scientific enterprise and perhaps even hinder the realization of its major goals. . . . Accordingly, it does not seem unreasonable to suppose that progress of psychology would be helped, and the level of its theoretical discussions raised, if psychologists were philosophically more knowledgeable than they usually are and had in particular competence in the logic of theory construction.

References

Boring, E. G. *A History of Experimental Psychology*. New York: The Century Company, 1929.

Boring, M. D., and Boring E. G. "Masters and Pupils Among the American Psychologists," *American Journal of Psychology,* 1948, *61,* 527–534.

Brett, G. S. *A History of Psychology,* Vol. III. London: George Allen and Unwin, 1921.

Broadhurst, D. E. *Behaviour—A Survey of Twentieth Century Theory in Behaviouristic Psychology*. New York: Basic Books, 1961.

Brody, N., and Oppenheim, P. "Tensions in Psychology between the Methods of Behaviorism and Phenomenology," *Psychological Review,* 1966, *73,* 295–305.

Conant, J. B. "Scientific Principles and Moral Conduct," *American Scientist*, 1967, *55*, 311–328.

Darwin, C. *The Expression of the Emotions in Men and Animals.* Chicago: The University of Chicago Press, 1965. (First published in 1872.)

Feigl, H. "The Mind-Body Problem in the Development of Logical Empiricism," in H. Feigl, and M. Brodbeck (eds.). *Readings in the Philosophy of Science.* New York: Appleton-Century-Crofts, 1953, pp. 612–626.

Hall, M. H. "An Interview with Mr. Psychology: Edwin G. Boring," *Psychology Today*, 1967, *1*, 16–19 and 65–67.

Hebb, D. O. *A Textbook of Psychology.* Philadelphia: W. B. Saunders Company, 1958.

Henle, M., and Baltimore, G. "Portraits in Straw," *Psychological Review*, 1967, *74*, 325–329.

Höffding, H. *Moderne Philosophen.* Leipzig: O. R. Reisland, 1905.

James, W. *Principles of Psychology*, 2 vols. New York: Henry Holt and Company, 1890.

James, W. *Essays in Radical Empiricism.* New York: Longmans, Green and Company, 1912. (For the essay dealing with the existence of consciousness, see pp. 1–28.)

Jones, E. *The Life and Work of Sigmund Freud*, Vol. 2. New York: Basic Books, 1955.

Kaplan, A. "Sociology Learns the Language of Mathematics," in J. R. Newman (ed.). *The World of Mathematics*, Vol. 2. New York: Simon and Schuster, 1956, pp. 1294–1313.

Merz, J. T. *A History of European Thought in the Nineteenth Century*, Vol. III. New York: Dover Publications, 1965. (First published in 1912.)

Nagel, E. "Psychology and the Philosophy of Science," in B. J. Wolman and E. Nagel (eds.). *Scientific Psychology.* New York: Basic Books, 1965, pp. 24–27.

Perry, R. B. *The Thought and Character of William James.* Briefer version. New York: George Braziller, 1954.

Peters, H. N. "Affect and Emotion," in M. H. Marx (ed.). *Theories in Contemporary Psychology.* New York: The Macmillan Company, 1964.

Pillsbury, W. B. "Joseph Jastrow," *Psychological Review*, 1944, *51*, 261–265.

Reymert, M. L. (ed.). *Feelings and Emotions.* New York: McGraw-Hill Book Company, 1950.

Seashore, C. E. *Introduction to Psychology.* New York: The Macmillan Company, 1923.

Steffens, L. *The Autobiography of Lincoln Steffens.* New York: Harcourt, Brace and Company, 1931.

Titchener, E. B. *Systematic Psychology: Prolegomena.* New York: The Macmillan Company, 1929.

Titchener, E. B. "Wilhelm Wundt," *American Journal of Psychology*, 1921, *32*, 161–178.

Warren, H. C. *Dictionary of Psychology.* Boston: Houghton, Mifflin Company, 1934.

Wundt, W. *Elements of Folk Psychology—Outlines of a Psychological History of the Development of Mankind.* (Translated by E. L. Schaub.) London: George Allen and Unwin, 1916.

Wundt, W. *Grundzüge der physiologischen Psychologie*, 3 vols., 5th ed. Leipzig: Wilhelm Engelmann, 1902.

Wundt, W. "Introduction: On the Methods in Psychology." (Translated by C. F. Winter.) In T. Shipley (ed.). *Classics in Psychology.* New York: Philosophical Library, 1961, pp. 51–78.

Wundt, W. *Outlines of Psychology.* (Translated with the cooperation of the author by C. H. Judd.) Leipzig: Wilhelm Engelmann, 1897.

Wundt, W. *Principles of Physiological Psychology*, Vol. I. (Translated from the 5th edition of 1902 by E. B. Titchener.) London: Swan Sonnenschein and Company, 1904.

Zaner, R. M. "Criticism of Tensions in Psychology between the Methods of Behaviorism and Phenomenology," *Psychological Review*, 1967, *74*, 318–324.

NAME INDEX

SUBJECT INDEX

absolute truth, 153

abstract concepts, 153–155, 451

abstract knowledge, recall of, 146

abstract logic, 608

abstractions, 30, 62, 63, 74; conceptual, 155; logical, 154; metaphysical, 329–330

abulia, 299 n.

academic psychology, 53, 60, 80 n., 85, 181, 430, 467–469, 472, 557; influence on Freud

accommodation, 518, 531

accommodative strain, 523

achievement: ego involvement in, 276; priority and, 66–68

act psychology, 84, 85, 96, 222, 271 n., 424, 463; associationism and, 82–84; intentionalism and, 79–82, 85, 96

active association, 377, 378

active attention, 487

active movement, Berkeleian emphasis on, 533–535

active powers, Reid on, 654–656, 659

Adlerian psychology, 93, 276–277, 408–410, 433

adolescent psychology, St. Augustine on, 137–138

adultomorphic fallacy, 136, 150

aerial perspective, 523; moon illusion and, 515–516, 519

affective values, psychical causality and, 849–850, 861–862

afferent impulses, 303, 342

afterimages, 86, 96, 623, 709

alchemy, 164, 165, 172

alternating personality, phenomenon of, 285

ambiguity, intolerance of, 22

American Psychological Association, 27, 40, 134, 182, 207 n., 219–220, 226, 456, 875 n.

Analysis of the Phenomena of the Human Mind, 702, 720, 721, 737, 792

anatomy, 100, 104–106, 165; brain, 668 n., 700; comparative, 156, 700; seventeenth-century, 321, 322

animal physics, 356

animal psychology, 75, 156, 157, 243, 252, 265, 335–336, 380, 656

animal spirits, Cartesian notion, 347–348, 350, 352, 674

animistic thinking, 181, 574, 576

anthromorphic fallacy, 136

anthropology, 5, 8, 66, 803 n., 869

antimonics, Kantian, 313, 314, 717

apatheia, 114, 116, 122

apperception, 481, 487–489, 498, 763–765, 844, 846, 863, 864, 871, 879

apperceptive mass, 763, 765, 767

appetite(s): Hobbesian view, 330, 333, 334, 412; Hume on, 598; psychic power of, 115; Spinoza on, 407

appetitive faculty, 192 n., 194

applied psychology, 117, 122, 249, 761, 873; opposition to, 251–252

applied science, 5, 10, 109, 251

Appolonian-Dionysian dichotomy, 429–431

approach-avoidance dichotomy, 329–330, 333

Arabian scholarship, influence of, 160–163, 168–170, 172–173

Arabic numerals, 161, 169

archetypes: collective unconscious and, 153; Jung's concept, 14–15, 358; Platonic ideas as, 60–63

Archimedes, principle of, 103–104

Aristotelian background, 71–97

Aristotle's illusion, 86–87, 388

armchair psychology, 20–25, 28, 42, 147, 340, 816–817, 855; Spinozistic, 433–434

asceticism, 115, 138, 443